W9-BHX-953

WHITEHALL

ALSO BY PETER HENNESSY

STATES OF EMERGENCY
(With Keith Jeffery)

SOURCES CLOSE TO THE PRIME MINISTER
(With Michael Cockerell and David Walker)

WHAT THE PAPERS NEVER SAID

CABINET

RULING PERFORMANCE
(Co-Editor with Anthony Seldon)

WHITEHALL

PETER HENNESSY

SECKER & WARBURG
LONDON

First published in Great Britain in 1989 by
Martin Secker & Warburg Limited
Michelin House, 81 Fulham Road, London SW3 6RB

British Library Cataloguing in Publication Data

Hennessy, Peter, *1947–*
Whitehall.
1. Great Britain. Civil service, to 1987
I. Title
354′.41006′09

ISBN 0–436–19271–3

Printed and bound in Great Britain by
Butler & Tanner Ltd, Frome and London

CONTENTS

ILLUSTRATIONS

PLATES

The author and publishers are grateful to the following for permission to reproduce copyright photographs: BBC Hulton Picture Library, Nos 1, 2;Keystone Press Agency, Nos 12, 19, 38; Central Press, Nos 3, 4; Times Newspapers Ltd, Nos 5, 8, 9, 11, 16, 17, 18, 20, 22, 24, 25, 26, 27, 28, 29, 31, 32, 33; Wide World Agency, No 15; Independent Newspapers Ltd, No 34; The Financial Times, No 36; The Sunday Times, No 21; Belinda Wilkinson, No 37; Douglas Glass, No 7; RAF Honington Crown Copyright, No 23; Associated Press, No 10.

DIAGRAMS

ACKNOWLEDGEMENTS

Thanks to Channel 4 Television for permission to quote from material gathered for Brook Productions' *The Writing on the Wall* and *All The Prime Minister's Men* and London Weekend Television's *Whitehall*; to David Higham Associates Limited for permission to quote from *The Castle Diaries 1974–76*; to George Weidenfeld and Nicolson Limited for permission to quote from *The Churchillians*; and to Professor Sir Douglas Hague for allowing me to make full use of our co-authored study, *How Adolf Hitler Reformed Whitehall*.

FOR NID

PREFACE

Society has become used to the standing armies of power – the permanent Civil Service, the police force, the tax-gatherer – organised on a scale which was unknown to earlier centuries.
Lord Radcliffe, 1951[1]

Nations begin by forming their institutions, but in the end, are continuously formed by them or under their influence.
Lord Hailsham, 1987[2]

Whitehall is the ultimate monster to stop governments changing things.
Sir John Nott, 1988[3]

This book has been a long time in the making. When I joined the team on the night desk of *The Times* in July 1974, Charles Douglas-Home, then the paper's Home Editor, told me to find a subject to write about in the quiet watches of the night, preferably in an area that the paper did not cover routinely. He promised to look at the result and, if it was up to standard, to place it in the paper. Without a moment's hesitation I chose Whitehall. My appetite for reporting this particular standing army of power was already considerable.

The man largely responsible for whetting it was the incomparable Anthony Sampson. In September 1965 I received a mint copy of his *Anatomy of Britain Today*[4] as a sixth form prize at Marling School in Stroud. Not only were his chapters on 'Prime Minister', 'Cabinet', 'Civil Service', 'Treasury', 'Diplomats' and 'Honours' eye-openers, the second volume of his *Anatomy* genre, it must be remembered, captured a rare moment of postwar elan in Whitehall – the excitement of the early Harold Wilson before the setbacks and the disillusionment had tarnished the bright promise of Labour's election victory in 1964 after thirteen years of Conservative government.

'For some weeks after the change', wrote Sampson, 'senior civil servants found themselves working a seventy or eighty hour week. To many, not necessarily Conservative ones, the new mood was exhilarating and full of new opportunity. "It's like champagne," one of them said to me. "I feel years younger," said another. And even the imperturbable secretary to the Cabinet, Sir Burke Trend, was observed to have a new look in his eye.'[5] Arthur Schlesinger, house historian of the Kennedy presidency (much in vogue as a dynamic, youthful style to be imitated in 1964–5), passed through London in the late autumn of 1964 and, in an *Evening Standard* article written in pure Camelot style, provided grist for the Sampson mill:

> London has suddenly come alive. Fresh winds are blowing. Whitehall, that once grey and depressing street, crackles with new spirit. There is the excitement which comes from the injection of new men and ideas, the release of energy which comes when men with ideas have the chance to put them into practice.[6]

And in the driving seat was the 48-year-old Harold Wilson, the supreme meritocrat, high-flying young don in prewar Oxford, Beveridge's brilliant assistant, a demon for statistics with a huge appetite for work, member of the War Cabinet Secretariat, Cabinet Minister at thirty-one. The grammar school boys had made it.

Wilson epitomised a new aristocracy of talent. I was a grammar school boy myself and I went up to Cambridge in October 1966 still believing every word of the Wilson legend despite the deflationary economic measures to which his Cabinet had resorted the previous July. Disillusion came slowly, and still, after nearly twenty years, causes a twinge.

Cambridge deepened my interest in the men who 'feel much happier . . . in a kind of back room', as Sir Robert Armstrong, Secretary of the Cabinet 1979–87, put it.[7] For example, reading Robinson and Gallagher on 'The Spirit of Victorian Expansion' in Africa one encountered senior Colonial Office civil servants like James Stephen speaking truth unto power, vainly as it turned out, with tart minutes to his minister like this one of 29 July 1840:

> I cannot but think that even if our National resources were far more potent than they at present are, it would be very bad policy to employ in Africa that part of them which is available for Colonisation. In North America and in Australia we have vacant continents to occupy, and every shilling well expended there may be made to yield a large and secure return. But in Africa we cannot colonise at all without coming into

> contact with numerous warlike tribes, and involving ourselves in their disputes, wars and relations with each other. If we could acquire the Dominion of the whole of that Continent it would be but a worthless possession.[8]

Preparation for the Modern British History Paper of the Cambridge Historical Tripos introduced me to formidable reforming officials – perhaps the best though not the most typical of the late Victorian breed – like Sir Robert Morant, a pioneer of state education and national insurance, whom Beatrice Webb described as 'the one man of genius in the Civil Service ... a strange mortal not altogether sane'.[9] So seized was I by the Civil Service theme that I devoted the essay paper of the qualifying test for the Civil Service Commission Assistant Principal Competition of 1969 to an (unfavourable) comparison of the recently published Fulton Report with the seminal Northcote–Trevelyan Report of 1854.[10] I think rather more highly of Fulton now (see pp. 206–8). The examiners clearly believed that such an opinionated temperament was not the stuff of which future assistant secretaries are made. Despite their low mark I was invited to attend the Civil Service Selection Board. I declined after receiving an offer of a graduate scholarship from the Ford Foundation tenable at the London School of Economics, a fortunate intervention which, with hindsight, proved a blessing both to me and to the higher Civil Service.

Research at the LSE into the origins of the cold war did not kindle my interest as much as it might. The thirty-year rule had not yet eaten into the postwar archives of the Foreign Office, the Ministry of Defence and the Service Departments. The primary material was dominated by American sources. Though reading FO material dealing with the Balkans and Eastern Europe in the last stages of the Second World War offered two benefits: I acquired a sense of how the policy-making hierarchy works, with a file crawling laboriously from Third Secretary to Deputy or Permanent Secretary and perhaps even the Secretary of State himself, attracting comment, redrafting and addenda as it progresses; the second benefit was personal – I plumbed the depths of tedium, it was the intellectual equivalent of National Service in the Armed Forces, which stood me in good stead when required to report certain aspects of the university and polytechnic systems for *The Times Higher Education Supplement* once free of the PhD treadmill (thesis still incomplete). The *THES* was my journalistic equivalent of National Service.

Reporting vice-chancellors for the paper, however, was good practice for the moment, some eighteen months later, when I began work on the permanent secretaries (the breeds are very similar). Life on the *THES* also introduced me to Maurice Kogan, Maurice Peston and John Vaizey who, in their different ways, were connoisseurs of the British Civil Service.

Maurice Kogan's excellent *The Politics of Education*[11] was brimming with material on high policy-making in the Department of Education and Science, the management of its huge building programmes in the fifties and sixties, and the impact of latterday Morants like Derek Morrell who illustrated the tension that can afflict a crusading policy entrepreneur inside what, according to its job specification, is a politically neutral career Civil Service.[12] While on the *THES* in 1972–4 I read Samuel Brittan's *Steering the Economy*,[13] a work which enhanced the residue I retained after reading Anthony Sampson eight years earlier. I could not have wished for a better primer on postwar economic policy-making and Treasury organisation or for a more readable introduction to the larger-gauge Treasury figures since 1945 like Sir Edward Bridges, Sir Frank Lee, Sir William Armstrong and Sir Douglas Allen (now Lord Croham).

My spell on *The Times* night desk was one of my happiest in journalism. In between the bombs (1974 was a year of IRA activity on the mainland), I would play Scrabble, drink tea and watch television with Colin Wilson, Brian Forbes, Neville Hodgkinson, Bob Parker and Stanley Baldwin. On the latest of the late shifts, 9 p.m. to 4.00 a.m., I would have the hours after 1.30 largely to myself, the silence broken occasionally by chattering teleprinters and my routine hourly calls to Scotland Yard, the London Fire Brigade and the Army in Lisburn, Northern Ireland. This was the perfect chance to plunder all the secondary sources prior to writing those stories I planned on Whitehall. (I had had two preliminary canters, a portrait of the post-Fulton Civil Service College for the *THES*[14] and a profile of the new head of the Central Policy Review Staff, Sir Kenneth Berrill, whom I had got to know while he was Chairman of the University Grants Committee, which I was in the process of preparing for *The Times*.[15])

The small hours of the morning in Gray's Inn Road found me head down in Richard Rose's reader *Policy Making in Britain*,[16] Paul Addison's *The Road to 1945*,[17] Tom Harrisson's *Living through the Blitz*,[18] Norman Chester's *Lessons of the British War Economy*,[19] and Hugh Heclo and Aaron Wildavsky's *The Private Government of Public Money*,[20] which achieved a degree of penetration inside Whitehall never previously accomplished, a feat all the more remarkable as the co-authors were American scholars. The combination of Brittan, Heclo and Wildavsky and Henry Roseveare's *The Treasury*[21] stood me in good stead as a reporter during the protracted sterling and public expenditure crisis of the mid-seventies.

In tackling Whitehall I was well aware that I was tilting at the hardest target in British journalism. My ambition was to do on a daily basis what Anthony Sampson did every few years with his anatomies. I knew what had happened to Anthony Howard when he was appointed Fleet Street's first Whitehall Correspondent by *The Sunday Times* in 1965 and was constantly reminded by fellow journalists and those inside Whitehall about how effective Harold Wilson's ban had been.[22] In the first week of December 1984, Wilson, installed once more in No. 10, paid me a similar compliment. Word of my intentions had reached Downing Street. A note went out, under the name, if my informants were right, of R. T. Armstrong (later Sir Robert), at that time Principal Private Secretary to the Prime Minister. The gist of it was simple. I was not to be spoken to by the Civil Service. The minute had quite a wide circulation, descending at least to Principal rank in the main departmental policy divisions.

Shortly after I had arrived on the night desk and, if memory serves, on Thursday, 5 December 1974, two people (one gave his name, the other did not) telephoned me at *The Times* to give me the contents of the minute. Pride mingled with panic. I was new to the game. Official Secrets Acts and D-notices were still a matter of awe to me. Charlie Douglas-Home had been the paper's Defence Correspondent. He would know what to do. Charlie was somewhat taken aback – why had Wilson done it? I told him I had found an area to write about – Whitehall. No. 10 had found out before my boss did and clearly did not like it. Charlie said it was magnificent and that I should hit them. He was – and remained – brave, boyish and infectious in his resolve.

The launch of my Civil Service operation owed a great deal to Harold Wilson. Thanks to his minute I became known down the length and breadth of Whitehall before I had put pen to paper (the profile of Sir Kenneth Berrill had still to appear). The general reaction in the senior levels of the Civil Service was that I was more sinned against than sinning (some later changed their minds). Wilson's ban gave an added thrill to the chase as did Mr James Callaghan's when his was issued to the permanent secretaries by Sir Ian Bancroft, Head of the Home Civil Service, at their regular Wednesday morning meeting on 15 February 1978 (a pair of stories, one on incomes policy, the other on contingency planning for industrial disputes, had caused particular offence in No. 10).

But there were more serious reasons for my journalistic obsession. Those long reading sessions in the empty *Times* news room in the early hours of the morning firmly reinforced the impression that the Sampson volumes and Cambridge reading lists had left. The Civil Service was one of the great estates of the realm, the 'permament government', as Anthony Verrier called it.[23] Its senior people exerted a formidable, continuous influence in the highest decision-making bodies in the land. Yet even the more politically sophisticated citizenry scarcely knew their names let alone where they came from, what they did, the values they espoused. There was the odd exception like Sir William Armstrong who in the early seventies to his credit had a thing about greater openness (to the chagrin of most of his colleagues) and by the mid-seventies had become a highly controversial figure as Edward Heath's virtual economic 'overlord'.[24] I took it upon myself with, I must admit, a degree of presumption and pomposity that ill became a twenty-seven-year-old even on what was then a genuine quality newspaper, to make the equivalent of Stephen, Morant, Bridges and Lee public figures while they still held high Whitehall office. There seemed little point to me in leaving them to be discovered, like some lost tribe, once the scholarly profession had got round to sifting the files declassified under the thirty-year rule. They seemed to me, and still do, to be far too important to be relegated to the status of historical curiosities. Which is not to say that the craft of the historian, the anthropologist and the archaeologist did not come in useful as part of the tool-kit for prising open the private world of Sir Douglas Corridor, as Bill Keegan used to call his composite permanent secretary. (When Bill was the Economics Correspondent of *The Financial Times* the Treasury was stiff with men called Douglas–Allen, Wass and Henley, to name but three.)

The task which I began in earnest on the night of 5 December 1974 was pursued from a variety of observation posts: *The Times* night desk, 1974–5; *The Times* Home News Room, 1975–6; from the Westminster Press Gallery as Lobby Correspondent of *The Financial Times* during the turbulent year of 1976; as Whitehall Correspondent back at *The Times* from October 1976 until January 1982; from St James's Street as a member of the Britain Section at *The Economist* for the bulk of 1982; from Gray's Inn Road once more as a *Times* leader writer from November 1982 to September 1984; from first Victoria and then Somers Town as a member of the Policy Studies Institute; and since the autumn of 1987 from the offices of BBC Radio 4's *Analysis* in Broadcasting House.

Gratitude almost amounting to a national debt has been acquired along the way as I have 'wheeled my pathetic little hobby-horse up and down the corridors of power' as a Conservative Cabinet minister, Angus Maude, once expressed it so kindly during a debate in the Oxford Union. I owe a great deal to my newspaper and journal editors, Sir William Rees-Mogg and his deputy, Louis Heren, at *The Times*, Andrew Knight at *The Economist*, Fredy Fisher at *The Financial Times*, the late Charles Douglas-Home at *The Times* once more, to John Lloyd at the *New Statesman* and Andreas Whittam Smith at *The Independent*. From 1983 I have built up a big debt to my wireless colleagues, to George Fischer, former Head of Talks and Documentaries at BBC Radio, who brought me into this branch of the business, to the cool and thoughtful David Morton, Editor of Radio 4's *Analysis* and to a superb group of producers, Anne Winder, Anthony Moncrieff, Mark Laity, Fraser Steel, Margaret Hill and Caroline Anstey, David Morton's successor. After writing, radio is my favourite medium. But I have been very lucky, too, in my television colleagues, Phillip Whitehead, Rob Shepherd, Stephen White, Mike Rossiter and Sally Anne Lomas when we worked together in 1986 on Brook Productions' *All the*

Prime Minister's Men and Julian Norridge and Nora Stein and their colleagues Karan Thapar and Jeff Morgan of London Weekend Television on whose *Whitehall* this book is heavily reliant. Between them, the two television series on Cabinet government and the Civil Service created a rich archive as, I hope, a glance at my end notes will confirm. For another form of compilation – the preparation of a statistical portrait of the Civil Service and for the raw material of the departmental summaries and organisation charts – I am greatly indebted to the painstaking work of Andrea Jones of Sussex University.

I have been very lucky in my institutional colleagues while preparing this book: John Pinder, Donald Derx and Bill Daniel, successive Directors at the Policy Studies Institute, and the Trustees of the Joseph Rowntree Memorial Trust who funded my senior fellowship there; Sir Frank Cooper, Sir Kenneth Stowe, Lady Wood, David Severn, Dr David Butler and all the Trustees and Advisers of the Institute of Contemporary British History and, in particular, to my co-director, Dr Anthony Seldon; Professor Jeremy Richardson and my ever-stimulating colleagues in the Department of Politics at Strathclyde University. Without Stephanie Maggin, first at the PSI and later the ICBH, I don't think I should ever manage to produce a word. For helping prepare the typescript of *Whitehall* I am also grateful to Mrs Sheila McNeil. When it comes to the production of books, pamphlets and journals Sue Johnson and Mary Cassels at PSI and Jane Henderson at the RIPA are without equal. On the documents front, Nick Cox, Helen Forde, Duncan Chalmers, John Walford and Hilary Jones have ensured that the Public Record Office remains my favourite government department. Other civil servants who have assisted me over the past fifteen years have to remain anonymous for their own protection. They know who they are and I am very grateful to them.

Giles Gordon of Anthony Shiel helped me lay the foundations of this book in 1983. David Godwin of Secker & Warburg helped me build it. From the outset I knew I was lucky in both of them. Events have confirmed it. Another, unexpected set of professionals played a part. I succumbed to a protracted illness in 1987 when the bulk of this volume was being drafted. Four doctors helped me to recover, Dr Dick Barrett and Dr Elspeth Holman of the Forest Surgery in Walthamstow, Mr Don Newling of Hull Royal Infirmary and Dr Malcolm Farr also of HRI and a brother to me since 1958. But for them I have no idea if and when *Whitehall* would have been finished. The book is dedicated to my wife Nid who does not share my fascination with the Civil Service but has tolerated it for some fifteen of the nineteen years of our married life.

Naturally the views expressed in this book are entirely my own and should not be associated with the Institute of Contemporary British History or any individuals involved in its work. The same applies to the other organisations and institutions with which I am connected. Responsibility is mine alone.

Peter Hennessy, Walthamstow, May 1988

INTRODUCTION

I confidently expect that we shall continue to be grouped with mothers-in-law and Wigan Pier as one of the recognised objects of ridicule.
Sir Edward Bridges, Head of the Civil Service, 1950[1]

It is a beautifully designed and effective braking mechanism. It produces a hundred well-argued answers against initiative and change ... If the positive forces – the forces of creativity and innovation and enterprise – were powerful, as they were in the late eighteenth and early nineteenth century Britain, it would be the best Civil Service that could be designed.
Mrs Shirley Williams, former Secretary of State for Education and Science, 1980[2]

The peculiar strengths and weaknesses of the Civil Service, and of the Treasury in particular, form a powerful contributory cause of our decline.
Professor Sidney Pollard, 1981[3]

Through a malign irony economic decline is a generator of parasitic growth industries. This volume is itself a by-product of this twisted phenomenon and, in my case, some of the pleasures of authorship have been soured as a result. I am at one with my political hero, Clem Attlee, in believing myself to be immensely fortunate to live in this country[4] and agree with my political friend, Douglas Jay, that nothing could be finer in one's twilight years than 'to cultivate private rather than public aspirations ... to live, love, garden [though I hate gardening] and die, deep in the English country'.[5] I have taken the economic decline of my country badly and personally. Its causes preoccupy me. I am convinced that before I expire somewhere deep in the English, Welsh or Scottish countryside, I shall have savoured the joy of chronicling its successful reversal. But in surveying contemporary Whitehall I have to say, if prejudice is to be declared as candidly as any author should, that I regard what I see as part of the problem rather than part of the solution – though the seeds of revival and reform are detectable.

Without our stunning relative economic decline, the great debate about Whitehall, its practices and its people, would not have taken off to the point where television producers treat it as a staple item in the endlessly recycled series of issues which coalesce into current affairs broadcasting at the deeper end of the market, where retired permanent secretaries regard an appearance in the lecture hall to reflect and prescribe (though never to recant) as part of their retirement portfolio along with knighthood and pension, and where publishers are prepared to commission volume after volume on the theme from Peter Kellner's and Norman Crowther-Hunt's *The Civil Servants*[6] by way of Leslie Chapman's *Your Disobedient Servant*,[7] Brian Sedgemore's *The Secret Constitution*,[8] Hugo Young's and Anne Sloman's *No, Minister*[9] and *But, Chancellor*,[10] Clive Ponting's *The Right to Know*[11] and *Whitehall: Tragedy and Farce*[12] through to this study.

The reason is inescapable. As Martin Wiener put it, 'the leading problem of modern British history is the explanation of economic decline'. Professor Wiener, himself the author of a contemporary classic in the 'great decline' literature, *English Culture and the Decline of the Industrial Spirit 1850–1980*,[13] explains:

> It has not always been thus. Until the later 1960s the generally accepted frame for the history of Britain over the previous century was that of a series of success stories; the bloodless establishment of democracy, the evolution of the Welfare State, triumph in two world wars, and the enlightened relinquishment of empire. Such a happy frame, however, became increasingly hard to maintain as, having steered clear of the rocks of political turmoil or military defeat, the British found themselves becalmed in an economic Sargasso Sea.

So established is the Great Decline as the dominant theme not just of modern history but of contemporary politics and economics that the best of the recent home-produced political science textbooks, Dennis Kavanagh's *British Politics, Continuities and Change*, starts its opening chapter on 'Understanding British Politics' with the following paragraph:

> Phrases like 'the sick man of Europe' or 'the British disease', and the many studies of 'what's wrong with Britain?' convey the sense of a people and a political system that have known better days. It may fairly be objected that there is nothing new about such self-criticism and that there has always existed a body of dissent about aspects of the British political system. What is new, however, is the scale of the present dissatisfaction.[14]

Correlli Barnett, a tireless prospector in the archival lodes of the Public Record Office, has turned up wartime files from the Board of Trade and elsewhere which indicate that the postwar travails of the British economy as an exporter,[15] a steelmaker[16] and a shipbuilder[17] were fairly accurately forecast (the economic recovery of Germany, crucial to these calculations, was correctly foreseen). And warning signals were conveyed from the Civil Service backroom to the ministerial frontroom in the shape of the War Cabinet Committee on Industrial Problems (Export Questions).[18]

But such prescience did not seep very far into the consciousness of those in the innermost foreign and economic policy-making circles. Take Sir Roger Makins (now Lord Sherfield), a great figure in the postwar Foreign Office, who was responsible for nuclear weapons policy and economic diplomacy and went on to the Washington Embassy (1952–6) and the headship of the Treasury (1956–9). Talking to Michael Charlton of the BBC about Britain's failure to join the European Coal and Steel Community (precursor of the European Economic Community), he said: 'the second thing which I certainly never foresaw [the first was the impact of General de Gaulle as President of France] and would not, I think, perhaps have credited at the time we are talking about – 1950 – was the economic and industrial failure of the United Kingdom in the 1960s. It was perhaps to be foreseen, but I certainly did not foresee it'.[19]

Employees of the Great Decline cottage industry have assigned more than a walk-on part to the senior Civil Service in the depressing, multi-instalment newsreel of economic, industrial and, as the consequences came home, social decay. Before lingering over some of the more vivid instalments, I ought to say that I do not subscribe to the 'I name the guilty men' school of history. To assign a disproportionate amount of culpability to the permanent bureaucracy is to offer a misleadingly monochromatic picture of a blurred and multi-coloured phenomenon. I have some sympathy for Lord Bancroft's view that 'We're all in the dock together. And the more that one tries to say, "Well, it's section A or section B or section C of the community that's to blame", I think the less chance there is of getting out of the mess we're in'.[20] The politics of scapegoating is a depressing feature of a nation in decline, and it leads nowhere – though, in a backhanded way, practitioners of the politics of scapegoating flatter the Civil Service.

For the Left the demonology embraces multinationals, the financial markets, the oil sheikhs (this diminished a bit with the slump in world oil prices), the International Monetary Fund, poor-quality management, the centre and right-wing parties, and the Civil Service; for the Right, responsibility for a disordered society and economy rests with the trade unions, monopoly public sector industries and services, the universities, teachers, social workers, the Anglican clergy, the left and centre parties, and the

Civil Service; for the centre, it is poor-quality management, badly led, unrepresentative trade unions, monopolies in the public and private sectors, the class bases of the two major parties, and the Civil Service. Whitehall is the multi-purpose alibi. When all shades of the spectrum agree, deep suspicion is the only response. It all seems just a little too pat, altogether too convenient to be plausible.

Civil servants, being human and much got at, are prone to retaliate in kind. As one permanent secretary put it to me in the mid-eighties, 'we live in an alibi society'.[21] I have never forgotten a senior Home Office official, during an off-the-record conference on open government in the late seventies at Ditchley Park, saying wearily to myself and other freedom-of-information advocates that he had a nightmare (no British civil servant would ever say 'I have a dream'): a decision on which he had advised a minister could already be the subject of a Parliamentary question, a select committee inquiry, an investigation by the Ombudsman, the Equal Opportunities Commission, the Community Relations Commission, or an appeal to the European Court on Human Rights. And here were we trying to make his life truly impossible by seeking to add a Freedom of Information Act whose workings might be reviewable by a select committee, an information ombudsman *and* the courts.[22] It was a totally different landscape through which he had to steer policy than the terrain he had entered as a young assistant principal in the 1950s. One almost felt sorry for him. Accountability was clearly a vast inconvenience.

Why not adapt and extend his nightmare for a moment? Let us gauge the pressures on an under secretary's desk in one of up to twenty ministries which, in their different ways, are seeking to grapple with the practical consequences of an economy in decline, for even those with only a remote connection to the condition of manufacturing industry have been buffeted by a tough climate of public spending restraint since 1975. Some of his (the under secretary grade is male dominated) preoccupations are timeless and will weigh on him much as they weighed on any predecessor since the 1880s: he will always have half an eye upwards on the views of his Civil Service superiors and his ministers (being human and ambitious he will want promotion and approval); the imperatives of confidentiality will matter as will the probity with which he deals with those outsiders who have a financial relationship to his department; he will ensure that whatever public money comes under his control is spent solely on the activity Parliament has ordained for it through the Vote system; precedent, statute and what Bridges called the 'storehouses of departmental experience'[23] count for a great deal in a cautious, traditional, hierarchical society like Whitehall; he must always bear in mind his regular 'clients' (they could be local authorities, trade associations, government suppliers, other departments, quangos, professional bodies or whole professions such as teachers or lawyers); there is always the tricky area of his own views and, even trickier, his own conscience, a problem the Ponting affair highlighted but did not solve.

The later 1960s and early 1970s generated additional pressures: the oil price explosion and the sustained underperformance of British industry has brought our official's manpower and money budgets into a condition of near constant crisis with irritating and time-consuming spin-offs such as increased union militancy among all sections of the Civil Service; a newer, more strident kind of single-issue pressure group has grown up; public service unions and the newer style pressure groups have become highly skilled at using the press as the megaphone of complaint and the recipient of leaks damaging to their negotiating partners; the House of Commons and its policy-orientated select committees have become much more assertive and intrusive, feeding through their activities an ever less deferential media increasingly keen to name the hitherto anonymous Civil Service counsellors as the true authors of this ministerial statement or that White Paper; increased overseas business, particularly that generated by the EEC, has come to absorb more Civil Service time and energy than running the Colonial Empire ever did; finally the polarisation of British politics, itself a child of decline, has made it ever more difficult to maintain the substance, not the shell, of that great nineteenth-century invention, a politically neutral and permanent career Civil Service. The landscape of Whitehall has been dramatically changed since our under secretary turned up in the mid-fifties to the Civil Service Commission for his final selection board, the key phrases from Bridges's *Portrait of a Profession* carefully committed to memory in order to impress the great and the good sitting on either side of the First Civil Service Commissioner. By the mid-eighties some were wondering whether they would have joined up had they known what was waiting for them. It is not much fun in your Indian summer to have to endure well-publicised claims from figures like Sir John Hoskyns that you have presided over thirty years of failure and that nothing short of a transfusion of new blood and new methods will suffice if your country is to survive the result of your life's work.[24]

A harbinger of what was to come appeared within five or so years of our under secretary's Whitehall apprenticeship. Preoccupation with the concealed influence of what Max Weber, that supreme theorist of bureaucracy, called the 'permanent residents of the house of power'[25] has a long tradition. Sir Patrick Nairne, when Permanent Secretary at the Department of Health and Social Security, sent me a copy of G. W. E. Russell's *Collections and Recollections*. As Sir Pat put it, 'GWER has an engaging Victorian flavour, but there are nice morsels of *la même chose*'.[26] One of these was a passage in Russell's chapter on 'Officialdom' in which he wrote: 'It would be beyond my present scope to discuss the composition and power of the permanent Civil Service, whose chiefs have been, at least since the days of Bagehot, recognised as the real rulers of this country.'[27] It was, however, to be nearly sixty years before another observer with a biting pen sought mercilessly to expose the malign consequences of the great reform of Bagehot's day – Britain's first aristocracy of talent in the shape of an administrative class recruited on the basis of competitive examination.

Its assailant was an outsider, a Hungarian-born economist, Thomas Balogh. Where others like A. J. P. Taylor[28] or Henry Fairlie[29] had tilted at a general target they liked to call 'the Establishment', Balogh went straight for Weber's permanent residents. In his celebrated essay of 1959, 'The Apotheosis of the Dilettante', Balogh inveighed against 'The Establishment of Mandarins', and the 'fatal myth' of 'a perfectly working Government machine', a myth 'not equalled since the divine right of Kings' which 'has found acceptance in the most select academic circles dedicated to a searching analysis of the essence of political relations'.[30] For Balogh the twentieth-century Civil Service had become the prisoner of its very real nineteenth-century success. But the handful of cultivated generalists needed by the 'Night Watchman State' (to borrow the brilliant phrase of the nineteenth-century socialist, Ferdinand Lassalle) to advise ministers on a very limited range of state activities were, by the end of the First World War, utterly inadequate to deal with the level and scope of state activity generated by total war and the transformation in the relationship it brought about between Whitehall and industry. 'In a planned economy', wrote Balogh, 'the crossword-puzzle mind, reared on mathematics at Cambridge or Greats at Oxford, has only a limited outlet. They must defend themselves against a system in which positive action is in order because they can only express themselves by transferring decisions from the realm of economic realities into the sphere of pseudo-moral philosophy.'[31] Balogh foresaw severe trouble for Britain in an increasingly competitive international economic climate if the 'two-tier dillettantism'[32] of amateur minister and amateur senior civil servant persisted. Labour, he declaimed, 'dare not fail' to remedy these shortcomings.

The experience of Labour in power between 1964 and 1970 showed just how complacently Balogh's friend and patron, Harold Wilson, dared to fail in precisely this area. Balogh's broadside is important as an early and brilliantly coloured piece in the growing mosaic of the 'great decline' literature. In this depressing corpus, the Civil Service ranks with the public schools as a culprit. Indeed, the two of them are, more often than not, bound tightly by the manacles of shared guilt. Correlli Barnett, in a 600-page dissection of the roots of Britain's economic and imperial decline, published in 1972, places great emphasis on the primacy afforded to the classics by the public schools and the preference of the reformed Civil

Service for taking classicists instead of insisting on a supply of candidates for the competitive examination mill schooled in disciplines relevant to a society already losing its technological and industrial lead to Germany and the United States. In an illuminating piece of research, Barnett conducted in his *The Collapse of British Power* an audit of questions set by the Civil Service Commission in the Class One examinations for the civil, foreign, Indian and colonial services which he judged to be 'a documentary record of the biases and myths of the late Victorian academic mind'.

> In 1870 possible marks for Greek or Roman studies were twice the totals for French or German studies or political economy – and taken together, a third more than allotted to the entire field of science. There was no paper on current affairs. A quarter of a century later the domination of the classics had only been slightly eroded, and the relative importance of science and modern studies only slightly enhanced. It was not until 1906 – too late for the generation of senior administrators of British power in the 1920s and 1930s – that political science, psychology and economic history were included.[33]

The result, given a past of decades of hierarchical life in a closed society, was, in a biting phrase of Sir Michael Sadler's coined in 1932, a Civil Service intellect consisting of 'Humanism with the sap dried out of it'.[34]

For Martin Wiener, probably the most influential of the recent school of decline scholars, the malign influence of the public school classical education was felt long before the cultivated aspirants from the Clarendon Schools submitted their applications to the Civil Service Commission. The sons of the unlettered entrepreneurs who gave Britain its world lead in the first steam-based industrial revolution proved incapable of sustaining their country's pre-eminence in the second simply because their socially ambitious fathers had deployed a portion of their new-won wealth in putting them through the gilded wringer of the public school: the result was a professional class imbued with aristocratic rather than commercial values, a class in which the Victorian Civil Service Commissioners found plenty of willing recruits.[35] According to this thesis, the seeds of our manufacturing decline actually blossomed into a top-flight Civil Service. This view found a pre-echo in a conversation I had with Denis Healey in 1977, four years before the Wiener book appeared. Quoting, or rather misquoting, Hannah Arendt's *The Origins of Totalitarianism*,[36] the Chancellor of the Exchequer said, jerking a dismissive thumb at the senior officials in his room, Arendt had argued that 'any nation whose best and brightest go into "number two" jobs like theirs rather than number one jobs like mine, is buggered – and she's right'.[37] His officials rather relished the brilliant, ebullient Mr Healey and were happy enough to put up with his jovial verbal brutality.

It is, however, a depressing and irrational thesis which suggests that a country with a Civil Service of intellectual aristocrats is on the road to decline. But a Cook's tour of the decline literature sees the men and women who are the subject of this volume popping up in a variety of villainous disguises. At best they appear, along with the British universities, as an asset that has been wasted or badly deployed when it came to serving 'great economic and social purposes', which was the view of the briefly influential report on *The United Kingdom to 1980* produced by the Hudson Institute, the famous private American think tank, in 1974.[38] At worst they star in Anthony Sampson's last and doom-laden *Anatomy* as an 'imperial bureaucracy' of the kind which brought down Pharaonic Egypt, the Ottoman Empire or the court of Imperial Spain. 'Of all the legacies of empire', wrote Sampson in 1982, 'the most dangerous is surely an immobile bureaucracy which can perpetuate its own interests and values, like those ancient hierarchies which presided over declining civilisations ... As the British mandarins reinforce their defences, awarding each other old imperial honours, do they hear any echoes from Castile or Byzantium?'[39]

For an economic historian like Sidney Pollard, the Treasury, the most scapegoated department in the Whitehall constellation, is the very incarnation of brilliant official minds utilised in defending the indefensible – 'one can only wish that an equal effort had gone into devising policies that would not be needed to be defended because they were successful'.[40] The perpetuation of what in Pollard's eyes 'was in many ways an ideal instrument for the later Victorian and Edwardian era'[41] has left the Treasury 'unprepared for the task of administering a complex economy ... even top administrators often lack a mathematical sense and a feel for quantitative relationships, preferring to trust their own alleged sense of values'[42]. For Pollard, the route to the top entrenches disastrous habits in he who was once young and promising:

> ... he quickly finds that what is rewarded is the ability to write good papers, the ability to compromise and the skill to avoid treading on too many toes; major innovative thoughts are not encouraged, particularly in junior administrators, and habits acquired then tend to stick. As far as the subject matter itself is concerned, he learns by the time-honoured method of 'sitting next to Nellie', or learning by doing what the others have done before him. It would be difficult to think of a system more designed to perpetuate the basic policies carried on to date and to inhibit their questioning.[43]

G. C. Allen, an economist with wartime experience of Whitehall policy-making,[44] writing several years before Martin Wiener's contribution to the perpetual inquest on national failure, produced a wider analysis of the socio-economic explanations for what Eric Hobsbawm called 'this sudden transformation of the leading and most dynamic industrial economy into the most sluggish and conservative, in the short space of 30 or 40 years (1860–90/1900) [which] is the crucial question of British economic history'.[45] Combining a knowledge of government, economics and education, Allen observed that 'the institutions created to serve one stage of development may prove to be intractable and frustrating at the next stage, but may survive none the less through the force of tradition and convention'.[46] Allen concentrated on the 'causes that converged to transform so many of the heirs of the great industrial innovators into complacent routineers'.[47] Inevitably, Allen's gaze, like so many before and since, lighted upon the public schools, the 'effective instrument for bestowing gentility on the sons of the rough and warty industrial pioneers'.[48] He recognised their good side. Indeed, he was eloquent on the point:

> They had great merits as the nursery of political leaders and administrators for several generations, and their products proved their mettle in the government of the British Empire. The standards of behaviour they inculcated were a marked improvement on those of the aristocracy in earlier times. The men they trained helped to bring order and a large measure of fair dealing over much of the globe . . .[49]

In that passage, G. C. Allen identifies one of the central themes to be treated in this book: the price paid for infusing the higher Civil Service with high-minded, classically educated 'routineers', apostles of orderly administration who brought probity and consistency to the conduct of public policy and who, in the process, came to be treated as the symbol of that very decline to whose orderly management they dedicated their lives. One does not have to go as far as Correlli Barnett in branding them the 'New Jerusalemers', who, through successfully marketing the welfare state and the mixed economy in 1940s, Whitehall brought about the collapse of 1970s and 1980s industry,[50] to recognise that Britain's first meritocracy may have developed a set of characteristics and skills which, once novel and refreshing, have decayed into innovation-sapping and convention-producing traditions. If this is so, it is, given the permanent proximity of the senior Civil Service to power, a particularly damaging example of what Mancur Olson has called 'institutional sclerosis'.[51]

Those with a knowledge of Whitehall could with justification complain at this point that this preoccupation with late-nineteenth-century elite schooling is itself an absurd and particularly damaging symptom of the British disease, given the early-twentieth-century rise of the grammar schools, the extended educational opportunity of the 1944 Education Act, the postwar 'reconstruction competitions' for the administrative class. My later look at the higher Civil Service – 'the regulars' – will not trace every blemish of British government to the Clarendon Schools circa 1870. But, to show at this stage that dissecters of the great decline are not without plentiful *prima facie* evidence for their sociological endeavours even in the mid-1980s, it might be instructive, for example, to examine the beautifully constructed and affectionate eulogy Sir Robert Armstrong, as Secretary of the Cabinet and Head of the Home Civil Service, prepared for the Memorial Service of his fellow classical scholar, permanent secretary and contemporary, Sir Anthony Rawlinson in April 1986, after Rawlinson's tragic death while climbing the Snowdon Horseshoe:

> There was an occasion when the then Permanent Secretary of the Home Office, waiting to temper the keen edge of the Treasury axe for expenditure on the prison programme, thought that it would be a good idea for his Treasury colleague to see for himself something of what the Prison Service was like. So one fine day I took Anthony to spend half a day going round Wormwood Scrubs, that microcosm of the splendours and problems of the Prison Service. I am glad to say that our expedition had the desired effect; and I shall never forget how, as the gates clanged behind us as we left, Anthony turned to me and said: 'Who would have thought, Robert, when we sat for the scholarship examination at Eton together, that forty years later we should come out of Wormwood Scrubs together?'[52]

There is a timelessness about that passage: here were two cultivated, influential men in their fifties who had progressed together from Eton, via Christ Church and the Civil Service competition, to the Treasury, to serve as career officials engaged largely, though not wholly, on the kind of jobs a pair of gifted Etonians might have filled in 1880s Whitehall in Gladstone's time. Indeed, the Wormwood Scrubs visit was wholly Victorian: it had to do with the economical expenditure of public money on capital spending for the penal system and the stately resolution of its proper level by a duo of high-principled, politically neutral civil servants prior to their ministers' ratifying their agreement. Mr Gladstone, old Etonian, classical scholar at Christ Church, sire of efficient and impartial administration and reformer of the Victorian Civil Service, could only have evinced pleasure at his enduring handiwork as he gazed down on the Scrubs from that mock-up of a Pall Mall Club into which St Peter decants former prime ministers.[53]

Things have changed, however, in 30 let alone 100 years. Even a relatively swift package tour around the decline literature[54] is sufficient to show how far the Civil Service has moved since it cohabited with Wigan Pier in Bridges's time. It is no longer a matter of comic banter in today's equivalent of music hall. The Service is seen as a particularly decayed estate in a seriously crumbling realm and a major element in the debilitating chemistry that has produced it. Again I must declare an interest. I share the view that the machinery of government matters and that its reskilling and retooling is a necessary, though not a sufficient, condition of recovery. I was co-author of a report, *Reskilling Government*, prepared in the winter of 1985–6, which stated as its major premiss: 'that the machinery of government does matter, and that its reform is an indispensable part of any strategy for bringing about an historic and lasting transformation in Britain's condition and prospects'.[55] The group which drafted that statement included Sir John Hoskyns and Norman Strauss from Mrs Thatcher's prototype Downing Street Policy Unit, Graham Mather, Head of the Policy Unit at the Institute of Directors where Hoskyns was by this time Director-General (Mather later moved to the directorship of the Institute of Economic Affairs), and Dr William Wallace, Director of Studies at the Royal Institute of International Affairs (Chatham House) and an adviser to David Steel, then Leader of the Liberal party.

Though it was not more than marginally conscious of the parallel when it began its work, the Reskilling Government Group was an informal successor to the Haldane Committee on the Machinery of Government of 1917–18, the last *official* inquiry to tackle the functions of the modern state and the apparatus and the people needed to fulfil them efficiently with 'zeal and discretion' and the 'spirit . . . essential to any form of government that is more than a machine'.[56] This is not the book of Sir John Hoskyns's latterday Haldane Committee, though I have drawn heavily on its thinking and discussions. But throughout I have written in the spirit of Haldane. This study is part history, part guidebook, part analysis and part reform tract written by an author in whom admiration and irritation vie constantly when contemplating the Civil Service. Its purpose is Haldanian in that each section of the book is a component in the case for reform.

Such lofty, even pompous, intentions may suggest several hundred pages of leaden reading. Indeed, the purpose is a serious one. I am at one with Sir Geoffrey Elton when he said during his inaugural lecture as Professor of English Constitutional History, that the purpose of constitutional history

> is to study government, the manner in which men, having formed themselves into societies, then arrange for the orderly existence, through time, and in space, of those societies. It is, therefore, like every other form of history, a form of social history, a form of the history of society. But it takes particular note of the question of government.
>
> It is concerned with what is done to make that society into a properly structured, continuously living body, so that what goes wrong can be put right, so that the political action of which that society is capable

> can be efficiently and effectively conducted. Machinery, yes. But also thought, the doctrine, the teaching, the conventional notions. What does the society think its government is, how does it treat it, what does it do to amend it? What forms of change are possible, what reforms . . ?[57]

These are heavy duty questions which, in one form or another, I have attempted to tackle in this volume. It may strike the reader as a grim prospectus. It strikes me that way, too, and reminds me of Norman Chester's farewell interview with Edward Bridges when he left the Cabinet Office after temporary service during the war. Chester, the bluff Mancunian grammar school boy, was asked by the classically educated Old Etonian Bridges what he had learned during his time in Whitehall. 'I have learned, Sir Edward, to distinguish between the various shades of grey', Chester replied.[58] I have written this book with the grey factor constantly in mind and have tried to dispel it wherever possible. The themes may be heavy but it is also the story of people, many gifted and some eccentric, of institutions, ancient and modern, with peculiar lives of their own. Behind the grey suits and stone walls issues clash and personalities throb. If by the end you feel you are merely distinguishing between shades of grey, I shall have failed.

I have arranged the book with the historical section at the front. This is both desirable and inevitable. It is impossible to understand the present, let alone to ponder what might be in the future, without an understanding of how we came to be where we are now. This is doubly so in a traditional, precedent-laden society like the British Civil Service. It is always difficult to know when 'history' ends and our current experience begins. Breaking the narrative story of the Civil Service is bound to jar wherever the barrier is placed. Given Mrs Thatcher's oft-repeated claim to have 'changed everything', I have picked the departure of the Callaghan Administration in 1979 as the terminus of the historical section. Part Two sketches the essentials of our Parliamentary and Cabinet system of government, takes a look at the conventions and rulebooks of 'the production engineers of the Parliamentary process' as Sir William Armstrong liked to describe his fellow professionals[59] and conducts the reader on a Cook's tour of the departments in which those rulebound official lives are lived out. Part Three is about three sets of players in the Whitehall game – ministers, career officials and the good and the great, Whitehall's territorial army, who undertake periodic service on Royal Commissions and committees of inquiry. Part Four assesses what some see as Mrs Thatcher's revolution in government. I doubt if it's quite that. But the lady *has* had a more profound effect on the Civil Service than any premier since Lloyd George, whom, in her anti-Establishment impulses, she closely resembles. The final section attempts two very difficult tasks: to estimate the degree to which the Civil

Service has contributed to the success or failure of our country as an economy, a society and a force in world affairs; and to gaze into the 1990s and beyond to see what it could and should become if it is to fully serve the public for whose benefit it exists and who, every man, woman and child of them, pay some £4.50 pence per head per week just to keep it in being.[60]

PART ONE | ORIGINS

Intellectuals are indispensable to any society, not just to industrial society, and the more complex the society, the more indispensable they are. An effective collaboration between intellectuals and the authorities which govern society is a requirement for order and continuity in public life for the integration of the wider reaches of the laity into society.
Professor Edward Shils, 1972[1]

Yes, I am a clerk in the India Office – having passed the medical with flying colours, balls and eyesight unusually perfect they said. My marks have arrived and left me enraged. Really, knowledge seems an absolute bar to success. I have done worst in the only two subjects of which I possessed a solid knowledge, Mathematics and Economics.
John Maynard Keynes to Lytton Strachey, 1906[2]

The Civil Service is a bit like a Rolls-Royce – you know it's the best machine in the world, but you're not quite sure what to do with it.
R. A. Butler, 1962[3]

The English and, more latterly, the British, have the habit of acquiring their institutions by chance or inadvertence, and shedding them in a fit of absent-mindedness.
Lord Hailsham, 1987[4]

The politician performs upon the stage; the historian looks behind the scenery.
A. J. P. Taylor, 1956[5]

There is an inevitable artificiality about institutional history. At its worst, it is as if the history of war were written in terms of rail warrants drawn up for a soldier's leave or the history of revolutions treated as a series of dockets containing requests for emergency spending on truncheons for special constables. Just occasionally, a rare example of the scholar/politician such as Roy Jenkins can deliver an attention-commanding *tour de force* on the condition of institutional life as he did in the House of Lords in March 1988.[6]

Yet, without a heavy 'front-end' investment in institutional history, an understanding of late-twentieth-century Whitehall would be impossible. I have tackled it by starting with Henry the Treasurer in Norman times, though the pace of narrative becomes less furious when we reach the formative period of the mid-nineteenth century. I have tried to compress without distorting, and to relate the dry life of the bureaucrat to the wider issues of war, economics and society shaping the Civil Service from the outside.

1 THE MAKING OF AN INSTITUTION

With some of the older Departments – The Treasury and Foreign Office are examples – there is no comprehensive statutory definition of duties ... the older and more fundamental powers ... are inferred from custom and long practice.

Sir Edward Bridges, 1952[1]

Our people are few compared with the multitudes likely to be arrayed against it and we must prepare for the trial by cultivating to the utmost the superior morality and intelligence which comprise our real strength. It is proposed to invite the flower of our youth to the aid of the public service.

Sir Charles Trevelyan to John Thadeus Delane, 1853[2]

They should have 'the best education that England affords: the education of public schools and colleges and such things, which gives a sort of freemasonry among men which is not every easy to describe, but which everybody feels ...'

Robert Lowe, 1873[3]

The functions came first. The names came later. Whitehall, that 'geographical expression', derived from a jumble of buildings on the road from Westminster to the City of London which comprised a royal palace. To be absolutely precise, the name was invented by King Henry VIII. When Thomas Wolsey, the great cleric-cum-bureaucrat, fell from grace, his master appropriated York House, the Cardinal's London town house, renamed it Whitehall and extended its grounds till it encompassed the area bounded by the Thames and St James's Park on two sides, Great Scotland Yard and Downing Street on the other.[4] It has a timeless and faintly romantic air when viewed from St James's Park which Neville Cardus captured in 1950: 'From the bridge looking towards Whitehall was accumulated nobility of dome and turret vanishing like white ghosts in the sky.'[5]

The terms 'Civil Service' and 'civil servant' came from the early Indian

Empire when it was run, as if on a franchise, by the East India Company, whose powers derived from a Royal Charter of 1599 renewed periodically until the mid-nineteenth century when Whitehall took complete control through the India Office. The company's civil service and its servants were so called to distinguish them from its military servants. The terms did not become current in Britain until the great Thomas Babington Macaulay penned his magisterial essays on Robert Clive and Warren Hastings for *The Edinburgh Review* in 1840 and 1841.[6] By the time Northcote and Trevelyan declared in their report 12 years later that 'it cannot be necessary to enter into any lengthened argument for the purpose of showing the high importance of the Permanent Civil Service of the country in the present day', the concept and the term were self-evident, though as late as the 1870s ministers and officials were reluctant to use it, preferring instead to speak of 'public offices' or the 'public establishments'.[7]

But the origins of the Civil Service lie a long way back before the makers of the Indian Empire and their brilliant portrayer and far away from the heat and dust of the sub-continent. They are to be found in that bedraggled, uncomfortable caravanserai of court servants which followed the Saxon Kings of England round from one primitive resting place to another. The Treasury function – money, its acquisition, recording and storage – was the inescapable fact which kept a small number of clerics in tow behind the royal procession. Intellectuals, people who could count and read (which in those days meant clerics) were, as Professor Shils pointed out, indispensable to any society however primitive. Picture them, huddled and embarrassed on the lower tables at feasts in great halls around the country, like shy actuaries present as guests on a raucous mess night, as their peripatetic monarch and his hangers-on consumed the victuals of their reluctant host. The King's extravagances were always greater than the wherewithal to pay. It was the function of his unfortunate priests to advise, to warn – and then to try and find more, which is presumably what Sir Edward Bridges meant when, in his stately address to the Imperial Defence College a millennium later, he said 'the older and more fundamental powers . . . are inferred from custom and long practice'.

The peripatetic priestly *cabinet* of the pre-Conquest kings must rank as our prototype Civil Service. But one has to await the arrival of the Normans – great organisers, great centralisers – to discover, with the Treasury historian, Henry Roseveare, the first properly identifiable civil servant:

> Fluidity certainly characterises the earliest history of the Treasury. As if in some dimly lit aquarium, where the personnel of the Norman royal household loom and disappear, ambiguous, enigmatic, historians have peered about in search of the origins of the great departments of State.

Fortunately, a shadowy figure seen flitting through Domesday Book appears to have been styled *thesaurarius*, and upon a consensus of learned opinion, the 'Henry the Treasurer', serving William the Conqueror and perhaps his successor, takes his place as the first identifiable officer with that title.[8]

Certainly, the files of the Public Record Office, possessor of the largest unbroken archive in the world, date from the Normans and their pipe rolls, the cylindrical parchments used by their Civil Service accountants. Indeed, the word 'Exchequer' derives from the half-yearly audits developed in the twelfth century when, in the equivalent of today's Budget ritual:

> Before the assembled dignitaries, on a table five feet by ten, lay the checkered cloth like the chess-board from which the institution took its name. Just as wooden 'tally sticks' served the Exchequer as receipts for money, with notches carefully graded from thousands of pounds – a handsbreadth – down to the merest scratch for a penny, so the cloth with its columns drawn for thousands, hundreds, scores and tens of pounds, for shillings and for pence, was a simple but foolproof accounting device in a largely illiterate society.[9]

The final account, the calculations on the checkered cloth completed, would be written on the Great Roll of the Pipe. The Norman ritual quickly acquired the sanctity and unreformability of Bridges's 'custom and long practice'. The tally-stick routine lasted for nearly eight centuries. When the wretched things were finally burned in incinerators beneath the House of Lords in 1834, they set fire to both the Lords and the House of Commons, reducing the entire Palace of Westminster to ashes – the most dramatic, if unintended, revenge the Treasury has ever taken on its parliamentary critics.[10]

In fact, the history of Whitehall is a story of long periods of routine punctuated by occasional orgies of reform when the system broke down, or, as in the greatest reform of all in the mid-nineteenth century, when scandal and outraged public opinion moved those in authority (who were already reform-minded, it has to be said), to inquire and then to act. The first of a long line of Whitehall reformers was Peter de Rievaulx, a Frenchman and close adviser to the young King Henry III. The Pipe Roll system had virtually crumbled under the weight of small debts and fines pouring into the Exchequer in the thirteenth century which, once Peter de Rievaulx was appointed to all the important financial offices under the Crown in 1232–3, 'witnessed some of those rare spasms of reforming initiative which have occasionally lifted English government, by its bootstraps, to a higher plane of competence'.[11] The Exchequer was overhauled and a more sophisticated system of record-keeping installed.

The next hundred years saw the development of another constant factor in the history of Whitehall when the rudiments of parliamentary control and consent over government, or other royal, finances began to emerge, a development recognised and incorporated by statute in 1340.[12] Only when Henry Tudor brought the medieval state out of the ruins of chaos and civil strife at the end of the War of the Roses did the importance of the ruler to the achievement of efficient administration become apparent.

Henry VII was a civil servant's ideal – orderly, cautious, hard-working and immensely careful with public money. Between 1485 when he seized the Crown and his death in 1509 the kingdom was exceedingly well-run. The sapping of royal power in the fifteenth century left the new King Henry with a shrunken revenue and, yet again, a furred-up financial machine graphically described by Professor Sir Geoffrey Elton:

> The financial department of State was the Exchequer, developed as a separate institution in the late twelfth century and therefore already 300 years old when Henry VII came to the throne. Its two parts – the exchequer of receipt where the money was received, stored and disbursed, and the exchequer of audit where accounts were audited and unpaid sums driven in – reflected a thorough desire for safety in bureaucracy. A multiplicity of officials and records, designed to prevent fraud and collusion, dealt with the finances. But while the King could be sure that the work of the exchequer was honest, he often had to wait a long time for the creaking machinery to do its work.[13]

Henry, like other subsequent rulers of the nation, attacked the problem of a creaking inherited machine unsuitable for his purposes by creating an alternative based on his own household, a kind of Tudor kitchen cabinet. The key official in this alternative machine was the Treasurer of the Chamber. Henry chose his treasurers, Sir Thomas Lovell (1485–92) and Sir John Heron (1492–1524), for their competence. Their impressive performance may have had something to do with the attention this accountant-on-the-throne paid to their work, signing each page of their accounts with the royal monogram once their arithmetic had been approved.

Henry's bureaucratic characteristics were clearly not conveyed in his genetic code, or not those parts of it that went into the making of Henry VIII. The hunt, the dance, philandering and the ostentatious display of conspicuous consumption marked his kingly priorities. In his reign, the bureaucrats, first Thomas Wolsey then Thomas Cromwell, took over – the original overmighty public servants – until regal wrath brought them low.

Both were what in C. P. Snow language would be called 'new men', selfmade people from outside the courtly ranks, a rare and early example of meritocracy and social mobility. Wolsey was the son of an Ipswich cattle-dealer and Cromwell's father was a Putney blacksmith. Wolsey rose through the Church and 'from 1515 to 1529 was not only the King's chief minister but virtually his only one. Though Henry never surrendered ultimate control over affairs, it was Wolsey who ruled.'[14] Wolsey knew about power and its uses. But administration and finance were closed worlds to him. Spending, not collecting, revenue was his forte.

It was a young solicitor in Wolsey's service, Thomas Cromwell, who engineered the Tudor revolution in government. 'Cromwell', wrote Professor Elton, 'was an administrator of genius. He could work harder at more details than seems quite believable . . . His temper was bureaucratic: he liked to organise and loved to record.'[15] Cromwell acquired offices as if it were a hobby – Clerk of the Hanaper (1532), Chancellor of the Exchequer (1533), Principal Secretary and Master of the Rolls (1534) and Lord Privy Seal (1536). In those days, there was no distinction between political and Civil Service posts. You were the King's servant and that was that, entirely dependent upon the monarch for patronage, honour and preferment. Not until the late nineteenth century did today's clear and much discussed distinction between the political and the administrative arms of government become accepted parlance. And even when the 'Civil Service' came into general usage as a term it tended, initially, to embrace both.[16]

Cromwell's accumulation of offices gave him a near-complete grip over the State machine; his rare intellectual equipment and application gave him a mastery of its detail. The result was a sustained burst of innovation in central government. He undertook the difficult task of obtaining a divorce for the King in defiance of Church and Pope and, in return, was given the chance of refashioning the English administrative system.

The essence of the Cromwellian revolution was twofold: it blended the simplicity of Henry VII's household system of financing with the more permanent, judicially based strength of the old, cumbersome medieval system it had superseded. By entrenching his reforms in a series of statutes he drafted himself, Cromwell ensured as much permanence as was possible in sixteenth-century conditions, protecting them from the vagaries of the occupant of the throne. In addition, he made 'the inner ring of the King's council into a proper institution known as the Privy Council'.[17] It was the Privy Council which, from the seventeenth century on, was to give birth to many of the modern Whitehall departments that began their lives as boards instituted under its aegis, as technically the Department of Trade and Industry still is.[18]

Thanks to Thomas Cromwell, by the time of William Cecil, Lord Burghley, Elizabeth I's Secretary of State, to whose job specification, as prescribed by the Queen, Sir Robert Armstrong turned for his personal code of ethics,[19] there was a recognised *national* as opposed to a household system of government. The departmental structure created by Cromwell (there were six departments, all dealing with revenue – Exchequer, Duchy of Lancaster, Court of General Surveyors, Court of Augmentations, Court of First Fruits and Tenths, Courts of Wards and Liveries) and his bagful of personal offices brought every governmental and policy activity into his hands – revenue and expenditure, home, defence and foreign affairs and, hugely important in Tudor times, religious affairs as well. Burghley, as Elizabeth's Principal Secretary of State, was no innovator apart from inventing the prototype British Secret Service, an instrument refined and developed by his protégé Sir Francis Walsingham. But he consolidated the Cromwellian achievement after nearly twenty years of uncertainty between the fall of Cromwell in 1540 and the accession of Elizabeth in 1558. He, too, was a Pooh-Bah figure bestriding economic, domestic and foreign policy.

Burghley grappled with some very familiar problems. He managed to beef up the revenue to nearly three times the yield in Henry VIII's time but inflation absorbed this and more. He battled to build up the navy – the contemporary deterrent against the contemporary threat, Spain – by stiffening the Navy Board, reducing corruption and backing John Hawkins' strategic preference for small, manoeuvrable fighting ships in preference to the 'traditional floating castles'. It was these little ships which later saw off the Armada. Burghley skilfully used the Spanish threat to extract ever larger sums from the Elizabethan parliaments. Elizabeth still managed to die £400,000 in debt. Burghley's personal assumption of the post of Lord Treasurer in 1572, and his faithful pursuit of his Queen's parsimonious appetites, drew forth the warmest commendation from mistress to civil servant – Elizabeth called him 'both her Treasurer, and her principal Treasure'[22] – till Mrs Thatcher described Sir Derek Rayner as 'a remarkable and wonderful person'.[21]

Like all natural administrators, Burghley relished routine, regularity, tidiness and good minute-taking. As a result the Elizabethan Privy Council, of which he was Principal Secretary, acquired a staff of four clerks, messengers and ushers and met on Tuesdays, Thursdays and Saturdays, which is three times as often as the present Cabinet. It handled a wide range of matters, great and small, as befitted the bureaucratic engine room of a nation somewhere between medievalism and relative modernity – 'war and peace, foreign affairs and diplomatic negotiations, military and naval matters, finance, religion and the Church, order and police duties, crown patronage in lands and offices, local government, private affairs, disputes and suits for favour'.[22] Star Chamber, perhaps the best known of Tudor institutions (it is the unofficial Whitehall name for MISC 62, Mrs Thatcher's regular autumnal Cabinet committee on public expenditure), was an off-shoot of the Privy Council much used, by Wolsey in particular, as a court for hearing petitions, for enforcing the King's or Queen's peace, censoring the press, regulating prices and controlling building in London.

Just as the age of the Tudors is seen as one of reformation in administration as much as religion, the age of the Stuarts is seen as one of profligacy and chaos. The Treasury, according to the standard view, may have done its best to curb excesses but it had no effective purchase on the rest of Whitehall. Patronage and corruption – targets of the nineteenth-century reformers – had already ensured that in the first half of the seventeenth century the needs of the State outstripped the capacity of the bureaucracy to meet them. Henry Roseveare has captured the dismal scene:

> Within the ramshackle empires of the great departments nothing could be done without bringing down the whole frightful debris of medievalism. The notion of reconstructing efficient, salaried departments was quite unthinkable. As it was, the widespread sale of official posts meant that the existing structure was held together by a web of property rights whose vested interest in conservation was virtually unassailable. Even in the few areas where this was not so the Treasury could do nothing unless it was supported by King and Council. Efforts were made in the 1620s and 30s to reform the fees and practices of several great departments – Navy, household, law courts – but the work was curiously sterile.[23]

Nor did the arrival of the puritan parliamentarians in Protectorate Whitehall bring in its train a spate of austere administrative reform, for all the symbolism of the street itself being the scene of the execution of Charles I. There were new committees aplenty but the only innovation the puritans brought was to insist that the Treasury's tally sticks should be inscribed in English rather than Latin![24] Yet the first half of the seventeenth century saw the beginnings of what were later to become important developments in the central government machine.

The making of peace with Spain in 1604 provided the impetus for the foundation of what became the first non-revenue-raising economic department in Whitehall. Peace brought new trading opportunities in European markets previously closed by conflicts. Pressure was applied to the Privy Council to do something about it and in 1621 it established a Committee for Trade and Plantations, the body to which today's Department of Trade and Industry traces its origins. King James I laid down its remit as to investigate the 'true causes of the decay of trade and scarcity of coyne [money] within this Kingdom, and to consult of the meanes for removing of these inconveniences'.[25] With the restoration of the monarchy, the job was divided between two councils, one for trade, the other for plantations (the early colonies). Reorganisation mania has often afflicted the trade and industry departments, none more so than in the 1970s and 1980s. It was present at the creation. The two councils were reunited in 1672. In 1696, that trade-minded Dutchman, William III, established as a permanent committee of his Privy Council, the Board of Trade and Plantations. Its revised remit had a distinctly modern and innovative flavour: 'To examine and to take an account of the state and condition of the general trade of England and of the several particular trades into foreign parts . . . to consider by what means profitable manufactures already settled may be further improved and how new and profitable manufactures may be introduced'.[26]

It would be wrong to read into those faintly dynamic terms of reference for the early Board of Trade anything amounting to an interventionist strategy. It was a hands-off, advisory department, though it did directly sponsor colonial development, looking after the colonists once they left and providing them with the professionals deemed necessary to a healthy community – a teacher, a doctor and a priest – once they arrived. Gratitude was expressed in what later became a traditional fashion. The capital of Nova Scotia was named in honour of Lord Halifax, an early President of the Board of Trade,[27] as later the Falkland Islands, Britain's most famous imperial residual, were named after a First Lord of the Admiralty, and, with a touch of ambivalence, Sydney in the penal colony of New South Wales took its name from the Home Secretary who had transported its early citizens.[28]

The most significant development in the embryonic Whitehall of the seventeenth century was the rise of the Treasury, the embodiment of the gerontocratic principle that age and power should go together. And it was the desire of Charles II for new blood, 'rougher hands', 'ill-natured men, not to be moved with civilities',[29] which wrought the transformation. The King placed the Treasury in the hands of five commissioners, three of them his own men, thrusters in their thirties, Sir William Coventry, Sir Thomas Clifford and Sir John Dunscome, with ballast from the good and the great civilian branch, the existing Chancellor of the Exchequer, Sir Anthony Ashley Cooper, and from its military branch in the person of the Duke of Albemarle who, as General Monck, had provided the military muscle which restored the monarchy.

But it was the man they appointed Secretary to the Treasury who truly gripped the ancient department by its throat; a state servant whose name is still a household word – Sir George Downing, who after his departure from the Treasury went into jerry-building and put up Downing Street. His name is scarcely ever committed to paper without a deeply insulting epithet, such as 'the treacherous and wretched George Downing'[30] attached to it. It was deserved. A clever puritan, son of a legal family, Downing was the second man to graduate from the newly founded Harvard University in Massachusetts. He clambered up the ladder of preferment as first a preacher to the puritan army, then Oliver Cromwell's spymaster in Scotland earning a fortune, £4 a day, for his black arts, a wealth-bringing marriage into the Harvard family, a diplomatic career abroad (a cover for spying on the deposed Stuarts), turning his coat at just the right moment to be of service to the restored monarch, exposing three senior puritans who had taken refuge in Holland and securing their extradition to England and the hanging and quartering that awaited them. He was made a baronet for his pains.

Downing is the greatest witness to the argument that niceness and decency do not necessarily accompany reform-mindedness. His achievement was to bring with him from the Hague to Whitehall the best Dutch administrative and accounting methods then far in advance of English techniques. The efficiency of government fund-raising from the City of London was greatly improved and the tax 'farmers' – revenue-raising was privatised into syndicates of collectors – were given a much tougher time by Charles II's Treasury Commissioners and their hard, energetic Secretary. Downing's greatest coup, however, was to establish the principle of Treasury control over the rest of Restoration Whitehall. As the institution's historian put it:

> After a brief tussle, an historic Order in Council of 31 January 1668 restated the extent of exclusive Treasury control over the revenue and departmental expenditure. All orders and most appointments relating to the collection and disbursement of the revenue must first pass the Treasury's scrutiny; grants, pensions and other royal bounty were to be checked and 'secret service' expenditure . . . was to be strictly confined.[31]

Downing and the Commissioners triumphantly carried off the Order in Council, inscribed it in a board and hung it up in their new premises, Treasury Chambers. No slouch at the geography of power, Downing had moved his department from the Exchequer rooms at Westminster to buildings adjacent to the King's chambers next to the Royal Laboratory. New artefacts of control were invented – minute books, order books, warrant books and letter books as much the state of the art in their time as ICL's computerisation of the Inland Revenue's Pay As You Earn system in the late 1980s. Downing established the Treasury as *the* leading department in Whitehall, a pre-eminence it has only very occasionally (and always temporarily) lost in the ensuing three-hundred years. Even that greatest of Whitehall diarists, Samuel Pepys, who had no love for Downing when he first arrived with his unloveable personality and Dutch technology, writing of his ability to raise loans for the public finances, said 'I do really take it to be a very considerable thing done by him; for the beginning, end and every part of it, is to be imputed to him.'[32]

It is salutary to ponder the career of men like Downing and the far nicer William Lowndes, whose Treasury career lasted for nearly 50 years (1675–1724). Painstaking and much respected, Lowndes prepared fresh financial legislation to meet the needs of each new year and can be cited as, in effect, the inventor of that great Whitehall ritual, the Budget. Downing and Lowndes showed that men of genuine talent could rise out of the mire of patronage and the mass of fifth-rate placemen to the top of the public service 150 or more years before their successor as Treasury Permanent Secretary, Sir Charles Trevelyan, co-author of the most famous Civil Service report of all time, sharpened his quill pen to denounce the evils of the patronage society in biting, unforgettable prose. Indeed, another Trevelyan – the great social historian, G. M. – felt moved to write that 'in the Treasury of the first twenty years after the [Glorious] Revolution we see the emergence of the best modern traditions of the permanent Civil Service',[35] a piece, I suspect, of exaggerated hyperbole from a marvellous Whig historian deeply immersed in the habit of writing the history of Britain as continuous progress after 1688.

In the years which spanned the public service career of William Lowndes, the central government machine – and its outstations in the colonies – grew to be a substantial force in the life of the nation and a major employer of its people. Revenue-raising, the oldest of all Whitehall activities, still absorbed the lion's share of public service manpower in the mid-eighteenth century, some 14,000 of the 17,000 people employed in government departments,[34] though it was to be another forty years or so until the first income tax was introduced during the Napoleonic Wars.[35] On top of the 17,000 another 10,000 or so worked in the Royal dockyards. If we add to the 1,000 staff of the Royal households, the Armed Forces of some 70,000 on average (a figure that would more than double in time of war) and, to top the total up, bring in crown servants in the colonies and *their* employees, it has been calculated that public employment accounted for about four to five per cent of the adult male population.[36] A contemporary Whitehall-watcher, John Douglas, was quite overwhelmed by the prospect:

> When we consider the vast body of persons employed in the collection of the revenue in every part of the Kingdom; the inconceivable number of placemen, and candidates for places in the *customs*, in the *excise*, in the *post office*, in the *ordnance*, in the *salt office*, in the *stamps*, in the *navy* and *victualling* offices, and in the variety of other departments; when we consider again the extensive influence of the *money corporations, subscriptions jobbers* and *contractors*, the endless dependence created by the obligations conferred on the bulk of the gentlemen's families throughout the Kingdom, who have relations preferred, or waiting to be preferred, in our *navy* and the numerous *standing army* ....[37]

'The inconceivable number of placemen' – the public service sagged under the weight of family, patronage and obligation. And once in, or 'preferred' as it was called then, they were unshiftable, as Sir Norman Chester has depicted in his fascinating snapshot of Whitehall's administrative system in December 1780:

> It was well accepted that an office constituted a form of property, particularly the longer and more certain its tenure and the more pronounced the rights and pecuniary benefits attached to it. By 1780, though some offices were still granted for life, most were granted at pleasure, i.e. at the discretion of the grantor. But in practice the difference was not very great. Apart from the holders of 'political' offices close to the King, who had no expectation of remaining long in them, for most office-holders, appointment at pleasure meant in practice appointment for life.[38]

For every Lowndes who deserved high office in the public service there were hundreds of incapables later savagely described by their would-be liquidator, Sir Charles Trevelyan, as 'sickly youths' whose 'parents and friends . . . endeavour to obtain for them employment in the service of the Government', as a soft option leading to an early public pension.[39]

Beneath the deadweight of patronage and inefficiency, the 1780s saw the emergence of two of the greatest modern departments of state, the Home Office and the Foreign Office, and the recrudescence of a third, the Board of Trade. Intriguingly, it was the King, George III, who realised the absurdity of maintaining the arrangement whereby responsibility for home and foreign affairs remained together in a single institution, the Office of the Principal Secretary of State, though the work was divided between two departments, the Northern and the Southern, each with its own minister. It was James Callaghan, one of ten Home Secretaries who later became Prime Minister,[40] whose politician's nose led him to describe the real reason for the split in a 1982 lecture to mark the Home Office's bicentenary, indulging in a little autobiography as he did so:

> When twentieth century Prime Ministers reorganise the machinery of government and split or abolish old departments or create new ones, they usually have a number of reasons whether avowed or not. They may believe that a department has got too big, or conversely that its interests overlap with those of another and should be observed; such change may come because of the incompatibility of Cabinet colleagues, or less worthily even to satisfy a Prime Minister's desire to make his mark.
>
> It was much the same in the eighteenth century. When the Home

> Office and the Foreign Office were first formed by separating the old Southern and Northern Departments of the Principal Secretary of State, there is little doubt that one of the reasons for dividing them was the mutual antagonism of Fox and Shelburne.[41]

The historic split occurred on 27 March 1782 when the Rockingham administration took office and the Prime Minister, sensitive to the incompatibility of his two Whig colleagues, took up, at last, the monarch's advice and, as Mr Callaghan put it, 'for reasons that would continue to appeal to twentieth century Prime Ministers ... created ... a logical separation in the handling of home and foreign affairs ...'.[42]

The first Home Office (the Home Secretary is still officially known as Secretary of State for the Home Department) under Shelburne, who became Prime Minister four months later, was a tiny ministry of thirty officials. It was mainly concerned with Royal affairs, Crown grants and appointments; the maintenance of the King's peace, 'the state's spinal cord down to this very day' (Mr Callaghan's phrase[43]) and colonial affairs. Then as now the Home Office was Whitehall's charlady mopping up the pools of activity that did not fit tidily into any other institutional container. As activities grew, they were spun off into separate departments or transferred to others, as happened with the 'first large shedding of responsibility' when colonial matters were transferred in 1801 to the third new Secretary of State to be created in the last years of the eighteenth century, the Secretary of State for War.[44]

That remarkable gambler, orator and trencherman, Charles James Fox, took the Foreign Office at the great divide in 1782. Indeed, the only formal acknowledgement that the split had taken place at all was his note to Britain's envoys abroad.[45] The FO swiftly became a bureaucracy apart, though to call it a bureaucracy gives a misleading impression of its size. By the mid-nineteenth century its numbers had only crept up to 30, and fifty years later its complement was a mere 41, though these figures exclude Britain's overseas representatives (the Foreign and Diplomatic services were not merged till 1919). Very little was asked of the early Foreign Office. As Valerie Cromwell and Zara Steiner discovered:

> Castlereagh did all his own work and ignored his staff. Canning did his own drafting but saw that despatches were accurately copied and circulated. Palmerston, while he neither sought the views of his officials nor permitted even his under secretaries to intervene in matters of policy, nevertheless wanted an efficient secretarial office and drove his clerks relentlessly ... he shaped the Foreign Office into an efficient office of scribes.[46]

Scribes they may have been, but blue blood flowed through those clerical veins. The FO remained 'the stronghold of the aristocracy'[47] in Whitehall well into this century. Blood and not brain was the criterion for admission to this 'last choice preserve of administration practised as a sport'[48] in a Foreign Office 'just easy enough to be agreeable, just ceremonious enough to possess distinction and just industrious enough to do its work'.[49] Two centuries later, though changed beyond recognition, the FO still possessed something of an aristocratic air, particularly when the much-missed Lord Carrington was its political chief (within days of its bicentenary he resigned, honourably, after the unexpected outbreak of war in the Falkland Islands).

The Board of Trade, or the Department of Trade and Industry, to be exact, celebrated its bicentenary in 1986 four years after the Home and Foreign Offices, which is a little odd, for, as we have seen, the Privy Council had turned its attention to trade and plantations nearly two hundred years before the founding date adopted by the DTI. The reason for this apparent error of calculation is that Edmund Burke, the formidable philosopher and parliamentarian, ran a campaign against its laxity and lassitude and succeeded in persuading Parliament to abolish it.

Burke launched his attack in a famous broadside of 11 February 1780, *A plan for the better security of the independence of Parliament and the economical reformation of the civil and other establishments*. Delivered in the Commons, it was published (there was no Hansard in those days) and went through a number of editions. It was as exquisitely phrased an attack as the Civil Service has ever had to endure:

> This board is a sort of temperate bed of influence; a sort of gently ripening hot-house, where eight members of Parliament receive salaries of a thousand a year, for a certain given time, in order to mature at a proper season, a claim to two thousand, granted for doing less, and on the credit of having toiled so long in that inferior laborious department ... This is the history of the regeneration of the Board of Trade.[50]

The Board fought back against the eloquent MP for Bristol. One of its members, William Eden, produced a long list of its achievements at home and abroad, its reports to Parliament and the Privy Council. It found an ally in George III who was a shrewd judge of politics and institutions and not the complete prisoner of fits of insanity which, according to the popular memory, have him filling his time talking to the trees in Windsor Great Park. After all, it was George who obliged the Hanoverian politicians to develop the practice of collective Cabinet responsibility, so adept was he at calling them in individually and interrogating them separately to find out what was really going on (hence their need to agree and memorise their collective line in advance).[51] Following Burke's attack, the King wrote to the Prime Minister, Lord North, 'I am sorry men should so far lose their reason and let the violence of the times or fears actuate them as to forget the utility of the Board of Trade.[52]

The King could not save it. Parliament abolished it with a clause in the Civil List and Secret Service Money Act 1782, in far from statuesque language which declared that the Board of Trade and its offices 'shall be; and are hereby utterly suppressed and taken away'.[53] Reality soon took care of this piece of Parliamentary self-indulgence. Its work was divided initially between the Home Office and the Privy Council. Two years after abolition an order in council recreated the Privy Council Committee on Trade and Plantations. The board itself was reconstituted by another order in council in 1786 which has run unbroken as its charter to this day and is the authority under which the Department of Trade and Industry functions. It was given two ministers, a President and a Vice-President, and a staff of seventeen, a chief clerk, seven other clerks, an office keeper and messengers and 'one necessary woman'.[54] The world's first industrialised nation achieved its economic take-off without significant help from a sponsoring department in Whitehall, a neat though trite and misleading piece of propaganda for the free market/small government school of political economy.

The early-nineteenth-century Board of Trade became an economic equivalent of the Home Office, a catch-all department in the front line of a wide range of governmental preoccupations – running the blockade in the Napoleonic War and coping with the dislocation of trade; overseeing the British merchant marine and the condition of the seamen working in it; assisting in the abolition of the slave trade; relaxing the Navigation Acts; and supervising the railway boom. Most significant of all, it became the bureaucratic cutting edge of the free trade movement which led eventually to the abolition of the Corn Laws in 1846. The department retains its free-trader reputation to this day.

The Board of Trade was, in many ways, the institutional epitome of the nineteenth-century reforming impulse which wove together free trade, individual liberty, a dash of benign enlightened intervention (protecting seamen, freeing slaves) and a constant eye to prevent the growth of the big state into something approaching an ideology often characterised, ironically, with the slogan of 'economical reform' advanced in Burke's great attack of 1782. It attracted and developed a high calibre of public servant commensurate with its growing scope and responsibility. In fact, they become the 'role model' for the small but vociferous lobby for Civil Service reform whose chief obsessional/philosopher/journalist was Robert Lowe, Vice-President of the Board of Trade 1855–8. Officials Lowe encountered there like Henry Thring, 'undoubtedly the most accomplished drafter of bills in mid-Victorian England',[55] and Thomas Farrer, a Board 'lifer' on whose memory and skill successive presidents relied, convinced Lowe (who saw them as examples of the near perfect public servant)[56] and others that if the best of the Whitehall breed could be replicated, indeed, standardised, the force of the Civil Service as an instrument of economical yet effective change would be enhanced beyond recognition.

For the Northcote–Trevelyan reforms and their gradual implementation over half a century *were* the greatest single transformation the British Civil service has ever undergone, and, in their day, they were wholly beneficial. But it must be stated from the outset that they were far from revolutionary in a democratic sense. For their most highly placed patron, W. E. Gladstone (no genuine Whitehall reform is possible unless the incumbent in No. 10 wishes it to be), the changes were intended 'to strengthen and multiply the ties between the higher classes and the possession of administrative power'.[57] Robert Lowe's 'true votaries'[58] were to be sought and found from the new, trained intellectual elite pouring forth from the reformed English universities (an earlier Gladstonian cause), but not all of them. As Asa Briggs succinctly put it, 'Whitehall was not to be surrendered to Manchester, but to Oxford.'[59]

The crusade (its fervour justifies the term) was pursued for the purpose of replacing one freemasonry with another. As H. G. G. Matthew, Gladstone's most recent biographer, puts it:

> A Civil Service hitherto appointed by patronage and influence would give way to a non-political administrative class educated in the moral values of a liberal education further developed by a reformed Oxford and Cambridge. It was a means of extending, confirming, cleansing, and legitimizing an existing elite. Whereas, Gladstone thought, the seventeenth century had been an age of rule by prerogative, and the eighteenth by patronage, the nineteenth would become a rule by virtue. For a liberal education attempted, above all, to produce citizens who were morally good, and such it was that would succeed in examinations.[60]

It worked. It created the country's first true meritocracy, a genuine aristocracy of talent. Its bone structure is clearly visible in the higher Civil Service of today. Despite two world wars, the complete extension of the franchise, a social revolution or two, the rise and fall of the British Empire and the decline of the country as the world's leading manufacturer and exporter, 'the Home Civil Service today' is, as the opening sentence of the 1968 Fulton Report expressed it, 'still fundamentally the product of the nineteenth-century philosophy of the Northcote–Trevelyan Report'.[61] The mid-Victorian Liberals built to last.

But this is to jump the gun. Once achieved, the principle of their great reform – that recruitment of the Civil Service should be determined by merit and not by connection – acquired the status of a self-evident truth.

It did not appear that way to substantial sections of Victorian society, from the Queen down, and it was long in the making, careful in the planning and hard fought for in the implementation.

The standard model for a present-day reform movement would run something along these lines: the appreciation among a small but intelligent and energetic group of people that an issue was important, far more important than generally appreciated and deserving of a higher place in the agenda of public debate; the framing of that issue in vivid terms to widen its appeal; the seizure and use of episodes and examples which illustrate the need for reform; publicity in newspapers; the search for allies in Parliament as well as Fleet Street and broadcasting; the attention of Parliamentary select committees would be attracted, pledges sought from opposition spokesmen; a coalition of forces would be sought before a final assault on the citadels of orthodoxy in Whitehall was mounted – the last redoubt of resistance being the permanent secretary's mind in the department dealing with the subject in question. In the case of the great nineteenth-century Civil Service reform, matters were reversed. The leading spirit and initiator was none other than the Permanent Secretary to the Treasury himself (then confusingly known as the Assistant Secretary), Sir Charles Trevelyan. Like most successful reformers he was abnormal, as Chapman and Greenaway, the leading pathologists of British administrative reform, recognised:

> In character Charles Trevelyan was the very reverse of the conventional picture of a mandarin. Energetic, incisive and intensely self-confident he was also impulsive, tactless and insensitive to the difficulties of others. Life for him was a battleground where the forces of enlightened, altruistic moral progress were to triumph over the dead weight of obscurantism and self interest.[62]

Trevelyan's is the epitome of a high-achieving Victorian life, a cocktail of evangelism, intelligence and family connection. Such people were earth-movers, knew it, and accepted it as both natural and divinely willed. It did not make them easy company. And unlike previous administrative reformers, such as Thomas Cromwell or George Downing, they were relatively free of graft and corruption. (Trevelyan was not averse, however, to easing the occasional relation into a public post.) They were comfortable, certainly, but not conspicuous consumers. And, unlike Cromwell and Downing, they would have found changing sides impossible, however glittering the prizes for betrayal and apostasy.

Charles Trevelyan, the maker of the British career Civil Service, was born in 1807 into an evangelical West Country family. In 1826 he joined the East India Company's civil service and married Macaulay's sister. At twenty-one he secured the dismissal of his superior for bribery. He returned to London and became Permanent Secretary to the Treasury at the age of thirty-two. Virtue had brought its own reward. His appointment in 1840 showed that the system he so despised could, even in its unreformed state, identify and promote the young and the meritorious in a fashion that would inspire sensation and disbelief today if a 32-year-old stepped into one of Whitehall's top three permanent secretaryships.

Once installed in the Treasury, Trevelyan set about creating efficiency in a single ministry rather like a whizz-kid suddenly put in charge of a staid family business. As with all missionaries or revolutionaries (he was a bit of both), for him boundaries existed to be crossed. By 1848 the reform of the Civil Service as a whole was his aim. He declared to the Prime Minister, Lord John Russell, that 'There was never a subject which promised so largely to reward the pains bestowed upon it, for there cannot be a doubt that the practical Executive Administration has, as a general rule, been very much neglected in this country.'[63]

Trevelyan was four-square in the grand Whig tradition of progress, the belief that society could be improved in a self-sustaining fashion if it nurtured certain values – free trade in manufactures, economy and efficiency in the use of state resources, merit in the recruitment of state servants. It was a noble and optimistic view. But it was flawed by a single great blemish – the fear that all this was too much for the incomprehending masses whose hands must be kept away from the levers of public power which were safe only in the hands of the enlightened few whose minds had been trained at public school and ancient university. He was, as Asa Briggs pointed out, not alone among Victorian reformers in appreciating the nation's 'need for a plentiful supply of informed gentlemen'.[64] Trevelyan deployed his formidable penmanship to express the point to Sir J. T. Coleman, the Lord Chief Justice, warning that 'when the irresistible tendency of the times is to bring into activity the political power of the lower classes of society' it would be dangerous for the 'higher orders' if they sank into intellectual sloth.

> It will not do to rest on traditions or on ancient privileges; if we will lead, we must make ourselves fit to be leaders; if even we will float with the current, and not be overwhelmed by it, we must, by discipline and training, learn to throw out our intellectual powers with the strongest and best trained . . . While all around us, the underwood of the forest is making vigorous shoots, our own growth must not stand still, lest we should be overgrown and stifled.[65]

In 1848 Trevelyan took his crusade to Parliament, arguing his case before a Commons Select Committee on Miscellaneous Expenditure. He tried to inject the notion of efficiency into MPs' customary preoccupation with economy. Trevelyan unveiled the second of his two *idées fixes*. Alongside his preoccupation with merit as revealed by examination, 'he believed a drastic improvement in morale and efficiency could be brought about by dividing work into routine and intellectual categories',[66] worthy clerks would perform the first and the young scions of his intellectual aristocracy the second. Trevelyan did not make converts among MPs.

Progress was possible, however, in-house in Whitehall despite Parliamentary indifference – again an intriguing reversal of the position in the 1980s. Trevelyan harnessed the Victorian passion for economy by using a series of *ad hoc* departmental economy reviews to pursue his wider aims. He was a tireless lobbyer of ministers. In September 1848, for example, Sir George Cornewall Lewis, Parliamentary Under Secretary at the Home Office, was being prodded by Trevelyan to adopt his plan for a thoroughgoing reorganisation of the Home Office not just for its own sake but because it would 'be a great help to us in dealing with other offices which want as thorough a revision as much as the Home Office'.[67] Trevelyan was not a man for the polite circumlocutions that can ease ministerial minds down the path of virtue. In many ways he richly deserved his unsympathetic portrayal as Mr (later Sir) Gregory Hardlines, Permanent Secretary at the Department of Weights and Measures, in *The Three Clerks* by that most literate of Post Office clerks, Anthony Trollope.

> To be widely different from others was Mr Hardlines' glory. He was, perhaps, something of a Civil Service Pharisee . . . He thanked God that he was not as those publicans at Somerset House . . . But now he was driven to a wider range . . . if he could promote a movement beyond the walls of the Weights and Measures; if he could make Pharisees of those benighted publicans in the Strand; if he could introduce conic sections into the Custom House, and political economy into the Post Office; if by any effort of his, the Foreign Office clerks could be forced to attend punctually at ten; and that wretched saunterer, whom five days a week he saw laughing in the Council Office – if he could be made to mend his pace, what a wide field for his ambition would Mr Hardlines then have found!
>
> Great ideas opened themselves to his mind as he walked to and from his office daily. What if the Civil Service, through his instrumentality, should become the nucleus of the best intellectual diligence in the country, instead of being a byword for sloth and ignorance![68]

Later Trollope, the inventor of the red pillar box, became friends with Trevelyan and his wife Hannah, though the novelist was never reconciled to the notion of competitive examination. Trollope's pseudonym for Trevelyan was adopted as a family nickname. 'We always call him Sir Gregory in the family', Hannah told Trollope.[69] It was a quaint pre-echo of the 1980s when more than one Cabinet minister would call his permanent secretary 'Sir Humphrey'.

Just how acute Trollope had been in his caricature became apparent when Jenifer Hart began work on Trevelyan's private correspondence in the late 1950s. In mid-Victorian days Parliament had the genuine right to call for official correspondence if it wished to see it. True feelings were reserved, therefore, for personal letters which took on a semi-official nature. From these Mrs Hart was able to construct a portrait of an unbending, unhumorous obsessional in her influential article carried by the *English Historical Review* in 1960. In character he appears almost the parody of a Prussian, admiring Germany and asking what were the English but improved Germans? The Irish famine of the 1840s, with whose relief he was officially charged, was to Trevelyan a calamity sent by God to teach the Irish the error of their indolent ways. Indolence he loathed in all its forms even when it was enforced by illness. Sick colleagues would be urged to improve their minds with Adam Smith's *The Wealth of Nations* or Edmund Burke's *Thoughts on Scarcity*. Detail preoccupied him as it does with many obsessionals. He opened all his letters himself. He was fanatical about creating a good record of his own activities as he went along and was appalled by the general condition of public records and peppered the Master of the Rolls, whose responsibility they were, with letters on the subject. Trevelyan's formidable energies were also directed literally to such minor economies in Government Offices as candles, wax and stationery. As a result of this absurd and self-imposed overload the Official Head of the Treasury would work through his lunchtimes and regarded holidays not spent in an improving fashion as sinful. Trevelyan was, in many ways, a monster, but a monster in the public interest. He was possessed by the spirit of improvement. 'He never saw,' wrote Jenifer Hart, 'any reason why the *status quo* should be accepted if it were not satisfactory.'[70] And the inefficient structure and practices of most Whitehall departments were quite unacceptable to him.

By the time Russell's Whig government fell in February 1852 economy reviews had been completed into the Home Office, the Foreign Office, the Colonial Office, the Irish Office, the War Office and the Treasury itself. Trevelyan or one of his Treasury people had been part of the review team. In each case Trevelyan pushed his pet reforms – the division of work into mechanical and intellectual labour and promotion on merit instead of time-serving. He won a breakthrough at the Colonial Office. Earl Grey, the Colonial Secretary, accepted the report. For Trevelyan, the Colonial Office became the very model of a modern government department, 'the first model for the constitution of a Public Office on the principle of making a proper distinction between intellectual and mechanical labour'.[71]

But, like all genuine reformers, Trevelyan encountered fierce resistance. The permanent secretaries of the Home and Foreign Offices rejected his recommendations and refused to permit the reports dealing with their departments to be published. The permanent secretary at the War Office counter-attacked vigorously. Even Trevelyan's own political chief, Sir Charles Wood, the Chancellor of the Exchequer, refused to implement wholly the division of labour by which his top official set such store.[72] The politics of reform were fluid and uncertain as were the rapidly changing administrations of 1852. But a crucial breakthrough was in prospect. A powerful, determined political patron was about to arrive – W. E. Gladstone, a figure as monumentally and evangelically monomanic as Trevelyan himself.

Gladstone arrived at the Treasury in December 1852 to begin the first of his two great terms as Chancellor of the Exchequer (1852–5, 1859–66). Happily for Trevelyan, the new Chancellor not only sympathised with his Permanent Secretary's ideas but boosted the Treasury's political clout relative to other departments, another indispensable ingredient in the accumulating preconditions of reform. 'As Chancellor', H. C. G. Matthew explains,

> Gladstone acted independently. He also acted aggressively. His years at the Treasury coincided with reform of that institution from within which Gladstone both shared and encouraged. The Treasury was asserting its right to control the activities and personnel of the Civil Service as a whole; Gladstone asserted the political position of the Chancellor in the Cabinet, in Parliament, and hence in the country generally.[73]

Gladstone pressed on with the individual departmental investigations which had so infuriated the traditional Whitehall baronies and fuelled the resentment against the 'Hardlines' characteristics of Trevelyan. It was Gladstone, too, who brought in Sir Stafford Northcote who was shortly to become the Marks to Trevelyan's Spencer. Northcote, though now a politician, had been a civil servant in the Board of Trade until he was forced by personal and domestic causes to relinquish his official career. Northcote suggested to Gladstone that he might help with the forthcoming inquiry into his old department. Gladstone agreed. The report into the Board of Trade which resulted was described by Trevelyan as a 'masterpiece',[74] which is not surprising as its findings were totally along Trevelyanish lines – division of labour into mechanical and intellectual work and recruitment on the basis of competitive examination. The Board of Trade inquiry was completed in March 1853 and Northcote entered into partnership with Trevelyan for a combined assault on the most difficult peak of all, the Civil Service as a whole. The man and the hour had come. For Henry Roseveare, Trevelyan was a 'bureaucratic hound of the Baskervilles ... born to do violence to all that was idle, wasteful and ungodly'.[75]

Once again, it was Gladstone, the crucial political patron of reform, who slipped the hound from its leash. He did it by that powerful bureaucratic device, the Treasury Minute (huge enterprises have been created solely by this method like the University Grants Committee in 1919). On 12 April 1853, Gladstone commissioned a Civil Service-wide review:

> For the purpose of considering applications for increase of salary, abolishing or consolidating redundant offices, supplying additional assistance where it is required, getting rid of obsolete processes, and introducing more simple and compendious modes of transacting business, establishing a proper distinction between intellectual and mechanical labour, and generally, so revising and readjusting the public establishments as to place them on the footing best calculated for the efficient discharge of their important functions, according to the actual circumstances of the present time.[76]

As terms of reference go, those were thoroughly skewed towards a particular outcome – indeed, one can feel already the kind of peroration likely to emerge in the final report. Such built-in bias is a fairly common feature of the Great and Good inquiry (see Chapter 13).

The second great twist of the Northcote–Trevelyan report involved identifying and recruiting 'the flower of our youth to the aid of the public service', as Trevelyan put it in a private letter to the Editor of *The Times*. The Treasury Minute took care of that, too, though in a way which suggested that the primary purpose was to keep out the halt and the lame rather than to let in the Victorian equivalent of the Renaissance prince. It was, the Minute declared, 'highly necessary that the conditions which are common to all the public offices, such as the preliminary testimonials of character and bodily health to be required from candidates for public employment, the examination into their intellectual attainments, and the regulation of the promotions, should be carefully considered, so as to attain every practicable security for the public that none but qualified persons will be appointed, and that they will afterwards have every practicable inducement to the active discharge of their duties'.[77]

Trevelyan and Northcote worked fast. They began in April 1853. Trevelyan produced the first draft in November. The final version was circulating within the Treasury in January 1854. It was published the following month. In its speed, the terseness of its presentation (it was only 20 pages long) and the vitality of its language it was an exemplary Great and Good production. But these very qualities have caused some, like the historian Henry Roseveare, to cast it in a rather unfavourable light. 'It was ostensibly based', wrote Dr Roseveare, 'on months of detailed inquiry into government departments, but it remains transparently a remarkable piece of propaganda, a brilliant manifesto for views by no means wholly based on an objective appraisal of facts.'[78]

This judgement, though understandable, is rather harsh. The Report's views were strong and expressed in far from bureaucratic language. But they were based on real, inside experience, the distillation, Trevelyan believed, of 'fourteen years continued labour',[79] and their dismissal as 'propaganda', therefore, is unfair. Yet the passion injected into the enterprise did make it a highly unusual phenomenon. It dominated the Treasury in 1853. It was 'by far the most important work we have before us'[80] Trevelyan wrote to Gladstone on 15 September before taking a month's leave to equip him for the supreme moment when his personal reform testament would be captured in words to be quoted from that day to this, Whitehall's equivalent of Lincoln's 'Gettysburg Address'. And the words were Trevelyan's, not Northcote's. Though valued by Trevelyan, Northcote devoted comparatively little time to the enterprise and was, as Sir Kenneth Wheare, the great chronicler of committee work, described him, 'a sober and cautious character; the politics of passion were not his field'.[81]

Trevelyan wrote his report as if it were a personal manifesto. Its purpose was boldly stated in the first paragraph: 'to obtain full security for the public that none but qualified persons will be appointed [to all the public establishments], and that they will afterwards have every practicable inducement to the discharge of their duties'.[82] Its opening premiss could be used, virtually unamended, in the preamble of a White Paper on the Civil Service today:

> It cannot be necessary to enter into any lengthened argument for the purpose of showing the high importance of the Permanent Civil Service of the country in the present day. The great and increasing accumulation of public business, and the consequent pressure on the Government, need only to be alluded to ... It may safely be asserted that, as matters now stand, the Government of the country could not be carried on without the aid of an efficient body of permanent officers, occupying a position duly subordinate to that of the Ministers who are directly responsible to the Crown and to Parliament, yet possessing sufficient independence, character, ability and experience to be able to advise, assist, and to some extent, influence those who are from time to time set over them.

Hindsight is a tempting but dangerous tool which is always lying close to hand on the historian's workbench. That job description for Trevelyan's 'efficient body of permanent officers' cries out for its application. Only when Trevelyan's ideal had been achieved for several decades did it become apparent to more than a handful that those with 'sufficient independence, character, ability and experience' would very often be in a position to do more, much more, than 'advise, assist and to some extent influence' ministers set over them. The British political class has never had – could and should never have – its equivalent of a Trevelyan calling forth, in Kipling's phrase, 'the best ye breed'. But if ministers are not top-flight themselves in intelligence, character and independence of spirit they are in constant danger of being overawed by the dozen to two dozen Northcote–Trevelyan types in their departments on whom they very largely rely for day-to-day survival and long-term succour. The seeds of *Yes, Minister* were planted in that second paragraph of the Northcote–Trevelyan Report. But this is to jump the gun on the grand scale. Trevelyan went on to contrast what was with what should be:

> It would be natural to expect that so important a profession would attract into its ranks the ablest and most ambitious of the youth of the country; that the keenest emulation would prevail among those who had entered it; and that such as were endowed with superior qualifications would rapidly rise to distinction and public eminence. Such, however, is by no means the case. Admission into the Civil Service is eagerly sought after, but it is for the unambitious, and the indolent or incapable that it is chiefly desired. Those whose abilities do not warrant an expectation that they will succeed in the open professions, where they must encounter the competition of their contemporaries, and those whom indolence of temperament, or physical infirmities unfit for active exertions, are placed in the Civil Service, where they may obtain an honourable livelihood with little labour, and with no risk . . .

Trevelyan painted a grim picture of parents foisting 'sickly youths' on government departments whose salaries and pensions were a lifetime burden on the taxpayer and whose inefficiency plunged the public service into public disesteem. He did, however, recognise islands of virtue in a sea of corruption and inefficiency:

> There are . . . numerous honourable exceptions to these observations, and the trustworthiness of the entire body is unimpeached. They are much better than we have any right to expect under the system under which they are appointed and promoted.

Trevelyan described a system which grossly under-used the talent which, despite everything, it did manage to recruit – a Buggins's Turn society of 16,000 public servants on which the bright, the young and the promising were reduced by repetitive, unnecessary mechanical tasks to shadows of their former selves, where promotion depended on length of service, not merit, where careers were channelled narrowly and permanently into the department the young man entered, where outsiders had to be brought in to the very top positions because the Civil Service was incapable of developing its own future leadership.

This description led Trevelyan to a passage of analysis which is the pumping-heart of the 'new blood' arguments advanced in the 1980s.

> The first question which here presents itself is, whether it is better to train young men for the discharge of the duties which they will afterwards have to perform, or to take men of mature age, who have already acquired experience in other walks of life?

Here Trevelyan, to my mind, introduced a desperate flaw into his argument, one which built weakness into his entire structure and which will, in the end, be the undoing of his remarkably enduring creation.

> Our opinion is that, as a general rule, it is decidedly best to train young men. Without laying too much stress on the experience which a long official life necessarily brings with it, we cannot but regard it as an advantage of some importance. In many offices, moreover, it is found that the superior docility of young men renders it much easier to make valuable public servants of them, than of those more advanced in life. This may not be the case in the higher class of offices, but it is unquestionably so in those where the work chiefly consists of account business. The maintenance of discipline is also easier under such circumstances, and regular habits may be enforced, which it would be difficult to impose for the first time upon older men. To these advantages must be added the important one of being able, by proper regulations, to secure the services of fit persons on much more economical terms.

If ever there was a false economy this is it. Sir Gregory Hardlines allowed his own fetishes about discipline, regular habits and economy to distort the shape of his greatest monument. The word picture of his *beau ideal* for the public servant was a mirror-like reflection of himself, the young man in the service of the East India Company who turned in his superior to the authorities. Whitehall was to be a life-long finishing school for classes of Charles Trevelyans. But to many of the true votaries, shaped by public school and ancient university, Trevelyan's words must have seemed a near-perfect job creation initiative, the most glittering youth training scheme ever devised by central government:

> The general principle, then, which we advocate, is that the public service should be carried on by the admission into its lower ranks of a carefully selected body of young men, who should be employed from the first upon work suited to their capacities and their education, and should be made constantly to feel that their promotion and future prospects depend entirely on the industry and ability with which they discharge their duties, that with average abilities and reasonable application they may look forward confidently to a certain provision for their lives, that with superior powers they may rationally hope to attain the highest prizes in the service, while if they prove decidedly incompetent, or incurably indolent, they must expect to be removed from it.

Trevelyan was creating the possibility for a gifted few of a sheltered, collegiate, gilded, fifty-year progression from entry into public school to departure from public department – and he knew it. He would have purred with pleasure had he been able to sit in the Senate House at Cambridge in 1950 to hear Edward Bridges speak of the Civil Service's 'corporate life' and 'general recognition that we are seeking to do something more important than the lives of any or all of us and something more enduring'. He would have understood, too, Bridges's regret that 'we are, unfortunately, lacking in the expressions of corporate life found in a college. We have neither hall nor chapel, neither combination room nor common room.'[83]

For Trevelyan, as for Bridges, the higher Civil Service would be a natural, career-long extension of the virtues and pleasures of intellectual and personal collegiate life in an ancient university. For Trevelyan, too, his report was intended to 'do more to quicken the progress of our Universities . . . than any legislative measures that could be adopted'. The instrument of this progress would be service-wide examinations supervised by a central board:

> We need hardly allude to the important effect which would be produced upon the general education of the country, if proficiency in history, jurisprudence, political economy, modern languages, political and physical geography, and other matters, besides the staple of classics and mathematics, were made directly conducive to the success of young men desirous of entering the public service.

This represented the confluence of two streams of thought from the Victorian intellectual aristocracy – Civil Service and university reform – which, in fact, proceeded in tandem. Macaulay, Trevelyan's brother-in-law, was the dynamo and the propagandist of the movement. Twenty years earlier Macaulay had been urging that the Indian Civil Service should be recruited by open competition. 'Look at every walk of life', he told his fellow MPs, 'at this House, at the other House, at the Bar, at the Bench, at the Church, and see whether it be not true, that those who attain high distinction in the world are generally men who were distinguished in their academic career'.[84]

In 1853, Macaulay's hour struck, like that of his brother-in-law. The charter of the East India Company was up for renewal. The Government recognised that India could no longer be run, as it were, by franchise. Macaulay was commissioned to report on the recruitment of the Indian Civil Service (the ICS). With him sat the great Dr Benjamin Jowett of Balliol, the determined protagonist of university reform at Oxford. Jowett wanted Oxford opened up, its horizons widened. Macaulay wanted the monopoly of Haileybury College broken as a provider of young men for the ICS. In July 1853 Trevelyan and Northcote travelled to Oxford to consult Jowett. Jowett was at his most persuasive. Speaking of the need to open up the ICS he said the new opportunities for graduates 'would provide us with what we have always wanted, a stimulus reaching far beyond the Fellowship, for those not intending to take [Holy] Orders'. It was to be a case of reform following the job in a new virtuous cycle. 'The inducement thus offered to us', the sage of Balliol (he was only thirty-six, mind you, in 1853) went on, 'would open up a new field of knowledge: it would give us another root striking into a new soil of society.'[85]

Jowett's advocacy worked. Both the Macaulay Report on the ICS[86] and Northcote and Trevelyan on the British Civil Service were suffused with his potent mixture of lofty idealism and hard-headed job creation. Never before or since has a British scholar been so supremely successful in founding professions to mop up pupils. Gladstone, the towering eminence in the Treasury, was equally convinced. Indeed, he pressed Trevelyan to recommend open competition as the only principle of entry when his permanent secretary, in early drafts of the report, appeared willing to countenance some accommodation with the old ways.[87]

The completed report was a charter for meritocracy – the determined recruitment of talent, its promotion on the basis of demonstrable merit and its efficient distribution throughout the public service to rid Whitehall of patronage, inefficiency and narrow departmentalism in one go. Northcote and Trevelyan did not need the services of copywriters to package the objects of their inquiry. The report was punchy to the last, its aims being:

1. To provide, by a proper system of examination, for the supply of the public service with a thoroughly efficient class of men.

2. To encourage industry and to foster merit, by teaching all public

servants to look forward to promotion according to their deserts, and to expect the highest prizes in the Service if they can qualify themselves for them.

3. To mitigate the evils which result from the fragmentary character of the Service, and to introduce into it some elements of unity, by placing the first appointments upon a uniform footing, opening the way to the promotion of public officers to staff appointments in other departments than their own, and introducing into the lower ranks a body of men (the Supplementary Clerks) whose services may be made available at any time in any office whatever.

Trevelyan had already spent nearly fifteen years pleading the cause of reform, seeking allies in Parliament and the Cabinet Room. He was determined to avoid his report treading what Professor Bernard Williams later called the 'pathway to the pigeon hole'.[88] He rounded it off, therefore, with a primer on its efficient and effective implementation:

It remains for us to express our conviction that if any change of the importance of those which we have recommended is carried into effect, it can only be successfully done through the medium of an Act of Parliament. The existing system is supported by long usage and powerful interests; and were any Government to introduce material alterations into it, in consequence of their own convictions, without taking the precaution to give those alterations the force of law, it is almost certain that they would be imperceptibly, or perhaps avowedly, abandoned by their successors if they were not even allowed to fall into disuse by the very Government which had originated them. A few clauses would accomplish all that is proposed in this paper, and it is our firm belief that a candid statement of the grounds of the measure would ensure its success and popularity in the country, and would remove many misconceptions which are now prejudicial to the public service.

Trevelyan was right to anticipate resistance. The rise of the meritocracy was not irresistible. Mid-Victorian England was not the opportunity society it may appear, given its devotion to economic *laissez-faire* and individual advancement. The sceptics were powerfully placed. They included the highest in the land, including the lady who gave the age her name.

Queen Victoria had grave reservations about 'opening up' the Civil Service, Trevelyan informed Gladstone a few days before the report was published.[89] Clubland was outraged. Macaulay reported an 'open-mouthed' reaction in Brooks's.[90] Northcote moaned to his wife about the 'terrible storm in the Civil Service about our plan'[91] when it was unveiled in

February 1854. Within the Cabinet, the patron of Northcote and Trevelyan, Gladstone, was largely isolated. Lord Palmerston, the Home Secretary, persuaded the *Morning Post* to run a series of critical pieces (of the press only *The Times* and *The Globe* were sympathetic). The Prime Minister, Lord John Russell, was horrified. Such reforms might be all right in India but not here. The result would be the substitution of 'talent and cramming for character'. The idea of professional bureaucrats was anathema to this scion of the great landed Bedford family. His aversion verged on the barmy. Russell saw in the report the seeds of republicanism, as revealed in a letter to Gladstone on 20 January 1854: 'In future the Board of Examiners will be in place of the Queen. Our institutions will become as harshly republican as possible, and the new spirit of the public offices will not be loyalty, but republicanism. I cannot say how seriously I feel all this, nor how averse I am to take part in such a change.'[92] Nearly thirty years later such nonsense was transmuted into delicious satire in Gilbert and Sullivan's *Iolanthe* when the Queen of the Fairies sets young Strephon 'running amok of all abuses' at Westminster to make their Lordships 'shake in their shoes'. In the finale of Act I, the Queen of the Fairies intones all the ghastly things that are to befall the House of Lords, the peers crying 'No' as each sentence is pronounced. The desperate climax is reached when the Queen declares:

> And a Duke's exalted station
> Be attainable by competitive examination!

To which the peers reply: 'Oh, horror!'[93]

Despite comparably noble histrionics from the real-life Lord John Russell in private in January 1854, the Cabinet decided six days after his republican nightmare to draw up a short Act of Parliament for the creation of an examination board for the Civil Service as a whole, which says a great deal about Gladstone's stature and powers of persuasion.

Those gifts were displayed in a 22-page letter to Russell, one of the most powerful to flow from the pen of that extraordinary man. It played ruthlessly on the Prime Minister's penchant for aristocracy. 'One of the great recommendations of the change in my eyes', wrote Gladstone,

> would be its tendency to strengthen and multiply the ties between the higher classes and the possession of administrative power. I have a strong impression that the aristocracy of this country are even superior in natural gifts, on the average, to the mass: but it is plain that with their acquired advantages ... they have an immense superiority. This applies in its degree to all those who may be called gentlemen by birth and training; and it must be remembered that an essential part of any such plan as is now under discussion is the separation of work, wherever it

> can be made, into mechanical and intellectual, a separation which will open to the highly educated class a career and give them a command over all the higher parts of the Civil Service, which up to this time they have never enjoyed.[94]

There has been an endless debate, reflecting the appalling British obsession with class, about which stratum of society was intended to benefit from Northcote–Trevelyan – the old aristocracy cleverly adapting to changed circumstances or the job-hungry, emergent middle classes.[95] From Gladstone's letter it is clear that the purest democratic principle was not the fuel of reform, and Peter Gowan is right to portray it as 'a means of providing a bulwark in the context of rising democratic and labour strength'.[96] One would not have guessed it, however, from the way the report was received in established circles.

The almost universally hostile reaction to the Northcote–Trevelyan Report on its publication took its toll. By May 1854 even the tireless Gladstone had to admit that there was no immediate prospect of legislation. External factors now took a hand. The reform coalition on the inside of Whitehall would not have prevailed but for a combination of war, scandal and public agitation on the outside. The war was in the Crimea; the scandal arose from the dreadfully inadequate equipping and provisioning of the British forces; and the public agitation largely, though not wholly, went under the banner of the Administrative Reform Association.

Once more the circumstances were full of paradox. Trevelyan was in charge of the commissariat, the supply organisation for the Crimea. The month his Civil Service Report was sending the Establishment into convulsions of rage he was assuring Lord Raglan that he would have 'as efficient a department as ever accompanied a British Army into the field'.[97] The story would have been hilarious if the human consequences had not been so appalling, as Mrs Hart explains:

> Then follows a mass of correspondence about every conceivable detail: the purchase of mules, the drying of oats, biscuit, beer, the merits of roasted and unroasted coffee ... But the general impression gained is that the organisation was very amateurish, and that Trevelyan wholly failed to realise the shortcomings of the commissariat. Thus he argued and fought fiercely against its transfer to the Secretary of State for War: the practice worked well on the whole, he said, though it could be improved; and one should not make a hasty change. This was six weeks after the first report of scandals in *The Times*, which Trevelyan regarded as unreliable ... The task was clearly beyond him, and his only remedy was to write more and more hectic letters, and to dissipate his energies

> on eccentric schemes such as getting pamphlets about Eastern Languages prepared for the troops, and in sending commissariat officers New Testaments in Bulgarian and Serbian ...[98]

Disasters in the Crimea, conveyed home in the scarifying despatches of *The Times*'s William Howard Russell, founding father of the war correspondents,[99] inflamed public opinion and baked hard existing views among the business and managerial communities about the inadequacy of the government machine. There is something in Roy Jenkins's view that the 1832 Reform Act nurtured an 'innovative flowering of mid-Victorian England' which expressed itself in pressure for institutional change.[100] Writing of the impulse for administrative reform post-Crimea, Olive Anderson claimed that 'warning rumbles of its advent can be heard from the time of the foundation of the Liverpool Financial Reform Association early in 1849, if not before'.[101] But it is the Administrative Reform Association of 1855 which has stuck firmly in the historical fly-paper.

The ARA is remembered because of the literary giants who provided its word-power. No other 'good government' movement has been able to claim the likes of Charles Dickens and William Makepeace Thackeray as its own. But it was not Trevelyanism by another means. These were the success stories of mid-Victorian England – self-made businessmen like the ARA's leader, the hosiery manufacturer, Samuel Morley – urging government to adopt business methods and keen to get more of their own kind into Parliament. Merit they certainly believed in, but not the kind revealed by competitive examination, which would, as Trevelyan intended, merely replace one kind of aristocratic stranglehold with another.

Nevertheless the fervour of the ARA's public meetings spilled over into the Parliamentary ferment stirred up by the Crimean War. Henry Layard, an ARA supporter on the backbenches, moved a motion blaming the traumas of the Crimea on 'the manner in which merit and efficiency have been sacrificed, in public appointments, to party and family influences, and to a blind adherence to routine'.[102] How Trevelyan must have blushed at this.

Trevelyan was mellowing. He found gratification in the creation of the first Civil Service Commission by order in council in 1855 by Gladstone's successor at the Treasury, Sir George Cornewall Lewis, though its remit fell far short of that recommended for Trevelyan's Board of Examiners. He was gratified by the 'intelligent, liberal interest' shown by the Commons and believed that 'that for which I had been labouring for so many years in obscurity and discouragement was all at once realised'.[103] Northcote, now an MP himself, was not deceived. The provisions of the Order, he told the Commons in June 1855, would not rid the Civil Service of the 'great bane of patronage . . . Unless they altered the whole code and *morale* of the service, they would do nothing.'[104]

The 1855 Order in Council instructed departments to appoint only those candidates for recruitment who had received a certificate of fitness from the three Civil Service Commissioners. The problem was the need for the Commissioners to clear the examinations to be applied with individual departments. Herein lay the weakening of the independent, centralist principle of Northcote–Trevelyan. Even the Treasury, Trevelyan's own department, were very dismissive of this. The field of candidates could be determined by the department and a favoured individual put up against a set of dullards. There is the famous, though uncorroborated, story of 'Hayter's Idiots', a pair of dense young men kept by William Hayter, Patronage Secretary to the Treasury, 1852–8, for the sole purpose of competing against his favourites. It was even rumoured that on one occasion the favourite performed so poorly that one of the 'idiots' slipped in and was duly certificated, as opposed to certified, by the Civil Service Commission![105]

Despite the alleged efforts of Hayter, there was some improvement in the post–1855 intake, as Henry Roseveare's survey of new Treasury men showed. Between 1856 and 1870, twenty-two of them joined the Treasury. Nine had been to Oxford and six to Cambridge compared with only six university men in the generations recruited between 1834 and 1856.[106] One of them, Sir Algernon West, later measured the flood of Etonians into Whitehall post–1855 who took the pick of the permanent secretaryships a generation later.[107]

It needed another fifteen years after the first Civil Service Order in Council before the Northcote–Trevelyan Report came into its kingdom. Trevelyan had long since left Whitehall, becoming Governor of Madras in India, that adventure playground of administrative reform, in 1859. The crucial year for *enduring* Civil Service reform was 1870. The reason? At last circumstance had placed obsessional reformers in No. 10 and the Treasury *simultaneously*.

When Gladstone formed his first ministry in December 1868, his surprise choice for the Exchequer was Robert Lowe. Lowe, a tormented soul, had achieved his heart's desire but managed to write to a friend on the day of his appointment: 'I am almost angry with myself for not being more pleased. One gets these things but gets them too late.'[108] Lowe was a slave of intellect and effort. His deeply unappealing manner and his striking albino appearance had not endeared him to his contemporaries at Winchester and Oxford. He was mortified when he missed a double first in classics and mathematics. Monumentally self-righteous, even by Victorian standards, Lowe was ill-equipped for political life. He could easily have become a kind of restless, striving, irritating public servant in the Trevelyan mould. He exulted in the company of the capable and the clever like the best of the Board of Trade officials with whom he worked as its Vice-President. He was formidable on paper and, when out of office, proved himself to be a superb leader writer with *The Times*, co-authoring in 1852 one of the best editorials that paper has ever produced when, fending off complaints from Lord Derby about its revealing coverage of foreign affairs, the 'Thunderer' declared: 'The duty of the journalist is the same as that of the historian – to seek out the truth, above all things, and to present to his readers not such things as statecraft would wish them to know but the truth as near as he can attain it.'[109] In those same columns Lowe had often railed against the corruption of an aristocratic, patronage society. Now he had the chance to do something about it.

In the autumn of 1869 Lowe took the cause of true open competition to the Cabinet. He got nowhere. Gladstone, naturally, was sympathetic but the old values still held many of the Cabinet in thrall. Lowe took up his pen and wrote to the Prime Minister: 'Something must be decided. We cannot keep matters in this discreditable state of abeyance.' If the Government did not act, 'we are in danger of retrograding to the days of Hayter's idiot'.[110] Gladstone concurred but proposed a compromise to ease the Cabinet doubters closer to change: establish the new system, but leave it up to individual departments to decide if they wished to use it. Lowe accepted this as stage one. He created virtue in one department by immediately placing all Treasury recruitment on an open competition footing.

Then Lowe, with the help of his permanent secretary, Sir Ralph Lingen (who had accompanied Trevelyan on his visit to Jowett at Balliol in the summer of 1852), launched a pre-emptive strike against the benighted in the rest of Whitehall. They drafted a new Civil Service Order in Council which gave the Treasury sway over recruitment procedures in all departments. It was put into effect on 4 June 1870, which stands as the day the Northcote–Trevelyan Report was implemented, apart, that is, from those citadels of the *ancien régime*, the Foreign Office and the Home Office, whose Ministers, Clarendon and Bruce respectively, produced the fatuous and now highly jaded argument that as their departments dealt with confidential material the first requirement of their officials was not intellect but character, a quality no exam could test.[111]

Lowe's biographer, James Winter, describes the 1870 settlement to which the rest of Whitehall, 'bewildered by the fast footwork at the Treasury', succumbed:

> The civil establishment would be divided into two classes, one for those involved in policy-making and the other for those doing routine work. The Civil Service Commission would examine all aspirants. A candidate for the higher grade could select as many subjects as he wished from a

list; each item on the list would be worth a given number of points; ratings would be calculated according to the number of points a candidate managed to accumulate. Lowe and Lingen did not leave the compilation of the list to the commissioners but drew them up at the Treasury. They saw to it that the subjects offered in the higher grade list corresponded to the curriculum of the universities. They were not, of course, averse to making a few improvements. They saw to it that the traditional subjects, classics and mathematics, received a proportionally high number of points but they also gave recognition to proficiency in the natural sciences, philosophy, modern languages, and modern literature. They assumed that this higher Civil Service would remain small in number and elite in character.[112]

They assumed correctly. This new public service 'freemasonry', as Lowe described it to the Commons Select Committee on Civil Expenditure in 1873,[113] was picked by some classic high Victorians including the great philosopher of the public schools, Matthew Arnold.[114] Little by little in the 1880s and 1890s, the new breed established their grip, though it took nearly forty years for it to become truly tight. Not until 1908, for example, when Sir Edward Troup was appointed, did the Home Office acquire its first permanent secretary who had been recruited initially on the basis of open competition.[115]

The new Civil Service families were linked with Bloomsbury. It was quite natural for the scions of WC1 to enter the service by the time Keynes sat for the competition in 1906. Henry Roseveare has described the pick of the crop which, naturally, was harvested by the Treasury itself:

> Excluding the first three men appointed in the period 1870–1913 (who were simply redundant products of the nominated competition system ...) fifty-seven of the remaining fifty-eight were university graduates – thirty-five from Oxford, nineteen from Cambridge, two from Trinity College, Dublin, and one from London University. Forty of them had received first class honours at some stage in their degree course, twenty-three of them double-firsts. Sixteen had come top in the higher Civil Service examination. Proof of their intellectual distinction need not stop there. Several, such as the brilliant Llewellyn Davies brothers, were Fellows of their College, with sheaves of university prizes. Others, such as Chalmers with his Sanskrit Studies, Heath with his editions of the Greek mathematicians, were to become eminent scholars as well as eminent permanent secretaries. The whole generation seems to carry the conventional, worldly emblems of an intellectual elite.[116]

Dr Roseveare's social analysis of this elite found a spectrum stretching from P. J. Grigg, the son of a carpenter (a future Permanent Secretary at the War Office and, later, Secretary of State for War 1942–5), to Sir George Murray, the heir to a dukedom who also inherited, on grounds of merit, the headship of the Treasury. In the main, however, the 'competition wallahs' were drawn from another great Victorian creation – 'the Treasury had at last become the perquisite of the professional middle class'.[117]

Bridges, that classic example of the Northcote–Trevelyan specification, talked of the new breed as being bound by a common bond, 'the bond of having entered by the same gate and of being of the same vintage, or perhaps a year more or less in bottle than Smith of the Department across the road'.[118] Seventy-five years after Lowe and Lingen penned their productive order in council, Bridges entered into a correspondence with his fellow permanent secretaries about the desirability of another dose of reform. He received a fascinating reply from Sir F. P. Robinson, Permanent Secretary of the Ministry of Public Building and Works, which caught neatly and accurately the eras through which the Northcote–Trevelyan breed had lived and served. 'There have been, as I see it,' Robinson wrote to Bridges on 1 March 1946, 'within our memories, three periods in the Civil Service':

> The first period was when Government activity was for the most part *regulatory*, giving effect, as it were, to the national conscience. The chief function of the Civil Servant then was to exercise a balanced and fair-minded judgement, and to dole out equality of treatment all round. The next period was the era of the Social Services which brought Civil Servants into the daily lives of the citizens. This work required staff of the type previously employed in Banks, Insurance Companies and, of course, in our own Revenue Departments. It was necessarily largely recruited initially from outside the Civil Service.[119]

The third of Robinson's periods, then of direct and immediate concern to Bridges and his fellow permanent secretaries, was the effect of Labour's nationalisation programme and of the continuing close relationship between Whitehall and industry which had developed during the Second World War, of which more later.

The Northcote–Trevelyan model was, in many ways, an ideal fit for the needs of the nation for a couple of decades, if one accepts that the 'nightwatchman state', a caretaker-regulatory establishment, was all that was necessary in the later Victorian years. Late-Victorian officials were high-minded, the national conscience incarnate, 'a corps of reliable umpires', as a Fabian pamphlet aptly described them three-quarters of a century later.[120] The problem was that from the 1880s onwards, Whitehall life became more complicated than that. The scope of departmental work gradually began to move beyond the reach of a great political figure aided by a handful of intellectuals and a relatively small number of clerks engaged in routine business. The hierarchical chain became just too long for a ministry to be run on the private country house model. As J. D. Gregory put it, departments no longer resembled 'a small family party' and became more a 'large insurance office or, in times of stress, a central railway station on a bank holiday'.[121]

As so often happens after a great surge of reforming activity, a period of quiet and consolidation sets in, whether justified or not, as if the problem had been solved for generations to come. The inquiries which followed Northcote–Trevelyan were wholly of this type. The Ridley Commission, chaired by the Conservative politician Sir Matthew White Ridley, was established in 1886 to investigate economy in Whitehall and stuck to its narrow brief. It made a feeble recommendation about more transfer between departments but it missed a golden opportunity to create a centrally managed, well-organised Civil Service. Departmentalism remained all. Whitehall was still Balkanised. As Chapman and Greenaway described it:

> The hours of labour remained unstandardised until 1910 and no attempt was made to introduce standard scales of pay. Clerks in the Foreign Office, the Home Office, the Colonial Office and the India Office – those ancient aristocrats of Whitehall – continued to enjoy salaries far above those of their less fortunate colleagues in the Local Government Board, the Board of Trade and the War Office. The result of this inaction was that the upper echelons of the service remained essentially fragmented until the reorganisation of 1919.[122]

The thirty years between the Ridley Report and the Armistice saw the total transformation of the British state. It ceased to be a mere regulator and became a doer. The nightwatchman disappeared for ever. Long before the Kaiser's War the human requirements of the state machine began to shift irreversibly as did its size: when Northcote and Trevelyan reported it was around 40,000; when Gladstone and Lowe implemented their recommendations in 1870 it was over 50,000; by the early 1890s it was nudging 80,000.[123] But no politician in office made the connection between manpower growth, new tasks and the new modes of thought, organisation and recruitment that might be needed to reflect them, and no late-Victorian or early-Edwardian Northcotes and Trevelyans were sought. By the turn of the century the 1870-model public servant was already a period-piece and ill-prepared for the demands that were about to be made on him.

2 WELFARE, WAR AND PEACE

We must bring the magic of averages nearer to the rescue of the millions.
Winston Churchill, frequently[1]

Men of push and go.
Lloyd George on the businessmen and experts brought into wartime Whitehall, frequently[2]

The [interwar] period is the one in which the higher Civil Service in Britain probably reached the heights of its corporate influence.
Professor Lord Beloff, 1975[3]

There are twin dangers in writing about central government in the two decades before the First World War: the first is to read back into its history too many of the preoccupations of the *last* decades of the twentieth century, particularly the corporatist relationships between government and powerful interest groups, especially the trade unions and employers, relationships whose deliberate rupture was part of the proclaimed political aims of Mrs Thatcher. The seeds were there, certainly. But there was nothing inevitable at that stage about their germination and growth. The second danger is linked to this: it is the writing of history in terms of the great and dynamic figures of the era. There are always more routineers than innovators in a bureaucracy and the late Victorian–Edwardian era is no exception despite its fluidity.

Nonetheless, while bearing such caveats in mind, the most illuminating way of perceiving the manner in which the nightwatchman official became something recognisably different is to examine the cases of two men who had made their personal, interventionist marks some years before the advent of the reforming Liberal administration of 1906 which is usually taken as the starting-gun for the growth of the big state. The first is Hubert Llewellyn Smith. Llewellyn Smith was first head (or Labour Commissioner) in the Board of Trade's newly created Labour Department in 1893. The man and the department were pathfinders. A. J. Mundella, the President of the Board of Trade, called it 'a big thing – larger and more important than the Government itself apprehends. It will do great work in the future.'[4] It was, in fact, the prototype of a modern ministry. It examined the causes of unemployment, the use of manpower and the condition of the labour market. It compiled statistics on strikes and lock-outs and accumulated a census of wages. It published its statistics and, from the start, a *Labour Gazette* 'to provide a sound basis for the formation of opinions' as Llewellyn Smith put it. It was Whitehall's first interventionist economic department and, according to the Board's official historian, it very largely created this role for itself with Parliament belatedly recognising the fact: 'Towards the end of the nineteenth century, having no statutory authority to do so, the Board intervened in various trade disputes, notably those in the coal, and boot and shoe trades, mainly because of the damage caused to industry. The 1896 Conciliation Act was passed to give the Board the necessary authority to negotiate settlement of trade disputes.'[5]

It was, perhaps, asking too much of clever, socially concerned officials to confine themselves to regulatory duties. They itched to be players as well as umpires. And the Botham of his day was undoubtedly Robert Morant at the Board of Education. Morant, Wykehamist, theologian and former tutor to the Crown Prince of Siam, was seeking to overturn the 1870 educational settlement, based on the elementary school, and to replace it with a national system of locally funded secondary schools. He laid siege to the issue, his ministers, the Cabinet – anybody he thought mattered. He even stooped to the clandestine, arriving at the Board's deserted offices on Boxing Day 1898 for a secret meeting with a local government figure crucial to his calculations.[6] As E. J. R. Eaglesham, author of a centenary tribute, put it, 'His station was indeed that of a civil servant; but . . . his ability, his personality and above all his sense of educational emergency made him plan as the master mind, and build as the master builder.'[7] The 1902 Education Act is always referred to as the Balfour Act, but it was Morant's progeny. A debate has long since raged about it as a contributor to national decline. Morant has been seen as the creator of the grammar school, the state-funded equivalent of the English public school with its classics and arts bias and as the man who deliberately turned his and, thanks to his ferocious advocacy in high places, the country's back on technical and professional education at the very moment when her economic competitors, the United States and West Germany, were about to surpass Britain as a productive power for exactly these reasons. Morant fell from influence for distinctly lesser reasons, however. His open contempt for the old elementary schools and those who worked in them, long the cause of personal hostility to him from the National Union of Teachers, burst into the open in a leaked Board of Education minute in 1910 and he was transferred to a new and natural home for the interventionist/activist – the embryonic National Insurance Commission.[8]

A policy entrepreneur with the magnetism and obsessional force of a Morant would fit ill in the Civil Service of the 1980s. Such figures, indeed, were rarities in peacetime Whitehall after the 1919 reorganisation (see above, pp. 71–5). The Civil Service was still remarkably fluid in the early years of the century, however, and not yet the rigid caste-for-life it was later to become. Of forty-seven permanent secretaries appointed between 1900 and 1919, fourteen (nearly 30 per cent) had begun life in another profession. They were very young by today's standards. The average age was just under forty.[9] And there was two-way movement between politics and administration of a kind unheard-of in Britain now though commonplace in France. As the Royal Institute of Public Administration's report on top appointments put it in 1987:

> At that time the distinction between political and Civil Service careers, although pronounced, had not the absolute clarity that it has today. To some extent, social background and connection helped to bridge the worlds of Whitehall and Westminster. A few successfully moved from one sphere into the other. In the sixty years after Northcote–Trevelyan, a handful of former MPs and junior ministers were appointed to permanent secretaryships, and as late as 1906 [Sir George Kekewich, Secretary to the Board of Education, 1900–3] a former permanent secretary was elected as a Liberal MP.[10]

It was not until Sir Warren Fisher's tidy, centralising mind was allowed full sway over the profession after the First World War that 'the higher bureaucracy emerged as a distinctive career Civil Service, one which was both highly centralised and which insulated its members from any systematic political influence over their careers'.[11]

The early Edwardian Civil Service is one of four periods when the profession was subject to a mixture of new blood and new methods. Each is of great importance to the would-be reformer of late-twentieth-century Whitehall, as opening-up the Civil Service – and keeping it open – is the key to a successful and long-lasting transformation. The first transfusion, as we have seen, was injected when the Northcote–Trevelyan reforms were implemented, particularly after 1870. The second was the era of the 'New Liberalism' associated with the 1906 government; the third, the First World War when businessmen and experts were brought in; and, most important of all, during the Second World War when Whitehall became an adventure playground for all the talents. But this is to jump the historical gun.

The 'New Liberalism' transfusion is the least known and the least appreciated. It occurred just as the men in the upper reaches of Whitehall were completing, in Jill Pellew's phrase, the transition from clerks to bureaucrats[12] when 'these competent and self-assured administrators had yet to become a closed caste'.[13] Even the Foreign Office, with its aristocratic disdain for the rest of Whitehall practice, did something in the early years of the new century about the historical time-lag in which it habitually found itself. At last it underwent its own version of Northcote–Trevelyan. Trevelyan's role was played by Francis Villiers, an assistant secretary, who lobbied his permanent secretary, Sir Thomas Sanderson, pointing out the gap between the calibre of the officials recruited and the tedium of the work they were required to perform. Lord Lansdowne, Foreign Secretary in A. J. Balfour's administration, was persuaded and 'the first steps were taken which led to a greater devolution of responsibility throughout the establishment'.[14]

But it was the Campbell-Bannerman and Asquith Cabinets which placed new demands on the state that were beyond the scope of the existing machine and its minders to meet. The outside expert, like the young William Beveridge, creator of the first Labour Exchanges, slipped naturally into the reforming Board of Trade under its immensely progressive President, Winston Churchill, in 1908. Llewellyn Smith, by this stage the Board's permanent secretary, saw nothing untoward in this. He had, after all, worked as an assistant to that great social surveyor, Charles Booth, before sitting the Civil Service examinations. Edwardian Whitehall was porous, not impervious, when it came to the flow of ideas, and the Fabians, in particular, were not slow to seize the chance of enhancing state activities in directions they regarded as wholly beneficial. The 'New Liberalism' was the Whitehall version of a wider European phenomenon captured by E. J. Hobsbawm in his *The Age of Empire*. 'The British Jurist, A. V. Dicey', wrote Hobsbawm,

> saw the steamroller of collectivism, which had been in motion since 1870, flattening the landscape of individual liberty into the centralised and levelling tyranny of school meals, health insurance and old age pensions. And in a sense he was right. Bismarck, logical as always, had already decided in the 1880s to cut the ground from under socialist agitation by an ambitious scheme of social insurance, and he was to be followed on this road by Austria and the British Liberal governments of 1906–14 . . .
>
> Dicey was also right in expressing the inevitable growth in the role and weight of the state apparatus, once the ideal of state non-intervention was abandoned. By modern standards bureaucracy remained modest,

> though it grew at a rapid rate – nowhere more so than Great Britain, where Government employment tripled between 1891 and 1911.[15]

The period delineated by Hobsbawm was, in its own way, as formative for the modern Civil Service as was Northcote–Trevelyan. It produced something of a revolution in tasks and staffing where they had achieved a transformation in the principle and practice of recruitment.

Regrettably, the Civil Service inquiry which ran concurrently with this promising fluidity of people and thought ignored it almost completely. The MacDonnell Royal Commission of 1912–14, as John Turner aptly expressed it, 'stands out, not only for the volume of evidence it reviewed, but for its towering reluctance to see the wood for the trees'.[16] It was a classic, painstaking pedestrian exercise by the great and the good with consolidation, not innovation, as its purpose. Its expressed aim, reflecting the sputter of parliamentary agitation which had preceded it, was to examine biases in recruitment. This it did, looking at the education system, recruitment, pay and grading. But it ignored the new demands on the Civil Service and the question of what, in the changing circumstances of state intervention and, by this stage, rearmament, it was there to do. Some of those it called to give evidence, like Lord Haldane in particular, tried to raise the sights of the MacDonnell Commission but to no avail.

The irrelevance of such periodic inquiries, particularly if they are treated as a matter of almost cyclical routine, is shown by what was happening – and, indeed, had already happened – in the Whitehall that the Royal Commission was pondering ('probing' would be too vigorous a verb). The crucial change agent was – as in the end, it has to be – a politician, David Lloyd George. The key to understanding Lloyd George as the twentieth century's greatest architect of governmental institutions is the appreciation of a paradox. 'He was', as John Turner noted, 'notoriously indifferent to detail in the machinery of government.'[17] Yet he was, as Kenneth O. Morgan described him, 'an artist in the use of power'.[18]

It was Lloyd George's arrival at the Board of Trade in 1906 which began the Edwardian revolution in government. In machinery terms, he was a Trotskyite, a bringer of perpetual revolution, and some of the effects were permanent. He was in office continually from 1906 to 1922, a feat rivalled by no contemporary. In those sixteen years he refashioned not only the Board of Trade but the Treasury, too, and the premiership. In addition he brought to birth one super department, the Ministry of Munitions (which did not last) and a tiny one, a co-ordinating brain for the whole system, the Cabinet Office (which did). It was the Lloyd George style, his methods and the people he attracted which wrought the transformations. It had nothing to do with carefully thought out blueprints or organograms. He was a pragmatist, a supreme improviser. John Turner has analysed the process behind the magic: 'More than any other contemporary politician of the front rank, he believed in the efficacy of state action; and by innovating in policy he brought about innovation in method.'[19]

At the Board of Trade Lloyd George found a kindred spirit in Llewellyn Smith. The new President knew how to make use of regular civil servants of drive and capability. He also liked to bring in his own people, often, though not exclusively, from the Welsh 'Taffiocracy', men like John Rowland, a South Wales schoolteacher and secretary of the Cardiff Cymmrodorian, who worked in the private office alongside (harmoniously it should be said) the career regular, the old Etonian, William Clark, 'clever, humorous and diplomatic' as LG's biographer, John Grigg, described him.[20]

Lloyd George relished juggling with the great interests in the land, regulating the shipping industry here, solving a potentially damaging dispute there. If these interests were not properly and formally represented in an institution or an association, they were encouraged to create one. It has sometimes been said that the British senior civil servant, compromise built into his genes, spends much of his time looking for someone to negotiate with. Lloyd George was the geneticist who began the disease – if disease it is. Its first Lloyd Georgian incarnation – carrying on where Llewellyn Smith had started in the 1890s – was Sir George Askwith, the government's Chief Industrial Conciliator, staff officer of what Keith Middlemas has called 'the new Liberal industrial concordat with labour'[21] (which met with but mixed success even when it was formalised into a National Industrial Council with Askwith in the chair during the severe labour unrest of 1911–12). The now much discredited phenomenon of 'beer and sandwiches' and what one No. 10 wag in the 1970s called 'the Chinese Electrician' (the 'chink of light' at the end of the negotiating tunnel) were very much Lloyd Georgian creations.

But it was the transfer of 'the people's champion' to the Treasury in 1908 which prepared the way for the mutation from the regulatory to the social service state, to reprise Sir F. P. Robinson's terminology. There were three pillars in the construction of the prototype British welfare state, the greatest creation of the New Liberalism: old age pensions which Asquith pioneered at the Treasury, his work being carried through by Lloyd George when Asquith succeeded Campbell-Bannerman in No. 10; Labour Exchanges introduced by Winston Churchill, LG's successor at the Board of Trade (there were 430 of them up and down the country plus a thousand small branch offices in rural areas – Whitehall's first regional network); and health and unemployment insurance, known as national insurance, Lloyd George's great personal contribution (though Churchill had tried to get in first at the Board of Trade, his bill failing when the House of Lords rejected LG's 1909 budget and Parliament was dissolved). Together, pensions, labour exchanges and national insurance created a great surge of state power in personal life and the national economy. Lloyd George and Churchill meant them to. Both were firm believers in the remedial properties of central government and the state, as Professor Eric Hobsbawm described it, as 'the only machine so far invented for changing the orientation of a national society in a fairly short time-span'.[22]

Lloyd George himself had visited Germany in 1908 to see how the Bismarckian system of state insurance operated. He determined, as he later put it in a speech in Birmingham, to join 'the Red Cross. I am in the ambulance corps. I am engaged to drive a wagon through the twistings and turnings and ruts of the Parliamentary road.'[23] The enterprise thereafter became known as 'Lloyd George's Ambulance Wagon.'[24] At the end of 1910 the Chancellor sent W. J. Braithwaite, an idealistic technocrat (a classically trained Wykehamist who lived at Toynbee Hall, the East End settlement which nurtured the social conscience of many others including Morant and Attlee), on another fact-finding mission. Lloyd George received Braithwaite's report with typical panache on the pier at Nice in the south of France where he was holidaying. Braithwaite himself described the scene where this 'curious genius', as he described his boss, sat surrounded by his political colleagues Rufus Isaacs and Charles Masterman plus wives, John Bradbury from the Treasury and Rowland, his special adviser in today's terminology:

> It was crowded. [LG] found a quiet and sheltered corner where he could not hear the band too clearly. He arranged a circle of chairs or got others to arrange it, fussing about over it all ... ordered drinks all round, put me on a chair in the middle – a straight stiff one I remember with a table against it on which I spread out a wallet – full of notes and papers – and when everyone was settled down in their lounge chairs – LG just opposite to me – with their drinks, he said: 'Now then, tell us all about it.'[25]

Poor Braithwaite reported on 'the Prussian thoroughness' of the German schemes and was subjected to two hours of questioning. A peculiar setting, Nice, for the birth of the British welfare state. Its gestation was almost as bizarre, with Braithwaite and his team 'scrambling round one large table in the Privy Council room',[26] though at least it was in Whitehall.

The scheme was an anti-poverty measure. Lloyd George believed that a third of the poverty in Britain was caused by sickness rather than unemployment. National insurance (he was a great coiner of phrases which stuck) was designed to tackle both. The Treasury was to raise £27m a year (a huge sum in those days) for its insurance fund, partly by state grants, partly from employers and employee contributions. Every worker receiving more than £3 a week would be compulsorily brought into the scheme. For its time it was revolutionary, the embodiment of Lloyd George's belief in the hands-on state.

The National Insurance Bill was introduced in the Commons in May 1911. After a very rough ride it received the royal assent in December. The scheme was to be implemented using existing friendly societies as the agency (the great nationwide Civil Service social security network was the creation of the next phase of the welfare state after the Second World War). Running it from the centre was a National Insurance Commission which grew from the chaos of Braithwaite's room in the Privy Council Office. To staff it Whitehall was raided for its best and brightest. In those days social security work was the place to be. Morant, as we have seen, was brought in to run it. The commission boasted no less than four Fellows of All Souls and was a veritable *Who's Who* of future Whitehall stars – Warren Fisher, Bradbury, John Anderson (prematurely grand and pompous as ever: 'Look here, Morant, how *can* I explain this thing to you if you constantly interrupt me in what I'm saying?'[27]) and Ernest Gowers, future author of the classic work *Plain Words* who, it is said, learned his linguistic craft during his national insurance days because Morant's people, for the first time in Civil Service history, 'had to explain novel and complex matters to the unlettered masses in plain and simple English'.[28]

By 1914 the task of explaining and administering the benefits conveyed by Lloyd George's ambulance wagon required no less than 1,800 civil servants divided between four commissions, one each for England, Scotland, Wales and Ireland.[29] By the time of the outbreak of war, the Civil Service had grown from 116,413 in 1901 to 282,420, an increase of 143 per cent. Sir Richard 'Otto' Clarke, that great technician of the machinery of government, noted the mixture of the old and new in Whitehall, as the great powers mobilised, and the lag between demands and capabilities. Despite the innovations and the imported experts, the 'new Liberal' state was stretched beyond its administrative reach before a shot was fired in anger:

> In 1914, there was a firmly established set of structures ... eighteen [major] departments, of which twelve were in the long-standing functions of treasury (money, taxes, government), overseas policy, defence, law and order and nationality: there were the Boards of Trade, Local Government, Agriculture and Fisheries; and the Office of Works and the Post Office. This was a straightforward structure, but already cracking at the seams. The Board of Trade had had a great expansion of its activities, particularly in the creation of labour exchanges and unemployment insurance ... the Insurance Commissions were establishing the health insurance system: the Local Government Board was clearly unequipped

> to be the base for the expansion of social and environmental services. The 1914 system was really suitable for the Britain of 1905, not 1914, and in this as in so many other things, the outbreak of war left much unfinished business behind it.[30]

And as if to demonstrate their sublime irrelevance to the task of rejigging the government machine, the MacDonnell Commission just had time before the 'new Liberal state' was tested to near destruction by total war to bemoan the use of non-Civil Service outsiders on the health insurance commissions.[31]

'Wars', wrote Professor Arthur Marwick in his classic study of total conflicts, 'are like weddings: essentially extravagant and unnecessary but a great stimulant in a convention-bound society.'[32] Already by 1914 the Civil Service was a convention-bound, precedent-laden, secretive society. The coming of war did little to change that initially. To be sure there were sections of the bureaucracy energised by the sense of emergency created by the possibility of war. The Committee of Imperial Defence, a kind of prototype national security council, on the initiative of its secretary, the former Royal Marine artillery specialist, Maurice Hankey, opened a War Book in 1911 (Whitehall has kept one ever since) a grim and detailed exercise in contingency planning for the purpose of co-ordinating the mobilisation of the civilian and service ministries on the outbreak of war.[33] But pre-1914, Hankey wrote later (as Whitehall began planning for a second world war) 'the Government had no national plan for an expansion of the army or for its armament. None of the problems had been worked out or thought of at all – exemption from military service of skilled or unskilled labour, machine tools, raw materials, and national industrial mobilisation generally.'[34]

The thinking was that the Royal Navy, the great blue water deterrent, would ensure that the German economy collapsed behind an economic blockade. Allied continental powers would be assisted by a small British expeditionary force and the strongest of the world currencies, the pound sterling. Such was its strength in 1914 that the entire overseas finance capability of the Treasury consisted of a black book and David 'Sigi' Waley. Once a week Waley would record the value of sterling in Paris, New York and other financial centres in the black book. He would convey it to his assistant secretary who would read it and initial it before it was replaced in its cupboard for another seven days.[35] It was Waley's political chief, Lloyd George, who minted the phrase 'business as usual' in August 1914 as the world went to war. It was, however, a verbal ruse. Between the middle of August and the end of December the government 'intervened in the insurance and financial markets on a massive scale ... [and] ...

pledged their own credit behind almost the entire financial system in order to re-establish confidence and to restart foreign trade'.[36]

Typically, once he had seen how ineffectual and fragmentary the partial mobilisation of national resources had been, it was Lloyd George who harried the Cabinet into action, telling his colleagues in February 1915: 'we could double our effective energies if we organised our factories thoroughly'.[37] The Cabinet allowed him to take powers to control the engineering industry. Lloyd George, in urging the Defence of the Realm (Amendment Number 2) Bill, containing those powers, on the Commons said, 'Instead of business as usual, we want victory as usual.'[38]

As so often, it needed a scandal to trigger the change that was really needed. By May 1915 the shortage of shells on the western front had reached scandalous proportions. Lloyd George, a persistent critic of Lord Kitchener and the War Office for their supply failures, was prompted by his old ally, Hubert Llewellyn Smith, Permanent Secretary to the Board of Trade, with whom he sat on the Munitions of War Committee. The shell scandal, he told LG on 21 May, 'has made possible a really comprehensive reform which even a week ago seemed impossible'.[39]

That scandal, as David French has expressed it, 'gave Lloyd George the opportunity to implement his vision of a total war economy'. The instrument of that vision was a new Ministry of Munitions, the first full-bloodedly interventionist department Whitehall had ever seen. It designed, built and presided over a command economy which shattered every standard economic nostrum of the age and created a clutch of new manufacturing capabilities, not least the British chemical industry (ICI provided a room in their headquarters for LG throughout his retirement as a thank-you offering). Lloyd George left the Treasury to run Munitions in June 1915.

His first day as Minister is the stuff of which legend is made. A. J. P. Taylor, in his famous Leslie Stephen Lecture at Cambridge University in 1961, 'Lloyd George: Rise and Fall', which sparked off a brilliant revival of LG studies, said:

> Any other man would have quailed at starting a Ministry of Munitions from scratch. Lloyd George rejoiced that when he entered the requisitioned hotel allotted to the new ministry, it contained a table, two chairs, many mirrors – and no civil servants. Alone among Liberal ministers, he appreciated that the War could not be conducted on the basis of *laissez-faire*.[40]

Like most legends, this has an element of myth. Lloyd George inherited quite a hefty supply organisation from the War Office. But it and its officials were dwarfed by what was to come. It grew into a mega-ministry, its headquarters staff mushrooming from nil to 12,000 in its first year, peaking at 25,000 when the war ended in November 1918. 'It encompassed, in part at least, the functions of an Ordnance Department, a Ministry of Supply, a Ministry of Labour, a Ministry of Science and Technology, the Board of Trade and the Home Office.'[40]

As usual, Lloyd George shook his own very personal cocktail of men and methods. Llewellyn Smith came to join his old chief. But it was as Whitehall's first businessmen's department that the Ministry of Munitions is remembered. In his memoirs, Lloyd George claimed that within a month there were 'at least 90 men of first class business experience' working for him.[42] Eric Geddes, who became a minister in the postwar coalition, was his favourite trouble-shooter, sorting out the lethargic supply of rifles and congestion at the Woolwich Arsenal. Geddes was the incarnation of push and go. Such men, with whom Lloyd George had become used to dealing in the prewar Board of Trade, were crucial to the pursuit of 'national efficiency', his self-proclaimed goal.

Not every corpuscle of the new blood contained the vigour and the capability of an Eric Geddes. It was not just a matter of some of the businessmen refusing to recognise any virtue in standard Whitehall drills and hierarchy (papers were lost; staff, pouring in, were left unorganised). Some of them took the opportunity of promoting their own firms' interests.[47] It was, in its way, a reversal to pre-Northcote–Trevelyan jobbery or an early example of insider trading. Their competitors, left outside the Ministry's walls, resented this, as well they might. The Labour movement, whose engineering wing had reached a concordat with Lloyd George in March 1915 when he was still at the Treasury – 'they agreed to drop restrictive practices for the duration and received in return some rather vague promise of industrial partnership'[44] – was far more content with his peculiar blend of patriotic corporatism. On the face of it, from the point of view of business, as John Turner has assessed it, 'The bargain was a simple one. Lloyd George and Addison [his successor] wanted munitions. The business community wanted, in the first place, money and recognition, and, in the second place, influence over the course of policy after the war. The first set of demands were readily met; the second was not, because the business community was itself divided about what it wanted'[45] – a factor which was to reappear time and again in that peculiar triangular relationship between employers, labour and government which dates from the Lloyd George era.

Putting the caveats to one side, the Ministry of Munitions delivered the shells, and much else. It brought modern machine tools and the electricity to drive them to large sections of already technologically backward British industry (in the new munitions factories 95 per cent of the machinery was powered by electricity[46]). It revolutionised industries and pushed new technologies. The Ministry of Munitions has even found favour with the arch fault-finder of the British historical profession, Correlli Barnett. He lovingly lists the cornucopia of products it developed or sponsored and produced in profusion – new types of steel, aero-engines, magnetos, ball-bearings, light bulbs, optical glass, rubber tubing, higher quality petrol and oil, dyer stuffs and chemicals . . .[47] In fact, the Ministry of Munitions demonstrated to future generations the formidable capability of well-organised and carefully channelled state power, while its founding father, Lloyd George, the most dynamic production minister in British history, knew what he wanted and what he was up against. In the month he moved into his requisitioned hotel in June 1915 he told a Manchester audience: 'We are fighting the best organised community in the world; the best organised whether for war or peace, and we have been employing too much the haphazard, leisurely, go-as-you-please methods which, believe me, would not have enabled us to maintain our place as a nation, even in peace, very much longer.'[48]

Yet another convulsion, the Cabinet crisis of December 1916, which deposed Asquith and catapulted Lloyd George into No. 10, enabled him to attack another redoubt of 'haphazard, leisurely, go-as-you-please methods' in the Cabinet Room itself. The country-house tone and procedure of pre-Lloyd George Cabinet meetings has not lost its power to amaze a modern technocrat of Cabinet government like Lord Hunt of Tanworth:

> Before the First World War Cabinet was a fairly leisurely process. The number of things that government was involved in was fairly limited – they were mainly single great homogeneous issues which could be looked at on their own. And Cabinets met rather infrequently, sometimes in great country houses, sometimes in London houses, without a secretariat and discussed these issues and took a decision.[49]

John Mackintosh, that supreme connoisseur of Cabinet government, described the pre-1914 arrangement (to call it a system would flatter) as operating 'in a delightfully simple manner. Including all the chief ministers, it discussed with little predigestion and no secretarial assistance all the issues of any importance and only in the restricted field of defence was the need for co-ordinated action appreciated.'[50] In essence what Lloyd George did on capturing the premiership was to reorganise the War Cabinet, its procedures and its back-up, along lines pioneered by the prewar Committee of Imperial Defence. So famous did this transformation become at home and abroad that it is said the creation of the US President's National Security Council in Washington in 1947 was consciously modelled on it, or, to be precise, its near identical progeny in the Second World War.[51]

As with other administrative revolutions, it is possible to exaggerate the novelty of the structure Lloyd George put into place inside a week in December 1916. Asquith's War Council, Dardanelles Committee and War Committee (which succeeded each other between November 1914 and November 1916), were steps in a similar direction, but Asquith failed politically to secure the personal domination of these bodies which was crucial to the higher direction of the war.[52] As has often been noticed since, prime-ministerial personality can be as important as institutional structures in shaping Cabinet government.[53] But John Grigg has described the crucial technology-transfer accomplished by Lloyd George as almost the first act of his premiership, when he created a War Cabinet of five ministers, only one of whom, the Conservative leader Bonar Law, had departmental duties, to pursue the supreme direction of the war uncluttered by routine ministerial responsibilities:

> No less significant than the creation of the War Cabinet – indeed more significant in the longer run – was the attachment to it of the old War Committee's professional staff under Hankey, which became the War Cabinet Secretariat. The War Committee had worked to an agenda, and a record was kept of its meetings. But at the same time the Cabinet continued to be run without a formal agenda and without minutes. Under Lloyd George's new model government the businesslike procedure of the War Committee was applied to the War Cabinet, and in due course the Cabinet Secretariat became, in peacetime, a permanent institution. No single change was more necessary to enable the executive to function efficiently, and it is one of Lloyd George's outstanding contributions to the modernisation of the British State.[54]

Hankey, the prewar secretary of the Committee of Imperial Defence, made himself as indispensable to the new secretariat and PM as he had been to the CID, the War Council, the Dardanelles Committee, the War Committee and Asquith. Churchill in his *Great Contemporaries* penned an unforgettable word portrait of A. J. Balfour making the transition from Asquith to Lloyd George in 1916. A. J. B. moved, wrote Churchill, 'like a powerful and graceful cat walking delicately and unsoiled across a rather muddy street'.[55] Hankey was Balfour's bureaucratic counterpart. In Asquith's last days, Hankey talked with Lloyd George about the deficiencies of the war machine at an allied conference in Paris[56] and, in greater detail, over lunch in London on 21 November 1916 when the two men sketched the outline of 'a new Inner War Committee'[57] which, inside three weeks, was to become the famed and fabled Lloyd George War Cabinet.

The start of modern, bureaucratised Cabinet government can be timed precisely: 11.30 a.m. on Saturday 9 December 1916, the moment when Lloyd George opened the first meeting of the War Cabinet. Hankey and

Colonel Dally Jones took the notes which became the first Cabinet minutes ever recorded and the first item of discussion was accommodation for the new Cabinet Secretariat across Whitehall in Montagu House at the bottom end of Whitehall Gardens and the need to augment its staff.[58] Nothing could have illustrated more graphically the importance the new Prime Minister placed on machinery-of-government questions. Hankey swiftly consolidated the War Cabinet's (and his own) exalted place at the apex of the new system of government by circulating 'Rules of Procedure for the War Cabinet' from one end of Whitehall to the other. Its fiat was to be all-powerful. Cabinet conclusions 'would become operative decisions to be carried out by the responsible Departments as soon as they had been initialled by the Prime Minister'.[59] The power and the majesty of the Cabinet minute was established that day and has survived undiminished to the present. Ministers are 'invited' to take a particular course of action, not instructed. But the import and impact is unmistakeable and brooks no argument. As Gerald Kaufman wrote of his experience in the Wilson and Callaghan governments of the 1970s, 'Cabinet minutes are studied in Government Departments with the reverence generally reserved for sacred texts, and can be triumphantly produced conclusively to settle any arguments.'[60]

Hankey's career was remarkable. A Royal Marine artillery officer by background and only a 'temporary' civil servant in his hierarchical terms (a cause of superior sniffiness on the part of some Civil Service regulars), he nonetheless shaped the Whitehall machine personally and permanently thanks to what was a genuine partnership with Lloyd George – though his creation, the Cabinet Office, only narrowly survived the fall of Lloyd George in 1922, thanks to Treasury jealousy, particularly from Sir Warren Fisher, its Permanent Secretary, and considerable scepticism about this revolutionary Lloyd Georgian creation on the part of the incoming Prime Minister, Bonar Law.[61] But Hankey was a natural when it came to machine-minding and easing the burden for intolerably busy ministers. In such prosaically consistent gifts lay the source of his continuing indispensability which was captured by Sir Robert Vansittart, Permanent Secretary to the Foreign Office, with whom Hankey conducted many a combined battle against Whitehall's appeasers in the 1930s. Looking back to December 1916, Vansittart wrote:

> A secretary was admitted to the arcana and it was Maurice Hankey, who progressively became secretary of everything that mattered. A marine of slight stature and tireless industry, he grew into a repository of secrets, a Chief Inspector of Mines of Information. He had an incredible memory . . . an official brand which could reproduce on call the date, file, substance

> of every paper that ever flew into a pigeon-hole. If St Peter is as well served there will be no errors on Judgement Day.[62]

Lloyd George would have concurred with this. After the War he placed Hankey's name on a list of fighting commanders from the Army, the Navy and the Royal Flying Corps which he recommended to Parliament for payment of a special gratuity (£25,000 in Hankey's case). There were protests at the inclusion of a desk-warrior like the Cabinet Secretary but Lloyd George 'insisted ... he was as essential to our success as any name in the list'.[63]

Though Hankey remained Cabinet Secretary until 1938, when he was succeeded by Sir Edward Bridges, and served briefly as a minister in Churchill's War Cabinet, he continued to be something of an outsider in the eyes of the career Civil Service[64] and was even threatened with the Official Secrets Act by his successor-but-two, Sir Norman Brook, when the Macmillan government wished to avoid the publication of Hankey's First World War memoirs which emerged eventually as *The Supreme Command*.[65]

The Lloyd George ascendancy is remembered for another legendary innovation, the Prime Minister's Secretariat, the famous 'Garden Suburb' so called because it was housed in temporary huts on the back lawn of No. 10. In essence it was a job creation scheme for a group of Lloyd George cronies who had not, as yet, benefited directly from the patronage fall-out occasioned by Asquith's departure.[66] The 'Garden Suburb' made a considerable impact at the time and left a lasting imprint on Whitehall folk memory for much the same reason as Mr Heath's Central Policy Review Staff more than half a century later. It was well served by the wordsmiths in the Press who found the notion behind its creation intriguing and appealing. H. W. Massingham, for example, did its inhabitants proud in *The Nation* when they had been in existence for less than two months. He called them:

> ... a little body of *illuminati*, whose residence is in the Prime Minister's garden, and their business to cultivate the Prime Minister's mind. These gentlemen stand in no sense for a Civil Service cabinet. They are rather of the class of travelling empirics in Empire, who came in with Lord Milner, and whose spiritual home is fixed somewhere between Balliol and Heidelberg. Their function is to emerge from their huts in Downing Street, like the competitors in a Chinese examination, with answers to our thousand questions of the Sphinx.[67]

'These gentlemen', as Massingham called them, were an odd collection brought together under the leadership of W. G. S. Adams, an Oxford don with an administrative record in the Irish Department of Agricultural and

Technical Instruction and the Ministry of Munitions. There was a Welsh flavour, inevitably, with David Davies, coal-owner, philanthropist and Liberal MP, and Joseph Davies, the statistician; an imperial flavour with Philip Kerr, Editor of *The Round Table* (as Lord Lothian he was Ambassador to Washington in the 1930s); and a dash of money and newspaper power in Waldorf Astor, the Conservative MP and proprietor of *The Observer*, and Cecil Harmsworth, Liberal MP and younger brother of Lord Northcliffe.

The suburbanites tended to play to their strengths and/or obsessions – Adams on agriculture, David Davies on supply matters at the Ministry of Munitions, Kerr on foreign and defence policy, Astor on controlling the 'beerage' (he was a temperance fanatic) and Joseph Davies on commodity statistics. Rather like the Mark II version of Mrs Thatcher's Downing Street Policy Unit they were intended to shadow clusters of departments, though this did not work out too neatly in practice.[68] However haphazard its methods and casual its mode of foundation, the Prime Minister's Secretariat was a significant administrative innovation[69] – a team of problem-solvers and progress-chasers for a prime minister attempting to run a Whitehall war machine of a size and complexity without precedent anywhere in the world at that time. As its historian, John Turner, has written:

> Another stimulant to the development of the Secretariat's functions was the sheer novelty of the problems facing government. Lloyd George had to take ultimate political responsibility for many things which neither he nor anyone else had even attempted to control before the war or even in its first years, such as the allocation of cargoes to merchant ships, the rationing of food, and the direction of industrial labour. Day-to-day executive responsibility was delegated to a gallimaufry of controllers, directors and ministers. This motley crew could only be managed, if it could be managed at all, with the help of personal advisers who had the skill and information to brief the Prime Minister at critical moments and thus relieve him of some of the burdens of a state of constant and universal emergency.[70]

Very early on it became apparent that the new Cabinet Office was a more powerful beast in the Whitehall jungle than the Prime Minister's Secretariat. Initially, the Secretariat was to filter reports from departments to the PM. But, on the sensible grounds that other members of the War Cabinet needed to see them as well, the flow switched to the Cabinet Office – a crucial matter in a paper culture. As Dr Turner expressed it, 'The Garden Suburb, consisting of five junior men without executive responsibility and with only five clerks and typists to assist them, could do little to maintain the comprehensive and continuous oversight of government demanded by this presidential concept of war-leadership.'[71] It might have led to something more. Adams told the Haldane Committee that a reorganised Prime Minister's Department, including the Whips' Office, should be incorporated into the Cabinet Office as an administrative intelligence organisation. Hankey argued against it. Hankey prevailed.[72]

It is easy to make too much of the Garden Suburb. Certainly it is the prototype for several later experiments – Churchill's Statistical Section during the Second World War (and its brief revival in 1951–3 during his 'Indian Summer' premiership), Attlee's Central Economic Planning Staff of 1947 vintage, Edward Heath's Central Policy Review Staff of 1970 and the Prime Minister's Downing Street Policy Unit created by Harold Wilson in 1974 and continued with modifications by his successors to this day.[73] It is surely overdoing it to suggest, as one political scientist has, that had the Prime Minister's Secretariat survived and not the Cabinet Office, the road would have been open to prime-ministerial rather than Cabinet government.[74] For a start, it was much more short-lived than is commonly supposed, disappearing when the war ended in 1918 rather than going out with the supreme technician of state himself in 1922.

But Lloyd George's 'administrative revolution' consisted of more than the Cabinet Office and the Garden Suburb. He followed up his first creative burst with another from which emerged in 1917 a new Air Ministry and a constellation of new departments spun off from the Board of Trade, a Ministry of Labour (forerunner of today's Department of Employment), a Department of National Service, a Ministry of Shipping and a Ministry of Food with William Beveridge as its querulous if gifted second secretary (he loathed LG's businessmen whom he believed could not, unlike regular civil servants, appreciate matters in the round). A month after the Lloyd Georgian revolution Beveridge wrote: 'For the time being . . . not only the last Government, but the whole Civil Service is out of office, and much of the subordinate government of the country is in the hands of amateurs.'[75] Despite the wailings of Beveridge, wartime Whitehall was acquiring at last the kind of planning and executive machinery for manpower, production and distribution that it had needed since the armies of the Central Powers mobilised in July and August 1914.

Ironically, one of the new departments, the Ministry of Reconstruction (or, to be precise, its immediate precursor, the Reconstruction Committee of the Cabinet), instigated a root and branch review of machinery of government *after* the great Lloyd Georgian upheaval when the *nouveau régime* was bedding down. Lord Haldane's famous committee, established in July 1917, found itself endorsing many of the recent innovations (particularly the War Cabinet and its secretariat) while suggesting more. By a double irony, its effect, despite the contemporary ferment, was less significant in the short term than in the long term. Indeed, the Haldane Report still shines like a beacon (see 'The Haldane Legacy', pp. 292–9, below). It was, perhaps, unfortunate for its immediate prospects that the document was published a month after the Armistice was signed.[76]

But one of the Haldane recommendations – tighter Treasury control over the rest of Whitehall – was an idea whose time had come now that the war was over and privateering wartime departments, the 'mushroom ministries'[77] as they were called, could no longer expect to roam free from central control of their staffs and budgets. As war engulfed the nightwatchman state, the MacDonnell Royal Commission, alarmed by the Treasury's lack of grip over the organisation and staffing of the rest of Whitehall, urged the foundation of a special section within the Treasury to supervise and control the remainder of the Civil Service.[78] The Kaiser put paid to that. The theme was taken up by the Parliamentary Select Committee on National Expenditure in 1917, alarmed by the consequences of the Acts of Parliament setting up the 'mushroom ministries' which vested control over spending and staffing in their individual ministers rather than the Chancellor of the Exchequer and Treasury[79] (an idea revived by that latterday admirer of Lloyd George, Mr Michael Heseltine).[80] Haldane's recommendation, therefore, of a section within the Treasury to oversee the Civil Service as a whole cut with the Parliamentary grain. Naturally, the Treasury was willing, on this occasion at least, to heed the prompting of MPs and the great and the good.

Planning for an extension of its imperium was already advanced inside the Treasury in the shape of an internal Inquiry into the Organisation and Staffing of Government Offices in the determined hands of Sir John Bradbury, one of its wartime triumvirate of permanent secretaries (the other two being Sir Robert Chalmers and Sir Thomas Heath). The Bradbury inquiry and its outcome represent a crucial moment – one of the true benchmarks – in the history of the modern Civil Service and a *locus classicus* for those who delight in tracing the imprint of the alleged dead-hand of Treasury orthodoxy. Ironically, the surge of Treasury power in 1919 – not to be turned back until the Second World War and then only temporarily – can be seen as the last bureaucratic convulsion caused by that prince of unorthodoxy, Lloyd George. In Whitehall terms, the Great War, to borrow a phrase of Max Beloff's, made it appear 'as though there [had been] a major acceleration in the entire historical process'.[78] Luckily for the Treasury, the brake was applied at the very moment it regained its supremacy over public spending, Civil Service manpower and Whitehall organisation. Bradbury's plan was to reshape the Treasury along functional lines, a concept very much in keeping with the Haldane Report. The 1914 Treasury was made up of six divisions of which only one, Finance, was function-based. The others shadowed various departments. The war had brought a pair of extra temporary divisions, one to handle foreign exchange and financial security matters, the other to deal with the new wartime departments. Bradbury's rationalisation divided the Treasury into three branches each with its own controller – Finance (both home and overseas), Supply to deal with public spending, and Establishments to take care of organisation, manpower and pay for the entire Civil Service. Bradbury unveiled his scheme to Sir Austen Chamberlain, the Chancellor of the Exchequer, the night before the meeting of the new Cabinet Committee on Finance on 5 August 1919. It went through 'on the nod'.[82] Ministers, including Lloyd George, were already deep into retrenchment and economy, a process which was to culminate in the notorious Geddes Axe when Lloyd George's star-find amongst the businessmen was unleashed on departmental budgets and the feather-bedding of those 'two mythical civil servants, Dilly and Dally',[83] in February 1922.

Treasury control over the rest of Whitehall, a crucial first step in the economy drive, was incorporated in a Treasury Minute of 4 September 1919 and distributed in a circular to all departments on the 15th. Paper changes, as we have seen, depend crucially on personalities to make them succeed at both ministerial and official level. The second prong of Bradbury's reform took care of that. The wartime 'top hamper' of three, co-equal joint permanent secretaries had ended the previous March when Chalmers retired. Bradbury was about to move on to become British Representative on the Reparations Commission and Heath was about to become Comptroller and Auditor General. Bradbury recommended that just one permanent secretary should replace them with the three new controllers beneath him. That one man turned out to be Sir Warren Fisher, another peculiarly obsessional bureaucratic animal who, like Trevelyan seventy years earlier, was to leave a permanent mark on his profession and British central government, thanks to his twenty-year headship of the Treasury. 'He was', wrote Henry Roseveare, 'the quintessential new broom, and he sustained this zest for years.'[81]

Fisher owed his preferment to Lloyd George to whom he was devoted.[85] A Wykehamist who did not fit at all the traditional image of desiccated calculating machinery into which Winchester College allegedly turns its scions who enter the public service, Fisher was only thirty-nine when he reached the summit of his profession and had been but sixteen years a civil servant. The bulk of them had been spent at the Inland Revenue, that monument to calculating machinery, though, as we have seen, he was among the Whitehall glitterati seconded to the National Insurance Commission in 1912. Time and again during his tenure at the top Fisher would emphasise that he was *not* a Treasury man. He was scathing, for example, about its practice of taking gilded youths as soon as they had emerged from the examination mill of the Civil Service Commission. 'If you do that', he said, 'they then get to work and take their little pens in their infant hands and they write away little criticisms of every sort and kind, very clever ones no doubt, but there is no training for constructive work, or work that would enable them to get the practical experience that might make them Heads of Department'.[86]

Fisher was, as we shall see, to change the circulation patterns of top Civil Service blood. But first, what was his inheritance? He had sat as a member of Bradbury's inquiry (he was Chairman of the Board of Inland Revenue at the time) and had a discernible impact on the recommendations which came out of it. But he was not responsible for the furore caused at the time, and for some years after, by part of the contents of the circular of 15 September 1919 incorporating the new powers of the Treasury, as he did not take up the job until 1 October. The passage which caused the trouble said that henceforth the Permanent Secretary to the Treasury was to 'act as Permanent Head of the Civil Service and advise the First Lord [i.e. the Prime Minister] in regard to Civil Service appointments and decorations'.[87] It seemed part of the increasingly presidential style of Lloyd George as Prime Minister of the Coalition of 1918–22, dominated, as it seemed to the more orthodox, by a group of brilliant, maverick cronies kept in power by the Conservatives, the Liberal Party being already on its way to electoral oblivion, thanks, among other things, to LG's destruction of Asquith in 1916. The reach of No. 10 in patronage matters (Lloyd George's use of the honours system, that other form of Whitehall patronage, had scandalised the kingdom from the monarch down) was further extended by a second Treasury Circular of 12 March 1920 which declared that henceforth the consent of the Prime Minister was needed for the appointment or removal of permanent secretaries, their deputies, principal finance officers and principal establishment officers in *all* departments, the Cabinet, on the recommendation of its Finance Committee, having approved the new dispensation the month before. Finally, the third of a triptych reflecting the Treasury's enhanced power and status emerged in the form of an Order in Council on 22 July 1920, entrenching the Treasury's right to 'make regulations for controlling the conduct of His Majesty's Civil Establishments, and providing for the classification, remuneration, and other conditions of service of all persons employed therein, whether permanently or temporarily'.[88]

As to the Headship of the Civil Service, Fisher was, as he told Ramsay MacDonald twelve years later, 'presented with a new fangled, indeed bizarre organisation the authorship of which is still unknown to me'.[89] But the extension of the Treasury's reach fitted exactly with his grand vision of the Civil Service as the Fourth Service of the Crown (the others being the Army, the Royal Navy and what became the Royal Air Force) with its general staff in Treasury Chambers. His passion to foster an equivalent of the Armed Forces' *esprit de corps* among the King's servants in civvies was absolutely genuine. Fisher told the Public Accounts Committee three years before he retired that 'I have myself to go round almost with a barrel organ and a monkey for these poor fellows to get things'.[90] Fisher, the barrel organist collecting for the benefit of the clerical classes, laid himself open to gentle parody from even as sympathetic a figure as his Treasury colleague, P. J. Grigg:

> The main instrument [of Fisher's purpose] was the careful organisation of Civil Service sport, the acquisition of spacious grounds at Chiswick as the headquarters of this and the arrangement of regular contests with the three fighting services. A not very successful effort was made to institute an annual Civil Service dinner, to be addressed by a senior Cabinet Minister and attended by the professional heads of the other services and *prominenti* from the outside world. Finally he always strove to ensure that the Civil Service should be treated on a par with the Forces in the matter of honours, decorations and customary privileges.[91]

It is easy to mock such efforts. Clerical armies have always and inevitably lacked the glamour of the real thing with their traditions, uniforms, regiments, messes and silver. The Armed Forces, for example, weathered their most acute period of ridicule in the 1960s far better than their Civil Service counterparts during their dog decade in the 1970s. Fisher, in fact, personally led the appeal, the 'Warren Fisher Fund' which launched Civil Service sports in 1921, and sheltered its Council within the Treasury.[92] There is a marvellous photograph, a real period piece in Samuel McKechnie's own period piece, *The Romance of the Civil Service*, of Fisher in front of the pavilion at Chiswick with George V in 1926 on the day the monarch opened the grounds (the picture beneath it of the Savings Bank Womens' Rowing Club's victorious eight of 1929 is even funnier).[93]

Fisher was a rarity in that he went beyond a mere rejection of the status quo. He developed a strategy for his own department and for the Civil Service as a whole and pursued it, year in year out, long after his patron, the supreme advocate of push and go, had departed for his own version of the political wilderness at Churt. In in-house Treasury terms it was a subtle one. 'He found himself', wrote P. J. Grigg, 'wanting to break the pride and the privilege of the Treasury while at the same time doing nothing to lessen its reputation and influence.[94] He laid it down that no longer should the Treasury take raw recruits from the Civil Service Commission. They would pick instead those who had shown promise and gained experience in line departments. This new practice was made easier by Fisher's creating for the first time a service-wide pool of talent from whom high-flyers and top appointees could be fished. In many ways it was the apotheosis of the process begun by Northcote–Trevelyan in 1853. The flaw in this otherwise admirable scheme for fluidity and mobility inside a rapidly circulating pool of talent was its cardinal characteristic of gifted amateurishness. It perpetuated, albeit now on a Civil Service-wide and not just a departmental scale, the phenomenon of the gifted dabbler. Those narrow professional men of push and go, so despised by Beveridge for their failure to appreciate the beauties of the bigger Whitehall picture, were extruded when peace returned.

For Thomas Balogh, founding father of the 1960s critics of the Civil Service, the years immediately following the First World War were when the rot set in. 'The establishment of a unitary Civil Service with vast powers was the result of the victory of the Treasury ... From the point of view of the permanent bureaucrats this was total victory. The threat of outsiders, of Lloyd George's Kindergarten (young men of great ability and expertise advising him directly ... his way of bypassing bureaucratic obstacles in the way of winning the war) was to be eliminated once and for all.'[95] This is not quite accurate. Fisher, after all, like Hankey, was an insider within the LG Kindergarten. Nor was his 'victory' complete. As we have seen, he failed to absorb the Cabinet Office. And the Foreign Office, whose top appointments he wanted to control, saw him off as it had seen off Trevelyan in the 1850s and Gladstone and Lowe in the 1870s. (Francis Hirst, the Editor of *The Economist*, was spot-on when he told the MacDonnell Commission in 1914 that: 'If the Foreign Office gave out a little more daylight, they might deserve a little more sunshine ...'[96]). But the core of Balogh's argument deserves to be taken seriously:

> It was only after 1918 that the system of Civil Service organisation planned by the Victorians became crystallised: a new corporation arose, vastly more important in the life of the nation than any other ... As the bureaucracy grew stronger they grew bolder. Yet, by that time the problems and needs of the nation had completely altered, leaving it with an outdated and rather unsuitable bureaucratic organisation. It became a vast, completely centralised service facing its ever-growing responsibilities with increasing insistence on a lack of expert knowledge. No Macaulay or Trevelyan arose to remedy this yawning insufficiency.[97]

This has the ring of truth. Fisher created finally the high bureaucratic caste, servants of the permanent government made up solely of Lowe's 'true votaries' anointed by the chrism of competitive examination. Not until Hitler and the prospect of war opened its arteries did the inward flow of new blood take place, not even in the twenties and thirties, those locust decades for the British economy and society, which cried out for the social scientists of the kind attracted into Whitehall in the fluid period of the

New Liberalism and for men of push and go capable of regenerating under-performing industry of the kind who had poured into the Ministry of Munitions. Whatever else the Fisher system may have been, it was free from political patronage. The taint of Lloyd George did not last, as an RIPA inquiry into top appointments in 1985–7 retrospectively assured us: 'Under Sir Warren Fisher the higher bureaucracy emerged as a distinctive career Civil Service, one which was both highly centralised and which insulated its members from any systematic political influence over their careers.'[98]

A close examination of Fisher's Civil Service reveals most of the closed caste traits against which 1980s critics rail, from the collegiality of the permanent secretaries, 'who got into the habit of seeking Fisher's advice or help on all their problems and not only those of staffing'[99], to that remarkable grapevine of information and fixing, the private office network. ('He [Fisher] abjured the earlier view that the official private secretary was a mere Post Office and insisted that he was a vital link between the Minister and the machine. His business was to see that the office knew all that was going on and might go on in the political world . . . and that the Minister did not decide questions without having considered official advice before him.'[100]

By 1930, the Fisher system had fully bedded down and he expressed satisfaction with it when giving evidence before the Tomlin Royal Commission on the Civil Service, whose secretary, incidentally, was Edward Bridges, a Fisher protégé and already a rising star in the now all-powerful Treasury.[101] Fisher's own evidence to the Tomlin Commission corroborates Balogh's description of a closed, self-perpetuating, amateur caste dominating the commanding heights of this commanding profession. Listen to his description of the choosing of permanent secretaries, those crucial setters of departmental tone and style: 'The Service estimate of the capacities of individual officers for higher promotion,' Fisher informed the Royal Commissioners, 'is obtained and collated by informal discussions between the Permanent Secretary to the Treasury and his senior Service colleagues.' He was proud of this informality:

> The less formal it is the greater the likelihood, in my opinion, of the eventual judgement being correct. My colleagues in departments, whenever they may come into my room, in the course of discussion sooner or later get onto this question, and they are themselves looking out for people. Names are canvassed . . . in the most informal way a trend of opinion gradually forms itself as to the suitability of people . . .[102]

After Lloyd George, interwar Prime Ministers (until Chamberlain began to prefer appeasers to non-appeasers) rarely used their prerogative to override the recommendations of Fisher and his college of Whitehall cardinals.[103] All this was immensely effective in keeping out new blood. The Whitehall plasma may have circulated more rapidly but it was rarely renewed above the cadet entry grade of assistant principal.[104] The system had truly become as monastic as its later critics claimed it to be. Fisher also saw the amateurism of his top men as a virtue. He told the Tomlin Commission:

> There is a good deal to be said for musical chairs . . . interchangeability or transfer on promotion is a healthy thing as a principle . . . It is not the business of these permanent heads to be experts; they are general managers . . . A man who has been running one of these huge business under inconceivable difficulties can run any of them. Ordinary businessmen do not have to deal with Parliament and the Press and all the things that these men have to deal with.[105]

To paraphrase Beveridge, the Civil Service was back in office – and how. All this was apparent to Fisher's colleagues and approved by them. Grigg wrote: 'When I went to India in 1934 I think it could be fairly said that Fisher had achieved most of his objects. The Civil Service was more homogeneous, more efficient and of greater influence than it had ever been, and all this without encroaching on the proper responsibilities of Ministers and Parliament.'[106] Grigg would say that, wouldn't he? The permanent government had truly come into its own, thanks to Lloyd George's last bequest to Whitehall (did he ever appreciate the result of his handiwork?) and Fisher's singular drive.

The interwar Civil Service and the Treasury in particular have long been in the historical dock, thanks to the 'guilty men' schools of writing which flourished in the post-Appeasement years. Fisher's men may have wielded great influence, but for a scholar who relishes 'men of hard mind and powerful will',[107] like Correlli Barnett, interwar Whitehall was a playground for soft, romantic idealists produced in abundance by late-Victorian public schools and universities who sought refuge in the public service from the ugly world of industry and the harsh world of international politics – the bureaucratic mirror of foppish Bloomsbury. Barnett believes 'the Home Civil Service . . . encouraged the steady, safe, orthodox man of academic approach'.[108] He was greatly impressed by the claim made by the retired civil servant, H.E. Dale, in his book on the higher Civil Service published during the Second World War, that he had only known four officials who displayed 'intense energy, great driving force and devouring zeal'.[109]

Again, it is fascinating to discover that what can strike a fiercely critical eye like Correlli Barnett's as a stark, self-evident blemish may just as easily appear a virtue to the eye of one of nature's insiders like Bridges who, in the span of the interwar period, rose from an assistant principalship in the Treasury to the Cabinet secretaryship. 'A civil servant's life', mused Bridges (a war hero and a connoisseur of literature – the incarnation of the romantic ideal),

> makes him, above all, a realist. He is less easily elated, less readily discouraged than most men by every-day happenings. Outwardly he may appear cynical or disillusioned, and perhaps to be disinclined to put up a fight for things which excite others. But that is because he has learnt by experience that the Walls of Jericho do not nowadays fall flat even after seven circumambulations to the sound of the trumpet, and that many of the results which he wants to see come about in the most unexpected of ways. Once the crust of apparent disillusion is pierced, you will find a man who feels with the fiercest intensity for those things which he has learnt to cherish – those things, that is to say, which a lifetime of experience has impressed upon him as matters which are of vital concern for the continued well-being of the community.[110]

For 'men of hard mind and powerful will' courtly passages of that kind explain how Bridges's successor but two, Sir William Armstrong, could unintentionally appal members of Mr Heath's Downing Street team in 1973 with the judgement that the business of the Civil Service was 'the orderly management of decline'.[111]

However allegedly effete or feeble (and it is a caricature so to dub them), the higher Civil Service of the 1920s and 1930s does represent the peaking of bureaucratic power in Britain, as Max Beloff intimated in his impressive assessment of 'The Whitehall Factor' between 1919 and 1939, small in number though they were (still only some 500 top generalists in 1939[112]). The key to this domination was the Treasury. 'The most salient fact about most of the domestic issues of the period', writes Beloff, 'is the priority attached to financial considerations and hence to the Treasury view. It is obvious that in this connection the fact that the unification of the Civil Service took place under the aegis of the Treasury and that throughout the period – from 1 October 1919 to 30 September 1939 – the same man, Sir Warren Fisher, was Permanent Secretary to the Treasury and in that capacity Head of the Civil Service is highly significant.'[113] That degree of Treasury control had the capacity to shock Treasury men themselves forty to fifty years later. I can remember one experienced official reacting with amazement to G. C. Peden's study of *British Rearmament and the Treasury: 1932–1939*[114] when it was published in the late 1970s. He could not believe how supine ministers had been in willingly submitting weapons programmes on whose need they were agreed to the Treasury as the final arbiter of whether or not they could be afforded.[115]

The story of the Singapore Base is a classic illustration of the combination of power, arrogance and amateurism which accompanied the new dispensation of Treasury control. Treasury men like Sir George Barstow, its Controller of Supply Services, never hesitated to wade in on strategic and foreign policy issues to do with the need for such a base or to have their say on the kind of weaponry needed to protect it despite having nil background or credentials in any of these fields. Any item would be seized upon as an excuse to kill the project. In February 1923, for example, Barstow argued that the outcome of the Washington Naval Conference, the debt settlement with the United States and the United Kingdom's current financial position all pointed towards cancellation. Fisher agreed and, as the archive shows, his manner of doing so once again demonstrates his conviction that the amateur above the fray and special-pleading is in the best position to judge. 'The question here', he minuted Barstow, 'is political on the largest scale and the sea-faring man is not an oracle about such a topic. *The expert is a good servant, but the last person to have the final word* [emphasis added].'[116] It does not seem to have occurred to Fisher 'that the Inland Revenue was hardly a better training ground than naval service for someone purporting to make judgements on such issues'.[117]

The Singapore Base was a story of stop–go, the minority Labour Governments of 1924 and 1929 freezing its construction, the Conservative and National Governments carrying on with it. Lord Beloff has produced an epitaph for the protracted and sorry tale:

> The Treasury's venture into defence planning ... landed it with the worst of all worlds. The Singapore programme went ahead as the political situation worsened; there was heavy expenditure on fixed heavy guns while supplementary air defences were also tried out. What could be argued was that the Treasury was largely responsible for the decision to give the main weight to the guns; by 1934 the basic pattern was fixed. The fact that the guns pointed seaward and the ultimate assault [in 1942] came from the land was something which the Treasury in its wisdom did not foresee at this juncture any more than did the service clients of whose judgement it was so doubtful.[118]

On imperial matters generally, not just questions of Empire defence, the Treasury were arrogant sceptics, heaping abuse on the Colonial Secretary, Leo Amery (a former official in the prototype Cabinet Office). For Sir Otto Niemeyer, a Treasury Controller of Finance, he was the 'Mad Mullah Minister'.[119] As for his ministry, the Colonial Office, there was 'not a glimmering of financial sense in the place'.[120] Amery's sin was to be an active minister pursuing a passion to improve the economic and social lot of His Majesty's colonial subjects. The Treasury presumed itself to have a greater insight into the needs of the Colonies than their sponsoring department in Whitehall. In 1931, for example, the Colonial Office argued in favour of developing the economy of British Somaliland with the long-term aim of ending its status as a deficit nation and, therefore, a permanent drain on the British Exchequer. This is how an official in the Exchequer treated that one: 'The Treasury could not contemplate the provision of additional funds for a forward development policy ... they would see no justification for continuing to incur expenditure on *medical and other services for improving the conditions of the natives, which the natives do not really desire and for which they are unwilling to pay* [emphasis added].'[121]

The personal contempt in which mandarin could hold minister is breath-taking even for the generation that has grown up with Sir Humphrey Appleby. Just listen to a senior Treasury man in 1929 on Leo Amery, a formidable, substantial character whether or not one sympathises with his passionate imperialism:

> Mr Amery's financial philosophy is based on the assumptions that idle funds are available in the market for Colonial investments, and that the Exchequer has surplus cash for subsidies to attract them into enterprises which offer no early return. From these assumptions it follows that if Mr Amery is given a free hand, the land will flow with milk and honey.[122]

The do-nothing Treasury, it should be pointed out, was no different when it came to developing the domestic economy and social infrastructure of interwar Britain.[123] Nor were such superior attitudes confined to Treasury officialdom. Other bureaucratic grandees, like the formidable Sir John Anderson at the Home Office, were equally capable of such haughty treatment of ministerial wishes. Attitudes of this kind were deeply engrained and could surface again even in a transformed Whitehall during the Second World War in highly achieving ministries with political masters to match. Douglas Jay, a wartime temporary in the Ministry of Supply, remembers its Second Secretary, George Turner (who had risen from the clerical grades in the War Office) referring to Supply's formidable Parliamentary Under Secretaries, Harold Macmillan and Duncan Sandys, as 'Our two parliamentary liabilities downstairs'.[124]

Yet compared to the interwar Foreign Office, the Treasury appears almost as a citadel of progressive democratic virtue attuned to the needs of a modern trading economy. The FO's extraordinary sense of specialness and its concomitant – a determined resistance to any external suggestions for improvement – were as manifest as ever. As we have seen, it beat off Fisher's attempt to acquire a determining say for the Treasury in its top appointments. Not until 1938 did it fall into line with every other department by making its permanent secretary its accounting officer.[125] Reform generated from within proved no easier to achieve. With force and prescience Sir Eyre Crowe pushed the notion in 1916 that: 'We are now committed to a national trade policy which will enter largely into the conduct of our foreign relations and may dominate them ... Trade and finance can no longer be things apart, outside the sphere of normal diplomatic work.'[126] The FO did not care to stoop to trade – the task was passed to a new hybrid, the Department of Overseas Trade, just at the point when, with Britain's economic supremacy no longer unquestionable, successful commercial diplomacy became a necessity, not a luxury. Personality, not intellectual attainment, remained the dominant criterion of selection after the First World War (the FO were quite open about this in their evidence to the Tomlin Commission[127]) though the Etonian supremacy was somewhat diluted by other public schools[128] and the requirement of private means for a diplomat (at least £400 a year) was dropped on the amalgamation of the Foreign and Diplomatic services in 1919.[129]

The advent of Labour governments made little difference to the exclusivity of the Foreign Office. Arthur Henderson, the Foreign Secretary, simply followed his departmental brief when pressed in Parliament in 1930 to amalgamate the diplomatic and commercial services to bring Britain into line with her counterparts.[130] The matter was of some importance and urgency in that era of recession and intense trade rivalries and it would not die. But socially, diplomats and consuls proved to be like oil and water – impossible to mix. Some nine months before the Second World War broke out it brought forth a classic statement of the FO ethos from a group which included a postwar permanent secretary, Sir Frederick Hoyer Millar. The spokesman for the group, Sir Hughe Knatchbull-Hugessen, addressed their opposition to a merger of the diplomatic and commercial services in a minute to the head of the Office:

> Though we would be far from suggesting that personality, 'address' and savoir faire are not of great importance in the Consular Service, it is in the Diplomatic Service that these rather intangible qualities are most essential ... He [a diplomat] must be able to deal as an equal with foreign colleagues, Cabinet Ministers, Prime Ministers and Heads of State; to hold his own with Sovereigns and other royalties and to fraternize with the governing class in no matter what country. This means that all suspicion of an inferiority complex must be absent from his make-up. It would be absurd to pretend that these qualities are exclusively the product of certain public schools and the universities or that they are in the slightest degree an exclusive attribute to the Diplomatic Service as at present constituted. The point we wish to emphasise is that in

> increasing the numbers and thereby widening the range of choice of entrants to the Diplomatic Service there is a danger that the Service may suffer by the admission of candidates who lack the qualities which we have tried to describe.[131]

These were *public* servants communing their true feelings in private. The language and the attitudes conveyed are scarcely believable in a mature democracy about to fight what became known as 'a people's war'. They may have been experts in 'abroad', but what did they know of the real Britain they were supposed to represent? Even in interwar Britain, it was surely apparent that British diplomacy, particularly in its commercial aspects, needed rather more skills in its human mixture than those possessed by polished diplomats of the old school.

Another important, though less immediately obvious, area in which Whitehall power waxed between the wars is in what retrospectively came to be seen as the creeping corporatism of British political and public life; a phenomenon totally visible in the First World War doer departments but still present in a muted form after Whitehall moved back in the direction of the 'nightwatchman state'. Professor Keith Middlemas, the great map-maker who has traced the 'corporate bias' in Britain from 1916, with precursor's in Llewellyn Smith's and Askwith's Board of Trade, deep into the 1970s, detects a movement towards increasing 'harmony in the political system'[132] in those years between capital, labour and government with the senior Civil Service as master of ceremonies at the proceedings as the British economy struggled to maintain its place in the world, and the political consensus, eruptions like the General Strike apart, sought to achieve social peace through accommodation. Middlemas's thesis is convincing whether one believes in corporatism's merits or that it left Britain 'a half-awake quangoland'[133] with an economy on a long, downward slide and an increasingly envenomed society.

Discussion of macro-themes like corporatism have a propensity to vagueness and opacity. What is certain is that the Civil Service was becoming more corporatist in its own internal industrial relations. Trade unionism made an uncertain start in Whitehall. The pioneers were to be found among officials serving the legal system. The County Courts (Clerks' and Officers') Association was formed in 1881 in solitary splendour. The 1890s saw a greater sputtering of white-collar unionism. In 1890 the Second Division Clerks' Association, precursor of today's executive officers' union, the National Union of Civil and Public Servants, was founded, quickly followed in 1892 by the Association of Tax Clerks, forebear of the Inland Revenue Staff Federation, and a brace of Customs federations in 1893 and 1894. The Assistant Clerks Association appeared in 1903 from which grew the biggest of today's Whitehall unions, the Civil and Public Services

Association, which represents the clerical armies of the non-Revenue departments and their outposts all over the country. Crown service was not easy ground in which to put down union roots. In Edwardian times, the associations could send petitions, or 'memorials' as they were called, to the Government about pay and conditions. The Treasury's practice was to reject them peremptorily.[134] Their lack of impact was pathetically revealed when Philip Snowden, Labour MP, former Revenue Clerk,[135] and member of the MacDonnell Royal Commission, questioned Sir Robert Chalmers of the Treasury in 1913 about the associations and their memorials. Sir Robert could not recall ever having heard of the Assistant Clerks Association.[136]

The First World War speeded up the historical processes of Civil Service trade unionism as it did of virtually everything else. The crucial lever towards status and full recognition was yet another sub-group of the Cabinet's Reconstruction Committee chaired by J. H. Whitley, Deputy Speaker of the House of Commons. It was established in 1916 in response to Government disquiet about labour unrest in heavy industry. Its first report appeared in June 1917 and recommended joint councils made up of employers and employees for every industry at national, district and works level to facilitate 'the regular consideration of matters affecting the progress and well-being of the trade from the point of view of all those engaged in it, so far as this is consistent with the general interests of the community'.[137] Whitleyism, as it became known, was the very essence of Professor Middlemas's harmony model. The War Cabinet endorsed it in September 1917.

The trade union movement as a whole was sceptical. But the Civil Service associations, to the alarm of the Treasury who did not want it applied to their own labour force, were enthusiastic. Whitley was asked if it did apply to the Civil Service and replied favourably. Whitehall resisted. Bill Brown of the Assistant Clerks, the towering figure of interwar Whitehall unionism, recalled the guile with which the associations pursued their course: 'The service associations jumped to the opportunity. Wherever a Government speaker appeared to commend the scheme to employers and employed, there was a pertinacious civil servant blandly inquiring why, if the idea was so good, the Government, which was the biggest employer of all, did not apply it in its own house.'[138] Eventually, under pressure from the new Ministry of Labour, the Treasury succumbed. Austen Chamberlain, the Chancellor of the Exchequer, accepted the principle of Whitleyism for the Civil Service at a packed meeting in Caxton Hall on 8 April 1919, saying it paved the way to a 'new era for understanding and contentment among the services of the State',[139] an entirely unjustified piece of hyperbole and wishful thinking, though Whitleyism did survive in the Civil Service in very much its original form until the Thatcher years.

It would be wrong to swallow whole the 'locust years' image of the 1920s and 1930s – of depression, stagnation and decline finding their counterpart in a static, penny-pinching state machine. The occasional innovation was attempted. For example, Baldwin established an institution with a decidedly Haldanian flavour – the Committee of Civil Research – with a brief to produce 'connected forethought from a central standpoint to the development of economic, scientific and statistical research in relation to civil policy and administration'.[140] To head it Baldwin picked the once great intellect of A. J. Balfour. The condition to which the ageing former prime minister had been reduced can be judged from the passion with which he told the House of Lords about the range of the committee's work from the life history of the tsetse-fly to the preservation of Australian apples on long sea voyages.[141]

With the installation of the second Labour Government in 1929, an enterprising official at the Ministry of Labour, H. B. Butler, persuaded Ramsay MacDonald of the need to create from the embryo of the Committee of Civil Research an economic equivalent of the Committee of Imperial Defence to tackle unemployment, with its own economic general staff and standing committees which would mix Whitehall insiders, industrialists and outside experts with a small secretariat of top-flight officials to pull it all together.[142] MacDonald, a political leader whom posterity has lampooned as a buffoon or, from the stance of the Left, vilified as a traitor to the Labour movement, was, whatever his faults, intellectually curious until his dreadful physical and mental decline in the mid-1930s. As his biographer, David Marquand, noted, the idea of an economic general staff appealed to Labour's first prime minister:

> For MacDonald, with his orderly temperament and touching faith in human reason, it had great attractions. He believed in getting up early, answering his letters promptly and reading his papers thoroughly; by the same token it seemed obvious to him that the way to solve a difficult problem was to set up a committee to marshal the facts, study them and come to a conclusion. Just as he believed that war could be avoided by arbitration and conciliation, so he took it for granted that economic conflicts could be resolved if the interests concerned could be persuaded to thrash out their differences round a table, in the light of an objective examination of the evidence.[143]

Fuelled by his faith in the power of intellect and reason, MacDonald moved swiftly and hosted a series of lunches at No. 10 in December 1929, entertaining an impressive array of talent under the suspicious, disapproving eyes of the Treasury (sometimes those of Philip Snowden, his highly orthodox and crabbed-minded Chancellor of the Exchequer; on other occasions the Treasury 'minder' at MacDonald's table would be Warren Fisher himself[144]).

MacDonald's guests at his economic lunches were heavyweights – top flight economists like Keynes, J. A. Hobson, G. D. H. Cole and Walter Layton and big figures from both sides of industry such as the steelmaster, Sir Andrew Duncan, and Walter Citrine from the TUC.[145] One secular saint was in attendance, the economic historian R. H. Tawney, author of *Religion and the Rise of Capitalism* and *The Acquisitive Society*,[146] who achieved immortality of a non-scholarly kind when, according to legend, he turned down the offer of a peerage from MacDonald with the words 'what harm have I ever done to the Labour party?'

The Downing Street lunches were a harbinger of things to come. Reason and light succumbed to passion and oft-rehearsed prejudice. The businessmen banged on about trade union restrictive practices; the trade unionists said such practices would not be relinquished without a quid pro quo; the engineering magnate, Lord Weir, hinted that the restoration of business confidence would require the Labour government to abandon its legislative programme.[147] There was no agreement on the remit of the proposed body. Goaded by Weir, the Prime Minister became almost evangelical in his rhetoric:

> In 1929 one section or interest is predominant, and brings pressure to bear on the Cabinet. In 1930 there will be another interest predominant. Hence inconsistencies and mess and no man can possibly stop it. You can have a body thinking, but it must think on actualities which cover the whole of the problem. Otherwise you will wiggle waggle from one side to another . . .[148]

But 'wiggle waggle' was exactly what the Economic Advisory Council did in terms of its influence over policy. Despite its collection of all the talents – just about the best problem-solving team that could be mustered at the time – its spell at the centre of events was confined to 'a few months in the summer of 1930'[149] when the economic position worsened and MacDonald was freed temporarily from his preoccupation with foreign affairs. But David Marquand is right to say of the EAC that 'In the history of British economic policy it deserves little more than a footnote; in the history of British Government it deserves much more.'[150] Marquand sees it as the spiritual precursor of two 1960s creations, the National Economic Development Council and the Department of Economic Affairs. And, with but a little stretching of the imagination, the blood-line of Haldane's principle of research and thought before action can be traced starting with Lloyd George's Prime Minister's Secretariat continuing through the Committee of Civil Research and the Economic Advisory Council to the Economic

Section of the War Cabinet Office, the Central Economic Planning Staff of the late forties and early fifties and, eventually, to the Central Policy Review Staff and Prime Minister's Policy Unit of the seventies and eighties.

Matters were not entirely static on the social policy front, either, in the 1920s and 1930s. Neville Chamberlain was Minister of Health in the first Baldwin Cabinets (Health covered both housing and local government at that time). His Housing Act of 1923, 'the one solid work of this dull Government',[151] extended state subsidy to both public and private house building. Chamberlain, raised in his family's grand tradition of municipal progress, firmly believed that the state had a duty to alleviate poverty. This, allied to his tidy-mindedness and administrative gifts, helped push through a substantial reform of local government in 1928–9 which abolished the Poor Law boards of guardians and brought poverty policy into the hands of public assistance committees answerable to county councils and county boroughs under the overall supervision of the Ministry of Health. Indeed, apart from the Post Office which paid out state retirement pensions and the Ministry of Labour's labour exchanges, local government was the welfare arm of the state carrying responsibility for education, public assistance, public health, housing, slum clearance, roads, town and country planning and the supply of electricity.

Important as these were to the quality of life of the ordinary citizen, it was the intellectual groundswell beyond Whitehall which gives the 1930s their lasting importance, for war and reconstruction in the forties gave the advanced thinkers of the thirties their opportunity to refashion the state machine in their own image, a chance they seized and used to great effect. Every intellectual climate acquires its own, lasting catch-phrase. In this case immortality (and a great deal of opprobrium from free marketeers) fell upon Douglas Jay when he wrote in his *The Socialist Case* of 1937 that 'in the case of nutrition and health, just as in the case of education, the gentleman in Whitehall really does know better what is good for the people than the people know themselves'.[152] In its bastardised form – 'the gentleman in Whitehall knows best' – the phrase has echoed for fifty years. Yet genuinely fruitful thinking about the use of state power and public money was forthcoming most famously from the pen of John Maynard Keynes in his *General Theory of Employment, Interest and Money* (1936)[153] but also from a galaxy of other sources – from Political and Economic Planning (founded in 1931 and precursor of today's Policy Studies Institute)[154] and the XYZ Club of progressive financiers and City men.[155] Harold Macmillan's political testimony, *The Middle Way*,[156] is a paean of praise to the beneficial effects of state planning for the economy, industry and the social services. In the immediate aftermath of the 1987 general election, Ben Pimlott looked back to these groups and individuals and hoped that

'Labour's paradoxical, strangely inspiring defeat could encourage a similar episode of fertility'.[157]

There were within late-thirties Whitehall one or two harbingers of a very modern theme – the politicisation of the Civil Service. Sir Robert Vansittart, a Germanophobe of the first water, became unsupportable as Permanent Secretary at the Foreign Office, given his implacable opposition to the Government's policy of appeasement. Even Anthony Eden, who was shortly to resign in protest at the appeasement of Mussolini, was persuaded that he needed a new top official, and Vansittart was removed on 1 January 1938 into a grand-sounding but entirely powerless limbo as Chief Diplomatic Adviser to the Government, to be replaced by the more congenial Sir Alexander Cadogan.[158] Instrumental in the removal of Vansittart was Sir Horace Wilson, who behind the camouflage of a wholly misleading Civil Service title, Chief Industrial Adviser to the Government, helped Neville Chamberlain run his very personal foreign policy from No. 10. He was, in effect, Chamberlain's *chef de cabinet* and in those crucial years of 1938–9 was the most loathed civil servant in the land. As an arch appeaser he went on a personal mission on behalf of Chamberlain to Hitler and accompanied his master to Munich. When Warren Fisher retired in 1939 Chamberlain appointed Wilson Head of the Civil Service. Beaverbrook was only going a mite too far when he wrote to a friend in June 1939, three months before the outbreak of war:

> ... politics have ceased to exist. In the old days active people in the House of Commons or men like myself who control great press interest were able ... to render their views effective. Today we are living under despotism by consent ... The Prime Minister has been able to establish a personal rule under which Parliament is practically ineffective and under which the Civil Service is silenced by the imposition of Horace Wilson. The power of this man can scarcely be exaggerated ... even the most minor appointments are contrived to fortify his position. The country at present is being ruled from the anteroom of Downing Street.[159]

A month later knowledge of Wilson's role reached a wider public when David Low published in the *Evening Standard* a cartoon of Wilson as a brolly-carrying boy scout traipsing behind Chamberlain as he inspects rows of 'Colonel Blimps' outside the offices of the pro-appeasement *Times* newspaper. Low was by no means the most savage critic of the man. Hugh Dalton, Minister of Economic Warfare in the Coalition Government, used to refer to him as 'Sir Horace Quisling'.[160] Probably no other crown servant in recent times has worked in such an intimate relationship as Wilson to Chamberlain. He would write notes to his boss whom he addressed as 'Neville, dear ...' He was counsellor and friend way beyond the call of duty. His spectre haunted his successors. William Armstrong, dubbed 'the deputy Prime Minister' by Bill Kendall of the Civil and Public Services Association during the Heath incomes policy of 1972–4 of which he was the key architect, confessed to me in retirement (he became chairman of the Midland Bank) that he 'was always determined not to be seen as another Horace Wilson, but that's what happened'.[161] Churchill, naturally, hated Wilson and ejected him the moment he became Prime Minister in May 1940. 'That fellow Wilson', he said to a member of his entourage, 'has he gone back to the Treasury?'

> 'Yes, Sir.'
> 'And is he settling down there?'
> 'I think so, Sir.'
> 'Does he ever come here now?'
> 'No, Sir.'
> 'Good, I won't have him come here.'
> 'No, Sir.'
> 'If he comes here any more I know what I'll do with him.'
> 'Yes, Sir.'
> 'Yes, Rmp! I'll make him Governor of Greenland!'[162]

Wilson served out his time with nil influence in the Treasury as Head of the Civil Service, to be succeeded in 1942 by Sir Richard Hopkins. His power was buried with Chamberlain. As the crowds left Westminster Abbey after Chamberlain's memorial service in November 1940, 'poor Horace Wilson . . . was seen alone, his face contracted with grief, praying for his dead friend'.[163]

The British Civil Service matured and came of age in the interwar years. It recruited its new blood young and kept it until well stale. By the late thirties Harold Laski, that great figure of the prewar London School of Economics, was urging sabbaticals for senior civil servants in characteristically forthright language.

> For what he needs, above all, is freshness of mind, the ability to make new contacts and to assimilate new experience. To be immersed year after year in an office where, inevitably, problems came to him very largely as issues on paper, is fatal to that freshness in all save a few remarkable men. Change of work and scene is fundamental to him. He must be able to free his mind from the embarrassment of detail, to put his travellers' pack, so to say, on the mountain peak from which the vast panorama of life unfolds itself as a whole, and not in the compartments that are his daily round.[164]

By the late 1930s the Civil Service was a staid organisation at virtually every level. A young tax clerk in the Inland Revenue, who read Laski avidly and later became something of a protégé of his, L. J. Callaghan (who forty years on rose to the premiership), has described the stifling, methodical 'rigidly stratified'[165] life in the Maidstone tax office in those years, part of a service in which the clerks were drawn from the secondary schools, the executive officers from the grammar school sixth forms and the administrators from the universities – careers for life with precious little movement from grade to grade. Not only did orthodoxy and hierarchy become entrenched in Warren Fisher's Whitehall – with the expert caged and the generalist roaming free – but the model spread throughout the British Empire and not just to India where, as we have seen, it started in the first place. Indeed, in former imperial territories, the Civil Service legacy has 'proved rather more tenacious than the Westminster system of Government'.[166] It took the collapse of Chamberlain's and Wilson's appeasement schemes to blow that model out of its pool of torpor – though plans for its detonation had been laid, perhaps partly unwittingly, by Warren Fisher and Maurice Hankey a year or two before the Chamberlain–Wilson partnership began to flourish.

3 HITLER'S REFORM

The theory before the war started was that the UK wasn't going to make the same mistake as in the First World War when some of our most brilliant scientists went in and were shot almost immediately.
Lord Penney, 1985[1]

Can it be doubted that this new blood would have benefited the Service even had there been no war?
Sir Norman Chester, 1951[2]

It's very unlike the Great and Good. They really were winners!
Sir John Winnifrith, 1985[3]

The war showed that the Civil Service could manage against objectives in time of crisis.
Clive Priestley, 1987[4]

The last person truly to reform Whitehall was that well-known expert in public administration, Adolf Hitler. He obliged the British Government to find new men and new methods almost overnight. Wartime Whitehall was a success story, a crucial factor in producing what became the most thoroughly mobilised society on either side, Allied or Axis, in the Second World War.[5] The mix of career regulars and outside irregulars blended between 1939 and 1945 represents *the* high point of achievement in the history of the British Civil Service.

How it was done is a fascinating story in itself. More important, it has lessons for the growing segment of the political nation which believes that British ministers need a new instrument if the country is to be successfully governed as it passes from the twentieth to the twenty-first century. In a convention-bound society, the would-be reformer can win an advantage by saying 'I've seen the past and it works.' At a time when Whitehall's critics look to France, the United States or Japan for a model, our own recent history suggests that we have something to learn from the day Whitehall threw open its doors to the capable and the innovative for the overriding purpose of licking Hitler.

The torrent of irregulars diverted from mainstream careers to help run Whitehall's war included a Cambridge scientist who was to become their house novelist. C. P. Snow had a name for the breed. He called them *The New Men*[6] – though Lewis Elliot, his earnest hero, the lawyer turned administrator of the British atomic bomb project, scarcely does justice to the glittering *grands corps* which grew up inside the shell of the traditional career Civil Service. Elliot found himself in what is clearly a fictional version of the real-life Department of Scientific and Industrial Research through 'some personal coincidences', not by virtue of his inclusion in any Whitehall head-hunting exercise:

> It was because the Minister knew me that I went into his department, and it was because of his own singular position that we saw the minutes of the scientific committees ... by 1939 he had become such a link as all governments needed, particularly at the beginning of a war, before the forms of administration had settled down: they needed a man like Thomas Bevill as the chairman of confidential committees, the man to be kept informed of what was going on, the supreme post-office.
>
> Just before the war began, he asked me to join him as one of his personal assistants. He had met me two or three times with the Boscastles, which was a virtue in his eyes, and I had been trained as a lawyer, which was another. He thought I was suitable raw material to learn discretion. Gradually, in the first autumn of the war, he let me item by item into his confidential files.[7]

Patronage of the Thomas Bevill type did find some of the real-life Whitehall irregulars, though it was frowned on at the highest levels in the Treasury and the Ministry of Labour.[8] In fact, by the time Lewis Elliot was hearing from his minister that 'some of these scientists believe they can present us with a great big bang',[9] Whitehall's planners had been working for over three years on the machinery of government and the people to man it should war come.

On 18 March 1936, eleven days after Hitler reoccupied the Rhineland, Hankey wrote to Fisher, noting 'we have learned so much from 1914–18 in respect of what our needs are likely to be for a major war, that it seems we should take advantage of that experience, in the comparatively quiet times of peace and do all we can in advance of another major emergency'.[10] As the historian of Lloyd George's Ministry of Munitions, R. J. Q. Adams, put it, 'While it can be fairly argued that rearmament came too late in the 1930s, when it did come, it demonstrated that Britain was not required to relearn all the lessons of 1914 and 1915.'[11] Harold Macmillan provided first-hand corroboration of this, recalling that 'when I was at the Ministry of Supply in the Second War, all we had to do was revive, with some modifications and adaptations to changing service demands, the machine which Lloyd George had constructed'.[12] Hankey, who after all had been LG's supreme Whitehall technician, sketched out a blueprint of the departments that wartime Whitehall might throw up:

Ministry of Food } thrown off by the Board of Trade
Ministry of Shipping }
Ministry of Supply
Ministry of National Service
Ministry of Blockade
Ministry of Information
Ministry (or Department) for the Redistribution of Imports[13]

Initially, the emphasis was on earmarking career officials in existing departments for possible transfer to new wartime ministries in an emergency to form a core staff. It was quickly realised at an interdepartmental meeting in the Treasury chaired by Fisher on 14 May 1936 'that certain Departments such as the Board of Trade would have a large number of war-time offshoots and would probably find it impossible to provide all the necessary higher staff . . . it was explained that in certain provisional plans proposals existed for employing outside experts either as actual members of the staff of the war-time Department or on Advisory Committees connected therewith'.[14]

These 'provisional plans' would have turned up in the War Book, that long-lasting Hankey invention. The latest exercise, triggered by Hitler's rearmament programme, was given considerable bureaucratic status at the end of July 1936 when a Treasury Minute, initialled by Fisher, Stanley Baldwin, the Prime Minister, and Neville Chamberlain, Chancellor of the Exchequer, put it on a formal footing, commissioning a Mobilisation (Civil Departments) Committee.[15] Progress, however, was desultory despite the interest of Hankey and Fisher, neither of whom was in the appeasement camp. There was bureaucratic overlap between Fisher's committee and a sub-group of the Committee of Imperial Defence, its Manpower Sub-Committee, chaired by Sir William Graham Greene. Greene was an old Whitehall warhorse who had been Secretary to the Admiralty and Permanent Secretary of the Ministry of Munitions during the Kaiser's war. He was brought out of retirement to produce, among other things, a report on the 'Employment in war of University Men'.[16] He sat in the summer of 1938 with selected good and great from the scholarly community, including the famous anti-appeasement candidate in the Oxford by-election later that year, A. D. Lindsay, Master of Balliol, W. M. Spens of Corpus Christi, Cambridge, Sir Hector Hetherington of Glasgow, Sir Franklin Sibley of Reading, Chairman of the Committee of Vice-Chancellors and Principals, and Ifor Evans of Aberystwyth. The CVCP had its own group under Spens shadowing Greene.

Greene signed his report on 31 August 1938. It had two main recommendations:

1. that undergraduates and graduates wishing to enlist should be treated primarily as a field for the selection of officers or for employment on special duties and therefore dealt with under special recruiting arrangements.
2. that those of them who have special technical qualifications should not be used for ordinary combatant services but should be retained with a view to their employment on technical work either with the services, in Government Departments, or in industry.[17]

The Greene report mentions 'the proposed central bureau' in the Ministry of Labour, the body dreamed up by the Treasury's man on the committee which, when it finally materialised post-Munich, was to be the pipeline carrying the transfusion of new blood into wartime Whitehall. In the 'voluntary period' before hostilities occurred, wrote Greene, university appointments boards, when they came across a suitably qualified chap, 'should send full particulars of his qualifications, including separate assessments of his personality and ability, to the Ministry of Labour for the use of the proposed central bureau which will deal with vacancies in administrative and technical posts both civil and military and should inform the man that he will be advised later as to the best way in which his services can be utilised'.[18]

Whitehall's most secret organisation, which in the end was to gather probably the greatest collection of first-class British grey matter ever assembled in one place, did not wait for Greene or Spens or Munich. That organisation was the Government Code and Cypher School, precursor of today's Government Communications Headquarters. And the place was Bletchley Park, a mock-Gothic mansion in Buckinghamshire, 'War Station' of the GC and CS. Its head, Commander Alistair Denniston, planned meticulously. He drew up an 'emergency list' containing 'men of the Professor type'.[19] By early June 1938 he had even been in touch with the Women's Employment Federation to find, as the Federation's circular to university appointments boards put it, 'a small reserve of young women with good language qualifications who would be available, at need, for unestablished service' at a time of emergency. Those interested were invited to get in touch with 'Miss Moore at the Foreign Office',[20] (the GC and CS used the cover of 'Room 47, Foreign Office'). Within three months, a skeleton staff was sent in haste from Room 47 in Broadway Buildings, home of MI6, the Secret Intelligence Service, to Bletchley.[21] The Czech crisis of September 1938 looked like the real thing. Trenches were dug in the London parks. Britain's fourty-four anti-aircraft guns were wheeled out. Thirty-eight million gas masks were distributed to regional centres.[22] Suddenly, Whitehall's planning for war ceased to be a leisurely affair.

Munich put flesh on the bones laid down by the Greene Committee. What had been a 3½-year paper exercise began to turn into people. Cards were despatched from one end of the kingdom to another to those whose professional background caused Whitehall to deem them potentially useful. Lord Franks, then Professor of Moral Philosophy at Glasgow University, remembers receiving his: 'In September 1938 we all had a bit of paper from the Ministry of Labour which said "Do you undertake to go wherever you are sent in the event of a national emergency?"'[23] H. M. D. Parker, the official historian of manpower policy in the Second World War, is highly critical of the Whitehall headhunters pre-Munich:

> During the crisis weeks over half a million enrolled in the ARP [Air Raid Precautions] services, and from the professional and scientific world so many offers of help were received that the Ministry of Labour was obliged to set up a special department – the future Central Register to record the names and qualifications of the applicants. Public opinion was thus forcing the government to more decisive action.[24]

H. M. D. Parker (not to be confused with Harold Parker, the Treasury's man on mobilisation policy in 1936–40), a Lecturer in Roman History at Oxford who entered the Ministry of Labour as a temporary in 1941, places the blame for the pre-Munich malaise squarely on the appeasement mentality of the Chamberlain administration:

> It was characteristic of the slowness or the unwillingness of the Government to accept the probability of war that virtually no steps were taken until the Munich crisis to ascertain the supply of suitable scientists, or, in the event of war, to prevent their diversion to other forms of employment where their specialised knowledge would be wasted. On the other hand, to meet the inevitable expansion of bureaucracy that war would involve, some steps had to be taken to identify and safeguard professional men of administrative experience whose services might be a valuable asset to the Civil Service.[25]

Those cards which popped through the letter-boxes of the young Professor Oliver Franks in Glasgow and others in the university world would have come as a complete surprise. Up to and including Munich, the vice-chancellors had been sworn to secrecy, a restriction they found irksome. In November 1938, Sir Franklin Sibley of the CVCP in a memorandum for Sir John Anderson, no longer a civil servant, but, by this time, Lord Privy Seal and the minister responsible for co-ordinating Civil Defence, said of the vice-chancellors:

> . . . in September last they were greatly hampered by the obligation of secrecy imposed by nearly every communication received by them from a variety of Government departments. It is impossible for the Head of a University to make necessary arrangements without consulting a number of his colleagues. It is also impossible to prevent members of the staff and students at a time of crisis from leaving the University and finding some sort of national service unless they can be told in advance what the Government desires them to do.[26]

Munich, it seems, energised the university establishment as much as it did Whitehall's. In October H. H. Wiles, the assistant secretary in charge of the Ministry of Labour's training branch, had approached Sir Walter Moberley, Chairman of the University Grants Committee, and asked him to chair a committee 'to advise the Minister on the utilisation in Government Departments or elsewhere, in the event of emergency, of personnel with scientific and technical and professional qualifications, and persons qualified for higher administrative posts'.[27]

The Moberly Committee blended Whitehall (Treasury, Admiralty, War Office, Air Ministry, Ministry of Labour and Department of Scientific and Industrial Research) with learned societies and professional bodies. They included the institutes of chemistry, mechanical engineering, civil engineering, electrical engineering and production engineering, the Royal Society, the Royal Institute of British Architects, three representatives from the universities, one apiece from the accountants' and employers' organisations plus a single representative from the auctioneers' and estate agents' institutes (to find people for requisitioning land, presumably).[28]

The Committee of Vice-Chancellors and Principals had produced its own skeleton plan by mid-November which was forwarded to Sir John Anderson on 23 November. It opened with a ringing declaration of purpose:

> The CVCP are of the opinion that the Universities and University Colleges can make a vital and specific contribution to the war-time needs of the country and they are prepared to undertake that duty.[29]

The vice-chancellors displayed a range of specialist services their people could offer. Departments of chemistry, physics, engineering, metallurgy and mathematics could help with problems of munitions supply, aviation and transport. The medics could offer assistance on safeguarding public health. The boosting of agricultural production was stressed:

> In addition many individual members of staffs possess skill in interpreting, translating, decoding etc. [the GC and CS brought some into Broadway Buildings in the autumn of 1938 for a bit of discreet cryptanalytical training[30]] and general administrative experience, readily capable of adapting itself to the needs of the Civil Service machine, as illustrated in the last war.[31]

That last, portmanteau category is interesting. It is the nearest anybody involved in mobilising the British thinking classes for war came to mentioning what we would now call social scientists. As for that 'general administrative experience', one wonders what it amounted to. The general administrator on the 'intellectuals' list' who did best (principal to permanent secretary in six years) was Oliver Franks. At the time of Munich he was thirty-three years old and, as we have seen, Professor of Moral Philosophy at Glasgow University. Until 5 September 1939 when he turned up at the Ministry of Supply, 'my filing system had been a draw in my desk and the two pockets in my jacket'[32] – though between Munich and the war he got in a bit of practice. 'I suppose the first committees I ever chaired were probably in Glasgow when I had to do with various pre-war precautions in the Munich year. The University and the City were arranging things and I was in charge of a few of them.'[33]

By December 1938, the hybrid outfit combining Whitehall, the universities and the professional organisations was up and running. Ernest Brown, the Minister of Labour (an ex-regimental sergeant major with the loudest voice in Parliament), signed letters of appointment. Soon there were little sub-groups, an 'Earmarking Committee', even a 'Journalists Committee'. Above all, there was a Central Register, thousands of filing cards with elaborate cross-references, stored at 569 Chiswick High Road in West London. Presiding over it was a distinguished-looking, 47-year-old ex-suffragette, Miss Beryl Millicent le Poer Power, only the second woman to reach the rank of assistant secretary in the Ministry of Labour.

Beryl Power's road to the senior ranks of the Civil Service had been a tough one. With her sisters, Rhoda and Eileen (the legendary medieval historian) she had been left in childhood, as her *Times* obituary put it, 'without any support from their father. It was hardly possible in 1909, when she left school, to get a Cambridge education on scholarships alone; Beryl had to take jobs – underpaid, as she always maintained, because she was a woman – and save money before she could go to Girton.'[34] Out of such experience sprang conviction. For three years Miss Power was an organiser and speaker for the National Union of Women's Suffrage Societies.[35] Success in the Civil Service examinations put paid to that, and in 1915 she entered the Board of Trade as an investigator appointed under the Trade Boards Act. A woman was a rarity in Whitehall's administrative class at that time. Miss Power encountered prejudice. A female colleague who entered the Civil Service in the 1930s recalled: 'She was one of those pioneering women who felt they had had a hard fight. It had, perhaps, left a bit of a scar.'[36] Another said, 'she kicked the door open for us'.[37]

This background and her steady rise in the Board of Trade and, after it was hived-off from Trade, the Ministry of Labour, had produced a 'very forceful person'[38] by the time war preparations obliged the department to transform itself into a Ministry of Labour and National Service. A lady colleague, who wishes to remain anonymous, has a clear picture of the newly promoted assistant secretary in the newly created national service department of the Ministry in the first days of 1939: 'solid rather than tall, dark hair, spectacles, good bust, she walked very upright. She was a little too forceful in saying what she thought without thinking too much of the effect on others'.[39] These characteristics stood her in good stead in the Blitz, however. Like many other women, Beryl Power would be accosted by men in the blackout. Her countermeasures were direct and effective. She would shine a torch on her face and say: 'Over forty and very busy' before striding on.[40] When serving in China after the war, she and another lady colleague were known as 'the British Dreadnoughts'.[41]

She owed her promotion as keeper of the Central Register to two things: the patronage of her deputy secretary, Humbert Wolfe (the poet who died in 1940), who thought very highly of her;[42] and her record as a vigorous and forceful executor of business (contemporaries reckon she was not too strong on policy).[43] The 'intellectuals' list', according to one, 'probably was her metier'.[44] Even Miss Power, however, found the task daunting and she made no secret of it to her friends:

> She told me over lunch she had a difficult time setting up the Central Register. I know it did bother her a lot. I have a feeling she had a slightly raw deal. There was a flavour of indignation. She was absolutely inundated with people offering their services.[45]

Miss Power's outfit, soon renamed the Central Register branch of the Ministry of Labour and National Service, consisted of twelve officials of staff clerk grade and above plus Sir Walter Moberly of the UGC as its Honorary Director and Supervisor.[46] It was something of a bureaucratic diaspora. Miss Power's superiors were in Montagu House in Whitehall. She was in Queen Anne's Chambers (co-located with the UGC) in Queen Anne's Gate. Her more senior staff were in Metropole Buildings, Northumberland Avenue. Her infantry were in Chiswick High Road, under the command of Mr Frank Gent, brought in from the Ministry of Labour's regional organisation for the purpose. They accumulated an archive of cards, some 80,000 of them by the time war broke out. Number 569, scene of the most successful personnel operation ever mounted by the British Civil Service, is now occupied by the Direct Tyre Company and consists of three houses combined into one shop with lots of little offices above.

One of the first waves to inundate Miss Power was caused by the Committee of Vice-Chancellors doing its stuff. For example, on 12 January 1939 returns for the University of London arrived. This is the only file to have survived which contains names, and among them is an entry which turned out to be a big one. Sir Henry Tizard, himself to become one of *the* great boffins of the Second World War, as Rector of Imperial College, compiled a list of his scientific and technical dons. There under Mathematics Department (Reader) is Penney, W. G.[47] If any single man can be called the father of the British atomic bomb, it is he. 'I think I got a little form I had to fill in about which subjects I knew. I said mathematical physics.' That 'little form' set the 29-year-old William Penney on a path which led to a knighthood, a peerage and the Order of Merit.

By February 1939, the Earmarking Committee was grappling with the snags which were bound to afflict a piece of improvisation on a scale represented by the Central Register. By its meeting on 23 February, one important decision had been reached. 'Miss Power said', the minutes record, 'that the Central Register could not guarantee to find a man a job carrying the same salary as his present one, and the voluntary nature of the Register permitted the refusal of jobs offered.' Harold Parker of the Treasury added that salaries would be based on Civil Service rates.[48] Other knotty problems appeared which would persist.

For example, intellectual dynasties had much to do with some of the most successful recruiting. Professor F. A. Lindemann (later Lord Cherwell), Churchill's intimate, brought in protégés from Oxford University's Clarendon Laboratory to fight the boffins' war. And what became the Prime Minister's Statistical Section was filled with economists known to the Prof.[49] A similar function was performed by Noel Hall, Professor of Economics at University College, London, who found, among others, an aspirant labour politician, Hugh Gaitskell, for the Ministry of Economic Warfare where Miss Power's brother-in-law, the economic historian M. M. Postan, was also installed.[50] Individual government departments went scouting independently of the Central Register for the best and brightest known to them. Parker was resigned to this. 'Departments', he wrote, 'might earmark "top notchers" without going first to the Central Register, though they should keep the Register informed of the names.'[51] Some ministries, however, went too far. The Admiralty was insatiably greedy. They were talking of needing 225 physicists, and the Central Register in

February 1939 had only 340 on its books. H. M. Phillips, one of Miss Power's principals, set out to investigate 'whether the Admiralty were drawing a long bow'. If they were not, it might be necessary to issue an appeal to British physicists living abroad.[52]

As war approached, the Ministries of Food, Economic Warfare and Information engaged in private enterprise, to the fury of the tidy-minded Miss Power. These were new departments. The Ministry of Food grew terribly fast from a headquarters staff of 300 to 30,000 officials dispersed in local offices throughout the country.[53] The Ministry of Supply became a mega-department of 60,000 with a labour force of 250,000 industrial employees working directly for it.[54] But some established departments transgressed the Power requirements. For example, the Air Ministry took on the artist Norman Wilkinson as an adviser on camouflage and the journalist Philip Hope-Wallace as a sub-editor without consulting the Central Register.[55] Such confusion appears to have irritated the universities as much as it did Miss Power. On 2 June 1939 she lunched with Sir Alexander Carr-Saunders, Director of the London School of Economics, and members of staff. She minuted J. M. Glen, her immediate superior, that:

> They mentioned amongst other things the great uneasiness felt by members of University Staffs in London, as well as at Oxford and Cambridge, at earmarkings which were obviously done by Government Departments without reference to the Central Register or to the qualified persons available. They gave as an instance the Department [sic] of Economic Warfare where they asserted that some of the persons earmarked were not as well qualified as members of University Staffs who had not been approached even though their names were on the Central Register.[56]

In April, Miss Power had attempted to raise the profile of her operation with departments when she circulated a minute to the effect that 'The Central Register is now rapidly taking form, and we should be glad to assist you through the Register by putting you in touch with any groups of professional people with whom you may wish to make contact with a view to their employment in time of war.'[57]

Some departments had a legitimate security reason for sidestepping the Central Register. We have seen how Commander Denniston set about finding his 'men of the Professor type' for Bletchley. At a meeting of the Earmarking Committee on 16 June 1939, the Foreign Office representative, J. W. Nicholls, said that his department 'had rather special requirements for men who were not specifically covered by the Central Register', by which he meant presumably recruits for the Secret Intelligence Service, M16.[58] Though Nicholls did not mention the problem of preventing hostile intelligence services spiriting their people inside as part of an influx of temporaries (Blunt and Philby are the best-known of the KGB/GRU plants), a prescient colleague had raised the question at the February meeting of the Committee. Colonel K. J. Martin was the War Office representative (the War Office at that time was responsible for the Security Service, M15). He said that it was impossible for the authorities to investigate the credentials of all persons registered. It was likely that 'the more dangerous element would have taken the trouble to obtain first-rate references'.[59]

The penetration problem was never cracked in the Second World War, not even to the extent of erecting rudimentary defences like positive vetting.[60] The privateering problem was only solved once the war started when the Treasury and the Ministry of Labour put their collective feet down. Ernest Brown, the Minister of Labour, to his credit, was concerned that 'jobbery' might rear its head.[61] Clearly, the normal Civil Service Commission procedures had to be suspended for the 'intellectuals' list'. Speed was of the essence. But the Central Register was, by and large, an adequate substitute as a defence against the early-nineteenth-century kind of patronage. Treasury reminders of the proper procedure helped. Miss Power prepared her own solution as 'the political situation worsened'.[62]

On Saturday, 2 September 1939, she was at her desk drafting the letter that would be sent to all departments 'directly war is declared between this country and Germany'.[63] It captures her brisk style, and a specimen copy is preserved in the files:

Instruction No. 13

CENTRAL REGISTER
Placing Procedure

Up to the present, the Central Register has been operated on the basis of the *peace time procedure* agreed in connection with earmarking orders from Government Departments, i.e., cards of suitable persons have been submitted direct to the ordering Department, the volunteers' willingness to be considered for the post under consideration being ascertained by the ordering Department, and not by the Central Register.

As from ...., the Central Register will be operated on the *War time procedure* set out in Appendix VIII to Chapter XVII of the War Book. Members of Earmarking Committees have been so informed in the letters attached, a number of copies of which have been sent to them for distribution within their Departments to persons authorised to give orders to the Central Register.

September, 1939[64]

At 9 a.m. on Sunday, 3 September 1939, an ultimatum to Berlin was delivered from the British Government. Unless German forces were withdrawn from Poland, Britain would be at war with Germany. At 11 a.m. the ultimatum expired and the Prime Minister, Neville Chamberlain, broadcast to the nation.[65] The Ministry of Labour had a fair scattering of staff at their posts as the Prime Minister approached the microphone, including Miss Power and two of her principals, C. J. Maston and Anthony Sutherland. Shortly after 11 o'clock, Sutherland's phone rang. 'Sutherland', said Miss Power. 'There's a war. Come to my office at once.'[66]

> When the alarm sounded at 11.15 – horrors, Miss Power had forgotten to bring her gas-mask! Maston and I had to decide which would risk his life for a lady by giving up ours![67]

Commander Denniston, head of the Government Code and Cypher School, and one of the best-informed people in Whitehall when it came to events in Europe, was also at his desk in Broadway Buildings that Sunday, drafting a letter to the Clerk's Department of the Foreign Office which controlled his manpower. Referring with sublime understatement to the activities of Hitler, he wrote: 'For some days now we have been obliged to recruit from our emergency list men of the Professor type who the Treasury agreed to pay at the rate of £600 a year. I attach herewith a list of these gentlemen already called up together with the dates of their joining. I will keep you informed at intervals of further recruitment.'[68]

The first list was pretty impressive:

Mr R. Bacon	15 August
Mr. L. W. Forster	24 August
Professor G. Waterhouse	29 August
Professor W. H. Bruford	29 August
Mr N. de Grey	29 August
Mr R. Gore Brown	30 August
Professor Vincent	30 August
Professor T. S. R. Boase	2 September[69]

The second list was even more glittering with some of the greatest names ever to work in the trade:

Mr. A. T. Hatto	4 September
Professor F. Norman	4 September
Mr. J. R. F. Jeffries	4 September
Mr W. G. Welchman	4 September
Professor F. E. Adcock	4 September
Professor A. H. Campbell	4 September

Professor H. M. Last	4 September
Mr A. M. Turing	4 September[70]

Never in the history of British cryptography has so much talent been recruited in a single day. Denniston's people, who could not be mentioned in Churchill's memoirs for fear of compromising the Ultra secret, and A. P. Rowe's radar experts at the Telecommunications Research Establishment at Malvern, fit perfectly with the mysterious, faintly menacing image used by the old warrior, Sir Winston Churchill, when he wrote that 'Unless British science had proved superior to German, and unless its strange sinister resources had been effectively brought to bear on the struggle for survival, we might well have been defeated, and, being defeated, destroyed.'[71]

Monday, 4 September was also the day on which the Power empire pressed its buttons. Her stiff note on the use of the Register was despatched to departments. The telegrams went out. One landed on the desk of Professor Franks in Glasgow. It read 'Go to the Ministry of Supply' as if it had come from the Community Chest in a game of Monopoly. He caught the night train to Euston.[72] Lord Franks does not fit the boffin category. He was picked to be one of 'the 100 Principals who will be required on the outbreak of war', a need identified by Miss Power in May 1939.[73] The Ministry of Supply, created only in July 1939, was essentially an initial amalgam of the production side of the War Office and the imports side of the Board of Trade. It was still desperately short of manpower in the last weeks of peace and applied for 'six dons' from the Central Register.[74] Five came from Oxford on the Monday. Professor Franks arrived on the Tuesday and found himself in a stimulating, urgent atmosphere in which 'we had to create our own ... rules and conditions and flavour. It was a very freewheeling exercise for the first two or three years and there was lots of initiative to get on with it.'[75]

The declaration of war meant that the Central Register was, at last, truly in business. Beryl Power was asked to produce a report for her minister. It stressed the virtues of the mixture of well-known names provided by the Treasury and the 'valuable qualities possessed by less well-known persons which might be put to good use'.[76] On 27 September, twenty-four days after the outbreak of hostilities, it was completed. In a covering note to Glen, she wrote: 'the flagrant abuses of the early days in respect of certain Departments should not re-occur'. According to the Power Report, 2,582 vacancies had been submitted by departments to the Register before 3 September, 1,839 since with a particular rush of requests from the Service Departments. She noted that the Treasury had submitted a number of 'well-known' names which would suggest that their famous List of the Good and Great had been trawled for her purposes. She was candid about shortcomings: 'Certain sections of the Register are deficient either because the demand exceeds supply (for example, telecommunications) or because many employers prevented their employees from coming on the Register (for example, electrical engineering)'. Her conclusion struck an optimistic note:

> It is reasonable to expect some dislocation in the first few weeks of the war when new Departments are getting into their stride. We have every reason to hope that, even though we must have missed many valuable opportunities of placing suitable people in certain of the big Departments which failed in the early days of the war to use the Central Register, we shall be increasingly used as the services we are able to supply get better known.[77]

There is evidence to suggest that Miss Power's forecast was vindicated. Her 'panels of experts' brought in to assist in placing people appear to have chosen well. The file records that 'a consulting engineer gave a week of his time voluntarily to the War Office "browsing" over the cards in the Central Register in order to pick out names of people who might be of value to that Department and to the Ministry of Supply. He subsequently said that he was much impressed with the Register and particularly with the method of classification adopted.'[78] Certainly, the services of the Power team were drawn on increasingly in the first months of the war:

	Placings per fortnight
SEP. 30, 1939	45
OCT. 14, 1939	38
OCT. 31, 1939	264
NOV. 15, 1939	745
NOV. 30, 1939	292
DEC. 15, 1939	733
DEC. 31, 1939	332
JAN. 15, 1940	404
JAN. 31, 1940	423
FEB. 15, 1940	248[79]

There were shortcomings, naturally. The national trawl for talent inevitably netted some unfortunates. H. C. Head, one of Miss Power's staff clerks, in a minute to A. A. Bytheway, staff clerk higher grade, dated 22 August 1940, noted:

> During the six months ended 30 June, 1940, the number of persons registered increased from 84,800 to 108,700 and quite a large proportion

of these fresh registrations were attributable to the broadcast statement in May which asked engineers who were immediately available to inform Central Register to that effect.

He went on in a world-weary manner familiar to clerical officers the world over:

> On every occasion where newspaper or broadcast by wireless has mentioned the Register or any posts in the national machine which are under consideration, the Register becomes deluged with correspondence from unfortunately unemployed, from cantankerous hardy annuals, opportunists, egoists and cranks. The amount of tracing and filing which falls to be done is therefore out of all proportion to any requirements of selecting officers and has increased tremendously in the six months under review.[80]

While Head was grappling with his fruitcakes, some pretty hefty talent was lying unused even though all the required particulars were held in Chiswick High Road. William Penney found himself at a loose end for the first six months of the war. Imperial College had been scattered – one part going to Edinburgh, another to Swansea while a small rump stayed in London, including those registered with Miss Power. Lord Penney had no teaching duties. So he took care of the finances of the students' union and rationing.[81]

Finally he received 'a letter from a civil servant' asking him to meet Sir Geoffrey Taylor, the legendary applied mathematician from Cambridge, in the Athenaeum. Taylor wanted Penney to join him on explosives research, a subject about which as 'a quantum man' he knew nothing at that time. He was asked to calculate the wave effect of underwater explosions, working in the main from home. Later he moved on to the effect of waves on the Mulberry Harbours being built for D-Day. After the invasion of Normandy he was transferred to the Department of Scientific and Industrial Research and sent to Los Alamos in New Mexico to work on the atomic bomb.[82]

Statisticians were like 'gold dust' in wartime Whitehall, according to Lord Croham who passed into the administrative class of the Civil Service in 1939 after taking a First in Economics and Statistics at LSE. (He was later to become Permanent Secretary to the Treasury and Head of the Home Civil Service.) Before he could take up his job, however, the University of London Appointments Board had sent him to the Army, ignoring entirely the purpose for which the Central Register had been established. He found himself an acting captain commanding anti-aircraft batteries in the London suburbs. His Brigade headquarters never forwarded the requests from the Ministry of Labour for statisticians. 'Never mind.

I've no regrets. The Army made me', he recalled.[83] Another statistician who also went on to higher things found himself working for the Ministry of Agriculture in Oxford until his patron, Sir William Beveridge, had him transferred to the Anglo-French Co-ordinating Committee in 1940 which led to a post in the War Cabinet Secretariat a year later. His name was Harold Wilson.[84] As for Beveridge, Master of University College, Oxford, where the precocious Wilson had been made a don at the age of twenty-one, his persistent attempts to find wartime employment in government took a long time to achieve results.

Beveridge, author of the best-read report of the Second World War (on social insurance in 1942) and probably the most famous piece of social policy analysis in official history, as we have seen had been a temporary civil servant in the First World War. He had been made Permanent Secretary to the Ministry of Food at the age of thirty-nine. However, he lacked charm and tact and that great Whitehall virtue, the ability to oil the cogs. He made enemies. According to conventional official and political wisdom, he was gifted but difficult. His offers of assistance were politely rejected. But, as his biographer José Harris noted, he was in exalted company:

> Beveridge's experience was shared by other veterans of First World War administration such as Keynes, [Walter] Layton and [Arthur] Salter; and throughout the autumn and winter of 1939–40 this group of 'ancient warhorses' met together at Keynes' house in Bloomsbury, where they denounced the Chamberlain government's lack of coherent policy, criticised the dispersal of Whitehall departments to the provinces, and devised alternative strategies for prosecution of the war.[85]

After Churchill's assumption of power in May 1940, 'one by one the other old war-horses were absorbed into government – Keynes into the Treasury, Salter into the Admiralty, Layton into the Ministry of Supply – but once again there seemed to be no place for Beveridge'.[86] He approached Churchill directly and received what Mrs Jessy Mair, his secretary and future wife, described as a 'very damping reply'.[87] Eventually, he secured a toehold. In July 1940, Ernest Bevin, Brown's replacement as Minister of Labour, asked Beveridge to make a quick survey of the Government's manpower requirements.[88] A year later, Bevin, anxious to be rid of this least congenial of social scientists, steered him out of the Ministry of Labour into what was expected to be a backwater, the chairmanship of the Committee on Social Insurance.[89] The rest, as the saying goes, is history.

How were Miss Power's people deployed in what H. C. Head called 'the national machine'? The answer is in pretty well every capacity except that of a minister. Some like Franks shone in the performance of traditional administrative class functions like policy advice while developing the managerial skill of ensuring that huge war industries delivered *matériel* for the Armed Forces. Some like R. V. Jones and Alan Turing proved to be geniuses at the rapid harnessing of original research to practical problems like the bending of radar beams in Jones's case or the need to speed up the decoding of communications with what are now regarded as the prototype computers in Turing's. Other like Keynes and Lionel Robbins played the classic role of economic adviser. Richard Stone invented a whole new system of national income accounts. A battery of irregulars in the Economic Section of the War Cabinet Office combined the functions of backroom and frontroom boy in designing and helping implement a rationing mechanism which, through its points system, preserved a measure of choice within the limits of a siege economy. Norman Chester, another member of the Economic Section, acted as secretary to Beveridge and his team of insiders.

Yet another, Harold Wilson, occasionally ministered to the great man himelf. 'I would not claim that I was in any way a member of Churchill's intimate circle. He found me a new element who could write a two-page document in language that he could understand ... To the end of his life I remained one of "his boys" and he was always very nice to me, despite my membership of the other Party.'[90] The War Cabinet Office left a lasting and important mark on Harold Wilson, according to Dr Bernard Donoughue, his senior policy adviser in the 1970s: 'He liked to display his intellectual skill and was ever respectful of the sleek Civil Service machine. Having served early on in the Cabinet Office secretariat, his respect for the hierarchy, with the Cabinet Secretary sitting at the peak, was established for life.'[91] But the fires of radicalism flickered in one part of the Wilsonian breast. A numerate social scientist himself, Wilson resented the exclusion of the professionals from the administrators' world. He moaned about it on the roofs of Whitehall while fire-watching to a fellow 'temporary' recruited from the university world. The name of that 'temporary' was John Fulton. A quarter of a century later Wilson invited Fulton to head an inquiry into the Civil Service.[92]

In a less dramatic fashion, other wartime irregulars were to leave their mark on peacetime policy. G. C. Allen, Brunner Professor of Economic Science at Liverpool University, joined the Board of Trade, and, using his detailed knowledge of British industry, combined with like-minded irregulars, such as Gaitskell, Ruth Cohen and Grace Coleman and one or two sympathetic insiders (most notably W. Hughes and C. K. Hobson), to pioneer anti-restrictive-practice policies. This bore fruit after the war in legislation creating the Monopolies and Restrictive Practices Commission.

Many of these activities and individuals have acquired a retrospective glamour. But wartime Whitehall needed its doers, its unsung heroes. Some six hundred of them were, for example, found to augment the Office of

Works, that Cinderella department, which almost overnight had to cover the country with Royal Ordnance factories to produce the sinews of war. W. L. Wilson, who has written their story, recalled that:

> Rumour had it that the 20 years of peace and limited funds had had an adverse effect on the skills, experience, outlook and opportunities of those engaged on the production of munitions. Certainly there was an old-fashioned air surrounding designs and attitudes in the halcyon days of 1936.
>
> But new men were brought in: Mitchell who was to deal with Filling Factories in a very effective fashion, Dally and Norrey who were to play leading parts in construction activities, Baker (later engaged on the PLUTO pipelines) who took on the construction of all power stations, and many others.
>
> Neilson and Sizer, permanent officers of the Department, grew in stature, and so a trickle of activity slowly swelled to a flood. In due course, to build a new factory became almost a casual event.[93]

A simple list of Office of Works constructions between 1939 and 1945 gives an indication of the prodigious performance required from regulars and irregulars alike:

Cordite factories
Bishopton (3)
Wrexham (3)
Ramskill (2)

TNT factories
Pembrey
Irvine
Drigg
Sellafield

RDX factory
Bridgewater

Filling factories
Chorley
Elstow
Bridgend
Brackla
Hirwaun
Glascoed
Thorpe Arch

Aycliffe

Miscellaneous
Patricroft (tanks)
Pendine (weapons)
Shrawardine (stores)
Ditton Priors
Beith (stores)
Chobham (tanks and technology)
Farnborough (wheeled vehicles)
Flax factories (5)
Hostels (miners, Land Army)
Hospitals (American and others)
Protected Accommodation (citadels)
Royal Observer Corps Centre
Prisoner of War Camps (250)
Warminster Ground Equipment Depot
Opencast Coal Screening and Washing Plants
Underground Storage (for treasures and strategic materials)[94]

W. L. Wilson's point about career officials growing in stature, as the tasks imposed upon them mounted, is significant. The Second World War enfranchised many gifted people previously consigned to the remotest of backrooms. One such was D. C. (later Sir Donald) Bailey, inventor of the famous military bridge which bore his name. He was thirty-seven when the war broke out and had been a War Office engineer for eleven years. It took Hitler to make the military and the Civil Service take his bridge seriously, as his *Times* obituary made clear: 'As early as 1936 he had worked out the broad principle of his invention but received no official encouragement.'[95] The principle of it was simple. The Bailey Bridge was made up of rectangular trussed welded steel units ten feet long and almost five feet high. Each unit could be handled by six men, and bridges of all sizes and shapes could be constructed piecemeal – an ideal instrument for pursuing armies which were dynamiting bridges as they retreated. But as the *Times* obituarist noted:

> His department sponsored several types of temporary bridge, but were developing a design of individual tubular members pin-jointed at the site. Bailey doubted its merits; he preferred unit panel construction and by 1940 had produced a completely detailed design ready to be made and tested.
>
> This the War Office were too busy to arrange until, in January 1941, the model tubular bridge failed under test at Christchurch. They then

> ordered a full-scale trial of Bailey's bridge to take place within three months.[96]

It worked. Mass production was ordered. Some six hundred companies making windows, greenhouses and bedsteads were converted to Bailey Bridge production.

The wartime emergency brought forward some highly unlikely Whitehall characters in totally unforeseeable directions. Take Martin Roseveare, a Cambridge mathematician who had taught at Repton and Haileybury before joining the Board of Education as an inspector of schools in 1927. When war broke out he was Staff Inspector of Mathematics. Lord Woolton, the Minister of Food, needed 'a civil servant with the highest possible mathematical qualifications to devise, if humanly possible, a fool-proof and fraud-proof ration book'.[97] Roseveare was produced and given the brief of compressing all the clever schemes devised by the brilliant economic irregulars in the Cabinet Office, the Ministry of Food, the Board of Trade and elsewhere into 'a volume of handy size for the housewife whose contents lasted for a year'.[98] Roseveare laboured mightily and tested his dummies on his wife and her friends. As his obituarist noted gently, 'Roseveare was wont to take a little pride in the fact that from being an apparently repressive document at the war's outset the ration book came through successive editions to be seen as a guide to balanced and healthy diet given the siege conditions of life in Britain at war.'[99]

Sir Martin Roseveare's fruitful partnership with the irregulars illustrates another significant trait of wartime Whitehall: a breakdown in those carefully polished peacetime distinctions between administrators and specialists, between one grade and another. The overriding need to solve problems and to implement solutions thoroughly and swiftly was a great solvent and a stimulant which pushed forward those who could deliver, wherever they came from and whatever their station. Lord Penney, for example, has no doubts about the quickening effect of new, young blood on the 'rather sedate older men' who had grown to maturity in prewar Whitehall R and D establishments.[100] Lord Franks has spoken about a similar process in the Ministry of Supply.

> The Ministry couldn't possibly have worked without the mixture, the civil servants some of whom were absolutely excellent and had been around a long time ... [but] ... one of the advantages of the outsiders, I think, was ignorance. They didn't know what they were expected to do so they got on with doing it as best they could according to their own insights. In this way, perhaps, they were more innovative and able to see ways of doing things which wouldn't have been so obvious to someone who'd spent twenty years in the Board of Trade.[101]

Before leaving the impact of Miss Power's protégés, it is worth examining a couple of the more successful cases – one Lord Franks, himself a general administrator, the other a professional – to see which factors were crucial in achieving effectiveness.

Douglas Jay, a former colleague, has written that 'there was nothing ambiguous about the reputation which Franks acquired as the most competent temporary civil servant in the war machine'.[102] The Ministry of Supply which Lord Franks entered on 5 September 1939 was in the process of growing from nothing (it was established the previous April, though Chamberlain did not get round to appointing a minister, as we have seen, till July[103]) to a super-ministry with hundreds of thousands of employees tackling *the* issue of the hour – the production of munitions. By the time Douglas Jay arrived at the Ministry's headquarters at Shell-Mex House in the Strand in December 1940, Franks was already a principal assistant secretary (equivalent to an under secretary today) and an Olympian figure with a reputation for speed, attention to detail and a natural judiciousness rare in one then so young (thirty-five) but of great value in resolving disputes. Franks's secret seems to have been an ability to work with the grain and to outperform the career officials without causing offence. He took to their culture like a file to a cabinet while bringing the freshness of the outsider. In his first few weeks, Jay was summoned to a meeting at which several of the best-known outsiders were in attendance. In fact, the impression given is that they were swamping the regular Civil Service:

> I was invited to attend for the Ministry of Supply, with Franks and Geoffrey Crowther [ex-*Economist*], a very superior meeting of the official Manpower Requirements Committee . . . presided over by Sir William Beveridge in person. Franks also told me that Beveridge . . . had brought in as secretary of the Committee a very young and very clever statistician from Oxford called Harold Wilson. There they both were across the table in a Whitehall committee room, rather like an owl and a sparrow: Beveridge, august, white-haired, venerable and dogmatic; and Wilson, diminutive, chubby and chirpy.[104]

Franks, 'who moved every few months on to a higher bureaucratic rank',[105] was not, according to Jay, by background 'the ideal choice, some might have thought, for the higher direction of an unparalleled wartime mobilisation. But Franks possessed not merely an outstanding talent for manipulating a huge organisation, but a rare intuition into the psychology of colleagues, high or low, and not least of those in the business world'.[106] Only once, it seems, did his intuition let him down. At the end of 1940, Jay was allocated a new assistant, Monica Felton, 'a young woman of marked ability, unhappily half crippled by polio. Her disability naturally excited the sympathy of all of us; and when I was told most confidentially that she was the mistress of the then Chairman of the House of Commons Select Committee on National Expenditure, I ignored this as wholly irrelevant.'[107] She turned out, however, to have a habit of 'inexcusably ignoring her job'.[108] She was transferred but the habit persisted. Franks and Jay fired her:

> We were somewhat surprised when after a few weeks she was appointed as a clerk to the Select Committee on National Expenditure; and even more surprised when some weeks later the Committee published a report on the Ministry of Supply Filling Factories. Next we were told there was to be a secret debate in the House on this Report, in which Duncan [Minister of Supply] and Bevin [Minister of Labour] would speak for the Government. Duncan, it was felt, must be told of the curious relationship involved. But should Bevin be told also?

The permanent secretary, Sir William Douglas, decided that he should.

> But who should tell him? Answer of course: Mr Franks. With much careful stage-management, it was contrived that Franks should meet Bevin absolutely alone in the latter's own personal office, and confide in him with due solemnity, in the greatest privacy, the terrible secret. On hearing it, Bevin replied: ' 'Undreds of people have told me that'.[109]

Bevin was a great admirer of Franks though their backgrounds (apart from the fact that both were west countrymen) were totally different, Bevin a product of the soil, Franks of the cloth. As Foreign Secretary, Bevin called Franks back from Oxford first to negotiate the Marshall Plan and later to be Ambassador to Washington. Bevin knew how to use his officials, regular and irregular alike.

Ministerial aptitude and capability were crucial in determining whether the talent found by Miss Power was turned to good effect or squandered, as another gifted irregular, a specialist this time, discovered. Professor Lionel Robbins was another immensely gifted scholar kept on the sidelines for the duration of the 'Phoney War'. By the spring of 1940, when the real war began, life in Cambridge – to which the LSE had been evacuated – became unbearable:

> Morning after morning brought news of fresh defeats and defections; and here we are, with all our potential unutilised, drooling out routine instruction which had suddenly seemed to lose all relevance. Of course, this was all wrong. It was very important to keep alive the lamp of learning and to maintain a sense of its significance among those who,

either because of extreme youth or some other disability, were unable to man the defences.

Nevertheless, a lack of patience was not unnatural in the circumstances. I am not ashamed of the intense feeling of relief with which, lifting the telephone one afternoon at home, I heard the voice of Austin Robinson [E. A. G. Robinson, Reader in Economics at Cambridge seconded to the Cabinet Office 1939], speaking on behalf of the assistant secretary responsible, inviting me to join the Office of the War Cabinet as an economic assistant. I need hardly say that I accepted there and then.[110]

Robbins, who rose rapidly to the Directorship of the Economic Section of the War Cabinet Secretariat in 1941, found himself part of an immensely talented team – Robinson, Richard Stone, John Jewkes, Harry Campion, Ely Devons, Stanley Denison, James Meade and Harold Wilson.[111] But there was a problem. They were led by Francis Hemming, a career official who had worked in the Economic Advisory Council and was now the assistant secretary on whose behalf Robinson had picked up the phone:

Hemming, although intensely ambitious, was not the man to organise such an enterprise successfully. He had his speck of inspiration in realising at an early stage that economists and statisticians would be needed at the centre. But he was extremely unwise in his relations with his equals and superiors in his own office and still more so with those in other departments. Furthermore, he was not a good administrator or a good manager of men.[112]

To complete his acid pen portrait, Robbins dwelt on Hemming's physical peculiarities and his tobacco stains, adding, for good measure, that 'Francis's acquaintance with the economic and statistical concepts of the national income must have been zero if not negative.'[113]

In the autumn of 1940, however, Robbins *et al.* were rescued both from Hemming and from ministerial neglect. The number crunchers were hived off into a new Central Statistical Office. A specific Economic Section was created. It found itself the instrument of some mighty and appreciative ministerial and bureaucratic patrons:

The economists . . . were made responsible to Sir John Anderson – Lord Waverley as he later became – the Lord President of the Council, with Norman Brook, at that time personal assistant to the Lord President, directly in charge, and Edward Bridges [Secretary of the War Cabinet], that fundamental connecting link of the whole war administration, with a friendly interest in our doings. This was delivery indeed.[114]

The Economic Section never looked back. Churchill effectively hived off the Home Front to Anderson and his Lord President's Committee while he and the Chiefs of Staff got on with the war. This was problem-solving at its best. They had the right blend of people. They knitted together some pioneering information systems. They had powerful patrons. They wielded clout. The Defence of the Realm Act, the rationing system and manpower controls gave them instruments of unparalleled efficiency for implementing policy. Norman Chester reckoned that 'in the sphere of general economic policy there were probably twenty to fifty people in Whitehall who, if their views coincided, could do almost anything'.[115] The Home Front became an adventure playground for conscripted social scientists.

There was change, too, on the diplomatic front. That ultra-hard target of reform, the Foreign Office, began to crumble before the battering-ram of war-induced change wielded, yet again, by that tank-of-a-man, Ernest Bevin. Bevin, impregnable in that commanding height of wartime Whitehall, the Ministry of Labour, never shrank from interfering in other departments' business. His formidable gaze quickly alighted on the Foreign Office as his 'inter-war experience as a trade union leader had forcefully demonstrated to him the importance for British industry and employment of international trading and economic conditions. He was particularly bitter that no British minister or Foreign Secretary had ever attended a meeting of the International Labour Organisation.'[116]

Bevin pressed his arguments in the autumn of 1940 on Cadogan and R. A. Butler, then the number two to Lord Halifax, the Foreign Secretary. He followed it up with a memo to Halifax himself arguing the case for a reform of the Diplomatic Service:

> My view has been that diplomacy has moved in far too narrow a circle and the reactions of our policy and the well-being of the people of other countries have not been comprehended. Neither, in my view, was there any sufficient understanding of the effect of our banking and financial policy in producing a feeling in other countries that, in fact, Britain was the cause of their economic troubles.[117]

Bevin was concerned about the narrowness of the social base from which the Foreign Office drew its recruits: 'The lives of ordinary people are strange to them as they are to all who have been accustomed to sheltered conditions.' He urged the appointment of Labour attachés and an interchange of officials with home departments. Modern diplomats should be picked for their ability to mix with all sorts and conditions of people and 'to express informed opinions on the strength and effect of organisations and movements in the countries in which they serve'.[118]

These views from a true aristocrat of labour education, as he liked to put it, the ''edgerows of experience',[119] were the exact obverse of those expressed a mere eighteen months before by Knatchbull-Hugesson and Hoyer Millar. But for the war they would have had as much impact as previous calls for a democratisation of the Foreign Service. After all, Lord Cranborne (better known in his later incarnation in 1950s Cabinets as Lord Salisbury), Eden's number two until their joint, honourable resignation in protest at appeasement in 1938, had written in a 1936 minute on recruitment: 'Personality counts for far more in diplomacy than in any other public service.' He went on: 'It is no question of enabling socially favoured candidates to obtain jobs. It is a question of securing suitable candidates for the very special work they have to do.'[120]

In fact, it fell to Eden, who replaced Halifax in December 1940, to make the first moves in response to Bevin's lobbying. As so often in instances of reform, the process was assisted by internal prodding from an improvement-minded insider. In this case it was Sir David Scott, head of the FO's Consular Department, who in the late thirties had been pressing persistently if fruitlessly for the members of his service to be given their due place in the bureaucratic sun. It was Scott's prompting of Eden which led him to commission an inquiry in January 1941 from Sir Malcolm Robertson, then Chairman of the British Council and a man with both business and diplomatic experience.[121]

Robertson worked swiftly and reported to Eden in four months.[122] War put the great and the good into overdrive. As the FO's anatomists, Valerie Cromwell and Zara Steiner, recorded:

> His proposals were clear and were very much along the lines sketched by Scott. Robertson recommended a foreign service separate from the home civil service. Existing services working abroad should all be merged with the exception of the commercial diplomatic service. In future diplomats must be made aware of the international economic situation and the economic implications of any foreign policy. A personnel department (long overdue) and an appointments board should be set up within the Office to handle promotions and appointments. Diplomatic missions abroad should be inspected regularly. Personnel department staff should be moved regularly. Specialisation should be encouraged. The difficulty of slow promotion and 'dead wood' at the top of the diplomatic service should be solved by the introduction of a system of early retirement.[123]

In less than a month the War Cabinet had approved the report as the basis for a postwar reform of the Diplomatic services. Embassies were informed that when recruitment competitions resumed in peacetime they would be choosing 'personnel more representative of the nation as a whole' for a single combined foreign service.[124] It all set a hugely progressive tone all the more impressive as Britain was still standing alone at the time Robertson reported; progressive, that is, unless one happened to be black, or a woman or afflicted by a speech impediment, for T. D. Dunlop, a former consular inspector, pressed hard for preliminary interviewing to weed out 'a man of colour, or having an intractable stammer'.[125]

Women had long vexed the Foreign Office. As we have seen from the career of Beryl Power, women had hardly stormed the Home Civil Service in the interwar years, but at least they had established a toehold. The aristocratic tradition kept the FO far behind in this respect as it did in so many others. The installation of Labour ministers made no difference (it should have done; Margaret Bardfield, Minister of Labour 1929–31, was the first woman to sit in a Cabinet). Hugh Dalton, FO junior minister 1929–31, commented on the performance of the FO's man, Hubert Montgomery, before the Tomlin Royal Commission in the following terms:

> I think you got away without being seriously hit. As to women, I prophesy that, before many years have passed, you will have to admit one or two into the Office, to placate outside opinion. I agree that they could only usefully serve abroad in one or two highly civilised, e.g. Scandinavian posts. Your arguments are weighty against the admission of many women; proportionately less weighty against one or two I think.[126]

Once more it took the admission of Bevin to the highest councils of the land for anything to happen. He minuted Eden urging him to 'take the bold line of admitting women to the service ... Go right out and accept terms of equality, purely on the basis of ability, it would be far better'.[127] After the war, women duly began to be admitted to the Diplomatic Service.

The final version of what should be known as the Eden/Bevin reforms appeared in a White Paper in January 1943[128] which ended the entrenched distinctions between the FO, the Diplomatic Service, the Commercial Diplomatic Service and the Consular Service, proclaimed the importance of an understanding of economics, finance, social policy and labour movements 'in forming a properly balanced judgement of world events', and foreshadowed the recasting of selection procedures.[129] The White Paper was a benchmark. Geoffrey Moorhouse has described it as 'a blueprint for the most radical change that British diplomacy has undergone' since the Foreign Office was founded in 1782.[130] Bevin would have agreed with that.

He had his own very special way of expressing his purpose which bore no relationship to the stately language of the Whitehall White Paper. For him, the Diplomatic Service had to recognise

> that the limited Court Circular society of the Chancelleries will never return; that if there is to be a reconstruction of the world, then that reconstruction has to be brought about by harnessing and utilising the rising mass of labour to whom the future really belongs, and who must be the dominant factor in any new democratic world. There must be an absolute broadening of the curriculum, and of the right of entry into the Diplomatic Service. If the boys from the secondary schools can save us in the Spitfires, the same brains can be turned to produce a new world.[131]

By an unexpected turn of political fate Bevin found himself in charge of the postwar Foreign Office. It didn't quite turn out to be the takeover by the grammar school lads fresh out of the Spitfires that those who had heard him in 1940 might have expected, but things were never so *ancien régime* again after the 1943 White Paper.

Without the war, the FO would have remained in the condition Knatchbull-Hugessen and co. so cherished. Only a total threat to its survival prodded that 'limited Court Circular society' into change, an observation equally true, if in a diluted fashion, for the rest of the public service. For the reform that Hitler forced upon Whitehall, the mixture of new blood with old, produced a state of the art bureaucracy – the logical and necessary next step after the Fisher reforms and their consolidation of the Northcote–Trevelyan model. Total war is a high price to pay for root and branch change in the central government machine. The double tragedy is that the resulting quantum leap was largely reversed in the years of peace that followed.

But, before turning to the missed opportunity of the early postwar period, a sketch is required of the Whitehall machine at war. In many respects it was, inevitably, a chaotic scene. Familiar divisions in traditional ministries found their staff diluted by call-up to active service or transfers to the new mushroom ministries which, as we have seen, grew to vast proportions where nothing had been before. These great new enterprises were a mixture of careful pre-planning and frenzied improvisation. The Ministry of Food, whose power reached every larder in the land when rationing was introduced in January 1940, is a case in point.

There was some past experience to go on. A National Rationing Scheme had operated for four months before the Armistice of 1918 brought the First World War to a close. With the prospect of a second conflict starting to preoccupy Whitehall in 1936, the ubiquitous William Beveridge, who had been a precocious permanent secretary in the Ministry of Food during the Kaiser's war, was brought in to advise on an updated scheme. The Beveridge Committee swiftly recommended that rationing must, if war came, be an early item in the apparatus of food control; that it should be linked to a system of national registration through identity cards; that the existing Civil Emergency Food Organisation be reorganised so that it could be reconstituted quickly into a fully fledged Ministry of Food if crisis came; that local authorities should set up a shadow system of food offices; and that the paperwork of rationing – ration books for the citizen, buying permits for the retailer – should be set up ready for mass printing by His Majesty's Stationery Office.[132]

The Board of Trade set up a Food (Defence) Plans Department for the purpose in November 1936. When war came almost three years later, there were snags and delays. But the target set by Beveridge of introducing nationwide rationing within four months was met. On 8 January 1940, sugar, butter and bacon were put 'on the ration'. Meat was added in March with tea, margarine and cooking fats following in July. By the turn of 1939 millions of ration books had gone out through the post. Food Offices were ready in every town. Elaborate sub-schemes for factories, military bases and restaurants were in place. Individual citizens registered with individual grocers and butchers to avoid chaos and the queuing nightmare which would have ensued from a free-for-all. Shopkeepers gave Food Offices estimates of needs. Food Offices totted them up and passed them on to the various commodity divisions at ministry headquarters. The ration coupon came to be as reliable as currency.

The Ministry of Food did not just pre-empt the material of the foodstuffs industry; it commandeered its key personnel as well and put them in some unlikely places. For example, control of the life-saving cuppa, which was to take on an almost mystical symbolism in the British war effort, was placed in the Ministry's tea division in its dispersed HQ at Colwyn Bay on the 'costa geriatrica' of North Wales where seconded tea traders and regular civil servants worked side-by-side.

Whether intentionally or not, fish control and potato control were billeted together in St John's College, Oxford, making this ancient seat of higher learning the biggest fish and chip shop the world has ever seen. Mr J. T. Bennett, a prominent London fish merchant, was appointed Director of Fish Supplies[133] and Captain Mollett, chairman of the Potato Marketing Board, was his opposite number on the chip side.[134]

The great apparatus of organised supply and demand was given a human face by a generally successful public relations assault on the consumers of reconstituted eggs and Woolton pies (meat pies without the meat named in honour of the most successful of the ministers of food). 'Dig For Victory', the yellow slogan on a black background beneath a gardener's basket bursting with vegetables, has entered the nation's folk-memory.[135]

Naturally there were problems, sometimes acute ones such as the breakdown of meat rationing in the early months of 1941. There was grumbling, too, about shortages and queues. But the postwar resentments exquisitely captured in Alan Bennett's *A Private Function*[136] should not be read back indiscriminately into the war years themselves.

Perceived fairness was the key to acceptance, as the Government's own surveys indicated. 'People', declared a Ministry of Information report in March 1942, 'are willing to bear any sacrifice if a 100 per cent effort can be reached and the burden fairly borne by all.'[137] Two months later another MOI report noted that 'the heavier penalties for black marketeers, the promise of restrictions on luxury meals, the extension of points rationing, the abolition of basic petrol . . . have been welcomed as real evidence that the Government is in earnest'.[138] The complaints files of the Ministry of Food itself tell a similar story. As its official historian, R. J. Hammond, recorded:

> The success of food rationing was something that the British people came to take for granted. Their satisfaction with control, speaking generally, varied directly with its completeness; it was the things amenable only partly, or not at all, to rationing techniques, like fish, oranges or milk, that evoked complaint. There could be no more powerful tribute to rationing than the demands that, say, cake should be rationed.
>
> They acknowledged the fairness of the system; but they also showed how well its limitations had been concealed not only from the public in general, but even from many in Whitehall and within the Ministry of Food itself. For it was from these latter enthusiasts – who would have rationed coffee and cocoa, for instance, in the name of equality – that those actually running the scheme had the hardest task to defend themselves.[139]

Writing thirty years after the war ended and twenty after the ration book finally disappeared from the housewife's handbag, Susan Briggs was able to sum up the case of wartime rationing in fine Lord Chief Justice style:

> Rationing was thought of as a *necessary* restriction during the war, and people happily turned the queue into a national institution. Memories of wartime shortages during the First World War were associated with unfair distribution and with profiteering. The Second World War was not to be a war like that. There were black markets – and country folk in Cumberland could fare better than town-dwellers in the Midlands –

> but the Ministry of Food, as much an innovation as the Ministry of Information, was the biggest (and fairest) shop in the world.[140]

But for me the greatest tribute to the Ministry of Food, its organisation and methods, was a backhanded one from no less a figure than Mrs Eleanor Roosevelt, wife of the President of the United States. Recalling her lunch with the King and Queen at Buckingham Palace in 1942, A. J. P. Taylor wrote, she 'was given a meal "which would have shocked the King's grandfather". It was served on a gold plate; and "spam on a gold plate" would be a good motto for the reign.'[141]

The other classic 'mushroom department' of the Second World War, the Ministry of Supply, did not, unlike the Ministry of Food, have a card on every mantelpiece to remind the citizenry of its importance. But it was crucial nonetheless. Few members of the workforce were unaffected by its control over the raw materials of industry. And, as the war progressed, every member of the uniformed services was clothed and armed by its output. In terms of regional policy and state intervention in industry, Supply was the biggest and most successful department of industry Whitehall has ever possessed or ever will.

As we have seen, it was created a mere one and three-quarter months before the war started. Its minister's powers were based on responsibility for supplying such military stores as the Government prescribed in a series of orders in council. Its official historians, J. D. Scott and Richard Hughes, were later to write, somewhat in the style of E. J. Thribb of *Private Eye*:

> So the Ministry of Supply was launched. To anyone who was not familiar with its origins and pre-history its functions seem a rather haphazard assortment; certainly its organisation was experimental. Many different forecasts were made about its development; few expected it to be regular, straightforward and free from surprises. Yet it fact the original conception weathered the storms of war with remarkable buoyancy. . . .[142]

That conception had been devised by its permanent secretary designate, Sir Arthur Robinson, a career man. The idea was to have a range of self-contained production divisions responsible for the entire sequence – 'design, development, production planning, provision of the necessary production facilities, ordering, "progressing", inspection and deliveries'[143] – which could be dispersed *in toto*. A headquarters secretariat would provide common services such as establishment work and dealings with Parliament. Atop of this structure would be the Ministry's own equivalent of the Service boards in the Service ministries – the Supply Council.

The Ministry of Supply was a genuine mixture of the insider/outsider. Until Franks was promoted into the job, the permanent secretary was an irregular. The Director-General of Finance, Patrick Ashley-Cooper, was recruited from the Hudson's Bay Company, and Sir William Rootes, the motor magnate, chaired the Supply Council.

As with the Ministry of Food there were shortfalls and problems. For example, Supply's equivalent of Food's meat crisis of 1942 was its jerrican crisis of 1943.[144] Nor did the structure of the department prove wholly advantageous. The Supply Council, to take one instance, never really developed into the forum of command it was intended to be. For a long time, with thirty-two members, it was far too big. The official historians sense a lack of positive activity about it. 'There was at all times a tendency to note information rather than to give decisions. The decisions indeed were made by the men who sat up on the Council, but they were not made *in* Council.'[145]

But from shells to surgical dressings, bullets to gaiters, it delivered what was needed not least because of the very close collaboration established with American industry even before the United States entered the war.[146]

Even the hyper-critical Correlli Barnett has acknowledged that in terms of planning, coordination and direction from the centre, the British war production machine, like its military counterpart, was noticeably superior to the German war effort (though Barnett vigorously maintains that down the line, in the front-line divisions and on the factory floor, the Germans man-for-man were far superior[147]). And the stories of Food and Supply had their equivalents throughout the Whitehall machine in the traditional as well as the mushroom ministries where, too, the gifted irregular penetrated. In a word, Whitehall as a whole, like the British people in general, raised its game admirably and dramatically between 1939 and 1945.

It *should* have been possible to keep it raised. Sustained high performance was critically dependent not just on the stimulus provided by the overriding need to bring the war to a successful conclusion, but on perpetual replenishment with new blood. When Keynes died in 1946, Otto Clarke, the gifted journalist who had joined the Ministry of Information in 1939 and moved to the Treasury by way of Supply, Production and Economic Warfare, wrote in his diary:

> Appalling news of the death of Keynes. Felt bereft as at death of Roosevelt and Alekhine [the chess champion]. He is the man whose career I would soonest match; I could never hope to match his all round genius, but I might hope to match his type of skill in the field of forensic economy ... his death leaves the Treasury in a terrible hole ... it

> will be interesting to see whether the Treasury relapses into habitual slovenliness and complacency or whether some new man is found for providing stimulus.[148]

Clarke might well have wondered. The answer was depressingly swift in coming.

4 THE MISSED OPPORTUNITY

Sir Edward Bridges ... thought all would be going back to normal, but of course this wasn't so.
Lord Franks, 1987[1]

They began their official lives believing that everything was achievable.
Lord Bancroft on the generation of senior civil servants recruited after the Second World War, 1984[2]

The average assistant principal entrant is a superior article to the average scientific officer entrant.
Background Treasury brief for the Priestley Royal Commission, 1954[3]

The reform Hitler forced on Whitehall was undone by the peace because neither the politicians nor the senior Civil Service tried or cared to devise its peacetime equivalent. This represents probably *the* greatest lost opportunity in the history of British public administration. The irregulars, one by one, went back to their universities, their companies, their law practices, their old professions, as if they were soldiers receiving a handshake and a demob suit. Some were offered permanent establishment. Franks could have had pretty well any post he liked. But from being the public servant who wielded the greatest ever powers over British industry, he seized the offer of the one job he had always wanted, the Provostship of his old College, Queen's, in Oxford, though within two years he answered the Foreign Secretary's call and returned to public service. R. V. Jones took the Chair of Natural Philosophy at Aberdeen. Gaitskell and Wilson stood for Parliament. Robbins went back to the LSE. Keynes negotiated the American Loan, came home to Sussex and died. Jay moved into No. 10 as Attlee's economic adviser until he stood for Parliament at a by-election in 1946.

Beryl Power had been transferred to the Ministry of Supply in 1941 to run its housing and welfare side. After the war she went to China as a consultant on administration and welfare policies for the United Nations Relief and Rehabilitation Administration. She remained in China and the Far East, though still officially on the books of the Ministry of Labour, until her retirement from the public service in 1951. In later life she chaired the Over Forty Association for Women Workers and died, an asthmatic, on 4 November 1974, her work forgotten, if it had ever been known outside a small Whitehall circle, and unrecognised in any Honours List.

Some of her people stayed on in postwar Whitehall. Penney and a few from the British contingent at Los Alamos came home to make a British bomb. Otto Clarke decided to remain, and rose to the rank of Permanent Secretary at the Ministry of Technology in 1966. Writing of the post-1945 Treasury, Sir Alec Cairncross judges him the only official with 'any real flair for general economic policy'.[4] Austin Robinson came back for a while to join Sir Edwin Plowden (a businessman brought in as a wartime temporary to the Ministry of Economic Warfare) in his new Central Economic Planning Staff created in 1947. The Economic Section carried on in the Cabinet Office first under James Meade and later Robert Hall. But elsewhere, the specialists dwindled:

> With the death of Keynes the Treasury were left without any professional economist to advise them and felt the loss very severely. The Board of Trade had an economic adviser up to 1950 and there were one or two professional economists in administrative or statistical posts. Other departments with the exception of Agriculture, Food and the Joint Intelligence Committee, had none or, at the most, one.[5]

What Alec Cairncross felt later Otto Clarke felt at the time. Even before Keynes's death, as David Hubback's article shows, Clarke was brooding in his diary in January 1946 about the human capital of the postwar Treasury. 'It is very worrying', he wrote, 'but what can one do if 90 per cent of senior officials are a generation behind in their economic thinking, egged on by the "professional economists"? The Civil Service is taking wonderful strides and is adapting itself readily to planning, but can it adapt itself fast enough?' For one fleeting moment a similar question was pondered by Clarke's superiors and the lessons of the war bureaucracy and their application to the long-term future of the peacetime Civil Service featured briefly on the agenda of the dispensers of Whitehall power and patronage. Even then it took the intervention of an outsider, a backbench Labour MP, Geoffrey Cooper, to propel them there. Cooper, in a letter to Attlee dated 12 February 1946, raised the question of whether the 'executive instrument' was capable of implementing the new bills rolling off the Parliamentary production line as the Labour Government got into its legislative stride, statutes 'which constitute a complete change of policy'. Cooper reminded the Prime Minister that Roosevelt, when introducing his New Deal, had appointed an inquiry into the administrative management capability of the Federal Government in Washington. 'Is there not a parallel here for our country at the present time?' Cooper urged Attlee to appoint a select committee to investigate, whose composition should include MPs 'with previous experience of scientific methods of busines organisation'.[6]

Attlee passed the letter to Bridges, who was never an enthusiast for the Parliamentary inquiry as he revealed in a letter to his fellow permanent secretaries of 26 February.

> Such a Committee could not get down to the business without an immense amount of enquiry into Government Departments and evidence from highly-placed civil servants; and I expect that we shall all feel that we have no time to spare for this. Moreover, even if we were convinced that an enquiry was necessary, I imagine that we should feel that a Select Committee was not the right kind of body to carry out the enquiry.[7]

Bridges, however, in his fair-minded way, conceded that Cooper had a point which should not be ignored and he launched into his own assessment of the wartime experience, starting, typically, with the precedent of 1918–19 when he was but a Treasury cub:

> Speaking for myself, I have been disposed to think of the change-over from war to peace, as it affects the Civil Service, largely in terms of what happened at the end of the last war. In that war, too, large numbers of business men, industrialists and others came into the Civil Service, and at the end of it, when the war problems came to an end, they packed up and went back to their businesses.
>
> It is true that in this war we have made far better use of the industrialists and others who have come to our assistance, and we have greatly regretted the loss of their help when the time came for them to go. But have others – like myself – been working on the general expectation that Civil Service problems would in a year or so resume more or less the same general pattern which they took before the war?
>
> That may or may not have been a reasonable working hypothesis a year or so ago [i.e. before the general election which brought Labour to power]. But is it not clear that the Government's legislative programme will more and more confront the Civil Service with problems which require a far closer degree of contact with industry than ever before, and

> that this will have important consequences on the experience and type of qualities which will be required in many sections of many Departments?[8]

Bridges went on to offer his fellow permanent secretaries more 'crude summaries of certain lines of thought'. Had they faced up to the consequences of the Government's nationalisation programme for the structure of the Civil Service and recruitment to its ranks? Should they bring into the service people with industrial experience? He summoned them to a Saturday morning meeting in his room at the Treasury to ponder such points.

Before they gathered, the thoughtful permanent secretary to the Ministry of Works (a crucial department in terms of Labour's reconstruction plans and not the cinderella department of popular repute), Sir F. P. Robinson, wrote Bridges the letter, from which I have already quoted, dividing the life of the service 'within our memories' into the regulatory phase, the social services phase and a new third phase currently unfolding in which Government was much more involved in productive industry. Robinson sensibly stressed the increasing importance to Whitehall of its in-house scientists and professionals, but the shadow of Warren Fisher intruded at this point: 'In any large organisation the need for special knowledge decreases from the bottom upwards ... At the top what is required is judgement and leadership, and the technical knowledge necessary can be quickly absorbed.'[9] It was as if the Second World War and its brilliant, persistent application of scientific and professional skills at *all* levels had not happened. For Robinson it was 'in the middle ranks that knowledge, as opposed to judgement or administrative capacity, becomes more important' and it was at this level that Whitehall should be recruiting anew. To be fair to him, Robinson argued that some civil servants needed to be trained 'to do what the industralist does, namely, look straight at his objective and brush aside all ancillary considerations instead of, as the civil servant is normally trained to do, look all round his problem in order to see the snags'.[10] 'Training', incidentally, was a misnomer. The art and craft of public service was learnt on the job. A wartime committee under the Conservative MP, Ralph Assheton, had recommended the establishment of a Civil Service College, but the proposal got nowhere.

When the permanent secretaries gathered round Bridges's table on 2 March 1946, most of them were sufficiently open-minded to recognise that, as Sir Cyril Hurcomb from the Ministry of Transport put it, 'the Civil Service had something to learn from business men particularly from their capacity for "economy in means"'.[11] Sir Frank Tribe from the Ministry of Food immediately pointed out the snags, as somebody invariably does at permanent secretaries' meetings. He 'doubted whether it would be possible to get many people from this source. In general, people from the world of industry and commerce were not attracted either by the pay or by the atmosphere of the Civil Service, and in present conditions it was unlikely that their firms could spare them.'

But it was Mr Oliver Franks, star of the wartime temporaries, then in his last days at the Ministry of Supply, who made the sole radical contribution to the crucial and so depressingly revealing meeting in the Treasury that Saturday morning. The problem, he said, was more fundamental than the seconding of industrialists:

> The real difficulty was that in recent years the functions of the Civil Service had changed from being purely regulative (functions for which the education and training the civil servant were ideally suited) and had become more and more those of management. Instead of analysing the problems of others, the civil servant now had to tackle those problems himself. This called for somewhat different qualities, of which the most important were nerve and ability to push a thing through to its conclusion. The old distinction between administration and execution no longer held good. The civil servant would thus have to acquire some of the qualities of the businessman. But the introduction of businessmen into the Service was not itself a solution. Public administration was on a far larger scale than any business, and this was a fact seldom appreciated by people outside the field of public administration.[12]

More than forty years later, Lord Franks remembered

> in a rather brash way saying I thought there was considerable need for change and ... that the role of the Civil Service in the war and from now on would be ... more managerial and less purely administrative. Now, some of my colleagues accepted this and others didn't. They believed that the thing would revert to normal and broadly they came from departments which had not been disturbed so much by the war and made to change their ways ... so that opinion was mixed and I suppose that the trumpet did not give a very clear sound to Edward Bridges.[13]

But Franks *had* spoken truth unto power and in a fashion that would have graced any submission produced as part of Mrs Thatcher's attempt to transform Whitehall management two Whitehall generations later. Bridges recognised it gracefully as 'a very fundamental question which should certainly be discussed'.[14] Lord Franks's contribution stimulated the 'congenital snag-hunters' (as Hugh Dalton is said to have called top civil servants).[15] Sir John Henry Woods from the Board of Trade said it was possible to exaggerate the degree to which the Civil Service was being drawn into management. There was no need to radically alter the pattern of recruitment. Training was the key. Sir Donald Fergusson from the Ministry of Fuel and Power doubted even that: 'Under the present system the civil servant was first and foremost the servant of his Minister, and so long as that was true his whole training and outlook would be coloured by that fact.' Sir Frank Tribe then gave a perfect illustration of Whitehall's failure-avoidance culture by pointing out 'that the outlook of the civil servant was inevitably influenced by the Public Accounts Committee and by the fact that what he did today would be the subject of an enquiry in two years' time. The qualities required for business management could not possibly develop under such conditions.' To round off a thoroughly negative morning, Woods and Franks suggested that 'there should be a better outlet for people of proved ability in grades below the Administrative Class' only to have 'other permanent secretaries' say they 'felt that this reserve had already been tapped to the full'.

This waterfall of negativism tumbled from one permanent secretary to another, only six months after the end of the Second World War which had shaken the Civil Service from top to bottom and created a world-beating bureaucracy, a crucial component in developing the most thoroughly mobilised society of any of the combatants. And this, Franks apart, was the way its lessons were gauged. It showed more than anything else I have come across in the literature or the files the perils of allowing the British Civil Service to conduct itself as a self-regulating organisation.

The system, however, provides elected politicians – ministers – as the antidote to such behaviour. How did they perform on this occasion? In a word, appallingly, even allowing for the huge weight of problem-solving and decision-taking that bore down upon Attlee and his colleagues in those early postwar years. Bridges was allowed to get away with his determination to keep outsiders out and 'that reform should be undertaken by the Civil Service itself rather than imposed from outside as the result of an enquiry'. He bought Dalton and Attlee off with warnings that an enquiry would impose more work on a Civil Service already 'working on a very narrow margin', a statement that 'you cannot solve the problems of the Civil Service simply by applying business technique', an observation that insiders 'can tell better than any outsider where the shoe pinches without any long process of collecting evidence' and a promise that working parties of officials would 'diagnose any existing weakness . . . in no spirit of complacency [as] my colleagues are well aware of the need to strengthen the machine to meet the growing tasks ahead'.[16] Dalton, to whom the minute was originally sent, who had railed in wartime against 'a jamboree of other ministers' officials in an irresponsible sub-ministerial underworld' and who loathed huge official committees as 'an indefensible excrescence on the British Constitution',[17] allowed Bridges to channel the reform impulse into a set of working parties on recruitment, training, accommodation, efficiency and the staffing of public boards from which precious little of substance emerged.[18] Attlee, whose one original foray into socialist thought was a short memo written in 1932 on the machinery of government and who had long shown a penchant for Haldanian views on the efficacy of scientific administration,[19] proved no better than his Chancellor at combating the congenital snag-hunters. Bridges had carried off *the* classic manoeuvre of professional self-preservation when, for once, the odds seemed stacked in favour of significant and lasting reform. That shrewdest of constitutional monarchs, King George VI, knew what he was saying when he told Aneurin Bevan and John Wilmot after swearing them in as privy counsellors in July 1945: 'Well, the Prime Minister has had a very difficult time, I'm sure. What I say is "Thank God for the Civil Service."'[20]

In its own way, the Civil Service thanked God for itself. There was an *internal* outcome to the permanent secretaries' broodings of spring 1946. A document labelled 'For Official Use Only' was circulated under Bridges's signature in January 1948 (I have been shown a private copy) containing extracts from the permanent secretaries' in-house inquiry into the efficiency of their profession. Entitled *The Conduct of Business in Government Departments*, its overall tone was self-congratulatory. 'Our main concern', it reported,

> has been with questions relating to efficiency of organisation in the Civil Service. We have given a good deal of thought to this and have heard evidence from a number of leading men in the business world who served in Government Departments during the war ... Neither we ourselves, nor those whom we have consulted, have been able to suggest any single or simple means of promoting greater efficiency in the Civil Service. There are, of course, many defects in the existing organization; but these vary between Departments and branches of Departments and we are satisfied that there is no single cure for them which would be universally applicable throughout the Service.

The contrast with the Rayner approach thirty years later is almost total (see Chapter 14). The document, however, did raise issues both relevant to the time and prescient in terms of the future. For example, it acknowledged that some ministries (it singled out Supply, Food and Works) were discharging functions 'similar to those of a large business organisation' and noted that 'the Civil Service must adapt itself to handle the increased volume of this class of business'. Similarly, the need to communicate better within ministries was stressed. In management terms, the O and M (Organization and Methods) branch of the Treasury, and the O and M divisions of individual departments, were to be the cutting edge of efficiency.

There were pre-echoes of Raynerism in the observation that 'too often imagination and initiative are lacking because these qualities have been stifled, or at least not developed, through lack of scope for their exercise during the first formative years in the Service'. Some of the remedies, too, have a Rayner ring about them:

* Every member of the staff – and particularly the junior staff – should be able to feel that he or she is a member of a small group, whose members from the most senior to the most junior are known personally to each other, which is working together for a common and well-recognized objective ...
* The written word is for the civil servant the chief tool of his trade. It is essential, therefore, that he should learn to use it properly .... If we could reintroduce a taut and muscular English as the normal means of official expression, in place of the flaccid jargon now in general use, we should substantially enhance both our efficiency and our reputation.

But as a reform charter for the times, *The Conduct of Business in Government Departments* fell far short of what was required in both intentions and means of implementing them.

Why the most radical administration between David Lloyd George and Margaret Thatcher failed to reform the Civil Service, as an integral part of its programme and as a necessary condition of its success, remains one of the great unstudied phenomena of the post-war period.[21] Attlee was proud to proclaim the virtues of the status quo, telling a conference of Asiatic socialists in Rangoon in 1953:

> that the same men who had worked out the details of Labour's Transport Act were now, at the behest of a Conservative Government, engaged in pulling it to pieces.[22]

Attlee went on to say he doubted 'if this impartiality is sufficiently realized even here at home. There were certainly some people in the Labour Party who doubted whether the Civil Servants would give fair play to a Socialist Government, but all doubts disappeared with experience.'

To find the answer to this surprising conservatism it is necessary to do more than to link it to Attlee's lengendary traditionalism about any of the great institutions he had belonged to or worked with. One has to delve back into the Second World War itself and the plans for postwar reconstruction that were being pieced together at the very moment Whitehall was improvising, innovating and managing by objectives as never before or since.

Strangely for a party whose effectiveness when in government is crucially dependent on the efficient use of state power, Labour has never really developed a theory of bureaucracy. Conservatives, on the other hand, have always had one – they don't like it, particularly the free marketeers among them who make a crude correlation between the tiny Civil Service and the world-beating economic performance of Britain during its nineteenth-century industrial apogee. During the 1987 general election, for example, Mrs Thatcher tackled a questioner at a Manchester factory who had asked about the North–South divide by replying: 'Just remember the North was made prosperous long before the South. The North was made prosperous by the initiative of the people long before there was any such thing as a Department of Industry or people from Government telling them about technology'.[23]

There was, however, an occasional intellectual foray on the bureaucratic theme from a Labour movement figure. Take the now almost totally forgotten and neglected Professor Harold Laski, who, much influenced by American notions of federalism and the separation of powers, developed a strain of thinking in the 1930s which sought to protect individual liberty from bureaucratic power within a socialist framework. Laski had been a member of the Donoughmore Committee on ministerial powers in 1929–32 'and became a fierce critic of the despotic implications of the quasi-judicial powers being annexed by faceless public servants in impenetrable government sanctums'.[24] But Laski's belief in a strong central state *and* a dispersal of powers within society seems to have overcome neither its inherent contradictions nor the disinterest of the wider Labour movement even during his decade of maximum influence. But time and chance put another socialist technician-of-the-state, Sir Stafford Cripps, in a position to give his theories a run on the inside track of government when the last ounce of productivity was being squeezed from the state machine in 1942, the year the wartime tide finally turned in favour of the allies.

The early setbacks of the Second World War had, to a certain extent, prepared the ground for Cripps' initiative on the machinery of government. There was, not for the first or the last time, a tendency in a crisis to blame Whitehall for a wider failure in the nation's performance. As Professor Michael Lee, the anatomist of the Second World War machine,[25] has written:

> As the Soviet model of economic planning was paraded before the popular imagination by Left-wing journalists and other critics of the British government's war organisation, the real presence of American economic power was becoming painfully apparent to the ministers and

> officials whose competence was in question. There was in addition for Britain the dreadful spectacle of the loss of the dependent Empire in the Fast East to the Japanese. From the fall of Singapore in February to the Battle of El Alamein in October 1942, much of the criticism raised against the structure of government organisation had an apocalyptic ring.[26]

These were pre-Beveridge days, but public thoughts were already turning to postwar reconstruction. Archbishop William Temple had popularised the concept of the welfare state (coined as a contrast to Hitler's warfare State). Into this promising compost of public opinion was inserted the austere, high-minded form of Cripps freshly returned from Moscow where he had been Ambassador to a regime shortly to peak in popularity in Britain at the time of Stalingrad. Absurd as it may now seem, Cripps appeared for a time to be an alternative to Churchill, not least to Cripps himself. He joined the War Cabinet as Lord Privy Seal and Leader of the House in February 1942 and used complaints about the machinery of government as a weapon of personal power.

Whatever else Cripps may have been, he was sincere in his convictions. Machinery of government was important to him. As Kenneth O. Morgan rather unkindly put it, for Cripps 'technology was all'.[27] With slightly greater charity, Douglas Jay, who worked under him at the Treasury, spoke of the 'strict bureaucratic rule of law under Stafford Cripps'.[28] A research chemist turned lawyer, specialising in highly technical briefs, he believed in the possibility of scientific administration and, like the Webbs, saw it as part of the motive power of the forward march of British socialism. From the War Cabinet Room, he pressed the case for 'another Haldane' to the horror of the senior Civil Service, who, to be fair to them, later came to appreciate what Cripps himself described as his tidy mind made up, as it was, of 'a series of well-fitted drawers'.[29] Churchill did not care for Cripps's suggestions either and grumbled about valuable ministerial time being wasted by 'academic and philosophical speculations which ought in these times to be the province of persons of leisure'.[30] Faced with such mighty opposition, Cripps's push for a new Haldane was diverted into an internal inquiry into practical machinery-of-government matters carried out by a small team of officials supervised by a Cabinet committee under Anderson. Parliament was to be kept out altogether. The recommendation of the Select Committee on National Expenditure that a standing select committee on the Civil Service be established got nowhere, as did Cripps's revival of Haldane's idea of select committees to shadow individual Whitehall departments. The war may have shaken British society from top to bottom but not Whitehall's capability for seeing off intrusive outsiders keen to scale what James Margach called 'the walls of Whitehall's forbidden city'.[31]

The insider review sparked off by Cripps lasted for ten years, well into the peace, coming to an end when Churchill was back in No. 10 once more. Very little came of it for the fundamental reason that the insiders' preoccupation with practical, limited matters and their horror of Haldane-like theorising, meant that their lengthy deliberations 'rarely took the form of explicit reflections on the Constitution or on constitutional behaviour'.[32] The tone of the ten-year exercise was very much set not by ministers but by Whitehall's 'higher divinities', as they were called, Bridges and Brook, who were central to the work throughout. Just how immune the higher Civil Service, baked hard by Warren Fisher, had become to outside influences even in a time of turmoil can be seen from Michael Lee's encapsulation of its defensive attitude, an attitude shared for the most part by the ministers who presided over it:

> Ministers and civil servants who experienced both war and reconstruction were genuinely ambivalent about the degree to which their more realistic approach could be shared with informed opinion outside. The traditional secrecy of Cabinet government was difficult to overcome. There were also a number of inhibitions which seemed to arise from the association of the science of public administration with socialism, or with 'rationalism in politics'. If the better 'human relations' in industrial personnel management would make capitalism more acceptable, a more systematic approach to public administration was the symbol of 'the New Deal' [Cooper's point to Attlee in his 1946 letter urging an inquiry into Whitehall] . . . Furthermore, insiders often found that the comments of outsider academic specialists in public administration were too naive and idealistic to carry conviction within the Civil Service. Inside realism was in large measure setting the attitudes of practical men against the propositions of the theorists.[33]

What a smug, unimaginative, insular world Michael Lee portrays! No trace there of Beveridge's declaration in December 1942 (as the Anderson Committee was beginning its work) in his famous report on social insurance that 'a revolutionary era is a time for revolutions not for patching'.[74] The key to understanding the lack of result is not timidity, however, but self-confidence. Ministers, just as much as Whitehall's 'higher divinities', knew they were running a machine that had worked in wartime and would continue to do so in the peace. The home front's performance, guided and goaded by the immense application of state power, had delivered the goods at a time of supreme national crisis and again in more tranquil times if the lessons of wartime organisation were learned and put into effect. Such feelings applied as much to Attlee and his ministers as to Bridges and his permanent secretaries.

The most important and durable example of this was the carrying over of the wartime model of strong Cabinet committees into the reconstruction period. The tiny War Cabinet was replaced by one of a normal size. But the strong underpinning of committees remained. This would have been publicly acknowledged by the Coalition if it had not broken up shortly before a planned White Paper on the machinery of government was due to be published. Instead, coalition thinking only trickled into the public domain when Anderson delivered the Romanes Lecture at Oxford in 1946 on the subject of machinery of government which, as Michael Lee expressed it, 'had the air of a substitute for the authoritative government report which was never completed'.[35]

The importance of Attlee's consolidation of the Cabinet machine was underlined by Lord Hunt of Tanworth forty years later:

> After 1945 you had another very big watershed with the government moving into areas which it didn't involve itself in before the war. This was the introduction of the welfare state, nationalisation, Keynesian economics – the feeling that the government was responsible for almost everything and needed to take a decision about everything. And this obviously imposed very great burdens on the old-style collective decision-taking by the Cabinet. The Cabinet couldn't remain in permanent session. The ministers had to be at their desks. And so the solution was to devise a system of Cabinet committees which was sufficiently representative of the Cabinet's views as a whole to take decisions in the Cabinet's name. And you had a proliferation of these committees which was a particular British innovation and I think was very successful at that time in coping with the problem of overload on government.[76]

The Second World War bequeathed to Whitehall, as we have seen, a remarkably rich and skilled mixture of public officials which it squandered, and a streamlined yet heavy-load-bearing Cabinet structure which it adapted and used to great effect. It also bequeathed to the Civil Service Commission the richest field of talent from which to pluck young high-flyers. Lord Hunt, after a war spent in the Royal Navy, was one of the young flyers brought into Whitehall by the reconstruction competitions which telescoped six years of suspended recruitment into three. Their combination of youth and war-induced experience made them unique. There will never be another generation like them. They were, as Ian Bancroft autobiographically put it, the Whitehall intake for whom 'everything was achievable'.[37] Their background, motivation and the cast of their minds made them ideal instruments for the Keynesianism, the public ownership and welfare programmes described by John Hunt – or nearly all of them. At least one candidate who appeared before Sir Percy Waterfield's pride and joy – the new Civil Service Selection Board modelled on the wartime War Office Selection Board for Officers[38] – saw his mission in totally different terms, as another future Head of the Civil Service, Sir Douglas Wass, remembered in his 1983 Reith Lectures: 'In the competition I took in 1946 to enter the Civil Service, the candidates were asked to give their reasons for applying. Most of us gave fairly conventional answers, but one, perhaps a little less orthodox with his background in the commandos, said quite simply, 'to stop the worst excesses of the Labour Government'.[79] The Civil Service Commission has photograph albums of the classes of 1945–8 – serious, mature young men (very few women still) in their mid-twenties in demob suits summoned for a selection of tests, exercises and interviews to the legendary country house at Stoke d'Abernon near Leatherhead.

Stoke d'Abernon also processed the new breed of diplomat foreshadowed in the Eden–Bevin reforms of 1943. Once installed in the Foreign Office Bevin set great store by these as, in the words of his biographer Lord Bullock, 'the foundation of the post-war foreign service'.[40] There were those at the top in the 1945 FO, 'still something of a world apart in Whitehall',[41] who expected to benefit, forcibly, from the early retirement provisions outlined in the 1943 White Paper, the Permanent Secretary, Cadogan, and his deputy, Sir Orme Sargent, among them.[42] To the surprise and fury of sections of his party, Bevin kept the 'Old Gang' in their place, preferring to bring in new blood for special assignments (like Sir Oliver Franks recalled to chair the Marshall Plan negotiations in 1947), to promote men of proven worth from within the office and to bed-out his cherished Labour attachés in embassy after embassy while waiting for his 1943 reforms to work their way through the system.

The FO may not have changed overnight from a stronghold of privilege to a citadel of secondary schoolboys and schoolgirls. Bevin didn't want it to. He was not class conscious. 'I am not one of those who decry Eton and Harrow', he said. 'I was very glad of them in the Battle of Britain – by God! I was.'[43] Merit was what he cared about from whatever social level it originated. The amalgamation of the various overseas services and the admission of women fostered meritocracy. (The second woman to be admitted to the Diplomatic Service, Cicely Ludlam, married the FO's junior minister, Christopher Mayhew, prompting a typical outburst of Bevinry: 'What does Chris think we are? A bloody matrimonial bureau?')[44] A number of senior postwar diplomats – such as the future Permanent Secretary, Thomas Brimelow, and the future Ambassador to Moscow, Terence Garvey – began their careers in the prewar Consular Service.[45] Bevin, wholly confident of his plans, beat off calls for political appointments to the Diplomatic Service made during the 1946 Labour Party Conference:

> It is said that these men do not carry out my policies. I deny that. I beg of you not to try to introduce the wrong principle into the Civil Service. I have had a good experience now for six years. What the Civil Service likes is a Minister who knows his own mind and tells the officials what to do. They will then do it. If it is wrong, the Minister must take responsibility and not blame the Civil Service. That I am prepared to do.[46]

It would be wrong to believe, as his left-wing critics claimed, that Bevin succumbed to the aristocratic embrace. He was in awe of no one. The foreign secretaryship has never seen a more self-assured figure who knew full well he was 'a turn up in a million'.[47] But he never forgot where he came from. He adored the FO's office-keepers and, as Bevin's private secretary, Sir Nicholas Henderson, remembers, 'the very English, not to say Podsnappian, way in which they would usher some foreign visitor into the Secretary of State's room. Flinging open the great door majestically they would proclaim His Excellency's arrival, as if he were some strange circus artiste from abroad.'[48] And Bevin's name is still blessed by the doorkeepers at the Park Door entrance to the FO (by which all diplomatic unfortunates summoned to hear the contents of a stiff note are filmed by the television cameras). Ernie insisted on the installation of a glass partition to protect them from the elements.[49] When he left, a dying man in March 1951, the news of his unwilling transfer to become Lord Privy Seal reached him during his 70th birthday party at the FO. Everyone, from the permanent secretary to the doorkeeper, had contributed sixpence to buy the present – a desk and a dinner service.[50]

The postwar FO, like the rest of Whitehall, benefited from the hard training that wartime service had given its recruits, so different from life in the examination crammer and the leisurely tour through Europe of the old days. But self-confident and experienced and sometimes highly decorated though they were, the postwar Whitehall intake had much to learn quickly as Mr Attlee's engine-room pushed forward the boundaries of state activity. They learned on the job. The Civil Service College was some twenty-five years away and its precursor, the Centre for Administrative Studies, nearly twenty. The learning process was Whitehall's equivalent of the school of hard knocks, as the lessons of politics, internal and external, were brought home to the young men. Sir Douglas Wass, a highly numerate Cambridge Wrangler who had worked in weapons research in the war, during his first week in Whitehall found himself presented by his Treasury principal, 'Mac' MacEwan, with a copy of the Army Estimates for 1946–7 and a request that he comment on them. Sir Douglas rejected the lot. MacEwan, a seasoned official with a Revenue background, complimented him on his precocious appreciation of the need for Treasury control but warned him that this was not the best way for a new assistant principal to proceed as the Estimates had only just been agreed after a lengthy negotiation between the department's defence matériel group and the War Office.[51]

Sir Leo Pliatzky, Sir Douglas's colleague in the Treasury's top hamper during the great currency and spending crises of the mid-1970s, joined the Ministry of Food in February 1947 after war service in the Army (he was one of those now myth-laden officers who lectured his men in the desert about the Beveridge report) and a spell as Research Secretary of the Fabian Society. The ministry was still presiding over 'a siege economy'.[52] Sir Leo progressed through the Alcohol and Yeast Division and the Home Grown Cereals Division in the MOF's grim office block in Portman Square. After a while he was made head of branch in the Animal Feeding Stuffs Division housed in Stanmore on the north-western edge of London. He found himself responsible, among many other things, for the National Pigeon Service (*everything* was conscripted in the war, even the birds of the air). This did not trouble him until the Labour Government began its 'bonfire of controls' as Harold Wilson, now President of the Board of Trade, called it on Guy Fawkes Day 1948.[53] A chain of events had begun that was to bring Sir Leo in from the bureaucratic cold of Stanmore to the fierce heat of political controversy at Westminster.

Pliatzky decided, Hitler having been defeated, that it was no longer necessary for His Majesty's Government to import maple peas and maple beans from Australia and New Zealand, a hard currency import it should be said, specially for the men of the homing pigeons unions whose birds had been on standby throughout the war in case the mails failed. Trained in Politics, Philosophy and Economics at Oxford Sir Leo thought, naturally enough, that reason was on his side. The Treasury agreed. The pigeon lobby did not:

> When this measure of decontrol was announced, there was strenuous resistance to it from the homing unions. Concerned at the possibility of higher prices and perhaps even a forced change of diet for their birds, they had 50,000 standard letters of protest printed, so that each of their members could sign one and send it to his Member of Parliament appealing against this measure of decontrol. The homing unions were particularly strong in coal-mining areas and, as the miners were held to have a good deal of clout, there were those who spoke gravely of this move. Members of Parliament simply sent these printed letters on in bunches to the Minister of Food [John Strachey, the leading socialist intellectual] so that he could let them have replies to send back to their constituents. All the letters were passed on to me so that I could provide the Minister's office with draft replies. The Ministry as a whole were

used to dealing with an average of a thousand letters of complaint a day ... but to me this avalanche of complaints was new.[54]

Thirty years later Sir Leo would tell this story with great glee, about how those sacks of mail paralysed his entire branch and taught him much about Parliament and pressure groups.[55]

Very swiftly the best and the brightest moved on to the fast inside tracks of Whitehall. Thanks to the thirty-year rule their progress can be traced in the official files. For example, the neat italicised handwriting of Sir Patrick Nairne catches the eye in Admiralty papers on Operation Zebra, the plan to use sailors to break the dock strike of 1948[56] and one I. P. Bancroft, as private secretary to the Treasury's Sir Henry Wilson Smith, turns up in the huge and well-preserved Treasury and Foreign Office archives on the 1949 Devaluation crisis.[57]

Postwar Whitehall was *the* place to be for the young and clever with a high personal charge of public duty. The beneficial capability of well-directed state power enjoyed an acceptance and an appreciation which peaked in the 1940s, for all the privations and crisis. And the crises were real enough, as was the self-confidence that they could be handled. For example, the grimmest file on the British economy I have encountered at the Public Record Office was a crash contingency plan prepared by the Treasury for Dalton during the Convertibility crisis of 1947 when, under the convertibility clauses of the 1945 American Loan, the country's gold and dollar reserves poured out across the exchanges. Otto Clarke, that highly gifted irregular who stayed on after the war, had within days to produce a survival plan for Britain if the dollars ran out and Marshall Aid failed to come on stream in sufficient quantities in time. Clarke and the very small, highly secret team working with him stared into the abyss. If the worst happened, said the report prepared for the Chancellor of the Exchequer, to survive Britain would need a 'famine food programme', conscription on to the land, 'radical interference with educational arrangements' to enable children to help with the harvest, drastic re-alteration of the sterling bloc and the creation of an autarkic trading system.[58]

When I encountered this file in 1979, I sent photocopies to the surviving members of the secret group of planners. One of them, Sir Frank Figgures, who had entered the Treasury in 1946 and finished his career as chairman of the Relativities Board during Mr Heath's winter crisis of 1973–4, replied with a revealing letter which captured perfectly the strange mixture of crisis and confidence of the late-forties Civil Service:

> I do not think that those who were taking part in these discussions felt very frightened ... I doubt whether many of those around that table ... felt that it was unmanageably dangerous. Although in the Treasury we

> perhaps more fully appreciated than most the state in which we had emerged from the war – very badly damaged – we were not at that time suffering from a major lack of confidence in ourselves. Most of those in senior positions in government had been engaged in the mobilisation of our economy in the war effort. On the whole those who had done it felt that it had been well done. We did not assume our economy was as strong as the Americans', but performance during the war years had been quite remarkable by our own standards. Whitehall knew a great deal about the details of foreign trade. Most raw materials and food stuffs were controlled, state trading covered a great area. I do not think that those who were involved in it wanted to continue it, but in the complex situation that could develop there were at hand instruments which had worked, and which no doubt in such circumstances could go on working.[59]

Certainly there was never a more seasoned team for running the country in crisis than the mix of ministers and officials in the Attlee years. But, as Sir Alec Cairncross, who witnessed events from the Cabinet Office and the Board of Trade, recalls, the politicans – for all their confidence and experience – depended heavily on their civil servants when the economic blows stuck:

> The economic problems encountered by the [Attlee] government were not, as a rule, those which it had expected. Equally, the solutions to those problems were rarely of the government's devising. There were exceptions, as when Bevin grasped at what became the Marshall Plan. But more commonly ministers were the reluctant pupils of their officials. On one economic issue after another – the American Loan, the coal crisis, the dollar problem, devaluation, the European Payments Union – they were slow to grasp the true options of policy and had great difficulty in reaching sensible conclusions.[60]

Sir Alec's judgement is undoubtedly accurate. It might, one would have thought, have inspired a degree of resentment on the part of Attlee's ministers, who, on the occasions he mentions, were the led rather than the leaders. There were isolated outbreaks of it. In the early days of the incoming Labour government, as we have seen, some of the top men of the Foreign Office expected to be purged by Bevin.[61] Bevin did not think highly of all of them. He did 'not think much'[62] of Sir Orme Sargent, for example, but nonetheless put up with him as his permanent secretary. At moments of high frustration, Cripps – whom most of the Treasury admired – was prone to outbursts against them as closet free-marketeers just biding their time for a Conservative restoration.[67] And there were vendettas pursued by younger Keynesian ministers against old-school Treasury officials such as Sir Wilfred Eady.[64] But, by and large, late-forties Whitehall approached the 'team model' of ministers and officials pulling in the same direction in an atmosphere of mutual respect. The system worked as it was intended to with very little of the mutual scapegoating that has characterised the two groups in periods when the outcome of public policy has been less successful. Even Hugh Dalton, who could be highly critical of his officials, was, on his return to the Cabinet in 1948, 'impressed once more with the freshness following a break, with the efficiency of the Higher Civil Service, making crisp sense of ministerial wavering diffuseness, and preparing admirable papers making it as easy as possible for ministers to choose between clear alternatives'.[65]

The reason for this was touched on by Paul Addison when he wrote 'that for a few critical years after 1945, the home front ran on without a war to sustain it, and Britain was reconstructed in the image of the war effort'.[66] The same applied to the huge adjustment of foreign and defence policy in response to the deepening cold war. Attlee and Bevin had been members of the key coalition Cabinet committees which tried to foresee and to plan the postwar reconstruction of Europe.[67] They were thoroughly familiar with the issues and with the senior diplomatic, Civil Service, military and intelligence advisers pondering those issues with whom they continued to work after VE Day. In short, Attlee and his senior ministers, despite being a radically intentioned government, did not embark on a reform of the Civil Service in 1945–51 because they knew the wartime machine personally and liked what they saw. They had seen the recent administrative past and it had worked.

For the purposes of immediate reconstruction it continued to work. The population was highly disciplined by the rigours of total war. Yet the task of demobilising the most thoroughly mobilised of the combatant nations was daunting. But it was carried out with a high degree of fairness and efficiency. New tasks were tackled in a wartime task-force fashion. For example, the huge school-building programme in which Sir Antony Part (another future permanent secretary recruited in the reconstruction competition) was crucially involved was successfully carried out with more than a dash of the wartime flair about it.[68] The spirit of 1939–45, which had so amazed old Treasury hands like Sir Richard Hopkins who led the service from 1942 to 1945 (public goodwill in accepting controls, wrote Hopkins, 'went beyond – in my judgement much beyond – any forecast which could reasonably have been made before hostilities began'),[69] was sustained deep into the peacetime years. The new breed recruited in the reconstruction competitions were thoroughly conditioned by it, which made the disappointments of the years after the late sixties so hard for them to take.

The new breed were not the crucial Whitehall figures of the early postwar period, however. For them we must look elsewhere. They have been captured but rarely on film or photograph. Two photogenic occasions come to mind however: VE Day when King George VI received his ministers, his military and his civil servants at Buckingham Palace. As they posed for pictures on the back steps, the King said to Bridges and 'Pug' Ismay (Military Secretary to the Cabinet) 'that he, Bridges and I [Ismay] ought to be taken together as the only three men who had kept their jobs throughout the war'.[70] The second photograph captured their last, sad hurrah at Sir Winston Churchill's funeral in January 1965. As the guardsmen carried the old warrior's coffin down the steps of St Paul's, that hugely successful political, military and Civil Service team waited and watched – Eden, Macmillan, a very frail Attlee perched on a chair, Menzies of Australia. Alongside were Slim and Portal, famous military men in full dress uniform. Between Menzies and Portal stood two grey, tired-looking figures to whom very few people could have put a name. They were Edward Bridges and Norman Brook, the 'higher divinities' of wartime and postwar Whitehall.[71] These were the men who set the tone and the pattern of the peacetime public service. These were the men upon whom, in the end, a reshaping of the Civil Service after 1945 crucially depended. Bridges, as we have seen, contemplated it briefly in 1946. Neither wished it or saw the need for it. Neither was a Trevelyan or a Fisher by another means. Why?

The most obvious answer is that Trevelyans and Fishers were rarities, that public services do not often throw up them or their like. It could also be argued that the tight, closed society created by Fisher made the recruitment, let alone the subsequent rise of fire-in-their-belly reformers even more unlikely than in the period before the gates of the Civil Service had closed so tightly against the heterodox and the irregular. It would not have occurred to Bridges or Brook that there was anything fundamentally wrong with the service over which they presided. Outside critics, as we have seen, were brushed aside as if they were ignorant and parasitical fleas on a flourishing, healthy body. Yet it would be misleading to see the two titans of post-1945 Whitehall as identical twins.

There was an informal in-house competition in Whitehall as to who was the greater. The Economic Section of the Cabinet Office came up with a balanced but revealing judgement: 'Bridges is the best of the poetry of the Civil Service, Brook the best of the prose.'[72] At the other end of the Civil Service hierarchy, less subtle standards applied. An old Treasury messenger watching the head of his profession disappearing down the long corridor of the New Public Offices said: 'Disgraceful, Sir Edward has holes in his socks!'[73] The loyal ancient would never have had any cause to criticise the appearance of Norman Brook, who was hyperfastidious about dress sense. His private office would not dare to wear tweeds to work unless Sir Norman was on leave.[74] One of his deputies, Sir George Mallaby, was warned not to attend Cabinet meetings in such a condition.[75]

Bridges was artistic, informal, intuitive. His preferred method of running the Civil Service was a discreet chat over tea and buns.[76] He subjected his fellow permanent secretaries and the newest Treasury assistant principals to this routine.[77] A summons to tea with Sir Edward was an awesome thing for the eminent as well as the lowly, as Sir Harold Kent recalls from an episode in Coronation Year, 1953, which captures to perfection the flavour of the Bridges style:

> When, at the beginning of March, I received a summons from the Head of the Civil Service, I walked round to Great George Street with mixed feelings. I knew of several cases of men with brilliant careers who had worked themselves into a nervous breakdown, or had become queer and difficult, and had been translated into some backwater where they could do no harm. I couldn't think of any reason why Bridges should want to see me, except a personal one.
>
> My fears subsided in the warmth of my reception by Tim Bligh, Bridges' private secretary who became Macmillan's principal private secretary. A condemned man would be received kindly, but not with this air of joyful expectation. He ushered me into Bridges' room, where I perceived that I was going to receive the VIP treatment of a cosy chat in two armchairs by the window.
>
> 'I want you to succeed Tommy Barnes next month as Treasury Solicitor', said Edward Bridges, beaming all over his face. 'Not to mention the Queen's Proctor.'
>
> I beamed too, but I was speechless. I had thought of many things but not of this . . .
>
> 'Do you really think I could do it?' I said.
>
> 'I don't know', said Bridges, 'but I want you to try. All the pundits say you're the man . . .'
>
> 'Yes, I'll try', I said soberly. 'Tommy Barnes will be a difficult man to follow, but I'll do my best.'
>
> 'Good man, that's settled then. And don't forget, Harold' – he used the Christian name of the Permanent Secretaries' club – 'I'm always here if you're worried about anything. That's what I'm for.'
>
> We had a cup of tea together and discussed the virtues of Tommy Barnes . . . We talked about the manifold things that could happen in the day of a Treasury Solicitor. 'You'll have a lot of fun', said Edward Bridges.[78]

Bridges used the word 'fun' a great deal. With the less august of his profession he would playfully land a mock punch on them as he said it;

another characteristic that distinguished him from Norman Brook who did not practise the bureaucratics of joy. When not engaged in business over tea, Bridges would tell his private office to 'shut up shop' while he edited the letters of his father, Robert, the Poet Laureate.[79] Brook's tea-time reading was the more interesting Foreign Office telegrams.[80] William Armstrong worked intimately with both Bridges and Brook, eventually succeeding to their mantle as head of profession. He once compared them for me in one of those word portraits which made conversation with him a pleasure. Typically for an English civil servant, power of the pen as revealed in draftsmanship was an important criterion:

> Brook was an immensely tidy person with very beautiful neat handwriting with a very much stronger sense of order and tidiness than Bridges. He had great clarity and was probably the best of the [first] three [Cabinet Secretaries] in sheer drafting ability. Hankey was a pretty awful draftsman. Bridges was a good natural stylist but Brook was very careful. Hazlitt was his favourite English author. Brook wrote a manual for the secretaries of Cabinet committees – very concerned that form should be clear and workmanlike without embellishment.[81]

As for Bridges, William Armstrong remembered: 'He believed in concentrating on the main issue not bothering too much about administrative tidiness or tying up loose ends, somebody else could do that. He was a very accessible person.'[82]

Bridges carried this informality of style into his crucial task of picking people for the highest Civil Service posts; not for him a committee of advisers or anything approaching the big board used by Sir William Armstrong or the elaborate 'succession planning' of post-Rayner Whitehall. Intuition was all. Bridges turned to the playing-field for an explanation of his philosophy:

> . . . the job of giving advice to the Prime Minister in these cases is not a matter of forming an order of merit of the candidates for a particular post, nor indeed of forming orders of merit of the candidates for a succession of several posts. The task is much more complicated. It is much more like that of placing the members of a cricket eleven in the field in the way which will give the strongest result for the team as a whole. It is no good settling that a particular man is the best slip field in the eleven if you find that you have got to ask him to keep wicket.[83]

Passages like that make Bridges prone to parody as did his 1950 tone poem to the gifted amateur, *Portrait of a Profession*, which was accurately described by Samuel Brittan as 'an inexhaustible quarry of quotations for radical critics'.[84] Bridges should not be underestimated, however. He was a formidable operator with a huge capacity for work and an acute sense of the permanent continuity of the state. This was perfectly illustrated in late 1941, one of the bleakest periods of the war. Despite the international outlook and the existing strain upon him, Bridges found time to set up a series of official histories of the war. Professor Sir Keith Hancock was recruited to edit them. He later recalled his initial meeting with Bridges:

> Was there any use or point, I asked him, in starting to write the history of war before we had won it? He replied that I would find ways of making myself useful in short term but I must also think in long term of the continuity of the State and the advantage of funding our war-time experience for future use . . . He told me about the [Cabinet Office's Historical Section] which hitherto had confined itself to military history; but the armed forces nowadays were no more than the cutting edge of the nation at war and their history had no higher importance than that of munition making and agriculture, of shipping, land, transport, mining and all the other civilian activities.[85]

Bridges, like Brook after him, had strong feelings about setting the record straight with top-flight official history, both military and non-military. Hancock's civil team numbered some thirty scholars in the late 1940s.[86] Subsequent Whitehall generations were lacking in this respect. By the late 1980s, the civil side of the Cabinet Office's Historical Section had dwindled to four authors.[87]

From 1945, when Hopkins retired, to 1947 when Brook replaced him at the Cabinet Office, Bridges held three jobs – Cabinet Secretary, Head of the Civil Service and Permanent Secretary to the Treasury – and all this after six punishing years of war in which, as we have seen, he was continually at the centre of events. As his friend and colleague, Sir John Winnifrith, noted:

> The strain on Bridges was terrific. It was not made easier by the lack of an easy relationship with Mr Churchill or by Mr Churchill's methods of work. The Prime Minister could never forget that Bridges had served Mr Chamberlain and, though he did not regard him as a man of Munich, there was not the same close rapport with him as there was with Ismay. This was partly a question of temperament. Bridges was shy and to those who did not know him, austere and almost prudish.[88]

After Churchill's death Bridges wrote his own account of their relationship.[89] In the period of the 'phoney war' when Churchill was First Lord of the Admiralty they had had a little spat over the Cabinet conclusions.

Churchill told Bridges 'that the Minutes I wrote were far too full and detailed. To all intents and purposes, he said, I was running a magazine. The Minutes should be far shorter.'[90] The transition from one prime minister to another can be difficult for a Cabinet Secretary to make. Bridges was no Horace Wilson, but would he be treated by Churchill as one of Chamberlain's 'Old Gang'? As he sat in the little waiting-room at Admiralty House on 10 May 1940 for his first interview he put his drafting skills to good use:

> ... as I sat and waited, I wondered what I should say to him. Twelve hours earlier I had been serving a different Prime Minister. It would not be becoming for me to be too effusive. And would congratulations be in place when one considered the desperate situation the country faced? So when I went into his room I said, 'May I wish you every possible good fortune?' He gave me one of the little grunts that one got to know so well, and after a long look said, 'Hum. Every good fortune! I like that! These other people here have all been congratulating me. Every good fortune!' As I was to learn later on, he was very conscious of the unspoken attitude of those he dealt with, and I am sure that he looked right into my mind, and knew why I had spoken as I did.[91]

Bridges learned quickly, too, that Churchill demanded that policy submissions be crammed into one side of typescript. The 'prodigious amount of intellectual effort'[92] often needed to meet this requirement frequently fell to Bridges. He had also to accommodate himself to Churchill's appetite for working through the night. Unlike Churchill, the Cabinet Secretary could not go to sleep as dawn broke. The resultant briefs had to be prepared for meetings the next morning. He gave himself twenty-four hours off each week from 6.00 p.m. on Saturday to 6.00 p.m. on Sunday.[93] The accumulated strain of this regime began to tell in the late 1940s when he developed 'a mysterious muscular nervous complaint'.[94] He was greatly looking forward to retirement at the general election of 1951 (he was fifty-nine when the government changed). Brook was to succeed him as Head of the Civil Service. Sir Thomas Padmore was to move from the Treasury to the Cabinet Office to replace Brook. Churchill's return to power scuppered this. The old warrior demanded familiar faces around him. Bridges stayed at his post for another five years.

Despite the fatigue, which was common to all those at ministerial or official level who had served as key components in Whitehall's war machine, Bridges remained a towering figure in the Attlee years, not just in the natural authority he wielded within the permanent secretaries' club but as an influence on the economic policy front too. Bridges was a classicist not an economist. He never presumed to give technical advice beyond his grasp. But he was a point of calm in an economic storm. He was despatched to Washington, for example, in December 1945 to ease Britain's negotiators, Keynes and Robbins, through the last stages of the American Loan discussions.[95] During the 1949 sterling crisis he made sure that Cripps, by this time Chancellor of the Exchequer, was properly apprised of the full width of advice from Keynesians like Robert Hall to anti-devaluationists like Sir Wilfred Eady.[96] Bridges seems to have stood somewhere between the two. His standard advice to ministers was that there were no easy answers to deep-seated economic problems like the dollar shortage and the need for greater productivity.[97]

This did not, as Churchill found in other circumstances during the war, always make Bridges the ideal dining companion.[98] The memory of his first lunch as Chancellor of the Exchequer in the Athenaeum with Bridges and William Armstrong, for example, burned itself into R. A. Butler's memory, a memory he expressed in his own singularly ironic style in his memoir, *The Art of the Possible*:

> We sat at a table in the window and ate what remained of the Club food after the bishops had had their run; for we were somewhat late, and the bishops attack the sideboards early. Both my singularly able advisers stressed the critical state of the economy and promised me a memorandum within a few days. Their story was of blood draining from the system and a collapse greater than had been foretold in 1931. I returned home in sombre anticipation of what was to be dished up to me, but already comforted by the personalities with whom I was to work.[99]

Butler, very much a permanent secretary *manqué*,[100] had no difficulty in instantly forming a team with the Treasury officials bequeathed him by Gaitskell; not for him any equivalent of Churchill's silly remark on surveying his No. 10 Private Office in October 1951 that they were 'drenched with socialism'.[101] He used them as allies when seeing off a variety of Churchill-inspired threats to the Chancellor's suzerainty on economic affairs.[102] Bridges's relationship with Churchill was less happy. They did not resume where they had left off in July 1945. During the war, as Sir John Colville, a close witness of their relationship, put it, despite their lack of warmth, Churchill 'had esteem for his judgement and put reliance on his advice'.[103] Six years on, things had changed:

> There were no disputes over official appointments, for Churchill was but little interested in departmental chiefs. There were occasional wrangles over the Honours List; but the distance which grew between the two men was due mainly to the fact that Bridges, after years of conscientious slogging in the service of his country, and one of the heaviest burdens

> of responsibility, was a tired man whose patience was tattered and whose acceptance of the new Government's economic and financial policy was always loyal, but by no means wholehearted ... [and] ... a new light was shining in Churchill's eyes. It reflected his liking and confidence in Bridges' successor as Secretary to the Cabinet, Sir Norman Brook.[104]

Sir John witnessed the Bridges–Churchill relationship from very close quarters in the No. 10 Private Office. It should be noted that nothing Butler wrote or said suggests that Bridges was lacking in sympathy for the economic policy of the incoming Conservative administration, which caused few problems for Whitehall, as Lord Croham, then an up-and-coming Treasury flyer, showed when he told Anthony Seldon that less change occurred in 1951 than at any other transfer of power since the war.[105] Bridges, however, could and did annoy Butler (an indecisive man) by not being being willing, or sometimes able, given his duties as head of profession, to drop everything to speak to the Chancellor.[106] Those duties could also cause friction with other key figures in the Cabinet like Sir Anthony Eden who did not enjoy being told by Sir Evelyn Shuckburgh, his private secretary, that 'Whitehall would not care for two Foreign Office private secretaries at No. 10' when Eden became prime minister. 'They can do what they are told', stormed Eden. 'I am not going to be run by Bridges!'[107]

Bridges's last quinquennium, for all the esteem in which his colleagues held him, was not altogether happy. The final great event in which he played a part – Suez – seems to have been a particularly distressing experience. He seemed tired even before the crisis broke. His designated successor, Sir Roger Makins, Ambassador to Washington (and a close confidant from wartime days in Algiers of Butler's successor at the Treasury, Harold Macmillan), called on him during a visit to London in April 1956. Talking about the two jobs that Bridges combined, heading both the Treasury and the Civil Service (the two were split in October 1956, Makins taking the Treasury and the headship passing to Brook who became joint Permanent Secretary to the Treasury while retaining the Cabinet Secretaryship), Sir Roger asked 'How do you manage it?' 'I don't', Bridges replied. 'I just catch one ball in four.'[108]

When the Suez crisis broke with President Nasser's nationalisation of the Canal Company on 26 July 1956, Bridges took responsibility for the 'Sterling War Book' and contingency planning to protect the pound from any consequences of international uncertainty and, if the worst happened, war. For one last time, he fulfilled the classic function of the civil servant – that of briefing, advising and warning the minister. On 8 August he minuted Macmillan on the Sterling War Book. Macmillan, a hawk until the very last moment when the United States applied its economic muscle to halt the Anglo-French invasion on 6 November, was warned by Bridges less than two weeks after Nasser seized the Canal that 'the trouble here is that the action to be taken is almost wholly different according to the situation which we are faced with – a limited war, or a not so limited war – a war in which we go it alone, or a war in which we have the Americans with us from the outset'.[109] Bridges told Macmillan that measures might be needed to protect sterling in the autumn even if there was no war. A month later the very circumstances which eventually halted the Anglo-French invasion were foreseen at the highest level in the Treasury and passed on to Macmillan by Bridges.[110] Less than a month later, Bridges, who had entered the Treasury as the British Empire peaked in territorial terms at the end of the First World War, went into retirement within weeks of its death-rattle in Egypt. He had done his duty to the last. For his pains he was kept out of Eden's inner circle of confidants and advisers. In his last days in Great George Street, Bridges sent his private secretary, Derek Mitchell, down the corridor to ask Brook for Cabinet committee papers dealing with plans for the Suez invasion. 'He was told by an embarrassed Brook that he had strict instructions as to who was to see the papers and Sir Edward was not one of them.'[111]

Though those instructions were laid down by Eden, not Brook, there could have been no more graphic an illustration of how and where the power in Whitehall had long since passed. The rise of Norman Brook baffled the high Tories in those class-conscious days. Eden's successor, Macmillan, gave lunch to Churchill's physician, Lord Moran, during the Parliamentary summer recess in 1959. The conversation turned to Brook. 'What do you think of Norman?' asked Macmillan. 'Do you think he looks better than he used to? I like to keep office hours. I don't keep him up half the night; Norman has most wonderful judgement. He is always right. Pure inborn judgement, because, as I expect you know, he had no background.'[112]

Brook went to Wolverhampton Royal Grammar School, a fine direct-grant institution. Presumably by having 'no background' Macmillan meant that he had not attended Eton or married a duke's daughter. Brook won a classical scholarship to Wadham. At Oxford he inspired, perhaps unknowingly, the worst kind of prejudice against the grammar schoolboy. Maurice Bowra, the legendary classical scholar much given to pronouncements on the social origins of those he encountered,[113] taught the young man from the Black Country.[114] Years later when Brook was Cabinet Secretary Bowra recalled his early impressions of Brook while accompanying a member of his college for a walk along the towpath. 'Very quick, Brook', recalled Bowra. 'Learned the tricks, learned the tricks. Came up with a front pocket stuffed full of pens. Soon disappeared inside. Learned the tricks.[115]

Brook clearly learned a trick or two from the fine if snobbish mind of

Bowra, taking a first in Mods. A scholarly career beckoned. As he later told George Mallaby, the authorities at Wadham said that if he gained a first in Greats he would be awarded a fellowship. He got a second and, as Mallaby put it:

> then felt he must look elsewhere. In this uncertain frame of mind, kicking his heels, as all of us have often done, in the College Lodge [Mallaby's circle, perhaps, was not of the widest], he observed a notice inviting applications for a competition for the Administrative Class. That very day was the closing date, and off he rushed to the Appointments Board, filled in a form, sent it off, and in due course sat for the examination, came out third in the list of successes and, after years of unremitting toil and absolute devotion, became Lord Normanbrook.[116]

Chance, it seems, can play its part in the career pattern of one of the most methodical minds ever to be shaped by the experience of Greats at Oxford. Brook's 'unremitting toil and absolute devotion' found its first official application in the Home Office which he entered in 1925 in its Andersonian heyday (Anderson was to be his patron and mentor both as a permanent secretary and as a minister). Brook advanced steadily through the Aliens Division, the Children's Branch, the private offices of two Home Secretaries (Herbert Samuel and Oliver Stanley) and the Criminal Division. He made his formidable reputation as a war planner revising the War Book and, under Anderson (back from governing Bengal by this time), as the reviver of civil defence. Even as a young man Brook was hugely impressive at interdepartmental meetings.[117] His *Times* obituarist had clearly seen Brook in action on many occasions and wrote down what obviously was a lexicon for success in that closed, decorous world:

> Norman Brook was a man of immense authority. The first impression was of size, with a head that was large even for such a heavy frame, and a calm gaze from heavy-lidded eyes. Then came the quiet, rather slow voice. At the start it might seem casual, even lethargic. But this illusion was dispelled as his voice took on a cutting edge and he shaped the words on which he wished to pivot his thought. And whether he was giving information, or advice, or instructions, his thinking was dominated by the need for good order in public affairs. Good order was also the characteristic of his personal work – the written word pared down to the minimum; the elegant, even hand; the clear desk, scrupulously punctual, responsive to the call of urgency, but never confused, never hurried.[118]

Brook, it seemed, had learned all the bureaucratic tricks – a paragon who rose effortlessly during the unusual conditions created by the war from assistant secretary at its outset to Cabinet Secretary in all but name (Bridges stayed on nominally to avoid a hierarchical clash between Brook and Ismay)[119] at its end. But to regard him as machine-man, the *compleat* neutral public servant of Northcote–Trevelyan specification, would be wrong. He was highly politically attuned and he did not shrink from pressing his own opinions in the steering briefs he penned for the prime minister before Cabinet or Cabinet committee meetings. For example, he cautioned Attlee against the abolition of capital punishment during preparation of the Criminal Justice Bill 1948[120] and, almost single-handedly, he talked the Labour Cabinet out of a thoroughly illiberal and unnecessary counter-subversive law during the Korean War.[121] But it was under Churchill that Brook became influential beyond a point that traditionalists would think proper. Colville captured the secret of Brook's influence over the old man:

> Brook had a less simple and straightforward personality than Bridges, but he was more adept socially and he was equally conscientious. Little by little Churchill came to rely on him in all things and to find his presence wholly agreeable. Unlike Bridges he was invited to be a member of the Other Club and he was regarded as an *ex-officio* companion every time Churchill crossed the Atlantic to confer with the Americans. Nothing was too much trouble for him and no details escaped his attention. He was wise in his advice and while appearing to fall in, at an early stage, with ideas that he privately thought wrong or extravagant, he presented the counter-arguments so skilfully and so tactfully that they were nearly always approved.[122]

Brook's first application of these formidable yet subtle powers of persuasion was to ensure that the new model Cabinet system was not jettisoned by an anti-bureaucratic premier, telling Churchill in the brief awaiting his return to No. 10 in 1951 that 'During the past ten years the system of Standing Cabinet Committees has proved its value as a means of relieving the Cabinet of a great weight of less important business.'[123] Temporarily, however, he lost the argument about 'overlord' ministers whom Churchill wished to see supervising clusters of ministries.[124]

Strong advice on such technical machinery-of-government matters was wholly in order. But it did not stop there, as Sir John Colville, who was present at meetings between Cabinet Secretary and Prime Minister, remembers:

> Brook did play a more active role in Cabinet and other ministerial appointments than had Bridges, although Bridges had often been asked

> for his advice. Brook gave his gratuitously and he did so in private so as not to upset the delicate sensitivities of the Chief Whip, Patrick Buchan Hepburn. For instance, when I was alone with Churchill at Chartwell [his country house in Kent] in June 1952, Brook joined us in the evening. The object of his journey was to suggest that Lord Woolton should abandon the chairmanship of the Home Affairs Committee and that Anthony Eden should take it over, relinquishing his portfolio as Foreign Secretary. Churchill was inclined to favour the proposal, but he remarked that Eden had become 'Foreign Officissimus' and would not be induced to change.[125]

As Colville drily remarked, 'Eden would have been even less amused than Queen Victoria if he had known what plots the Prime Minister and the Secretary to the Cabinet were hatching behind his back.'[126] Had the extent of Brook's influence over such wholly political matters become known at the time it would have placed him in the unfortunate category occupied by Horace Wilson before him and William Armstrong after him. As Colville's diary shows, after Churchill's stroke in 1953 (which was kept secret even to the extent of doctoring a medical bulletin on the premier's condition[127]) the country was virtually run for a month by a triumvirate of Colville, Brook and the Prime Minister's Parliamentary Private Secretary, Christopher Soames, Churchill's son-in-law, in the old man's name.[128] By the end of July, Churchill had recovered sufficiently for 'Christopher and I [to return] to the fringes of power, having for a time been drawn perilously close to the centre' wrote Colville.[129] As it was, all Brook had to contend with during his career were some rather laboured jokes linking Cabinet-making with his private passion – carpentry (see picture no. 8).

For all his closeness to the centre in Churchill's last years, there were some boundaries Brook would not cross. At a meeting of the Cabinet's Defence Committee in 1954, called to discuss the possible manufacture of a British hydrogen bomb, Churchill tried to get the Cabinet Secretary to confirm that Attlee had decided to make the atomic bomb without informing the full Cabinet. Brook stared out of the window and said nothing.[130] However, his image as the stern, unbending guardian of proper procedure took a bit of a battering when Sir Evelyn Shuckburgh's diaries were published nearly twenty years after Brook's death. Shuckburgh, as Eden's Foreign Office private secretary, was on the innermost of inner circles in 1951–4. He records the chit-chat among the initiated at the private secretaries' cocktail party in the Cabinet Office in March 1954 in terms which convey the unforgettable flavour of that tiny but influential world as well as revealing a surprisingly bitchy side to Brook:

> Talked to Norman Brook, George Mallaby and [Tim] Bligh (Bridges' Private Sec) and they all complained about the Chancellor. He is moody and impossible to deal with, having his Budget shortly ahead. Norman attributes his character to the fact that Mrs Butler [the formidable Sydney Courtauld] ought to have been a man – is a man – so that Rab has become a woman. I said pity both the Chancellor and Foreign Secretary should be women.[131]

Yet Brook's gift of appealing to all sorts and conditions of men, political and official, was remarkable. For a Labour politician, Douglas Jay,

> Norman Brook ... was probably, with Edward Bridges, the most accomplished permanent civil servant of my years in the government service. He blended suavity with sagacity in a way which somehow made work pleasant, and seemed to possess a hardly ever failing instinct for a compromise or a procedural device which would resolve the worst ministerial deadlocks. He adjusted with charm. Nobody could draft a more masterly minute, letter or parliamentary answer.[132]

Some officials admired him almost to the shores of idolatry. One young civil servant who rose high in the Home Office took to smoking a pipe in calm imitation of the great man.[133] Even after his death, Brook's style cast a long shadow. A stickler for confidentiality and orderly procedure, he was cited by Dame Evelyn Sharp (by this time Lady Sharp) shortly after the publication of the Diaries of her former minister, Richard Crossman, had driven a coach and horses through all Whitehall's cherished conventions. 'This would never have happened in Norman Brook's time', she said.[134]

Bridges and Brook were policy men, masters of procedure and managers of ministers rather than managers in the business sense. And the young flyers recruited in the late 1940s, the successors of Bridges and Brook well into the 1980s, were groomed in their tradition, which was, as Bridges's *Portrait of a Profession* showed, the pure late-nineteenth-century tradition of Northcote–Trevelyan. As Sir Douglas Wass put it, 'When I was a young man in the Treasury, the concentration of the training I received was really on ... the delivery of excellence, it was the supplying of a service to ministers which was as near Rolls-Royce as you could make it. You were not encouraged to think of the cost of delivering that service.'[135] Sir Douglas, though nowadays thoroughly seized of the idea of better management at the highest levels of the Civil Service, remains thoroughly imbued with the ancient guild principles in which he was steeped in the Bridges–Brook era:

> The outsider frequently ... has considerable difficulty in understanding what I call the craft of government. It's a completely different activity from the making of profits, from the developing of entrepreneurial skills – I'm talking now of the policy advisers rather than the managerial function.
>
> But in policy formulation you have a multiplicity of issues to take into account of anything you look at. The political dimension is always there ... both with a small 'p' and a capital 'P'. When a businessman looks at the sort of issues that confront him they are very rarely the same sort of political issues, the constraints which the political system imposes on the Civil Service. And in my experience businessmen are not good at handling those political constraints, they become impatient of them and if one's impatient of those constraints, the likelihood is that one would get things wrong and irritate the Opposition. One will fail to achieve what finesse and diplomacy can. Finesse and diplomacy are an essential ingredient in public service.[136]

That would have fitted without a hiccup in delivery into Bridges's *Portrait of a Profession* lecture nearly forty years earlier. And Sir Douglas's oft-quoted remark in his 1983 Reith Lectures that he doubted the place of enthusiasm in administration – 'It can colour judgement and lead to unwise decisions. Even the politically committed should be wary of enthusiasm. But energy is a different matter.'[137] – is very similar to Bridges's warning that 'the Walls of Jericho do not nowadays fall flat even after seven circumambulations to the sound of the trumpet'.[138] The reconstruction generation were deeply steeped in the timeless traditions of the Civil Service, as Bridges meant them to be. The Elders taught well. When Sir Ian Bancroft became Head of the Home Civil Service in 1977 he let it be known that he wanted to set a tone as Sir Edward Bridges had done. Six years later in a public lecture at the London School of Economics, which became famous for its flimsily concealed attack on the Thatcher Government he had so recently served ('The ritual words of praise, forced out through clenched teeth in public deceive no one if they are accompanied by noisy and obvious cuffs round the ear in semi-private'), Bancroft contrasted the contemporary malaise of his profession with 'the then self-confidence' of those golden postwar years. Sir Ian painted a remarkable personal portrait of the young man who presented himself at the Treasury as a winter crisis enveloped the government and the country:

> The weather on 20 January 1947 was bitter, and rapidly becoming worse. It was the cruellest winter ... The Earl's Court bed sitting-room soon had no heat, no light, no water ... 20 January was the day I joined HM Treasury reasonably fresh from the 7th Armoured Division and a brief

return to Oxford. It was twenty months after Hitler's suicide. Harry S. Truman had still to face his first US Presidential election. Frederick S. Trueman was still only fifteen years old. Dalton was Chancellor of the Exchequer. Wilson was Parliamentary Secretary to the Ministry of Works. Let me extend the perspective, for it is important to get the context. As a boy, I knew my mother's family housekeeper. She had been born when Wordsworth and Wellington were still alive; before the Crimean War . . . before, too, the birth certificate of the modern Civil Service had been filled in, namely, the 1853 Northcote–Trevelyan report. Time takes more spin than some spectators realise.

The Treasury I joined was a small community. The most vivid impression I had of it was self-confidence. I had come from a regiment (the Rifle Brigade) and a college (Balliol), neither deficient in self-esteem. Treasury staff, and their peers in other departments, seemed well-endowed with it, too. One could dismiss the remark that they had been modest, good-humoured men and that it was Whitehall which had made them insufferable. There was nothing insufferable about them. There were legendary figures in other departments too. If they were proving difficult they were invited to take tea with Bridges or the appropriate Second Secretary. If they were extra difficult they were given cake with their tea. But as then seen from more junior levels in the Treasury, some of these legendary figures . . . seemed monsters.[139]

It would be wrong, however, to depict these impressive 'monsters' of the postwar years as wholly backward-looking and traditionalist in the immediate postwar years. They were improvement-minded if not reform-minded. We have seen how Brook championed the enhanced Cabinet machine to the returning Churchill in 1951. He had done the same in 1946 when Attlee, goaded by the ever machine-minded Cripps, attempted to cut down the Cabinet committee workload endured by ministers.[140] In the Autumn of 1946, Brook minuted Bridges about his wish to put 'to the Prime Minister some of the arguments *in favour* of handling business through Cabinet Committees. I suspect at the moment he sees all the disadvantages and none of the advantages of committee work.'[141] Brook clearly had his way. Attlee's Cabinet paper on Cabinet committees circulated on 26 September 1946 was imbued with his Cabinet Secretary's philosophy.[141]

Bridges and Brook worried, too, about the public-expenditure implications of the Attlee administration's policies. Two months after Labour was returned, albeit with a slim majority of six in the 1950 general election, Brook minuted to Bridges:

> It is curious that in modern times the Cabinet, though it has always insisted on considering particular proposals for developments of policy and their cost, has never thought it necessary to review the development of expenditure under the Civil Estimates as a whole.
>
> It is remarkable that the present Government have never reflected upon the great increase in public expenditure, and the substantial change in its pattern, which has come about during the past five years in consequence of their policies in the field of the social services.[142]

Brook recommended a system of twice yearly forecasts on future spending to be prepared for the Cabinet and the designing of a review procedure to examine the distribution of spending between various services. Very little came of this initially. Two months later the Korean War cast all forecasting to the winds, stimulating, as it did, an eventual quadrupling of the defence estimates. Five years later, though, the Treasury developed something along these lines for the Conservative Chancellor, R. A. Butler, as part of his examination of social service spending.[144]

Bridges and Brook, however, swiftly developed a close and effective working relationship with the one bureaucratic innovation of the Attlee years – the Central Economic Planning Staff – after an initial skirmish with Herbert Morrison about the Whitehall location of the Chief Planning Officer, Sir Edwin Plowden, a successful businessman and wartime temporary brought back into government in March 1947.[145] Plowden was Franks-like in his ability, though an outsider, to get on with the people and the institutions with whom he was brought in to work. After the reorganisation of economic portfolios and the structure of economic decision-taking which followed the Convertibility crisis of July – August 1947, the September ministerial reshuffle and the resignation of Dalton, after leaking budget secrets to a journalist, in November, Plowden formed a remarkable and enduring partnership with the new Chancellor, Sir Stafford Cripps. The two men suited each other – intelligent, high-minded and production-minded, as Douglas Jay, who saw them at close quarters, noted:

> As Chief Executive of the Ministry of Aircraft Production in the War, he [Plowden] had gained an impressive reputation as a practical organiser, and his sympathy with Cripps' religious beliefs gave him great persuasive power with the Chancellor. Sometimes it seemed to some of us that Plowden's inclination to share Cripps' faith in strength through sacrifice might push this moral maxim too far. But in 1947–51, as we have all learnt since, it was certainly a fault on the right side.[146]

Plowden had a gift for getting on with ministers which survived the change of government (there had been some nervousness about the CEPS's chances of survival, and Bridges, who strongly wished it to carry on, had been in touch with the Conservative Opposition about it).[147] Butler swore by Plowden: 'I depended on Edwin Plowden . . . to interpret and give practical edge to the advice generated by the less voluble and extrovert Hall [Sir Robert Hall, Chief Economic Adviser], to act as *vulgarisateur* or publicist for his ideas. Plowden was to become my faithful watchdog-in-chief.'[148] As a scion of the great and the good (see pp. 551–2) Lord Plowden remained a quietly influential figure for forty years after he returned to Whitehall to lead the CEPS.

The Central Economic Planning Staff has been almost entirely neglected by scholars as a body worthy of study in its own right. The best work on it is a fine unpublished undergraduate thesis written by Charles Andrew.[149] It has been ignored, I suspect, because Labour's vague but grandiose ideas about planning – 'nebulous but exalted',[150] as Cairncross describes them – came to very little. The Economic Planning Board, which Plowden chaired and the CEPS serviced, was an early National Economic Development Office bringing together government, employers and unions. It produced one four-year plan in 1948 but it had no real power. That lay with the Cabinet and its Economic Policy Committee. As Joan Mitchell, the historian of British economic planning, put it, 'A committee of this kind could not plan in the proper sense. It had no power to make any direct impact on the allocation of resources. Neither industrialists nor trade unionists *per se* can forecast the structure of the economy in a technical way . . . What they can be expected to do, however, is to comment in a general way on economic policies which may be required to carrry out forecasts or plans presented to them.'[151] The Economic Planning Board began work just as the Labour Government began to shed many of the physical controls bequeathed by the war in favour of fiscal controls and demand management along Keynesian lines.

The CEPS, however, had a proper job to do in two areas: it took the lead in co-ordinating the British side of the Marshall Plan; and it acted as a problem-solving capability for the Government on matters great and small from the dollar import programme and the balance of payment to the making of briquettes from coal slurry and the economics of egg production. Like its spiritual successor, the Central Policy Review Staff, the CEPS was demand-led, a pattern set, as Charles Andrew has shown, 'during the economic crisis conditions of the first few months of the CEPS' existence [when] their job was essentially that of short-term crisis management: increasing the production of aluminium houses and opencast coal, scrutinising steel requirements, looking into building project delays, and estimating future electricity demand'.[152] Like the Attlee Government as a whole, the CEPS was very production-minded.[153]

The CEPS was a bit bigger than the CPRS – 25 as opposed to 17. It mixed outsiders and insiders, specialists and generalists. It was particularly strong on trained economists – like Eric Roll, a wartime temporary who had been persuaded to stay on,[154] Austin Robinson, who had been a key figure in the War Cabinet Economic Section and the young economist, Ken Berrill, a future head of the CPRS. The CEPS regulars, too, often possessed highly relevant skills. Douglas Allen, Plowden's private secretary and a future Head of the Home Civil Service, had a degree in economics and statistics. The CEPS worked well and closely with kindred spirits like Otto Clarke in the Treasury,[155] that 'forceful and ingenious man' with his 'disruptive magnetism', as Bridges put it.[156]

In its way it was a *cabinet* for successive Chancellors – Cripps, Gaitskell and Butler. Like good *cabinets* should be, it was a flexible instrument. During the Korean War it was central to the economic mobilisation of the country and instrumental, as Bridges noted at the time, 'in seeing how a very considerable increase in the rearmament programme can be put into effect promptly and quickly with the least damage to British industry'.[157]

The key to its success was Plowden and his fruitful relationships with his ministers, career regulars like Bridges and fellow professionals like Robert Hall with whom he worked closely and influentially during the 1949 Devaluation crisis. Plowden's departure for the new United Kingdom Atomic Energy Authority in 1953 was seen as a severe blow by Butler which 'undoubtedly weakened my position and that of the British economy'.[158] With Plowden gone, the CEPS became marginalised and subject to dismissive criticism from within Whitehall, particularly from the Economic Section (now housed in the Treasury, too). By the end of 1954 it had been absorbed into the regular Treasury machinery.[159]

The CEPS, though for a time it found a place on the inside track of economic policy-making, was rather puny, as machinery-of-government changes go, given the huge change war and reconstruction had wrought in the nature and scope of government. The permanent consolidation of the wartime Cabinet committee system was genuinely significant. But it amounted to a somewhat meagre result from the thousands of hours of top people's time absorbed over a decade by the Anderson Committee and its successors before the machinery-of-government initiative started by Cripps petered out when the Conservatives returned to power and 'there was a strong official reaction against central MG [machinery-of-government] work when it seemed no longer viable as a guide to the tasks of institutional development or as a corollory of government intervention by physical controls'.[160]

In some areas, postwar Whitehall could be forgiven for expecting, albeit wrongly, that current conditions were a temporary dislocation. It would have been an arch-pessimist even by Civil Service standards who assumed that the problems of what Sir Paul Gore-Booth, the economic diplomat, called 'a thinly lined Exchequer'[161] would continue to blight policy-making for most of the postwar period or that Britain's standing as a world power would diminish so swiftly and starkly, particularly after Suez, that 'terrible setback for British arms and influence',[162] as Sir James Callaghan called it. Indeed, postwar economic and diplomatic planning was predicated on Britain's restoration as a great power. It was the basis of Bevin's policy at the Foreign Office and Cripps's at the Treasury. It explains why the development and manufacture of a British atomic bomb was an 'of course' decision in 1947[163] and why the Chief Scientist Adviser to the Ministry of Defence, Sir Henry Tizard, was treated 'with the kind of horror one would expect if one made a disrespectful remark about the King'[164] when he provided his superiors with a highly unpalatable piece of analysis which, to hindsight-laden eyes, reads in a remarkably prophetic fashion:

> We persist in regarding ourselves as a Great Power, capable of everything and only temporarily handicapped by economic difficulties. We are not a Great Power and never will be again. We are a great nation, but if we continue to behave like a Great Power we shall soon cease to be a great nation.[165]

Officials who speak truth unto power in terms as stark as that inevitably court the brusquest of rebuttals from their political chiefs. Lord Rothschild suffered a similar fate when he did a Tizard twenty-four years later during the Health premiership, despite the accruing tribulations of the country's society and economy during the ensuing generation.[166]

It was all very understandable that those in authority in what was still, despite sterling crisis and austerity, Europe's leading economic power and the world's third military power, after the United States and the Soviet Union, would not see plainly the dramatically changed international and economic circumstances in which Britain and her Empire were living and the fundamental adjustments that would have to be made either voluntarily or under duress. Having said that, there were changed circumstances visible and seemingly permanent even to the undiscriminating eye, let alone to Whitehall sophisticates in the permanent secretaries' club.

For a start there was the phenomenon of great new state industries which exercised Geoffrey Cooper MP and, thanks to his letter to Attlee, the permanent secretaries themselves for a time. It is easy to forget the magnitude of this economic shift, particularly in recent times when Labour's then trade and industry spokesman, John Smith, declared that 'the Morrisonian principles on nationalisation are outdated'[167] and the Treasury's former privatisation desk-man, Gerry Grimstone, claimed that 'if the present political climate is sustained, there seems nothing to stand in the way of the eventual demise of the British nationalised industry'.[168] At the time, the extension of public ownership had an air of massive permanence. Only the nationalisation of steel aroused genuine controversy between the parties. The extension of public enterprise moved a workforce of 2,304,200 people from the private to the public sector between 1945 and 1951.[169] The statutes rolled from Parliament as if off a production line – the Bank of England, civil aviation, Cable and Wireless, coal, railways, gas, electricity, road transport and steel. The model was the London Passenger Transport Board created in 1934 by Herbert Morrison during his London County Council salad days.[170] Whitehall departments would sponsor public corporations. Ministers would appoint efficient, expert people to boards which would run the industries at arm's length from Whitehall, Westminster and the work-force[171] (there was no question of industrial democracy marching shoulder to shoulder with nationalisation until Tony Benn made the running when Labour found itself in opposition in the early 1970s).

The extra workload on the sponsoring departments in Whitehall was immense both in quality and quantity. The arm's-length relationship proved a pipedream. The distribution of scarce investment was too crucial even under Labour's semi-planning to permit it. What was needed were half-way house ministries somewhere between the all-hands-on wartime Ministry of Supply and the all-hands-off departments of the interwar years, with hybrid staffs of insiders and outsiders, generalists and professionals to match. Instead, it was Whitehall business as usual. As in the 'New Liberalism' years, the scope of the state overreached its Whitehall grasp. The double tragedy is that in the recent wartime experience Bridges and his colleagues had all the experimental data to hand for a new bureaucratic strain to be developed – fluid, capable and managerial; and it even reached the formal agenda of the permanent secretaries' club. A great opportunity was squandered and much lost in Bridges's room on that Saturday morning in March 1946.

Prior to that meeting Sir F. P. Robinson in his letter to Bridges had contrasted the previous social services phase of Civil Service development with the new industrial/managerial responsibilities now befalling it. The postwar period saw a dramatic and permanent extension of the social-service workload. Again, it was a qualitative as well as a quantitative shift. The welfare statutes began to roll even before the wartime coalition government relinquished office with the Family Allowances Act, 1945. Labour's intention was to implement the Beveridge Plan for a comprehensive welfare state within three years of taking office.[172] It did exactly that with the Industrial Injuries, the National Insurance, the National Assistance and the National Health Service Acts of 1946 with the National Health Service, the jewel in Labour's crown, coming into being as if on cue on 5 July 1948, the third anniversary of Labour's victory at the polls, nationalising 1,000 voluntary and 2,000 local authority hospitals and embracing 95 per cent of the population within its care.[173] Not only did this rolling welfare programme produce a surge of expenditure, as Brook pointed out to Bridges in his 1950 minute on spending control, it brought into being a nationwide social security organisation run directly by central government,[174] unlike the Lloyd George welfare state which relied on other agencies such as the friendly societies.

The Benefits Office joined the Labour Exchange as the visible symbol of the state in every high street in the land, a formidable management task in itself for the minister, Jim Griffiths, and his small team of advisers in Carlton House Terrace.[175] But there was more. The welfare state required its clerical factories to process an ever more complicated mesh of entitlements. The pioneer establishment, now DHSS Newcastle Central on its huge site at Longbenton, started life as the Ministry of National Insurance outstation in a converted warehouse in the Team Valley, Gateshead.[176] The creation of what Griffiths called his 'nation-wide administration'[177] changed the face and the configuration of the Civil Service as a whole – to a younger, non-London-based corps with many more women among its (lower) ranks, a 'two nations Civil Service', as one historically minded official called it in the 1980s.[178] The unions grew in size and strength. Thanks to Whitehall's new welfare machine, the Civil Service Clerical Association had by 1948 doubled its pre-war size to stand at 153,000.[179] It quickly became and has remained the largest and, usually though not invariably, the most militant of the Civil Service unions. This, too, changed the nature of Civil Service management once the precedent of official industrial action was set in 1973,[180] peaking in the then record-breaking 22-week Civil Service strike of 1981. To the traditionally minded official in Whitehall it must have seemed as if the welfare state had created a new clerical proletariat of its own. Indeed, during the 1987 industrial action, the Civil and Public Services Association claimed that parts of its membership were forced by low pay to become supplicants from the benefits system they themselves ran.

Sadly, international circumstances forced a continuation of a substantial warfare state after 1945 as, almost without a pause, the menace of Stalin's Red Army replaced Hitler's Wehrmacht as the preoccupation of Whitehall's military planners. The Ministry of Supply's network of ordnance factories shrank but did not disappear. A substantial number of industrial civil servants were retained in the peace to be Britain's cold war armourers in a world where technological leaps occurred as a matter of routine from one generation of weapons to another with the new, costly and huge enterprise of atomic weapon production siphoning off the best, the brightest and the most highly skilled.[180]

This wholesale requisitioning of scientific brainpower, begun, as we have seen, by the compilers of the Central Register in 1938–9 and continued on a lesser but still substantial scale after 1945 (the Conservative Government of Mrs Thatcher declared publicly in 1987 its view that too much national talent was absorbed in defence research[182]) might, if reason was any guide, at last have catapulted the Civil Service professionals into a place in the Whitehall sun. Reason is not a guide. War enfranchised the government scientists. The image of the brilliant, slightly batty boffin producing war-winning-wonders from a chaotic Nissen hut became firmly etched in the national consciousness. A. P. Rowe, superintendent of the radar research establishment evacuated from vulnerable Swanage on the Dorset coast to Malvern College in Worcestershire, said that the Napoleonic Wars may have been won on the playing fields of Eton but this one would be won on the playing fields of Malvern.[183] (Malvern, as it happened, was not an ideal site for the Telecommunications Research Establishment. The ancient igneous rocks of the Malvern Hills have magnetic properties which affect its instruments. Folklore at the now renamed Royal Signals and Radar Establishment, still based at Malvern, has it that their original destination was Marlborough College in the chalky Wiltshire Downs until a clerical error in the over-stretched Whitehall of 1940 did its diversionary work.[184])

Thanks to Hitler, those pressing the cause of science, like the anonymous authors (in reality the legendary figures Solly Zuckerman and J. D. Bernal) of the 1940 Penguin special, *Science in War*[185], were 'pushing at a door which was already half open, and which would soon be torn off its hinges by the pressure of events'.[186] Such pressure pushed the boffinry on to the agenda of the Cripps-inspired machinery-of-government review. Naturally, administrators dominated this, though, to be fair, Sir Alan Barlow, the Treasury official most closely involved, 'had cultivated scientific interests, particularly through friends and acquaintances in the Athenaeum'.[187]

The fundamental appetite for applied science created by war was not the only advantage enjoyed by Civil Service professionals. They had a uniquely placed lobbyist in Lord Cherwell, Churchill's beloved 'Prof', for whom, as his biographer put it, the war inaugurated 'an extraordinary period of power without responsibility, power greater than that exercised by any scientist in history'.[188] The Prof's submissions on the celebrated one side of A4 often stimulated the sending of a Prime Minister's Personal Minute, the most potent piece of paper in Whitehall then as now, on scientific matters. Events and personalities can suddenly enfranchise lobbies even when, as in the case of the scientific community, they were fragmented. Its grander figures, the presidents of the scientific institutes, quite rightly warned in a letter of *The Times* in the summer of 1943 that the degree to which social problems could be solved by scientific methods alone was limited and that 'a scientific and soulless technocracy would be the worst form of despotism',[189] a pre-echo of Harold Macmillan's pithy aside seven years later that 'We have not overthrown the divine right of Kings to fall down before the divine right of experts'[190] – never a danger in Britain except, perhaps, in public housing, the very area in which Macmillan subsequently made his political reputation. Whitehall's professionals themselves showed no desire to take over the political and administrative world, however great the opportunities presented by the demands of total war. As Michael Lee discovered in his researches, 'Although it was important to many specialists that they should have as easy an access to ministers as the administrative class, they hesitated to put their argument within a machinery of government context, and concentrated on the forms of recognition which better pay and conditions could express.'[191]

Little had come of the scientific side of the machinery-of-government review by the time the Coalition fell. In December 1946, the Attlee Government published a White Paper which created the Scientific Civil Service as a separate entity.[192] This was largely the work of Lord Hankey, the former Cabinet Secretary, who was far from happy with subsequent progress on improving the standing and numbers of scientists and technologists, writing as much to the Minister of Labour, George Isaacs, in 1949.[193] Just how meagre was the impact of war on the long-term status of Whitehall's professionals can be found in a Treasury brief prepared almost a decade after hostilities ceased. It took the form of a background paper drawn up by the Establishments Division for Bridges prior to his appearance before the Priestley Royal Commission on the pay and conditions of the Civil Service. The note, which reflected the views of 'various permanent secretaries', was dated 1 November 1954 and entitled 'Points in favour of the Administrator, as contrasted with the Specialist'. It reads:

> Wider view-points. Duty to keep in mind greater variety of considerations. The specialist's contribution to policy (if any) is confined to specialist considerations: administrator must take account of these and others too.
>
> Greater versatility: must be capable of being switched from one job to another with quite different content.
>
> More wear and tear. Takes main impact of Ministerial, Parliamentary and PAC [Public Accounts Committee] requirements. 'Cushions' and 'carries the can for' the specialists.
>
> Recruitment is much more selective: the average AP entrant is a superior article to the average SO entrant.[194]

Of all the Treasury files I have read that one takes the prize for smugness, narrowness, arrogance and restrictive practice. If it had fallen into the hands of a French civil servant, schooled in one of the *grands corps*, he would have thought it quite mad. If Lord Cherwell had seen it (he had left government the year before) his comments would have been unforgettable. It was fortunate for Bridges that Churchill (still in No. 10) did not see it.

It would, however, be quite wrong to brand an entire profession for a whole era on the basis of memoranda like that. As we have seen, the Bridges–Brook generation possessed superb qualities of the kind Northcote–Trevelyan prized. They were intelligent, admirable, hard-working men, high-minded and proper. To accuse them of missing an opportunity to reshape their profession in response to new circumstances is not to diminish that. Though I never knew that generation personally, my admiration for them is more than sneaking. They had, after all, worked themselves into the ground during a world war which, if the Axis powers had won, would have resulted in my generation being born into a tyranny.

It would be equally wrong not to recognise that the postwar Civil Service contained among its most senior ranks administrators with a generalist background, as well as professionals, whose zest and foresight would have graced any public service at any time anywhere. At the very highest level there was, for example, Sir Frank Lee, permanent secretary successively at the Ministry of Food, the Board of Trade and the Treasury. He was short and unprepossessing in appearance, but his officials adored working for him. Lord Croham, his successor-but-two at the Treasury, said of him, 'A lovely man, good humoured, good company, very sensible and very down to earth. He wouldn't pull rank on those below him and was not intimidated by those above him whoever they were.'[195] There was nothing desiccated about Frank Lee. If he believed in a policy he would argue it through with his ministers. He could be very persuasive. At the Board of Trade in the early 1950s he weaned his President, Peter Thorneycroft, away from that traditional Tory cause, imperial preference, and converted him into a free trader. Thorneycroft, primed by Lee, persuaded the Cabinet and – much more difficult – the Conservative Party Conference. Later in the fifties Lee more than any other civil servant was responsible for the decisive shift of opinion in Whitehall in favour of the Common Market.[196] Lee's independence of spirit may have had something to do with his background in the Colonial Service as a district commissioner in Nyasaland where he fostered football as an alternative to tribal strife.[197] A colonial blooding into the public service could not have been more different a formative experience than the traditional rise from Treasury assistant principal.

Another public servant, self-confident and entrepreneurial in the Lee mould, who deserves an honourable mention in any *galère* of the postwar period is Sir Andrew Cohen, known in the Colonial Office as 'the King of Africa'. Cohen, with Attlee's Colonial Secretary, Arthur Creech-Jones, providing the crucial ministerial support, more than anyone else began the remarkable process of decolonisation (the Indian sub-continent, a different and a special case had, of course, preceded this process) by preparing the way for an eventual transfer of power in the Gold Coast (Ghana from independence day when it eventually came in 1957). The process was a remarkable political and administrative feat by any standards – one of the greatest, though nowadays least-mentioned, of Whitehall's postwar success stories. Between 1947–8 (India, Pakistan, Burma and Ceylon) and 1980 (Rhodesia/Zimbabwe) forty territories were granted independence by the United Kingdom. It was a feat unprecedented in international experience as 'no nation had ever before voluntarily given away pieces of its empire (except the United States giving away the Philippines in 1935)'.[198] In bureaucratic terms this was hugely ironic. The Colonial Office only really became a large department during the Second World War when the human and material resources of the Empire were thoroughly mobilised in the anti-Axis cause. From their base in Church House, Westminster, Creech-Jones and Cohen set in train a geopolitical revolution. Brian Lapping has painted a bright portrait of Cohen, the Cambridge classicist, member of the Apostles in its legendary/notorious 1930s phase, who became head of the Colonial Office's Africa Division in the late 1940s and 'Britain's most effective anti-colonialist'.

> He was physically huge, like an elephant, always bursting into rooms, his hands full of stuffed briefcases and his keys or the rim of his Homburg clenched between his teeth. Unlike Creech Jones, Cohen came from a wealthy and well-connected background. The modest, quiet minister, who was hopeless in the House of Commons but clear on the principles he was determined to pursue, and the superior, self-confident civil servant, who was equally dominant in committees and at dinner parties, made an odd but highly effective couple.[199]

Whatever else can be said about interwar Cambridge, which proved such a fertile recruiting ground for the Russian intelligence service, it also provided postwar Whitehall with many of its genuinely dynamic figures like Frank Lee, Andrew Cohen and Otto Clarke. It was the zest they brought to the service of the state which made them unusual. A colleague's comment on Lee could have applied to all three – 'the curious thing about Frank is that he has never become aware of the fact that there is such a thing as uninteresting work'.[200] There were others like them. The personnel to work a rebored Whitehall machine were there after 1945. The plans and the production engineers to carry out the task of reboring were not – or not in the key ministerial and Civil Service positions.

To have avoided missing the postwar opportunity for reform would, depressingly, have probably required the nation to experience a degree of trauma unlikely to be experienced by a victorious power. It was defeat, occupation and the subsequent collaboration of large tracts of its ruling elites that led to the post-1945 transformation of the French Civil Service – a price for progress too appallingly high to be wished on any country, let alone one's own. To illustrate the postwar French administrative spirit and to contrast it with the Bridges–Brook era, it is only necessary to quote from its moving spirit, Michel Debré, and the purposes he outlined for his elite civil service school in Paris, the legendary Ecole Nationale d'Administration, intended to provide, as it duly did, a new young generation to replace the tainted *ancien régime*:

> The school must teach its future civil servants the sense of the state; it must make them understand the responsibilities of the Administration, make them taste the grandeurs and appreciate the service of the profession. It must do more. By a sustained effort of its best teachers, by recalling the great examples and the great men of its history, it must give to its pupils the awareness of some master qualities; the sense of humanity which gives life to all work; the sense of decision which allows them to take risks, having weighed them; the sense of imagination, which is not afraid of any boldness, or any grandeur.[201]

Even if Whitehall's wartime machinery-of-government exercise had managed to publish its planned White Paper before the Coalition fell it would not have – could not have – come up with anything like that!

One of the many reasons for this arises from the DNA of the British civil servant since Northcote–Trevelyan. Passion for policy is not supposed to be a part of their genetic code. That is what, in their different ways, made officials like Lee, Cohen and Clarke different, as it had Vansittart and Morant in previous generations. The orthodox professional requirement has been put most succinctly by a former professional head, Lord Bancroft: 'Conviction politicians, certainly: conviction civil servants, no'.[202] His friend and successor, Sir Douglas Wass, as we have seen, said that officials must show energy but not enthusiasm in the pursuit of ministerial wishes.[203] The reason was given by both heads of profession: to preserve the paramount principle of a permanent Civil Service able to transfer its loyalty from one elected government to the next, that enduring nineteenth-century principle.

A price can be paid for this. Sometimes it can be more than flesh and blood can stand. There was a tragic case with a senior DHSS official who, it is thought, may have committed suicide in 1970 when a cherished piece of social policy did not survive the change of government.[204] It is an unresolved dilemma at the heart of the Civil Service's (unwritten, as yet) ethic. It has never been better expressed than by Derek Morrell, a gifted, inspirational maker of progressive social policy at the Department of

Education and Science and the Home Office where he was the moving spirit behind the original urban programme in the late sixties.[205] Morrell's impassioned speech is remembered as if it were yesterday by those who heard it at the 1969 annual conference of the First Division Association shortly before his tragically early death. He began what must be one of the most unusual and thoughtful speeches ever delivered at a trade union conference with a simple statement of the Civil Service ethic as understood by someone who had risen though its postwar ranks:

> We stand committed to neutrality of process. We profess that public power is not to be used to further the private purposes of those to whom it is entrusted. It is to be used solely for the furtherance of public purposes as defined by constitutional process.[206]

With one aspect of this Morrell had no quarrel:

> We have evolved rules for the appointment and promotion of staff, for the control of public money, and for other formal accountabilities, such that even the *temptation* to use public power for private ends has, in these areas, been very largely eliminated.

It was the all-embracing nature of 'neutrality of process in Whitehall' which aroused Morrell's singular *cri de coeur*:

> So far as concerns our private aspirations in the field of public policy, we cling to the myth which science has now abandoned. We still do not accept the reality of our individual humanity; we have not therefore evolved rules of procedure such that we can contribute all that we are to a process having public and not private outcomes. And the price which we and the public pay for pursuing a myth is heavy.
>
> Speaking personally, I find it yearly more difficult to reconcile personal integrity with a view of my role which requires the deliberate suppression of part of what I am. It is this tension, and not overwork, which brings me, regularly, to the point where I am ready to contemplate leaving a service which I care about very deeply.

Morrell's speech was hung on the peg of the Fulton Report, published a year earlier, of which he was highly critical (see p. 205). But the problem of a job description which required them, to use Nye Bevan's unforgettable phrase, to be desiccated calculating machines[207] was there throughout the postwar period, however latent. Only once did it surface in the immediate postwar period and that was at the moment it reached its close during Suez, *the* great political crisis of the 1950s. This stretched the Northcote–

Trevelyan fabric to the point where it began to tear in private if not in public in an uncanny pre-echo of the dilemma faced by Clive Ponting almost thirty years later.

The moral dilemma of many civil servants in both the home and the diplomatic services about the Anglo-French assault on and invasion of Egypt in October–November 1956 and the collusion with Israel which preceded it (which only a handful of them knew of at first hand) seeped out only gradually. Their protest was not public, unlike Flying Officer Kenyon, a Canberra pilot in Cyprus, who pulled up his undercarriage and incapacitated his bomber rather than take off on a mission against Egypt (he was court-martialled, imprisoned and dishonourably discharged from the RAF).[208] William Armstrong's protest was visible, just, inside the Treasury but he did not make it public until nearly twenty years later in a celebrated television interview with Desmond Wilcox shortly before his retirement:

> 'Would you resign over any issue that you felt strongly about?'
>
> 'I've often wondered that. I've never come up against a case where I felt so strongly that I even got within striking distance of resigning. I think I would find it very hard not to resign if a Government tried to abolish the liberty of the subject in some way or other – to abolish trial by jury, to get rid of habeas corpus, something of that kind.'
>
> 'Has there been any time in your own experience when you might have been close to some similar gesture of protest?'
>
> 'At the time when it was decided to put an army ashore at Suez and, as was said at the time, to divide the Israelis from the Egyptians, I felt that that was not only a bad move, in policy terms, but that I personally had been duped, because I had been sent to discuss with the American State Department something quite different – the introduction of a Suez Canal Users' Association which would deal with the Egyptians over the Canal and so on. I was very angry indeed at, as I thought, being used as part of a cover plan while the ... preparations were being made. So I wore a black tie until the operation ended.'
>
> 'Did anybody notice?'
>
> 'One or two chaps noticed, yes. It was the equivalent of letting off steam. I now think it was rather a juvenile gesture ...'[209]

Armstrong was not alone in the Treasury in feeling that way. Indeed, one of its ministers, the Economic Secretary, Sir Edward Boyle, resigned in protest at the invasion. At official level few seem to have sympathised with the hawkish Chancellor, Harold Macmillan. As we have seen, Bridges peppered him with prescient warnings. His successor, Sir Roger Makins, thought ministers were 'running in blinkers'.[210] Younger men like Leo

Pliatzky and Ian Bancroft (who had moved from the Treasury with Butler in 1955 to run the private office of the Lord Privy Seal) were horrified. For Bancroft, it was a failure of Cabinet government: 'There was a little committee ... everything seemed to be conducted in a hurried, reactive, almost furtive way ... it seemed to me to typify the dangers of trying to run something as if it were a private laundry and not, as we then were, a major country on the world stage engaged in a singularly difficult adventure.'[211] For Pliatzky, Suez was 'quite exceptional' in postwar administrative history because of the issue of conscience it raised: 'This was the only occasion in my time in the government service when I had to reflect how the British Civil Service, with its commitment to work for the government of the day, irrespective of its policies, differed from officials in Hitler's Germany who had helped to carry out the Nazi atrocities.'[212]

But it was officials in the Foreign Office, all but a handful kept in the dark about the secret treaty with France and Israel on the personal instructions of the Prime Minister, Sir Anthony Eden,[213] who experienced the most intense pressure on their professional ethic. Several contemplated following their minister of state, Sir Anthony Nutting, into the honourable wilderness of resignation.[214] In the event only Evan Luard, a young diplomat who later became a junior Foreign Office minister, and Peter Mansfield, the distinguished scholar and commentator on the Middle East, resigned from the FO, though the ebullient William Clark, Eden's Press Secretary, left No. 10 in protest.[215]

It was another young diplomat, Hugh Thomas, who left the Foreign Office in 1957, owing to 'more a general distaste for official life' than in protest at Suez[216] (he wrote an entertaining, cathartic novel, *The World's Game*, once free of Whitehall)[217] who pieced together the first inside account from the British side. His *The Suez Affair*, published ten years after the event, talked of 'a group of [FO] under secretaries, the architects of the "special relationship" [with the United States] over ten years, [who] signed a round-robin criticising the operations', citing 'a Foreign Office official' as his source.[218] Still later, Lord Gore-Booth, the FO's deputy secretary on the economic side in 1956 who later rose to head the Diplomatic Service, admitted authorship of the 'round-robin' which, in fact, took the form of a memo signed only by Gore-Booth and forwarded to the permament secretary, Sir Ivone Kirkpatrick.[219] After Gore-Booth's death, the memo was made available by his widow to the Bodleian Library at Oxford. It was written on 2 November 1956, four days after the Anglo-French task force sailed from Malta, three days after the air assault on Egyptian airfields on the day the United States General Assembly called for a ceasefire. Gore-Booth told Kirkpatrick:

I believe it to be only right to make you aware of the following. In the course of the week's business I have seen a lot of members of the Office of all ranks, and have been deeply impressed with the dismay caused throughout our ranks by HMG's action. People are doing their duty but with a heavy heart and a feeling that, whatever our motives, we have terribly damaged our reputation.

I have not sought this opinion, but it is only honest to add that I myself, with my USA, UN and Asia background have been appalled by what has been done – even granted the gravity and imminence of the Nasser menace.[220]

Gore-Booth's memo may not have possessed the drama of the protest sent the same day to the Prime Minister by Lord Mountbatten, the First Sea Lord: 'I am writing to appeal to you to accept the resolution of the overwhelming majority of the United Nations to cease military operations, and to beg you to turn back the assault convoy before it is too late'[221] – but it was highly unusual, possibly unprecedented, for a deputy secretary to communicate in such terms with his permanent secretary. Kirkpatrick, 'a very loyal public servant . . . [and] . . . also a combative Irishman',[222] and one of the handful of diplomats apprised of the full story, was wholly behind Eden's Suez policy, telling Shuckburgh as the crisis deepened that 'the PM was the only man in England who wanted the nation to survive; that all the rest of us have lost the will to live; that in two years' time Nasser will have deprived us of our oil, the sterling area fallen apart, no European defence possible, unemployment and unrest in the UK and our standard of living reduced to that of the Yugoslavs or Egyptians'.[223] Kirkpatrick, nonetheless, took note of his senior colleagues' dissent. On the morning of Monday, 5 November, the day Nutting and Boyle resigned and British and French paratroopers dropped on Port Said and Port Fuad at the mouth of the Suez Canal, Kirkpatrick, in Gore-Booth's words, called 'an urgent top-level meeting . . . at which [he] did his best to answer questions to which there was no answer. For instance, if we and the French occupied the Canal and marched on Cairo, and Nasser escaped to a neighbouring Arab country, what was supposed to happen then?'[224]

It would be misleading to infer from Kirkpatrick's personal view that those civil servants in the know about Suez and the collusion with France and Israel for the purposes of providing the cover-story for Anglo-French military intervention thought differently from the Gore-Booths, Armstrongs and Pliatzkys. Sir Richard Powell, Permanent Secretary at the Ministry of Defence, who was privy to the full story, told me thirty years later: 'I think all officials were doubters. They all felt doubt and hesitation. You know officials as well as I do and that would be typical of them – to have doubts but to carry out instructions.'[225] Full insiders like Sir Richard only felt able to speak after the Suez archive was opened at the Public Record Office when BBC Radio 3 was putting together its Suez documentary, *A Canal Too Far*.[226]

Some, like Brook, were dead and could not speak. From other sources, we know Brook thought the invasion to be 'folly',[227] that if the task force sailed from Malta, Britain would be committed because it could neither turn back nor sit offshore,[228] that he had serious doubts about Eden – 'Our Prime Minister is very difficult. He wants to be Foreign Secretary, Minister of Defence and Chancellor'[229] – and that Brook himself was, professionally, 'in a very difficult position. He had to be loyal to his Cabinet *and* the repository of people's worries in Whitehall.'[230]

Only when old loyalty oaths were suspended after the publication of official papers could those civil servants completely in the know be asked about 'the Ponting dilemma' – what do you do if you think your minister is considering misleading Parliament? In the case of Suez in 1956, unlike that of the Ministry of Defence, its ministers and the sunken Argentinian warship, the *General Belgrano*, in 1982–4, the dilemma is clear-cut. Sir Anthony Eden lied knowingly during his last appearance in the House of Commons on 20 December 1956. Under questioning the Prime Minister said: 'There were no plans got together [with Israel] to attack Egypt,'[231] . . .

Sir Donald Logan, private secretary to the Foreign Secretary, Selwyn Lloyd, and the only man from the British side to have attended both secret meetings at the villa in Sèvres in the Paris suburbs where the protocol binding Britain, France and Israel was signed, was in the Officials' Box in the Chamber of the House of Commons when Eden uttered those words. I asked him how he reacted to the Prime Minister's words:

> 'I felt that at that moment his attempt to justify his intervention to separate the forces simply exploded.'
>
> 'Did you feel at all that you should have done what Clive Ponting in another generation did?'
>
> 'In those days civil servants were not expected to betray their ministers and I certainly did not feel this, no.'
>
> 'You don't regard lying in the House of Commons as a cardinal sin on the part of an elected politician?'
>
> 'Whatever I may think, it is, I think, for ministers to decide their own conduct in the House of Commons and for the House of Commons and the public to judge ministers on their performance. I think the idea that a civil servant should get up and say "The minister is not telling the truth" any time that this is likely to happen is a recipe for chaos and certainly for disloyalty.'[232]

Sir Guy Millard, Eden's private secretary, who, on Brook's instructions, wrote up Whitehall's secret history of Suez in 1957,[233] took an identical line to Logan when interviewed for *A Canal Too Far*, saying he 'didn't feel the need to strike political or moral attitudes ... [as] ... I don't somehow see that as the function of a civil servant'.[234] Sir Guy, a charming and cultivated man, later wrote to Mark Laity, producer of *A Canal Too Far*, thanking him for a tape of the programme and 'the BBC for drawing my attention to an ethical dilemma of which I appear to have been unaware at the time'.[235]

None of the surviving insiders took anything other than a hostile view of Clive Ponting and his actions in 1984. The Prime Minister may have lied to Parliament about Suez but not one of them even contemplated blowing the whistle on Eden. Nobody blew the whistle on the British side until Sir Anthony Nutting published his *No End of A Lesson*[236] in 1967 in the teeth of Cabinet Office and Foreign Office objections (even Gore-Booth tried to dissuade him)[237] – though a year after Suez the Brombergers' book[238] published in Paris took the lid off the affair, and Moshe Dayan's memoirs[239] had given chapter and verse on collusion before Nutting published his account.

Suez was *the* greatest professional trauma experienced by the British Civil Service before or since 1957. Yet discipline held. Nobody flouted the rules or spilled the beans. In its way it was a remarkable tribute to the ethos of the profession. Would it be the same today in identical circumstances? I doubt it. Most would bite their lips and think of England, but not all – and it only takes one mouth to blow a whistle.[240]

5 CRITICISM, INQUIRY AND REFORM

What we get . . . is a two-tier dilettantism. It may well happen that both the Permanent Secretary and the Minister arrive simultaneously at a new department. Neither of them has made an intensive study of the problems with which they have to deal . . . How purposive positive policy can be formed under these conditions is a mystery, or rather it would be a mystery if purposive policy were formed.
Thomas Balogh, 1959[1]

I had now spent over twenty years in Whitehall and Westminster watching, and wherever possible, countering the wily and dominating ways of the Treasury. I was determined that this department should be cut down to size with a new machinery of government to handle economic affairs in a Labour Cabinet.
Lord Wilson of Rievaulx recalling 1963 in 1986[2]

The idea failed because the Department that was set up didn't really have either the expertise or the flow of information that the Treasury had and . . . it was then very swiftly relegated into a very agreeable form of adult education.
Lord Lever, former junior minister, Department of Economic Affairs, 1986[3]

The Fulton Committee was very much a product of its time. Its time was the brief period of Harold Wilson's technological revolution.
John Garrett, MP, 1980[4]

I was very, very careful, very careful indeed, to say that the appearance of the Fulton Report was a great opportunity. I called it on television 'an ice-breaker'. What I meant was that it was a catalyst and enabled all kinds of ideas to come through.
Lord Armstrong of Sanderstead, 1977[5]

Suez, 'the supreme crisis of the 1950s',[6] did more than prick the private conscience of the permanent government: it stimulated a protracted period of national re-examination, which grew steadily in the late 1950s and peaked in the 'what's wrong with Britain?'[7] years of the early 1960s. Inevitably, the Civil Service was an early target of this prolonged institutional autopsy with its real-life equivalent of Gray's *Anatomy* – Anthony Sampson's anatomies of Britain which went through edition after edition,[8] becoming ever more preoccupied with the theme of Britain as a latter-day Imperial Spain locked into an irreversible decline, trapped by its ancient institutions including 'the unloved Establishment', as he called the Civil Service.[9]

It would be wrong, however, to assume that the Civil Service fell from the heights to the depths of public esteem during the post-Suez years. Even in their 1940s glory days the profession felt got at. In 1946 Sir Henry French, Permanent Secretary at the Ministry of Food, telegrammed the economist and wartime temporary Eric Roll (himself to become a permanent secretary) in Washington inquiring, 'Will you now authorise me to go straight ahead with view your joining much harassed, much maligned but on the whole useful and necessary body of permanent civil servants?'[10] A year later a Cabinet committee on Civil Service manpower, chaired by the Home Secretary, James Chuter Ede, reported to the full Cabinet in the following terms: 'In conclusion, we wish to emphasise one point to which we attach great importance – the morale and standing in public esteem of the Civil Service.' The Cabinet committee, its examination of Whitehall's workload completed, forecast a further increase in manpower and that:

> Therefore, especially during these next 12 months, we may expect that the Civil Service will be even more heavily under fire than it has been in recent months. This is a matter on which the Government must take a definite line. No organisation can long sustain morale or attract the right type of recruit if it is publicly or privately stigmatised as consisting of parasites on the community or unjustly criticised in other equally opprobrious terms; and if, being debarred from replying for itself, it is left undefended.

The Cabinet committee urged Attlee to take an early opportunity 'to underline the part which the Civil Service plays and its contribution to the public good. Then other ministers, on suitable occasions, should do the same with the result that the Civil Service will be encouraged by those responsible for its direction to take a proper pride in its work and the heart will not be taken out of the new entrants on whom the building up of a more efficient service largely depends.'[11] Three years later Bridges himself delivered, with a resignation appropriate to his station and an endearing familiarity with the music-hall, the line for which he is probably best remembered: 'I confidently expect that we shall continue to be grouped with mothers-in-law and Wigan Pier as one of the recognised objects of ridicule.'[12]

Post-Suez, British institutions ceased to be the butt of the music-hall comedian and the gentle satire of Ealing comedy of the *Passport to Pimlico* variety. The mood became nastier, more anguished, more recriminatory, a by-product of the politics of decline. Over three decades it spawned the huge 'decline' literature we have already encountered. It infected the fiction market, too, again in a way altogether different from the earlier, Angela Thirkell *genre* pining for a past gentility. That brilliant chronicler of the secret bureaucracy, John Le Carré (did the Foreign Office recruiters at CSSB realise what they were unleashing when he passed through their special competition in the early fifties?), captures it in almost every opus to come off his formidable production-line. In *Tinker, Tailor, Soldier, Spy* (1974) he has Connie, the brilliant, booze-sodden ex-MI6 researcher, pining for her 'Poor loves. Trained to Empire, trained to rule the waves. All gone. All taken away.'[13] In *A Perfect Spy* (1986), Le Carré places a sequence of thoughts in the head of the veteran agent-runner, Jack Brotherhood, as the British Intelligence establishment ponders the wreckage caused by Magnus Pym who has been spying for the Russians through all the years between Mr Attlee and Mrs Thatcher: 'Tonight they were one voice and one dead hand. They are the body corporate I once believed was greater than the sum of its parts, he thought. In my lifetime I have witnessed the birth of the jet aeroplane and the atom bomb and the computer, and the demise of the British institution. We have nothing to clear away but ourselves.'[14]

Post-Suez the Civil Service was swiftly in the frame of criticism, not because of anything it had or had not done during the crisis. Eden and his inner group of ministers took the blame for that (though it did nothing to prevent Harold Macmillan, first-in and first-out at Suez as Harold Wilson delighted in saying, from winning a 100-seat majority for the Conservatives at the 1959 General Election). It was an obvious target, as one of the great institutions in the land, for the more general mood of self-questioning.

Decline was the spur for the pioneering polemic directed by Thomas Balogh at 'the myth of a perfectly working government machine' in his seminal essay 'The Apotheosis of the Dilettante'. 'Britain's power', he wrote, 'has been declining at a rate unparalleled since the crash of the Spanish Empire, and the decline cannot be explained by the venality of the voters, or the folly of politicians acting in a democratic system, or even the harshness of the world.'[15] Balogh declared that in attacking the myth of the perfectly working Whitehall machine he was tackling a fatal myth of a kind which served 'to blind people to their problems and in their complacency to destroy all hopes of solving them'.[16] The 'very success of the boldness of the effort of the Victorian reformer'[17] has saddled Britain with an entrenched administrative class of non-specialist dabblers renewed, generation after generation, by a recruitment process 'favouring the smooth, extrovert conformist with good connections and no knowledge of modern problems'.[18]

Balogh argued that this essentially Victorian model of a 'Mandarin's paradise'[19] was outdated by Armistice Day 1919. Balogh, for all his brilliant assaults on past practice and omissions, had his eyes firmly on the future – on the day Labour would be returned to power. He pitched his climactic claim very high and very wide:

> Civil Service reform alone will not restore parliamentary democracy or Cabinet responsibility in Britain. It cannot by itself create the basis for a successful Socialist Government. It is, however, one of the most essential and fundamental pre-conditions of both ... It is a challenge to Labour to achieve this and it dare not fail.[20]

Balogh was obsessional about the Civil Service. Even when Labour had regained power in the 1960s he erupted on the subject regularly, as the diaries of his friends, Richard Crossman, Tony Benn and Barbara Castle, record.[21] But obsessionals have their value, particularly in keeping issues alive in the wilderness years of opposition. And the issues Balogh raised in 'The Apotheosis of the Dilettante', and the context in which he dissected them, started a trail which led to his friend, Harold Wilson, commissioning the Fulton Committee in 1966. Indeed, when Dick Crossman turned up as Lord President of the Council and Leader of the House to present his evidence to Fulton and his colleagues in their Treasury committee room in January 1967 he 'fired off a considered broadside which started with the declaration that before I became a Minister I had found Tommy Balogh's chapter on the Establishment the most important statement on the Civil Service. Now I had some experience I was even more impressed by it.'[22]

Balogh was an influential member of the Fabian Group on Civil Service Reform in the early 1960s, an exercise which resulted in one of the Society's most superbly crafted pamphlets, *The Administrators*, which pre-echoed not just the preoccupations of Fulton a few years later but many of the themes and remedies advanced by reform-minded study groups on the machinery-of-government twenty years later. The group was a pretty star-studded collection. In the chair was the Cambridge economist Robert Nield, who entered the Treasury with Labour as a special adviser in October 1964 and sat on the Fulton Committee. Shirley Williams sat on both groups, though appointment to ministerial office removed her from

Fulton after the first meeting. Anthony Crosland, already a formidable political figure, was a member. The Fabian group included serving civil servants like Maurice Kogan (shortly to leave for university life), David Henderson, the economist (then at the Ministry of Aviation), the head of the Treasury's historical branch, James Ogilvy-Webb, and two future permanent secretaries.[23]

The Fabians followed Balogh in describing the Northcote–Trevelyan service as the world leader of its day. But they bemoaned, in particular, the re-emergence, with minor modifications, of the pre-war Civil Service after 1945 despite the assumption by government of new and permanent responsibilities (at least from the perspective of 1963–4 when the pamphlet was drafted) for full employment, nationalised industries, economic growth and a wide range of health, education and welfare responsibilities and town and country planning. It was particularly hard on the Attlee administration for failing 'to draw up any long-term plan, apart from a four-year programme required under the Marshall Plan as a means of obtaining aid. A planning machine – the Central Economic Planning Staff – was established, but it seemed to assume the colours of the rest of the machine, and no plan emerged. This was the time when in France M. Monnet succeeded in establishing his Commissariat du Plan, and enlisted the advice and help of a number of British economists in the process.'[24] *The Administrators* was all the more persuasive for being even-handed. It had none of the 'I name the guilty men' flavour of undiluted Balogh. Some of its paragraphs were worthy of comparison with the best kind of judicial summing-up. The following passage conveys its tone:

> The permanent Civil Service proved itself adaptable to the job of setting up the new social services after the War – notably the Health Service – and expanding the new ones in a pretty short time, but not so adaptable to the more novel tasks of forward economic planning and the modernisation of the national economy and industry. The Civil Service is traditionally good at judicial and negotiating functions – administering rationing schemes and dealing with local authorities, trades unions and other associations and pressure groups. It is traditionally bad at creative financial management and any activities with direct involvement in new technological developments (but its large scale use of computers is an exception to this). It may be claimed that it was thoroughly at home in building up the new social insurance schemes and thoroughly at sea in such matters as energy policy.[25]

To improve matters the Fabians concentrated on both people and structures. Their pamphlet recognised that the occasional outsider like

Lord Franks or Lord Plowden had managed to 'shimmer in and out of government service',[26] but for the most part Whitehall remained a world apart, a closed, secretive society with little direct experience of the economy and society with which it was concerned, a society of largely untrained, narrowly recruited generalist all-rounders, 'as closed and protected as a monastic order,'[27] dominated by a 'preponderant' Treasury with little interest in management and 'a positively masochistic attitude to office staffing and equipment wholly inconsistent with efficiency'.[28]

Four months before the general election which returned Labour to office in October 1964, the Fabians published their reform plan. Ironically, the Prime Minister, Sir Alec Douglas-Home, was privately working on his plans to shake up the bureaucracy if the electorate returned him to power (his aim was to cut down the Cabinet and Civil Service workload, and he planned to ask Mr Enoch Powell to rejoin the Government for the purpose,[29] though Mr Powell never knew of this[30]). Unlike Sir Alec, the Fabians did not believe in Parkinson's Law, which suggests, as the Fabians summarised it, 'that the Civil Service, like other hierarchies, grows too fast, inventing work for itself as it does so'.[31] Their plan for a Civil Service fit for implementing a Labour government's programme envisaged:

* The removal of Whitehall personnel and management policy to a beefed-up Civil Service Commission.
* An inquiry by the Commission into the alleged bias in recruitment to candidates from Oxford and Cambridge with arts degrees with a view to widening the trawl.
* The movement of new blood into the Civil Service and the movement of old blood out for refreshment in local government, the public and private sectors.
* The establishment of a 'School of Administrative Studies' to train top officials and personnel from nationalised industry, public agencies and the private sector.
* 'The better articulation of careers so that people acquire a progressively widening range of experience and are not jumped about to unrelated jobs.'
* The abolition of 'class' distinctions between generalists and specialists plus greater access for professionals to top jobs and the recruitment of more specialists.
* 'Greater openness so that outside study and discussion of long-range policy issues are encouraged, not discouraged by excessive secrecy, and fuller use is made of outside research.'

* Provision of ministerial *cabinets* of the French type and the recruitment of two kinds of outsider – the policy expert and the political aide – to staff them.[32]

The Fabians acknowledged that their inquiry was limited and had 'not dealt with the division of responsibility for economic policy as between Ministries, which we regard as a separate issue from the question whether Establishments should be in the Treasury'[33] as indeed it was. The machinery of economic policy-making was the other great issue of the hour and a prime preoccupation of that star of prewar Oxford PPE, Harold Wilson.

As so often happens to Opposition policy-makers, Labour's shadow spokesmen were not dealing with a static picture on the economic front (the Fabians very largely were, though the Treasury had made a gesture towards modern training by establishing the Centre for Administrative Studies in Regent's Park in 1963 with a view to making Whitehall's assistant principals more numerate and economically literate[34]). Macmillan's government had undertaken quite a substantial overhaul of the economic policy machine by the time the political and personal crises erupted which brought down the old advocate of planning and the middle way in 1963.

The most significant development of the 1950s was a gradual transformation of the mechanics of long-term public expenditure planning and control, the absence of which had stimulated Brook's minute to Bridges of April 1950. As so often in the private history of the permanent government, it required a combination of individuals and circumstances to kindle the chemistry of progress. The elements began to react in the autumn of 1953 when Otto Clarke, that most restless of officials 'ruthless in the pursuit of effective solutions, ruthless in the demolition of soft advice, soft decisions, soft colleagues and soft Ministers', as Douglas Allen (now Lord Croham) called him,[35] was transferred from overseas finance, where he had grappled with dollar gaps and import programmes since the end of the war, to head the Treasury's SS Division responsible for controlling expenditure on the social services. He remained the Treasury's controversial but undisputed public spending king until he departed to head the Ministry of Technology in 1966. By this time his brainchild – the Public Expenditure Survey system, known as PESC from the initials of the committee of finance officers which ran it initially – was an established and absolutely crucial part of the central machinery of state.

Otto Clarke remains a controversial figure – a great tribute to a public servant who died in 1975. For one young Treasury colleague, Peter Jay, he was quite simply 'the greatest of all the civil servants'.[36] Yet for Sir Leo Pliatzky, another strong-willed lover of argument who inherited the Clarke mantle in the crisis-embattled and inflation-beset Treasury of the mid-

1970s (and to whom it fell to modify the PESC system in a counter-inflationary direction), the legend is not wholly glittering:

> Otto Clarke stands out as its [PESC's] architect and master builder. He was a large man, both physically – at any rate he had a large dome of a head – and in the scale of his ideas, in which he believed with a force and a passion which was sometimes a little surprising in relation to the nature of the issue or the facts of the situation. The creation of the new system was a great conceptual achievement. To secure its acceptance by Whitehall was a feat of will and organisation. I say this as someone who – to understate the point somewhat – owed nothing to patronage from that quarter. Whether the new system was something *sensible*, and whether our last state was better or worse than our first, are questions on which judgement has to be deferred for the moment.[37]

In the autumn of 1953 Clarke's political chief was another great technician of state, the Chancellor of the Exchequer, R. A. Butler (not until 1961 did the Treasury invent the Chief Secretary as its custom-appointed spending minister). Butler, who in old age liked to remark, 'The Treasury's hell, isn't it?'[38] saw burgeoning public spending on health and the social services as part of his ministerial torment and made frequent attempts to instil a similar sense of disquiet among his colleagues, as the Cabinet minutes and papers show.[39]

Clarke's own account of his partnership with Butler is a little classic of the speed and the vagaries of Whitehall and ministerial life. Writing of SS, he recalled:

> This was a heavy and varied division at the heart of the Treasury's 'Supply' work. This was a remarkable education both of Whitehall, and in finding the nerve-centres in this immense size and range of spending by central and local government. Coming from the fast-moving world of the balance of payments, I found myself in an arena in which today's decisions were determining the development and cost of the services several years ahead. So when in July 1955 . . . Mr R. A. Butler got his colleagues' agreement to a Five-Year Survey of the Social Services, we were ready, and it appeared in November. The sequel shows the hazards of public administration, for both Mr Butler and I were immediately transferred to different fields, leaving this unfinished business.[40]

Clarke's new job, however, as head of the Home and Overseas Planning Staff, the latest mutation of the Central Economic Planning Staff now wholly absorbed by the Treasury though it was not formally dissolved until 1958,[41] enabled him to pursue his Holy Grail of improved long-term planning. With Burke Trend and Frank Figgures as his under secretaries he was, over the next four years, able to assess the investment needs of industry and manpower in the light of a five-year forward economic assessment as a whole. Coupled with changes inside the Ministry of Defence, in the middle of its perpetual long march to a unified structure, chain of command and budgeting system (which did not end with the abolition of the service departments and their absorption into a single giant department in 1964, see pp. 417–9), the huge budgets of Whitehall's big spenders were, one by one, beginning to be assessed through a new prism.

This very much accorded with the 'middle way' philosophy by Macmillan who replaced Eden in No. 10 in January 1957. Clarke himself saw the period between Macmillan's accession and his triumph at the polls in October 1959 as 'a turning-point in Britain's post-war economic history ... we were passing from the expansionist economic liberalism of Mr Butler's time at the Exchequer towards the interventionist policies of indicative planning and incomes policy which dominated both Conservative and Labour Governments in the 1960s'.[42] So, when Sir Godfrey Nicholson and his fellow MPs on the Select Committee on Estimates began an inquiry into Treasury control of public spending with a view to improvement in late 1957, they were very largely pushing at an open door.

As so often, inquiry was in response to rather than ahead of a changing reality. The Conservative governments of the mid-fifties were very investment-minded. The Cabinet minutes groan with discussion of huge capital schemes of public investment – the railway modernisation plan, the roads programme,[43] the first civil nuclear power programme – all of which changed the face of Britain (replacing steam with diesel, meadow with motorway and coal with atom). All were planned by a Whitehall almost bereft of professional economists. The Fabians were right to make much of this in *The Administrators*. They noted in 1964 that 'the Government is using, to assist it in the whole country's economic policy, about the same number of senior economists and statisticians as are employed by a big progressive firm'[44] and were particularly harsh on the Ministry of Transport, *the* great infrastructure department as, 'until recently [it] has not contained a single economist [and] that it has had almost no planning organisation and that only last year [1963] was the first report ever published which looked at road and rail transport together'.[45]

By the time the Estimates Committee reported in July 1958, the Macmillan administration was openly set on a high public spending course for which the newer Conservatives of the 1970s and 1980s never ceased to upbraid it. The Chancellor, Peter Thorneycroft, and his entire Treasury team (Enoch Powell, the alleged Svengali of the scene,[46] and Nigel Birch) had resigned the previous January (Macmillan's famous 'little local difficulty'[47]) over the Cabinet's unwillingness to cut the Estimates by £50m, a small but symbolic amount.[48] For those on either side of the political divide always willing to ascribe motives and designs to the 'guilty men' in the Treasury, officialdom was neutral in the matter.[49] The episode so impressed the prospective parliamentary candidate for Finchley, a certain Mrs Margaret Thatcher, that she made Thorneycroft chairman of the late-seventies Conservative Party she was engaged in reconstructing in her own image.

But by the time the Nicholson Committee reported six months later, the Treasury resignations seemed like prehistory in the cornucopia of consumer goods with which Macmillan's economic policies seemed to be swamping the electorate. Equally, in such an economic climate, the techniques of public spending control were strictly for the cognoscenti. The findings of the Estimates Committee were not the stuff of which headlines were made:

> The system appears to work reasonably well. But it would be idle to pretend that your Committee is left entirely without disquiet . . . Your Committee have reached the conclusion that further inquiry, at once more detailed and more expert, is required. Accordingly they recommend that a small independent committee, which should have access to Cabinet papers, be appointed to report upon the theory and practice of Treasury control of expenditure.[50]

According to Clarke, who like the famous schoolboy inventor of Rugby Football simply picked up the ball and ran, 'the proposal for another enquiry was naturally unwelcome'.[51] But, eventually, the Chancellor of the Exchequer, Derick Heathcoat Amory, appointed a hybrid committee of insiders and outsiders under Lord Plowden, who, Jeeves-like, once more shimmered back into Whitehall to lead it.

The Plowden Committee of 1959–61 was the subject of a brilliant parody by one of the giants of postwar British political science, W. J. M. Mackenzie, offering what he called 'a translation' of its findings opening with a 'spoof' preamble by the chairman:

> 1. For various political reasons we were asked to attempt the impossible; to accept criticisms without accepting them, to have a public inquiry which is not public.
>
> 2. At first I was expected to carry the can alone. Then I got them to add three pretty safe people [here he names: Sir Sam Brown, City solicitor and ex-wartime temporary; Sir Jeremy Raisman, Vice-Chairman of Lloyds Bank and ex-ICS; J. E. Wall, a director of EMI and ex-wartime temporary].

3. Naturally, there was a great wrangle about what should be published, and this was ended by a nonsensical compromise embodied in this document. The Civil Servant members of the inquiry (who are officially nameless, but you can easily find out who they were) do not agree to this paper, but they did not disagree in any respect whatever.

Plowden
Chairman[52]

In fact, the Plowden Report deserves none of the standard strictures directed against futile exercises by the great and good. By locking many of the key Whitehall figures who would have to implement the findings into membership of the committee (officials such as Burke Trend from the Treasury and Evelyn Sharp from the Ministry of Housing and Local Government, see p. 437) it had effectiveness built in. Otto Clarke, however, was its theologian, its life-force and the man who made the report flesh (though he claimed that discussion of its basic principles was well under way by the time he became an assessor, as the official members were called, in January 1960[53]). The crucial recommendation, as Sir Leo Pliatzky rightly describes it, was (in Pliatzky's paraphrase) 'that arrangements should be introduced for making surveys of public expenditure for a period of years ahead, and that all major individual decisions involving future expenditure should be taken against the background of such a survey and in relation to prospective resources'.[54]

The key to the Plowden Report was its mixture of the constitutional, the practical and the efficient. Otto Clarke described its trio of core principles:

1. Effective collective responsibility of Ministers for public expenditure, so that the Chancellor no longer carries the weight alone [three months after Plowden reported, Macmillan gave a second seat to the Treasury in the Cabinet Room by creating the post of Chief Secretary].
2. Regular Ministerial appraisal of public expenditure as a whole, over a period of years ahead, and in relation to prospective resources. Decisions involving substantial future expenditure should be taken in the light of these appraisals.
3. The greatest practicable stability of decisions on public expenditure when taken, so that considerations of long-term economy and efficiency throughout the public sector have the best possible opportunity to develop.[55]

The system lasted for fifteen years until brought low amid a welter of criticism (see above pp. 251–2) during the 'stagflation' (the malign combination of economic stagnation *and* inflation) of the mid-1970s.

High and growing public spending is the dividend of an expanding, productive economy. The other reforming thrust of the Macmillan administration in terms of economic machinery was devoted to this in terms of a British version of the French Commissariat du Plan so beloved of the Fabians. The British embodiment of the French-style indicative planning mentioned by Otto Clarke was the National Economic Development Council, or Neddy, which was brought into being in the year after Plowden reported (though the trade unions did not agree to serve on it until January 1962). Not everyone in the Treasury was keen on this shift towards an interventionist strategy. Sir Frank Lee, that most persuasive of permanent secretaries who had succeeded Sir Roger Makins in 1960, was a free competition man to his last fibre and, as can happen, a far more dynamic figure than the Chancellor of the Exchequer, Selwyn Lloyd (who had replaced Heathcoat Amory after the 1959 election). Macmillan backed Lloyd, though many in the Cabinet were sceptical about going down the planning road (or the corporatist road as it would now be called), bringing employers and unions into an institutionalised partnership with government. Macmillan and Lloyd prevailed in Cabinet and, therefore, in the Treasury too which, despite what its critics sometimes claim, must always yield in the end to the force of a Cabinet minute. Its permanent secretary behaved impeccably and put duty above scepticism as Samuel Brittan, Treasury-watcher *sans pareil*, recorded:

> Without Sir Frank Lee, NEDC would have remained a paper dream. He was ill in Paris during the July [1961 economic] crisis; when he came back to London and found that the planning 'decision' had been taken, he spared no effort to make it work, whatever he might personally have thought about 'planning'. Lee was fully behind Lloyd's insistence, against the advice of many senior Treasury officials, that the NEDC office must be distinct from the Treasury if the unions were to have confidence in its independence.[56]

The innovations of 1961–2 on economic planning and spending control and the Treasury reorganisation, particularly the creation of the Public Sector Group (the rejigging was done according to a joint Otto Clarke–William Armstrong blueprint),[57] which embodied them, could as easily have been introduced by a Labour government under Hugh Gaitskell as a Conservative government under Harold Macmillan. But once Wilson had replaced Gaitskell in January 1963, the search was on for a new model.

Harold Wilson has had a career-long animus against the Treasury, though he was offered a permanent, established job there after the war.[58] His dislike of Whitehall's commanding height was not diminished by the mellowing that normally accompanies retirement. Almost a decade after he left government Wilson told me: 'They're still at it. Recently, we were having a debate in the Lords and we got on to nationalisation and I said that the one thing we need to nationalise in this country is the Treasury, but nobody has ever succeeded.'[59] During his last premiership Bernard Donoughue noticed that in contrast to Jim Callaghan, 'Harold Wilson seemed over-respectful towards the Treasury, perhaps even a little frightened, and kept himself more at arm's length from his Chancellor.'[60] Naturally, this is not quite how Wilson saw it when I asked him about it in February 1985: 'Some of us have had more success than others. I had the advantage of having been in the Civil Service in the war . . . Anyone who had had that knew a bit about the Treasury and knew a little bit about fighting back and working round them . . . They still wheedled and played their little tricks.'[61] 'Working round them' was the essence of Wilson's strategy as he began in 1963 to plan the shape of a Whitehall fit to be the powerhouse of the New Britain, to use the language he favoured in those heady days. Balogh was recruited to help him. Within three months an outline plan was ready, as Balogh reported to Tony Benn:

> At Harold's request he has prepared a major document on Civil Service reform which he claims could be started within two weeks by dividing the Treasury into two halves and giving half of it over to a Ministry of Expansion or Production. The rump of the Treasury would handle financial matters and would act as a Bureau of the Budget. The Prime Minister's office would then be expanded to absorb the National Economic Development Committee [presumably Benn meant Council] and all disputes between the Treasury and the Ministry of Production would automatically be settled by the Economic Committee of the Cabinet, under the chairmanship of the Prime Minister.[62]

Though it is hard to realise it a quarter of a century later, 1963–4 did have something of a radical dawn about it, certainly for Tony Benn: 'Tommy [Balogh] gave me this document to take away and read and I am delighted to think that Harold is working on such radical plans. If we get fundamental parliamentary, Civil Service, local government, legal and education reorganisation we shall have gone a long way to reshape Britain.'[63] If they had got them, they would, but they didn't.

Though Wilson's machinery-of-government changes when power gave him the chance to act in 1964 were plentiful – a Ministry of Technology, of Land and Natural Resources, of Overseas Development and a Welsh Office (only the Welsh Office survives with its own Cabinet minister, Overseas Development is now under the wing of the FO and led at minister of state level).[64] But the keystone in the arch was to be a top-flight, modern ministry of the kind Balogh wanted, to break once and for all the paralysis caused by the dead hand of the Treasury. The Department of Economic Affairs was Labour's secret weapon for countering 'the mighty Treasury departmental power' as Harold Lever called it.[65]

The appellation may have been part of Wilson's penchant for his 1940s salad days. Cripps, after all, had briefly been Minister for Economic Affairs, with the CEPS under his wing, in 1947 until Dalton's budget indiscretion enabled him to enter the entire economic kingdom when he moved into the Treasury proper. Wilson in 1963 wanted to counter 'the wily and dominating ways of the Treasury' by building a new balance of power within the Cabinet, as he told his unenthusiastic shadow Chancellor, Jim Callaghan, who was never persuaded by Wilson's notion of 'creative tension' between the Treasury and the DEA.[66] Callaghan maintains to this day that the reorganised post-1962 Treasury under William Armstrong 'had sloughed off a number of their old ideas, and were anxious to try to ensure non-inflationary growth. But when there was a department set up like the DEA that was wholly devoted to growth and nothing but growth, then the Treasury rather retreated into its shell and found itself fighting a defensive battle.'[67] Wilson, therefore, was addressing a sceptic when he told Callaghan 'that, while the Chancellor of the Exchequer would be responsible for all actions necessary in the monetary field, foreign exchange, internal monetary management and government expenditure and taxation, Britain could hope to win economic security only by a fundamental reconstruction and modernisation of industry under the direction of a department at least as powerful as the Treasury [which] would be concerned with real resources, economic planning and strengthening our ability to export and save imports, with increasing productivity and our competitiveness in domestic and export markets'.[68]

For such a short-lived department (it survived for less than five years) the DEA acquired a formidable legend, part of which rested on the celebrated story that it was born in the few minutes it took a London taxi to carry Wilson and George Brown from a meeting with the TUC in the St Ermin's Hotel, Westminster, back to the House of Commons. The tale fits neatly into the British habit of reshaping their constitution on the back of envelopes. But, sadly, it is not true. The idea was well advanced before the cabbie picked them up, though Brown was offered the job of running the new department, with the peculiar title of First Secretary of State, as the taxi crept round Parliament Square.[69]

The permanent secretary picked to head the new department, Sir Eric Roll (then the Treasury's man in Washington), learned his destiny in an equally bizarre fashion:

While I was spending a few days in New York on my way to Washington in 1963, I was walking along Fifth Avenue with my wife and daughters when to our surprise we met George Brown. In the short conversation we had he urged me 'not to put down deep roots' in the USA: there would be an Election the following year and I might be wanted in London. A further hint came a few months later when Harold Wilson on a visit to Washington, at a luncheon party at the Embassy, talked about his intention to create a Department of Economic Affairs and, winking at me, said, 'And we have even picked the Permanent Secretary'.[70]

Under the newly minted Douglas-Home rules, which allow the Opposition access to Whitehall in advance of an election to put their planned changes to the permanent secretaries (see p. 284), William Armstrong and Sir Lawrence Helsby, who had become Head of the Home Civil Service on Brook's retirement in 1963 (Burke Trend had taken the Cabinet Secretaryship), drew up a blueprint of the new department ready for Brown's arrival, the electorate permitting.[71]

The blueprint was not comprehensive. It lacked, among other things, any provision for such basics of the Whitehall trade as desks, chairs and telephones, as George Brown discovered when he turned up at the Storey's Gate entrance to the New Public Offices (the Treasury occupied the Whitehall end). It was a day his private secretary, Tom Caulcott, will never forget, as he told Susan Barnes, biographer of Anthony Crosland, her husband and Brown's minister of state:

'Here was George, who legitimately believed his was the No. 2 job in the Government, finding he had Eric Roll, Donald MacDougall [Director of Economics, ex-Churchill's Statistical Section who had come from NEDO] and me. And one Diary Secretary'. Except for the First Secretary of State, who had a chair, everyone sat on the floor like buddhas. By Monday Caulcott, who'd hardly slept for three days, had got together a Private Office. He himself had tramped over to the Treasury, seized a typewriter from the Chancellor's Private Office, carried it away in his arms. But there still wasn't any DEA writing paper. The chaos was terrible, George erupting the whole time.[72]

There was a rough equality about the early DEA. Life was equally grim amongst the other ranks who included Samuel Brittan, author of the acclaimed *Treasury Under the Tories*, recruited as part of a gifted group of 'irregulars' as he called them.[73] Mr Brittan, the famed economic commentator of the *Financial Times* who, with Peter Jay (then still along the corridor as a Treasury regular), was later credited with inducing a sea-change in British economic thought, is a convinced believer 'that the injection of new men and ideas will always be necessary to bring a breath of fresh air into Whitehall'. He also brought a journalist's eye to the high thinking and the low living in a department carrying such great hopes, confining his observations to a fascinating diary.

The first entry in his 'diary of an irregular'[74] opens with a lament on the atrocious working conditions:

> Gloomy toilet with no soap or towel. I donated a piece of soap to the toilet, which afterwards vanished. Apparently suggestion of modern type ticking roller towel has never got anywhere in Whitehall! . . . There were no telephone directories in the so-called 'suite' of offices in which I was or at the entrance to the Ministry . . . No tea was being provided. This was a privilege of the messengers, but there were no messengers allocated to our corridor . . . Found cupboard in my room which wouldn't open. Told about stringent security precautions. But there was no security cupboard in my room yet![75]

Every so often Mr Brittan would jot down 'Reflections'. A week after his arrival he is already questioning the effectiveness of Wilson's strategy for transforming Whitehall.

> A ministeral *cabinet* might be better than having these extra Departments. The Wilson solution is no substitute for a thorough reform of the Civil Service to make it natural for people to go in and out at all stages. The system operates through the Private Offices and through the Treasury control of establishments (e.g. Caulcott). It would have been better not to have had the Economics Ministry, but to have hived off the control of the Civil Service. It is Treasury control of establishments that determines the real loyalties of civil servants.[76]

By mid-November, Mr Brittan is having trouble gaining access to the documents, as, he discovers, are his fellow economic irregulars, Thomas Balogh and Michael Stewart. Turf fights are breaking out. Sir Alec Cairncross, Chief Economic Adviser to the Treasury, was away ill when the new Government was appointed. According to a future chief economic adviser, Sir Fred Atkinson (as reported by Brittan), Labour would have to make up its mind whether to sack him [Cairncross] and introduce the spoil system.[77] (Sir Alec survived and worked closely with Callaghan; it was Cairncross who persuaded him that devaluation of the pound was inevitable in 1967.[78])

Within a month of Labour taking office, Samuel Brittan was convinced the DEA-Treasury 'split can only work: *either if Economic Affairs reduced to NEDC floating in the air away from immediate policy, or if Treasury is reduced to supervision of public expenditure and details of tax system*'. He quotes Tom Caulcott as saying 'Power still with the Treasury'.[79]

The body of the DEA was prodded and poked from the start as if an autopsy was being performed while the patient was still alive. Indeed, the process began before it was born. Early in 1964 Wilson had recorded a BBC radio conversation with Norman Hunt (later Lord Crowther-Hunt of Fulton fame) about Labour's plans for Whitehall. He outlined at considerable length his plans for a 'Ministry of Production or Planning' as he was calling the DEA at that stage.[80] Bridges, long since retired and now chairing the Arts Council, was offered the chance of replying in a radio talk of his own. Wilson's wartime boss, the man who had taught him how to take the minutes at War Cabinet committees, was deeply disturbed by the direction of his protégé's thinking. Bridges thought splitting the Treasury 'would make the job of any Chancellor of the Exchequer extremely difficult and would inevitably result in some tension, if not actual confusion between the two departments. I would have thought that some one minister must be responsible for the oversight of the totality of our resources, and for deciding, under Cabinet authority, how that totality is to be assigned and allocated'[81] – a view undoubtedly shared by the two chancellors, Jim Callaghan and Roy Jenkins, who had to cohabit with the DEA.

Whatever else it was, the DEA was a rip-roaring place to be. George Brown, alone, made sure of that – aflame with his mission (and, on occasion, the drink), he roared his way from meeting to meeting, enraging ministerial colleagues and outraging his officials, several of whom he would sack periodically, only to restore them, with contrition, when calm returned. According to encrusted legend, even the courteous John Burgh (a future director-general of the British Council), who succeeded the long-suffering Caulcott as private secretary, was reduced to hurling an apple at the First Secretary's head, though he missed. Like so many legends, it is not entirely accurate. The true story, however, is very revealing of DEA life under George Brown. In Sir John's own words:

> It had been a very long day in the private office with no time to eat. About nine George came out of his room not drunk but under the influence which made him much more difficult. He started arguing about something I had done or not done. We had a major row. I was eating an apple when he came out. I continued to eat it as I was very hungry. He shouted, 'This shows the respect you have for the Secretary of State that you continue eating an apple!' I deliberately kept eating it. He stormed out. Determined not to be outdone and to have the last word, I followed him. Bill Rodgers [junior minister DEA] thought I was going to assault George. He put his back to the door while I tugged at the

> handle. Then I really lost my temper. I had the core of the apple in my hand and threw it at the window meaning to break it. But it landed in the wastepaper basket – not something it would normally have done.[82]

It was one of the most lowly ranked Whitehall officials who put Brown, the former trade union leader, most firmly in his place – his driver. The men and women of the Government car pool should never be underestimated. They know a great deal because they hear a great deal. They are said to gather in one of the bigger limousines in Downing Street to hold their own Shadow Cabinet while the real one is meeting in No. 10. Brown's driver in 1965 (whose name, sadly, is not recorded) suffered mightily from his minister's abusive tongue in the small hours of a morning when the ancient Austin Princess allocated to the First Secretary broke down. According to Sir Donald MacDougall, who was in the car at the time, he 'pulled himself up to his full height and said, "I, too, am a member of the Transport and General Workers' Union"'.[83]

But, for all the tantrums, the DEA was a serious attempt to meet a longstanding criticism that the Treasury sustained a stop-go economy by deflating every time the pound and/or the balance of payments hit trouble, a criticism, to Bridges's mind, 'of the way in which the Treasury have done their job: not of what their job is, or ought to be'.[84] Where the Treasury had displayed what Sidney Pollard called its 'contempt for production'[85] the DEA would demonstrate a pro-production bias. The incarnation of that bias was to be Brown's pride and joy, the National Plan of 1965.

Brown strained every fibre of his remarkable personality to weld an agreement between capital, labour and government (including a famous night-time dash in an ancient vehicle from the Government car pool to bully sceptical captains of industry around a private dining table[86]). The key element in the policy was restraint in the rise of prices and incomes out of which would emerge an export-led growth rate of some 3.8 per cent a year and that elusive postwar economic miracle. It was an attempt to do for the British economy what Monnet's Commissariat du Plan had done for the French after 1945. It formed the basis of Labour's appeal to the electorate which returned Wilson with a 90-seat majority in March 1966. It survived for another four months till it was wrecked by the sterling and balance of payments crisis of July 1966, when the persistent underlying weaknesses of the British economy were exposed by a seaman's strike. Brown argued in vain for a devaluation of the pound, 'The Unmentionable' in mid-1960s Whitehall as Tony Crosland called it[87], as an alternative to traditional deflation, lost and left for the Foreign Office and an unsuccessful attempt at Ernest Bevin impressions.

The DEA staggered on under first Michael Stewart and then Peter Shore until Roy Jenkins, who replaced Callaghan at the Treasury after devaluation had eventually come, finally persuaded Wilson to kill it off in early 1969 despite Wilson's decision to place himself in overall command of the DEA when Shore replaced Stewart in August 1967.[88] But it was never the same after July 1966. The triumph of crisis-induced Treasury orthodoxy had taken the stuffing out of it. The great experiment was reduced, as Harold Lever said, to 'a very agreeable form of adult education'. Why did it fail? Lord Lever believes it was because knowledge is power and the DEA 'didn't really have either the expertise or the flow of information the Treasury has'.[89] From Samuel Brittan's seat in the boiler room similar thoughts were emerging by October 1965 (a month after the National Plan was launched with great fanfare):

> *Reflection. Scarcest commodity in the Civil Service is information.* Like all scarce commodities it is not freely exchanged. Quite wrong to think that someone in another Department (or even in one's own) will give freely of knowledge. Therefore there is a premium on those with the knack of finding out.[90]

Sir Douglas Wass, that great Treasury-lifer, is, perhaps, the cruellest of all about the DEA: 'I'm not sure that the Treasury ever vulgarly saw the DEA as a rival . . . The Treasury did, in fact, export some of its most able people to the DEA [including Douglas Allen and the bulk of its National Economy Group] – not something it would have done if it had really feared the DEA.'[91] Though the Treasury's nickname for the DEA – 'the Department of Extraordinary Aggression'[92] – suggests that the new ministry was not regarded as being entirely toothless. Sir Douglas Wass is brutally accurate about the weakness of the DEA from day one:

> All the important operational tools of economic management were in the hands of the Treasury (external financial relations, managing the balance of payments, operating monetary policy, controlling public expenditure). The Department of Economic Affairs, although it had a more senior minister in charge, did not have departmental responsibilities for anything apart from prices and incomes that really affected day-to-day decisions. It really [was] left beached studying the longer term problems of the British economy.[93]

The most bizarre epitaph for the DEA came from its inventor, Harold Wilson, when I interviewed him for BBC Radio 3 in February 1985: 'Why couldn't you break the power of the Treasury and get your beloved Department of Economic Affairs to take off?' I asked. 'Moles,' Wilson replied, 'moles. "Moles" was a phrase we very often used about the Treasury and it's been used many times since. The Treasury were very,

very skilled chaps in more or less stopping you doing anything.'[94] For the Oxford historian and Labour loyalist, Kenneth O. Morgan, 'Somehow, the tone [of Wilson's reply] recaptures the frustration and the paranoia of government in that era.'[95] The DEA, however, long after its demise remained an object of affection for those who had worked in it. They would meet regularly, usually in the Two Chairmen, a pub within walking distance from Storeys Gate. Its nameplate was kept on the wall there. When the Two Chairmen was refurbished in the late 1970s, it disappeared, lost in a builder's skip – a last sad blow for a bureaucratic innovation of noble intention and thwarted hope.

Reflecting for Susan Barnes on the chaos of those pioneering DEA days in the autumn of 1964, Tom Caulcott said: 'The Civil Service didn't appreciate how much thirteen years in Opposition had made the Labour Party dubious of the official machine. In fact, there was good will for the incoming Labour Government, and Jim Callaghan's great strength, after a slow start, was to learn to use it. George never did.'[96] Caulcott's judgement is confirmed by somebody who was present at one of Sir Henry Hardman's famous election night parties at his home in North London, occasions when permanent secretaries would have let their hair down had it been allowed to grow long enough. In October 1964, after thirteen years of Conservatism, change was keenly awaited not so much for any pro-Labour reasons as for the human and understandable desire for fresh pastures.[97] Ian Bancroft expressed the feeling well when he observed that 'even if the same administration gets back in you may find that the daily dose of castor oil is spiked with a drop of political vodka which makes it all rather more exciting'.[98] Despite Labour's manifesto pledge to renegotiate the Nassau Agreement under which US Polaris missiles were to be purchased for the Royal Navy, nobody at the senior levels in Whitehall really expected the Wilson Government to turn Britain into a non-nuclear power; if it had, that could well have caused a crisis between advisers and advised.[99] There may have been a degree of nervousness about Wilson's plans to bring in some temporaries with him, some assistant secretaries into the Cabinet secretariat,[100] some top-level technologists and industrialists into the Ministry of Technology, economists into the DEA, scientists into the Department of Education and Science[101] plus a smattering of principals in other departments.[102] Wilson, however, ruled out *cabinets* – 'there is a danger that you get a false division between his [the minister's] political *cabinet* ... and the civil servants'[103] – and undertook 'to see any experts [were] properly dovetailed into the administrative machine ... not floating about in an irresponsible way'.[104] There would, Wilson told Norman Hunt, be no '*eminences grises* or Rasputins or court favourites'[105] to advise the Prime Minister.

In the event, a relatively small number of irregulars were recruited. The

1. Sir Charles Trevelyan: designer of a great estate of the realm.

2. David Lloyd George: an artist in the use of the machine.

3. Lord Haldane: arch engineer of the machinery of government.

4. Sir Maurice Hankey: titan of the pigeon-hole.

5. Sir Warren Fisher: masterbuilder of the career Civil Service.

6. Andrew Arends and the author outside 569 Chiswick High Road, scene of Whitehall's most successful personnel operation.

7. Sir Edward Bridges: the twentieth century incarnation of the Victorian ideal.

8. Sir Norman Brook: Cabinet-maker at work and at home.

11. Right: Sir Edwin Plowden on his first day as top planner.

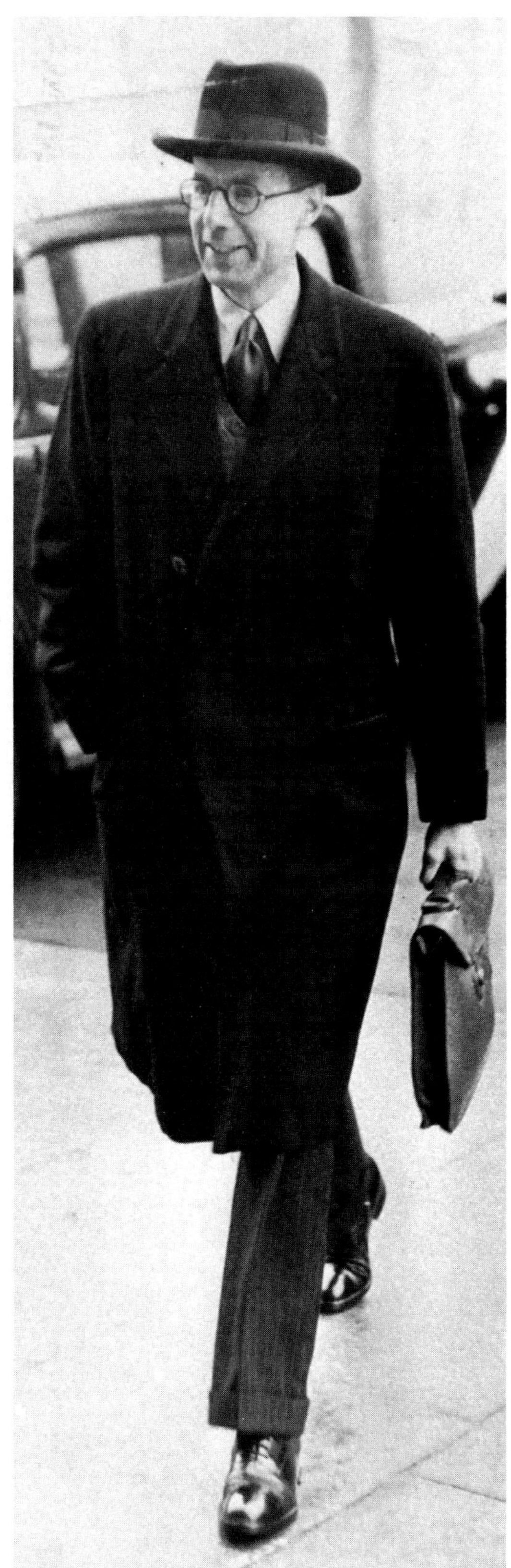

9. Above left: Sir Oliver Franks: shuttling effectively across the Atlantic.

10. Below left: Dr William Penney at home shortly before the bomb went up.

12. Sir Richard ('Otto') Clarke: a sparkling temporary who stayed.

most important concentrations were, in addition to the DEA, the duo of economists Nicholas Kaldor and Robert Nield brought in to help Callaghan at the Treasury, Balogh brought into the Cabinet Office to assist Wilson, and Sir Patrick Blackett sent to the Ministry of Technology to work with Frank Cousins. (C. P. Snow, chronicler of the *Corridors of Power*,[106] also joined up for a time as a minister, Parliamentary secretary to Mintech, after Wilson had made him a peer.) For some Whitehall regulars, this appeared, still does, to be the thin end of a wedge of politicisation which has advanced ever since. One seasoned Treasury man, for example, traces to October 1964 a growing tendency among some career officials to trim their advice to ministerial preferences. Certainly there was a degree of mutual wariness in Whitehall between the old and the new blood, which produced some choice stories that have long since passed into Whitehall lore and legend – the most famous involving Wilson's Political Secretary, Marcia Williams (now Lady Falkender) and the Principal Private Secretary, Derek Mitchell, inherited by the new premier from Alec Home. Mitchell, the epitome of elegance and irony, is said, in his deceptively angelic fashion, to have told Mrs Williams that she could indeed accompany the Prime Minister to Washington on his visit to President Johnson paid for by public funds provided she travelled as Mrs Wilson's maid.[107] Equally celebrated, though probably apocryphal, is the story of the Hungarian twins, Kaldor and Balogh, meeting on the steps of the Reform Club in the first days of the new administration with Kaldor expostulating: 'Tommy, those bastards in the Treasury tell me I know fuck nothing about economic policy. I tell them they are wrong, I know fuck all!'[108]

On a more serious level, the lack of specialist professionalism among the Whitehall regulars was very apparent to some of the irregulars. Towards the end of his first year in the DEA, Samuel Brittan reflected on the gaps in his book, *The Treasury Under the Tories*. He wrote: 'Should have kept in phrase about "one ounce of financial radicalism worth one ton of physical planning". Even more sceptical about expertise now. There is no salvation in Bridges' amateurs. Need is for economic types who will think things through and press policy dilemmas.'[109] Brittan, and those on the inside who thought like him, found an influential public echo outside in a report on Civil Service recruitment from the House of Commons Estimates Committee chaired by Dr Jeremy Bray, a former ICI technocrat. Early in 1964 they recommended, as a first step, the appointment of a Plowden-style committee containing a mixture of insiders and outsiders, with full access to the files, 'to initiate research upon, to examine, and to report upon the structure and management of the Civil Service'.[110] Bray, a mathematician by background, had a strong animus against Whitehall's 'hard core of public school, Oxbridge, upper-class classicists with second-class honours degrees'.[111] His committee, in rather more measured tones, reported: 'We find it hard to accept that the task of Government justifies the unique significance attaching to the Administrative Class, and that only a select few are fitted to undertake this work.'[112]

Wilson, as we have seen, was receptive to this stream of thought. He chose not to follow the Plowden route. Instead, he adopted the traditional great and good (G and G) approach and a departmental committee of inquiry, with the Treasury itself as sponsor, was commissioned, though Wilson, not the Chancellor, Callaghan, announced its formation to the House of Commons in February 1966. Its chairman was to be his old wartime fire-watching chum, Lord Fulton, Vice-Chancellor of the new and, then, hugely fashionable Sussex University.

Wilson's words in the House that day repay careful scrutiny. The small print of G and G terms of reference can be critical to the eventual outcome. They were in this case. Fulton's terms were simple enough – to 'examine the structure, recruitment and management, including training, of the Home Civil Service and to make recommendations'. It's what wasn't there, as opposed to what was, which is significant. Wilson said that the Fulton Committee would not deal with 'machinery of government questions'. In other words, it was not to be a new Haldane, posing and answering fundamental questions about the adequacy of the Whitehall machine to cope with the increasing workload which it was required to bear. Equally fundamentally, Wilson told MPs that the Government's willingness to contemplate changes in the Civil Service 'does not imply any intention on their part to alter the basic relationship between Ministers and civil servants'. Wilson continued: 'Civil Servants, however eminent, remain the confidential advisers of Ministers, who alone are answerable to Parliament for policy; and we do not envisage any change in this fundamental feature of our parliamentary system of democracy.'[113] Fulton, in other words, was steered away from the start from fundamental, fascinating and important questions which, to my mind, needed to be settled before the second-order questions such as recruitment, training and management were addressed. The specifications of the machine and the ground-rules for its operation surely should have been considered before the choice and man-management of its minders were pondered. Fulton, therefore, never had a chance of joining Northcote, Trevelyan and Haldane in the select club of ground-breaking inquirers.

According to one of Fulton's colleagues, Norman Crowther-Hunt, this gelding was deliberate, a pre-emptive strike from the permanent secretaries' club, displaying once again their genius for damage-limitation as they conceive it. Exclusion of machinery-of-government questions, wrote Norman Crowther-Hunt a decade later, 'which was badly wanted by the mandarins, enabled Sir William Armstrong, when he subsequently became head of the Civil Service, to argue that the Committee's work was thus unduly circumscribed and, as a consequence, that there were considerable doubts about most, if not all, of its recommendations. His view was that until "machinery of government" questions had been settled, you could not really know what sort of civil servants you needed and how they should be organised.'[114]

To Norman Hunt, Armstrong's view was 'nonsense'.

> The tasks of government were going to be pretty much the same ... however many departments you had, or whatever their size and however they were organised, and irrespective of whether or not, for example, the Prime Minister needed a department of his own. So the Committee's main recommendations were concerned with the type of civil servant you needed to undertake the tasks of modern government irrespective of the precise way Whitehall might organise itself to carry out those tasks. So this was a sterile controversy; but it is a nice illustration of the way the Civil Service helped to narrow the Committee's terms of reference – and later was able to argue that this restriction invalidated much of what the Committee said![115]

It was not a sterile controversy. Its enforced removal from machinery-of-government questions *and* minister/civil servant relationships made Fulton a one-dimensional inquiry rather than the three-dimensional investigation that was needed. Ironically, some of the individual evidence to the committee preserved in Fulton's five fat volumes illustrates the shortcoming to perfection. Some of the best evidence came from former officials, still young and recently departed such as that gifted trio William Plowden, Nicholas Deakin and James Mayall[116] and Peter Jay who wrote his memorandum at the moment he departed the Treasury for *The Times* at Easter 1967 with its appeal to a teamwork approach to problem-solving in Whitehall and its *cri de coeur* about the lot of the young high-flyer: 'Not for him the pride of authorship, the spur of reputation or the joy of creation which is the stuff of life to the writer, the scholar, the research scientist, the artist, the entrepreneur or even the journalist ... [thanks to the] ... suffocating layer-cake of successive administrative generations filtering every initiative to purest innocuity.'[117]

But the most impressive submission of all – a mini-Haldane, in fact – came from a serving official, William Ryrie, an assistant secretary in the Treasury (a decade later he was the Treasury's man at the IMF during the great sterling crisis of 1976) who rose to lead his own department, Overseas Development, and might well have headed the Treasury if Keynesianism had not acquired the status of heresy, at ministerial level at least, by the early 1980s. In the opening paragraph of his memorandum, 'The Role of the Civil Service in Modern Society', Sir William, as he now is, raised the debate to the level it required as opposed to the one it was kept to by Wilson's corset in Fulton's terms of reference:

> There is a general feeling about the Civil Service – both inside and outside it – that 'something is wrong'. Indeed a great deal is wrong. But diagnosis is difficult because the root of the trouble is not in the Civil Service itself but in the fact that the whole machinery of government is ill adapted to the tasks of government in society today. The ideas put forward in this paper certainly go beyond the [Fulton] Committee's terms of reference; but I think it is impossible to discuss the structure and management of the Civil Service constructively without giving some thought to its role, and indeed to the changed role of government itself in modern society.[118]

Ryrie's submission is flawed in only one respect to 1980s eyes (and that is not his fault). In 1967 he believed that the party battle about the role of the State was, in an extreme form anyway, over for the foreseeable future and that 'the new consensus should make it easier to find a generally acceptable basis of ideas for remodelling the machinery of government, and the Civil Service as part of it'.[119] The Treasury at Ryrie's level would have known of Mrs Thatcher in 1967. She was, after all, a junior member of Iain Macleod's front bench team shadowing Treasury affairs and during the previous year's Budget debate had delivered herself of the remark (in the context of selective employment tax) that 'The Chancellor needs a woman at the Treasury'.[120] But not even the most perceptive assistant secretary can have been expected to see the seismic shifts in personal fortunes and British political economy which propelled her into No. 10 and precipitated a (so far) nine-year attack on the boundaries of the State.

Yet the core problem as dissected as William Ryrie remains as he described it twenty years ago – a government machine designed for nineteenth-century needs, when the State 'was responsible for a very limited number of purely national matters and answerable in detail for them to Parliament', buckling under a late-twentieth-century workload:

> A great deal of the cumbersomeness and inefficiency of government can still be traced to the doctrine of a minister's responsibility for all the detailed operations of his department and, in many cases, subordinate organs; and the right of Members of Parliament to enquire into them. It is not just that answering Parliamentary Questions takes up much of the time of the Civil Service: the possibility of the Parliamentary Question or debate hangs over all public departments as an inhibitor, curbing initiative and stifling the will to take responsibility.
>
> Far too many issues are referred to the top not because they are

> intrinsically important but because they could be brought up in a political encounter in Parliament. A large proportion of the time of Ministers is taken up in delving into small issues for this reason, or guarding against this danger. Consequently far too little time and energy is given to the important work of framing basic and long-term policies and objectives.[121]

In a remarkably prescient passage, Ryrie foretells exactly what was to happen in the 1970s, writing some eight years before Professor Anthony King developed the theory of 'overload' (see pp. 318–9).

> If this [the lack of time for long-term policy development] is true now, it must get progressively more serious as time goes on unless the machinery of government is changed. The process by which the government is involved in more and more areas of collective planning and decision-taking and the growing technical complexity of problems will heap heavier burdens on Ministers. If at the same time they have to cope with a growing volume of detailed work there is a serious danger that the whole machine will simply come to a standstill for lack of drive from the top.[122]

Ryrie's was a voice from the Treasury engine room. At the time he was its desk man on international monetary affairs. He thinks 'William Armstrong issued a general permission for Treasury officials to submit personal views as evidence to the [Fulton] committee. He did not personally vet and approve my evidence.' Ryrie, writing to me twenty years later, could 'not recall William Armstrong making any particular comments at my evidence although I was a member of a small group of youngish people in the Treasury who had occasional discussions over sandwiches and beer with him away from the office. I think he was a little sceptical of my ideas of a degree of specialisation within the Civil Service.'[123] The singular thread in his analysis was its linkage of an over-burdened, top-heavy decision-taking system with 'the dissatisfaction which civil servants feel about their work and the dissatisfaction which the public feels about the Civil Service' because:

> It is a matter of common experience amongst civil servants that they feel they have little or no responsibility, because ultimately everything seems to go to the top. We see our political masters over-burdened with detailed work on day-to-day issues, and unable to give proper attention to the basic long-term issues of policy which should be their main concern. At the same time we feel frustrated ... Officers at the level of assistant secretary and principal feel they have much less responsibility than their predecessors twenty or thirty years ago, and they are right.[124]

The other crippling malady diagnosed by Ryrie was the mania for co-ordination caused by too many departments with overlapping responsibilities leaving too many officials devoting an excessive amount of time to liaison and 'co-ordinating the views of departments which have to be consulted just because they exist and have Ministerial chiefs who can take a disagreement to the Cabinet'.[125]

It is a tragedy that the Ryrie plan which grew out of these thoughts was relegated to the obscurity of a scantily read background volume to Fulton. The whole contribution, though only eight printed pages long, deserved almost as much exposure as the main Fulton Report itself. In essence Ryrie wanted civil servants to be better trained, more expert, *and* imbued by the feeling that they alone could not possess all the answers – that Whitehall should not aim at self-sufficiency but realise that it needed the constant help of outside experts if it was not to 'grow more and more cumbersome, and more and more out of touch with the rest of the community ... the 19th-century notion of the intelligent layman, able to turn his hand to anything, relying if necessary on the experts but relegating them to an advisory role, is now frivolous and irresponsible'.[126] In this Ryrie's views were very much along the same lines as Fulton's. But for Ryrie the solution was two-dimensional. Equally important was 'a drastic reorganisation and simplification of the central departments' which if successful in terms of 'rationalisation and streamlining [must make it] possible to bring about a substantial reduction in [Civil Service] numbers'.[127] He signed off with a personal note on 'the vocation of a civil servant' which has even more bite in the late eighties than it had in the late sixties:

> The morale of the Civil Service, once a rather self-satisfied *elite*, has suffered sadly since the war. A new sense of vocation is badly needed. A re-statement of the role of the civil servant in the second half of the 20th century on the lines of this paper, combined with reforms to enable us to carry out that role more effectively, would, I think, do much to restore our drooping spirits.[128]

On its lower plane, far below the strategic level of machinery-of-government and civil servant/political master relations, the Fulton committee ground away, processing reams of evidence, commissioning bulky social surveys of the constituent classes of official and their social backgrounds plus a management consultants' inquiry which Norman Hunt took sabbatical leave from his Oxford college to lead. The committee was not, by most accounts, either happy or well-run. At a 'Fulton: twenty years on' seminar organised by the Institute of Contemporary British History, Robert Nield said, 'There was no strategy whatever. There was more anarchy than strategy', while Lord Allen of Abbeydale (the former Sir Philip Allen) declared that Fulton 'was the worst report I have ever been concerned with, and I've sat on very many committees in my time, and we left so many loose ends untied. Nevertheless it did make people start thinking.'[129] This, from a twenty-year perspective, was true enough, though the result, published in June 1968, was a treatise and a prescription whose contents, far from building a new and lasting consensus on the model of Northcote and Trevelyan, are hotly debated to this day.

Fulton came up with twenty-two recommendations. For all the controversy they aroused, they have become something of a sacred text in the history of the British Civil Service and, therefore, deserve to be reproduced unvarnished and in full:

1. The Home Civil Service today is still fundamentally the product of the nineteenth-century philosophy of the Northcote–Trevelyan Report. The problems it faces are those of the second half of the twentieth century. In spite of its many strengths, it is inadequate in six main respects for the most efficient discharge of the present and prospective responsibilities of government:

   (a) It is still too much based on the philosophy of the amateur (or 'generalist' or 'all-rounder'). This is most evident in the Administrative Class, which holds the dominant position in the Service.
   (b) The present system of classes in the Service (there are over 1400, each for the most part with its own separate pay and career structure) seriously impedes its work.
   (c) Scientists, engineers and members of other specialist classes are frequently given neither the full responsibilities and opportunities nor the corresponding authority they ought to have.
   (d) Too few civil servants are skilled managers.
   (e) There is not enough contact between the Service and the community it is there to serve.
   (f) Personnel management and career planning are inadequate.

   For these and other defects the central management of the Service, the Treasury, must accept its share of responsibility.

2. We propose a simple guiding principle for the future. The Service must continuously review the tasks it is called on to perform; it should then think out what new skills and kinds of men are needed and how these men can be found, trained and deployed.

3. A new Civil Service Department should be set up with wider functions than those now performed by the 'Pay and Management'

group of the Treasury, which it should take over. The new department should also absorb the Civil Service Commission.

4. The new department should be under the control of the Prime Minister. We hope that he will retain direct responsibility for senior appointments, machinery of government and questions of security. Outside this area, we suggest that the Prime Minister should delegate day-to-day responsibility to a non-departmental Minister of appropriate seniority who is also a member of the Cabinet.

5. The Permanent Secretary of the Civil Service Department should be designated Head of the Home Civil Service.

6. All classes should be abolished and replaced by a single, unified grading structure covering all civil servants from top to bottom in the non-industrial part of the Service. The correct grading of each post should be determined by job evaluation.

7. The Service should develop greater professionalism both among specialists (e.g. scientists and engineers) and administrators (i.e. the new counterparts of the present Administrative and Executive Classes). For the former this means more training in management, and opportunities for greater responsibility and wider careers. For the latter it means enabling them to specialise in particular areas of government. We identify two such areas and accordingly recommend the development of a group of economic and financial administrators, and a second group of social administrators.

8. Employing departments should have a larger role in recruitment and there should be a speeding up of procedures. A majority of us consider that in the recruitment of graduates for one or other of the groups of administrators more account should be taken of the relevance of their university courses to the job they are being recruited to do.

9. A Civil Service College should be set up. It should provide major training courses in administration and management and a wide range of shorter courses. It should also have important research functions. The courses provided by the College should not be restricted to civil servants; a proportion of places should be set aside for men and women from private industrial and commercial firms, local government and public corporations.

10. More resources should be devoted to the career management of all civil servants. All must have the opportunity to progress as far and

as fast as their talents and appropriate training can take them. This involves major changes in promotion procedures.

11. While the Civil Service should remain predominantly a career Service, there should be greater mobility between it and other employments. We, therefore, recommend an expanded late entry, temporary appointments for fixed periods, short-term interchanges of staff and freer movement out of the Service. These proposals involve substantial changes in the pension scheme and the replacement of 'established' status by new terms of employment.

12. In the interests of efficiency, the principles of accountable management should be applied to the organisation of the work of departments. This means the clear allocation of responsibility and authority to accountable units with defined objectives. It also means a corresponding addition to the system of government accounting.

13. Management services units with highly qualified and experienced staff should be set up in all major departments.

14. Departments should establish Planning Units.

15. In addition to the Permanent Secretary, there should also be in most departments a Senior Policy Adviser to assist the Minister. The Senior Policy Adviser would normally be head of the Planning Unit. His prime job would be to look to and prepare for the future and to ensure that present policy decisions are taken with as full a recognition as possible of likely future developments.

16. In some of the big technical departments, there may be a need for a further senior post: a chief scientist, engineer or other specialist.

17. We do not propose that the Senior Policy Adviser and chief specialist, together with the Permanent Secretary, should constitute a formal board. The working arrangements should be informal and variable from department to department and from time to time; different Ministers' individual ways of working will do much to determine the pattern.

18. There should be one man who has overall responsibility under the Minister for all the affairs of the Department and he should continue to be the Permanent Secretary.

19. A Minister at the head of a department should be able to employ on a temporary basis such small numbers of experts as he personally considers he needs to help him.

20. We have suggested a number of further inquiries. Their subjects among others, should be:

    (a) the desirability of 'hiving off' activities to non-departmental organisations;
    (b) ways and means of getting rid of unnecessary secrecy both in policy-making and in administration;
    (c) the new pattern of joint consultation that will be appropriate for the Civil Service in the light of the Government's decisions on our report. This inquiry should be conducted jointly by the Civil Service Department and the staff associations;
    (d) methods of making recruitment procedures as speedy and objective as possible.

21. If our proposals are accepted, we hope that the Government will take steps to see that the progress made in their implementation is reviewed. This could be by an annual report to Parliament during the next five years. A small committee might be set up at the end of that period if needed.

22. We have seen that the Service has men and women with the ability, vision and enthusiasm needed to carry our proposals through to success. A Civil Service reconstructed on the basis of these proposals will, we believe, make possible the progressive and efficient conduct of our affairs.[129]

Intense politics imbued the final draft of Fulton. It looked at one stage as if the committee would divide between majority and minority reports. In the event only the veteran social scientist from Liverpool University, Professor Lord Simey, took up his pen to draft a note of reservation which, according to Whitehall talk, reflected the view of William Armstrong and the Treasury. (Whitehall felt that Wilson had his men on the committee – Fulton and Hunt who would sometimes call at No. 10 before committee sessions – so, presumably, felt unashamed at speaking through the sympathetic Simey.) Lord Simey felt that Fulton's opening chapter had been 'unfair to the Civil Service', failing 'to recognise, in my opinion, the contemporary relevance of the great contribution the Service made to the successful conduct of the war and, subsequently, in the transition from war to peace'.[130] Simey did not accept Fulton's strictures about gifted amateurs and maintained 'that we have in the existing Civil Service an asset which it would be utterly foolish to discard. Its potentialities provide a more than adequate basis for any reforms that may be necessary both in the immediate and the long-term future.'[131]

The word in Whitehall was that the 'conservative' elements on Fulton, including the two permanent secretaries Sir Philip Allen and Sir James Dunnett, had calculated that a unanimous report would be less extreme than a majority report and that this would be important particularly if Labour won the next election in 1969 or 1971 and found itself in a position to implement what might have been, had the committee split, a strongly anti-Civil Service prospectus.[132]

The politics of implementing Fulton began from the moment when, in the spring of 1968, as William Armstrong recalled, 'There was a little ceremony with the four of us – Harold [Wilson] and myself for the Government, and Fulton and Hunt for the Committee – when the report was handed over. Harold and Fulton started reminiscing about the early years of the war. I never knew this, but they both worked as temporary civil servants in the Board of Trade.'[133]

The battle for Fulton took place at both the political and official levels. Its ministerial frontline can be traced with the help of the Crossman and Castle diaries. In essence, Wilson wanted a pair of Fulton's core proposals – a separate Civil Service Department and the abolition of classes – accepted instantly and implemented quickly; his Chancellor of the Exchequer and minister responsible for the Civil Service, Roy Jenkins, wanted a period of delay for reflection before the Government announced its response. Both Wilson and Jenkins lobbied potential allies. The Prime Minister used the faithful and committed (to Civil Service reform, that is) Tommy Balogh to make the first approach to Mrs Castle, Employment Secretary and a big figure in Wilson's Cabinet in the summer of 1968. Her diary entry for 19 June records that:

> Tommy phoned to say Harold wanted me to know there was likely to be a row over Fulton at Cabinet tomorrow and he wanted me to back him up. Roy, though he liked the report, was expected to argue the need for delay while we considered it. This would give the appearance of indecision and would give time for the Civil Service to get round us. Harold was keen to go ahead, as was Tommy. There were some points on which Tommy thought we should go further but 'this is the minimum'.[134]

Two days earlier, after a row about spending cuts in the social services between Jenkins and Crossman (by this time installed in the mega-department, the DHSS, specially created for him), the two of them struck a deal over Fulton which, such is the nature of Cabinet government, had nothing to do with the merits of the Report's proposals. Wilson, according to Crossman, had circulated a paper proposing the removal of the Treasury's pay and establishment divisions into a new Civil Service Department without consulting Jenkins. '"Now, Dick, let's be practical"', Crossman records Jenkins as saying. '"If I agree with you about postponing the decision on Social Service cuts for a week will you give me your full support on Fulton?" "Yes", I said, "if you will support me on [House of] Lords' reform as well." And that, roughly speaking, was the deal we came to.'[135]

Crossman took a dim view of the Fulton Report and expressed it in his customarily patronising fashion: 'It's a second-rate report written in a very poor style by Norman Hunt. He and Harold are tremendous buddies, who live in the same world of uninspired commonsense. The report is perfectly sensible but, oh dear, it lacks distinction.'[136] Before the first Cabinet discussion on Fulton, Crossman had a chance to talk to William Armstrong about it (they met to discuss a successor to Sir Arnold France as Permanent Secretary to the Ministry of Health): 'Then William got on to the Fulton Report where of course he knew of the tension between the Chancellor and the Prime Minister. He told me it was very unpopular in Whitehall but that although he had informed the Prime Minister he didn't think the information would be passed on to me. Armstrong is a very good man but he is worn, exhausted, and he wasn't going to inject himself into a battle between the Chancellor and the Prime Minister.'[137]

The battle, such as it was, took place at a meeting of the full Cabinet on 10 June. Discussion was delayed by that great, time-consuming side-show of the late 1960s – House of Lords reform. Wilson was clearly very personally committed to Fulton. Crossman thought he knew why: 'I haven't asked him but I'm pretty sure that the reason he has committed himself to this report so early and so personally is partly because he has a strong liking for Fulton and even more for Norman Hunt and partly because he thinks this way he can improve his image as a great moderniser.'[138] Crossman went on to describe the discussion in a manner, I am sure, much more vivid than Burke Trend's minute (which will not be released until January 1999).

> He [Harold] put his case for immediately accepting the main recommendations of the report, including the creation of a Civil Service Department. Then the Chancellor put his case against what he described as precipitate action. Denis Healey [Defence Secretary], Michael Stewart [Foreign Secretary] and I supported Roy and all the support Harold got was from Wedgy Benn [Minister of Technology] and Peter Shore [Secretary of State for Economic Affairs], his two hirelings. He was so upset that at this point he stopped the meeting and asked that it should be resumed later.[139]

Barbara Castle, so little importance did she attach to Whitehall reform at that time, left Cabinet after the opening contributions to have lunch with the Editor of *The Times*, William Rees-Mogg, despite Wilson's Principal Private Secretary, Michael Halls, a keen advocate of Fulton (his death in April 1970 deprived the 'inner circle' pushing for its implementation of a key member[140]) rushing after her and saying 'Are you going? There's Fulton.'[141]

Prior to the Report's publication after what Norman Hunt described as 'a great deal of high level ministerial lobbying' by the Committee, Wilson and Halls developed the strategy of pushing for the swift acceptance of three recommendations – a CSD, a Civil Service College and class abolition – while leaving the rest for later.[142] Jenkins's counter-lobbying thwarted that. But Wilson did not give up. Mrs Castle was summoned by the Prime Minister after her evacuation to *The Times* from the first Cabinet discussion.

She found him upstairs at No. 10 'in a new study which he said he had taken over from the Church Commissioners! He was on the brandy – talkative and affectionate, saying he liked my TV make-up and not to show my knees at him. He kept repeating how well I am doing, and was as usual obsessed with conspiracies.'[143] Wilson, typically, banged on about leaks to the press. Mrs Castle, herself a former journalist, continued:

> I begged Harold not to bother with these press comments – he could never prove anything anyway – but he kept repeating, 'I've got them this time'. I sometimes think he is going mildly off his rocker.
>
> But I discovered that his main purpose was to get my support at Cabinet tomorrow for his announcement accepting the Fulton Report. Just what his passion for Fulton springs from I'm not clear, except that he said the classics boys have always been against him and that he prefers the earthy, elementary school types like Michael Halls. I said I was all in favour of his announcing acceptance in principle but that I wasn't going to agree to any reference to 'phasing in' the expensive parts of Fulton unless and until we had announced the phasing in of equal pay in the industrial field about which I was in touch with the Chancellor . . . Harold replied, 'Work me out a formula for this side of my statement.'
>
> I left Harold still brooding about what he believes are Dick's conspiracies with Roy against him though I'd told him flatly it was nonsense: Dick had been very scathing to me about Roy's dilettantism. 'Yes', said Harold somewhat comforted, 'Roy only works a four-day week.'[144]

Such is the nature of high Cabinet politics! A crucially important long-term issue like Whitehall reform – vital to all ministers at all times, central to their permanent back-up system, policy intelligence service, the lot – is treated as a lever for quick deals on other issues and the lightning conductor for paranoia and rivalry. No wonder it is so hard to change the British Civil Service.

At the 'special Cabinet'[145] on Fulton on 25 June Wilson delayed proceedings while he ranted on about leaks from the Cabinet. 'Then', as Crossman recorded, 'he glared at us and stopped. There was no discussion and Harold started on the Fulton Report, where we gave him a very easy time . . . Harold needed a success for himself and Cabinet consented to his getting it with a Statement tomorrow.'[146]

So much for Roy Jenkins's attempts to delay matters. Unknown to the Cabinet, William Armstrong was busily engaged in a private debate with Wilson about one of three key elements of Fulton that the Prime Minister wished to accept instantly, a debate that Norman Hunt (who died almost twenty years later believing the permanent secretaries had wrecked his beloved report) later made much of. Armstrong, according to Hunt's co-author, Peter Kellner, had no objection to a Civil Service College or a separate Civil Service Department. (Otto Clarke, now at Mintech, had: 'I never dreamed that the responsibility for financial control of departments would be separated from that for management control . . . because the non-responsiblity for management control drives the Treasury back to the worst kinds of financial control of departments, which not only loses sight of the wood for the trees, but also loses sight of the forests.'[147] 'What Armstrong did not like', wrote Kellner, 'was the third, but most crucial proposal – the unification of the classes. Yet this was what Wilson most keenly wanted to announce.'[148] In an interview with Kellner in the mid-1970s, Armstrong said:

> They [Wilson, Fulton and Hunt] wanted a timetable for common grading announced in the Commons. I told Harold, 'No, no, you'd regret that; it isn't practicable and if you give me a chance I would hope to be able to demonstrate it. I'm with you on getting rid of unnecessary obstacles from bottom to top. But it isn't on for doctors, lawyers or engineers to become administrators. The traffic would be all one way. I think you want to think about this.'[149]

So much for the Armstrong of Crossman's imagining too worn and exhausted to do battle over Fulton. According to Armstrong, he and Wilson were at cross-purposes about what kinds of class they were talking about. 'What Harold was thinking about was nothing to do with different Civil Service classes, but class with a capital C – upper class, middle class and lower class.'[150] In other words, the Prime Minister was talking about a ladder of opportunity for bright officials whatever their social origins; Armstrong about the myriad of 1,400 separate Civil Service classes. The two men agreed on a compromise. The statement which Armstrong drafted for Wilson to make on 26 June talked about 'consultations with the staff associations . . . so that a practicable system can be prepared for the implementation of unified grading'.[151] Armstrong told Kellner: 'We both knew what the other would make of it. It was push and shove.'[152] Wilson duly announced to the Commons that 'the three things that [he] regarded as of prime importance', as Armstrong told the Commons Expenditure Committee in 1977, were 'to set up a Civil Service Department, taking it out of the Treasury ... to set up a Civil Service College, and ... the abolition of the classes'.[153] As Wilson put it at the time, in that 'New Britain' style of language so familiar then and so heavily criticised since,[154] the new mobility flowing from the abolition of classes 'will mean that for everyone in the Civil Service, whether from a college of technology or from a university, whether he or she comes in from industry or from a profession – all in future, the school-leaver, the graduate, the accountant, the engineer, the scientist, the lawyer – for all of them there will be an open road to the top which, up to now, has been in the main through the Administrative Class.'[155]

A debate of almost theological proportions has raged about Fulton since its publication a generation ago. The report found two tireless and fluent defenders in Norman Hunt and John Garrett, the management consultant who worked with Hunt on Fulton and later became a Labour MP. Hunt incorporated his protracted lament for 'the lost reforms' of Fulton in the volume he co-authored with Peter Kellner. Garrett's testimony was published in 1980 as part of his *Managing the Civil Service*.[156] Wilson, too, remained proud of Fulton and liked to point out the changes it had led to. When he founded his Downing Street Policy Unit in 1974 under Dr Bernard Donoughue (an institution that has grown and adapted under his successors both Labour and Conservative) it represented a conscious implementation of the Fulton recommendation for Planning Units – 'the right solution, following the recommendations of the Fulton Report' was how he put it.[157] So proud of it was Wilson that he treated the Commonwealth Prime Ministers, gathered in Jamaica in 1975, to a little seminar about it.[158] I can remember a conversation with Wilson shortly after his retirement from the premiership in 1976 when he mentioned with pride the appointment of James Hamilton, ex-Royal Aircraft Establishment, Farnborough, former leader of Whitehall's Concorde team and head of the Cabinet Office economic secretariat, who was shortly to become Permanent Secretary at the Department of Education and Science – the first professional post-Fulton to tread that open road to the very top. At the time I described Hamilton in *The Times* as being 'widely regarded as the finest flowering of "Fulton Man", because he is that rare phenomenon among civil servants, a man as good on paper as on his slide rule'.[159]

Sadly, that crucial insider participant in the post-Fulton debate, William Armstrong, died before he got round to his long-planned memoirs.[160] His reflections on Fulton have to be gleaned in fragments from interviews and appearances before select committees. The core of his defence was that he did what Wilson had wanted him to do,[161] particularly the 'horizontal barriers' between the administrative, executive and clerical classes (now all part of the same Administration Group), 'the ones, in fact, Mr Wilson was most interested in',[162] as Armstrong told the Expenditure Committee, as opposed to the 'vertical barriers' between specialists and generalists, which, according to Kellner and Crowther-Hunt, were the ones Fulton was most concerned with, and which remain in the shape of the professional and technology and science groups.

Peter Kellner, using internal papers and the memory of Norman Hunt, has traced in detail how Armstrong, aided by all but one of the Civil Service unions, the specialists' Institution of Professional Civil Servants, maintained the distinction (apart from the top three grades of permanent, deputy and under secretary – some eight hundreds officials – renamed the 'open structure') between specialists and generalists. The battle raged in an 'inner circle' of William Armstrong, Norman Hunt and Michael Halls till Halls's tragic heart attack two months before Wilson's surprise defeat in the general election of 1970.[163] Halls, who had worked with Wilson in his Board of Trade days in the late 1940s, was described by his chief as 'the epitome of the new management type envisaged by the Fulton Committee but, more than this, his main preoccupation in the latter years of a distinguished career was Civil Service reform and the speediest possible implementation of Fulton'.[164]

The defenders of Fulton would be wrong to make Armstrong the sole villain of the piece. Wilson himself struck down a key recommendation, the so-called 'preference for relevance' when choosing the young administrators of the future. This had one defender – albeit a powerfully placed one – in Sir Douglas Allen,[165] Permanent Secretary to the Treasury once Armstrong moved across in October 1968 to lead the new Civil Service Department and head the profession on the retirement of Sir Lawrence Helsby. Allen had taken a first in economics and statistics at the London School of Economics just before the war and was once described to me by a leading economic commentator as 'by far the most economically literate permanent secretary ever'.[166] Armstrong and Lord Shackleton, the Lord Privy Seal and first ministerial chief of the new CSD, had taken seriously the possibility of Wilson accepting a preference for relevance. Lord Shackleton, a delightful, self-ironic man, who had described his relationship with Armstrong as 'he was the head and I was his political adviser',[167] told me how the pair of them 'had a great game deciding what was relevant and we decided Greats was because you learnt about politics in microcosm in Greece and Rome. [We] produced a great thing on "relevant man" [but] we needn't have bothered. He [Wilson] dismissed it out of hand.'[168] Even amongst 'relevant men' already in the specialist ranks of Whitehall a touch of ennui afflicted some in post-Fulton discussions though, on the face of it, they had the most to gain from its wholehearted implementation. Sir Donald MacDougall, by 1969 Head of the Government Economic Service, confessed in his memoirs that:

> The Report contained some good ideas, but a lot of it was ... rather general and even woolly; and I was obliged to read, and sit through discussions of long papers by the CSD which I thought were sometimes like sermons. First there was the text – a paragraph from Fulton; then ten pages discussing what it might mean; then another ten considering what might be done about it; and a final section quite often saying why nothing was possible or, worse still, with no conclusion at all.[169]

The swiftest and heaviest flak Fulton encountered in terms of public reaction stemmed from the report's description of the administrators as 'amateurs' – 'the decisive tactical mistake' as Peter Kellner called it.[170] The House of Lords debate on the report within a month of its publication was dominated by the amateur factor. Even C. P. Snow, himself a scientific temporary in the 1940s and house-novelist of that war-shortening breed, said: 'I much regret that this absurd stereotype was not criticised out of existence during the process of drafting.'[171] It inspired Derek Morrell of the Home Office, as we have seen, to deliver his magnificent oration at the FDA conference in 1969, though he was 'wholly in agreement' with much of it. But referring to 'the famous – or infamous – first chapter of Fulton', where the amateurism taunt was inscribed, he said:

> I reject the diagnosis there recorded. We are not amateurs. We are professionals. Ever since the great reform of the last century, we have exhibited the two primary characteristics of a true profession. We profess an ethic regulating our work: and we possess knowledge and know-how specific to that work.[172]

For a decade and more, the Fulton report continued to be the butt of private abuse from many, though not all, administrators – most of it infinitely less reasoned than Morrell's and often imbued by the kind of snobbery and arrogance that goes with an entrenched ruling group secure in the tradition of a century. I encountered a representative sample of this while preparing a 'Times Profile' of the Civil Service in 1975.

> Fulton was a joke. The Civil Service is much too smart to worry about Fulton. They accepted everything he said then did what they wanted to.[173]
>
> Oh, there have been loads of changes. We have renamed everything.[174]

Twenty years after its publication Robert Armstrong was more balanced in his put-down – Fulton had been an important milestone on the road to the lasting reforms of the 1980s – but 'not for the first or last time the Service felt that it was being criticised more for its formal description of itself than for the reality'.[175]

Norman Hunt, who lost no opportunity to remind the political nation of 'the lost reforms',[176] was a particular target of superior wit. I remember an assistant secretary saying over the lunch table in the late 1970s how tiresome it was, 'like a cracked 78 from the Big Band era – Norman Hunt and the Fultonaires'.[177]

Yet a run-through of Fulton's main proposals from the perspective of the late-1980s produces, in my case at least, a much more favourable audit than those slick seventies dismissals would suggest. Taking them as Fulton and Hunt wrote them, there remains an urgent need for Whitehall to make better use of the riches locked up in its specialist and technical staff. Since the Rayner reforms (see Chapter 14) the Civil Service has begun to fulfil the Fulton requirement of 'continuously review[ing] the tasks it is called on to perform; it should then think out what new skills and kinds of men are needed and how these men can be found, trained and deployed'.[178]

The Civil Service Department was established within four months of Fulton reporting and the Civil Service College within two years. The CSD had a chequered life, as we shall see, and was abolished by Mrs Thatcher in 1981. The college, after a shaky start (it was heavily criticised by a two-man inquiry, consisting of Sir Leslie Williams, former general secretary of the National Staff Side, and Neville Heaton, a retired deputy secretary, in 1974)[179] found its feet in the late 1970s and is very much a part of the 1980s thrust for improved financial management. There have, too, been considerable associated efforts to instil professionalism in management at all levels. A senior official whose candour I admire said of Fulton in 1987, 'It allowed us to lose the polish without acquiring the managerial efficiency.'[180] But it strikes me as unfair to complain of an unfinished revolution in the context of a report which was only half-heartedly implemented and not acknowledged as an input into the more determined drive for improved management in the 1980s. Unified grading has now been extended down to principal rank, embracing 18,500 officials instead of the original 800 in the old open structure. Mobility has improved between Whitehall and the outside world though to nothing like the extent Fulton wanted or what is needed. The Financial Management Initiative since 1982 has extended considerably the principle of units of accountable management. Planning units, the No. 10 Policy Unit apart, have failed to materialise. A number of departments – Defence, Education, DHSS – established them in one form or another, but they have not turned out to be the force intended. There has been a great deal of hiving-off of functions into agencies and commissions (the Heath administration was very strong on this). As to 'ways and means of getting rid of unnecessary secrecy both in policy making and administration',[181] there have been the inquiries Fulton wanted (Franks on official secrets 1971–2, Allen on Open Government in 1976–7) but precious little tangible came of either (see Chapter 9).

As for Fulton's recommendation that 'a Minister at the head of a department should be able to employ on a temporary basis such small numbers of experts as he personally considers he needs to help him'[182] – the *cabinet* idea – it seems to have had a promising, though ultimately fruitless, run in post-Fulton Whitehall. Mrs Castle records in her diary one of a series of meetings on the report held between CSD officials and individual ministers in the spring of 1970. 'Spent nearly three hours at the Civil Service Department', she wrote on 13 April,

> talking to Eddie's [Shackleton's] and William Armstrong's little group of 'thinkers' who are discussing with selected Ministers what Ministers expect from the Civil Service and what they get. All part of their post-Fulton activities. Apparently Wedgie [Benn] went along last week full of enthusiasm and charts and details of how he communicated with his Department. I don't find it so easy to sit down in a circle at 4.30 pm and hold forth on these subjects in cold blood. However, I gave them some frank thoughts which they assured me they enjoyed enormously. They were an impressive lot, including Philip Rodgers and John Hunt . . . I was particularly pleased when Hunt said that after I had been six months at MOT [Ministry of Transport] the change that came over my civil servants was most marked. They were the same people and yet their approach was entirely different because they knew what they were supposed to be doing.
>
> Eddie assured me that it was the best discussion they had had so far. All this confirmed me in my belief that the best civil servants are so reasonable and enlightened and intelligent that a Minister needs more political reinforcement against them, not less. The elite embrace can be the most dangerous of all. William, of course, was as rational and progressive as they come. He said he particularly sympathised with my concept of the political isolation of a Minister, what I had called 'the loneliness of the short-distance runner'. We discussed for some time what form political 'cabinet' might take.[183]

Twenty-seven years later the discussion, as rational and progressive as ever, continued. Shortly before the 1987 General Election Sir John Hoskyns's Reskilling Government Group put out a detailed plan, costed by the First Division Association, for 'an experimental *cabinet* system [to] be introduced immediately after the General Election, for four secretaries of state and five other ministers'.[184] Mrs Thatcher was returned to power. Nothing happened. Matters remained where they had been at that spring afternoon meeting at the CSD in 1970.

The Fulton legacy, then, is mixed, but time *is* changing the balance between lost and found Fulton reforms. Perhaps 'Norman Hunt and the Fultonaires' will have the best tunes in the end and gradually become rather more treasured objects from a past era like a Glenn Miller LP.

6 EXPERIMENT, CRISIS AND DISILLUSION

What was most important was for the Cabinet to be in a position to take strategic decisions. I had seen Cabinets which had all the time seemed to be dealing with the day-to-day problems and there was never a real opportunity to deal with strategy ... What I wanted to do was so to change things that the Cabinet could do that.
Edward Heath on his new 'style of government', 1972[1]

Ted Heath had some of the best ideas of any postwar prime minister. He ... was a rather radical person.
Dr David Owen, 1983[2]

[Ted] believes there is an answer to all problems which can be worked out by proper bureaucratic means – I'm not using that word abusively for once – by the proper approach. If all the relevant facts are assembled and put together by competent people, and logical analysis is made, then that will provide the answer.
Enoch Powell, 1984[3]

The programme analysis and review system created a great deal of work but not much in the way of results.
Lord Hunt of Tanworth, 1984[4]

As time went by it [the Central Policy Review Staff] concerned itself less and less with central issues and became a meddler in departmental business.
Sir Douglas Wass, 1983[5]

Bernard, it is all falling apart. I do not trust the Whitehall machine. I think Ministers and their departments are quietly selling out.
James Callaghan to Bernard Donoughue, January 1979[6]

When Lobby Correspondent of The *Financial Times*, I prepared a piece speculating where Harold Wilson and Edward Heath would have been had Wilson in 1945 accepted Bridges's offer of a permanent established post in Whitehall and had Heath been sent to the Treasury instead of the Ministry of Civil Aviation after passing out joint top of his reconstruction competition in 1946.[7] 'It is a nice point for historians to ponder', I wrote, 'how different the country would have been if both men had remained and risen to the top in Whitehall. By the 1970s, one could well have seen Sir Harold as Cabinet Secretary and Mr Heath as Permanent Secretary to the Treasury.'[8] This remark prompted one official who had worked with Wilson to tell me, 'You're quite wrong about Harold wanting to have been Cabinet Secretary had he stayed in. The job he would have wanted would not have been John Hunt's but the Head of MI5!'[9] I thought it was intriguing at the time, but little did I realise, given the subsequent claims of MI5 plots to destabilise Wilson in the mid-1970s, just how pregnant it was.

Wherever they might have ended up in the Whitehall hierarchy, one permanent secretary *manqué* replaced another in No. 10 after the surprise result of the 1970 general election. Heath had firm, thought-out views on the machinery of government. He found a sympathetic ear in William Armstrong, who made the transition from one administration to another as effortlessly as he always had. Armstrong, as he later told the Expenditure Committee, believed

> that there were quite a lot of things in the Fulton Report that either were slightly misconceived or, in any event, could not be done in the way that he said, because his terms of reference put the cart before the horse. In my opinion, which obviously was not taken, the first inquiry should have been into the machinery and organisation of government and, after that had been done, an inquiry into the Civil Service would have made sense.
>
> But Fulton started off on the one without the other having been done so that we had to embark on a sort of 'do-it-yourself' programme of machinery of government changes to get the thing into a shape that made sense.[10]

There was nothing DIY or improvised about Heath's ideas for the machinery of government. He was, in such terms, the most managerially minded prime minister since Attlee. As leader of the Opposition he had commissioned a depth of detailed planning unmatched by any premier before or since. Mr Heath began the work even before he succeeded Sir Alec Douglas-Home as party leader in 1965. After the Conservatives lost the 1964 general election Heath assumed the chairmanship of the party's policy group which 'had devoted much attention to the machinery of government'.[11] Once Heath became party leader, the chairmanship of the group passed to Sir Edward Boyle who was appointed a member of the Fulton Committee the following year. The group was, as Christopher Pollitt put it, 'discreetly advised by several ex-civil servants, including Lord Normanbrook'.[12] By the end of 1965 the departmental parameters of what was to become Heath's new style of government were already discernible:

> There was to be one economics department (not two as – with the DEA – Labour was then operating), and considerable amalgamation of other departments to produce a pattern of fewer, larger units. The latter were to include a single large industry department (similar in responsibilities to the Department of Trade and Industry as it emerged five years later). The whole exercise was closely directed and co-ordinated by Heath, and its recommendations received the approval of the Shadow Cabinet.[13]

Heath, as he later told two journalists from the *Evening Standard*, found 'this [the machinery of government] of extraordinary interest'.[14] He did not stop at departmental boundaries. Techniques, the very detailed stuff of process and analysis, also fascinated him. He established a Public Sector Research Unit under that veteran dynamo, Ernest Marples (legendary moderniser of the railways while at the Ministry of Transport). Marples sent his young men, David Howell and Mark Schreiber, to Japan and North America to scour the think-tanks and the agencies in search of modern management methods. Retired public servants would be summoned to Heath's flat in the Albany to be shown the results – plans for American-style zero-based budgeting to prevent spending programmes staggering on beyond their natural life, the blueprint of a prime minister's think-tank – an idea which grew from Mark Schreiber's idea of a 'Crown Consultants Unit'.[15] Lord Plowden caught the flavour of the Albany sessions when recalling a visit he paid to Heath with Robert Hall (now Lord Roberthall), his friend from CEPS days:

> We went one morning to his apartment in the Albany where we found a consultant. This firm of consultants had drawn up a plan. He had also dotted lines of where businessmen would be drawn in. One thing I do know about Whitehall is, if you do have people floating about in it, they will do no good and probably do harm. Robert and I said we did not believe this is the way to do it. I suppose Ted said, 'What do you think?' So we wrote down on a piece of paper something we thought would be a useful body.
>
> I think we described it as something that should be in the Cabinet Office to serve all ministers, to take an overall view of problems put to it (not to take a departmental view) and to come up with recommendations that were not the usual Cabinet Office brief of 'On the

> one hand, on the other'. I don't know how much influence it had on Ted. But he did set up the CPRS something along those lines.[16]

Bringing businessmen into government was a characteristic Heath theme. In 1969 he put together a Businessmen's Team under Richard Meyjes of Shell. By the autumn those recruited included Richard East from GKN, David Cruikshank from Bovis, Ken Lane from RTZ, Tim Sainsbury from Sainsbury's and Richard Hutton from Hambros. Most significant of all in terms of the future history of the Civil Service was the recruitment of Derek Rayner from Marks and Spencer. The businessmen worked for Mr Heath in their spare time on the understanding that if and when the Conservatives won the election their companies would loan them to the government for two years. In the meantime their efforts were devoted to specific projects, East working on decision-making procedures, Rayner on public purchasing and so on.[17] By the spring of 1970, in collaboration with the Conservative Party machine, the businessmen had helped produce a 'Black Book' containing the strategy for taking over the Whitehall policy-making machine, integrating the businessmen plus specific suggestions for structural changes.[18]

The Tory planners, like everyone else, were surprised when Wilson called a June election in 1970. But Heath made a more extensive use of the Douglas-Home rules than he had in 1966 (or Wilson in 1964 for that matter).[19] Rayner went to see the Head of the Home Civil Service, as did Meyjes who, in Christopher Pollitt's words, 'found a well-briefed Armstrong ready to comment on the advantages and disadvantages of the businessmen's "projects"'.[20] Schreiber called on the Cabinet Secretary and found Trend ready to explain 'the difficulty of having the "central capability" [the Conservative manifesto contained a reference to the prototype think-tank which it called the "central capability unit"[21]] reporting to the Prime Minister rather than to the Cabinet as a whole'.[22]

The reaction of Armstrong and Trend to Heath's emissaries in 1970 was a classic example of the permanent government at work acting like powerful but low-profile tugs nudging the ocean liner of a great political party into different berths than those on the bridge had intended. Bridges would have called it dipping into 'the storehouse of departmental experience ... [or letting] ... the waves of the practical philosophy wash against ideas put forward by his ministerial master'.[23] In the later 1970s critics like politician Brian Sedgemore (himself a former member of the administrative class) would call it an application of the 'Civil Service veto'.[24]

Trend and Armstrong were to the 1960s and early 1970s what Bridges and Brook had been to the 1940s and 1950s – the dominant duo of their generations. As individuals they were closer than Bridges and Brook who had become a bit distant from each other, particularly after Bridges 'developed a mysterious nervous complaint', as Sir John Winnifrith put it,[25] when, it has been suggested privately to me, Brook thought his old colleague ought to have retired.[26] No such friction grew between Armstrong and Trend. Trend was the senior in age and experience (Armstrong had succeeded him as private secretary to the Chancellor of the Exchequer in 1949). Armstrong used to refer to Trend as 'Pasha'.[27] They held the central machine together for a decade. When Lord Rothschild arrived to run the Think-Tank later on in 1970, he confided to a friend: 'Until this week I never realised the country was run by two men whom I'd never heard of'.[28]

Trend was educated at Whitgift in Croydon a few miles from Armstrong's grammar school in Tooting. He took a double first in Greats and entered the Board of Education in 1936 (Armstrong followed him there from Oxford two years later). Within a year Whitehall's talent spotters had switched him to the inside track to the Treasury. He stayed on that inside track until his retirement in 1973. Burke Trend, a tall, spare, thoughtful pipe-smoking man, was reminiscent in appearance of the style John Le Carré once characterised as incarnating 'the best tradition of the Anglo-Saxon administrative class' – 'his stride was agile, his body forward-sloping ... in the same attitude, whether static or in motion, Englishmen have hoisted flags over distant colonies, discovered the sources of great rivers, stood on the decks of sinking ships'.[29] Trend was a great fan of Le Carré. In his 'retirement' job as Master of Lincoln College he brought Le Carré, who had been an undergraduate there, back to talk to the young men, listening himself at the back, fascinated.[30] Burke Trend knew all about the secret world. Like Hankey, he genuinely was a man of secrets. As a young principal in the Treasury he had been put in charge of the 'secret vote', came to love the work and the men in it and took the job with him as he rose up the hierarchy. As Cabinet Secretary he became something of a shop steward for the secret servants of the state in lieu of the union they cannot join or form. He made sure they got their fair share of honours and allowances and, naturally enough, became a great favourite with them.[31] A year after his retirement Wilson brought him back in the deepest secrecy to investigate claims that the former Director-General of MI5, Sir Roger Hollis, had spied for Russian military intelligence. One day a week for a year in 1974–5 he caught the train from Oxford to Paddington and sat in his special room in the Security Service headquarters in Curzon Street just like George Smiley hunting Gerald the Mole, going forwards and backwards through the most secret files in Whitehall.[32]

Trend was a natural for the discreet back-rooms of Whitehall. Hugh Dalton, whose private secretary he became in 1945, once told him that those interested in government had to decide whether they liked 'the glare of the footlights or to work backstage'.[33] Burke Trend was always a backstage man. Unlike Armstrong he was never really attracted by notions of more open government and was a stickler for Cabinet confidentiality (he had the misfortune to take the minutes at some of the leakiest Cabinets ever in the Wilson years, 1964–70). Cabinets for him were dignified occasions, the difference between a Cabinet committee and a meeting of the full Cabinet being, as he once put it, that 'Cabinet is a more formidable business. Ministers are on their best behaviour. They are less relaxed, it's like the difference between playing on your own club ground or at Twickenham.'[34]

Trend, like many of the most accomplished officials of his generation, had a nice line in self-mockery. As we have seen, he was crucially placed in the Treasury when the first civil nuclear power programme was put together and had sat with Plowden and Clarke during the remoulding of the public spending system. Yet in retirement he would insist that he was innumerate and unable to read The *Financial Times* because of the figures.[35] Trend was a deeply patriotic man again in that quiet, understated way which was his trademark. As Cabinet Secretary he never forgot that the Cabinet Office was the progeny of the Committee of Imperial Defence. A fellow permanent secretary once said of Trend in the early 1970s, 'I've heard him utter some absurdly imperialist sentiments.'[36] He saw Suez from the inside as Brook's deputy. (John Hunt was also deeply embedded at the secret heart of government during that dreadful autumn of 1956 as Brook's private secretary; there is a kind of apostolic succession in the Cabinet Secretaryship!) Suez distressed him deeply. For Trend it was a pyschological watershed, the moment when it became apparent that Britain was no longer capable of being a great imperial power.[37] He tried his hardest when Cabinet Secretary to persuade Sir Anthony Nutting not to spill the dirtier beans of Suez in his *No End of a Lesson* but only succeeded in removing references to the views of a pair of diplomats, Sir Derek Dodson and Sir Humphrey Trevelyan.[38] Nutting was not prosecuted but, in an intriguing sidelight on Trend's interpretation of the constitutional conventions, Crossman's diary for 4 May 1967 disclosed that:

> This evening at my business meeting with the PM Burke raised the matter and made it perfectly clear that he and he alone had taken the decision about Nutting's book because the Prime Minister, like any other Labour minister, must be denied access to the minutes of the other side and doesn't therefore know whether Nutting's account of the Suez Cabinet is correct or not. So the Secretary to the Cabinet becomes the independent arbiter in such affairs and in this respect he's played a role as important as that of the monarch a hundred years ago.[39]

Quite apart from his *ex officio* position as custodian of Cabinet confidentiality, Sir Burke would have felt genuine personal pain about the scars of Suez being re-opened. Someone who knew him particularly well once told me, 'Burke feels very deeply the loss of Empire. They [his Whitehall generation] all do. After the war they had to dismantle it, to do something they didn't want to do. They felt they were betraying the Victorian legacy. And yet they knew it was right and that they had to do it with great delicacy and care.'[40] I always felt he had taken the decline of his country badly, almost personally. I admired him for it. Trend was a great believer in the Anglo-American 'special relationship' as a way of shoring up Britain's waning power. After his death in July 1987, his successors, John Hunt and Robert Armstrong, wrote to *The Times* to underline this. 'At a time', they wrote, 'when successive governments were working towards membership of the European Community, he was determined to do all he could to ensure that the development of closer relations with our European partners was not at the expense of keeping in the best possible repair the close political, military and economic links forged during and after the Second World War, which he saw not just as essential for Britain but as a foundation for world peace and stability.'[41]

As Henry Kissinger's memoirs show, this belief saddled Trend with some particularly delicate missions during the last days of his Cabinet secretaryship when the European-minded Edward Heath found himself at odds with President Nixon at the time of the European Summit at Copenhagen in July 1973. In the aftermath of Copenhagen, Trend arrived in Washington for one of his regular talks as Heath's link-man with Nixon. 'In the light of the Copenhagen decision [about the best way to pursue *Ostpolitik* negotiations with the Soviet bloc]', wrote Kissinger.

> he [Trend] had nothing to talk about. There was a painful session with my wise and gentle friend. We both realised that if these tendencies continued, we were at a turning point in Atlantic relations. For the sake of an abstract doctrine of European unity and to score purely theoretical points, something that had been nurtured for a generation was being given up. Atlantic – and especially Anglo-American – relations had thrived on intangibles of trust and consultation. They were now being put into a straitjacket of legalistic formalisms. Trend had lived too long in the old framework, based on mutual confidence, to be anything but uncomfortable with his brief. He came as close to showing his distress as the code of discipline of the British Civil Service and his high sense of honour permitted. But matters had gone beyond his level in the hierarchy.[42]

Trend had been a natural successor to Brook in 1963 though, as we have seen, Brook's headship of the Civil Service passed to Lawrence Helsby –

one of Macmillan's more eccentric appointments, in the considered view of the permanent secretaries' club.[43] According to legend, Macmillan invited the four contenders down to Birch Grove (Trend was not one of them). After dinner, one who had drunk too much fell asleep during Macmillan's monologue about the trenches of the First World War and inter-war unemployment, the two Treasury men were victims of Macmillan's anti-Treasury bias, and the fourth, Helsby, puffed his pipe and nodded sagely. Macmillan thought he was the wisest man he had met in Whitehall for years and gave him the job![44]

Armstrong had been afforded similar treatment. He had been summoned to Admiralty House (No. 10 was being rebuilt) for lunch with Macmillan and Sir Roy Harrod, the Oxford economist and biographer of Keynes.[45] Macmillan told Armstrong he had asked three other Treasury men to the lunch but they could not make it. Macmillan then goaded Armstrong and Harrod into a debate which he sat back and observed.[46]

Armstrong had no idea that he was being considered as Sir Frank Lee's replacement. He was a third secretary in the Treasury and two ranks from the top. I remember him telling me over lunch at Odin's restaurant how the news had been broken to him:

> A few weeks after the lunch I was at home in bed waiting for an appendix operation. On the Saturday Norman Brook rang and said could he come and see me as he had something to discuss which was too important to be mentioned on the phone. I was baffled. The Queen's income was always handled oddly and at that time, Brook and I did it together. I thought something must have come up on this.
>
> Norman arrives, towers over my bed, shakes my hand and says, 'I must congratulate you. The Queen has been pleased to approve your appointment as Permanent Secretary to the Treasury.' He explained it wasn't meant to happen till the autumn, but there had been a leak and *The Sunday Telegraph* were going to publish it the following day.[47]

When Trend replaced Brook at the Cabinet Office the following January, the duumvirate that was to dominate Whitehall for ten years was in place. It was to be a turbulent decade for both of them – brimming with political crises, sterling crises and industrial disruption. Trend's first year at the Prime Minister's right hand in the Cabinet Room saw the Profumo crisis, the departure of Macmillan and the arrival of Sir Alec Douglas-Home. (Trend would never indicate a preference for his premiers, but one sensed a particular warmth for Home which was reciprocated.)

Trend was always calm under pressure and had an acute sense of the dividing line between the administrative and the purely political. If he judged that Cabinet discussion was moving from one to the other he would put down his pen, shut his notebook, put both his hands on the Cabinet table and make sure the two other note-takers did likewise. Occasionally he would nod and all three would slip away out of the room.[48] Wilson, a connoisseur of Cabinet secretaries, rather relished Trend and the quiet, Rolls-Royce service he provided from the first day of their partnership when he presented the new prime minister, fresh from Buckingham Palace, with a minty draft Queen's speech. 'It was a first class draft', Wilson later wrote. 'All our major policy commitments were there, and we felt it right to endorse them.'[49] On one occasion, Wilson told Barbara Castle that Trend was 'the best civil servant I've known'.[50] The Cabinet Secretary, however, was the subject of deep suspicion on the part of some other Labour ministers who believed he had too much influence on Wilson. On one celebrated occasion, Crossman accused him of cooking the Cabinet minutes. In the early months of the 1964 Labour Government, Crossman took exception to the way Trend had recorded a discussion of nuclear proliferation. Trend had recorded as an aim of British policy 'the aim of satisfying the nuclear aspirations of the Federal German Government'. 'Harold can't have said this', Crossman told Trend:

> To which he replied, 'Ah, of course he never said it, we never do give verbatim what people say. We precis the sense and give the substance of what they say'. To which I replied,'This is not the substance of what he said, and if it had been the substance, he would have divided the Cabinet'.

Trend, according to Crossman, offered him the words 'deal with' instead of 'satisfy'. Crossman accepted.[51]

In one very peculiar passage, Crossman portrays Wilson's closeness to Trend as a kind of proof of the Prime Minister's devotion to conventional virtue:

> He [Wilson] has a number of moral convictions: he's a perfectly sincere Sunday Methodist; he's against the legal reforms to deal with homosexuality or abortion. He has a conventional respect for the BBC as a public corporation and won't allow advertising. He likes playing golf with ordinary businessmen; he's devoted to the Queen and is very proud that she likes his visits to her. He's really fond of Burke Trend and sees him as a close personal friend and confidant. In all these ways his moral values are extremely conventional.[52]

Shortly before Christmas 1966, Trend called on Crossman, then Leader of the House, to discuss Parliamentary reform (which he favoured, incidentally, believing that specialist select committees would strengthen the

Executive as well as the Legislature) and was rewarded by this pen portrait: 'He's a strange character – a nanny-like, very able, very sweet, very shy man. He strengthens Harold in all his most establishment tentativeness, making him on the whole less abrasive and less radical. On most things he's the opposite extreme to me in his influence on Harold.'[53] By the following spring, Crossman, ever tempted by hyperbole, was writing: 'If I had to describe the essence of this Government I should say that whereas the first Wilson Government was a troika [presumably of Wilson, Brown and Callaghan], this one is a Wilson–Burke Trend axis.'[54]

By the time the 'quiet revolutionaries' of Heath's 'new style of government' paid their pre-election calls on the permanent secretaries in 1970, Burke Trend had been Cabinet Secretary for seven years and had served three prime ministers; his detailed knowledge of Whitehall, its ways and its mechanics had been slowly accumulating for thirty-four years. In a different way, William Armstrong was an equally awesome figure to the political class. Reginald Maudling, who worked with him in a Chancellor–Permanent Secretary relationship in 1962–4, had known him since Oxford days where, as was customary for the best and the brightest of their generation, they read Greats, as Maudling recalled forty years later:

> There is no doubt in my mind that in the 1930s, at any rate, Greats was a remarkable school. Being of a rather lazy disposition, and not a meticulous scholar in any sense at all, I took Pass Moderations instead of Classical Honour Moderations, and went straight on to the ancient history and philosophy which constituted Greats. Fortunately one was not expected to do well in both of them. Examples of people who could were rare, though I do remember William Armstrong . . . who took his degree and his oral examination at the same time as I did, being congratulated by the examiners on 'the consistent excellence of his papers throughout the examination'. Was there ever a man more clearly destined to become Head of the Treasury?[55]

Reggie Maudling was clearly not a preference-for-relevance man. Armstrong had risen from the grammar school (in the pre-Butler Act days when it was much more difficult to do so) on to the ladder of opportunity prized by the scholarship boy, and the classics ladder was the most prized of all. I can remember Sir Hugh Casson once quoting the great Oxford scholar, Wade-Gery, to the effect that everyone should read the classics for two reasons – they were the language of the gospels and, secondly, they led to positions of great emolument.[56] Armstrong was the son of Salvationists. Much was made of this after his illness and collapse during the 1973-4 winter crisis (see p. 240). Armstrong was asked shortly before his retirement if his evangelical background accounted for his keenness on openness. 'Are you a bit of a showman?' the interviewer inquired. 'Well, my father was', Armstrong replied. 'As an officer of the Salvation Army he had a message to proclaim and he proclaimed it. He would do that either at the Cenotaph, shortly after it was put up, or in the forecourt of Buckingham Palace or on a white horse going down Plymouth Hoe. I suppose I've inherited a certain amount of that from him.'[57]

Armstrong was, insofar as these things are discernible in Whitehall, regarded as being somewhat left of centre, whereas Trend's attitudes struck others apart from Crossman as small 'c' conservative. From my conversations with him I would judge Armstrong to have been the very incarnation of Butskellism, that brilliant, apt invention of *The Economist*'s Norman Macrae.[58] I remember William telling me one day how, though still private secretary to Stafford Cripps whom he 'adored', he was with Hugh Gaitskell (then Minister of Economic Affairs) in New York in 1950 when the news came through that Cripps had resigned for reasons of ill-health and that Attlee had chosen Gaitskell to replace him. William recalled Gaitskell, in his elation, outlining the Labour Party of the future as he saw it – it would become like the Democratic Party and the Conservatives like the Republicans, with large areas of agreement between the parties and elections fought on which side was the more competent. Gaitskell, William added, had he become Prime Minister, would have been 'Labour's Heath'. I remember thinking, as Armstrong recalled that evening with Gaitskell twenty-six years earlier, that Gaitskell's vision was Armstrong's also and I asked him if he agreed that when you scratched a senior civil servant you found a Gaitskellite. 'Butskellite', William replied. 'After all those years you tended to be within a narrow line either side of the centre. Most of them [this was in July 1976] would like a government with Heath as Prime Minister and Jenkins as Chancellor.'[59]

I remember also the first time I met Armstrong a year after he had left Whitehall[60] appreciating instantly why so many politicians of all parties had sworn by him as a confidential adviser. As he sat in his peaceful, deep-carpeted, wood-panelled office in the Midland Bank, his quiet voice almost purred as it emerged from the wreaths of ever-present cigarette smoke recalling with care and precision this or that point about the Civil Service of old. His charm was tangible, the calmness quite returned after his illness of the previous year. I liked him straightaway and until his death five years later would look forward keenly to the next conversation. For his part, Armstrong seemed to pine for Whitehall. From 1940 when he joined the Home Defence Executive, he once told me, right up until he left the CSD he had been in receipt of confidential papers. Only when he left thirty-four years later and had to rely on *The Times* and The *Financial Times* for his daily intelligence about what was going on in government did he realise how little the ordinary citizen knew.

By the time Heath emerged the surprise victor at the polls in 1970, Armstrong was a mighty figure in Whitehall terms with a growing public reputation as a moderniser of the bureaucracy. Post-Fulton he had cultivated a higher public profile than any of his predecessors as head of profession. In 1968–9 he had done the round of union conferences. He was a regular performer in learned lecture halls. The first time I set eyes on him was in the turbulent forum of the Old Theatre at the London School of Economics while the enraged left tried, successfully as it turned out, to prevent him delivering the annual LSE Oration in December 1969. Lord Robbins, the great economist and chairman of the LSE's court of governors, appealed vainly for calm, a young academic, one Dr Bernard Donoughue, whispering advice in his ear as the uproar grew.[61] Armstrong sat on the platform with a calm but pained expression on his face appropriate to a public servant under duress. When he could get a hearing, Armstrong was a thoughtful and vivid phrase-maker. He told one Civil Service union conference, for example, 'We are not a debating society, a private army, or a social club; we are the instrument through which our fellow countrymen seek to exercise their collective wills – for their benefit, and only, incidentally, for ours.'[62]

Armstrong's influence was quite extraordinary for a civil servant. One of Heath's ministerial colleagues described him as 'one of the philosopher kings'.[63] For another, Heath's Home Secretary, Reginald Maudling, 'wherever Armstrong's name is on the door, that is where power will be'.[64] When he died, that supreme Whitehall-watcher, Samuel Brittan, said of Armstrong: 'his personal impact was a great deal stronger than that of many politicians who fill the headlines'.[65] In the Heath years William Armstrong was to rise to truly dizzy heights which made his fall – which predated Heath's by a month – all the more dramatic.

Naturally, none of this nightmare was foreseeable when Heath inherited his political and bureaucratic kingdom in June 1970. A large slice of the best talent in Whitehall was deployed on turning his plans for the machinery of government into reality. In addition to Armstrong and Trend, those involved included Peter Baldwin in the Treasury, John Hunt, Frank Cooper and Ian Bancroft at the CSD and Peter Carey in the Cabinet Office.[66] There were three elements to Heath's 'quiet revolution': a reduction in the workload of Cabinet achieved by the amalgamation of work into a smaller number of bigger departments *plus* the hiving-off of large blocks of work into executive agencies; the creation of a new, vigorous and institutionalised system of policy analysis; and the foundation of a central capability unit. It amounted to the most thoroughgoing review of the Cabinet system, its back-up and support service since Haldane (see pp. 292–9). There has been nothing comparable attempted since.

Between June and October 1970, when the final blueprint was published as a White Paper, *The Reorganisation of Central Government*,[67] a great deal of work was shifted with much haggling between the regulars and irregulars. In many ways, Mr Heath's reformers were preaching to the converted. As we have seen, William Armstrong was keen on this kind of exercise and believed that it should have been undertaken *before* Fulton. And Burke Trend later spoke of 'a quite remarkable coincidence of diagnosis' as he and Armstrong had been thinking along similar lines to the Heath team about the central capability unit idea: 'I think that the Conservative Party were thinking of it rather more in a practical sense than we were in Whitehall. We were thinking of it more in terms of the deficiency in the constitutional machinery. Whereas they were thinking of it more in terms of what a prime minister would actually need when he took office, what sort of immediate buttons would he need to have at his disposal.'[68]

Heath's own view of the hole he wanted the new unit to fill was outlined to members of its first staff when they met him on the lawn in the garden of No. 10. 'He said that in Opposition', recalled the economist Hector Hawkins, a founder member, 'he had been very struck that it was possible for the Shadow Cabinet to consider its strategy as a whole, to take a slightly longer-term view of things. But as soon as they became a Government, it was impossible to do that. And he had set up the Think Tank in order to remedy that.'[69] Douglas Hurd, at that time Heath's political secretary in No. 10, put it even better when he later wrote that it 'rubbed ministers' noses in the future'.[70] For all the 'remarkable coincidence of diagnosis' detected by Burke Trend, there was a battle for the soul of the capability unit between the drafting of the Conservative manifesto in May 1970 and the promulgation of the White Paper in October. David Howell and Mark Schreiber, now installed in the CSD as junior minister and special adviser respectively, saw things differently from Trend when it came to the capability unit. 'Frankly', says Howell, 'some of us actually wanted that to be a staff for No. 10, for the Prime Minister . . . and less a general body to serve all the Cabinet.'[71] Trend wanted it the other way round. Trend won. The Cabinet Secretary also prevailed on the much less important matter of a name for the new outfit, though here his antagonist was the Prime Minister himself. 'I wanted it call it "the Think Tank",' Heath told an RIPA lecture audience a decade later. 'The Secretary of the Cabinet won and we called it the Central Policy Review Staff.'[72] Why did Trend object to the Prime Minister's wish?

> It became known as the Think Tank, but they weren't quite the words you could see on the front of a White Paper. I remember scratching my head and sucking my pencil and thinking, 'What on earth are we going to call this thing?'
>
> And then it seemed to me that if you took the words which we finally

> did adopt, they came as near as I could come to being accurate about it. It *was* central, it *was* concerned with policy; and it *was* concerned with reviewing policy centrally and it consisted of a staff, not a political unit.[73]

So, when the White Paper appeared, the Central Policy Review Staff it was. It was, in fact, pure Burke Trend who had long amazed his contemporaries with his ability to draft such documents in his head.[74] The Tank may have been intended to be the new style of government made flesh, but the charter of the CPRS was couched in phrases of traditional courtliness. 'Governments', the White Paper observed, 'are always at some risk of losing sight of the need to consider the totality of their current policies in relation to their longer term objectives; and . . . of evaluating . . . the alternative policy options and priorities open to them.' The remedy was the foundation of a 'small multi-disciplinary central policy review staff in the Cabinet Office'. It would operate under the supervision of the prime minister, and it would also serve ministers collectively, enabling them 'to work out the implications of their basic strategy in terms of policies in specific areas, to establish the relative priorities to be given to the different sectors of their programme as a whole, to identify those areas of policy in which new choices can be exercised and to ensure that the underlying implications of alternative courses of action are fully analysed and considered'.[75] There was a clear echo in all this of Churchill's Statistical Section. Like his predecessor in No. 10, Mr Heath had been irritated as a Cabinet minister by Whitehall's tendency to produce conflicting data which blurred the process of decision-making as ministers haggled over facts and their interpretation. This most rational prime minister wanted the Think-Tank to produce a common data base before Cabinet or Cabinet committee met to find a solution.[76]

The entire White Paper was a monument to reason in Whitehall – an outline for a thinking, efficient system. Events were to undo much of it within a generation. Unlike Lloyd George's reforms, *The Reorganisation of Central Government* did not change the bone structure of central administration for ever. But it was a bold attempt. Apart from creating the CPRS and giving it its charter, the White Paper established a pair of giant departments, the Department of the Environment and the Department of Trade and Industry; foreshadowed the creation of important agencies, the Property Services Agency and the weapons Procurement Executive which Derek Rayner went off to design and then to run till Marks & Spencer claimed him back in 1972; and created a new system of scrutiny and action, Programme Analysis and Review, or PAR, which would ruthlessly question existing commitments and put brain behind the crude brawn of PESC, the annual public expenditure survey round.

It was the Think-Tank which captured – and retains to this day – the public and political imagination. The British have long had an imaginative weakness for the brilliant backroom boffin ever since the reading public became aware of Sherlock Holmes's brother Mycroft, who did something very secret and very clever for the government. The other reason for the lasting glamour of the CPRS was the man recruited to run it, Lord Rothschild, research scientist, ex-MI5 bomb disposal expert during the Second World War, don and banker, a man who always had an air of mystery about him long before his alleged role in the Peter Wright affair emerged in a courtroom in Sydney, New South Wales, in 1986. His name was announced two weeks after the White Paper was published. Burke Trend, who had long been worried about ministers' abilities to take complicated decisions on science policies,[77] came up with his name. 'I don't think I'd known him very well or very closely. But what I knew of him made me think that this was the right sort of man.'[78]

Lord Rothschild had just retired at the age of sixty as Research Co-Ordinator of the Royal Dutch Shell Group. Between 1948 and 1958 he was Chairman of the Agricultural Research Council. Lord Rothschild is the kind of man who has an immediate impact on most people who have encountered him. For one social scientist wise in the ways of Whitehall, 'Physically a big man, he has verbal wit and great intellectual curiosity expressed in a mellow voice – he has great presence, like General de Gaulle.'[79]

Media coverage was important to the CPRS and its status in Parliament and Whitehall which partly explains why its demise in 1983 caused considerably more excitement and discussion than the disbanding of another thirteen-year-old, supposedly reformist institution, the Civil Service Department, two years earlier. Lord Rothschild, his personality and record were the key to the early visibility enjoyed by the fledgling CPRS. He was natural profile material. Witness the opening paragraphs of Ivan Yates's *Observer* portrait shortly after his appointment:

> It would take a C. P. Snow to do justice to Lord Rothschild's appointment to head the Prime Minister's new 'think tank' or 'central capability unit'.
>
> Hardly more than a week ago, this unusual, unorthodox, brilliant man was looking forward with some dismay to his sixtieth birthday. He had to retire from his job at Shell. He had no plans for the future. Nothing was on offer. It seemed as if he might have to settle for something at the family bank, where in the early 1930s he had spent five depressing months.[80]

The call from Heath changed all that. Ivan Yates concluded with a piece of prophecy:

What is tolerably certain is that Lord Rothschild is going to be in his element probing, thinking up the questions, teasing out the answers. The only foreseeable source of trouble is that the civil servants are not going to be in their element being subjected to the abrasive intentions of this twentieth-century original.[81]

On entering his new domain, the 'Lord of the Think Tank' found John Mayne, an MOD principal recruited by Trend to help design the CPRS, and a secretary. Lord Rothschild was not sure about Mr Mayne. It became a standing joke in the Tank that he had been planted by the Cabinet Secretary but that 'Burke's Spy' had been turned by his new boss[82] who was, after all, a former MI5 officer. Lord Rothschild, in his customarily elliptical fashion, referred to this episode in his *Random Variables*:

> We had an excellent start because, on D-Day, Sir Burke injected into the Tank Dick Ross, the distinguished economist, and two young, top-class civil servants, John Mayne and Robin Butler. In one case, the injection was made somewhat earlier than D-Day. It never passed through our minds, of course, that any of these had been planted in the Tank for more Byzantine or Smileyesque reasons. Had that been the case, some of us knew a bit about turning people round, *and* round.[83]

Despite the Conservative manifesto, the thoughts of Sir Burke and Sir William and the ground-work undertaken by Mr Mayne, Lord Rothschild had no idea of the boundaries, the powers and the contents of the kingdom he was inheriting.

> When I accepted Mr Heath's invitation, conveyed by the Cabinet Secretary, Sir Burke Trend . . ., to become the first head of the Government's Think Tank, I had no idea what it was intended to be or do in spite of the characteristically sonorous prose in which its future activities were described in the inevitable White Paper. Nor did anyone else seem to have much idea, such phrases as 'long term strategy', 'trans-departmental problems', 'not the rate of exchange', or 'not the Office of the White House' being bandied round.[84]

His first meeting with the Prime Minister did little to clear the confusion, though it rattled Sir Burke and Sir William as Lord Rothschild has recorded:

> *Mr Heath*. 'It's funny we have never met before.' Then there was a sort of row of dots. I could not think what to say; after a while I said

rather desperately: 'Prime Minister, do you think it would be better to have an economist in charge of this Unit?'

Mr Heath. 'I did economics at Oxford.' Another row of dots. Again after a while, I said rather desperately: 'Prime Minister, could you give me an example of the type of problem you want the Unit to tackle?'

Mr Heath. 'Concorde.' At that moment I thought, perhaps wrongly, that I detected some anguished vibrations emanating from Sir Burke Trend and Sir William Armstrong ... who were hovering in the background. There was some justification for their anguish, if I did not imagine it, because an hour beforehand they had told me it was precisely things like Concorde that the Government Think Tank would *not* be expected to study.

While I was still feeling the vibes, a Secretary came in and handed the Prime Minister a piece of paper which he read with some signs of displeasure, and said, 'Oh well, I had better see him.' Turning to me he concluded the interview by saying, 'Let me know if there are any other points.'[85]

Lord Rothschild then did a milk-round of Cabinet ministers to find out what they thought the CPRS should concentrate upon. For example, Sir Alec Douglas-Home, the Foreign Secretary, said: 'You couldn't reduce the amount of paper that comes on to my desk, could you?'[86] One Cabinet minister confused the new head of the CPRS with Sir Solly Zuckerman, the Government's Chief Scientist, with predictably absurd results.[87]

It took about six months of argument inside the prototype Tank before its functions and methods were established. It was assumed from the start that the head of the CPRS and his deputy would have the right to attend and speak at ministerial committees of the Cabinet. There was no argument about this, which is surprising at first sight. But the Tank, after all, was a part of the Cabinet Office whose main business is to service Cabinet committees. This important right enjoyed by the two top men in the CPRS was not appreciated outside Whitehall until 1979 when Dr Tessa Blackstone disclosed that 'The head of the CPRS and his deputy are unique among civil servants in that they are able to speak at meetings of ministers.'[88] Whilst other officials had and have spoken at such gatherings, they have not done so on a regular basis and of right.

Lord Rothschild was insistent that the members of the Tank should enjoy the stimulus and excitement of being involved in advising ministers on pressing issues of the hour. For them to concentrate solely on dry intractables like regional policy would be disastrous. In conversation with me in 1983, Lord Rothschild said he had in mind a phrase of Aldous Huxley's to describe his strategy (one maintained by his three successors as head of the CPRS) of blending quick-dash productions dealing with current Cabinet business and long-term policy reviews. It was to be a case of 'routine punctuated by orgies'.

There was much vagueness in the Treasury, the Civil Service Department and the Cabinet Office about how much this was going to cost. In real terms, the CPRS budget turned out to be remarkably stable, hovering around £1m a year (in 1983 prices). On a less strategic plane, the early Tank was given an expense allowance of £100 a year. Mr (now Sir) Peter Carey, a senior official on secondment from the Departments of Trade and Industry, used it to finance a couple of sandwich lunches for industrialists.[89]

Lord Rothschild invited his team to produce their own definitions of what the Tank was for. Out of this came Professor Ross's famous aphorism: 'You must think the unthinkable, but always wear a dark suit when presenting the results.' Mr (now Sir) Robert Wade-Gery,[90] a Foreign Office diplomat on loan to the Tank, produced a synopsis which became something of an unofficial charter for the CPRS urging it to:

> Sabotage the over-smooth functioning of the machinery of Government.
>
> Provide a Central Department which has no departmental axe to grind but does not have overt policy status and which can attempt a synoptic view of policy.
>
> Provide a Central reinforcement for those Civil Servants in Whitehall who are trying to retain their creativity and not be totally submerged in the bureaucracy.
>
> Try to devise a more rational system of decision-making between competing programmes.
>
> Advise the Cabinet collectively, and the Prime Minister, on major issues of policy relating to Government's Strategy.
>
> Focus the attention of Ministers on the right questions to ask about their own colleagues' businesses.
>
> Bring in ideas from the outside world.

The Wade-Gery prospectus was the polished product of one of the Monday morning brainstorming sessions which were a feature of the Rothschild Tank. (Preceding them was a regular and rather more stately occasion when Lord Rothschild took coffee with Sir Burke and discussed the forthcoming week's Cabinet business.)[91] He kept the team deliberately small. It was never more than the sixteen to twenty people who could be accommodated round his table on a Monday morning. Throughout its thirteen-year life, the Tank's membership fluctuated between thirteen and twenty with a rough half-and-half division between insiders from Whitehall and outsiders from industry, the universities and the professions. The mix of outsiders varied a little from administration to administration and director to director. As one would expect, recruits from the private sector were rather more prominent under Heath and Thatcher. The academics peaked in the Callaghan years. Ideology seems to have had little to do with the proportion of public sector recruits to the CPRS. These peaked in the Sir Robin Ibbs/Thatcher era and probably reflected the priority afforded to the nationalised industries in that period of the Tank's life.

At the beginning Lord Rothschild inherited three people – John Mayne, the future Cabinet Secretary Robin Butler and Dick Ross. Finding the rest was up to him. Recruiting to the CPRS was crucial to its fortunes but never easy. Lord Hunt of Tanworth recalls:

> It's obviously very difficult because you are asking the head of the CPRS to find a team of outstandingly talented people who have the capability of coming up with original perspectives and original questions which departments, with all their back-up and resources, haven't found.
>
> It very much depended on the head of the CPRS and his deputy to go and ferret out these bright young people, which wasn't easy. It wasn't easy not only in Whitehall, not only to identify them, but then to persuade departments to release them. It was even harder but more important when you were looking outside Whitehall.[92]

Hunt, who succeeded Trend as Cabinet Secretary in 1973, is clear that in Lord Rothschild himself the Cabinet Office had found exactly the person it needed to run the Tank:

> I remember Victor Rothschild sort of ambling into my room from time to time and saying 'How much time have you spent in the last month thinking about X?' And he would go out again because, as you know, he had a rather Delphic approach. But a few months later, I would realise that X was a very important subject. That is the sort of capability you're looking for. You don't find it easily.
>
> Are we in this country worse at it? Yes, I think we are. Much worse. In the States people in academic life, in business life ... they are all terribly interested in coming in, feeding in the right questions. Talk to academics here, they're very often not interested ... We are a very fragmented society, both vertically and naturally.[93]

Filling the Tank as a whole, and not just its headship, proved difficult throughout most of the thirteen years. According to CPRS-watchers inside Whitehall, Lord Rothschild had the easiest time of it with his connections in universities, the energy world, the City and the bureaucracy itself.[94] The cynics were prone to see it as a kind of job creation scheme for the gifted friends and contemporaries of his daughter Emma.[95] Mr William Waldegrave, fresh from Harvard, was suggested to Lord Rothschild by

Lord Jellicoe, then Lord Privy Seal, with the question, did he want a messenger-cum-tea-boy?[96] Mr Waldegrave shone in the CPRS, went on to join Mr Heath in No. 10 as his Political Secretary and in the mid-1980s found himself a junior minister at the Department of the Environment trying to sell the Thatcher administration's local government financial reforms to Parliament and the public.

Compared to Lord Rothschild, his successors had a much tougher time in recruiting the right 'boys and girls', as Sir Kenneth Berrill would invariably call them. Sir Kenneth was *au fait* with the universities and Whitehall. Sir Robin Ibbs knew industry, and Sir John Sparrow the City. But none possessed a network to match Lord Rothschild's. Rothschild's Tank was helped by the word spreading that it was *the* place to be. It had glamour, glitter and almost fell into the ghastly category of radical chic, particularly after some near-eulogistic coverage in *The Sunday Times* Colour Magazine in 1973.[97] Lord Rothschild would take his team to dinner at the Mirabelle. They had the ear of the mighty daily, weekly and six-monthly at their famous strategy sessions at Chequers. It was heady stuff. From the moment Lord Rothschild set up shop to the oil crisis of autumn 1973, these were the salad days of the CPRS. Life was never quite so buoyant or such fun after the Arab–Israeli war and the quadrupling of world oil prices.

Much of what the Rothschild Tank did remains locked in the Cabinet Office registry. Detective work has uncovered a fair span of its activities, however. The list reads something like this:

Airships.
Better presentation of information to ministers.
British computer industry.
Building society mortgages.
Canals.
Concorde.
Construction industry.
Counterinflation.
Criteria for public expenditure priorities.
Decision-making under stress.
Early retirement.
Effect of a shorter week, year or life on unemployment.
Electric cars.
Empty office blocks.
Energy conservation.
Fast breeder reactor.
Fertiliser and lime subsidies.
Gas and electricity prices.

The Good and the Great.
Helium.
Land and property speculation.
Maplin Airport.
Miners' wages.
Northern Ireland.
Nuclear reactor safety.
Oil economics and supplies.
Open cast mining.
Pensions.
Race relations.
Regional policy.
Relations between government and nationalised industries.
Rolls-Royce.
Treatment of offenders.
UK coal industry.
UK population trends.
Worker participation.[98]

Lord Rothschild's memoranda had bite. They are remembered with affection in the grey world of Whitehallese. He had a brilliant way with statistics, applying them to the most surprising phenomena. For example, when he gave up smoking in August 1986 on doctor's orders, he told me he had smoked 24.6 miles of Turkish cigarettes in his lifetime. As one permanent secretary put it: 'What distinguished Victor's memos from all the others was that they were totally free of bureaucratese and all on two-thirds of a page saying virtually all that needed to be said. A great man.'[99] Another permanent secretary was less flattering: 'Victor was silent in committees and couldn't write [a judgement not borne out by his two volumes of essay and memoir]. He would get bright stars like William Plowden to prepare papers. Then Victor would make them controversial and insert the flashies.'[100]

The way in which the Rothschild memoranda are recalled can be misleading. In 1981, when the CPRS celebrated its tenth birthday, yet another permanent secretary lamented: 'Gone are the days when a CPRS paper would begin with the words "Concorde is a commercial disaster". Its all very dull and worthy now.'[101] This left the impression that the Tank had recommended the killing of Concorde. Three years later, in a radio interview, it emerged that it did not when I asked Lord Rothschild: 'Didn't the politics override your Concorde presentation because Whitehall legend has it that it began with the sentence "Concorde is a commercial disaster"? He replied: 'Whitehall is comparatively accurate on this occasion. But I think I am allowed to say that the paper in question went on "in spite of that you have got to go on". And, if it's of any interest to you, it also said, "and for God's sake stop bellyaching about it, just get on with it" '[102]

Assessing the impact of the CPRS under any of its directors is difficult. The Tank's was only one of many ingredients in a haphazard mix of prejudices, pragmatism, and analysis which is flattered by the name of policy-making. Among Whitehall insiders, a pattern is discernible – the CPRS and Lord Rothschild were a good thing when dragging up other people's prize blooms; when they invaded your back garden, that was another matter. Here is a senior official in the Home Office recalling the CPRS study of penal policy:

> Lord Rothschild was rather well suited for the job. He was absolutely fearless and not tied down by orthodoxy. His great virtue was the way he would upset Ted Heath by telling him the truth.
>
> When they turned their attentions to prisons it was not very good. It seemed to us that their paper rehearsed the problems which were only too familiar to us, without being very helpful.[103]

One long-serving member of the CPRS is not surprised by the 'It's fine for everyone else, but it could tell us nothing new' syndrome. Part of the Tank's funtion, he says, was to act as an outside consultant, to focus on the solution that reform-minded insiders had been pressing for in vain for years and, by operating as an external catalyst, help achieve its acceptance and implementation.[104]

In a television interview with Bernard Levin, Rothschild described the Tank's method of educating ministers and achieving impact. His examples ranged from 'a pifflingly elementary thing' like the retail price index ('a lot of members of the Cabinet of both parties didn't know what the RPI was') to a hugely complicated subject such as nuclear reactors:

> To be able to explain the problems associated with different sorts of nuclear reactors to a lay audience requires, on the one hand, considerable analytical ability to understand them yourself, on the other hand another type of ability to explain it in simple language.
>
> I'm not saying that I did all this, of course. I had a team of people. And, indeed, I've always tried whenever possible to get the present Prime Minister's Principal Private Secretary [Robin Butler] to make presentations because in those days . . . [he was a] . . . rather good looking young man who looked like a well scrubbed head prefect. And I thought that they would be more attracted by somebody looking like him, than an elderly gent like me.[105]

Lord Rothschild took the issue of presentation sufficiently seriously, the

Levin interview revealed, to summon his old friend, the actress Dame Peggy Ashcroft, to the Cabinet Office to coach Wade-Gery and his team on how to speak before an audience to the greatest effect. Sometimes it succeeded.

On at least one strategic issue, Lord Rothschild is given credit for influencing an outcome which he insists was the work of others – the Heath Government's U-turn on economic policy in the autumn of 1972. 'It is quite untrue, though I was present in No. 11 Downing Street when Ted Heath did the U-turn. The CPRS was not consulted about that particular operation. We never presented any paper on it.'[106] The origins of the incomes policy of autumn 1972, according to one insider who was closely involved, can be traced to 'the early summer of 1972 when William Armstrong asked Ted Heath if we could start preparing contingency plans for a new counter-inflation strategy in case inflation topped 10 per cent. Ted said "yes".'[107] At least two participants (neither members of the CPRS) reckon that one of the Tank's regular six-monthly strategy sessions at Chequers on a Saturday afternoon in September 1972 was crucial in shifting opinion inside the Cabinet about the need for a new interventionist strategy. 'The message filtered through', said one attender of the CPRS presentation that day. The divergence of view of the Tank's impact on economic strategy in the summer–autumn of 1972 seems to be one of those episodes that requires the workings of the thirty-year-rule to resolve.

Energy is one policy area, however, where all agree that the Rothschild CPRS made a direct and important impression. It forecast a steep rise in the price of oil in 1971 way ahead of the Arab–Israeli War of October 1973 and the subsequent application of muscle by the Organisation of Petroleum Exporting Countries. In Whitehall terms, such prescience brought the Tank much kudos and is frequently cited as the classic example of how such a body can win respect and influence by being ahead of the regular government departments. Lord Rothschild puts it less dramatically:

> I don't know that we formally alerted the Cabinet. But it was quite clear to me that there was probably going to be an oil crisis in the sense of a price hike. And I suppose I learned this from my ten years in the Royal Dutch Shell Group. And I certainly let it be known that this was my view and that we should, therefore, be taking certain measures to counteract that possibility.[108]

In another area the direct influence of a Rothschild production is demonstrable. After his 1972 report on the organisation of research and development in Whitehall, government science *was* reorganised on the basis of the customer-contractor principle. Sir Burke Trend would not allow the R&D report to be published under the Tank's imprimatur. So it came out as a White Paper.[109]

Trend took great pains to keep the CPRS away from foreign and defence policy issues – terrain he judged unsuitable for outsiders. This irritated the Tank. Some of its members were particularly keen to have a go at Northern Ireland. Heath by-passed the Cabinet Secretary and asked Wade-Gery to report on the province.[110] It is not known if Trend discovered this piece of private enterprise. It is probable that he did. Little escaped him. Wade-Gery's paper failed to impress those living with the Irish question from day to day for rather the same reasons given by critics of the operation on penal policy. Sir Frank Cooper, who was Permanent Secretary at the Northern Ireland Office, 1973–6, reckons:

> It was probably very unlikely that some relative newcomer could come and throw some brand new light on the whole situation ... Certainly there was no opposition in the Northern Ireland Office to the Think Tank having a look. We didn't have any great hopes that it would bring some blinding flash of new insight ... simply because the people who were working in the Office were totally immersed in it. They'd found it difficult enough to get to know something about it. And although Robert Wade-Gery is a man of outstanding ability, I think it's unlikely that he or anyone else involved could have produced something which gave an absolutely revolutionary view of the situation which was going to work.[111]

For good measure, Sir Frank, an old Air Ministry hand who was Permanent Secretary at the Ministry of Defence 1976–82, buttresses the Trend view of those parts of Whitehall the Tank should not reach:

> They are not areas where there is a great deal of widespread expertise in this country. In defence in particular there are very few other experts and [the Ministry of] Defence has a near monopoly. In terms of foreign affairs? Well, people certainly write history and write pieces about foreign affairs. But again there is a limited knowledge of the real relations that one country has with another.[112]

Lord Rothschild has challenged the Trend–Cooper view of the CPRS's fitness to examine foreign and defence matters. In his 'Epistle to a Prime Minister' about the shape and remit of a future Think-Tank prepared for BBC Radio 3s *Routine Punctuated by Orgies*, he wrote:

> No particular class of investigation, such as those concerned with foreign affairs, defence, the Budget or the exchange rates, should be barred. This may, from time to time, pose security problems as not all members of the CPRS, even though p.v'd [positively vetted], may be cleared to see papers with the highest classification.

> But this need not present problems as the head of the CPRS must, after due indoctrination and consultation, be allowed to be selective in regard to which members of the CPRS may have access to particularly sensitive material.[113]

In an intriguing aside he added: 'It may even on occasions be appropriate for some classes of material to be seen by a particular member of the CPRS and not by its head. This has happened.'[114]

The Budget to which Lord Rothschild alluded was another area in which he operated secretly, so secretly, in fact, that even Mr Heath did not know of it. Lord Rothschild asked Anthony Neuberger, who had joined the CPRS straight from university, to take the previous year's Budget and see what real harm would have been done if it had been leaked *in toto*. He found that 50 per cent of its contents could have been disclosed prematurely without damage, despite the genuinely obsessional security which surrounds any document with the special marking 'Budget-Secret'. The Neuberger report was shown to no one outside the CPRS.[115]

There were other private CPRS operations. Lord Rothschild had a preference for the idea of pilot studies. You would pick an area with a suitable mix of industry and agriculture, city and country dwellers – Warwickshire was his favourite candidate – and try out schemes and policies. This was not pressed upon the Tank's customers as it was felt they would not be prepared to buy.[116]

As part of its authorised activities, the Rothschild CPRS examined what were then regarded as some of the greatest policy intractables, including nationalised industry policy. His team had two attempts to persuade the Heath administration to disengage from detailed interference in the state enterprises. They failed. Lord Rothschild had a horror of another perpetual intractable – regional policy. According to one insider, he likened it to a 'black hole',[117] but the Tank studied it nonetheless.

There was one timeless issue on which Lord Rothschild believed that the CPRS could work with profit – the machinery of government. William Armstrong regarded this as his private turf and saw Lord Rothschild off with the words: 'Victor, if it's the last thing I do, I'm going to do that.'[118] He never did. And Lord Rothschild still hankers for the chance to have a go himself.[119]

During the autopsy performed on the CPRS by commentators and retired permanent secretaries after its demise in 1983, it became a truism to remark that the relationship between the head of the Tank and his patron, the prime minister of the day, was absolutely crucial. The Rothschild–Heath partnership was probably the most successful of them all. But it was punctuated by one spectacular row in the early autumn of 1973 held deliciously and uproariously in full public gaze.

It was a tale of two speeches. The date was 24 September 1973. Lord Rothschild had accepted an invitation to open a new seminar room at the Letcombe Laboratory in Wiltshire run by his old outfit, the Agricultural Research Council. He drafted a short address along what he confidently believed were platitudinous lines, so platitudinous, in fact, that he forgot to submit them for routine clearance by the Downing Street Press Office.[120] His theme was that unless the country pulled itself together, by 1985 Britain could be producing about half of the output of Germany or France. Unknown to Lord Rothschild, the press officer of the Agricultural Research Council telephoned a few paragraphs to the Press Association, the London-based national news agency. In a matter of minutes teleprinters in news rooms the length and breadth of the land were tapping out the stark message.

Lord Rothschild prefaced his remarks to the research scientists by saying that he would avoid 'the circumlocutory half-truths and understatements normally, but often unjustly, expected from a civil servant writing a report'. He went on:

> These general issues can be summed up by ventilating a fear I have, which I believe has virtually nothing to do with the politics of the left, right or centre, about the future of this country. From the vantage point of the Cabinet Office, it seems to me that unless we take a very strong pull at ourselves and give up the idea that we are one of the wealthiest, most influential and important countries in the world – in other words that Queen Victoria is still reigning – we are likely to find ourselves in increasingly serious trouble. To give just one unpalatable example, in 1985 we shall have half the economic weight of France or Germany, and about equal to that of Italy.[121]

The diagnosis got tougher, as did the prescriptions. The Letcombe speech is worth examining at length for two reasons: it represents the considered view of Lord Rothschild after examining from the inside for two years the priorities and operations of British central government; and it amounts to a warning cry uttered two months before the oil price hike engendered a more general sense of crisis across the nation. Rothschild turned to the difficulty of persuading the British public that they were in a condition of emergency which

> ... depends on something that seems very difficult to achieve in this country. It is the knowledge that our difficulties and dangers are as severe and ominous as they were in World War II, though, of course, of a different sort ... every man and woman in the country must be

made aware of the dangers and difficulties ahead and of the need to contribute to their solution . . .

. . . if we are to solve or even ameliorate the problems and dangers we are facing, there must be a major national change of orientation. We have to think twice about the desirability of courses of action which, in the distant past, were ours by right. We have to realise that we have neither the money nor the resources to do all those things we would like to do and so often feel we have the right to do.[122]

This performance of Lord Rothschild's in the obscurity, as he thought, of the Wiltshire countryside had a bite which took it far beyond platitude, all the more so given who he was and for whom he worked. As Lord Rothschild noted retrospectively: '. . . by a coincidence the Prime Minister was making a speech on the same day in another part of the country. In it he referred to the number of people in the United Kingdom who had colour television sets and other signs of comparative affluence.'[123]

The Press had a field day. Mr Heath was livid. Lord Rothschild was summoned to No. 10. 'He gave me a rather unpleasant dressing-down. I apologised. And in a very typical Heath-like way there came a moment in the interview when he said, "Well, now let's discuss nuclear reactors". And that was the end of it. The matter was never raised again and our relationships were perfectly OK afterwards.'[124]

Writing in 1976–7, Lord Rothschild noted: 'Re-reading what I said [at Letcombe], it is somewhat ironical to find that so far from having to wait until 1985 for my gloomy predictions to come true, they have, unfortunately, already done so to a large extent.'[125] A decade later Rothschild inscribed what he called his 'new motto' in my copy of *Random Variables.* I always thought it had an indirect bearing on the Letcombe incident. It read: 'Quick to give, and quick to take, offence'.

Within two months of the Letcombe speech there began a chain of political and economic events which administered a severe shock to the country's industrial base and lit a five-month fuse beneath Heath's premiership. But this is to jump too far too fast.

Sadly, the story of Heath's 'quiet revolution' is of one revolutionary element after another being taken away and shot or allowed to expire because of neglect. The sickliest of them was what was supposed to be the vigorous system of policy and programme review, PAR. The Treasury never liked it. (PAR was once described to me as 'a bloody excrescence' by a senior Treasury man crucial to its fortunes.[126]) Their first step towards smothering it was to remove it from the grasp of Heath's businessmen in the CSD and to draw it into their own citadel in Great George Street from which it never emerged alive. The crude reality of power over PAR was revealed for all to see when John Hunt, then a Treasury deputy secretary, introduced Richard East (the GRN, the businessman brought in by Heath) and his Treasury colleague, Ken Couzens, to the Expenditure Committee at the start of their hearings on PAR in early 1972: 'Mr East,' he said, 'will say how we ought to go about it and Mr Couzens will say what we are in fact doing.'[127]

PAR has been one of the most intensely studied of the Heath innovations with immensely thorough works from a pair of teams, Hugh Heclo and Aaron Wildavsky[128] and Andrew Gray and Bill Jenkins,[129] and a fine individual contribution from Colin Campbell.[130] But to be brutal and brief about it, PAR became slow, top heavy and the victim of the relentless, interdepartmental grind, complete with its own steering-committee, PARC, a classic example of what Derek Rayner (whose arrival in 1979 saw the final demise of the moribund PAR) would later call a 'stifling committee'.[131]

On the committee front, Heath was forced into one innovation which he would rather have been without even though it was and remained a high-level and formidably efficient body crucial to the survival of his entire administration. He called it his 'Winter Emergencies Committee'.[132] Its official title was the Civil Contingencies Unit, the CCU, an immensely secret body whose existence was only revealed in a newspaper article two years after Heath's departure.[133] It was the first national miners' strike since 1926, and the invention in early 1972 of massed secondary flying picketing by a little-known official of the Barnsley area strike committee of the National Union of Mineworkers, one Arthur Scargill, which changed the face of industrial relations in Britain (until, that is, the miners' strike of 1984–5) *and* the Whitehall machine for handling industrial emergencies. This highly secret central government capability had existed, in one form or another, since Lloyd George set up the Supply and Transport Organisation in 1919 and persuaded Parliament to give it sinew with the Emergency Powers Act 1920.[134]

After his humiliating climbdown in the face of the miners' demands, Heath ordered a thoroughgoing review of the old Home Office Emergencies Organisation which was not deemed to have fulfilled its task satisfactorily when faced with the physical and economic consequences of Arthur Scargill who, symbolically, turned the tide against the Government when, in the company of 15,000 massed secondary pickets, he closed the Saltley Coke Depot in Birmingham on 10 February 1972. The review was put in the hands of the Cabinet Office, with Trend's deputy, John Hunt, in the lead and a ministerial group under the Lord Privy Seal, Lord Jellicoe, to process its findings. Home Office men, still resentful of Cabinet Office imperialism, maintain to this day that Heath's was a crisis of confidence in a political colleague, Maudling, the Home Secretary, *not* in an institution, the Emergencies Organisation.[135]

The result was the CCU, a mixed Cabinet Committee of ministers and officials of the kind favoured by the executive-minded Heath and frowned upon by purists (who included Harold Wilson) who think ministerial and official committees should be kept distinct, though nobody quibbled about the CCU operating as both in a fast-moving industrial emergency. The contingency planning machine in its new streamlined form was firmly in the hands of the Cabinet Office in time for Heath's final, fatal winter crisis of 1973–4. The CCU, despite the political outcome, is still seen by those involved, like David Howell, as having been 'run very well indeed. I am enormously impressed. It's fashionable, and always has been, to sneer at civil servants. I think the way in which they organise that side of things is quite brilliant.'[136]

It was economic and industrial troubles which pushed Heath, as his critics have never ceased to recall, away from the manifesto pledges of a free market economy and into increasingly detailed interventionist policies after his 1972 U-turn, policies incarnate in the Industry Act 1972 and the return of incomes policy. The political demonology of the new Right makes much, too, of Heath's ever deepening retreat from his political colleagues and into the arms of the senior civil servants. The image conjured up is 'of Heath surrounded by Douglas Allen (Head of the Treasury), Robert Armstrong (his principal Private Secretary), Burke Trend . . . and William Armstrong. This was the Treasury mandarinate, which nourished Heath's belief in lonely Prime Ministerial power, and was fortified by a leader who seemed to share some of their contempt for the average politician.'[137]

That image has something in it, but it is too simple. Heath was certainly close to the two Armstrongs (William had picked Robert for the private secretary's job as he knew Heath could be distant and cold and assumed, rightly, that a shared love of music between the Premier and the former conductor of the Treasury Singers would be the basis of personal warmth and a good working relationship.)[138] Heath respected Douglas Allen but did not warm to either him or the Treasury, whose forecasts he thought over-gloomy generally, and was not convinced that they shared his views about the great economic benefits that would accrue from British membership of the EEC, Heath's Holy Grail.[139] Allen had a brusque, apparently cynical style. He would not spare ministers the realities as he saw them. Not for Douglas Allen the beguiling, comforting phrases of a William Armstrong.

Nor did Heath warm to Trend. The Cabinet Secretary, a classic Northcote–Trevelyan man, did not see it as part of his duty to tell the Prime Minister what to do. Like the Greats scholar he was, Trend preferred the Socratic approach in his steering briefs for the Prime Minister – a series of questions from which, in Trend's view, the political chief could be expected to draw his own, and hopefully correct, conclusion. This could infuriate Heath. One official witnessed this prickly relationship in the odd form of messages from one to the other tapping off the Cabinet Office teleprinter as the workaholic Heath sent down from Chequers, where he was spending the weekend, requests for information and advice to his Cabinet Secretary. As the official remembered it, the last message from Heath expressed anger at Trend's unwillingness to state his view of what should be done. Trend replied that it was not his job to do so.[140] Trend took the apolitical nature of the British civil servant so seriously that, throughout his Whitehall career, he never cast a vote in a general election. John Hunt, the man chosen by Heath to replace Burke Trend on his retirement in 1973, had a very different style, 'a great gripper of issues' as a colleague described him,[141] never reluctant to give his views when asked.

Heath was critical of the Civil Service as a whole for its reticence at moments of crisis. Douglas Hurd reflected his master's impatience when he wrote of the Heath years that there were three occasions on which 'at a crucial moment they fell below what was required'.[142] The three episodes were in the aftermath of 'Bloody Sunday' in Londonderry in 1972, during the discussions on inflation in the summer of 1973, and in the deepening oil/industrial crisis in November 1973. 'No-one who was present at any of these three meetings', wrote Hurd, 'could believe that the Civil Service runs this country.'[143] The duty of the officials, according to the diplomat-turned-politician, is, at confused moments, 'to force the discussion into some coherent channel'.[144] Heath had long hankered after a French-style Civil Service with highly trained officials not afraid to take a strong line.[145] When Prime Minister he despatched Mark Schreiber and a CSD official, Tony Hart, to Paris to report on the adaptability of the *cabinet* for British purposes. Their finding was surprisingly wishy-washy – 'If British Ministers feel the need for some personal reinforcement . . . there are features of the *cabinet* system which could be adapted to fill the need'[146] – and nothing happened.

William Armstrong, however, appeared, by 1973 at any rate, to be Heath's French-style *chef de cabinet*. During the Civil Service industrial action of that year (which Armstrong took very personally, sending a letter to every civil servant in the land[147]) it was Bill Kendall of the CPSA, the greatest phrase-maker in the trade union movement (and probably the best read), who first called him 'the deputy prime minister'.[148]

Armstrong regretted the 'deputy PM' impression – 'when honest people can use the words "deputy prime minister" of one, then clearly something's got slightly askew'[149] – and in August 1972 dismissed talk that Heath was planning on Trend's retirement to establish a Prime Minister's Department with him at the head of it as 'silly season stuff'.[150] But at least one close observer of the Whitehall scene believes 'Armstrong was very glad to leave Civil Service reform when Heath asked him to run counterinflation policy.'[151]

There was a pre-echo of Armstrong's economic overlordship the previous year when he was put in charge of an official committee whose brief from Heath was to plan for industrial expansion and full use of the economic opportunities which would be available when Britain joined the EEC in 1973. It was highly secret. The free-marketeers among the ministers at the Department of Trade and Industry knew nothing about it despite the detailed Industry Bill which was to emerge. Sir Leo Pliatzky, a member of the Armstrong Committee, recalled that 'when conclusions were reached, and the wraps came off, it was a very great shock to some of the other members of the government, and some of those who were most committed to the market economy philosophy were really quite taken aback by the whole thing'.[152]

It was the fear of unemployment topping the then unthinkable level of one million that pushed Heath into the U-turn for which he is still routinely derided in Mrs Thatcher's Conservative Party – the announcement on 6 November 1972 of a statutory incomes policy with a ninety-day freeze on pay, prices, dividends and rents. He announced it at a presidential-style press conference in Lancaster House rather than in the House of Commons. Armstrong made the huge mistake of allowing himself to sit alongside the Prime Minister with the cameras upon them both. The impression of an overmighty, political civil servant dates from that day. For his part, Armstrong, as he neared retirement, took pains to counter that impression:

> It really developed quite naturally. I'd been engaged on a big reform of the Civil Service following the Fulton Report, and, by the spring or early summer of 1972, most of the effort that I could personally put into that reform had been done. The job had passed, as it were, from the generals down to the company commanders. So I had more time on my hands, and that seemed to coincide with a need on the part of Mr Heath to have someone in a direct relationship with himself. It was not me alone – I was merely the head of a team of officials who worked with the corresponding team of Ministers on the talks with the CBI and TUC.[153]

What is certain is Armstrong's personal belief in the need for Heath's prices and incomes policy. Phillip Whitehead described him as 'a political civil servant not so much in the ideological sense as in his ambitious desire to embrace a policy without the civil servants' ultimate detachment'.[154] In this Armstrong was four-square in the Morant tradition and a one-man battleground for those personal-official impulses so brilliantly described by Derek Morrell a few years before. I once suggested to Armstrong that he was trying in 1972–4 to recreate the success story of the home front during his formative years working with Bridges and Brook in the War Cabinet Office but without the crucial tools of manpower and material controls. He said there was something in that but it was not quite right.[155]

It was stage three of the cherished incomes policy which broke Armstrong and the Heath Government despite their secret attempt at a meeting in the garden of No. 10 with Joe Gormley of the NUM in July 1973 to shift the rock, or rather the coal seam, on which it shattered. As the problems piled one on another after the Yom Kippur War in October, Heath and Armstrong battled to hold the breach. The strain began to tell. Douglas Hurd has described the 'Tchekovian' atmosphere of a weekend conference with visiting American Congressmen at Ditchley Park, the choicest contemporary watering-hole of the British Establishment on 26–7 January while the miners were balloting on their strike call: 'We sat on sofas in front of great log fires and discussed first principles while the rain lashed the windows. Sir William was full of notions, ordinary and extraordinary.'[156] Phillip Whitehead, when preparing his superb television series on the seventies, pieced together a picture of the sad, alarming final days of William Armstrong's Whitehall supremacy:

> He had been at Ditchley on 27 January, talking wildly of coups and coalitions to his alarmed fellow guests. Campbell Adamson [Director-General of the Confederation of British Industry] remembers himself and the president of the CBI being harangued by Armstrong at this period.
>
> 'We listened to a lecture about how Communists were infiltrating everything. They might even be infiltrating, he said, the room he was in. It was quite clear that the immense strain and overwork was taking its toll ...'
>
> Downing Street insiders talk of him as '... really quite mad at the end ... lying on the floor and talking about moving the Red Army from here, and the Blue Army from there.' The smoothest piece of the Whitehall machinery had broken down.[157]

The final collapse came at a meeting of permanent secretaries on 1 February 1974. Armstrong told them all to go home early and obviously that afternoon to convince the public that the government was coping. He went silent. Douglas Allen got up and gently led Armstrong from the room.[158] Shortly after he left for the West Indies to rest at Lord Rothschild's villa in Barbados.[159] By the time Wilson replaced Heath in No. 10 in March, Armstrong had decided to leave. As Joe Haines, who went into No. 10 with his boss, noted, 'his decision to become chairman of the Midland Bank – which greeted Harold Wilson when he became Prime Minister again –

prevented a very awkward situation arising'.[160] In a farewell interview with Mike Horsnell published in *The Times* the day he retired, Armstrong admitted he 'must have put a foot wrong' to have become so closely identified with Heath and incomes policy and that he had since reverted to his 'proper' role.[161] In his last days Desmond Wilcox, in a wonderfully revealing exchange, asked Armstrong, 'What do you go home and say at moments of economic crisis?'

'Thank God the Government's influence is so little.'

'Would you expand on that?'

'I have a very strong suspicion that governments are nothing like as important as they think they are, and that the ordinary work of making things and moving things about, of transport, manufacture, farming, mining, is so much more important than what the Government does, that the Government can make enormous mistakes and we can still survive.'

'As long as we have our Civil Service?'

'No, no. Even in spite of it'.[162]

For me William delivered his own sad epitaph as we lunched in the summer of 1976: 'I was always determined not to be seen as another Horace Wilson, but that's what happened.'[163] It was a genuine tragedy – a truly productive and glittering career of almost forty years tarnished beyond repair in its last months. Armstrong collapsed at Ditchley Park on 11 July 1980. He died in Oxford the following day at the age of sixty-five. Though I only knew William in the last five years of his life, I still miss him.

The economic and industrial crises which afflicted the Heath administration in 1972–4 claimed other casualties, the new style of government among them. The CPRS was diverted from its long-term function into the desperate casework of survival. Every horizon contracted to the short-term as the OPEC crisis required every forecast and forward plan to be rewritten. Sir Kenneth Berrill transferred from the University Grants Committee to the Treasury to take up the post of Chief Economic Adviser just days before the Yom Kippur War. Very soon, his working hours became exhausting and extended. His only consolation was on the way home to take a pint in the pub just before closing-time. Listening to the bar-room experts laying down the law about the economic crisis he would turn to them, as he drained his glass, and say:

'It's not quite as simple as that, you know.'

'Who the hell are you?'

'I'm the Chief Economic Adviser to the Treasury.'

'And I'm the Queen of Sheba!'[164]

Another casualty of the oil crisis was the Heath-patented mega-ministry, the Department of Trade and Industry which had absorbed the Ministry of Technology which, in turn, had swallowed up the old Ministry of Fuel and Power. In January 1974 it was split up with a new Department of Energy being created under Lord Carrington to tackle the issue of the hour. The hiving-off process continued as planned however. The same month as the DTI crumbled also witnessed the birth of the Manpower Services Commission out of the Department of Employment. It was tragically appropriate that the organisation which was to become in the 1980s the mega-ministry of unemployment should have emerged in the middle of industrial and economic crisis.

There was a less obvious casualty of Heath's growing preoccupation with the economy which has been identified by David Howell. For him 'the thing that unravelled it [the new style of government] all was . . . that after 1972 the pressure for tight control of public spending was really off'.[165] For Howell the objective of the new style was less but better government. To achieve it a sharp pair of scissors was needed – one blade being administrative reform, the other being 'a pretty mean and tight approach to public spending'.[166] Mr Heath's U-turn and dash for growth changed all that. 'After 1972', Howell later explained,

> the word came through from No. 10 and senior ministers and even from the Treasury, incredibly, that retrenchment was no longer the order of the day. On the contrary, 'expansion' was the word. So those very able civil servants, who'd risen to prominence in departments as analysts, saying 'Look boys, for years I've thought we were wasting money. We could cut this out or do it different', suddenly found they were in the pending tray, got a rather smaller office, pushed down the corridor, didn't get called into the permanent secretary so often. And the whole bit of Whitehall that had been geared to this terrific, thrusting reform rather got put on a back-burner.[167]

The Heath reforms, the most ambitious deliberate attempt at reshaping the machinery of government since Lloyd George, were hugely unlucky in the circumstances of their crucial formative years. When launched in 1970 there was no crisis atmosphere to 'speed up the historical process' and enable a determined premier to sweep away the slow bureaucratic accretion of decades. When crisis did come it struck a system far from fully run-in, and, inevitably, diverted ministerial – and, particularly, prime-ministerial – eyes and attention elsewhere. In combination with the failed experiments of the Wilson years, it resulted, too, in a fashionable dismissal of all structural solutions to any governmental problems which was still apparent in the late 1980s. During the 1987 election campaign, for example, Peter

Jenkins, by this time the influential political columnist of *The Independent*, could loftily describe sections of the Liberal-SDP Alliance manifesto as demonstrating a touching faith in the machinery of government, a relic of the Wilson era'.[168] Thanks to the continuing animosity within Tory ranks about the legacy of the 1970–4 government, Heath as PM has still to receive his historical due. When he does, the potential importance of his administrative reforms, and the care with which they were prepared in Opposition, will be a substantial element in the 'revisionist' literature.

Harold Wilson did not expect to be returned to No. 10 by the 'who rules?' election of 28 February 1974. 'On polling day', Bernard Donoughue has written, 'Mr Wilson clearly feared defeat and he had certainly made no preparations whatsoever for victory . . . he had made quite bizarre secret preparations to go into hiding should he be defeated'.[169] But the Wilson who strode into No. 10 on 4 March 1974 (Heath had tried and failed to create a Conservative–Liberal coalition in the interim) to be greeted by an applauding staff led by Robert Armstrong,[170] was very different from the Wilson who had crossed the same threshold in October 1964 to be greeted by Derek Mitchell (whether applauding or not, I don't know, but suspect not). Wilson, who seemed to many to have lost his zest for power, had told Donoughue during the campaign that 'if elected, he planned to be a very different Prime Minister from how he had been . . . in 1964. There would this time be "no presidential nonsense", no "first hundred days", and no "beer and sandwiches at No. 10" to solve crises. He said that Ministers would run their own departments and as Prime Minister he would try not to interfere.'[171] This time there was no clutch of new ministers reflecting a new 'purposive' (that awful word, the taste for which Wilson shared with Balogh) style of government. He broke up the DTI still further, mainly to meet his need to find sufficient Cabinet portfolios – Tony Benn went into the new Department of Industry, Peter Shore to the Department of Trade (though a traditionalist, Wilson did not revert to 'Board') and Shirley Williams to a new invention, the Department of Prices and Consumer Protection.

Over-concentration on structural change, however, can mislead. Wilson made one ministerial change of considerable importance in March 1974. He brought Harold Lever into the Cabinet as Chancellor of the Duchy of Lancaster with a tiny staff in the Cabinet Office and a roving brief across financial and industrial affairs. Lever roamed freely across both, which, as Leo Pliatzky noted, 'was to prove a nuisance to the Treasury from time to time, as no doubt it was meant to be, since Harold Lever was no believer in hair shirt policies but a man for ingenious solutions rather than hard choices; and the Cabinet, impressed by his reputation for financial wizardry in his private affairs, invariably supported his ingenious, even if expensive, solutions for problems of public finance'.[172] Micro issues, such as the

Chrysler rescue in 1975, and macro issues, such as the handling of the public sector borrowing requirement and the exchange rate throughout the entire 1974–9 period, bore traces of the Lever thumbprint. When Callaghan institutionalised his role as a one-man counter-Treasury task force inside his highly secret economic seminar after the IMF crisis of 1976 (see p. 260), Harold Lever's influence on policy was probably greater than that ever achieved by the Department of Economic Affairs. For Sir Leo Pliatzky, 'he was such an engaging person, and one so free from malice, that there was nothing in the atmosphere of the "creative tension" of the DEA days'.[173] Sir Douglas Wass, the Treasury permanent secretary throughout virtually all the Lever years, painted a vivid picture of the Lever technique and the Lever effect in a conversation with me for the Channel 4 documentary, *All the Prime Minister's Men*:

> 'His technique frequently was to invite what he regarded as . . . key people in the Treasury to go to the Cabinet Office and take tea with him and discuss some important issue. I remember I had a very agreeable afternoon with him talking about the problems of building societies in the middle of 1974. He was very gifted at getting information out of people even though you might not have wanted to give it to him.'
>
> 'You make him sound a far more effective counterweight than the DEA.'
>
> 'Mr Lever set out to be involved in all these issues – the issues of the balance of payments crisis, the recycling of oil surpluses, counter-inflation policy and so on – whereas the DEA did not. The DEA concentrated principally on two issues: one was prices and incomes; and the other was the National Plan. And neither of them brought [it] into the central area of Treasury policy, namely controlling public expenditure, budgetary matters generally and monetary policy. Mr Lever, by contrast, saw those were the two critical areas to become involved in, and he did [become involved] very successfully . . . [his] gift was to go on asking Socratic questions of those who formulated policy.'[174]

Despite setting up Harold Lever with his roving brief in the Cabinet Office and founding the Downing Street Policy Unit under Bernard Donoughue, his one enduring innovation, Harold Wilson, to the surprise of some, kept the CPRS – though never again would Lord Rothschild, as Douglas Hurd once described him, 'roam like a condottiere through Whitehall'.[175] His and the Tank's great days were over, though Wilson did send him one of the funniest Prime Minister's personal minutes ever penned:

In view of the current economic crisis, I would be grateful if you would give consideration to the following figures:

Population of the United Kingdom	54,000,000
People aged 65 and over	14,000,000
People aged 18 and under	18,000,000
People working for the Government	9,000,000
The Armed Forces	2,300,000
Local Government employees	9,800,000
People who won't work	888,000
People detained at Her Majesty's pleasure	11,998
Total	53,999,998
Balance left to do the work	2

You and I, therefore, must work harder, especially you, as I have felt no evidence of your considerable weight since I took office.

1 April 1974 HW.[176]

The CPRS had not been an election issue, though some of its members thought its future was at stake. But Lord Rothschild had been told privately in October 1973 that Labour would not wind up the CPRS, as he disclosed three years later:

When Mr Wilson became Prime Minister, some members of the Think Tank were quite worried lest it should suddenly be liquidated, several important people in the Labour Party having previously said the Tank was a joke, that they did not need anyone to think for them, and so on.

I could not relieve the members of the Think Tank of their anxiety, although I knew, in confidence, before Mr Wilson became Prime Minister, that he was not going to liquidate us: I had met him at luncheon six months before the Labour Party came into office and, at the end of it, he said to me 'when we win the election I do not intend to make any institutional changes at the centre'.[177]

Bernard Donoughue *is* convinced, however, that the life of the CPRS was in danger.

When we went in, there was enormous political hostility to the Tank from Labour ministers. They saw it as a Heath creation and political. The fact that William Waldegrave [who at the end of the Heath administration had moved into No. 10 as the PM's political secretary] and Adam Ridley were there was a demonstration that it was a Tory Party operation at the taxpayers' expense and it should be abolished. I came

> across nobody who saw it as a contribution to administration. Tony Benn went on at great length to me about it. The new Policy Unit was seen as Labour's. We were coming in and they were going out.[178]

Donoughue, though subsequently critical of some of its tactics and papers, was and remains a supporter of the idea of a CPRS and in March 1974 he lobbied for its survival:

> I rather surprised Wilson after we got into No. 10 by saying I hoped we would keep it. He obviously assumed he was going to get rid of it. He had also assumed that I would want to get rid of it because it was competition. Wilson had a little chat with me about it and then, I think, he took Victor for lunch at the Athenaeum.[179]

Harold Wilson's study, *The Governance of Britain*, published in 1976, gives no hint of ambivalence about the value of the CPRS or its head. He even described the Tank as 'a project that was being worked up before Labour left office in 1970' (which corroborates Lord Trend's account of his discussions with William Armstrong prior to the election). Heath, according to Wilson, showed 'Inspiration in the appointment of its first head'.[180] A few pages later his praise becomes unstinted:

> Edward Heath made a first-class appointment in Lord Rothschild, and the quality of the top appointment was reflected in those lower down ... Experience with two successive governments of different parties suggests that they have come to stay, an integral part of the decision-making centre of government.
>
> Their work closely follows the White Paper remit: they stand aside from day-to-day in-fighting and departmental issues – and their reports are utterly fearless, related to strategy and singularly unworried about upsetting Establishment views or producing conclusions extremely unpopular with those who commission them.[181]

Shortly after Labour's return to power, William Plowden, an old friend of Bernard Donoughue's inside the CPRS, urged him to clarify the relationship between the Tank and the new Downing Street Policy Unit. Donoughue had a couple of meetings with Rothschild to reassure him about the Tank's survival. Rothschild seemed concerned about the plan to recruit an oil expert to the Policy Unit, a field of great importance to the CPRS. Donoughue recalled: 'I cancelled that as a gesture to the CPRS. I tried very hard in various ways to establish good relations with Victor. I think it worked. Victor and I got on actually quite well.'[182]

The new Government noticed Lord Rothschild's gloom about prospects for the future. Events since the controversial Letcombe speech had reinforced his fears. He felt it was time to leave. Bernard Donoughue remembers: 'He was terribly gloomy. Wilson noticed how gloomy he was and Wilson didn't like gloomy people. I don't think he was too sorry to see him go.'[183]

But Lord Rothschild did not leave without sounding another warning note. Modelling himself on ambassadors whose last despatch before retirement consists of a *tour d'horizon* for the Foreign Secretary, which invariably begins with the words, 'With great truth and respect', Lord Rothschild sent Mr Wilson a letter entitled 'Farewell to the Think Tank'. Unlike the standard diplomat's valedictory, this was published, with his permission, in *The Times*, on 13 October 1974.[184] In his elliptical fashion, he skewered politicians as a breed:

> Politicians often believe that their world is the real one: officials sometimes take a different view. Having been a member of this latter and lesser breed, it is, perhaps, inevitable that I should have become increasingly fearful about the effects of the growing political hostility between and among our people. To what extent is this blinding us, preventing us keeping our eyes on the real ball assuming there is one? I think there is and I have said before what I believe *it* to be: that the people of Britain must now agree to the necessity for a period of national sacrifice. . . .
>
> There is no chance at all of us maintaining our standard of living, of keeping up with inflation, even though politicians and other national leaders seem to think it is axiomatic that this is both a possible and an essential right of the people. We, the people, have no divine rights; only those that a democratic society can afford and has the will to provide. So if, in the interests of the future, democracy requires a freeze, rationing and harsh taxation of luxuries, it is no good saying that such measures are acceptable in war but not in peace: Because we are at war, with ourselves and with that neo-Hitler, that arch enemy inflation.[185]

In fact, Lord Rothschild waited another twenty months before tearing into the British political class. His Israel Sieff Memorial Lecture, 'The Best Laid Plans . . .', delivered in May 1976, carries the unmistakable whiff of 1974 and the first months in office of the new Labour Government. He quoted 'a very distinguished civil servant' on the difference between the two parties to the effect that: 'Conservative Cabinet ministers grunt, and Labour Cabinet ministers give us out of date lectures on economics' adding that 'my occasional contacts with Cabinet ministers have not made me feel that this apophthegm was totally false'.[186] Then Lord Rothschild really let his old bosses have it in a passage brimming with indirect observations on the difficulty of placing non-partisan political analysis of the CPRS variety before newly elected ministers:

> Something really should be done about this problem of the party's first few months in office, which are without doubt the worst. This prolonged festival, a mixture of the madness of Mardi Gras and Auto da Fe, celebrated by burning anything of a political character which is regarded as inimical, can be a great nuisance, to put it at its mildest.
>
> Governments can do dreadful things in their first heady months of office. I wish there could be a law against a new Government doing anything during its first three or so months of existence. Apart from their constituency and parliamentary duties and, of course, their ritual appearances at hospitals, new power stations, Strasbourg and the like, new ministers, even if they have been in office before, should read documents, listen to expert opinion, ask questions and refrain, unless absolutely essential, from taking positive or negative action, activities which, at the beginning of a new term of office, almost invariably create new problems. There should be a period of purging and purification – a kind of political Ramadan.[187]

The quality of ministerial decision-taking and the problem of 'overload' preoccupied Lord Rothschild for a decade after he left Whitehall. (Before departing, he himself experienced this particular industrial disease and suffered a mild heart attack as the Heath winter crisis gathered pace in mid-December 1973.[188]) A few months after leaving the Cabinet Office he published in *The Times* his famous test for policy-makers suffering from jet lag and drink which had formed the core of the Tank's study of decision-making under stress.[189] It took the form of a logical set of questions involving the letters 'A' and 'B'. Candidates were required to tick 'True' or 'False' beside each one and were invited to answer as many items as possible in three minutes. As Lord Rothschild recalled a decade later, the idea was not greeted with acclaim in Whitehall:

> It was very unpopular with the permanent secretaries on whom I tried it first and it really wasn't worth going on and trying to persuade ministers to do this three minute test. As a matter of fact, the person who did best at it was Field Marshal Lord Carver. Every time he tried my test after a long trip ... and perhaps a couple of Martinis on the aeroplane, he got 97 out of 100.[190]

The scholarly former Chief of the Defence Staff was miffed at Lord Rothschild's indiscretion. He told the *Times* Diary: 'Victor set it because he was horrified at the way some ministers took decisions. He said quite firmly at the time the results would be extremely confidential.'[191] Sadly, Rothschild's attempt to persuade Britain's politicians that exhaustion and overwork were not assets when it came to the conduct of public business seems to have been a complete failure.

Lord Rothschild believed the headship of the CPRS was the best job he ever held.[192] In October 1974 it passed to an old friend of his, Sir Kenneth Berrill, an academic amphibian who had hopped between Whitehall and the universities since as a young man he had followed his teacher, Professor Austin Robinson, into Lord Plowden's Central Economic Planning Staff. Before taking over the Tank, Sir Kenneth was, as we have seen, Chief Economic Adviser to the Treasury. At the same time he served as unofficial economic adviser at weekends to his Cambridge neighbour who just happened to be Lord Rothschild.[193]

Berrill was, in many ways, a sharp contrast to Rothschild. Physically smallish and compact, he exuded an air of bustle and jollity and, for one so senior in public life, a kind of matiness. Berrill was not an original thinker. His great skill as an economist was to synthesise the work of others, to select and blend that which was practical. This was very much his style at the CPRS. In conversation he was down-to-earth, fast talking and sparse rather than grand, direct rather than elliptical. He was very similar to Sir Douglas Allen, who as Permanent Secretary to the Treasury had in 1973 been instrumental in transferring Berrill from the University Grants Committee to the post of Chief Economic Adviser and Head of the Government Economic Service. Both men were professional economists trained at the London School of Economics, meritocrats who had risen by the scholarship route. Neither had acquired the Oxbridge manner, though Sir Kenneth had for many years been Bursar of King's College, Cambridge.

The change of government in March 1974 affected Berrill's tenure as Head of the Government Economic Service directly, not because incoming Labour ministers found him unsympathetic, but because of an ancient feud in the Cambridge University Economics Faculty, for accompanying Denis Healey on his arrival at the Treasury as his special adviser was Professor Lord Kaldor. Berrill and Kaldor, as was well known, did not get on. Lord Rothschild's informing Mr Wilson of his intention to retire in the autumn provided a neat solution to the Treasury's Cambridge problem, though it upset the careful career planning of Whitehall's Senior Appointments Selection Committee. The Committee, which since Fulton had consisted of the six most senior permanent secretaries, had foreseen the succession of Douglas Wass to the headship of the Treasury (it actually happened in 1974 shortly after Labour's return to power) at a relatively young age. The idea was to have Sir Kenneth, a seasoned old Keynesian, in post as Chief Economic Adviser while the new permanent secretary found his feet.[194] The Cambridge factor, the early retirement of William Armstrong and the consequent transfer of Douglas Allen from the Treasury to the Civil Service Department ruined the whole scheme. Everybody seemed content with the Berrill appointment to the CPRS, however, as *The Times* profile of him noted:

> It is widely thought that he was Lord Rothschild's hand-picked successor and that his lateral promotion was a move which killed several birds with one stone . . . The esteem in which he is generally held . . . was well illustrated by one civil servant who said 'I believe both leaders of the major political parties think he was their choice, and I believe there are several high-up civil servants who think he was their choice'.[195]

Bernard Donoughue in the No. 10 Policy Unit was made uneasy by the enthusiasm with which Sir Kenneth's move was greeted by senior officials. He believed Berrill was essentially their choice, a Civil Service appointment rather than a political one:

> It was in July 1974, at the private secretaries' party in the garden of No. 10, John Hunt was talking very excitedly about what a marvellous chap he had got, a reliable man to replace Victor. He was making it clear that this was excellent for the Cabinet Office. I went and broke into the conversation. He told me it was Ken Berrill.
>
> I had mixed reactions. I had negative reactions. I feared because of the way Hunt described it that the Civil Service had got the CPRS under control. But I had dealt with Ken at the UGC. I knew he was an able man. I knew personally I would be able to get on with Ken.
>
> But I was a bit worried about the future of the Tank. I spoke to Wilson about it. He had basically left Hunt to do it. He didn't seem very interested.[196]

Sir Kenneth, however, had one significant advantage when he moved into Lord Rothschild's suite in the Cabinet Office in October 1974. He could start the job running. As Chief Economic Adviser he was intimately familiar with the post-OPEC problems of surging inflation and a public spending system largely out of control. Nor did Labour ministers have any illusions about Sir Kenneth's willingness to speak his mind. Earlier that year, while giving evidence at the Commons Expenditure Committee, he had been asked how inflation could be controlled if a statutory incomes policy was an impossibility. He replied, in his ironic and brutal fashion: 'I don't think I can answer that question because the Government, and therefore, of course, the Treasury, believe a voluntary policy will work.'[197]

Economic crisis overshadowed Wilson's administration as it had Heath's. The Treasury, as well as Wilson's ministerial team, seemed paralysed in the face of it for the first year, at least, of the new government's life. Whitehall as a whole had been shaken rigid by the winter crisis of 1973–

4, the naked application of trade-union power and Wilson's settlement of the miners' strike on the miners' terms. The lunch tables were very gloomy in 1974 with Spenglerian talk about 'the decline of the west' and 'tides in the affairs of men'.[198] For the Treasury the fall of Heath was a particular blow not because of any Conservative sympathies, but because their incomes policy – the most sophisticated they had constructed since they first embarked on the art for Cripps in 1948 – had also crashed in ruins. Pride of authorship, not anti-Labour sentiments, lay at the root of it.

To some, the Treasury appeared shell-shocked to the point of passivity between the two elections of 1974. As Bernard Donoughue told the makers of Channel 4's *The Writing on the Wall*, there was an 'almost complete absence of discussion of economic policy. I think it's true that the Cabinet never really discussed economic policy before the October election; indeed didn't, as I recall, discuss it until early 1975.'[199] Donoughue went on to recall a lunch 'with a very senior Treasury official' during which he asked him why there were no Treasury papers on the surging rate of inflation. He said, 'Oh no, of course not, Bernard. Politicians never deal with serious issues until they become *the* crisis. So at the Treasury we're waiting till the crisis really blows up.'[200] By midsummer 1975, with inflation at 26 per cent, its postwar peak, unmistakeable crisis forced the Wilson Cabinet back to incomes policy. Until Labour fell four years later, the Treasury and the clutch of Whitehall departments which were sponsoring ministries for the nationalised industries were once more deeply and intricately involved in wage determination by direct means. Labour's original social contract, a surrogate for incomes policy, was a casualty of hyperinflation. There was another, less public, economic casualty – the post-Plowden public expenditure machine.

The Treasury in the mid-1970s was *the* scapegoat department as the economic setbacks crowded in, just as the Foreign Office found itself in the dock in the post-Falklands early 1980s. Public expenditure control, or the apparent lack of it, was the motor which drove public and political abuse. The Commons Expenditure Committee, thanks to some sharp econometrics from that ex-Treasury temporary, Wynne Godley, now at Cambridge, 'discovered' in December 1975 the legendary 'lost five billion' – the difference between the real out-turn of public expenditure in 1974–5 and the figure that had been allowed for (inflation included) in the 1971 spending White Paper.[201] This led to huge, adverse publicity for the Treasury and put the select committee firmly on the journalistic map.

The Treasury, in fact, was planning a much tougher regime for spending control when Sir Leo Pliatzky – who, in his own words, 'was no lover of the PESC system and had never served as one of its high priests'[202] – succeeded Sir Douglas Henley as second permanent secretary on the spending side at the end of 1975. Pliatzky, who 'had never expected to inherit responsibility for Otto Clarke's creation and found a certain irony in this situation',[203] changed the nature of that system for ever by driving, with firm ministerial support from Denis Healey and Joel Barnett, strongly forward on the cash limits project, bringing to an end what was, in effect, inflation-proofed public spending. As Sir Leo later put it: 'Instead of waiting to see what the rate of inflation turned out to be and providing extra cash to cover it when the time came, the government would, in snooker terms, be calling its shots on inflation and declaring in advance what cost increases it would be prepared to finance.'[204] No longer would ministers and officials have to deal with 'the funny money of constant prices'.[205]

Pliatzky was one of the most talked-about characters of his Whitehall generation. A good-hearted man, he nonetheless gave the impression of having eaten a tin of razor-blades for breakfast. Rab Raphael, the former head of information at the Treasury, created a little cameo portrait of Pliatzky in his novel, *Treasury Alarm*. Writing under the pseudonym 'Jocelyn Davey', Raphael transmogrified Pliatzky into 'Bert Prescott', a 'rough diamond' from the North of England, symbol of a new 'no-nonsense Treasury'.[206]

Pliatzky's rebuilding of the public spending system in 1975–6 was not confined to the construction of cash limits. After discussions with Sir John Hunt, the Cabinet Secretary, a proposal was developed whereby neither the Chancellor nor the Chief Secretary could be overruled on a spending matter in a Cabinet committee. Only full Cabinet could do that. And 'shifting the onus of appeal on to the spending minister would make a great deal of psychological difference'[207] as, in Wilson's words, it would give the Treasury 51 per cent of the votes.[208] Wilson, in fact, accepted it, and it is now a fixture of Cabinet procedure. Sir Leo was justified in describing it as 'quite a significant constitutional change'.[209]

Away from the front-line of the economic and spending battlefield, the Wilson government encountered other changes made since its senior men left office. One was Heath's development of mixed Cabinet committees. These offended that old Cabinet Office hand, Harold Wilson and, with the exception of the Civil Contingencies Unit, they were swept away.[210] Other changes he kept. There was no alternative after Heath's imposition of direct rule in Northern Ireland in 1972 but to keep the instrument of it, the Northern Ireland Office, Whitehall's own front-line department then under Sir Frank Cooper and enduring a particularly grim and bloody phase of the Troubles.

The arrival in Belfast of Merlyn Rees as Wilson's Secretary of State for Northern Ireland in March 1974 produced one of the best minister–civil servant stories in years. After the first meeting between the Social

Democratic and Labour Party and the new minister, one of its leaders, Paddy Devlin, was asked for his impression. He replied: 'During the war, Merlyn Rees was a fitter on Sir Frank Cooper's Spitfire and the relationship is exactly the same today.'[211] Mr Devlin was a bit off-beam. Sir Frank was indeed a Spitfire pilot in the war and was in contact with Mr Rees at one stage when he, Rees, was the squadron leader administering a set of airfields on one of which Sir Frank's aircraft was parked.

The other great change agent in the bureaucracy was Europe. Britain had acceded to the Community in January 1973 and our membership had been confirmed by the referendum of June 1975 (supervised by Sir Philip Allen, the former Home Office Permanent Secretary who had sat on Fulton) after a renegotiation serviced by a special European Unit in the Cabinet Office (led by Sir Patrick Nairne). The European dimension in Whitehall is as important as it is unexciting. Harold Macmillan once said that Europe 'isn't just about fixing a price for prunes and a suitable method of marketing bananas'.[212]

But, for all the fervour it engenders now that the great membership debate has subsided, that is precisely the level on which it is perceived. Hugo Young and Anne Sloman described the United Kingdom Representation, or UKREP, as 'the hidden arm of Whitehall . . . in Brussels'.

> It is 'hidden' not because of any great secret about British membership of the European Community but because hardly anyone understands how deeply this fact has imposed itself on the way our governing classes spend their time. For some departments, like the Foreign Office and the Ministry of Agriculture, it is *the* dominating premise of their professional lives. In others – Energy, Industry, Trade – it gives work to a lot of officials who wouldn't otherwise have been needed.[213]

In emotional terms it may not be the surrogate for Empire for which Dean Acheson once claimed we were searching, but in bureaucratic terms it is.

'Those cardinals of bureaucracy',[214] as Lord Rothschild once described the permanent secretaries, had changed a good deal, too, between 1970 and 1974 and were to change again between 1974 and 1976 as the generation for whom everything was achievable[215] came into its own. Shortly before Labour returned to office some of the big figures of the generation recruited just before the war had departed – Burke Trend from the Cabinet Office and Philip Allen from the Home Office. (Otto Clarke, the legendary wartime temporary, left shortly after Heath took office to write a book on the organisation of central government.[216]) Within a few months of Labour's arrival William Armstrong went from the CSD and Sir James Dunnett, a Fulton veteran who had headed Transport, Labour and, latterly, Defence, retired. Douglas Allen replaced Armstrong at the CSD and was succeeded at the Treasury by Douglas Wass. The following year Ian Bancroft became Permanent Secretary at Environment. In 1976 there was a further re-ordering of what used, archaically, to be called the 'top hamper' when Sir Michael Cary, Dunnett's harpsichord-building successor at the Ministry of Defence, died suddenly and was replaced by Sir Frank Cooper. Sir Patrick Nairne became Permanent Secretary at the DHSS in succession to Sir Philip Rodgers. For some reason, the generations tend to leave the impression of having changed in a flurry.

As the seventies progressed, in so far as a duumvirate developed in succession to the Bridges–Brook, Trend–Armstrong combinations, it was a Hunt–Cooper axis. Both were tough, no-nonsense fixer-operators well suited to a period when central government was under acute stress. John Hunt was tall and athletic in appearance. When he walked through the arch between Horse Guards Parade and Whitehall, the soldiers of the Household Division in their dress uniform guarding the London District Headquarters would regularly clatter to attention, mistaking him for a general in civvies.[217] As a journalist I was rarely unnerved by people to whom I talked, but I can remember sensing the slightly menacing air of power about John Hunt as we stood opposite each other on a January afternoon in 1976 talking about his war service on corvettes in the Western approaches while his photograph was taken by Harry Kerr of *The Times* with the door linking the Cabinet Office and No. 10 in the background. (He presumably learnt how to look strong and formidable when, at a young age, he accepted the sword of a Japanese general in surrender on a remote Pacific island.[218])

People on the inside who had seen Hunt in action tended to reach for images of power when describing him:

> Burke was feline; John is a Borzoi.[219]
>
> Trend was Byzantine, like Rothschild; Hunt is a sixteenth century cardinal with a touch of the Borgias.[220]
>
> Fascinating man, a Jesuit with a total belief in the state and its objectives. Nothing, neither friendship nor anything else, would come before that. In many ways he was a frightening man in his devotion to the Hegelian concept of the state. He was only interested in two things – the [Roman Catholic] church and the state. He had extraordinary energy. He pulled power to himself and the Cabinet office. He intervened in twice as many things as Robert Armstrong [his successor].[221]
>
> Sir John Hunt . . . made the Secretary to the Cabinet the most powerful man in Whitehall.[222]

Hunt was certainly formidable in committee. He wrote the standard work on Whitehall chairmanship. No detail is left uncovered; everything is calculated, calibrated:

> If things get sticky remember there are different ways of taking the heat out of an argument, for example:
> (a) Introducing a new factor into the discussion.
> (b) Asking for the views of someone who is not already involved in the argument.
> (c) A light-hearted remark.
>
> Any of these is better than appealing for moderation.[223]

John Hunt, ever cool and courteous, would, when the opportunity presented itself, take pains to counter his image as a granitic servant of the state and an accumulator and wielder of power on a scale unmatched since Thomas Cromwell. In an interview with Desmond Quigley to mark his retirement at the end of October 1979, he said of the Cabinet Secretary: 'He should not be an *eminence grise*. We are here to help.' And went on to say: 'My role in advising the Prime Minister has certainly grown over the years, and over the years before me. But quite honestly I have not sought to exercise influence nor have I really been conscious of doing it. I have never sought to push a Prime Minister in the direction he or she does not wish to go. It is not my business to argue.'[224]

In an interview with me for *All the Prime Minister's Men*, Hunt was hugely dismissive of the Crossman thesis that the Cabinet Secretary cooks the Cabinet minutes – 'absolute nonsense', he called it; and the view 'that civil servants rig everything behind the scenes is a grossly exaggerated theory'.

And he simply could not understand why so many former ministers have complained about their ignorance of the existence of this or that Cabinet committee: 'I think in most cases, if they'd bothered to find out they could have done ... there certainly used to be a Cabinet Committee Book which contained a list of all Cabinet committees and which was available to departments.'[225]

But from the same interview it was clear how the impression grew abroad that Hunt's tenure as Cabinet Secretary – 'the most fascinating job in the Civil Service', he called it[226] – was perhaps the zenith of the power of that office, certainly since the Brook–Churchill years of 1951–5: 'Grip' is the great Hunt word:

> Slowly over a period of six to seven years I found I was devoting more of my time to servicing the Prime Minister in one way or another, as compared with my normal duties of servicing the Cabinet ... I can think of a lot of examples, they will normally be subjects where the Prime

Minister judges them important, where he thinks that the normal machinery [is] not going to produce the right options for ministers quick enough and he wants the thing gripped from the centre.[227]

Nor was Hunt the kind of public servant to reach for the antiseptic at the mention of politics:

It is very important for the Cabinet Secretary to have a political nose. I think, under our system, it would be a great pity if the Cabinet Secretary were too committed to a particular political view because he has got to serve governments of different political complexions. But that doesn't mean he can be a sort of political neuter and uninterested. He's got to be . . . passionately interested in the political scene. But above all he has got to have a nose for trouble ahead and what the next issues to hit the Prime Minister or the Cabinet are going to be.[228]

John Hunt had a great feel for power, the efficiency of its flow and deployment. He grew increasingly concerned about the load on central government and the capacity of the machine to bear it. At his last permanent secretaries' Sunningdale (every October they repair to the Civil Service College for a thoughtful weekend in the countryside) shortly before his retirement he shared his concerns with those he would soon be leaving behind. He talked particularly of ministers' need for 'advice given earlier and in greater depth'.[229]

Once free of Whitehall, with a new career at the Banque Nationale de Paris and the Prudential, Hunt, surprised at the lack of withdrawal symptoms ('I'm a person who lives in the present'[230]) though missing Whitehall's superb briefing facilities, or 'nanny service' as he called it,[231] nonetheless found time to develop his thinking about the deficiencies of central government and the Cabinet system. He had always shunned the image of the thinker – 'I certainly don't think I'm an intellectual. I like to think that I get on with things'[232] – yet his considered thoughts, delivered to a conference of accountants at Eastbourne on election day 1983 proved to be a modern classic on the problems and realities of Cabinet government. He talked of a 'hole in the centre' of government 'which an overworked Cabinet seemed incapable of filling'.[233] He would return to the theme of 'a Cabinet which has collective responsibility without sufficient information or power to exercise it'[234] at seminars and in the occasional interview. He was concerned, too, that his successor, Robert Armstrong, suffered from an individual overload problem in having to carry the headship of the Civil Service *and* the Cabinet secretaryship.[235]

For all the stress of mid-seventies government, Hunt never gave the slightest sign of being overwhelmed by it. Nor did his friend Sir Frank

Cooper. Cooper, small, combative, always capable of an explosive bravura performance whether it was before a select committee (here he was the best and wiliest performer of his generation – he once defused a particularly threatening Public Accounts Committee hearing by suggesting they meet in the ward room of a nuclear submarine at Chatham; they did and were like schoolboys on a treat[236]), in Cabinet committee or bashing together the heads of MOD's warlords. He was a highly unusual civil servant, more a combination of industrial tycoon (he became one on retirement) and Spitfire pilot (which, as we have seen, he had been). His singularity made Cooper one of the most effective politicians since the war, though nobody ever elected him to anything. One of his colleagues explained his influence by saying 'he gets away with it because he is more of a politician than the politicians themselves. They've never met a civil servant like that before and they don't know how to handle it.'[237] Perhaps the greatest compliment ever paid to Sir Frank came from that heavyweight of postwar Labour politics, Denis Healey, with whom he had formed a formidable partnership at the MOD in the 1960s. In a television interview, Healey, irritated by something Cooper had said about nuclear weapons policy in another interview, said: 'I wouldn't treat Sir Frank's evidence as totally impartial. He is an extremely intelligent, able politician as well as a civil servant.'[238]

Cooper joined the Air Ministry in 1948 just as the British atomic bomb project was moving into its stride. Virtually throughout his career – which spanned the planning period of the 'V' force to the planning for Trident – he was one of the 'exceptionally limited circle of people who were privy to the innermost details of nuclear thinking and nuclear technology'.[239] He built a formidable reputation within the defence world as a policy-maker and a negotiator. He engaged in marathon sessions with Archbishop Makarios in 1959 in pursuit of the agreement which left the aircraft of the Royal Air Force on the tarmac of the UK sovereign bases in Cyprus. It was another set of delicate negotiations, conducted at one stage removed this time, which brought him, controversially, into the public eye when the Northern Ireland Office arranged a cease-fire with the IRA in 1975.[240] 'Did you talk to the Sinn Fein yourself?' he was later asked. 'No, but I organised the people who talked . . . The object was to get rid of internment and bring back the rule of law.'[241]

Cooper was recalled to Whitehall, on Michael Cary's sudden death, in time to implement the defence review of 1974–5. He began a ferocious manpower economy drive three years before the cutting edge of Raynerism bit into departmental staff. By the time he left in December 1982, 55,000 others had gone before him[242] (the MOD stood at 298,104 when he took over in 1976[243]). At the same time he launched an equally ferocious battle against the Treasury to change the basis of their spending control. Victory came shortly after he left when a substantial degree of carry-over of underspend from one year's budget to the next was permissible. He fought like a tiger till the end. His last appearance before the Public Accounts Committee saw him as the squaddies' friend pitted against an unfeeling Treasury, arguing that if he could budget two to three years ahead on capital projects instead of one, he could, among other things, achieve enough savings to pull down the Second World War huts in which the bulk of the Army lived, putting them in brick buildings like the rest of the population.[244] Then Cooper and Joel Barnett, the PAC chairman, took a fond leave of each other like a pair of bantamweight prizefighters on the verge of retirement. Few others have ever made the defence budget interesting.

Part of Cooper's clout came from the surprise factor. He was incapable of talking like a White Paper on legs. His conversation would be peppered by highly personal phraseology such as his remark on a well-known political commentator to the effect that: 'Old X, he's moved to the right of barbed wire.'[245] (Cooper, with his Manchester Grammar School background, was proud of the provincial radicalism which remained with him throughout his career.[246]) Not that he, any more than Hunt, would accept at face value the image others projected of him. 'I don't think,' he once told me, 'I am what you call a political fixer. I think I'm quite a good operator, but then I never think very much about myself.'[247] In his last days at MOD, however, he did admit to having been a '"Perhaps, Minister" man'.[248]

The greatest and most immediate strain on the new men of the mid-seventies fell on the Treasury team as the economic blizzard struck. The most exposed of the permanent secretaries was Sir Douglas Wass. He was also the most thoughtful, ever donnish even under duress. A very orderly man, he pressed ahead with a management review of the Treasury. The resulting division between the overseas finance sector, public services sector and the new domestic economy sector (designed to get a greater Treasury purchase on the real economy), each with its own second permanent secretary, he believed helped the department to weather the fiercest of its recent storms – the great sterling crisis of 1976 and the visitation of the International Monetary Fund.

Wass had his problems with the Treasury barons beneath him, all formidable characters – the svelte, witty Derek Mitchell who was deeply (and wrongly) suspected by some ministers of selling Labour and sterling short abroad, the abrasive Pliatzky and the equally abrasive Alan Lord, who had made a formidable reputation as an Inland Revenue principal when, with Nicholas Kaldor, he designed corporation tax for Callaghan in 1964–5.[249] Lord, fresh from a spell at the Department of Industry, was put in charge of the new domestic economy sector. He had a strong mind and he always spoke it. Had he not left Whitehall first for industry, then the City, Alan Lord would have been the obvious successor to Wass in the

1980s. Pliatzky has alluded to his relationship with Lord (Lord has kept silent):

> The Treasury reorganisation [of 1975] had led to another Second Permanent Secretary appointment, which I would have preferred and hoped to get, in charge of a new grouping which brought together all aspects of Treasury work which were related to industrial policy, including some expenditure programmes as well as taxation. The Treasury's leading role in industrial strategy and incomes policy, with a strong personality in charge of that side, together with the absence of any established guidelines about relationships between the two sides, was bound to create some ambivalence about the relative priority of the Treasury's objectives in these various fields and to add a fresh complication to the thankless task of trying to bring public expenditure under control.[250]

The economic crisis, which befell James Callaghan less than six months after he had succeeded Harold Wilson in No. 10, enforced a kind of power-sharing in Whitehall at two important levels. In perhaps the finest recent exhibition of classic collective Cabinet government, Callaghan, mindful of the need to carry his senior colleagues as a whole, took the IMF loan and its terms to no fewer than twenty-six meetings of the full Cabinet.[251] Prime ministers are normally highly reluctant to take such market-sensitive financial discussions in so large a forum.

For its part, the Treasury was obliged to share some of its insider preserve not just with socratically questioning Harold Lever but with the Cabinet Office. Hunt, who himself had a Treasury background, skilfully used Berrill as virtually his own chief economic adviser and the professional economists of the CPRS as his own economic service. The Cabinet Office input into the IMF discussions was crucial. Those discussions took some utterly bizarre turns. On Callaghan's instructions the IMF team were left in Mayfair 'kicking their heels in Brown's Hotel for several weeks'[252] while the politicians and the departments manoeuvred against the background of a sliding currency. At the end of November William Simon, Secretary to the US Treasury, came to London to move matters along to a conclusion at a series of secret meetings with the Treasury and the Bank of England. 'Unfortunately', he later recalled, 'the press was hounding me everywhere I went and as a result I had to devise something rather devious.'[253] That 'something' was a secret meeting in Wells, the Mayfair tailors, a venue which, no doubt, stretched even Sir Derek Mitchell's delicious sense of the absurd. 'We met the Treasury people', Simon continued, 'and there was generally a small parade of folks in and out of this tailor and I ended up buying three suits I didn't need; but nonetheless we pretty well set the parameters.'[254]

John Hunt, that great cartographer of concealed power, later analysed the change in the Treasury's position *vis-à-vis* the rest of Whitehall in the 1970s:

> When I joined the service just after the Second World War the Treasury was virtually all powerful. It was in a different league to other departments, not only as *the* big economic department but also as a co-ordinator. Its power was felt very strongly in every department. And if the Treasury view was known to be so-and-so, this tended to get reflected throughout Whitehall. That has changed partly because the co-ordinating role is divided between the Treasury and the Cabinet Office.
>
> I think it's also changed because Chancellors of the Exchequer are less able to take big economic decisions on their own, and, therefore, the power and the awe attaching to the Treasury is less. Chancellors are being forced to discuss economic policy with their colleagues, and this has stripped some of the mystique of the Treasury.[255]

After the IMF had departed, Callaghan institutionalised part of this power-sharing. The Cabinet's salad days as the key economic forum were past. But the Treasury's did not return. Instead the key discussions on exchange rate policy, interest rates and monetary policy were moved into a group Callaghan camouflaged beneath the innocuous title of the 'Economic Seminar'. Three ministers attended: Callaghan, Healey and Lever. The official back-up consisted of Gordon Richardson and Kit McMahon from the Bank of England, Wass and Ken Couzens from the Treasury, Hunt from the Cabinet Office, Berrill from the CPRS, Ken Stowe and Tim Lankester from the No. 10 Private Office and Donoughue from the Policy Unit.[256] Callaghan, unlike Wilson, 'showed absolutely no deference towards the Treasury'.[257] He wanted the divisions of opinion normally locked up inside the Treasury and the Bank to be ventilated in front of him. 'I liked to hear what they all had to say . . . and try to weigh up what were the different views they had. All very helpful to me . . .'.[258] Callaghan made it all sound matey and almost routine. But it was more than that – it was a skilful manifestation of an old pro bringing ancient satrapies to heel. It was also highly secret. Probably the first the majority of the Callaghan Cabinet heard of the Economic Seminar was when it was 'blown' after they had left office.[259]

It was not just the Treasury that endured a crisis of confidence in the mid-1970s: it was the Civil Service as a whole. They became the scapegoat for national failure. For the Right they were a great shuddering blancmange smothering and stifling an otherwise healthy nation (the unions and the nationalised industries apart). For the Left they were centrist-minded and cautious. For the managerially minded centre they were traditional and amateur, quite incapable of performing the technocratic feats of their French counterparts where, even in the dog days of fifties political instability, the technically proficient *grands corps* in Paris were widely credited with having laid the foundations of the French economic miracle of the 1960s.

Anthony Keating, hero of Margaret Drabble's *The Ice Age*, which captures better than any other novel the bleak despair of 1975–6, is moved to an explosion of rage against the breed from which he was bred:

> Enough apology, enough politeness, enough self-seeking high-minded well-meaning well-respected idleness, enough of quite-well-paid middle-status gentlemen's jobs, enough of the Oxbridge Arts graduate. They had killed the country, sapped initiative, destroyed the economy. This was the new line of the new Anthony, Oxbridge arts graduate turned property dealer.[260]

A later, still brooding Keating asks, 'who, in a recession, can afford the luxury of Greek, who can afford the luxury of a Civil Service staffed by those who have first-class degrees in classics?'[261]

Into this climate was born the report arising from the last of William Armstrong's initiatives, the Wider Issues Review (meaning wider issues than pay). The document, *Civil Servants and Change*,[262] published in February 1975, with its emphasis on better office conditions, health, welfare and promotion prospects, had no chance in a freezing climate compounded of a public expenditure crisis and deepening public hostility towards the public service. This hostility intensified when Sir Geoffrey Howe, the Shadow Chancellor of the Exchequer, made the running on public service pensions, inflation-proofed since the Superannuation Act 1971 linked them to movements in the retail price index. The impression, fostered relentlessly by the popular press, grew apace of a group of people insulated from the economic consequences of their own incompetence. The politics of envy is a potent force. Rarely did politicians point out that their pensions, too, were protected in an identical fashion.

In 1975, the postwar Civil Service peaked (if you exclude throughout the Post Office which became a public corporation in 1969) at 747,000. An economy drive was begun with the CSD's Cost of Central Government Review. The aim of the review when completed in 1976 was the shedding of 35,000 jobs by 1978–9, a saving of some £140m, though Sir Douglas Allen made clear his view to a Commons Select Committee that 'I don't think it [growth of the Civil Service] is the reason why public expenditure has gone up rather rapidly. The staff element in it has not been the driving force.'[263]

Sensing the prevailing public and political mood in the opening days of

1976, the general sub-committee of the Commons Expenditure Committee launched what promised to be the most protracted Parliamentary inquiry into the Civil Service since the Second World War. Its chairman, the Labour MP Michael English, said that: 'As public expenditure now represents more than 50 per cent of the gross domestic product and these are the people responsible for spending it, it makes sense to look at them. Two-thirds of the cost of central government goes on salaries.' Mr English added that he and his all-party colleagues were well aware of recent criticisms of the Civil Service. 'We have a completely open mind at this stage.'[264]

The English hearings were a lengthy business, lasting a year from May 1976 to May 1977. There were some moments for connoisseurs to savour. Harold Wilson appeared before them in February 1977 and indulged in an uncharacteristic outburst of *mea culpa*ism almost worthy of that arch hand-wringer, Sir Keith Joseph. As for his Inner Cabinet, or Parliamentary Committee – 'I am not sure that it was a very good idea'[265]; merging Health and Social Security in 1969 – 'Looking back on it, I think that perhaps it was the wrong merger'[266]; on the post-Fulton drive for reform – 'I think there was an immediate burst of activity after Fulton came out and it was very much under Prime Ministerial direction. I got the impression . . . that by about 1969 it was tailing off a bit . . . with so many urgent problems at that time, I was not able to give my mind to it sufficiently'.[267] Listening to Wilson, as I did from the press bench in the Commons Committee Room, helped crystallise the growing conviction in my mind that he treated Whitehall as a kind of adventure playground-cum-laboratory with departments as so many pieces of Lego to be stuck together this way and that almost as the mood took him. He certainly gave rejigging the machinery of government a bad name as an activity.

Edward Heath, who had given his evidence a week before Wilson, delivered a vigorous defence of his 1970 reforms, regretted the diversion of the CPRS into 'these instant surveys' of the motor and power plant industries and the review of overseas representation then being carried out – 'it was not the purpose for which I set up the CPRS'.[268] Ever the systems analyst, Heath speculated on 'the question of the inertia of Whitehall' and, without going into detail, gave an account of the thinking that had lain behind the Cabinet committee cull he had ordered Sir John Hunt to carry out in 1973 and the thinking behind those mixed committees of which Wilson so disapproved:

> I have sometimes thought we have got what is, I know, the admiration of many people . . . a 'Rolls-Royce' Cabinet Secretariat and Cabinet Committee system. But it is so highly developed and so finely tuned that it can, of itself, take a long time before it produces results because it is

so devoted to securing argeement between those round the table . . . Can you change that? Well, you can do so if you say to the Secretary of the Cabinet, 'We cannot afford to have so many committees. It is using up far too much ministers' time. We must concentrate items in fewer committees.'[269]

Life on a press bench in a year-long series of select committee hearings has about it the kind of tedium that used to be associated with National Service in the Armed Forces. There are few memorable moments. One of them happened on 24 January 1977. It was the first time I had set eyes on the large, cheerful, yet peculiarly authoritative figure of Derek Rayner. It was the day William Armstrong also appeared before the English Committee. Armstrong went first. As he finished he saw Rayner waiting to take his place. I noticed the genuine warmth with which the two men greeted each other. Rayner told me later that Armstrong in the early 1970s had given him 'wholehearted support' for the changes he proposed in defence procurement.[270]

Rayner's evidence was not particularly long. But from his brief opening statement he left a strong impression upon me with his description of failure-avoidance as *the* dominant trait of the Whitehall culture:

Efficiency in the Civil Service is dependent, as in business, on motivation, and whereas in business one is judged by overall success, in my experience the civil servant tends to be judged by failure. This inevitably conditions his approach to his work in dealing with the elimination of unnecessary paper work, and in eliminating excessive monitoring, and leads to the creation of an unnecessary number of large committees, all of which leads to delays in decision-taking and the blurring of responsibility.[271]

Rayner went on to say that the Civil Service had been required to take on substantial new management tasks: 'No sensible business would undertake them at this rate without attracting new blood to help deal with them. I do not believe that the present top rates of pay in the Civil Service will attract the top management from industry who can come in and deal with some of these senior management tasks.'[272]

Rayner did not spare the MPs themselves. Replying to a question from Nicholas Ridley he said:

I hope that I am not speaking out of turn, but I really cannot overemphasise the effect that Parliamentary committees have upon the conduct of the average civil servant. They continually have in mind that one day they may be asked to account for what they have done, and it

> is a very powerful force in the way in which they conduct their lives . . . if the only time they appear it is to be censured, their motivation is to avoid mistakes.[273]

He ended with a pre-echo, though nobody could know it then, of the essence of Raynerism when that other 'ism' – Thatcherism – gave him the chance to do something about the Whitehall culture. Talking about 'the whole paraphernalia of working within the Civil Service' Rayner concentrated his fire on those two prime artefacts of bureaucracy, 'the inevitable piece of paper and the almost inevitable committee'.[274] In that interminable series of grey hearings, Derek Rayner seemed, and was, a breath of fresh air.

Another enlivening feature of the English Committee's sessions, though in a very different way, was the aggressive questioning of Brian Sedgemore, the Labour MP who had the unusual distinction of being radicalised as a young man by his experience as an assistant principal in the old administrative class.[275] When the English Committee finally reported in July 1977, it was Sedgemore's alternative draft which captured the headlines, much to the fury of the bulk of the Expenditure Committee, a majority of whose members had voted it down, 15–11.[276]

The main report, it must be admitted, was workmanlike rather than exciting. It was Fulton-like in tone, urging 'a determined drive to introduce accountable units in all areas of executive work and, where possible, in administration work',[277] though it wanted to partly undo Fulton by putting back into the Treasury the CSD's manpower and efficiency work.[278] Again the *cabinet* notion surfaced – 'A Minister should be free to adopt any organisation he thinks fit for the efficient discharge of business, including a group of advisers, or even backbench MPs, with executive authority in the department.'[279]

Brian Sedgemore's alternative report, whatever the merits of its contents, burned through the page by comparison with the one adopted. It opened with an unrestrained attack on the distribution of power in society:

> Politicians exist to improve society by facilitating social change. That they are not very successful at this is in part due to the structure of power in our society which is undemocratic and hence unresponsive to changing needs and circumstances.[280]

The senior Civil Service was the unmistakable villain of the Sedgemore piece:

> There is a conflict between their superior intellect and the little that they have to offer in a practical way. There is, or should be, no role in

our society for people with little to offer in a practical way, but civil servants have got round this stumbling block by inventing a role for themselves. The role that they have invented for themselves is that of governing the country. They see themselves, to the detriment of democracy, as politicians writ large. And of course as politicians writ large they seek to govern the country acccording to their own narrow, well-defined interests, tastes, education and background, none of which fit them on the whole to govern a modern, technological, industrialised, pluralist and urbanised society.[281]

It is hard to recall a piece of select committee literature to match the Sedgemore declaration of 1977. His remedies were the conscious construction of a countervailing power based on elected people (MPs in *cabinets*), political appointments to the top three grades of the Civil Service, a dramatic diminution of official secrecy and the creation of 'powerful investigatory committees on a systematic basis covering the work of each department by the House of Commons'.[282] Brian Sedgemore went on to elaborate his thesis and his prescriptions for 'a country where democracy has gone to sleep'[283] in a spirited book, *The Secret Constitution*, published in 1980 after he had lost his seat in the general election of the previous year.[284]

None of this appealed to the cautious former Inland Revenue officer in No. 10 (the third former civil servant in succession to fill the premiership, an unprecedented run which is unlikely to be surpassed). Callaghan was, however, interested in the question of rejigging the central departments and changing that mobile but always unsatisfactory frontier between the Treasury and the CSD. The most dramatic of the English Committee hearings took place on 14 February 1977 when John Hunt, in a carefully prepared presentation that can only have been compiled with the knowledge and permission of Callaghan, rehearsed the machinery-of-government options for the central departments. Though his personal preference was surrounded by caveats it seemed clear enough:

I ought to declare a personal interest in that for a very long time – and let me say that this was the case when I was within the Treasury – I was a believer in the idea of a Bureau of the Budget, combining expenditure and manpower. I think that there is a very strong case for this, but whenever I discussed it I was always convinced at the end of the day that because of the size of our public sector and the importance of it in balancing the economy, you could not really separate this from managing the economy ... I have always felt that it was arguable that over time, this objection would become less strong, because macroeconomic policy, I think, is becoming increasingly a matter of argument.[285]

The 'old tank' in the Treasury, as Roy Jenkins once called Denis Healey,[286] was not pleased by such headlines as 'Dismantling of the Treasury is Suggested'[287] in the following day's newspapers. At a meeting of the Cabinet's economic strategy committee that morning he was reported as greeting Hunt with the words: 'Morning John, I'm going to appear before the select committee and suggest the Cabinet Office is split up!'[288] As Desmond Quigley later wrote after an interview with the retiring Hunt, 'Sir John concedes that he did not make himself popular with his suggestion, but he is unrepentant and with a slightly mischievous smile suggests that it at least "stirred the pot".'[289]

Healey's view of the proposal was blunt and unequivocal: 'You don't take out a man's appendix while he's lifting a grand piano'[290] – the 'grand piano' being economic recovery and stabilisation after the punishing IMF autumn. It became plain that Callaghan, sensibly enough, would avoid a battle with Healey. It was simply not worth jeopardising their relationship over it. The Economic Seminar was the alternative way of opening up economic policy, albeit within a very limited circle, though, as Bernard Donoughue later disclosed, the remarkably resilient Healey during the IMF weeks seemed virtually to collapse at one point and the possibility of appointing a new Chancellor was floated.[291] Had Callaghan won the 1979 general election, those privy to his thinking are convinced, Healey would have moved to his career's desire, the Foreign Office, and Callaghan, the main obstacle gone, would have split the Treasury along the lines favoured by Hunt into a Ministry of Finance and an Office of Management and Budget, destroying the unloved CSD in the process.[292]

The other part of the machine which attracted the Prime Minister's attention was the Foreign Office. The story, which began when Callaghan was still Foreign Secretary in 1975, is a little classic as it was immensely revealing of the FO, the British Establishment and the post-Rothschild CPRS which carried out the Review of Overseas Representation, or ROR as it was known, and suffered a huge, largely self-inflicted, wound as a result. Those involved still carry the scars. David Young, the tough man of the CPRS team which conducted it (he was on secondment from the Ministry of Defence), said six years later: 'It was a devastating experience, and one that I found it difficult to talk about for two years afterwards.'[293] For Sir Kenneth Berrill, 'It was an own goal. It was one of those cases where, when asked to do a piece of work, frankly, as Head of the Tank, I should have found a reason for not doing it.'[294]

The affair began innocuously enough in 1975 when the CPRS sent a paper to Callaghan saying it was time to have another review along the lines of the Duncan Report of 1968. Callaghan replied to Berrill saying, 'Yes, I think you're right and you'd better do it.'[295] The alarm bells should have rung when it became apparent that the Review of Overseas

Representation was going to absorb a substantial proportion of the Tank's manpower (six of them to be precise) for eighteen months both in London and on an extensive series of fact-finding trips abroad. Berrill later admitted that in 1975 he did not 'think through adequately whether we were the right people to do it and what it might involve in terms of time, effort and [the] incredibly detailed recommendations which it in fact led to'.[296]

The CPRS immediately encountered difficulties with the Foreign Office as the idea was that the ROR would go further than any previous review and examine *all* aspects of overseas representation at home and abroad and not just those managed by the Diplomatic Service. The clear implication of this approach was that the very survival of the Diplomatic Service as a separate entity was open to question. Berrill explained it in these terms: 'Do remember that it was the role of the Think Tank – as Victor Rothschild said – to think the unthinkable, to take a whole history and experience apart and hold it up and see if it was right.'[297]

The terms of reference of the ROR eventually emerged in Parliament on 14 January 1976 as:

> To review the nature and extent of our overseas interests and requirements and in the light of that review to make recommendations on the most suitable, effective and economic means of representing and promoting those interests both at home and overseas. The review will embrace all aspects of the work of overseas representation, including political, economic, commercial, consular and immigration work, defence matters, overseas aid and cultural and information activities, whether these tasks are performed by members of Her Majesty's Diplomatic Service, by members of the Home Civil Service, by members of the Armed Forces or by other agencies financially supported by Her Majesty's Government.[298]

But, according to a book published before the ROR itself, the original CPRS submission to Mr Callaghan in November 1975 indicated that the Tank wanted to go much further. It was, wrote Joe Haines, then Wilson's Press Secretary, doctored by FO officials before it reached the Foreign Secretary's desk. He indicated that such matters as the number and cost of cars used by diplomats was included in the original submission.[299]

The manner in which the Diplomatic Service mobilised to defend itself between the winter of 1975 and the summer of 1977 was very impressive. At the highest level, its head, Sir Michael Palliser, Permanent Secretary to the Foreign and Commonwealth Office, fought his corner strongly in a steering committee chaired by Hunt (and including Berrill and Douglas Allen, Head of the Home Civil Service) which met to review progress and discuss drafts.[300] At the intermediate level, Sir Andrew Stark was recalled from the embassy in Copenhagen to run a liaison group inside the FO which became known inside the CPRS as the 'anti-Tank unit'.[301]

At the lowest level, a great deal of scuttlebut and disinformation was spread among MPs and sympathetic journalists. To one Whitehall-watcher, it showed that the FO had not forgotten the arts of black propaganda it displayed in the days of the Political Warfare Executive in the Second World War.[302] The female members of the ROR team were singled out for particularly vicious treatment. Miss Kate Mortimer and Dr Tessa Blackstone endured more vilification than any woman public servant before or since. Dr Blackstone, an educational sociologist, later recalled:

> 'Dark-eyed evil genius' was the term that was used. I think that I was singled out for perhaps two or three different reasons. Firstly, because I came from outside Whitehall . . . [secondly,] I came from the London School of Economics which was seen as a radical institution that bred presumably radical people who had outrageous ideas. Thirdly, I was a woman working in an area where there are very few women. The people concerned were understandably a bit defensive at being asked rather fundamental questions about their role . . . by two youngish women. Perhaps my style is somewhat abrasive, and that's something they were also unused to.[303]

By early 1977, MPs, on the Conservative side mainly, began to receive highly sophisticated breakdowns of the manpower and budget of the Diplomatic Service. The British FO, it seemed, cost no more to run than Wandsworth Borough Council, the implication being that a Rolls-Royce system of overseas representation came cheap at that price.[304] Occasionally, the anti-Tank briefing descended into farce as it did in the spring of 1977 during a lunch at the Traveller's Club in Pall Mall, popularly known as the 'FO's Canteen', involving a clutch of senior men and pair of journalists from a quality newspaper.

The FO team, spread out as they were around a huge circular table in the Club's dining room, scored two unforgettable own goals. Gentlemanly scorn was poured upon the Tank's scepticism about the value of political reporting from embassies abroad. It was simply not true that all that ministers needed to know could be found each morning in the foreign news pages of *The Times* and the *Financial Times*. Occasionally, such a view had validity. For example, there was no way Mrs Gandhi could lose tomorrow's general election in India. One did not need the Head of Chancery in the High Commission in New Delhi to remind one that the Congress Party had not lost an election since independence in 1947. Mrs Gandhi went down to defeat the next day.

The second own goal showed just how easily the most careful planning and attention to *placement* can backfire. At the end of this disquisition on the indispensable subtleties of top-flight political reporting, there was an explosion from a representative of the 'other ranks' of the Diplomatic Service brought along to show just how democratic and representative an outfit it was. The man in question, who bore a marked physical resemblance to the late Ernest Bevin, the greatest (in every sense) of postwar foreign secretaries, erupted. It was all very well to go on about sending beautifully drafted telegrams back home. People forgot what the bulk of Diplomatic Service life was like, the awfulness of the other ranks' existence in hardship posts. Nobody ever talked about what it was like being stuck for days on end at a port in the tropics with the stinking body of a dead expatriate waiting for a freighter to take it home to England. At this point, there was a great deal of cutlery-rearranging and a sweeping of crumbs from the tablecloth by the officer class as 'Ernie Bevin' slumped back into his chair.[305]

As the ROR team travelled the world – the pair with the highest security clearance and the requisite foreign and defence background did the secret intelligence part which was never published – a backcloth of ever deepening economic crisis unfolded at home. This was the era of the IMF visit and the 'Fortress Britain' exercise which examined for the Cabinet the pros and cons of a siege economy and in which the two economists on the ROR, John Odling-Smee and Kate Mortimer, were closely involved.[306] This had two effects which influenced the final product. First, it made the reviewers perhaps excessively pessimistic about Britain's future diplomatic and foreign policy role; second, according to his many defenders in the regular Whitehall machine, it distracted Sir Kenneth Berrill's attention from the ROR until the spring of 1977 when drafting was well under way, the argument being that some of the report's more controversial sections would have been diluted had he been directing his peripatetic half-dozen more closely.[307]

The scene was set at the drafting stage for the Establishment explosion that was to come when *The Guardian* leaked the Tank's preferred option – that the Diplomatic Service should be abolished as a separate entity, its functions grouped along with trade, overseas development and the rest as a foreign specialism within the Home Civil Service. The report, when it finally appeared on 3 August 1977, was a mammoth 442 pages. Roger Berthoud, son of an ambassador and brother of a diplomat, crammed its essence into an economically worded, yet all-embracing opening paragraph in the 'splash' story on the front page of *The Times* the following morning: 'A smaller, more specialised, less hospitable Diplomatic Service containing fewer diplomats and more home civil servants is called for in the long-awaited *Review of Overseas Representation* carried out by the Central Policy Review Staff published today.'[308]

The pent-up outrage of the FO was released. The Civil Service unions summoned another *Times* man to a sandwich lunch in the duty clerk's flat high up in the eaves of the Foreign Office building. There, with the strains of a military band floating up from St James's Park below on a perfect English summer's day, they let fly. One senior figure, who went on to become prominent in public life, said that when it came to defending his members' interests, he was as militant as Mr Arthur Scargill of the National Union of Mineworkers.[309] Another senior man declared: 'The epitome of the awfulness of the report is its pessimism. It is not what ministers have said. It is not what we believe. Sir Kenneth Berrill is well known in Whitehall for his pessimistic economic views.'[310]

This was a mere foretaste of what was to come. By concentrating on the entire span of overseas representation, as required by its terms of reference, the Tank touched several sensitive nervous systems – the Diplomatic Service, the Defence Attachés, the British Council, the BBC External Services – each with its own lobby of defenders, almost without exception of the Establishment variety. The correspondence columns of *The Times*, fondly known in those days as the 'Tom-Toms of the Establishment', reverberated for weeks. Far from the vested interests of British overseas representation passing through the wringer, it was the CPRS team which was put through it from the outset – hence David Young's inability to talk about it for two years.

Their ordeal was, in fact, spread over twelve months with difficult sessions at Chatham House before the stalwarts of the Royal Institute of International Affairs and, in the New Year of 1978, a grilling before a sub-group of the Commons Expenditure Committee whose members were very shirty about the relative youth of the team (Sir Kenneth deftly pointed out that their average age was thirty-seven, the same as that of Dr David Owen, then Foreign Secretary). Behind the scenes Dr Owen was engaged in his own operation to geld the ROR. Its battleground was GEN 89, a Cabinet committee chaired by Mr Callaghan, now Prime Minister, who, as Foreign Secretary, had commissioned the enterprise.[311]

More than five years later, the memory of the ROR could still arouse David Owen's ire:

> I thought it was hopeless, actually, because from the moment I arrived in the Foreign Office there was nothing you could do because everybody was waiting for the CPRS. So there was a great excuse not to take action. And then, of course, you were presented with this report which for a variety of reasons was immensely difficult to implement.
>
> I think it was a fatal, flawed decision, actually, to put the CPRS on to the Foreign Office. They're not geared to that type of investigation. It went wider than their proper brief. I think it damaged the CPRS and

it made it very much harder for me as Secretary of State, to make the changes that I actually wanted to make.[312]

The Owen reform plan was simple and narrowly focused: 'You cannot have dud ambassadors ... The able ones have got to be able to be promoted much earlier. People of 35, 38, ought to be having important ambassadorships and those people who do not meet the high requirements have got to be able to be golden-bowlered generously ... And if I had not had the CPRS report, I would certainly have got it through in my first year.'[313] Dr Owen concluded a secret deal with those at the summit of the Diplomatic Service hierarchy: 'I did make a sort of slight trade-off for the Foreign Office – okay, I'll ditch the report if you then support me on this up-and-out business.'[314] And ditch its main recommendation he did in the confines of GEN 89 where Sir Kenneth Berrill, who attended its meetings, found himself an isolated figure.[315]

The Callaghan Government's response to the ROR came in the form of a reply to the Commons Expenditure Committee report on the subject in August 1978. Far from accepting the ROR's philosophy of a foreign policy rethink to adjust traditional ambitions to straitened economic circumstances, Dr Owen's *The United Kingdom's Overseas Representation* opened with a statement of global ambition almost worthy of Ernest Bevin in the 1940s:

> The geographical and economic facts of life make it inevitable that today, as in previous centuries, British interests should extend round the world. The Government believe that Britain has the assets to defend her interests and effectively to promote her objectives. These assets include our economic and military strength as a nation; our historical ties with many members of the international community; the binding force of the English language; our unquestioned standing in the arts and sciences and our contribution to the world's cultural heritage; the example of British values and our country's democratic way of life; but above all the influence which we derive from co-operative and co-ordinated action with our partners in democracy.[316]

No trace of Little Englandism here. If the White Paper it approved was any guide, GEN 89 believed that Britain had the men, the methods and the money, too, for a first-class diplomatic effort:

> Politically, too, the position which we occupy in the principal areas of international affairs gives us a more than adequate springboard for an imaginative and effective foreign policy, and our resources can support

> the system of overseas representation which such a foreign policy entails.[317]

The White Paper demolished another central premise of the ROR. The Diplomatic Service would survive as an entity separate from the Home Civil Service. But the enterprise to which the CPRS had devoted such a disproportionate amount of manpower and time was not totally in vain. The Callaghan Government did propose a few marginal changes:

* A beefed-up system of interchange between the FO and seventeen home departments to produce 100 more secondments within five years and thought to be given to extending the process to industry, commerce, banking and the trade unions.
* A review of training for commercial officers in the Diplomatic Service.
* More mini-diplomatic missions abroad and a reduction in the size of posts; six subordinate posts to be closed with five more under review.
* The FO Research Department to be cut by 17 per cent, overseas information staff by 16 per cent and defence staff by 25 per cent.
* The British Council to be reviewed but not abolished.
* A management review of the Ministry of Overseas Development.
* A review of the BBC External Services' vernacular broadcasts but a world-wide 24-hour schedule to be maintained.

The White Paper's final put-down of the ROR was blandly dismissive:

> These changes are deliberately evolutionary in character. They aim to build on that which is already good, efficient and of proven value; yet also to establish a pattern capable of adapting to the future on the basis of a realistic but confident assessment of Britain's role in the world.[318]

The reaction of others was less politely phrased. The reputation of the CPRS as an institution, not just its one-off on overseas representation, sank like a stone. Sir Frank Cooper, who watched the exercise closely from across Whitehall in the Ministry of Defence, believes:

> The outcome did the CPRS a lot of harm, both within itself in relation to its own confidence and more particularly in and around Whitehall and Westminster. It lacked . . . skill in presentation. It manifestly looked wrong and felt wrong and was wrong on a number of important aspects.

And it was not . . . produced in such a way as to win friends and influence people.[319]

David Young agrees with much of that assessment by his old boss. He believes the main message of the report was lost:

I think that the argument at the beginning of the report about the relationship between economic power and influence in the world was wrong in fact and was certainly tactically wrong because it didn't lead to anything. I mean that time-scales were much longer than we supposed and it was something that offended politicians unnecessarily. I think some of the language in the report was unfortunate and I also myself think that we made a strategic error . . . in going for too many things at once and managed, therefore, to form an unholy alliance of the British Council, the External Services and the BBC, the Foreign Office, the Defence Attachés and so on.

All we were saying is that when you're dealing with complex economic [or] technological issues that the same people should be dealing with it around the world. Therefore, the chap who in Tokyo is talking to the Japanese Ministry about the need to rationalise the international car trade should be somebody who's actually done a spell in the Department of Industry office in Birmingham and understands the British motor car industry . . . you've got to bring London and overseas closer together.[320]

No one has dared tackle the FO from that day to this.

Callaghan was Attlee-like in the care he took of his time and energy. John Hunt was to remark later that 'he [Callaghan] did not want to involve himself in every issue; he would have liked almost an Attlee role – presiding as Chairman of the Cabinet and concentrating his efforts on the things of greatest importance and interest to him. He found this was impossible, however, and he had to get involved in all sorts of detail.'[321] Given his preoccupation with incomes policy and counter-inflation strategy it is not surprising, in those tough, pre-North Sea oil days, that Callaghan should have given a low priority to reforming the Diplomatic Service and to machinery-of-government matters generally, though he did dislike Heath-style mega-departments and took the opportunity of his reshuffle in September 1976 to winnow out Transport from Environment.[322] The impending retirement of Douglas Allen at the end of 1977, however, obliged him to ponder it. There were three candidates for the succession – Bancroft, Callaghan's former private secretary at the Treasury, Cooper and Nairne.[323] He saw all three before making up his mind.[324] Cooper, never a fan of the CSD, was not keen on inheriting the existing structure. He had long had a preference for a strong, freestanding and overtly independent Civil

Service Commission which would be led by the Head of the Home Civil Service. In Cooper's view, the Commission had been incorporated into the CSD in 1968 'largely to make up numbers'.[325] Callaghan, as we have seen, had no plans to rejig the machinery of government that side of an election, so Bancroft it was.

Bancroft, who hoped to set a tone like Bridges had done,[326] took over in January 1978 in very un-Bridges-like circumstances. The public portrait of his profession was harsher, nastier, than in 1950. Bancroft, sensitive and artistic, was a very different kind of man from the hard-boiled, no-nonsense Allen, though the exterior – 'smooth as monumental alabaster' according to one Civil Service union leader[327] – could be deceptive. One official who worked very closely with him described him as 'very much the mailed fist within within the velvet glove'.[328]

Bancroft always seemed to me to take the attacks on the Civil Service very personally – almost as if he was interposing his body, Lytton Strachey-like, between his profession and a hostile world. It was a noble but painful spectacle for those who knew him and liked him (though we had our differences – he was not an open government man and did not pretend to be – I came into that category). He did a good deal of work on the Civil Service's public profile and presided over a review of the Civil Service image led by a CSD under secretary, Mike Power, a former district commissioner of great charm who joined the Admiralty (he came from a naval family) after Kenya obtained its independence in 1963. The work had started after an initiative of Sir Patrick Nairne's in the autumn of 1977 while Douglas Allen was still in post. By the time it was completed in May 1978, Bancroft had succeeded him. As a result of the Power Report an Image Unit was set up in the CSD. It would meet early in the day to pluck the previous night's news bulletins and current affairs programmes off its video and tape recorders and to read the morning papers. If there was criticism and it was unfair, the permanent secretary of the affected department would be urged to write a letter putting the miscreant right; if it was justified, the permanent secretary would be asked to put his house in order.[329] The Image Unit did not survive the 1979 general election. Mike Power's video was sold off as part of the CSD's post-election cuts exercise – the first piece of State property to be privatised under Mrs Thatcher.

Whitehall was directly and grimly affected by the 1978–9 winter crisis which led to the fall of Callaghan as surely as its predecessor of 1973–4 had led to the fall of Heath. As happened in the IMF autumn, crisis led some officials to be asked to do some bizarre things as part of their service to ministers. The Civil Contingencies Unit, product of the Heath–Jellicoe rethink of emergency planning in 1972, increasingly became the focus of ministerial and official attention – and the symbol of their weakness, too, as the Labour movement seemed ever more hellbent on destroying the Labour Government. During the lorry drivers' strike of 1978–9, Sir Clive Rose from the Cabinet Office, Peter Lazarus from the Department of Transport and John Moss from the Ministry of Agriculture would file grimly into Transport House each afternoon to take up with the Transport and General Workers' Union all too many breaches of their voluntary code on picketing.[330] Apart from anything else, this was an odd constitutional position in which the civil servants found themselves, treating almost as mendicants with Mr Alex Kitson of the T&G.

The Government slowly subsided in a welter of bitterness and despair while a helpless Civil Service looked on. Callaghan wanted to declare a state of emergency but his ministerial colleagues talked him out of it: 'My instinct was in favour of doing so as a demonstration of our determination, but it was argued that it was very uncertain whether a declaration would do much practical good.'[331] His Transport Secretary, William Rodgers, later gave a graphic account of the meeting on 13 January 1979 at which the powerlessness of central government was apparent to all:

> When ... I urged the need to move vital medical supplies out of Hull docks, defence ministers were adamant and bland: 'It will take days to put a suitable convoy together'. Nor did they have available any detailed plans of the docks to tell them where to go ... The Home Secretary, advised by the Cabinet Office, was no more eager for the risks involved. The declaration of a State of Emergency had been considered by the Prime Minister but rejected, and it was to be considered and rejected again.[332]

Whitehall was waiting for the Callaghan administration to expire, and the Prime Minister knew it. He told Bernard Donoughue the day before he flew off to Guadeloupe for the World Economic Summit that 'it is all falling apart ... I think ministers and their departments are quietly selling out. We are going to wake up soon and find that everybody in the public sector is settling for 20 per cent and the pay policy has been sunk.'[333]

It was the issue of devolution to Scotland which finally sank Callaghan when his Government lost a vote of confidence on 28 March 1979. But the *real* Exocet was clear to all. As Bill Rodgers wrote:

> The trade unions had defeated the Labour Government and opened wide the doors to Mrs Thatcher. They had also defeated themselves. A Conservative Government would ensure that they were never the same again.[334]

The change of government in 1979 also ensured that the Civil Service was never the same again. Before we see how and why, it would be sensible to examine the contemporary system of central government and the people who staff it, run it and advise it.

PART TWO | SYSTEM

Almost entirely, the functions and working of this intricate mechanism, perhaps the most perfect, efficient and disinterested the world has ever seen, is the product of convention, tradition and administrative practice.
Lord Hailsham on 'The Government Machine', 1978[1]

All new governments inherit a system, well-oiled and well run-in. Mrs Thatcher was no exception in 1979. Having brought the story of the Civil Service from, to take its top men of the day, Henry the Treasurer to Ian Bancroft, it is a good idea to pause before taking a detailed look at *very* recent history, and to acquire an idea of the constituent parts of this 'intricate mechanism', as Lord Hailsham called it. In the course of doing so, I shall examine the Thatcher effect on the practice of Cabinet government, which is a different, though related, question to her treatment of the Civil Service.

7 POLICY-MAKING IN OPPOSITION

Parties come to power with silly, inconsistent and impossible policies because they have spent their whole period in opposition forgetting about the real world, destroying the lessons they learnt in government and clambering slowly back on to the ideological plain where they feel happiest.
Sir Adam Ridley, former Director, Conservative Research Department, 1985.[1]

The Liberal Party has repeatedly talked about 'preparing for government' but it has never actually begun to do so . . . we ought to be scared stiff of arriving there unprepared.
William Wallace, adviser to David Steel, 1985.[2]

They [the political parties] rely on pamphlets written on wet Sunday afternoons by somebody in his spare time who doesn't really give all his devotion to it . . . this is academics doing things free . . . somebody travels down from Glasgow or York or Oxford on the train. The scribble out a few notes about what they're going to say in the policy discussion later that evening.
Dick Taverne, SDP policy adviser, 1986.[3]

This room is standard for members of the Shadow Cabinet. It's totally inadequate for our needs . . . My secretary . . . my research assistant and I have to co-exist in a space, what, about ten by twelve feet. This is simply no way to run a parliamentary democracy.
Dr John Cunningham, Labour spokesman on the Environment, 1986.[4]

When you are in a government, five years is a very short time. When you are in opposition it is a hell of a long time.
Mrs Margaret Thatcher, 1987.[5]

> The promises and panaceas which gleam like false teeth in the party manifestos.
> **Lord Rothschild, 1976.**[6]

New British governments do not simply arrive raw in Whitehall like some triumphant resistance army hardened by years in the mountains avid for the soft life of the plains. They descend with manifestos, policy papers of varying degrees of sophistication and, in the case of the more zealous new ministers, a conviction that some of the great intractables will at last yield to the force of correct policy and political will. 'Manifestoitis', as Professor Finer calls it, is a peculiarly British phenomenon. Opposition parties on the continent are immune to it. There 'parties produce broad, bland statements of intent which don't have to be researched'.[7] Here manifesto pledges can acquire the status of Holy Writ to be defended against all-comers – our trade competitors, international bankers and hostile military powers abroad; the City, the chiefs of staff and the permanent secretaries at home.

Policy-making in opposition is an area relatively neglected by scholars. It should not be. A long, long road winds from initial idea to royal assent for the statute which embodies it. Flaws built in during the opposition stage can take a great deal of removing, particularly if they are enshrined in a manifesto and become a symbol of party machismo. There are those who recognise this and argue that a broad-brush approach to opposition policy-making is the only sensible course, as the party research departments, without the resources to undertake original research, cannot hope to succeed where Whitehall, royal commissions, research institutes and professional economists have failed on issues like economic growth and the reduction of unemployment. This is roughly the position of the Finer school. It is a view that enjoys the weighty support of no less a figure than Sir James Callaghan.[8] It has its advantages. It avoids hostages to fortune and parties taking power burdened with pledges on the dotty or the undoable. Support for such a view can be found in surprisingly technocratic quarters. Professor John Ashworth was a member of the CPRS and the Cabinet Office's Chief Scientist 1976–81. He believes that shadow cabinets should concentrate their time and energy on strategy, not detail:

> Once you've convinced yourself those strategies are right, and remember they have to be right politically as well as administratively . . . it's best then to throw the detail away because the actual detail which will face you when you come into government will almost certainly be different from the detail that you have had access to and that you've used in forming those opinions . . . What you are dealing with here is a mixture of administrative constraints and political imperatives that colour your

strategic choices. It's concentration on those which makes a government effective or ineffective.[9]

To allow day-to-day tactics to drive strategic policy is 'the route to disaster', says Professor Ashworth.

The minimalist school of opposition policy-making tends to point to the experience of the Heath administration of 1970–4 to buttress its case. Never had a government been better prepared for office. Edward Heath was a permanent secretary *manqué*. Indeed, his friends had the impression that had he been posted to the Treasury rather than to the Ministry of Civil Aviation as an assistant principal in 1948, Mr Heath could well have eschewed a political career, stayed in the Civil Service and served governments of both kinds as Sir Edward Heath KCB having reached the rank of permanent secretary round about 1965, the year he became Leader of the Conservative Party.[10] A very senior permanent secretary once said to me, 'Ted would have made a super permanent secretary'.[11] One product of this was the thinking which emerged from the Public Sector Research Unit which Mr Heath had set up under Ernest Marples.[12] As the 1970 election approached, plans were well advanced for the new style of government later embodied in the White Paper, *The Reorganisation of Central Government*.[13] After the famous Selsdon Park conference, a 'future legislation chart' was prepared by the Conservative Research Department which stipulated which bills the new government would introduce and in what order.[14] For the sceptical Professor Finer the question is:

> But what came of it? Well, one thing came of it I suppose and that is that the European Communities Act was passed which took Britain into the EEC, this is the one enduring monument of that administration ... A lot of the bills got put on the statute book, like the Industrial Relations Act, as planned. But two comments are worth making: the first is that the election was fought by the Conservatives on the issue of inflation. Inflation happens to be the one area that had not been researched in that period; the other point [is that] it all went by the board because by late 1972 Heath got very worried about rising unemployment and it's from then on that you have to date a complete U-turn, a wholly new direction of policy which made all that preparation – or most of it – irrelevant.[15]

The lesson, according to Professor Finer, is: 'let them be warned that futurology is, by definition, very tricky'.[16] The Finer thesis brings a heated rebuttal from some of those actually engaged in the business. Sir Adam Ridley, a civil servant in the Government Economic Service in the 1960s, was a member of Lord Rothschild's CPRS and became a key figure in the Conservative Research Department 1974–9. He writes:

> Professor Finer's views about the scope for making policy in the most vague and general terms of high principle are demonstrably bosh! It is easy to refute them with many counter examples ... When the Conservative Party was considering its immigration policy before the 1979 Election, it was quite clear that one could not undertake to implement any general philosophy or principles without determining first, whether these principles were compatible with the legal framework, and second, whether they were demonstrably feasible. Neither of these issues could be resolved even tentatively without some hard analysis and expert knowledge. In the event, one of the necessary instruments was a new nationality law. How one could have confidently asserted a general principle in a manifesto or an election campaign without that kind of groundwork being undertaken is beyond my comprehension! Countless other examples could be given.[17]

The Finer philosophy is also the butt of a practising opposition leader, Dr David Owen, a self-confessed 'detail man' ('I am obsessed by policy; probably too obsessed by it'[18]). For Dr Owen, sticking to generalities is not an option in the eighties:

> In the olden days, people would say, 'Ah well, politicians should stick to principles', and you hear some of the politicians talking like that. But I don't think they've any idea of the pressures that are now put on ... You go to a meeting with CND these days and you talk about minimum deterrence and you'd be eaten alive if you're not capable of arguing with them what the weapons systems are – the range of a missile, the megatonnage, they know the ABM [the Anti-Ballistic Missile Treaty 1972] inside out. They know all the details of these things. And that could be mirrored in many other areas. You talk about housing policy, you talk to Shelter, they're experts ... The old days of the generalist politician who came in with a sort of broad brush approach to life was over. It was probably finished by the end of the sixties.[19]

Sir Adam Ridley was intimately involved in the one example of opposition policy-making that has surpassed that of the Heath period in the late sixties. A decade later, the Conservative Party in preparing for power went along two tracks: the detailed policy-making of the Conservative Research Department and the heady combination of evangelism and policy which emerged from the private, free-market think-tank, the Centre for Policy Studies, founded by Mrs Margaret Thatcher and Sir Keith Joseph in 1974 (with Mr Heath's approval, ironically). Policy planning *and* philosophy became intertwined as the Conservative Party thought anew about the lessons of 1972–4, the period after Mr Heath's U-turn.

When Mrs Thatcher arrived in Downing Street in May 1979, as we have seen, she struck Whitehall with the force of a tornado. The Civil Service does what it can to find out what an Opposition is up to, though formal contacts were taboo until the Douglas-Home Rules, drawn up in 1964 when Sir Alec was Prime Minister and Labour had been out of office for thirteen years, permit meetings between shadow ministers and permanent secretaries in the immediate run-up to an election. But in 1979 Whitehall was taken unawares. The Bank of England knew of the intention to abolish exchange controls because, with the permission of Denis Healey, the Labour Chancellor of the Exchequer, the Conservatives had been to see Gordon Richardson, Governor of the Bank, before the election. But the determination to stick to its monetary policy and the detail of its public expenditure planning came as a surprise to the Treasury.[20] Of the activities of the Centre for Policy Studies (two of whose most energetic adherents, Sir John Hoskyns and Norman Strauss, went into the No. 10 Policy Unit) the Civil Service machine knew even less.[21]

The Whitehall drill for acquiring intelligence on an Opposition party has an overt and a covert side. It scans pamphlets, party statements, speeches, parliamentary questions and transcripts of interviews. This is rather akin to Kremlinology, learning about personality and policies at several stages removed: paper intelligence for a paper culture. In addition there is a clandestine network which attempts to remedy this unsatisfactory state of affairs, which has been described by William Wallace, an adviser to David Steel, when Leader of the Liberal Party. Thanks to his post as Director of Studies at the Royal Institute of International Affairs (Chatham House), Dr Wallace is plugged in to this informal network:

> We are back to all of the awful mechanisms of the British Establishment which are the only way to operate – Oxford dinner tables, country cottages, dinner tables around London where people can talk without being seen – that has to be the main area of operation. The institute world, the conference circuit, provide other areas of contact . . . you have to talk when you can.[22]

It is a very chancy business, depending as it does on who knows whom sufficiently well to risk the wrath of those in authority in the Shadow Cabinet and the real Cabinet. It has an air of John Le Carré's 'Moscow Rules'.[23] You would not think that those involved were fellow citizens of a free society with a common interest in good government. It is an area crying out for the attention of any serious reformer.

More important still is the quality of what Norman Strauss calls policy research and development that goes on in Opposition. There is a barrage of criticism about this from back-room boys like Dick Taverne ('it was by and large a shambles'[24]) or Adam Ridley who contrasts the strength in numbers of the three hundred top officials in the Treasury alone with the two dozen young graduates in the Conservative Research Department;[25] from a front-room person like David Owen who thinks the £62,000 of public money the SDP received each year (pre-split) for its parliamentary work was 'totally inadequate to even pay for the Leader's office and the bare essentials of parliamentary activity';[26] and from a former top civil servant like Sir Frank Cooper who, having experienced five changes of government during his Whitehall career, describes the output of the party research departments on his speciality, defence and foreign policy, as 'patchy', adding, 'but I'm perhaps being too generous, there were more dull patches than bright patches which is not very surprising because, obviously, in a number of areas, access to data is not very great'.[27]

The result is not at all healthy if one subscribes to the view that in a democracy, the wishes of elected people, ministers, should in the end prevail over those of appointed people, civil servants. The two sides who, at the flick of the electorate's wrist, can be transformed into intimate partners at the highest level of government, prepare for this eventuality like two rival armies watching each other in the night. Papers are prepared for presentation to each other on day one of government or, if machinery-of-government changes are involved, at the 'Douglas-Home' meetings in the run-up to the election. There is a grave imbalance here. Whitehall has the best information bank in the country; it has experience, continuity, current knowledge often of a highly classified kind and 4,000 top Civil Service policy-makers to assess and make use of it. An Opposition party has between ten and twenty front bench shadows, an overstretched research capability of thirty often inexperienced people at the maximum and an information bank almost wholly restricted to open material in the most closed information society in the advanced western world. The problem is particularly acute where genuine security is involved as it can be in defence or foreign policy and it can be compounded where a new minister is entirely fresh to the field having shadowed something else in Opposition. The result was described in a BBC radio interview in 1986 by Sir Frank Cooper:

> HENNESSY: Sir Frank, the Ministry of Defence . . . is one of the most complicated of all government departments, in the sense that it has deeply technical issues and very complicated strategic issues, on which ministers must decide collectively. What is it like for a raw untrained minister with no particular background in the defence field, who suddenly finds himself thrust into your old world, how unprepared are they for the tasks which immediately confront them?
>
> COOPER: Well, I think it's a very very difficult job for anybody new to do, even though they might be well prepared. But the great majority of

them, of course, are not well prepared. You can count really on the fingers of one hand the number of defence ministers since World War II who'd really studied the subject deeply, and the turn-over rate, of course, is extremely high.

HENNESSY: Has it got worse in recent years, where the technical and technocratic problems that your ministry threw up for its ministers were getting worse in the span that you served there from the late forties to the early eighties?

COOPER: No doubt they are getting worse, and they will go on getting worse, when you look at some of the problems themselves. Just look, at the moment, for example, at the AWACS airborne early warning aircraft, it's a terribly difficult problem, even if you've studied that kind of issue all your life, you'd find it extremely difficult. And one must have, I think, the greatest sympathy with any secretary of state, who has that coming across his desk. It's difficult even if you were in one of our large major industrial high-tech companies. But for somebody who's also got to put it in a political environment, it's even more difficult.

HENNESSY: Did you notice the politicians themselves trying to raise their game to match these new circumstances as it were to try and get better preparation in the opposition years for these problems?

COOPER: Not really because I think most prime ministers and putative prime ministers keep a lot of their team on edge by wondering which job, who is going to get [it] and the number who really are quite clear that they're going to get a particular position, I think, is quite small.

HENNESSY: What's the practical penalty of this lack of preparedness when they come in, how does the Civil Service, the military and the scientific community and the ministry of defence help them up their learning curve? It must be a crash course in many ways?

COOPER: Oh, it is very much a crash course, and I think the Civil Service as a whole does prepare very carefully for a change of government. They have massive briefings of all kinds ready for any incoming administration. The problem is that it's a terribly indigestible mess for somebody to try and absorb let alone digest within a very short period of time. The learning curve in a complex department, a big department, is very long indeed, and even if you'd been sort of professional in Whitehall, it's very very difficult for somebody to come from another Whitehall department to Defence and be effective within it. That's always been the case. So for a minister it really is hard work and don't forget he's got a lot of other things to do as well as run the department.

HENNESSY: Doesn't it mean almost inevitably that a new secretary of state for defence and his ministers of state are prisoners of the machine, prisoners of the departmental orthodoxy?

COOPER: I think if you go into any kind of new job in any kind of

> environment, to some extent you are prisoners, which is a somewhat emotive word, I think, of the new machine, you're bound to rely on skilled advisers and after a little period of time, which I think depends very much on the ability of the minister concerned, he or she will find out and put some personal value on the ability, or otherwise and the helpfulness or otherwise of those advisers . . . A great number of ministers go through exactly that process when they attain office.[28]

What is so galling about the problem of policy-making in Opposition is that, apart from Labour in 1945, which had a near-complete ministerial team hardened by the realities of wartime coalition government, *au fait* with issues and well past the learning curve stage,[29] every new administration is hobbled by the same factors. Foreseeable problems should be so much more remediable than unknowable ones. This particular cyclical problem can be broken down into four parts: money, people, secrecy and customers.

Opposition policy-making is a shoestring affair. In December 1986, the party research effort consisted of the following:

Conservative Research Department
24 'desk officers'[30]
Budget not disclosed. An informed 'guesstimate' put it around £500,000 a year.[31]

Labour Party Research Department
17 researchers
Budget: £360,000 per annum.[32]

SDP Policy Department (Pre-split)
3 researchers (normally 5)
Budget: £75,000 per annum.[33]

Liberal Party Research Department (Pre-split)
3 researchers, 1 information officer
Budget: £46,000 per annum.[34]

In addition to this there is the Short money alluded to by David Owen, so-called after Edward Short, now Lord Glenamara, the Labour Leader of the House of Commons who established the principle of public subsidy to political parties in 1975. It is allocated solely for parliamentary work but it can be used in ways which augment research capability. The Short money, since the most recent rejigging of the rules in 1985, is allocated on the basis of £1,500 for each seat in Parliament plus £3 for every 200 votes won at the previous general election, with an overall ceiling of £450,000 per party per year. This broke down as follows:

Labour	£440,000
Liberal (Pre-split)	£88,000
SDP (Pre-split)	£62,000
Others	£40,000[35]

In Labour's case, the distribution of Short cash enables each frontbench shadow spokesman to receive £9,000 a year for the purposes of hiring a research assistant, but, as its environment spokesman, Dr John Cunningham, explains, 'it would be impossible for me to work anything like effectively without a full-time person, so I have to raise the additional resources to pay a full-time researcher myself'.[36] For the SDP, an additional input from Westminster research assistants was a significant contribution, according to Dr Owen: 'The policy unit of our party [has] never been more than three and sometimes down to two and [they] work appalling hours ... [they have] been helped by having some research assistants to MPs who've also produced a great deal of effort'.[37]

Geoff Bish, Labour's veteran Policy Director, who, in Peter Kellner's words, 'has spent much of his adult life trying to instil common sense into the party only to see his efforts crushed between party dementia and electoral hostility',[38] has no doubts 'that all my researchers are overworked in terms of being able to do policy development properly'.[39] When Labour was in office in the seventies he had high but vain hopes of organising formalised links between Transport House and ministers' special advisers, *cabinets* no less.[40] Not that he was overawed by the weight and majesty of the massed brainpower of Whitehall. 'Where the Civil Service falls down', he told me, 'is its lack of understanding of what makes ordinary people tick. The experience needed in a policy adviser is not necessarily reflected in the level of a university degree. My people are active in the Labour Party and the trade unions. Their reactions to events are likely to be more intelligent and realistic than those of a bright young thing straight from Oxbridge.'[41]

But bright young things, whatever their provenance and familiarity with ordinary people, have to be paid for by the political parties themselves without the benefit of more than a trickle of Treasury support. If you add the Short money and the party research budgets together, the tally is about £1,611,000. It cost £27m, almost seventeen times that amount, to hold the 1987 general election.[42] The taxpayer is skimping on democracy.

For a complete research picture to be drawn, one must include the services of the House of Commons Library, which are available to all 650 members on an individual basis. The Library as a whole is funded to the tune of nearly £2.5 m, 'a very cost-effective use of resources', according to the Top Salaries Review Body's review of Parliamentary allowances in

1987.[43] Of that about £630,000 is allocated to the research division of some twenty specialist senior staff deployed as follows:

Economic affairs	4
Statistics	5½
Education and social services	4
Home affairs	4
Scientific affairs and defence	2½[44]

In party political terms, experienced researchers do not come cheap. Sir Adam Ridley has vividly expressed the problem using the public ownership/privatisation issue as his example:

> If you consider the position of an opposition spokesman, with perhaps his secretary, half his research assistant, occasional background papers from the House of Commons Library and a third of the time of a very harassed 24-year-old English graduate somewhere in his research department, and then ask yourself how is he going to plan the nationalisation of steel and pharmaceuticals and the commanding heights of the economy? Or how, indeed, is he going to plan the denationalisation of the British National Oil Corporation or ICL or whatever it may be, you can see straight away that the challenge is enormous.[45]

If, taking Sir Adam's example, one needs to buy the time of a person with powerful analytical skills *and* first-hand experience of industry, the sum required is around £50,000 a year. At the other end of the scale, £10,000 a year will buy a powerful but inexperienced young university-trained intellect. Under-funding Opposition research effort has two consequences: over-reliance on young people whose high political charge makes them willing to work for a low return (a combination of burning political faith and inexperience is not the ideal make-up for a researcher facing issues of immense complexity); and a resort to seasoned academics cobbling up position papers on wet Sunday afternoons, the dons-on-trains syndrome described by Dick Taverne.

It was Dick Taverne's exercise on tax and benefits undertaken for the SDP in 1985–6 which most graphically illustrated the high price the country pays for excessive Whitehall secrecy. The overlap between tax and benefits, whereby one bit of Whitehall, the DHSS, gives, only to have another part, the Inland Revenue, claw it back, has long been recognised as a messy, wasteful absurdity. However, it is the blackest of the black holes of British social policy into which past governments have ventured never to return. The problems are huge and genuine. Sorting it out is a problem to tax a technocratic genius. Any solution requires one to slaughter an abattoir full of sacred cows in the form of cherished benefits or tax reliefs. There will be gainers *and* losers, and losers have votes.

In many ways the conditions were auspicious for the Taverne enterprise. He himself relished the task. A former Labour Financial Secretary to the Treasury in the late sixties, Mr Taverne was experienced in the ways of politics and administration, highly numerate and the founder of a superb private think-tank, the Institute for Fiscal Studies. He was also reporting to a political leader, Dr Owen, who had made a virtue of being both a no-sacred-cows man and a detail man.

The IFS, 'an alternative Civil Service', as Mr Taverne calls it,[46] had done a great deal of work on tax and benefits. It is a non-party organisation offering its services to all-comers. One of its staff was seconded to the Taverne working party – 'if it hadn't been for that we wouldn't have produced what I think was one of the best researched and well-thought-out proposals for reform that had been produced certainly by the SDP and I'd say almost any party'.[47] There were snags. When the document was published in the summer of 1986[48] the press concentrated on the losers and bursts of unfortunate phraseology. Refinements were promised. There were fears that a clear-cut strategic solution would be fudged by a welter of special cases.

Quite separately, there was another problem. *The* great experts on implementation are not in the IFS but in Whitehall, a phone-call away. Such is the taboo on contacts between Opposition and Civil Service that neither side could pick up the telephone.

> It would have saved us an awful lot of time if we'd had civil servants there ... because we would have not had to work all these things out very elaborately ourselves. The Civil Service could have given us the answers on the spot. You gain an awful lot by having the Civil Service there. They're very good about pointing out the snags. IFS ... knows probably more about tax than the DHSS. It knows probably more about social security than the Inland Revenue. But the Inland Revenue will still know more about tax and the DHSS will still know more about social security ... What is really needed is first, really well-researched proposals which draw on the alternative civil service [i.e. the IFS] and then a public discussion of these proposals in which, preferably, civil servants should take part. It's said that twenty civil servants are now [autumn 1986] beavering away at the DHSS and in the Inland Revenue to try and prove how awful they are, or what they would cost, or who's going to lose. Now why shouldn't this be done publicly?[49]

Why not, indeed? Tax and benefits policy is of no interest to the KGB. It is of vital concern to the public whom both Civil Service and political parties claim to serve. The secrecy argument can be taken further. Without an easing of the rules, much of the raw material of informed policy-making is kept inside those Whitehall departments who use public money to gather it, tilting still further the imbalance of forces between government, its wholly legitimate competitor parties and the House of Commons select committees who have done much but could do much more to enrich the supply of data on which Opposition policy-makers can draw.

There is a final problem here. Do Opposition policy-makers really want to apply their minds to the hard grind of top-class policy analysis? If they do not, no amount of extra money, high-calibre people and improved information is going to make any difference. The prospect can be dispiriting for would-be suppliers like Sir Adam Ridley:

> The thing that strikes one above all, if you've been through the process of working with a party recently, arriving in Opposition, is the following unsurprising phenomenon.
>
> When politicians retreat to Opposition, they retreat to the familiar ideological high ground where they're happiest. And why do they feel happiest there, and how does this come about? Well, partly because the role of an Opposition is ideological. It is preaching. It is pummelling the table on matters of principle. It is evangelism. It's partly negative things. When you're a minister, you see the reality of day-to-day decision making, the complexity of ordinary life, the need to argue things with countless groups. All these things you get distanced from as you become an ordinary MP on the back benches. The officials aren't there, the departments aren't there, the papers aren't there.
>
> In addition, you have other little considerations, which subtly change the scheme within days of a government going into Opposition. New shadow spokesmen are promoted. They may not have had much direct responsibility for the department that they speak for. They may have had no formal government responsibility at all. And to support them, you have a really modest staff, not the enormous resources of the Civil Service. You may have almost none at all, indeed. Therefore, if you look at it from the point of view of the eager, aggressive individual, keen to make his name, he's unfettered, he has an open field before him. He has only one natural place in which to make his mark, and that is parliament; that is by advocacy; that is by talking. It is not so much by analysis.[50]

All in all, Opposition policy-making is a bleak prospect unless one believes (which I do not) that it is unwise to attempt more than generalities couched in a philosophical overlay by way of preparing for a manifesto to put to the electorate. Manifestos can be greeted in Whitehall with all the enthusiasm that awaits a plague bacillus. Senior civil servants do comb them, says Sir Frank Cooper:

> I'm sure they think about them very constructively in all cases. They think, 'Oh my God, is this really going to happen?' But being a decent, hard-working bunch of people, they will then scratch their heads and do at least some preliminary thinking if the minister really does insist on this happening ... how could this actually be brought about, what are the pitfalls, what are the consequences?[51]

When temporary minister meets the permanent government, a tussle royal can begin. Unless the politician has a rich personal past experience on which to draw or is particularly well prepared thanks to painstaking Opposition staff work, the contest, in the initial stages at least, can be as unequal as that between a small territorial army and regiment after regiment of crack regular troops.

Just fifteen hours of voting can wreak the most fundamental transformation in a politician's life – from rags to riches, from powerlessness to power. An entry ticket to government office, courtesy of the electorate and the prime minister in that order, is an awesome thing. The system sweeps you up and keeps you in motion until the electorate and/or the prime minister lets you down again. That system – its conventions, its relations to Parliament, to the public, to pressure points of all kinds – will govern a minister's life for the duration. Yet very few politicians give more than a moment's thought to its nature before they are part of it – and once they are part of it, they are too busy. The occasional exception is a rare spirit. The rarest spirit of all was R.B. Haldane who has acquired a form of political immortality. For any sensible discussion of the twentieth-century system of British central government must start, even now, with the man and his report.

8 CABINET, PARLIAMENT AND PRESSURE

THE HALDANE LEGACY

Above all, it is our political institutions and decision-making procedures which require to be looked at for they represent the litmus test of the credibility, competence and acceptability of government. Are these not at risk in today's Britain? Should we not stop living in the past? Can we afford any longer to have a political Establishment which feeds on division? Do we not need to look for some more Haldanes?
Sir Frank Cooper, 1986[1]

A comprehensive job on the Haldane model badly needs to be done, not least because it could offer an opportunity, which is becoming overdue, to reassess the machinery of government in terms not simply of tinkering with departmental structures and organisation but of tackling the conceptual problem of the correct relationship between a government's social and economic policies and its administrative machinery which will take us into the twenty-first century.
Lord Trend, 1986[2]

Richard Burdon Haldane cast a long shadow over twentieth-century Whitehall. The philosopher, lawyer and Liberal-turned-Labour politician would have been immensely gratified in the week before Christmas 1918, one month after the First World War ended, when he submitted his report to the Lloyd George Coalition had he been able to foresee a conversation nearly seventy years later in the Westminster flat of a former Secretary of the Cabinet, Lord Trend. Burke Trend, elaborating on his call for a new Haldane, said he had always been 'a great admirer' of the man 'though I didn't read him attentively until I was thinking about the Central Policy Review Staff in 1970'.[3] Lord Trend said no government since 1918 had had the benefit of such a report and proceeded, at my request, to think aloud about where a new Haldane should start – 'with an analysis of society as we're still operating a central machine that belongs to the great manufacturing and imperial age of Britain'.[4]

Who was this singular intellectual-in-politics, the translator of Schopenhauer and biographer of Adam Smith,[5] and what was the genesis and the product of his inquiry that his work could be so emphatically called in aid by seasoned public servants concerned about the condition of British government at the turn of the twentieth and twenty-first centuries? Haldane, a squat, dumpy figure who held his cigars in a two-pronged silver fork, was a product of what Paul Johnson has called 'that unique civilisation created by the British Liberal movement in the later part of the nineteenth century . . . [a] civilisation . . . based upon Free Trade, classical scholarship, strict religious observance, public probity and reformist zeal'[6] – precisely that mixture, as we have seen, which created the modern career Civil Service after 1870. Haldane and his close friend Herbert Henry Asquith were the most prominent intellectual scions of this tradition in the last Liberal government to dominate the House of Commons. From an upper-middle-class family in Perthshire, Haldane's nonconformity caused him to become an undergraduate at Edinburgh rather than Oxford of whose Anglicanism his father firmly disapproved. He went on to study at Göttingen and Dresden which left him with what Roy Jenkins rather unkindly describes as 'a strong and persistent taste for rather cloudy metaphysics'[7] and a spectre that was to come back and haunt him – his love of Germany – which caused him to be hounded out of the War Office by the worst kind of Tory prejudice as the price of Conservative participation in Asquith's wartime coalition government in 1915.[8] Burke Trend believes that Haldane's fascination with the principles and practice of administration, rare in a politician, was born of a marriage between philosophy department and War Office. 'He'd been Secretary of State for War. He thought in terms of military planning . . . [and] . . . he was a philosopher, a Hegelian.'[9] The best remembered product of Haldane's fertile mind is the creation of the Territorial Army and the British Expeditionary Force. Less well known is his chairmanship of a pair of sub-committees of the Committee of Imperial Defence from which sprang MI5, MI6 and the now notorious section 2 of the Official Secrets Act, 1911.[10]

It was Haldane's personal experience in that legendary Liberal Cabinet of 1906–10, so brimming, according to folk memory, with character and talent, that turned his tidy mind to the problems of Cabinet government and the Whitehall machine. 'Looking back,' he wrote in his memoirs,

> I think I ought to have taken a more active part in the general business of the Cabinet. But my hands were quite full with military affairs, and, while I was ready to suggest fresh ideas, I could only prevail in counsel when the conditions existed for which I was best fitted, those of working

> with two or three colleagues who knew me. Moreover, the Cabinet was organised on an old system which I hope will never be restored. It was a congested body of about twenty, in which the powerful orator secured too much attention. The Prime Minister knew too little of the details of what had to be got through to be able to apportion the time required for discussion. Consequently, instead of ruling the Cabinet and regulating the length of the conversations, he left things much to themselves. We had no Secretary, no agenda, and no minutes in those days. The evils prevailed that we described in the Report of the Reconstruction Committee on the Machinery of Government, over which it fell to me to preside afterwards, in 1918. Indeed I got the Government of that day to appoint this Committee because I was keenly conscious of the necessity of bringing these and other evils to light.[11]

As Haldane's reflections remind us, the machinery-of-government inquiry was but one of a number of sub-groups spawned by the Reconstruction Committee of Lloyd George's coalition government. It met not in the sparse Whitehall committee room which has been the drab lot of later manifestations of the great and the good, but in Haldane's comfortable bachelor home at 28 Queen Anne's Gate, Westminster, Haldane's 'Doll's House' as the Kaiser called it – from the street it looks exactly like that – on a visit to London in 1911[12] (his much feared and hugely exaggerated intelligence service in Britain would not have been able to tell him of Haldane's institution building in the secret world). Twice a week the Haldane Committee would consume tea, muffins and cigarettes in Haldane's dining-room at No. 28 summoning and questioning Cabinet ministers and permanent secretaries and 'discussing the theory and practice of government . . . It is a pleasant sport', wrote one committee member, the formidable Beatrice Webb in her diary for 14 November 1917.[13]

Haldane's tea-time companions in that last winter of the war were an odd bunch. Apart from Mrs Webb, who was quite open in her motives – 'I tell them that I am discovering the land of Whitehall for the future Labour Cabinet'[14] – the leading spirits, in addition to Haldane, were the committee's secretary, a senior civil servant by the name of Michael Heseltine (secretary of another Reconstruction sub-committee which led to the foundation of the Ministry of Health in which Heseltine served for the bulk of his career) and the remarkable, tormented Sir Robert Morant, former permanent secretary at the Board of Education. 'A strange mortal,' wrote Mrs Webb of Morant, 'not altogether sane but in spite of his malicious tongue and somewhat tortuous ways, he has done more to improve English administration than any other man.'[15]

The other members were MPs Jimmy Thomas for Labour, Colonel Sir Alan Dykes for the Conservatives, Edwin Montagu for the Liberals (though he was quickly removed to Delhi on his appointment as Secretary of State for India) and a pair of permanent secretaries, Sir George Murray from the Post Office and Sir Claud Schuster from the Lord Chancellor's Department. Mrs Webb appears to have bombarded the rest with memoranda which she prepared with the help of Heseltine whose capabilities she regarded as 'brilliant'.[16]

Diarists, particularly those like Beatrice Webb, who deploy their pens as weapons are both a bane and a boon to the historian. Theirs is often the only insider source that conveys the smell and feel of an operation (more formal official records rarely do). Yet the events they depict are refracted through a highly personal and highly misleading prism. Mrs Webb presents all these problems, though she knew her weaknesses and she found the committee instructive as 'Haldane, George Murray, Schuster and Morant know far more about the workings of Cabinets and Government Departments than I do, but I try to make them face the newer problems of combining bureaucratic efficiency with democratic control – they are forever insisting that the working of Parliament makes sensible, leave alone scientific administration, impracticable.'[17] In one strange passage earnestness is matched with modesty: 'I wish I were stronger-brained – the subject matter of the Machinery of Government Committee is immense and the importance of the questions raised vital to the success of the Equalitarian State'.[18] She was fairly pleased with the result. The final report of the Haldane Committee pretty well followed her line: 'But these ideas appear in nebulously-phrased hesitating propositions: a concession to Murray's vested prejudices and Sykes's vested interests and Haldane's incurable delight in mental mistiness – it has been a pleasant and interesting experience examining, over tea and cigarettes, in Haldane's comfortable dining-room, a succession of the chiefs of the Civil Service and gossiping with them . . . about different Cabinets and Cabinet Ministers.'[19]

There is a timelessness about the view of Whitehall that formed from the gossip and through the cigarette smoke:

> This informal review of our bureaucracy leaves an impression of good temper and good manners of native capacity and no systematic training, of philosophical indifference to ends, tempered by a moderately felt loyalty to the ideals of the British ruling class. Contempt for Parliament and a disdainful dislike for the newly imported 'business man', a steady depreciation of Parliamentary chiefs, are almost universal in the higher ranks of the Civil Service. There is no contemporary statesmen [sic] for whom Murray, Morant and their fellows have any considerable admiration, and many for whom they have contempt frequently expressed in unparliamentary language.[20]

The Haldane Committee's brief was reformist. Its terms of reference were 'To enquire into the responsibilities of the various Departments of the central executive Government, and to advise in what manner the exercise and distribution by the Government of its functions should be *improved* [emphasis added].'[21] The Haldane inquiry accords again with Arthur Marwick's dictum that 'Wars are like weddings: essentially extravagant and unnecessary but a great stimulant in a convention-bound society.'[22] Haldane's reforming eye surveyed a profession and a system clogged by what we would now call 'institutional sclerosis',[23] the besetting disease of big bureaucracy. The Committee's first finding set the tone for the whole report:

> Our investigations have made it evident to us that there is much overlapping and consequent obscurity and confusion in the Departments of executive Government. This is largely due to the fact that many of these Departments have been gradually evolved in compliance with current needs, and that the purposes for which they were thus called into being have so gradually altered that the later stages of the process have not accorded in principle with those that were reached earlier. In other instances Departments appear to have been rapidly established without preliminary insistence on definition of function and precise assignment of responsibility. Even where Departments are most free from defects we find that there are important features in which the organisation falls short of a standard which is becoming progressively recognised as the foundation of efficient action.[24]

Those judgements in that style of language could as easily have emerged from Mrs Thatcher's Efficiency Unit in 1987 as from Haldane's dining-room in 1917.

The Haldane Report itself was a model of tidiness and logic, proceeding methodically – principles in the first part, application in the second – from one essential to the next, defining and delineating as it went and deploying a strength of language and a felicity of phrase that puts the Whitehall draftsmen of the 1980s to shame. Part I tackled the two mistresses of the Civil Service – Cabinet and Parliament. The section on Cabinet was thoroughly Haldanian and reflected the frustration of those tedious hours the former War Minister had spent in the Cabinet Room while Asquith, half an ear on the business, drafted letters to his *amoureuse* Venetia Stanley. It also reflected the views of Hankey, the Cabinet Secretary, whom Haldane, while at the War Office, had made Secretary of the Committee of Imperial Defence.[25] Haldane plunged in with a definition of Cabinet which would make today's political scientists, who delight to see how many differing interpretations can dance on the head of a pin, recoil from its boldness. 'Cabinet', wrote Haldane, 'is the mainspring of all the mechanism of

Government'.[26] He went on to lay out the main functions of the Cabinet:

(a) the final determination of the policy to be submitted to Parliament;
(b) the supreme control of the national executive in accordance with the policy prescribed by Parliament; and
(c) the continuous co-ordination and delimitation of the activities of the several Departments of state.[27]

Haldane laid down five conditions which were 'essential or, at least, desirable', if these three functions were to work:

(a) the Cabinet should be small in number – preferably ten, or, at most, twelve;
(b) it should meet frequently;
(c) it should be supplied in the most convenient form with all the information and material necessary to enable it to arrive at expeditious decisions;
(d) it should make a point of consulting personally all the Ministers whose work is likely to be affected by its decisions; and
(e) it should have a systematic method of securing that its decisions are effectually carried out by the several Departments concerned.[28]

Haldane assumed, rightly as it turned out, that the prewar system of Cabinet without agenda, minutes or secretary would not return (though in 1922 Bonar Law, as we have seen, came within an inch of closing down the Cabinet Office then seen as a revolutionary Lloyd Georgian creation rather than as the citadel of orthodoxy it is today).

Next on the Haldane agenda was the formulation of policy. Juxtaposing the modern methods developed by the Committee of Imperial Defence to the procedures and practices of civil administration which trailed far behind, Haldane came up with the one-liner with which his name will always be associated. It was embedded in a paragraph of contrived understatement. '. . . we have come to the conclusion . . . that in the sphere of civil government *the duty of investigation and thought, as preliminary to action*, might with great advantage be more definitely recognised [emphasis added]'.

This phrase has been something of a beau ideal in the British Civil Service ever since. The degree to which it is cherished explains why, almost to an official, the higher bureaucracy decried Mrs Thatcher's closure of the Central Policy Review Staff, a thoroughly Haldanian institution, in 1983. On that autumn afternoon in Westminster spent discussing the

Haldane legacy, Burke Trend, with considerable passion, continued to denounce the abolition of the CPRS as 'a disastrous mistake'.[30]

Again in an uncanny pre-echo of the Hoskyns group on Reskilling Government, Haldane recognised 'the proved impracticability of devoting the necessary time to thinking out organisation and preparation for action in the mere interstices of the time required for the transaction of business'.[31] His suggestion was the creation of intelligence and research branches (what nowadays we would call 'think-tanks') for each ministry pulled together by a single central department, a Ministry of Research, under a senior minister, preferably a trained thinker, as 'science ignores departmental boundaries ... [and] ... success or failure in a particular field of inquiry will ... often depend upon the presence or absence of a fertilising contact with another field'.[32] Great care should be exercised, said the report, in finding the right people for these jobs, people whose 'primary duty' should be to keep in touch with 'scientific workers in various fields throughout the country'.[33] And senior administrators should have more time to devote to the research and intelligence side of their departments. Rounding off the scheme and the argument for it, the Haldane Committee reckoned 'A Cabinet with such knowledge at its disposal would, we believe, be in a position to devolve, with greater freedom and confidence than is at present the case, the duties of administration, and even of legislation.'[34]

Large sections of the report bear the imprimatur of 44 Grosvenor Road, the London home of Sidney and Beatrice Webb whence poured forth a stream of memoranda to the committee prepared jointly by this extraordinary duo. As Mrs Webb's diary shows, the dilemma of increasingly scientific administration supervised by a slimmed down and efficiency-minded Cabinet confronted across Parliament Square by a far from scientific or administration-minded House of Commons and House of Lords was never far from the committee's mind. It reported:

> We have throughout our deliberations borne in mind the fact that any action directed to this end [the efficient and economical working of the public service] would fail to achieve its purpose if it were to have the effect of disturbing the balance of authority between the Legislature and the Executive. It would, we think, be generally felt that any improvement in the organisation of the Departments of State which was so marked as substantially to increase their efficiency should have as its correlative an increase in the power of the Legislature as the check upon the acts and proposals of the Executive. We need scarcely say that we adhere without reserve to this view.[35]

The committee had been much impressed by the young permanent secretary to the Ministry of Shipping, John Anderson, already on his way to becoming a mighty though publicly little-known figure in twentieth-century government striding from interwar Whitehall, via the Second World War Cabinet Room to a predominant position in the post-1945 great and good.[36] Anderson, according to Mrs Webb's diary, told the committee 'that the perpetual sniping at Government officials in Parliament and the Press bred a wrong sort of Civil Servant – it developed the critical faculty instead of the constructive. The man who was prized in a department was he who kept his minister out of trouble and had a smart answer to an awkward question.'[37] Anderson's remedy had to wait till the St John-Stevas reforms of 1979 for its implementation – parliamentary committees shadowing the subject matter of government. The Haldane Report did not presume to tell Parliament its business but suggested that such committees might be a good idea.[38]

As is so often the fate of official reports, very little was extracted and implemented from the Haldane Report, to its author's chagrin, by the postwar Lloyd George Coalition. Poor Haldane, who grandly called his team 'the Great Reform Committee',[39] expected its report to open the door, once more, to a Cabinet position for himself. Lloyd George had dined with him at Queen Anne's Gate in April 1917, leaving with the words: 'You must come in. All the difficulties must be put aside, for the nation wants your brains badly.'[40] The call did not come till, Lloyd George long gone, Ramsay MacDonald invited Haldane to be Lord Chancellor in the first Labour Government of 1924. However, in 1919 the Treasury reorganised its financial relationships with departments on a more systematic basis; establishment officers were appointed in departments to supervise personnel policy research councils began to appear, though the current set of five took from 1918 to 1965 to create.[41] But, in its peculiar way, the report that grew from those tea-time discussions in Queen Anne's Gate shone like a beacon – its scope and lucidity unemulated in the intervening years – and illuminated the mid-eighties dinners, discussions and conferences at the Institute of Directors in Pall Mall a quarter of a mile away across St James's Park. And any 'new Haldane' would have to start where he did with the two demanding mistresses of the Whitehall machine – Cabinet and Parliament.

CABINET

> The underlying principle is, of course, that the method adopted by Ministers for discussion among themselves of questions of policy is essentially a domestic matter, and is no concern of Parliament or the public.
> **Miscellaneous Questions of Procedure,**
> **Note by the Prime Minister, 8 August 1945**[42]

It is easier to know what the Cabinet was than what it is now.
Professor Colin Seymour-Ure, 1971[43]

The history of post-war British Cabinets has been a continuous story of people trying to do too much, believing that they had power over events which in fact they lacked, treating national circumstances as entirely within their control and twirling the wheel on the bridge as though every move would produce an instant response in some well-oiled engine-room below.
David Howell, 1987[44]

The Prime Minister is a very determined person and thank goodness for this country that she is so. But, at the same time, she has always been prepared to listen. She has always been prepared to modify her views if there is a good reason for doing so.
Lord Whitelaw, 1987[45]

'One would have thought', wrote Lord Trend, Cabinet Secretary to four prime ministers, writing in the aftermath of the Westland affair, 'that it was easy enough to understand. Twenty or so individuals sit round a table and try to agree on the solution to some difficult problems, on the basis that they are accountable for their decisions; that it is therefore better to hang together than to hang separately; and that hanging together implies being pretty reticent about their methods of doing business.'[46] A century ago it *was* easy enough to understand. With the emergence of disciplined political parties organised to appeal to a mass electorate, effective power over policy-making was lifted from the chambers of the Houses of Parliament and deposited in the Cabinet Room.[47] For a leading Whitehall-watcher of the day, G. W. E. Russell, one reality was clear and instantly understandable: 'The Cabinet is the Board of Directors of the British Empire.'[48] For Haldane, as we have seen, it was 'the mainspring of all the mechanism of Government'.[49] Since 1945, thanks to the huge and seemingly irreversible expansion of central government activity, life for the anatomist of Cabinet has ceased to be so simple. As doubts about its ability to cope with the strains of big government have grown, definitions of what 'it' really is have grown longer, more qualified and opaque – studies of Cabinet government litter the years since 1945 like a street market, the latest to set up a stall being myself with the predecessor of this volume.[50]

As recently as 1985 a former prime minister like Lord Home could continue to depict Cabinet government as 'designed to concentrate the attention of a small number of people, rather like the board of directors of a company, on the essential business to be done'.[52] Yet Professor Colin Seymour-Ure, fourteen years earlier, had been reduced by a study of the first Wilson Cabinets to the view that 'the importance of the Cabinet as an institution appears to have diminished to the point where it ought properly to be described as no more than *primus inter pares* among other government committees, just as the Prime Minister used to be called *primus inter pares* among his colleagues'.[53] Pushing his train of thought further down the line he suggested 'that the Cabinet is becoming a *principle* of government and barely an institution at all'.[53] Intriguingly, the third group participating in the great postwar Cabinet debate, the retired civil servants, throw their weight behind Seymour-Ure's abstraction. Sir Frank Cooper, for example, describes the essence of Cabinet government as 'discussion before decision'[54] and his friend and colleague, Lord Hunt of Tanworth, Cabinet Secretary 1973–9, said in a famous lecture on election day 1983 (the timing was coincidental): 'I accept that Cabinet Government must always be a somewhat cumbrous and complicated affair and that this is a price well worth paying for the advantage of shared discussion and shared decision provided the system can keep up with the demands put upon it.'[55]

Indeed, one of the fascinating features of the 'mainspring' of our system of government is the free-flowing debate its current condition has triggered among practitioners (former prime ministers and Cabinet ministers), production engineers (retired civil servants) and observers (academics and journalists). And the discourse is of more than scholarly interest. That there should be such debate and confusion about what Cabinet is and does matters directly to the Civil Service, the instrument for turning its minutes into tangibles such as white papers, bills, treaties, and sometimes, new institutions. Cabinet is supposed to be the command and control post of our system. Continuing contemporary confusion about its methods, even its purpose, would have hugely distressed the tidy-minded Hegelian of Queen Anne's Gate.

The confusion and debate about Cabinet arise from a number of factors. A crucial one is the quintessential British aversion for writing down matters constitutional on a single sheet, or even several sheets, of A4. For petty rulebooks we have a genius (see Chapter 9). When it comes to big issues and grand principles we are paralysed by the fear, in George Dangerfield's vivid metaphor, of setting 'down in writing a Constitution which for centuries had remained happily unwritten, to conjure a great ghost into the narrow and corruptible flesh of a code'.[56] The law is no guide; indeed, it misleads. Parliament vests power in secretaries of state, that is, ministers, rather than the prime minister or Cabinet. As A. W. Bradley, the latest renovator of the classic volume Wade and Phillips on *Constitutional and Administrative Law*, puts it, 'Like the Cabinet, the office of prime minister has evolved as a matter of political expediency and constitutional practice rather than law.'[57] As a legal entity, the British prime minister is a Peter Pan figure glimpsed fleetingly in successive Ministerial Salaries Acts and the Chequers Estate Act 1917, dealing with the Buckinghamshire country annexe of No, 10.[58] Yet to compile an audit of prime-ministerial power by the weighing of statutes would be, to adopt a phrase of Neil Kinnock's, a piece of 'political science fiction'.[59]

The British way is to use procedure as a surrogate for the 'great ghost' of an unwritten constitution. As Sir Kenneth Pickthorn, that formidable constitutional expert-turned-Member of Parliament, put it in the House of Commons in 1960, 'Procedure is all the constitution the poor Briton has.'[60] Cabinet does have a kind of highway code, *Questions of Procedure for Ministers*, a lengthy list of 'do's' and 'don'ts' (mainly 'don'ts) which has grown piecemeal and mightily since 1945.[61] '*Questions of Procedure for Ministers*', said its former custodian, Lord Trend, 'is not a constitution, merely some tips for beginners – a book of etiquette.'[62] But it *is* the only guide the poor Cabinet minister has in a system without maps.

The Westland affair, from which a score of PhD theses are certain to bloom, shows how inadequate that multi-paragraph book of etiquette can be when crises crowds out the constitutional niceties and how the Whitehall machine can be crippled by uncertain and confused messages pouring out of its control room. Westland did raise genuine constitutional issues. Each side claimed that the other was breaking the rules. Both sides were right.[63] As December 1985 progressed, Mr Michael Heseltine, the Secretary of State for Defence, pressed the case for a European rescue of the floundering British helicopter firm, Westland. The Prime Minister and Mr Leon Brittan, Secretary of State for Trade and Industry, favoured an American saviour in the shape of the Sikorsky Company. Heseltine tried to run his solution up the Cabinet hierarchy – informal *ad hoc* ministerial group, the standing Cabinet committee on economic strategy to the full Cabinet itself. He was, he maintained, thwarted at every level. He took his case to the public and he did it very well. In doing so, he drove a tank through the section of *Questions of Procedure* dealing with collective Cabinet responsibility which reads:

> Decisions reached by the Cabinet or Cabinet Committees are binding on all members of the Government. They are, however, normally announced and defended by the Minister concerned as his own decisions. There may be rare occasions when it is desirable to emphasise the importance of a decision by stating specifically that it is the decision of Her Majesty's Government. This, however, should be the exception rather than the rule.
>
> It is important to avoid giving any indication of the manner in which the Minister has consulted his colleagues before any decision is announced. The principle of the collective responsibility of Ministers, upon the maintenance of which the Cabinet and Cabinet Committee system depends, requires opportunities for free and frank discussion

between Ministers; the method adopted by Ministers for discussing among themselves questions of policy is essentially a domestic matter, and such discussion will be hampered if the processes by which it is carried on are laid bare. The growth of any general practice whereby decisions of the Cabinet or of Cabinet Committees were announced as such would lead to the embarrassing result that some decisions of government would be regarded as less authoritative than others; critics of a decision reached by a particular Committee could press for its review by some other Committee or by the Cabinet itself, thus impairing the constitutional right of individual Ministers to speak in the name of the Government as a whole.[64]

Heseltine had spared no effort in making the Government line on Westland appear 'less authoritative than others' and was vigorously pressing for a review.

But the Prime Minister was sinning against custom and practice in her treatment of Heseltine. There are no written rules covering the right of a dissenting minister to take an issue to full Cabinet. The normal conventions were explained by Lord Hunt of Tanworth, when interviewed for the television programme, *All the Prime Minister's Men*:

HENNESSY: How about Cabinet Ministers having a right to put an issue on to the agenda of full Cabinet, that's been controversial in the Westland affair as well, what's your understanding of the constitutional practice there?

HUNT: The constitutional practice is that the agenda is produced by the Secretary of the Cabinet and approved by the prime minister. Any minister can ask for an item to go on. In the ordinary way his department will have asked. And if it is the right time for it to come to Cabinet, if there is room on the agenda, it'll be on. But if a minister is unsatisfied and wants an item included which isn't on, he can always ask. And I've known that happen, and in the ordinary way the prime minister will agree.

HENNESSY: But prime ministers have the right to keep things off the agenda if they want to, for whatever reason?

HUNT: I have never known a prime minister keep an item off an agenda for what one might call a disreputable or tactical reason. I mean there have been times where I've known a prime minister say, we have ten items next week, there simply isn't time, or it is not the right time to discuss this because ... but where you've had a position of a minister who is unhappy and unsatisfied that an issue is not being given a hearing, I've never known a prime minister refuse to have it on the agenda.[65]

Under the parameters outlined by Lord Hunt, Heseltine should have had his full Cabinet discussion. He was a political heavyweight and, with Leon Brittan at Trade and Industry, one of the two lead ministers on the Westland issue. He had reason to be aggrieved. The one ploy he might have tried but did not was to insist on his right as a Cabinet minister to circulate a memorandum to his colleagues. One experienced Whitehall figure is convinced that it would have been very difficult for Sir Robert Armstrong, the Cabinet Secretary, to refuse to distribute it.[66]

A third convention was smashed to smithereens when that now immortal helicopter crashed on to the Cabinet table – the standard constitutional view of the role of civil servants and ministers: that civil servants are accountable to ministers and ministers are accountable to Parliament. Heseltine's flair for publicity led to this particular piece of demolition. The chief weapon in the Whitehall war over Westland was the non-attributable briefing to the press. The Ministry of Defence and the Department of Trade and Industry used it systematically. Downing Street has a press machine which provided a daily service on this basis – the controversial lobby system[67] – which it could deploy on Westland duties at will. In late December 1985 and early January 1986 combat by competitive letter took to the field of battle. As part of this process, Heseltine wrote to Mr Horne of Lloyd's Merchant Bank, an adviser to the European consortium seeking to rescue Westland, including material that the Ministry of Defence had wanted inserted in an earlier letter from Mrs Thatcher to Sir John Cuckney, Chairman of Westland. It had been rejected. As the subsequent report from the all-party Commons Select Committee on Defence indicated, Heseltine's note to Horne raised the temperature to boiling-point, the select committee commenting that 'the effect of such a letter upon the Prime Minister and the Secretary of State for Trade can have been nothing short of incendiary'.[68]

Over the Christmas period, the Thatcher–Brittan camp had consistently lost the battle of the headlines to Heseltine. His letter to Horne produced a weekend of feverish activity in No. 10 and the Department of Trade and Industry over the period 4–5 January. Mrs Thatcher read the exchanges between Horne and Heseltine on the Saturday. Realising that Heseltine's reply had not been cleared by the Government's Law Officers she sent a message to Brittan suggesting that he 'as the sponsoring Minister for Westlands . . . should ask the Solicitor General to consider . . . the Defence Secretary's letter and give his opinion on whether it was accurate and consistent with my own letter to Sir John Cuckney'.[69] By mid-morning on Monday, 6 January Sir Patrick Mayhew, the Solicitor General, had completed his reply. By mid-afternoon Collette Bowe, Brittan's Head of Information at DTI, a career civil servant, though troubled about the propriety of her action, had leaked selectively parts of the Mayhew letter most damaging to Heseltine to Chris Moncrieff of the Press Association news agency after obtaining 'cover' from Bernard Ingham, the Prime Minister's Chief Press Secretary, and Charles Powell, the Downing Street private secretary specialising in foreign and defence matters. Like Miss Bowe, Ingham and Powell were career civil servants.

Miss Bowe's leak backfired more damagingly than any Whitehall press operation in recent memory. It produced an instant Parliamentary furore, and a farcical leak inquiry by Sir Robert Armstrong (he must have known who was responsible before he started, but the Law Officers might well have resigned if the inquiry had not been set in motion);[70] it refuelled an existing Commons Select Committee inquiry[71] and started a second. Controversy raged for months and the suspicion remained that undisclosed material lay hissing like an unexploded bomb beneath Mrs Thatcher's Downing Street.[72] The subsequent inquests and their outcome had critical constitutional implications for the Civil Service.

As we have seen, the standard constitutional view of the role of the civil servants and ministers is as familiar as it is banal: civil servants are accountable to ministers, ministers are accountable to Parliament. This simple chain had already been broken routinely by select committee inquiries when MPs, at public hearings, had questioned named officials about individual items of policy on which they had advised ministers. The officials never disclosed that advice, but they became personally associated with areas of departmental activity. Westland, according to a former permanent secretary, moved civil servants from a difficult position into 'an impossible position'.[73] For a start, said the aggrieved retired official, it was the Prime Minister herself who had named the five civil servants involved in the leaking of the Mayhew letter during her Commons statement describing the result of the Cabinet Secretary's leak inquiry. Mr Brittan had, in the end, accepted ministerial responsibility for his officials' actions and resigned. The Prime Minister had not. And ministers had prevented the five named officials from defending themselves before the Commons Defence Committee. For this particular seasoned public servant, Westland had changed the constitutional landscape beyond recognition. No official in future would know where he or she stood.

By a nice irony of timing, the Government published its reply to the Treasury and Civil Service Committee's report on the duties and responsibilities of civil servants on the same day (24 July 1986) that the Defence Committee released its outspoken criticisms of 'improper' ministerial and official behaviour over Westland. Its section on accountability was worded as if Westland had never happened:

> The Government endorses the committee's two basic propositions on accountability: that ministers and not officials are responsible and accountable for policy; and that officials' advice to Ministers is and

> should remain confidential. Constitutionally, Ministers are responsible and accountable for all actions carried out by Civil Servants of their departments in pursuit of Government policies or the discharge of responsibilities laid on them by Parliament.[74]

The top civil servants' union, the First Division Association, was far from satisfied with this restatement of traditional doctrine as the Government's attempt to fill the breach caused by Westland. Its general secretary, John Ward, writing in the Union's journal in September 1986, said:

> It . . . seems that the conventions regarding accountability are no longer accepted. Individual civil servants have been placed in an intolerable position, both in relation to their own conduct and by being asked to account for the veracity of minister [s], and there is no reason to believe this may not happen again. One should not underestimate the effect that this has on general as well as individual morale. Senior civil servants are not shrinking violets. They are perfectly capable of giving a robust account of themselves and rebutting criticism if allowed to do so. At present they are not.[75]

Formal representations along these lines were made to Sir Robert Armstrong by the Council of Civil Service Unions in a letter from its secretary, Peter Jones, in October 1986.[76]

Crises can be very revealing of the true condition of a system or an institution. What in the end does Westland show? It illustrates beyond doubt that ours is a system without maps. Its epitaph was pronounced by that veteran observer of British government, Professor J. G. Griffith, the distinguished public lawyer at the London School of Economics. While waiting to give evidence to the Commons Treasury and Civil Service Committee on 5 February 1986, I bumped into him in the Committee corridor at the Palace of Westminster. With the smoke of the Westland affair still coursing through the building, John Griffith confessed himself to be wholly baffled, 'The constitution,' he said, 'is what happens.'

His confusion was, in its way, a kind of clarity. For despite the grand constitutional language in which much of the Westland debate has been couched inside Parliament and out, it was raw politics and not matters of convention or probity that prevailed throughout. Managing a difficult colleague, not *Questions of Procedure for Ministers*, determined Mrs Thatcher's initial decision to let Michael Heseltine go rogue and prepare a European alternative to Sikorsky. Damage limitation and not the imperatives of collective responsibility lay behind her efforts to rein him in in mid-December 1985. Assertion of her political supremacy explains her determination to foreclose discussion in the Economic Strategy Committee of the Cabinet. The need to turn the tide in the battle for public opinion led (by whatever route history may eventually uncover) to the leaking of the Solicitor-General's letter on 6 January 1986.

It was the Prime Minister's attempt to gag Heseltine by insisting at the Cabinet of 9 January that in future he clear all his statements on Westland with the Cabinet Office which finally triggered his resignation. Pressure from Conservative backbenchers, not the requirements of ministerial responsibility, forced Leon Brittan to follow Heseltine out of the Government. The need to preserve the position of the Prime Minister and not constitutional doctrine led the Conservative majority on the Commons Defence Committee to 'clear' Mrs Thatcher. The Defence Committee's naming and blaming the civil servants involved in leaking the Solicitor-General's letter was done without a moment's pause to consider the conventions of ministerial and official responsibility. Procedure may be all the constitution the poor Briton has, but in the Westland affair it provided not one jot of protection or guidance for the system or the people who work in it. The constitution really was reduced to what happened.

Westland, for all its drama, was but one scene in a play that had been unfolding since May 1979 – the impact of Mrs Thatcher on the British Cabinet system. Mrs Thatcher is an antidote to consensus and none is remotely in prospect on this issue. But her reshaping of the constitutional plasticine is unquestionable. Even her current and former Cabinet colleagues were actively engaged in the debate while the lady was still firmly installed in Downing Street to a degree unprecedented in the history of the premiership (Lloyd George included). The debate Mrs Thatcher's stewardship has inspired is important to our theme because it has added to the confusion about what Cabinet government is and should be.

Let us start with the Cabinet ministers themselves and take the most venerable and experienced of them first. When it comes to the condition of Cabinet government, Lord Hailsham, the former Lord Chancellor, is a prime witness. He may have found it difficult to remember the names of some of his colleagues around Mrs Thatcher's Cabinet table[77] (his dignified bulk rested right opposite the Prime Minister, perfectly placed for catching her eye[78]), but he sat at it for seventeen years, a postwar record. He saw in action Sir Anthony Eden in the dreadful months of Suez (Lord Hailsham was First Lord of the Admiralty in 1956, just below Cabinet rank[79]). Harold Macmillan brought him into the Cabinet in January 1957 and there he remained through the Macmillan and Home years till October 1964. He was on the Woolsack for the duration of the Heath government and the first two Thatcher governments. His judgement of the Thatcher style is, therefore, a collector's item.

It is breathtaking. She reminds him of the late Lord Chief Justice, Lord

Goddard, according to legend the hardest judge to have sat on the bench since the war (Lord Hailsham remembers him as 'a sweet man').[81]

> I don't think the critics have got it quite right when they say that she doesn't like people who differ from her. She reminds me very much of some judges before whom I've appeared who form their own opinion by arguing with counsel. Now Lord Goddard was one such judge. And you would think for a time he was really against you and had made up his mind that you were wrong before you'd had your say. And indeed if you laid down on your back with your paws in the air and wagged your tail, you'd lose the case . . . I think the present Prime Minister is somebody who likes to test her steel in real argument and I don't think she holds it against you even if you hit back pretty hard.[81]

Lord Hailsham is but one of many Cabinet ministers to have delivered his verdict on Mrs Thatcher's style in the Cabinet Room while she is still the occupant of No. 10. It is yet more evidence that Mrs Thatcher has performed a minor miracle – she has made the study of government and public administration interesting again. Before analysing the insider intelligence this has produced, it is sensible to begin by taking the material raw. In a now famous interview with Kenneth Harris of *The Observer* shortly before becoming Prime Minister, Mrs Thatcher issued a declaration of intent.

> It must be a conviction government. As Prime Minister I could not waste time having any internal arguments.[82]

As such declarations go it was unusual in its tone and the fact that it was made public. Harold Macmillan, by contrast, began his premiership by pinning to the Cabinet Room door a passage written in his own hand from Gilbert and Sullivan's *The Gondoliers*:

> Motto for Private Office and Cabinet Room.
> Quiet, calm deliberation
> Disentangles every knot. HM[83]

Mrs Thatcher's early Cabinet contained an acknowledged expert on the subject, Norman St John-Stevas, Leader of the House of Commons and editor of the collected works of Walter Bagehot. For him, 'There is no doubt that as regards the Cabinet the most commanding Prime Minister of modern times has been the present incumbent, Mrs Thatcher. Convinced of both her own rectitude and ability, she has tended to reduce the Cabinet to subservience.'[84] Other victims of her Cabinet purges hum a similar theme. One veteran did it unattributably: 'She was not really running a team. Every time you have a prime minister who wants to take all the decisions, it mainly leads to bad results. Attlee didn't. That's why he was so damn good. Macmillan didn't. The nearest parallel to Maggie is Ted.'[85] The Westland affair brought Sir Ian Gilmour on to the television news telling the viewers of both major bulletins on 19 January 1986 that being a good listener was not one of Mrs Thatcher's virtues[86] and that there had been 'a downgrading of Cabinet government'[87]. Gilmour, like St John-Stevas, had written on the subject in the past in his *The Body Politic*.[88] A dissenter-in-place, Peter Walker, expressed his feelings through a merry quip at after-lunch speeches. He would quote the Duke of Wellington's reaction to his first Cabinet meeting as Prime Minister: 'An extraordinary affair. I gave them their orders and they wanted to stay and discuss them.' Then he would pause and say, 'I'm so glad we don't have prime ministers like that today.'[89] Perhaps the most outspoken Whitehall critic of the Thatcher style, however, is not a sacked minister but a former official, Lord Bancroft, Head of the Home Civil Service, who was despatched into early retirement when she disbanded the Civil Service Department in November 1981. 'Amongst the prime ministers that I have come across,' said Ian Bancroft, 'either closely or not so closely, the two who have inspired most fear have been Mr Churchill and Mrs Thatcher. As a result the grovel count amongst ministers, and some officials, has been much higher than normal.'[90]

Of course, Mrs Thatcher's most famous critic is Michael Heseltine. But his 'grand remonstrance of protest', as *The Observer*'s leader writer called it,[91] was, at least in its public dimension, a dispute about procedure, not personality. And the Westland affair deserved the special, separate treatment we have given it. But the Prime Minister as manager of Cabinet had her defenders both before and after the immortalisation of the small aircraft company in the west of which the political nation, till December 1985, knew little. Though critical of her lack of interest in reforming the machinery-of-government,[92] Sir John Hoskyns, the head of Mrs Thatcher's Downing Street Policy Unit 1979–82, believes that her style and temperament have been crucial to her success as 'a remarkably effective agent of change'.[93]

> She's done that for two or three reasons. I think first her temperament and background make her impatient with the whole sort of Establishment culture and way of thinking, even way of talking. And that, I think, is extremely healthy because I happen to think that the Establishment ... is absolutely at the heart of the British disease ... she's gone further than that because she has been prepared to be extremely unreasonable in order to get change – impossible on occasions and many people of a

more gentlemanly and old-fashioned upbringing were rather shocked at the way she carried on.[94]

Sir John Nott, who served Mrs Thatcher at Trade and later at Defence, enjoyed what he called 'a process of combat' in the Cabinet Room. 'It is possible', Sir John said after leaving Whitehall for the City, 'for the critics to say that Mrs Thatcher was not a particularly good chairman. I don't think she's a natural chairman, she's more of a managing director . . . but the fact is that she's perceptibly moved the country away from an accelerating decline . . . and by being a very good chairman, as opposed to being a thrusting, aggressive managing director, she would not have been able to do it.'[95]

Leon Brittan, who held three Cabinet posts under Mrs Thatcher till Westland brought him down, reacts strongly to the charge that Mrs Thatcher packs the Cabinet room with compliant placemen. The Prime Minister is quite right to turn her back on 'a system of running the Cabinet on a basis of Buggins' turn, and that nobody can get anywhere unless they've been this that or the other for a very long time'.[96]

There were some in the 'permanent government' who relished the Thatcher style. Sir Frank Cooper, Permanent Secretary at the Ministry of Defence until the end of 1982, was happy to speak publicly about it: 'I think she's changed a number of things. She certainly leads from the front. No one would argue about that and she believes it's the duty of any prime minister to lead from the front. And I would have a great deal of sympathy with that view, quite frankly.'[97]

Mrs Thatcher is aware of her Cabinet Room personality and the debate it has aroused. In accepting Jim Prior's resignation in 1984 she wrote: 'I take your point about frankness! That's what Cabinets are for, and lively discussions usually lead to good decisions.'[98] And, with the smoke of Westland still swirling round Whitehall, while her Home Secretary, Douglas Hurd, was telling one television audience 'I think it is very important that people should see we are under Cabinet government',[99] the Prime Minister was telling another: 'Some said that I should, in fact, have dealt with it and asked Mr Heseltine to go earlier. I can only tell you that had I done that . . . I know exactly what the press would have said: "There you are, old bossy-boots at it again."'[100]

It could be argued that the Prime Minister's personal style does not matter. The electorate knew what she was like in 1979, 1983 and 1987 and liked what they saw. But style can clash with system in a way that has important implications. As Lord Hailsham put it, 'There are two functions in the prime ministerial duties: one is to be a chairman and the other is to be a leader, and they are not always compatible.'[101] Mrs Thatcher has proved incapable of imitating Attlee and using silence as a weapon. She cannot overawe her Cabinet by a great set-piece *tour d'horizon* in the manner of Churchill. She cannot make them purr with pleasure like Macmillan with his aphorisms, quotations and reminiscences. She cannot hang back and score at the last minute like Jim Callaghan. It is almost as if she abhors collectivism in any form, including collective discussion as the indispensable prelude to decision. She goes against the grain of traditional Cabinet government. But does it matter? Is it an efficient way of conducting business? Is it unconstititional? These are the questions that count.

Any systems analyst allowed free access to the Cabinet Secretary's registry (there is no chance of that; the performance of Cabinet government is the one area that *will not* be the subject of a Rayner efficiency scrutiny)[107] would find the physical manifestations of a decline in collective discussion, the essence of Cabinet government if one accepts the judgement of Lord Hunt 'that Cabinet government must always be a somewhat cumbrous and complicated affair and that this is a price well worth paying for the advantage of shared discussion and shared decision'.[103] The raw statistics of Cabinet business tell part of the story.

It is rare for Mrs Thatcher to have more than one meeting of the Cabinet per week.[104] Allowing for Parliamentary recesses, that amounts to between forty and forty-five meetings a year – not a particularly significant statistic if more business is being taken in committees (more of that in a moment). Attlee and Churchill logged twice that figure and Macmillan was in the habit of calling two Cabinet meetings a week. The flow of Cabinet papers is well down too, to between sixty and seventy a year, about a sixth of the totals accumulated in the late forties and early fifties. Far from more being taken in Cabinet committee to compensate, workload is down there as well. Mrs Thatcher's Cabinet engine room consisted, when I last conducted an unofficial audit late in 1985, of some 160 committees. She accumulated some 25 standing committees and 125 *ad hocs* in 6½ years; in 6¼ years Attlee totted up 148 and 313; Churchill 137 and 109 in 3½ years; the Macmillan and Home years remain a mystery as, very largely, do the period of Wilson Mark I (1964–70) and the Heath era. Wilson Mark II, between March 1974 and March 1976, ran up a total of somewhere around 120 *ad hoc* groups; Callaghan in the three years between April 1976 and April 1979 commissioned about 160 *ad hoc* committees, a similar growth rate to Attlee's. Without doubt Mrs Thatcher is running the slimmest Cabinet machine since before the Second World War.[105]

Structure is one thing, content another. Our systems analyst, had he been able to sit in on Cabinet and Cabinet committee meetings at various moments in the postwar period, would have found the quality of discussion changing. Mrs Thatcher is as brisk as Attlee in curbing wafflers but, in the process, appears to some to syringe the collective marrow out of the proceedings. Sir John Nott may have relished the style but to other ministers it was like vinegar on an oyster. David Howell, a Cabinet minister in the first Thatcher administration at Energy and Transport, was a backroom architect of Edward Heath's attempt to bring more reason and analysis to Cabinet business. He did not enjoy his spell with the Thatcher colours.

> If by 'conviction government' it is meant that certain slogans were going to be elevated and written in tablets of stone and used as the put-down at the end of every argument, then, of course, that is indeed what happened ... Of course there is a deterring effect if one knows that one's going to go not into a discussion where various points of view will be weighed and gradually a view may be achieved, but into a huge argument where tremendous battle lines will be drawn up and everyone who doesn't fall into line will be hit on the head.[106]

This style of discussion may not be the best way of solving problems of immense complexity which will not yield to sheer ministerial will, political conviction and what Lord Rothschild once called the 'promises and panaceas that gleam like false teeth in party manifestos'.[108] Her abolition in 1983 of the Central Policy Review Staff, the Cabinet's Think-Tank of which Lord Rothschild was the first head, was taken rightly as further evidence of the Prime Minister's dislike of traditional policy analysis as a precursor to decision taking. As Professor John Ashworth, a former Chief Scientist to the CPRS, expressed it, 'Of its very existence it sort of encapsulated a view about government for which she had no great sympathy. She was what she called a conviction politician. There is a difference between being a conviction politician and being a rationally guided politician.'[108] Sir Frank Cooper, as we have seen an admirer of Mrs Thatcher, believes conviction politics are fine for slaughtering sacred cows which genuinely deserved the abattoir but not so good for constructing new policies from the offal.[109] This is likely to be one area where, once the shot and shell of current controversy is stilled, future historians of government will fault Mrs Thatcher compared to Mr Heath. It is already a conventional wisdom virtually across the political spectrum that some kind of Central Policy Review Staff needs to be restored. Prior to the 1987 general election all three leaders of the Opposition parties were committed to it[110] and the idea finds favour with some members of Mrs Thatcher's administration, most notably Douglas Hurd.[111]

The throughput of Cabinet and Cabinet committees is down. What does go through is conducted in Cabinet and the committees the Prime Minister chairs in a brisk, no-nonsense, often combative style which will be long remembered in Whitehall. Nobody could say that Mrs Thatcher's governments have been passive administrations. So, where is the business being done? A fair amount is conducted by ministerial correspondence, a perfectly acceptable method in constitutional terms. The Franks Report on the Falklands gives an indication of just how much this goes on. One reason, for example, why the Falklands issue figured so infrequently on the agenda of the Cabinet's Oversea and Defence Committee before the Argentine invasion of April 1982 is that Lord Carrington, then Foreign and Commonwealth Secretary, disliked bringing FO business before committee meetings of his colleagues.[112] Another swathe of high-level business is tackled by Mrs Thatcher in *ad hoc* groups which fall outside Sir Robin Butler's Cabinet Committee Book.

The most important of these is her version of the 'Economic Seminar' set up by Mr James Callaghan after the sterling crisis of 1976 to handle sensitive, market-related issues like exchange rate policy.[113] Though it no longer has that name, it handles similar subjects to his – monetary policy, delicate decisions affecting the money markets. Early in her first premiership it caused her a moment of acute embarrassment. One Cabinet minister, a member of the Economic Strategy Committee but not of this most secret inner group which was meeting straight afterwards, was a bit slow to gather his papers. As he is about to leave, Sir Geoffrey Howe, then Chancellor of the Exchequer, launches into his paper on the plan to abolish exchange controls. 'Oh,' says the laggardly minister, 'are we going to do that? How very interesting.' Embarrassed silence. Then Sir Geoffrey says, 'X, I'm afraid you should not be here.' X departs Cabinet door left.[114]

Under Mrs Thatcher the 'Economic Seminar' remains highly important. But it is flexible, an amoeba-like group whose composition changes according to circumstances. 'It's a habit of working, not an approach', explains an insider. 'If there is a problem or a proposal, she'll call a meeting involving those immediately concerned. She may also invite someone who will be important when it comes to selling it in Cabinet – someone [before his retirement] like Willie Whitelaw.'[115]

Other *ad hoc* groups beyond the reach of MISC series, as recognised *ad hoc* groups are known in Cabinet Office nomenclature, can have a considerable impact even though they only meet once or twice. For example, Mrs Thatcher convened a meeting of ministers to consider the now legendary minute entitled 'It Took a Riot' prepared for her by Michael Heseltine, then Secretary of State for the Environment, based on his experiences in Merseyside following the inner city riots of July 1981. It proposed an ambitious programme of investment and the designation of Cabinet colleagues as ministers for various decaying areas. Mr Heseltine had evangelised Whitehall on behalf of his cause like a latterday John the Baptist. He held a secret dinner at Locket's restaurant in Westminster for several influential permanent secretaries, including Sir Robert Armstrong. They were impressed.

The Prime Minister, however, prevailed. In September 1981 she convened an *ad hoc* group on inner cities and stacked it against Mr Heseltine. It consisted of the two of them, Sir Geoffrey Howe, Chancellor of the Exchequer, Sir Keith Joseph, Industry Secretary, and William Whitelaw, then Home Secretary. Whitelaw, concerned as ever to be the mediator, strove to find a middle way between Heseltine and those who did not want a penny extra for the cities for fear of being seen to reward rioters. Heseltine was isolated. There was an increase in the urban programme but on nothing like the scale he wanted.[116] On this occasion, he succumbed to the verdict of a loaded ministerial group in the full knowledge that if he took the issue to full Cabinet he would be defeated there as well.[117]

Mrs Thatcher conducts a great deal of business in gatherings like that. The pattern varies but is often along these lines. Mrs Thatcher will ask a particular Cabinet colleague to prepare a paper on a particular issue just for her, not for the Cabinet or a Cabinet committee. This explains why the tally of Cabinet papers is so low. The minister is summoned to No. 10 with his back-up team. He sits across the table from Mrs Thatcher and her team which can be a blend of people from the Downing Street Private Office, the Policy Unit, the Cabinet Office and one or two personal advisers. She then, in the words of one insider, proceeds to 'act as judge and jury in her own cause'.[118] It is this practice more than anything else which causes those on the inside to speak of 'a devaluation of Cabinet government' and her 'presidential style'.[119] The build-up of leaks and stories from such occasions creates a cumulative impression of a truly overmighty premiership.

So powerful did this impression become that Mrs Thatcher's style of Cabinet government became an issue in its own right during the 1987 general election. David Steel, the then Liberal leader, began it two days before the election was called, accusing the Prime Minister of 'having virtually abolished Cabinet government and replaced it with personal autocracy'.[120] Later, after she had sent a letter to David Owen criticising Alliance defence policy, Mr Steel said, 'You would think she is trying to treat us though we were members of her Cabinet.'[121]

Labour took up the refrain. For Neil Kinnock the Prime Minister was, as he put it in a radio interview, a practitioner of 'one person government',[122] though, as he later explained, it was not entirely her fault as 'the sycophants and assorted doormats' around the Cabinet table allowed her to get away with it.[123] For Denis Healey it was 'a matter of legitimate public concern that she is concentrating power in No. 10 Downing Street and in a most dictatorial way'.[124]

The cumulative attacks from the Opposition parties were significant as it is rare for constitutional proprieties to become a mainstream issue, especially at election time. There was no precedent for it since the backbench revolt that brought down Lloyd George in 1922.[125] But the element of genuine surprise came from John Biffen, whose days in the Cabinet were terminated straight after the election, who was reported as saying that if purged, 'I would sooner leave on my feet than crawl on my knees. I cannot guarantee to show the same contrition as my predecessors.'[126]

But was that cumulative impression of overmightiness accurate? A case can be made for both its constitutional propriety and its administrative efficiency. Take first Mrs Thatcher's version of the 'Economic Seminar'. David Howell is a critic of the Thatcher style but he sees nothing wrong in it:

HOWELL: I don't think one would have expected, not being in the Treasury, to be involved. One would have assumed that, indeed I think it was generally known, that the Prime Minister and Treasury ministers and her Chancellor kept in very close touch with the financial authorities and the central monetary authorities which means the Bank of England among other people and that all would go on. I don't think one would assume anything else. If it had a name, or a code word, well that sounds like civil servants playing games. Ministers would assume that went on. Occasionally other ministers might be called in to those discussions. But of course the nexus of any government in this country is No. 10 and the Treasury and with the Bank of England as the Treasury's appendage which unfortunately it is. I say 'unfortunately' because I would like to see a more detached monetary authortity myself. Therefore one assumes they're very hugger-mugger all the time. Under this government and under the regime that emerged after '79, which wasn't quite the one we planned for before '79, but after the one that did emerge after '79 the nexus between No. 10 and the Treasury is decisive, it overrules, it's everything. The Treasury always knows they can win. That is why they're able to go for these very precise figures of public spending, scientific precision about estimates for the years ahead and then say 'all argument hereafter ceases. Anyone who wants to change anything will have to somehow change it without altering the figures because they're settled and we know that if we ever go back to No. 10 or the Cabinet we'll always get the backing of the Prime Minister and the appellant will always be overturned.'

HENNESSY: Going back to the 'Economic Seminar', you seem to accept these things are bound to exist, these small inner groups. Doesn't it rather vitiate the nature of Cabinet government, though, if a decision, like the one to remove all exchange control, a very fundamental one for any economy, is in fact worked up, although it goes to full Cabinet in the end, in such a body? Doesn't it mean that you're presented with a set of *faits accomplis*? You're meant to be collectively the highest strategic decision making body in the land and here are all these great slices of crucial economic decisions done in a group in which ministers are outnumbered three or four to one by officials.

HOWELL: Yes, well, you say 'meant to be' and you're right to say 'meant to be' because, of course, Cabinet government is only a layer of the government and there is a kind of inner Cabinet government, whether it's called that or not, under different prime ministers, it always tends to develop. On top of that there must be an even more inner kind of government concerned with very very sensitive issues of which exchange control is one. It would have been inconceivable for exchange control to be tossed around and knocked around in Cabinet.

HENNESSY: Why?

HOWELL: Because of the numbers of people involved and because of, well, I suppose I have to say it, the inevitability of leaks.[127]

Senior civil servants, the inside connoisseurs of prime-ministerial style and procedure, tend not to be purist about the operational implications of Cabinet conventions, apart from their routine deployment in the occasional public lecture. They seem, in practice, to treat Cabinet government as a chunk of modelling clay to be pummelled and fashioned by the prime minister of the hour. This is the kind of reasoning you hear when senior men think aloud in private about the theme of Cabinet government:

> The Cabinet system has been different for Heath, Wilson and Mrs Thatcher. There's a reaction, which we can get in our constitution, to suit the PM of the day and his or her working relationships. The decisions get taken in the way in which people want to take them.
>
> Mrs Thatcher is very clear about her views, very much a leader. Because of that she doesn't need or want to resolve things by collective discussion. She knows what she wants to do about almost everything. But it *is* a collective machine because they all sink or swim with her. She uses the Cabinet as a sort of sounding board. It restrains her when restraint is necessary. She has her own instinct when she cannot carry her colleagues with her. She lets them know what she thinks. Then they try and adapt and mould it. She has very acute antennae. She's very quick to take the signals if she can't carry it.[128]

Mrs Thatcher's method of conducting business is highly efficient in its use of precious ministerial time and nervous energy. She has a bias towards decision. She has found her own highly distinctive solution to the problem of governmental overload identified by Professor Anthony King in 1975[129] and a staple item in the lore of political science ever since. It is reminiscent of Harold Wilson's well-known line about the Labour Party needing to be driven fast like a stagecoach so that the passengers are too exhilarated or too sick to object.[130] A fast driver like Mrs Thatcher can get away with it as long as her Cabinet colleagues acquiesce or concur. The seasoned Lord Hailsham, a few days after he left the Cabinet having 'had a good innings and ... without complaint',[131] exempted Mrs Thatcher from blame for the new style of Cabinet government:

> The volume of work that has to be carried out means that the Prime Minister has tended to govern through smaller sub-groups of ministers ... instead of working through the full Cabinet, or one of the formal groups like the foreign affairs committee, choosing the group of ministers with whom she works.
>
> Intrinsically it is bad ... [but] ... it would be a great mistake to assume it's confined to this particular Prime Minister.[132]

Certainly there is nothing unconstitutional about her approach. The style of conducting Cabinet business is very much putty in a prime minister's hands, much more a matter of personality than convention or tradition. There have been outbursts of objections. After the 1981 Budget she was obliged to hold periodic economic Cabinets to discuss strategy.[133] But her ministers had proved remarkably acquiescent towards Mrs Thatcher's manner of conducting business until that helicopter crashed, metaphorically speaking, through the skylight in early December 1985.

As we have seen, when corners are cut in relation to what is generally understood to be standard practice, a very high price can be paid eventually, as it was over Westland when two Cabinet resignations, a prolonged diversion of precious time and energy at the highest level in the land and a lingering taste of incompetence and chicanery (which found its most trenchant expression in the subsequent report on the affair from the all-party Commons Select Committee on Defence) left the Government looking tatty and tarnished through much of 1986.

It was generally expected that the trauma of Westland would squeeze the Thatcher style of Cabinet government into a more traditional mould, collective rather than presidential in configuration. The handling of the proposed sale of Land Rover and BL Trucks division in the early spring of 1986 suggested that this had happened when the planned sale to General Motors was abandoned in the face of backbench hostility and Cabinet doubts. But the Prime Minister granting permission for United States F-111's to fly from British bases in a raid on Libya in April after minimal ministerial consultation suggested to her routine critics at least that the Old Adam of an overmighty premiership still afflicted Mrs Thatcher. The need for tight security to surround a special operation of this kind can always be advanced in exoneration. But the first most of the Cabinet heard of the raid was when its completion was announced on BBC radio on the morning of Tuesday 15 April 1986 as the bombers were returning to Upper Heyford and Lakenheath. At a Cabinet meeting that morning, several senior ministers are reported to have cavilled, including the veteran Lord Hailsham[134] – though, as he said later, 'I don't think anyone resigned over it, and I think therefore one must take it that it is not an affront to Cabinet government.'[135]

That such a negative definition of the meaning of Cabinet government was needed from so seasoned a figure was an eloquent reflection of the battering the more reassuring notions of collective responsibility had taken in the Thatcher years. But to depict her era in stark colours as an unconstitutional premiership would be wrong. Progress towards a stronger, more assertive premiership 'had its origins in small sparks eating their way through long historical fuses before the detonations began' in a dramatic fashion, to borrow a metaphor Professor Jack Gallagher used to describe another process (the decline of the British Empire) in another era.[136] Temperament and, arguably, necessity combined to make Mrs Thatcher a managing director rather than a chairman in the Cabinet Room. Whoever succeeds her in that chair is unlikely to wholly reverse that process, though, no doubt, much political capital will be made in the early broadcasts from No. 10 of a style born out of Stanley Baldwin and James Callaghan with a smattering of Harold Macmillan. As Baldwin was determined to be anything but Lloyd George and Mrs Thatcher was to imitate anybody but Ted, her successor, of whatever party, will assuredly be, in style at least, anybody but Margaret. In its perverse way that is a rare compliment, and the Prime Minister, when safely in the Lords as Viscountess Grantham, should draw genuine comfort from it.

In looking at the Thatcher years we briefly touched on the first factor which for some forty years had been placing the Cabinet system – and its production engineers – under increasing stress. By the mid-1970s, Vernon Bogdanor was not the only observer to sense that 'We seem to be gazing at a system built long ago, for a different age, which survives only by adopting one expedient after another. It is a nineteenth century system, vainly attempting to operate in the latter half of the twentieth century.'[137] Bogdanor's 'uncomfortable impression that *all* of our political institutions are obsolescent'[138] arose from a reading of the first volume of Richard Crossman's *Diaries of a Cabinet Minister* published in 1975,[139] the year in which the 'overload' theory of government took off.

The political scientist with whose name the theory is associated is Professor Anthony King of Essex University. In that period of hyper-inflation, wafer-thin or non-existent Parliamentary majorities, an all-powerful trade union movement and pressure for devolution, Tony King captured the mood of the age when he wrote: 'Today our image of government is more that of the sorcerer's apprentice. The waters rise. The apprentice rushes about with his bucket. And none of us knows when, or whether, the magician will come home.'[140] By a fascinating coincidence, as King was marshalling his thoughts on overload in East Anglia, the Cabinet, then presided over by Harold Wilson in his last premiership, was acting out a real-life version of the thesis a hundred miles away in the Chilterns. The place is Chequers; the date Sunday, 17 November 1974; the subject a CPRS review of the British economy after the quadrupling of prices by OPEC (electoral considerations had prevented the Wilson Cabinet from facing up to the magnitude of the crisis between the February and October elections in 1974);[141] the source, Mrs Barbara Castle's Diary.[147] Her note of the occasion, which took place in the library at Chequers, is a graphic illustration of the malign combination of overload and the politics of economic decline:

> Though the CPRS had drawn up an agenda in four parts, starting with our relationship with the external world, we soon found ourselves in the middle of a second reading debate over the whole field. Ken Berrill [Head of the CPRS] introduced the discussion succinctly, setting out the problems (the threatening world slump, the petrodollar crisis, etc.) rather than attempting to answer them. Harold Lever then spoke to his own paper. 'We have only a 50 per cent chance of avoiding world catastrophe', he told us. Getting some international machinery to recycle the petrodollar was the only hope. Everything else, like petrol rationing, was only 'frolics at the margin'. We should broadly back the Americans. Denis [Healey] admitted that it was very unlikely we could close the whole of the balance of payments gap by 1978–79, even if things went well. But unless we improved our competitiveness our balance of payments position would become disastrous. There was a strong case for an energy conservation programme, if only on psychological grounds.
>
> Roy [Jenkins] ruminated: 'Your memory is better than mine, Prime Minister, but I believe it is ten years ago this very day that we sat in this room discussing the Defence Review. The world has changed out of all recognition since then.' He then talked about the changes in the power blocs, adding that those like himself who had expected the coherence of Europe to develop strongly had found the reality 'disappointing'. The Middle East situation was full of menace and he believed a pre-emptive strike by the USA was possible. Eric [Varley] talked about energy extremely competently, though he insisted that looking for major energy savings was likely to be 'extremely disappointing'. He was 'very opposed' to petrol rationing and maintained that rota cuts, organised systematically, would be the only effective method –

and they were out of the question. The only hope was to move to energy self-sufficiency. But the miners' attitude was frightening. He had been speaking only a day or two ago to a miners' meeting attended by what he called the 'Scargill Mafia'. When he told them that the Government could have used more oil at the power stations this summer and so built up coal stocks for the winter against a possible strike, but hadn't, they merely retorted, 'More fool you' and thanked him for letting them know how strong their position was. He concluded sadly: 'Don't let us frighten the oil companies away.' We needed their investment.

Wedgie [Tony Benn] then made what I found a very effective speech, pointing out that we had got to look at the problem in domestic as well as international terms. A devolution of power had also been going on at home and all our policy must take account of it. 'We cannot win consent to a technocratic solution. We must redistribute power in this country by peaceful means. Beyond the slump must be the perspective of a better society.' He did not believe the solution lay in bigger and bigger units: he had been immensely struck by the emphasis which Jim [Callaghan] laid on devolution in his paper. 'We must show what sort of Government we are.' Were we going to go for impersonal macro-solutions, or were we going to realise that the people were looking for us as their leaders to provide an answer to their difficulties? To them their leaders seemed utterly remote. 'Without consent no solution we work out round this table will have a chance.' Mike [Foot] said wryly that if, as Harold Lever said, we had only a 50 per cent chance of avoiding catastrophe, we had better work out a contingency plan in case that chance did not come off. Roy [Mason] made a fluent contribution about the added danger of war in the Middle East.

The gathering gloom was compounded by Jim [Callaghan] acting Cassandra as usual. 'When I am shaving in the morning I say to myself that if I were a young man I would emigrate. By the time I am sitting down to breakfast I ask myself, "Where would I go"?' (Laughter).[143] Mike had talked about contingency plans for catastrophe, he continued. If we ever got to a siege economy he, Jim, dreaded the effect on our democracy. He didn't think that the US would do a Suez in the Middle East. The more likely prospect was our declining influence. 'One prospect is that we shall lose our seat on the Security Council.' Jim concluded gloomily that in his view we should go on sliding downhill for the next few years. 'Nothing in these papers makes me believe anything to the contrary. I haven't got any solution. As I said, if I were a young man, I should emigrate.'

But the Chancellor of the Exchequer, the combative Denis Healey, would have none of this defeatism:

> Denis rallied the defeatists with a robust speech: what everyone had said showed how pretentious were some of the demands made by the party for us to interfere here, there and everywhere. 'It is no good ceasing to be the world's policeman in order to become the world's parson instead.' But he would have nothing of Jim's gloom. 'If we do join the Third World it will be as a member of OPEC.' He wasn't as pessimistic as Harold L. (who by this time had gone home, pleading that he was suffering from gastric flu). We could not sensibly plan ahead for a doomsday-type catastrophe. He agreed with Wedgie about the dissolution of the power blocs. He rejected the conspiracy theory of foreign affairs. 'International Communism has as much or as little significance as the Commonwealth.' By this time it was nearly 1.00 pm. Harold summed up by saying the discussion had been first-class: 'the best I have ever heard in this type of gathering'.[144]

This was not Wilson indulging in a burst of black humour. More than a decade later when I reminded him of that autumn Sunday at Chequers, he said: 'it meant that I'd got through all my policies . . . [they] all had a little bit of fun and expression and there was no change in policy. I was quite pleased with it.'[145] But before his ministers dispersed for home, there was worse to come. The afternoon session found Tony Crosland, incarnation of the intellectual-in-politics and a trained economist, saying that nobody knew how our relative decline had taken place. 'All we can do is press every button we've got. We do not know which, if any, of them will have the desired results.'[146]

It all seemed a far cry from the Labour Government of Clement Attlee, the postwar model against which other administrations tend to be judged in terms of efficiency and effectiveness.[147] It was Tony King's benchmark, too, in his seminal article on 'overload'. In commenting on 'the increasing difficulty that both major political parties seem to have in carrying out their election manifestos' he looked back to the Attlee years: 'The fit between what the Labour Party said it would do in 1945 and what the Labour Government actually achieved between 1945 and 1951 is astonishingly close. Most of *Let Us Face the Future* reads like a prospective history of the immediate post-war period. Since about 1959, however, the fit has become less close.'[148] Caution is needed here. The Attlee governments should not be placed atop a pedestal of administrative impeccability. Even Mr Attlee's engine room showed signs of wear and tear. By 1946 Sir Stafford Cripps, the organisation-minded President of the Board of Trade, had become concerned about the cumbersome nature of the Cabinet's back-up machinery and the taking of too many minor decisions at Cabinet and Cabinet committee level. His worries were shared by his permanent secretary, Sir John Woods, and by Bridges and Brook.[149] Despite the Prime

Minister's efforts, the conduct of Cabinet business could still appal the tidy-minded ex-civil servant, Hugh Gaitskell, the young Minister of Fuel and Power, who confided to his diary in October 1947 that 'sometimes Cabinet meetings horrify me because of the amount of rubbish talked by some Ministers who come there after reading briefs which they do not understand'.[150]

Attlee, particularly after his reorganisation of economic decision-taking with the creation of an Economic Policy Committee of the Cabinet in the autumn of 1947, did run a tight, well-organised government.[151] But the suspicion remains, as Sir John Hoskyns puts it, that 'since 1945 government has been writing itself an undoable job specification'.[152] The growth in the workload of the central government machine is a running theme of our historical chapters dealing with the twentieth century. Sir John's view remains pertinent even for the most anti-statist administrations since the war, the Thatcher governments of 1979–83 and 1983–7.

The dilemma of a self-proclaimed radical government striving for a simultaneous withdrawal from state activity *and* a boosting of efficiency in those activities that remain within the public perimeter was classically illustrated within the space of a week during the 1986 Party Conference season. On 8 October, Mr Norman Lamont, Financial Secretary to the Treasury (its minister responsible for privatisation policy), told the Conservative Conference at Bournemouth that since 1979 £8,000 million had been raised from the sale of state assets and that by the end of 1987, 600,000 workers would have moved from the public to the private sector. After eight years of Conservative Government the state sector would have shrunk by more than 40 per cent.[153] This was not, as it was sometimes portrayed, the greatest shift in ownership in British industrial history. That politico-economic rosette remains pinned to Attlee's lapel. When the ratchet effect was moving the other way, a labour force of 2,304,200 was shifted between the private and public sectors by the nationalisations of 1945–51.[154] But it was a formidable achievement, a more radical adjustment than the Conservatives expected or planned for in 1979 and one of the factors likely, in the eyes of posterity, to make the Thatcher years historic rather than historical, to use a distinction made by Professor Sammy Finer.[155]

Such a record could only bring a glow of pleasure to subscribers of 'Taylor's Law of Painful Proximity' ('Taylor' being Stephen Taylor, civil servant-turned-management consultant) that 'the performance of any organisation improves in proportion to its distance from political control'.[156] Yet as if to illustrate *the* greatest single paradox of the Thatcher years, evident almost from the start in its ever more interventionist approach to local government, the Government announced five days before Mr Lamont's triumphalism at the Conservative Party Conference that a minister was, for the first time since its creation by Aneurin Bevan almost forty years earlier, to take full political control of the National Health Service – Taylor's Law in reverse. Mr Tony Newton, the Health Minister (a post that did *not* at that time carry Cabinet rank), was to chair the key management board of 'the world's largest employer after the Soviet Army and the Indian State Railways System'.[157] It was little noticed, though no minister had wielded such direct power over so large a proportion of the British labour force since Sir Andrew Duncan left the Ministry of Supply in 1945.

The border between the public and private sectors, as befits a nation whose two major political parties are obsessed with the ownership of industry, has been almost continuously mobile since 1945, as has the scope of central government. It must be remembered that in terms of workload on the Cabinet, getting out of state activity is just as difficult and time-consuming as getting in. Preparing a privatisation is just as intricate as arranging a nationalisation. The politics of it is equally fractious with sniping from the Opposition about the need for any change in existing ownership and from the governing party's own zealots dissatisfied with the pace of progress. The same applied, intriguingly, in the withdrawal from Empire. Disposing of imperial possessions was far more absorbent of Cabinet time in the thirty-five years from 1945 to 1980 (from India to Zimbabwe) than acquiring them ever was over a 300-year period (from Cromwell to the Versailles peace treaty or Ireland to Tanganyika).

What does seem to be constant, however, from administration to administration, is the personal overload experienced by the British Cabinet minister. This, as Chris Patten, the capable and respected Minister for Overseas Development, has observed, is another stress-making paradox at the heart of the Cabinet system. 'It is extraordinary,' says Mr Patten, 'that in our system of government we both have more ministers than others and, in my experience, more tired and put-upon ministers than others.'[158] Apart from titanic figures like Mrs Thatcher, who can get by on four hours' sleep and eat a red box and a permanent secretary for breakfast every morning, most ministers are aware of the problem and have a string of horror stories they are prepared to tell about the quagmire of detail into which the British ministerial class is sucked. Take the tale of two graveyards. The first involves Sir Winston Churchill's resting-place in Bladon Village, Oxfordshire, and Richard Crossman as Minister of Housing and Local Government. The busy schedule of this senior Cabinet figure was obliged to accommodate in 1965 a meeting with 'the Clerk of Oxfordshire County Council and the chairman of planning, Alderman Wise, [to] deal with that splendid subject, the toilets in Bladon village'. Objections had been raised to planning permission for a car park to cater for visitors to the old warrior's grave 'on the grounds that the toilets and the car park were in the wrong place' and necessitated 'a hot summer afternoon ... passing the distance from the car park to the grave'.[159] The second ministerial elegy in an English churchyard involves a middle-ranking minister who has since risen far, Sir Geoffrey Howe. Sir Geoffrey, as Minister of Trade and Consumer Affairs, was responsible in the early seventies for aspects of the Heath government's incomes policy. Holding the dam against inflation obliged a busy minster of the Crown to telephone in person the vicar of Trumpington in Cambridgeshire to ask him not to increase the charge he made for burials under the terms of the Prices and Incomes Act, 1973.[160] Intervention on this micro scale is an absurd waste of scarce ministerial time and nervous energy, and of their officials' time and energy too.

But how does one explain the macro phenomenon described by Chris Patten in which Britain has more ministers than comparable Western governments, who, nonetheless, appear more tired than their overseas counterparts? Obviously it has a great deal to do with managing big government in hard times, coping with the industrial and social consequences of decline, propping up State welfare and defence machines under-engined because of the inadequate performance of the British economy. It is equally revealing to examine how many jobs the British Cabinet minister is expected to perform. He or she must (apart from the two to four Cabinet ministers in the House of Lords) deal with constituency duties. A politician's postbag becomes heavier when he becomes a minister: constituents expect him to be able to deliver more.[161] He must keep in close touch with his party nationally and undertake a fairly continuous round of speaking engagements. He must maintain his links with his party's backbenchers in Parliament and burnish his press image, the hard currency of reputation and standing. He must within his ministry be policy-maker-in-chief and, since the Rayner reforms, chief executive in the managerial sense as well. What is left from this formidable job description has to be divided between collective duties in Cabinet and Cabinet committees and private life and relaxations among family and friends. It is a schedule to exhaust a superman or superwoman. And, as Sir William Rees-Mogg has opined in another context (that of the Director-General of the BBC), 'impossible jobs tend to be done badly'.[162]

These problems have long been recognised. Had Sir Alec Douglas-Home been re-elected Prime Minister in 1964, reducing the Cabinet's workload was to have been a priority.[163] Had Harold Macmillan not been forced by illness to make way for Home in 1963 *his* work-plan for 1964 involved, as his Press Secretary, Harold Evans, noted in his diary, 'an entirely new routine . . . He would be taking off time from the Cabinet (the Lord Chancellor could preside) in order to concentrate on the things that really needed doing.'[164] Lord Hailsham, whose personal solution to the overload problem as Secretary of State for Education in the Macmillan and Home Cabinets was to refuse to take home any red boxes of papers,[165] devoted his opposition years of the mid-seventies to writing an account of the clogging-up of British central government in which he declared:

> I am myself a real believer in Cabinet government as essential to a democratic constitution. But I would immediately require to make a number of qualifications. In the first place, Cabinet ministers have ... a great deal too much to do and much more to do than ministers in other countries. Overwork is the mark of a bad system of administration or a bad administrator. Since I always managed to acquire a greater amount of leisure than my British colleagues, I do not believe the fault lay in myself. I believe simply that our system of government is inefficient partly because it is overcentralised. Ministers should have plenty of time to think, and plenty of time to go about visiting their own outstations and comparing experience in this country with that abroad, and should spend far less of their time in the House of Commons dancing attendance on the division bells.[166]

It is more than twenty years since Lord Home toyed with his plans for counter-attacking against the deluge of business flooding Cabinet and ten years since Lord Hailsham pondered the problem. It has not abated. Douglas Hurd devoted his keynote address to the RIPA conference at Durham University in September 1986 to the theme of 'a government machine clogged with matter'.[167] There seems to be an iron law of overload in Whitehall which grips administration after administration. The Home Secretary said to his expert audience at Durham:

> The colleagues I admire are those who have managed to organise their lives so that the matters which come for collective discussion are not to them residual, after they have signed all the letters and dealt with all the submissions from their own departments, but take their proper place at the centre of their working lives. If collective decisions are to be of the right quality then collective decision-making has to be a principal, and not the last call on the time and energy of ministers.[168]

For Mr Hurd, a minister with a near-unique width of Whitehall experience (professional diplomat, political secretary to a prime minister, junior, middle-ranking and Cabinet minister), overload clearly threatened the efficient performance of the cardinal functions of Cabinet government. He sought remedies for the problem inside Whitehall ('It is up to us to find the time and energy needed for effective collective discussion') and, like Haldane before him, across the square in Westminster ('I believe that one day Parliament is going to have to get a grip on itself').[169]

PARLIAMENT

The House of Commons is the greatest closed shop of all ... For the purposes of government, a country of 55 million people is forced to depend on a talent pool which could not sustain a single multinational company.
Sir John Hoskyns, 1983[170]

His first impression is that he is in Church. The vaulted roofs and stained glass windows, the rows of statues of great statesmen of the past, the echoing halls, the soft-footed attendants and the whispered conversation, contrast depressingly with the crowded meetings and the clang and clash of hot opinions he has just left behind in his election campaign. Here he is, a tribune of the people, coming to make his voice heard in the seats of power. Instead, it seems as if he is expected to worship; and the most conservative of all religions – ancestor worship.
Aneurin Bevan, 1952,
recalling his arrival at Westminster in 1929[171]

Mr Livingstone told a one-day seminar in North London ... that he had never realised how much he was going to dislike being in Parliament until he had attended the meeting [of the PLP]. He said it was like going back in a time machine to the days of King Alfred – the atmosphere was 'absolutely tribal'.
Newspaper report on Ken Livingstone's
first days as an MP, 1987[172]

That mob at Westminster.
Alfred Milner, 1902[173]

Parliament has a curiously mellowing effect on men and women.
Lord Hailsham, 1987[174]

Power is a mercurial concept in a mature democracy. It slips through the fingers of those who would hold it and trickles down a myriad of crevices before going underground. Its elusiveness was appreciated by Nye Bevan, himself an 'artist in the use of power' when a member of the Attlee Cabinet,[175] as a very young man and far away from those vaulted halls in the valleys of industrial South Wales. Drawing on a Commons speech of Bevan's in December 1943, his biographer, Michael Foot, captured the motivating force of the young Bevan in Tredegar:

'Very important man. That's Councillor Jackson', his father had said to him. 'What's the Council?' he asked. 'Very important place indeed and they are very powerful men,' his father had replied. When I got older I said to myself: 'The place to get to is the Council. That's where the power is' so I worked very hard and, in association with my fellows, when I was about twenty years of age, I got on the Council. I discovered when I got there that power *had* been there, but it had just gone. So I made some enquiries, being an earnest student of social affairs, and I learned that the power had slipped down to the County Council. That was where it was and where it had gone to. So I worked very hard again and I got there and it had gone from there too.[176]

Bevan never recorded whether he caught up with the coat-tails of power when he took his seat in the Commons Chamber in 1929 or when he arrived for his first Cabinet in 1945. One suspects he saw them slipping out of the door each time.

Apart from a perpetual shortage of money, Parliament is by far the most ancient of the influences on the state bureaucracy. The British Civil Service, whether they be priests, place-men or meritocrats, have had to live with the beast since the knights of the shires were summoned to London to be the Communities' (or Commons') representatives and to report on how much taxation their communities could bear in the mid-thirteenth century.[177] The power of Parliament has waxed and waned *vis-à-vis* the Government ever since. It has usually adopted the posture of the whingeing underdog, apart from the Cromwellian Protectorate when the Parliamentarians temporarily usurped the monarchy.

Parliament is a place of paradoxes. It is totally infused with the richest resin of historical romanticism, which captivates most who go there, not least foreign observers. Listen, for example, to the view of a 'Czech Anglophile' in 1939 just before he and his country were engulfed by totalitarianism. I have never encountered a more poetic rendition of the romantic theme:

The character of a [British] Member of Parliament should be so upright that the faintest breath of scandalous suspicion perishes at once through its absurdity. He should have the courage of Cromwell so that he is never silent through the discretion bred of fear; whenever he has to make a decision he will shun expediency and ask only 'Is this right?' His skin should be thick enough to resist the countless mean things that will be said and written about him; but he should be sufficiently sensitive to recognise fair criticism and, like John Bright, to heed the cry of genuine distress. He should possess a deeply founded knowledge of all the main political issues and expert knowledge of at least one or two. His culture, like Haldane's, should ensure that his interest are Catholic. Like Arthur James Balfour, his mind should be open to new ideas, free from any confusion of prejudice with principle. He should be so intelligent that

> he should be able to meet the best informed on terms of ease if not of equality. He should be so eloquent that he can speak spontaneously for an hour, and his audience should long for more when he sits down. His silences should be as eloquent as his speeches. He should be the reverse of a bore or a prig. He should be so witty that he can illuminate the most laborious subject and the most pompous occasion with appropriate flashes of humour. He should be equally at home with mineworker and millionaire. Like Gladstone, his physical health should be so sound that it easily endures the strain to which his unflagging industry subjects it. He should be the diligent and accessible friend of his constituents, but should never forget that the Nation must come before the parish.[178]

A Parliament of paragons would solve two ever-present problems of the British system: the pool of talent from which ministers are fished would be more than adequate for the regular, renewable supply of twenty-two Cabinet members capable of coping with that impossible workload *and* having sufficient extra time and energy to move beyond mere coping and into the realms of problem-solving and creative thinking; those that remained in the pool would be more than capable of calling ministers and the Civil Service to account in fulfilment of Parliament's classic scrutiny function. Reality, inevitably, bears no relationship to the romantic illusion. During the 1987 general election, a senior civil servant said to me that of all the complaints made by the critics of the British system of government, the meagreness of the Parliamentary pool of talent was what worried him most, a worry which recurred time and again as he sat in on ministerial meetings.[179]

The public, however, according to what survey evidence exists, seems reasonably content with the performance of its MPs. Philip Norton noted in 1985 that 'in Almond and Verba's classic study published in 1963,[180] more Britons expressed pride in their governmental and political institutions than in any other feature of the nation that was mentioned. Perceptions of the House of Commons as an effective working body have shown no significant decline since that time.'[181]

But amongst the 'political nation', particularly the former insiders, sharp criticisms can be heard. As so often, Sir John Hoskyns heads the lists of the most merciless dissecters of the institutionalised inadequacies of our system of government; speaking in 1983 he turned his verbal firepower on Conservative MPs as a Conservative Government was in office at the time:

> Conservative MPs (and probably MPs of other parties, too) are uninterested in method. This is ... because they are, at heart, romantics. They see Britain as a canvas on which the young MP, a sort of Dick Whittington figure, can paint his political self-portrait; making his way

> in the world, until he holds one of the great offices of state, finally retiring full of honour and respectability. Political life is thus about the triumphs and disasters of personalities; living biography. The old legends fascinate them ... obsessed with tradition, Conservatives often forget that, like period houses, today's traditions were once innovations by bolder spirits. For most of them, questions of policy analysis and formulation are thus of secondary interest, until it is too late.[187]

Sir Frank Cooper speaking in 1985 was marginally kinder. He recognised there were times 'when the House of Commons has a profound and sensitive feel for the gravity of the occasion and, indeed, for the mood and feelings of the nation as a whole'. But his overall appraisal was as stark as Hoskyns's. 'Have not,' he asked, 'the Mother of Parliament image, the ability of the British to govern themselves effectively, and the efficacy of the Parliamentary process, like the British bobby, became fantasy and myth rather than reality or truth?' Sir Frank answered his own question:

> One has only to enter the Houses of Parliament to sense the magic and past glory of our Parliamentary history. One has only to watch the proceedings on the floor of the Lower House often to feel ashamed by the behaviour of its members, by the inability of the Opposition to influence the Government, by the tremendous premium put on the style of speaking and the scoring of debating points rather than the real issues and the matters of substance. The frequently noisy proceedings lack dignity and responsibility. To whom are they an example in these days of almost instant media coverage?[183]

To any list of the factors hobbling a high and sustained Parliamentary performance – the quality of MPs, the burden of tradition, the adventure-playground aspects of procedure, the bias towards the trivial and the transient against the weighty and the long-term – must be added another paradox: that at one level Parliament tries to do too much, getting bogged down in a wealth of detail far better handled at national level (if one favours devolution to Scotland and Wales), at regional level, or at local level – if one resents the new interventionism in central–local relations by economy-minded administrations since 1976 when a Labour Environment Secretary, Tony Crosland, told the local authorities 'the party is over'.[184] Yet on a different plane, Parliament has been unable to raise its game to the new heights required if it is to cope with another, rival focus of sovereignty, attention and rule-making, the supra-national European Economic Community. At the individual level, too, the workload of an MP has increased substantially. In the 1950s an MP could expect to receive between twenty and thirty letters a week from constituents. In the 1980s the figure was well over 100.[185]

These are big themes, important but not central to this volume. Of the three core functions of Parliament singled out by that indefatigable observer of the Westminster scene, Philip Norton – providing the personnel of government, legitimisation of the decisions of government and scrutiny and influence over government decisions[186] – it is the last which matters most to Whitehall. And here Westminster really has tried to raise its game in the past decade with the new select committee system created in 1979.

Shortly after the Conservatives returned to power, Mr Norman St John-Stevas, historian, parliamentarian, constitutionalist and, in the best sense, showman, persuaded a sceptical Cabinet of the need to implement a version of the reforms adumbrated a year before by the all-party Commons Select Committee on Procedure.[187] The kernel of the reform idea was the creation of new select committees to shadow and monitor individual Whitehall departments, or clusters of them, on their performance both as policy-makers and as deliverers of public services. St John-Stevas moved swiftly before the cares of office had dimmed the euphoria and optimism of electoral victory. Shrewdly, he sought and won the support of the two veteran eminences of Mrs Thatcher's Cabinet, Mr (as he was then) William Whitelaw and Lord Hailsham, the Lord Chancellor. Hailsham's support was conditional on the Law Officers remaining exempt from select committee scrutiny, which explains the continuing absence of a committee with this function.[188] Most ministers have come to rue this rash of reforming zeal, none more so than Mrs Thatcher, always sceptic, who, at one stage removed (a serving prime minister does not attend hearings), herself had to endure trial by select committee over the Westland affair.

Announcing the reform of the House of Commons on 25 June 1979, Mr St John-Stevas acknowledged the contract between the romantic view and the reality of Parliament and made two bold claims:

> Today is, I believe, a crucial day in the life of the House of Commons. After years of discussion and debate, we are embarking upon a series of changes that could constitute the most important parliamentary reforms of the century. Parliament may not, for the moment, stand at the zenith of public esteem. There are tides of fashion that rise and fall as there are tides of opinion that move. We should not be too concerned about that. One truth abides and that is that parliamentary government has been one of the great contributions of the British nation to the World's civilisation ...
>
> ... That is not to say that I believe that Parliament is impeccable ... it has been increasingly felt that the twentieth century Parliament is not effectively supervising the executive and that while the power and

effectiveness of Whitehall has grown, that of Westminster has diminished. The proposals that the Government are placing before the House are intended to redress the balance of power to enable the House of Commons to do more effectively the job it has been elected to do.[189]

Was 25 June 1979 a crucial day? Were those parliamentary reforms the most important of the century? Did they progressively redress the balance of power between Whitehall and Westminster? In the spring of 1983 a gathering of experts met at Southampton University to ponder the St John-Stevas tests shortly before the fourth anniversary of the select committee's birth. (Mr St John-Stevas had been despatched to the backbenches by Mrs Thatcher more than two years earlier; a reformer is rarely honoured in his or her own lifetime.) Gavin Drewry conducted an efficiency audit worthy of Lord Rayner. He noted that in 1918 Haldane had been keen on standing committees of Parliament to cover 'the main divisions of the business of government'.[190] Indeed, the St John-Stevas reforms could be treated as the implementation of yet another Haldane improvement after a mere sixty years in which the British body politic had become slowly accustomed to the idea. But Drewry turned to the natural world rather than that of Hegelian philosophy for the inspiration of his impulse towards managerial investigation – to the Mercalli Scale for measuring earthquakes from force I to force XII:

I: Just detectable by experienced observers when prone. Microseisms.
II: Felt by few. Delicately poised objects may sway.
III: Vibration but still unrecognised by many. Feeble.
IV: Felt by many indoors but few outdoors. Moderate.
V: Felt by almost all. Many awakened. Unstable objects moved – and so on, up to XII (Damage total. Vibrations distort vision. Objects thrown in the air. Major catastrophe.) Various opinions are held about the seismic significance of select committees, but the first four or five points on the scale are more than enough to encompass the credible range of such variations.[191]

Drewry's verdict was as bleak as St John-Stevas's hopes had been lush: 'Committees may produce some vibration, which causes delicately poised objects to sway and is felt by many indoors, but by few outdoors. Few are awakened.'[192]

I disagreed with this at the time. As the Whitehall watcher at this period of first *The Times* then *The Economist* then *The Times* once more, I produced periodic audits of my own based on many hours spent along the Committee Corridor of the House of Commons. For a start, personal observation gave me a different impression. Almost from the beginning, the mere existence of those dozen new committees raised the level of the *Whitehall* game as well as the Westminster one in a benign cycle of mutual reinforcement. One should not have been surprised. Since Gladstone's time, the queen of the select committees, the Public Accounts Committee, had by *its* very existence exerted a cleansing effect in all governnment departments. The knowledge that, on its day, the PAC could put the most seasoned permanent secretary, in his role as departmental accounting officer, through the wringer over some aspect of procurement, expenditure and, increasingly, value-for-money, inspired a high degree of preparation at the highest level in a ministry prior to a PAC appearance even if, in the event, the committee concentrated on minnow-matters instead of sharks and whales. Whitehall reputations could be made or broken in the PAC. They still can.

The key to the PAC's pre-eminence was and remains the formidable back-up provided by the Exchequer and Audit Department, another Gladstonian creation when the Grand Old Man was at the Exchequer in the mid-1860s (he may have cut down every tree within reach at home in Hawarden but he was a master planter of sturdy oaks when at his desk in Whitehall). Reconstituted in the early eighties as the National Audit Office with a staff of 650 under Sir Gordon Downey, an experienced Treasury-hand who was, for a time, No. 2 in the CPRS (he was succeeded by an MOD-hand, John Bourn, in 1987), the old E and AD tradition of meticulous filleting of the files continues, conducted by a battalion of relentlessly tidy-minded accountants who make a habit of winning the Civil Service bridge competitions when not fashioning ammunition to place in the hands of MPs on the Public Accounts Committee.

The new select committees have nothing comparable to the National Audit Office. Where Mr Robert Sheldon, Chairman of the PAC, can call upon John Bourn's Own, even Mr Terence Higgins, chairman of the prestigious Treasury and Civil Service Committee, has to rely on a handful of clever generalists from the House of Commons Clerk's Department and a fluctuating team of specialist advisers recruited on a modest daily rate of. Even so, the knowledge that some difficult but gifted MP on this committee, like Dr Jeremy Bray, ex-ICI and highly numerate and economically literate (who has since left on his appointment as a Labour frontbench spokesman), might embark upon a series of desperately difficult questions one twilight afternoon in Committee Room 15 was enough to keep the lamps in the Treasury burning late, thinking through the nuances of departmental policy, to avoid the Chancellor, the permanent secretary, or even a deputy or under secretary, being slowly pinned to the wall in front of appreciative eyes on the press bench conveniently placed between interrogator and interrogated. The potential power of those committees could be felt constantly where I sat hour after hour with Richard Norton-Taylor of *The Guardian* and Robin Pauley of the *Financial Times* even on afternoons when the MPs cudgelled their grey cells in vain to drive a penetrating question the fifteen or so feet between them and the witness.

These were not seismic occasions where volcanoes beneath the glaciers suddenly melted the icebergs of Whitehall secrecy and reticence, the accumulation of centuries. But it was a climatic and ecological change sufficient to open up the occasional crevasse from which the sounds of creaking and groaning would emerge. The best evidence that St John-Stevas's tests were more than the routine rodomontade of parliamentary exchanges came from his colleagues who increasingly cursed what he had done and their civil servants complaining about increased workload and exposure. Shortly after the Treasury and Civil Service Committee had investigated monetarism, the philosophical core of the then Government's economic strategy, Sir Leo Pliatzky, recently retired from Whitehall, spoke for many of his former colleagues on BBC Radio 4's *Analysis* when he said in August 1980:

> My impression is that the pips are beginning to squeak in the Treasury in meeting all these demands, not simply for appearances but for asking questions and submitting memoranda. Let me not for one moment suggest that this is resented or that there's any half-heartedness in meeting this on the part of my former colleagues. But when, for instance, you get a situation in which the select committee has more advisers on monetary policy than the Treasury has working on monetary policy in the Treasury, you can see there's a danger of these people being distracted from the actual work of monetary policy to coping with the select committee's requirements for explanations, discussions etc. on monetary policy.[193]

New realities need thunderstorms and flashes of lightning to illuminate the changed landscape. What Suez was for foreign and defence policy in the fifties, Arthur Scargill Mark I was for industrial and trade union policy in the seventies and Scargill Mark II for yet another shift in the eighties, Westland was for the Parliamentary select committees in 1986. As we have seen in our section on the Cabinet, an existing Treasury select committee inquiry into the relations between ministers and civil servants swung its beam on to Westland and the purpose-built Defence Select Committee inquiry brought tranche after tranche of inconvenient material (from the Government's point of view) into the public domain between January and July 1986. The Government's attempt to remove civil servants from beyond the reach of the select committees in its reply to the Defence Committee in October 1986 produced another constitutional storm with the rights of select committees at its epicentre. The offending paragraph, issued in the Prime Minister's name on October 1986, read:

> The Government does not believe that a select committee is a suitable instrument for inquiring into or passing judgement upon the actions or conduct of an individual civil servant. As a witness the civil servant is liable to be constrained in his answers by his instructions from or his accountability to his Minister or by his duty of confidentiality, and therefore unable to speak freely in his own defence. The fact that a select committee's proceedings are privileged does not absolve him from the obligation to comply with those instructions and that duty. There is a further risk that the process of questioning may be affected by political considerations, particularly if politically controversial matters are involved. A select committee inquiry into actions and conduct of an individual civil servant, conducted in public and protected by privilege, would give the civil servant concerned no safeguards and no rights, though his reputation and even his career might be at risk. These considerations reinforce the case for not blurring or cutting across the lines of accountability – from civil servants to Ministers, and from Ministers to Parliament – and confirm the Government in its view that *it is not appropriate for the inquiries of select committees to be extended to cover the conduct of individual civil servants* [emphasis added]. Accordingly the Government proposes to make it clear to civil servants giving evidence to select committees that they should not answer questions which are or appear to be directed to the conduct of themselves or of other named civil servants.[194]

The Government's reply – a blend of the Prime Minister's philosophy and the drafting skills of Sir Robert Armstrong and Mr John Wakeham then Mrs Thatcher's Chief Whip[195] – quelled the doubts of the First Division Association rumbling since Mrs Thatcher named the Westland Five in the Commons the previous January. Their people were once more behind the fireproof shield of ministerial accountability to Parliament.[196] But it caused an earthquake in the House of Commons of at least force V. The nature of the television and Fleet Street news coverage meant that it was felt 'by almost all'. Many were awakened, perhaps for the first time, to the perpetual tussle between Westminster and Whitehall. Several unstable objects (politicians, commentators, journalists) and perhaps some highly stable ones (permanent secretaries and the like) did move.

The Government was condemned from all sides, the FDA apart. Almost as soon as Parliament returned from the summer recess a debate was forced. It was billed, inevitably but justifiably, as a showdown, a test case of the relative power of the executive and the legislative. In a leading article the day before the Commons debate, the *Financial Times* declared that the Government's reply to the Defence Committee 'smacks of the arrogance of power ... It is a matter for Parliament as a whole. If MPs have any self-respect they should make their views known in tomorrow's debate. Otherwise a once admirable attempt at parliamentary reform will have been effectively aborted by the very party which in its halcyon days sought to introduce it.'[197] For Hugo Young of *The Guardian*, the Government's redefinition of the rules of Parliamentary accountability was nothing less than a tawdry talisman of tarnished times:

> Accountability is a word most people understand. It means explaining and justifying one's actions and inviting a verdict upon them. In most worlds it is not theoretical, not merely a word. In politics it has degenerated into an abstraction, and become part of the debauchery of language and government characteristic of out time.[198]

The language of outrage was not confined to political commentators or the Opposition benches. During the Commons debate on 29 October, Sir Edward du Cann, whose credentials cluttered the page – Conservative MP for Taunton, former Chairman of the 1922 Committee of Tory backbenchers and no less than four premier select committees, the old pre-1979 Expenditure Committee, the Public Accounts Committee, the Treasury and Civil Service Committee and the Liaison Committee (the shop stewards' committee of all select committee chairmen) – recalled St John-Stevas's assurance in 1979 that the Government would be accountable to the Commons through the new select committees. 'From these clear and specific assurances the Government now seeks to renege,' he said. 'The Government asserts that it will henceforward limit the effectiveness and authority of this Parliament. "Be damned if you will", would be my reply.'[199] Only with difficulty did John Biffen, Leader of the House, defuse the atmosphere at the end of the debate by promising to consult the Liaison Committee before the revised instructions to civil servants went out.[200]

The Westland breakthrough was very largely the work of one committee, Defence, and one of its members in particular, Labour's Dr John Gilbert. In recalling it for an interview with *Contemporary Record*, he talked like a prizefighter: 'In the depths of Westland I was walking up and down my bedroom and rehearsing how I'd get the sonofabitch, how I'd box him, as I was convinced he was trying to mislead the committee.'[201] The 'sonofabitch' was none other than Sir Robert Armstrong, showing, incidentally, that greater love hath no civil servant than to lay his reputation on the line for the woman he serves. The Gilbert–Armstrong duel was *the* classic confrontation of the new select committees in the first two parliaments of their life. His experience led Dr Gilbert to claim, justifiably in my view, that 'the select committee is by far the most powerful instrument for getting the truth out of ministers. It's much more powerful than Parliamentary Question Time or correspondence with ministers.' He explained why:

> When questioning a minister in a select committee, as opposed to the chamber of the House of Commons, you can ask supplementary after supplementary. He can't run away.
>
> You have certain advantages and disadvantages compared to a prosecuting barrister. A barrister in court can go on for days and days. People get bored in a committee if one person hogs the questioning and sessions only last for two or two-and-a-half hours. But on a select committee you have the advantage of sitting there and listening to your colleagues asking questions and you can suddenly see the openings they may not have spotted.[202]

There is convincing evidence that Gilbert's views are shared by his fellow MPs. After the 1987 general election the competition for a select committee place was fiercer than ever.[203]

The post-1979 select committees were the new frontline in the near-constant struggle between the legislature and the executive (whether monarch or Cabinet/Whitehall) since the mid-fourteenth century. But the traditional longstanding instruments of accountability should not be forgotten, despite Dr Gilbert's remarks: the Parliamentary Question, some 47,000 a year at an average cost of £75 per oral answer and £45 per written reply; MPs' letters to the Minister, the private word in his ear; even the old-fashioned public speech; Enoch Powell's notorious 'River Tiber foaming with much blood'[204] speech on immigration policy in April 1968 brought forth 100,000 letters.[205]

The revival of another traditional instrument much beloved by Mr Powell, the House of Lords, was a remarkable phenomenon of the 1980s. The object of repeated ridicule since Gilbert and Sullivan sent the peers strutting across the stage of the Savoy Theatre singing:

> Bow, bow, ye low and middle classes,
> Bob, bow, ye tradesmen, bow ye masses,

the Lords, in its unreformed condition, was virtually written off by no less a figure than Lord Hailsham in the mid-1970s as 'arguably less persuasive than a powerful leading article in *The Times*, or even a good edition of *Panorama*'.[206] Mrs Thatcher endured more than a hundred defeats at their Lordships' hands during her first two terms. Ministers and civil servants began to take the Upper House very seriously indeed[207] and Lord Whitelaw, Deputy Prime Minister and Leader of the Lords, found himself in a great deal of trouble when he predicted in November 1987 that the Government might be defeated in the Lords on key clauses of its Education Bill.[208] Pressure groups were quick to latch on to the value of the Lords, with its

244 often very expert cross-benchers and near permanent condition as a hung Parliament, as *the* forum in which to press their specific causes.[209]

Indeed, Parliament, or, more specifically, the House of Commons, by virtue of its being elected, is *the* legitimate pressure group. It was not the first – the church and the barons had been engaged in the business for years before Simon de Montfort rode into town – but Parliament became and, despite vicissitudes and much justified criticism, remains the most important pressure group with which Whitehall has to deal. The moment the appointed public servant ceases to walk in fear of the elected member of Parliament, the system and the constitution really will be in a state of disequilibrium.

PRESSURE

> We are treated to the premasticated speech, tossed back and forth across the floor of the House, blocs who have already formed their opinions in secrecy. This secrecy, this twilight of Parliamentary debate envelops the Lobby in its own obscurity. Through this, the lobbies became – as far as the general public is concerned – faceless, voiceless, unidentifiable; in brief, anonymous.
> **S. E. Finer, 1958**[210]

> It is not a healthy or even a genuine democracy in which the individual takes responsibility for a decision once every four or five years ... Pressure groups are a way whereby people can exercise their right to know and comment on what is happening, and to argue for different policies and priorities throughout a government's term of office.
> **Des Wilson, 1984**[211]

> Members of Parliament and Ministers both ... need to shake themselves free to some extent from the embrace of pressure groups and interest groups ... They are like serpents constantly emerging from the sea to strangle Laocoön and his sons in their coils.
> **Douglas Hurd, 1986**[212]

Pressure grouping is like Jim Callaghan's famous definition of leaking when giving evidence to the Franks Committee on Official Secrecy in 1971: 'Leaking is what you do; briefing is what *I* do.[213] It's fine when I do it for legitimate purposes wholly in the public interest which only the benighted powers-that-be fail to recognise as self-evident truths to be acted on instantly. When you do it it's log-rolling, devious, taking the gullible for a ride, distorting the will of the people as expressed at election time, overriding the general good in favour of an imbalanced, single-issue obsession. It is as old as political life though in Haldane's time it did not, as it does now, intrude into any primer on our system of government. Some politicians recognise it and use it for their own purposes. One of the sayings attributed to Franklin Delano Roosevelt when President of the United States is: 'You've convinced me. Now go out and put pressure on me.' Clem Attlee, shortly after he had ceased to be Leader of the Opposition in the mid-fifties, was visited by a pair of political scientists pursuing the study of extra-Parliamentary influence. 'Pressure groups,' said Lord Attlee, 'we don't have those in this country.'[214] He was speaking at a time when, as a result of highly successful pressure from the commercial television lobby, the face of British broadcasting and, by extension, its culture, too, was in the process of being changed for ever.

To be fair to Attlee, he may have been making the justified and necessary distinction between commercial lobbies in favour of independent television or better roads and pressure groups, to take other examples from the time, *for* colonial freedom and *against* capital punishment. Whitehall has to deal with innumerable variants. Though difficult to measure, their growth seems to have been exponential since Professor Sammy Finer penned *Anonymous Empire*, his pioneering work on the Lobbies (not to be confused with the Westminster Lobby of Parliamentary journalists of whom more later). Just occasionally, however, one can observe a reverse ratchet effect in the pressure group that failed to materialise. For example, in 1981 Britain's forty-seven universities were subject to an average cut of 17 per cent in their budgets and subject to extreme financial pressure in the six years thereafter. The alumni, by definition among the most literate and professionalised people in the land, failed to rally round. Ministers responsible for higher education noticed this, and one of them, Robert Jackson, himself a former Fellow of All Souls College, Oxford, went public on the reasons why, as he saw them:

> by the end of the seventies, people had a picture of unattractive, unappetising students, complacent dons and a university system in particular which had become so entirely bound up with state support as to be irrelevant to the concerns of a lot of other people out there in the system ... That's the reason why, when the troubles came, the dogs didn't bark.[215]

Higher education was an aberration which highlighted the norm. Just as political parties became hugely more sophisticated in deploying their propaganda in the eighties, so did the pressure groups. The literature on pressure groups is now substantial and this is not the place to replicate it.[216] It is not a simple picture. For example, Des Wilson, prince of the single-issue pressure groups, who believes they extend democracy rather than distort it, operates on two fronts – against the commercial lobbies such as the car lobby, 'which,' he says, 'is as powerful as any in Britain ...

it consists of the car manufacturers themselves and their trade unions',[217] and against ministers and the central government machine. Whitehall tends to complain much more about the Des Wilson-style pressure groups than about the commercial lobbies. The single-issue groups have often been quoted at me by senior civil servants as an important reason for moving carefully on the open-government issue for fear of providing more ammunition to those who would use it for their narrow interests, not the wider public interest as a whole (it is a prime characteristic of the pressure group debate that all the protagonists claim to be defending the wider public interest).

One of the most successful and, in Whitehall terms, most loathed of recent pressure groups is that motley assortment of politicians, industrialists and post-Imperial romantics – the Falkland Islands lobby. (I must admit to marching at least partly to the same drumbeat.) 'A totally uncompromising lobby', Lord Greenhill, the former Head of the Diplomatic Service, called them.[218] Its 'spearhead', the Falkland Islands Committee, was established in the late 1960s when the Wilson government was toying with the idea of ceding sovereignty to the Argentine. Its prime mover was an ex-diplomat turned Lincoln's Inn barrister, William Hunter Christie. 'I don't like seeing minnows chucked out into a pond full of pike, that's all' he told the BBC's Michael Charlton.[219] Mr Hunter Christie and his all-party supporters (men of utter sincerity and passionate rhetoric like Sir Bernard Braine for the Conservatives and Mr Peter Shore for Labour) saw off all attempts at peacefully changing the status of the Falklands from the late 1960s to the early 1980s, whether it be the total cessation of sovereignty or the half-way house of leaseback. Michael Charlton was right to characterise them as 'one of the most effective lobbies in modern British politics'.[220]

Some of the greatest and most constant pressures on Whitehall, it must be remembered, have nothing to do with the power of lobbies (though they are heavily involved) when it comes to measuring the true sources of their clout. The most important of these is the 'Buy British' impulse which is built into the genetic code of every politician with a constituency to face. The impulse is paramount and ubiquitous when the Government needs a new computer for its paying-in or paying-out functions or, most significant of all, when it is purchasing a new weapons system. The economists can debate the virtues of buying British till their calculators melt,[221] but it is – and will remain – a primary seismic force in terms of pressure on Whitehall. For example, the Ministry of Defence's Procurement Executive spends 95 per cent of its £9 billion equipment budget on British industry. It is British industry's largest single customer. Some 700,000 jobs depend on it.[222] It accounts for the output of 45 per cent of the country's aerospace capability, 30 per cent of its shipbuilding and 20 per cent of its electronics.[223] As Sir Frank Cooper put it, 'You should never forget [that] the Secretary of State [for Defence] is a politician and a lot of the difficulties about these choices has got very little to do with defence. They've got everything to do with social, economic, industrial and Parliamentary elements. No-one wants to lose a factory in the South of England, the Midlands, the North or in Scotland, or, indeed, Northern Ireland, at the expense of having to buy from the United States or Toulouse.'[224] Lord Weinstock, Chairman of GEC and a formidable pressure group in himself despite losing the Nimrod airborne early warning contract to the United States in 1986, knows there is power in every word when he says:

> If you don't buy British, you don't have a British industrial defence capability. And if you don't have a British industrial defence capability, I don't see that you have, in the end, any capability at all which is independent. If you cannot supply the essential needs for the defence of the country, as part of the [NATO] alliance or independently, you will be dependent on a foreign power to supply. And if you displease the foreign power, they may decline to supply you [and] your independence of action in foreign policy and, maybe, even in domestic policy, will be prejudiced.[225]

A figure like Lord Weinstock or Sir Raymond Lygo of British Aerospace carries more clout in his person, when the Private Secretary shows him in to see the Defence Secretary (and, sometimes, the Prime Minister), than any of the institutions that embody the fifty-seven varieties of organised pressure. These, however, should not be ignored.

There are some institutions with a capital 'I' which, in their own way, are as influential as the biggest British defence contractor. The Royal Opera House, Covent Garden – garden of the permanent secretaries' delight – is one of them. When Clive Priestley, Rayner's chief-of-staff, turned up to talk efficiency with its board in 1982 as part of his scrutiny, he found himself faced not only by incarnations of the great and the good like Lord Goodman, but by a former permanent secretary, Sir Claus Moser, and in the guise of minute-taker number one, his boss, Sir Robert Armstrong, and, as minute-taker number two, Robin Butler, at that time the Prime Minister's Principal Private Secretary.[226] In 1987, when the board was involved in pushing through an environmentally controversial expansion scheme, it was rightly described by Lawrence Marks as 'a glittering concentration of wealth, power and social authority ... [with] ... enough establishment warheads to wipe out the entire environmentalist movement of south-east England several times over'.[227]

Any list of the organised pressures pushing through the walls of Whitehall and on to the ministers' and officials' desks would include:

Sectoral commercial lobbies such as the Society of Motor Manufacturers and Traders and the United Kingdom Petroleum Industry Association.

Single-issue pressure groups like Shelter and the campaign for Nuclear Disarmament.

Producer lobbies, permanent powers in the land – employers' organisations like the CBI and the Institute of Directors, employees' organisations, individual unions and their collective pressure group the TUC, the National Farmers' Union.

Charities can prove formidable at exerting pressure on policy as, for example, in 1985–6 when various aid charities, most notably Bob Geldof's Live Aid, persuaded the Government to extend Royal Air Force food relief flights in Ethiopia. Another is what Sir Adam Ridley calls the 'heritagenous lobby' which is very active in pressing the Treasury for tax concessions for ancient houses and estates.[228]

Consumer lobbies. Parent power can be formidable, however loosely organised, in educational matters, as the Government discovered in 1984 when it toyed with the idea of upping the parental contribution to university fees.

Professional lobbyist. Public relations firms of increasing sophistication are used by companies and interests as pressure professionals to influence new policy-making at every stage until a bill is given royal assent.

Personal lobbies. Perhaps the most anonymous empire of all arises, in the words of Professor John Ashworth, former Chief Scientist of the CPRS writing in the context of rulers as lonely people, from 'the temptation to look to wives, lovers, husbands, chauffeurs, hairdressers, old school chums and especially relatives for advice and support in fields other than the emotionally/personal [which] is ever present and often disastrous'.[229]

The activities of these groups are known about. Some, notably the charities and the single-issuers, live by maximum publicity, though they can have their own air of cultivated mystery. It took six years before the remarkable partnership of Des Wilson, king of the single-issues, and property millionaire Godfrey Bradman, was publicly appreciated.[230] The spoor of some of the others, notably the professional lobbyists, can be more difficult to detect publicly, though the men and women in the Whitehall policy divisions feel it acutely enough when a measure like the 1986 Financial Services Bill is on the stocks. It is on such complicated matters of acute and, literally, vital interest to a host of moneyed organisations (if your regulatory body does not recognise you, you cannot trade in the City of London), that the skilled, modern lobbyist comes into his or her own. Charles Miller of Public Policy

Consultants, a great exponent of what he calls the 'logic lobby'[231] – a quiet word with the people who matter, not just the minister but the assistant secretary managing the bill – as opposed to the razzmatazz of advertising and public campaigning, did the outsider a great service in 1987 when he published what amounted to his firm's operating manual in *Lobbying Government*.[232]

Quite apart from its value as a bible of 'do's' and 'dont's' and, to borrow Lord Trend's phrase, tips on etiquette (it could well be seen as the equivalent of *Questions of Procedure for Ministers* for those who would influence the mighty), *Lobbying Government* seeks to do something I have never seen done before: to rate on a scale of 1 to 10 those individuals and groups that comprise 'the components of power'. Charles Miller singles out sixteen. Propping the list up at the feeble end are individual MPs who rate 1, the Commons Chamber, all-party (non-select) committees and individual peers all on 2. The top four in ascending order are ministers 7, officials 8, Government whips 9 and the Prime Minister 10.[233]

Miller further lists the strengths and the weaknesses of each power group. For the officials he deems their strengths to be:

* Command of facts
* Advice to ministers often conclusive
* Ministers can't survive without them
* Draft and formulate legislation
* Control consultative processes
* Put words into ministers' mouths.

As for their weaknesses, these are that they are:

* Usually defensive
* Often poor commercial understanding
* Must work within overall manifesto/ministerial brief.[234]

I would quibble with some of Miller's ratings (the whips' figure seems overly high) but of the veracity of the high count he awards the permanent government there can be no doubt. Peter Kellner and Norman Crowther-Hunt were engaging in hyperbole, but only just, when they described civil servants, in the sub-title of their books, as 'Britain's ruling class'. And I would add to the list the most concealed, the most powerful, the most permanent pressure groups in our society, better placed than any in the geography of power to exert continuous and concealed influence – the military as represented by the Chiefs of Staff of the Armed Forces (who have yet to suffer exposure by television situation comedy and who deserve a book to themselves). The most subtle pressure groupers know this and target accordingly. The truly skilled seekers after influence know that it can often be more productive to approach the man who drafted the departmental letter (the civil servant) rather than the man who signed it (the minister). The in-house Whitehall pressure group may, despite a hugely popular television series, remain a closed world to those it has never admitted, but as closed societies go, it has an abundance of published or publicly available rules. They speak volumes about its culture, and it is to them that we must now turn.

9 SECRECY, NEUTRALITY, PROBITY

Civil servants are under an obligation to keep the confidences to which they become privy in the course of their official duties; not only the maintenance of trust between Ministers and civil servants but also the efficiency of government depend on their doing so. There is and must be a general duty upon every civil servant, serving or retired, not to disclose, in breach of that obligation, any document or information or detail about the course of business, which has come his or her way in the course of duty as a civil servant.
Sir Robert Armstrong, Head of the Home Civil Service, 1985[1]

Cabinet secrecy has in reality nothing to do with the making of plots . . . is there anything offensive to enlightened and constitutional ideas of today that such a group, committed to the conduct of the central government, should expect to keep to themselves the details of the process of formulation and that each should be able to rely on the other for the observance of such an understanding?
Report of the Radcliffe Committee of Privy Counsellors on Ministerial Memoirs, 1976[2]

With confidence and competence so much lower than they should be, it is not surprising that Whitehall fiercely defends its tradition of secrecy. The Official Secrets Act and the Thirty Year Rule, by hiding peacetime fiascos as though they were military disasters, protect ministers and officials from embarrassment. They also ensure that there is no learning curve.
Sir John Hoskyns, former head of Mrs Thatcher's Downing Street Policy Unit, 1983[3]

When an Old Bailey jury acquitted Clive Ponting, a Ministry of Defence assistant secretary, of charges laid under section 2 of the Official Secrets Act, 1911, after a celebrated trial in January–February 1985,[4] the then head of Mr Ponting's profession did what he does best and performed as if pre-programmed according to some nineteenth-century manual of correct mandarin conduct. He moved swiftly to fill the breach opened by the Ponting acquittal in Whitehall's defences against the outside world. For ballast and concrete he turned to the files and the accumulated wisdom of his predecessors, Sir Warren Fisher in the 1930s and Sir Edward Bridges in the 1950s.[5] Damage-limitation and a devotion to precedent are dominant characteristics among the higher Civil Service. The result, issued with the full approval of Sir Robert's forty-one fellow permanent secretaries, was a classic restatement of a tradition dating back to the Privy Counsellor's Oath of Confidentiality in the mid-fourteenth century. So consistent a theme has it been that administrative secrecy – Whitehall's cardinal value and dominant characteristic – picks itself as the starting point for any study of its rule-books. Indeed, Sir Robert's favourite definition of a civil servant's job (though he omitted to mention it in his post-Ponting guidelines) is lifted straight from the sixteenth century. 'I'm not sure', Sir Robert told Hugo Young in a BBC Radio interview in 1985 a few days before the publication of his note on the duties and responsibilities of officials, 'that the underlying requirements of the civil servant have changed really in four hundred years.'

> When Queen Elizabeth I appointed Sir William Cecil to be her Secretary of State in 1558, she said: 'This judgement I have of you, that you will not be corrupted by any manner of gift and that you will be faithful to the State, and that without respect of my private will, you will give me that counsel that you think best'.
>
> I think that summed it up pretty well. I think that is what we still expect of our Civil Service and I think that's what we still get out of it. And I have every confidence that it will continue to provide good public service, an outstanding public service, on that basis.[6]

More than mere antiquarianism requires the Whitehall-watcher to linger long and carefully over the Armstrong guidelines and a near shelf-full of other, mutually reinforcing rules and regulations. In the absence of a written constitution, rules of conduct and procedure for servants of the Crown, be they ministers or civil servants, are the nearest thing we have to a surrogate. As the leader-writer of the *Financial Times* put it in a leading article to mark the Queen's sixtieth birthday, 'the trouble with the unwritten British constitution is that it is based on the assumption that in the end practically everything turns out all right'.[7] That assumption no longer holds, as the Armstrong guidelines themselves showed when they were the subject of a lengthy inquiry and a critical report from an all-party select committee of the House of Commons in 1985–6.

The outstanding feature of Sir Robert's restatement of the timeless verities of the Civil Service is the absence of caveats. Take, for example, his emphatic declaration that:

> Civil servants are servants of the Crown. For all practical purposes the Crown in this context means and is represented by the Government of the day ... The Civil Service as such has no constitutional personality or responsibility separate from the duly elected Government of the day.

Armstrong's predecessor as Head of the Home Civil Service, Ian Bancroft, put it rather differently in a public lecture a year earlier. In a passage in praise of Sir David Serpell, Lord Bancroft said:

> I was trained in the Treasury for good or ill by a man who still ferociously pursues the public good. Those were the golden days when 'monitor' was still a noun. He showed me how to negotiate, how to draw breath in mid-sentence so as to discourage interruption, how to draft, *and why the Service belongs neither to politicians nor to officials but to the Crown and to the nation* [emphasis added].[8]

Quite apart from its value as an example of how the mandarin craft is conveyed from one generation to the next, the italicised section contains a distinct difference of emphasis to Armstrong's constitutional treatise which is all the more impressive as Bancroft is not an open-government man and a fierce critic of leakers, as that same Royal Society of Arts lecture showed.[9]

Secrecy is the bonding material which holds the rambling structure of central government together. Secrecy is built into the calcium of a British policy-maker's bones. Of all the values incorporated into the culture that moulded Bancroft and Armstrong, secrecy is *primus inter pares*. It is the very essence of the Establishment view of good government, of private government carried on beyond the reach of the faction of political party, the tunnel-vision of pressure group and the impertinent curiosity of the journalist. The rule is that the fewer people who know, the better, including insiders. During the Second World War Naval Intelligence did a study which purported to show that when more than *four* people knew a piece of information, its security could not be guaranteed.[10] Secrecy suffuses the text of the Armstrong guidelines. Of all the rules, secrecy is the most sacred. It is also the most criticised among the ranks of the excluded. Any treatment of the house regulations of a convention-laden, traditional hierarchy like the British Civil Service must start with secrecy, the breach of which for a nineteenth-century permanent secrecy, Sir Ralph Lingen (and for at least one successor in the late 1970s)[11] was comparable only to cowardice in a soldier. For reasons of fairness and perspective, it should be admitted at the outset that secrecy is as much a part of the English landscape as the Cotswolds. It goes with the grain of our society. Its curtailment, not its continuity, would be aberrational. Whitehall, another traditional part of the landscape, is only its greatest, not its sole, monument.

Why is this? Partly because it is packed into the genetic code of any bureaucracy. Max Weber discovered this particular kind of official DNA more than seventy years ago and, expressed it in brilliant, instantly comprehensible prose:

> Every bureaucracy seeks to increase the superiority of the professionally informed by keeping their knowledge and intentions secret. Bureaucratic administration always tends to be an administration of 'secret sessions': in so far as it can, it hides its knowledge and action from criticism ...
>
> The pure interest of the bureaucracy in power, however, is efficacious far beyond those areas where purely functional interests make for secrecy. The concept of the 'official secret' is the specific invention of bureaucracy, and nothing is so fanatically defended by the bureaucracy as this attitude which cannot be substantially justified beyond these specifically qualified areas. In facing a parliament, the bureaucracy, out of a sure power instinct, fights every attempt of the parliament to gain knowledge by means of its own experts or from interest groups ... Bureaucracy naturally welcomes a poorly informed and hence a powerless parliament ...[12]

But in the British case there is more to it than that. Social scientists are not allowed by their peers to invoke anything so commensensical as national character as an explanation. But journalists can. And one of Britain's finest ever reporters, George Orwell, captured the essence of the problem in his *The Lion and the Unicorn* when he spoke of an 'English characteristic which is so much a part of us what we barely notice it, and that is the addiction to hobbies and spare-time occupations, the *privateness* of English life'.[13] Privacy is the bright, the acceptable face of the coin; obsessive secrecy its regrettable obverse.

It is as natural for the secretary of a village cricket club to stamp the minutes of its committee meetings 'confidential' as it is for Sir Robin Butler to write 'secret' at the top of his dry account of yesterday's Cabinet. When I was a leader writer on *The Times*, I was once ticked off by the Editor for admitting on the BBC Radio 4 *Today* programme that had the paper been published that day (it was off the streets because of a strike) I would have written the leading article on the subject Brian Redhead wished to discuss with me. The fiction was that he, the Editor, wrote *all* of them – a myth on a par with collective responsibility in the Cabinet Room – which is why the list of tomorrow's leaders, with name of author alongside subject matter, bore the marking 'confidential' when circulated round the *Times* building on a need-to-know basis.

Outside observers tend to ascribe many of our secrecy ills to the elite nature of British government, particularly its administrative class – small, narrowly recruited, traditional and permanent – and to the deferential nature of British society which either does not notice it or puts up with it. The American sociologist, Edward Shils, who knows Britain intimately, has written of the differing results of the competition between the impulses of privacy, publicity and secrecy here and in the United States. Observing the Britain of the mid-fifties he found a complete contrast to the assaults on the government, the muckraking and hyperpatriotism of Washington in the McCarthy years. Britain's immunity from such trauma Professor Shils explained in terms of the tradition of centuries:

> Although democratic and pluralistic, British society is not populist. Great Britain is a hierarchical country. Even when it is distrusted, the Government, instead of being looked down upon, as it often is in the United States, is, as such, the object of deference because the Government is still suffused with the symbol of monarchical and aristocratic society . . .
>
> The acceptance of hierarchy in British society permits the Government to retain its secrets, with little challenge or resentment [that much, at least, has changed in thirty years]. The citizenry and all but the most aggressively alienated members of the elite do not regard it as within their prerogative to unmask the secrets of the Government, except under very stringent and urgent conditions . . .
>
> The deferential attitude of the working and middle classes is matched by the uncommunicativeness of the upper middle classes and of those who govern. The secrets of the governing classes of Britain are kept within the class and even within more restricted circles. The British ruling class is unequalled in secretiveness and taciturnity. Perhaps no ruling class in the Western world, certainly no ruling class in any democratic society, is as close-mouthed as the British ruling class. No ruling class discloses as little of its confidential proceedings as does the British.[14]

Another close observer of Britain, the Canadian civil servant D'Arcy Finn, told me shortly before he became head of Canada's equivalent of MI5 that he reckoned it was Britain's being a small island off the north-west coast of Europe, ever vulnerable to more powerful continental neighbours, that had produced a secrecy mentality for understandable military reasons and that, over the centuries, this had spilled into civilian life.[15]

Centuries old it certainly is. Administrative secrecy is as old as Parliament. The birth of the Privy Counsellor's Oath is dated as 1250 by the Privy Council Office. Mr (now Sir) Neville Leigh, Clerk to the Privy Council, when I asked its press officer to age the oath, obliged willingly enough but added, 'Of course, you won't quote Mr Leigh'. Sir Neville, it seems, was operating a 730-year rule, so the information had to be transmitted non-attributably![16] The oath, though, couched in medieval legal language, bears an uncanny resemblance to the passage in the Armstrong guidelines quoted at the head of this chapter. Every new member of the Cabinet, the more senior appointees at minister of state level and the leaders of the opposition parties, swear the oath on their knees in front of the Queen. It can go hilariously wrong. After Dick Crossman's first Privy Council meeting as Lord President at Balmoral in September 1966, the then Clerk, Sir Godfrey Agnew, told him

> an extraordinary story of a Privy Council which went fantastically wrong when Sir Edward Bridges was there with four politician privy councillors. Somehow they got themselves kneeling on the wrong side of the room facing Sir Edward. He waved them away and they crawled across the room on their hands and knees. In the process they knocked a book off the table and it had to be rescued by the Queen, who looked blackly furious. After the Privy Council had gone out Sir Edward crept back into the room and she said something very pleasant to him. He said how terribly sorry he was and she said, 'You know, I nearly laughed'. Then he realised that when she'd looked terribly angry it was merely because she was trying to stop herself laughing.[17]

The oath the wretched politicians had, somehow, to swear runs as follows:

> You will, in all things to be moved, treated and debated in Council, faithfully and truly declare your Mind and Opinion, according to your Heart and Conscience; and will keep secret all Matters committed and revealed unto you, or that shall be treated of secretly in Council. And if any of the said Treaties or Counsels shall touch any of the Counsellors, you will not reveal it unto him but will keep the same until such time as, by the consent of His (Her) Majesty, or the Council, Publication shall be made thereof.[18]

The key words are '*all* Matters' in the PC's oath and '*any* document or information or detail about the course of business' in the Armstrong guidelines. *Total* reticence is required for *all* time by those affected by both. Like the Mafia's system of *omerta*, only the grave can bring release. The oldest and newest of our secrecy provisions breathe as one.

One cannot help noticing the coincidence of the Privy Counsellor's oath with the summoning of the first English Parliament. I've long harboured an historical fantasy on what had happened to nurture the first official bloom of what has proved to be a longstanding national genius for confidentiality. It runs something like this. Imagine the shock administered to the cloistered world of the cleric-bureaucrats of the Court of King Henry III when the men from the shires arrived at Westminster and began demanding the redress of grievances before they would help the monarch syphon money from the provinces to fund the royal exchequer. Their rough ways and country accents would have grated on those priestly ears attuned to the elegant precision of Church Latin. Imagine what happened the day a far from deferential MP put down the first Parliamentary Question: 'Would the Chancellor of the Exchequer confirm that the groat is about to be devalued relative to the franc?' The Cabinet Secretary equivalent of the day would seek audience with the King to complain that the Tam Dalyell of the day was on to something. Somebody at the court had been talking. It was not good enough. It had to stop. 'What can I do?' the King would complain. 'Some of the barons are constantly three sheets to the wind. They leak like sieves. Gossip and drink is what gets them through the day. How do you think we can stop it?' 'I just happen to have a draft here, Sire' ... says the cleric. (Sir Humphrey Appleby has his medieval origins too.)

Enough of fantasy. Back to reality and to today.

The Privy Counsellor's oath is not some antiquarian residual kept for reasons of ceremony and no more. It has life and bite. Lord Radcliffe, when inquiring into the rules governing the publication of ministerial memoirs in 1975 after Volume One of the Crossman Diaries had driven a coach and horses through the thirty-year-rule, stressed its importance. I have heard Dr John Gilbert describe how, when he was Minister of State at the Ministry of Defence, there was a sudden increase in the amount of sensitive documentation that passed across his desk once he was admitted to the Privy Council. One permanent secretary described it as 'the ministerial equivalent of the Boy Scout's oath'.[19] Leaders of the Opposition parties, even if, like Neil Kinnock, they have never held ministerial office, are admitted into the Privy Council so that they can be given classified information on 'Privy Counsellor terms' should the need arise on a matter affecting national security. This became controversial for a time during the trial in Australia of Peter Wright, the former MI5 officer. Conservative MPs were enraged when Neil Kinnock admitted that he had been in touch with Wright's lawyer. After seeming to side with her backbenchers, Mrs Thatcher made it plain that the normal courtesies would be maintained. Some ten years earlier, to the disgust of some Labour Ministers, Len Murray, General Secretary of the TUC, was made a Privy Counsellor during the years of the 'social contract' so that he could be consulted on the policy of the Labour government at its formative stage in the mid and late 1970s.[20] That medieval bureaucrat who drafted the oath for Henry III created something truly enduring.

For the purposes of preparing a study of secrecy, I once drew up a checklist of its weapons in an attempt to measure the forces operating towards closed government in public life. The Privy Counsellor's oath was the natural starting point. The next addition to Whitehall's usable, and still used, past in secrecy terms is the development of the doctrine of collective Cabinet responsibility. It is a multi-purpose weapon: an ever-present justification for telling Parliament and the public only what is convenient about current government business. Few prime ministers can resist wrapping themselves in its dignified folds to conceal their rather less dignified needs in the arena of competitive adversary politics; it was the redoubt on to which Mrs Thatcher and Mr Leon Brittan clambered as they sought to rise above the ruins of Westland; it is, as we have seen, the fail-safe mechanism, the control room of *Questions of Procedure for Ministers*, intended to protect against constitutional meltdown. Thanks to Westland, this desiccated constitutional doctrine became a live issue, the common currency of political debate, and the spark of a memorable sketch in Central Television's *Spitting Image* in which Douglas Hurd attempted to reintroduce the concept in the Cabinet Room only to be browbeaten into submission by Mrs Thatcher. There was, post-Westland, a postcard on sale in London shops and kiosks – a dozen smiling Mrs Thatchers, shoulder to shoulder, under the caption 'My Cabinet is completely behind me'. It was entitled 'Collective Responsibility'; the first time, surely, that a constitutional nostrum has acquired postcard status[21].

A glance at the origins of this all-encompassing constitutional principle, this muscular sinew of British secrecy, is instructive. It was a typically English, highly practical political invention during the reign of George III to combat residual royal attempts to intrude in Cabinet business (the last known appearance of the monarch at Cabinet was in 1784) as Richard Pares explained in his *King George III and the Politicians*:

> The King did nearly all business with the Ministers in the room called his closet. He normally saw them one by one ... A Minister had no strict right to discuss anything in the closet but the business of his own department; but a senior Minister – especially if he were Leader of the House of Commons or had pretensions to consider himself as Prime Minister – could range more freely ... The business of the closet does not appear, at first sight, to have afforded the Ministers much opportunity for collective action. But they knew how to counteract the tendency to separate and confine them. On any question of general

> political importance, they would agree beforehand what to say, and then go into the closet, one by one, and repeat the identical story.[22]

A weapon that had served so well to thwart the inquisitiveness of the King could, with great and enduring ease, be turned against Parliament and public. Even monarchs can be victims of official secrecy!

It was another century before the concept of official secrecy was made into the flesh of a statute. Until then, breaches were filled by exhortations fashioned from what Clive Priestley, former chief of staff in Mrs Thatcher's Efficiency Unit, has called Whitehall's 'good chaps theory'.[23] When leaks appeared in the press, the Treasury would issue stiffly worded circulars. Very often the leaks were trivial, disclosing, for example, the organisation of the Exchequer and Audit Office and the likelihood of pay rises for suburban letter-carriers.[24] Such breaches could bring forth magisterial rebuke, as in Sir Ralph Lingen's note of 1873 which is the classic expression of the official mind's devotion to confidentiality: 'The unauthorised use of official information', wrote the Permanent Secretary to the Treasury, 'is the worst fault a civil servant can commit. It is on the same footing as cowardice by a soldier. It is unprofessional.'[25] Three Treasury circulars of this kind, those of 1873, 1875 and 1884, were bound together and presented to Parliament as a Command Paper.

Appeals based on the 'good chap' theory failed to work. Two more serious leaks in 1887, one involving the sale by a dockyard draftsman, Young Terry, of confidential designs of warships (he was dismissed but could not be prosecuted), pushed the Government into drafting a 'Breach of Official Trust Bill'. When it finally emerged as the Official Secrets Act, 1889 it was in two parts: Section 1 dealt with spying and Section 2 with breaches of official trust. Under the terms of Section 2 it was an offence for a crown servant to communicate official information 'corruptly or contrary to his official duty' to a person to whom it 'ought not, in the interest of the State *or otherwise in the public interest* [emphasis added], to be communicated at that time'.[26] In the first of our four Official Secrets Acts, what the lawyers call 'a public interest test' (the core of Clive Ponting's defence at the Old Bailey in 1985) was incorporated into the statute. In the second of our secrecy laws, the one that still bites, it was removed.

Why, after the 'good chap theory' had been fitted with a set of teeth in the shape of criminal penalties contained in the 1889 Act, did the guardians of official secrecy feel the need to trouble the Parliamentary draftsmen once more? To the Whitehall mind, happy with nothing less than 100 per cent confidentiality, 'even the passage of legislation providing criminal sanctions as a means of protecting government did not prove wholly effective . . . For instance, in 1900 there was a premature leakage to the press of the Home Secretary's decision to authorise an increase in the pay of the Metropolitan

Police.'[27] But the real impulse towards ever tighter secrecy in Edwardian times was the fear of German espionage. A sub-committee of the Committee of Imperial Defence was established as a kind of task force on the problem with, as we have seen, Lord Haldane in the chair. As Section 2 of the Official Secrets Act, 1911, the most controversial and notorious result of the committee's labours, is now derided as the acme of clumsy and illibertarian legislation conceived in panic and passed in haste, it is as well to appreciate the climate in which Haldane and his colleagues deliberated. Whitehall was shaken rigid by the swift emergence of Germany as a blue-water naval power in the first years of this century – the first real threat to Britain's military supremacy since 1815. The mania for national security it engendered in official circles, far from outraging public opinion, went with the grain. Popular agitation was the very reverse of CND's today. The Dreadnought battleship was, as Jonathan Steinberg described it, 'yesterday's deterrent'[28] and the cry was 'We want eight and we won't wait.'[29] Keeping the Kaiser's spies out of Portsmouth, Chatham and Devonport dockyards was a highly popular cause,[30] particularly after the war scare of the Agadir crisis which gave the guardians of national security their chance to rush a bill through the House of Commons in a single afternoon in August 1911.[31]

Section 2 of the new Act is the foundation upon which layer after layer of administrative secrecy have been built from that day to this, its essence captured and reproduced in rulebook, memorandum and leak inquiry. The all-embracing nature of Section 2 has a completeness of which any totalitarian would be proud. No caveats, no mention of the public interest this time. The interests of the state, as defined solely by the state, were henceforth to be supreme. The Franks Report of 1972 (which recommended a narrower, more clearly drawn secrecy law – a recommendation that has still to be acted upon) conveys the enormity of the statute:[32]

> Section 2 is short but it is in very wide terms and it is highly condensed. It covers a great deal of ground, and it creates a considerable number of detailed offences. According to one calculation over 2000 differently worded charges can be brought under it. It is obscurely drafted, and to this day legal doubts remain on some important points of interpretation . . .
>
> The main offence which Section 2 creates is the unauthorised communication of official information (including documents) by a Crown servant. The leading characteristic of this office is its catch-all quality. *It catches all official documents and information* [emphasis added]. It makes no distinctions of kind, and no distinctions of degree. All information which a Crown servant learns in the course of his duty is 'official' for the purposes of Section 2, whatever its nature, whatever its importance, whatever its original source. A blanket is thrown over

> everything; nothing escapes. The section catches all Crown servants as well as all official information. Again, it makes no distinctions according to the nature or importance of a Crown servant's duties. All are covered.[33]

Indiscrimination has been a hallmark of administrative secrecy and of those who enshrine it in the Whitehall rulebooks since the cleric's quill pen first scratched the words 'all' and 'any' on the page as the Privy Counsellor's oath took shape. The medieval church distinguished between mortal and venial sins. Not Whitehall. It still can't, as the swiftest glance at David Hooper's authoritative *Official Secrets* shows[34], though in the spring of 1988 the Home Secretary, Douglas Hurd, seemed about to try.

The press ran a campaign against the legislative offspring of Haldane's committee when first it saw the light of day in 1908 and it was withdrawn.[35] Press silence when it reappeared in 1911 has been explained by the anonymous author of the historical appendices of the Franks Report: 'their attention was elsewhere, monopolised by the Parliament Bill and the associated constitutional crisis'.[36] It is richly ironic that the most illiberal measure to pass through the Commons this century should have been sponsored by the last Liberal administration behind the progressive smoke-screen thrown up by its determination to take on the Lords over Irish Home Rule. Lingering guilt at its inadvertence might, one could suppose, have led to a press campaign to undo the damage of Section 2 once the wartime emergency was passed. Instead, there was a further tightening of the rules with the third of our quartet of secrecy statutes, the Official Secrets Act, 1920. The impulse for it came from MI5 who were keen to preserve as much as they could in peacetime of the Defence of the Realm Act (DORA) which held sway during the First World War. As Harold Kent, the Parliamentary draftsman who specialised in security matters in the interwar period, noted: 'For them [MI5] it was a sad thing that the only crumbs from the rich table of DORA 1918 were some minor additions to the Aliens Order and the Official Secrets Act.'[37] The 1920 Act dealt mainly with spying, and its provisions, therefore, chiefly affected Section 1 of the 1911 statute. But new provisions covering codes and passwords were inserted in Section 2.[38]

The degree to which MI5 was suffering from security mania even alarmed the senior Civil Service in the interwar period. At the time of the Abyssinia crisis in 1935 MI5 succeeded, by lobbying inside the Committee of Imperial Defence, in getting a working party established on a new DORA. Its membership included Kent with Sir Claud Schuster, Permanent Secretary at the Lord Chancellor's Department (who had sat on the Haldane Committee), in the chair, and Norman Brook, then a rising young star at the Home Office, as its secretary. MI5 so irritated the other members of the War Legislation Committee that Brook and Kent's colleague, Jack Lindsay, set a trap for the Security Service in which the MI5 Director-General, Sir Vernon Kell, duly fell. MI5 was determined to control the use of wireless telegraphy as every modern spy was equipped with a secret transmitter. This was a very difficult requirement to frame in terms of a DORA regulation. Brook and Lindsay drafted one 'to the effect that no person should, without a written permit granted by the competent authority, make any sound transmissible by wireless telegraphy'.

When the Regulation came up for consideration by the Committee, satisfaction was expressed by MI5 and Naval Intelligence. There was an expectant hush, with all eyes on the chairman.

'It looks like being a very silent war,' said Schuster. There was a ripple of laughter round the table.

'Of course,' said the head of MI5, 'we should only prosecute in really suspicious cases.'

'Oh no,' cried Schuster, 'not that again!'

The head of MI5 came out of his strange world inhabited more or less exclusively by potential enemies and their spies and sympathisers. He looked for a moment at that other world of innocent persons pursuing their comparatively innocent avocations.

'I suppose it won't do,' he said regretfully.[39]

It is all too easy, in any disquisition on the malign effects of the British secrecy obsession, to belittle MI5 and the country's security and intelligence apparatus. I am unwilling to do that for the simple reason that as long as a country, because of its status as a world power, its possession of advanced weaponry, and its geographical location, is engaged in diplomacy, alliances and defence planning, it needs such an apparatus. The cold war cannot yet be dismissed as history. It was not the product of fevered imaginations in the Chiefs of Staff suite in the Ministry of Defence, the oversea and defence secretariat of the Cabinet Office or the private offices of the directors-general of MI5 and MI6. That said, it is especially vital in a democratic state that such agencies are subject to taut ministerial control and are prevented from usurping one ounce more of the citizen's individual liberty than is absolutely necessary.

MI5 are never reluctant, for example, to be drawn into a Whitehall leak inquiry, however trivial the seepage of information. Cabinet Office files released by mistake at the Public Record Office show MI5 tapping the phone of Paul Einzig, the political correspondent of the *Financial Times* in the late forties, because he published advance information dealing with the Attlee government's forthcoming White Paper on iron and steel.[40] When I was operating on a daily basis as a Whitehall correspondent I would often gaze at the photograph of my own MI5 desk-officer. He was pinned above my desk, rather as Monty kept a picture of Rommel in his desert campaign caravan, conveniently placed to see what I was writing and the source material I was using. I usually discovered which MI5 man or men were conducting the leak inquiries into my stories. If it was not my usual – of whom, at a distance, I became rather fond – I would be concerned for his health. So, even bearing in mind their necessary functions in an evil, cold-war-ridden world, MI5 must be depicted since their creation in 1909 (Kell was their first chief who endured till 1940) as an accretion to the forces of closed government.

A similar view has to be taken of the D-notice system, the arrangement by which the British press censors itself voluntarily in peacetime on certain defence and intelligence matters. Again, I have to confess to a degree of ambivalence. At the time of the Falklands crisis – a limited and local as opposed to a total, global war – the system had its justifiable uses. D-notices were another invention of that fertile period of security institution-building under our last Liberal government. The Committee of Imperial Defence, its members prone like the rest of us to table talk, were haunted by Bismarck's assertion over dinner to Prince Louis of Battenberg that he acquired all the intelligence he needed in the Franco-Prussian war from French local newspapers which obligingly published the whereabouts of regiments in which local men were serving.[41] The Edwardian guardians of national security were determined that the British press should offer no comparable service to Bismarck's successors in Berlin. The press, to its credit, proved far from compliant when the idea was floated in 1906. But, as Alasdair Palmer's researches uncovered, the man of the hour was a shrewd assistant secretary at the War Office, Reginald Brade. And the hour, once again, was the Agadir crisis of 1911 which had created the climate in which Section 2 passed through the House of Commons as if on oiled castors. Brade knew he would get nowhere with the journalists. So, advised by Reginald Nicholson, managing editor of *The Times*, he went directly to the proprietors. Not for the last time, the ploy worked.[42] The D-notice system, in modified fashion, survives to this day monitored by a joint Whitehall–Fleet Street committee.

Before Hitler gave MI5 the opportunity to work, once more, with a full-blooded Defence of the Realm Act, the Chamberlain government was persuaded to introduce a fourth Official Secrets Act. This 1939 measure did not affect Section 2 – clearly, as amended in 1920, this was by now sufficiently all-embracing to satisfy even MI5. The latter was confined to Section 1. It did, however, affect the practice of journalism in permitting the prosecution of persons who failed to give information about unlawful disclosures. A journalist could, therefore, be required to commit his equivalent of a mortal sin – naming his source.[43]

Wartime *is* different. Even the most liberty-minded journalist has to accept that restrictions are necessary. But the Treasury in 1942 managed, to my amazement when I discovered it, to find the time in between mobilising the Civil Service to help lick Hitler, to tighten up and revise its own mammoth internal rulebook, then known as *Estacode*, now called the *Civil Service Pay and Conditions of Service Code*.

This is a monster of a volume, the Civil Service's Bible of 'do's' and 'don't's' – one of the greatest monuments, perhaps even the Albert Memorial of British achievements in the field of confidentiality. Paragraph 9904 is a passage to be savoured and rolled on the tongue, as it rivals Section 2 of the 1911 Act as the tightest definition of administrative secrecy ever to flow from an official's pen. It states:

> Under the Official Secrets Acts, 1911 and 1920, it is an offence for an officer to disclose to an unauthorised person, either orally or in writing, any information he has acquired through his official duties unless he has received official permission.

At this point, an unexpected dose of liberalism is injected.

> There is, however, no objection to his repeating information which has already officially been made public.

But, lest the crown servant fear hallucination, the iron grille of secrecy falls once more.

> The Official Secrets Acts cover material published in a speech, lecture, radio or television broadcast, in the Press or in book form; they cover non-secret as well as secret information, and apply not only during an officer's employment but also when he has retired or left the service.[44]

A masterpiece of draftsmanship! Perfect. It catches the crown servant from the cradle to the grave. He regains his civil rights only when he is six feet under. Nobody this side of the Iron Curtain has ever done it better. The beauty of it is that it does not simply apply to secret information, but to *anything* he picked up while receiving a salary from the Paymaster General.

Estacode is not alone in being drenched with the backwash of the 1911 Act. Successive versions of *Questions of Procedure for Ministers* are similarly affected.[45] Each department has its own custom-drafted security manual pumping out the same indiscriminate message. One of my favourite departmental productions is the Cabinet Office's *Talking About the Office* which gives 'guidance to staff of the Office on the line they should take in answering questions about their own work from friends or other contacts outside the public service'. If you live in Esher, Wimbledon, Leatherhead or any of the areas in which senior civil servants reside, don't be fooled by the anonymous-looking kind of man you might meet at parties. He could be something quite important in this crucial department of state bursting with secrets. They have been coached by *Talking About the Office*[46] in what to say on such occasions.

> No details should be given of the chain of command within the Office, other than those which are clearly deducible from official publications such as ... *The Civil Service Year Book*. Staff working in the common sections should not say what section they are in and should describe their work in some such general phrase as providing executive (or clerical, typing, etc.) support for Cabinet Committees. The staff supporting the Joint Intelligence Committee became part of the Cabinet Office in 1957. But it is not widely known publicly that the JIC is a Cabinet Committee or that its assessment machinery is located here; and this should not be mentioned in conversation with outside contacts.[47] Members of the Joint Intelligence Organisation should say simply that in the Cabinet Office they are concerned with a number of committees on the defence and oversea side (or the economic side, if they come from an economic department), adding, if necessary, that the servicing of committees necessarily includes the assembly and assessment of information required for determining policy.

The symmetry of these monuments to the god of confidentiality is impressive. Minutiae, such as the form of words to be used on social occasions, are related to the grand constitutional themes of Cabinet government:

> The work of the [Cabinet] Secretariat ... [is] ... essentially confidential. This stems directly from the secrecy which properly surrounds Cabinet business and the advice given to Ministers, and, by extension, the business of Cabinet Committees. It has always been maintained by successive Administrations that disclosure of the processes by which Government decisions are reached weakens the collective responsibility of Ministers, which is what welds the separate functions of Government into a single Administration.
>
> The first rule, therefore, is that even the existence of particular Cabinet Committees should not be disclosed – still less their composition, terms of reference, etc. This is so even though on occasion the Government *finds it convenient* [emphasis added] to make a public reference to an individual Committee (for example, the Defence and Oversea Policy Committee has been mentioned in successive Defence White Papers). It follows that members of the Secretariat should describe their work in the broadest terms, referring only to the side of the Office in which they are principally engaged – e.g. the scientific and technological, defence

and oversea, European communities, economic or home and legislation side . . .

To be fair to the keepers of Cabinet secrecy, Mrs Thatcher has made it a practice at the start of her premierships to acknowledge the existence of three more Cabinet committees in addition to the Oversea and Defence group – economic strategy, home affairs and legislation.[48] In the autumn of 1986, however, openness was taken a step further. The existence of an *ad hoc* Cabinet committee on the disease Aids under the chairmanship of Lord Whitelaw, Lord President of the Council, was disclosed initially as a classic newspaper scoop in *The Independent*[49]. So urgent was the public concern about Aids and so great the Government's need to be seen to be acting, that less than a fortnight later, Norman Fowler, Social Services Secretary, in what *The Independent* called an 'unprecedented step', briefed the press outside No. 10 on the outcome of an Aids Cabinet Committee meeting before the Cabinet Secretariat had even had time to type the minutes.[50] Ministers felt able to practise such openness as, mercifully, the urgency of coping with Aids was not a controversial issue between the parties.

Despite such advances, the apparatus of secrecy remained almost wholly intact in the late eighties, though under assault from a remarkable range of people including some former MI5 officers, of whom the best-known was Peter Wright. They made unusual bedfellows with the normal open-government lobby, their motivation being the need, as they saw it, to show publicly that the Security Service had been penetrated far more seriously in the post-war period than the Prime Minister was prepared to admit.[51] It should be remembered that not all bureaucrats follow Weber's iron law of bureaucratic secrecy. There is secrecy within and between departments. The 'need-to-know' principle is strictly adhered to. The junior and the gifted can feel almost as excluded and in the dark as an outsider. Samuel Brittan put it very neatly in his diary during his days as a DEA 'irregular' when he wrote in one of his 'reflections': 'Top people meet in Top Secret and no contribution possible from lower down!'[52]

In the early months of 1988, Whitehall once more went into protracted convulsion in another attempt to deliver a secrecy settlement which would command respect. The *Spycatcher* story, and its spin-offs in the guise of injunctions preventing the press from publishing reports or extracts, plus further spin-offs in the form of contempt of court actions, had produced a situation which was recognised as unsatisfactory all round. Lord Scarman, the most respected liberal jurist in the land, argued in a letter to *The Times* that

> If we were not plagued with the panic legislation of 1911, which carries the secrecy of governmental information so far beyond the needs of national security that it has become unenforceable, we would long ago have legislated not by an unconditional assertion of press right (as in the US) but by a carefully-balanced protection of freedom of speech and information along the lines of the European Convention on Human Rights, which fully recognises the national security exception.
>
> The confusion and obscurity of our public law have led the Government to use (abuse?) the private law protecting confidential information. For heaven's sake legislate now before our law, our courts and our reputation as a free country become the laughing stock of the world.[53]

Lord Scarman's advice reflected that of Mr Justice Scott in his High Court judgment on *Spycatcher* delivered on 21 December 1987. 'It is open to Parliament', he said, 'if it wishes to impose guidelines.... Parliament has not. And so it is for the courts to strike the balance.'[54]

Indeed, the quickest way for Britain to acquire a well-sprung constitution on the secrecy side would have been the incorporation of Article 10 of the European Convention on Human Rights into English and Scottish law. Article 10 reads as follows:

> 1. Everyone has the right to freedom of expression. The right shall include freedom to hold opinions and to receive and impart information and ideas without interference by public authority and regardless of frontiers.
>
> 2. The exercise of these freedoms, since it carries with it duties and responsibilities, may be subject to such formalities, conditions, restrictions or penalties as are prescribed by law and are necessary in a democratic society, in the interests of national security, territorial integrity or public safety, for the prevention of disorder or crime, for the protection of health or morals, for the protection of the reputation or rights of others, for preventing the disclosure of information received in confidence, or for maintaining the authority and impartiality of the judiciary.

Parliament, in its pure, unwhipped form, was carefully kept away from providing guidance to the judiciary on secrecy matters. Without, that is, a firm steer from the Government. The Conservative Whips used the 'payroll' vote of ministers and their parliamentary private secretaries to vote down Mr Richard Shepherd's private member's bill on secrets reform in January 1988 on the grounds that the Home Office was not yet ready to come forward with its own proposals.[55]

It was clear, too, that the wholesale adoption of Article 10 was not a solution favoured by Whitehall. The age-old caution about opening the floodgates was as prevalent as ever. A tidying-up operation was what ministers had in mind rather than any extension or even recognition of a public right to know, as became plain in a conversation I had with the Home Secretary, Douglas Hurd, for the Radio 4 *Analysis* programme *The Need to Know*. 'We will certainly try,' he said,

> 'to define clearly the three kinds of information which civil servants have: one, over which there need be no protection although it is protected at the moment by the Official Secrets Act; secondly, there is the category where there needs to be protection but where, quite reasonably, that can be done by ordinary discipline, you don't need the criminal law; and thirdly there is the area . . . which is a small minority of the whole, where there is . . . a section which does need the protection of the criminal law.'
>
> 'Can you give me three very quick examples from each of those categories?'
>
> 'Yes. I don't think we've offered you a cup of tea. But if you saw the details of the teabag and the tea served in the Home Office, technically . . . you might well be in breach of the Official Secrets Act. That is nonsense – no reason why that should be protected at all. When officials brief me for this interview, give me advice as to what it should contain . . . I would be displeased if they immediately said that I hadn't taken their advice. But I wouldn't think that was a matter where they should be prosecuted. But there might be a disciplinary point there. But if supposing that someone was to rush after you as you caught the lift down from this interview and said, "Oh, by the way, the actual truth about this or that Security Service operation is so-and-so," then I would think that that disclosure to you might require criminal action.'[56]

A world in which teabags may safely brew – only in Whitehall would that be considered an advance!

But, appropriately enough, it was Parliament which willy-nilly took over the open-government running another guise in the wake of the Westland affair, as we have seen in our Cook's tour of the system. At issue in this instance was a document entitled *Memorandum of Guidance for Officials Appearing before Select Committees*, issued on 16 May 1980 in obscurity by E. B. C. Osmotherly, assistant secretary in charge of the Civil Service Department's machinery of government division, who answered to Sir Ian Bancroft, then Head of the Home Civil Service, a stickler for confidentiality. Circulated through Whitehall as 'General Notice GEN 80/38', it carried, as if a Papal Bull, a menacing footnote to the effect that it was 'valid indefinitely'. The Civil Service Department, so ingrained and routine is the confidentiality impulse, were quite happy to let me, then a *Times* journalist, have a copy. To the eternal chagrin of Edward Osmotherly it became a controversial document in our constitutional history and its sixty dry paragraphs afforded him immortality by becoming known as the 'Osmotherly Rules'.[58] The trouble arose because the Osmotherly Rules seemed to run counter to the St John-Stevas spirit – 'to redress the balance of power between Westminster and Whitehall' – imbuing the new select committee structure. It appeared that what Whitehall had conceded with one hand it could claw back with another.

The Westland problem – the question of what an official could or could not be asked to give evidence upon – was anticipated from the start:

> Officials appearing before Select Committees do so on behalf of their Ministers. It is customary, therefore, for Ministers to decide which officials (including members of the Armed Services) should appear to give evidence. Select Committees have in the past generally accepted this position. Should a Committee invite a named official to appear, the Minister concerned, if he did not wish that official to represent him, might suggest that another official could more appropriately do so, or that he himself should give evidence to the Committee. If a Committee insisted on a particular official appearing before them they could issue a formal order for his attendance. In such an event the official would have to appear before the Committee. He would remain subject to Ministerial instructions as to how he should answer questions.[58]

Yet, the document started promisingly enough.

Officials, said the Osmotherly Memorandum, were to be as helpful as possible to the new committees. 'Any withholding of information', he wrote, 'should be limited to reservations that are necessary in the interests of good government or to safeguard national security.' The snags arose with the Bancroft–Osmotherly definition of 'good government'. It precluded, for example, all discussions of:

* interdepartmental exchanges on policy issues;
* Civil Service advice to Ministers;
* the level at which decisions were taken and the manner in which a Minister consulted his colleagues;
* questions 'in the field of political controversy'.

In short, elected MPs were to be denied any real knowledge of the inside workings of the Whitehall machine and any chance of making the bureaucratic brokers of concealed power accountable to the sovereign Parliament.

With their professional attention to detail, Bancroft and Osmotherly carefully closed off any back routes to information. MPs might be reluctant to accept Whitehall refusals to release reports from departmental committees on which it was known that outsiders were sitting. So officials must be careful 'in deciding how much publicity should be given to the establishment of committees of this kind'. A good deal of material is given to some select committees, the Defence Committee, in particular, which does not appear in their published reports. The process of censorship is known as 'sidelining'. Committee chairmen, Bancroft and Osmotherly warned, might be reluctant to agree to sidelining information that was not itself classified! Finally, they offered officials an all-purpose safety net to protect themselves in awkward moments. If all else fails, stall and 'ask for time to consider the request and ... promise to report back'.[59]

The Osmotherly Rules struck me at the time (and still do) as an attempt to stymie the reforms of the 1980s with the rules of the 1940s or even the 1250s if one were uncharitable enough to detect a kind of papal succession between the draftsman of the Privy Counsellor's oath and Edward Osmotherly. And, naturally, Sir Robert Armstrong's post-Ponting guidelines were four-square in this grand tradition. Reforming this Byzantine edifice would be a supreme task. Between the general elections of 1983 and 1987 all three of the then Opposition party leaders – Mr Kinnock, Mr Steel and Dr Owen – were pledged to do just that.[60] If reform is to succeed, all the post-1250 guidelines, codes, rulebooks and statutes will have to be rewritten.

The secrecy sections of the Whitehall rulebooks are ludicrously overdone. James Margach, the legendary political correspondent of *The Sunday Times*, described it as a 'conspiracy of secrecy, to preserve the sanctity of Government behind the walls of Whitehall's forbidden city'.[61] Given the unwillingness of governments of all kinds to open the forbidden city since its first rampart was thrown up in the thirteenth century and the tendency of most civil servants to follow Weber's law of bureaucratic secrecy, it fell to my and Jimmy Margach's profession to do something to sap and mine those ever accumulating defences on behalf of the citizenry as a whole. As that famous *Times* leader of 1852, of which Robert Lowe was co-author, put it: 'The duty of the journalist is the same as that of the historian – to seek out the truth, above all things, and to present to his readers not such things as statecraft would wish them to know but the truth as near as he can attain it.'[62]

It was bound to be an unequal struggle, as Lord Radcliffe, who ran wartime censorship as Director-General of the Ministry of Information in the 1940s, knew full well. Governments, he said, always tend to want not really a free press but a managed or well-conducted press. I do not blame them. It is part of their job. It is equally part of the job of the press to be wary about responding to these sometimes subtle, sometimes rather obvious inducements. Do not let us think of the Government as being powerless or ill-equipped in this issue. They have all the resources of modern public relations at their beck and call, they have the subtle acts of pressure, the nods and the winks, the joggings of the elbow, the smile at what is called the responsible reporter, and the frown at the man who does not see quite clearly the Government's point of view.[63]

Far from squaring up to the challenge, the British political press succumbed to the Whitehall embrace in 1884 – when, in Stephen Koss's phrase, 'representatives of the press were accredited by the Speaker to patrol the corridors of power'[64] – at the very moment when Britain staggered towards mass adult male suffrage, and a properly informed electorate served by an independent media became more vital than ever. By organising themselves into the Westminster Lobby (the collective name given to the corps of political reporters in Parliament, from the Members' Lobby outside the chamber where they are allowed to await their contacts), Britain's political journalists availed themselves of an increasingly tightly organised system of mass, non-attributable briefings by ministers or their spokesmen. It was – and remains – a cosy arrangement which suits, like all monopolies, the insider traders, the losers being the consumer, in this case the reader, the public, the electorate.[65]

Some of the most biting critics of the system have been found inside the walls of the Whitehall citadel. Humbert Wolfe, the poet who doubled as a deputy secretary in the Ministry of Labour, wrote in 1930:

You cannot hope to bribe or twist
Thank God! the British journalist,
But seeing what the man will do
Unbribed, there's no occasion to.[66]

But it was Francis Williams, former Editor of the *Daily Herald*, who published, while Attlee's Press Secretary in No. 10, the most blistering denunciation of Britain's system of political and specialist reporting – strictures that still have force today when specialist groups of accredited correspondents continue to exist in the political, diplomatic, defence, industrial (i.e. labour) and education fields. Fresh from wartime censorship work in Radcliffe's Ministry of Information, Williams wrote in 1946 in his little classic, *Parliament, Press and the Public*, that it had become

> normal practice for some of the big Departments to hold regular background and news conferences with the Press. At these conferences information is given sometimes by the Minister, sometimes by the Public Relations Officer and sometimes by other senior officials of the Ministry. In a number of cases only correspondents belonging to a recognised group, with its own officials and rules, are now invited to these conferences ... It is easy to see the advantages of such a system to a Department.[67]

Williams's account of the practical consequences and ethical blemishes of such practices, though more than forty years old, has never been bettered. 'Such a system', he wrote;

> also means that the newspaper correspondents concerned give up much of their independence. Some of them tend to depend so largely on official sources for information and to develop such obligations to the officials with whom they work, that they become mouthpieces of authority, taking their 'line' from the Minister or his officials and undertaking to hold up the news to suit the convenience of the Department. They are known as 'trustworthy' by the Department with whom they work.
>
> But a journalist's trust is not to any government Department but to the public. Some of these groups include men of ability and independent judgement who do in fact take their own line [which is still true today, it must in fairness be said]. Their presence does not alter the general principle that anything which ties newspapers too closely to official sources of news, or sets up obligations which may conflict with a newspaper's primary responsibility to the public is a bad system and ought not to exist.[68]

Whitehall's own declassified files attest to the premium placed on the Lobby by those on the inside who would set the agenda, week-in, week-out, for mainstream political discussion and the supinely grateful attitude of the Lobby for the pabulum provided. One of the most revealing was released at the Public Record Office in January 1985. Churchill, no less, had asked for a note on the Government's relations with the Lobby, then a much more mysterious and largely unknown body rather than the 'extremely secret organisation that everyone at Westminster knows about', as Gerald Kaufman wittily described it nearly thirty years later.[69] The brief for Churchill was duly provided on 29 October 1954 by Fife Clark, Director-General of the Central Office of Information, into which the Ministry of Information had transmogrified in peacetime.

There was some question about which government minister should be the regular briefer – Lord Swinton or the Chancellor of the Exchequer, the enigmatically revealing R. A. Butler. Swinton, wrote Fife Clarke, has been the Lobby's 'friend and advocate for $2\frac{1}{2}$ years and the Lobby are very grateful to him, just as they have become very fond of him personally. Their gratitude has been expressed not once but many times in the secrecy of the Lobby Room.'[70] 'The secrecy of the Lobby Room' – it sounds something between a confessional and a Masonic temple. In the early days of the 1951 government, Fife Clark continued, bad Lobby relations had 'undoubtedly poisoned reporting and comment'. Thanks to Lord Swinton, matters were much improved. 'Three years ago Ministers were not sure that they could "trust the Lobby". Now they know they can.'

What a cosy comfortable world, so very clubby and so convenient to all concerned, both the briefers and the briefed, a world for which the older generation of politicians like Lord Whitelaw continued to pine in the late 1980s.[71] There was but one shadow over these discreet and decorous proceedings. Fife Clark told Churchill that these golden opinions 'would, I am sure, be shared by the majority of the Lobby Journalists, and could be confirmed by confidential reference to the Chairman and the elders such as S.W. Mason of *The Times*. There is a minority headed by Derek Marks and Robert Carvel of the *Daily Express*, but it is fair to say that this group is dissident on most issues and it would not be easy for any Minister to provide them, week in week out, storm or calm, with all the news they think they ought to have.'[72] Good for Marks and Carvel. Bob Carvel was down at the PRO for the *Standard* in late December 1984 for the press preview of the 1954 papers when this little gem was uncovered and I can still see the glee on his face when he was shown it.

The Lobby is a very venerable institution, older than complete adult suffrage and almost as old as the post-Northcote–Trevelyan Civil Service. The menu of its centenary lunch had a Cummings cartoon of Mr Gladstone and Mrs Thatcher atop a birthday cake, with 'The Lobby 1884–1984' iced upon it, the Grand Old Man about to pass the torch to the not so grand or so old lady.[73] On that occasion at the Savoy Hotel in London, Mrs Thatcher was the guest of honour. In her speech she first teased the Lobby, saying it was 'the first time that the Fourth Estate has avowed its Secret Service', before moving on to congratulate all 150 of them on a 'successful hundred years in pursuit of press freedom'.[74] I still can't make up my mind, not having been present, if Mrs Thatcher was being deliberately ironic in making that remark. I think probably not. It was all too reminiscent of the early Harold Wilson describing the Lobby as 'the golden thread' in Britain's parliamentary democracy[75] – that same Harold Wilson who, deeply embittered by his treatment at the hands of Fleet Street, allowed his Press Secretary, Joe Haines, to suspend Lobby briefings during his last premiership.[76]

Two years after its orgy of centenary self-congratulation the Lobby was plunged into crisis by the refusal of the newly-founded *Independent* to subscribe to the system and by *The Guardian*, its conscience pricked by the new paper,[77] threatening to attribute the statements of Mr Bernard Ingham, Mrs Thatcher's Press Secretary, and his deputies. After an inquiry and a series of votes, the Lobby correspondents decided to maintain the status quo, keeping the No. 10 briefings non-attributable (the Opposition Leaders, to their credit, were by now briefing on-the-record) with sourcing kept to vague 'Whitehall sources' rather than the infinitely more precise 'Downing Street spokesmen' as *The Guardian* wished.[78] The Fourth Estate was as far away as ever from storming Jimmy Margach's Whitehall citadel on behalf of the public.

For its part, Whitehall's regulars remained protected not merely by the sturdy if, by now, ivy-covered ramparts of the citadel but by row after row of information officers, several of whom were ex-journalists themselves. As long ago as 1950 Bridges had noted, 'It is the ... absence of direct responsibility which makes the average civil servant uncomfortable and infelicitous in his relations with the Press.' Bridges continued:

> The direct quick reply may be the only thing which will satisfy the Press inquirer, but it may result in headlines the next morning which will be far from pleasing to his ministerial master. The tendency of many civil servants is, therefore, to hedge or confine themselves to what has already been said. This disease is so endemic that we have had to call in gentlemen from Fleet Street to help us out of our difficulties. I see no remedy for it, unless it be accustoming the younger generation of civil servants to face the rigours of the press from their early years.[79]

Bridges's proposed remedy went largely unheeded. The bulk of Whitehall press work remains in the hands of its specialist information class. The Foreign Office has always been the exception. The best of its top diplomats staff up the FO News Department. They always have done. The wittiest remark ever made by a Whitehall Press Officer falls to an unknown member of the News Department. On the day the Molotov–Ribbentrop Pact was concluded in August 1939, the FO's spokesman produced the unforgettable reaction, 'All the 'isms are wasms'.[80] Since the early 1970s, the Treasury, too, has routinely made an administrator its Head of Information. Its current Permanent Secretary, Sir Peter Middleton, shone in this role in the mid-1970s (he had entered the Civil Service as an information officer in the Central Office of Information). Occasionally, other departments belatedly follow Bridges's advice, as when David Wilkinson, an assistant secretary, became Head of Information at the Department of Education and Science in 1986.

Despite much lip-service to open government by successive administrations – James Callaghan had even promulgated an open government directive, named after Lord Croham who had drafted it, in 1977, but the results it yielded were meagre[81] – Whitehall's secrecy rules remained as tough as ever in the late 1980s.

Yet there are other parts of the rulebooks, equally tightly drawn, where tautness is a virtue. One of these, crucial to the character of the Civil Service, is the requirement, since the creation of the Civil Service Commission in 1855, that it be politically neutral. If this characteristic is to be modified, even in part, it must be done openly after discussion and careful consideration. The section of the *Code* dealing with Political Activities opens with a ringing, high Victorian 'Statement of Intent':

> Civil servants owe their allegiance to the Crown. In its executive capacity, the authority of the Crown is exercised through the Government of the day. Civil servants are therefore required to discharge loyally the duties assigned to them by the Government of the day of whatever political persuasion. For the Civil Service to serve successive governments of different political complexions it is essential that ministers and the public should have confidence that civil servants' personal views do not cut across the discharge of their official duties. The intent of the rules governing political activities by civil servants is to allow them the greatest possible freedom to participate in public affairs without infringing these fundamental principles. The rules are concerned with political activities liable to give public expression to political views, rather than the privately held beliefs and opinions.[82]

The *Code* identifies ten activities, five at national/international level and five at local level, as 'political activities subject to restriction'. The list was agreed between the Management and Personnel Office and the Civil Service unions in negotiations which followed the Armitage Report on Political Activities of Civil Servants published in 1978,[83] though the ground had been broken, for rule-making purposes, a generation earlier by a committee under the great wartime exponent of the double-cross system and M15 luminary, Sir John Masterman.[84] They are:

National level

* public announcement as a candidate or prospective candidate for parliament or the European Assembly;
* holding, in party political organisations, offices which impinge wholly or mainly on party politics in the field of Parliament or the European Assembly;
* speaking in public on matters of national political controversy;

* expressing views on such matters in letters to the press, or in books, articles or leaflets;
* canvassing on behalf of a candidate for Parliament or the European Assembly, or on behalf of a political party.[85]

Local level

* candidature for, or co-option to, local authorities;
* holding, in party political organisations, offices impinging wholly or mainly on party politics in the local field;
* speaking in public on matters of local political controversy;
* expressing views on such matters in letters to the press, or in books, articles or leaflets;
* canvassing on behalf of candidates for election to local authorities or a local political organisation.[86]

For the purposes of political activity, the Civil Service, like Gaul, is divided into three parts: a 'politically free' group, including industrial civil servants and everybody in the non-office grades, messengers and the like; a 'politically restricted' group, administration trainees and everyone above the rank of principal, who are debarred from *all* national political activity but who can, if the parent department grants permission, participate in local political activities; and an intermediate group, clerical and executive officers and professionals below the rank of principal equivalent, who can take part in national and local political activity, though if they become candidates for Parliament or the European Assembly they must resign.[87]

For those in the grey area of the restricted category political activity will normally be prohibited if they are working closely with ministers in a private office or a policy division 'or areas which are acutely politically sensitive or subject to considerations of national security'. Similar self-denial is expected of officials who speak for the government in dealings with overseas governments or home-based commercial bodies, pressure groups or public authorities. And that sizeable army of indispensable, if lowly-graded, officials who have regular face-to-face contact with the public in benefit or tax offices must also forego the joys of political life.[88]

Even where political activity is permitted, for a civil servant the freedom is qualified. They are subject to a 'code of discretion' which implies a duty to moderation:

> Even when permission, either individually or en bloc, is given to staff in the intermediate or politically restricted group, a civil servant's political views should not constitute so strong and so comprehensive a commitment to the tenets of one political party as to inhibit or appear to inhibit loyal and effective service to Ministers of another party.[89]

This invocation strikes me as immensely difficult to enforce. Presumably it is a fall-back sanction for use if, say, a clerical or executive officer active in local politics attracted the notoriety of a Derek Hatton – though the withdrawal of permission to engage in political activity would, in those circumstances, inevitably become a national *cause célèbre*. Indeed, the fine print of the 'code of discretion' could be interpreted as a catch-all for those with views on the extremities of political life, with a personality and a command over words to match.

* Individuals in the intermediate and politically restricted groups undertaking political activities should bear in mind that they are servants of the Crown, working under the direction of Ministers forming the government of the day. While they are not debarred from advocating or criticising the policy of any political party, comment should be expressed with moderation, particularly in relation to matters for which their own Ministers are responsible, and indeed all comment avoided if the departmental issue concerned is controversial. Personal attacks should be avoided.
* Every care should be taken to avoid any embarrassment to Ministers or to their departments which could result, inadvertently or not, from the actions of a person known to be a civil servant who brings himself prominently to public notice in party political controversy.
* Permission to participate only on local political activities is granted subject to care being taken by the officer concerned not to involve himself in matters of political controversy which are of national rather than local significance.[90]

Similar rules govern trade-union activities. Apart from MI5, MI6 and, controversially since 1984, the Government Communications Headquarters, 'civil servants do not need permission to take part in activities organised by their trade unions'. MI5 and MI6 personnel have never been allowed to join a union. GCHQ now has its own in-house staff association though, at the time of writing (early 1988) a handful of people employed in communications intelligence are clinging to their union membership in defiance of the ban. But for those free to join unions who become union officials, the regulations of the Code are in cloud-cuckoo-land. Paragraph 9937 states:

> This section of the Code in no way denies their right to pursue the legitimate interests of their members; but when this involves commenting on Government policy they must make it clear that they are expressing views as representatives of the Union and not as civil servants and must

put them over in a reasonable way, bearing in mind their position as civil servants. In cases of doubt advice should be sought from the Establishment Officer.

A glance through the cuttings of the Civil Service Union conference season any April or May, not to mention the record 21-week Civil Service strike of 1981, will show just how much notice is taken of paragraph 9937. The Establishment Officers' waiting rooms are not cluttered up with union activist mendicants.

If a civil servant is sufficiently politically charged to crave election to Parliament or the European Assembly, he or she must, if in the restricted or intermediate category, resign the moment they are adopted as a prospective candidate. Those in the politically free group have to go only when formally nominated in the run-up to an election.

To prevent political patronage moving in a reverse-flow into the Civil Service, the Victorians invented the Civil Service Commission created by Order in Council in 1855. It has operated on the basis of order in council ever since, and answers to the Queen, *not* the Prime Minister, as an institutionalised guarantor of merit and probity against the corrupting forces of political favouritism and patronage. The Commissioners' weapon is the certificate of qualification which only they can award. Their function has been a constant in public service life for as long as anyone, minister, civil servant or public administration specialist, can remember. Like most constants it was taken for granted with an occasional flurry of interest as in 1978 when the rules for temporary civil servants had to be amended to accommodate special advisers, like Dr Bernard Donoughue in the Downing Street Policy Unit, in case Mr Callaghan delayed calling an election and their period of service went beyond the stipulated cut-off point of five years.

The Commission and its powers shot into prominence, however, in December 1984 when Michael Heseltine, then Secretary of State for Defence, decided to appoint his former special adviser, Mr Peter Levene, chairman of United Scientific Holdings, as Chief of Defence Procurement, an *established* not a temporary post of second permanent secretary rank. Two factors caused a furore: the size of Mr Levene's salary, £95,000 a year, then way above, more than double in fact, the going rate for the grade; and the nature of the appointment, which tore through the Civil Service Commission's protective shield. Mr Dennis Trevelyan, First Civil Service Commissioner, let it be known that the commissioners had been taken by surprise and had considered resignation *en masse*.[91] In fact, Mr Trevelyan had learned of the appointment from Sir Robert Armstrong the evening before it was announced.[92] The indications were that Sir Robert himself had only learned of it that day,[93] which is very surprising as he chairs the Senior Appointments Selection Committee which advises the Prime Minister and secretaries of state on *all* appointments at that level. The Levene appointment, all the more bizarre because there was a sitting incumbent some way off retirement, Mr David Perry, was, it appeared, an enterprise kept wholly within the Ministry of Defence. Ignorance of the rules, rather than defiance of them, was offered as the explanation and even then in private.[94]

It was not that Mr Levene was unqualified for the job. His experience was rich, his drive singular and his aptitude for the pursuit of value for money remarkable. Once in the job his zest for competitive tendering won reluctant plaudits from defence contractors whose profit margins and delivery dates had suffered at his hands. Mr Levene's patron, Mr Heseltine, went so far as to claim in his political testament, published in the spring of 1987, that he 'will have saved, by now, hundreds of millions of pounds for the Defence budget. If he has saved 8 per cent of the equipment programme – and he has said that he expects to save 10 per cent – he will have paid for the Trident programme single-handed.'[95] It was doubly damaging, therefore, to those who argued that Whitehall needed new blood at the top, that the manner of Mr Levene's preferment, which was bungled, distracted attention from the value of it, which was considerable.

When the Levene appointment was announced, it was stated that it was outside the scope of the Civil Service Order in Council of 1982 (the latest in the unbroken line from 1855). The Civil Service Commissioners sought legal advice. The advice was that an appointment on secondment like Mr Levene's 'was capable of amounting to an "appointment to a situation" in the Home Civil or Diplomatic Services as covered by Article 1(1) of the 1982 order'.[96] And Article 1(1) is quite explicit. The qualifications of a person proposed for such an appointment must have prior approval of the Civil Service Commissioners 'whose decision shall be final, and no person shall be appointed to such a situation until a certificate of qualification has been issued by the Commissioners'.[97] Mr Levene was granted such a certificate in time for his taking up the post of Chief of Defence Procurement in March 1985.

The Civil Service Commission, with its great tradition and direct link to the Sovereign, carries clout. To flout it is tantamount to acting unconstitutionally. Mrs Thatcher acknowledged its powers – indeed, she extended them – in the backwash of the Levene case when she announced in the Commons on 18 March 1985, as the Commission's 1985 annual report paraphrased it,

> that measures were being taken to provide that future appointments to the Home Civil Service which took the form of secondment from an outside organisation would be made in compliance with the Civil Service

> Order in Council and any regulations made thereunder. It was immediately clear that these developments represented a significant widening of what was considered to be the scope of our responsibilities, given the increasing use of inward secondments, often at senior levels in recent years.[98]

These secondments had grown from 60 in 1977 to 150 in 1985. And an even greater inward flow is crucial to most of the reform plans being mooted in the late eighties, which is why the post-Levene arrangements are of more than historical interest. The Commissioners recognised past confusion at departmental level and 'regularised' (their word) previous appointments, including that of Mr Levene, in a new Civil Service Order in Council issued from Buckingham Palace on 15 May 1985.[99]

The Commissioners, after further deliberation and consideration of legal advice, reached an important compromise between 'appointments . . . made on merit on the basis of fair and open competition' and appointment where 'it may be known that the sort of knowledge and expertise for which a department is looking can be found only among the employees of one or two organisations [the Levene example]; or the proposed secondment is part of an exchange programme with an identified organisation'.[100]

The new settlement which came into effect on 1 May 1986 allows departments to make their own arrangements, in accordance with Commission guidelines, except where an appointment is for more than five years or is to a post at under secretary rank or above. In those cases the commissioners must examine the appointment and satisfy themselves that, in the absence of an open competition, the 'secondment was a suitable way to fill the post on the terms proposed and that the individual was the best qualified candidate available'.[101] Clearly, Mr Trevelyan and his four fellow Commissioners believe that in this fashion the essentials of the great nineteenth-century Northcote–Trevelyan reform can be reconciled with the late-twentieth-century need for a more rapid circulation of talent. The 1986 settlement had a tentative, somewhat experimental, air, however, as the Commissioners 'recognise that this is an area of considerable public interest. We shall, therefore, keep the new arrangements under close review to see whether they require adaptation or modification in the light of experience.'[102]

Movement in the other direction, civil servants leaving Whitehall not on secondment but to take up outside business appointments, was substantially more controversial a subject in the 1980s than inward flows, the Peter Levene case notwithstanding. The Treasury and Civil Service Select Committee mounted no less than two investigations into the subject in its first six years of life. But the issue has a long history of its own. In 1936 the Royal Commission on the Private Manufacture of and Trading in Arms[103] criticised the movement of civil servants and members of the Armed Forces to weapons manufacturers. The Royal Commission pre-echoed the select committee reports of the 1980s in its fear that the independence of the Civil Service might be impaired if it was thought likely that officials' behaviour could be influenced while in the public service by the prospect of future employment with government and suppliers and in its emphasis on the importance of allaying public anxiety on this score. The National Government responded the following year with a memorandum on the acceptance of business appointments by Crown servants.[104] It established the rule which still holds that officials or officers at the top levels, and more junior people with special technical expertise, need to apply for clearance if they wish to take up a job in business within two years of leaving their service.

The issue lay dormant until the Poulson Affair in the early 1970s brought corruption high on to the political and media agenda. The bankruptcy hearings involving the prominent architect, Mr John Poulson, in 1972 uncovered an alarming network of corruption in the awarding of public building contracts. It reached to very nearly the highest level at the Scottish Office. Mr George Pottinger, Secretary of the Department of Agriculture and Fisheries for Scotland, an under secretary, was convicted in February 1974 of offences under the Prevention of Corruption Acts. As the subsequent Royal Commission on Standards of Conduct in Public Life pointed out, 'over the years Mr Poulson had succeeded in corruptly penetrating high levels of the Civil Service, the National Health Service, two nationalised industries and a number of local authorities'.[105] In this renewed climate of concern, the Labour government of Harold Wilson tightened up procedures dealing with business appointments for officials, an area tangential to the Poulson case, though related. All permanent secretaries in future would be obliged to wait for three months between resignation or retirement and the taking up of a business job. And an Advisory Committee on Business Appointments was established to advise the Prime Minister on prospective appointments covering the top three Civil Service grades (under secretary and above) and their equivalents in the Forces.[106]

This arrangement did not satisfy everybody. The issue began its long march through the Commons select committees. In 1977 the Expenditure Committee, as part of its general inquiry into the Civil Service, noted that 'there has been public criticism implying that the prospect of ... outside jobs can be dangled before civil servants as an influence upon them before they leave the service'.[107] It was puzzled at the absence of legal sanctions to back the rules. The Labour government of James Callaghan was not impressed. The number of applicants for clearance was small and evidence of abuse nil. The Government, said Lord Peart, Lord Privy Seal and Minister for the Civil Service in 1978, 'could not justify setting aside time amid a crowded Parliamentary timetable for a Bill to inhibit a mischief which appears to be largely theoretical'.[108] In 1980, however, the Civil Service Department tightened the wording of the rules, making particular reference to job offers from firms enjoying a contractual relationship with government.[109]

In the same year the new Commons Treasury and Civil Service Committee opened a specific inquiry into business appointments. Unable to agree among themselves, the committee issued what amounted to a Green Paper in 1981 floating the possibility of tighter controls, including legislation, and inviting comment.[110] In 1983 it returned to the theme. This time the recommendations were tougher. The Thatcher government had made an important modification in response to the previous inquiry. Two outsiders – Sir David Orr and Sir William Duncan, businessmen both, had been brought on to the Advisory Committee. With their presence, no longer did retired crown servants make up a majority of the membership.[111] The select committee was not placated. Its sub-committee, under the chairmanship of Mr Austin Mitchell, a Labour MP and a tough critic of the Establishment and its values (including the honours system), began a series of protracted hearings, some of which involved combative exchanges between MPs and top officials now in business like Mr John Lippitt (ex-Department of Industry), Mr Alan Lord (ex-Treasury), Sir Frank Cooper (ex-Defence) and Lord Hunt of Tanworth (ex-Cabinet Office) plus a clutch of retired military.

When it reported in 1984, the Mitchell committee, much less riven by faction than its predecessor, urged significant reforms. The MPs were exercised by the surge in the number of applications over the five-year period 1979–83, particularly from the Ministry of Defence (118 in 1979 to 535 in 1983), and far from satisfied with assurances from Sir Robert Armstrong that current arrangements were adequate. The select committee wanted an extension in the maximum delay period from two to five years, a more systematic role for the Advisory Committee particularly on the Defence side, a written undertaking from those accepting posts that for five years they would not represent their new employers on matters for which they had once held official responsibility, the withdrawal of pension as a sanction if rules were flouted, a ban on officials discussing jobs with prospective employers within the last twelve months of service before retirement and the appointment of two senior backbench MPs to the Advisory Committee.[112]

In a word, the select committee got nowhere. In its White Paper replying to the report in March 1985,[113] the Government ruled out extending the possible limbo period from two to five years as current knowledge on contracts and technical information erodes rapidly, certainly within two years; as there was no evidence of abuse, sanctions were unnecessary; it would be both restrictive and impractical to debar discussion about possible retirement jobs in an official's final year; and there was nothing wrong with placing two senior backbenchers on the Advisory Committee but it was normal practice to have two ex-ministers now in the House of Lords on it, and was that not sufficient as a link with Parliament? The issue, however, will not – and should not – die, not because subliminal corruption is coursing through the veins of senior civil servants and high-ranking officers in the Armed Forces, but because a greater exchange of people, experience and ideas is a prerequisite of *any* reform of Whitehall worthy of the name. It may be that the price of this increased mobility is tighter rules more intensely policed. But, that much greater movement, not just at retirement age, is highly desirable should not be an issue between the Treasury and Civil Service Committee and the Government.

Naturally, it is as impossible as it is undesirable to take a consistent stand on Whitehall rules. In some areas it is a great public boon that it is a regulation-bound society. Corruption, the prevention of, is one of these. Its absence is a hallmark not only of a proper public service but of a modern one. Patronage has to be slain as does graft. In the first, as we have seen, the Civil Service Commission plays St George. In the second it is the Establishment Officers, the heads of personnel in each ministry, keepers of the *Civil Service Pay and Conditions of Service Code*, and the *Establishment Officers' Guide*, with the back-up of three statutes, the Public Bodies Corrupt Practices Act, 1889, and the Prevention of Corruption Acts, 1906 and 1916.

The Code is phrased in admirably strong and principled tones on the matter:

> The high standard which the Service sets itself goes beyond the normal standards of personal honesty and integrity; the civil servant must not only be honest in fact, but also he must not lay himself open to suspicion of dishonesty.[114]

Detailed guidance on the implications of such standards are specific, as officials must 'always have in mind the need not to give the impression to any member of the public or organisation with whom they deal, or to their colleagues, that they may be influenced, or have been influenced, by any gift or consideration to show favour or disfavour to any person or organisation whilst acting in an official capacity'.[115] For example, it is fine to attend trade dinners and working lunches and, up to a point, to reciprocate hospitality. But 'acceptance of frequent or regular invitations to lunch or dinner on a wholly one-sided basis even on a small scale might give rise to a breach of the standard of conduct required'.[116] Gifts are another tightly controlled area. Under the Prevention of Corruption Act, 1906, it is an offence for a civil servant to corruptly accept a gift as an inducement or a reward for doing, or refraining from doing anything in his official capacity or for showing favour or disfavour to any individual. Under the 1916 Act any money or gift received by a civil servant from an individual holding or seeking to hold a government contract will be deemed by the Courts to have been received corruptly unless the official can *prove* the contrary.[117] The vexed question of gifts from overseas governments on foreign trips is also covered. They can be accepted but must be given up to the Crown unless the official pays the Treasury a sum equivalent to their value or the 'gift is a small and inexpensive article of a personal nature to which the application of the general rule would be either impracticable or excessively complicated'.[118]

I have always found these anti-corruption statutes and rules utterly admirable and one of *the* greatest virtues of the British Civil Service. Are they effective? From my own observations I know they have a powerful effect on the ethos and culture of Whitehall. Corruption cases come before the courts from time to time. The Property Services Agency, the government's estate manager, has been the main area of trouble in recent years for obvious reasons as it is a big provider of publicly funded work. The Department of the Environment, its parent department, has very detailed guidelines on gifts, hospitality, private interests, contracts and contractors.[119] But an inquiry by Sir Geoffrey Wardale, a former DOE permanent secretary, in 1983 gave cause for concern.[120] Sir Geoffrey examined 40 cases of alleged corruption and fraud. He found 13 of them to be serious, another 18 less so (fiddling of expenses, that kind of thing).[121] As a result, twenty persons were committed for trial at the Old Bailey, nine civil servants from the PSA, one former officer with the Greater London Council and ten building contractors. (At the time of writing the final outcome of the series of trials was unknown). Such committals justified Anne Mueller's statement in the autumn of 1986 'that standards of conduct in the public service are high and that recent prosecutions for corruption indicate a high state of vigilance and a high concept of what is and is not permissible'.[122] The problem with such cases is that they may be the tip of the iceberg. The Poulson case is haunting in this respect. The Royal Commission on Standards of Conduct in Public Life reckoned that he 'first resorted to corrupt methods' in 1949–50.[123] But for his filing a bankruptcy petition *twenty-two years* later, his widespread graft would probably never have emerged. But for the remarkable tenacity and forensic skill of Poulson's interrogater at the bankruptcy hearing, Mr Muir Hunter QC, the appalling tale contained in Poulson's papers and files might not have yielded the material needed by the Director of Public Prosecutions to bring his long list of prosecutions under the Prevention of Corruption Acts.[124] Similar 'tip of the iceberg' unease was aroused just before Christmas 1986 when Department of Trade and Industry investigations of insider trading in the

City turned inward upon the department itself when Mr Paul Channon, the then Trade Secretary, appointed inspectors to investigate allegations that some of his own officials within DTI, the Office of Fair Trading and the Monopolies and Mergers Commission had contravened the Company Securities (Insider Dealing) Act 1985.[125]

The Civil Service Code and the *Establishment Officers' Guide*, its routine and corruption paragraphs apart, had a somewhat impermanent air about them in the mid-1980s. Several possible changes were on the horizon any one of which would have required them to be rewritten substantially. Freedom of information, based on a code or a statute, would demand a very thorough rethink of that rule mountain of paragraphs based solely on the philosophy and the provisions of Section 2 of the Official Secrets Act, 1911. The responsible minister, the Home Secretary, Douglas Hurd, was planning changes in this area on the grounds that nobody, as he reminded an RIPA conference, 'is satisfied with the present condition of the Official Secrets Act'.[126] (Mr Hurd was due to publish an Official Secrets White Paper in the summer of 1988.)

Another area on which Mr Hurd touched in his address at Durham – the relationship between ministers and civil servants – is certain to remain live. For Mr Hurd, the Armstrong memorandum after Clive Ponting's acquittal is 'an adequate framework for the relationship'.[127] But the Government recognised the scope for debate, if not for immediate change, and discussions began in the autumn of 1986 between Sir Robert Armstrong and leaders of the Civil Service unions. If parts or versions of the FDA's draft Code of Ethics[128] were incorporated into the Civil Service, rather more would be needed in the Civil Service 'Bible' than its all-embracing, indiscriminate opening claim that 'the first duty of a civil servant is to give his undivided allegiance to the State at all times and on all occasions when the State has a claim on his services'.[129] No longer could all the partners in government, including senior officials themselves, be expected to swallow whole and unqualified Sir Robert Armstrong's assertion that 'for all practical purposes the Crown [i.e. the State] in this context means and is represented by the Government of the day'.[130] But ethos and culture, the keys to any institutional genetic code, are made up of far more than clusters of rules and regulations, codes and laws. History, as we have seen, is what shapes them, custom and practice, the passing on of skills and habits from one generation to the next, the survival of structures and departments whose functions have so altered, as Haldane put it, that the later stages of their existence 'have not accorded in principle' with the purposes for which they were initially created.[131]

Above all, tradition and convention are added to and subtracted from by each generation through whose hands they pass, and it is the possessors of those hands – the people who make up the Whitehall team – to whom we must turn shortly. But first, a detailed examination of the institutional sub-groups into which the system is physically broken down – a glance at the geography of administration – is required.

10 THE GEOGRAPHY OF ADMINISTRATION

The first thing to be noted about the central government of this country is that it is a federation of departments.
Sir William Armstrong, 1970[1]

What is often underestimated is the extent to which departments have characteristics and, indeed, even characters. Departments are to a very great extent coloured in their attitudes by the last major reform that they undertook.
Shirley Williams, 1980[2]

In the first of his legendary Ford Lectures on 'the Troublemakers' at Oxford in 1956, A. J. P. Taylor began by emphasising a truth which must never be allowed to sink beneath the gaze of any observer of government. 'We may remind ourselves over and over again', he told his capacity audience,[3] 'that the foreign policy of a country is made by a few experts and a few rather less expert politicians ... We write "the British" when we mean "the few members of the Foreign Office who happened to concern themselves with this question".'[4] Taylor's Law, at a slight risk of oversimplification, can be applied to virtually every area of policy-making in which the state plays a role sufficiently substantial to have it institutionally enshrined in the stone, brick or plate glass of a central government department. Departments matter. They lead lives of their own. As Shirley Williams put it, they have banners to defend on which the departmental traditions and orthodoxy are emblazoned like fading regimental colours in a cathedral – and these are defended against all-comers whether they be pressure-groups, select committees, international organisations or other ministries. Among the other departments the 'auldest enemies' can often be found. The Treasury is the 'auldest' of them all. I can remember over lunch one under secretary with a vivid imagination likening his Treasury colleagues to sentries on the ramparts at night gazing down on the fires around which huddled their assortment of departmental foes waiting for the dawn assault upon their walls.

Any book on Whitehall needs a Baedeker guide to the banners and the battlements of the departmental satrapies. For most of them I have drawn up, with the help of Andrea Jones of Sussex University, a departmental chart encapsulating a core of information – numbers, budgets, functions, management system – and attaching an organogram. For each I have added a brief essay on the department's soul, its lore and legend. No tabulation can be perfect as functions can overlap (the Department of the Environment, for example, is both an economic and a social ministry and the Treasury is both a central and an economic department). But, for the sake of convenience, I have divided the departments up as follows:

Central
Prime Minister's Office
Cabinet Office
Treasury

Overseas and defence
Foreign and Commonwealth Office
Overseas Development Administration
Ministry of Defence

Social
Department of Health and Social Security
Department of Education and Science

Economic
Department of Trade and Industry
Department of the Environment
Ministry of Agriculture, Fisheries and Food
Department of Energy
Department of Transport
Department of Employment
Manpower Services (now Training) Commission

Territorial
Home Office
Scottish Office
Welsh Office
Northern Ireland Office

Secret
Security Service, MI5
Secret Intelligence Service, MI6
Government Communications Headquarters

Money-raising
Board of Inland Revenue
Board of Customs and Excise

The geography of Whitehall is never static. But the geomorphology of its 1980s bedrock would be recognisable to any set of postwar ministers and officials who had lived their careers atop of it. Even if substantial swathes of executive functions were hived off, the current departmental boundaries would most likely remain with their in-house functions largely reduced to policy-making and regulation.

THE CENTRAL DEPARTMENTS

Prime Minister's Office

> No. 10 Downing Street has a more modest face than any of the world's great buildings ... From the street outside it is a classic example of British understatement, hiding the treasures of art and history and experience that are within ... Today it harbours only Britain's crises, but it was once the eye of the storms that shook the world.
> **Joe Haines, 1976**[5]

> The door shuts in the small closed world of prime ministerial power.
> **Bernard Donoughue, 1987**[6]

> At the end of the day the decisions that matter are taken not in the Whitehall village but in the castle of No. 10 Downing Street and the Cabinet Room.
> **Sir Leo Pliatzky, 1982**[7]

James Callaghan was in No. 10 for only three years but he always managed to convey the impression of a shrewd and seasoned politician who had been at the top for a generation and seen it all before. He developed a theory 'that it is the small problems that upset government and not the large problems'.[8] He would illustrate the point by talking about sea-power and the Falklands, a subject close to his heart as a former naval person:

> ... because of my background, I asked the Admiralty every week to send me a map of the world, about the size of this blotter in front of us here, which set out the position and disposition of every ship in the

British Navy, including all the auxiliaries, so that I could know exactly what we could do and how long it would take us to get to the Falklands and where we needed to be. That is the kind of thing I think a Prime Minister must do. There are small things he must do, and large things. That's one of the small things he must do that can save a very large catastrophe.[9]

The power of the British Prime Minister is truly awesome in matters great and small. All the power lines lead to No. 10. The armoury of personal power is immense – the right to hire and fire all ministers; control of the Cabinet agenda; the creation, composition and subject matter of its committees; the right to intervene on *any* issue in *any* department. The Prime Minister's Personal Minute, that most potent of dockets, is an artefact crying out for a political archaeologist. A study of it from Churchill's 'Action this Day' to Macmillan's elegant and witty disquisitions, via Attlee's terse one-liners and Eden's fussy initiatives, is perfectly possible from the files. It would demonstrate the long antecedence of Callaghan's law of all issues great and small.

There have been a number of attempts to assess the relative clout of the castles, the stately homes, the semis and the terraces of the Whitehall village, the most recent being by Professor Richard Rose of Strathclyde University and Charles Miller of Public Policy Consultants. In Rose's table of the 'Political Status of Ministries', twenty departments are divided into three leagues. The Prime Minister's Office inevitably tops League Division One,[10] as it does Miller's measure of influence and strength in his target appraisal for those who wish to bring pressure on government.[11] Whoever made the calculation and whatever the indices on which it was based, the answer would be the same.

The number of staff buttressing this pinnacle of power in the British system is modest in comparison to the back-up available to premiers, chancellors or presidents in other democratic systems.[12] In 1986 Mrs Thatcher was assisted by a staff of twenty-seven split between the Private Office, the Press Office, the Political Office and the Policy Unit. When secretaries, telephonists, messengers and all the various kinds of support staff were added in, the total reached 63.[13]

The Private Office, 'the single most important section' of the PM's back-up,[14] consists of two senior career officials – the Principal Private Secretary and the Foreign Affairs Secretary – and three juniors covering the economic, home and parliamentary fronts plus the diary secretary, junior in status but crucial as the controller of access to the PM. All these are crammed into two offices next to the Cabinet Room. Bernard Donoughue has mapped their locus as a commanding height in the geography of power:

> Virtually all official communications to or from the Prime Minister, written or verbal, are channelled through the Private Office. The Private Secretaries sift through the flow of papers and decide – based upon their experience of central government and upon their knowledge of a particular Prime Minister's interests and priorities – which to put before him urgently, which to delay, and which not to bother him with but to answer themselves. They fill the Prime Minister's red boxes for his nightly or his weekend reading. The senior secretaries will periodically sit with him in the study or in the flat discussing how to respond on certain issues. Usually a close bond of trust builds up between the Prime Minister and his Private Office, which organises the whole routine of his governmental working day.[15]

Even the briefest of spells in the Downing Street Private Office is usually a launch-pad to the highest Civil Service posts.

But it is not a risk-free path to the top, as one former principal private secretary told me. 'It's very heady,' he said. 'There you are sitting in the cockpit of the United Kingdom in an atmosphere that is friendly and close. You can say what you think. You don't lightly override the advice of your elders and betters but you can if you want. You can tell the PM "this is nonsense" and deftly guide him to something better. But if you are demonstrably wrong just once you have had it.'[16] Those who excel at the job must, in effect, get inside the PM's skin. One Principle Private Secretary said the relationship should develop so that neither should need to finish a sentence to be completely understood by the other.[17] Such a bond is fostered by permanent intimacy with the Principle Private Secretary who undertakes a wide spectrum of tasks from high policy adviser, honest friend and personal nanny. They have to be highly political animals without ever forgetting the canons of Northcote and Trevelyan. It is rather like riding two horses at high speed.

The Press Office can play a surprisingly influential role. Under Bernard Ingham it probably peaked in terms of its postwar influence on the Prime Minister and the flow of policy-making, though Sir Tom McCaffrey (Callaghan), Joe Haines (Wilson) and Sir Harold Evans (Macmillan) ran Mr Ingham hard on that criterion. The Press Secretary's job has oscillated between politically appointed outsiders like Francis Williams (Attlee) and Haines and career regulars like Evans and Ingham. The regulars are normally drawn from the ranks of the Government Information Service. Ingham was a hybrid: after leaving *The Guardian* he belonged to the information class, but by the time he replaced Henry James at No. 10 in 1979 he was an under secretary on the policy-making side at the Department of Energy. Heath preferred the Foreign Office News Department system and appointed a pair of career diplomats from outside the information group to run his Downing Street Press Office in the persons of, first, Sir

Donald Maitland, and later Sir Robin Haydon. The Downing Street Press Secretary is not normally the top information officer in Whitehall. That titular honour falls to the Director-General of the Central Office of Information who doubles as Head of the Government Information Service. But the PM's man is the crucial figure in real terms. Ingham had considerable influence over top information appointments in Whitehall, not as great as the Secretary of State in the department concerned but certainly more than the Head of the GIS. He also chaired the Monday evening meeting of MIO, (Meeting of Information Officers) the body which co-ordinated the timing and flow of what official information it was deemed safe to divulge attributably.

There remains in No. 10 one deliciously Trollopian function a world apart from the gloss and hype of political public relations. It has to do with that timeless appendage of power – patronage. The Patronage Secretary is the one career post in the Civil Service that has to be filled by a practising Anglican because of the Prime Minister's continuing role in the choice of bishops of the Church of England. Perhaps for this reason the three patronage secretaries I have met – Sir John Hewitt (1961–73), Mr Colin Peterson (1974–82) and Mr Robin Catford (since 1982) – have been the incarnation of courtesy and charm. The other distinction they share is their occupation of the finest room in No. 10,[18] and periodic but vain attempts have been made to turf them out of it.[19]

In the forties and fifties the job was filled by one of the greatest eccentrics in Whitehall history, Sir Anthony Bevir. Bevir, an old Etonian with a scholarly air, was inherited by Churchill when he replaced Chamberlain in No. 10 in May 1940, as Sir John Colville (whom Churchill similarly acquired) remembered:

> Anthony Bevir had been badly wounded at the end of the First World War, through the whole of which he fought meritoriously (itself a strong recommendation in Churchill's eyes) ... He was ill at ease in the speed and clatter of Churchillian life and temperamentally unsuited to serve an unpredictable master. So he was relegated to handle the ecclesiastical patronage on the grounds that I, who had become acquainted with all the characters in Trollope's Barchester novels during the previous nine months, was too juvenile to deal with bishops. 'On the other hand,' said Eric Seal [the Private Secretary Churchill brought with him from the Admiralty] when he broke the news to me, 'I think you might be better than Tony Bevir at dealing with the Prime Minister.'
>
> Bevir took infinite pains to help anybody in trouble and often thought of original ways to do so. Indeed he was one of the kindest and least self-seeking of men. He continued to serve Church and State, to the benefit of both, under Attlee after 1945, under Churchill once again and

under Anthony Eden. In 1952, Churchill, who had developed an affection for him, decided that his faithful service merited a reward. He proposed to recommend him for a KCB in the new Queen's Birthday Honours List. He was, it appeared, of the wrong seniority in the Civil Service for a knighthood of any kind and the Secretary to the Treasury, Sir Edward Bridges, descended in wrath on No. 10. He had a blazing row with the Prime Minister: at least Bridges blazed, but to my surprise Churchill remained icily calm. Fortunately the Queen, quite independently, had decided that Bevir's long and helpful connection with Buckingham Palace on episcopal matters deserved a KCVO. The Prime Minister at once concluded that a personal gift of this kind from the Queen was even more distinguished than the Order of the Bath. So with a mischievous smile he told me to let Bridges know he would withdraw his proposal.

By an unhappy chance Bevir then proceeded to lose his key chain in a taxi. Attached to it were all the important box-keys in Whitehall and that of the garden entrance to 10 Downing Street. So the locks had to be changed with great speed and at great expense.

When the Honours List was published a few days later, the Treasury were dumbfounded. They had been outwitted by their own First Lord and their Sovereign. However, they had the last word. On the morning the list appeared my telephone rang. It was Sir Burke Trend, future Secretary to the Cabinet. 'Do you know,' he asked, 'what KCVO stands for? Keys Can Vanish Overnight.'[20]

Bevir also features as the butt in one of the best Attlee stories to have survived his stewardship in No. 10. Its teller, Sir George Mallaby, recalled the Downing Street habit of referring to Attlee as 'the little man':

There was perhaps an element of the patronising about this but it never implied any lack of respect. At this time he had a private secretary named J. T. A. Burke – before the war with the Victoria and Albert Museum and now Professor of Fine Arts at the University of Melbourne – and the patronage secretary was, and remained for many years to come, Tony Bevir – later Sir Anthony Bevir. Burke had a very small son for whom he betrayed much paternal solicitude and, like all fathers, supposed that his friends were almost equally solicitous and interested. Upon return from leave in Ireland on one occasion Tony Bevir enquired of Burke, 'And how is the little man?' To which Burke replied, 'He is all right now but we have a lot of trouble with him.' 'Trouble?' said Tony Bevir. 'What sort of trouble?' 'Well,' Burke explained, 'he gets strange notions into his head and nothing will persuade him that they are false.' 'Dear me!' said Tony, 'this sounds very serious. I knew there might be some anxieties at first but I hoped that time and experience would teach him stability and caution. But can you give me an example of these strange notions?' 'Well, the other day,' said Burke, 'he said that he had swallowed nails and drawing pins.' 'Swallowed nails and drawing pins! Whatever did you do?' 'We rushed him off to hospital and they X-rayed him but there was nothing to be seen. So they gave him a good dose and he seems to be all right again.' Tony Bevir's amazement was extreme – 'You've told Bridges, of course, haven't you?' 'Told Bridges? Why ever should I?' said the astonished father – and at that point, but not before, the cross-purposes became plain.[21]

Bevir and his descendants have been dubbed 'heaven's talent scouts'.[22] But their work embraces a wider circle than divines – the regius professorships, the mastership of Trinity College, Cambridge. The Appointments Secretary runs charities for old actors and for sculptors and poets in danger of penury. Since Bevir's day, they have also acted as establishment officer for the junior staff in Downing Street and as custodians of the fixtures and fittings of No. 10 and Chequers.[23]

The Political Office is a far more fluid entity than either the Private Office, the Press Office or the Appointments side. Its shape bore the very personal imprint of the PM. In Mrs Thatcher's time it has been headed by a chief of staff who advises her on party and electoral matters and usually plays a crucial role in speech-writing. Her Political Secretary relieves her of much of the burden of constituency work. The Parliamentary Private Secretary – her sounding-board and intelligence officer on Westminster matters, a role brought to triumphant heights of devotion and application by Mr Ian Gow in 1979–83 – is a part of the Political Office. Equally shaped by the PM's style and priorities are the network of personal policy advisers within the Policy Unit or floating free alongside it who are described in detail in Chapter 15 (see pp. 651–5).

Oddly enough, under the British system the Prime Minister's 'Permanent Secretary' is not located in No. 10 but through a connecting door to the Cabinet Office. For almost twenty years a debate has raged about the desirability on constitutional or practical grounds of creating a more logical structure in the form of a Prime Minister's Department. John Hunt liked to quote the solution to this perpetual dialectic proposed by a fellow permanent secretary at one of their annual autumn conferences at Sunningdale. 'It's perfectly obvious,' he said, 'we need a Prime Minister's Department – so long as it is still called the Cabinet Office.' 'I think that', Hunt added, 'may be the answer.'[24]

The Cabinet Office

> The Secretary of the Cabinet is, in a sense, the 'Prime Minister's Permanent Secretary' to use a phrase of ... [Burke Trend's] ... on handing me my first brief in 1964; but his loyalty is no less to Cabinet and the doctrine of Cabinet Government.
> **Harold Wilson, 1976**[25]

> Your concern is to see that the issues are processed up properly and that they finally reach Cabinet, when they've got to go to Cabinet, in a sufficiently compact, intelligible, clear form for the Cabinet to know what it is they've got to decide, what are the pro's and con's.
> **Lord Trend, 1976**[26]

> Throughout its history ... there has been a clear thread: the Cabinet Office has seen itself and has been seen as the servant of the Cabinet and of the Government collectively, its purpose being to promote and assist the discussion and resolution of issues that transcend departmental boundaries and the reaching and disseminating of conclusions and decisions commanding the collective assent of ministers. It is not a 'Prime Minister's Department'.
> **Sir Robert Armstrong, 1986**[27]

> The machine can actually influence and limit policies while nominally going through the merely administrative function of processing ... The Cabinet Office in particular may constrain (or accelerate it) because it establishes the agenda for policy discussion and selects and co-ordinates the participating departments, thus shaping the structure, balance and timetable of policy debate.
> **Bernard Donoughue**[28]

Founded: 1916.

Ministers: Prime Minister, Minister of State for the Civil Service.

Responsibilities: Co-ordination of policy briefing for Cabinet and Cabinet committees, co-ordination of the security and intelligence services, preparation for economic summits, Civil Service security, top Whitehall and public appointments, honours, official histories.

Budget: (1987–8) £49 million.

Staff: 1,690.

Management system: MAISY (the Treasury's computer-based management accounting system).

'Every department is about something,' an astute Whitehall observer told me when I first became interested in the Cabinet Office in the mid-1970s. 'The Treasury is about economics and finance, Environment is about housing and roads [this was before Callaghan split Environment and Transport]. The Cabinet Office is powerful because it is pure bureaucracy.' 'It is', he added for good measure, 'a rapidly expanding power and reflects the times in which we live.'[29] The Cabinet Office was certainly perceived as an expanding imperium during the tenure of John Hunt, a man whose style and bearing exuded power. It threw into sharp relief the somewhat jagged boundary that always exists between the Cabinet Secretary's domain and the Principal Private Secretary's, as Bernard Donoughue observed from his eyrie in the Policy Unit. In describing the ambiguous question of whether the Cabinet Secretary or the Principal Private Secretary 'is actually the Prime Minister's primary official adviser' he wrote:

> Certainly the Cabinet Secretary, Sir John Hunt, had ambitions and claims to be Mr Wilson's and Mr Callaghan's chief adviser. He was a senior permanent secretary, the only senior permanent secretary within the Prime Minister's central capability. He ranked above everybody in No. 10 and he commanded the Whitehall machine. However, although he had the status, he was not based at No. 10 and he did not therefore have automatic access to the Prime Minister. The Cabinet Secretary by convention had to telephone the Principal Private Secretary in order to receive clearance to come through the locked door to No. 10. On the other hand, the Principal Private Secretary – who in 1974–9 was first Robert Armstrong and then Kenneth Stowe – was always either an under secretary or a deputy secretary. He therefore had the access but not the seniority.[30]

Donoughue, who is like a mobile radar-station-made-man, was transfixed by the signals and pulses which radiated from this most fluid of relationships:

> Watching the relations between the distinguished Cabinet Secretary and the rising Principal Private Secretary was absolutely fascinating. It was a game about territory. Some of the boundaries were clearly defined, not least by the locked green baize door between the two offices. But there was a grey area of common land which each sought to occupy. This led to subtleties of behaviour and finesse of language which aroused my amused admiration: the total courtesies of address; the softly veiled hints of status from the Cabinet Secretary when telephoning to say 'I am coming through to see the Prime Minister about a highly important and secret issue, but of course I am phoning to let you know'; the politely deferential tone of the Principal Private Secretary to his senior, while

even so sometimes stating, 'This is not a convenient time but I will give you a ring when he is ready to see you . . .' On the important issues, of course, these officials usually worked together in impressive tandem, serving both of my Prime Ministers to their great satisfaction. However, the status relationships and ambiguities at the margin led to perennial tension, which Mr Wilson always relished and seemed occasionally to provoke.[31]

Turf fights aside, whoever fills the Cabinet Secretary's chair, the Cabinet Office will always be powerful in the Whitehall scheme of things, as Hankey and Lloyd George intended it to be when they installed its internal wiring in 1916. The Cabinet Office is *the* crucial junction box of the central government system. It does not command the money lines like the Treasury. But when it comes to formulating policy at the critical stage just before it goes to ministers collectively, all wires lead to No. 70 Whitehall. Roughly speaking, the wires run into six plugs known as secretariats. They are largely self-explanatory.

The Economic Secretariat deals with economic, industrial, energy, industrial relations and inner cities policy.

The Oversea and Defence Secretariat is the old Committee of Imperial Defence organisation, on which the prototype Cabinet Office was modelled, in its modern guise. It blends foreign and defence policy-making with the output of the intelligence agencies. It also handles Northern Ireland and Anglo-Irish relations.

Housed within the Oversea and Defence Secretariat is one of the most crucial of state capabilities – that of maintaining, as far as possible, the essentials of life (food, fuel, water) when they are disrupted by acts of God or acts of trade unions.[32] The Cabinet Office acquired this function from the Home Office in 1973 with the foundation of the Civil Contingencies Unit. The unit, as Sir Clive Rose, its head during the 1978–9 winter of discontent now said, is 'not to keep the government going, but to keep the country going'.[33]

The European Secretariat was established in the early 1970s. It handled negotiation and re-negotiation of Britain's membership of the EEC, then remained as a permanent addition to Cabinet Office capability to handle an ever-widening trans-departmental range of business offices mixing high political sensitivity with immense complexity.

The Home Affairs Secretariat is the Cabinet Office's charlady mopping up social policy, law and order, environmental matters (unless they have a high economic content), education, housing and local government. It also plans the Government's legislative programme.

The Science and Technology Secretariat has enjoyed successive boosts under Mrs Thatcher, the first scientist to fill the premiership. It was spun off from the Central Policy Review Staff in the early 1980s and lustily survived its demise. It now boasts its own Technology Assessment Office, and since July 1987 it has enjoyed the clout of a Cabinet committee chaired by the Prime Minister herself.[34]

The Joint Intelligence Secretariat is the most sensitive of all the 'black boxes' in the Cabinet Office. The Cabinet Secretary is accounting officer for the secret vote and the PM's principal adviser on security and intelligence policy (which is why Sir Robert Armstrong spent those uncomfortable weeks in Australia in 1986 during the *Spycatcher* hearings). The Security and Intelligence Secretariat is his back-up in this area and it also services what internal oversight there is of the secret agencies (see p. 473). Its bread and butter, however, is the work of its Assessments Staff which collates intelligence from all sources (our own and our allies') for discussion at the weekly meeting of the Joint Intelligence Committee before its onward transmission to selected ministers in the shape of the highly classified 'Red Book'.[35]

The sheer mechanics of shifting the raw material of collective discussion through the committees and distributing the product to those who need to know is immensely time-consuming. The flow is calibrated by a forward planning meeting at the end of each week chaired by the Cabinet Secretary and attended by the heads of his six secretariats, the PM's Principal Private Secretary and the Head of the Policy Unit. It is, to use an overworked metaphor, the bureaucratic equivalent of painting the Forth Bridge. In its way, it is strangely comforting. One former Cabinet Secretary told me how reassuring it was, no matter how great the political turbulence breaking round his head, to know that the traditional green vans carrying the minutes would go out conveying the Cabinet and Cabinet committee minutes and papers at eight, one and five precisely.[36]

The Cabinet Office also houses the Central Statistical Office, the number crunchers of the system. Its staff and their works are not as dull as they sound. Considerable figures like Sir Claus Moser and the floral-tied Sir John Boreham, who held famous and delicious parties for statisticians, their customers and friends at his Kent home,[37] have run it in recent years. It grew apace in the 1960s and 1970s. I once pointed this out to a particularly hard-boiled policy-maker, with the observation that as they had waxed so had the British economy waned. 'I know,' he replied, 'but it does mean that we're going to have the best-measured decline in economic history.'[38] The Raynerism of the 1980s, however, and the demise of statistics-hungry Keynesianism, saw them carrying a 25 per cent cut with a similar economy falling upon their colleagues in the Government Statistical Service bedded out across the whole range of departments.

When Robert Armstrong assumed the joint Headship of the Civil Service in 1981 (he became sole head on Wass's retirement in 1983), a large chunk of ex-Civil Service Department work was absorbed by the Cabinet Office. Some fitted quite naturally. Civil Service security (positive vetting and the rest) was an example. Other responsibilities Armstrong relished; the honours system was particularly welcome. He always took it very seriously and applied consistent attention to it despite his myriad of other responsibilities. It is a fascinating and elaborate world of its own with a well-oiled organisation under the Cabinet Office's Ceremonial Officer, the whole being supervised by a Main Honours Committee chaired by the Cabinet Secretary himself. His job is to keep it efficient and respected (quotas exist to stop modern premiers debasing it as Lloyd George did) and he has the help of a blue-riband Political Honours Scrutiny Committee to help him keep it clean.[39] However, one of the most criticised parts of the system has been the automatic flow of patronage to top civil servants – peerages to retiring Cabinet secretaries, knighthoods to permanent secretaries, commanderships to deputy secretaries – from their two custom-minted Orders, the Bath and the St Michael and St George. Mr Callaghan reduced the flow a little and Mrs Thatcher stopped the automatic award of peerages to retired heads of the Treasury and the Diplomatic Service.[40] But that did little to assuage the critics who tended to link gongs and inflation-proofed pensions in a seamless cloak of privilege.

Apart from its security and honours work, other accretions to the Cabinet Office after the demise of the Civil Service Department exuded a temporary air. The rump of the CSD – known as the Management and Personnel Office – always had a patina of impermanence around it and much of it transferred to the Treasury in the autumn of 1987.

The Treasury

The Treasury never sleeps.
Michael Heseltine, 1987[41]

It's wrong to attribute to the Treasury as an institution a lot of power when the power really derives from the subjects it's responsible for . . . It's always difficult for any individual to set himself up against an institution, even the head of the institution. Even I as Permanent Secretary could never get the better of the Treasury. There were too many clever people in it who knew more about any one subject than I did for me to be able to assert my own private preferences.
Sir Douglas Wass, 1986[42]

The Treasury is a bunch of bank clerks who think they are mandarins.
Lord Beloff, 1987[43]

Parliament is incapable of exercising its financial responsibilities. We must do it for them.
Anonymous Treasury official, 1987[44]

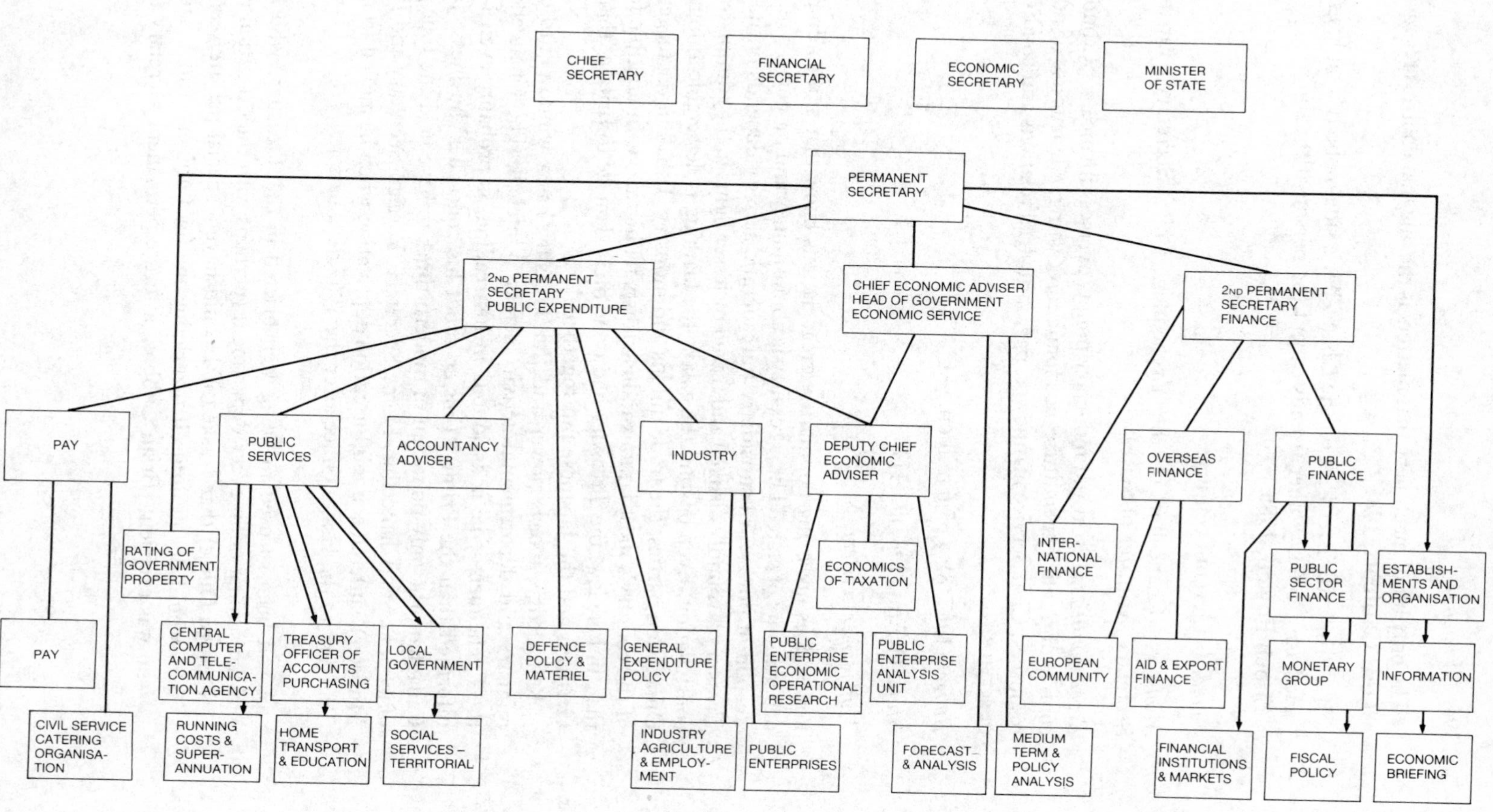

Fig. 1. H M Treasury

The only bit of machinery that matters is the one that controls resources.
Tom Caulcott, 1987[45]

If a Prime Minister isn't on the Chancellor's side, nobody's on his side. He hasn't got any other friends except the person at the top.
Enoch Powell, 1986.[46]

Founded: Eleventh century.

Ministers: Chancellor of the Exchequer, Chief Secretary, Financial Secretary, Minister of State.

Responsibilities: Fiscal and monetary policy, overseas finance, EEC budget, control of public expenditure, economic forecasting, efficient use of public resources; Civil Service manpower, pay, industrial relations and conditions of service.

Budget (1987–8): £65.6 million.

Staff: (1 April 1987): 3,417.

Management system: MAISY.

Power does not bring popularity: great nations know that and so do great departments of state. The Treasury is about money and money is a mighty weapon of power. All subsidiary bureaucratic activity depends on it. The Treasury is roundly disliked and feared by lesser lights in the administrative constellation. Even beyond the galaxy the loathing is detectable among the Opposition parties, the trade unions and industry. I shall never forget one of the country's most famous industrialists telling me, with tangible force, that, in his view, the Treasury had done more damage to Britain 'than the Germans and the Japanese put together'.[47]

Knowledge, too, is power and the Treasury has a window into every ministry and departmental activity across Whitehall. The Chancellor of the Exchequer, if he is assiduous in his reading, is probably even better informed than the Prime Minister about his colleagues' business. James Callaghan, the only politician in modern times to have held the four great offices of state (Chancellor, Home Secretary, Foreign Secretary and Prime Minister), suffered acute information deprivation when he moved from the Treasury to the Home Office after the 1967 devaluation:

> I had been so used to being well briefed in the Treasury, who know what's going on in every department (perhaps with the exception of the Foreign Office) that I asked if I could have a special private secretary who would devote himself to briefing me for Cabinet. And I had one who was excellent [Brian Cubbon, a future permanent secretary in the

department] ... But the Home Office, by virtue of its constitution, couldn't get me briefs, couldn't get me information the same way that the Treasury had it. The Chancellor always has, and needs to have, a real advantage.[48]

Given that the performance of the British economy has been *the* central problem of successive sets of ministers and officials operating at the summit of government since 1945, the Treasury has been in the eye of virtually every storm since the war. Always small in number and hugely well endowed in having the pick of the Civil Service's finest, it has, given persistent economic failure relative to most of the world's advanced economies, been a constant battleground for conflicting ideas and approaches and the major scapegoat for overall national failure on the part of highly charged political partisans of the Left, Right and Centre. It would be quite wrong, for example, to see the three decades of Keynesian ascendancy (from the 1944 Employment White Paper to Mr James Callaghan's speech to the Labour Party conference in 1976) as a period of stability for the Treasury. As we have seen, it endured successive assaults on its monopoly of economic decision-making. And its structure was frequently reshaped to reflect new priorities.

From 1947 until the mid-seventies there was, however, a tendency for new, more sophisticated and interventionist capabilities to be added to its superstructure. In November 1947, Plowden and his planners arrived as part of Cripps's portmanteau to be followed from the Cabinet Office in 1953 by Robert Hall and his Economic Section. Throughout the fifties Otto Clarke built up the Treasury's public expenditure apparatus piecemeal until the Plowden report gave him his chance at master-building on the grand scale. The sixties and early seventies – the William Armstrong years – saw, as part of the Keynesian apotheosis begun in 1941 when the Treasury swung to the new economics, the expansion and sophistication of the Treasury's economic forecasting capability without which, self-evidently, attempts to fine-tune the economy would be as successful as a symphony orchestra without a score. There were those who believed that a policy cacophony would result however many computers were installed in Treasury Chambers and however bright the members of the rapidly expanding (21 to 317 between 1964 and 1975) Government Economic Service who manned them.[49] Denis Healey, in the Treasury cockpit during the great currency and expenditure crises of the mid-1970s, used to apply his jovial thuggery to the hapless forecasters reeling from the quadrupling of the oil price: in benign moments he would liken their accuracy to that of the weather forecasters; when feeling really uncharitable he would declare that his aim was to do for economic forecasters what the Boston Strangler had done for door-to-door salesmen!

The Boston Strangler turned up all right, but not in the guise of Denis Healey. It was Mrs Thatcher's pursuit of her priority task of turning round the British economy after 1979 that made the most difference to forecasters and forecasting (though it survived in modified form) as it did to all the accumulated baggage of Keynesianism, including the Treasury's interventionist industrial arm – the domestic economy sector – created as part of Wass's 1975 management review.

The Treasury's endurance, in fact, has been remarkable. In many ways its relative power surged to renewed heights after 1979 despite the process of de-Keynesianisation. David Howell ruefully explained why in a radio interview a couple of years after he lost his seat in the Cabinet:

> . . . the nexus of any government in this country is No. 10 and the Treasury, with the Bank of England as the Treasury's appendage . . . Under this Government and under the régime that emerged after '79 . . . the nexus between No. 10 and Treasury is decisive, it overrules, it's everything. The Treasury always know they can win. . . . On the whole, the spirit of the '79 Government . . . has been, 'No, don't bother me with the facts. The Treasury's figures are settled. Good afternoon.'[50]

The only time the Treasury has genuinely lost power since Gladstone led it to its Victorian apogee was in the period of the two world wars when the imperatives of survival obliged the principles of good housekeeping, as Keynes put it, to be jettisoned for the duration.

Yet the argument that the Treasury's anti-production bias, whose current intellectual high priest is Professor Sidney Pollard, is an important contributor to our relatively poor economic performance has almost as much staying-power as the object of its strictures. That bias, as we have seen, was given institutional shape in the mid-sixties in the Department of Economic Affairs. Roy Jenkins saw it off, and, incidentally, restored another Gladstonian artefact, the battered red leather budget box which his predecessor, James Callaghan, had replaced with a standard, Government-issue black leather briefcase. In the late 1980s the anti-production charge rides again mounted by such impressive figures as John Smith, Labour's Shadow Chancellor,[51] and Michael Heseltine,[52] both of whom favour a beefed-up Department of Trade and Industry as a production-minded counterweight to Treasury orthodoxy.

The Treasury Thousand, perpetually in the dock, absorb such charges with the equanimity that comes from long familiarity. It is a surprisingly self-confident department with a strong collective identity which, as Douglas Wass admits, even its permanent secretary can do little to reshape. Roy Jenkins described it in terms which make it sound a bit like a republic of the intellect in which the bright young principal is free to frisk in the policy paddock beneath the benign gaze of his superiors. Comparing it to the Home Office he wrote:

> The Treasury, as I knew it, was more self-confident, less centralised, more relaxed. It operated upon the basis of an easy informality. Christian names were always used. All my private secretaries automatically called the permanent secretary by his. There was never the slightest difficulty in provoking argument and disagreement at meetings. Most people had plenty to say and didn't mind to whom they said it, or whether the recipient of their views agreed with them or not . . .
>
> A hostile critic would argue that all this easy informality and confident delegation of authority was based on the assumption of an aristocracy of talent and an essential community of outlook and view. It was open and democratic only in the sense that Whig society in 1780 was so. There is something in this, but not very much.[53]

I think there is rather a lot in it from what I have seen of the Treasury and its lifers. I was reminded of it in a very lifelike reconstruction of a hypothetical spending issue involving that perennial heart-tugger, hospital building, staged by London Weekend Television for its *Whitehall* series. (Sadly, this sequence was not shown in the broadcast version.) Michael Folger, the ex-Treasury man playing the assistant secretary in the Treasury's social services division, rebutted his DHSS opposite number with the phrase: 'My withers remain unwrung.'[54] They are proud of those cast-iron withers. In a perverse way, they take pride in the harshest of criticisms. For Churchill, another former Chancellor, they were 'like inverted Micawbers, waiting for something to turn down'.[55] For Sir Bruce Fraser the Treasury exists 'in order to curtail the natural consequences of human nature'.[56] Fraser delivered that remark to the old House of Commons Estimates Committee.

It is when these aristocrats of talent extend their Whiggishness to contempt for Parliament that I part company with them. The worst example I have encountered is that unnamed Treasury official who, to Sue Richards and Les Metcalfe, described the Treasury's techniques of expenditure control as 'delegated democracy' as 'Parliament is incapable of exercising its financial responsibilities. We must do it for them.'[57] This is so rich as to be indigestible, coming as it did from a department which will not, except under severe duress, concede one inch of power to elected MPs or Parliament's backbenchers. Yet there is something in the argument that the public good, given the pressures for increased public expenditure, requires this most ancient of departments to behave as the Treasury *contra mundum*. As that veteran of Treasury control, Sir Leo Pliatzky, put it in 1986, 'A lot of people, including some Prime Ministers, don't like the force of circumstances, they don't like the force of reality. They think "if only somehow I could get a different sort of Treasury". Okay, why don't they abolish the Treasury instead of trying to set up a counterpoint? Well, they can't because the Treasury stands for reality.'[58] There speaks the authentic, timeless voice of Treasury power.

Such pomposity from Treasury Man would be unendurable without the self-irony that, in the end, is their saving grace. I can remember hearing about the story told by a veteran Treasury under secretary at his retirement party in the early 1980s. As retailed to me it ran something like this:

> When I was a young man and first joined this department just after the war I thought the Treasury was Whitehall's equivalent of the signal box at Clapham Junction – we pulled the levers and guided activities and politics on to this track or that. I spent several happy years manipulating those levers. Only after a very long time did I realise there were no wires underneath them – they were connected to nothing at all.[59]

Treasury men enjoy telling stories like that. It is a kind of comfort to them.

It was another old Treasury warlord who demonstrated this to perfection when I asked him one day, in my days with *The Times,* whether the Treasury, even if it had had the services of a thousand Maynard Keyneses instead of a thousand normal human beings since the war, could have got the British economy right. 'If you'd had a thousand Keyneses instead of a thousand human beings there would have been no bloody work done at all,' he said. 'Why not?' I asked. 'Because they would have all been too busy buggering each other,' he replied. The private secretary dropped his pen; the press officer lit his pipe; I was speechless. The comment was quite unusable in *The Times* – and he knew it.[60]

OVERSEAS AND DEFENCE DEPARTMENTS

The Foreign and Commonwealth Office

> The British developed their system of decision-making in foreign policy in a period of world power and at a time of limited democracy at home . . . Only a dynamic and determined Prime Minister or Foreign Secretary can strike out in new directions. Even where the diplomats have been forced to yield pride of place, every effort is made to keep decision-making within a restricted body of participants.
> **Zara Steiner, 1987**[61]

> Keeping the nation's nerve.
> **Lord Gore-Booth's definition of the FO's function, 1974**[62]

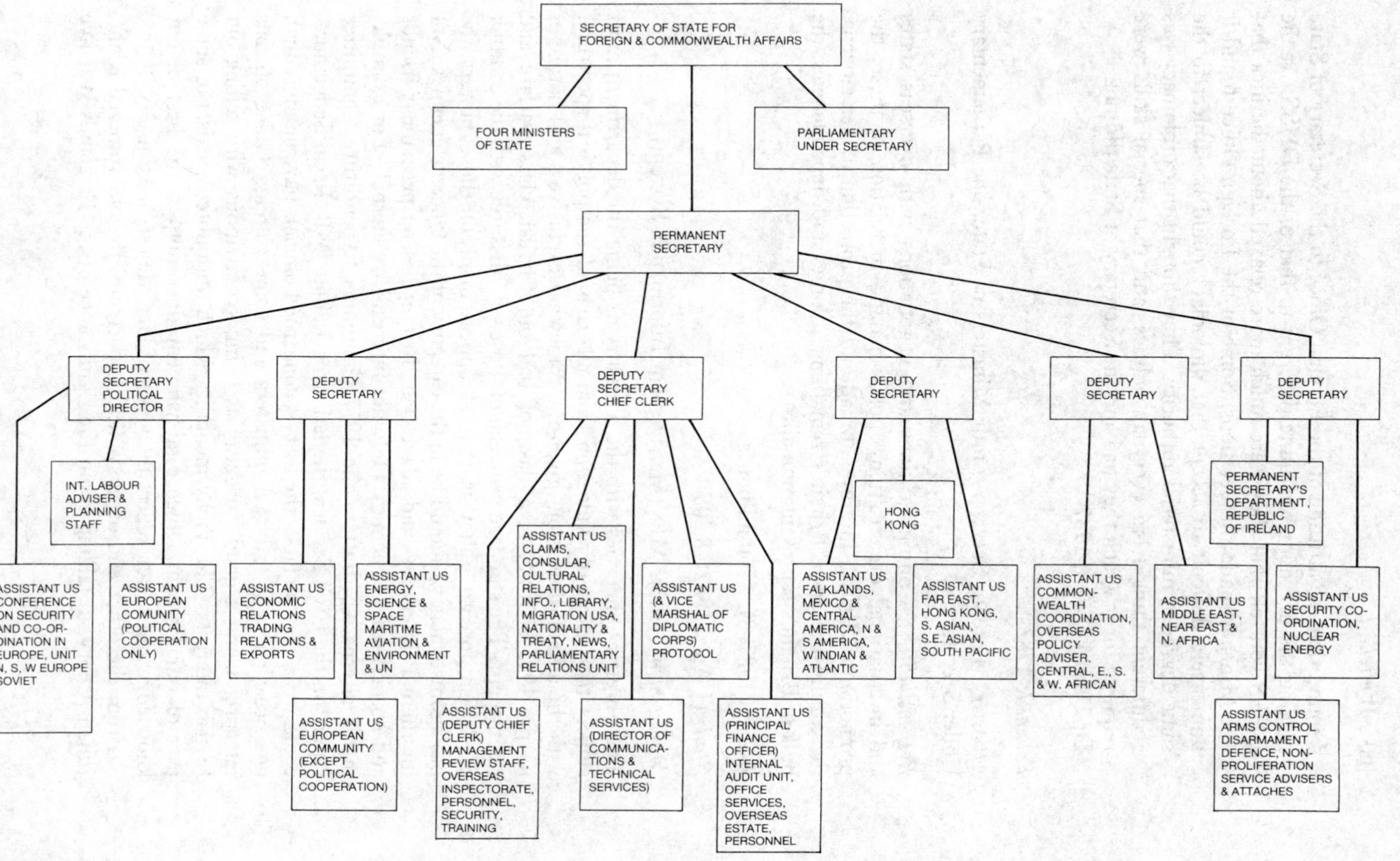

Fig. 2. Foreign and Commonwealth Office

> I found that the attitude of the Foreign Office to the Secretary of State making the decisions was quite different to that of the DHSS. At the DHSS you felt that they were much more relaxed about the idea that one Minister made the decisions. Some of the Foreign Office found it immensely difficult to accept that diplomacy could be subject to the same degree of ministerial authority. They thought that diplomacy was a different thing from everyday politics, and that special skills were required for it which they had and the Secretary of State did not.
> **Dr David Owen, 1987**[63]

Founded: 1782.

Ministers: Foreign Secretary, four Ministers of State, one Parliamentary Under Secretary.

Responsibilities: Communications and negotiations with overseas states and international organisations; policy-making in relation to these; the promotion of British interests abroad and the protection of her citizens; the administration of Britain's remaining colonies and dependencies; the bulk of Britain's representation abroad.

Budget (1987–8): £700 million.

Staff: (1 April 1987): 8,305.

Management system: MIS (Management Information System).

The Foreign Office vies with the Treasury as being the department most subject to streams of vilification from all parts of the political spectrum, with the added dimension, given the somewhat exclusive social nature of its pre-1945 staffing, of a dash of bad old English class warfare and resentment. The standard criticism of those who disagree with the conduct of British foreign policy is that of appeasement of those powers the protagonists believe should be in the category of the Queen's enemies. Not for them Palmerston's old adage that 'Britain has no permanent friends and no permanent enemies. Only her interests are eternal.' For example, in his alternative draft to the 1977 Commons Expenditure Committee report on the Civil Service, the left-wing Labour MP, Brian Sedgemore, could write that 'so far as the EEC is concerned officials have on more than one occasion badly advised ministers and some Foreign Office officials interpret being a good European as being synonymous with selling out British interests. The Vichy mentality which undoubtedly exists in some part of our Foreign Office establishment does not, to the best of our knowledge and belief, reflect the views of Her Majesty's Ministers.'[64]

From the other end of the political spectrum, the old Imperial Right, Julian Amery, in talking about the significance of the Falklands War five years after the victory won by the British Armed Forces, could tell Michael Charlton in his superb BBC Radio 3 documentary series, *The Little Platoon*, that '... After Suez there was a great streak of defeatism [which] entered into the hearts and minds of the British Civil Service establishment, which didn't enter into the gut feeling of the representatives of the British people in the House of Commons ... After the terrible psychological shock of our defeat – I wouldn't use any other word – at Suez, it was an element of redemption.'[65]

Even those prone to mock the views of a latterday member of the Milner Kindergarten like Julian Amery on such historical questions as Suez and the Falklands (and I am not one of them) would have to concede that, whether true or not about the spunk of the post-Suez Foreign, Colonial and Commonwealth Offices (there is a 'great debate' under way about this),[66] it *was* the impression conveyed to individuals like Admiral Anaya, the hawkish commander of the Argentine Navy at the time of the invasion of the Falklands. Anaya, when interviewed by Admiral Harry Train of the United States Navy for a classified study of the Falklands conflict, took the story back to 1956, as Train told Michael Charlton, 'by pointing out that in the Suez crisis of 1956 the United States failed to support the United Kingdom, and when you add that to his perception of an eroding national will and eroding maritime capability on the part of the UK, he had a political-military situation where at best he could hope for United States neutrality ...'[67] That shrewd calibrator of world forces, Dr Henry Kissinger, underscored the plausibility of Anaya's calculation when he wrote of Suez: 'I have always believed that many of our later difficulties have stemmed from our insensitive conduct towards our allies at that time, which both stimulated a long-festering resentment and fostered a sense of impotence that accelerated their withdrawal from overseas commitments and added to American burdens.'[68]

Whatever the precise impact of Suez on British power and on the formulation and conduct of foreign policy, since 1956 policy had been made against a backcloth of diminishing economic and military power. 'The object of policy', wrote Paul Gore-Booth, the Suez dissenter who rose to head the Foreign Office in the 1960s, 'had to be to ensure that a great nation could stop half-way down and establish itself as a second-level power with real tasks to perform and obligations to fulfil.'[69] Whether this amounts to defeatism or realism depends on one's prejudices and one's conception of the figure Britain could or should cut in the world. It is undeniable that Britain's foreign and defence policy-makers for three decades, through force of circumstance, have been engaged in what William Armstrong called 'the orderly management of decline'. An institution to which such a task falls is a prime target for the politics of scapegoating and it becomes the inevitable butt of the patronising aside of the type Tony

Benn, as Postmaster General visiting Japan, committed to his diary in 1966. 'It is the final end of the public school man,' he wrote, 'now that the Empire has gone – to finish up in British Embassies around the world, representing all that is least dynamic about British society, although no doubt they have first-rate intellects and a fundamental decency.'[70]

Putting the cruder attacks to one side, the Foreign Office still strikes outsiders as a department apart, perhaps *the* classic example of a ministry feeding deep off its own storehouse of wisdom. David Owen had a bruising relationship with all its grades. (It is said that he set some kind of record for the number of drivers he got through in just over two years. This is impossible to verify, though he did say later, 'I'm sure I was as much of a problem to some people in the Foreign Office as they were to me. If I had those years over again there is no doubt that I'd be more emollient.'[71]) He was convinced that they were policy entrepreneurs, particularly on Europe:

> The pro-European officials had been given too much freedom during the years when we had been fighting the battle for entry, when they had been involved in, and too often allowed to make, political decisions and political judgments over the Community calculated to help us get in. Successive governments had allowed them too much leeway. The result was that these Foreign Office civil servants had been acting almost as politicians, making political concessions and judgments, working very closely with ministers and having great influence with ministers . . .
>
> Some of the ablest and brightest of the people involved in the European Community negotiations over the whole twenty-year timespan had come to think that opposition to the EEC on any matter was motivated by anti-EEC sentiments. This was not so: sometimes they were being opposed on the merits of the case. Some of these civil servants used to contribute a lot to counter-briefing directed against Tony Benn on the assumption that he being anti-Europe everything he said should be resisted. I disliked this intensely. This kind of official politicking is one of the most unattractive aspects of the Civil Service.[72]

Naturally, the career-lifers would not see it in quite such stark terms. They have a way of recoiling gracefully from the assaults of bruiser Foreign Secretaries like George Brown or David Owen while waiting for the restoration of more graceful times under a Lord Carrington or the soothing emollience of a Sir Geoffrey Howe. But there is something in what David Owen says. Listen to Sir Antony Acland talking as Head of the Diplomatic Service to Simon Jenkins:

> I think that if a government were to decide to take Britain out of Europe, that would be very unsettling and worrying for a large number of

members of the Foreign and Commonwealth Office, and I think for home civil servants as well. But there are other issues too which would cause them great anxiety: I think the withdrawal from NATO, or going wholly unilateralist, would also cause great anxieties in the minds of quite a number of us. But I suppose in foreign affairs there has been a greater tradition of bipartisan policy over the years than on other issues, and it may have been comforting and consoling for us.[73]

But such comfort and consolation could not be presumed in the 1980s on nuclear weapons policy. Bipartisanship had broken down. Michael Foot offered Britain a non-nuclear defence policy at the 1983 general election, and in 1987 Neil Kinnock undertook to call the Polaris submarines home on the first day of his premiership,[74] a move which prompted the former Chief of the Defence Staff, Lord Bramall, to state publicly that 'I and my colleagues are very concerned particularly over the recent Labour statement that Polaris would be recalled on day one. That means there would be no time for consultation with allies and no time even to improve conventional forces. We feel this is something new.'[75]

Ironically, had Labour won in 1987, the difficult task of explaining its defence plans to the Reagan administration would have fallen to Sir Antony Acland, by this time Ambassador to the United States. Sir Antony's remarks to Simon Jenkins can only be interpreted in one way – that the career men in the FO can only work easily if the essentials of the foreign and defence policy consensus hold, which does not square with the ethic of a politically neutral Civil Service capable of serving any administration chosen by the British electorate in a free and fair poll. Between Labour's two unilateralist elections, I asked Neil Kinnock about this on Granada Television's *Under Fire*. He struck me as more complacent than the Acland statement warranted. In the autumn of 1985 I asked Mr Kinnock

> . . . whether Whitehall would actually carry out your instructions on day one to bring Polaris home, because Sir Antony Acland, Permanent Secretary to the Foreign Office, said publicly it 'would create "great anxiety" in Whitehall. Can you be so sure that you'll get the chiefs of staff and the permanent secretaries to collaborate?'
>
> 'On the day,' he replied, 'that senior civil servants and chiefs of staff in Britain do not follow the elective will of government, we will live in a very different kind of society. I think you do both the chiefs of staff and junior officers and senior civil servants and their juniors a disservice in believing that they are so prejudiced against the ideas of government – an elected government – as to try and frustrate its will especially in an important area of activity. So I don't think they would change the habit of a lifetime, which . . . is . . . admired throughout the world, for the purpose that you suggest.'[76]

There is, I suspect, in British diplomats a trace of the phenomenon detectable in members of the Armed Forces – that they work for the Queen. Constitutionally, it is plain that this means the Crown as embodied in the Queen's ministers. But the ambience of being the Queen's representative in some distant capital is genuinely felt and is subtly different from being the Cabinet's or the Foreign Secretary's man-on-the-spot. This, I reckon, has something to do with the long view of Britain's interests taken by some members of the Diplomatic Service.

The special nature and separateness of the Foreign Office should not be exaggerated. The social mix is far less exclusive than before the Eden–Bevin reforms and much of the work is not so different from that of the Home Civil Service. In one of the FO's biggest growth areas of the past fifteen years – the United Kingdom representation to the EEC in Brussels – the Diplomatic and Home Civil team is very much a joint affair with a wide range of domestic departments – Agriculture, Energy, Trade and Industry and the Treasury – having deep and enduring interests in the conduct of Community business. A great deal of the work is conducted through shuttle-diplomacy. About two hundred officials a month travel to Brussels from the Ministry of Agriculture alone.[77] But, in bureaucratic terms, the chief beneficiary of Britain's membership of the EEC has been the Foreign Office. The diplomats have found a new place in the sun, if that is not too vivid a climatic metaphor for Brussels, Luxembourg and Strasbourg.

This line of argument can be overdone. Europe is not a surrogate for Empire, though Tony Benn, at least, speaks of it in terms of a new Imperium managed by the FO:

> I think the Foreign Office in a deep way has transferred its allegiance from Britain to Brussels . . . I think the Foreign Office influence on Whitehall is now quite pernicious because the Foreign Office can properly claim that every bit of economic policy, industrial policy, social policy is now European policy and has to be fed through them. If they think it will interfere with our relations with our partners in the Community they will veto it, if they can, in Whitehall. If it isn't vetoed in Whitehall, they will be party to the process by which the Brussels Commission might veto it. And that is a fundamental change in allegiance.[78]

Again, there is something in this. Roy Hattersley was a pro-EEC number two at the FO during the Foreign Secretaryship of James Callaghan in the mid-1970s which saw the re-negotiation of Britain's terms of membership. 'The Foreign Office,' he once said,

> holds two views about Europe: one is on the national interest of being in, the second is on what Europe does for the Foreign Office. The Foreign Office has been transformed by our membership of the EEC. It now interferes in and is concerned with subjects which were not its proper province ten years ago [Mr Hattersley was speaking in 1981]. Foreign Office civil servants are interfering in agricultural prices; they're interfering in economic policy; they're interfering in energy policy. Naturally enough, the Foreign Office has an enthusiasm for continuing an institution that gives them this very substantial increased power . . .[79]

Certainly that influence is fiercely defended when periodic attacks are mounted upon it, as happened briefly in 1987 when, after yet another dispute between No. 10 and the FO about Britain's contribution to the EEC budget, Mrs Thatcher toyed with the idea of hiving-off European policy into a separate department.[80]

Certainly, the Foreign Office has never liked any individual or any institution interfering with its monopoly of dealing with 'abroad' on behalf of Whitehall and interpreting 'abroad' for the Cabinet and other departments. It has great confidence in the superior wisdom of its thinking when compared to that of others – including ministers. As Sir Paul Gore-Booth put it with a timeless loftiness: 'Never forget that in the two great crises of my time, Munich and Suez, when, by later universal consent the judgment of a British government was grievously wrong, the sense of the Foreign Office was right.'[81] As the unofficial motto of Foreign Office man, that cannot be bettered. It combines the hauteur of the aristocrat and the conceit of the swot. No wonder so many politicians make them a scapegoat. Naturally, a British diplomat can spot a scapegoater or an axe-grinder a mile off and can dismiss them accordingly.

In-house critics are not so easily brushed aside. When Sir Ham Whyte retired as High Commissioner to Singapore in 1987 he devoted his traditional valedictory despatch to a bitingly-phrased critique for the Foreign Secretary, Sir Geoffrey Howe, on just what was wrong with the service of which he was political chief. Sir Geoffrey – and Sir Ham's colleagues – took it seriously. Sir Ham was highly unusual as diplomats go. A thoroughly unstuffy person with a slightly bohemian air, on his several tours of duty on the news side of the FO, he seemed actually to like journalists and to believe that they had a real job to do in keeping an open society open. Sir Anthony Parsons, Whyte's boss at the United Nations during the Falklands War, once said, 'Ham is different. He's not cut along the ordinary pattern of bureaucrats. He's got imagination and flair and is very good at getting on with all sorts of people without distorting his own personality.'[82]

'Whyte's Farewell', as one might call it, opened by telling the Foreign Secretary:

> My time has spanned three decades of Britain in relative decline, recently arrested, too soon to say reversed. Some vilify you for your past. Others bemoan that you are no longer what you were. Many have expectations that you cannot fulfil.
>
> The resources of the Service diminish while the tasks increase. Staff have been cut since 1968 by 18 per cent, while Britons travelling abroad have gone up by 307 per cent. The planet shrinks and the interconnections multiply. Add in drugs, terrorism and Aids. We *need* a smart Foreign service.

Sir Ham gave credit where it was due.

> We have not responded badly. We are a whole lot more professional than we were thirty years ago. Gone is the smug satisfaction that we were, after all, the Rolls-Royce of the British bureaucracy. A better model now would be a land cruiser, proof against bugs and bombers (impossible) and packed with state-of-the-art navaids, IT and secure communications (expensive but essential). But we should do better.[83]

The key to doing better, according to Ham Whyte, was to apply to the Diplomatic Service the kind of 'up-and-out' early retirement scheme long operated by the Armed Forces, a notion, as we have seen, dear to the heart of Dr David Owen when he was Foreign Secretary.

Those at the top of the 4,700-strong Diplomatic Service did not throb with reformist impulses when confronted with the Whyte valedictory. They did, however, react to it. They had to. The FO's ministerial team asked questions about it when Sir Ham's despatch was made public.[84] With the deftness which comes from years of sophisticated advocacy, they poured cold water on the 'up-and-out' idea as applied to them.

They pointed out that early retirement was already possible if officials wished to go or the service's management required them to; that 300 officers had gone early in the past eight years since 1979; and that, in career planning terms, the FO's personnel side had not found retirement at 60 a barrier to the efficient deployment of its human capital. The insiders went further and argued that the already considerable task of completing a perpetual appointments jigsaw – in which experienced officers had to be fitted into 145 embassies and 60 consulates overseas – would be made more difficult if the kind of seasoned, all-round career experience that men and women in the Diplomatic Service acquire was disrupted.

Cash was the other argument used against the Whyte idea. The FO calculated that to retire a senior grade ambassador at 55 after 33 years of service would cost the taxpayer £180,000 more than routine retirement at 60.[85]

The FO listened to Sir Ham – but nothing happened. However, there was a spin-off. The Head of the Diplomatic Service, Sir Patrick Wright, who had been Gore-Booth's private secretary in the 1960s, updated for me his old bosses' view about the need to halt decline half-way. 'For much of my career,' Sir Patrick told me in March 1988,

> for post-imperial and other reasons, we have been in the business of managing decline and adjusting to Britain's position after the war. What encourages me, and I tell this to the new entrants to the service, it seems to me that we are out of that period of managing decline. This is not a party political point. Our job is to promote the development of British interests in an era in which Britain has a new political and economic strength and respect in the world. This opens up new opportunities.[86]

Intriguingly enough, almost as Sir Patrick was delivering his refreshingly bullish assessment, a pathologist of international decline over centuries, Professor Paul Kennedy of Yale (a British brain drained to the United States), published an influential book, *The Rise and Fall of the Great Powers,* which maintained that Britain's priorities in the foreign and defence field were still way out of line. 'The divergence', he wrote, 'between Britain's shrunken economic state and its overextended strategical posture is probably more extensive than that affecting any of the larger powers, except Russia itself . . .'[87] The FO, however, had by the late eighties lived with forty years of critiques of that kind – though few so well researched or presented as Professor Kennedy's.

Like the Treasury's, the FO's core function is so central to state activity that it will remain high in the departmental constellation whatever the priorities and configuration of a government. Like the Treasury it has been much criticised and much inquired into (by Lord Plowden in 1962–3,[88] Sir Val Duncan in 1968–9,[89] and the Central Policy Review Staff in 1976–7[90]); like the Treasury it remains immensely resistant to change.

Overseas Development Administration

> We had been heartened by Harold Wilson's creation of new Ministries, reflecting our Manifesto aims . . . [including] . . . the Ministry of Overseas Development with a seat in the Cabinet as a guarantee that overseas aid was no longer to be regarded as a charitable donation from rich to poor but as an essential motor to world development.
>
> **Barbara Castle, first Minister of Overseas Development, 1984**[91]

Founded: 1964.

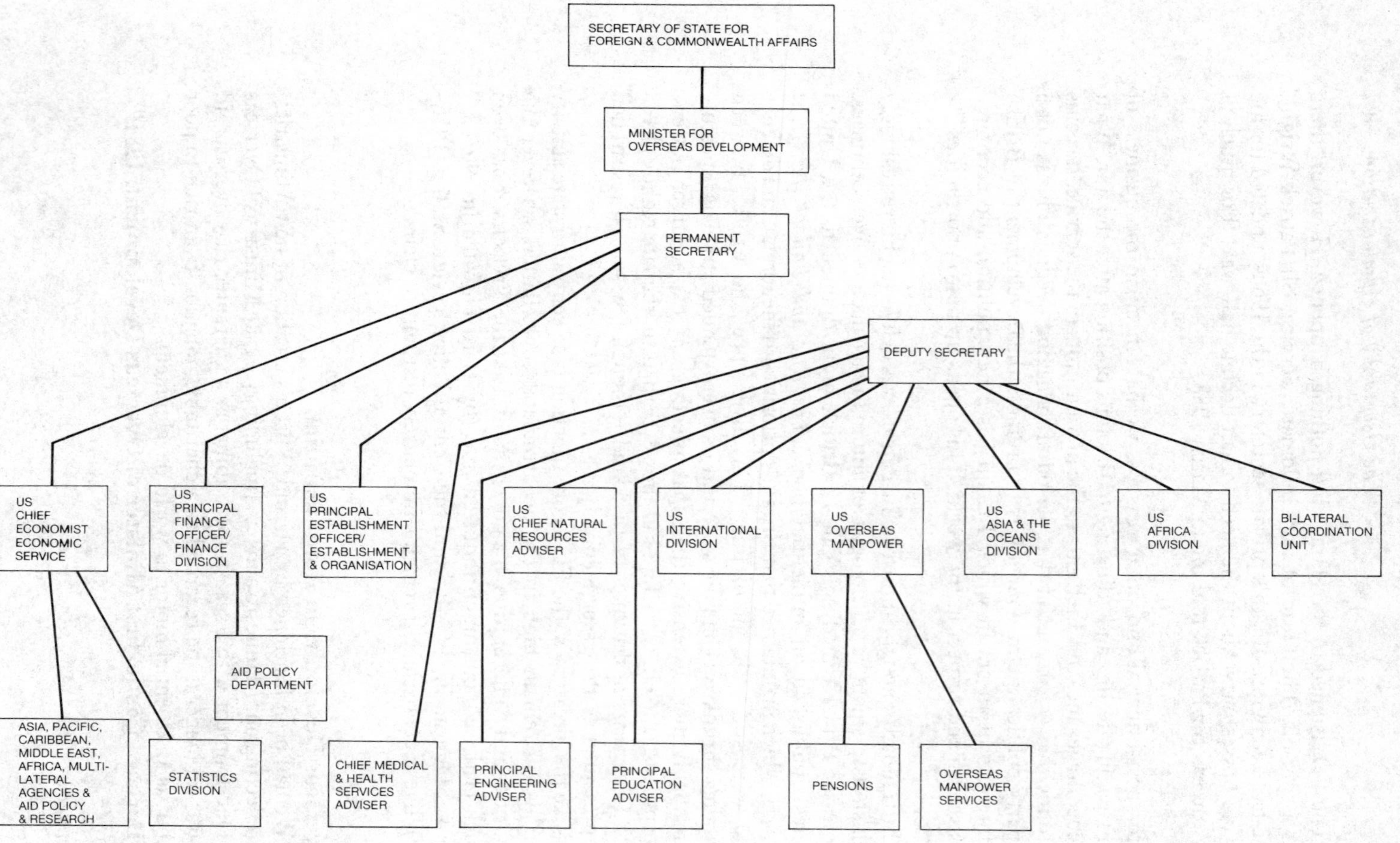

Fig. 3. Overseas Development Administration

Ministers: Foreign Secretary, Minister for Overseas Development.

Responsibilities: Formulation of UK policy towards the economic and social development of less developed countries. Management of the British aid programme, its disbursement direct to individual recipient nations and via international agencies; the appointment of British aid experts to serve overseas.

Budget (1987–8): £1,355 million.

Staff: (1 January 1987): 1,535.

Management system: MINIS. [Management Information System for Ministers.]

Whenever I hear mention of the Ministry of Overseas Development I think of Labour's election victory in 1964. More than any other of Harold Wilson's artefacts, it seemed to embody above all the mobilisation of practical altruism, the finest of the 'send forth the best ye breed' side of the old imperial impulse. Wilson gave it life, a budget, a place round the Cabinet table and one of the most energetic and persuasive members of his ministerial team, Barbara Castle. As if to link the old altruism with the new, the ministry's first permanent secretary was to be Sir Andrew Cohen, the 'King of Africa' we have already encountered in his great Colonial Office days (see pp. 160–1).

Almost immediately, its star began to wane, eclipsed by the travails of a British economy moving further and further away from its imperial glory. The Ministry of Overseas Development never recaptured the promise of 1964 or fulfilled the hopes of its early days, valuable work though it did and continues to do in its truncated form of an Overseas Development Administration tucked away in the shadow of the mighty Foreign Office.

The Ministry of Overseas Development was constructed according to specifications laid down in yet another blueprint from the Fabian Society in the early 1960s, an extraordinarily productive period in the history of that 'ginger group of gradualism' as the Webbs called it. When Mrs Castle arrived at the Ministry, a despatch rider was sent to the Society's headquarters to collect six copies of the relevant pamphlet.[92] Yet within nine short months, the writing was on the wall, as Mrs Castle recorded in her diary entry for Sunday, 4 July 1965:

> One of the bleakest days in my political life. I had Andrew Cohen and Martin Lynch of the Department over to the cottage to tighten up my brief for the Public Expenditure Committee [a precursor of Mrs Thatcher's 'Star Chamber'] which met all day. Set off after lunch to take my turn . . . My careful preparation of an opening submission went

for nothing: Jim [Callaghan, Chancellor of the Exchequer] didn't want to hear it. Instead they jumped into hostile cross-examination. I have never been in a more unfriendly crowd. George Brown [Secretary of State for Economic Affairs] on my right and Frank Cousins [Minister of Technology] on my left joined in attacking our figures. In vain I pointed out that our basic allocation would mean a cut-back on present policies. When I said that if we didn't get the additional for which we asked (and we had fiercely pruned our figure [for 1966–7] down to £250m to try and meet them) it would mean either no general purpose aid for India or the abandonment of Durgapur [aid for the third phase of an Indian steel plant], Frank said viciously 'India never wanted Durgapur till we put it into their heads.' And when I pointed out that if Durgapur was abandoned the UK steel plant-making industry would be in the soup, George Brown said savagely, 'Perhaps they would go out then and look for some real exports.' They obviously couldn't care less about the Party's commitment to 1 per cent of GNP. They dismissed aid as irrelevant. I crawled home exhausted and dispirited. Andrew's worst fears have been realised.[93]

It has ever been thus when hard economics have clashed with institutionalised altruism. But the enterprise has survived more than two decades of relative economic decline. Labour salves its conscience by recreating it as a separate ministry, usually, though not invariably, with its minister in the Cabinet, in the full knowledge that the returning Conservatives will reduce it to dominion status within the FO.

The Ministry of Defence

I am beside myself with anger at the FCO for lining themselves up with the Whitehall official view. Gutless is what they are, whereas the MOD are malign.

David Owen, Foreign Secretary, to Peter Jay, Ambassador to Washington, 1978 [94]

The fiercely protected prerogatives of the Royal Navy, the Army and the Royal Air Force had produced and sustained for twenty years something which was indefensible not only by modern standards of management in the world beyond the services but by every rule of command taught to the humblest uniformed recruit.

Michael Heseltine, former Secretary of State for Defence, 1987[95]

We have people within the Ministry of Defence, within the Civil Service, who I would have given my right arm for in industry.

Peter Levene, Chief of Defence Procurement, 1987[96]

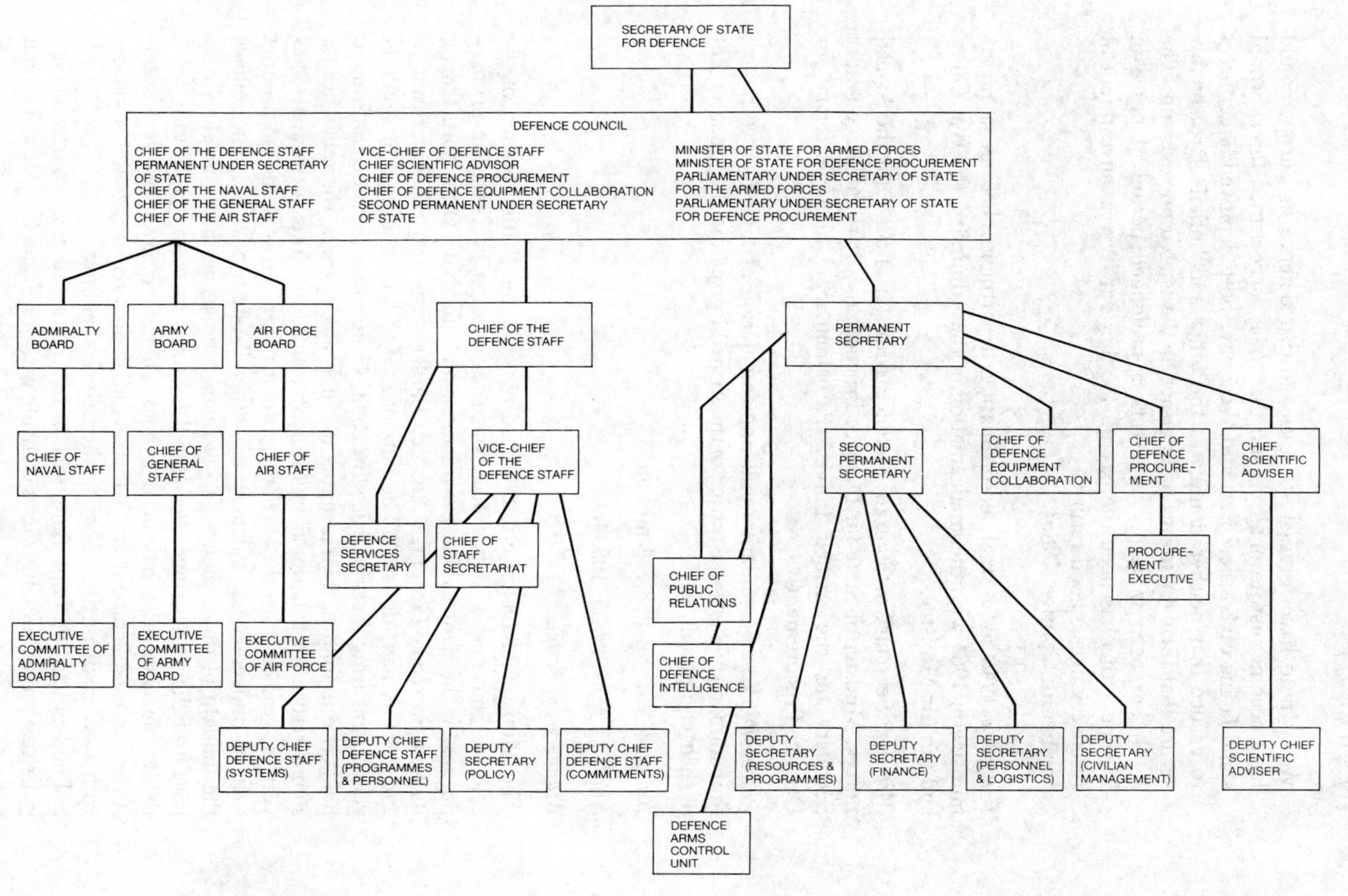

Fig. 4. Ministry of Defence

> Who would have forecast 40 years ago that defence in Europe would have become institutionalised and that today large armed forces would stand facing each other? East and West have both deployed large forces to ensure that neither dominates the other and both feel reasonably secure that their territories will neither be devastated nor overrun. The result has been in terms of history a prolonged period of peace in Europe – this has been the pay-off for the year by year investment of resources. It is a good return.
> **Sir Frank Cooper, 1986**[97]

Founded: 1946 as a small co-ordinating department; became a mega-ministry in 1964 with the amalgamation of the Admiralty, the War Office and the Air Ministry.

Minister: Secretary of State for Defence, Minister of State for the Armed Forces, Minister of State for Defence Procurement, Parliamentary Under Secretary for the Armed Forces, Parliamentary Under Secretary for Defence Procurement.

Responsibilities: Formulation and implementation of UK defence policy, the command and administration of the Armed Forces and the procurement of their equipment.

Budget (1987–8): £18,784 million.

Staff: (1 April 1987): 165,000.

Management system: MINIS.

The Ministry of Defence is the head office of the British branch of the cold war business and has been since its creation in 1946. Its primary purpose is the same as that provided privately for NATO by Lord Ismay, its first Secretary General – 'to keep the Russians out, the Americans in and the Germans down'.[98] The bulk of its £18 billion annual budget still goes on ensuring that the truce lines of 1945 in central Europe continue to hold. If one follows the reasoning of Sir Frank Cooper, there has been a sound return on a national investment which, the Americans apart, has year in, year out absorbed a higher proportion of gross domestic product than its budgetary equivalent in any other Western power. If one follows the thought of those such as Tony Benn, who argue that it is 'absolutely false' to believe that since 1945 'the Russians were waiting to invade us',[99] the whole enterprise has been a hoax on the taxpayer by the Anglo-American establishment and a forty-year dissipation of national resources with a severe distorting effect on the British economy.

Fond as I am of Tony Benn (one of the nicest and most courteous men in British public life), my views coincide with Sir Frank Cooper's. Though

13. Sir Frank Lee: steered Whitehall away from Empire and towards Europe.

14. Sir Burke Trend: in *the* corridor of Cabinet Office power.

15. Sir John Anderson (Lord Waverley): skating effortfully to the top of public life.

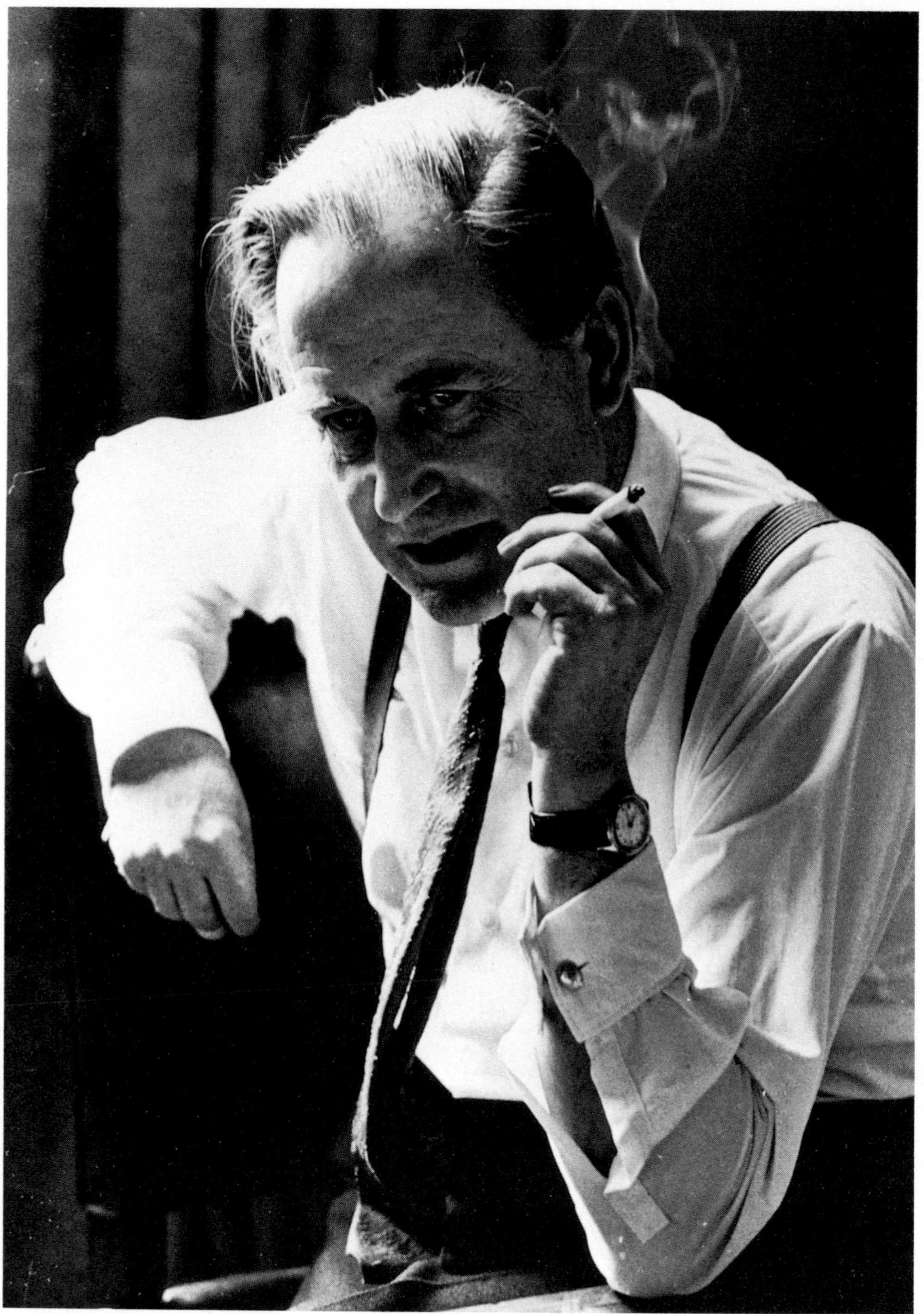

16. Sir William Armstrong: soothing words through the cigarette smoke.

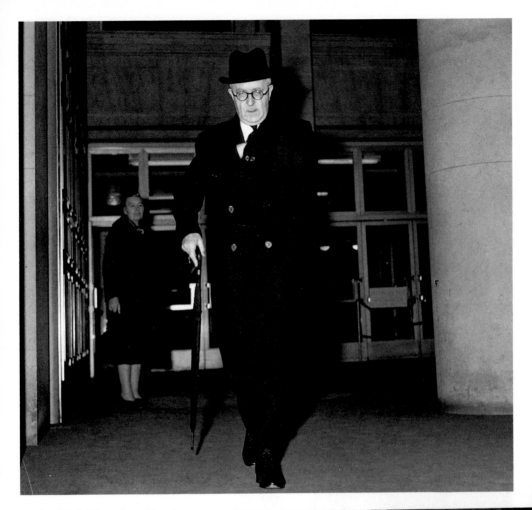

17. Lord Radcliffe: eminent Victorian and pillar of the Good and Great.

18. Lord Fulton: launching his report against a tide of Establishment fury.

19. Sir Paul Gore-Booth and wife: off to tackle Moriarty.

20. Sir Douglas Allen (Lord Croham) and wife: a cockney sparrow takes to the courts.

21. Bernard Donoughue: about to join Harold Wilson and Joe Haines in No 10, at the Huyton count in the general election, February 1974.

22. Sir John Hunt: sentinel guarding the door between the Cabinet Office and No 10, with the author.

23. Sir Frank Cooper takes to the air in a Tornado.

24. Sir Douglas Wass: kept his intellectual curiosity till the last.

25. The Treasury team during the IMF autumn: L to R, Sir Derek Mitchell, Alan Lord, Denis Healey, Sir Douglas Wass, Sir Bryan Hopkin, Sir Leo Pliatzky, Joel Barnett.

26. Sir Ian Bancroft: chronicler of the generation for whom everything was possible.

intrigued by the writings of revisionist historians like William Appleman Williams,[100] Walter La Feber[101] and Gar Alperovitz,[102] who suggest that with greater subtlety and less xenophobia on the part of Western policy-makers in 1944–7 the cold war might have been averted, I cannot accept their thesis. For me the cold war was a tragic inevitability, and I cannot fault the account Lord Bullock has given of what actually transpired in the late 1940s as the Labour government, British foreign and defence policy and the British people moved reluctantly into the cold war mould which, given the vote-losing capacity of Labour's defence policy in the 1980s, would appear to have endured longer than the party's adherence to it. In the third volume of his life of Bevin, Alan Bullock wrote:

> The most important factor in the criticism of Bevin between 1945 and 1947 was the reluctance of the British to contemplate the possibility of renewed conflict now that the war was over. This makes it all the more impressive that the strong lead which Bevin gave in foreign affairs in 1947 steadily gathered support to the point in 1947–9, when it came as near consensus as any British foreign secretary has been able to count on in time of peace.
>
> This change could never have taken place if British public opinion had not come independently to the same conclusion Bevin had already reached, that there was a real danger of the Soviet Union and other Communists taking advantage of the weaknesses of Western Europe to extend their power. We know now that this did not follow, but nobody knew it at the time. This was a generation for whom war and occupation were not remote hypotheses but recent and terrible experiences. The fear of another war, the fear of a Russian occupation, haunted Europe in those years and were constantly revived – by the Communist coup in Czechoslovakia, by the Berlin blockade, and the outbreak of war in Korea in 1950 . . . It is unhistorical to dismiss those fears as groundless because the war and occupation did not occur.[103]

In January 1981, the MOD declassified a survey of 'the threat' as it is known these days, which had been prepared for the Chiefs of Staff by their Joint Planning Staff shortly before the Korean War broke out and updated quickly thereafter.[104] I sent a photocopy of it to John Ledlie, one of the most imaginative men to have filled a Whitehall press officer's chair, with the request that I be given an account of the current version of that 31-year-old brief on the grounds that the annual Defence White Paper, then under preparation, and the several billion budget therein contained, were largely based on the premise that such a threat still existed in albeit modified form. Ledlie arranged one of the best briefings I have ever had. It was laid on by six members of the Defence Intelligence Staff, an often forgotten and frequently underestimated branch of the intelligence community. They covered all their major inputs – weapons, technical/scientific, political and economic intelligence.

I asked them whether they had read the revisionist studies of the cold war. They had. How did they rate them? Had they ever wondered if the whole huge and costly enterprise of the British defence programme was based on a misconception? 'No' came the confident answer. The revisionist literature was irrelevant to their business – the assessment of Soviet intentions and capability – because one thing mattered and they were certain of it. Whether or not the Soviet Union was or had been after world domination, its leadership was determined that if war in Europe erupted again it would start not in their territory but in somebody else's. Therefore since 1945 they had pursued a 'forward' policy and continued to do so.[105] This required, and would do for the foreseeable future, a Western response in strategy and weaponry that would contain that 'forward' policy. I still cannot make up my mind whether that was hard-nosed reality or a brilliant piece of casuistry from people who were not keen to dismantle decades of thought-patterns even if Soviet behaviour gave serious grounds for a rethink.

But, undeniably, it is still the bedrock argument that sustains the MOD and its cold war machine despite *glasnost*. That machine is the biggest, though not the costliest, in Whitehall (the DHSS budget is more than three times the Defence Estimates) and in its mix of administrators, scientists and other professionals and members of the Armed Forces in civvies on temporary desk-work ('driving a desk' as they self-derisively like to put it) it is the richest and most varied of any department. The MOD produces a distinctive type of civil servant – a particularly tough breed, though not because war planning requires the harder type. It has more to do with constant battles with project-rolling scientists and gold-plating officers ever keen to put the latest and costliest modification upon their weaponry. The quintet of ministers nominally in charge of this huge and often fractious operation have their work cut out to achieve any real impact upon the perpetually jostling scene of in-fighting bureaucrats, boffins and politicians-in-uniform. Those politicians who do make an impression normally have to pre-empt policy-making in a very personal way as Duncan Sandys did during his 1957 defence review and as John Nott did during his in 1981.

The Ministry of Defence ties up a significant proportion of the nation's best scientific and technological brainpower, a proportion the Thatcher government declared itself determined to reduce in 1987.[106] It shapes the output and configuration of a large part of the country's manufacturing industry, too. The Defence Secretary runs an industrial policy, however non-interventionist the Cabinet in general. Ninety-five per cent of the MOD's equipment budget is spent on contracts with British firms, supporting some 700,000 jobs in the United Kingdom. The ministry's Procurement Executive, which lets out 40,000 contracts a year, is the customer for 45 per cent of the UK's aerospace output and 20 per cent of its electronic industries.[107] In short, it is British industry's largest single customer. Britain's defence industrial base, as it is called, is huge and crucial to the national economy as a whole. Its output is largely devoted to the cold war which has proved to be a nasty and regrettable but highly effective Keynesian multiplier since the end of the Second World War. A great debate has raged about whether this has fatally distorted the British economy or kept it afloat in increasingly hostile seas.

For forty years the natural buy-British impulses of every minister of defence has made the British defence industries the country's most effective pressure group (see pp. 339–40). There are signs that this might be changing as the MOD inches, reluctantly, towards the eighth defence review since 1945, for two problems have bedevilled the British defence community since the ceasefires of 1945 – organisation (which I will turn to shortly) and money. Defence commitments and aspirations have consistently run ahead of the British economy's capacity to fund them. The list of postwar defence reviews since Attlee appointed a neutral official, Sir Edmund Harwood from the Ministry of Food, to chair an economy committee of the Chiefs of Staff in the late forties, tells its own story:

Review	*Date*	*Government*
Harwood Review	1949–50	Attlee (Lab.)
Radical Review	1953–4	Churchill (Con.)
Sandys Review	1957	Macmillan (Con.)
Healey Mark I	1964–5	Wilson (Lab.)
Healey Mark II	1967–8	Wilson (Lab.)
Mason Review	1974–5	Wilson (Lab.)
Nott Review	1981	Thatcher (Con.)[108]

Like so many other postwar stories, this one would not have been self-evident to the defence planners of the late 1940s even after their thinking and their work had moved to a thoroughly cold-warlike stance. If it could have been assumed that by the late 1960s the bulk of the British Empire would have been relinquished, including the substantial presence maintained East of Suez by the Royal Navy and the Royal Air Force, then at last the pressure could have been expected to ease on a largely NATO orientated UK, particularly if collaboration with the United States on nuclear weapons technology had been restored (as it was in 1958).

Yet pressure on the defence budget continued. Why? The answer is successive leaps in the sophistication and, therefore, the cost of defence equipment. For example, in the late 1950s the RAF's Lightning interceptor was the embodiment of advanced technology. Its mid 1980s replacement, the air defence version of the Tornado (a collaborative project with Germany and Italy, as advanced aircraft increasingly were) was seventy-five times more complicated a piece of equipment than the plane it succeeded on the aprons of East Anglia.[109] My old mentor at the London School of Economics, Professor Donald Watt (who is also the MOD's official historian on the organisation of postwar defence policy-making), shared with me his vision of the future in 1981 as John Nott was grappling with yet another defence review. He foresaw the British defence budget of the mid-twenty-first century as being capable of purchasing just one weapon on the frontier of advanced technology. Inter-service rivalry would be reduced to fights about who had the right to parade with it outside Buckingham Palace.

Michael Heseltine's answer to the relentless pressure of equipment costs was, controversially – though, in my view, justifiably – to recruit Peter Levene of United Scientific Holdings from the private sector, to become the Chief of Defence Procurement. Levene finally put paid to old-style defence contracting whereby the suppliers were guaranteed their costs plus an agreed profit virtually irrespective of how well or poorly the company performed in meeting the requirements of quality and time. Fixed price contracts were henceforth to be the order of the day. The maximum amount of competition was injected: where only one British supplier was in existence, the MOD developed ground-rules to maximise competition among the sub-contractors of that monopoly manufacturer. As Heseltine put it in his enthusiast's way, 'if he [Levene] has saved 8 per cent of the equipment programme – and he has said that he expects to save 10 per cent – he will have paid for the Trident programme single-handed. Not a bad achievement for one entrepreneur!'[110]

Mr Levene is a formidable operator, a born bargainer, who got on the telephone the day in December 1986 when the British Government clinched its deal for radar early-warning aircraft from Boeing to wrest another £40 million from the American manufacturer.[111] But there are those who argue that even his efforts cannot save the MOD's system for procuring weapons, with its 10–15-year cycles between an idea and its manifestation in a usable tank, plane or frigate. For an ex-insider like former Chief Scientific Adviser Professor Sir Ronald Mason, these interminable timescales are so rigid that new and cost-saving technologies which come on stream in the meantime in the civil sector are frozen out of its military equivalent. To avoid this, he says, the length of the procurement cycle has to be halved. There must, he believes, be a more rational system of decision-taking, with still more collaboration amongst the Western allies, as 'the mileage left in salami-slicing must be negligible'.[112]

That more rational system of decision-taking has been the second Holy Grail pursued by the British defence community since the war. After Herculean lobbying of the kind only he could mount throughout the Macmillan years, Lord Mountbatten, as Chief of the Defence Staff, secured the merger of the Admiralty, the War Office and the Air Ministry into a single Ministry of Defence in 1964. The key figure, however, in terms of preparing the blueprint was that brilliant back-room boy of defence policy-making, General Sir Ian Jacob. Jacob had been one of the architects of the tiny prototype MOD in 1945–6. Seventeen years later he was commissioned, with that other Second World War veteran, Lord Ismay, to prepare plans for a unified department. The Ismay–Jacob Report has yet to be declassified, but naval historian Eric Grove is clearly familiar with its contents:

> Jacob did most of the work, interviewing over two dozen ministers and officials. The report, 'Principles for Defence Reorganisation', was completed in six weeks . . . It diagnosed 'discord, uncertainty and malaise' in top British defence decision making and recommended making a significant, but not complete, move to an integrated Defence Ministry under a single powerful secretary of state . . . It was duly announced in July 1963 that a unified Ministry of Defence would indeed be created, although, in accordance with the Ismay–Jacob recommendations, the separate armed services would retain their identity as departments right up to Chief of Staff. Nevertheless, they would now be in a single building, responsible to a single Defence Council chaired by the Secretary of State for Defence. The Defence Council would delegate its authority to individual service boards.[113]

To the critics, this merely transferred inter-service rivalry, the bugbear of rational decision-taking and weapons procurement, to a different if tidier playing-field. The reform did not go as far as Mountbatten wished in the direction of service integration. Grove accurately captures the magnitude of the problem which still vitiated policy formulation at the highest levels:

> . . . it was specifically recommended by Ismay and Jacob, against Mountbatten's wishes, that the Chiefs of Staff should continue to express their views collectively to the Cabinet. Only if there was disagreement could the CDS [Chief of the Defence Staff] state his own views and, in such a case, he also had to transmit all the views set out by the three separate Chiefs of Staff. Although the CDS [Mountbatten] now had a strengthened staff of his own, he had not received official sanction for the independent line he had been taking on some issues, based on the advice of his own personal staff. This had caused much friction with the

three services. The situation was compounded also by the decision not even to follow the Ismay–Jacob recommendations that all senior officers should be carried on a single list responsible to the CDS alone. This made it certain that any senior officer who did find himself on the Defence Staff would have, at best, divided loyalties. His commitment to the centre might well be in conflict with the loyalties demanded by his own service hierarchy.[114]

The next serious attempt to tackle the central organisational problem of institutionalised service rivalries had to wait until the early 1980s and the aftermath of the 1981 Defence Review in which John Nott lost one of his juniors, Navy Minister Keith Speed, for publicly dissenting from the planned cuts, the bulk of which were to fall upon his service. Single junior ministers for each service were dispensed with and the present arrangement was instituted of a pair of ministers, a minister of state and a parliamentary under secretary, for all three Armed Services combined. Simultaneously, the Chief of the General Staff, the First Sea Lord and the Chief of the Air Staff lost their right to attend meetings of the Cabinet's Oversea and Defence Committee. Henceforth, only the Chief of the Defence Staff would go and would represent opinion on a tri-service basis.

The seismic shift in service power and relationships, however, occurred when Michael Heseltine was transferred to MOD from the Department of the Environment in January 1983 to apply his managerial enthusiasm to the defence machine. Heseltine compiled a Strangelove-style big board of the organisation – civilian, military and scientific. John Mayne was picked from within the department to develop an MOD version of the MINIS system that Heseltine had pioneered at DOE.[115] Heseltine's first impression of his new domain was not favourable. 'The very size of the MOD and its loose federal organisation, with central co-ordinating staff placed alongside single service structures, was a recipe for wastage of effort; and the military and civilian staffs tended to report upward through separate chains, blurring responsibilities.'[116] Gazing at his big board cleared his mind – 'There is no better way to learn about the department for which you are responsible than to ask somebody to draw lines of accountability on a sheet of paper and put names into boxes'[117] – and he decided to complete 'the reorganisation of the Ministry which had been contemplated for about thirty years'.[118]

Flying home in an RAF VC10 from a visit to Kuwait, Heseltine sketched out his new organisational structure:[119]

> It was clear that my target must be the independent powers of the three single-service planning and equipment requirement staffs. I decided to bring them together in central planning and systems staffs with a new post of Vice Chief of the Defence Staff to take charge. He would also have

under him the key policy and operations staff. To put the realignment of power beyond doubt the Vice Chief was to be of four star rank – the same seniority as the service chiefs – and all of them became answerable to the CDS. On the civilian side, the fragmentation of responsibility for finance and budget issues was also ended. The aim was a new machinery for reaching the key resource allocation decisions on a defence-wide basis, rather than by a process of fair shares for three competing service interests.[120]

Warrior-politicians like the Chiefs of Staff know all about power. They did not succumb without a struggle to the Heseltine plan which was outlined in the 1984 Defence White Paper.[121] Shortly before the White Paper was published, the First Sea Lord, the Chief of the General Staff and the Chief of the Air Staff exercised their right of direct access to the Prime Minister. Mrs Thatcher granted them a small concession – the right to maintain a small single-service staff in order to present alternatives to the Secretary of State.[122] Heseltine wrote later that designing his new structure in the VC10 without consulting the Chiefs of Staff 'was without doubt the least comfortable position I adopted in government'.[123] But he won his reform and it is likely to stand as the new status quo for quite a time. The same cannot be said about the configuration of the defence budget. When Francis Pym was Defence Secretary, he would sometimes wonder if there was a better way of funding the defence programme than endless tussles with the Treasury. There probably is, but the ground-rules only change when war is approaching, and that is too high a price to pay for rationality.

SOCIAL DEPARTMENTS

The Department of Health and Social Security

I had a little talk with the Queen who knew that this afternoon I was to be appointed Secretary of State for Social Services and she asked where I was going to be. I said, 'the Elephant and Castle'. 'Oh', she said, 'What a with-it address.' A funny remark, showing how completely out of touch she is, because of all the places that are not exactly with-it that dreary part of South London is the worst, brand new and yet unpopular and unmodish. However, perhaps she meant to be nice to me.
Richard Crossman, 1968[124]

When ... after consulting the civil servants, I merged the two – Health and Social Services – I think that that was probably the wrong step. In fact, soon afterwards – I take full responsibility for it – they were saying to me that they were not sure they ought not to have advised me to merge social services with the Home Office ...
Lord Wilson, 1977[125]

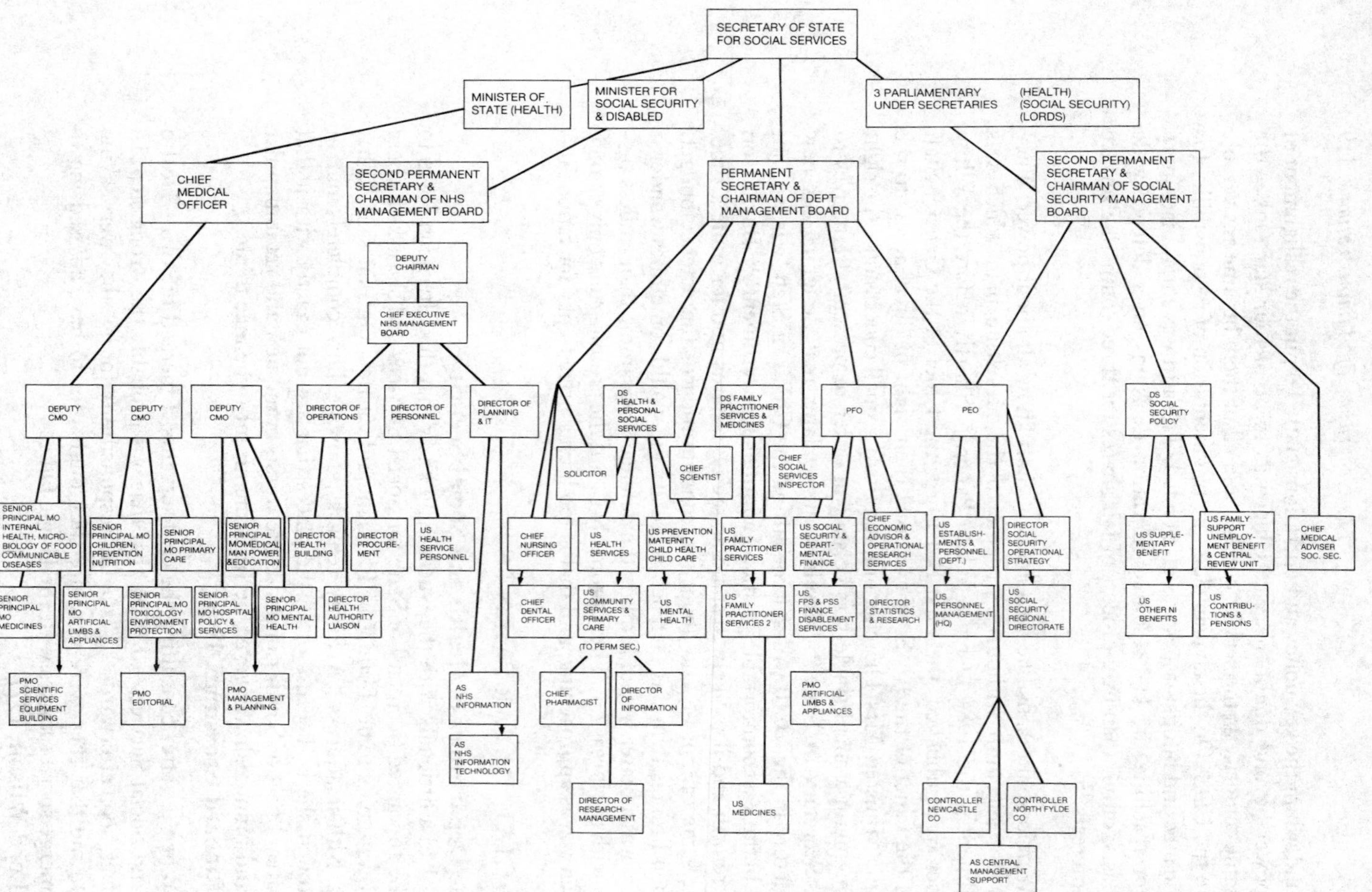

Fig. 5. Department of Health and Social Security

Dealing with the doctors is even worse than negotiating with the French.
Senior DHSS official, 1976[126]

I am surprised that civil servants should be associated with such stuff. It's like something out of *New Society* – a magazine I fortunately do not have to read.
Treasury official to DHSS official on the Annual Report of the Supplementary Benefit Commission, 1975[127]

We cannot go into liquidation; but neither can we dispose of unattractive subsidiaries or get out of the often unrewarding markets we are operating in.
Sir Kenneth Stowe, Permanent Secretary to the DHSS, 1986[128]

Founded: 1968.

Ministers: Secretary of State for the Social Services, Minister for Health, Minister for Social Security and the Disabled, three Parliamentary Under Secretaries.

Responsibilities: Hospital and community health services through the agency of 14 regional health authorities, 191 district authorities, 1,900 hospitals and 8 special health authorities covering the London postgraduate teaching hospitals; family practitioner services delivered through 54,000 independent contractors including general practitioners, dentists, opticians and pharmacists; personal social services through the local authorities, and the department's own central and regional staff (covering, for example, special hospitals, public health laboratories, grants to voluntary bodies); social security, directly managed by the department through two central offices in Newcastle and the Fylde and 509 local offices; between them they disburse benefit to five out of six households in the UK and collect contributions under the national insurance and industrial injuries schemes; wider health and social responsibilities, e.g. health education, relations with the private health sector, evaluating the safety of medical equipment, sponsoring the pharmaceutical and medical equipment industries; regulation of the medical professions (with the Privy Council Office).

Budget (1987–8): £65,125 million.

Staff (1 April 1987): 95,850.

Management system: DMA (Divisional Management Accounts).

The DHSS is *the* big spending department, some £16 billion on health and £45 billion on social security, well over a third of public expenditure as a whole. It has, after MOD, the biggest of the bureaucratic battalions to man it. If the 'public choice' school of political theorists were right in arguing that public money and manpower in abundance were what every bureaucrat craved, as that way lay real power, the DHSS would be the elite ministry for politicians and civil servants alike. In fact, it is the reverse, a cinderella department widely regarded as too big and as bringing together two huge public businesses which should be separate. Conventional wisdom has it (and I agree) that it was an organisational nonsense put together quickly and clumsily by Harold Wilson to keep Dick Crossman quiet – a monument to the 1960s, a kind of bureaucratic tower block. For the rest of Whitehall it is a black hole into which financial and human resources disappear, a policy-maker's and manager's nightmare. A posting to the Elephant and Castle is Whitehall's equivalent of a Siberian power station.

And yet, the DHSS *matters*. It touches everyone's life directly. The life chances of millions depend on it and will continue to do so no matter how hard Mrs Thatcher and her ministers strive to reduce what they call the 'dependency culture'. The best way of conveying the scope and the reach of the DHSS is to chart it:

DHSS annual activity

* 800,000 new claims for retirement pension;
* 900,000 new claims for other contributory national insurance benefits;
* 6 million new claims for supplementary benefit;
* 1,040 million separate payments, mostly by order book and Giro at the Post Office;
* 1,400 new drug product licences issued;
* 12,500 adverse reaction reports on drugs;
* 5 million hospital in-patient cases in England;
* 37 million hospital out-patient attendances in England;
* 5 million childhood immunisations in England;
* 31 million courses of dental treatment in England;
* 320 million prescriptions dispensed and paid for in England;
* 10 million sight tests in England.[129]

DHSS monthly turnover

* raises £1,861 million;
* spends £4,500 million;
* makes 80 million cash payments to individuals;
* reimburses chemists for 27 million prescriptions;
* enters 3 million records of national insurance contributions;
* pays for 800,000 employees of the health authorities in England;
* pays 95,000 departmental staff.[130]

Together, its health and social security activities make the DHSS almost certainly the largest business in the world. Every bit of it is politically charged, some of it highly so.

DHSS annual accountability turnover

* 6,400 Parliamentary questions;
* 100 Parliamentary debates;
* 35,000 letters from MPs needing a ministerial reply;
* 63,000 letters to its headquarters from members of the public;
* 50 deputations to a minister led by an MP or a peer;
* 100 cases investigated by the Ombudsman requiring a response from the permanent secretary.[131]

The DHSS is the institutional embodiment of the explosion of the welfare state, not just since the prototype Ministry of Health was created in Lloyd George's day, but since its Attleean reconstruction was completed. Attlee's welfare state was fairly simple with less than half-a-dozen core benefits.[132] The DHSS now disburses over thirty different benefits, a fivefold increase in forty years. These, and many other of its activities, have a statutory basis. The DHSS's work is governed by 100 laws and 1,500 statutory instruments.[133] The scope for judicial review of disputes between government and governed is almost infinite, not to mention the likelihood of Parliamentary scrutiny via the Public Accounts Committee and the National Audit Office.

Until the creation of Wilson's folly, separate ministries took care of health and social security. Since 1968, 'the difficult part', as Sir Kenneth Stowe put it in his understated fashion, 'is to try to make it all fit together'.[134] His predecessor, Sir Patrick Nairne, put it more bluntly.

> All my time at DHSS, I felt you had to be ready as permanent secretary for one of those lightning strikes in the autumn ... We were one of the elephantine departments that had survived: but were we in the process of becoming a dinosaur? I have always found it difficult to answer the question 'If you started now would you create the DHSS?' It was an extraordinarily difficult department to run ... the benefit offices, the relationship with the NHS who were not civil servants, the social services administered by local authorities and the public health role.[135]

In the 1980s, the DHSS's big businesses have been reorganised at the top. The two key bodies are separate management boards for health and social security, each bringing in outsiders with business experience and each chaired by a minister of state. Insofar as is humanly possible, all the activities of the department's fifty-one operating divisions are pulled together by a departmental management board with the DMA management system as its tool. I am constantly amazed that the 1968 structure has lasted as long as it has. In ministerial and Civil Service terms, the DHSS is a political and a management impossibility. The problem can be tackled either by undoing the 1968 merger and recreating separate ministries, by hiving off large chunks of executive work in the manner prescribed by the Efficiency Unit's 1987 report, *The Next Steps* (see pp. 619–21), or by dramatically reducing state involvement in health and welfare. Until one of those three changes is made, the engine room of the welfare state – the DHSS – will remain the single most overloaded component of the Whitehall machine.

At the time of writing (spring 1988) the political misfortunes of Mr John Moore as Secretary of State for the Social Services,[136] then embroiled in the immediate consequences of implementing a more streamlined system of benefits *and* a fundamental review of the National Health Service, were causing a revival of speculation that the unloved department would be split in two at the next reshuffle with social security placed in an Ibbs-style public agency.

The prospects of an undoing of the 1968 merger twenty years on were unknowable. What was undeniable, however, was the revival of press interest in the immense difficulty of keeping the social security system in motion. Under the changes planned by Norman Fowler and implemented by John Moore, some 3.7 m claimants were to lose out, nearly three-quarters of a million of them by more than £5 a week.[137] Protective grilles went up in benefits offices up and down the land to separate DHSS officials from those they served. Such things can be overdone, but it was, in its way, a tangible sign of Beveridgism going into reverse.

Even in the prosperous south-east the benefits machine – the modern-day version of Lloyd George's ambulance wagon – was visibly failing to cope. The day before the new benefits came into force in April 1988, *The Observer*'s Carmel Fitzsimons described the daily spectacle 'around the draughty skirts of North London's Archway Tower Office [where] the snaking queue assumes its shape by seven in the morning. The shuffle of feet moving slowly into the [DHSS] office will be halted abruptly by the guards at lunch-time when the shutters come down through overcrowding. Many claimants bring vacuum flasks and sandwiches in preparation for a long vigil on this nouveau breadline.'[138]

The true test of bureaucratic health is such spots – the point of delivery remote from the private offices and the committee rooms where the grand strategic rethinks take place. Improving matters here depends not just on computerising the system or splitting the DHSS in two or an ambitious office improvement scheme, helpful though these would be. Real, lasting improvement depends upon a buoyant and humane political economy and society in the creation of which the DHSS is but a part, albeit an important one. For me one of the most crucial qualitative tests of any state is the manner in which it treats those, to borrow Ken Stowe's phrase, who, for whatever reason, fall into its sump.

> **The Department of Education and Science**
> It's spiritually a bit on its own.
> **Sir Edward Boyle, former Secretary of State, 1971**[139]
>
> If it's the last thing I do, I'm going to destroy every fucking grammar school in England and Wales and Northern Ireland.
> **Anthony Crosland,**
> **Secretary of State for Education and Science, 1965**[140]
>
> The problem for all of them [Ministers of Education] was that their department had little power. Education policy was conducted by the local authorities and the teachers' unions, with the Department of Education, as Harold Wilson once commented to me, being little more than a post box between the two.
> **Bernard Donoughue, 1987**[141]
>
> The truth is that our education system is not the product of a single directing mind – a Napoleon or a Bismarck – let alone the expression of a single guiding principle. It has grown by a process of addition and adaptation. It reflects a good many historical compromises. In short, it is a bit of a muddle, one of those institutionalised muddles that the English have made peculiarly their own.
> **Kenneth Baker,**
> **Secretary of State for Education and Science, 1987**[142]

Founded: 1899, as the Board of Education.

Ministers: Secretary of State for Education and Science, Minister of State, three Parliamentary Under Secretaries.

Responsibilities: Formulation of national policy for education in England and for the forty-six universities in the UK as a whole; the funding of 101 local education authorities; the supply and training of teachers; Her Majesty's Inspectorate of Schools; standards of school building; the five research councils (medical, agricultural, science and engineering, natural environmental, economic and social).

Budget (1987–8): £16,604 million.

Staff (1 April 1987): 2,450.

Management system: TRIDENT.

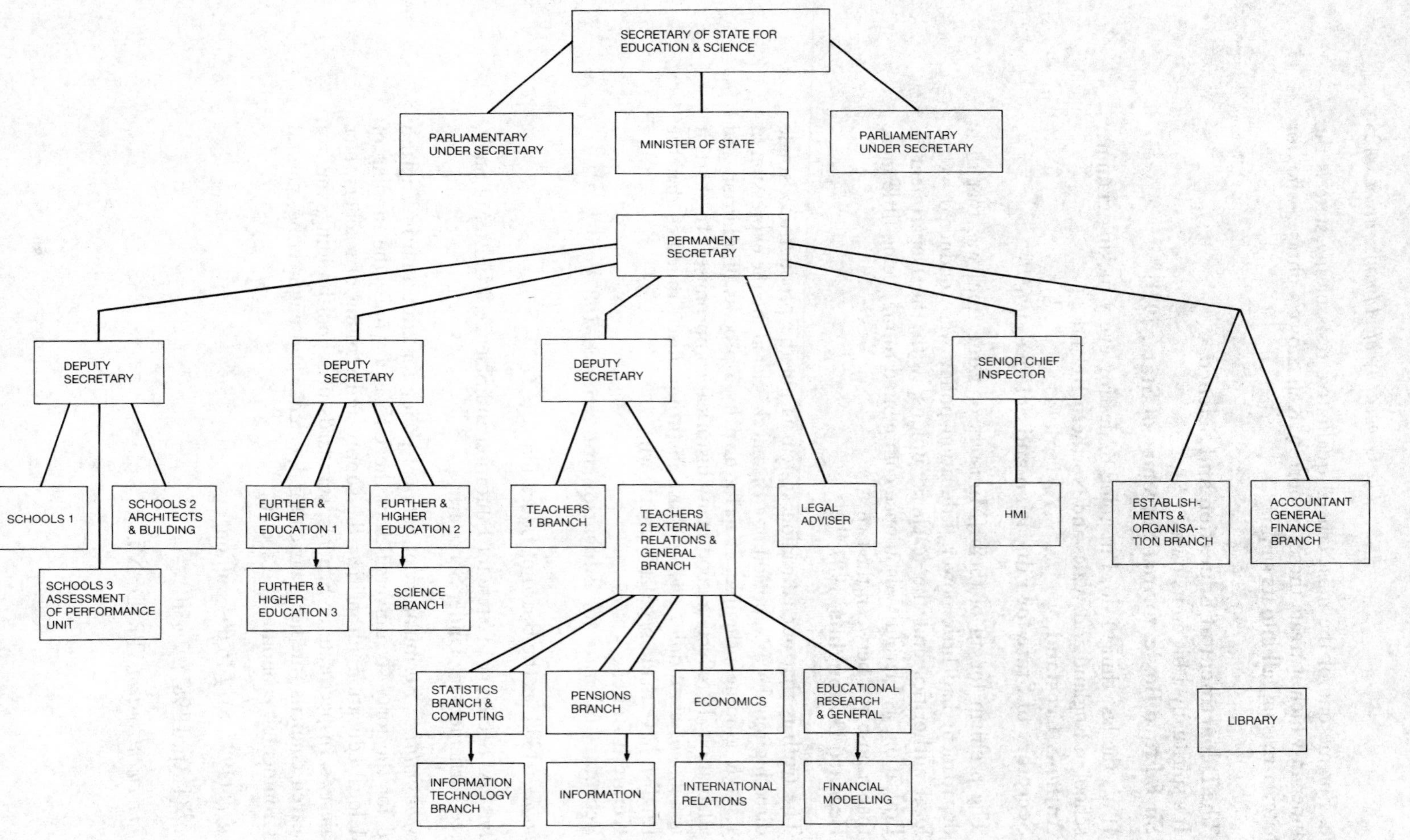

Fig. 6. Department of Education and Science

The DES is widely regarded as another cinderella department. Officials from other ministries are the subject of commiseration when posted there. It is seen as an institution in which bureaucrats turn grey. Yet every generation or so, this particular cinderella gets to go to the ball. When the tide of reform runs, education floats to the top of the Cabinet's agenda as it did in the mid-1940s under R. A. Butler, in the early to mid-1960s under Hailsham, Boyle and Crosland and in the late eighties under Kenneth Baker, the would-be Bismarck unifying an agglomeration of provision.

The traditional ambivalence of the mighty to the education portfolio is enshrined in the legend of the exchange in 1941 when Churchill offered it to Rab who expressed unalloyed pleasure at the offer. 'Just like you, Rab', the grand old man is alleged to have said. 'I only offered it to you as an insult.' Though it is certainly true, as Paul Addison noted, that 'in Churchill's eyes the Board of Education in wartime was a political backwater of no possible significance, and he thought Butler peculiar for wanting to take it on',[143] the reality of their exchange was rather different though very revealing in what it tells us about the 'hands-off' tradition in British state education, a tradition that Mrs Thatcher and Mr Baker have challenged head-on. Rab tells the story as only Rab could:

> He [Churchill] saw me after his afternoon nap and was purring like a tiger. He began, 'You have been in the House fifteen years and it's time you were promoted ... and I now want you to go to the Board of Education. I think that you can leave your mark there. You will be independent. Besides,' he continued, with rising fervour, 'you will be in the war. You will move poor children from here to there', and he lifted up and evacuated imaginary children from one side of his blotting pad to the other; 'this will be very difficult.' He went on: 'I am too old now to think you can improve people's natures. Everyone has to learn to defend himself. I should not object if you could introduce a note of patriotism in the schools.' And then, with a grin. ... 'Tell the children that Wolfe won Quebec.' I said that I would like to influence what was taught in schools but that this was always frowned upon. Here he looked very earnest and commented, 'of course not by instruction or order but by suggestion'. I then said that I had always looked forward to going to the Board of Education if I were given the chance. He appeared ever so slightly surprised at this. ...[144]

It has fallen to very few education ministers since the Board of Education was spun off from the Privy Council's Education Committee in 1899 to make or to consolidate their reputations there. Butler made his reputation with the 1944 Act. By establishing secondary provision for all and ending, at last, the religious controversies that had dogged the system for so long, he placed himself on a trajectory of progressive policy achievement which made him an outstanding figure in postwar politics. Crosland won his reputation with his 1965 DES circular enshrining comprehensive education as the new norm and his Woolwich speech foreshadowing a great expansion of the polytechnics in the wake of the great surge in university expansion inaugurated by his Conservative predecessors, Hailsham and Boyle on the recommendations of the Robbins Report.

In between such innovatory spurts, the DES has remained one of the largest spenders in Whitehall but with miniscule say in the detailed disposition of its resources compared, for instance, to the DHSS or the MOD. The department has dispensed cheques to the University Grants Committee for the universities and to the local authorities for schools and polytechnics with guidelines sometimes attached but virtually nil powers of enforcement. Traditionally, as Butler reminded Churchill, the state has been very wary of interfering directly in what is taught in the classroom, spoken in the lecture hall or attempted in the lab.

In the 1980s all that changed. It was one of the great ironies of the Thatcher administration, a self-proclaimed hands-off government, that, at the very moment when it was withdrawing the state from as many areas of economic, industrial and social activity as possible, it should push forward state power so far and so firmly in the education field. As Professor John Ashworth, the former CPRS Chief Scientist who became Vice-Chancellor of Salford University, said to Robert Jackson, the minister responsible for higher education in 1987, 'They are privatising everybody else and nationalising us.'[145]

By the late autumn of 1987 the thrust of Mr Baker's intentions were plain:

* the right of schools to opt out of local authority control with funding directly from the DES;
* a range of city technical colleges funded jointly by government and industry;
* a core curriculum in which the basics of every child's education would be laid down by the state;
* new funding councils for the universities, for the polytechnics, with strong reserve powers for the DES, in which managerial efficiency and the direction of the higher education system towards meeting the country's economic needs will be secured through the award of competitive contracts.

Taken together, these policy initiatives placed the DES, along with Environment, in the van of the movement to by-pass local government wherever possible and, in crude Whitehall terms, activity plus high and sustained ministerial attention = high relative status.

One thing was plain, however. Its new status was not going to cause a huge growth in the DES as a piece of bureaucratic machinery. Work on the great Education Reform Bill pushed its complement up to around 2,500 staff. Once the bill became law, the permanent increase in staff needed to handle the new financial arrangements with local authorities was thought to be a matter of tens rather than hundreds, though on the 'opting out' side it would clearly depend on how many schools chose to do so and the kind of 'trust' or 'quango' set up to oversee the new sector.[146]

In the late 1980s the DES found itself a place in the Whitehall sun for the first time in twenty years but at the cost of abandoning its quietist mixed tradition of high spending and great self-restraint. From now on, DES money was to talk. Whether the Baker years will leave its civil servants permanently changed is still an open question. They probably will because new functions often breed a new type of official and, barring a seismic and unforeseen change in the political landscape, the department's functions will have been transformed, probably permanently, before the tenth anniversary of Mrs Thatcher's assumption of the premiership.

ECONOMIC DEPARTMENTS

Department of Trade and Industry

You have to have some body which wants to develop public enterprise but our present Civil Service is not interested in growth. It is geared to care and maintenance.
Tony Benn, 1965[147]

I have a very simple rule of thumb: my department should spend far more of its time finding ways to help industry to trade than it should do inventing and enforcing rules and regulations to stop industry trading.
Lord Young, Secretary of State for Trade and Industry, 1987[148]

The contempt for production ... is what distinguishes the British government from all others ... Britain, sacrificing her productive power on the altar of monetary symbols, suffered not only in real welfare, but in the end damaged also the symbols for which it had been sacrificed.
Professor Sidney Pollard, 1984[149]

No one questions the need for the Treasury to play the central role in the macro-economic management of our affairs. The weakness is that there is not sufficient challenge to Treasury judgements which may frustrate the strategic industrial objectives of the Government and the work of the DTI.
Michael Heseltine, 1987[150]

The central role in British strategic planning must be performed in a

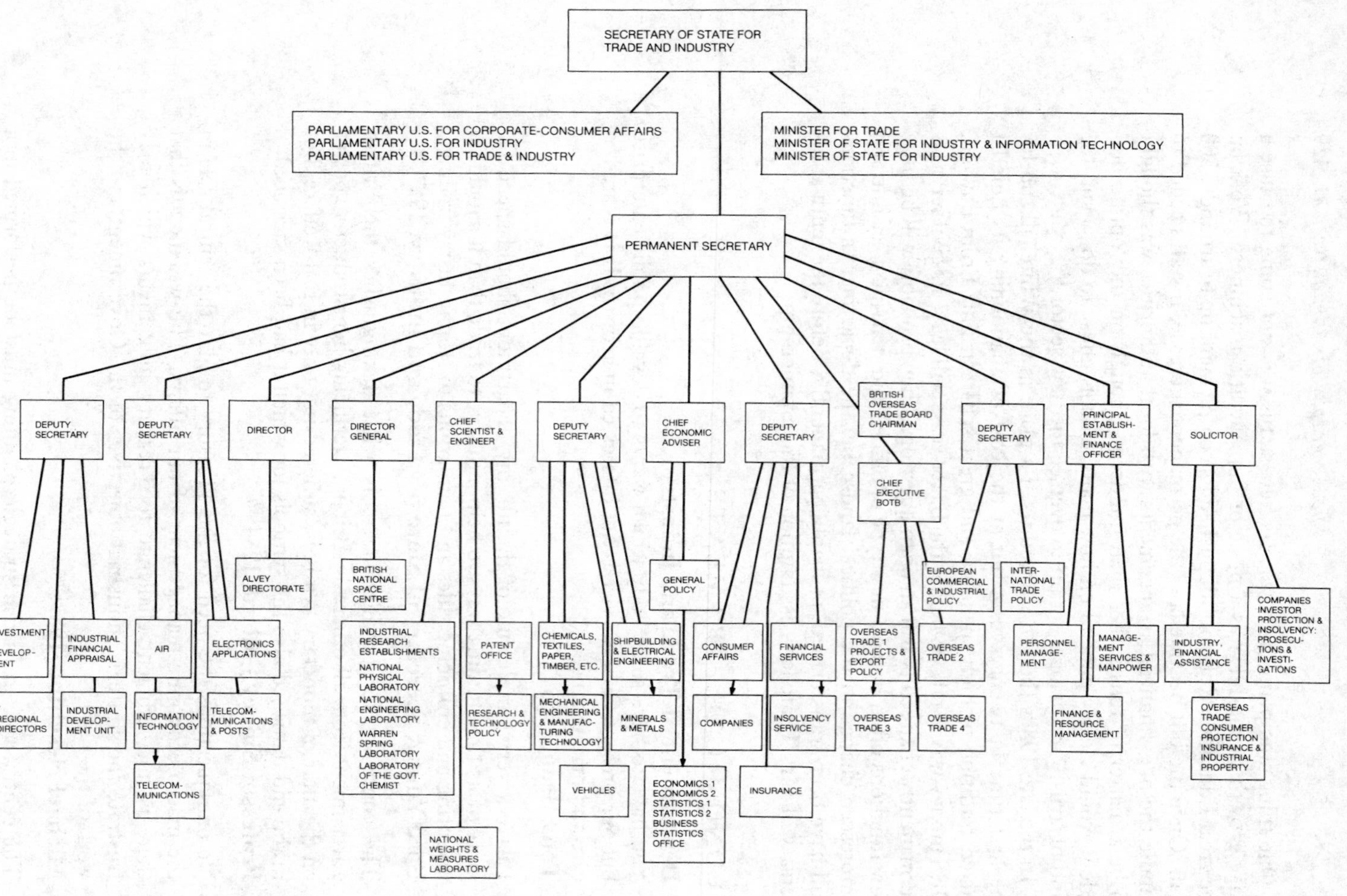

Fig. 7. Department of Trade and Industry

> Department of Trade and Industry – but it must be a rather different DTI from the edifice we have at present.
> **Neil Kinnock, 1986**[151]

Founded: As Board of Trade in 1786, as Department of Trade and Industry in 1970, split in 1974 and reconstituted in 1983.

Ministers: Secretary of State for Trade and Industry and President of the Board of Trade, Minister of State (Cabinet member), Minister of State, three Parliamentary Under Secretaries one of whom designated Minister for Corporate and Consumer Affairs.

Responsibilities: International trade policy, the promoting of British interests and exports; industrial policy; regional policy; co-ordination of inner cities policy; monopolies via Monopolies and Mergers Commission; fair trading in Office of Fair Trading; policy towards technology and civil research and development; supervision of company legislation; the insurance industry; patents; radio frequency regulation.

Budget (1987–8): £1,272 million.

Staff (1 April 1987): 12,843.

Management system: ARM (Activity and Resource Management).

The DTI is the Ethel Merman of the Whitehall scene – it has had more comebacks than can be counted. The latest relaunch came after the 1987 general election when Mrs Thatcher's favourite 'can do' minister, Lord Young, declared, 'Fundamentally we are the department for enterprise. We want to help industry and commerce become better equipped to meet the challenge of the next century and to lay the foundations of a more productive and prosperous society.'[152] Lord Young wanted an end to the DTI as the vet's surgery of the British economy treating a succession of lame ducks. He commissioned a thorough review of the department's structure, with every activity to be questioned along zero-based budgeting lines,[153] which promised to change it beyond recognition – to a management consultancy serving industry as a whole instead of a ministry divided into vertical, functional specialisms, a promise fulfilled, in rhetorical terms at least, by the White Paper, *DTI – the Department for Enterprise,* in January 1988.[154]

Oddly enough, Tony Benn, who had two spells in Lord Young's seat as Minister of Technology 1966–70 and Industry Secretary 1974–5, wanted his departments to do the same kind of thing for public enterprise. The Morrisonian model of nationalisation, he said, only permitted you to do what the public ownership statutes said you could do.[155] Mr Benn wanted a more entrepreneurial form of public enterprise and, as his diaries show, a more entrepreneurial kind of civil servant to help Labour ministers achieve it.

Given that the relative performance of British industry has been *the* central policy-making problem since the war, it is not surprising that the temptation to tinker with the Whitehall machinery designated to cope with it has been so overwhelming so frequently. Until fairly recently, wartime apart, the Board of Trade used to do virtually all the policy-making successive governments wished done. After 1945 large chunks of new industrial policy were apportioned to departments such as the Ministries of Fuel and Power and Transport as sponsoring bodies for the nascent nationalised corporations.

Since the late 1950s, as Dr Brian Hogwood has shown, the sponsorship of industry has shifted across a bewildering array of central government departments.[156] Success, in terms of sustained growth in the British economy, might have brought stability. Relative failure did not. The most important organisational benchmarks were the creation of the Ministry of Technology in 1964 which, by 1970 when it disappeared, had become a super ministry incorporating a battery of traditional sponsorship functions as well as incarnating Wilson's faith in the white heat of science-based industries as the motor of expansion; and Heath's creation of another kind of super-ministry by merging 'Mintech' and the Ministry of Fuel and Power and the Board of Trade into a Department of Trade and Industry in 1970.

There were tensions in this new arrangement flowing from a clash of departmental traditions. The Board of Trade was the embodiment of the free-trade impulse, Mintech of intervention. Fuel and Power did not fit either and the Department of Energy was spun off as the fuel crisis mounted in 1973–4. Wilson split up the rest of the DTI after his surprise election victory, not to resolve the tension between Trade and Industry but to find portfolios for the ministers appointed, in a particularly delicate balancing act between left, right and centre, to his last Cabinet. Though this did not prevent a year-long tussle between Wilson and Benn about the direction of industrial policy.

The agony of the conflicting *laissez faire* and *dirigiste* traditions was made manifest in the martyred features of Sir Keith Joseph who arrived at the Department of Industry in 1979 armed with copies of Adam Smith which he urged his officials to read. He wanted Whitehall to pull out of industrial intervention altogether and for his Industry Department to be wound up and re-merged with Trade. A genuinely humane man, Joseph could not, however, let the companies – state or private – which were wheeled into his casualty ward simply be shunted towards the mortuary. It led him to produce what one senior official remembers as perhaps the most bizarre Cabinet paper of the early 1980s. It argued for the closure of

British Leyland but went on to point out the appalling consequences to the company's workforce and those of its myriad of small suppliers in the already hard-hit West Midlands. All the evidence so graphically displayed pointed against the conclusion reached. Never before, said the official, had he seen a Cabinet paper written in a way which so obviously invited its rejection.[157]

After the 1983 general election Sir Keith's wish was fulfilled. Industry and Trade were reconstituted under Cecil Parkinson who was almost instantly obliged to resign because of personal scandal. Norman Tebbit replaced him, to be succeeded by Leon Brittan. Westland destroyed Brittan's career. Paul Channon's tenure was brief. After the 1987 election, David Young, who had entered the Department of Industry in 1979 as Joseph's special adviser, inherited the kingdom as the fifth Secretary of State in four years. All this was no way to treat the ministry presiding over the deepest-seated of all the country's problems.

One of Young's first acts was to remove himself and his political team from the fray for a weekend at Saltwood Castle, near Folkestone, home of Alan Clark, his Minister for Trade, to ponder the DTI's future. Out of this came its rebirth as the department of enterprise and the intention, as the *Times* reporter who was given the scoop put it, of making 'the department the Whitehall motor of economic growth and change and gradually to shed its reputation as a provider of blanket grants to depressed regions and smoke-stack industries'.[158] Young, who prides himself on his communication skills, circulated the new objectives of the department to every member of its 12,000 staff:

* to produce a more competitive market by encouraging competition and tackling restrictive practices, cartels and monopolies;
* to secure a more efficient market by improving the precision of information to business about new methods and opportunities;
* to create a larger market by privatisation and deregulation;
* to increase confidence in the working of markets by achieving a fair level of protection for the individual consumer and investor.[159]

Such departmental objectives are suffused with politics. The DTI will remain highly fluid in functional terms as long as the civil war between the political parties continues to range about the precise mix of the mixed economy and the most beneficial strategies for making that economy grow – in other words, as long as Britain remains an open political society. Any major political figure with an alternative strategy in his or her pocket has a particular plan for the DTI. Michael Heseltine wants its power boosted *vis-à-vis* the Treasury with the Secretary of State for Trade and Industry in charge of a Cabinet Committee on Industry;[160] Neil Kinnock and John

Smith want something very similar to that, though their purposes are somewhat different from Heseltine's.[161]

Few changes are more dramatic for the career civil servant than those which the political pendulum can bring for the DTI official: one party requires him to be a surrogate entrepreneur of the kind bred by the French *grandes écoles*; the other demands the skills of a management consultant-cum-midwife of the enterprise culture. DTI is, perhaps, the most schizophrenic of all departments. If any ministry demonstrates the case for a different, more fluid and wider flow in the stream of recruitment it is Trade and Industry.

As a piece of bureaucratic territory, the DTI will continue to be fought over as if it were a disputed border unless British industry regains something approaching its effortless superiority in world terms of 1840–70 (which cannot happen, however divine a future British economic miracle) and a policy consensus emerges among the political parties (which is unlikely if not impossible). If importance was the criteria which determined status, the DTI would be high in the departmental hierarchy. But it has never matched the Treasury or the Foreign Office. It is not seen by officials as offering a gilded track to the top. Being in the front line in terms of national problems does not guarantee glamour. The place and stature of the DTI is proof that, even within Whitehall, Martin Wiener's thesis of a flight of talent from manufacturing has force. If Lord Young can do for the DTI in the eighties what Bevin did for the Ministry of Labour in the forties his achievement will be genuinely formidable.

If evangelism were enough, there would be no doubt that the prize is within his grasp. Visitors leaving his office in Victoria Street found him thrusting a tract into their hands which encapsulated the DTI's enterprise objectives. I found him quite happy to accept the suggestion that he was engaged in an attempt to convert the DTI into a bureaucratic version of the Institute of Economic Affairs. He appeared to be Cripps and Benn by another means, a comparison he found interesting as they were both socialists.[162]

Like them Lord Young applied a long historical perspective to current economic problems. In the opening section of his enterprise White Paper, which he had written himself, he dug deep into the bedrock of the past:

> The seeds of economic decline can be traced back over a hundred years. After 1870 the UK's growth rate was persistently below that of the United States, France, Germany, Italy, Sweden and Japan. The enterprise of the nation appeared to have been lost. The education system discouraged young people from working in business and neglected the skills of management and innovation. No training was available for the

great mass of people at work; such training as did exist was too often rigid and anachronistic.[163]

It was an unmistakable compound of Martin Wiener and Correlli Barnett. Whether it encouraged British industry to greater exertions remained to be seen. It certainly encouraged people who write books about the condition of contemporary Britain.

Department of the Environment

The person who dominates all the proceedings is ... Dame Evelyn [Sharp]. She's been permanent secretary now for ten years ... She is a biggish woman, about five feet ten inches with tremendous blue eyes which look right through you ... Last Saturday, when I was appointed, she drove back from her country cottage at Lavenham and told me the moment she got to London that, largely owing to me, the Department [Housing and Local Government] had been sold down the river by Harold Wilson's decision that Fred Willey should be in charge of planning and that I should do housing ... As soon as she realized this Dame Evelyn got down to a Whitehall battle to save her Department from my stupidity and ignorance ... When on Wednesday afternoon at a meeting I turned to her and said, 'Well, Dame Evelyn, you've won,' she replied ... 'Of course, I always win. But it was exhausting.'
Richard Crossman, 1964[164]

Founded: 1970 with the merger of the Ministry of Housing and Local Government (an environment ministry in all but name since 1951) and the Ministry of Public Building and Works.

Ministers: Secretary of State for the Environment; Minister of State for the Environment, Countryside and Water; Minister of State for Housing and Planning; Minister for Local Government; four Parliamentary Under Secretaries one of whom is Minister for Sport.

Responsibilities: Development and implementation of policy on housing, local government, planning, inner cities, new towns, urban development corporations, water, environmental protection, countryside, sport and recreation, conservation, royal palaces and parks, historic buildings and ancient monuments. The Property Services Agency (PSA) is responsible for the accommodation and buildings of government departments and the Armed Forces and the Crown Suppliers.

Budget (1987–8): Housing, £2,380 million.
Other environmental services, £3,530 million.
PSA, £110 million.

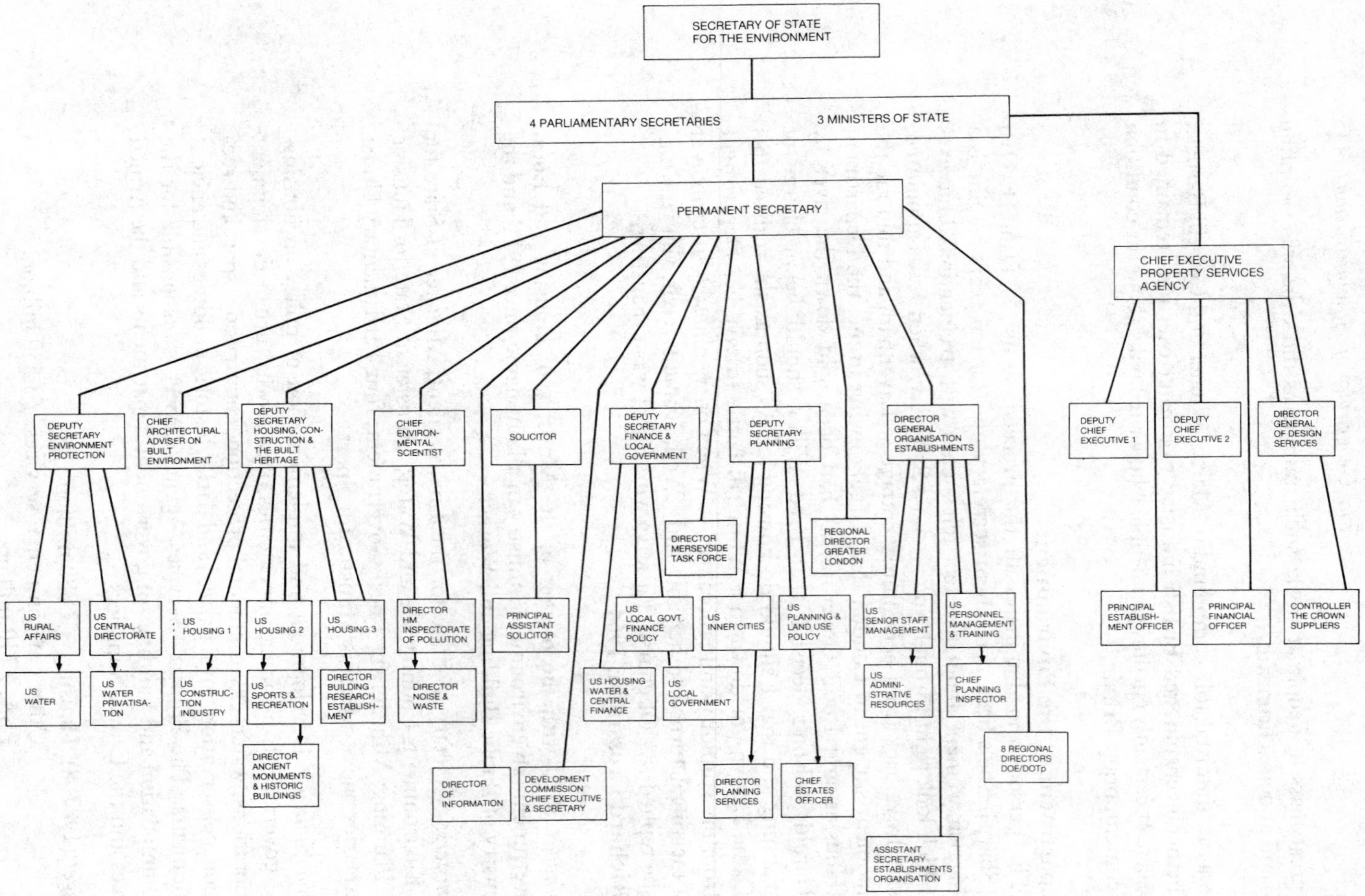

Fig. 8. Department of the Environment

Staff (1 April 1987): DOE, 6,405; PSA, 25,099.

Management system: MINIS.

Harold Macmillan put the Ministry of Housing on the political map when he pushed housebuilding up to 300,000 homes a year in the early 1950s, the happiest patch of his political life he would call it in his glorious anecdotage – 'the Ministry of Housing was like cricket, you could see the runs, the houses were built'.[165] But it took Dick Crossman to make it famous and the only reason he was able to do that was the magnetic field which surrounded the marvellous woman who greeted him that autumn Saturday in 1964. Evelyn Sharp entered the senior Civil Service in 1925, when it was exceedingly rare for a woman to aspire to such a career, let alone to contemplate a rise to the very top. One of the surprises of the serialisation of volume one of the Crossman Diaries in *The Sunday Times* in 1975 was the tremendous appeal of the Dame to the mass readership which encountered her for the first time. Assiduous readers of the first *Anatomy of Britain* would have caught a fleeting glimpse of her as 'one of the most formidable characters in Whitehall, the daughter of a political clergyman, a keen walker and hiker. She is an expert on town and country planning, a fierce opponent of litter and defender of green belts, and she has a reputation – very rare in Whitehall – for calling a spade a spade.'[166] The more the arrogant and bullying Crossman railed against the Dame, the more the reader sided with her. And, though it was not intended to be flattering, there was something both grand and appealing about Crossman's portrayal of her.

> pale, un-made up face, uncoloured lips. She is dressed as middle-or-upper-class professional women do dress, quite expensively but rather uglily. She is really a tremendous and dominating character. She has worked with a great many ministers before me. She was under the 1945–51 Labour Government in the Silkin Ministry of Town and Country Planning . . . She is rather like Beatrice Webb in her attitude to life, to the Left in the sense of wanting improvement and social justice quite passionately and yet a tremendous patrician and utterly contemptuous and arrogant, regarding local authorities as children which she has to examine and rebuke for their failures. She sees ordinary human beings as incapable of making a sensible decision.[167]

That passage from Crossman on the urge towards improvement and social justice is, I think, an accurate reflection of the dominant impulse of the senior Civil Service in the postwar period.

The Department of the Environment, which gained transport in 1970 and lost it six years later, is very much the beast the Dame knew – a ministry of local government finance and a ministry for the built environment in the form of houses, new towns and, more recently, urban development corporations.

What has changed since the Dame's day is the frontier between the DOE and the local authorities, the location of its boundary and the nature of its policing. The old attitude may have been slightly patronising but it was close and warm with the Ministry of Housing acting as local government's agent in Whitehall like some domestic equivalent of the Colonial Office. These days, to the regret of many of the officials, it is more like NATO and the Warsaw Pact, a cold war broken by outbursts of hot words. With the metropolitan counties come and gone, ratecapping and the progressive writing of local government out of the script of inner cities (with parallel moves at the DES on schooling), central–local government relations are at their most envenomed in living memory. In fact, they have probably never been so poisonous. One of Mrs Thatcher's more profound alterations to the political landscape has been to terminate the State's reliance on local government as its partner in delivering important services at the local level – the tradition bequeathed by the Chamberlains, Joe and Neville. Living through the years 1979–87 was a genuine wrench for civil servants reared in the old tradition.

But, as Peter Jenkins put it, politicians of the Thatcherite persuasion 'were of the opinion that reversing Britain's decline was too serious a business to be left to the sort of people who these days got themselves elected to the town and county halls'.[168] And in macro-economic terms local authority spending mattered, absorbing as it did some 25 per cent of public spending as a whole. Central government through its fiendishly complicated system of rate support grant provided about half of it, but in this instance money did not equal power. Ministers had precious little control over how the DOE's, DES's, DHSS's and Department of Transport's subventions were spent, hence the resort to crude devices such as ratecapping to put a lid on the local authority gusher. Everybody, except a handful of far-left local authorities who brought many others, wrongly, into disrepute, accepted that something must be done. It was the relish and self-righteousness with which the Thatcher administration turned on the local authorities – treating them as a kind of enemy within, albeit an incompetent one – which caused offence among more traditional Conservatives who did not welcome the extension of central government power that this inevitably involved. In these conditions it was impossible for the DOE to continue the traditional role as local government's friend and advocate within Whitehall and, in the other direction, as the dispenser of advice and benign guidance as well as money.

The DOE, in addition to its core functions of local government and housing, is a bit like a Whitehall holding company in the range of activities

TABLE 1

DOE-SPONSORED NON-DEPARTMENTAL PUBLIC BODIES

Body	*Staff (1984)*	*Expenditure 1983/84*
	Numbers	£m
Audit Commission	524	13
Tower Armouries	63	1
British Board of Agréement	73	2
Countryside Commission	98	13
Council for Small Industries in Rural Areas	303	7
Development Commission	39	12
Historic Buildings & Monuments Commission	60	40
Housing Corporation	535	1,358
New towns – 14 including Letchworth Garden City & Commission for New Towns	5,901	743
London Docklands Dev. Corp.	90	63
Merseyside Dev. Corp.	50	33
National Heritage Memorial Fund	5	15
Nature Conservancy Council	606	13
Royal Commission on Historical Monuments (England)	126	2
Sports Council	545	28

Source: Harrison and Gretton.[169]

it supervises to a greater or lesser extent at arm's length. It is the classic quangoid department operating through a network of statutory bodies, some of which are big spenders and employers. Michael Whitbread, a former economic adviser to the DOE, illustrated this phenomenon of secondary bureaucracy, freeze-framing it in its 1983–4 incarnation (Table 1). Since Whitbread prepared that table, four more urban development corporations have come into existence in Tyne and Wear, West Midlands, Teesside and Manchester/Salford and still more are planned.

Taken together with its traditional functions, its quangoid empire makes the DOE one of the hardest departments to run, particularly when the huge management problem of the Property Services Agency (the old

Ministry of Works) is added. Yet the DOE was in the van of the movement for managerial improvement after 1979. This was entirely due to the posting there of Michael Heseltine, perhaps the only minister in recent times for whom management is a pleasure not a chore.

In his *Where There's a Will,* Heseltine proudly reproduces the illegible plan for office management, staff and policy which he scribbled down, literally, on the back of an envelope, prior to his first meeting with the DOE's top official. He later wrote:

> I was lucky that my first permanent under secretary was Sir John Garlick, a dedicated civil servant whom I had known and with whom I had worked in the Ministry of Transport nine years before. I invited him out to lunch, and there we renewed our relationship on the right footing, meeting outside the department, not on neutral ground but on my ground.
>
> Sir John came, as I knew he would, unarmed. There was not a file in sight although, to the best of my recollection, there were references to the briefing that awaited me in the office. I was not quite unarmed: I came with the outline of my programme on the back of an envelope. I gave it to him and forgot it, but when I left the department after four of the happiest years of my life I had a kindly note from Sir John, who had by then retired. He wished me well and said that perhaps now I might like to have back the envelope which he enclosed.[170]

Sir John was no Dame Evelyn. He was quiet, assiduous and unassuming. I first met him when he was heading the Cabinet Office's Constitution Unit and struggling with the intricacies of the, so far, never-to-be devolution of power to Scottish and Welsh assemblies. He is the only permanent secretary I know to have discussed with me, without prodding, the question of the point at which a civil servant should resign if a British government slipped into tyranny.[171] In an on-the-record interview to mark his retirement in 1981, Sir John told me the indefinite suspension of *habeas corpus* in peacetime would represent a 'classic' breaking-point. But, short of that, he wondered if he would recognise the benchmark and resign in protest in time. 'There could come a point,' he said, 'theoretically, where civil servants found themselves so out of sympathy with the broad political framework that a Government was trying to create, that they were no longer able to serve it.'[172]

In that same interview, Garlick said he had enjoyed his last two years working in the service for 'an extremely radical administration' and that it was absolutely right that his minister, Michael Heseltine, should take a direct role in managing the DOE rather than simply concentrating on policy. Heseltine's first act was to compile the equivalent of a Domesday Book on the kingdom he inherited. He reviewed its baronies, no less than sixty-six directorates, and reduced them to fifty-seven. He set in train a programme of vigorous manpower economies and instructed officials to construct a new management system for himself and his ministerial team – a system which emerged as the famous MINIS, prototype for the Government's financial management initiative (see Chapter 14).

The official construction team on the MINIS project led by Geoffrey Chipperfield, won high reputations in the course of their work which was extended in 1983 by MAXIS, a cost-centre-based system for managing administrative expenditure. Heseltine, like Harold Macmillan before him, never ceased to pine for his Environment days, particularly its inner-cities work. It is an interesting phenomenon derived, I reckon, from the tangibility of the job – creating real things in the shape of bricks and mortar – which more than compensates for the pain of dealing with the intractability of local government finance.

Ministry of Agriculture, Fisheries and Food

> The Ministry of Agriculture looks after farmers, the Foreign Office looks after foreigners.
> **Norman Tebbit, undated**[173]

> Public opinion would have it that MAFF conspires with foreigners in the EEC and farmers at home to squander public money on vast stockpiles of food and destroy England's green and pleasant land in the process. As this is precisely what MAFF officials are striving to avoid, they quickly develop a thick skin or a persecution complex.
> **FDA Administration Trainee panel, 1987**[174]

Founded: 1889 as the Board of Agriculture.

Ministers: Minister of Agriculture, Fisheries and Food; one Minister of State; two Parliamentary Secretaries.

Responsibilities: Administering government policy for agriculture, horticulture and fisheries in England; administering the EEC's common agricultural and common fisheries policies; offering an Agricultural Development and Advisory Service; sponsoring the agricultural, fishing, food manufacturing and distributive industries and ensuring the maintenance of safety and public health.

Budget (1987–8): £2,258 million.

Staff (1 April 1987): 11,646.

Management system: MINIM (Ministerial Information in MAFF) supported by MAIS (Management Accounting Information System).

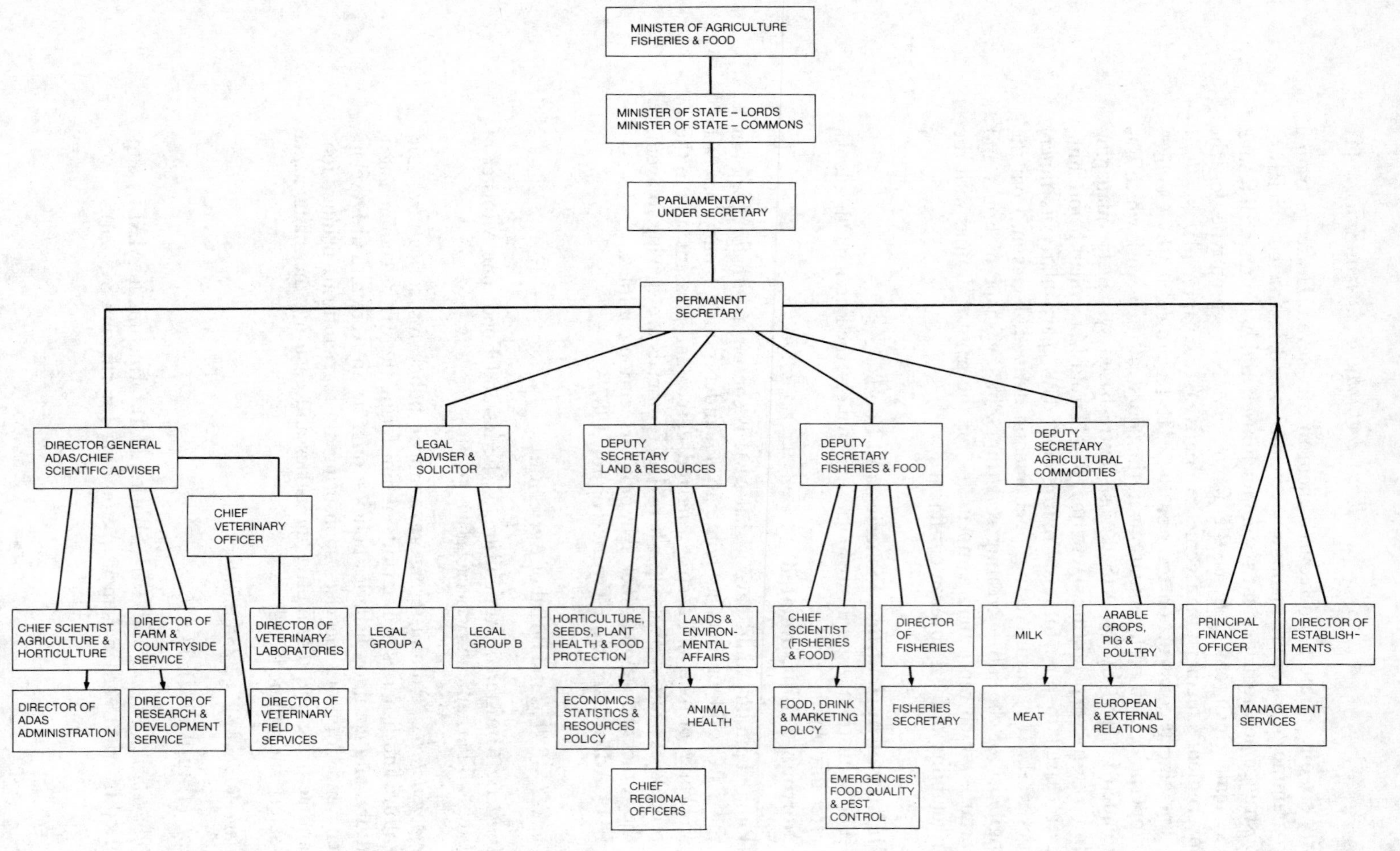

Fig. 9. Ministry of Agriculture, Fisheries and Food

The Ministry of Agriculture shows that if you are a government department, you cannot win. It has presided for forty years over the most consistent and conspicuous success story in British industry and yet it is surrounded by carping and controversy. In terms of efficiency, manpower use, capital investment and output, farming has shown since the war what a mixed economy can do given the right circumstances and good management in both its public and private sectors.

Like most of the other major enterprises of the mixed economy, the system of farm price support is a product of the 1940s. It was a self-evident truth in wartime that every scrap of food had to be squeezed from every pocket of land. Even the verges of trunk roads were put under the plough. In the first years of peace, the system of support through subsidy pioneered by bodies such as the Milk Marketing Board in the 1930s was extended to agriculture as a whole and enshrined in the Agriculture Act of 1947, steered through the Commons by an elderly ex-miner, Tom Williams. If ever a minister of agriculture deserved the title the 'farmer's friend' it was Labour's Williams, though his beneficence did little or nothing to dent the solidly Conservative rural vote.[175]

Thanks to Williams's system, which enjoyed bipartisan political support, farmers had assured markets for about three-quarters of their produce.[176] Under such arrangements, long-term and stable planning was possible on the part of fiercely capitalistic farmers operating within a market whose main parameters were controlled by the State. It was the special position of British agriculture, far and away the most efficient in Europe, which was one of the main stumbling-blocks to British membership of the EEC and, at best, left important politicians like R. A. Butler (who represented a rural seat in East Anglia) ambivalent about the whole European enterprise.

Once British membership was achieved, much of the odium of the Community's Common Agricultural Policy fell upon MAFF in the era of beef mountains, milk lakes and barley barons. Joining the EEC pushed MAFF much more into the front line in Civil Service terms, thanks to its crucial importance in Whitehall's annexe in Brussels. For many farmers, the EEC was a bonus almost comparable to the 1947 shot-in-the-arm. As a Cambridgeshire farmer, Oliver Walston, put it:

> In the 1970s farming did better than it has ever done before in the history of agriculture ... Going into the Common Market in general and the CAP in particular ... meant that we were told by Brussels to produce regardless of cost and regardless of quantity, because Brussels, God bless them, thought that self-sufficiency was the name of the game ... We went into surplus in this country around 1980, for the first time since the Middle Ages.[177]

The results were impressive. The march of subsidy and science (in both of which MAFF led the way in partnership with the British chemical industry) did indeed transform the picture both in output and in appearance: stubble-burning in the new hedgerow-bereft British prairies to the east of the A1 raised a howl of protest from the environmentalist and amenity lobbies.

Not every section of the farming community continued to bless Brussels. From the mid-1980s dairy farmers suffered real cuts in milk production, thanks to EEC-imposed quotas. And success, generally, brought its own problems for MAFF which had to plan and manage a 10 per cent cut in output as a whole. Overproduction forced a dramatic rethink in land usage policy and some fairly acid turf fights between MAFF and DOE. As the Minister of Agriculture, John MacGregor, put it in 1987, the move 'from 60–70 per cent self-sufficiency to over 80 per cent self-sufficiency in the things we grow', though good for the country and the consumer, obliged MAFF 'to look at the rural economy as a whole' to a much greater extent 'when the prime need was to get agricultural production up'.[178] This process brought MAFF closer to both the DTI, the sponsor of small business, and the DOE, the nearest entity in Whitehall to a 'green' department. The policy was fraught with controversy and brought the department face-to-face with highly articulate pressure groups of all kinds and not just the immensely powerful National Farmers' Union to which MAFF had been bound with hoops of steel for forty years. But the problems it brought to Mr MacGregor's desk would have been regarded as luxury items, the problems of success, by Tom Williams and John Strachey who presided over the system in the age of the ration card.

Department of Energy

> We do not produce coal at the Ministry of Power. People seem to think we do. Coal is not produced by statistics, or by Government departments, or even by speeches however eloquent they may be. Coal is produced by miners working underground.
> **Emanuel Shinwell, 1947**[179]

> The Department of Energy – our nearest equivalent to a Siberian power station.
> **Peter Jenkins, 1987**[180]

> There should be no commitment to a large programme of nuclear fission power until it has been demonstrated beyond reasonable doubt that a method exists to ensure the safe containment of long-lived, highly radioactive waste for the indefinite future.
> **Flowers Report, 1976**[181]

Founded: 1942 as Ministry of Fuel and Power, disappeared into the DTI in 1970 but re-emerged as the Department of Energy in 1974.

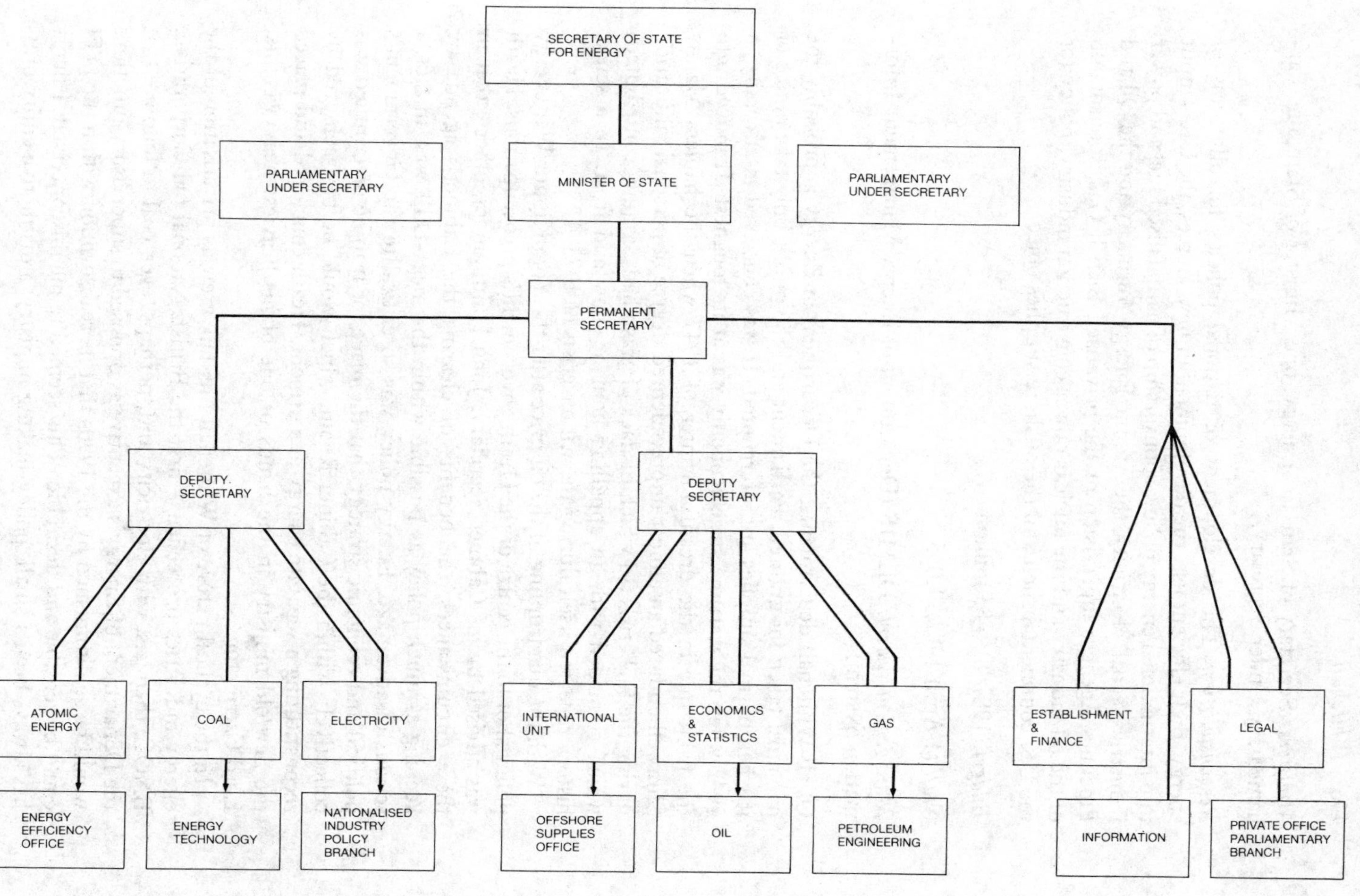

Fig. 10. Department of Energy

Ministers: Secretary of State for Energy, one Minister of State, one Parliamentary Under Secretary.

Responsibilities: The development of national policies for all forms of energy, their efficient use, the development of new sources; the UK's input into international energy policy; sponsorship of nationalised fuel and power industries – coal, electricity, the Atomic Energy Authority and the Oil and Pipelines Agency; supervision of the privatised British Gas; sponsorship of the oil industry and the nuclear power construction industry; policy for the UK continental shelf and the offshore supplies office.

Budget (1987–8): £85 million.

Staff (1 April 1987): 1,055.

Management system: DEMIS (Department of Energy Management Information System).

Of all Whitehall departments, the Department of Energy is probably the one most taken for granted. Parliament and the public only take notice of it when normal supplies are interrupted. It was conceived in adversity in 1942 when the wartime siege economy was at its toughest. It moved into the front line in the dreadful winter of 1947 when the hapless Manny Shinwell endured an almost unprecedented degree of personal vilification during the fuel crisis (to which his lack of grasp had certainly contributed) which coincided with an appalling bout of snow and frost. In a sense, history repeated itself during the winter crisis of 1973–4.

With the quadrupling of the oil price after the Yom Kippur War energy policy shot to the centre of the Heath government's preoccupations. Heath was advised by his Cabinet Secretary, John Hunt, among others, that in these circumstances, the benefits of clearing the Cabinet's agenda by keeping as much policy as possible within the mega-DTI was, in fact, a serious disadvantage. Energy policy was so critical to the Government's political and economic strategy that the place for it to be determined was collectively within the Cabinet Room, which would be best achieved by reconstituting a separate energy department. Heath concurred and placed the new/old ministry in the hands of one of his heaviest heavyweights, Lord Carrington.

In the cyclical nature of Whitehall life, talk grew as privatisation of the energy industries proceeded – first the British National Oil Corporation, BNOC, then gas, with electricity and, perhaps, even coal to follow – that the Department of Energy's executive as opposed to supervisory functions would be so diminished by the 1990s that its reabsorption within the DTI could be sensible and desirable. This seemed to me misconceived. Energy has always been a small, policy-making ministry, a distinctive entity of its own, with its eyes fixed, by necessity, on the long term. It is the lead department in formulating policy on fiendishly complicated procurement decisions, equalled only by those on Defence, involving, in the case of civil nuclear power, vast sums and considerable risks in terms of public opinion and, if Lord Flowers's warnings about the 'plutonium economy'[182] are to be believed, of safety as well. It has a considerable international side to its work through bodies such as the International Energy Authority. The crucial importance of energy in a modern, industrialised society will remain, however well the British economy performs. The history of energy policy since the 1940s – not least its nuclear side – requires a small, high-quality but separate ministry, however great the temptations of administrative tidiness.

Department of Transport

> At the Ministry of Transport, I was to become the twenty-sixth Minister in fifty years, an average tenure of office of only two years . . . it seemed I was to become a sort of political public relations officer dealing with seat-belts and speed limits . . . Most ministers of transport have made their reputation out of the nation's strange obsession with the motor car.
> **Sir Richard Marsh, 1978**[183]

> Transport is a great bore.
> **Anthony Crosland, before Christmas 1975**[184]

> Had forgotten Transport was so interesting.
> **Anthony Crosland, after Christmas 1975**[185]

Founded: 1919.

Ministers: Secretary of State for Transport, Minister of Public Transport, (Minister of State), Parliamentary Under Secretary for Roads and Traffic, Parliamentary Under Secretary for Aviation and Shipping.

Responsibilities: Development of policy for public transport and freight; shipping, marine and ports; road and vehicle safety and licensing; highways and traffic; aviation; international transport; deregulation and increased competition; transport and the disabled.

Budget (1987–8): £5,142 million.

Staff (1 April 1987): 14,725.

Management system: MAXIS (Management of Administrative Expenditure Information system).

Transport is another of Whitehall's cinderellas. Yet it is immensely newsworthy, highly political in its vulnerability to lurches in policy on changes of government, and, like the Home Office, prey to bolts from the blue,

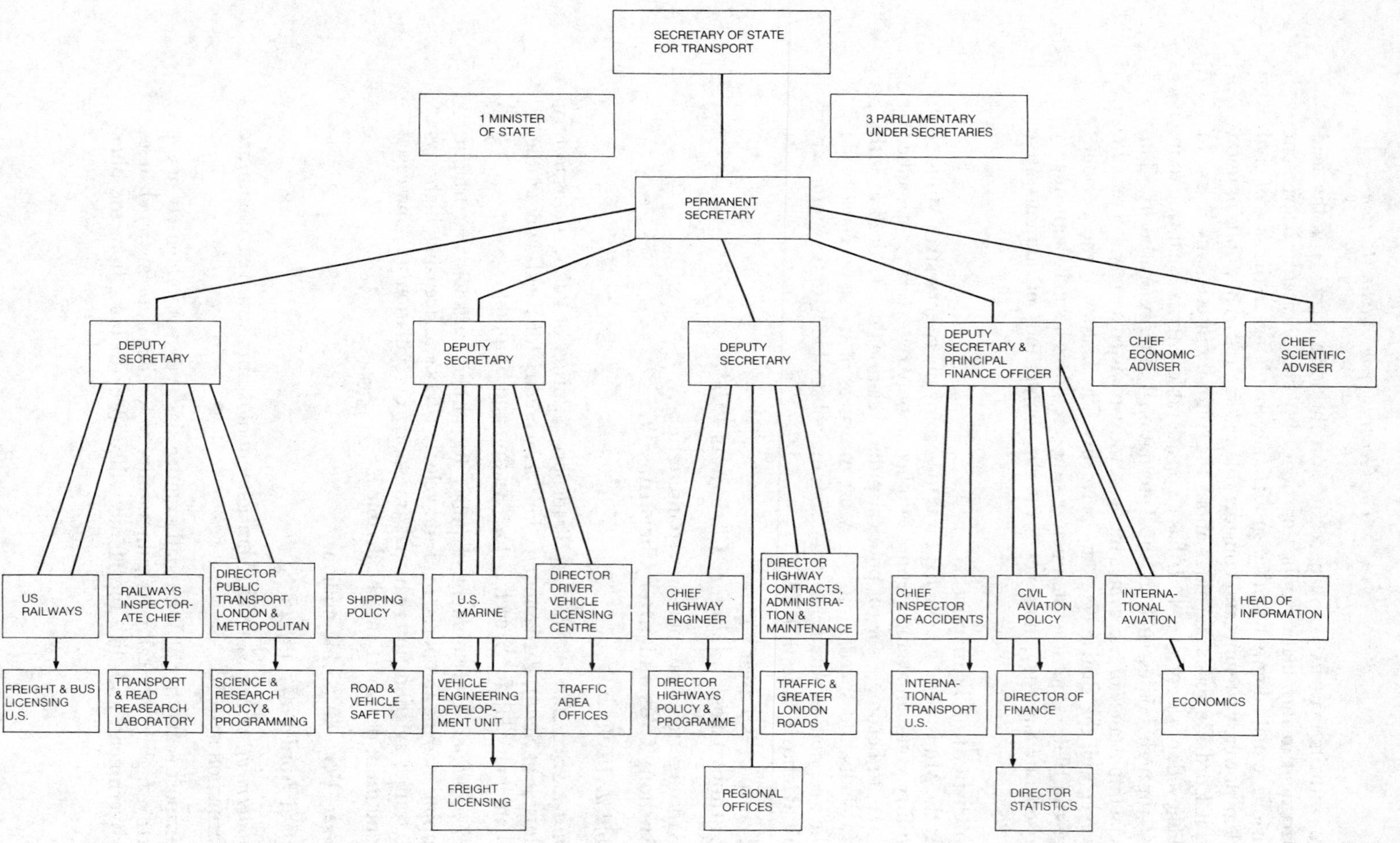

Fig. 11. Department of Transport

such as a Zeebrugge disaster or a King's Cross Underground tragedy, which project it to the top of the news bulletins and across all the front pages.

It has, too, a dramatic impact on everyday life. The British landscape changed when rural railways went and motorways came in the 1960s. For a romantic like me, my countrymen are divided into those who can remember steam and those who cannot, rather as for the generations older than me, the population is cleft by those who lived through the Second World War and those who did not. Judged by this standard, the politician who had one of the greater impacts on the changing face of postwar Britain is John Boyd-Carpenter, the Minister of Transport who steered the first motorway programme through the Cabinet and paved the way for the modernisation (or de-steaming) of the railways in the mid-fifties.[186]

Transport truly is a life-shaper for the citizen, as Tony Crosland pointed out by quoting in his 'Orange Paper' on Transport in 1976 Marcel Proust's observation that 'Since railways came into existence the necessity of not missing the train has taught us to take account of minutes whereas among the ancient Romans, who had not only a more cursory science of astronomy but had less hurried lives, the notion not of minutes but even of fixed hours barely existed.'[187] (Astronomers would contest this slur on ancient Roman skills, it should be said.) A systems failure in any of transport's main carriers can inconvenience voters by the thousand. A clogged M1 between London and the West Midlands is a daily reminder of the planners' persistent habit of underestimating demand despite the disappointing growth rate of the British economy. The under-use of the Humber Bridge is another daily reminder of how a by-election (Hull North shortly before the 1966 general election) can have a permanent monument in a piece of fixed capital investment.

But the politics of transport has always been greater than the product of the pork barrel. For the centre left it has acquired since the war something approaching theological status with an integrated transport policy as it Holy Grail. If passing a law could secure such a mystical article, Labour's Transport Act of 1947 would have purchased it. The Attlee government under that statute created a body designed to achieve integration – the British Transport Commission brigading all forms of transport, rail, road haulage, canals. Only air was excluded. In addition, area transport schemes were prepared to achieve integration on the ground.

The BTC was treated by the Conservatives as a tarnished talisman of socialism. On regaining power in the 1950s, they sold as much of British Road Services as the market was willing to take and in 1962 they disbanded the Commission altogether. On Labour's return to power, particularly after Mrs Castle's appointment to the Ministry, energetic efforts were made to extend once more the concept of public ownership of public transport with two new bodies, the National Freight Corporation, the National Bus Corporation – a process reversed yet again when the Conservatives returned to office after 1979 and Mr Norman Fowler and, later, Mr Nicholas Ridley deregulated the long-distance and local buses and disposed of state road haulage through a management buy-out.

Transport is one of the most highly politicised subjects. The department which embodies it in Whitehall is, by extension, probably the most vulnerable ministry in terms of swinging political fashions and the application of ideology to policy and administration. It is also a department where reputations can be made and a kind of immortality achieved. It is often said (rightly) that the political career of Leslie Hore-Belisha will be remembered for only one thing, belisha beacons, those orange balls that wink atop black and white poles by zebra crossings. Jim Callaghan once remarked (wrongly) that history would remember him as the junior transport minister in the late forties who forced through the use of life-saving 'cat's eyes' on British roads.[188]

Department of Employment

> A bed of nails.
>
> **Ray Gunter, frequently**[189]

> He [Wilson] asked me if I had thought over his Ministry of Labour suggestion which had increasingly grown on him. He could see me handling industrial correspondents as well as the lobby, getting my picture in the papers and on TV and generally helping the Government's image.
>
> **Barbara Castle, 1968**[190]

Founded: 1916.

Ministers: Secretary of State for Employment, One Minister of State, two Parliamentary Under Secretaries.

Responsibilities: Employment policy; promoting enterprise, growth and jobs; policy on industrial relations and trade-union and labour law; equal opportunities; training (through the agency of the Manpower Services Commission); the resolution of disputes (through the independent Advisory Conciliation and Arbitration Service); the collation and publication of key statistics on unemployment and the retail price index; payment and administration of unemployment benefit.

Budget (1987–8): £3,686 million.

Staff (1987–8): 36,600.

Management system: RIS (Resource Information System).

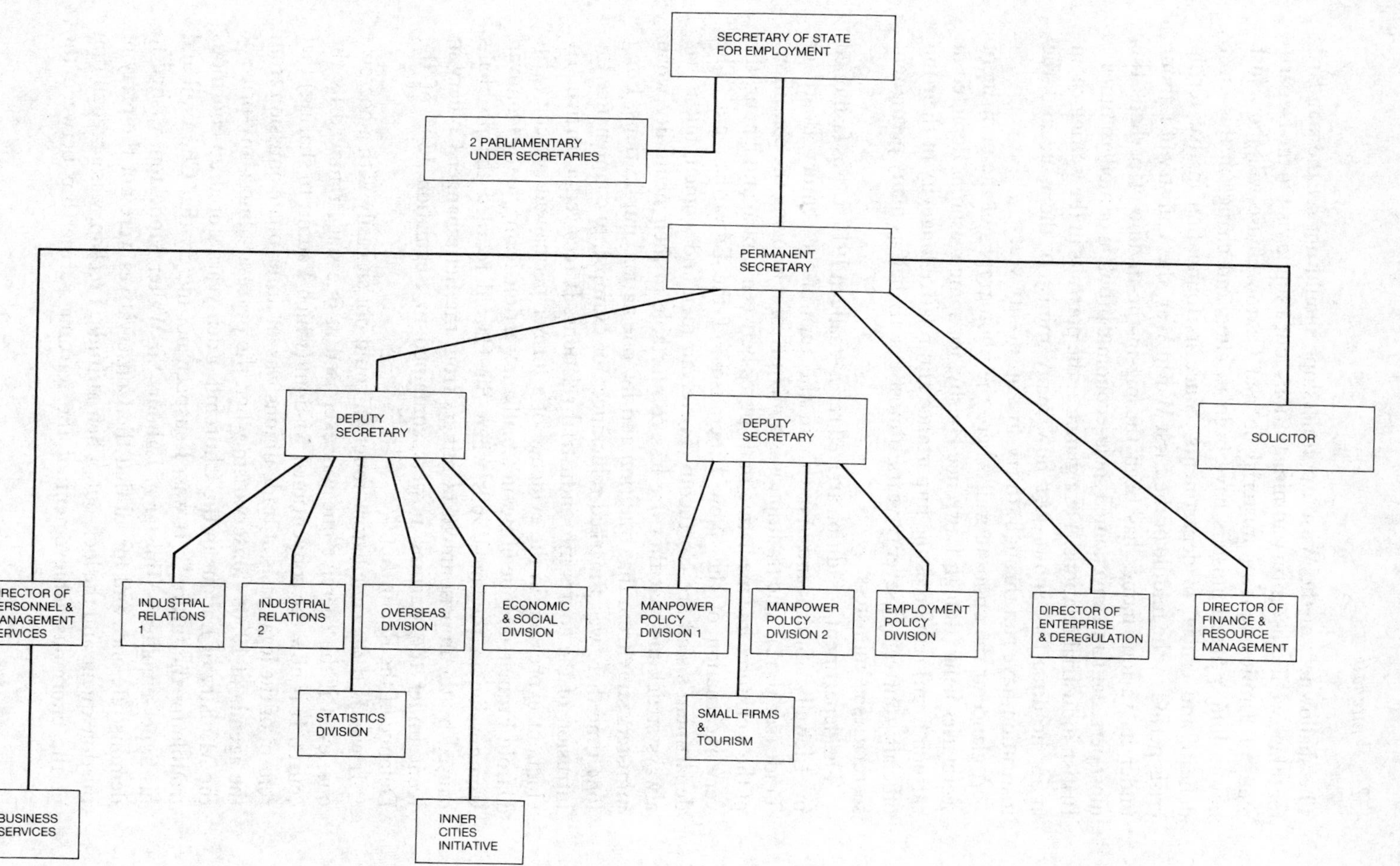

Fig. 12. Department of Employment

The shallowness of the Wilson premierships should not set the standard for other twentieth-century administrations, but a single visit to the Department of Employment's ministerial floor at Caxton House will show just how willing prime ministers have been to chop and change in this most delicate and crucial of departments. Since its foundation in that fertile crisis period in the middle of the First World War, the Ministry of Labour under its various names has been the pig-in-the-middle of perhaps the most persistent and envenomed socio-economic problem of modern times – British industrial relations. Yet a glance at the portraits in the waiting room at its headquarters shows just how many ministers the issue and the institution have run through: thirty-five in seventy years.

A glance at the opposite wall where the photographs of the permanent secretaries hang (though Lawrence Helsby, for some reason, is depicted in cartoon form) reinforces the importance and relative longevity of their top officials: fourteen in seventy years, almost exactly half as many permanent secretaries as ministers.

The department's tradition arrived ready-made in 1916. It was fashioned by Llewellyn-Smith and Askwith in the turn-of-the-century Board of Trade (see p. 52). The tradition was a mixture of improving the conditions of the workforce *and* mediating in disputes between capital and labour, the very incarnation of the 'New Liberalism' of the Edwardian era. The department's staff are Northcote–Trevelyan men and women, but it has always struck me that they are less comfortable in their neutrality when ministers stray from that tradition and its 'one nation' implications. For a long time there was a marked reluctance, for example, to countenance the intrusion of the courts into industrial relations. It received a particularly eloquent expression in the evidence of a former permanent secretary, Sir Harold Emmerson (one of Bevin's brilliant wartime team), to the Donovan Commission in the mid-1960s when Sir Harold recalled the problems caused by the imprisonment of miners from the Betteshanger Colliery in Kent under the wartime powers contained in Regulation 1305 of the Defence of the Realm Act.[191]

It was as if the conciliatory function could not sit easily with a coercive one, even if the coercive one was exercised at one stage removed by the courts. It is now the conventional wisdom (which I admit to sharing) that reform of the legal basis of trade unions was an unfortunate omission from the agenda of 1950s Conservatism when the peace-at-almost-any-price of the Ministry of Labour in the Churchill–Eden years stored up enormous trouble for the future.[192] It was, I suspect, not merely that Churchill and his hyper-emollient Minister of Labour, Sir Walter Monckton, wished to demonstrate once and for all that the Conservatives were not the party of the dole queue and the lock-out. Their attitude, I reckon, was a recognition of the enormous achievement of the wartime partnership between the

Labour movement and the state personified by the greatest-ever Minister of Labour, Ernest Bevin, and a reluctance to recognise that times and the trade union movement had changed.

The transition period, when the ministry's old tradition was discarded, cruelly brutalised by events (wild-cat strikes in particular), was the late 1960s when Wilson, Mrs Castle and Roy Jenkins attempted to drive through a recast policy for relations between labour and the State. The story of their ill-starred *In Place of Strife* White Paper has been fully and frequently told.[193] It was for different reasons, however, that the Heath government developed a plan to hive off the conciliation function from the rest of the department. It was part of his managerial revolution, a grand design which, in the Department of Employment's bailiwick, meant the creation of separate agencies not just for conciliation but for health and safety, manpower and training. It was a design inherited and implemented by the last Wilson government which has survived the 1980s and the rewriting not just of trade-union legislation but of the Department of Employment's job description as well – a surprising residue of bipartisanship given the shot and shell exchanged in a near-unceasing barrage since 1979 between the department's traditional clients, the Labour movement, and the ministers to whom the civil servants owe their primary loyalty. Bevin and the official breed who served him would not recognise either today's battleground or its rules of engagement.

An unforeseen consequence of great magnitude of the hiving-off exercise of the early 1970s was the crucial and growing importance of the Manpower Services Commission. So central is it as a Whitehall entity and as a big spender that it deserves equal treatment with the department to which it answers, though, like the Health and Safety Executive, it was conceived as, and in theory remains, a tripartite body involving government, unions and employers, the embodiment of the much vilified Heath-style corporatism.

Manpower Services (now The Training Commission) Commission

The Commission ... has set itself the long-term aim of developing a comprehensive manpower policy with a dual function: to enable the country's manpower to be developed and to contribute fully to economic well-being; and to ensure that there is available to each worker the opportunities and services he or she needs in order to lead a satisfying working life.

MSC Corporate Plan, 1975[194]

The MSC is not omnipotent. We cannot create jobs as such and change the economy ... The purpose of the Manpower Services Commission is to provide training and act as a part of the economic regeneration of the country.

David (now Lord) Young, 1984[195]

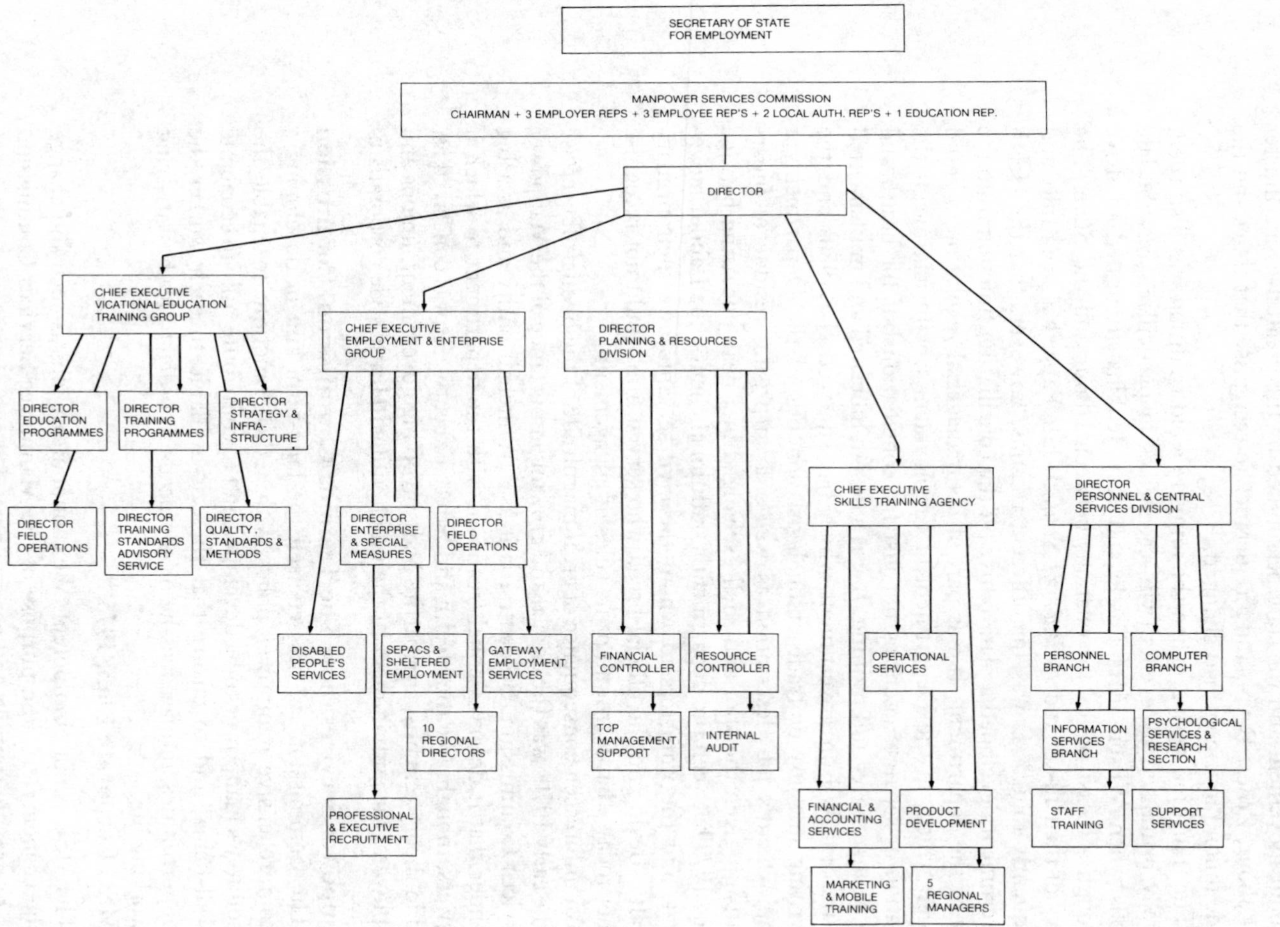
SECRETARY OF STATE FOR EMPLOYMENT
MANPOWER SERVICES COMMISSION
CHAIRMAN + 3 EMPLOYER REPS + 3 EMPLOYEE REP'S + 2 LOCAL AUTH. REP'S + 1 EDUCATION REP.
DIRECTOR
CHIEF EXECUTIVE VICATIONAL EDUCATION TRAINING GROUP
DIRECTOR EDUCATION PROGRAMMES
DIRECTOR TRAINING PROGRAMMES
DIRECTOR STRATEGY & INFRA-STRUCTURE
DIRECTOR FIELD OPERATIONS
DIRECTOR TRAINING STANDARDS ADVISORY SERVICE
DIRECTOR QUALITY, STANDARDS & METHODS
CHIEF EXECUTIVE EMPLOYMENT & ENTERPRISE GROUP
DIRECTOR ENTERPRISE & SPECIAL MEASURES
DIRECTOR FIELD OPERATIONS
DISABLED PEOPLE'S SERVICES
SEPACS & SHELTERED EMPLOYMENT
GATEWAY EMPLOYMENT SERVICES
10 REGIONAL DIRECTORS
PROFESSIONAL & EXECUTIVE RECRUITMENT
DIRECTOR PLANNING & RESOURCES DIVISION
FINANCIAL CONTROLLER
RESOURCE CONTROLLER
TCP MANAGEMENT SUPPORT
INTERNAL AUDIT
CHIEF EXECUTIVE SKILLS TRAINING AGENCY
OPERATIONAL SERVICES
FINANCIAL & ACCOUNTING SERVICES
PRODUCT DEVELOPMENT
MARKETING & MOBILE TRAINING
5 REGIONAL MANAGERS
DIRECTOR PERSONNEL & CENTRAL SERVICES DIVISION
PERSONNEL BRANCH
COMPUTER BRANCH
INFORMATION SERVICES BRANCH
PSYCHOLOGICAL SERVICES & RESEARCH SECTION
STAFF TRAINING
SUPPORT SERVICES

Fig. 13. Manpower Services Commission (renamed Training Commission)

Founded: 1974.

Ministers: Secretaries of State for Employment, Scotland and Wales.

Responsibilities: The development and management of public employment and training services.

Budget (1987–8): £3,300 million.

Staff (1 April 1986): 21,075.

Management system: COMIC (Corporate Management System).

It is one of the tragedies of contemporary Britain and contemporary Whitehall that an agency intended to enhance the skills of the British workforce should within five years of its conception have become, in effect, a super-ministry in its own right, the unacknowledged and unnamed department of unemployment, a far cry from the original concept of the MSC as a kind of holding company to look after the employment and training services of the old unified ministry.[196] As high unemployment become endemic to the British economy and not a passing epidemic, the MSC grew like a 'mushroom ministry', as the temporary wartime departments had been called.[197] In its way, it was the peacetime equivalent of the Ministry of Supply.

The mushrooming really began in 1978 with the first of the 'special programmes' to assist the unemployed and to remove them, temporarily at least, from the unemployment register. The MSC's budget doubled between 1976 and 1981.[198] But true take-off occurred under the fruitful partnerships of, first, Sir Richard O'Brien as Chairman and John Cassels as Director-General, and those of their successors David Young (the second stage of his dazzling rise to the top) and Geoffrey Holland. The aerodynamic element was the £1 billion programme, the Youth Training Scheme, designed not just to ease youth unemployment but to make up the training gap which had yawned for generations between Britain and her chief economic competitors. In effect, absorbing the 16–17-year-old age bracket *in toto* (or that part of it not already in work or higher education), the Thatcher government 'virtually nationalised Youth', in John Vincent's judgement, and showed themselves to be the greatest collectivists since Attlee.[199]

In 1987 the new Employment Secretary, Norman Fowler, attempted to control his departmental mushroom. He renamed it the Training Commission, removed its responsibilities for Job Centres, put them back inside the Department of Employment, rationalised a clutch of training schemes and announced that in transmuting to the new Training Commission the

MSC would lose half its staff. The wheel turned back half a circle from where it had been pre-1974.[200]

TERRITORIAL DEPARTMENTS

Home Office

> Even for unadventurous spirits the Home Office can never provide a rest cure. It is residuary legatee of every problem of internal government not specifically assigned to some other department, and many of these problems are politically sensitive, straddling the controversial borderline between liberty and order.
> **Lord Butler, 1971**[201]

> The climate ... of the Home Office is one of tropical storms that blow up with speed and violence out of a blue sky, dominate the political landscape for a short time, and then disappear as suddenly as they arrived. When they are on it is difficult to think of much else. When they are over it is difficult to recall what all the fuss was about.
> **Roy Jenkins, 1971**[202]

> The Home Office, the graveyard of free-thinking since the days of Lord Sidmouth, early in the nineteenth century, is stuffed with reactionaries ruthlessly pursuing their own reactionary policies, which is not so bad when reactionary governments are in power but less good otherwise.
> **Brian Sedgemore, 1977**[203]

> I like to feel that one or two members of the Home Office actually cut themselves shaving in the morning while thinking about some problem.
> **Sir Brian Cubbon, 1981**[204]

Founded: 1782.

Ministers: Home Secretary, three Ministers of State, one Parliamentary Under Secretary.

Responsibilities: Sustaining the rule of law, maintaining the quality of justice; prisons; police; probation; the running of magistrates' courts in England and Wales; fire services; civil defence; immigration and citizenship; criminal injuries compensation; the Metropolitan Police; dealings with the royal family; the care and maintenance of instruments for declaring war; official secrecy.

Budget (1987–8): £5,543 million.

Staff: 37,172.

Management system: APR (Annual Performance Review).

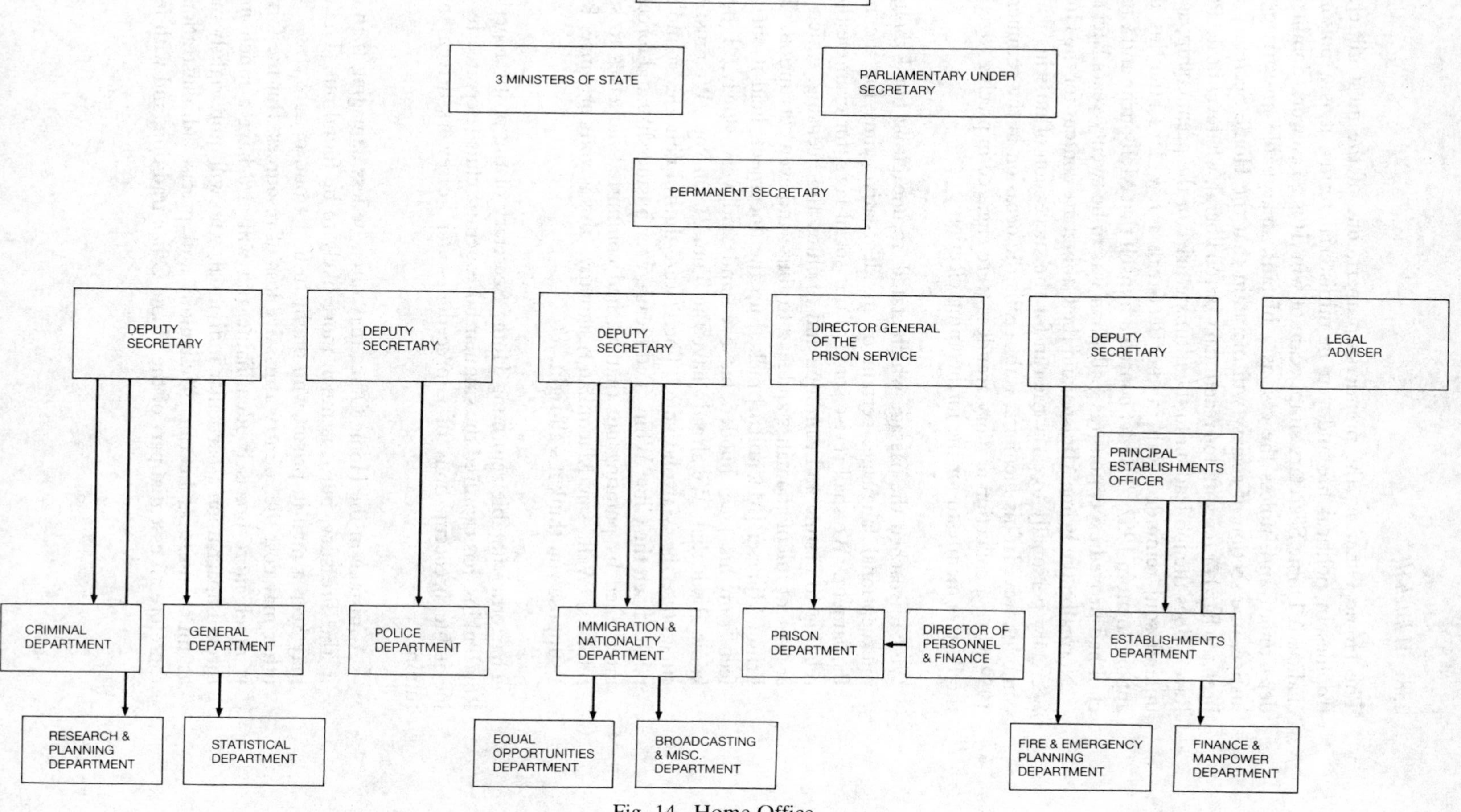

Fig. 14. Home Office

The Home Office is, the premiership apart, one of the most glittering trophies in political life and yet, in ministerial terms, it is a poisoned chalice. A Home Secretary simply cannot win. It is a casework-dominated department and, unless the case is a blatant, unarguable miscarriage of justice, one section of society will maintain that the Home Secretary has been too hard or too soft, too reactionary or too liberal, whatever he decides. Rarely does the job lead on to the ultimate prize of the premiership, as an unkind soul reminded Rab in the Beefsteak a few days after his disappointment in 1957.[205] Butler consoled himself that Melbourne and Churchill had proved exceptions (as Callaghan was to be twenty years later).

Normally, the Prime Minister and the Cabinet are content for the Home Secretary personally to carry the can for the succession of no-wins which come his way. In his memoirs, Rab recalls the occasion in the summer of 1959 when a collection of Tory grandees were engaged in piecing together the Party's manifesto for the forthcoming election:

> We had reached the passage which stated, in unexciting but I thought unexceptional language, certain of my legislative aims for the next Parliament. 'We shall revise some of our social laws, for example those relating to betting and gambling and to clubs and licensing, which are at present full of anomalies and lead to abuse and even corruption.' The Prime Minister [Macmillan] picked up the document, held it out two feet from his face, hooded his eyes and said very slowly, 'I don't know about that. We already have the Toby Belch vote. We must not antagonise the Malvolio vote.' There were dutiful chuckles round the table. Then the Chief Whip, Ted Heath, ever businesslike and forceful, intervened by pointing out that we had committed ourselves to such reforms. 'Well,' said Macmillan resignedly, 'this is your province, Rab. I suppose you think it's all right.'[206]

That other notable reforming Home Secretary of the postwar period, Roy Jenkins, has captured the singular bureaucratic climate created by the inevitable preoccupations of a precedent-laden, casework-driven institution:

> A mistake in the Home Office may often be less damaging than one in the Treasury, but it is much more likely to be found out. The one may keep a man in prison who ought to be let out, or *vice versa*. The other may cost the country a massive loss of resources. But the former is much more precisely identifiable and will also have a much more direct impact upon a particular individual, who will quite rightly make as much noise as he can. Meticulous and precise administration is therefore an essential part of the Home Office tradition, and with it, as

the reverse side of the same coin, tends to go a certain rigidity of outlook.[207]

The rigidity and institutional reaction of the Home Office can be exaggerated. If the conventional wisdom of the liberal left on this were to be believed it would be impossible to account for the occasional spurts of reform that have occurred under Churchill before the First World War, and under Chuter Ede, Butler and Jenkins after the Second. Jenkins himself has explained how this apparent paradox can be reconciled:

> In the Home Office it is more difficult for a Minister to make small changes, but perhaps easier for him to affect the general climate. Because of the great importance attributed to consistency he will find more resistance to granting a free pardon in a motoring case where the conviction looks to him odd, if the Department does not agree, then he will to the initiation of a new policy on race relations or the law relating to homosexuality.[208]

The tyranny of case-work and short-term crisis management can all too easily drive out the long-term in the everyday life of the Home Office. Leon Brittan managed to offend the hard and the soft elements in society during his ill-starred Home Secretaryship in the mid-1980s, but in attempting to solve this perpetual problem he excelled and his efforts have been recognised by knowledgeable outsiders.[209] Brittan, by this time on the backbenches as a consequence of the Westland affair, described his Home Office reform to me in the summer of 1987:

> It's true you can be having a quiet time and then something comes that is totally absorbing and highly emotionally charged and highly controversial and that's entirely right. And it's because I knew that's bound to happen ... that [the conclusion that I came to] was to have a very carefully structured and organised programme of reform ... which would be deeply embedded in the Home Office because you'd thought it through and discussed it, and indeed, even published it, and which would therefore, have a momentum of its own. So that if for a day [or] a week the Home Secretary personally was diverted to crisis management, his thrust and the momentum of his long-term, longer range work would continue because he'd made sure it was embedded in the system.[210]

A great deal of Home Office work is keeping-the-show-on-the-road management and administration of huge enterprises such as the Prison Service which accounts for three-quarters of its manpower. The system of justice, however, is beyond its remit and is overseen by the Lord Chancellor's Department in England and Wales and the Lord Advocate's Department in Scotland while the Government's law officers, the Attorney-General and the Solicitor-General, have their own office as part of the Law Courts in the Strand.

For all the strictures one tries to observe about stereotyping Whitehall, its departments, its tribes and its individuals there remains a distinctive Home Office type, a compound of dourness and hard work. The Home Office itself fosters it. In the glossy brochure distributed to mark its bicentenary in 1982, there was a section of departmental characters. Two extracts, I thought, captured the place. One was a delicious clerihew dealing with its granitic permanent secretary of the late forties and early fifties:

> Frank Aubrey Newsam
> Affected to look gruesome.
> This carried great weight
> With successive Secretaries of State.[211]

The other was a deputy secretary (unnamed) of recent vintage who was

> remembered for his excellent health (as well as the decrepitude of the carrier bags in which he transported files between office and home): so much so that on returning from a single day away with the 'flu he had many kindly enquiries in the corridor. A characteristic reply was reported as: 'Oh, quite recovered, thank you. I spent the day in bed. Disposed of twenty-two files and read five novels.'[212]

Scottish Office

Without Scotland the English would be sunk.
Lord Boothby on 'Scots at Westminster', 1957[213]

He [Churchill] used to look upon all our politics as 'drains'.
Lord Home recalling his days at the Scottish Office, 1985[214]

In the absence of convincing evidence of advantages to the contrary, the machinery of government should be designed to dispose of Scottish business in Scotland.
Royal Commission on Scottish Affairs, 1954[215]

Scotland ... [is] ... the biggest pressure group in Britain.
Michael Fry, 1987[216]

Founded: 1885.

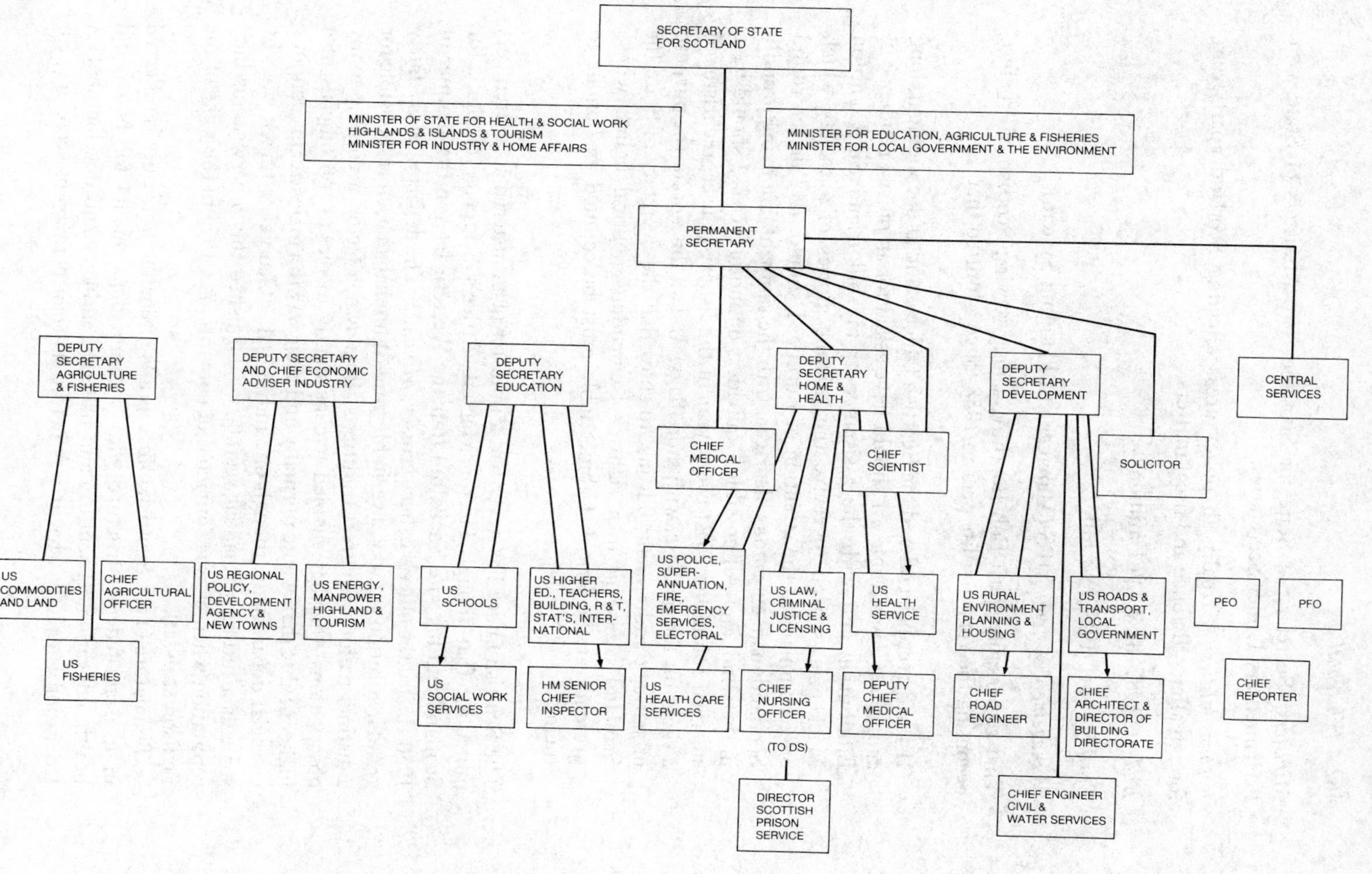

Fig. 15. Scottish Office

Ministers: Secretary of State for Scotland, two Ministers of State, two Parliamentary Under Secretaries.

Responsibilities: Virtually all policy areas affecting Scotland apart from foreign affairs, defence and fiscal matters.

Budget (1987–8): £7,961 million.

Staff (1 April 1987): 12,140.

Management system: MPS (Management Planning System).

That remarkable spirit Bob Boothby, a long-serving Scottish MP before becoming the very first life peer in 1958, once admitted that

> If I had ever been offered the Scottish Office – and at one moment, long ago, it was conceivable – I should have asked for an official residence in Edinburgh; and with the assistance of my old friend Sir Compton Mackenzie, striven to revive the pristine glories of a society which once commanded the attention of Europe. I should have driven round Scotland in an enormous black car, with the rampant lion flying proudly in the wind, and – if possible – outriders on motorcycles. I should have steamed round her coast every year in the fishery cruiser, rechristened a yacht for the purpose, with more flags. And all this not for the purpose of self-aggrandisement; but just to show that the Secretary of State for Scotland is, in his own right, a tremendous political figure, whose presence at the British Cabinet table must be counted an honour to them.[217]

The Scottish Office has never had a minister or ministerial accoutrements quite like that though Hector McNeil, Attlee's Secretary of State for Scotland and his wife Sheila did tour the Western Isles in the summer of 1950 aboard the office's fishery cruiser, *Minna*.[218] The department is a fairly grand institution anyway, a veritable mini-Whitehall in itself responsible for a distinct nation with great traditions all its own, a factor, according to my observations, that has enabled it consistently to recruit top officials of a higher calibre than would normally find their way to a mainstream economic or social department (though one individual – George Pottinger, seen by some as a future permanent secretary – tarnished this otherwise justified reputation when he was convicted of corruption in 1974 in the wake of the Poulson scandal).

The nature of the Scottish Office as a Whitehall in miniature is reflected in its semi-federal structure with separate departments for home and health, education, agriculture and fisheries, industry and development. A federation is exactly what it was before its then permanent secretary, Sir

Douglas Haddow, deliberately meshed the office more tightly together in the late 1960s and early 1970s.[219] By the 1980s the Scottish Office was being seen as a microcosm of the old Whitehall fast disappearing in London – interventionist in economic and social matters, a kind of Keynesian satrapy (along with the Welsh and the Northern Ireland offices) in an otherwise monetarist nation. This was an exaggerated and oversimplified view. But it is true that the capacity of the Scottish Office in general and the Scottish Development Agency in particular to co-ordinate effectively the work of a wide range of public and private bodies in the task of urban renewal was praised and envied by those such as Mr Michael Heseltine who craved a more hands-on strategy in England.

The compact nature of the Scottish Office has always brought both personal and administrative advantages denied to Civil Service colleagues in the Whitehall diaspora. As Sir Charles Cunningham, a Scottish Office veteran until summoned south in the 1950s to head the Home Office, put it:

> We were all working in the same building in St Andrew's House and we'd daily contacts of an informal kind. We would lunch together, we would have informal discussion about points of mutual interest and so on, both by formal weekly meetings, when the agenda included any topic of importance which was of current interest, and through informal contacts from day to day, we were all in the fortunate position of knowing what the others were up to, and up to a point, being able to contribute with a detached view about how agricultural policy, or educational policy, ought to develop – and what the impact might be on the work of our own department.[220]

The advantage of living on top of each other in what is now New St Andrew's House is somewhat dissipated by the presence in Dover House, the office's magnificent London outstation in Whitehall, of the Secretary of State and the Permanent Secretary for three or four days a week when Parliament is sitting. All this, however, seemed set to change in the late 1970s when substantial though still partial devolution (taxation powers were to remain with the Treasury) seemed about to happen with the prospect of a Scottish Assembly in Edinburgh. Had it happened, the Scottish Office would have been obliged to scramble out of its familiar chrysalis and emerge as a bureaucracy of a very different kind. It still might.

Devolution, despite the hours of ministerial and official time lavished on it in the late seventies, always had a Never-Never Land feel about it in stark contrast to the shrewd practicality which had characterised the Scottish Office since the wartime stewardship of Tom Johnston, probably the most effective voice Scotland has ever had in the scrabble for resources in Whitehall.[221] Michael Fry, the Scottish political economist, as Conservative as Johnston was Labour, had him firmly in mind when describing his country as Britain's greatest pressure group:

> Scotland has so organised itself as to get absolutely the best out of this system. We were, in a certain sense, lucky in having a minister in the Scottish Office in the 1940s, Tom Johnston, who realised exactly what was going on ... who saw that the welfare state was coming, who conceived of Scotland as an entity in its own right . . . He set up various administrative and lobbying arrangements at the Scottish Office . . . which have [got] Scotland consistently higher levels of public expenditure than are available for other parts of the United Kingdom.[222]

Michael Fry maintains that the 'pressure group' system remained intact in the late eighties even when the Scottish Secretary, Malcolm Rifkind, was engaged in making speeches about an end to the dependency culture.

I had a chance to assess this tartan factor while making *Adam Smith's Children* for BBC Radio 4's *Analysis* in the spring of 1988: I put the thesis to Bob Calderwood, Chief Executive of the overwhelmingly Labour Strathclyde Regional Council.

> 'There are always arguments about whether the Scottish Office is there to represent Scotland in the Cabinet or whether it's somebody to represent the Cabinet in Scotland.'
>
> 'What do you think?'
>
> 'I think it's an enormously valuable asset to Scotland and it would be a great pity if that link between Scottish local authorities and the Scottish Office were divorced. I was Town Clerk of Manchester before I came to Strathclyde and I had nothing like the relationship with the permanent secretaries [in Whitehall] that I have had with the permanent secretaries in the Scottish Office . . .'
>
> 'What you've just said reminds me [of the description of Scotland] as the greatest single pressure group in Britain . . .'
>
> 'Why shouldn't it be?'
>
> 'So, despite being Chief Executive of a very heavily Labour dominated regional council, you think that Conservative Malcolm Rifkind is Scotland's megaphone in the Cabinet Room?'
>
> 'Yes, and I think Malcolm Rifkind would see that role for himself as well.'[223]

Does he? 'Oh, there's an enormous amount in that pressure group argument,' said Mr Rifkind, 'and I'd be less than honest if I suggested otherwise. You're quite right, all Scottish Secretaries seek to promote the Scottish interest and that's part of their job . . .'[224] In real power and real bureaucratic terms, some things surpass both personality and party.

Welsh Office

> The analogy of Scotland has been advanced . . . I think, however, that it must be recognised that the two cases are not parallel. For Scotland has always had different systems of law and administration from those in force in England . . . Wales, on the other hand, since Henry VIII's Act of 1535, has been closely incorporated with England and there has not been, and is not now, any distinct law or administrative system calling for the attention of a separate minister.
> **Neville Chamberlain, 1938**[225]

> Harold Wilson greeted me cordially and invited me to become – in his own words – 'the Charter Secretary of State for Wales'.
> **James Griffiths recalling October 1964, 1969**[226]

> We will fly into Wales this time [sometime in the twenty-first century], up the estuary of the Dyfi, the Dovey, half-way along the western coast, and there, clustered among green water-meadows below the mountains, stands the national capital of Machynlleth. It is not a very big capital – the smallest in Europe, in fact, except possibly Reykjavik – and it looks, as it always did, like a small market town: but the Red Dragon flies everywhere above its rooftops, a cosmopolitan crowd swarms among its pubs and cafés, and sometimes a big black car with Corps Diplomatique plates weaves a cautious way through the market stalls of Stryd Marchnad.
> **Jan Morris, 1984**[227]

Founded: 1964.

Ministers: Secretary of State for Wales, one Minister of State, one Parliamentary Under Secretary.

Responsibilities: Policy and expenditure for Wales on industry, social services, agriculture and fisheries, roads and transport, health, education, housing, tourism, local government, water, sewerage, land use, the Welsh language and culture, environmental protection and countryside, urban programme, new towns, historic buildings and ancient monuments.

Budget (1987–8): £3,192 million.

Staff (1 April 1987): 2,280.

Management system: Cost Centre Coding Structure.

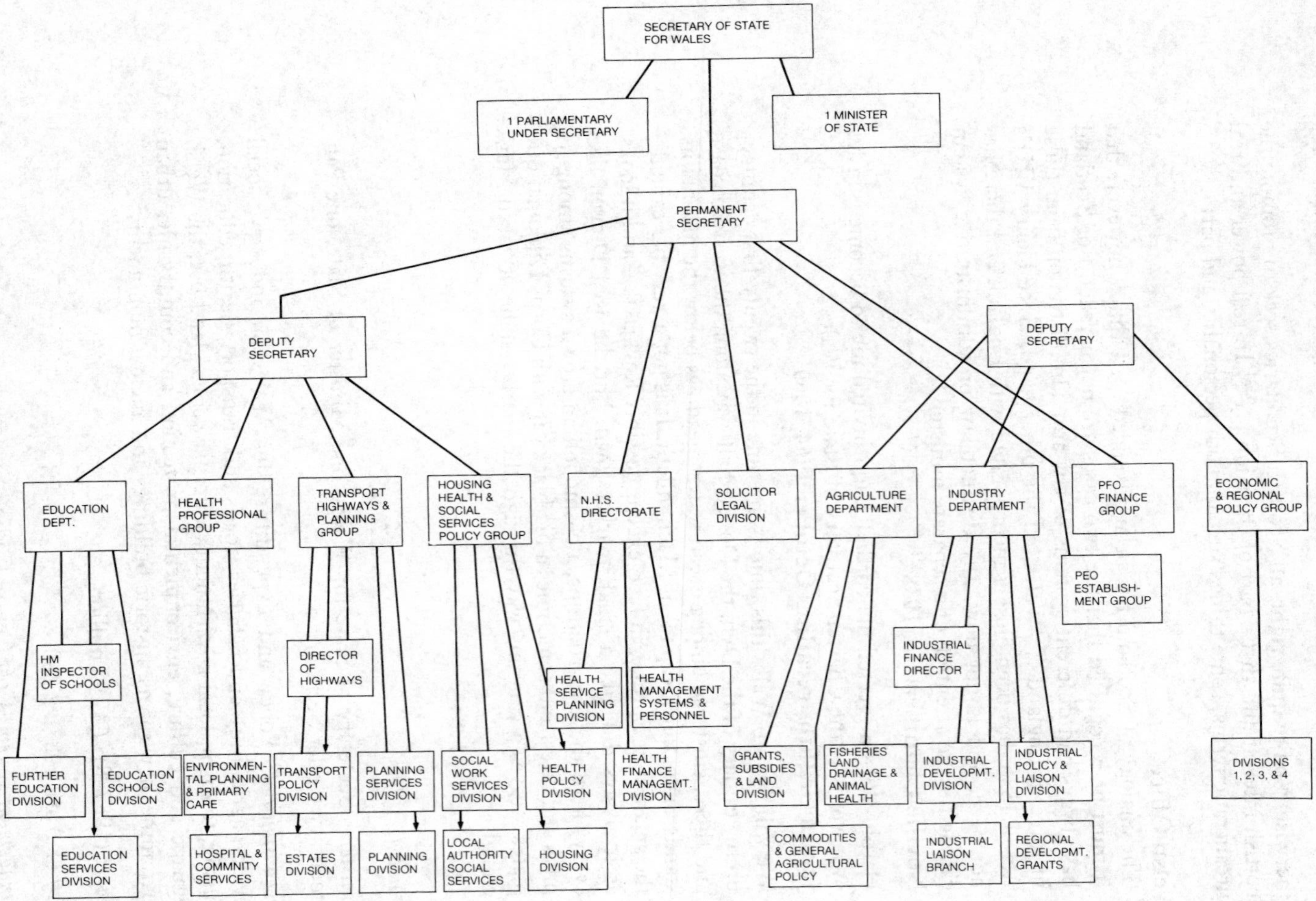

Fig. 16. Welsh Office

Whitehall has always been reluctant to recognise the claims of the Welsh. In Norman times they were crushed by force; for the first half of the twentieth century they were smothered in the cotton wool of a benign, condescending phraseology of the kind Neville Chamberlain used to rebut the suggestion from the Welsh Parliamentary Labour Party that there should be a Secretary of State for Wales. Not that the Labour Party was united on this issue any more than it was on the question of Welsh devolution forty years later. Their greatest ever wordsmith, Aneurin Bevan, was never really convinced, as Jim Griffiths (who was) recalled:

> Nye's doubts about the wisdom of the creation of a Welsh Office went beyond considerations of administration. He has related how he came to realise that if he was to achieve his objectives, and his burning desire to create a Socialist society, it was imperative to reach out from the valley, and beyond the county, to the centre where the levers of power were operated. He was impatient of nationalisms which divided peoples and enslaved nations within their narrow geographical and spiritual frontiers. He feared that devolution of authority would divorce Welsh political activity from the main stream of British politics, as he felt was already happening in Scotland.[228]

Progress towards a Welsh Office with its own minister was painfully slow. The Attlee government established in 1948 an appointed body of the Welsh good and great – the Council for Wales and Monmouthshire. Churchill in 1951 designated the Home Secretary, David Maxwell-Fyfe, as Minister for Welsh Affairs (he became known as 'Dai Bananas' in the less deferential parts of the Principality presumably because of the presence of Fyfe's bananas in the greengrocers').[229] Gaitskell was persuaded to place a pledge to create a Secretary of State for Wales in Labour's manifesto for the 1959 general election. Wilson repeated it in 1964 and, on the Saturday after the poll, sent for Griffiths and made him ministerial chief of a new Welsh Office. The idea had been canvassed that Griffiths should sit as a kind of pooh-bah-cum-watchdog with a ministry of his own but overseeing the Welsh elements of other departments' work. He was against that idea as was his old permanent secretary from National Insurance days, Sir Tom Phillips, who told him: 'You must be, of course, a watchdog for Wales as a whole, but in order to do this effectively you ought to have a department of your own with a competent Civil Service staff.'[230]

Whitehall was trawled for the competent and the Welsh; Sir Goronwy Daniel was brought over from the Ministry of Fuel and Power to be permanent secretary, Ken Pritchard came from the Admiralty to be Griffiths's private secretary and Lloyd Thomas transferred from the Home Office where he had worked on the Welsh affairs side of the department.

Like the Scottish Office, the Welsh Office was split between Cardiff and Whitehall. The Welsh lobby had, at last, prevailed. The office was in business.

It was a tiny entity to start with, a mini-ministry of just over two hundred officials. It has expanded tenfold in just over twenty years as more and more responsibilities have been transferred from Whitehall to add to its original core of roads, housing, planning, water, tourism and national parks and ancient monuments. Health and welfare followed in 1969, primary and secondary education in 1970, child care the year after, substantial industrial powers in 1975 followed by higher education, agriculture and manpower policy in 1978.[231]

Yet the Welsh Office still has to fight harder for its place in the central government sun than any other ministry. It is newer and smaller than the Scottish Office, has fewer MPs in Parliament to lobby the Welsh issues and, like the Scottish Office, has to spread its fire, like buckshot, where one of eight or nine functional equivalents in Whitehall can unloose a single bullet. All too often it appears to be treated as marginal in political and administrative terms (unjustifiably, in my view). It was said (wrongly, I'm sure) that when Mrs Thatcher appointed Peter Walker Secretary of State in 1983 she thought his Worcester constituency *was* in Wales. An English Secretary of State may have been a far cry from Griffiths's limited vision of the 1950s and 1960s and a world away from Jan Morris's twenty-first century dream, but matters are never static and the Welsh have the admirable trait of thinking in centuries. As David Lloyd George, Wales's greatest gift to British politics and administration, once put it:

> Two thousand years ago the great Empire of Rome came with its battalions and conquered that part of Caernarvonshire in which my constituency is situated. They built walls and fortifications as the tokens of their conquest and they proscribed the use of the Cymric tongue. The other day I was glancing at the ruins of those walls. Underneath I noted the children at play, and I could hear them speaking, with undiminished force and vigour, the proscribed language of the conquered nation. Close by there was a school, where the language of the Roman conquerors was being taught, but taught as a *dead* language.[232]

Wales and the Welsh Office will survive an English Secretary of State.

Northern Ireland Office

I refuse to prejudge the past.

Mr William Whitelaw arriving in Belfast as the first Secretary of State for Northern Ireland, 1972[233]

> Certainly in the early part of . . . 'the troubles', successive Cabinets paid a great deal of attention to Northern Ireland. But I think it then got into the 'too difficult' category. What happens in the British Cabinet system of government is that people will try over a period of time to deal with a particular issue. Then it gets too difficult. You're not going to have a solution. So they put it, to use an old Irish phrase, 'on the long finger' . . .
> **Sir Frank Cooper, 1985**[234]

Founded: 1972.

Ministers: Secretary of State for Northern Ireland, one Minister of State, four Parliamentary Under Secretaries.

Responsibilities: Law and order, security policy, constitutional developments, liaison with the Republic of Ireland under the terms of the 1985 Hillsborough Agreement and for a wide range of economic, industrial and social policies through the agency of the separate Northern Ireland Civil Service.

Budget (1987–8): 4,310 million.

Staff (1 April 1987): 175 (plus 26,565 for the Northern Ireland Civil Service).

Management system: MIS (Management Information System).

As with Scotland in 1885 and Wales in 1964, the Secretary of State came first and the department to support him came second. The office of the Secretary of State for Northern Ireland which, as an NIO official put it, 'one could say . . . is one that no one, either in Northern Ireland or Westminster, ever wanted',[235] was created because in 1972 the Heath government judged the public order position in the six counties to be so parlous that only the imposition of direct rule from London offered a way forward. Law and order is what brought the Northern Ireland Office into life. Security policy has remained its core purpose ever since. Its prototypical staff, reflecting this, were drawn from the Home Office, the Ministry of Defence and the Foreign and Commonwealth Office, with – unacknowledged, naturally – an important input from both secret services, MI5 and MI6.

Yet more and more the NIO has come to resemble the Scottish Office as Westminster politicians took over the functions formerly exercised by politicians from the disbanded provincial parliament at Stormont. In the existing Northern Ireland Civil Service they had a tried and tested machine for this and the transition proved to be remarkably hitch-free. Roy Mason,

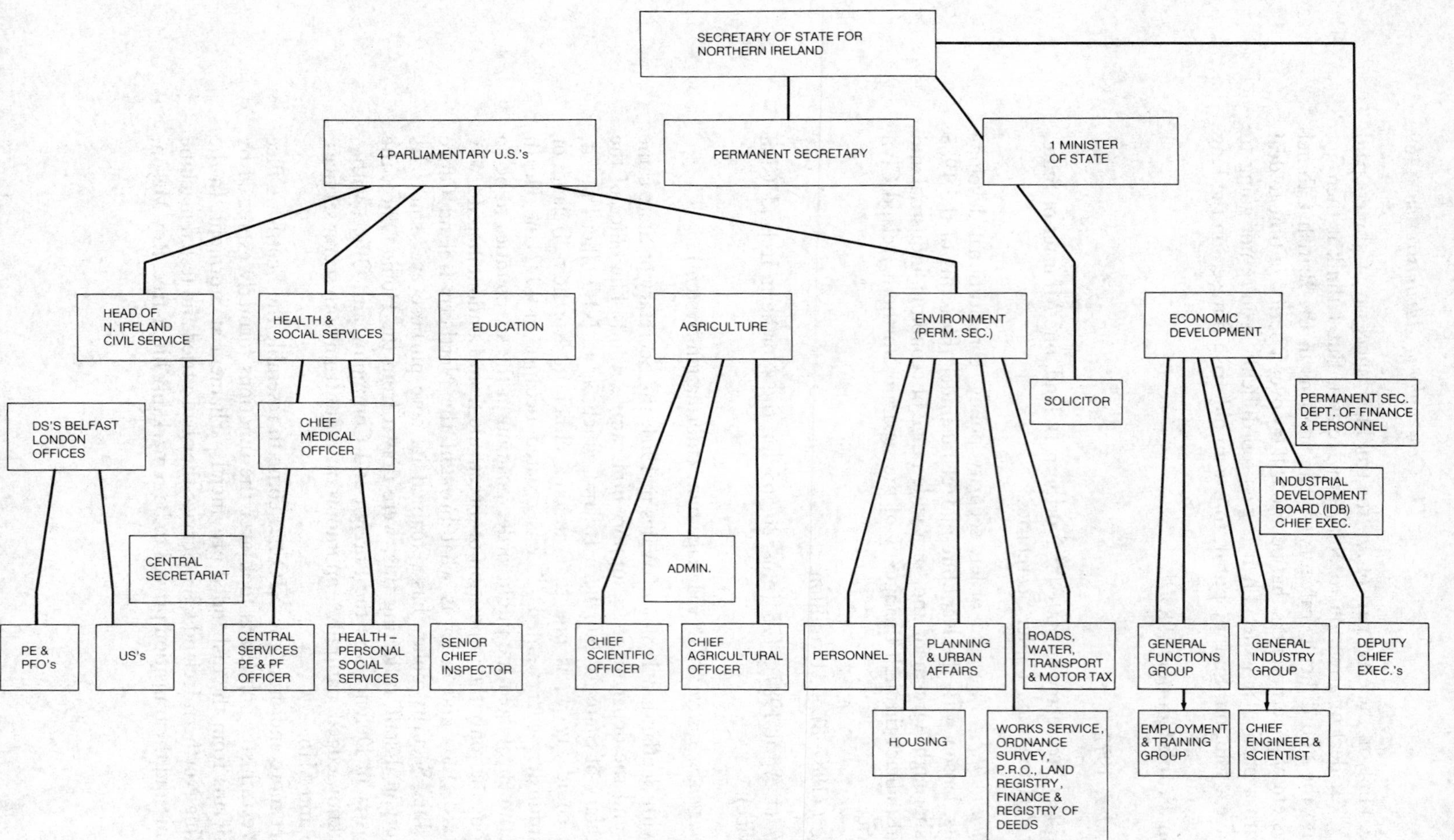

Fig. 17. Northern Ireland Office

Secretary of State 1976–9, was by the late 1970s likening himself to a mini-prime minister presiding over a team of colleagues.[236]

The NIO, however, has always retained a deliberately temporary air. As P. N. Bell put it from his insider's perspective, an 'important constant is that the violence and political uncertainty accompanying the institutions of Direct Rule has obliged successive secretaries of state to give priority to stemming violence and to political developments, with administrative problems to the rear, a ranking of priorities reinforced by the original belief that Direct Rule would not last long'.[237] At the time of writing, it has lasted over 16 years and the NIO has seen a succession of permanent secretaries who returned to play significant roles in the Whitehall constellation as a whole (Cooper, Cubbon and Stowe).

The arrival of mainland officials and mainland methods in Stormont Castle after 1972 had a beneficial impact on the work of the Northern Ireland Civil Service, as its former Head, Dr John Oliver, acknowledged:

> Direct Rule has given an enormous impetus to inter-departmental work as the British Ministers and officials understandably seek to acquaint themselves not only with the problems of departments but with the problems that cut across boundaries and in particular those that may affect security ... The British officials seem to have a much more highly developed sence of teamwork and cohesion than we have ...[238]

That teamwork, according to the guardians of public spending in the Treasury, makes the NIO second only to the Ministry of Defence when it comes to successfully raiding the public till. Crisis and emergency creates operators. And, in departmental terms, crisis comes nowhere more often or more seriously than in Stormont Castle.

SECRET DEPARTMENTS

> God even loves secret policemen.
> **Sir William Rees-Mogg, 1977**[239]

> He [Roger Hesketh] treated journalists' efforts to pump him for his story with contempt; he knew that sound secret services remain secret.
> **M. R. D. Foot, 1987**[240]

Successive prime ministers have agreed with Roger Hesketh. Mrs Thatcher was entirely consistent with all her predecessors when she maintained throughout the *Spycatcher* affair that members and former members of the security and intelligence services must never divulge their secrets 'because if they did there would soon be no secrets or intelligence services'.[241]

Despite the behaviour of Peter Wright, that policy of secrecy has succeeded to the extent whereby, in my judgment, it is not possible to offer routine portraits of the clandestine agencies. A general picture can be offered, however, of the kind I essayed in *The Independent* in December 1986 with the help of its graphic artist, Donald Hounam.[242]

Security and intelligence is not an activity, either, where manpower and budgets are easy to estimate unless one is privy to the accounts and ledgers of the Cabinet Office's security and intelligence secretariat which manages the secret vote on behalf of the Cabinet Secretary. In very round terms, the Government Communications Headquarters probably employs some 10,000 staff at Cheltenham and its outstations across the United Kingdom and around the world. MI5, the Security Service, probably employs about 1,500, and MI6, the Secret Intelligence Service, roughly the same. Each has its sponsoring minister and department (GCHQ and MI6 come under the Foreign Secretary and Foreign Office; MI5 answers to the Home Secretary and the Home Office). But their budgets bear little relationship to these lines of accountability. The secret vote is dispensed by the Cabinet Office, but the Ministry of Defence pays for the bulk of GCHQ's very advanced capital equipment for signals and electronic intelligence, which is where the big money goes. Budget decisions are made by an inner group of ministers on the basis of advice from the Permanent Secretaries Committee on Intelligence and Security.

The intelligence product, too, bears little relationship to the departmental chains. Its pooling and assessment are chiefly in the hands of the Cabinet Office, its Joint Intelligence Committee and the Assessments Staff which services it through a network of area-based current intelligence groups. The final product is presented to selected ministers in the form of a weekly 'Red Book'. A vital, in fact an overwhelmingly important input is the pooled produt of the very special intelligence relationship which has existed since the late 1940s between the United Kingdom, the United States, Canada, Australia and New Zealand. (New Zealand's input ceased after the Lange government went non-nuclear.)

Bearing that in mind, it is possible to piece together the likely order of intelligence priorities for Britain in the 1980s. They read like this:

Constant priorities

* East–West Cold War

Strategic capability, both political and military, of the Soviet Union and her allies in the Warsaw Pact.

The political and military intentions of the Soviet Union and allies (this became Whitehall's most urgent priority when *glasnost* broke out in Moscow.

New developments in their weaponry, offensive and defensive.

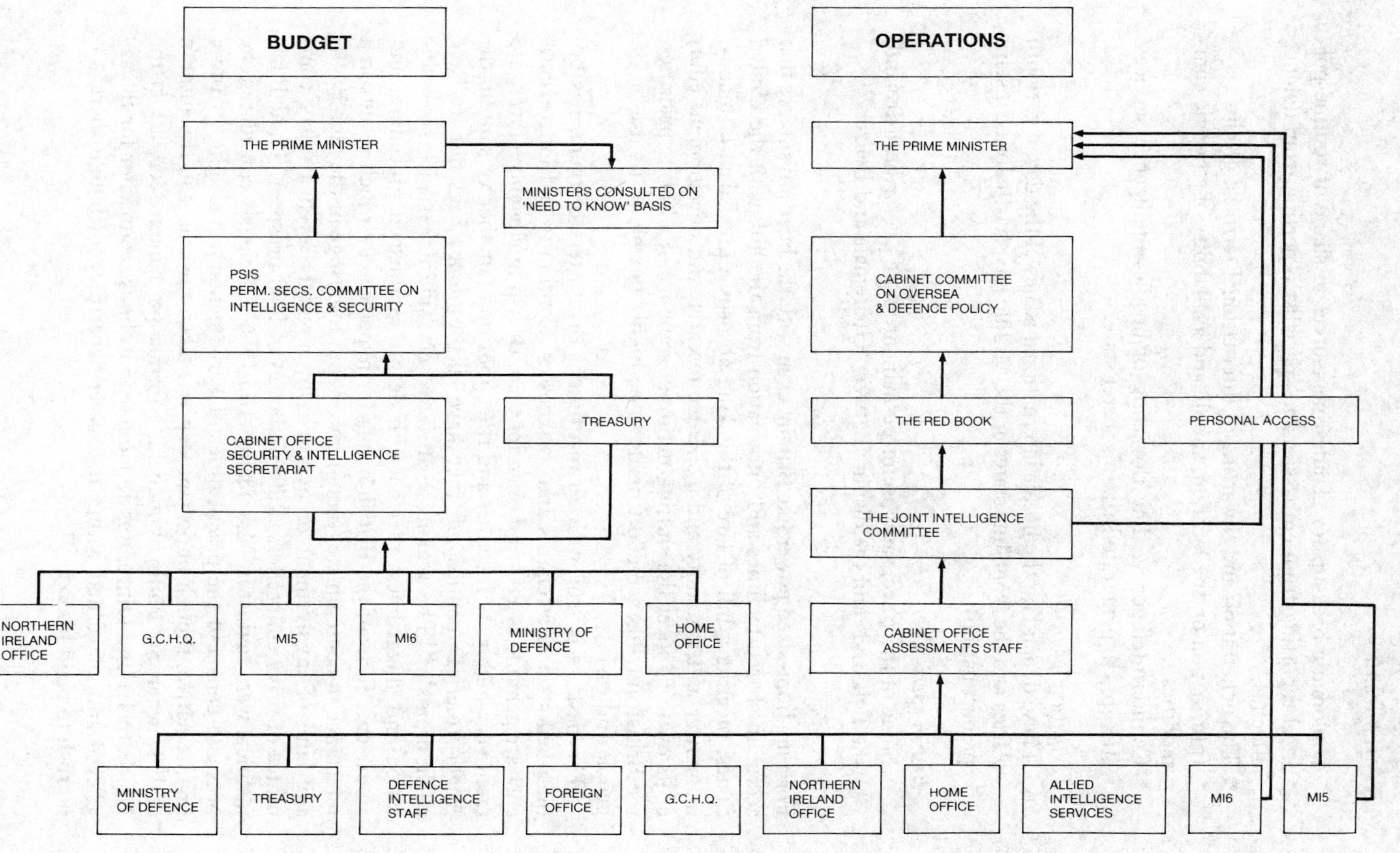

BUDGET
THE PRIME MINISTER
MINISTERS CONSULTED ON 'NEED TO KNOW' BASIS
PSIS
PERM. SECS. COMMITTEE ON INTELLIGENCE & SECURITY
CABINET OFFICE SECURITY & INTELLIGENCE SECRETARIAT
TREASURY
NORTHERN IRELAND OFFICE
G.C.H.Q.
MI5
MI6
MINISTRY OF DEFENCE
HOME OFFICE
OPERATIONS
THE PRIME MINISTER
CABINET COMMITTEE ON OVERSEA & DEFENCE POLICY
THE RED BOOK
PERSONAL ACCESS
THE JOINT INTELLIGENCE COMMITTEE
CABINET OFFICE ASSESSMENTS STAFF
MINISTRY OF DEFENCE
TREASURY
DEFENCE INTELLIGENCE STAFF
FOREIGN OFFICE
G.C.H.Q.
NORTHERN IRELAND OFFICE
HOME OFFICE
ALLIED INTELLIGENCE SERVICES
MI6
MI5

Fig. 18. The Whitehall Intelligence System

* Diplomatic back-up for clandestine sources in shape of routine political reporting from embassies and specialist reporting from defence attachés.
* The penetration and thwarting of international terrorist groups.
* Information on the location, supply and availability of strategic commodities.
* Counterintelligence. The thwarting of hostile intelligence services' attempts to penetrate Britain's secret state.

Temporary priorities

These depend on the hotter international issues of the day, e.g. South Africa and the front-line states or the Middle East (virtually a constant preoccupation).

British specialities

Some of these are, sadly, semi-permanent too, e.g. Northern Ireland, the Falklands and the dispute between Guatemala and Belize.[243]

For a medium-sized power like Britain, even with the huge advantages that accrue in shared facilities and information from the link with the United States, meeting a bill of fare of this kind absorbs a great deal of money, manpower and ingenuity and a sizeable research and development effort of its own. To meet the shifting nature of some if not all of its priorities, the British intelligence effort needs to be highly flexible in its use of kit, people and cash.

The past, as is true with all institutions or clusters of them, has bequeathed a set of strengths and weaknesses. Continuity and long experience are genuine assets. And, man for man, British intelligence officers are rated very highly by the allies and the opposition (another version, in the Anglo-American context, of 'they have all the money bags but we have all the brains').[244] The weaknesses are the reverse side of that coin – the ossification and sluggishness that go with deeply established procedure, and an extreme form of the British mania for hypersecrecy which results in a reluctance to contemplate (though this began to change in the mid-1980s) any kind of involvement or oversight by anybody, even a select committee of privy counsellors. Reform, however, is in prospect. Though her instincts were against it, Mrs Thatcher in 1986–7 seriously considered the pros and cons and the practicalities of Parliamentary oversight.[245] And a first, tentative, though important step was taken towards it in the autumn of 1987 when Sir Philip Woodfield, a former permanent secretary at the Northern Ireland Office, was appointed an in-house counsellor for the aggrieved and concerned within the secret departments (though there was no rush to bend his ear).[246]

MONEY-RAISING DEPARTMENTS

Board of Inland Revenue

Idolatrous adoration.
W. E. Gladstone on his attitude towards the Inland Revenue, 1860s[247]

As I gained experience I found that members of the Tax Service regarded themselves as belonging to an elite which had no equal among the other clerical grades of the Civil Service.
James Callaghan on the 1930s, 1987[248]

Founded: 1849.

Minister: Chancellor of the Exchequer (though no ministerial control over individual cases).

Responsibilities: The collection and management of taxes levied directly on income or capital; the collection of national insurance contributions; advice to the Treasury on proposals for changes in direct taxation or stamp duty.

Budget (1987–8): £1,242 million.

Staff (1 April 1987): 68,250.

Management system: SMS (Senior Management System).

Whitehall's money-raisers, the Inland Revenue and Customs and Excise, make everything else possible. Without their labours no central government activity would happen. Yet nobody since Gladstone has had a good word to say for them and even he did not care for Customs.[249] One might expect the taxpaying public to whinge but not Treasury ministers. Even the affable Joel Barnett puts the boot in. Recalling his service at the fiscal colours between 1974 and 1979, he wrote:

> I had a long running battle with the Inland Revenue over the whole of my period in office about the sheer length of their briefs. On the smallest of issues, I would receive a ten- or twelve-page brief. When I was working on my boxes at night, and opened a folder to see an Inland Revenue brief, my heart sank. I like to think that my constant complaints eventually had some effect, but I am dubious.[250]

Even in the best-informed accounts of Whitehall life, such as Young and Sloman's portrait of the Treasury, the money-raisers exist in a rather sad half-life. 'We were let into a [pre-Budget] meeting', they wrote:

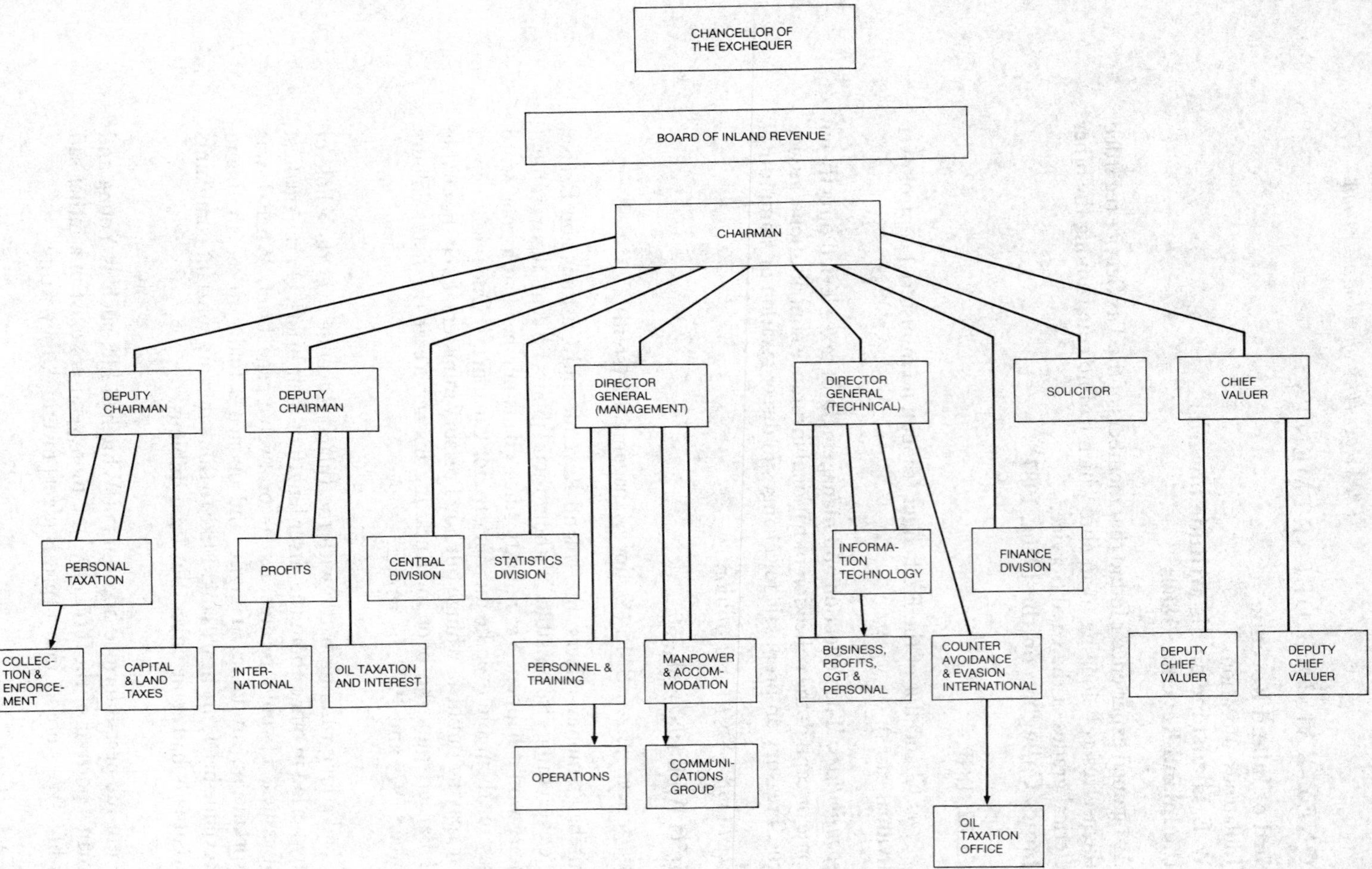

Fig. 19. Board of Inland Revenue

> A delegation of economists from the Inland Revenue and Customs and Excise trooped in to meet their Treasury counterparts, in another of those unadorned committee rooms, essentially to see if they could agree. What would 2p on beer duty or 5p off the standard rate (these are notional examples) actually mean? The meeting was halfway between a seminar and a seance. Government economists have to cultivate this weird mixture of extreme meticulousness and a talent for blind stabs in the dark, assisted by well-remembered ghosts from the past. Half the time we were there was spent discussing beer, and those present seemed, rather charmingly, to have little more idea than anyone else why beer consumption had gone down, and what this should mean for the beer tax.[251]

Even the inmates talk themselves down. The young administration trainee who helped prepare the Revenue's entry in the first 'alternative' First Division Association guide to Civil Service careers wrote: 'This is a genteel and academic department slightly segregated from the rest of Whitehall mainly by geography.'[252]

This remoteness from the mainstream is, in a way, Whitehall's equivalent of the contempt for production identified by Sidney Pollard. It is as if the hewers of wood and drawers of water who keep the rest supplied were a sort of necessary outsider. And yet the remote antecedents of the men and women of the money-raising departments have been crucial to the state since those mendicant pre-Conquest kings went on their grasping travels. As a recognisable entity they go back to 1694 when the Board of Commissioners of Stamps was founded to collect stamp duty. The modern Board was created in 1849 with the merger of the Board of Stamps and the Board of Excise (though Excise split off to join Customs in 1909).

And unlike those notional or phantom 'boards' (Trade, Local Government and Education and the rest) which floated from the Privy Council in the eighteenth and nineteenth centuries, the Board of Inland Revenue is a real one, consisting entirely of civil servants known as 'Commissioners' with the very real purpose of keeping ministers' sticky fingers off the tax returns of the citizenry. Or, as the Revenue itself truly genteely puts it,

> The Board has a distinct constitutional existence of its own. This is because its members, unlike most other civil servants, hold statutory appointments made by the Crown ... The Board is, in fact, specifically and directly entrusted by law with the 'care and management' of the Inland Revenue taxes and is given the powers needed for that purpose – for instance the power to prescribe the form of tax returns. The advantage of this system is that Ministers are spared the burden of responsibility for the detailed administration of tax law, and at the same time the

> administration is kept free from any possibility of political intervention in particular cases.[253]

The Revenue with its national network of offices and huge staff (it is Whitehall's third largest department, after Defence and the DHSS) is a huge enterprise to manage. In the 1980s it pioneered the extension of information technology in Whitehall on the grand scale with the £70 million computerisation of the Pay-As-You-Earn system with more than 20,000 desk-top terminals for the department's tax office network. Gladstone, ever the apostle of efficient administration, would have adored that.

Board of Customs and Excise

> It was a distinguished member of the French Civil Service who remarked to me enthusiastically, at an early stage in our own planning, that we should find VAT an intellectually interesting tax.
> **Dorothy Johnstone, 1975**[254]

> We positively boosted manpower to track down abuse of the welfare system; yet at the same time we insisted on economies on the policing of VAT and tax evasion. To which the honest answer was that there was widespread public concern about abuse of social welfare; whereas there was not the same belief in generalised abuse of the tax system.
> **Jock Bruce-Gardyne,**
> **Economic Secretary to the Treasury, 1981–3, 1986**[255]

Founded: 1671.

Minister: Chancellor of the Exchequer (in same hands-off fashion as with the Revenue).

Responsibilities: The collection and administration of customs and excise duties and value added tax; enforcement of a range of prohibitions on the importation of certain goods; the collection of customs and agricultural levies for the EEC; the compilation of overseas trade statistics.

Budget (1987–8): £445 million.

Staff (1 April 1987): 25,918.

Management system: BMP (Board's Management Plan).

No department that devised and runs VAT can expect the hosannahs of a grateful nation. Nor can an institution whose most conspicuous servants at ports and airports rifle a selection of the citizenry's luggage in search of excess alcohol or tobacco. The Customs, however, has one factor going for it which the Revenue must envy: it catches the drugs fraternity and that

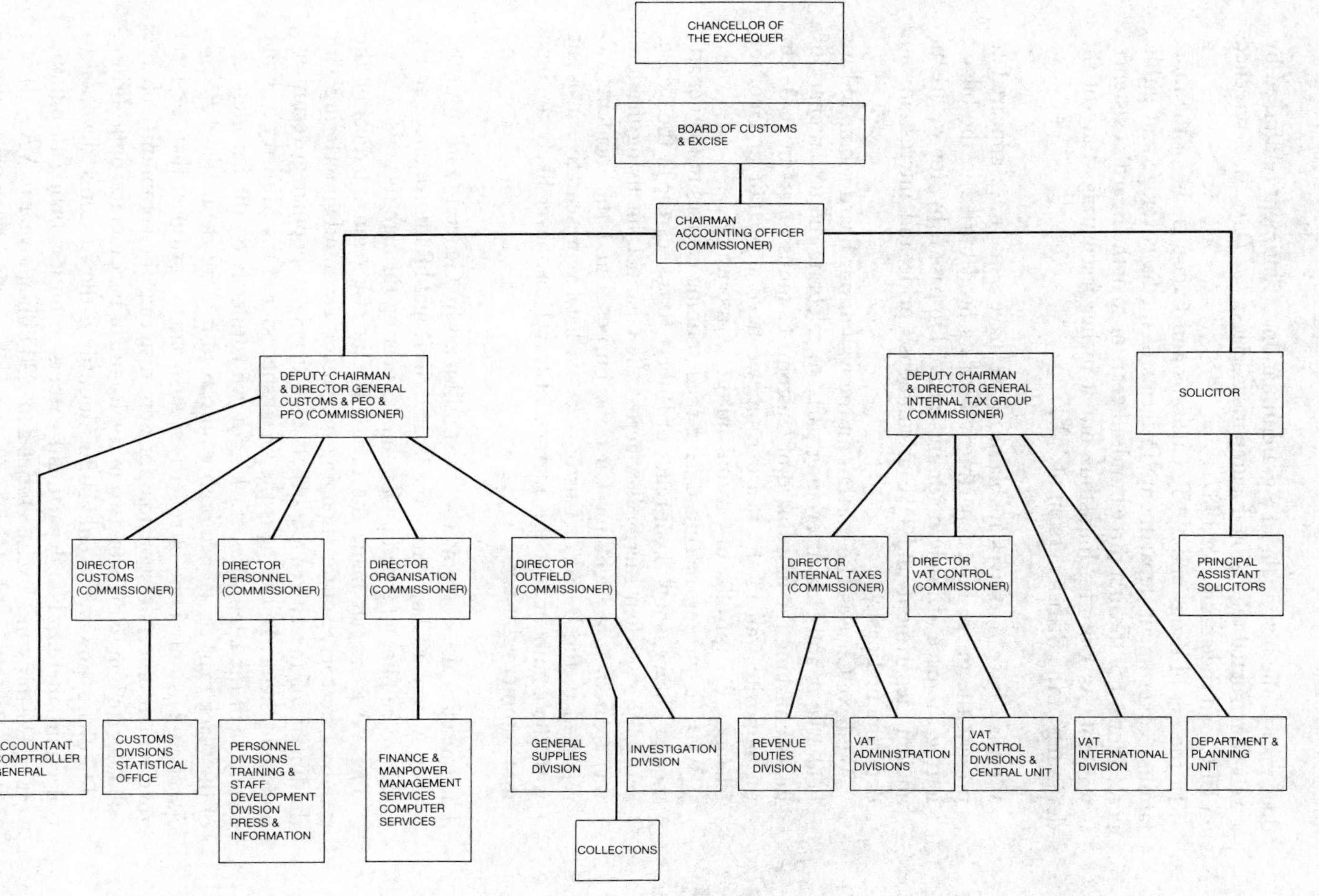

Fig. 20. Board of Customs and Excise

does inspire the hosannahs of a grateful nation, a sentiment reinforced by a well-constructed television documentary series, *The Duty Men,* screened on BBC 2 in the autumn of 1987.

In the era of drugs and VAT, Customs and Excise is one of the more familiar government departments in terms of media coverage and public perceptions. For the first three hundred years or so of the Board's existence, it was not. As Dorothy Johnstone put it in her fascinating study of the designing of the British version of VAT:

> We may have ourselves to blame if we have sometimes appeared to present the image of a department with its head buried in the bilges, letting the pace of modern administrative life pass it by, for we are an ancient department and take an immense pride and interest in our departmental past . . .
>
> We have Charles II's portrait on the wall of our board room, and we held a large and elegant evening party to celebrate the tercentenary of his establishing the first Board of Customs Commissioners in 1671. On the opposite wall of the board room we have a portrait of Geoffrey Chaucer, Comptroller of Customs in the 14th century . . .
>
> We take our new recruits during their training courses to the departmental library, show them relics of Robert Burns' career in the excise, and tell how, when Blériot flew across the Channel, his flying machine was treated as a yacht for Customs purposes and the incident was reported to the Board of Customs by its local representative in Kent with the comment that this method of travel was never likely to come into commercial use.[256]

The museum also contains the illicit still used by General Gordon in the Sudan. A former Chairman of the Board, Sir Ronald Radford, once gamely agreed to be photographed by *The Times* peering through its coils.

The VAT era has made the Customs official a regular target for the standard stereotype of the snooping bureaucrat constantly interfering with the liberty of the citizen on behalf of a deeply unpopular government-imposed scheme. In this he is the lineal successor of the Ministry of Food inspector of the late forties cracking down ruthlessly on the harmless end of the black market, as memorably portrayed in Alan Bennett's *A Private Function.* His only hope of relief is, I suspect, the prospect that the local government officers responsible for administering the community charge will relegate him to division two in the league of bureaucratic opprobrium.

The State, however, would suffer mightily if the Customs' devotion to collection faltered. The department gathers in no less than £16 billion a year in Customs and Excise Duties and £20 billion a year in VAT. It is a vital but thankless task. History has never been kind to the tax gatherer and it never will be. Yet the probity and efficiency of Whitehall's money-raisers is a major factor which distinguishes our bureaucracy from most of those in the rest of the world.

PART THREE | PEOPLE

The nature of long experience defending ministers tends to give the culture of the Civil Service a certain defensive aspect – 'At all costs, my boy, keep the minister out of trouble' is the kind of early advice one tends to get.
Sir Patrick Nairne, former Permanent Secretary, DHSS, 1987[1]

The soul of our service is the loyalty with which we execute ordained error.
Lord Vansittart, former Permanent Secretary, Foreign Office, 1958[2]

I don't think the good and great do make policy . . . they are much more like a governor on a motor . . . what they do is to help iron out some of the excesses of policy and to persuade people that you can do a certain number of things at a certain speed but it's no use racing the engine.
Sir Reginald Hibbert, ex-Ambassador to Paris, 1984[3]

No description of a system is adequate without a detailed treatment of the people who operate it, so before turning to the here-and-now and completing the history of the Civil Service with an account of the Thatcher years, I shall take a look at the players in the Whitehall game – the political, the neutral and the high-minded.

11 MINISTERS

I long for those boxes; I crave for those boxes.
Winston Churchill, 1945[1]

It's endlessly stimulating, there's no question about that. And there is a kind of flow of energy that all Cabinet ministers have to have in order to deal with the workload which is truly enormous.
Peter Shore, 1985[2]

Conviction politicians, certainly: conviction civil servants, no.
Lord Bancroft, 1983[3]

The nature of political competition in democracies emphasises criteria that have little correlation with qualities needed for some of the main tasks of rulers, especially policy-making . . . The game of politics certainly does not assure the high moral fibre of people who reach the top.
Professor Yehezkel Dror, 1984[4]

A minister usually has hobby-horses that officials will groom and train.
Dudley Seers, ex-civil servant, 1967[5]

A great deal has been written about ministers and civil servants. Much of it falls into the *Woman's Own* category – the relationship of a minister to his permanent secretary should be like that of husband and wife in a successful marriage; or into the regimental memoir genre – 'fine body of men', 'best Civil Service in the world'; some of it, particularly since the 1970s, reads like submissions in a divorce case – 'hamstrung by my officials', 'Whitehall applied the Civil Service veto'.

It will always be a precarious relationship. Politics and administration as careers attract very different kinds of people. The recruitment processes could not be more different. This is as it should be in a healthy democratic society. An equivalent of the Civil Service Selection Board for ministers would be ruinous. Neither Lloyd George nor Churchill, Attlee nor Bevin would have got through. Some would (Butler and Eden), and some have (in recent times most notably Douglas Hurd, who entered the Foreign Office in 1952, and Edward Heath, Ministry of Civil Aviation 1946). Roy Jenkins, a permanent secretary *manqué* if ever there was one, brilliantly illustrated the point in his *Nine Men of Power*. Writing of Bevin as Foreign Secretary, he said: 'there was no other position in the Foreign Office, unless it was that of a rather truculent liftman on the verge of retirement, which it would have been possible to imagine his filling'.[6] Yet Bevin was the Foreign Secretary most prized by the Foreign Office certainly since 1945, probably of all time. I can recall Sir Antony Acland, its permanent secretary in the early 1980s, shedding his habitual reserve and flowing with pleasure while talking about Bevin when I interviewed him in 1983.[7] Bevin, the Bristol carter turned titanic minister, was, however, the 'turn up in a million' that he liked to describe himself as.[8] They are scarce in any political system and ours places particularly heavy burdens on its ministers, as any career official as experienced and as candid as Lord Croham will testify:

> Being a minister in the British government is not something that comes naturally like breathing when you're born. It has to be an experience you grow into and that's usually the difficulty – that they really can't cope with the range of problems they find for the first time when they become ministers ...
>
> I am absolutely certain the ministers are overloaded even though many ministers don't think that they are ... You have to remember that ministers are pursuing about four or five different roles – they are constituency MPs; they are members of a party; they are members of a government; they are policy leaders for a department; and, quite often, they are representatives in international bodies. This is an impossible load and it's not surprising that usually after three or four years most ministers are exceptionally tired.[9]

It is very easy at the best of times to be beastly to the political class, our elected rulers as opposed to our appointed ones. It has to be remembered before launching into a torrent of strictures that the mere fact that they are elected by votes freely cast in genuinely competitive circumstances is the greatest single safeguard of a healthy political and administrative system. And the requirement that, in the end, their wishes prevail over those of non-elected people is cardinal. It is truly perilous if this is forgotten at any time by anybody, particularly by the appointed servants of the state, which is why Peter Wright's allegations about MI5 plots against Harold Wilson in the mid-1970s were truly shocking.

With such constitutional verities constantly flashing as if in neon lights, it is salutary nonetheless to take a warts-and-all look at the pool from which our elected rulers are fished on the hook of prime-ministerial patronage. The most ruthless professional for this purpose is Professor Yehezkel Dror of the Hebrew University of Jerusalem whom I once described as '*the* world expert when it comes to putting rulers and their advisers on the couch and exploring their inadequacies, self-delusions and evasions'.[10]

Dror, like all good social scientists, likes to enumerate his points. When you read them in a section labelled 'Rulers are Defective', coldly numbered from one to seven, you fear for yourself, the citizenry, the country and the future. It is John Ashworth's treatise on the powerful and the giving of advice minus the humour that brings a modicum of relief (see p. 341). The 'inherent defects' of rulers, according to Dror, include:

* Quantitative work overload, with many vital activities taking up a great deal of time and energy and super-saturated decision agendas producing great fatigue.
* Qualitative overload, with perplexing quandaries combining with time pressures to result in stress.
* Strain and stress, which produce particularly dangerous defects in crisis decision-making, where important and sometimes momentous choices have to be made under extreme stress and distress . . .
* Court politics and the 'corridors of power' syndrome, with a constant struggle for access to the ruler and for gate-control, which easily becomes mind-control. As time and attention are among the scarcest of the ruler's resources, court politics significantly influence and often distort his world pictures and options.
* A preponderance of positive feedback. Deference to the ruler and often fear of him, as well as court politics and competition for his support, result unavoidably in the ruler's being surrounded by 'mirrors on the wall' which tend constantly to tell him how wise he is and how well realities fit his biases and prejudices . . .
* Option manipulation, which can involve overly limited options being presented to rulers, often with 'raïl-roading', such as presenting a number of options in such a way as to support a single favoured one.
* The pomp and ritual surrounding rulers, which also occurs in many democratic countries, cannot but further distort perception of reality and augment ego-hypertrophy.[11]

As if this check-list were not disturbing enough, there are some peculiarly British factors which can darken the picture still further. That great practitioner of comparative studies, Jean Blondel, has shown that of politicians in the western democracies, British ministers are among the least likely to be picked for their specialist knowledge and background.[12] As Richard Rose puts it: A [British] minister is a professional politician before he is a Secretary of State . . . Advancement in politics requires the cultivation of political skills, and does not require many skills valued in other professions and occupations ... From the perspective of an individual politician, what a ministry can do for his career is as important as what he can do for the ministry.'[13]

The fact that the overwhelming proportion of ministers are drawn from the 650 MPs in the House of Commons is another limitation in any audit of intrinsic capability. Some outsiders, businessmen in particular, have been scathing about what Sir John Hoskyns called 'a talent pool which could not sustain a single multinational company'.[14] Sir Michael Edwardes, the former chairman of British Leyland, was even more cutting: 'When you think of it, we put government ministers in enormously powerful positions, yet nobody tries to measure their intelligence, leadership, drive or any other damn thing. They go in cold and they're changed only when they've made a mess of it. Maybe you can run a country like that. But it's no way to run a business.'[15]

But to treat all 650 MPs as the talent pool is to magnify it. A modern government has just under 100 posts on offer, four-fifths of them filled from the House of Commons. These 80–85 ministers or whips are drawn from the 326+ MPs in the majority party. If you remove the elderly, the undeniably incapable, the unambitious and the irrefutably callow, the pool is pretty tiny. A majority of MPs elected three or more times sooner or later receive office.[16]

Few habitats have received as much scrutiny as the political world. Political scientists, however much they like individual politicians or defend their profession as an honourable and necessary calling, write about them as anthropologists do of a family of chimps in the jungle. Listen to that veteran observer of the British and American political scenes, Professor Richard Rose, on 'being a minister':

> Experience in the Commons does not lead naturally to the work of a minister, as primary school leads to secondary school. Becoming a minister is as much a change for an MP as going out to work is a change for a school boy. The chief skills that an MP must cultivate are dealing with people and talking about ideas. These are important for a minister, but he must have other skills too. A minister must know how to handle the paperwork required at the top of a large organisation; how to analyse problems so that the political essentials are abstracted from a welter of detail; how to delegate tasks to others; and how to relate personal priorities to those of other ministers, and especially the Prime Minister.

As a backbench MP, a politician can repeat empty or impossible slogans popular in the party. As a minister, a politician must say what is consistent with government policies, even if this is unpopular in the party.[17]

To be fair, some members of the political profession recognise the severe problems that can arise from the lack of a specialist background. When Harold Wilson promoted Tony Benn from the Post Office to the Ministry of Technology in 1966, he despatched him to his new post with a Wilsonian version of Rothschild's Law that ministers should subject themselves in their first three months to 'a kind of political Ramadan' in which they confine themselves to briefing, the asking of questions and harmless activities such as opening power stations or hospitals.[18] In this instance, Wilson told Benn: 'Now you must start learning and for six months you will have to keep your head down and read, and no gimmicks.'[19] To his credit, Benn recognised 'that my big problem is that I am so ignorant of industry'[20] and, after his first month of grappling with the departmental embodiment of Wilson's 'white heat' of the technological revolution,[21] that 'Just at the moment Mintech is becoming a little too much for me. All the decisions are so complicated and technical and I'm not really qualified to judge them. No doubt it'll get better later but it's all very worrying.'[22]

The politico-anthropologists do not leave off at this initial point in a ministerial career. Their passion for labelling takes over once the trace of a ministerial record can be followed. Bruce Headey is the Tonto of the profession. Once he has followed and caught them, he rounds British ministers up into three pens:

1. Policy initiators. In here one finds Harold Macmillan as Housing Minister 1951–4 putting up 300,000 dwellings a year; Iain Macleod pushing on the pace of independence as Colonial secretary 1959–61; Anthony Crosland comprehensivising the schools as Education Secretary 1965–7; Roy Jenkins as a reforming Home Secretary on individual liberties and racial equality 1965–7; Barbara Castle as an energetic breathalysing, infrastructure-building Transport Secretary 1965–8; and Robert Carr as a trade union reforming Employment Secretary 1970–2.
2. Executive Ministers. Rubbing shoulders in this pen are Henry Brooke at the Ministry of Housing 1957–61 and the Home Office 1962–4, Denis Healey at Defence 1964–70 and Peter Walker at Environment 1970–2.
3. Ambassador Ministers. Bleating loudly in their corral one finds the public relations specialists Ernest Marples at the Post Office 1957–9 and Transport 1959–64 and Tony Benn at Technology 1966–70.[23]

This is supermarket political science – everything with a label and its own single space on the shelf. It does not work like that. To take the penned ministers, Macmillan and Castle were brilliant at publicity. Healey was no mere executive. Conducting two defence reviews in six years is a matter of policy initiation first and management second. Peter Walker's pioneering work on inner-city deprivation puts him high amongst the initiators and he was no slouch at publicity either. Marples was a self-conscious modern manager who was responsible for the Beeching review of the railways. Tony Benn at Technology was much more than an evangelist of progress through gadgetry. This is not to decry the value of political scientists as anthropologists descending and pronouncing upon what Hugh Heclo and Aaron Wildavsky called 'village life' in Whitehall.[24] The task of sifting anecdote, memoir and episode and detecting some kind of pattern is very necessary, provided the imprint imposed does not itself distort, as, from a journalist's point of view, over-emphatic labelling or modelling is prone to do.

Turning from the anthropologists' perspective of ministers to that of their keepers, there is at first sight a degree of unanimity between keepers and kept, permanent official and transient politician. The cliché is shared – both stress the joy and pleasure of having/being a strong minister. Of all the one-liners a new minister carries in his or her head, that which dominates day one belongs to Arthur Henderson, Ramsay MacDonald's Foreign Secretary in the second Labour Government and a venerable figure in Labour movement hagiography. 'The first 48 hours', said 'Uncle' Arthur, 'decide whether a new Minister is going to run his office or whether his office is going to run him.'[25] A more recent Foreign Secretary, Dr David Owen, has updated the Henderson nostrum. When writing about Mrs Barbara Castle, under whom he served at the DHSS 1974–6, he said, approvingly, that 'more than any Cabinet minister she knew the need to be able to dominate civil servants – who by the limitations of their job cannot be bold or innovatory'.[26]

The officials' version of Henderson's Law is based on a rather longer period than forty-eight hours. A fair sequence of Cabinet committee meetings must pass before it is made, with a set of grade A inter-departmental battles thrown in for good measure. Lord Croham, who spent nearly thirty years in the Treasury and saw fifteen chancellors of the exchequer in action, put it with characteristic directness:

> Without any hesitation civil servants like strong ministers. They are much easier to deal with for a number of reasons ... They are more likely to get their own views across and, therefore, if you work hard to do something for a minister it's not wasted. The other point is that if you're dealing with a minister and he doesn't like your advice, you know

> pretty clearly ... He decides on his own line ... which gives it the maximum chance of succeeding ... and [he's] most unlikely to turn round and blame the department if it doesn't work. Every civil servant I know likes strong ministers.[27]

This is not the same thing at all as an insecure minister brandishing Henderson's Law and throwing his weight around in the first two days, changing things for the sake of it, treating sensitive policy decisions as instruments of his own gratification and generally being rude to the civil servants. The 'we are the masters now' syndrome is depressingly common. Robert Armstrong put it rather well before the Commons Treasury and Civil Service Committee in November 1985 when he said of ministers: 'Their duty, if they have a duty in relation to civil servants or a responsibility, is to read, mark, learn and digest the information and advice which the Civil Service has to offer, to put it together with whatever advice or information they have from other sources, and to take that seriously. Then they take their decisions.'[28]

Lord Callaghan in the same series of hearings on 'Civil Servants and Ministers: Duties and Responsibilities' said his code for ministers would contain but a single paragraph: 'It is your responsibility to be polite, to be courteous, to listen to what is said to you and absorb it and be loyal to your Private Office so they can serve you to the best of their ability.'[29] It sounded to me as if Callaghan had remembered the behaviour of George Brown at the DEA and put in his code everything the volatile George failed to do. His list of requirements produced a memorable generation clash with Austin Mitchell, the effervescent chairman of the select committee inquiry.

> 'It sounds like a Boy Scout code ...'
> 'What is wrong with the Boy Scouts?'[30]

Courtesy and a willingness to read and to listen are perpetual virtues on the part of a minister. The link between strength and virtue, however, is not so straightforward. As Douglas Croham put it, 'A minister who is strong but wrong is going to damage.'[31] His successor at the Treasury, Douglas Wass – ever a monument to the pursuit of reason in high political places even after nearly forty years of seeing how often, in reality, such a quest is doomed – devoted a portion of his 1983 Reith Lectures to the problem of the overmighty departmental minister, the ace policy-initiator to use Bruce Headey's terminology. It comes back to what the politicians joined for. Wass declared:

> The form and structure of a modern Cabinet and the diet it consumes almost oblige it to function like a group of individuals, and not as a unit. Indeed for each minister, the test of his success in office lies in his ability to deliver his departmental goals. Mr Macmillan's 300,000 houses provided him with the initial success which eventually took him to No. 10. No minister I know of has won political distinction by his performance in Cabinet or by his contribution to collective decision-taking. To the country and the House of Commons he is simply the minister for such-and-such a department and the only member of the Cabinet who is not seen in this way is the Prime Minister.[32]

Wass sees the mighty and capable minister as a menace who can distort a government's overall strategy, as 'No mechanism exists to enable the Cabinet to challenge his view unless the interests of another minister are involved, and even then the challenge itself may be partisan. Cabinet can too easily be railroaded.'[33]

Civil servants are far more prone to ponder the long-term than are the ambitious itinerants the prime minister sets in temporary charge over them. This can cause them acute worry. Lord Young of Graffham, Mrs Thatcher's find who was plucked from obscurity to become her ministerial fireman (where Wilson would create a new ministry Mrs Thatcher would send in David Young as a new minister), was cherished by his officials because of his penchant for the long-term. As one senior man put it, he did not belong to the 'let me make Prime Minister first and I'll fill in the details later' school of political thought.[34] They are exceptions and there are perils for them, too, as Lord Croham explains:

> There are always a few ministers who really want to change things a lot, and know it takes a long time. The danger for such ministers is that they forget the short-term. But, in general, the minister is so captivated ... by the day-to-day affairs of being a minister and making the impression in Parliament, making his speeches in the constituency and elsewhere, that he really finds the long-term issue is something he'll do tomorrow – and tomorrow never comes.[35]

The problem of endemic short-termism is compounded by the habit of British premiers of circulating their ministerial talent around Whitehall at an excessive rate of knots. Douglas Hurd has been eloquent about the 'amazingly haphazard' way top ministerial posts are filled.[36] They do not remain filled for long. Pre-1939, a minister would stay put on average for four years. Now it is less than two.[37] And government has taken a quantum leap in complexity in the interim. Richard Rose has captured the consequence: 'Even when a minister is not reshuffled, the prospect of being posted to another ministry or being dismissed by the Prime Minister or the electorate discourages a politician from identifying with the long-term concerns of the ministry. When looking ahead, the one constant is that a minister must look to his own career.'[38]

The rare luxury of a third successive term of office enabled Mrs Thatcher to let it be known in June 1987 that her new ministerial dispositions represented 'a major exercise in career development' for the young and the promising in her party.[39] She was not sure, however, that her successor was in the Cabinet. 'They will need to be different in some respects,' she told Rodney Tyler a few days after the election. 'It takes a different capacity to turn round a great ship of State going in one direction: first to turn the whole thing round and then get it through in another. So, perhaps the one who keeps it going will not have to be quite so combative as me, because by then the ship will have its own momentum.'[40] The plan was 'to get lots of young people starting on the first rung of the ladder so they can be promoted upwards, so all the available talent is ready'.[41]

The politicians themselves, naturally, do not see the ministerial life in the same way as their domestic staff in the departments or the academic anthropologists poking them through the bars of the Whitehall cage. There are a few – a very few – who think in such a civil-servantish fashion that they appear to wish they themselves were public servants rather than politicians. The classic example of this was R. A. Butler. He did not pass Croham's decisiveness test. Sir Nicholas Henderson, his private secretary at the Foreign Office, recalled that he could fuss all day about whether to attend a minor diplomatic function at the Moroccan Embassy (in the end he went).[42] As his biographer, Anthony Howard, put it, Rab 'never believed in building a Chinese wall between a minister and his official subordinates'.[43] When he received a particularly good brief from a civil servant 'he would simply draw a little Valentine – a heart with an arrow going through it pointing directly towards the initials of the writer'.[44] Ian Bancroft, his private secretary in the mid-fifties, 'was the most regular recipient of this signal mark of favour'.[45] On his last day as a minister in October 1964 'he took his leave of his [Foreign Office] Private Secretaries making them an eloquent speech on the theme of how he envied their continuing careers in the Government service before leaving by a side-entrance to walk alone across St James's Park to his flat in Carlton Gardens'.[46]

Roy Jenkins was another imposing Cabinet figure one could have imagined as official head of his department as easily as its political chief – perhaps even more so than Rab as Jenkins in office was a more decisive character. Jenkins was a true connoisseur of ministers, ministries and officials. He had drunk deep in political biography and produced a rich vintage himself before becoming a minister.[47] And he entered the Cabinet with some practical lessons as a result. For example, he was determined 'not to spread one's energy too widely but to concentrate on a limited number of major issues at any one time'.[48] Lord Jenkins wrote later in disapproving tones of Barbara Castle for having 'made exhaustion into a political virility symbol and [for being] foolishly critical of those who did not believe that decisions were best taken in a state of prostration'.[49]

Jenkins wrote a deliciously elegant essay in 1971 'On Being a Minister', largely based, as we have seen, on a comparison of life in the Treasury and the Home Office. In it he corroborated the Croham thesis almost word for word. Ever the time-budgeteer, Jenkins noted that a substantial portion of a chancellor's or a home secretary's time is 'consumed in discussion and argument within the department'.

> This does not mean, except in unusual circumstances, that a Minister has to batter his head against a brick wall of determined departmental opposition. If he knows what he wants to do he will not in general have much difficulty in getting his policy carried out. Most civil servants, including the most able, prefer it this way. If a minister is putty in their hands they have a nasty suspicion that he will be putty in the hands of everybody else too, and that policy will not so much be made by the civil servants as never properly made at all.[50]

Lord Jenkins clearly accepts the Northcote–Trevelyan style official with tenure, willing to speak truth, as he sees it, fearlessly unto power:

> It is . . . the duty of civil servants to point out to a minister the likely consequences of his actions. As 'likely' consequences frequently involves judgement and not merely objective fact prejudices can obviously enter the picture. But it is for the minister to make up his own mind about this. If he has any will of his own he will do some things against advice, but after considering the argument more carefully than if he were going with the tide. Equally, unless he is incredibly rash and pig-headed, he is bound to be deflected by the weight of argument from certain causes to which he was originally attracted. Were this otherwise there would be no point in having advisers.[51]

Roy Jenkins really could be a permanent secretary talking. Sir Paul Gore-Booth on the role of the Civil Service adviser is a clear echo: 'If they [ministers] take decisions without first taking advice, they may decide things of great importance without knowing the full background of detail, of opportunity and danger. There is no other source from which they can expect to find such advice presented in an orderly, convenient, comprehensive, and, as far as possible, unbiased form. That is what professional advisers are for.'[52] Intriguingly, Gore-Booth noted that 'in general Conservatives tend to be less touchy about advice than their opponents'.[53] For him, ministers ignore official advice 'at the nation's peril',[54] and he notes the tragic irony 'that on the occasion of our two foreign policy disasters in my time, it was the Conservatives who did not so much reject advice as decline to hear it ... Just as Mr Chamberlain did not choose to have full advice from the Foreign Office in 1938 [Munich], so did Sir Anthony Eden tragically avoid it in 1956 [Suez].'[55]

On the Gore-Booth touchiness measure Roy Jenkins does not seem to have been entirely typical of the Labour Party he later left. Indeed, to show how life in one house of the Whitehall village can be totally different to the domestic ecology of another, it is only necessary to travel from the Jenkins Treasury of the late sixties to Crossman's Department of Health and Social Security at the Elephant and Castle. Twenty years later the memories were still green, as became apparent during the discussion after a paper presented by Dr Janet Morgan, editor of the *Crossman Diaries*, to a seminar at the Institute of Contemporary British History.

His friend and Minister of State at the DHSS, David Ennals, described Crossman as 'less than fair to most civil servants'.

> I suppose he didn't treat civil servants that much worse than he treated other people, but civil servants were not able to treat him as other people could treat him. No civil servant would ever answer back to a Secretary of State. Dick would complete their sentences for them and sometimes get it wrong, he would berate them implying they were incompetent, they hadn't thought, he would never let them finish their defence. When he asked them to state a case and they were half way through it he would try and demolish it. I thought this was cruel and it was borne of this intellectual arrogance which he didn't ever seem to be able to grow out of. He couldn't see that civil servants were at a disadvantage and he just exploited the position. Sometimes he would have a session with civil servants and they would almost fall out of the room as if they had been battered.[56]

Sir George Godber, Chief Medical Officer at the DHSS in Crossman's time, corroborates the Ennals portrait but, remarkably, can still see virtue in Crossman's tenure at the Elephant:

> He was a curious character. He made it very difficult for the person who wanted to present a coherent argument to get through with it, because he would interrupt, having picked up something from the beginning of the presentation ... He would go swiftly off on some intellectual tangent of his own, and reach a conclusion which might well not have been

> reached if he'd listened just a couple of minutes longer ... Discussions could get very rough. But I think he was right to say that the department, when he came to it, was complacent with the situation it had. He made us look again at a lot of things, and was a stimulus that the department needed.[57]

Crossman's permanent secretary at the DHSS, Sir Clifford Jarrett, believed that 'if only he had been less conspiratorial, above all, less rude to people, they would have probably come to like him more'.[58] Sir Richard Powell, who was Permanent Secretary at the Board of Trade and saw Crossman in action at Cabinet committees, said, 'he did not understand how to use the departmental machine ... [and] ... knew little or nothing about economics and finance'.[59]

In Crossman's case, it was temperament more than ideology which produced the sound of conflict and offered a cacophonous contrast to the calm, sweet reasonable world depicted by Roy Jenkins and Paul Gore-Booth. In Tony Benn's, it was his belief that the Civil Service can work happily only with ministers who operate within the central lowlands of British politics and keep away from the highlands of conviction on either side. Mr Benn's thesis is Bridges's storehouse-of-departmental-wisdom philosophy viewed through a different prism:

> It would be a mistake to suppose – as some socialists have suggested – that the senior ranks of the Civil Service are active Conservatives posing as impartial administrators. The issue is not their personal political views, nor their preferences for particular governments, though as citizens they are perfectly entitled to hold such views and to vote accordingly. The problem arises from the fact that the Civil Service sees itself as being above the party battle, with a political position of its own to defend against all-comers, including incoming governments armed with their philosophy and programmes.[60]

The senior Civil Service would blench at the phraseology and thrust of that paragraph of Tony Benn's. But, surely, they would recognise something of themselves and their profession in this one?

> Civil Service policy – and there is no other way to describe it – is an amalgam of views that have developed over a long period. It draws some of its force from a deep commitment to the benefits of continuity and a fear that adversary politics may lead to sharp reversals by incoming governments of policies devised by their predecessors, which the Civil Service played a great part in developing. To that extent, the permanent secretaries could be expected to prefer consensus politics and to hope

that such a consensus would remain the basis for all policy and administration.[61]

Though Mr Benn did not give an example in that passage, his supporters like Brian Sedgemore in his book *The Secret Constitution*[62] make much of his time as Industry Secretary in 1974–5 when, as they see it, Labour's commitment to public ownership, public investment and planning agreements with large private companies as the basis of industrial regeneration was resisted by Whitehall. Senior officials, naturally, did not see it that way at all and regard the Benn–Sedgemore thesis as a conspiracy theory without foundation. It created a delicate and, in many ways, unprecedented situation. I can remember at the time a Labour minister in the Trade–Industry–Prices group telling me of the combination of horror and fascination with which they witnessed the debate between two highly principled (and immensely courteous) men – Tony Benn and his permanent secretary, the highly experienced Sir Antony Part.

The key to the outcome – a much watered-down policy when the White Paper, *The Regeneration of British Industry*, appeared in August 1974,[63] precursor of the Industry Act 1975 – lay outside the battleground of the Department of Industry across Parliament Square and up Whitehall in the Cabinet Office and No. 10. Wilson removed the issue to a Cabinet committee under his chairmanship and much of the groundwork into the Cabinet Office economic secretariat under Jim Hamilton. The No. 10 Policy Unit became, in essence, an anti-Benn unit with its economist, Richard Graham, put on something of a Benn-alert. The Unit's head, Bernard Donoughue, later said: 'I'm sure that Tony Benn felt himself betrayed by his Prime Minister, because the moment the word got around, as it rapidly did in Whitehall – and the Cabinet Office made sure that it got around – that the Prime Minister was not giving his support to Tony Benn, then the civil servants began to back-off from their Minister. Although, in this case, Mr Benn had backed off from them in the beginning.'[64] Mr Benn, an immensely sharp observer of village life in Whitehall, knew exactly what had happened to his industrial strategy in 1974. Not for nothing did he later produce a plan for 'a constitutional premiership'[65] alongside one for 'a constitutional Civil Service'.[66]

Tony Benn is a singular man and a singular politician. Most ministers in both parties prefer to work with the grain in the belief not merely that Whitehall life is more comfortable that way but that more can be achieved as well. And there are ways of cutting against the grain without causing offence or driving people into foxholes behind heavily defended positions. Bevin's remark as Minister of Labour is still part of Whitehall folklore: 'You've just given me twenty good reasons why I can't do this; I'm sure that clever chaps like you can go away and produce twenty good reasons why I can.' Of course, it is not as simple as that, as Bevin himself understood. He knew how to use his officials and was big enough to take their criticism – indeed, he encouraged it. A few days after entering government in 1940 he called the senior officials of the Ministry of Labour into his office and told them: 'I shall have a lot of ideas: it's your job to tell me which of them are good and which of them are bad.'[67]

If civil servants have a besetting prejudice when it comes to the fifty-seven varieties of minister they are required to serve, it is for the tidy-minded despatcher of business who gets his work done neatly and methodically. This is why Sir Geoffrey Howe, with his dull, lawyer's ways, has always been beloved by the officials in the ministries through which he has plodded. Sir David Hunt, an official in No. 10 in the early fifties, used to dine out on his version of the private secretary/minister story and the contrast between Churchill and Attlee:

> Very soon after the changeover . . . everybody asked me, 'Well now, do tell me about the differences. [As] a sort of party piece I would say, 'Oh, you can't imagine the difference between them, it's extraordinary. On the one side, decision, firm answers, everything down just like that – bang, bang. And, on the other side, hesitation, uncertainty, 'Oh, I'll look at that at the weekend' or 'I'm not going to deal with that now, this ought to come to Cabinet' or sometimes he'd say 'Ah, breeze down to Chartwell and I'll look at it there'.
>
> And when I got to the word 'Chartwell', they'd all do a sort of double-take because hitherto they'd all been saying 'Ah, just what I thought, you know' [and] shaking their heads. And then they suddenly realised that the decisive and rapid one was Attlee, and the man who used to put things off was Churchill.[68]

Once more labelling is shown to be a dangerous trade. It can be so, too, in less grand circumstances than stories of great men in No. 10. There was an example in the 1987 general election. Kenneth Baker at the Department of Education may have had a penchant for the radical policy departure announced before the policy ground had been broken, let alone thoroughly tilled. But he was good with his officials (his father had been a middle-ranking civil servant in the Ministry of Supply).[69] He said of them, and his style justified it, that 'I am a very open man. I believe in having a good team about me and I don't encourage my senior civil servants to say, "Yes, sir, no, sir". I dislike malice and I'm not a dictator.'[70]

But during his election tour, Mr Baker asked officials, via a minute from his private secretary, Chris de Grouchy, for details on the local education authorities through which he would be passing. He wanted statistics, details on the teachers' action being taken there (the long-drawn-out teachers' dispute was still in train). But it was in asking for details of achievements and problems that he set alarm bells ringing.[71] It struck some officials that they were being asked to step over the line between the administrative and the political. They raised it with their union. Within a few days the permanent secretary, Sir David Hancock, reassured his staff that provision of the material Mr Baker wanted was within the guidelines which applied at election time, though he asked them to beware of tailoring information in a way which distorted it.[72]

It is easy but wrong to take away the impression from reading the literature on Whitehall that officials do behave rather like keepers at the zoo watching the antics of their charges – ministers – with a mixture of familiarity, superiority and detachment. A good antidote to this is a new genre of literature in which the ministers bite, or at least write, back. Labour's Gerald Kaufman is the founding father of this school and Jock Bruce-Gardyne its most prominent Conservative member. Their *How to be a Minister* and *Ministers and Mandarins*[73] are little gems of observation, irony (Kaufman) and cynicism (Bruce-Gardyne). Such books are reminders that ministers, too, can 'collect' civil servants and apply their own ranking to them. Mrs Thatcher was famous for this. Long-servers like Harold Wilson prided themselves on it. Dick Crossman, in a well-known passage in his diaries, compared his two principal private secretaries at the Ministry of Housing and Local Government: 'Under George Moseley it was a good solid Rover of a Private Office, under John Delafons it was a Rolls-Royce. He was the man I selected myself, having seen him at work at one or two meetings. Under him the Private Office provided the machine I needed for controlling the Department, as well as help with writing my speeches.'[74]

In a grey Whitehall world, the line official with a bit of sparkle in his or her prose can brighten an otherwise burdensome red box. At the Department of Industry, Gerald Kaufman used to wait for the offerings of one civil servant in particular:

> The system has its own stately rituals. One of the most formalised relates to communications between officials and ministers. Officials will put an issue to ministers in a document known as a 'submission'. Some officials are exceptionally prolific with submissions. The most prolific I ever knew – I suspect the most prolific there ever has been or possibly ever will be – was a superb deputy secretary at the Department of Industry – brilliant, inventive, humorous, loyal – called Ron Dearing.
>
> When my private secretary used to tell me that a submission was on its way – for private secretaries know in advance everything that is going to happen – my reply would simply be 'of course'. I once even contemplated writing a novel in the style of E. M. Forster called 'A Submission from Mr Dearing'. It was eventually decided that Ron

> Dearing's formidable if idiosyncratic skills could be put to more fruitful use and he was appointed head of the nation's postal services, so reaching his apotheosis in supervising the safe and speedy transmission and delivery of other people's submissions ...[75]

Ministers are very good, also, at distinguishing the private impulses, which are not necessarily the same thing as the personal politics, of the officials with whom they work most closely. Joel Barnett, as a self-confessed 'new boy at the Treasury' in 1974, noticed that an

> area where officials were quite brilliant was in the different ways they had of 'fudging' figures, particularly on expenditure decisions. It was more understandable if you started from the same standpoint as officials, which was conservative with a small 'c', although this would by no means apply to all of them. Many were obviously sympathetic to the need for more to be spent on improving public services, or even had vaguely Labour sympathies. Sir Leo Pliatzky, my most fascinating permanent secretary, had been in the research department of the Fabian Society before joining the Civil Service.
>
> Nonetheless, the prevailing belief among them was that our poor industrial and economic performance meant we must restrain the growth of public expenditure. Consequently, all their considerable efforts in presenting the figures would be geared to that end. My main complaint was not about the 'fudging', or, as they occasionally put it, 'massaging' (there was 'light' and 'deep' massage) of the figures, but that it should be clear to *me* just what they were doing.[76]

Books of ministerial reflections, too, are necessary reminders that ministers *do* matter. It is all too easy for policy analysts to concentrate on the huge rolling budgets of departments – the mints that fund the welfare state either directly (social security) or at one stage removed (education), or the defence programme and the Armed Forces that people it – and to conclude that ministers are, at best, marginal to the process. There is something in this. I can remember Sir John Nott at the time of the 1981 Defence Review feeling very much a prisoner of his ministry's long-term costings and attempting to carve out for himself a smallish budget which he could use on new initiatives shaped by his own hand.[77]

Yet even a glance at those big programmes shows how much a government determined to change the balance of priorities can do if the electorate gives its ministers sufficient time and those ministers stick, largely if not wholly, to their original intentions. For example, shortly before the 1987 general election it was possible to calculate the major changes in the pattern of public expenditure since Mrs Thatcher had become Prime Minister eight years earlier. Much higher, and deliberately so, in real terms were defence (+28 per cent), law and order, as measured by the Home Office budget (+50 per cent). Down, equally deliberately, were Housing (−60 per cent), Trade and Industry (−65 per cent) and Britain's contribution to the EEC (−24 per cent). To paint a fair picture, recession and unemployment had pushed some budgets far higher than ministers would have wished, Employment (+90 per cent) and Social Security (+39.5 per cent), in particular.[78] And the merest glance at the chart of nationalisations and privatisations since 1945 shows just how much activity was concentrated within the life-spans of the two most radically inclined postwar governments under Attlee and Thatcher (Table 2).

Ministers also matter on the micro as well as the macro policy level. The

TABLE 2 THE SHIFTS OF PUBLIC OWNERSHIP 1946–87

Nationalisation		*Privatisation*	
Bank of England	(1946) Attlee	Iron and Steel	(1953) Churchill
Civil Aviation	(1946) Attlee	Road haulage (partly)	(1953) Churchill
Coal	(1947) Attlee		
Railways	(1948) Attlee	Thomas Cook	(1971) Heath
Road haulage	(1948) Attlee	State breweries	(1971) Heath
Waterways	(1948) Attlee	State holdings in Ferranti	(1980) Thatcher
Hospitals	(1948) Attlee	Fairey Engineering	(1980) Thatcher
		British Aerospace	(1981) Thatcher
Electricity	(1948) Attlee	Cable & Wireless	(1981) Thatcher
Gas	(1949) Attlee	Amersham International	(1982) Thatcher
Iron and Steel	(1950) Attlee	National Freight	(1982) Thatcher
		Britoil	(1982) Thatcher
		Assoc. British Ports	(1983) Thatcher
Iron and Steel	(1967) Wilson	British Rail Hotels	(1983) Thatcher
National Bus	(1967) Wilson	Enterprise Oil	(1984) Thatcher
		Inmos	(1984) Thatcher
Rolls-Royce	(1971) Heath	Jaguar	(1984) Thatcher
		Sealink	(1984) Thatcher
British Leyland	(1975) Wilson	British Telecom	(1984) Thatcher
		Yarrow Shipbuilders	(1985) Thatcher
British Shipbuilders	(1977) Callaghan	British Aerospace	(1985) Thatcher
British Aerospace	(1977) Callaghan	Vosper Thorneycroft	(1985) Thatcher
		Swan Hunter	(1986) Thatcher
		Vickers Shipbuilding	(1986) Thatcher
		National Bus	(1986) Thatcher
		BA Helicopters	(1986) Thatcher
		British Gas	(1986) Thatcher
		British Airways	(1986) Thatcher
		Royal Ordnance	(1987) Thatcher
		Rolls-Royce	(1987) Thatcher
		British Airports	(1987) Thatcher
		Leyland Bus & Truck	(1987) Thatcher
		British Petroleum	(1987) Thatcher

buck stops with them on a host of decisions that affect the citizen as an individual (an immigration case decided within the Home Office) or as part of a collectivity (on the Department of Energy's recommendation, the Cabinet decided to pursue a third generation of British nuclear power stations based on the pressurised water reactor).

For the Civil Service the buck-stopping question is of crucial importance. Under the doctrine of ministerial responsibility, ministers are the ultimate can-carriers for *everything* done by the Civil Service in their name. But life is never as clear as it seems. The moment a first principle has been stated, the fog descends made up of droplets of caveat and nuance. It is no longer possible, for example, to regard Sir Thomas Dugdale's honourable resignation in 1954 over the Crichel Down case as the *locus classicus* of ministerial responsibility in action, an act described by Churchill, the premier who accepted the resignation, as 'chivalrous in a high degree'.[79]

The story is a tangled one and developed over sixteen years. In 1938, with war in prospect, the Air Ministry acquired 725 acres of agricultural land on Crichel Down, a corner of north-east Dorset just off the road between Blandford Forum and Salisbury, as a bombing range. It was purchased from three owners. When the bombs ceased to fall after the war, the land was transferred from the Air Ministry to the Ministry of Agriculture, then in a sustained drive to ease austerity by maximising the domestic production of food. In 1950, the ministry's Agricultural Land Commission decided to let all 725 acres as a modern, fully equipped farm rather than disposing of it in smaller, less efficient parcels. The son-in-law of one of the original owners, Lieutenant Commander George Marten, attempted to purchase the 328 acres which would, if returned to the original owners, now belong to his wife. The ministry stuck to its original policy. Commander Marten sought and found help from his local MP and the National Farmers' Union. His case became a *cause célèbre* – of the individual versus the state, of private enterprise versus state bureaucracy – and a lightning-conductor for the accumulated atmospheric electricity that had gathered as sections of the nation seethed at the prolongation of postwar controls. Crichel Down itself became the most famous farm in British constitutional history.

Into the storm after the Conservatives returned to power in 1951 stepped Sir Thomas Dugdale, an honourable, pedestrian, rather old-fashioned Tory whom Churchill appointed Minister of Agriculture. The hue and cry over Crichel Down led to an inquiry by Sir Andrew Clark QC, a former Conservative candidate, who conducted what now appears to be a thoroughly partisan inquiry which ended up by publicly pillorying several named civil servants. Dugdale, after an appalling hounding by his own backbenchers, resigned in July 1954.

Subsequent revelations by Mr I. F. Nicolson in his deeply researched book, *The Mystery of Crichel Down*, based on declassified papers at the

PRO, a rethink (based on a reading of Nicolson and the documents) by Professor John Griffith, whose article in *The Modern Law Review* in 1955[80] helped create the standard interpretation, and a contribution from the late Lord Boyle have changed the picture of the Dugdale resignation significantly. Lord Boyle, seems to have been Dugdale's confidant as to his true motives for going. 'Sir Thomas Dugdale', he wrote in 1980, 'did not resign because he accepted responsibility for an act of maladministration; he resigned because he was not prepared to abandon a specific . . . decision – the decision that his Department should retain and equip Crichel Down as a single farm unit – which was unacceptable to an influential sector of his own party in Parliament, as well as to certain individuals and interests outside . . . I happen to know from first hand that [he] never changed his view that his stand had been right.'[81] This was the view of Dugdale's predecessor at the Ministry of Agriculture, the wing-collared farmers' friend, Tom Williams, who refused to take part in the Commons debates on Crichel Down and maintained that Dugdale was hounded from office on the wholly fictitious issues of Crichel Down'.[82] Herbert Morrison in winding up the second of the debates for Labour accused the Churchill government of having succumbed to pressure from its own backbenchers, 'happy that they have the scalp of a Minister'.[82] Professor Griffith has now come to the conclusion that it was the hounding from his backbenchers which drove Dugdale from office, not his clinging to that pillar of the constitution, the doctrine of ministerial responsibility.[84]

But that sour and combative Commons debate of 20 July 1954 lives on as the setter of the standard benchmarks of ministerial responsibility. The statement of Sir David Maxwell-Fyfe, the Home Secretary who wound up for the Government (he had chaired the Cabinet committee on Crichel Down), was quoted as *the* definitive constitutional statement by the Commons Treasury and Civil Service Committee in its post-Ponting and post-Westland inquest into the accountability of ministers and officials to Parliament.[85] Maxwell-Fyfe distinguished a quartet of cases in which the doctrine applied, outlining the course of proper conduct for the minister in each:

* Where there is an explicit order [to an official] by a Minister, the Minister must protect the civil servant who has carried out his order.
* Where the civil servant acts properly in accordance with the policy laid down by the Minister, the Minister must protect and defend him.
* Where an official makes a mistake or causes some delay, but not on an important issue of policy . . . the Minister acknowledges the mistake and he accepts responsibility although he is not personally involved. He states that he will take corrective action . . . He would not, in those circumstances, expose the official to public criticism.

* Where action has been taken by a civil servant of which the Minister disapproves and has no prior knowledge, and the conduct of the official is reprehensible, then there is no obligation on the part of the Minister to endorse what he believes to be wrong, or to defend what are clearly shown to be errors of his officers. The Minister is not bound to defend action of which he did not know, or of which he disapproves.[86]

The trouble with constitutional doctrines, even when spelled out as precisely as in the Maxwell-Fyfe formulation, is that they never seem quite to fit each new instance as it arises. By their very nature, each occasion on which questions of ministerial responsibility feature prominently is a special case. We have examined the tortured ethics and responsibilities which dropped on the Commons as part of the fall-out from Suez. The nearest there has been to a re-run of Crichel Down was the Vehicle and General Affair of 1972. The tribunal of inquiry accused a named senior official in the DTI's insurance division, of negligence following the collapse of the cut-price insurance firm.[87] No DTI minister resigned to carry the can for its insurance division, less than one per cent of whose work was referred to ministers.[88]

The V and G tribunal advanced the novel concept that merely by occupying senior positions, civil servants 'hold themselves out as persons exercising special skill in that particular field'.[89] William Armstrong bore the brunt of the First Division Association's complaints about the confusion left by the V and G inquiry. He sympathised with the view that the 'special skill' factor was unsatisfactory. In an aside that can only have brought a wry smile to the protagonists of the Fulton Report, Armstrong later said: 'That did not make any sense at all to civil servants. We didn't think that we held ourselves out as competent. We were just appointed because other people thought we were.' Characteristically, Armstrong added, 'We might have had private doubts about it.'[90]

The Falklands invasion of April 1982 saw three Foreign Office ministers resigning but no officials. Lord Carrington, ironically, had been one of Dugdale's junior ministers in 1954. He had offered his resignation but Churchill had refused to accept it.[91] In 1982 he offered his resignation to Mrs Thatcher who did not want it either. He insisted and departed along with Sir Humphrey Atkins and Mr Richard Luce. That night he told a television interviewer that he was going because the invasion of the Falklands 'is a national humiliation'.[92] But again, matters were not so straightforward as they appeared. He was taken aback by attacks on the Foreign Office from Tory backbenchers at a meeting which followed the famous Commons debate on Saturday, 3 April 1982 (shades of Dugdale). And press attacks compounded his belief that he had to go.[93] And Charles

Douglas-Home's most famous *Times* leader, 'We are all Falklanders Now' on the morning of Monday, 5 April, which called upon Carrington to 'do his duty', was undoubtedly a factor.[94] He left later that day, enhancing his already high public reputation.

As if to show there is no consistency in these things, eighteen months later Carrington's friend and colleague, Jim Prior, stayed after the mass break-out of thirty-eight Republican prisoners from the Maze prison in Northern Ireland. He offered his resignation but Mrs Thatcher refused to accept it on the ground that 'the escape was a risk that was inherent in the unique conditions of Northern Ireland's prisons', as Mr Prior paraphrased her.[95] He himself 'took the view that I should not resign unless it was clear from the Report [of Sir James Hennessy, Chief Inspector of Prisons] ... that a policy change or directive had been the direct cause of the escape ... [when published] it showed that no policy decisions contributed to the escape'.[96]

A very practical definition of ministerial responsibility, that. At first glance the next eruption of the issue should have been clear-cut during the Westland affair but it wasn't. When Leon Brittan resigned as Secretary of State for Trade and Industry he did not go because, on his instructions, his officials had leaked part of a confidential letter from the Solicitor-General. He went in January 1986 because of the strength of backbench Tory feeling against him, as both Dugdale and Carrington had before him.[97]

The baffling accumulation of precedents may be one thing, but ministerial responsibility *does* always involve a degree of can-carrying even if it usually falls short of resignation. At the very least, the minister has to stand his or her ground under intense fire in the House of Commons (the Lords are usually much more forgiving and forbearing). And here a genuine community of interest exists between ministers and officials. In the end, it is in the interests of neither party to the contract if one or other goes too deeply and too publicly into the manure. That contract, though unwritten, is fully understood. It is graven on all official hearts, apart from a few whistleblowers, and was given perfect articulation by John Welser of the Foreign Office in 1970 during the official secrets trial involving *The Sunday Telegraph* and its reporting of the Nigerian civil war. 'It is no business of any official', said Mr Welser, 'to allow the government to be embarrassed. That is who we are working for. Embarrassment and security are not really two different things.'[98]

Oh yes they are. But, in saying that, John Welser was taking us quite close to the unspoken job description of the British civil servant – to make the minister, however ill-suited he is for high office or however hopeless and helpless he is once office is attained, to seem and to be that much better and more competent than he actually is. This calls for a singular mixture of abilities and attributes on the part of the civil servant. It is to these that we now turn.

12 REGULARS

The proper soil for the bureaucratization of an administration has always been the specific developments of administrative tasks ... In the field of politics, the great state and the mass party are the classic soil for bureaucracy.
Max Weber, 1916[1]

The administrative class ... numbers no more than some 3000 highly intelligent men and women who decided to make non-electoral politics their professional career.
Lord Zuckerman, 1985[2]

Civil servants are the production engineers of the Parliamentary process.
Sir William Armstrong, early 1970s[3]

We keep civil servants to perform somersaults. They're selected and trained to perform that as part of their job.
Enoch Powell, 1984[4]

I've only had three days training in my career. That's not a boast. That's a confession.
Sir Robert Armstrong[5]

As people of power go senior civil servants are, at first glance, underwhelming individuals in a rather dowdy habitat. The buildings, or some of them, may be rather grand on the outside. Within, a seedy austerity in furniture, decor and atmosphere tends to prevail. The men amongst them are not snappy dressers, neither truly smart like the military nor tycoonish like the top businessman. Their language is understated as are the claims they make for their work. They can, in a word, be a great disappointment for those unfamiliar with the breed expecting to find, at last, the repositories of real power in British society.

This camouflage comes quite naturally. Even at the moment of retirement it stays with them, a decorous fixture, a permanent protection. For example, when Sir Brian Cubbon left the Home Office in the spring of 1988 he spoke of the permanent secretary as 'the reciprocal of the minister, there to produce coherent effort between the department and ministers. If there is incoherence or friction or lack of understanding, it is the permanent secretary's fault.'[6] The nearest he came to acknowledging the often formidable personal influence of a man like himself was when he told David Walker of *The Times*, 'I have been philosopher to pragmatists and realist to the cerebral.'[7]

Don't be fooled. These people are not as dry or as reticent as they make out. And there are occasions on which this becomes apparent. General elections are always an interesting period in Whitehall terms. The transient government takes to the road, the rails and the air. The permanent government can be observed in near-perfect laboratory conditions. The political element in Whitehall is reduced to the minimum. A Cabinet group, the Election Business Committee, a shadowy body consisting of the Lord Chancellor and a handful of minister/peers who, by definition, have no constituencies of their own to go to, comes into existence to mind the shop.[8] It will only meet if a minor emergency arises. (A major one – a collapse of the pound, an Argentinian invasion of the Falklands – would swiftly bring the Prime Minister and her senior ministers back to London.) John Biffen, that rare and deliciously ironic spirit among politicians, said to me the day the 1979–83 Parliament was dissolved: 'The civil servants are the professionals. It's much better run when they're in charge.'[9] Whitehall, in fact, goes on to automatic pilot.

During the 1987 election Lord Bancroft gave a relaxed interview at his home in Putney to Michael Crick of *Channel 4 News*. It turned out to be a miniature classic, wonderfully revealing about the culture of the permanent government, though only a fragment of it was broadcast by ITN on 11 June, election day itself. He had noticed, Bancroft told Crick, that the Alliance leaders had already visited the Head of the Home Civil Service to discuss their plans for government. (They had been filmed for television turning up outside No. 70 Whitehall.) The occasion, incidentally, was of some significance, though Bancroft did not refer to it in these terms. In an interview with me some seven months earlier for BBC Radio 4's *Analysis*, David Owen said of the possibility of a pre-election meeting: 'I can see nothing that Sir Robert Armstrong could contribute to the debate personally ... I think he's become a civil servant who's very much seen as a supporter of the Government. I think his credibility is at a very low ebb ...'[10]

Bancroft is a firm believer in the value of contacts under the Douglas-Home rules. 'It would be ... a dereliction on both sides if that did not happen', he said.[11] In fact, everybody made use of the facility in May–June 1987. Neil Kinnock and his shadow spokesmen paid their visits to the permanent secretaries, unlike Michael Foot and his team who had not bothered in 1983.[12] Elections, as described by Lord Bancroft, were bitter-sweet occasions for 'the policy-managers in Whitehall'. It was a call on their ingenuity.

> Change is in the air and civil servants, despite appearances to the contrary, are, on the whole, human beings and they quite like a bit of change. It's tempered, though, by a feeling of sadness because most of them know that they are going to lose their Minister [because of a reshuffle] even if the same administration get in then, nevertheless, this may well mean a new Minister and if you've been working for the same Minister for two, three, five, six years, then it's a great personal sadness.[13]

So far, so bland. But the surprise came when Michael Crick asked the former Head of the Home Civil Service, Permanent Secretary to the Department of the Environment and private secretary to a fistful of chancellors of the exchequer, about manifestos. There was a hint of what was to come in a remark (with which I wholly sympathised) about 'the party conferences, which are vexatious affairs in which normally sensible people temporarily lose their marbles'. With an elegantly rotating right hand, he warmed to his theme of discussions between permanent secretary and newly arrived minister about

> how best those policies might be implemented. And here the permanent secretary might have to tread very delicately perhaps suggesting modifications of a relatively minor nature in the priority given to those policies . . . because the permanent secretary must steer a course in which he retains or gains the trust of the new Minister but, at the same time, carries out his responsibilities of bringing to the attention of the new Minister . . . the difficulties of implementing some of the policies which are in the manifesto . . . It's not that the permanent secretary wants to get in the way of the wishes of the electorate, but he has got, in the words of one of my predecessors, to be 'faithful to the facts'.

Such nuance and delicacy of phrase is the stuff of the Crossman and Castle Diaries, the richest ingredient of *Yes, Minister*. But it was in speaking as an old Whitehall pro that Ian Bancroft forsook nuance for plain speaking:

> In earlier days, manifestos were written in general terms. They tended to be written in what I might call disappearing ink . . . Now they have tended, over the last 15, 20 years to be written in indelible ink in a fine

> italic hand with great particularity. And they have had rather quaint persons called 'guardians' appointed who tick off the fulfilled pledges ... They are written on the whole, without disrespect, by amateurs ... without the benefit of the advice of the old pros ... [the next passage was used in Michael Crick's election day report] ... There are occasions when one looks at a manifesto ... where a balloon comes out of one's head which says 'Garbage! God!' and then it's a question of handling matters so that, somehow or other, the garbage is made into something edible.[14]

Few moments are so revealing of our system of government as when temporary minister meets permanent secretary. Tony Benn, as one might expect, sees such moments in a very different light. Speaking of senior civil servants he told Hugo Young:

> During an election campaign they really de-couple themselves from their ministers, disconnect except for day-to-day business. They read the manifestos, then they prepare papers designed to show how part of them could be implemented and how part of them can't be implemented. They dress it up so that an incoming government will feel that there is a sympathetic Civil Service. In effect what they do, however, is to write massive briefs, which are the most important documents to be found in Whitehall, in which – and it's the only time it happens – they actually set out the Civil Service policy.[15]

Mr Benn tells the hilarious story of October 1974 when the Department of Industry prepared two briefs for Labour, one for Mr Benn returning Secretary of State, another for 'An incoming Labour Minister if not Mr Benn'. By mistake he was given both![16] Tony Benn has developed his own theory about the post-election process described by Lord Bancroft:

> The deal that the Civil Service offers a Minister is this: if you do what we want you to do, we will help you publicly to pretend that you're implementing the manifesto on which you were elected. And I've seen many ministers of both parties, actually fall for that one ... They are always trying to steer incoming governments back to the policy of the outgoing government, minus the mistakes that the Civil Service thought the outgoing government made.[17]

When one stands back from these two impressionist paintings of the same scene created by those two veterans of the Whitehall School, Benn and Bancroft, it dawns on one that the configurations of this celebrated portrait of public life were drawn more than a hundred years before the episodes they were describing. They can be found in that celebrated passage in which Northcote and Trevelyan stated in 1853:

> It may safely be asserted that, as matters now stand, the Government of the country could not be carried on without the aid of an efficient body of permanent officers, occupying a position duly subordinate to that of the Ministers who are directly responsible to the Crown and to Parliament, yet possessing sufficient independence, character, ability, and experience to be able to advise, assist, and to some extent, influence, those who are from time to time set over them.[18]

The words convey, as they were meant to, an impression of constitutional impeccability. But it surely could have been no surprise to Charles Trevelyan, at least, that these intelligent Whitehall paragons would, as years and experience grew with their grey hairs, exert more than a passing influence on the temporary masters the electorate placed in charge of them. Northcote and Trevelyan mapped out a remarkable system, a network without equal, upon which every minister after 1870 was obliged to depend. The power of that network to steer or to absorb those political chiefs whom the constitution supposes are there to direct it, never ceased to amaze the likes of Tony Benn, Dick Crossman and Thomas Balogh. The last two, though supposed experts in government, had no idea that official committees existed to shadow ministerial ones[19] and, subsequently, were to see conspiracy behind every filing cabinet.

Such a network exists and it is a kind of Frankenstein's monster created initially by the Victorian politicians themselves and often threatened but never broken by generations of politicians ever since. It is the very stuff of *Yes, Minister*, the constant refrain of nearly all ministerial memoirs and the quintessence of the Whitehall culture. The best description of it I have ever read was penned by one of Britain's leading cultural historians and a former wartime intelligence officer, Noel Annan. 'The spy system of the Mandarins', he called it. Writing for an American readership, as part of his attempt to provide the background to Peter Wright's *Spycatcher*, Lord Annan explained:

> The mandarins are the permanent secretaries who are at the head of each Ministry. The spies are the young civil servants who are the private secretaries of the Cabinet Ministers. Every meeting a minister has is attended by his private secretary, who logs it; every conversation he makes on the phone is recorded; every appointment he makes in Whitehall is monitored.
>
> If a Secretary of State starts to throw his weight about, or adopts a policy the civil servants regard as dangerous, the warning bells ring, and

in an emergency the top civil servant of all, the Secretary to the Cabinet, will intervene with the Prime Minister. If a Minister brings a political adviser into his ministry and the adviser does not toe the line, the mandarins cut off his information: he will appear at a meeting and discover that his rivals possess certain important memoranda that mysteriously have never reached his desk. He therefore appears to be badly briefed and loses credibility.

Each Tuesday morning before the mandarins meet in the Cabinet Offices [in fact, it's Wednesday morning] they are briefed by their spies to hear what is cooking. If you try to bend a Minister's ear in his office, what you say will be round the Civil Service within forty-eight hours: the only way is to catch him at dinner in the evening when his attendant nurse from the mental clinic, his private secretary, is no longer observing his patient.[20]

Lord Annan exaggerates in his asylum analogy, but only slightly. The Civil Service does take over a minister's diary and, if the minister permits it, a great deal of his or her life as well, from the Prime Minister – particularly the Prime Minister, as Bernard Donoughue's biopsy of Wilson's and Callaghan's appointments shows[21] – down.

Of all forms of power, private power is the most seductive for a certain sort of intelligent person – the sort who tends to become a civil servant and will continue, I suspect, to do so despite the disdain of public opinion and on the part of some ministers for the profession or the lure of alternative careers more attractive in material terms. In October 1987 I attended the reunion dinner held to mark twenty-one years of Kennedy Scholarships which, since 1966, had despatched a dozen or so young British graduates to Harvard or the Massachusetts Institute of Technology as a kind of living memorial to the late President, JFK. A particularly gifted civil servant of my acquaintance, surveying the well-heeled bankers and lawyers around the table in the Middle Temple, said that despite the difference in salary he would not swap his job for their's, as nothing could match the interest and variety of his own.

Though many of his peers had demonstrated their disagreement with my friend by evacuating Whitehall for the City, it remained true that the profession of private adviser to the wielders of governmental power remained inherently attractive, particularly for those who entered into its fast stream. The gateway to that stream since 1945, as we have seen, has been the Civil Service Selection Board – the key body in renewing the profession and, unless things change, picking its dominant figures some twenty-five to thirty years in advance. CSSB is one of the most intensively examined of all the Whitehall artefacts. In so far as it has a popular image it is of a gilded funnel through which a smooth arts-educated elite from the public schools and the ancient universities pour into a secure job for life insulated from outside influences, part of what Bernard Donoughue in a brilliant phrase called the 'velvet drainpipe'[22] phenomenon in the British Civil Service. CSSB, in this characterisation, is the cloning mechanism by which the *grand corps* created by Northcote and Trevelyan reproduces itself generation after generation. This already potent image received a powerful boost in 1986 when a BBC television documentary team, allowed to film the CSSB processes right through to the Final Selection Board, followed the fortunes of two candidates, both Oxbridge educated as it happens, in which the charming and beautiful ex-public schoolgirl is admitted to the Foreign Office despite demonstrating appalling ignorance of foreign affairs and the spiky ex-comprehensive schoolboy brimming with passionate views is turned down for the Home Civil Service.[23]

The post-1945 CSSB method was based, as we have seen, on techniques pioneered by the War Office Selection Board during the Second World War. Although, as I shall explain in a moment, I have long been impressed by the essentials of the method, one fact from its R and D phase has left me with lingering doubts: one of the guinea pigs used by WOSBEE, as the military precursor of CIZZBEE was known, was none other than the novelist Evelyn Waugh, who left an unforgettable account of it in his diary.

> The Army has become alarmed at the poor type of officers coming away from the OCTUs [Officer Cadet Training Units], a large proportion of whom, after passing out, are sent away from their regiments as unsuitable. So, like Romans consulting Sibylline books, they decided in despair to call in psychologists. As these unhappy men had never met an officer in their lives and had no conception of what they were supposed to look for, they were set loose on us with the idea that we are presumably more or less satisfactory types. I think they found us very puzzling.
>
> I was interviewed by a neurotic creature dressed as a major, who tried to impute unhappiness and frustration to me at all stages of adolescence. He had presumably been cautioned to keep off sex, as no word was said of it. He also neglected to mention religion and I gave him a little lecture about that at the end. He was chiefly surprised to learn that I chose my friends with care and drank wine because I like it ... We had a series of intelligence tests, printed forms with simple questions to be answered, such as are, I believe, issued to elementary schoolchildren. On another occasion he had a magic lantern and displayed a series of blotches which we were supposed to find like objects. Most of us made a mockery of this.[24]

Poor Waugh was a year later to cease to be a 'more or less satisfactory type' himself and was asked 'to leave the Special Service Brigade for the Brigade's good'.[25] Between this episode and his restoration to active service behind the lines in Yugoslavia, he was to write his masterpiece, *Brideshead Revisited*.[26]

I first encountered the organisation which had matured from the prototype described by Waugh when I took the qualifying test in 1969 for what was still the assistant principal competition for the Home Civil Service. I just cleared the first hurdle and was invited to CSSB but turned down the invitation as I had won a research scholarship to the London School of Economics in the meantime. In 1969 two recruitment systems were running in parallel, the old Northcote–Trevelyan competition based on a hefty series of tough, subject-based written examinations (known as Method I) which was to disappear in a few years, and Method II, the WOSBEE derivative. In 1957 the Civil Service Commissioners had reviewed the merits of the two systems and decided to keep both. Their report produced a classic little 'Prime Minister's Personal Minute' from Harold Macmillan. 'I have read your minute about the Civil Service Commissioners with great delight,' he told Norman Brook.

> I was brought up in a period when Method I, competitive examination, was regarded as the *sine qua non* of honest and effective administration. Method II was just patronage. Method I is the glory of the 19th century. Method II is the gift of the 18th century. I am glad to see that they are both being used in the 20th century. I think this is what modern theologians call the higher synthesis.[27]

Macmillan was, of course, entirely wrong about Method II, which had nothing to do with the eighteenth century and everything to do with the 1940s.

The next time I came across CSSB in 1976, the encounter was more direct than in 1969. The Director of CSSB in the mid-1970s was a Scottish psychologist, Ken Murray, a formidable advocate of the system who pursued a policy of exemplary openness and would proudly tell visitors of the many foreign governments who envied the British way of recruiting its top officials. I remember his telling me how he endeavoured to avoid the cloning syndrome whereby an existing administrative elite sought to reproduce itself by ensuring that one third of CSSB's assessors had never been civil servants themselves. He wanted them to watch out for signs of intellectual and personal arrogance on the part of the candidates. 'I do not like anything that marks them at the beginning as "The Lord's Anointed" like the old Indian Civil Service.' The job of the assessor, he explained, was to 'be analytical without being too cold-blooded right up to the end', he said.[28]

And that 'end' could be pretty bitter not because of bias or hostility, but from the sheer exhaustion of completing all the tests and exercises prepared for the would-be civil servant by CSSB's examiners. The system has been refined a little in the past decade but, naturally, my first impression of it (when I sat in on the entire procedure apart from the psychologist's interview which had so enraged Evelyn Waugh) was the freshest and most immediate. This is how it struck me in 1976:

> Last year 3,100 aspirants presented themselves to the commission seeking a toehold on the ladder to the most elevated posts in the Civil Service. A qualifying test, designed to measure their innate literacy and numeracy, reduced the field to 1050 candidates who were invited to undergo the 'mangling experience', to borrow the phrase of a now eminent public servant, of the two-day event at CSSB.
>
> The aim of CSSB is to compile as complete a picture of each candidate as possible. A series of cognitive tests provide an objective element. A further series of written appreciations, drafting tests and simulated committee work, examines in a very direct fashion the candidates' skill in handling the day-to-day duties they are likely to perform in a government department. Candidates are separated into groups of five, though they do not compete against one another, but against an overall standard. Their performance is monitored by three assessors, a psychologist, an observer (usually a civil servant in his late twenties) whose job it is to gauge their 'mental horse-power' and a chairman who is very often a retired public servant of great eminence. Individual assessors interview each candidate in turn and compare notes throughout the two days.
>
> The core of this year's CSSB programme involves an imaginary Whitehall brainteaser dealing with British aid to a notional developing country (a piece of inspired fiction whose ramifications were quite beyond the wit of this reporter) drafted, with frequent touches of whimsy, by an official on secondment from the Foreign and Commonwealth Office. Candidates are required to write an appreciation for the minister outlining the merits of the various options.
>
> The assessors then select a drafting test, which usually takes the form of a letter for the minister dealing with one area of the aid problem, and a committee test which requires each candidate to take the chair in an interdepartmental discussion on an aspect of the programme. Each test is selected with the intention of probing the candidate on what the assessors deem to be his or her stronger or weaker points.
>
> Finally the assessors draw all the strands together and award a mark on a numerical scale for penetration, fertility of ideas, judgment, written expression, oral expression, personal contacts, influence, drive and determination, emotional stability and maturity. These marks are collated on

> an alphabetical scale. Last year, 54 of the 1,050 hopefuls went forward to the Final Selection Board with an 'A' mark, indicating that CSSB saw them as future 'high fliers', 94 with a 'B' suggesting they might well 'fly' and 127 with 'C' on the ground that CSSB saw them eventually reaching the rank of assistant secretary but at a rather slower pace.[29]

I sat through CSSB on two more occasions in the late 1970s and the mid-1980s. On all three occasions I was impressed by the attention to detail, the determination to be fair right to the end even to candidates who after the first day had clearly performed so badly that they had no hope of reaching the standard required to go on to the last stage of the competition, the Final Selection Board, the mixed panel of insiders and outsiders usually chaired by the First Civil Service Commissioner himself. Only once was I shocked and it was a double shock at that. I may have been showing the kind of personal bias the assessors strive to avoid as the individual concerned was from a very similar background, in terms of university, degree subject and interests, to my own. After the mock committee exercise which he had chaired with aplomb, though it dealt with a tangled decision on where geographically to target industrial aid, the aspirant administration trainee (the assistant principal had ceased to be the entry grade in 1971) gathered his papers and said: 'Well, colleagues, I think we have based our advice to ministers on a thoroughly rational analysis but we should have no illusions. Whether the area actually gets the money will depend entirely on how many by-elections are pending in the region.' For this jovial and wholly realistic quip he was heavily marked down by the chairman of the assessors, a retired permanent secretary, who recommended the Inland Revenue as the place where such levity might be extracted from the young man concerned. Some time later I mentioned this to a serving permanent secretary in an economic department. He agreed that the candidate had been thoroughly justified in making that observation but added, to my horror, that 'old X was quite right to mark him down – cynicism in one so young is deeply distressing'.[30]

By the time of my third and last visit to CSSB, the Civil Service Commissioners had commissioned a rethink of their own. In 1982 Sir Alec Atkinson, a former second permanent secretary at the DHSS, was brought out of retirement to examine the selection system. When he reported in 1983 Sir Alec gave CSSB a clean bill of health – it 'continues to enjoy a high reputation and need not fear comparison with any other'[31] – though it was an expensive one. It cost some £11,000 to find a successful candidate. However, as Sir Alec points out, the pay and pensions of a successful candidate who entered at twenty-four, reached the rank of assistant secretary, and retired at sixty cost the Exchequer a total of £430,000,[32] so 'it would be imprudent to secure savings on the lesser amount which imperilled the value received on the greater'.[33] (A classic piece of Civil Service wordmanship, that.)

Atkinson urged the Commissioners to greater efforts in three areas that had been of outstanding concern:

* enhanced attention to bringing on insiders in the executive grades so that they could compete more effectively for fast-stream places with high-flying graduates from outside;
* more scope for late entry recruitment of men and women with outside experience;
* greater emphasis on attracting candidates from beyond Oxbridge – 'the main scope for improvement lies outside Oxford and Cambridge Universities'.[34]

But the most striking of his recommendations was 'reinstating the guidance to CSSB assessors that candidates of forceful and thrusting personality should be welcomed provided that they are able to work as members of a team, and continuing to stress the importance of giving full weight to personal qualities as well as to intellect'.[35]

My last visit to CSSB postdated Atkinson and I detected genuine efforts to imbibe those critically important criteria within the system and the equally important need to look for managerial as well as policy-making potential. The Oxbridge element continued to predominate post-Atkinson despite the determined missionary work of the First Civil Service Commissioner, Dennis Trevelyan, who toured assiduously around the polytechnics, the redbrick and the plate-glass universities. In 1986 357 Oxbridge and 2,030 non-Oxbridge candidates sat the Qualifying Test (15% to 85%). Of those attending CSSB 125 were from Oxbridge and 207 from elsewhere (38% to 62%). Of those attending the Final Selection Board 59 were from Oxbridge and 70 from elsewhere (46% to 54%). Oxbridge, however, overtook the rest at the final hurdle. Passing successfully from the FSB were 54 Oxbridge candidates and 45 non-Oxbridge (55% to 45%). Of the 78 men and women who took up administration trainee (AT) or higher executive officer (development) (HEO (D)) appointments in 1986, the final tally was as shown in Table 3.

Nick Gurney, Trevelyan's deputy, was to my mind accurate in the way he dissected the forces which continue to drive the Oxbridge candidates to the top of the competition, when questioned for LWT's *Whitehall*:

First, selection to the Civil Service is on merit. Second, the standards of this competition are very high. Third, I think most educationalists, parents and others agree that Oxford and Cambridge take a lot of very able people. And, fourth, there is a long tradition of such people applying

TABLE 3. AT AND HEO (D) ENTRANTS 1986

	University			Degree subject		
	Total entrants	*Oxford and Cambridge*	*Other university or polytechnic*	*Arts*	*Social Sciences*	*Science and Technology*
Men	55	30	25	32	14	9
Women	23	6	17	15	6	2
Total	78	36	42	47	20	11

	Degree class			
	Class I	*Class II*	*Class II i*	*Class II ii*
Men	20	4	22	9
Woman	5	2	15	1
Total	25	6	37	10

Source: *Civil Service Commission, Annual Report 1986*

> for the fast stream in the Civil Service. Now, if you put that together . . . it is barely surprising that we're going to get quite a few successful people coming into the fast stream from Oxford and Cambridge and I'm glad to see that . . . There is no preference for Oxbridge. There's no question of background being more important than ability . . .[36]

Now I, as an arts graduate from St John's College, Cambridge, may be showing personal bias when I admit to never having worried unduly over the question of Oxbridge domination of the Civil Service intake. As a grammar school lad who enjoyed, even relished, my own ancient university, I have never felt such places to be utterly unrepresentative citadels of privilege. Meritocracy was the dominant strain at Cambridge by the time I arrived in 1966.

Far more worrying to me than social origins, school and university is the element of self-selection in the kind of people who apply to the Civil Service Commission in the first place. It worried another grammar school – ancient university man, Bernard Donoughue, too. Donoughue has spoken of a 'personality inhibition . . . the kind of person who chooses the Civil Service as a lifetime career is possibly more conservative and cautious than some others and, certainly, it's someone who will need great convincing of the need to take risks on change because they're not taking risks on their career'.[37] The dominance of the safety-first type can only have been increased at a time when, as Civil Service Commissioner Gurney admitted, the Civil Service in job-market terms was 'meeting more competition than in the past from the accountancy profession, the City and so on',[38] and suffering from a severe image problem stemming from political and media attacks which he did not mention. All the more reason, one would have thought, for CSSB and FSB to search more fully for Atkinson's thrusters. 'In terms of originality,' said Commissioner Gurney in his LWT interview, 'we most certainly do wish to attract such people ... and I rather suspect we're not attracting enough because, after all, our candidate population selects itself. And they, perhaps, select themselves against an image of the Civil Service which, I would say wrongly, but in their eyes might be seen as traditional, safe, conservative ...'[39]

Some time after his television interview, Mr Gurney explained that in terms of 'originality and pronounced character', his 'main concern was to demonstrate that these were more difficult attributes to assess than I have found to be commonly realised, and that they need to be complemented by other, equally important attributes such as commonsense, pragmatism and ability to rub along with a wide variety of different people, to listen and to compromise where necessary.'[40]

Gurney's fellow Commissioner, Teddy Morgan, who directed CSSB until 1987, emphasised the practicality requirement. Passing the pre-CSSB Qualifying Test, he says, demonstrates a candidate's intellectual horsepower, but sometimes, with 'the very highly intellectually agile ... man or woman ... you can hear the engine purring away up in the front, but [there is] nothing connecting it to the wheels, no clutch'.[41] But Mr Gurney went further than his 'wrecker-of-the-inner city' in parodying the sober Sir Alec Atkinson's prescription. 'Pronounced character' he found a difficult concept. 'In the Civil Service, like any other large organisation, we must have people who will relate well to others ... we don't have room for bullies, for autocrats, for ego-trippers.'[42]

CSSB, however, is a self-critical organisation. Ken Murray, Teddy Morgan and Clarence Tuck, who held the job between Murray and Morgan, were not complacent people. But, for me, CSSB is attempting the impossible for two reasons. Firstly, it is beyond the scope of anyone to predict the kind of Civil Service that ministers, Parliament and the public will need twenty-five to thirty years on, which is the moment at which CSSB's successes will be entering their kingdoms as permanent, deputy and under secretaries. In 1950 when the young Robert Armstrong entered the Treasury as an assistant principal it would have been impossible to foretell the delineations of the economy and the society which he was to survey on entering the Cabinet Office in 1979. Secondly, even if the needs of the Civil Service *could* be foreseen thirty years in advance, it would be impossible to predict which of the young men and women successfully negotiating the tests and exercises of CSSB and the extended interview of

FSB will be best suited to meet them. Teddy Morgan, CSSB's tester-in-chief, was very honest about this: 'The most difficult thing of all is to forecast what kind of civil servant they will make in the various options which they've chosen over quite a long period because, although there is much greater mobility of labour nowadays than there used to be, there are still a fairly sizeable number of people who are aiming to join the Civil Service because they intend to stay there.'[43]

Mr Morgan's remarks in 1987 were significant as they seemed to contradict the findings of a follow-up survey of the 421 men and women recruited as assistant principals in the reconstruction competitions of 1945–8, the results of which had been published by the Civil Service Department in 1976. The statistical analysis of the reconstruction competitions was undertaken by Dr Edgar Anstey, head of the CSD's Behavioural Sciences Research Division. It led him to claim that the CSSB procedure in the immediate postwar period achieved 'probably the highest validity coefficient that has ever been obtained for high-grade selection in any country'. Dr Anstey acknowledged that the FSB marks had been disclosed to the successful candidates and the departments to which they were posted. 'This practice', he said, 'may have helped new entrants with very high marks to get off to a good start – the self-fulfilling prophecy – but it is hardly likely to have continued to affect their progress after the first two or three years, by which time departments would have formed their own opinions.'[44]

My criticism of the reliance placed on CSSB as the selector of saplings from which future Whitehall oaks will grow is that it artificially restricts the richness and variety of the forest that may be required if government, politics, the economy and society change as much in the period 1987–2017 as they have, say, between Suez and Mrs Thatcher's third election victory. CSSB does an impossible job well, but it is impossible nonetheless. Many of its persistent or alleged deficiencies – the reproduction of yesterday's elite, the Oxbridge and arts biases, the difficulty of predicting and the cost if duds get through at over £11,000 per time – would be remedied if it figured less large in the recruitment scheme of things, as I think it could and should (see pp. 725–7).

CSSB for all its importance is only the start of Whitehall's grooming of its young thoroughbreds. Its toughness and competitiveness can make successful candidates feel part of an elite, which, indeed, they are. The positive vetting that so often follows enhances a feeling of specialness, as do the induction courses and security briefings new recruits receive. And even if CSSB does avoid the recruiting-in-its-own-image trap, the process of acculturation thereafter can produce much the same result, as the Civil Service's No. 2 gatekeeper, Nick Gurney, readily admits:

> We have to remember that recruitment is merely the first stage of the process of becoming a civil servant. And, after twenty or more years in the Civil Service, you're bound to have been moulded and influenced to some extent by the ethos and culture in which you've been working as well as influencing and moulding it in your own turn. So, when somebody points a finger at a civil servant who's been in twenty or thirty years and says, 'Ah, typical civil servant' – a term, by the way, which I personally take as a compliment not an insult – you have to remember that he might be quite a different person from the one who was recruited.[45]

The Civil Service, it must be admitted, is very proficient at moulding its bright and its young. They very quickly rub shoulders with the great, the seasoned and the established in the upper ranks and are indulged in the way that dons treat bright, sparky undergraduates who are fun to teach. Fairly quickly, a proportion of them move into the private office of a permanent secretary. There the process of a generation recruited thirty years earlier shaping one that will still be there thirty years later is at its most intense. In this way, the Holy Grail of Northcote–Trevelyanism and all its sub-cultures is transmitted in almost pure extract.

As so often, the most eloquent depicter of this private process was Ian Bancroft in an address to the Royal Society of Arts in 1984, which I have partially quoted earlier.

> I was trained in the Treasury for good or ill by a man who still ferociously pursues the public good. Those were the golden days when 'monitor' was still a noun. He showed me how to negotiate, how to draw breath in mid-sentence so as to discourage interruption, how to draft, and why the service belongs neither to politicians nor to officials but to the Crown and to the nation. It is an odd irony that this intensely private man should have given railway language a new word. His name is Serpell [Sir David Serpell who chaired a review of railway financing in 1982]. He has been a life-long friend and will not thank me for mentioning him.[46]

And when a group of similarly accultured young men and women spend the next three decades rising, more or less in parallel, up the Civil Service hierarchy, they will, by the time they gather each Wednesday as mature persons in their fifties at the regular permanent secretaries' meeting, be more or less indistinguishable from each other whatever the stratum of society into which they were born, the school they attended or the subject they read at this or that university. Their habits, modes of thought, patterns of speech, style of drafting will have rubbed off one to the other to the point where but a few free or tough or independent spirits resist mutation into a sludgy administrators' amalgam.

It is this blending, this marinating of the new generation in the juices of the old, their gradual maturing over decades which produces the phenomenon on which a battery of 1980s critics have fixed their gunsights. For John Hoskyns they are a generation demoralised and defeated by presiding over thirty years of policy failure.[47] For Norman Strauss they are natural compromisers 'who have not missed a consensus yet'.[48] For Bernard Donoughue, the result of stuffing bright 22-year-old graduates into Whitehall's velvet drainpipe is that 'they emerge at the top as senior civil servants thirty-odd years later and not much light has come in along the way. . . They've become associated with ministerial attempts at change and if [they] fail, they become bruised by it, they think "Well, I tried that last time when I was younger and I wasted a lot of time and energy and I sat up all night and it came to nothing." '[49] Conversations with officials who have spent many unbroken years grappling with the tougher of the intractable problems of Britain's economy or society can be a hard-boiling experience. Even when there is public largesse to be distributed, the gloom sometimes fails to lift. 'Government is always about the losers. The gainers never thank you' is a philosophy I have frequently heard. Career lifers very easily drift into such attitudes.

Mind you, large doses of sceptical realism are sometimes justified. Stephen Taylor likes to tell the story at management conferences of his time in the Department of Transport's Policy Review Unit in the bleak days following the OPEC crisis of 1973:

> One day we got a letter from a poultry farmer in Dorset, saying that he had the answer to the oil crisis in the shape of an engine that ran on chicken slurry and would we like to come and see it. Normally that kind of thing got the reply 'thank you for your interesting letter, the contents of which have been duly noted'. But matters were pretty serious, so I arranged for one of our vehicle inspection engineers to go down and have a look. I have kept the minute he sent me afterwards, which I have here and which I shall read to you.
>
> 1. As requested, I have been to see the poultry farmer near Bournemouth.
> 2. His equipment consists of a hopper mounted on the roof of a 1956 Morris Minor, into which slurry from his chicken shed is piped, a methane converter on the back seat, and a methane-burning engine in the boot connected to the drive shaft.

3. A day's slurry from 75 chickens is sufficient to charge the converter, start the methane engine and propel the vehicle, and I have seen this done.
4. However, I think it right to point out that the vehicle would go faster, and much further, if instead the chickens were harnessed to the front bumper and obliged to pull it along.

To be fair to the Civil Service, it has come increasingly to accept the validity of Donoughue's 'velvet drainpipe thesis' and has deliberately driven holes into it. These take two forms: two-way secondments between Whitehall and outside professions; and the development of the Civil Service College as both a meeting place and a two-way mirror. In 1986 secondments with industry and commerce of three months' duration or more were running at 189 into the Civil Service and 280 out, a total of 469, a substantial (almost fourfold) increase over ten years from 123 in 1977 (60 in, 63 out).[50] In 1986 the detailed breakdown was as shown in Table 4. A substantial programme exists alongside the industrial/commercial traffic of exchanges with other bodies such as local authorities, regional health authorities, quangos, universities and European institutions. In 1986 this particular flow measured 394 out and 95 in, a total of 489 in all.[51] At the highest levels of assistant secretary and above, a select group of forty officials in 1986 were given permission to acquire experience as non-executive directors or observers at the board meetings of private companies. Such appointments are unpaid and, as the Cabinet Office puts it, 'care is taken to avoid conflicts of interest'.[52]

What impressions are gained from those involved in this two-way human traffic? Will Pedder left his merchant bank, Lazarde Brothers, for a two-year spell in the DTI. He found that there was 'still a big gulf of understanding between the public sector and the private sector arising really from the difference in culture. The civil servant is thinking of his public duty, his responsibility upwards to ministers, whereas the private sector person is thinking of how to get their company to survive in a competitive environment.'[53] Mr Pedder's testimony is weighty because, far from harbouring an animus against those civil servants with whom he worked, he warmed to their virtues:

> I was very surprised coming in as a secondee to find how dedicated – I think that's not too strong a word – a lot of staff (certainly the high fliers) ... are to the concept of public service, of doing the job well because it's good for the country, working very long hours on occasions; [I] find that really a very pleasant contrast from the private sector where people are more out for their own good, trying to jockey for position

TABLE 4. INTERCHANGE WITH INDUSTRY AND COMMERCE, 1986

	Secondments out of Dept	*Secondments into Dept*	*Total*
Ministry of Agriculture, Fisheries and Food	4	1	5
Cabinet Office	1	3	9
HM Customs and Excise	1	0	1
Ministry of Defence	141	63	204
Department of Education and Science	2	4	6
Department of Employment	24	5	29
Department of Energy	5	8	13
DOE/Transport/PSA	28	21	49
Department of Health and Social Security	10	2	12
Home Office	5	9	14
Overseas Development Administration	1	2	3
Scottish Office	4	3	7
Department of Trade and Industry	36	46	82
HM Treasury	15	12	27
Welsh Office	3	1	4
Export Credits Guarantee Department	0	2	2
Registry of Friendly Societies	0	2	2
TOTAL	280	189	469

Source: Cabinet Office

> within their companies, trying to demonstrate that they're doing better than their colleague down the corridor. Civil Service sense of duty is very strong and very very surprising to an outsider.[54]

Given such warmth, his criticisms have bite. His chief one is directed at 'the Whitehall game of arguing one's own department's policy through the system ... at times it's reminiscent of a university debating society ... Their real interest lies in the political interaction with ministers ... that's where the fun lies and management is considered a secondary objective to policy-making.'[55]

The outward flow of secondee civil servants is a tacit recognition of the validity of Mr Pedder's point. John Taylor left the DTI for a spell with the construction firm, Balfour Beatty. He reckons there is no substitute for officials actually working in industry for a time, particularly those in a ministry like DTI where 'most of my colleagues have gone straight from university not via industry. They have been attracted to the Civil Service not for the same reasons that people are attracted into industry. Yet they are in a department which has to work closely with industry, has ideally to establish the framework and environment in which industry can flourish without having any direct experience of that industry and, therefore, the only way that it can be overcome is to go out on these secondments.'[56] John Taylor, like Will Pedder, is an enthusiast for secondments but he feared that on returning to his department, he would not be posted to the division dealing with the construction industry, where his experience would be of direct relevance, and 'I'm sure that once I go back, I will be gradually absorbed back into the existing ethos of the Civil Service and it will be very easy for me to forget, unless I go out again on a regular basis, the lesson and experiences that I've learned.'[57]

Those who live in it have no doubt about the power of the Whitehall culture and the ethos entrenched by a century or more of experience. The growth in secondment is admirable but, clearly, it is not enough to transform substantially the attitudes and practices of Lord Zuckerman's '3000 highly intelligent men and women' who chose 'to make non-electoral politics their professional career', let alone the 600,000-strong army they supervise and manage.

The other institutionalised syringe for injecting new thought and outside experience into Whitehall is that enduring creation of the Fulton Report, the Civil Service College. The college was formally opened by Edward Heath in 1970 as one of his first engagements after winning the general election. William Armstrong once told me that Wilson wanted Norman Hunt to run it. Armstrong wanted Pat Nairne, then an under secretary in the Ministry of Defence. A compromise was agreed. The choice would be delegated to the Civil Service Commission under its First Commissioner, John Hunt. In an open competition, an accomplished social scientist, Eugene Grebenik, a demographer from Leeds University, was chosen. 'Grebby', as he was universally known, used to complain later that his brief was an impossible one – to create an institution which combined the functions of All Souls and a mechanics' institute.[58]

There was some justice in 'Grebby's' lament. The college was intended to cater for the elite, not for the masses huddled over the ministry desk. The commentating classes and some backbench MPs active in the select committees continued to hanker after a British version of L'Ecole Nationale d'Administration in Paris to do for the Crown Services in grey what the Staff College at Camberley does for the Crown Services in khaki. In the event, the early college tended to fall between all the stools.

It enjoyed something of a revival in the late seventies and early eighties under the successive principalships of Barbara Sloman and Brian Gilmore. But it was the coming of the financial management initiative (the FMI) and the new emphasis on personnel management, in which training was a key element, and the close interest taken in training by Mrs Thatcher, which projected the college at long last into a place in the Whitehall sun, a position confirmed by the appointment of a young rising star from the MOD, Roger Jackling, as its Principal in 1986. (Jackling had impressed Mrs Thatcher during the Falklands War and subsequently served for a brief spell in No. 10 as her defence adviser.)

The vast bulk of Civil Service training is undertaken by departments themselves. The college supplies only 5 per cent and there are no plans to increase its market share, though its market share of training provided for principals and above is between 70 and 80 per cent.[59] And 'market' is the right word. One of the changes imposed on the college in the Thatcher years was the obligation on departments to pay it for course places provided. Ministries, therefore, could choose to train their people themselves or to send them outside to business schools in preference to the college. The new financial regime caused a dip in placements, from 89,000 student days in 1985–6 to 82,000 in 1986–7, but the college more than covered its costs.[60]

Its reshaping to meet the requirements of the post-Rayner Civil Service was evident from the breakdown of its courses in 1986–7. Systems training (information technology and management services) topped the bill with 505, followed by management studies with 241, public administration and social policy with 144, accountancy and internal audit with 130, statistics and operational research with 101 and economics with 59.[61]

What was particularly impressive about the Raynerisation of the Civil Service College was the inclusion of the top ranks within the process. In its early years it was rare for the college's work to penetrate the stratosphere. The permanent secretaries would use its facilities in Sunningdale for their annual conference every autumn, but that hardly amounted to a course. There was an occasional seminar for officials at assistant secretary level but little else, the unspoken assumption being that at that stage of their careers they knew what the job of a civil servant was about.

The most dramatic symbol of the change is the Top Management Programme through which all officials must pass in the transition from assistant secretary to under secretary. It was designed by John Mayne, a member of the prototype CPRS, who was brought over to the Cabinet

Office from the Ministry of Defence to put the new course together. Mayne toured the business schools and the staff colleges in 1985 plagiarising the best existing practises for Whitehall's use. Ironically, the college was not wildly keen on having Mayne's 'Flying Circus',[62] as I once called it, given its peripatetic nature moving from a public–private-sector joint session at a country house to a purely Civil Service phase at Sunningdale. Luckily for the college's overall reputation, the Top Management Programme was eventually integrated with its existing provision as it won high praise from all sides, including Rayner himself. Rayner described it as 'an excellent course' on the basis of reports from Marks & Spencer executives who had taken part in it.[63]

The under secretaries' course lasts for six weeks in all, the first three of which are spent with an equal number of the fast-rising from the private sector. Hayden Phillips, a high-flyer from the Home Office, who succeeded John Mayne as course director in 1986, in true FMI style breaks its purpose down into specific objectives:

> To enable quite senior people to get a better understanding of what is going on in a whole series of environments – economics, technology, society; interchange between the public and private sector and learning from each other; to help senior managers develop a real sense of strategy about the management of their organisations; it's about value for money and quality of service – and finally it's about leadership and learning the important tasks that senior civil servants have in motivating and encouraging their staff.[64]

The training programme is broken up into four parts: tutoring by outside speakers from the public and private sectors, the business schools, the universities and the media, the 'going back to school' element, as Phillips calls it;[65] sessions led by course members in which they dispense insights based on their own work experience; problem-solving in syndicates; and finally, 'sets of seminars where we bring together two or three distinguished visitors . . . in slightly more relaxed surroundings with slightly less pressure to discuss current issues'.[66]

The current philosophy of Civil Service career development is, in Phillips's words, 'a constant process of re-education . . . to make sure that one wasn't just using [the Top Management Programme] as . . . a remedial injection for people in their middle age who had not had a good deal of training before'.[67] What this means is that the young flyer emerging from the Civil Service Commission's Final Selection Board can expect between the ages of say twenty-two and forty-two to experience a sporadic, though planned, programme of training with the prestigious under secretaries' course at its apex.

At the bottom is the often-changed Administration Trainee Course for the new entrant, first introduced in 1971. It never was intended to be a British version of ENA. It still isn't. Roger Jackling, the college's principal, is quite explicit and open about this:

> We don't see our job [as being] to train people in the way that the French do at ENA which is, in a sense, postgraduate education preparatory to entering government. What we do here is a little bit of induction which is necessary on first arrival, and then short courses which are designed to train people up in particular areas as and when that training will be useful to them and will reinforce what they are doing in departments ... ENA, it seems to me, is an extension of the selection process ... I suspect that once [it is] behind them, its influence on their competence is less than that of short bursts of job-related training which is what we provide.[68]

The initial burst the ATs receive in the college's London headquarters in Belgrave Square near Victoria Station within a few months of joining their department tells them, in Mr Jackling's words, 'where the Civil Service fits into the system of government and politics in the UK'.[69] From my own experience of teaching ATs a bit about Cabinet government on this course, it is a good mix of outsiders and insiders with an emphasis on candour about such matters as ministerial/official relationships (the Crossman Diaries are an ingredient) and Whitehall's dealings with the press. Like most other outsiders, I have found the ATs a highly stimulating audience, though, naturally, not as tough or as funny as the senior executive officers with years of experience in Customs or the Revenue that one encounters in middle management courses.

The idea is to give the ATs about eighteen weeks of training in their first five years. After the initial course, the programme is broken down into specific modules of practical relevance such as economics and statistics. The college tries not to burden them with heavy, lengthy courses of the kind they have so recently experienced at university. But some problems still bedevil the modular stretch of the AT programme. As Roger Jackling explains, they are intended to take these 'after they've been in their departments for two years or three years, which is when they are quite likely to find themselves in private offices or in busy divisions and the line managers find it difficult to spare them. That is a problem we have responded to by making the modules more intensive and shorter ... Departments should respond to it by being a bit more determined to see that their people get all the training they're meant to.'[70]

Linking the AT and the under-secretaries' courses over that twenty-year time span is another recent innovation, the Senior Management development programme in which principals and assistant secretaries receive a mere five days' training a year from the college or an outside institution, such as a business school, in job-related skills like personnel management or investment appraisal which both they and their establishment officers agree to be beneficial. It is a very weak link in the chain linking the rookie and the old sweat, but a good deal better than the void which preceded it.

Another link in that chain, which the college has been valiantly forging since the early post-Fulton days, is the Senior Professional Administrative Training Scheme, known as SPATS. The idea behind it is twofold: to enable promising scientists and professionals of grade 7 (principal equivalent rank) to transfer to administration and policy work and to equip those who remain in their specialisms to cope better with its increasing administrative content as they rise to the top posts in their laboratories and research establishments. Some twenty specialists a year were put through a six-week course on government, parliament, the law, personnel and financial management.[71] So great was the demand when unified grading was extended downwards to principal level in 1986 that the college was obliged to put on two courses a year and to cram the content into three weeks. The SPATS net catches an impressively wide trawl. The autumn 1987 course, for example, included a theoretical physicist, an electronics engineer, a civil engineer, an accountant, a statistician, a photo scientist, an information officer, a data processor, a planner, a chemist, a factory inspector and an official receiver.[72]

As the twentieth anniversary of the Fulton Report drew near, the Civil Service College found itself in better condition than at any time since its foundation. But it still remained more marginal to mainstream Whitehall life than it should have been, as shown by the continued reluctance of departments to make the time needed to release their best and busiest staff for courses. In this it worked in total contrast with the Armed Forces. And the reason was candidly explained by Roger Jackling himself. 'The fundamental philosophy', he said, 'is that you learn to do your job in government at your desk, not in a school.'[72] As long as that doctrine holds true in all its purity and starkness, Civil Service training and the college which embodies it will remain valuable but peripheral.

Training an organisation of the size and the variety of the British Civil Service is a daunting prospect. In fact, it is impossible to think of any institution which contains such a kaleidoscopic mixture of people and skills within its boundaries. The best way to appreciate the panorama is to examine it section by section.

The picture on 1 January 1987 looked like this. The Civil Service in its crudest division can be separated into two main categories: 500,419 non-industrial officials, and 105,593 industrials (of whom nearly 30,000 were craftsmen of various kinds). The non-industrials divided almost evenly between men and women, though the bulk of the women work in the lowest two grades of the administrative hierarchy. The open structure embracing all types of non-industrial official reached down to principal rank of grade 7, as shown in Table 5.

TABLE 5. CIVIL SERVICE UNIFIED GRADES

Grade	*Men*	*Women*	*Total*
1 (Permanent Secretary)	38	1	39
2 (Deputy Secretary)	133	3	136
3 (Under Secretary)	467	22	489
4 (Supervising grade)	163	7	170
5 (Assistant Secretary)	1,955	153	2,108
6 (Senior Principal)	3,483	251	3,734
7 (Principal)	10,909	983	11,892

Source: HM Treasury

Below the rank of principal, the Civil Service explodes into a mass of categories and special classes. The general category shelters the big battalions of executive and clerical officials, and the professional groups not included in the scientific or technical categories, as shown in Table 6.

Such is the huge and remarkable collection of men, women and skills at the disposal of the party to whom the electorate entrusts power. The Prime Minister, its chairman, and the Cabinet, its board, pay a tidy wages bill for the privilege, though when broken down into particles it is far from lavish (see Table 7). For the purpose of pay and conditions, this army of crown servants, members of the secret services apart, organise themselves into seven unions which reflect either the grades of their membership, such as the First Division Association for the mandarinate, the National Union of Civil and Public Servants for the executive ranks, or specific functions, like the Institution of Professional Civil Servants for the scientists and specialists or the Inland Revenue Staff Federation for the taxmen and women below the ranks of the Inspectorate.

TABLE 6. CIVIL SERVICE GENERAL CATEGORY

ADMINISTRATION GROUP

Rank	*Men*	*Women*	*Total*
Senior Executive Officer	7,237	907	8,144
Higher Executive Officer (D)	150	66	216
Higher Executive Officer	19,163	6,163	25,326
Administration Trainee	70	21	91
Executive Officer	25,408	21,811	47,219
Administrative Officer (used to be known as clerical officer)	26,866	58,149	85,015
Administrative Assistant (used to be known as clerical assistant)	16,575	48,818	65,393

ECONOMIST GROUP

Rank	*Men*	*Women*	*Total*
Senior Economic Assistant	56	9	65
Economic Assistant	48	16	64

INFORMATION OFFICER GROUP

Rank	*Men*	*Women*	*Total*
Senior Information Officer	253	47	300
Information Officer	282	154	436
Assistant Information Officer	60	55	115

LIBRARIAN GROUP

Rank	*Men*	*Women*	*Total*
Senior Librarian	28	22	50
Librarian	61	88	149
Assistant Librarian	57	140	197

STATISTICIAN GROUP

Rank	*Men*	*Women*	*Total*
Senior Assistant Statistician	52	38	90
Assistant Statistician	22	23	45

TABLE 6. CIVIL SERVICE GENERAL CATEGORY—*contd*

SECRETARIAL CATEGORY/GROUP

Rank	*Men*	*Women*	*Total*
Manager grades	3	1,640	1,643
Personal Secretary	26	4,588	4,614
Typists	92	17,961	18,053

SOCIAL SECURITY CATEGORY/GROUP

Rank	*Men*	*Women*	*Total*
Local Officer 1	7,511	9,821	17,332
Local Officer 2	8,358	24,693	33,051

SCIENCE CATEGORY/GROUP

Rank	*Men*	*Women*	*Total*
Senior Scientific Officer	2,684	176	2,860
Higher Scientific Officer	2,801	406	3,207
Scientific Officer	2,062	671	2,733
Assistant Scientific Officer	1,321	593	1,914

PROFESSIONAL AND TECHNOLOGY CATEGORY

Rank	*Men*	*Women*	*Total*
Senior P & T Officer	5,039	53	5,092
Higher P & T Officer	6,932	77	7,009
P & T Officer	13,567	153	13,720
P & T Officer IV	1,512	11	1,523
Graphics Officer Group	346	68	414
Marine Services Group	470	—	470

RELATED PROFESSIONAL AND TECHNOLOGY GRADES

Rank	*Men*	*Women*	*Total*
Technical Officer B	5	—	5
Trainees (all categories)	456	74	530
Technical Grade 1	72	291	363
Technical Grade 2	11	70	81

TABLE 6. CIVIL SERVICE GENERAL CATEGORY—*contd*

SECURITY CATEGORY/GROUP

Rank	*Men*	*Women*	*Total*
Security Officer I	2	—	2
Security Officer II	10	—	10
Security Officer III	41	3	44
Security Officer IV	321	13	334
Security Officer V	1,337	83	1,420

TRAINING CATEGORY/INSTRUCTIONAL OFFICER GROUP

Men	*Women*	*Total*
5,021	115	5,136

LEGAL CATEGORY

Men	*Women*	*Total*
53		
31		
84		

MUSEUMS CATEGORY

Men	*Women*	*Total*
58	30	88

POLICE CATEGORY/GROUP

Men	*Women*	*Total*
3,638	263	3,901

RESEARCH OFFICER CATEGORY

Men	*Women*	*Total*
146	70	216

TABLE 6. CIVIL SERVICE GENERAL CATEGORY—*contd*

GENERAL SERVICE CLASSES

	Men	*Women*	*Total*
Actuaries	25	3	28
Cartographic and Recording Draughtsmen	2,489	508	2,997
Cleaners	79	1,440	1,519
Medical Officers	460	104	564
Messengers, Office Keepers and Paper Keepers	4,765	4,267	9,032
Pharmaceutical Officers	56	28	84
Photographers	428	19	447
Photoprinters	896	1,927	2,823
Process and General Supervisory	1,221	45	1,266
Psychologists	137	75	212
Stores Officers	1,632	81	1,713
Telecommunications Technical Officers	853	2	855
Telephonists	263	1,447	1,710
Teleprinter Operators	363	212	575

DEPARTMENTAL CLASSES

HOME OFFICE GRADES

Rank	*Men*	*Women*	*Total*
Immigration Service	1,285	313	1,598
Prison Governors	519	79	598
Prison Officers	17,497	971	18,468

INLAND REVENUE GRADES

Rank	*Men*	*Women*	*Total*
Tax Inspectorate	3,958	844	4,802
Tax Officer (higher grade)	5,917	5,078	10,995
Tax Officer	3,979	9,685	13,664
Collector	1,927	1,178	3,105
Assistant Collector	1,470	3,053	4,523
Professional Valuation grades	982	192	1,174
Non-Professional Valuation grades	1,292	1,034	2,326
Capital Taxes Examiners	80	27	107

TABLE 6. CIVIL SERVICE GENERAL CATEGORY—*contd*

COURTS SERVICE

Rank	*Men*	*Women*	*Total*
Bailiffs	818	13	831

DEPARTMENT OF TRANSPORT

Rank	*Men*	*Women*	*Total*
Driving and Traffic Examiners	1,811	74	1,885

HEALTH AND SAFETY EXECUTIVE GRAPES

Rank	*Men*	*Women*	*Total*
Factory Inspectorate	749	95	844
Mines and Quarries Inspectorate	84	—	84

Source: HM Treasury

Ever since the Whitley system was established after the First World War (see p. 81), the staff associations have been a part of the regular establishment, though in many cases and most decades since then they have expressed far from Establishment opinions. Yet the FDA is the nearest the British Establishment has to a trade union affiliated to the TUC. With 7,609 members, including the Association of HM Inspectors of Taxes with which it merged in the mid-1970s, it has a majority of the permanent secretaries within its ranks. They, like many other FDA members, are in a particularly delicate position when strikes are called. A degree of professional schizophrenia is involved in acute cases, as during the 1981 strike when Mike Fogden as FDA Chairman took part in inter-union planning for the dispute and, as deputy controller of the DHSS Newcastle Central Office, was deeply involved in contingency planning to reduce the impact of the dispute on the payment of benefits.[74] The FDA in the 1980s was as much a professional body as a trade union pursuing steady and thoughtful campaigns on issues such as open government and a code of ethics for public servants.

The boffins' union, the Institution of Professional Civil Servants, at 85,689 members more than eight times the size of the FDA with which it has sought unsuccessfully to merge in the mid-1970s, was equally impressive in its own specialist fields. No other British union could match the IPCS for the quality of its conference debates on issues like nuclear safety in which members from the Atomic Weapons Research Establishment or the

Atomic Energy Authority would debate with delegates from the Natural Environment Research Council. The IPCS pursued a steady, moderate and restraining course during the outbreaks of Whitehall militancy in the 1970s and 1980s. In 1987 it finally broke ranks with the other unions and reached a new pay agreement with the Treasury which went some way to recognising the scarce skills many of its members possessed.

The National Union (formerly the Society) of Civil and Public Servants, the union of the executive grades, has long been in stark contrast to the IPCS. Its membership is generalist where the IPCS ranks are specialist and its bargaining stance militant where the IPCS, in the end, is conciliatory. The old hard left has always had a firm foothold in the Society and its conferences exude a fieriness which sits oddly with the sober citizenry of office managers, customs officers and prison governors which make up its ranks.

At 90,397 members the Society is second in size only to the 147,189 Civil and Public Services Association representing the massed clerical grades. Periodic attempts have been made to merge the two. Yet the NUCPS and the CPSA are different not just in the sense that the National Unions members are the managers of the CPSA's big battalions in the clerical factories and the diaspora of local offices. The CPSA is a more volatile union swinging dramatically in its politics from left to right and back again. Its membership is young and changes fast. The National Unions is older and relatively stable. And the CPSA's left is new left, not old. In the late eighties the Militant Tendency was its dominant strain, making it an establishment officer's nightmare.

Yet the panoply of Civil Service unions also possessed the nearest the British Labour movement has to a hard right union – the 25,575-strong Prison Officers' Association – another nightmare at least to the establishment officers of the Home Office's Prison Service and the Scottish Office. Their membership, in general terms, had less in common with the CPSA's militants than Mrs Thatcher has with Mr Gorbachev. Completing the union picture is the 54,057-strong Inland Revenue Staff Federation, a tough professional body which moulded the young Jim Callaghan and the 36,135-strong Civil Service Union which, after a crippling loss of membership when its radio operators at GCHQ were forcibly deprived of their union membership, sought the shelter of eventual merger with the NUCPS.

The Civil Service unions, plus the Northern Ireland Public Service Alliance, operate through an umbrella body, the Council of Civil Service Unions, which, under the genial secretaryship of Peter Jones, has the difficult task of formulating common positions from such an extraordinarily mixed bag of memberships, a task only exceeded by that of the United Nations General Assembly. Yet despite such problems, the failure of the

21-week strike in 1981 and the de-unionisation of GCHQ three years later, on average some 75 to 80 per cent of non-industrial civil servants remained in membership of a trade union in the mid 1980s.[75]

The modern British state had by the last decades of the twentieth century accumulated piecemeal a large regular army of crown servants in civvies, much criticised, difficult to manage and yet formidable in its capability. I remember telling Burke Trend of Lord Home's brilliant idea, had he won the 1964 election, of letting Enoch Powell loose upon it.'Ah,' said Trend, 'not even Enoch could have won. Nobody could. The machine wins every time.' The machine is daunting in its history, its traditions, its restrictive practices and, above all, in the proportion of our national talent it recruits and locks within itself. More and more in the 1980s its critics pressed the case for freeing up the Whitehall labour market – for letting the lifers out and the outsiders in. The traditionalists within could and did reply by pointing to Whitehall's long tradition, when faced with particularly vexing, complicated or controversial problems, of looking outside to its reserve army of auxiliaries, the men and women of the royal commission and the committee of inquiry. It is to these worthies that we must now turn.

TABLE 7. RATES OF PAY IN THE HOME CIVIL SERVICE

OPEN STRUCTURE

Grades 1–1A	*Grade 2*	*Grade 3*	*Grade 4*	*Grade 5*	*Grade 6*	*Grade 7*
£59,500–65,000	£43,500–54,000	£34,000–41,000	£28,975–30,475	£24,765–28,215	£18,786–25,335	£15,030–20,292

GENERAL CATEGORY

SEO	*HEO D*	*HEO*	*Admin. Trainee*	*EO*	*Admin. Officer*	*Admin. Assist.*
£12,150–15,500	£10,900–13,900	£9,900–12,650	£8,000 10,150	£5,820–10,100	£3,664–7,247	£3,314 5,799

ECONOMIST GROUP

Senior Economic Assistant	*Economic Assistant*
£10,900–13,900	£8,000–10,150

INFORMATION OFFICER GROUP

Senior Info. Officer	*Information Officer*	*Assist. Info. Officer*
£12,093–15,200	£9,798–12,407	£5,455–9,821

LIBRARIAN GROUP

Senior Librarian	*Librarian*	*Assist. Librarian*
£12,093–15,200	£9,798–12,407	£6,942–9,821

TABLE 7. RATES OF PAY IN THE HOME CIVIL SERVICE—*contd*

STATISTICIAN GROUP

Senior Assist. Statistician	*Assist. Statistican*
£10,900–13,900	£8,000–10,150

SECRETARIAL CATEGORY

Manager Grades	*Senior Personal Secretary* (Inc. Trainee PS)
£8,400–12,650	£5,600–10,150

SCIENCE CATEGORY

Senior Scientific Officer	*Higher Scientific Officer*	*Scientific Officer*	*Assist. Scientific Officer*
£11,557–15,214	£9,219–12,505	£7,816–10,154	£4,004–7,816

PROFESSIONAL AND TECHNOLOGY CATEGORY

Senior PT Officer	*Higher PT Officer*	*PT Officer*	*Graphics Officer Group* Trainee→G1	*Marine Services Group* G3→G1
£13,005–15,823	£10,154–13,005	£8,284–11,089	£3,892–15,309	£7,930–15,309

RELATED PROFESSIONAL AND TECHNOLOGY GRADES

Technical Officer B	*Trainees* (*All Categories*)	*Technical Grade I*	*Technical Grade 2*
£13,005–15,214	£7,349–9,219	£6,388–8,370	£3,592–6,498

SECURITY CATEGORY

Security Officer I	*Security Officer II*	*Security Officer III*	*Security Officer IV*	*Security Officer V*
£10,203–11,729	£9,493–10,817	£6,856–7,683	£5,635–6,437	£5,199–5,916

SOCIAL SECURITY CATEGORY

Local Officer 1	*Local Officer 2*
£5,550–10,097	£3,664–7,547

TRAINING CATEGORY

GA	£10,842–12,624	GII	£8,769–10,382
GB	£10,534–11,707	GIII	£8,155–9,946
GI	£9,992–11,151	GIV	£7,285–8,964

LEGAL CATEGORY

Senior Legal Assistant	*Legal Officer*
£17,336–23,534	£10,387–14,587

MUSEUMS CATEGORY

Grades D–G
£3,568–15,200

TABLE 7. RATES OF PAY IN THE HOME CIVIL SERVICE—*contd*

POLICE CATEGORY

Constable	£7,752–12,936
Sergeant	£12,372–14,193
Inspector	£14,193–16,116
Chf. Inspector	£16,116–17,928
Superintendent	£21,924–23,805
Chf. Superintendent	£24,372–25,878

RESEARCH OFFICER CATEGORY

SRO	£10,960–13,988
RO	£6,942–10,103

Source: HM Treasury

13 AUXILIARIES

THE ESTABLISHMENT NOTION

A secret tome of *The Great and the Good* is kept, listing everyone who has the right, safe qualifications of worthiness, soundness and discretion; and from this tome came the stage army of committee people.
Anthony Sampson, 1965[1]

Nor ought one exclusively to rely on the Civil Service Department's famous 'List of the Great and Good', all of whose members, if I may be allowed to indulge for a moment in my propensity to exaggerate, are aged fifty-three, live in the South-East, have the right accent and belong to the Reform Club.
Lord Rothschild, 1976[2]

I would welcome new names. I seek new names.
Paul Channon, Minister of State, Civil Service Department, 1980[3]

It is part of the British gift for public administration to ensure freedom to extra-governmental bodies by placing them in the hands of men and women who can be trusted to exercise it [power] disinterestedly in the public good. If this did not continue, no amount of superstructure, guardians and guardians of the guardians could avert or cope with the resultant trouble.
Sir William Haley, former Director-General of the BBC, 1977[4]

All paid-up members of the Establishment know that we are born to be figures of fun, the perfect target for a custard pie.
Sir William Rees-Mogg, Chairman of the Arts Council, former Editor of The Times, ex-Vice-Chairman of the BBC, 1986[5]

Whitehall's regulars have long realised that they cannot make policy entirely on their own. For nine hundred years, beginning long before the first

English Parliament was summoned, the permanent government has mustered and kept in reserve a territorial army ready to answer its country's call. They have a generic term – the Great and the Good – from the unofficial title of the Whitehall list (now a set of computer disks) on which their names are kept. William the Conqueror started the whole very English business while spending his Christmas holiday at Gloucester in 1085. He decided to assess the national income of his kingdom. The noblemen he despatched as commissioners to do the work – men like Remigius, the Bishop of Lincoln, and the Barons Henry de Ferrers and Walter Giffard[6] – were the prototype great and good of old England and the Domesday Book of 1086 was their first report. They have been a standard prop in the scenery of government ever since.

The great and the good form an important segment though not the whole of that other great British breed and fixation, the Establishment. Those who are members of it, the self-ironic Sir William Rees-Mogg apart, tend to loathe the term and to deny its validity. Lord Radcliffe, a pillar of the postwar G and G, once declared in a Cambridge Lecture, 'Let a fairy grant me my three wishes, I would gladly use them all in one prayer only, that never again should anyone using pen or typewriter be permitted to employ that inane cliché "Establishment" '.[7] It is, however, a notion that will never die and it is worth examining the phenomenon itself before examining its G and G mutation.

'The Establishment' is a fluid, mercurial concept, infuriating in its imprecision to minds as tidy as the late Lord Radcliffe's. It was not always so. Lord Radcliffe himself quotes the toast common amongst the rural Anglican clergy in the early nineteenth century – 'Prosperity to the Establishment and confusion to all Enthusiasts'.[8] Those sound and comfortable clergy were referring, no doubt, to the Established Church, that is, their own, and to the vulgar enthusiasms of the non-conformists. But had their targets been secular the toast would have seemed equally apt. For their period was the tail-end of the Whig autocracy when the Establishment knew who it was and the non-established did, too. They were the Whig grandees, landed men who possessed huge estates and elegant mansions which exuded, as Lord David Cecil put it, 'an extraordinary impression of culture and elegance and established power'.[9]

For Cecil, the Whig aristocracy 'was before all other things a governing class. At a time when economic power was concentrated in the landed interest, the Whigs were amongst the biggest landowners; their party was in office for the greater part of the eighteenth century; during this period they possessed a large proportion of the seats in the House of Commons; they produced more ambassadors and officers of state than the rest of England put together. And they lived on a scale appropriate to their power.'[10] The eighteenth-century Establishment ran England, which, as we have seen, was still very largely a patronage society, from those marvellous country estates – 'their houses were alive with the effort and hurry of politics. Red Foreign Office boxes strewed the library tables, at any time of day or night a courier might come galloping up with critical news, and the minister must post off to London to attend a Cabinet meeting.'[11]

The nineteenth century saw a blurring of the boundaries of political and financial power, beneficial, no doubt for the British economy but highly inconvenient for the cartographer of the Establishment. The progressive shift of money and influence from country to city, from agriculture to manufacturing, the blossoming of a professional middle class, their representation in a new kind of politics, led to a seepage of power from those 'cream and gilt libraries piled with sumptuous editions of the classics'[12] and littered with official papers from Whitehall, and its dispersal throughout a thoroughly confusing diaspora which, by Edwardian times, had even begun to embrace the trade-union movement.

It is typical of the development of language that the vocabulary of power took about a century to catch up with what by the end of the First World War was a thoroughly faded Whig ascendancy, though the country-house phenomenon, its attendant habits and morals, remained quite capable of capturing the politically, socially and economically mobile on their way up. The noun 'establishment' begins to make its sporadic appearance just as the Conservative Party of Stanley Baldwin and the Labour Party of Ramsay MacDonald were about to bury the fragmented husk of the old Liberal Party into which the Whigs, with some difficulty, had eventually deliquesced. In 1923, in R. Macaulay's *Told by an Idiot*, the following sentence appears containing not just *that* word but an enduring truth as well: 'The moderns of one day became the safe establishments of the next.'[13]

But its usage in our time is largely the responsibility of that most diverting and intellectually fertile of postwar political commentators, Henry Fairlie. In his regular 'Political Commentary' column in the *Spectator* in September 1955, shortly after Guy Burgess and Donald Maclean, the notorious pair of defecting British diplomats, had turned up in Moscow, Fairlie suggested that the 'Establishment' would continue to cover up for two of its own:

> . . . what I call the 'Establishment' in this country is today more powerful than ever before. By the 'Establishment' I do not mean only the centres of official power though they are certainly part of it – but rather the whole matrix of official and social relations within which power is exercised.
>
> Somewhere near the heart of the patterns of social relationships which so powerfully control the exercise of power in this country is the Foreign

Office . . . At the time of the disappearance of Maclean and Burgess, 'the right people' moved into action . . . No one whose job it was to be interested in the Burgess–Maclean affair from the very beginning will forget the subtle but powerful pressures which were brought to bear by those who belonged to the same stratum as the two missing men.[14]

Fairlie, for all his excellent contacts, cannot have known just how fully he would be vindicated when papers from Sir Anthony Eden's Cabinet were released under the thirty-year rule in January 1986. A combination of the reappearance of Burgess and Maclean and the revelations in Australia of the KGB defector, Vladimir Petrov, had created something of a frenzy in Westminster political circles, particularly as Petrov had pointed to the existence of a Third Man who had tipped off Burgess and Maclean that MI5 was closing in. It was clear to ministers that a parliamentary statement would be required promising action of some kind. The Foreign Secretary, Harold Macmillan, was the urbane incarnation of those values, mannerisms and social connections Fairlie had in mind in his article. In a Cabinet paper circulated on 18 October 1955, Macmillan recoiled from the prospect of a public inquiry for which the Labour Opposition was pressing as 'Nothing could be worse than a lot of muck raking and innuendo. It would be like one of the immense divorce cases which there used to be when I was young, going on for days and days, every detail reported in the press.'[15]

He told the Cabinet on 20 October 1955, 'he was concerned that there was nothing to be said for holding an inquest into the past. This would give currency to a stream of false and misleading statements which could never be overtaken and corrected in the public mind.'[16] Macmillan favoured instead an internal inquiry into security procedures. The Cabinet concurred and a committee of Privy Counsellors was summoned for the purpose, chaired by Lord Salisbury, Lord President of the Council. Lack of incriminating evidence obliged Macmillan to clear the name of Kim Philby, the former MI6 officer, during the Commons debate that ensued. This later proved embarrassing to Macmillan as Prime Minister in January 1963 when Philby himself defected to Moscow.

There is a timelessness about this rich cocktail of Establishment values, spy scandals, public prurience and allegations of cover-up. Macmillan's 1955 memo on Burgess and Maclean had been declassified for less than a year when an 'immense case going on for days and days, every detail reported in the press' brought an almost identical cast of characters into play when the British government tried to suppress the publication of Peter Wright's memoirs in Australia. The British Establishment, claimed Wright, had never accepted that it was 'en masse penetrated by the Russians'.[17] Sir Robert Armstrong was treated by Wright's lawyer, the aggressive Malcolm Turnbull and the extraordinary New South Wales trial judge, Mr Justice

Powell, as a surrogate for the entire British Establishment. The Cabinet Secretary irresistibly reminded me of Sidney Carton on the scaffold in Charles Dickens's *A Tale of Two Cities*.[18] It was this spectacle which inspired a vintage article from the pen of my old boss from *Times* days, Sir William Rees-Mogg, in which he wrote of Armstrong: 'I have every fellow feeling for him. We would both have to confess to being members of the Establishment – indeed he is probably the leading figure of the Establishment. He is also a kind, sensible, intelligent, moderate and highly cultivated man . . . to go to give evidence in ockerish Australia is as certain to invite farcical retribution as for a Victorian missionary to try to impose trousers on a cannibal island'.[19] Henry Fairlie's *Spectator* piece thirty-one years earlier provided the thought and the phrases for the 1986 eruption surrounding the Wright trial as it had for much of the comment which greeted the appointment a month earlier to the chairmanship of the BBC of Mr Marmaduke ('Duke' Hussey)[20] another man I remember with affection from *Times* days. Fairlie's must rank as one of the most seminal columns ever printed.

Fairlie may not have shamed the Foreign Office into candour in 1955, but he struck an immediate and enduring chord with the more irreverent members of the political nation. The phrase 'Establishment' stuck to an extent that infuriated Lord Radcliffe. Before enumerating Fairlie's followers in the late 1950s, natural justice requires me to risk the charge of unfashionability by claiming that one aspect of Establishment supremacy in Burgess and Maclean territory was probably beneficial. The fact that Britain's cold-war security purge of its public service was kept inside the family, as it were, did ensure that we avoided any serious outbreak of home-grown McCarthyism at least until Peter Wright and the MI5 'Young Turks' began spiriting names into the public domain after the exposure of Anthony Blunt. The occasional oddball, such as Sir Waldron Smithers MP, would regularly press for a Select Committee on Un-British Activities. But the answer, whether it was from Mr Attlee or Mr Churchill, was the same.[21] The permanent secretaries, with the backing of ministers, kept tight control over the purge to avoid making martyrs.[22] Neither political party sought to make security the kind of issue at the polls it had become in the United States after the 1948 presidential election.

Such a claim in mid-fifties England would have been dubbed an irredeemable statement of Establishment wisdom and derided accordingly. The names of the derisors who followed Fairlie make for glittering reading. Lord Altrincham (better known as the journalist and political biographer John Grigg) launched his broadside against the Establishment in *The National and English Review* two years after Fairlie's opening salvo.[22] As Obituaries Editor of *The Times* he later became their unofficial gravedigger. The gilded, though not so youthful, C. P. Snow, in *The Conscience of the*

Rich, published in 1958, had his interwar journalist figure refer to 'that gang', by which he meant 'the people who had the real power, the rulers, the establishment.'[24] And in 1959, the year of Macmillan's electoral triumph (though some two years ahead of the satire boom), the Fairlie genre was crowned when Anthony Blond published *The Establishment: A Symposium*[25] edited by the young Hugh Thomas, a top-flight historian, working at that time on his classic study of *The Spanish Civil War*[26] after employment as a diplomat in the Foreign Office and as a lecturer at the Royal Military Academy, Sandhurst.

Thomas himself contributed an essay on the class system; the economist John Vaizey opened his discussion with a typically Vaizeyian squib – 'Intelligent discussion of the public schools is handicapped by the fact that they are indescribably funny';[27] the novelist Simon Raven turned his formidable word-power on the military; the economist Thomas Balogh, as we have seen, made the most quoted and longest lasting contribution in his famous attack on the senior Civil Service, 'The Apotheosis of the Dilettante'; stockbroker Victor Sandelson dissected the City Establishment; the former Tory MP, Christopher Hollis, brother of Sir Roger Hollis of MI5, Peter Wright's chief quarry, tackled 'Parliament and the Establishment'; while founding father Henry Fairlie rounded the volume off with an attack on the BBC; 'of all the voices of the Establishment', he wrote, 'the British Broadcasting Corporation is the most powerful'.[28]

Three of the contributors were themselves to benefit from what Michael De-La-Noy called 'the establishment bounty'[29] – the honours system. Balogh was created a peer by Harold Wilson as was Vaizey, though he died a convinced supporter of Mrs Thatcher, who ennobled the symposium's editor as Lord Thomas of Swynnerton. Lord Thomas now runs the Prime Minister's private think-tank, the Centre for Policy Studies. Their collective ennoblement might be construed as proof positive of Macaulay's doctrine whereby the moderns of one day become the Establishment of the next, though a peerage does not necessarily confer honorary membership of the Establishment. Indeed, only one member of the House of Lords, Lord Franks, is on record as acknowledging his inclusion among its ranks: 'If anybody likes to label me in that way, I don't object, because what it means is that I have done public duties from time to time. That's by definition being a member of the Establishment – so, yes.'[30]

For our purposes, the Franks criterion – that of performing 'public duties from time to time' – is the benchmark to be used for tracing the contours of the Establishment. It cannot be a complete map. Each profession has its own Establishment and not all of those involved engage in wider public duties. Each sport has its own Establishment. Alan Watkins once unforgettably described Mr Peter May, Chairman of the Test Selectors, as 'one of those who view the world from behind a collar-stud'.[31] For some it is all a question of political attitudes. Ronald Butt reckons that 'the great and the good among political commentators' are those 'whose idea of political neutrality resembles the collected words and deeds of Mr Roy Jenkins and Mrs Shirley Williams', an 'establishment which Mrs Thatcher had the effrontery to challenge with some of the common sense of the suburbs'.[32] For others, like Tim Heald, it is a question of networks, clusters of old boy networks to be precise, based on family, school, college, club.[33] All this illustrates the impossibility of doing for the contemporary British Establishment what Lord David Cecil did for the Whigs.

The Franks criterion, however, does help to isolate and identify an important and ancient slice of it – the great and the good, the men and women whose names are kept on the famous List of the Great and the Good in the Cabinet Office to which ministers and permanent secretaries resort when searching for people to sit on royal commissions, committees of inquiry, the boards of nationalised industries plus assorted advisory councils, Britain's 'half awake quangoland', as Peter Jenkins rather cruelly characterised it.[34] Who are the 'great', who are the 'good'? How are they found? What is their utility? Are they an elite? If so, of what kind – an aristocracy, a gerontocracy, a meritocracy or merely a 'legitimate mafia'.[35] As, traditionally, they have mattered so much to Whitehall and its regulars, it is important to find out.

FINDING THE GREAT AND THE GOOD

> Once, when Giant Reason still ruled in old England, they used an archaic device, called a Royal Commission or a Committee of Inquiry.
> **Professor Peter Hall, 1985**[36]

> There is a fashion in these things and when you are in fashion you get asked to do a lot.
> **Lord Franks, 1977**[37]

> Committees are the oriflamme of democracy.
> **Harold Macmillan, 1953**[38]

The origin of the phrase 'the great and the good' is lost in the Establishment mists, though it is highly unlikely that one of their own invented it, given its ironic, faintly comical overtones. I encountered it as a child in the 1950s when, in common with thousands of Roman Catholic youths at Benediction, I would trill 'God bless our Pope, the great, the good'. But this is to confuse matters. Whatever the progress of ecumenism, His Holiness will never be invited to chair a British royal commission. The phrase 'great and good' conveys an aura of wisdom and benevolence. Its ambience is apolitical, high-minded, non-partisan. The activity it suggests is one which eschews short-term gain for long-term benefit, putting the strategic above the tactical.

The 'List of the Great and the Good', however, suggests that a hierarchy exists among committee people in the eyes of ministers and senior civil sevants who do the choosing. As Tom Schuller, an Associate Member of Nuffield College, Oxford, has suggested, 'The Great' are the Lord Franks's of this world, people of chairman potential, and 'The Good' are the rest who fill the chairs either side of the green baize tables.[39] A month after he uttered it, the Schuller distinction acquired the kind of sanctity that only an official document can confer. At the preview of the 1955 Cabinet papers granted to the press on 30 and 31 December 1985, the story of how the Eden Cabinet authorised the preparation of a draft Commonwealth Immigrants Bill, designed to restrict the inflow of coloured people from the colonies, attracted much attention. Particularly appreciated by journalists at the table around which sat representatives of *The Times, The Guardian* and *New Society* was a collector's item which offered a rare insight into the decorous hierarchical world of the great and good.

The Home Secretary, Gwilym Lloyd George, a convinced protagonist of control, argued that parliamentary and public opinion in mid-1955 was not generally aware that unrestricted coloured immigration from the colonies was causing difficulties in certain parts of the inner cities and that the problem would worsen unless curbs were applied on the waterfront and at the airports. As Sir Norman Brook, Secretary of the Cabinet, explained in a steering brief to Sir Anthony Eden, drafted on 14 June 1955, 'the Home Secretary proposes a committee of enquiry. Its purpose would be, not to find a solution (for it is evident what form control must take), but to enlist a sufficient body of public support for the legislation that would be needed.'[40] Three days earlier, Lloyd George had circulated a Cabinet paper suggesting 'the following for the composition of the committee':

Chairman: Lord Radcliffe, or failing him, the Earl of Crawford and Balcarres, or Mr John Sparrow (Warden of All Souls) or Sir David Lindsay Keir (Master of Balliol).
One Conservative, One Labour and One Liberal MP.
One representative of employers' organisations.
One representative of the TUC.
One person familiar with Commonwealth problems, to be nominated by the Commonwealth Secretary.
One person experienced in colonial administration, to be nominated by the Colonial Secretary.
One person (preferably a woman) well known as a social worker.
One economic expert.

One member of a local authority concerned with housing and public health questions.

At least one of the members should be chosen from Scotland and one from Wales.[41]

The terms of reference for this committee of eleven, chaired by a big name and peopled by a carefully balanced ballast encompassing political parties, capital and labour, relevant experience, a woman and persons from Scotland and Wales, were to be:

> To consider and report whether, having regard to the importance of maintaining traditional ties between this country and other parts of the Commonwealth, any, and if so, what?, changes in the law relating to the admission to the United Kingdom of British subjects from overseas (or any class of them) and to their subsequent stay in the United Kingdom, are necessary or desirable in the national interest and in the interests of the immigrants themselves.[42]

Norman Brook, himself an experienced Home Office hand, told the Prime Minister: 'I think that most members of the Cabinet now agree that a report by an independent committee is necessary for this purpose.'[43] But, showing where *real* patronage lies in the system, he applied a very superior version of quality control to the names dished up by the Home Secretary, confirming in the process Lord Radcliffe's position as unofficial No. 1 on the List of the Great and Good. Brook wrote to Eden:

> Of the Chairmen suggested, John Sparrow seems the best. Lord Radcliffe, who is in great demand, should be reserved for subjects which are more complex or difficult intellectually. Lord Crawford also would do other things better. John Sparrow is a lawyer: though he is untried, I think, as a committee chairman, it would be quite a good thing to bring him into this sort of work.[44]

All Brook's careful sifting came to naught. No committee on coloured immigration was commissioned. Cabinet discussion proved inconclusive and Eden booted the issue into touch by establishing a Cabinet committee on the subject chaired by Lord Kilmuir, the Lord Chancellor.[45] And when Parliament eventually legislated on the matter with the Commonwealth Immigration Act in 1962[46] it did so without the benefit of prior advice from a committee of the great and good.

The reaction of officials involved in the G and G operation in the 1980s to the publication of that 1955 document was twofold: 'nothing changes', said one;[47] 'You're very lucky to get that', said another; 'it doesn't very often get on the file.'[48] Indeed, the thirty-year rule does not seem to apply to the list of the Great and the Good. Its custodians in the forties and fifties (the List was a Bridges invention) were part of the Treasury's Establishment side. But no trace of the List or the running files of its compilers have reached the Public Record Office, which means that the systems analyst of the G and G must rely on occasional pieces of flotsam to follow the real power of patronage through its underground channels.

Mercifully, as that anonymous insider put it, 'nothing changes', at the top level at least. There have been important improvements in the engine room, if not on the bridge, since the mid-1970s, changes to which we will turn later. What other beams of light exist to illuminate patronage at the top? The ultimate locus of power in No. 10 is, in fact, laid down in the secret rules of the Cabinet system, the now familiar document *Questions of Procedure for Ministers*. The relevant paragraph in the most recent version to reach the public domain, the 1976 marque, reads as follows:

> The Prime Minister should be consulted in advance about appointments of chairmen and deputy chairmen of nationalised industries and public boards; he should be informed in advance about appointments of chairmen and deputy chairmen of the more important departmental committees of an independent or semi-independent nature; and he should be given the opportunity to comment before the appointment of members of boards and commissions in cases where they are likely to have political significance.[49]

The second tier of patronage, one below that of the prime minister, is beautifully laid bare in Mrs Castle's Diary dealing with the period 1974–6 when she was Secretary of State for the Social Services. In 1975, the Wilson government was keen to buy time on the controversial issue of private beds in National Health Service hospitals. The remedy, sanctified by long Wilsonian practice, was to establish a royal commission. The next requirement was to pick a chairman who would increase the chances that its final report would go with the grain of ministerial prejudice. On Wednesday 5 November 1975, Mrs Castle held a private dinner at the Old Russia restaurant for her Health Minister, Dr David Owen, her special advisers, Jack Straw and Professor Brian Abel-Smith, and some of her allies in the public service unions. She takes up the story:

> Over drinks before the meal, I had casually raised the question of the chairmanship of the Royal Commission on the Health Service. Had they any suggestions? To my surprise, Audrey [Audrey Prime of NALGO] said enthusiastically, 'Yes, Merrison' [Alec Merrison, then Vice Chancellor of Bristol University]. David and I were rather taken aback, but

as she had served with him on the Merrison Committee [the Committee of Inquiry into the regulation of the medical profession, 1973–5], she was in a better position than any of us to judge his attitudes to the NHS and *the things in which we believe* [emphasis added]. She was emphatic that he was a dedicated supporter of the NHS and she was sure he would have no truck with private financing and all that nonsense. David and I agreed afterwards that this made Merrison a very serious contender for the job.[50]

Alec Merrison duly got the job – and a knighthood. Ten years later, David Owen was quite candid about the episode. In an interview for BBC Radio 3, the following exchange took place:

OWEN: Sadly, politicians have rigged Royal Commissions ... I've been party to that myself, I'm afraid, so I plead guilty.

HENNESSY: Which one did you rig – the Merrison one on the National Health Service?

OWEN: The National Health Service, that's the one, yes. That was rigged basically. I mean it was ensured that [it] was not going to come out with a powerful minority report [which] would oppose the basic principles of the National Health Service ... I would claim it was done for higher motives. But it was rigged.[51]

Sir Alec Merrison is a highly regarded scholar and administrator-cum-chairman. It is unfair to infer from Mrs Castle's Diary and Dr Owen's recollection that he was or is an unqualified placeman and a creature of crude political patronage. But other documentary fragments from the postwar private life of the G and G do attest to the kind of amateurism which led Sir Michael Edwardes, in the context admittedly of private companies, to rail against the absence of 'a system for appraising the calibre and performance of people' which, Sir Michael said, switching to the example of government ministers, means that 'nobody tries to measure their intelligence, leadership, drive or any other damn thing'.[52] What would Sir Michael have made of this gem from the Cabinet minutes for 1954? The issue is the composition of the new Independent Television Authority, precursor of the Independent Broadcasting Authority, which was to preside over a great engine of commercial and media growth in the 1950s and 1960s. Peopling it was a standard G and G exercise overseen at ministerial level by the Postmaster-General, Earl de la Warr. The matter reached Cabinet, the highest decision-taking forum in the land, on 26 July, 1954:

The Postmaster-General said that it was important that the Authority should be appointed and should set to work without delay. Unless it could hold its first meeting before the end of the summer the Authority might not be able to initiate the programmes until towards the end of 1955. The Authority would have an advisory function, and *the qualities required in the Chairman and members were tact and sound judgement rather than energy and administrative ability* [emphasis added].[53]

Matters did not change much over the next thirty years. A permanent secretary exploded over the lunch table in the early 1980s, when speaking of the G and G, '*They* are the real amateur element in the system, *not* us; and they're not even gifted amateurs'.[54] The G and G themselves can be disarmingly frank about their lack of specialist qualifications. Lord Wolfenden was chairman of the Home Office's Departmental Committee on Homosexual Offences and Prostitution, in popular newspaper terms the spiciest of all the postwar committees (and, serious though its findings were, the one most vulnerable to *comédie noire* as when a deputation of street ladies declined to cross the threshold of the Home Office to give evidence[55]). Wolfenden, a classical don and university administrator, was offered the job in 1954 by Sir David Maxwell Fyfe, the Home Secretary, an overcoat slung over his pyjamas, in a sleeping car on a train somewhere between Liverpool Lime Street and Crewe.[56] In his memoirs Lord Wolfenden confessed himself baffled as to why he was chosen, being an expert on neither subject, supposing the reason to be 'that if a government wants somebody to examine as objectively and dispassionately as possible some area which is likely to be controversial it is not a bad thing to look to the universities to provide him'.[57]

The Committee on Homosexual Offences and Prostitution was inevitably more of a poisoned chalice than a glittering prize of public life. But we have seen the high politics and personality of the deployment of the patronage weapon at prime-ministerial and ministerial level. Its philosophy, as adumbrated by Earl de la Warr, defies parody. But how are the 'other ranks' found? In the 1950s the Treasury possessed both advantages and disadvantages in fulfilling its head-hunting responsibilities. Its operation seems to have been a rather hit-and-miss affair. Lord Plowden, himself never far from the top three of the G and G in the last thirty years, remembers as head of the Treasury's Central Economic Planning Staff in the early 1950s that 'the list of the great and the good was fairly short. Some of the people on it were dead. No one knew who to go to. I sent a private memo to Norman Brook saying that an attempt must be made to widen the list and keep it up to date.'[58]

Yet Lord Plowden's pedigree illustrates perfectly the rich endowment of human capital the G and G embodied in his generation, thanks once again to Adolf Hitler. As a young businessman he was recruited to the Ministry of Economic Warfare in 1939. By the end of the war he was at the age of thirty-eight Chief Executive at the Ministry of Aircraft Production. He was recalled to Whitehall in 1947, as we have seen, to run the Attlee administration's new Central Economic Planning Staff. Lord Plowden's G and G record passes through the chairmanship of the United Kingdom Atomic Energy Authority 1954–9 where he played 'a vital part' in the crucial 1958 agreement restoring the exchange of nuclear information between the United States and Britain,[59] the Treasury's Committee of Inquiry into the Control of Public Expenditure 1959–61, the Foreign Office's Departmental Committee on the Organisation of Representational Services Overseas 1963–4, swiftly followed by the Committee on the Future of the Aircraft Industry 1964–5, and the Standing Advisory Committee on the Pay of the Higher Civil Service 1968–70. In 1987, at the age of eighty, he was still active as chairman of the Top Salaries Review Body, which once a year projects him into the newspaper headlines, as whatever recommendations the TSRB produces for the remuneration of permanent secretaries, judges and generals, the result is invariably one of public and parliamentary outrage. The Plowden family are, in fact, the nearest post-war Britain has come to possessing a Whig dynasty: Lady Plowden is a former chairwoman of the Independent Broadcasting Authority and has a fistful of influential reports to which her name is attached; son William was once a member of the Central Policy Review Staff and now runs the Royal Institute of Public Administration which, under his leadership, has spawned several important inquiries of its own; son Francis, of Coopers and Lybrand, has been an influential shaper of the Thatcher administration's financial management initiative as a consultant to the joint Treasury/Management and Personnel Office Financial Management Unit.

Postwar Whitehall drew deeply and frequently for its G and G chairmanships on the pool of talent channelled initially by Miss Beryl Power. One senior Treasury man, Sir John Winnifrith, who was responsible in the forties and fifties for the List, pined for Miss Power's operation. 'It's very unlike the Great and Good. They really were winners', he said.[60]

In the postwar G and G roll of honour the names of Oliver Franks (Ministry of Supply 1939–46), Cyril Radcliffe (Ministry of Information 1939–45) and John Maud (Ministry of Food 1941–4) crop up repeatedly, in Franks's case until the early 1980s. Herbert Morrison coined an apt phrase to describe the breed. He called them 'the useful people'.[61] Postwar Whitehall also failed to repeat in bureaucratic terms the feat of Mr Frank Gent and his team in 569 Chiswick High Road, as Lord Plowden's memo to Sir Norman Brook bore witness – though to be fair, the postwar list of the Great and Good in the Treasury should *not* be confused with Beryl Power's Central Register in the Ministry of Labour. They were compiled by different people for different purposes even though no doubt some of the names overlapped.

For a large part of the period since 1945, the G and G were managed by Miss Mary Bruce, a Treasury principal who reported direct to successive Heads of the Home Civil Service. Miss Bruce was described by a former colleague as 'a silver-haired diminutive lady with sewn-up lips'. She is remembered as 'an institution, the repository of all knowledge, she would only speak to those who needed to be spoken to. Everyone was terrified of her. It was said that she liked horses more than people. She would come into the office on Saturdays wearing jodhpurs.'[62] For Miss Bruce the process of selecting the great and good required absolute secrecy. She dealt very much on a personal basis with her permanent secretary. 'It was all very *ad hoc*', said one insider, 'names were on different lists – for example there was a nationalised industries list – but it was never brought together.'[63] Miss Bruce took over the list in 1950 and died in harness in 1973 at the age of fifty-seven.

Some twenty years after Lord Plowden's attempt to stimulate reform, another Whitehall amphibian tried again. Acting on a suggestion from Reginald Maudling, Home Secretary in the Heath administration, Lord Rothschild, the first head of the Central Policy Review Staff, examined the system. 'I may be wrong,' Lord Rothschild recalled, 'but I thought I detected some resistance on the part of the authorities to the Think Tank studying this subject. Patronage is ... a very precious and delicate commodity, and the list of the Great and Good is jealously guarded, no doubt for good if not great reasons.'[44] The Tank took a look anyway. Its report remains classified. A hint as to its contents can be found in a lecture Lord Rothschild delivered after leaving Whitehall:

> Obviously, the selection of the right people for these critical posts should be hived off ... from the politicians and the Civil Service; and the independent selection panel should not be headed by an emeritus member of either class. But this pipe-dream won't come true. To paraphrase Clemenceau or Talleyrand, patronage is too serious a matter to be left to outsiders.[65]

The initiative was chewed up by the Whitehall machine. 'They did set up a committee,' said one insider, 'and that killed it.'[66]

After the fall of the Heath government in 1974, reform of the G and G found another powerfully placed patron in Dr Bernard Donoughue, head of Harold Wilson's new Downing Street Policy Unit, who acted without knowledge of the Rothschild initiative:

> I had no idea Victor had done that. I was just appalled by the lists that came out of the Civil Service Department [which had taken over responsibility for the G and G in 1968] of people for jobs – the same

> old names and the same old hacks. So I discussed it with Richard Graham, a member of my unit. He said 'what we need is a little unit whose job is to travel and advertise and actively look for good people'. I drafted a paper to the Prime Minister suggesting a public appointments unit. The PM supported it.[67]

Sir Douglas Allen, then Head of the Home Civil Service, commissioned an internal review in response to the impetus from No. 10. Mr Richard Poland, a retired under secretary from the Department of the Environment, was recalled to the colours to undertake it.[68] As a result of the Poland Report, a Public Appointments Unit (PAU) was established in the Old Admiralty Building, headquarters of the Civil Service Department. As its founding Director, Sir Douglas Allen chose Jonathan Charkham, a businessman who had come late to the Civil Service as a direct entry principal and who had, by 1975, reached the rank of assistant secretary. Mr Charkham, an immensely personable man, had an open and engaging style. His own version of this job description – 'to find chaps of both sexes for posts'[69] – contrasts vividly with the dry, formal remit of the PAU, the latest marque of which reads as follows:

> 1. Maintain the Central List [the formal name for the List of the Great and Good] of people who might be considered for full or part time public appointments; pursue all appropriate ways of strengthening the Central List by seeking and receiving advice from all sources including the public representative organisations and government departments.
>
> 2. Provide advice to departments whose Ministers are responsible for public appointments by suggesting against their specifications names of people from the Central List, or by advising on candidates under consideration who have been recommended to departments from other sources.
>
> 3. Provide advice to the Head of the Home Civil Service on public appointments (other than Civil Service appointments).
>
> 4. Co-ordinate, as necessary, policy and information relating to public appointments; advise departments on procedures; and other miscellaneous tasks.[70]

On taking over the legendary list, Mr Charkham was told a cautionary tale: 'During the war, in response to suggestions from Mr Churchill for a particular appointment, Lord Halifax minuted "Prime Minister: of the three candidates you suggested I much prefer the two who are dead."'[71] In his seven years as Director of the PAU Mr Charkham always managed to heed that warning – just.

HENNESSY: Did you in your time make any frightful mistakes like serving up a stiff or a member of the criminal classes who got through the net?

CHARKHAM: (Pause) None that we weren't able to retrieve at the eleventh hour.[72]

The list was at a low ebb when Mr Charkham inherited it. A team of six had been engaged on the work in what was very much a backwater on the personnel management side of the Civil Service Department. It consisted of about 3,000 names. The Charkham brief was to find new blood. Some blood groups were at a particular premium – under forty, women, and people from outside the golden triangle of the South-East. He toured the country like a latterday Wesley preaching the new message about 'chaps of both sexes' to professional and public organisations. Mr Charkham opened the whole process up. He gave interviews to the press. He was photographed leaning against the filing cabinets in which the particulars of the G and G were stored.[73] 'Jonathan Charkham', said a colleague, 'demystified the list. It is now a working tool.'[74] Bit by bit, the list improved in the desired directions. By 1981 it contained 3,900 names, 16 per cent of whom were women.[75]

In one area the momentum of reform broke on the rock of ministerial prejudice. Bernard Donoughue and Richard Graham had wanted both a wider trawl *and* an advertising programme. Plans were prepared for notices to be placed in post offices encouraging people to nominate themselves or their friends for possible inclusion on the Central List. When the idea reached Cabinet committee, it was killed by Labour ministers led by Peter Shore, Secretary of State for the Environment, as Lord Donoughue remembers:

> Whether it was the views of the sponsoring ministers themselves or whether it was their departmental briefing or a mixture of the two, but certainly the sponsoring ministers, especially from the social service and housing and that side, resisted it. I think that they didn't want to give up a piece of power, although in general it was not a power that they had the time or the energy or the knowledge to exercise very well . . . I remember Peter Shore very strongly resisting and making the . . . totally conservative case for the tried and trusted procedures.[76]

It needed a change of government before phase two of the reform could be implemented. In February 1980, when facing questions from the all-party House of Commons Treasury and Civil Service Committee, Mr Charkham was asked if the idea of opening up the public appointments system through advertising had borne fruit. 'Not yet', he replied; 'nor is it dead.'[77] The notion eventually blossomed at the unearthly hour of 6.17 a.m. on the morning of 5 August 1980 during an all-night debate in the House of Commons. Replying to a speech on ministerial patronage from that devoted observer of the G and G, Bruce George, Labour MP for Walsall South, Paul Channon, then Minister of State at the Civil Service Department, told a near-deserted chamber:

> The list is always capable of improvement and expansion, and I would welcome suggestions from the Hon. Gentleman [Mr George] of suitable people to be put on the list. Indeed, I would welcome that from any Hon. Member or from any member of the public. If they want to suggest the names of people who would be valuable in the public interest, I shall ensure that they are carefully considered.[78]

The most dramatic democratic breakthrough in nine centuries of great and gooding went unnoticed for several days until *The Times*, whose publication had been stopped by a journalists' strike, finally ran a story on 30 August.[79]

The immediate result of the Channon declaration was that 150 people wrote to Mr Charkham. 'All the applications were serious and were carefully considered', he said later. 'There was no evidence whatever that cranks wrote in. Probably about half went onto the list immediately.'[80] By November 1981, a further 450 had written in.[81] Following the Channon reform, self-nomination forms were sent to all inquirers. So from the summer of 1980, to the search for more women, more under-forties and more provincials was added something of an open-page policy. A great deal had been done in procedural terms to allay criticism of elitism and the closed door, though misunderstandings which created a deeply unfortunate impression could sometimes arise. For example, the Central List does not seek to include trade unionists *as* trade unionists. Since an agreement between the Wilson government and the Trades Union Congress in 1968, the Department of Employment has fed in all the names drawn from organised labour, a fact which Mr Colin Peterson, who suceeded Mr Charkham, in 1982, took pains to point out.[82] Under Mr Peterson, who had previously served in No. 10 as Appointments Secretary helping successive prime ministers pick bishops (he was affectionately described as we have seen as one of 'heaven's talent scout'[83]), the new system containing the 1975 and 1980 reforms bedded down. In 1984, Mr Peterson left the Civil Service to become Assistant to the Bishop of Winchester. Mr Charkham is now a Chief Adviser at the Bank of England, which led one Cabinet Office wag to remark that 'one has gone to God, the other to Mammon'.[84]

The current PAU team in the Cabinet Office consists of Mr Geoffrey Morgan, Director, an under secretary who manages the list in addition to other duties; Mr Geoffrey Wollen, Deputy Director, an assistant secretary who, like his chief, performs his G and G tasks part-time; and Mr David Barrows, Assistant Director, who is, at principal rank, the most senior official in the team devoted whole-time to appointments work. Supporting Mr Morgan, Mr Wollen and Mr Barrows are three executive officers and four clerical and secretarial staff. The whole operation costs £146,000 a year.[85]

The latest data I have (January 1986) supplied by the PAU shows that the number of names on the Central List has increased from 3,900 in 1981 to 4,500 in 1983, 4,954 in 1984 and 5,143 in 1988. Its ingredients are as shown in Table 8.

TABLE 8. THE CENTRAL LIST (JANUARY 1986)

Total number of names – 5,143		
Men	4,212	
Women	931	
Those aged 40 and under (i.e. born in 1945 or later) – 239		
Men	128	
Women	111	
Geographical distribution		
London and South-East	2,348	(gross 3,475*)
Rest of the United Kingdom	2,795	

*including those who work in London and the South-East but reside elsewhere.

Source: Public Appointments Unit

The impact of the Channon reform is now strongly visible. Some 20 per cent of those on the current list have nominated thmselves, another 10 per cent have been nominated by other outside individuals. A further 20 per cent have been nominated by representative bodies such as professional associations. The remaining 50 per cent have come through the official Whitehall sieve as before,[80] though some names arrive on Mr Morgan's desk by more than one route. The PAU remains highly impressed by the quality of people flowing in through the self-nomination channel. Fears that the self-important would dog the system have not been realised. 'English modesty', suggested one insider, 'has proved to be the safeguard. Some self-nominees are interviewed and it has been found in some cases that modesty has caused them to take too narrow a view of their potential.'[87]

In addition to the 5,143 names on its active list, the PAU keeps another 15,000 in reserve on its micro-computer, some of whom may be needed to replenish the 40,000 public appointments which need to be filled at any one time. The reservists, for example, consist of the over–65s and categories of people whose skills and experience are already in plentiful supply on the active list. Names on the list are kept confidential. The 238 categories fed in to the PAU computer, to enable it to reply convincingly to a wide combination of individual requirements, are not released either. But the general headings include the sponsoring source, that is, department, professional body or ministerial (the list is not politically segregated; skill and experience rather than prejudice are the criteria for inclusion, though what ministers do with names supplied by the PAU is another matter); language and professional qualifications; overseas interests, special characteristics, such as an individual belonging to an ethnic minority (though no specific questions are asked here) or taking an interest in the elderly or the treatment of offenders; functional specialisms like industrial relations, farming, management or research and development. Most of the computer categories fall under employment characteristics which distinguish between manufacturing and service industries, public service and education, the entertainments industry and the arts, politics and trade unionism. There is a code for job status, where applicable, and finally the suitability of an individual is entered on the computer which distinguishes between deliberative function (i.e. committee of inquiry or royal commission), executive action (for example, a senior job in a nationalised industry), or an appointment of special responsibility (which can cover a host of one-offs).[88] Those whose names are on the list can, if they wish, check how they and their particulars are recorded. And these days, all the G and G, the 'great' as well as the merely 'good', are on the computer for the sake of completeness.

The imperatives of the 1975 and 1980 reforms are still felt by the Cabinet Office's talent scouts. The proportion of women on the list continues to increase. It rose from 16 per cent in 1983 to 18.1 per cent by January 1986 (intriguingly, a higher proportion of those actually holding public appointments are women – some 20 per cent of the 40,000). Still more are being sought. Mr Wollen is applying his past experience at the Civil Service Commission, and the continuing assistance of the Women's National, Council and other professional bodies is being applied to the search. 'Women', says one insider, 'are a reservoir we need to tap.'[89] Readers keen to take the initial step into Whitehall's world of patronage should write to: The Director, Public Appointments Unit, Cabinet Office, Whitehall, London SW1.

It is hugely ironic that just as the reforms of the G and G began to pay off in the size and mix of the list, ministers, and the Prime Minister in particular, should go off the whole idea of royal commissions and committees of inquiry as an instrument of policy-making. But before turning to the freezing out of the great and the good, it is instructive to examine the biographies of three of their grandest figures in the postwar period.

A TRIO OF GRANDEES

That's all right, we can leave it for a day or two to the automatic pilot.
Churchill to Attlee, 1944, on allowing Sir John Anderson to run the country in their absence[90]

Cyril Radcliffe was in the super league. He had everything, intellectual ability, balance, the lot.
Dennis Trevelyan, First Civil Service Commissioner and former secretary of the D-Notice Inquiry, 1986[91]

If Britain became a republic, Oliver Franks would have to be president. No one else would be acceptable.
Former senior civil servant, 1982[92]

To whom at moments of crisis do the powerful in our deferential society defer? The Queen, certainly, and a handful of eminent figures, highly respected, both high-minded and practical, undeniably above the heat and dust of the political day. The first name that floats across the mind is, by a process of elimination, *the* number one on the List of the Great and the Good. Not being creatures of fashion or of the cruder kind of political patronage, longevity is a characteristic. In fact, it can be argued that there have been only three since 1945: John Anderson, Viscount Waverley, 1945–52; Viscount Radcliffe, 1952–77, and Lord Franks from 1977 to the present day. All three were Victorians in that they possessed what Ian Bradley has described as 'a call to seriousness';[93] all three at one time or another were accomplished civil servants, and all three were possessed of a presence which made them immensely difficult to gainsay in a committee room; all three were meritocrats in that brain, not blood, was the substance which accounted for their pre-eminence; and all three would have made superb Viceroys of India.

They are worth singling out for a number of reasons: it is intriguing to map the career path which can project a man to the summit of public life while raising him above political taint (our grandees have been indispensable to every post-war premier from Attlee to Thatcher); the personal characteristics and committee-room techniques which make up their G and G tool bag are revealing; the assumptions and nostrums that constitute their mind sets even more so; if the G and G is to reach its millennium, where is the successor generation to come from in the absence of Empire and a wartime Civil Service?

The Apostle of Orderly Administration[94] Lord Waverley, 1882–1958

There can be no doubt that it is the Prime Minister's duty to advise

> Your Majesty to send for Sir John Anderson in the event of the Prime Minister and the Foreign Secretary [Sir Anthony Eden] being killed.
> **Winston Churchill to King George VI, 28 January, 1945**[95]

> When it comes down to serious business there is, I have found, little room for fads and fancies or for those political nostrums that merely make a transient and meretricious appeal.
> **Sir John Anderson,**
> **Election Address to the Scottish Universities, 1938**[96]

John Anderson was the complete servant of the state, a man for whom one could feel admiration but never warmth. Whether it be in Dublin Castle during the Troubles, the Home Office during the General Strike, the Governor's residence in Bengal during the riots or the Treasury during the war, he persisted in viewing life from the wrong side of a collar-stud. His idea of light, dinner-time conversation was an earnest discussion of Dicey's *Law of the Constitution*.[97] The pomposity of the address to his electorate in 1938 sprang not only from the aloof manner which dogged him throughout life, but from a genuine conviction, also lifelong, that he was above politics. 'John', wrote his biographer, 'steadfastly refused to recognise that he had in any way descended to the level of election canvassing. This he felt was beneath him; it was a part of that vulgar side of party politics for which he had neither liking nor affinity.'[98] As we shall see, his political opponents did not see it that way – a perception which was eventually to end his No. 1 rating on the G and G scale.

If any political figure deserved Nye Bevan's withering description as 'a desiccated calculating machine'[99] it was Anderson. For he was that rarity among senior civil servants, not to mention politicians, a first-class scientist, a chemist and a mathematician, who followed the classic scholarship boy's route from George Watson's to Edinburgh University and a spell of research at Leipzig into the chemical properties of uranium. He was proud of his intellectual equipment, but conscious of the limitations of even the most accomplished intellectual athletes. He once remarked that he did not believe anyone could really concentrate for more than twenty minutes at a time.[100]

Anderson trod the meritocratic path into government, taking the Civil Service examination in 1905. He secured the second highest mark ever achieved.[101] Appointed to the Colonial Office he promptly penned, for the benefit of his old school, a homily on how to succeed in the competition. Published in *The Watsonian*, it is stunning in its pomposity and suggests that Anderson never had a youth. How about this for a chatty intro from a 23-year-old to his erstwhile school chums:

> As this joint examination for the three dignified services of the Home Country, the Great Dependancy, and the Crown Colonies is beyond doubt the most severe competitive test in the country, both on account of the scope and variety of the subjects, and from the fact that success in it is a cherished ambition of many of the most earnest students in every one of our universities, a few suggestions from one who has had occasion to give the matter some thought may be of service to young aspirants.[102]

For all the gravitas, which led him to be nicknamed 'Old Jehovah', Anderson fitted perfectly the lofty Northcote–Trevelyan ideal of the high-minded, disinterested servant of the state, calm, swift and efficient, which explains Whitehall's tendency to move him from one area of high and/or difficult activity to another. Sir John Bradbury commandeered him form the Colonial Office to join the immensely gifted team of officials constructing the embryonic welfare state with Lloyd George's National Insurance Act, 1911, as their charter.[103] By 1920 he was in Dublin Castle and under secretary in the Irish Office, attempting to manage the unmanageable as the southern counties endured the successive convulsions which ended British rule. By January 1922, at the age of forty, he reached permanent secretary rank as Chairman of the Board of Inland Revenue.

Within three months he had moved to the Home Office as its permanent secretary. The man and the institution suited each other to perfection. Jehovah had come into his kingdom and he was to stay there for ten years. His was the mind which fashioned the instrument – the Supply and Transport Organisation – that enabled Baldwin to defeat the General Strike.[104] Anderson ran the Home Office almost as a personal fiefdom. Even in Roy Jenkins's time as Home Secretary in the mid-sixties, the legend lived on. Jenkins, writing of his own permanent secretary, Sir Charles Cunningham, said:

> He was firmly in the tradition of strong, long lasting Home Office permanent secretaries. This tradition dated back at least to Sir John Anderson and probably well before that. It was epitomised by a story relating to Anderson in his heyday. A paper originating with an assistant principal bearing the initials (let us say) of HMT worked its way up to the Secretary of State. The minute from HMT recommended course A. This was not merely opposed but excoriated by everyone else on the way up. The general tenor of the subsequent minutes was that any man in his right mind must clearly accept course B. But not the Secretary of State. He was not one of the more distinguished occupants of this post. But on this occasion he allowed an element of daring to creep through his habitual timidity. 'I think I rather agree with HMT' he somewhat

tentatively wrote. The next minute was less tentative: 'I have spoken with the S of S. He no longer agrees with HMT. JA'. Anderson had intervened. The file was closed.[105]

In 1932, Whitehall's supreme fireman was drafted to Bengal to douse an incendiary mixture of nationalism and Muslim–Hindu animosity. As Governor, sixty million citizens of the 'Great Dependancy', as he had described India in his disquisition in *The Watsonian*, came under his care, a population nearly twenty million greater than that of the United Kingdom at that time. His biographer describes Anderson's five years in Bengal as 'A record of unqualified and almost unparalleled success',[106] with disorder quelled, bankruptcy averted and the condition of the rural poor improved. Having turned down Neville Chamberlain's offer of the High Commissionership in Palestine he returned home to be made a Privy Counsellor. While on board the P. & O. liner on the way back, Anderson was invited to let his name go forward as a possible successor to Ramsay MacDonald, who died in November 1937, as MP for the Scottish Universities. After some hesitation he accepted and was elected to Parliament in February 1938. Within eight months he was a Cabinet minister.

Anderson was a brilliant contingency planner. Chamberlain made him Lord Privy Seal in October 1938, one month after Munich, to organise civil defence in case of war. When war came he was promoted and became Home Secretary and Minister for Home Security. Anderson survived Churchill's purge of the 'Old Gang' in 1940 simply because he had become indispensable. When in 1943 there was talk of his being sent to Delhi as Viceroy, Smuts told Attlee: 'Don't let Churchill send Anderson away. Every War Cabinet needs a man to run the machine. Milner did it in the First World war, and Anderson does it in this.'[107]

From the autumn of 1940, Anderson in effect ran the Home Front as Lord President of the Council. To all intents and purposes, Churchill, with the Chiefs of Staff and General Sir Hastings Ismay, took care of the war and devolved everything else to the Lord President's Committee which became the Cabinet for home affairs. For all his dryness and lack of social warmth Anderson was an official's dream. As we have seen, the hugely gifted group of economists drawn into the War Cabinet Office's Economic Section in 1939–40 had languished for lack of patrons and customers. Anderson's assumption of the Lord Presidency changed all that. Thereafter, home front Whitehall became an adventure playground for the cream of British social science with Anderson presiding like a benign, practical umpire over their competing schemes.

Unknown to his batteries of economists and statisticians, Anderson assumed ministerial responsibility in 1941 for an awesome corner of Whitehall's war-making theme park – that devoted to the development of an atomic bomb. Rarely, if ever, can a minister have possessed exactly the right specialist background for a complicated administrative and technical assignment. As Wheeler-Bennett put it in his ever so slightly eulogistic style, 'John's first love had been science, a field in which he had shown considerable promise as a student. Was there not his brilliant paper on explosives written at Edinburgh University and the remarkable coincidence that he had investigated the radio-activities of uranium while a post-graduate student at the University of Leipzig?'[108] Anderson from the start was part of that 'smallest possible circle of ministers and advisers' privy to the bomb project, wrote Professor Margaret Gowing, its official historian, and 'only two of them, Sir John Anderson and Lord Cherwell, knew continuously and in detail about the whole business'.[109]

Even more remarkable than the conjunction of Anderson's scientific background and his ministerial responsibility for Tube Alloys, as the bomb programme was codenamed, is the manner in which his pivotal role continued in a G and G capacity after the change of government in 1945 when he was no longer a minister (Anderson had become Chancellor of the Exchequer in 1943 but had kept his atomic brief until Churchill's defeat at the polls). The day Japan surrendered, Attlee's Cabinet committee on atomic energy, known as GEN 75 from its Cabinet Office classification, met and agreed that an Advisory Committee on Atomic Energy should be commissioned. Attlee proposed Anderson as its chairman. It consisted of scientists associated with the bomb and representatives of the Armed Forces and the Civil Service. Its terms of reference were twofold: '(a) to investigate the implications of the use of atomic energy and to advise the Government what steps should be taken for its development in this country for military or industrial purposes; (b) to put forward proposals for the international treatment of the subject'.[110] As Professor Gowing explained, 'the committee was indeed responsible for making the recommendations which led to the first decisions on the shape of Britain's atomic programme and the attitude to international control'.[111]

Anderson, while a member of the Opposition front bench (though he continued to remain an Independent MP outside the Conservative Party) was a key arc in the innermost of inner circles on a project which did not even go before Mr Attlee's full Cabinet.[112] This was an influence and a *placement* without parallel in the history of the great and good before or since. As Professor Gowing put it:

> The position of Sir John Anderson as Chairman was especially important. He returned to an office in the Cabinet Office, enjoyed the services of its secretariat and was a quasi-minister. He was consulted on all important telegrams before they were sent off and on most questions of policy that had to be submitted to the Prime Minister. The High

Commissioner in Canada and the British Ambassador in Washington continued to address telegrams personally to Sir John on atomic matters of special secrecy or importance, and it was Sir John who accompanied the Prime Minister on his atomic energy talks with President Truman in Washington in November 1945.[113]

Anderson was not interested only in destructive force. The creative had a high place in his scheme of things. Like most top-flight G and G, he diverted part of his administrative energies into artistic channels. In 1946 he succeeded Keynes as chairman of the Covent Garden Trust and in 1950 he chaired a committee established by the Treasury to examine the export of works of art.

When the Conservatives returned to power in October 1951, Churchill wanted Anderson to become 'Overlord' of his economic ministries – the Treasury, Board of Trade and Ministry of Supply. Anderson declined. The 'Overlord' idea did not accord with his traditional concept of Whitehall organisation in peacetime. And he had acquired a desire to make money and did not relish the prospect of having to relinquish the chairmanship of the Port of London Authority and his several directorships.[114] He did, however, accept a peerage and entered the House of Lords as Viscount Waverley. His reluctance to return to government freed him to trigger what in retrospect looks like an explosion of Great and Good activities in the early 1950s.

His pre-eminence at the time produced one of the best G and G stories in its nine-century life, even though the tale is apocryphal. The Russians, the story ran, sent a high-level delegation to Britain at the height of the cold war. They were conveyed from Tilbury, where they had disembarked, to Westminster by launch and were met at the pier by Lord Waverley, chairman of the Port of London Authority. An early engagement in their programme was with the chairman of the United Kingdom Advisory Council on Atomic Energy and, to their mild surprise, they found themselves shaking hands with Lord Waverley. That evening at a reception in Buckingham Palace they just happened to come across one of the Sovereign's most trusted Privy Counsellors, Lord Waverley. The next day, having expressed a particular interest in Britain's defences against coastal flooding, they found themselves in East Anglia with Lord Waverley who was busy running an official Home Office inquiry into this phenomenon following the east coast floods. That night, as a farewell present, the Russians were taken to Covent Garden for a gala performance. There they were met by the chairman of the Board of the Royal Opera House, Lord Waverley. The exhausted delegation returned to the Soviet Embassy and cabled its report to Moscow: 'Comrade Stalin, Britain is not as we thought a democracy. It is an autocracy run by a man called Waverley.'[115]

But at the very apogee of his dignity and his G and G influence, crude politics dealt Anderson a blow which dislodged him from his No. 1 position. In November 1951, the chairmanship of the Royal Commission on Taxation of Incomes and Profits fell vacant, owing to the resignation of Lord Justice Cohen. Anderson, a former Chancellor of the Exchequer and chairman of the Board of Inland Revenue with a mind like an adding machine (computers, though in production in Manchester, had yet to infiltrate the popular imagination), was a natural choice to succeed him. Churchill and his Chancellor, R. A. Butler, pressed him to accept. When the appointment was announced in the Commons by Churchill on 26 February 1952 there ensued, to Anderson's horror, an outcry from the Labour benches led by a pair of former chancellors, the two Hughs – Dalton and Gaitskell. The critical motion they tabled made plain their objections. Anderson's attack on the size and cost of the welfare state and Labour's interventionist economic policies between 1945 and 1951 had left scars. For all his insistence on his independence as a parliamentarian, Labour could not accept him as an impartial figure. 'He was particularly pained', wrote Wheeler-Bennett, 'that these accusations should have been made by men with whom he had worked as a loyal colleague in the National Government of 1940–1945.'[116] He wrote to Churchill offering to resign the chairmanship and Churchill, reluctantly, accepted it. 'No event', said his biographer, 'in the otherwise serene and successful postwar life of John Anderson caused him such offence and spiritual laceration as this episode.'[117] His notion of public service was total. He could never accept that he had ever stooped into the minefield of political partisanship. His last publicly known words speak volumes about the man. As he lay dying in St Thomas's Hospital in December 1957, the Order of Merit he was due to receive in the 1958 New Year Honours List was brought forward by a few weeks. On hearing that he was to be honoured personally by the Queen in this fashion, Anderson, ovecome with pleasure and gratitude said, 'The Civil Service will be pleased about this.'[118] Only Anderson could have thought that, said it and believed it.

The Eminent Victorian Lord Radcliffe, 1899–1977

It is not the easiest thing to argue with people like Lord Radcliffe. It is rather like dealing with God.
Privy Counsellor on the Radcliffe Committee on Ministerial Memoirs, 1976[119]

Education has gone wrong. It paralyses rather than inspires. People have lost the sense of tragedy in life that gives quality to action and thought. A sense of gravity is part of the make-up of society.
Lord Radcliffe, 1976[120]

Lord Radcliffe spoke those words to me at his country home, Hampton Lucy House in Warwickshire, on a freezing January morning in 1976. As a young reporter on *The Times* I had driven from London to see him to talk about the report on ministerial memoirs he had published five days earlier with the help of a team of privy counsellors commissioned by Harold Wilson to repair the breach in the dyke of Cabinet confidentiality caused by the publication of Volume One of the Crossman Diaries.[121] The report had been accepted instantly by the Prime Minister. Wilson must have taken great comfort from a typically Radcliffian paragraph in which the old judge spoke of past ministers of the Crown regarding themselves 'as bound by the rule to keep their discussions secret and to respect the confidence that each reposed in the other that this should be so'. Lord Radcliffe went on to remark that few people could have thought such a rule had been obeyed in every instance. There had been breakdowns. 'What matters is that it came to be restated.'[122]

It was the first and last time I met Lord Radcliffe. He took over as unofficial number one on the List of the Great and Good when he replaced Lord Justice Cohen as Chairman on the Royal Commission on Taxation of Incomes and Profits in 1952 after the Labour Opposition had, to all intents and purposes, vetoed John Anderson. He remained at number one till his death in 1977, apart from a short interruption after his magisterial denunciation in the House of Lords of Harold Wilson's interpretation of his report on the D-notice Affair in 1967.[123] As Hugh Noyes wrote at the time, 'In a 25 minute speech he took apart the Government's case with the artistry of a surgeon and at the end left it scattered about the operating theatre headless and limbless.'[124] My first impression of him was a trifle odd. He welcomed me and my photographer colleague, Bill Warhurst, with the words that he and his wife were very glad we had come as it gave them an excuse to put the central heating on. Hampton Lucy House is a big country mansion. But, after all, the Radcliffes had a bit of money. He left £351,082 net[125] and when Lady Radcliffe died in 1982, her estate was valued at £587,639 net.[126]

The second impression swiftly brushed notions of eccentricity aside and has remained to this day – of a high-minded, highly intelligent man deeply out of sympathy with his age; and of a singular faculty, a gift with words in which his every sentence was perfectly phrased as if it were a precise, measured judicial summing up. He spoke warmly of the Victorian era. 'I have lived through all sorts of denigration of Victorian ideas and achievements', he said. 'I have seen the weight of feeling changing. People are beginning to realise what astounding achievements they were.'[127] He drew a distinction between the great nineteenth-century royal commissions and his inquiry into ministerial memoirs. 'This committee was a discussion committee, not a fact-finding committee', he said.[128] He talked about running committees, the need to avoid starting with preconceived ideas. If you had them, your colleagues would be 'less susceptible' to your chairmanship. He spoke highly of the quality of the Civil Service. (He was a bit of a hero to his secretaries, officials such as Robert Armstrong, who worked with him on his Committee of Inquiry into the Monetary and Credit system, 1957–9, Dennis Trevelyan, secretary of the D Notice Inquiry, and Michael Moss, who assisted at his inquiry into ministerial memoirs.)

Of all the G and G's output, only those reports bearing the names of Lord Radcliffe and Lord Annan (Chairman of the Home Office Committee on Broadcasting, 1975–7) bore the unmistakable marks of their chairmen's personal draftsmanship. In the absence of a written constitution, the thoughts of Lord Radcliffe are something of a surrogate:

> Cabinet secrecy has in reality nothing to do with the making of plots ... Is there anything offensive to enlightened and constitutional ideas of today that such a group, committed to the conduct of the central government, should expect to keep to themselves the details of the process of formulation and that each should be able to rely on the other for the observance of such an understanding?[124]

Whatever the contemporary historian might think of that rather stuffy justification of traditional British secrecy, it is far more elegantly phrased than any of the lifeless paragraphs in *Questions of Procedure for Ministers*. Lord Radcliffe, in the same document, had something to say about history and historians. 'At some point', he wrote, 'the secrets of one period must become the common learning of another.'[130] But 'Government is not to be conducted in the interests of history .... the historian cannot have as of right a smooth highway constructed for him through the intricate plans of public administration and statecraft ... There is no sudden flash of light that illumines the whole landscape: we should be surprised if historians would wish that there were.'[131] The Radcliffe guidelines on ministerial memoirs now occupy a section of their own in *Questions of Procedure for Ministers*. They were incorporated in time for the revised version prepared when Mr Callaghan acceded to the premiership.[132]

As I left Hampton Lucy, Lord Radcliffe gave me a copy of his *Not in Feather Beds*. Its contents gave an indication of the background and interests which moulded his personal marque of statecraft: essays on India (he had never really recovered from his impossible task as the drawer of boundaries between India and Pakistan in 1947 and the bloodshed which ensued); the law; the ancient universities; the arts; Kipling; 'The Dissolving Society'. This last essay illustrated his acute sense of tragedy in a postwar society whose condition, in one way and another, he had spent long hours dissecting in committee rooms:

We take so much for granted in modern society and by so doing we impose such heavy strains on our good sense. We steam ahead, carefree navigators as if the conduct of democratic society was an easy art. 'Look, no hands.' It is, on the contrary, the most difficult in the world.[133]

It was war service in the Ministry of Information which brought Cyril Radcliffe, a KC with a genuinely brilliant record at the Bar, to the attention of the dispensers of patronage. When the war ended, Sir Edward Bridges tried to tempt Radcliffe to stay on as permanent secretary in one or other of the major departments.[134] After some thought, he decided to return to the bar. Repeated attempts were made to lure him back into quasi-government service. Attlee asked him to chair the newly created National Coal Board.[135] He declined, though duty took him to India as Chairman of the Punjab and Bengal Boundary Commissions. In the fifties, the demands of being number one on the list left him little time for sitting as a Lord of Appeal. The roll-call is relentless: inquiries into tax; recruitment to the secret intelligence service;[136] security procedures; the Vassall case; Chairman of the BBC General Advisory Council; Constitutional Commissioner for Cyprus; the Board of Trustees of the British Museum; Chancellor of the University of Warwick. No wonder that by 1955 Norman Brook advised Eden to hold him in reserve for the most complex and intellectually demanding inquiries.

In January 1976, he told me that he retained his intellectual curiosity. He had suffered from ill-health but remained a stocky figure with a large, imposing face and a forceful delivery. 'I do not mean to do anything again,' he said. 'I'm nearly 77 and you get out of touch.' Back in the *Times* office I wrote, 'But few in Whitehall would be surprised if he were summoned once more from the tranquillity of Hampton Lucy. No doubt, like Fu Manchu, we shall hear of him again.'[137] I was wrong. He was right. Lord Radcliffe died, inappropriately, on April Fools' Day, 1977.

University Man
Lord Franks, 1905—

My life is my university.
Remark attributed to Lord Franks, 1948[138]

One day the temperature was over 100 and all of us were sweating like horses. I looked at Sir Oliver. He was sweating too, but in a different, special way. A drop of moisture formed near his right cheekbone and, simultaneously, another near his left. Then those two drops moved neatly down his face in perfect alignment. 'Can you beat that', I said to myself. 'He even sweats symmetrically.'
Remark attributed to a member of the United States delegation at

the Marshall Plan negotiations, Paris, 1947[139]

Lord Franks is a monument to the English genius for understatement. It comes out in the most famous Franks story, which dates from his spell as Ambassador in Washington 1948–52. A local radio station had the sharp idea of asking the representatives of the great powers what they would like for Christmas. The resulting broadcast was hilarious. It cut into a tape recording of a Parisian voice, pregnant with sincerity: '"Pour Noël, I want peace throughout all the world". Then we asked the Ambassador of the Soviets what he would like most of all today ... A dogmatic voice on the tape this time: "For Chreesmas I want freedom for all the people enslaved by imperialism, wherever they may be". ... Finally folks, we asked Her Majesty the Queen's Ambassador from London, Sir Oliver Franks, what he would prefer this day ... The diffident tones of Bristol Grammar School and Oxford came on the air: "... Well, as a matter of fact, it's very kind of you, I think I'd quite like a small box of candied fruit."'[140]

His shunning of the limelight is genuine. He has consistently given the impression that each time the call to public duty has sounded – from the Ministry of Labour in 1939 with its instruction to 'Go to the Ministry of Supply',[141] from Ernest Bevin in 1947, this time the destination was Paris and the subject the European Recovery Programme,[142] and from Clement Attlee in 1948 with a request that he accept the Washington Embassy[143] – he would much rather have stayed in his university. He believes in universities in a way which is immensely unfashionable in the 1980s. But then fashion, intellectual or othewise, has never bothered Lord Franks. If, as a journalist, you pay him a visit in his old farmhouse in North Oxford, he will greet you in a magnificent double-breasted suit straight out of the big band era. Though he is a shy man, he has no qualms in the presence of journalists. He once told me that his experience in Washington taught him familiarity with the media. Only once was he nonplussed. It was at the press conference to launch NATO in 1949. A propos of nothing, a lady representing an American women's magazine asked 'Sir Oliver, were you breast-fed or bottle-fed?'[144]

Listening to Lord Franks one is constantly reminded of the title of the memoirs of his great friend, Dean Acheson, US Secretary of State in the Truman administration. Franks has invariably been *Present at the Creation*.[145] He joined the Ministry of Supply when 'if you had an idea of what you wanted to do, there was very little to stop you doing it'.[146] Just after the war, as Permanent Secretary to the Ministry of Supply, he motored with the atomic scientist Sir John Cockcroft to a disused aerodrome in Berkshire near Harwell. Cockcroft had said his team working on atomic energy needed to be near a university or they would wither on the vine. As Lord Franks told a seminar nearly forty years later, 'there on the windswept Berkshire Downs, with rainclouds scudding, Cockcroft said "This is where it will be". And that was the beginning of Harwell.'[147] We have already encountered him sweating symmetrically at the Marshall Plan negotiations. The reason Attlee and Bevin prised him out of the Provost's Lodge at Queen's College, Oxford (the provostship being the summit of his ambition) in 1948 was to help secure a more permanent alliance between Europe and North America. He was intimately involved in the negotiations which led to the North Atlantic Treaty in 1949.

There are parallels with the G and G career of Lord Radcliffe. Like Radcliffe, Lord Franks was offered a permanent post at permanent secretary rank after the war and the top job at the National Coal Board. At various stages British Railways, BP and the Atomic Energy Authority had been floated at him: even the legendary White Fish Authority has been deemed a suitable outlet for his talents. And when he returned home from Washington in 1952, the editorship of *The Times*, the director-generalship of the BBC, a top post in the Treasury and the eventual succession to Bridges were all offered.[148] His heart's desire – the Provostship of Queen's – was filled. So he decided to launch out on a completely different career in the City and chaired a clearing bank, Lloyds, from 1954 to 1962. I once asked Lord Franks why he thought there had been so many attempts to turn him into the Pooh Bah of British public life. 'There is a fashion in these things', he said, 'and when you are in fashion you get asked to do a lot. I was in fashion for ten or twelve years.'[149]

In the 1950s, part of the fashion was to offer grandees like Lords Franks and Radcliffe the microphone in the shape of the BBC Reith Lectures. Lord Radcliffe's set on 'Power and the State' were still being quoted thirty years later. For example, Sir John Hoskyns began his biting attack on the conservatives of the political establishment in 1983 with Lord Radcliffe's observation that 'The British have formed the habit of praising their institutions, which are sometimes inept, and of ignoring the character of their race, which is often superb. In the end they will be in danger of losing their character and being left with their institutions; a result disastrous indeed.'[150] Franks does not possess Radcliffe's linguistic firepower. His Reith Lectures on 'Britain and the Tide of World Affairs', delivered in 1954, were a carefully composed but rather conventional tour of the international scene. But, two years before Suez, he did seize the opportunity to bring home the reality that was all too apparent to him at that Marshall Plan meeting in Paris in 1947. With Byrnes of the United States on one side of him and Molotov of the USSR on the other (until the Russians walked out and turned their backs on the Plan), he realised that Britain still had a voice 'but it was a junior voice'.[151] His script on the radio seven years later reflected this perception, which, pre-Suez, was not widely shared by his fellow countrymen. Britain's decision-taking since 1945, said Lord Franks, flowed from an accepted principle that:

> Britain is going to continue to be what she has been, a great power. This is something the British people assume and act upon. Once they see that some action or decision is required by this first principle of national policy, they accept it and do not question further. What is noteworthy is the way that we take this for granted ... Yet what we have taken for granted has not been taken for granted abroad. This is one of the things I discovered in the United States ... It was felt by many Americans that a new pattern was emerging in world affairs. It was the age of nations on a continental scale. There were really only two Great Powers – the United States and Russia.[152]

Though no longer seated at the high tables of international diplomacy and having deliberately kept out of Whitehall's inner circles and away from highly visible editorships at the BBC and *The Times* in favour of a less public profession, Lord Franks continued to imbibe the private pleasures of the G and G, chairing the Committee on Administrative Tribunals and Inquiries 1956–7, the Commission of Inquiry into Oxford University 1964–6, and the Home Office Departmental Committee on Section 2 of the Official Secrets Act which sat in 1971–2. He admits he enjoys the work:

> I do enjoy it. I think the first reason is that I have always found myself with very able members of the committees I have been on, with minds as good or better than my own very often bringing expert deep knowledge into it, and trying to match them; trying to keep up with their minds. And trying to bring them into some sort of agreed unity about the way to tackle a problem. It is to me an exciting form of endeavour. I do enjoy that.[152]

He was philosophical, too, about which of his endeavours found favour with those in a position to implement his recommendations and which did not:

> Let me draw a comparison between the official secrets committee and the committee on tribunals and inquiries. In the second case, tribunals and inquiries, a very great deal of what we recommended was acted on very quickly and in the case of the official secrets committee it wasn't acted on at all. Now, I have always thought that in regard to the outcome of any committee's work it depends in part on the quality of what's done, on whether it is in readable English that a layman can understand if he is willing to give some attention. But it is also in a large part – say

> 50 per cent – a matter of whether public opinion is ready for it at the time. Now it happened with tribunals and inquiries that public opinion was ready to make changes and therefore our report was favourably received and acted on with speed. In the case of the Official Secrets Act, the opposite was true. Because every government in power is very reluctant to give up any weapon of power.[154]

There is a timelessness about Lord Franks when he talks in this vein. He strikes one as a combination of fireman and umpire on whose services virtually all postwar premiers have had to draw. When I first met him at Blackhall Farm in 1977 I scribbled in my notebook: 'Tall, statuesque, austere looking in grey pin striped suit'. Six years later, on another January day, as we chatted about his forthcoming report on the origins of the Falklands War I scrawled 'in very cheerful, chipper, sparkling form'. What one Oxford friend called his 'sphinx-like' qualities[155] became less apparent on successive encounters.

The mid- to late-1970s saw Lord Franks sitting with Lord Radcliffe on ministerial memoirs repairing the breach opened by the Crossman Diaries and with Lords Shackleton and Carr as 'new blood' on the Political Honours Scrutiny Committee filling the metaphorical breach made by Sir Harold Wilson's notorious 'lavender notepaper' Resignation Honours List. His committee touch remained impeccable. I sat beside him for a weekend as rapporteur to chairman at a Ditchley conference on confidentiality and privacy in November 1978. It was not a sweaty occasion, but the proceedings were wholly symmetrical. One official, later very highly placed in Whitehall, purred with pleasure at Franks's performance. With Lord Radcliffe recently dead, it was quite clear who had become the new number one.

The day after the Ditchley conference broke up, Lord Franks travelled to the Civil Service College in Sunningdale where the Official Cabinet Committee on Official Information, GEN 146, masquerading as 'a seminar on open government', was in session. He was in his element, teaching once more and deploying his philosopher's precision: 'Knowledge is power', he told the deputy and under secretaries. 'It is important to recognise that the issue of open government is about power, political power, a shift in power, it's redistribution.'[156] He updated for them his 1972 report on official secrecy published before freedom of information had lifted the issue to a newer and more administratively troublesome plateau.[157] The Franks solution for the problem of grafting FOI to the British system of Parliamentary and Cabinet government was unveiled: a commons select committee on Open Government to bring pressure on government while avoiding the courts or an information ombudsman.[158] The Green Paper on open government, published on 30 April 1979 in the dying days of the Callaghan government, floated the idea of a select committee to monitor a code of conduct on openness.[159] Lord Franks had been heeded once more.

The Anderson–Radcliffe–Franks phenomenon may strike those under the age of seventy as a peculiar way of injecting advice from gifted outsiders into mainstream policy-making. It cannot be seen as a by-product of the 'great man' theory of government. All three were 'great' in the sense of being 'larger gauge people', as one senior civil servant put it.[160] But none of them fits Sir Isaiah Berlin's definition of a 'great man':

> A great man need not be morally good, or upright, or kind, or sensitive, or delightful, or possess artistic or scientific talent. To call someone a great man is to claim that he has intentionally taken (or perhaps could have taken) a large step, one far beyond the capacities of men, in satisfying or materially affecting, central human interests.[161]

Writing of Chaim Weizmann, whom he does dub a great man, Sir Isaiah says that such a person seems capable, almost single-handed, of transforming radically the 'outlook and values of a significant body of human beings'. And the transformation he or she wreaks must be 'antecedently improbable – something unlikely to be brought about by the mere force of events, by the "trends" or "tendencies" already working at the time'.[162]

It cannot be said that any of our trio of grandees came into that category. Anderson was involved in managing the Anglo-American venture which produced the first atomic bomb and Radcliffe had to work at great speed on the new boundaries between India and Pakistan which affected the lives of millions. But neither Anderson nor Radcliffe created the events with which their names are associated. And, by its very nature, no royal commission or committee of inquiry is ever going to be in a position to release forces which transform a society by cutting in a completely uncontrollable way against its grain. Upright, moral and sensitive the best of the G and G may be, but they are not in business to make reformations. They are, or were, no more and no less than top-flight permanent secretaries *manqué* (all three, after all, held the rank for a time) with an overlay of wider experience, great presence, natural dignity and considerable gifts at running committees and other committee people. This makes them highly valuable but not great.

Are they, then, the physical embodiments of some kind of consensus, cartographers of the middle way? Not really. Anderson was uncomfortable with the postwar world. Remember it was his outspoken attacks on the extent and cost of the welfare state which, among other things, caused Labour front benchers to attack his appointment to the Royal Commission on Taxation. He was not one of those 'New Jerusalemers' Correlli Barnett excoriates as destroyers of native British industrial enterprise.[163] Radcliffe, as his essays and his reverence for the nineteenth century show, clearly found the pursuits of many postwar men of political power trivial, damaging and distressing. Of the three only Franks, who took the Liberal whip when raised to the peerage in 1962, seems part of the Beveridgite-Keynesian post-war consensus. To be top flight G and G, then, capacity as a mould breaker or sympathy with current political and economic orthodoxies was not *de rigueur*. The ability to shift business and to find a way through administrative thickets was the key – until Mrs Thatcher's time, that is.

CRITICISM AND DECLINE

Heath consciously reacted against the Wilson style of buying the hours with beer and sandwiches at No. 10, and the years with royal commissions.
Phillip Whitehead, 1985[164]

Probably what she [Mrs Thatcher] objects to about the classical Good and Great is that by their very nature – by the fact that they all know each other, there are 'clubby' people, they frequent the same environment – they do tend to reach moderately balanced medium conclusions about whatever matter they are dealing with.
Sir Anthony Parsons, 1985[165]

When ruling classes are on the run, their womenfolk wear the trousers.
Professor Norman Stone, 1984[166]

Criticism of the Great and Good and their venerable artefacts, the royal commission and the committee of inquiry, did not wait upon the arrival in No. 10 of the most anti-establishment prime minister of recent times. Virtually every scholarly examination of official inquiries contains the obligatory quote from A. P. Herbert, usually an extract from his delightful poem, 'Sad Fate of a Royal Commission', published over fifty years ago:

I saw an old man in the Park;
I asked the old man why
He watched the couples after dark;
He made his strange reply:
I am the Royal Commission on Kissing
Appointed by Gladstone in '74;
The rest of my colleagues are buried or missing;
Our minutes were lost in the last Great War.
But still I'm a Royal Commission.
My task I intend to see through,

Though I know, as an old politician,
Not a thing will be done if I do.[167]

A glance at the list of royal commissions since 1945 shows none of the thirty-seven to be quite in the kissing category, but the 1946 Royal Commission on Awards to Inventors (which took a decade to report)[168] and the 1951 Royal Commission on University Education in Dundee[169] look, as subjects go, a trifle peripheral for such grand treament. And, in the last year of his premiership, Sir Winston Churchill circulated a note to the Cabinet urging a more sparing use of the device. Sir Ernest Gowers's Royal Commission on Capital Punishment, Sir Winston wrote, 'occupied four and a half years and cost £23,000. It seems to me that the latter figure should be borne in mind when other proposals for Royal Commissions are presented to us.'[170]

Sir Winston's injunction had but a minor impact. Taking simply royal commissions and not the vastly more plentiful committees of inquiry, six were set up during the six and a quarter years of Labour rule after 1945 – Awards to Inventors (1946); Justices of the Peace (1946); the Press (1947); Lotteries, Gaming and Betting (1949); Capital Punishment (1949); and University Education in Dundee (1951). Twelve royal commissions were established during the thirteen years of Conservative government which ensued – Taxation of Profits and Income (1951); Marriage and Divorce (1951); Scottish Affairs (1952); the Civil Service (1953); the Law Relating to Mental Illness and Mental Deficiency (1954); Common Land (1955); Doctors' and Dentists' Remuneration (1957); Local Government in the Greater London area (1957); the Police (1960); the Press (again) (1961); National Incomes (1962); and the Penal system (1964). Harold Wilson turned royal commissions into a growth industry. Extract Lord Pearson's Royal Commission on Civil Liability and Compensation for Personal Injury (1973), founded during the Heath interlude, and Wilson's creations accumulate remorselessly: Reform of the Trade Unions and Employers' Associations (1965); Medical Education (1965); Prices and Incomes (1965); Local Government in England (1966); Tribunals of Enquiry (Evidence) Act 1921 (1966); Assizes and Quarter Sessions (1966); Industrial Relations (1969); Environmental Pollution (1970); the Press (the *third* time since the war); Standards of Conduct in Public Life (1974); the National Health Service (1976); Gambling (1976); and Legal Services (1976). James Callaghan established one, the Royal Commission on Criminal Procedure (1978). Mrs Thatcher has created precisely *none*, though the Royal Commissions on Environmental Pollution and on Historical Manuscripts are permanent bodies and continue to produce reports.[171]

For the waxing and waning of postwar royal commissions *and* departmental committees, the figures are bulkier (see Fig. 22), tell a slightly different story and give a more complete picture. Mrs Thatcher has had resort to the departmental inquiry and the committee of privy counsellors, but, before treating the Thatcherian onslaught on the G and G, the impact of Wilson must be assessed. For by debasing the coinage through an inflation of commissions, Wilson induced a reaction not only from the prime ministers who succeeded him but from the G and G themselves. They tired of sitting to no purpose.

Lord Rothschild began the revolt of the grandees a fortnight before the report of his Royal Commission on Gambling landed on the Home Secretary's desk. Addressing the annual dinner of the British Academy at the Middle Temple on 29 June 1978[172], Lord Rothschild questioned the utility of such exercises. After quoting A. P. Herbert – 'a Royal Commission is generally appointed, not so much for digging up the truth, as for digging it in' – he asked, 'can a system which relies on the goodwill, the evenings and the weekends of hard-pressed people be viable in the Seventies and after?' He tilted at the compilers of the List of the Great and the Good and the Home Office who, between them, had come up with his commissioners:

> None of the members of the Royal Commission on Gambling is a hardened or experienced gambler (indeed few of us indulge in it at all), and there seems to be no particular reason why a philosopher, a sports commentator, a specialist in office organisation, an ex-scientist, an Olympic medallist, a trade unionist, a journalist and two practising barristers should be any better qualified to pronounce on the particular subject than any nine members of the Cabinet; except that the latter are known not to have time, whereas the former are assumed, for some obscure reason, to have the time, the energy and the capacity to learn an entirely new subject and become expert on it.[173]

He found it difficult to understand why the Home Office had set him and his commission in operation, as its own research unit had undertaken its own review of gambling literature and 'while our Royal Commission was labouring – and parturition has occasioned much labour – a Select Committee of the House of Commons made an investigation in depth into one important aspect of gambling, the Tote, which for obvious reasons, we were also studying. Is there not something incomprehensible about such prodigality, such overkill?'[174] Within a year the fountains of patronage in No. 10 were firmly turned down, if not off, by a lady who substituted rationing and parsimony for prodigality and overkill.

By the late 1970s, when Lord Rothschild uttered his lament before the British Academy (not all of whom appeared to relish it,[175] presumably because a high proportion of the decorations which enlivened their evening dress had come from national service in the ranks of the Queen's own G

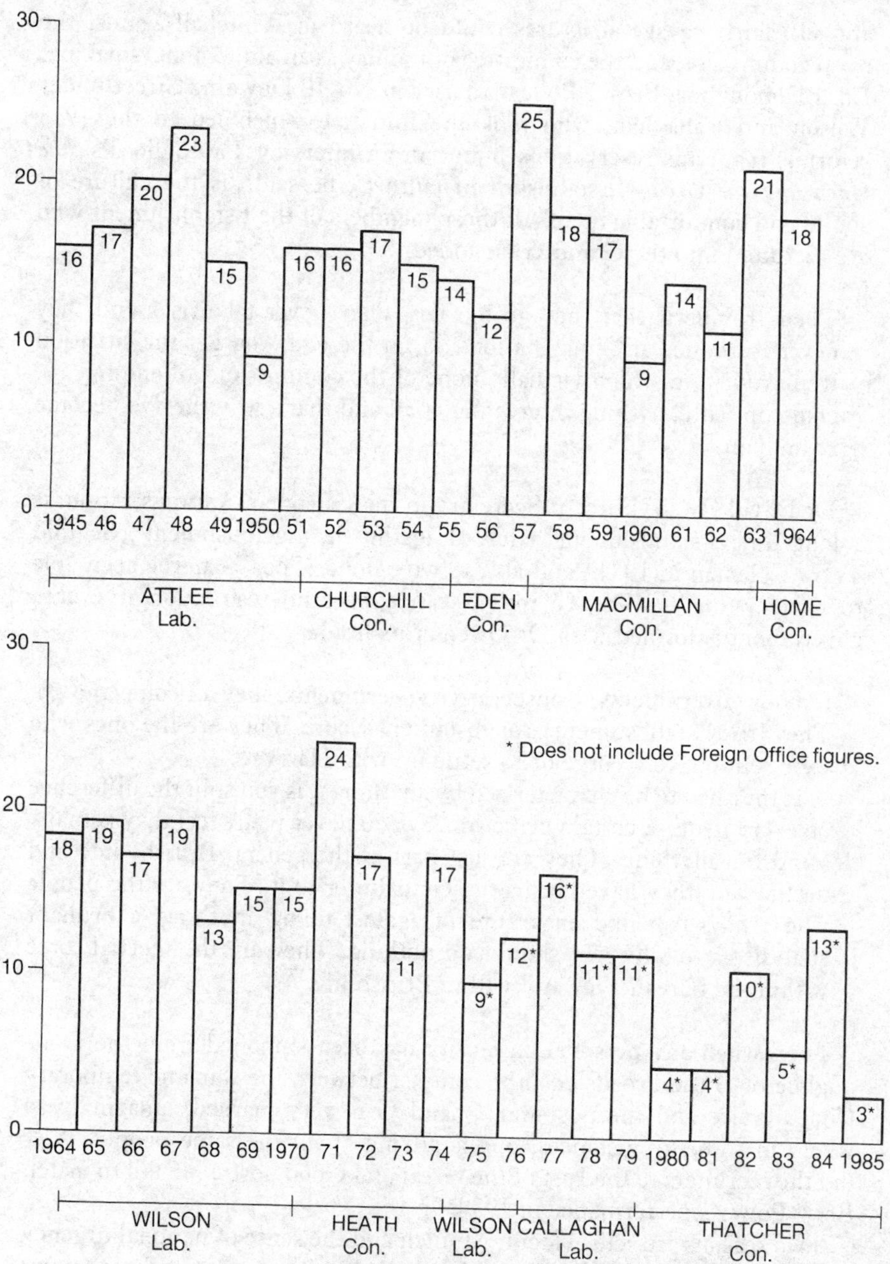

Fig. 21. ROYAL COMMISSIONS AND COMMITTEES OF INQUIRY NEW STARTS, 1945–85

and G), fairly savage strictures could be heard in Whitehall against the royal commission and the committee of inquiry as an aid to policy-making. Lord Donoughue, Senior Policy Adviser in No. 10 Downing Street under Wilson and Callaghan, who took the initiative which led to the 1975 reforms, made his reservations public in an interview for Radio 3's *The Good and the Great*. 'Establishment culture', he said, 'is the culture of sound and comfortable men.' Of those members of the Establishment who are recruited into the G and G he added:

> Their trouble is that they go too far. They never take risks and they never introduce any imagination. So, in the end, you get the situation we have had in which virtually none of the commissions of enquiry ... come up with anything interesting at all and that's why they've become redundant.[176]

Dr David Owen, Foreign Secretary in the Callaghan Administration, is a long-time Establishment hater. 'I loathe the Establishment', he told Terry Coleman in 1984, 'and always have done. They've never been able to envelop me.'[177] The G and G can expect no restoration if ever a government is formed with Dr Owen at its head:

> Labour governments, Conservative governments, they all come and go. They [the Establishment] are absolutely secure. They are the ones who were sent out to George or to settle up with Harry ...
>
> If they had to be characterised by anything it is you split the difference on every issue. A certain cynicism ... You never really feel they actually stand for anything. They are just part of the general British slide and decline and they have been a big contributor to it. They are the people who always can find an argument against doing anything, a brilliant analysis as to why you should do nothing. They are the inertial force within the bureaucracy and within British life.[178]

Even when any personal animosity has been siphoned from the Donoughue or Owen broadsides, the contrast between the wartime temporary Civil Service and the post-war G and G is very marked, amazingly so when, in so many instances, one is talking about the same people. Why did the recruiters to the List of the Great and Good post-1945 fail to match Beryl Power's performance in 1938–9?

Two reasons are self-evident. Munich and the sense of national urgency it created allowed the Ministry of Labour's headhunters to suck up talent, like some giant vacuum cleaner, wherever it was concealed in the British Isles. Secondly, the posts the wartime irregulars filled were essentially practical jobs with direct executive responsibilities – running a division of the Ministry of Supply in the case of Douglas Jay,[179] creating a utility furniture scheme in the case of Gordon Russell[180] or designing a more bearable form of rationing with a points system in the case of that formidable collection of brainpower in the Economic Section of the War Cabinet Office.[181] The post-war G and G were deployed almost exclusively on *advisory* tasks, not executive functions. However apt or timely their reports, their recommendations had to grind through the Whitehall mill of inter-departmental working parties and Cabinet committees and to endure that peculiar blend of prejudice, hunch and political calculation of which policy-making so often consists at ministerial level. Lord Wolfenden was warned by the Permanent Secretary to the Home Office in 1957 that his recommendations on homosexual law reform aroused such passion that fourteen years could be the time lag between recommendation and legislation. In the event it took ten.[182] Even where a royal commission or committee of inquiry consisted of experience in depth with a proven graduate of Miss Power's academy at its head, its product could appear utterly ineffectual, whatever its intrinsic merits, as adoption and implementation lay in entirely different hands.

This phenomenon, which Bernard Williams immortalised as 'pathways to the pigeonhole', was what fuelled the revolt of the G and G themselves. Professor Williams, a member of the Royal Commission on Gambling (Bernard Williams was the philosopher Lord Rothschild referred to in his address to the British Academy) and chairman of the Home Office's Committee on Obscenity and Film Censorship, delivered his Grand Remonstrance at the Royal Institute of Public Administration's conference on public influence and public policy at Sussex University in April 1981.[183] Commissions and committees, said the then Provost of King's College, Cambridge, 'characteristically involve a great deal of work for unpaid participants, and that . . . work often seems to be wasted'. He swung into line with A. P. Herbert:

> This is not simply the point that a report very often fails to lead to any legislation. More than that, the appointment of such a committee seems often designed not to lead to legislation, and to be diversionary. Moreover, although there are ways in which a report can be useful and indeed influence opinion even though it does not lead to legislation, the system is largely designed to prevent those further effects coming about.[184]

Professor Williams offered a remedy. No government can be committed in advance to accepting the recommendations of a committee. Its report 'may be divided, or idiotic'. And the government may have changed while it was sitting. 'But any administration should be committed to saying why it does not accept the recommendations, if it does not, and if it is the same administration, it should be institutionally required to show that the committee was set up in good faith, namely out of interest in its answer, and not merely as a way of removing the question.'[185] One way to do this, he added, would be to oblige a government to make a reasoned response to the report in a publication *and* a debate in the House of Commons.

Two years later a similar line was taken by two of the last royal commission chairmen the country has seen, Lords Rothschild and Benson. In his British Academy Lecture, Lord Rothschild noted that the last time royal commissions themselves had been inquired into was 'as recently as 1910'.[186] He was referring to the Home Office's Departmental Committee on the Procedure of Royal Commissions on 1909–10 which sat under the chairmanship of Lord Balfour.[187] Lords Rothschild and Benson, while making it plain that the person who should be updating the work of the Balfour Committee was the Secretary of the Cabinet, not them, proceeded nonetheless to do an inquiry of their own which they presented in the form of an obituary, calling it 'Royal Commissions: A Memorial'.[188]

Royal commissions, said their lordships, now cost in excess of £1m (remember the £23,000 for the Royal Commission on Capital Punishment mentioned by Churchill). They laid down four conditions that should be met before a commission was established: the problem to be tackled must be significant but not urgent as royal commissions took time; Whitehall did not already possess sufficient information to put before ministers; the evidence needed could only be gathered by research or interviewing a significant number of informed people; when a royal commission was established it should be stated publicly that there was an intention to act when its report was published.[189] They lingered on the importance of picking the right people as commissioners. They had to possess wide general experience, average or above average intelligence, integrity, grasp, a determination to reach a balanced judgement and a moderate political outlook. They must not have intense political or doctrinaire views, prior commitment to a stated view or the views of an organisation or pressure group.[190] Lords Benson and Rothschild warned of the perils of second-rate minds being let loose on serious matters of public policy:

> Many commissioners, particularly if they are of second quality, start their work in the belief that they will not be doing their job unless they recommend radical changes ... They should be disabused of this idea ... A wise commissioner is the person who only recommends a change when one is clearly needed and then he is satisfied that the new organisation will be better than the one which now exists, particularly if the latter is repaired or strengthened.[191]

Finally, in the manner of one of Lord Rothschild's celebrated CPRS reports, they displayed a set of terse conclusions that fitted nearly on one side of A4:

> 1. A review of Royal commissions appointed in the last twenty years should be made in order to prevent a waste of public monies in the future.
> 2. The quality of commissioners appointed is crucial to success...
> 3. The number of commissioners should be small and should not exceed ten. The chairman should be consulted before appointments are made.
> 4. Guidelines for the use of prospective commissioners should be made ... commissioners should undertake to give up the necessary time before being appointed.
> 5. A nucleus of experienced staff of a sufficiently high grade should be appointed to the secretariat. The present *ad hoc* appointments are not satisfactory.[192]

Shortly after the Rothschild–Benson obituary was published, the RIPA held a wake in a basement room, just across the road from the Treasury on 15 December 1982.[193] The occasion left a deep imprint on me. It was dominated by the Williams–Rothschild–Benson theses. There was talk of 'the deafening silence syndrome'. I described the seminar as 'a collective whinge' and its participants as 'The Lost Tribe of British Public Life'.[194]

For the men and woman in that basement room, loaded with honours and dripping with gravitas, knew that since 1979 they had been pretty well frozen out, that talk of reforming the committee/commission system was largely irrelevant for the foreseeable future. Mrs Thatcher, on this issue at least, breathed as one with Dr Donoughue and Dr Owen. Clive Priestley, who, as Lord Rayner's chief of staff in the Prime Minister's Efficiency Unit, worked closely with her, said that Mrs Thatcher 'does have a particular view of the sorts of people who can help her on the missions which she regards as important. Broadly speaking, but not exclusively, she is against the "golden oldie" type, and, I dare say, that would tend to cut out quite a number on the List of the Great and the Good.'[195] The Rayner Unit was an example of her preferred method of operating. Mrs Thatcher, as we have seen, had no wish to commission a variation of the Fulton Committee on the Civil Service of 1966–8.

But even an anti-G and G premier like Mrs Thatcher has to empanel some committees of inquiry and appoint, whether she likes it or not, a small army to the boards of quangoland. In December 1986 there were 37,748 of them sitting on 1,658 public bodies of various kinds.[196] And it is in this latter sector of patronage that she has aroused the fiercest criticism.

The Thatcher effect in this area is difficult to document (as it is in the field of senior promotions in the Civil Service). There is a feeling abroad that 'conviction politics' as practised by a prime minister with powerful temperamental likes and dislikes has, to put it no higher, altered conventional procedure, though, as we have seen, 'rigging' went on in the 1970s as Mrs Castle's Diary and Dr Owen's recollections bear witness in the case of the Royal Commission on the National Health Service. But for scholarly purposes, hearsay and supposition are no substitute for documents. Unless or until an equivalent to the Castle Diaries for 1979–87 is published, or a senior figure, whether politician or civil servant, who had participated in the patronage business comes clean in public about this or that appointment, a drizzle of complaint from traditionalists and some *prima facie* evidence is all we have to work with.

The *prima facie* material is fairly plentiful. The most convincing comes from Ronald Butt of *The Times*, a supporter of Mrs Thatcher, who revels in the offence she has caused in the ranks of 'the great and the good among political commentators – whose idea of political neutrality resembles the collected words and deeds of Mr Roy Jenkins and Mrs Shirley Williams'.[197] Mr Butt's fire was aroused by the snobbery he detected behind much of the fashionable hostility to the Prime Minister:

> There was the intellectual snobbery which resented her non-acceptance of an establishment which had become unused to challenge. There is a strong whiff of class snobbery. You might think this absurd since Grantham and Somerville is no worse than a mining valley and Balliol [Roy Jenkins's pedigree]. But it all depends on willingness to join the establishment which Mrs Thatcher had the effrontery to challenge with some of the common sense of the suburbs.[198]

And it is the BBC, which, according to Henry Fairlie in 1959, was 'of all the voices of the Establishment, the most powerful',[199] and which had now in Mr Stuart Young (until his untimely death in 1986) a Thatcher appointee brimming with the common sense of the North London suburbs (Woodhouse Grammar School, North Finchley), that has brought the criticism of current prime-ministerial patronage to the fore. Another *Times* columnist, the late David Watt, former Director of the Royal Institute of International Affairs and an unashamed defender of 'some of the virtues of the old paternalism',[200] claimed that:

> By far the most influential group ... [of the BBC's enemies] ... is made up of those who have a visceral objection to the BBC as the perfect embodiment of the old establishment, the paternalist expression of traditional middle-of-the-road consensus. Thatcherism and the Prime

Minister herself, being in iconoclastic reaction against just these things, are naturally hostile to the BBC; they have also helped to create a polarised political and cultural climate in which Reithian aspirations find it hard to survive.[201]

But it was the decision of the BBC Board of Governors, after pressure from the Home Secretary, to ban the showing of the *Real Lives* television documentary on political extremism in Northern Ireland which led in the summer of 1985 to the more perfervid accusations about supine placemen in the BBC hierarchy. A somewhat bizarre spin-off from this was the paean of praise to the old establishment which poured forth from the pen of the *Observer*'s leader writer:

> . . . to blame Mr Young exclusively for the quite unnecessary shambles the Governors have created would be unfair. He had, after all, to work with the material at his disposal; and the days have long since departed when the BBC's Board comprised people of the independence and calibre of, say, Lady Violet Bonham Carter, Sir Harold Nicolson or the redoubtable . . . Baroness Wootton.[202]

Even an outspoken critic of the G and G like Lord Donoughue maintains that a regrettable precedent has been set by the pattern of patronage since 1979:

> When I was in Downing Street, both prime ministers [Wilson and Callaghan] would make sure that able people from the Conservative side were utilised in public appointments. I think what's very wrong and worrying is the way the present government has made appointments on the basis of only people who agreed with them politically. That is not only bad because the advice is not very valuable; but it's also a very bad precedent for the future . . . If you got in a left wing government, they could put up just as many people. I think Mrs Thatcher might come to rue the consequences of that precedent.[203]

It is hard to see how the Good and the Great idea can run unless it is lubricated by a cross-party, if not an above-party, philosophy. Clive Priestley believes that it could become difficult to persuade people that a period of public service is time well spent because of 'a very unfortunate and damaging polarity of political opinion and activity in the country at the moment. I think the public generally feels itself demeaned by this and let down by it.'[204]

Richard Hoggart has made the running among those who believe 'the two Thatcher Governments have steadily undermined one of our more useful democratic devices', which he describes as 'arm's-length or buffer committees'.[205] He shares with Professor Ralf Dahrendorf (a German citizen who, while Director of the London School of Economics, sat on Lord Wilson's inquiry into the City and Lord Benson's Royal Commission on Legal Services) the view that such bodies, in the way they are peopled as well as the way they operate, are a peculiarly British phenomenon. Hoggart wrote:

> Few foreigners understand them, or if they understand the words used, can take them at face value. The idea of a committee set up and funded by government which contains members from right across the political spectrum and is ostensibly free to report as it wishes must be a trick, one of Old Albion's characteristically humbug-based forms, a type of repressive tolerance which will in the end not seriously disturb any government or will do so at the peril of its own life.[206]

Hoggart, who suffered what he called a 'manipulated departure' from the vice-chairmanship of the Arts Council – 'it was a political decision, a response to what was felt to be the wish of "No, 10" '[207] – was undoubtedly reflecting accurately the tendency to read the PM's mind in the higher reaches of Whitehall departments where patronage decisions are processed. In one non-defence department, for example, there was some nervousness about a particular chairmanship going in the early 1980s to a highly qualified individual because he had spoken against the cost of the Trident missile programme, an issue which had absolutely nothing to do with the post for which he was eventually picked.[208] Richard Hoggart (writing in December 1985) added his torch to the searchlight on the BBC Board of Governors: 'Never before has . . . [it] . . . had both a Conservative Chairman [Stuart Young] and a Conservative Vice-Chairman [Sir William Rees-Mogg, who also chairs the Arts Council].'[209] And he rounded off his tirade in defence of the G and G and the arm's-length principle by saying that under Mrs Thatcher 'the process is a reflection of the Prime Minister's unshakeable faith in the individualised, centripetal, one-of-us system of government. Against such operations, the old-style quangos, weaknesses and all, shine like a Christmas candle in an imperfect world.'[210]

The problem as perceived by Richard Hoggart persisted even when the guard had changed at Broadcasting House. The hugely respected Sir Denis Forman of Granada Television in the 1987 Dimbleby Lecture, speaking of the BBC and the IBA, said: 'Above all it behoves the chairmen of the two authorities to guard against the packing of their boards with an undue proportion of members who are responsive to the views of the government in power. The pressure is bound to be applied; they are bound to resist.'[211] His words, if *The Guardian*'s Media Editor, Peter Fiddick, is a guide, did not fall on unreceptive ears. He reported the BBC's new chairman, Duke Hussey, as being 'among those who hope to persuade the Government to return to a broader view of potential candidates, not just in their apparent political allegiances, but also in their age and capacity to contribute through personal achievement in their fields to the working of the board'.[212]

Nonetheless, one has to treat the widely purveyed image of Mrs Thatcher as Queen Boadicea driving a chariot of conviction politics through traditional conventions and institutions with a degree of scepticism. To take it at face value, it suggests that the majority of permanent secretaries appointed since 1979 share the values of the Grantham corner shop and believe the Beveridgite-Keynesian consensus to have brought Britain to the brink of disaster. In all probability, the Prime Minister, even if those were her criteria of preferment, would, as we have seen, find it hard to muster a single true believer from the top three grades of the Civil Service. The same applies to Cabinet government. It has not been put on a shelf in the No. 10 Registry along with decaying volumes of Sir Ivor Jennings and the late John Mackintosh. The same applies to patronage. The BBC Board of Governors may have appeared to be the Government's catspaw when the *Real Lives* affair began. But a sensible and widely acceptable solution was found in a matter of weeks which projected the programme on to the screen albeit with a carefully phrased preamble. But take that other grouping crucial to the future of British public broadcasting, the Peacock Committee. True, its remit – to examine alternative ways of financing the BBC including advertising – would not have been laid down by any previous government, Labour or Conservative. But the Peacock Committee was not packed by people the Prime Minister would deem 'one of us'.[213] Alastair Hetherington is a former editor of *The Guardian* and ran BBC Scotland before taking up a chair at Stirling University. Mr Samuel Brittan, Economics Editor of *The Financial Times*, may be the brother of Leon, the former Home Secretary who commissioned Peacock, but he is one of the most independent-minded people in British journalism.[214] Mr Jeremy Hardie was an SDP candidate. At a push it could be suggested that Professor Peacock, Miss Judith Chalmers, the television personality, Sir Peter Reynolds of Rank, Hovis McDougall and Lord Quinton of Trinity College, Oxford, cut with the Thatcherite grain, but there would be inaccuracy and injustice in such a remark. And their report when published was not exactly what the Prime Minister had in mind. It offered market solutions, certainly, but those based on long-term deregulation rather than taking in advertisements in the short term.[215]

The most convincing evidence that the G and G, as they approached their nine-hundreth anniversary, were down but far from out came in the mopping-up operation after the greatest single crisis of Mrs Thatcher's premierships, the Falklands War of 1982. She promised the Commons an inquiry into its origins. Before appointing a chairman to lead a team of Privy Counsellors, the Prime Minister had to consult the leaders of the Opposition parties. At such moments all roads lead to North Oxford and Lord Franks. It was clearly a job for the No. 1 on the List. Sir Robert Armstrong, Secretary of the Cabinet and a long-time admirer of Franks the man and the Franks style, called at Blackhall Farm one Saturday morning to check that Attlee and Bevin's favourite fireman was able and willing to travel on the G and G flyer from Oxford to Paddington once more. Lord Franks was willing, and his committee, after (as Mr Callaghan later put it in the Commons), painting 'a splendid picture' in the first 338 paragraphs of their report, behaved in paragraph 339, the last one, as if Lord Franks had 'got fed up with the canvas he was painting and ... chucked a bucket of whitewash over it',[216] a charge Lord Franks firmly denied.[217] Whatever the justice of the former prime minister's complaint, the Franks report on the origins of the Falklands War effectively laid the matter to rest in the approach to the 1983 general election. Lord Franks was and remains the safest pair of hands at Whitehall's disposal.

But, for a strict Haldanian, harder utilitarian tests must be applied to the commissions, the committees and the advisory councils as aids to high-quality and timely policy-making. Is there a place for them in the terrain identified by Samuel Brittan, fresh from service with the Peacock Committee, as 'a middle ground between the highly technical reasearch typical of contemporary social science ... and the mere representation of interest groups and political views'?[218] I think there is – that the G and G in a repaired, strengthened and modernised form *do* have an important place in a new system of central government for the twenty-first century. But before turning to the sinews of that system we must try and assess the system we have and the manner of its reshaping under the most commanding prime minister of recent times.

PART FOUR | MRS THATCHER'S WHITEHALL

> Why has Mrs Thatcher had this impact . . . ? I think it is force of will combined with intolerance, and combined with this ability to see a number of limited things; like Neville Chamberlain to see them very clearly but not to be assailed by doubt or excessive respect for views one does not agree with . . .
> **Roy Jenkins, 1988**[1]

Lord Jenkins, in reaching that judgement, was considering Mrs Thatcher as a practitioner of Cabinet government. But the judgement, in the view of many people, including some on her own side, fits her approach to central government as a whole. This part of the book deals with events that are very recent and very controversial. Perspective is therefore difficult to achieve. To increase the chance of achieving it I have split the story in two and have taken the least controversial and probably longest-lasting aspect of her stewardship – the reform of Civil Service management – first, to avoid its becoming distorted by the high-frequency clutter of other issues.

14 RAYNERISM

My view of the Prime Minister, or Thatcherism ... is that they reflect the qualities of real leadership. She has vision, she has faith in her mission, and she has the determination and the guts to carry it out. To me the only argument arises as to whether her policies are right or not.
Lord Rayner, 1986.[1]

A remarkable and wonderful person.
Mrs Thatcher on Lord Rayner, 1980.[2]

My great strength was the unquestioned support I had from the Prime Minister. They all knew that I did carry the authority equivalent to the then Head of Civil Service and the Head of Treasury.
Lord Rayner, 1987[3]

If you think of the great reform movements of the past, they have all been attended by long periods of pain and agony. The movement which triumphed is that which had power for long enough and was bloody-minded for long enough. Thos of us who are committed to reform just have to grit out teeth and put up with a certain amount of flak, misunderstanding and misrepresentation.
Clive Priestley, 1984.[4]

At first sight, Clive Priestley, Whitehall chief of staff to Derek Rayner, Mrs Thatcher's Efficiency Adviser, 1979–83, is an unlikely-looking candidate to be the cutting-edge of a tough new management drive in the Civil Service. A careful and polished speaker, a wearer of beautifully groomed suits of a timeless design and a watch chain, he carries something of the air of a Lord Peter Wimsey. He is, however, a man who believes with a degree of passion unusual in a career civil servant that the state, wherever its boundaries are drawn by the politicians, must be superbly managed.

Justice to the taxpayer and the consumer of public services, and a proper pride in his work by the public servant himself, demands no less.

Priestley, like a number of his colleagues, was not happy with the quality of Whitehall management in the 1970s which he witnessed from its supposed cockpit, the Civil Service Department, where he had been engaged, among other things, in departmental management reviews including the Treasury's in 1974–5. For a variety of reasons – speech, dress, personality and experience – he is one of the few people who can genuinely hold an audience on such a subject. It was at the Adam Smith Institute's Anglo-American seminar on bureaucracy at St George's House, Windsor, in May 1984, that he first outlined his philosophy of the 'well managed state' in public:

> By the time Mrs Thatcher took office in 1979 . . . there was an extensive but vague political conviction about the scale, cost and efficiency of the state . . . A major reason for this vague conviction at this time is that the theory of the welfare state . . . has not actually until recently included any emphasis at all on efficiency, effectiveness or value for money. This is a very curious philosophical omission, and the fact that it exists is a comment on the relatively slack intellectual time in which we live as compared with, say, political philosophy one hundred years ago.[5]

Priestley described the growing hostility of press and public opinion in the 1970s about the size of the bureaucracy and 'what was thought to be the privilege of officialdom'.[6]

Though he had a vested interest in contrasting the achievements of Raynerism after 1979 with what had preceded it, Mr Priestley's description accords with the views of many other officials and, for what they are worth, my own observations of the mid to late seventies:

> The period immediately before 1979 did not do enough to encourage efficiency in the Civil Service. Firstly, neither political nor official leadership in central government had come to regard the efficiency of central government as a policy in is own right. Secondly, the development of the higher Civil Service was, with a few exceptions, still along instinctive, intuitive and empirical lines, with not enough value placed on education and training. . . .
>
> There were consequently very few positive prizes for determined management or cost control. Public services were free, the unions were very powerful, and for most of the 1970s were dealing with a government that was pro-union and preferred to increase staff numbers than to precipitate discontent. The machinery for efficiency in government was either cumbersome or ineffective, and not much improved even after the

IMF intervention of 1976: we still had fairly laborious public expenditure survey machinery; the PAR machinery had become bureaucratic, time-consuming and slow; and manpower control was being operated sluggishly.[7]

Clive Priestley had a quarter of a century's practice in drafting the carefully weighed word when he assembled that judgement. Mrs Margaret Thatcher's views on the subject were not shaped and refined by a lifelong career in the administrative class.

The best intelligence on the anti-Civil Service bias that Mrs Thatcher brought with her to Downing Street came from a commentator who shared it, Patrick Cosgrave:

> She was already, when she came into office, profoundly suspicious of the Civil Service. 'Do you', a friend asked her in 1980, 'hate all institutions?' She frowned and replied. 'Not at all. I have great respect for the Monarchy and Parliament.' But for the City, the trade unions, the Civil Service and the Church of England she has a dislike that some would call hatred and certainly veers regularly over into contempt.[8]

Cosgrave was, in Opposition days, in a position to assess her feelings at first hand:

> This ferocious attitude to the Civil Service, which she rarely bothers to justify in terms of greater efficiency or savings made, is one she has held for a long time. I recall an occasion in 1977 when I was helping her to prepare a speech in which there were to be a number of references to Churchill. I told her that when I had been working on a book on Churchill some years previously I had interviewed General Sir Ian Jacob, in 1940 a deputy military secretary to the War Cabinet. I knew from the papers I had read that Sir Ian had been highly critical of Churchill before he became Prime Minister, and highly supportive afterwards. I asked him if there was any particular time when he had changed his mind. 'Yes', he replied, after a moment's reflection, 'it was on the thirteenth of May 1940. I saw a permanent under secretary in a corridor in Whitehall in his shirtsleeves, *running*. Then I knew that Churchill could shake up the machine.' The anecdote gave her enormous pleasure.[9]

Her dislike of the official culture she encountered at the Department of Education and Science during the Heath government is well known as is her formative and far from favourable experience at the Ministry of Pensions in the Macmillan years.

Mrs Thatcher is a great believer in the 'guilty men' theory. In her demonology it is the protagonists of the failed Keynesian-Beveridgite consensus who have brought Britain low. She appears to treat them, almost as a Marxist might, as a class with their own values. And those with the biggest horns in this demonology are the permanent politicians, the senior civil servants who assisted at the birth of that consensus and who had succeeded in capturing every Cabinet, Labour or Conservative, for its cause from the mid-forties to May 1979. It is easy to see why Correlli Barnett's *The Audit of War* enjoyed such an instant vogue amongst those who share her views, like Keith Joseph,[10] when it was published in 1986. Always ready to exempt those who have served her closely and personally, Mrs Thatcher nonetheless detests senior civil servants as a breed. As one permanent secretary put it to me, 'She doesn't think clever chaps like us should be in here at all. We should be outside, making profits.'[11]

It is not surprising that, bearing in mind this set of attitudes, the strictures contained in Leslie Chapman's *Your Disobedient Servant*, with its account of his thwarted efforts to pursue better management inside the Property Services Agency, should have fallen upon sympathetic ears inside the office of the Leader of the Opposition when the book was published in 1978. As Clive Priestley later put it, rather loftily:

> The proposal was for a new audit department to replace the Exchequer and Audit Department [now the National Audit Office], which would be staffed up with detectives, forensic analysts, barristers, inquisitors and others, who would go round and find out where the bodies were buried. They would then bring the offending bureaucrats before a Committee of the House of Commons which would sit in judgement while these offenders were grilled by the high-powered inquisitors. Here was a senior level civil servant providing parables about the working of the service and saying that they could not be trusted.[12]

During the 1979 general election campaign, Mrs Thatcher was advised on Civil Service efficiency by Mr Chapman.[13] Why then was it Rayner and not Chapman who joined Mrs Thatcher in Whitehall to lead the crusade against waste and inefficiency once the election was won? Clive Priestley is as tactful as he is delphic in providing the answer:

> Sir Derek was a member of a firm [Marks & Spencer] which she greatly admires, and uses. He had been in government before; he had reorganised defence procurement, and had been in an official position as the first head of the Defence Procurement Executive; he was a trusted political adviser, and not a political adviser who was *parti-pris* to the point of prejudice, but one who would speak his mind as a decent human

> being should; and, of course, Mr Chapman was not well known to the Prime Minister.[14]

What Mr Priestley said of Derek Rayner as an adviser remains true. He is probably the only one of Mrs Thatcher's circle whom it is possible to imagine advising a prime minister of a quite different political philosophy, including a PM of another party. His techniques are as useful for a politician wishing to expand the role of the state as they are for one pursuing smaller government. It is, whatever one's political views, wasteful to divert to Whitehall a single pound or a single official surplus to requirements with so many other priorities clamouring for public resources. Indeed, there was a coded plea from Whitehall to Labour that the Rayner reforms should be persisted with eight months before the 1987 general election when Miss (now Dame) Anne Mueller of the Management and Personnel Office told an Institute of Personnel Management Conference: 'The conclusion I must draw from continuing pressure on resources and rising expectations is that it must be in the interest of all political parties to secure better value for money from the resources available.'[15] In addition to such rational factors, Derek Rayner has the kind of personality and temperament (and shape) which appeals to people of all sorts and conditions and prejudices. His 'ism' could be, should be, independent and freestanding of the 'ism' of the prime minister he served. And, when you think about it, it is quite a feat for a man of Rayner's background to become an eponym of British political life.

Like Mrs Thatcher, Derek Rayner carried strong views formed by prior experience into the office set aside for him overlooking Horse Guards Parade, previously occupied by Harold Lever. (On his arrival at the Cabinet Office on 8 May 1979 he found Lever's assistant, a young member of the Government Economic Service, David Allen, and decided to keep him on – a good move from both their points of view.) His experience working on procurement for Heath remained vivid in Rayner's mind:

> When I first arrived in a ministry in 1970 I was amazed that in the defence department with enormous expenditure that there were no kinds of financial management that I knew in business and that the head of finance was certainly not an accountant by training or experience ... and yet we were dealing with 10-year forecasts involving billions of pounds ... [When I asked] about new projects, I was assured there was space for them in the long-term costings. My natural request was to see the long-term costings. I was told 'They're not for you.' I said 'But I wish to see them.' In due course, a large, wheeled skip arrived containing these very documents. Needless to say, in that form they were not much good for senior management to make any judgments at all as to whether there was room for expenditure or not.[16]

Rayner rightly described the MOD's procurement programme as 'one of the biggest general management jobs I know of in the country and yet, until I came along in 1970, it was done by a senior civil servant, often brought in from the Treasury, who'd had no experience at all of industrial matters, R and D which had to precede or accompany most defence issues. The job of that man was to make sure the rulebook was in force.'[17] What Rayner was in fact describing was the classic 'umpire' function being pursued by a classic product of the Northcote–Trevelyan Report.

Between leaving the Procurement Executive in 1972 and answering Mrs Thatcher's call in May 1979, Derek Rayner had kept in touch with life inside the citadel's walls as an outside member of 'one or two management review committees' whose practices he faulted because 'there was always a tendency to look at everything, and I know perfectly well from business you cannot look at everything – that is not possible, you have to pick those things that you believe are worthy of investigation in depth and then, from what you learn, apply them on a wide area'.[18] This philosophy underlay the scrutiny programme, the examination of specific blocks of work by young officials – 'Rayner's Raiders', as they became known – working to a strict timetable and reporting to him as well as to their permanent secretary.

Rayner likes management to travel light but to dig deep. He applied this to his own organisation the day he arrived in No. 70 Whitehall and found Dave Allen pondering his fate. He quickly accepted Ian Bancroft's offer of Clive Priestley as his chief of staff. Building his own team, however, did not take long. In addition to Priestley and Allen it consisted of a single secretary. They were the Whitehall equivalent of the Long Range Desert Group in North Africa during the Second World War – tiny but of high quality. Rayner prefers a biblical metaphor:

> I had no interest in creating a pseudo-Treasury or Exchequer and Audit Department of my own. I would waste time trying to get the staff I needed; having a large organisation would, ironically, add to bureaucracy rather than lessen it; and I would no doubt be seen off by the real Treasury and by departments. Goliath should be matched with David, not with a small version of himself.[19]

The Rayner approach was in complete contrast with the Grace Commission, President Reagan's 1981 equivalent in Washington with its 161-strong executive committee and its 'wallpapering'[20] of all departments of the Federal Governments. But, large or small, he and his outfit would have had minimal to nil influence from day one but for what Rayner called 'the unique political imperative' created by Mrs Thatcher, as 'support for the initiative was not extensive among other ministers or at the higher echelons of the Civil Service'.[21] Upon their wall the Rayner Unit placed a framed copy of an extract from Machiavelli's *The Prince*:

> It must be considered that there is nothing more perilous to conduct or more uncertain in its success than to take the lead in the introduction of a new order of things. For the reformer has enemies in all those who profit by the old order, and only lukewarm defenders in all those who would profit by the new order.[22]

The Rayner experience has one thing in common with the Fulton experience – both demonstrate how absolutely and utterly crucial is the patronage of the occupant in No. 10: Wilson lost interest; Thatcher did not.

Stripped to its core, Raynerism is the belief that 'the two most important instruments are money and people',[23] the single greatest enemy is 'paper, the tyranny of the past'.[24] There exists in the Cabinet Office registry an official encapsulation of the Rayner philosophy in the shape of a Cabinet Paper entitled *The Conventions of Government*, dated April 1980, which, under the conventions of secrecy, we cannot see until the first week of January 2011 – though Derek Rayner, by temperament an open-government man, has spoken about it since:

> I recommended to Cabinet a series of actions. There were three: a short-term getting rid of paperwork; a medium-term getting down to individual activities or discrete parts of government and improving the way they perform; and thirdly, lasting reforms, bringing about the changes and the education and the experience during the career of a civil servant which would ... [enable] ... him to manage the substantial amounts of work that would unquestionably come his way.[25]

I conducted my first interview with Rayner a few weeks before *The Conventions of Government* went to the Cabinet and was struck by the passion with which he attacked Whitehall's paper culture:

> The books of rules and regulations grow every time a mistake is made. Initiative, common sense and anything that smacks of the entrepreneur goes out of the window because failure is always noticed and success is forgotten. The workload is very largely created by the rule books.
>
> I was in a Department of Health and Social Security office before Christmas where the clerks have to work with 50 volumes of rules created since 1948. Unless the rules are cut down and allowance is made for a percentage of error, we will not get to grips with the numbers.[26]

He talked enthusiastically about his scrutiny programme – digging bore-holes into areas of activity and applying lessons from the detritus across the whole of the Civil Service landscape. He was determined it would not suffer the fate of PAR which he had persuaded the Cabinet to kill off the previous October.[27] PAR failed, Rayner believed, because too many senior civil servants could get at its findings before they reached ministers, erasing any traces of radicalism.[28]

Rayner circulated his PAR replacement to ministers and officials on 2 November 1979. It took the form of a note of guidance on the scrutiny programme. It was written in his spare, Marks & Spencer style: 'The purpose of the scrutinies is action, not study. It is therefore (a) to examine a specific policy, activity or function with a view to savings or increased effectiveness and to questioning all aspects of the work normally taken for granted; (b) to propose solutions to any problems identified; and (c) to implement agreed solutions, or begin their implementation, within 12 months of the start of the scrutiny.'[29]

The work was to be completed within 90 working days. True to the philosophy he had outlined to the Expenditure Committee three years earlier, Rayner told his scrutineers not to look for 'bad news only. Where there is a good story, Ministers may wish to tell it and it would be reasonable for the reports to reflect this.'[30] Rayner was convinced that Whitehall was rich in officials wishing to probe and to innovate who found themselves smothered by the system. 'The greatest waste I found in government,' he once told me, 'is so much talent at the service of the nation that, for one reason or another, is not being harnessed to bring about the kind of improvements with which my name is associated.'[31]

The key to the scrutinies was the discovery and enfranchisement of that suppressed talent. By giving them an unambiguous charter, backed by the ever present shadow of 'she who must be obeyed' as the Efficiency Unit liked to refer to Mrs Thatcher,[32] Rayner hoped to release it. He said in his note to ministers and permanent secretaries:

> The officials selected should be free to examine the specified part of their Department's functions in detail, seeing such colleagues and making such visits as are necessary within their own Department; consulting other Departments . . . and going right outside Government where appropriate. They should ask radical questions, e.g. 'Why is this work done at all? Why is it done as it is? How could it be done more efficiently and effectively at less cost?'[33]

While he was at it, Rayner struck a blow for equality and meritocracy: 'The quality of the officials selected is more important than their age or present occupation. An experienced and hard-headed 50-year-old is as acceptable as a "flyer" and a good professional as a good administrator;

intellectual capacity and personality are more important than grade or group.'[34]

The 'philosophy' of the programme, as Rayner outlined it, was the exact reverse of Leslie Chapman's inquiring 'outsiders'. This was to be an 'insider' job:

> The reasoning behind the scrutiny programme is that Ministers and their officials are better equipped than anyone else to examine the use of the resources for which they are responsible. The scrutinies, therefore, rely heavily on self-examination. The main elements are the application of a fresh mind to the policy, function or activity studied; the interaction of that mind with the minds of those who are expert in the function or activity; the supervision of the Minister accountable to Parliament for its management and for the resource it consumes; and the contribution of an outside agency in the shape of my office and me.[35]

Rayner made it plain that the 'outside agency' would not let minister or permanent secretary get at the scrutineer or the scrutiny. He would involve himself at all stages to avoid a repetition of PAR. Ian Beesley, an early scrutineer who later joined the Efficiency Unit and succeeded Clive Priestley as its chief of staff, described what it was like when Rayner would brief his raiders before they were unleashed:

> He's a very big man physically and he's quite a demanding personality, slightly larger than life . . . He would [say] to them, 'For the first time in your life, you're not going to be dominated by the in-tray. If you let the flow of paper in your in-tray tell you what to do then the Empire will actually strike back and will prevent you doing that job you have been put there to do.'[36]

Ian Beesley, naturally, is an enthusiast and a 22-carat Rayner man. But he conveys convincingly the stimulating novelty for a career official of working under licence from Rayner:

> It was exhilarating . . . you knew you had an opportunity to show that the Civil Service could improve itself and that that was a fairly rare opportunity. The second thing was that you were asked to apply your own judgment to a situation. You were asked to look at a topic. You were asked to write a report. It would have your name on it. It would go in front of the Minister with your name on it.
>
> Nobody would be allowed to alter those words .. What he [Rayner] said . . . was 'let the facts speak for themselves and then the conclusions

> will follow.' That was very rare because it was an exercise in personal responsibility [and] it was done under a timescale that was fairly tight.[37]

Norman Warner, a DHSS scrutineer, discovered that Rayner could deliver the support he promised: 'He certainly had a capacity to ensure that doors were opened when we needed information.'[38]

Acquiring information, analysing it, presenting a radical report to ministers and persuading them of its merits is one thing. Getting them to implement it is quite another, as Norman Warner found after he had completed the most famous Rayner scrutiny-that-got-away. Warner and his colleague, Gerry Grimstone, looked at one of the many big businesses the DHSS runs – the payment of pensions and child benefits weekly through post offices. They identified the considerable savings that could be made if such benefits were paid monthly and automatically into bank accounts. They presented their findings to Mrs Thatcher and later to the Cabinet, as Mr Warner recalls:

> In the course of the discussion with the Prime Minister we did explain that what we were proposing would mean that fewer people would have pensions paid less frequently through post offices and that there was likely to be a row with the sub-postmasters who would lose income from this change in payment arrangements. And, as I recall, I was fixed with a fairly firm, clear stare and told that 'political will was something that this government didn't lack, young man'.[39]

Other wills soon came into play, however. The plan leaked. The outcry was formidable. The rural economy itself would be jeopardised and rustic life never the same again if country post offices had to close. Norman Warner describes the epitaph of his and Gerry Grimstone's endeavours:

> Rather like Wat Tyler, the sub-postmasters marched on London and deputed to the House of Commons. And in the general uproar which followed, I'm afraid that at one Question Time, the Prime Minister did in fact concede that benefits would continue to be paid weekly . . . so the main plank of the scrutineers' report was actually lost.[40]

By the time Rayner decided to devote virtually all his time to Marks & Spencer after December 1982, 130 scrutinies had produced £170 million savings and economies of 16,000 posts a year, plus £39 million more in once-and-for-all savings with another £104 million worth of possible economies identified.[41]

Not everybody was impressed by these results. Professor Richard Rose, noting they were less than 0.4 per cent of total public expenditure in 1982–3, said 'the rewards of efficiency efforts are paltry, compared to the total cost of contemporary government'.[42] This is not a fair picture. If you compare the savings with the running costs of central government, some £16.5 billion in 1983–4[43], rather than the £109.5 billion of public expenditure as a whole (and it was reducing running costs that the early scrutinies were all about), matters look rather more impressive – as they do when compared to the years of relative profligacy in the 1970s. Lord Rayner has his own retort to those who belittle the scrutiny-yield. It 'may be tiddlers' for some, 'but as a modest businessman [it] is a hell of a lot of money to me'. [44] It certainly seemed more than 'tiddlers' by the time Mrs Thatcher won her third election in a row. In just over eight years, more than 300 scrutinies had generated savings of over £1 billion,[45] which is highly impressive when one considers what a billion would buy in the eighties (the M25 motorway, 22 new hospitals or the Chevaline improvement to Polaris.[46]) In addition, further continuing economies worth another £325 million a year had been implemented.[47]

The National Audit Office, however, had concentrated in its investigation on one aspect of the pioneering period and, in his undemonstrative way, that old Treasury and CPRS hand, Sir Gordon Downey, was quietly impressed with Rayner's design and management of the early scrutiny programmes. Downey, by this time Comptroller and Auditor General, examined the programmes from their origins in 1979 to the point where Rayner severed his last remaining connections with them altogether after the 1983 general election when he was succeeded as Mrs Thatcher's Efficiency Adviser by Sir Robin Ibbs, the ICI man who had replaced Berrill as head of the CPRS in 1980 (see p. 643). By the time Rayner left for good, departments had conducted five waves of scrutinies, 155 in all, which had identified potential savings of £421 million a year.[48]

Downey 'did a Rayner' on Rayner in the sense that he drove bore-holes down into selected scrutinies with a view to drawing general lessons about them all. He looked at 20 per cent of them and concentrated on four departments, the Inland Revenue, Home Office, FCO and DHSS. The bottom line of the National Audit Office's investigation of this key component of Raynerism was its endorsement of 'the continuing usefulness of the scrutiny process as a high level management technique to improve value for money'.[49] The body of Downey's report certainly showed that most of the key factors outlined in Rayner's note of guidance to scrutineers of November 1979 had been carried out:

> The scrutiny officers generally adopted working methods closely modelled upon Sir Derek Rayner's advice. Their examination was thorough....
>
> The scrutiny reports indicated that key issues had been identified and

that radical departures from accepted practices had been considered ... including additional expenditure to secure larger savings.

Most conclusions and recommendations were explicitly related to the ascertained facts and the analysis included estimates of present costs and future savings ... The range of conclusions and recommendations tended to confirm Sir Derek Rayner's belief that departmental management was well placed to improve efficiency in the use of resources. Their effectiveness in doing so through the scrutiny arrangements depended on the choice of topics.[50]

Downey found that the time taken to follow up scrutinies varied widely, that ministers did not accept all recommendations, that some were overtaken by events or conflicted with government policy. He noted, too, that the Government's drive to reduce the Civil Service numbers substantially (it surpassed its target in fact; between 1979 and 1984 108,000 posts were saved, more than the planned reduction from the 732,000 officials they inherited to 630,000[51]) provided an important external incentive for pursuit of Rayner-identified economies, a view Sir Derek shared. ('I knew the numbers would go on growing unless a very stern attempt was made to bring them down ... I did not want to bring them down with a mallet; I wished to bring them down with a scalpel.'[52]) Downey also pushed another standard Rayner line, 'that the full potential for improvement and development through successful use of scrutiny techniques can be realised only if there is a commitment at the top of each department – specifically on the part of Ministers and Accounting Offices [i.e. permanent secretaries] – to bring this about'.[53]

The National Audit Office inquiry threw up a number of suggestions for improvement and noted the refinements and developments made by Rayner's successor, Sir Robin Ibbs (the NAO reported before the appearance of *The Next Steps*, see pp. 619–22). But, all in all, it can only be seen as a probe which gave the scrutiny slice of Raynerism an excellent bill of health.

Not that Rayner needed such belated endorsement to make an impact. He was very good at personal public relations (superb, indeed, when compared with standard Whitehall practice). Early on, he had pledged himself to a policy of openness. Asked on the BBC 1 Television programme, *Platform One*, in January 1980, 'if you think you are being frustrated and fooled, led down the garden path, will you throw in your hand and say so publicly?', Rayner replied, 'If I was sidetracked I would certainly seriously consider how far this should be allowed to become yet another secret in the file.' Earlier in the interview he had remarked: 'I am very much for ending secrecy where, in fact, it does not mean secrecy, but silence.'[54]

Rayner was very forthcoming with Parliament in the shape of the

Treasury and Civil Service Committee and with journalists and interviewers too. His cause was greatly helped by his Unit's facility for coming up with the memorably fashioned statistic. For example, when his team produced their first estimate of the cost of central government in 1981 they ensured that it could be presented as the fact that 'it costs each man, woman and child about £3 a week to support the running costs of the Civil Service before a single benefit is paid, Parliamentary question answered, Bill drafted, weapon procured or Cabinet minute typed'.[55]

When Rayner announced the result of one of his trans-departmental reviews or mega-scrutinies it always helped if an eye-catching story could be produced. For as long as the Rayner experience is written about, the £30 rat will scurry across the page. This notorious rodent was uncovered at the Ministry of Agriculture's veterinary laboratory at Weybridge in Surrey. The government's vets, it seemed, reared their own rats for research purposes at £30 a time. A private enterprise rat, Rayner's Raiders discovered, could be purchased commercially for £2.[56] Rayner himself could talk in a fascinating way for ages about the absurdities, anomalies and plain fossiled practices he uncovered as if in a modern imitation of the works of Charles Dickens's famous 'Circumlocution Office'. He managed to persuade the Inland Revenue, for example, to abolish 'one tax form which occupied 400 people's time which was not used any longer. It had been designed for much earlier times in history and it ceased to have any value.'[57]

Rayner used his attack on one of the raw materials of bureaucracy – administrative forms – as a vehicle for delivering his and Clive Priestley's philosophy of the well-managed state and the proper relationship between governors and governed. 'An administrative form', said Rayner in February 1982, 'is a means by which the citizen or the firm on the one hand and the Government on the other talk to each other over an immensely wide range of business . . . a household will deal in the course of a year with forms like the Income Tax Return and the renewal of the TV licence and Vehicle Excise Duty on a car.'[58] He dug into Lord Salter's memoirs to show how the builders of the prototype welfare state, when constructing the apparatus to implement the 1911 National Insurance Act, had chosen 'an ordinary mortal' to edit all the circulars which were to go to the public.[59] 'Too few forms now in circulation', commented Rayner, 'seem to have been submitted to a similar test.'[60]

Again, the Rayner Unit came up with the kind of bright language and vivid metaphor normally absent from the modern White Paper. 'Forms', they declared, 'deserve special attention as the face and voice of Government for many people.'[61] And there was a multitude of 'faces' and 'voices' on offer:

> Over 2,000 million Government forms and leaflets are used by the public each year. That is 36 for every man, woman and child in the country. The price to the taxpayer is not known; but if each form costs just 10 pence in all, it would be in the region of £200 million. There is also the substantial cost to the people who use the forms. Even good forms impose some burdens. Bad forms make for worse problems and extra costs. They also damage relations between Government and the public and undermine the efforts of civil servants, particularly those in local offices, to provide an efficient and helpful service.[62]

Rayner sought the aid of the Plain English Campaign to make forms more comprehensible and was able to promise a 25 per cent reduction in the number of statistical forms sent to businesses as a result of the trans-departmental review of the Government Statistical Service.[63] It was this review, led by a member of the GSS, Ian Beesley, which initially brought Priestley's successor as chief of staff into the Efficiency Unit. Five years later, Richard Luce, as Minister of the Civil Service, announced the result of the quinquennial war on paper which Rayner had declared – 27,000 forms scrapped, 41,000 redesigned at a saving of £14 million.[64]

Rayner was very loyal to his staff both in the Unit and among the ranks of the 'Raiders'. Scrutinies of which he was particularly proud would be paraded before the Prime Minister and sometimes the Cabinet with the young scrutineer taking the spotlight. One of them was Clive Ponting who was later awarded the OBE for his scrutiny of the supply of food to the Armed Forces:

> I had found glaring examples of waste and inefficiency everywhere – warehouses full of food that was stored for years, three separate distribution organisations, and nobody in charge of the system. It even took two months to answer a basic question such as the cost of running the system. My report suggested immediate savings of about £12 million and annual savings of about £4 million.[65]

Ponting, after chronicling the less than triumphant progression of his recommendations, concluded that, in general, 'some small victories had been won, but Whitehall had absorbed Raynerism, as it had all the other schemes for reform and improving efficiency',[66] a judgment on my friend's part which, in this instance, I do not share.

When Clive Ponting went on trial in 1985, Rayner had no hesitation in supplying the court with a glowing character reference, speaking of his 'strength of character' and saying 'he handled [his] difficult task with distinction'.[67] Rayner told me later, 'Clive Ponting was an excellent Rayner scrutineer . . . he came up with an outstanding and detailed report.'[68]

Rayner was particularly pleased when scrutiny results turned up an 'unsung hero' of the vast middle ranks of the Civil Service whose virtues could be paraded in front of the Prime Minister. Mr Eric Turtle, a senior executive officer in the Reading office of the Property Services Agency, was a classic example. Rayner, in his early days, had discussions with Leslie Chapman about his experiences in the PSA. He decided to put down a probe, and the place chosen for a maintenance economy review was the Bath District Works Office (there are big MOD facilities in Bath and district). Turtle, who had been involved in one of Chapman's pioneering maintenance economy reviews, was picked for the job.[69]

The Turtle Report, one of the initial 29-strong batch of Rayner scrutinies, illustrated with precision the Rayner style of determining the detailed points through which the taxpayers' money was flowing, in this case by accumulating a list of decay-prone window frames and excessively tended rose-beds, for the purposes of item-by-item economy with lessons drawn for wider application.[70] Turtle's investigation cost £12,000. It identified possible capital savings of over £6 million, plus current economies of £230,000 for the PSA and £162,000 for its client departments. As a result another 30 maintenance economy reviews were commissioned.[71]

But it would be wrong to see Rayner as carrying all before him in early eighties Whitehall backed by 'she who must be obeyed'. He certainly did not see it that way. He was asked by Hugo Young in a BBC radio interview in June 1981 if there had been any real change at the top of the Civil Service 'under the whip of Thatcherism and, indeed, Raynerism'. 'Taken as a whole, I must be frank and say "No"', he replied.[72] One reason for his midsummer blues was the failure at that stage of his 'crusade against the Civil Service Department'.[73]

Rayner believed that:

> Unquestionably from the early days when the Civil Service Department was set up until the time that it was abolished, it gradually lost steam and momentum as this new creation became part of the Establishment ... I thought it was another cog which had to be taken account of in decision-taking ... The people who worked in the Civil Service Department [CSD] were very high quality and I believed ... that by placing them elsewhere – in the Treasury, partly; in the Cabinet Office, partly – they would be able to deliver their task more effectively.[74]

At the first time of asking, Mrs Thatcher decided to keep the Civil Service Department. On 29 January 1981 she told the Commons that she would strengthen and improve it.[75] Nine months later she changed her mind. She disbanded it and scattered its staff between the Treasury (its manpower divisions) and the Cabinet Office where its establishment functions were housed in a new Management and Personnel Office.[76] After a very frank exchange of views with Sir Ian Bancroft, who fought like a tiger for his department and his Service, Bancroft and his deputy, Sir John Herbecq (a man of quiet charm who had risen from the clerical grades), were despatched by the Prime Minister into early retirement, the headship of the Civil Service passing jointly to Douglas Wass at the Treasury and Robert Armstrong at the Cabinet Office. The cutting edge of Fultonism had been scrapped almost 13 years to the day after its foundation.

There were other battles, unlike the fight for the CSD, which Rayner never won. He wanted to abolish the grade of under secretary. As a result of the chain of command review conducted, at Rayner's prompting, by Sir Geoffrey Wardale, former Second Permanent Secretary at the DOE, the 'open structure' embracing the top three grades was trimmed by 10 per cent but the rank of under secretary remained. Of the other items on the menu of his *The Conventions of Government* Cabinet Paper, there were only sporadic examples of accelerated promotion and, to date, the experiments with merit pay have been limited.

The most important area where the Marks & Spencerisation of the Civil Service has failed, despite Rayner's best efforts, is the improvement in staff working conditions that was always a key component in the Sieff family's approach to the successful running in their retail chain. On his early series of visits, Rayner in 'going round local [DHSS] offices ... found that the conditions under which staff worked were deplorable ... The staff were confronted with interpreting endless rules which [it] was almost impossible for them to do, so innumerable mistakes occurred and the number of justified complaints were quite substantial.'[77] He cited a specific example of poor conditions when interviewed for London Weekend Television's *Whitehall*:

> The average [DHSS] claimant's amount of money was over £30 yet a rule still stood that cheques issued must not be over £30. So most claimants were therefore paid by using two cheques. That would not be too bad on a very modern machine. But they were being printed on machines that I thought were museum pieces and the poor ladies who operate them were covered with ink and they were continually breaking down ... The frustration that came out of this absurd system need not be described and yet, having mentioned it, I got this chang[ed] overnight.[78]

Rayner, however, in general terms got no further with his attempt to raise Civil Service morale through improved working conditions than William Armstrong had with his *Wider Issues Review* a decade earlier. It was an item from his 'lasting reforms' that he picked out in his farewell 'Unfinished Agenda' lecture at London University in 1984:

27. Rayner's Raiders. L to R, Jean Craig, Lynn Holmes, Lord Rayner, David Allen, Elizabeth Thoms, Jean Sullivan, Ian Beesley, Clive Priestley.

28. The 'notorious' Think Tank team which took on the Foreign Office – and lost: L to R, Marrack Goulding, David Young, John Odling-Smee, Sir Kenneth Berrill, Kate Mortimer, Tony Hurrell, Tessa Blackstone.

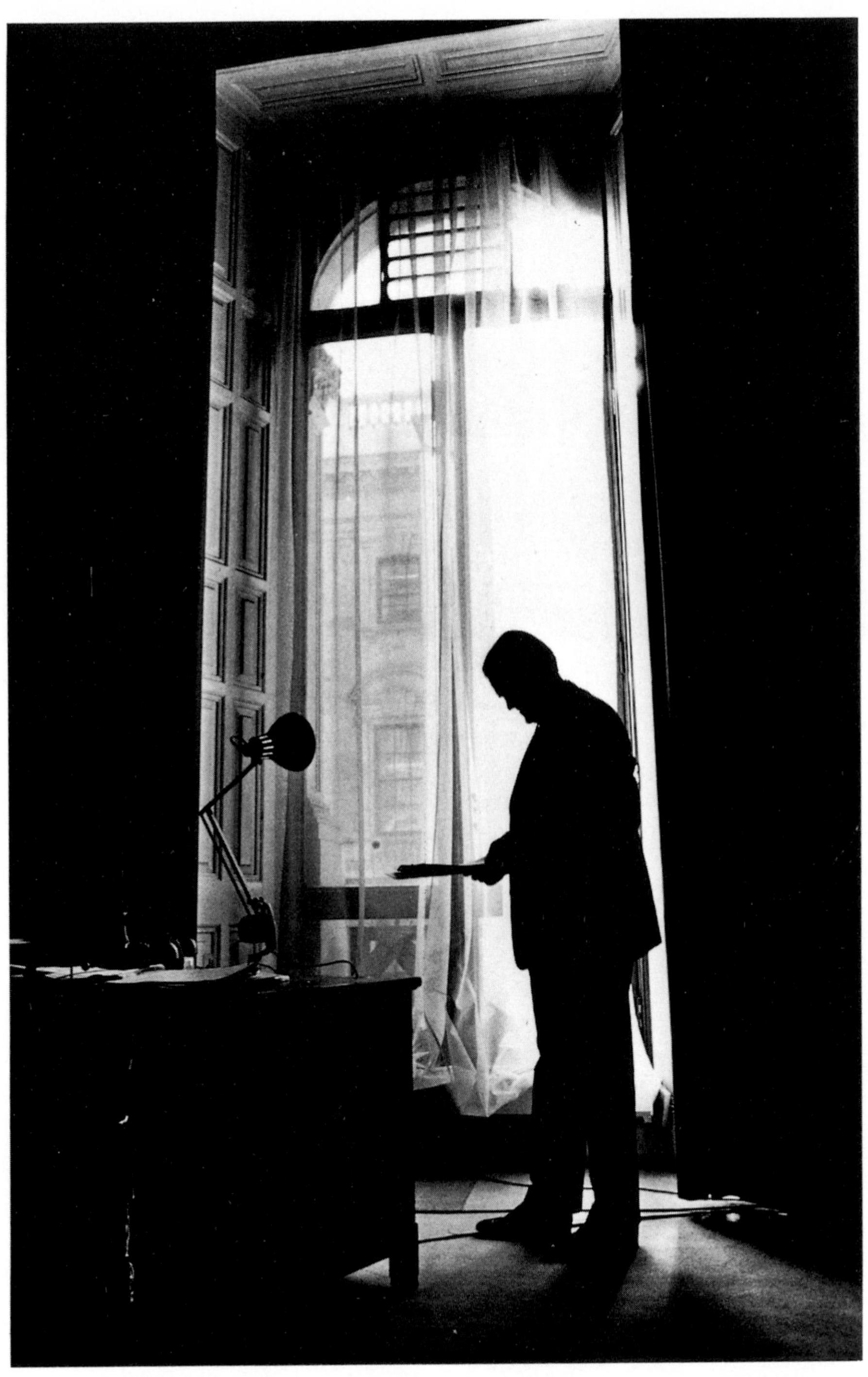

29. Sir Robert Armstrong: it took *Spycatcher* to draw him from the shadows.

30. Norman Strauss: determined to dynamite the Whitehall culture.

31. Sir John Hoskyns outside the Cabinet Office, a citadel he failed to storm.

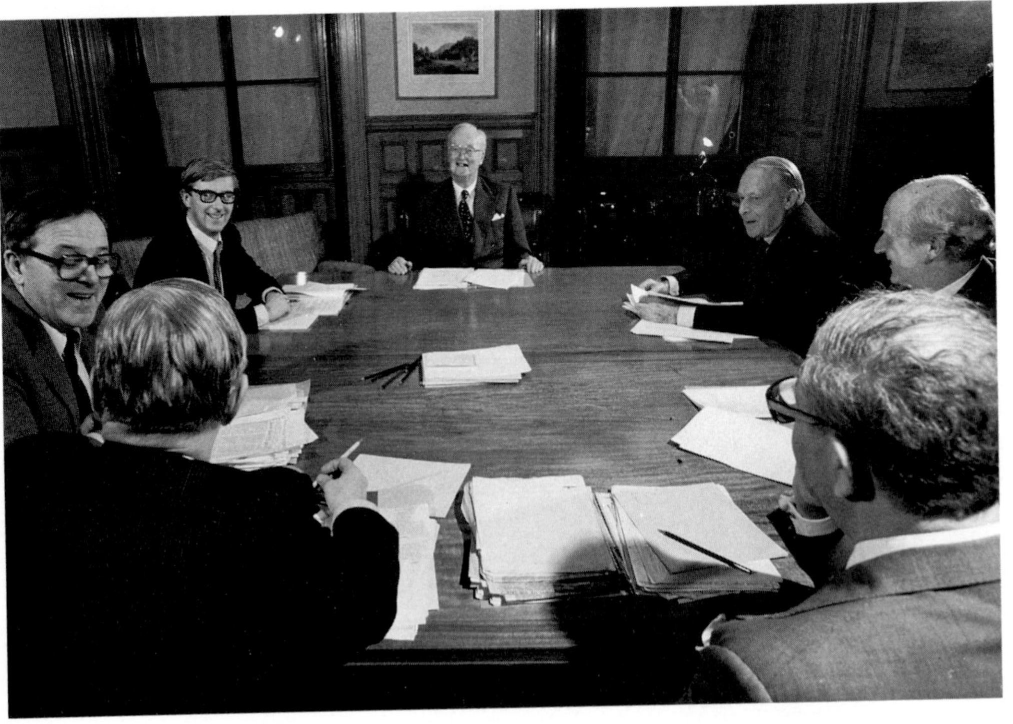

32. Lord Franks (centre) plus Falklands Good and Great, L to R, Merlyn Rees, Sir Patrick Nairne, Anthony Rawsthorne, Lord Watkinson, Lord Lever and Lord Barber.

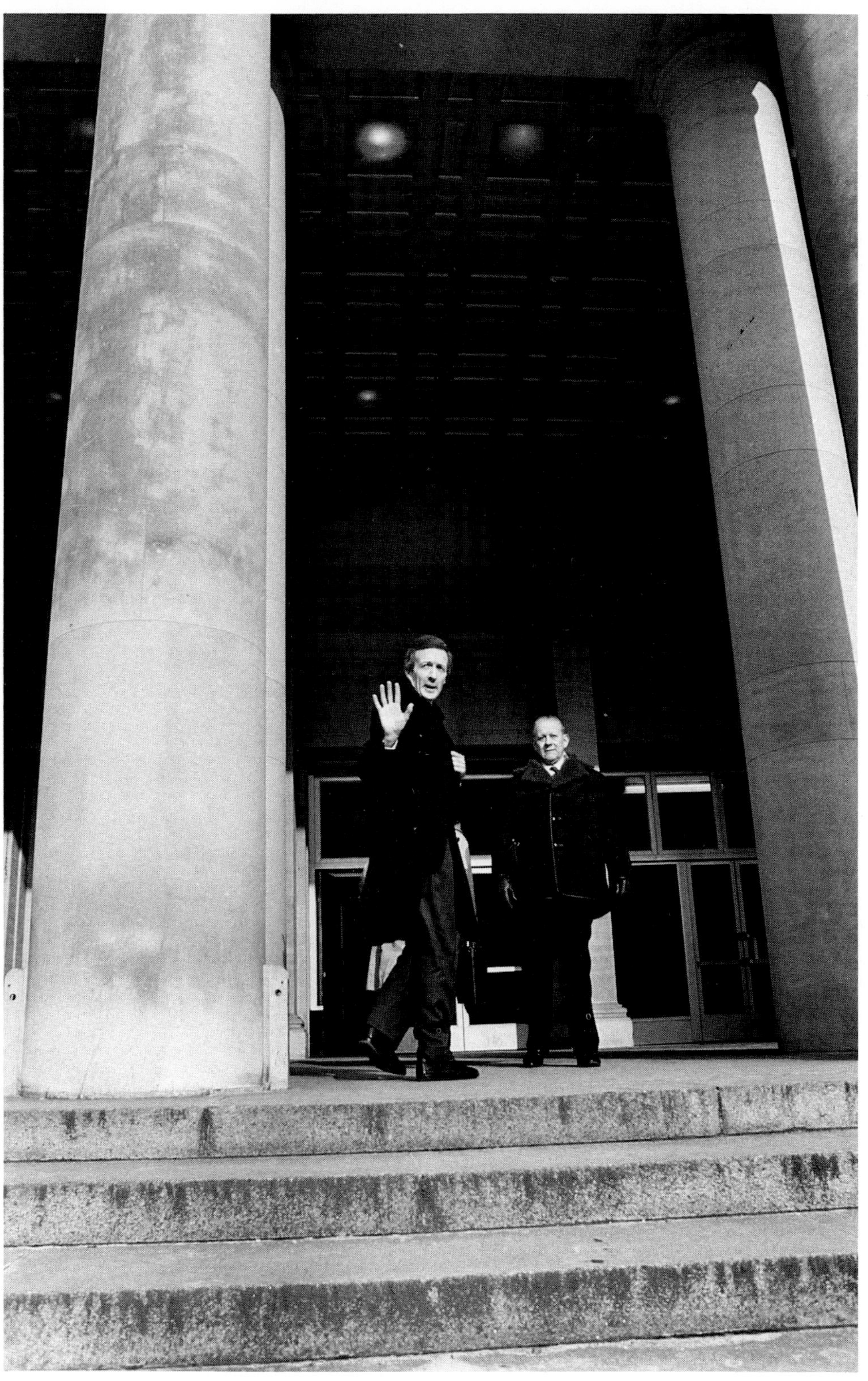

33. Clive Ponting: last day at the Ministry of Defence.

34. Sir Robin Butler and Sir Robert Armstrong: passing the torch with a smile.

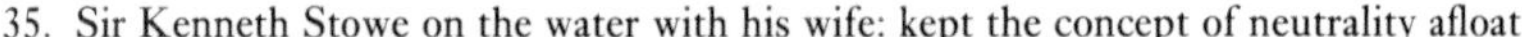

35. Sir Kenneth Stowe on the water with his wife: kept the concept of neutrality afloat.

36. Sir Robin Ibbs: not the grey consolidator he seemed.

37. Kate Jenkins: a plan to shift the foundations.

38. The old guard pays its last respects at Churchill's funeral in 1965. L to R, Lord Attlee (seated), Lord Avon (formerly Sir Anthony Eden), Lord Slim, Lord Portal, Lord Bridges, Lord Normanbrook, Sir Robert Menzies, Mr Harold Maxmillan.

> I ... wanted a more specific and comprehensive recognition of and response to the quality of the talent available at more junior levels. This quality had impressed me in the early 70s and did again during my second tour. It seemed to me that a large part of this recognition must consist in ensuring that staff had the right equipment and the right conditions in which to give of their best and that any other course was a false economy. I cannot claim that this part of my programme had much success.[79]

The critical element in Rayner's compound of lasting reforms was a solvent intended to melt and then alter the traditional culture of the Civil Service from top to bottom. Rayner was always eloquent on this theme which centred on two of the three key instruments of government, as Richard Rose has succinctly defined them, money and people (the third being laws)[80]. 'In any large business', Rayner once told me, 'when you go down a different route, you are, in fact, changing the culture in part of that organisation. And cultural changes are not brought about even by good desires. They're brought about by acquiring new habits and being able to observe that those new habits are effective and enjoyable to perform.'[81]

He delayed his full return to Marks & Spencer to set the elements in place for the chain reaction that would dissolve old Whitehall bonds and precipitate new ones. The name of the policy, in total contrast to the magnitude of its purpose and the fluency of its progenitor, was (and remains) the financial management initiative, now universally known as the FMI. It was conceived inside the Efficiency Unit but another small body was created to run it in, the Financial Management Unit, or FMU (later, confusingly, known as the Joint Management Unit). Sandy Russell, an MPO under secretary, was chosen to run it. Russell had been closely involved with the Thatcher government's efficiency strategy from its outset, running the CSD's functions and programmes group,[82] before heading the management and efficiency divisions of the MPO after the abolition of the CSD.

Russell was a quite, pertinacious man with a lovely dry sense of humour, which he once used to great effect against me. In July 1984 I had written a leader in *The Times* criticising the lack of literary flair in one of the JMU's productions, a White Paper entitled *Progress in Financial Management in Government Departments.*[83] I said its members, had they drafted it, 'would have made the Sermon on the Mount sound like a reading from the Jerusalem telephone directory'.[84] A few weeks later at a conference of scholars and administrators at York University, Sandy Russell, giving a presentation in his quiet, slow Scottish voice, alluded to this leader (which he knew I had written) and begged to differ. 'Where I come from,' he said, 'sermons are things to be endured not enjoyed. And for the inhabitants of

Jerusalem and its environs, the Jerusalem telephone directory is a thing of great utility.'[85]

Sandy Russell led a team of six, a mixture of Civil Service regulars and management consultants. In addition to Russell himself, it consisted of Vincent Watts from Arthur Andersen, Francis Plowden (son of Edwin and Bridget, brother of William) of Cooper Lybrand, plus two part-timers, Barrie Collins from Peat Marwick and Stephen Taylor from Hay MSL. The other two career civil servants were Denis Northrop, an assistant secretary on loan from MOD and David Jamieson, a Treasury senior principal.

With Rayner's guidance and the Prime Minister's approval, they produced what was intended to be the charter of the Civil Service management revolution. It was not, however, in the class of Lincoln's Gettysburg Address or Lenin's words at the Finland Station. As if to compound the quietistic impression, the wordsmiths of Whitehall only managed to come up with *Financial Management, Note by the Treasury and MPO* by way of a title.

Its publication date, 17 May 1982, was equally unfortunate, though that was the fault of the far from efficient or effective General Galtieri in Buenos Aires, not of the Financial Management Unit in Whitehall. For it was the height of the Falklands War, the troopships were about to rendezvous with Admiral Woodward's Task Force off the Islands, and the plan to put an invasion force ashore at San Carlos was about to go to the full Cabinet.[86] The quality of Whitehall management was not in the forefront of the public's or ministers' minds.

The FMI was meant to be a fast breeder reactor which would achieve a permanent, self-sustaining reaction the length and breadth of every Civil Service chain of command, whether a management or a policy-making hierarchy. As its core were three fuel elements to produce 'a system in which managers at all levels have: (a) a clear view of their objectives; and assess and wherever possible measure outputs or performance in relation to these objectives; (b) well-defined responsibility for making the best use of their resources including a critical scrutiny of output and value for money; (c) the information (including particularly about costs), training and access to expert advice which they need to exercise their responsibilities effectively.'[87]

Such language cried out for the attentions of a Beveridge or a Radcliffe. It was as utterly forgettable as it was important. As Sir Frank Cooper later put it, 'The written description of the financial management initiative was a masterpiece of using every relevant phrase – it was all things to all people – but it represented a genuine symbol.'[88] Ironically, one member of the FMU, Vincent Watts, did eventually come up with a memorable metaphor to describe the FMI's purpose of entrenching the early Rayner advances. 'Rayner's is the hunter-gatherer economy', he told me. 'We are trying to turn it into an agrarian state, to domesticate the animals.'[89]

In essence, the FMI was the bureaucracy's surrogate for private-sector stimuli. Referring to its core elements, the FMI charter admitted:

> There are obstacles to the application of these principles in the public service. The yardstick of profitability is lacking. Many government objectives are generalised, and the test of their success is often acceptability rather than a quantified measure of output. In some areas, final measures of output are elusive and only partial indicators of performance can be devised. The task of applying the principles will therefore take time, and complete success in every particular is not to be looked for. Nevertheless, the principles are fundamental to good management and the effective use of resources. They should be applied to the maximum practicable extent.[90]

The FMI made flesh was to be development plans produced by 31 government departments. The model for them was MINIS, the management information system for ministers pioneered, with Rayner's help, by Michael Heseltine when Environment Secretary. MINIS was without precedent in Whitehall. It was a kind of bureaucratic Domesday Book itemising every activity in the giant DOE, the manpower and money devoted to it and the priority afforded it.

Heseltine was, in both senses of the word, a Whitehall 'freak'. He was – is – fascinated by the machine, avid to trim it and supercharge it simultaneously. I can think of no other politician who would devote, as Heseltine did, the first two chapters of his political testament to the subject. Not even that supreme technician-of-state, Lloyd George (whose portrait Heseltine carried round with him from department to department), would have placed so heavy an emphasis on Whitehall. Just how unusual he was for a political animal became apparent at a meeting in a No. 10 dining-room in 1982 when, at the Prime Minister's request, Heseltine outlined before his less than admiring colleagues the subtleties and benefits of MINIS.

'My fellow Cabinet Ministers', Heseltine wrote in *Where There's a Will*, 'sat in rows while I explained my brainchild, each with his sceptical permanent secretary behind him muttering objections, or so I suspected. Any politician knows when he is losing his audience's attention, and I knew well enough. When I had done there were few takers and absolutely no enthusiasts.'[91] What Mr Heseltine did not record in his book was how Mrs Thatcher, confronted with collective Cabinet ennui and disdain for his (and Rayner's idea) of the minister-as-manager, pleaded for 25 minutes with her colleagues to take MINIS seriously and to emulate it in their own departments.[92] In the end 'she who must be obeyed' was obeyed. The FMI charter of May 1982 locked them in. From now on, ministers had to be chief executives in their ministries as well as policy-makers-in-chief.

Mrs Thatcher's ministers, Heseltine apart, tended to believe they had enough to do without becoming managing directors of some of the country's largest businesses too. It was not what they joined up for. Those who had survived from earlier Conservative Cabinets were baffled by the techniques, the jargon and the acronyms that enshrined them. Until he was purged in the September 1981 reshuffle for allegedly mishandling the Civil Service strike of that year, Lord Soames was the lead minister on Whitehall efficiency. Bluff, affable and intuitive in his approach to high politics with more than a dash of his father-in-law, Winston Churchill, about his style, he seemed less than convincing when interviewed for the radio about the new style of Whitehall management.

> There is much more management going on today; but I suppose this is true in the country as a whole. I mean there is much more emphasis on tight-ship management all over the country than there was, I think, in those days [in the 1950s when Soames was first a minister].
>
> I mean there are a lot of expressions which never existed then which have become part of the jargon, like 'management control' and . . . What? I don't know, well anyway, there is. There is a lot of jargon around today.[93]

The sceptical ministers gathered in the No. 10 dining-room to listen to presentations from Rayner and Heseltine and that call-to-management from Mrs Thatcher had plenty of support from past and present members of the permanent secretaries' club. Sir Peter Carey, ex-permanent secretary at the Department of Industry, took the view that 'Ministers are amateurs of management: it is not their skill or, frequently, inclination. Extremely few have had experience in genuinely managing a large organisation over a prolonged period. And in the isolated cases where they have, they have not been notably successful as politicians – which is what they essentially need to be.'[94] John Hunt, now in retirement, was another sceptic:

> I'm all for ministers managing but that isn't their prime role . . . In many ways it would be better if the Civil Service was left to get on with the management job. What ministers need to do is to take more time and have better advice on the political direction in which they want to go and have a coherent strategy which hangs together and will stick. And, on the whole, if the Civil Service knows what the policy is and the strategy is, it will make quite a good fist at carrying it out.[95]

The most suprising fount of scepticism about the minister-as-manager concept came from the most management-minded permanent secretary of his generation, Frank Cooper. He regarded himself as managing director of the MOD and estimated that he spent 70 per cent of his time on management.[96] When interviewed for *All the Prime Minister's Men* he was highly dismissive of this aspect of Raynerism:

> Personally, I regard the minister-as-manager as nonsense. Ministers are not interested. It's not part of the ministerial stock-in-trade . . . It's not what they went into politics for. They went into politics because they're interested in politics and the use of political power and political authority, and management isn't really very much about any of these things.
>
> Now this doesn't mean to say that departments shouldn't be accountable to ministers and indeed to Parliament for management . . . [the] . . . parallel is very close with industry . . . You have the chairman of the board, who is very concerned about the strategy of the company and, indeed, the policy of the company – but he has a managing director to carry it out and report to him on how he's carried it out.[97]

Cooper's views are particularly intriguing as he was the man Rayner wanted to succeed him as head of the Efficiency Unit.[98] (Rayner returned to Marks & Spencer a few days before Cooper, who had no desire to remain in Whitehall in any capacity,[99] retired.)

Rayner was equally outspoken in rebutting Cooper's attitude towards the minister-as-manager:

> Sir Frank Cooper's views, I'm afraid, are quite different to my own. The idea that you can develop politics – politicial policies – and . . . have the vision and the qualities of leadership that presumably politicians have, without managing the resources that are needed to bring those changes . . . about, is ridiculous.
>
> Of course everybody doesn't have to be a good manager. The heads of very large businesses may not manage in detail, they may not be finance directors . . . or lawyers. But the idea they can abdicate from a responsibility of ensuring that the right people are in post to carry those functions out and to take an interest in their achievements, frankly, I find ludicrous.[100]

Cooper reserved his most telling shaft against the policy so dear to Rayner and the Prime Minister for a piece on the Ministry of Defence in the Thatcher years published almost five years after he left Whitehall:

Over the seven-year period there were four Secretaries of State and, importantly, no less than six Ministers of Defence Procurement who were required to deal with much of the most difficult part of the Ministry, both in terms of policy and of management. The scale of ministerial change made a mockery of the Government's claim that ministers should be regarded as managers. Apart from being overloaded – Cabinet and its committees; Parliament and its committees; constituency work; party work – and unpractised in management, the plain truth is that the rate of turnover was such that even the most reputable outside business would have lost the confidence of its investors if it had changed its top management on even a fraction of the scale that ministers changed from 1979 to 1986.[101]

But from the Falklands spring onwards, ministers had, at the very least, to go through the motions of management and acquire a patina of jargon which seemed to be quite beyond the unfortunate Lord Soames who appeared, and was, much more at home in bringing Rhodesia/Zimbabwe to the final stage of independence. The FMI charter gave them eight months to design the equivalent of Heseltine's MINIS for their own departments. Elements of the prescribed ingredients of each system had a decidedly Fultonish air – accountable units and a heightened emphasis on management – though this was nowhere acknowledged.

The FMI charter, in its way, was even more ambitious than Warren Fisher's attempt in 1919–20 to extend Treasury control and financial uniformity across Whitehall. In 1982–3 it was the Treasury's job to ensure that the FMI systems were fully integrated with the existing public expenditure survey processes. There were five key elements to the centre's early 1980s attempt to disperse virtue to the periphery:

1. The system should not only meet the needs of higher management for aggregated information for estimating and control, but should also provide managers at successive levels down the line with the information about their resources which, together with information about performance and outputs, will help them to do their job properly. Unless the system, meets the second criterion as well as the first, managers will not use it and its accuracy will degenerate.

2. The responsibilities of managers should be specified systematically for the control of the resources they consume and, whenever feasible, the results they achieve. Each department should therefore examine the scope for breaking its structure down into cost-centres or responsibility-centres to which resource costs can be allocated and for which, where appropriate, measures of output can be devised and monitored.

3. Whatever the pattern of their other expenditures, all departments incur the costs of their own administration. All departmental plans should include a system for the budgeting and control of administrative costs. Where outputs are difficult to assess, the identification of costs will still pose questions of value for money.

4. The management accounting system should be used within the department for the purposes of planning and control. If it is relegated to the status of an optional extra for the display of information only, again the information fed into it will not be accurate and the system will not be used. . . .

5. The development of performance indicators and output measures which can be used to assess success on achieving objectives is no less important than the accurate attribution of monitoring and costs. The question to be addressed is 'where is the money going *and* what are we getting for it?'[102]

The word went out from the Treasury and MPO in May 1982. It was reinforced in September 1982 by the Government's White Paper replying to the efficiency and effectiveness inquiry of the Commons Treasury and Civil Service Committee (the Committee was very keen on Heseltine's MINIS being deployed across Whitehall).[103] By the end of January 1983 all departments had submitted their plans on time and according to specification.[104] After detailed discussion with the Treasury and the FMU the 31 plans were refined and finally published in another White Paper, *Financial Management in Government Departments*,[105] which was coupled with a Government announcement of a £35 million programme in direct costs for the computer systems and the people to run them which the FMI schemes would require over the next two years.[106] Whitehall, once again, was deluged with acronyms – MINIM, RIS, DMA, MAXIS, ARM (see Chapter 10).

With Rayner 'the hunter gatherer' back in his retailing pastures, the task of placing the FMI keystone in the arch of Raynerism fell to another familiar Whitehall in-and-outer, Sir Robin Ibbs, who had replaced Berrill as head of the CPRS in 1980 and had stayed for two years until his parent company, ICI, had summoned him back (see p. 645). Sir Robin was a very different character from Rayner. Where Rayner was an open-government man in thought and deed, Ibbs was a closed-government man to his last fibre not only in the CPRS (where there was some justification for it) but also very largely in the Efficiency Unit (where there was not). Ibbs commands respect. He does not, as Rayner did, dispense inspiration. As a young man Rayner had considered the Church as a profession. If his career *had* taken a religous turn Canterbury would surely have been its destination and the Church of England would have brimmed with fervour and gleamed with efficiency. Ibbs, by contrast, was the corporate planner incarnate.

Yet in many ways he was a good choice for Raynerism phase two once its heroic, pioneering, evangelising stage was over. Quiet, a good listener, with a great sense of purpose and a gift for seeing the essentials and how to achieve them – all these qualities, plus a great loyalty to Mrs Thatcher and her purposes, were the qualities Ibbs brought to the Efficiency Unit in 1983. And there was, as we shall see, a strong if concealed strain of radicalism in the retiring Sir Robin. His ICI background, too, gave him first-hand knowledge of managing change in big organisations.[107] Like Rayner, Ibbs did the job part-time. Like Rayner he relied greatly on his full-time chief of staff, who in his first three years was Ian Beesley after 1986, Kate Jenkins, herself a former member of the CPRS.

It was typical of the Ibbs style that the Efficiency Unit should conduct a scrutiny of scrutinies, and to their great credit they actually came up with an interesting and lively title, *Making Things Happen*, for the finished product.[108] The scrutiny of scrutinies was proud of achievements to date – 266 scrutinies since 1979, cumulative savings of around £750 million a year and an extension of the technique to the National Health Service and the Universities.[109] But it had a 'could do better' air about it. The scrutiny team, which was led by Kate Jenkins, estimated 'that as much as £300 million more might have been saved if decisions had been taken more quickly'.[110]

The report was candid about where Raynerism pinched. Understandably, if implementation was left to headquarters managers, there might be a lack of drive as the implicit criticism of the scrutinies was directed at them. And a diminution of urgency was likely after the 90 days of investigation were past.[111] New ground-rules were laid down – an action manager responsible for implementation should be named at the outset, the permanent secretary should be responsible for implementation, and results should be achieved within two years of the scrutiny starting. Scrutinies, therefore, had to be 'realistic as well as radical'.[112] New guides were sent out on managing scrutinies to ministers and top officials. An updated primer on 'How to do a scrutiny' was prepared for scrutineers. The Prime Minister, for whom the report had been prepared, ensured that any sceptics at ministerial and permanent secretary level took its 'sensible and straightforward' recommendations (Mrs Thatcher's adjectives) seriously by commending them unequivocally in a Foreword which restated the principle that 'Value for money from government spending is vital to the nation and scrutinies are a powerful way of improving it – provided that action follows analysis.'[113]

Prime ministerial power, unequivocally expressed, was then, as throughout, crucial to Raynerism being taken seriously at the highest bureaucratic levels and to its capacity to overcome what Sue Metcalfe and Les Richards called Whitehall's 'disbelief system' – the scepticism about tinkering with institutions, the conviction reinforced by experience that reforms fail and the refusal to take seriously long-term concepts to do with management improvements.[114] And there genuinely was a degree of pride and scepticism intermingled at the top of the hierarchy certainly in the early days of Raynerism. The Efficiency Unit sometimes saw it manifested *en clair* as when one top person replied to their request for job descriptions from each permanent secretary by quoting Elizabeth I to Robert Cecil (the Virgin Queen seems to have been a plentiful source of one-liners): 'Must! Is *must* a word to be addressed to Princes?'[115] Even Whitehall princes must, in the end, succumb to the wishes of 'she who must be obeyed' and who has been elected – particularly when it has happened three times in a row.

The minister-as-manager argument was squarely addressed in *Making Things Happen*. The Jenkins team found:

> The attitude of the Permanent Secretary is crucial: in particular the extent to which he or she is seen to be committed to action – and how he or she checks that results are really delivered. . . .
>
> Ministers have a specific role in the scrutiny process and we saw that when their interest is both clear and clearly expressed, scrutiny teams feel they have the support to enable them to be tougher and more radical. If that support is not continued into implementation the results suffer.[116]

But in their specific apportionment of responsibilities between ministers and permanent secretaries, the Efficiency Unit came close to Frank Cooper's chairman/managing director division:

> The political priority lies with results not with process. The continuing interest of ministers in charge of departments in improving value for money by using scrutinies is important. But once the minister has indicated the main targets for improving value for money it is a matter for the permanent secretary to ensure they are delivered, and that the necessary scrutinies are successfully carried out on his behalf and implemented.[117]

Shortly after his appointment as her Efficiency Adviser, 'the Prime Minister asked Sir Robin Ibbs to help ministers to use their top management planning and information systems to set targets for improvement in value for money in specific areas and to commission scrutinies and other work to bring about the improvements'.[118] This he appeared to do, though such matters are difficult to demonstrate. Sue Richards and Les Metcalfe, outsiders with insider experience (Richards in the Treasury and Metcalfe in the Efficiency Unit), believe that:

> Under Sir Robin Ibbs' guidance the Efficiency Strategy has moved on from relying on the demonstration effect of scrutinies to placing more emphasis on their role as one among several means of upgrading departmental management and performance. As part of the effort that Ibbs has led to inculcate a value for money ethos in government, departments have been encouraged to take a more integrated approach and – an important break with the past – to manage for year-on-year improvements in performance.[119]

Ibbs was a patient, persistent missionary. Once a year with his chief of staff he visited every minister and his permanent secretary for a quadrilateral session of progress chasing.[120] Ibbs's quiet work was given the public recognition it deserved when Gordon Downey (who had served as his number two in the CPRS) produced his Comptroller and Auditor General's seals of approval of the scrutiny programme and the FMI ('real progress is being made in the development of suitable systems')[121] in 1986.

Inevitably, there were difficulties and frustrations. Success can bring its own problems. Expectations and appetites increase as the scope for dramatic advances decreases. This is precisely what Julian Norridge and Nora Stein of London Weekend Television discovered when they conducted their own Rayner-style scrutiny on the FMI by sinking a shaft into its bedrock in 1987. The shaft was sunk in Sheffield at one of the Department of Transport's 53 vehicle testing stations, run by its Vehicle Inspectorate. Its manager, Brian Andrew, was eloquent about the improvements the FMI had brought to his operation, from greater control over his budget, much increased flexibility in the organisation of tasks, even the ability to have his paperwork typed on site rather than despatched to a Civil Service typing pool in Leeds. 'We are now aware', Brian Andrew told Nora Stein, 'that when we're going to spend anything, have we budgeted for it, are we covered for it? So it's a major change for us. It's a change that we like.'[122] The workforce were equally fluent before the camera on the benefits of the new regime. Productivity was up. Morale was up. Where then were the snags?

The snag was that Brian Andrew and his colleagues wanted more where that had come from – freedom to make even more decisions over matters like the hiring of staff and accommodation. Tom Stratford, another manager at the Sheffield testing station, said: 'We've . . . tried . . . to . . . think ahead of what the organisation is wanting from us and have pursued that right down the line. And we're getting to a point now where they're actually putting brakes on us at the moment. I think they we're moving a little bit . . . faster than they might want us to at this stage.'[123]

Norridge and Stein did what a Rayner scrutineer would (or should) have done at this stage. They examined another piece of the service-delivering public sector where matters were arranged differently. They chose Eastbourne on Britain's 'costa geriatrica' where East Sussex County Council had pioneered new methods of providing care for a town with possibly the largest percentage of elderly people in Western Europe. The solution devised by Ken Young, then its Director of Social Services, assisted by Norman Flynn of the London Business School, was to push decision-taking on the use of resources to case-workers at the local office level. Young offered his staff three things:

> One, we've given away the power to make decisions to the lowest possible level in the organisation to spend money, to develop services, to distribute staff resources. Second, we've given away the need to always double check with someone in the hierarchy. And thirdly, we've opened up opportunities for new developments by giving people pockets of money that they are free to use in any way they like.[124]

Such delegation has its risks in any social policy area where mistakes swiftly lead to heart-rending horror stories in local newspapers. Crucial to the policy's success was the willingness of the politicians on East Sussex County Council to back it and to trust its professionals, and the politicians, after all, are the eventual can-carriers in local government as much as central government. Yet the East Sussex example, in terms of genuinely devolved financial and personally responsibility, did eclipse the Sheffield vehicle inspectorate, FMI success story though Sheffield genuinely was.

Whitehall's high command was well aware of this and did not shirk the issue. When interviewed for the same television programme, Anne Mueller, then a Second Permanent Secretary in the Management and Personnel Office, admitted:

> ... there's still a long way to go in terms of giving greater freedom and discretion to individual departments and, within departments, to individual line managers. We are working on it. We're working quite hard on it. But it will take time just as it's taken time to set up the original systems for the financial management initiative then the delegated budgets.
>
> But, at the end of the day, there is a limit. And it's a different sort of limit from the sort you'll find in the private sector, where you can simply rely on the profit measurement to determine what is and what is not acceptable for an organisation as a whole.[125]

Gordon Downey's investigation of the FMI, which was conducted between September 1985 and February 1986 and covered twelve government departments,[126] uncovered both the continuing frustrations of Civil Service middle managers and the limits imposed by the constitutional constraints of the Whitehall–Westminster system. He wrote:

> The NAO Study suggested that middle and lower management had reservations about the benefits of the new arrangements. These reservations appeared to reflect mainly the extent of their power, as they saw it, to control many of the costs for which they were held responsible in their budgets . . . If the FMI is to succeed at these levels, it is essential that managers should feel personally responsible for achieving targets which contribute to ministers' overall objectives. To this end, managers should, within the limits inescapably imposed by the ultimate responsibility of ministers and by the maintenance of common rules and standards across the Civil Service, be aware of their full costs and be given as much personal responsibility as possible with powers closely matched.[127]

It was not just 'middle and lower management' that had to wrestle with the contradictions of devolved responsibilities in a system whose accountability genes all reflected a genetic code in which the minister was supreme and, for the health of democracy, had to account personally for every penny and every activity in Parliament. It affected some very senior managers, too – men like Hayden Phillips who, as a 41-year-old under secretary in 1984, was in charge of the Home Office's first Rayner-style 'responsibility centre' which also happened to be probably the greatest of its plentiful political minefields, the Immigration and Nationality Department. The case work was immense, parliamentary interest high and, therefore, ministerial sensitivity acute. I once described the effervescent Mr Phillips, a high-flyer who had, for a time, followed his old boss and patron, Roy Jenkins, to the EEC Commission during the Jenkins presidency, as 'Whitehall's super district commissioner wrestling with the problems that have accumulated since the Empire came home with the large-scale immigration of the 1950s'.[128] His bureaucratic empire consisted in 1984 of a staff of 3,000 and a budget of £45 million, his clients the taxpaying immigrants already in Britain, the 34 million people who pass every year through British ports, those abroad who want to settle here and taxpayers who live in Britain but come and go.[129] Again, one serious slip in this vast minefield and a political explosion and a barrage of headlines were guaranteed.

The greatest conceptual and practical problem of the FMI, however, was in extending its principles beyond the 13 per cent of central government expenditure absorbed by administration into the remainder – the big billions largely absorbed by programmes. The designers of the FMI had no illusions about this either. The problem was appreciated from the outset as the hard target to be penetrated by the FMI. This was the area where the big beasts of the Whitehall jungle roamed, both the ministerial and the Civil Service varieties. Here raged the political conflicts where individual muscle rather than reason tended to prevail, to the constant distress of rationalists like Douglas Wass. The crudity of the annual scramble for the millions, if not the billions, during the last-minute battles within the 'Star Chamber' Cabinet committee went on as before.[130]

In the prototype Financial Management Unit Vincent Watts was put on to this problem from the start. Francis Plowden tackled the running costs side. Watts was given the poisoned chalice of programme expenditure and the meshing in of the new system with the Public Expenditure Survey and the traditional forms of accounting to Parliament.[131] It was a major preoccupation of the Robin Ibbs/Ian Beesley partnership at the Efficiency Unit.[132] It remained one within the Joint Management Unit under Valerie Strachan, an under secretary on loan from Customs and Excise to which that loather of sermons, Sandy Russell, had departed to help achieve progress. The JMU devised a system whereby, in Mrs Strachan's words, 'ministers have agreed that whenever there is a proposal for a new policy or whenever there's a policy review, the departments should state in putting up the policy for consideration by ministers what's to be achieved, by when, at what cost and how that achievement is going to be measured subsequently'.[133]

There is widespread agreement, within Whitehall and without, that, in the words of Sir Gordon Downey, there is a 'need to hasten the extension to programme expenditure of those features of budgetary systems which will assist achievement of improved inefficiency and effectiveness'.[134] Yet Whitehall remains highly sensitive about it. Julian Norridge and Nora Stein could not find a department willing to let LWT film the FMI on policy programmes in action.[135] Ian Beesley, by this time at Price Waterhouse in the City, was able to explain why. Speaking of the FMI he said:

> It is very important in introducing a significant change of this sort to start small and to build on success . . . One of the quite deliberate ideas was to start with the running costs of government which is far less threatening than to look at the policy content of government. . . .
>
> Policy and politics are very closely related. Looking, therefore, at policy is a fairly intimate thing to do. In a way, it's an unnatural practice best done in private by consenting adults because it's very close to the persona of those who are putting themselves up for judgment on the basis of those policies . . . [It] is a tremendous thing to be happening that ministers are prepared to talk to each other about the success or otherwise of their policies and to adjust. But I think it would be foolish

> to bring that into the full glare of public opinion particularly in view of politics which would almost certainly kill it off at the very early stages.[136]

The agenda, therefore, remained, in Rayner's phrase, very much unfinished even after Mrs Thatcher won a third term for her administrative revolution. 'We will press on with long-term management reforms in order to improve public services and reduce their cost', said the 1987 Conservative manifesto.[137]

Just before the 1987 election Ibbs had enlarged that agenda substantially and significantly. He presented Mrs Thatcher with his equivalent of Rayner's *The Conventions of Government* paper of 1980. It was called *The Next Steps* and was so laden with sensitivities and implications that it was kept secret on the Prime Minister's personal instructions.[138] Its prognosis, which seeped out drop by drop in the autumn of 1987, was truly revolutionary by Whitehall standards. The big businesses of Whitehall were to be recognised for what they were and treated accordingly – as large enterprises with different and special needs best managed by their own chief executives with *real* power to determine pay and recruitment policies as well as developing their own styles of management. If implemented in full, *The Next Steps* would undo Warren Fisher's revolution of 1919–22 which, through common standards of pay, recruitment and finance, created for the first time a genuinely unified Civil Service under tight Treasury control. Naturally, the Treasury were immensely reluctant to see those bonds – the sinews of their power – snapped. A battle royal ensued in the autumn of 1987 which raged for several months.

But, even allowing for uncertainty surrounding the future of *The Next Steps*, the signs of genuine change and progress since 1979 were apparent along the lines developed by Rayner and his team in their first year of activity, pretty well wherever one looked in 1987 from manpower figures, the style and quality of management of people and money, to the content and bite of training on offer particularly at the Civil Service College with its FMI-orientated courses and its Top Management Programme. The pioneering Rayner phase had been succeeded first by the consolidating period of Ibbs phase one and then by the radical proposals of Ibbs phase two in the shape of *The Next Steps*, though the Marks & Spencer touch was still apparent in important initiatives such as the establishment in the Treasury of a Central Unit on Purchasing. In 1986–7, its first full year of operation, the unit's use of the government's muscle as a big buyer achieved value-for-money improvements of £286 million, some 4.7 per cent of the total spend of £6 billion on non-defence goods and services.[131]

Despite very real efficiency advances in techniques and procurement, the human side of the Civil Service was far from a success story. Morale remained a widespread problem at all levels. The crudity of Mrs Thatcher's anti-bureaucratic approach had exacted a price. But the well-informed and far from adulatory Les Metcalfe and Sue Richards, the most authoritative of the chroniclers of post-1979 efficiency politics, had no hesitation in concluding their 1987 study by stating:

> Looking back, the Efficiency Strategy has achieved a good deal more than was expected at the start. Many people were prepared to write it off as an electoral fashion that would fade rapidly from the scene as soon as more pressing political issues surfaced. There was a widespread belief that the forces of bureaucratic inertia would soon emasculate it.
>
> The early achievements of the Efficiency Strategy have exceeded pessimistic forecasts because it gave a sharp edge to the politics of efficiency without overstretching the limited Civil Service capacity for managing change. Quick results established a measure of political credibility that earlier reform efforts lacked. Starting small, with narrowly focussed scrutinies, increased the probability of success, and at the same time helped develop the confidence and the competence needed to undertake more ambitious projects.[132]

Metcalfe and Richards were justified in adding at that stage the observation that 'there are some serious questions about whether the Efficiency Strategy is evolving in the right direction to rise to new and greater challenges'.[133] But it would be as churlish as it would be inaccurate to pretend that the first eight years of Raynerism represented anything but a formidable achievement in absolute terms as well as in comparison to anything that had gone before. Equally, it would be as misleading as it would be partisan to lump Raynerism with any crude bundle of policies and attitudes labelled as 'Thatcherism'. The experience has demonstrated, as Rayner and Priestley wished it to, and successive inquiries by all-party Commons select committees had confirmed, that the concept of a well-managed state was valid in its own right and worthy of adoption as policy and practice by *any* democratically elected British government whatever its political colouration. And, perhaps most significant of all, from about mid-1984, the permanent secretaries got as close as they ever do to enthusiasm when talking about administrative matters. Over lunch one day, one of the biggest of the bureaucratic power-brokers said of the FMI, 'I never realised what an effort it would be turning this tanker around. But over the past year it has become clear that it [the FMI] will endure. If there was a change of government, we would still want to do it for our own purpose.' That was genuine progress.

Even greater progress seemed possible, if not inevitable, when *The Next Steps* was finally published in February 1988.[135] Its production was a fascinating and revealing story in itself which changed fundamentally the picture of Ibbs as the grey consolidator where Rayner had once sparkled and pioneered. The path to that transformation started in the autumn of 1986 when he unleashed Kate Jenkins and her colleagues, Karen Caines and Andrew Jackson, on a truly radical inquiry.

The Jenkins team was asked to discover what had been achieved by the scrutiny programme since 1979 and by the FMI since 1982; to identify which obstacles stood in the way of substantial improvements in efficiency; and to state what kind of explosive was needed to dynamite them. After consulting a wide range of ministers, senior and middle-ranking officials and, significantly, talking to a batch of gifted high-flyers who had left Whitehall in various stages of disillusion, they came up with a truly damning report.

Despite the real achievements of the Rayner years, it showed how little in the way of *real* financial and management responsibility had been devolved down the line; how meddlesome the Treasury and Cabinet Office remained; how dominant was the Whitehall culture of caution; how great was the premium placed on a safe pair of hands; and how rarely were proven managerial skills perceived as the way to reach the top of the bureaucratic tree.

By May 1987 the report was in the hands of Mrs Thatcher. It is easy to see why she ordered it to be kept secret. An election was imminent and, in so many words, it spelled out how little her much-vaunted Whitehall revolution (itself a prominent feature in the 1987 election manifesto) had achieved in eight years. And its recommendations were scarcely less palatable. *The Next Steps* proposed fundamental change on two levels:

* a real devolution of power over budgets, manpower, pay, hiring and firing to executive agencies in areas of activity embracing the 95 per cent of the Civil Service involved in the delivery of services as opposed to advising ministers or policy;
* a change in the British constitution, by law if necessary, to quash the fiction that ministers can be genuinely responsible for *everything* done by officials in their name.

The report's selling-point was the relief its implementation would bring to overloaded ministers burdened by the tasks the British system of government imposes on them to the point where they are incapable of managing their departments in anything but the most nominal way. The salesmanship failed. The Ibbs report was sat upon for months and then diluted liberally.

When it appeared it was instantly clear that Treasury power was intact. The Ibbs revolution of 1986 had failed to undermine the Lloyd-George/Warren Fisher revolution of 1920. The centre had not yielded one ounce of real power to the periphery. One suspects that Mrs Thatcher, under whom the Treasury had enjoyed a purple patch of imperial power, did not want it to.

Her announcement in the Commons of the Government's response to *The Next Steps* on 18 February 1988,[136] and the press conference given immediately afterwards by Richard Luce, Minister for the Civil Service, and Sir Robin Butler the new Head of the Home Civil Service, made it plain that constitutional changes in ministerial responsibility were out as were any attempts to end Treasury control over budgets, manpower and national pay bargaining. Furthermore, the initial list of candidates for executive agency treatment left the big tax-raising and benefit-paying empires intact, though there were a few substantial chunks of work included, most notably the Employment Service, HMSO, and the Driver and Vehicle Licensing Centre in Swansea. A Treasury lifer, the formidable Peter Kemp, was transferred to the Cabinet Office to become project manager.

All in all, it seemed to be the revolution-that-never-was.[137] The Prime Minister's statement on *The Next Steps* left open the possibility of some Civil Service work proceeding, via the agency route, to eventual privatisation. But Sir Robin Butler's comments a month later before the Treasury and Civil Service Select Committee seemed to capture the tentativeness of it all. Answering questions on the accountability angle of any changes he said:

> 'An announcement about agencies and *The Next Steps* is designed primarily to apply to activities that remain within the Civil Service and the Prime Minister, I think, used the word that they would "generally" remain within the Civil Service. If they were to go outside, either by a non-departmental public body or perhaps a limited company being set up, that would normally have to be covered by legislation and, in the course of that legislation, the arrangement for accountability would be a matter to be determined by Parliament.'
>
> 'It has not yet been considered within the Civil Service?'
>
> 'No. In the case of each agency the set-up of these matters will have to be specifically considered and negotiated. The Prime Minister's announcement was about a general direction and she announced each of the areas of activity where it was hoped to apply this approach. But the detailed arrangements in each of these cases, and, in deed, the decision about whether it goes ahead in each case has yet to be taken.'[138]

What did *The Next Steps*, its contents and its fate reveal about the achievements and the future of Raynerism? Clive Priestley drafted his own assessment for *The Independent*:

On the plus side, a lot of the systemic reform begun or reinforced since 1979 producing benefits. The Financial Management Initiative, the Treasury's main contribution, may be unloved but it is also unavoidable. The Prime Minister's conviction that people do not want a poorly managed state is unshaken. In Robin Butler . . . and in Peter Kemp . . . she will have a formidable, youthful duo on her side. There is a groundswell in the mass of the Civil Service to deliver better service. Much of Government is already in, or could be put into, agency form.

On the minus side, the report shows that even after seven years of Prime Minister-led reform, 'management' has not yet caught on generally in the upper echelons of the Civil Service. The distinction between 'policy' and 'management', although not unique to Whitehall, has a peculiar strength there. Ministers' lack of interest in management is echoed by many Parliamentarians, much of the media and, alas, much of the public.

So, as Sir Robin Ibbs contemplated his retirement from the Efficiency Unit,[140] the agenda of Raynerism, more than five years after its founder's departure, remained unfinished despite the gradual though undeniable trickle down of its nostrums and procedures into virtually every Civil Service crevice.

15 THE THATCHER EFFECT

The Civil Service is a great rock on the tide-line. The political wave, Labour or Conservative, rolls in, washes over it and ebbs. The rock is exposed again to the air usually virtually unchanged. But Mrs Thatcher has been applying sticks of dynamite to that rock.
Clive Priestley, 1984[1]

I think I have become a bit of an institution – you know, the sort of thing people expect to see around the place.
Mrs Margaret Thatcher, 1987[2]

The grovel count amongst ministers in this administration and, I think, necessarily, therefore, in some officials has been much higher than normal.
Lord Bancroft, 1986[3]

Never let anyone say I am laissez-faire . . . We are a very strong government. We are strong to do those things which government must do and only government can do.
Mrs Margaret Thatcher, 1987[4]

Finally among the institutions, Whitehall [by 1989] will have become a thoroughly Thatcherised satrapy.
Hugo Young, 1986[5]

Sometimes a single phrase really does say it all. In this case it was four words: 'Deprivilege the Civil Service'. They were to be found in the annexe to a Cabinet committee paper on strategy and priorities drawn up for the new Conservative administration in 1979 by John Hoskyns, then head of the Downing Street Policy Unit.[6] Another priority was a diminution in the power of the Civil Service unions.[7] Such phrases were coined by John Hoskyns but they came to be seen within the higher Civil Service as words which clearly reflected HMV, His Mistress's Voice.

It would be wrong to conclude that the Civil Service had an animus, a prejudice, against Mrs Thatcher from the start. In some departments she was positively welcomed. The Ministry of Defence was an example, as Sir Frank Cooper explained:

> In the spring of 1979 the Ministry of Defence looked forward to a change of Government. The reason was self-interest, not political. The resources allocated to defence had been declining in the latter part of the 1970s. The Services believed themselves to be both underpaid and unloved – morale was not good. Major decisions, including the future of the nuclear deterrent, lay ahead.[8]

According to Ian Bancroft, such feelings were not confined to the MOD:

> When it [the Thatcher administration] came in in 1979, in a totally non-party way the Civil Service, I believe I detected, welcomed its arrival because as professional administrators, as professional managers, they had been pretty hamstrung during the previous two or three years of a Labour Government without an adequate majority having to govern necessarily from day-to-day and hand-to-mouth and . . . the officials' job was really to help the Government survive. . . But in exchange for that rather debilitating experience to have a government coming in with a thumping majority [and] a strong, reforming manifesto was, I repeat, welcomed by the civil servants.[9]

But, for Bancroft, the relationship between the new Government and its servants was quickly 'soured' by three words in 'an unpublicised item in the unpublished Conservative Manifesto which was "deprivilege the Civil Service"'.[10] Bancroft believed the phrase had been coined by Sir Keith Joseph and that it 'did his luminous intelligence less than justice', and, as a concept, the notion that you 'come into office on the basis that you are going to try and worsen the conditions in which your senior staff work seemed to me at the time, and seems to me now [1984], populist and silly'.[11] Bancroft, as he later explained, was not merely reacting on behalf of his own kind – the senior policy adviser in Whitehall. The candour of his reflections on those he had so recently served was without precedent among the five Heads of the Civil Service who had preceded him:

> If you come in as the head of any enterprise expecting continuing commitment over a period of many years to a radical programme of reform, you don't come in and say to the people you expect to carry it out '(a) we think you're privileged and (b) we're going to strip you of those privileges'. This showed terrible confusion on the part of those who dreamt up that magic phrase. It confused the 3000 policy-managers

> in Whitehall who advised ministers on policy (who might be regarded as privileged or not – I don't think they were or are) with the 597,000 people who are actually carrying out the politics at the sharp end. And to tell a twenty-year-old girl in a DHSS office in Merseyside that she's over-privileged and she's going to have her privileges stripped from her seems to me insulting to her intelligence. And I said so.[12]

Mrs Thatcher did not get on with Ian Bancroft during the two and a half years that elapsed between her election and the disbandment of the Civil Service Department and his early retirement. That the last of his professional partnerships should be so sour must have been galling for so sensitive and decent a public servant who had worked closely and successfully with the likes of Butler, Callaghan and Crosland. The Prime Minister treated Derek Rayner as if he were a surrogate Head of the Civil Service and, as we have seen, made it plain that his status was on a par with that of Bancroft and Sir Douglas Wass at the Treasury.

For her part, Mrs Thatcher had strong views on the likes of Sir Ian and his profession. These had been formed some eighteen years earlier when she became Parliamentary Under Secretary at the Ministry of Pensions and National Insurance. The memory of those early years as the lowest form of ministerial life under Harold Macmillan (who did not care for her, describing the Thatcher Cabinet Room as containing 'a brilliant tyrant surrounded by mediocrities'[13]) could bring on an attack of the Iron Ladies even after two decades, as her friend, Sir Laurens van der Post, discovered when he interviewed her in 1983. Speaking of official advice Mrs Thatcher remembered:

> I saw it vary from Minister to Minister. I used to sit there sometimes and say 'That's not what you said to my last Minister. You are giving him totally different advice. Why?' And gradually they said 'Well, the last one wouldn't have accepted that advice.' I said, 'Well you're now trying it on with my present one.'[14]

An under secretary said to me in the mid-1980s, 'Civil servants make a great mistake if they patronise junior ministers. After all, all prime ministers have been junior ministers once – even the junior minister at Pensions and National Insurance.'[15]

Mrs Thatcher's spell at the Department of Education and Science in the wilderness years of 1970–4, when she said very little in Cabinet and was placed by Ted Heath in the 'blind spot' on the other side of the Cabinet Secretary,[16] did nothing to lighten her dim view of permanent officials. Her permanent secretary at the DES, Sir William Pile, said of Mrs Thatcher:

> Within the first 10 minutes of her arrival, she uncovered two things to us. One is . . . an innate wariness of the Civil Service, quite possibly even a distrust; and, secondly, a page from an exercise book with 18 things she wanted done that day. Now these were two actions quite unlike anything we'd come across from predecessors and we later on, I think, saw that this was only the beginnings of the revelation of a character that we'd have to get used to and that we hadn't run into before.[17]

Sir William's colleague, Richard Jameson, said of Mrs Thatcher in 1970 that 'her handwritten note of matters for immediate action took away the breath of her officials'.[18]

Pile was a genial, quiet, pipe-smoking official, an old Ministry of Education hand who had had a spell running the Prison Service before returning as permanent secretary. (He finished his career as Chairman of the Board of Inland Revenue.) He liked to look on the bright side. He said to me once at a *Times Higher Education Supplement* lunch, 'Young man, you are the kind of person who would say that "this [wine] glass is half empty". I would say that "it is half full".' (I was berating him for his department's failure to implement fully some report or other.) His reflective temperament was thoroughly different from Mrs Thatcher's. He once said:

> She is the only person I know who I don't think I ever heard say 'I wonder whether . . .?' Most of us at moments of uncertainty or faced with a lot of conflicting circumstances and confusion of objectives will say 'Well, what's it all about? What should we do? Any ideas? Should I do nothing? Should I do this?' . . . Her self-sufficiency amounted to having already the answer in herself springing from her character.
>
> Equally, for that reason, she never seriously delegated anything. I asked her on several occasions, 'You know, this is quite a trivial matter. One of us can do that for you. If we get it wrong, you can kick us on the bottom.' She said, 'No, I'll do it myself.' She worked to all hours of the day and night. She always emptied her box with blue pencils and marks on. Every single bit of paper was attended to the next day.[19]

The female touch, so often lacking at the senior levels in government – whether ministerial or official – could also take the department by surprise. When she was first its Secretary of State, the DES was housed in Curzon House in Curzon Street, Mayfair, now the headquarters of MI5. Sir William Pile recalls:

> I was briefing her alone on a Wednesday before the Thursday's Cabinet, when she suddenly stopped and said 'What's the time?' I said, 'It's ten to five.' She said, 'Oh, I must go and get some bacon.' And I said, 'What

do you mean?' She said, 'I must get Denis some bacon.' And I said, 'Well, the girls in the office outside can get it for you.' 'No', she said, 'they won't know what kind of bacon he likes.'

So she got up and she went down, put her hat on and put her coat on. I remember she put her gloves on because it was, after all, November, and she walked down to Clarges Street, across the road into Shepherd's Market, bought . . . a pound of streaky bacon, came back into the office, took her gloves off, took her coat off, put the bacon down, sat down on the chair and said, 'Now, where were we?' So we resumed discussing the Chancellor's proposal that £30 million should be cut off the Education public expenditure bid.[20]

Pensions and education were a very narrow base of ministerial experience for a future prime minister. But the commanding fact of her premiership, in Whitehall terms, was the ideological passion she brought to Civil Service matters most unusual in a non-ideological country and in what used to be an intuitive rather than an ideological political party. As an institution the Civil Service was seen as one of the great obstacles – part of an inflated public service/state industries sector with overmighty trade unions to match – to the creation of a more dynamic enterprise society. Whitehall, too, was high on that long list of established institutions which, Parliament and the Monarchy apart (see p. 59), she instinctively mistrusted.[21]

As for Whitehall's staff officers in the upper vaults of the hierarchy, they fell prey to her version of the 'guilty men' theory. In Mrs Thatcher's demonology, it is the protagonists of the failed Keynes-Beveridge consensus who have brought Britain low. And those with the biggest horns are the senior civil servants who assisted at the birth of that consensus and who had succeeded in capturing every Cabinet, Labour or Conservative, for its cause from the mid-forties till May 1979. She was proud to assert the economics of the domestic household – you can't spend what you don't have – against the 'funny money' of even the modified PESC system. A woman who left her desk to buy bacon for her husband could better be trusted with the nation's finances – 'our money' as she liked to call it in the context of the EEC budget – than the permanent secretary taken aback by her behaviour. Equally she could not stand that trademark of the career official – the high-minded ability to see every side to a question, or, as George Jones put it, the urbane sceptic who finds problems to every solution.[22] Her world was in black and white, not the shades of grey of those paid to serve her. She was not, by the wildest stretch of the imagination, a permanent secretary *manqué*. Indeed, in Roy Jenkins's game of where would the minister be if he or she were in the Civil Service hierarchy, Mrs Thatcher is even more difficult to place than Ernie Bevin. Though always ready to exempt those who have served her closely and personally, she nevertheless detests senior civil servants as a breed. Mrs Thatcher simply does not believe that people of flair and enterprise should sign up for a job in the public service.

The senior Civil Service network is a highly sensitive membrane. Mrs Thatcher's attitude was quickly apparent in the spring of 1979 and the word spread fast through the Whitehall grapevine. Within a year a fair-minded and seasoned senior official was telling me over the lunch-table that 'to be told by politicans that they don't want whingeing, analysis or integrity, that we must do as we are told and that they have several friends in the private sector who could do the job in a morning with one hand tied behind their back – is a bit much. It seems to be injudicious to attack the people on whom you rely.'[23] Reading this quote in a piece I prepared for *The Times*,[24] Patrick Cosgrave, who, as we have seen, was close to Mrs Thatcher in her Opposition years, declared: 'that official gave Hennessy a very fair picture of the Prime Minister's attitude to the Civil Service in general'.[25]

Turning to the particular, Mrs Thatcher relied greatly on first impressions when judging individual officials. Several were written off – wrongly – on first acquaintance. This was quite a frequent occurrence in her first term when she embarked upon a series of departmental visits, occasions that were anticipated with about as much enthusiasm as an American embassy waited for Roy Cohn and David Schine, Senator Joe McCarthy's aides, to drop by in the early fifties. The best officials, none-theless, still spoke the truth as they saw it, and one in particular, Donald Derx, was widely felt in ministerial and Civil Service circles to have lost his chance of a permanent secretaryship as a result. Derx is a tough, no-nonsense official in the Douglas Allen mould, totally without ingratiating ways or false deference. At the time of Mrs Thatcher's visit to the Department of Employment he was a deputy secretary dealing with industrial relations policy, a key item in the Prime Minister's political agenda. Derx's Minister, Jim Prior, witnessed the occasion for which his department had been readying itself with the utmost care:

> Before she came to the Department of Employment we spent days preparing a brief for her visit. It was to be divided into three sessions, one before lunch with senior officials during which policy issues would be raised, a buffet lunch for her to meet various people, and then a visit round certain groups.
>
> The first session showed her at her worst, as she got into an argument with one of the best and most dedicated civil servants I have ever met, Donald Derx. She insisted on picking an argument without knowing the facts or the legal position on secondary industrial action. Even when Patrick Mayhew [Minister of State and a lawyer] intervened in utter

frustration she still wouldn't stop. It ended by Donald Derx saying, 'Prime Minister, do you really want to know the facts?'

I suspect that, as a result of this, Donald had a black mark against his name and appeared to be passed over for promotion. It was a pity that she was not able to accept that, by standing up to her, he was displaying qualities which a civil servant must have if he is to serve his Minister properly and which she of all people used generally to accept. . .[26]

With the 'other ranks' of the service, Mrs Thatcher was utterly different on that day at the Department of Employment[27] and generally. The warmth was as intense as if they had been, as it were, part of the family at No. 10. Jim Prior himself noticed and admired it as 'when her driver, George, having just retired, sadly died very suddenly. She went out of her way to go to the funeral. It was a gesture of respect and kindness which I liked very much.'[28]

Other colleagues besides Jim Prior were concerned about her hostility to the permanent-secretary class. Willie Whitelaw, her deputy and the Cabinet's professional peacemaker, was one. He got on exceedingly well with his senior officials, as a general would with his chief of staff or a landowner with hs steward. He believed it was because she only saw the permanent secretaries on formal, official occasions that the Prime Minister had such a dim view of them. Whitelaw suggested an informal dinner at No. 10 at which everybody, in pleasant and non-stiff circumstances, could get to know each other better. It was a disaster all the more tragic for being well-intentioned.

Thanks to a variety of private sources, an account of the evening can be pieced together. The chemistry was wrong from the start. More than forty men (the permanent secretaries' club plus Whitelaw and Rayner) and one woman is not a good mixture. The Prime Minister made a speech, hectoring in tone, of the 'you've all got to pull your socks up' variety. Bancroft replied in his quiet, courteous way and was defensive in tone. It was not well received by 'she who must be obeyed'. The atmosphere was devoid of hilarity until Frank Cooper left to relieve himself. His department had been in the news recently when the Army had rescued hostages trapped in the Iranian Embassy in London. As Cooper departed, permanent secretary A said to permanent secretary B, 'Thank god! Frank's gone to get the SAS to get us out of here.' According to my information, 'permanent secretary A' was Lawrence Airey, the irreverent Chairman of the Board of Inland Revenue, though Sir Lawrence has never confirmed this. The evening dribbled on and ended abruptly at ten when the Prime Minister said 'Gentlemen! Your cars are waiting.'

Such stories tended to confirm the impression that Mrs Thatcher, with a few exceptions, disliked the permanent secretaries she inherited and was keen to use her chance to replace them with a different breed as the post-war generation for whom, in Bancroft's words, 'everything was achievable', retired in the early eighties in the same concentrated manner with which they had entered in the late forties. Episodes like the clash with Donald Derx tended to buttress the impression that 'is he one of us?' was a key criterion in her selection of a name from the short-list provided by the Senior Appointments Selection Committee consisting of the Head of the Home Civil Service and half-a-dozen seasoned colleagues under their standard post-Fulton procedure.

Internal and external evidence suggests that matters were nothing like so clear-cut. The issue is an important one, particularly given Mrs Thatcher's longevity at the top. Between 1979 and 1985, 43 permanent secretaries and 138 deputy secretaries (the two grades in appointments to which the PM has a direct say) departed the scene, which is virtually a complete turnover, as the current strength of these grades was 38 permanent secretaries and 134 deputy secretaries (some of the appointments were lateral transfers rather than promotions).[29] Certainly, some flew higher and faster because of her patronage. She has her favourites. Peter Middleton, her choice to succeed Douglas Wass in 1983, was one. If SASC had been left to its own devices, the mantle would have fallen most likely on Sir David Hancock (who went to Education instead) or Sir Brian Hayes (who moved from Agriculture to Trade and Industry).[30] Middleton was a convinced monetarist who had been crucial in putting together the Government's medium-term financial strategy.[31] Mrs Thatcher and those ministers who thought like her (as the Treasury team did) preferred dealing with Middleton rather than the ever-courteous but ever-sceptical Wass.[32] Middleton, however, has a sparky style and a 'can-do' approach which appealed hugely to Labour ministers in the Wilson and Callaghan years. It is possible, but far from certain, that he would have become No. 1 under a Labour Chancellor (though he would certainly have been on the SASC short-list). Middleton's detractors in Whitehall believe that, deep down, he is a mercurial figure capable of showing great elan in implementing the policy of the hour whatever its political provenance. One Treasury figure once told me that he could see Middleton, under a left of centre Labour government, implementing a siege economy with as much relish as he was currently pursuing a free market approach,[33] though I find that hard to believe. His intensive reading in the late seventies did genuinely seem to have made him a monetarist. It was his roguish side, his slightly raffish appearance and his open enjoyment at basking in the sunshine of prime-ministerial approval that stimulated the accusations of opportunism. And Middleton is very much a hands-on, can-do type of official of the kind that appeals to Mrs Thatcher whatever their views. For a fellow permanent secretary this was wholly compatible with the traditional ethic of the profession. 'Peter is a

Northcote–Trevelyan man,' he said, 'but he does believe in getting from Ministers what the policy is and getting on with it.'[34]

Apart from Middleton, it is hard to see any 22-carat 'one of us' figure benefiting from her preferment. Robert Armstrong's politics, in so far as they are discernible, are closer to those of Harold Macmillan than to those of Margaret Thatcher.[35] And the views of Michael Quinlan, who became permanent secretary at Employment instead of Derx, on such key matters as trade-union reform were not known, almost certainly because he did not have any. Though a deputy secretary in the Treasury when promoted, Quinlan was a Defence man by background and he returned to the MOD in 1988. Mrs Thatcher was particularly impressed with his work on strategic nuclear weapons and was said to have been especially taken by his (anonymous) disquisition on deterrence theory and the British strategic nuclear force in the 1981 Defence White Paper.[36] Sir Clive Whitmore, who replaced Cooper at Defence, was appointed at the age of forty-seven, early by Whitehall standards. His preferment was widely thought to have been on the 'one of us' basis. It was not. Whitmore was clearly going to make it at some stage. Sir James Dunnett, at a party to mark Whitmore's departure from his private office in the early 1970s, spoke of him warmly as a future permanent secretary of the MOD.[37] Whitmore may have got it sooner. The Prime Minister, like Lord Rayner, was keen to lower the age of permanent secretaries. To that extent, but to no other, was there a Thatcher factor in the Whitmore appointment.

Yet the accusations that the senior Civil Service was progressively becoming, in Hugo Young's phrase, 'a thoroughly Thatcherised satrapy' have to be taken seriously as they were widely held to be true. At least one member of SASC in the early eighties, Douglas Wass, urged that the question should be looked at as one part of the agenda of the Royal Commission on the Civil Service for which he called when free of the Treasury.[38] He told me in 1986 that 'my own feeling is that the public disquiet on this is exaggerated, probably grossly exaggerated. Nevertheless, one only has to glance at the informed newspapers to see that there is a good deal of discussion of this as a development.'[39] In the same interview I tried unsuccessfully to pin him down on just how much of a problem this was under Mrs Thatcher. The conversation switched from looking back to looking forward.

> Looking to the future, what are the bench-marks that we ought to be concerned about once we're on the way to the politicisation of the senior Civil Service? What are the danger points?
>
> Well, the danger of politicising our senior posts is that we would destroy... one of the great values that a permanent career Civil Service has which is that it presents its advice and counsel to its political chiefs

> in a fearless and frank way . . . I think the big losers in a politicised Civil Service will be Ministers themselves. . . The worst of all worlds would be to have the semblance of a permanent Civil Service but with the deep knowledge that political acceptability in rather narrow and specialised senses was required on the part of those civil servants.[40]

For Robert Armstrong, who sat with Douglas Wass on the Senior Appointments Selection Committee for nearly four years' worth of appointing, there was absolutely no problem at all. Not for Armstrong the careful caveats and qualifications of his old friend:

> There is no question of political considerations entering into the choice. The Prime Minister is ultimately responsible for the appointments of permanent and deputy secretaries, and she takes a keen interest in them. She attaches much importance, as I do, in making recommendations to her [Armstrong was Chairman of SASC when making these observations], the skill and effectiveness in management as well as in the traditional role of policy advice. She is not concerned with, and I can vouch for the fact that she does not seek to ascertain, the political views or sympathies (if any) of those who are recommended. Nor do I. She wants, as I want, to have the best person for the job.[41]

Armstrong's view was corroborated by Rayner (who was not a member of SASC but certainly knew the Prime Minister's mind on appointments). 'I have no evidence', he told me, 'that the Prime Minister has a view about senior civil servants on the basis of their political persuasion. But I'm certainly very conscious . . . that she is interested in the qualifications that they have by way of experience, training and track-record to carry out the tasks which are involved in the proposed appointments.'[42]

Evidence in its hard form is elusive and very difficult to come by. Ian Bancroft, whom Robert Armstrong replaced as chairman of SASC in 1981, has been eloquent about the 'grovel count' which is always present among ministers and officials. He has noted, too,

> a degree of personal ascendancy by the Prime Minister over her colleagues which is unusual . . . But I think that the idea that Permanent Secretaries, for example, are being appointed because they're of the same political persuasion as the present government . . . is wholly misplaced. There's never one particular chap who is the only God-given candidate for a particular post. There's always a field of two or three people and in none of the appointments that I know, that have been made since I retired [Lord Bancroft was speaking in 1986] has an appointment been made from outside that field.[43]

But Bancroft, ever skilled at fine-tuning, puts his finger on the *real* problem which also, in my view, is the source from which the *impression* of politicisation under Mrs Thatcher has arisen. Bancroft went on to say that 'the dangers of politicisation are rather more subtle and rather more insidious' than the matter of appointments at permanent secretary level: 'The dangers are of the younger people, seeing that advice which Ministers want to hear falls with a joyous note on their ears, and advice which they need to hear falls on their ear with a rather dismal note, will tend to make officials trim, make their advice what Ministers want to hear rather than what they need to know.'

Frank Cooper, who sat on SASC from 1976 to 1982, believes it is chemistry rather than politics which determines Mrs Thatcher's attitudes to individual officials. 'What she likes to see and what she likes to hear about ... is that X or Y is being pretty fusty or dynamic ... about this particular issue or that particular issue, and she has made it her business to get to meet ... far more younger civil servants than many of her predecessors.'[45] Cooper does not believe that Mrs Thatcher has appointed her top Whitehall people on a political basis. But his description of the pragmatic way in which her greater than usual interest in top appointments has been accommodated is the clue to the way in which the appearance of politicisation has arisen:

> The question of who should be put forward as a short-list to the Prime Minister ... is always something which is very difficult ... Permanent Secretaries do get a pretty good idea of who should be on a particular short-list and, obviously, one element of this is how effective officials are at dealing with Ministers, including the Prime Minister. It's no use having a very senior official in a particular seat who hasn't got the confidence of his Minister, who is ineffective at dealing with that Minister, who is not going to get his views across to that Minister and is a source of discord within the whole organisation ...
>
> It's not simply that the present Prime Minister – people do watch how she reacts to particular officials – they do it also with individual Secretaries of State ... I don't see this as an issue of any great moment. What I would see as very damaging is if you had to have a political signature on your cheque when you went forward. That would totally and utterly change the nature of the Civil Service and ... would be utterly corrupting in the full sense of the word.[46]

It is this watching of Mrs Thatcher's reactions to individual civil servants wherein lies the rub. It would be alarming if the reaction depended wholly, in Ian Bancroft's words, on whether the official's words 'fall with a joyous note' because of their political tone or because of other factors. There are certainly those she admires because they have the gift of expressing inconvenient or contrary views in a style she admires. Equally there are those who would not say 'boo' to the prime-ministerial goose but do not shoot up the ladder of preferment because they lack drive, or because the bell, however pleasantly it tinkles superficially, rings hollow in the last analysis. Equally, there are instances, of which the Donald Derx case is the best-known, where Whitehall and ministers judge an injustice to have been done by a Prime Minister in an 'off-with-their-heads' mood. The hostile-minded could so order the picture as to make it appear that informal and unacknowledged 'one of us' tests are being applied in a genuinely political manner. But it is not as clear-cut as that, by any means.

An impressive group of the great and the good, convened by the Royal Institute of Public Administration under the chairmanship of Professor David Williams of Wolfson College, Cambridge,[47] effectively cleared Mrs Thatcher of the charge of politicising the senior Civil Service, though the Williams Committee did detect an unprecedented level of interest in top appointments from the incumbent in No. 10 after 1979:

> To some extent, the appointment process has become more personalised in the sense that at the top level 'catching the eye' of the Prime Minister (in a favourable or unfavourable manner) may now be more important than in the past. Evidence to our group suggests that personal contacts and impressions play a role in promotion decisions. Downing Street communicates more opinions about the performance of civil servants, even down to quite junior levels, based on impressions made at meetings with the Prime Minister... However, we do not believe that these appointments and promotions are based on the candidate's support for or commitment to particular political ideologies or objectives.'[48]

So the permanent secretaries' club is nowhere near becoming an appendage of the Carlton. Neil Kinnock, in effect, acknowledged this, albeit with a degree of agnosticism, during a television interview with Peter Jay in 1985:

> I don't know about the permanent secretaries. We obviously have to examine the degree of enthusiasm and loyalty that they are prepared to demonstrate in support of a Labour government and in the implementation of the policy of that government. I'm prepared to work on ... the conventional basis, which has stood us in good stead in Britain, about the way in which civil servants are prepared to work.[49]

Within a month, Robert Armstrong had found occasion to 'welcome' Kinnock's statement and to tell him: 'He can be sure that ... the Civil

Service would serve the government of which he was the head with no less energy and loyalty, and goodwill than they have served the present government and its predecessors.'[50] There was not a single permanent secretary who did not welcome Kinnock's statement and Armstrong's response to it.

Mrs Thatcher may not have usurped tradition and squandered the bequest of Gladstone and Lowe by contaminating the principle of a career meritocracy in Whitehall, but she constructed alongside it something of a counter-Whitehall of her own. The Rayner Unit was, literally, an anti-CSD in 1979–81. By recruiting Rayner in the way she did and placing him in the Cabinet Office with a tiny staff she achieved her main efficiency purposes without causing the major eruption that would have ensued if she had sacked Ian Bancroft in May 1979 and installed Derek Rayner in his stead. Another area in which she moved cautiously was along the fuzzy borderland between the CPRS and the No. 10 Policy Unit.

When the government changed in May 1979, the CPRS – not for the first time – doubted its portability from one administration to the next. As one senior figure put it, 'We all thought that Ken Berrill was for the high jump one day after the election and so did he. They [the incoming Conservatives] had it in for Ken because he was a Keynesian and because of the hangover from the *Review of Overseas Representation*. It was uneasy for a few weeks. Then the Prime Minister was putting enormous pressure on him to stay. She began to appreciate Ken's merits and how useful the organisation could be.'[51] The image of the Tank and its head had indeed suffered after the ROR. The CPRS had made a remarkable recovery after its 1977 disaster with a steady stream of briefs for Callaghan and his ministers on public expenditure, energy, the aircraft industry, social policy, information technology and trade with the Third World.[52] But the trauma of the ROR had put Berrill firmly off publicity, and the Tank's recovery was appreciated internally but not publicly; most important of all, it had gone unnoticed in the office of the Leader of the Opposition. Ironically, it was the man who was to head her Downing Street Policy Unit, John Hoskyns, who saved the CPRS, arguing, as Donoughue had done with Wilson, that it should be retained. It was no thanks to Rothschild that Hoskyns reached the conclusion he did. He had had 'a long afternoon discussion with Lord Rothschild at Mrs Thatcher's suggestion shortly before the election to find out his experience and his view of it. He was at that time .... rather negative about the Tank. I think he felt that it had probably served its purpose and there wasn't really any need for it any longer.'[53]

Rothschild's views did nothing to abate Mrs Thatcher's anti-Tank sentiments, as Hoskyns recalled: 'There was a period when I think she felt it had no real purpose ... partly the influence of Lord Rothschild ... and partly because I think she felt that the Tank was perhaps politically unsympathetic to her ... She was a little worried that it was, so to speak, part of the rather fuzzy left-of-centre consensus which she felt ... was behind so many of the country's problems.'[54]

Mrs Thatcher was more than 'a little worried' by her image of the Tank. Her first meeting with Berrill, whom she knew from DES days when he was Chairman of the University Grants Committee, shortly after taking office in May 1979 quickly became the stuff of Whitehall legend. She harangued him on the awfulness of the ROR and on the pinkness of the Tank's political colouration.[55] It was not an auspicious beginning. The sensation of prime-ministerial disdain and suspicion instantly spread throughout the CPRS membership. But it had survived to fight another day. Mrs Thatcher, in fact, decided to keep it going on a trial basis before the 1979 election and Hoskyns had been instrumental in the Tank's being granted parole: 'It might have been that she would come in and the first thing she would do was to close it down. Certainly I and other people urged her to keep it and at least to see what it could do. Because ... you can always close it down if you find it's an encumbrance. But it's very difficult to reconstitute it once you've closed it down.'[56]

The bulk of the advice from career officials in closest contact with the new Prime Minister, most notably John Hunt and Kenneth Stowe, her Principal Private Secretary, seems to have been to save the CPRS. But its workload changed quickly and substantially. Public expenditure, a staple activity present since the creation, went. No longer did the CPRS partake as of right in the meetings of the Public Expenditure Survey Committee.[57] The social policy slice of the CPRS workload, a hefty segment since the inauguration of the Joint Approach to Social Policy, withered into insignificance. Work on relations with the Third World went, too.[58] Some aspects of the Tank's output survived after fierce arguments with its new patroness. Microprocessors were an example. This was later to blossom as the Thatcher administration's information technology initiative, first, in private, as an official Cabinet Committee on Information Technology chaired by Professor John Ashworth, the Tank's Chief Scientist, and later, through the very visible Minister for IT, Mr Kenneth Baker.[59]

Indeed, the Berrill CPRS came in from the cold before Berrill left for the City in March 1980. There were a number of reasons for this. One of the first CPRS submissions to Mrs Thatcher was, naturally enough, on economic strategy. It warned her against raising VAT and was ignored. She later came to believe the Tank had been correct.[60] Similarly, it stated very firmly that the Government should not think indefinitely in terms of having to index-link every benefit for ever.[61] This was music to Mrs Thatcher's ears. In fact, Whitehall noticed how swiftly in some areas the CPRS became almost more Thatcherite than the Cabinet. One Tank member reckons that Whitehall was well served by the transformation of those Mrs Thatcher had so recently written off as prisoners of a failed orthodoxy. He admitted they 'had been taken over by the machine' in the early Berrill years. But with the change of government, that became a virtue. The Tank was able to lead the machine itself into adapting to the new orthodoxy.[62]

Their quick immersion in Thatcherism, after the shock of Berrill's initial encounter with the Prime Minister, was in the forum of an *ad hoc* Cabinet committee on innovations chaired by Sir Geoffrey Howe, Chancellor of the Exchequer. It was one of the earliest *ad hoc* groups to be established by the new government and was known as MISC 14. Berrill himself chaired MISC 15, the official committee which serviced it.[63] MISC 14 was given the task of charting the undergrowth stifling industrial enterprise in Britain and coming up with suggestions for cutting it down and helping create a true market economy. The CPRS undertook a battery of investigations of taxes, regulations and restrictive practices. By midsummer of 1979 it was deeply immersed in Thatcherite preoccupations. And, as had happened after the change of government in 1974, it established a closer partnership with the Downing Street Policy Unit now headed by Hoskyns.[64] By the end of the year it was heavily involved in a study on the possible de-indexation of benefits, feeding an inter-departmental committee on the subject.[65]

By the time Berrill left at the end of March 1980, the CPRS had virtually transformed itself into an advisory unit on economic and industrial policy. It was active on all the major examples of case work such as British Leyland and civil nuclear policy (a pair of old faithfuls) and industrial problems such as the steel strike.[66] Berrill said in 1983 that he conceived his job post-May 1979 as that of showing the new prime minister that in the CPRS she possessed a 'valuable piece of equipment'. In the end, 'I think she thought it was valuable', he said.[67]

The man who had helped save the CPRS and, thereby, kept Berrill in Whitehall for another year reached the inner sanctums of policy analysis and advice-giving by a very different route from Berrill's thirty-year shuttle between the universities and the Civil Service. By the mid-seventies John Hoskyns was an unusual combination of Establishment pukka (Winchester and professional soldier with the Green Jackets) and whizz-kiddery (IBM and the foundation of his own software group). If anything, he had been apolitical until the economic and industrial crises of 1973–4. He had voted Labour in 1970 and Tory in 1974.[68] The troubles and dislocations of that period made him fear for the future of his country and he decided to sell his business in 1975, but 'I wasn't even certain at that time that the Conservative Party were the people I could best help.'[69]

Hoskyns became involved with the Centre for Policy Studies, the private free-market think-tank established by Mrs Thatcher and Sir Keith Joseph in 1974. It was the centre's director, Sir Alfred Sherman, who gathered around him many if not all of the people who were to comprise Mrs Thatcher's early counter-Civil Service in the years after 1979. Another was Norman Strauss, ex-Unilever, who, like Hoskyns, was drawn into political activity by the mid-seventies crisis. Strauss is an ebullient, combative businessman who cannot see a conventional wisdom without wishing to puncture it or a vested institutional interest without trying to expose it. He is as abrasive as Hoskyns is smooth. Sherman, wisely, thought undiluted Strauss would alarm Mrs Thatcher, who is a far more cautious and conventional person than she is often given credit for being. He sent Hoskyns with him when Strauss visited Mrs Thatcher to outline his ideas on the need to think in radical strategic terms when formulating policy.[70] Hoskyns and Strauss made an odd but effective pair with Strauss fizzing like a catherine wheel and Hoskyns identifying, isolating and refining the most promising sparks. Together they developed the 'stepping stones' approach to planning for the Conservative restoration – picking out first-order problems, such as curbing the power of trade unions, beating down inflation and restoring financial stability, which had to be tackled and solved before the wider spectrum of political ambitions had a realistic hope of being achieved.

Their work sat uneasily with the Opposition policy-making being undertaken by the Conservative Research Department, though their thrusts – the freeing of the labour market and the creation of an enterprise society – ran very much in parallel. It only became clear a month or so before the 1979 general election that Hoskyns would lead the No. 10 Policy Unit and not the Research Department's Adam Ridley, who went to advise Sir Geoffrey Howe at the Treasury instead. Hoskyns accepted, subject to two conditions – that he could write his own terms of reference (she agreed) and that he never became involved in speech writing (no absolute assurance on that).[71] What attracted Hoskyns to Mrs Thatcher's approach to government was 'this absolute commitment, this sort of slightly reckless feeling that ... she had got to achieve real change even though that meant, as a politician, living dangerously'.[72]

The terms of reference Hoskyns agreed with the newly elected Mrs Thatcher were 'that the Policy Unit should not be a sort of in-house consultancy waiting to be told what to do, waiting for jobs and problems to crop up. What it should be doing is thinking ahead and saying to her and her colleagues "These are the important issues which have to be thought about in roughly the following sequence ... There are other things which people may be trying to make you spend a lot of time [on] ... but which are not actually central in a strategic sense."'[73] Hoskyns later revealed what that 'thinking ahead' agenda turned out to be in the three years he spent in No. 10 between May 1979 and April 1982:

> The Unit's work was concerned entirely with financial stabilisation as the over-riding objective for the first term: making public sector pay fit the MTFS [Medium Term Financial Strategy] framework; ending the old Civil Service pay comparability system; de-indexing other elements of public spending; switching from a volume to a cash basis for public expenditure; trade union reform; handling the public sector strikes which were inevitable in the face of such a programme; the 1981 Budget [over which there had been a great battle, at the depth of the recession, between reflationists and deflationists with Hoskyns siding with the 'dries' who prevailed]; challenging the 'Macmillan doctrine'[74] of the invincibility of the NUM [National Union of Mineworkers]; and the decision to start preparing for a coal strike.[75]

In pursuing this programme, Hoskyns and Strauss (assisted by one career official, Andrew Duguid) experienced the usual turf fights with the regulars, as Hoskyns recalled:

> She [the Prime Minister] may find that ... she is being perhaps misled a little bit – probably quite sincerely misled – by people in a department with [a] much larger staff who have great mastery of all the detail and will say to No. 10 ... 'We really don't believe this is the right way to do it.' So ... she's got to have some people there who've got the time to do that sort of thinking and say 'We don't agree.'[76]

Hoskyns encountered resistance in the early days – '"Who the hell is this man, knows nothing about politics you know, he's a businessman'", which is practically the worst thing you can say about anybody in the political world even in the Tory Party.... the Civil Service assume that you're really just a sort of bag-carrying hack who can, with a bit of luck, be shunted into a siding ... while they get on with really helping the Prime Minister to solve her problems. It takes a bit of a while to break through that.'[77] One way Hoskyns broke through that was by being as bloody-minded as the lady he served:

> I can remember a particular point where I had put a minute to the Prime Minister which was extremely critical ... of a very distinguished and I think actually rather outstandingly good permanent secretary. And, immediately, one of his minions came to see me and said that, for some reason that wasn't clear, the minute had not yet actually found its way into the Prime Minister's box. There were one or two things arising

from it which they would like to discuss and in the light of that discussion was I still so sure that I really wanted this minute to go to the Prime Minister?

... I said 'yes' because it was an absolute test case. He [a Downing Street official] wanted to stop me sending someting which was critical of a senior civil servant to the Prime Minister.[78]

Hoskyns also acquired access to important ministerial meetings. He could attend any meeting of the Cabinet's economic strategy committee, the key body in terms of the Policy Unit's priority issues. 'I could speak by arrangement or she [Mrs Thatcher] might ask me to speak if she wanted to.'[79] Hoskyns attended but did not speak at each year's 'two major economic Cabinets... one a general review of the economic strategy [before the Budget] and another on public expenditure [just before the summer recess]'.[80]

The issue for which he became best known within the political nation – Whitehall reform – does not feature in the list of priority business with which the Policy Unit busied itself in 1979–82. As Hoskyns later revealed, 'Norman Strauss recognised the need for reform much sooner than I did, but neither of us did any work on it until after we had left Downing Street. I never discussed Whitehall reform with Mrs Thatcher, nor wrote a sentence to her about it during the five years [1977–82] during which I advised her. With the critical social and economic situation facing the incoming Government in the wake of the "winter of discontent", it would have been absurd even to broach such a subject.'[81]

He judged the Prime Minister's mind well. In her pre-election discussions under the Douglas-Home Rules Mrs Thatcher let it be known among the permanent secretaries' club that, as one of them put it, 'her job was to turn the economy round; she was not going to muck around with the machinery of government'.[82] It is a view to which she has adhered. As David Willetts, former member and unofficial house historian of the Policy Unit in its later variant, put it in 1987: 'This Government has rightly been constitutionally conservative –unless there are exceptional circumstances it is more productive for Ministers to use their limited time and energies to get on with the real job of pursuing their policies rather than the less fruitful game of reorganising Whitehall.'[83]

Norman Strauss had been brooding on the Civil Service as a barrier to change since the mid-seventies. He began his attempt to persuade Mrs Thatcher of his theme even before the electorate placed her in No. 10:

What was clear [in 1977–8] was we were moving into turbulent times ... and we had to have a mechanism for managing in turbulent times and creating change. I tried to make Mrs Thatcher understand that it

> was one thing to gain power but quite another to exercise it effectively ... I tried to alert her to the fact that the Whitehall culture had to be managed and that meant change and in many cases it was going to mean thought. And I said to her 'You must understand what we're getting into here. This is a very powerful culture. It's been built up over the years. It's a very proud culture and this pride can sometimes manifest itself as arrogance and complacency and we must be able to shake it up.'[84]

Strauss believes that in Opposition she listened and in office she did not. The bitter memory of the experience has spurred him to further reformist exertions ever since:

> I can only say that from the very first day she was in Downing Street, as far as I could tell, she ignored all that advice about the government machine ... because her own advisers confirmed her in her mind as Leader of the Opposition whereas the Civil Service advisers confirmed her as Prime Minister. And since then I [have] formed the view that the real prize political parties have fought for in the past is the Civil Service because that's what tells them that they're Ministers and in power. I find that, I have to say, an utterly despicable and sickening thought that this is what the game is about and it certainly doesn't seem to be about improving the lot of citizens.[85]

Mrs Thatcher's reluctance to espouse radical Civil Service reform was a key element in Norman Strauss's decision to leave No. 10. His own experience in No. 10 began to push Hoskyns's thinking in a similar direction, particularly the 'We've seen it all before syndrome' in Whitehall:

> At meetings to discuss difficult problems – sometimes even on things as crucial as the Budget, sometimes on legislation – there would be ... people round the table who were saying 'You know, we've tried all these things before' or 'you know, they tried that in 1973 and it didn't work' [or] 'Jenkins tried this in 1968 and it didn't work'. There is never the feeling, which I've experienced a lot in business, of excitement, of brainstorming – producing perhaps half-baked ideas out of which people suddenly begin to see that maybe we've got something here.[86]

Hoskyns was keen to beef up the alternative Civil Service. For a time it looked as if the Policy Unit might merge with the CPRS with Hoskyns in charge of the new entity when Sir Robin Ibbs returned to ICI. The idea was appealing to some members of the CPRS. One of them said of Hoskyns, 'He was just the kind of man we'd have been glad to have worked through the night for.'[87] But the idea met with stern opposition from the permanent secretaries and Mrs Thatcher dropped it.[88] Hoskyns has not spoken publicly about the CPRS–Policy Unit merger-that-never-was and the degree to which it influenced his decision to leave, but he has alluded to it indirectly:

> I didn't attempt to change the Civil Service ... while I was there ... some people feel that I put forward proposals and then realised that I couldn't get them accepted. That isn't in fact correct. I really only started thinking about it hard after I left.
>
> The reason why I left was slightly related to that ... I could see the long-term thinking about strategy which really had to be done and had to be started then [1982] for the latter half of the decade, was not going to be possible inside Whitehall because of the lack of people with the right time and organisation to do that thinking.[89]

Hoskyns had good relations with what then comprised Mrs Thatcher's alternative Whitehall, particularly Professor (later Sir) Alan Walters, the ex-London School of Economics free marketeer whom Mrs Thatcher persuaded to return from Johns Hopkins University, Baltimore, to be her Downing Street economic adviser. Partly paid for by public funds and partly by the Centre for Policy Studies, Walters operated separately from the Policy Unit, but he and Hoskyns thought very much alike on economic matters.

Alan Walters was rated highly by his fellow professionals, particularly on transport economics, though he was no friend of British Rail (who were keen on a number of capital projects in the early 1980s). In 1981 the *Daily Mail* pictured him in a second-class compartment on a train between St Pancras and Leicester where he was to receive an honorary degree from his old university. 'I don't intend giving money away to British Rail', he said. 'First class travel is far too expensive. I don't know how people can afford it.' (Professor Walters was earning £50,000 a year at the time.[90]) One well-placed Whitehall figure said of him 'Alan is very good on big public expenditure projects ... He's done exactly the job he was appointed for – to see all the economic stuff going to the PM and stopping the nonsense. He's given her a great sense of security about the Treasury. It's good for the Treasury too. They can talk to him before putting stuff up to her.'[91] Walters himself confirmed his function as a nonsense-stopper in a lecture at the Conservative Party Conference in 1981. 'The Minister needs protection,' he said. 'The adviser must provide the Minister with a critical account of various ideas and propositions which are fed to him or her. In its most elementary form it is, of course, identifying nonsense and economic error in the propositions which are put forward. His job is to expose the quack cures.'[92]

Given her priority of turning the economy round, Mrs Thatcher was well served by the trio of Hoskyns and Walters in No. 10 and Ibbs at the CPRS after April 1980. Hoskyns reckoned the CPRS 'came to its full, or as near as it had probably got to its full potential, under Robin Ibbs. It began to focus on strategic issues . . . the things that he was looking at with the Tank were central.'[93] In fact, the Prime Minister and the new head of the Think Tank suited each other admirably. Mrs Thatcher wanted the CPRS to operate under closer political direction, which suited Ibbs with his industrial background. Berrill's university origins were reflected in the free-and-easy manner in which his Tank worked (though this was less true after the change of government in 1979). For some like Professor John Ashworth, a bit of the fun went out of Tank life after April 1980. He put it down partly to the male–female ratio inside the CPRS:

> Lord Rothschild never made any secret that . . ., other things being equal, he would rather work with women than with men, and I had a lot of sympathy with that. And so, I think, did Sir Kenneth Berrill. So the number of females in the Tank . . . I always thought profoundly affected the sort of atmosphere and general gaiety of life. The fun tended to decline, I thought, under Robin Ibbs' leadership.[94]

The Tank's number one customer, Mrs Thatcher, is not an exponent of joy through government. Ibbs's *modus operandi* found favour. As part of his new-style CPRS, he instantly became involved in another ancient policy debate, the relationship between Whitehall and the nationalised industries. A year later this was to develop into a major CPRS study. It started in a piecemeal fashion with an early submission about the need to relax the cash limits of the Central Electricity Generating Board in order to facilitate the stockpiling of coal at power stations as insurance against a future miners' strike.

Another public sector issue in which the early Ibbs Tank became active was the question of state industry and Civil Service pay, a preoccupation of the Prime Minister's Cabinet Committee on Economic Strategy in 1980–1.[95] By the end of 1980, the Tank was well into the details of nationalised industry operations, including the role of non-executive directors and the possibility of merit pay for board members. Some of its old talent for the heterodox surfaced when it looked at how the more successful Eastern bloc economies ran their nationalised industries.[96] After the Cabinet's climb-down on pit closures in February 1981, coal became a CPRS preoccupation. It was directly involved in MISC 57, the special official Cabinet committee commissioned by Mrs Thatcher to advise ministers on the possibility of withstanding a prolonged coal strike.[97] Other offshoots of its state-sector work included an alliance with the Treasury (and Alan Walters) to kill British Rail's electrification programme.[98]

In March 1981, the CPRS was formally commissioned by Mrs Thatcher to review Government–nationalised industry relations and to make recommendations within two months.[99] It produced four main proposals:

* a clearer set of financial controls and policy objectives for each industry from its Whitehall sponsoring department;
* boards to have a majority of non-executive directors who would have specific responsibilities, for productivity, say, with a direct link to ministers and officials;
* each sponsoring department to set up a business group of outside industrialists to monitor state industries. Each group would be led by an experienced figure from business;
* a new Cabinet committee on nationalised industries, chaired by the Prime Minister, to whom the groups would report.[100]

The Ibbs Report stimulated a battle royal in Whitehall. Senior officials, some of the sponsoring ministers and virtually all the nationalised industry chairmen formed an alliance to kill the business groups idea. It did produce some results, however. By December the new Cabinet committee was in being. It was known as Economy (Nationalised Industries), or E(NI). Mrs Thatcher rather took the glitter off it by opening its first meeting with the words: 'Oh no. Not the boring nationalised industries again.'[101] There was, too, a tightening up of efficiency monitoring through the Monopolies and Mergers Commission and new bureaucratic devices like the Treasury's Public Enterprise Analysis Unit.[102] The Ibbs Report had been gelded. But it was not an own goal like the ROR four years earlier.

Another leaked report from the Ibbs era fell into a similar category of limited though far from complete influence. A study of Merseyside by Quentin Thompson and Eileen MacKay, commissioned by Mrs Thatcher herself with the intention of drawing lessons for inner-city policy in general, was mentioned in *The Times* in July 1981 in the middle of the urban riots. It had been completed a month earlier after the Brixton disturbances but before Merseyside's own eruption in Toxteth. *The Times*, particularly sensitive towards the story given events on the streets, approached Ibbs via the Downing Street Press Office and asked if he would like to speak to two of its reporters before the story was published. Even the disturbances in Toxteth and Moss Side failed to persuade him to drop his policy of total non-communication with the press.[103]

The Thompson–Mackay report warned of increasing social tension in urban areas experiencing high unemployment and poverty and foresaw a threat to law and order arising from them.[104] The main thrust of the document was that central government could not simply wash its hands of Merseyside. To pursue a policy of managed decline would be politically and socially unacceptable as well as expensive.[105] The study had no illusions about the difficulty of regenerating industry in Merseyside. It was not just a matter of industrial recession and poor industrial relations continuing to produce a spiral of decline. Technological change meant that even a pronounced upturn was unlikely to restore unskilled manual jobs in anything like the proportion of those that had been lost in the 1960s and 1970s. A substantial effort on service industries and tourism (the Beatles connection) was recommended.[106]

There is evidence that at prime ministerial level the CPRS report on Merseyside would have fallen on particularly deaf ears, but for events in Toxteth. Michael Heseltine, Secretary of State for the Environment, rushed to Merseyside with a supporting team which included Quentin Thompson, one of the report's authors. Mrs Thatcher herself paid a flying visit. Some of the CPRS analysis was incorporated in Heseltine's famous *It Took a Riot* minute to the Prime Minister in August 1981, which, in diluted form, constituted the core of the Government's new inner-city policy announced in the autumn (see pp. 702–4).

At the turn of the year, there was talk of a new head of the Tank. ICI wanted Ibbs back as soon as his initial two-year appointment was up in April 1982. He was judged in Whitehall to have done well in his pleasant, undemonstrative but pertinacious fashion. As one experienced insider put it, 'On industrial matters, it's a matter of "Call for Robin."'[107]

His successor, John Sparrow, was a quiet, courteous merchant banker from Morgan Grenfell who turned out to be the fourth and last head of the CPRS. But in April 1982 nobody's eyes were on the Think Tank or the No. 10 Policy Unit where the engaging author and *Spectator* journalist, Ferdinand Mount, replaced Hoskyns. All attention was focused on the South Atlantic where Argentine forces had invaded the Falkland Islands, putting Whitehall on a war footing for the first time since Suez and stimulating the machine to one of its best patches of peak performance in the postwar period.

The Falklands crisis, the lack of warning and the inadequate performance of the overseas and defence policy side of Whitehall so graphically chronicled in the Franks Report, shook what faith Mrs Thatcher had in the machine and the Foreign Office in particular. The FO, in fact, became *the* scapegoat department for bureaucracy-baiters in the eighties as the Treasury had been throughout the sterling and public spending crises of the seventies.[108] For a time after the Falklands War Mrs Thatcher was in the market for new remedies or, to be more exact, new versions of old ones. The idea of a Prime Minister's Department surfaced and papers were prepared for her by Sir Alfred Sherman and Ray Whitney, ex-Foreign Office, then an MP but not yet a minister.[109] It seemed a runner for a while, but the constitutional row which would have ensued in Parliament and the certain resentment of several Cabinet colleagues already disturbed by signs of an overmighty premiership seem to have caused caution to prevail. A PMD was not worth the row. It was, to paraphrase Beveridge, to be a time for patching, not for a revolution in the machinery of government, and the patches were put in place in stages during 1982 and 1983.

The first patch was a brightly coloured one and its name was Sir Anthony Parsons. Parsons, a career diplomat but a distinctly unorthodox one, had impressed Mrs Thatcher hugely during the Falklands crisis when he was approaching the end of his career as Ambassador to the United Nations after having endured the trauma of serving in Tehran as the Shah's regime collapsed around him.[110] After the Falklands she persuaded him to join her in No. 10 as her foreign affairs adviser, separate, like Walters, from the Policy Unit. Parsons was an Arabist by background and a considerable scholar of the Middle East with a fund of good stories about the last days of Britain's informal empire there which always appealed to a district commissioner *manqué* like myself, particularly the one (if memory serves) of Sir John Troutbeck sitting in the Baghdad embassy in the early fifties as a howling mob gathered outside and turning to the young Tony Parsons to remark, 'I fear our prestige is dangerously high.'

Parsons was always a bit suspect within the FO, partly because of his irreverence and slightly raffish air and partly because he was 'unsound' on the Anglo-American special relationship, believing we should be a good ally to them in areas where reason prevailed in Washington's foreign policy-making – NATO/Europe – and a sceptical one where internal US pressures and lobbies distorted the process as in the Middle East.[111] He was certainly not an Establishment man. In the autumn of 1984 after Parsons had left No. 10 I asked him to help me with a radio documentary on the great and the good and received the following entirely characteristic reply: 'I would be most interested in participating in your search for the Establishment. I might find out if I belong to it or not. I think not. Clubs are an essential feature and I hate them!'[112]

The Establishment, however, has a soft spot for Parsons. He is the stuff of which legends are made. John Gale, recalling his days in the Transjordan Frontier Force in the forties, wrote of his squadron commander, Parsons, that he was 'a brave and clever man... He taught me a lot. Sometimes he fought guests invited to the mess with a sabre; and once he had a duel, using full bottles of champagne, in which he nearly severed his wrist... he would quote pages of Latin prose and verse; and then sing "Cocaine Kate and Morphine Sue" at the top of his voice.'[113] He won his spurs with Mrs Thatcher during one tense Falklands weekend at Chequers by saying to her, in exasperation, 'Prime Minister, will you please not interrupt me until I have finished.'[114] Parsons is no Thatcherite when it comes to economic or domestic policy (he was not hired for his views on those).

Equally, his views on foreign policy are very much his own. Almost certainly this was the quality which attracted her, and Parsons admires similar traits in Mrs Thatcher, though, even in retirement, he was cautious when I questioned him about it:

'[Mrs Thatcher is] not known to be a lover of the good and the great style, she goes for doers rather than thinkers ... rather than the old grandees. Do you think that's a fair assessment of her? How does she pick her chaps to do her one-off jobs?'

'Have to answer that obliquely. I think probably what she objects to about the classical good and great is that by their very nature, by the fact they all know each other, they are clubby people, they frequent the same environment, they do tend to reach moderate, balanced, medium conclusions about whatever matter they are dealing with. I think that the Prime Minister prefers people who are prepared ... to think the unthinkable and to reach logical conclusions automatically.'[115]

At the time, Parsons's appointment as Downing Street foreign affairs adviser was portrayed in the quality press as 'a setback to one of Whitehall's proudest departments'.[116] One former ambassador greeted him in a London club with a 'How are you, Sir Horace?' – a malicious (and unjustified) reference to the Wilson–Chamberlain partnership.[117]

Francis Pym, who had replaced Lord Carrington as Foreign Secretary when the Argentines invaded the Falklands, took it badly and saw it as direct prime-ministerial inteference in Foreign Office matters.[118] Parsons was sensitive to this and worked closely and well with Pym's permanent secretary, Sir Antony Acland.[119] Equally important, he took his place as the PM's man at Wednesday morning meetings of the Joint Intelligence Committee while Lord Franks and his fellow Privy Counsellors probed the failings of that committee and its supporting apparatus during the run-up to the Falklands War.[120] For a time Parsons was joined in No. 10 by Roger Jackling, an MOD assistant secretary who had been closely involved in the Falklands operation. Jackling, a sharp yet affable operator, was Mrs Thatcher's eyes and ears on defence policy and weapons procurement but soon felt there was insufficient work to justify his *and* Parsons's presence, and returned to the MOD after the 1983 general election. The Franks Report on the Falklands, when published in January 1983, led to a further tightening of the Prime Minister's grip on the intelligence machine. The chairmanship of the JIC was removed from the Foreign Office and placed in the hands of Sir Antony Duff, the Cabinet Office's co-ordinator of security and intelligence, whose direct lines to Mrs Thatcher were emphasised.[121] She was later to send him to reform MI5.

1983 was the year of the great shake-up in Mrs Thatcher's counter-

Whitehall and will long be remembered for the demise of the CPRS, a move that was almost universally criticised. Bancroft was speaking for many in both the political and the administrative classes when he called it 'a sad blow by prejudice against enlightenment'.[122] John Sparrow's was an ill-starred stewardship of the Tank. It began promisingly enough in the spring of 1982 with Sparrow starting with a candour and an openness which was in stark contrast to Ibbs's silence. *The Economist* described Sparrow as 'chatting freely' and went on to report:

> Mr Sparrow has been advising Mrs Thatcher on City matters intermittently for some years (surprisingly, he sees Mrs Thatcher as in the mould of his political hero, Iain Macleod). But he enters the Whitehall jungle with little knowledge of the beasts who roam there. And it is these beasts, ministers and mandarins ... who have been responsible for battering much of the Think Tank's recent work (see for instance what they did to Mr Ibbs's recommendations for the nationalised industries).[123]

The Economist concluded, prophetically, that 'Mr Sparrow starts at an unfair advantage, with too much to learn both about politics and about Whitehall'.[124] He started, however, with a hefty programme of work inherited from the Ibbs era. There were studies of unemployment, regional policy, education and training, alternatives to domestic rates, and central government–local government relations, to be carried through. Above all, there was the follow-up to the Ibbs report on the nationalised industries.

The Prime Minister's E(NI) committee was in regular session in the spring of 1982. Sparrow's contribution was to supervise a further study of which state monopolies could be broken up and how best to regulate the fragments. Its focus was beyond the general election expected in 1983. It fitted blended in with the post-1979 CPRS curbing the power of monopoly trade unions. This, naturally, was seen as a beneficial by-product of dismembering nationalised industries.[125] The Tank turned its attention to the preparation of performance criteria for each public industry and service.[126] Sparrow's inaugural months also saw the early stages of what was intended to be a major study of the labour market and its rigidities. But little had come of this by the time of the Tank's demise in July 1983.[127]

The Sparrow era, however, will be remembered for one thing – the tremendous row which developed when *The Economist* leaked its study of long-term public expenditure in September 1982, just in time for the story to dominate the party conference season. The CPRS paper, which went to the Cabinet on 9 September, was essentially a technician's report. Its genesis was a Treasury exercise on the tax and spending implications of a range of economic scenarios up to and including the early 1990s assuming some economic growth, low growth, no growth and so on. When the Cabinet discussed this before the summer recess it was decided that the CPRS should put flesh on the statistical bones. They were asked to spell out what would have to happen to the big spending programmes in a nil or low growth economy if public spending was not to absorb an increased proportion of gross domestic product. The study looked at education, social security, health and defence and produced options, *not* recommendations.

* Education. An end to state-funding of higher education with fees set at market rates and some 300,000 state scholarships a year backed up by a system of student loans. At the schools level, the old faithful of vouchers was given another airing plus the possibility of allowing pupil–teacher ratios to rise.

* Social Security. De-indexing of all payments.

* Health. The replacement of the National Health Service with a system of private insurance.

* Defence. This flummoxed the Tank somewhat, though it was suggested the defence budget should be frozen as a proportion of gross domestic product once the Government's existing commitment to NATO to increase defence spending by three per cent a year ran out in 1986.[128]

Several ministers were taken aback by the radical implications of the document when it went before the Cabinet on 9 September. So was the political nation when it was disclosed in detail by *The Economist* nine days later. The Cabinet, from the Prime Minister down, spent the next few weeks denying that the Government had a plan to dismantle the health service. Thanks to the leak, the Tank's paper effectively killed all Whitehall debate about long-term spending and taxation until after the 1983 general election, by which time its authors had been scattered.

The effect of the leak on the CPRS was traumatic. As a result of an inquiry, the Prime Minister knew but could not prove that the disclosure had been a political act by a politican. [129] Uninformed circles attributed the indiscretion to the Tank itself. Mr Sparrow retreated further into his shell. When *The Times* leaked the story that the CPRS was working on plans for fragmenting the state monopolies on 1 November, he asked Robert Armstrong to call in MI5 to discover who was the source of this very mundane piece of news. The leak inquiry failed.[130]

Ironically, *The Times* appended to its 1 November story a favourable account of Sparrow's immersion into the world for which *The Economist* had judged him to be so unprepared. Recalling April 1982, the paper said:

> Sceptics gave him little chance of making an impact. So far, they have been largely confounded. Senior civil servants have been impressed by his energy and ability to fight his corner in discussions. He has achieved a good working relationship with ministers in general, and the Treasury team in particular.[131]

Certainly the members of the CPRS liked working for the new man: 'It was marvellous working for John Sparrow because he let you do what you wanted, unlike Robin Ibbs, he would pass it on as a CPRS paper unamended.'[132] But one member of the Tank thought this pleasant trait was Mr Sparrow's 'great mistake':

> He allowed other people's work to go forward when he did not understand it. He lacked self-confidence. This was not helped when he had to tell Mrs Thatcher why we thought something should or should not be done particularly as she had a habit of asking tough questions. It would have been much better if John Sparrow had said from the start: 'I'm no Rothschild. We're going to concentrate on these three areas which I know about. We're going to do it my way.'[133]

The shadow of Rothschild still fell over his successors a decade after he left the CPRS. As one 1980s member put it: 'The Rothschild aura affected everybody – the feeling that he had been so marvellous and the members of his CPRS so bright. I wonder if they really were?'[134]

Early in the new year of 1983, with the election in mind, Mrs Thatcher's thoughts returned to the question of her personal briefing and policy support. By the spring of 1983, Mrs Thatcher's thinking had reached the idea of a beefed-up Policy Unit headed by a chief of staff who might be a non-departmental minister or a heavyweight figure who could run an expanded Downing street team. By the time of the election, she had not made up her mind on precise details of the stretched version of Downing Street. But she had decided to kill the CPRS.[135]

There were two main reasons for the sentence of death. Mrs Thatcher had always had a thing about manpower economies. She could not be seen to be building up her staff without a concomitant saving. Secondly, the Tank had ceased to give real satisfaction. The leak of its spending document had left a scar. Was it worth risking another huge political embarrassment for an output that did not really make much difference to Government strategy? The price was not deemed worth paying.[136] As one well-placed observer put it:

> The CPRS was not delivering the goods. The conclusion in No. 10 was, therefore, that it had become a part of the Cabinet Office and was politically starved. John Sparrow saw Mrs Thatcher regularly and got on well with her. But it wasn't like being part of her office. He did continue to deliver the goods on technical aspects like nationalised industry pricing. But on anything that had a political dimension, the Tank found itself rather isolated.[137]

There was a deeper reason for the abolition. Professor Ashworth, who had predicted it, reckoned that Margaret Thatcher and that sort of policy analysis simply do not mix:

> Of its very existence it [the CPRS] sort of encapsulated a view about government for which she had no great sympathy. She was what she called a conviction politician. There is a difference between being a conviction politician and being a rationally guided politician.[138]

After reading of the Tank's demise in *The Times*, Mr Sparrow made a last-ditch effort to save it. He appealed directly to Mrs Thatcher.[139] She was unmoved. Not a single minister spoke up for it at Cabinet when the agenda reached its abolition.

The prospect of death concentrated Mr Sparrow's mind wonderfully, if belatedly, on talking to the press. After the official announcement of abolition from No. 10 he agreed to be interviewed by *The Times*. The policy analysis work – the quick briefs for Cabinet – had 'been done consistently well', he suggested. But the longer-term inquiries, the 'think tank function' Mr Sparrow called it, need not be done in-house and, in fact, might be better done outside government. His overall judgment on advising ministers in general was that 'the job has been done well throughout the life of the CPRS'.[140] Four years after the Tank's death, David Willetts, fresh from service as one of the Prime Minister's men in the No. 10 Policy Unit, published what can be seen as the definitive view of the demise when he wrote of the 'four crucial reasons' underlying the Prime Minister's decision to abolish it.

> First, this Prime Minister is better aware than most that a strategy is nothing without the right tactical decision. The strategic direction of her government has been clear from the start –the reduction of inflation, extending the operation of markets, and allowing greater scope for personal responsibility and choice. The challenge is to ensure that the day-to-day decisions coming before ministers fit in with these strategic objectives. Yet the CPRS seemed to become more donnish and detached from hard day-to-day decisions.[141]

Willetts suggested that the latterday Tank had lost its earlier ability to put on the short, sharp and timely Cabinet paper and was, by the end, 'more orientated towards providing a 100 page report within 3 months', work it did well but work which departments thought they could do themselves. He was candid about the leak factor, too:

> The CPRS was a Cabinet Office body serving all of the Cabinet. So any major review would get wide circulation. It was very likely that at least one minister would have such an interest in opposing the CPRS's recommendations that he would be sorely tempted to leak against them. Unfortunate episodes like this afflicted the CPRS in its later years.[142]

David Willetts's third reason for the Tank's death sentence would, if I had been its judge, have led to instant pardon and restoration on the grounds that it was fulfilling the independent role enshrined in its charter:

> CPRS papers could divert the conduct of Cabinet and Cabinet committee business in a way unwelcome to other departments as much as to the Prime Minister. If a department circulates a paper with a major policy proposal, it legitimately expects that its paper will form the centrepiece for ministerial discussion. But a CPRS paper, circulated to all ministers attending the meeting could overshadow the original work and itself set the framework for the meeting; whilst this might seem . . . an advance – the neutral central body setting the terms of debate – in the long run it could undermine the department's morale and sense of lead responsibility for policy in their areas. The Policy Unit, by contrast, only briefs the Prime Minister, leaving the relevant minister (and maybe the Treasury with a counter proposal) much more influence over the agenda.[143]

David Willetts's last reason for abortion has a universal and perpetual validity when it comes to evaluating institutionalised antidotes to orthodoxy: 'perhaps most importantly, institutional innovations at the centre may have an inherently short life. The grit in the machine is worn smooth.'[144]

What is certain, however, is that the Policy Unit drew sustenance, vulture-like, from the corpse of the CPRS. Two of the Tank's members transferred immediately to the Unit. But it was the arrival of the merchant banker, John Redwood, from N. M. Rothschild in November 1983 and his replacement of Ferdinand Mount two months later which led to the construction of what Willetts calls the 'new model Policy Unit'.[145] It was an altogether bigger, more structured and institutionalised outfit and the new model continued under Professor Brian Griffiths, recruited from the

City University Business School in 1985 when Redwood was adopted as a prospective Parliamentary candidate (he was elected in 1987).

Mount is intelligent, cultivated and original but not a bureaucrat *manqué* and certainly no empire builder. He left his mark with a spirited but largely unsuccessful attempt to place the family at the centre of social policy (he had written a much-praised book on the subject[146]) and as a speech-writer, an important function in an election period. Under Redwood, the Policy Unit became a Whitehall in miniature with each member shadowing a cluster of policies and departments. It avoided Whitehall's propensity to create hierarchies and to put up walls between divisions by deliberately cultivating a style that 'is collegiate and friendly – the whole unit will discuss any major bone before advice is sent to the Prime Minister'.[147] In this sense it is very similar to the CPRS: 'Peer review helps to keep the Unit's advice sharp and purposeful. The range of experience and skills of its members is crucial to the Unit's success. A lawyer, an economist, a management consultant, an industrialist can all give their angle on a problem. In this respect the Policy Unit is very different from the Civil Service which recruits early and for life.'[148] One difference between the Tank and the CPRS was the imprimatur on its submissions to the customer-in-chief:

> Neither John Redwood nor Brian Griffiths behaved at all autocratically, though they have provided the leadership. Above all, the head of the Unit acts as a quality controller. Important pieces of work are, if time permits, shown to him so he can ensure [they are] up to the Unit's normal standards of clarity and vigour. But each member of the Unit establishes their own character with the Prime Minister and the department in the areas they cover. Work goes in under their signature, not that of the head of the Unit.[149]

Another difference between the CPRS and the Policy Unit which mattered in the Thatcher–Rayner era was running costs. The Tank was always twice as large as the Unit even in its larger marque. In its last year the CPRS cost just under £1m at 1983 prices;[150] by comparison the Hoskyns era Unit was bargain basement £66,147 in 1981–2. In 1986–7 the expanded Unit absorbed £344,490 of public money (at 1987 prices),[151] about one third of the cost of the CPRS in its final incarnation.

But the acutest and most important difference between the CPRS and the Policy Unit is that the Policy Unit was *hers* to its last paperclip. There was no question of its serving other Cabinet ministers or some notion of the wider interest. David Willetts was candid about this when he wrote that 'The pattern of the Policy Unit's work is largely determined by the papers and meetings coming up for the Prime Minister. Liaison with the

[No. 10] Private Office helps ensure that the Unit sends the Prime Minister work that is relevant to her immediate preoccupations.'[152] The Private Office forwards to the Unit all papers covering domestic policy except those dealing with appointments and security matters. Foreign policy papers go to Sir Percy Cradock, the seasoned FO Chinahand who replaced Parsons as her foreign affairs adviser in 1983.

What happens to those papers when they reach the Policy Unit shows how closely it functions (as did its Wilson and Callaghan incarnations before it) as an extension of its boss's priorities and prejudices. As Willetts put it,

> When a department puts a paper to the Prime Minister the relevant member of the Unit can ask himself some basic questions such as: Is there a less interventionist solution which has not been properly considered or has been wrongly rejected? Is there a less expensive option? Are the arguments consistent? What is the evidence to back them up? Are there other relevant facts which the Prime Minister needs to know?[153]

Such a function has a long pedigree. It was, after all, what Adam's team did for Lloyd George, the Prof's for Churchill and Donoughue's for Wilson and Callaghan. Mrs Thatcher's 'Garden Suburb' also fulfilled that other classic function of such a body – progress-chasing. As Willetts, a Treasury regular by background after all, shrewdly observed, 'Departmental ministers are so enormously busy that once one policy problem has been resolved, they then move on to the next one. Civil servants may encourage them in this – much higher status is accorded to conceiving fresh new policy advice than to ensuring that an existing agreed policy stays healthy and vigorous.'[154]

The customer-is-queen principle is put into practical effect by close liaison with the regulars in the Private Office, a routine Friday morning meeting between the PM and the head of the Unit, and the team members meet on Monday and Thursday mornings 'to review the Prime Minister's diary, discuss business coming up and allocate tasks'.[155] Willetts in his tidy. Treasury-trained fashion, itemised seven functions carried out by the fully-fledged Unit in the Redwood–Griffith incarnation:

1. As 'a small, creative think tank', Unit members were on the look-out for new policy ideas and angles to put to the PM and to send in 'free-standing think pieces'.
2. Policy adviser commenting on the input from departments to the PM.
3. Progress reporting on where a policy is heading.

4. To raise issues likely to be by-passed or ignored by standard inter-departmental machinery. [This, too, was an old CPRS speciality.]
5. Lubricating relations between departments and No. 10 to focus on crucial issues and avoid unnecessary conflict.
6. To provide 'a non-Whitehall' perspective on departmental advice to the PM.
7. To act 'as a grand suggestions box' for the PM drawing on ideas from the universities or the 'frustrated reformer' within the Civil Service.[156]

Like the Tank it superseded, the Unit was proud of its licence to be heterodox. 'A crucial achievement of this Government', wrote David Willetts in 1987, 'has been to roll back the frontiers of the "politically impossible." The Policy Unit, because it is directly subordinated to the most senior and astute politician of the lot, is not afraid of putting forward what might initially appear to be politically far fetched.'[157]

Intriguing though a small team operating on the fringes of the politically thinkable might be, they are few and the more cautious regulars are many. And sheer weight of numbers, tradition, continuity and the geography of power ensure that certain regulars share a considerable influence even on the most anti-bureaucratic premier of modern times. The first person a new PM sees is the Principal Private Secretary of the outgoing rival. The second is the Cabinet Secretary. The third is the Director-General of MI5 who arrives and departs discreetly, after, equally discreetly, leaving a dossier on the background of some Parliamentary colleagues which the new PM might like to read before making final ministerial dispositions.[158] On 4 May 1979, the first official to greet Mrs Thatcher after she had quoted St Francis of Assisi to the crowds outside No. 10 was Kenneth Stowe, who had served both Callaghan and Wilson before her.

Ken Stowe is a great believer in and an eloquent advocate of public service and has spoken of a particular strength of the British Civil Service as being 'a commitment and conscientiousness to the public service which will not require personal gain or personal advantage to generate high motivation and sustained performance'.[159] He fits to perfection the second postwar recruitment wave which followed the reconstruction competition generation – meritocratic scholarship boys with a high public service charge keen to run and improve the newly constructed welfare state. Stowe moved from Dagenham County High School (he grew up in a London County council overspill estate and, as he put it, 'you cannot get more non-U than that'[160]) to History at Exeter College, Oxford, and back to the East London suburbs as an assistant principal in the National Assistance Board where he began his official life cycling round Romford with cash and blankets for those in need, a rare initiation for a future permanent secretary.[161]

In machinery-of-government terms Ken Stowe likened the National Assistance Board to 'the sump of the engine – it contained the necessary lubricant but it got all the debris'.[162] He stayed there until the Social Security Act 1966, which he helped frame, united the NAB and the Ministry of Pensions and National Insurance into a new Ministry of Social Security which was, as we have seen, itself merged with the Ministry of Health two years later to accommodate the requirements of Richard Crossman. He had his first taste of Whitehall's commanding heights in 1973 at the relatively late age of forty-six when he became the Cabinet Office under secretary who prepared the briefs and took the minutes for the Cabinet's Legislation Committee, then chaired by Jim Prior. A set of curious chances moved him to the innermost circle in 1975 when Robert Armstrong was about to move from No. 10 to the Home Office. Harold Wilson, as usual, displayed an animus against the Treasury men served up as possible successors (though he always exempted Robin Butler, then a junior private secretary in Downing Street, from such taint). Wilson asked John Hunt of the Cabinet Office if he had anyone suitable to become Principal Private Secretary. Hunt recommended Stowe. Edward Short, who had succeeded Prior as Leader of the House in 1974, spoke of him with great warmth. At two hours' notice, Stowe found himself trying to talk Wilson out of appointing him on the grounds that he had spent his life on the periphery and had never been a private secretary, which made the idea of appointing him all the more appealing to the Prime Minister.

Ken Stowe's four years in No. 10 are of some importance and not just for the usual reason that an unusual degree of influence falls on an under secretary when he takes the job (they are invariably appointed to deputy secretary while in post). If, as is widely and, I think, rightly assumed, British politics polarised in the 1970s and if, as I also think, this makes it harder though not impossible to sustain the Northcote–Trevelyan specification of a neutral career service, Stowe's tenure in Downing Street between 1975 and 1979, under three very different premiers, is worth examining. Stowe himself becomes a man of secrets when asked about his prime ministers. He has, as far as I know, ventured only one public comment which was when I asked him in 1981 what was the art of being principal private secretary to the prime minister in rough times and he replied, affirming first that 'it is an art, not a science', that it 'is clear thinking, a sense of priority, coupled with a sense of urgency, an acute awareness of where the rough or sensitive point is going to arise. Coupled with that is a knowledge of how to get the best out of the resources of Whitehall.'[163]

That job description excluded the personal element, a crucial factor in the chemistry of the successful private secretary–prime minister relationship. For Stowe managed to get on well with all three and was fond of all three beyond the call of duty, though the relationship was warmest with

Callaghan whom he served the longest. According to Bernard Donoughue, 'Mr Callaghan thought the world of him.'[164] According to Callaghan, 'Perhaps the best illustration I can give of our close relationship [PM and the Downing Street private secretaries] is that although the No. 10 team has long been dispersed, some serving abroad as ambassadors or in high positions at home, we still enjoy a regular reunion to renew our friendship and exchange our news.'[165] Callaghan particularly admired Stowe's 'awesome capacity to distil the essence of conversations with visiting heads of government, without seeming to lose any nuance. His skill was that he not only remembered accurately but he also understood the inner and sometimes unspoken meaning of what had been said.'[166]

But the key to Stowe's success in becoming and remaining close to his three premiers, according to those who watched them in operation, is that he was totally loyal to each one, was utterly free of the grandeur which can sometimes afflict the higher official at the centre and was never the manipulator or entrepreneur of a particular policy line, though he was no lover of inflation and each of his trio of PMs (he joined Wilson *after* he had performed his U-turn on incomes policy) pursued as a priority their own versions of counter-inflation policy. Bernard Donoughue put his finger on the Stowe style when contrasting him with his predecessor in No. 10, Robert Armstrong: 'Stowe was an easier and simpler man, entirely without side... His great virtues were his calmness, his openness and his directness.'[167] Thanks to these virtues he did demonstrate that the career official still could move from one PM to another without strain even though the rending of the traditional fabric of British politics was approaching the deafening. After No. 10 Stowe went to head the Northern Ireland Office, returning to the DHSS, after an absence of eight years, as its permanent secretary in 1981. His last job was to inquire, at Mrs Thatcher's and Robert Armstrong's behest, into that perpetually vexed question, the distribution of Whitehall management functions at the centre. The outcome in the autumn of 1987 was the transfer of the Civil Service Department's old functions to the Treasury with the winding up of the Management and Personnel Office half-way house and its management and efficiency functions flowing where manpower, pay and pensions had already gone in 1981, back into the mightiest of the Whitehall departments,[168] though Stowe recommended a far more radical approach to the management of central government (see p. 732).

The second official to brief Mrs Thatcher on 4 May 1979 was Sir John Hunt, the Cabinet Secretary. Hunt had worked for even more premiers than Stowe. Mrs Thatcher was his fourth in six years and he had been appointed by Edward Heath, the man Mrs Thatcher was shortly and unsuccessfully to try and banish to the Washington Embassy as Churchill had done with Halifax in 1941. Hunt, as we have seen, was a great machine man, a great gripper of business, as his model, Norman Brook, had been. As Brook had with Churchill in 1951, Hunt had to explain the value of the modern Cabinet committee system to the new PM. Mrs Thatcher arrived with a firm prejudice against Cabinet committees. She would do business with her fellow ministers free of the curse of committees. Reality soon modified that prejudice.[169] Within a couple of months Mrs Thatcher had to pick Hunt's successor and chose the front-runner, Robert Armstrong, whom, when he took up the post in 1979, she found a bit of a relief after the brisk style of Hunt. As one close observer put it, 'Mrs Thatcher had an enormous respect for John, but she thought he tended to push her along when she was not quite ready ... John was always sorting things out; Robert behaves in a less autocratic manner.'[170] For his part, Hunt relished his six short months as Mrs Thatcher's Cabinet Secretary. He told his friends it had been a fascinating experience which he would not have missed.[171] When Hunt had left to pursue a second career in banking and insurance Mrs Thatcher continued to speak highly of him and regarded him as her mentor when she took up the premiership.[172]

The other partner in the Hunt–Cooper duo also relished the Thatcher phenomenon and had considerably longer to witness it in operation. He approved of her leading-from-the-front style,[173] and appreciated the value of a period of conviction politics in No. 10. 'What I think conviction politics do,' he said after his retirement, 'and do very well – and not before time in many cases – is get rid of sacred cows.'[174] But he was not convinced that 'constructive policies' were being created from the offal. Of the Thatcher governments he said in 1986 they had 'been less good at working out how and where [they go] from here and offering some kind of future which [they have] been successful in persuading people to believe in'.[175] A few months before he retired at the end of 1982, Cooper, who had, one way or another, been involved in all the limited wars fought by the British Armed Forces since 1945, was closely involved in the exercise of (if you stand where I do on the issue) conviction politics at their best in the Thatcher administration's response to the Argentine invasion of the Falklands. He was in the inner circle of the advisers to the 'War Cabinet' and involved, as one insider put it, 'in a good deal of hand-holding with the Prime Minister'[176] as the precarious military operation proceeded. He was and remained unrepentant at giving the press the impression, just before the San Carlos landings, that a D-Day style operation was not contemplated (which, in miniature, is exactly what was planned) on the grounds, with which even as a journalist I entirely sympathise, that when lives are at stake the enemy must, if possible, be deceived even at the cost of temporarily deceiving the press.

Of all the 'old guard' permanent secretaries Mrs Thatcher inherited in 1979, Sir Douglas Wass was probably the most suspect on ideological grounds. He never concealed his Keynesianism which was, in its effect on the new prime minister, rather like holding a crucifix to Dracula. He had, too, the misfortune that candour can bring when during a lecture at his old college in Cambridge in 1978 he made public his scepticism about the value of over-precise monetary targets.[177] The shadow chancellor, Sir Geoffrey Howe, was not impressed and made discreet soundings about the desirability of moving Wass if the Conservatives were returned to power.[178] For his part, Wass seemed determined to show that a principle was at stake – that an incoming government could not just sack a permanent secretary whose views it did not care for.[179] If Howe and Thatcher *had* removed Wass in May 1979, the Northcote–Trevelyan settlement would have been publicly destroyed. Wass remained until retiring age and never trimmed his views, which were always delivered in that quiet, courteous, donnish fashion of his. Mrs Thatcher and her ministerial team appeared, for their part, to quietly bypass him, taking their advice from Alan Walters in No. 10, Terry Burns, the young and influential Chief Economic Adviser recruited from the London Business School in January 1980, and Peter Middleton, Wass's eventual successor. Wass did not seem to mind too much. Indeed, before he retired at Easter 1983 the Thatcher administration had genuinely warmed to him. He had not, after all, proper old-fashioned civil servant that he was, tried to sabotage the policy. He had merely not enthused about it. (He did not care for enthusiasm in officials, as he said in his 1983 Reith Lectures.[180]) For one Thatcher intimate he became simply 'Good old Douglas, whose heart was never really in the policy'.[181] When he was about to retire, Mrs Thatcher summoned the first meeting of the now totally ceremonial Treasury Board (over which she presided as first Lord) since the 1920s to bid him farewell and to welcome his successor. Wass wore morning dress. Middleton turned up in a lounge suit.[182]

Rather meanly, Mrs Thatcher did not award Wass the peerage that has customarily gone to a retired Head of the Home Civil Service. She behaved in an identical fashion to Sir Michael Palliser who retired as Head of the Diplomatic Service in 1982, to whom she had not warmed either (though she did ask him to stay on to run the Falklands Unit in the Cabinet Office during the 1982 crisis). But Wass had remained true to Northcote–Trevelyan and to his own belief which he put rather nicely in his Reith Lectures when he said 'I like to think that our Civil Service resembles the ancient Netherlands Order of the Golden Fleece, a company whose duty it was to give advice to the Dutch ruler and to be bound by solemn oath to speak freely, honestly and under privilege.'[183] Wass, in Mrs Thatcher's terms, was never 'one of us'. But he was as true to his profession as she was to hers, a conviction official to her conviction politician.

But *the* civil servant whose name will always be synonymous with the Thatcher years is Robert Armstrong. Alone amongst the Cabinet secretaries he served but one political chief. That is not the reason why his name will ring down the years with hers as surely as does Horace Wilson's with Neville Chamberlain or William Armstrong's with Edward Heath. Though neither Wilson nor William Armstrong held the post of Cabinet Secretary. The reason is, as a fellow permanent secretary put it as the Robert Armstrong years drew to a close, 'this awful series of stinkers – GCHQ, Ponting, Westland and Wright'.[184] It is often said that permanent politicians have a secure, quiet and predictable life compared to elected ones. But who could have predicted in July 1979, when it was announced that Armstrong was to be appointed to the job for which at least the last decade of his official life had seemed a preparation, that the de-unionisation of an intelligence establishment, the trial of a disillusioned MOD assistant secretary, the financial troubles of a small helicopter firm and, above all, the obsessions of a disgruntled MI5 man would make the quiet, retiring Armstrong, while still in post, the most famous public servant since Cardinal Wolsey?

It was a family friend, that star of the wartime temporaries, Sir John Maud, who set the young Robert Armstrong on the long road to unwanted notoriety when, in the late forties, he urged him to seek a career in the Home Civil Service. Armstrong has always had a warm admiration and respect for the good and great, men like Franks and, above all, Radcliffe. As one figure who knows him well put it:

> Robert's hero is Radcliffe and Franks, too . . . I think perhaps he's tried to model himself on Radcliffe. Robert is the epitome of the Establishment. I don't think Robert would go out and risk his career for anything [this conversation took place before the Wright Affair reached the New South Wales courts]. Ian [Bancroft] and Frank [Cooper] would. They were two giants. They had fire in their bellies. Neither could be pushed over at all. Robert is a well-oiled machine man.[185]

Maud had spotted a natural. Robert Armstrong glided up the hierarchy as if on motorised castors. His great skill was as a manager of great men – secretary to the Radcliffe Committee, private secretary to Roy Jenkins, Edward Heath and Harold Wilson – rather than as a manager of great enterprises. The only faint question mark over his succeeding Hunt was the feeling that he had not, by his standards, done terribly well at the Home Office between No. 10 and the Cabinet Office. (There was a brief possibility that Palliser or Cooper might fill the Cabinet Secretaryship for a few years.[186])

As always when there is a change, comparisons between the recently departed and the new incumbent were a commonplace of the Whitehall lunch tables. People warmed more to Armstrong than they had to his predecessor, who was certainly respected and sometimes feared.

John was a man of great charm but Robert is a far nicer man in every way. People do things more readily for him. But Robert is not quite the hand John was at getting things done. John was the iron hand in the iron glove. Robert produces so much affection that everyone works well for him. He's a sympathetic figure.[187]

The physiology of the two men, oddly enough, reflected their temperamental differences. Armstrong had a boyish air (like Bridges he contrived to appear like a schoolboy almost to the end of his career). Slightly stooped and with a somewhat rolling gait, Armstrong, unlike Hunt, would never have been mistaken for a general by the sentries in Horse Guards. Both Hunt and Armstrong, however, possessed the one characteristic indispensable to those upon whom the Hankey mantle falls – a devotion to the Wells Fargo principle of always getting the Cabinet minutes through on time. I remember a conversation with a senior man about Armstrong who, like many others, found him an enigma even after three decades in Whitehall. It went as follows:

'Can you think of anything he'd resign for?'

'Nothing within the bounds of credibility. If there were a take-over by the National Front I think he would probably quit. His view of duty is "I've got to make the system work." '

'Is that enough?'

'I don't think it's enough to be a human being. It's enough to be a civil servant.'[188]

That conversation made me worry a little about the make-up of Northcote–Trevelyan man, as the man with whom it took place had also done very well by making the system work.

To be fair to Armstrong, he was well aware of the problems the crumbling of political consensus caused for the nineteenth-century model career official. Like Ken Stowe in 1979, Armstrong as Principal Private Secretary in No 10 had had to cope with a particularly sharp switch of policy when Wilson replaced Heath in 1974 and the counter-inflation strategy, by which Whitehall, too, set great store, foundered on the rock of the National Union of Mineworkers. He was worried, also, by the possibility of a British withdrawal from the EEC. In an interview with Marcel Berlins he said that if after the 1975 referendum 'Mr Wilson had taken a decision, or the Labour government of the day had taken a decision to leave the Community, I think I should have said to him "I had better not be your Principal Private Secretary any more because if I go into Europe ... associated with a programme for coming out of Europe, I shan't be credible. I've just spent $3\frac{1}{2}$ years doing the other thing. You had much better have somebody who will have more credibility." '[189] The referendum went the way Armstrong wished. He was not confronted by the dilemma and, indeed, he won high praise from Wilson's circle, Bernard Donoughue calling him 'a warm, complex and very sensitive man [who] comes professionally from the best Civil Service tradition of integrity and public duty'.[190] This 'Rolls-Royce in Whitehall' (Donoughue's description[191]) showed in 1974 as Stowe was to show in 1979 that there was genuine life left in the Northcote–Trevelyan model.

Ten years after his dilemma-that-never-was over Britain's membership of the EEC, Armstrong reflected publicly in a radio interview with Hugo Young about the difficulties political polarisation can bring. For one so cautious and discreet it was remarkable that he answered Young's probings at all. Armstrong told him:

> One difficulty I do see, I have seen, stems from what appears to be the greater degree of polarisation in British politics. If you look back, on the whole what one government did tended to be left in place by another government. That government might change direction but it didn't try to undo what its predecessors had done. That's not quite as true now as it was 30 or 40 years ago.
>
> And the polarisation has meant that the difference between – the gap between – the two main parties who provide the alternate governments is greater than it was. And I think that the business of being a professional, non-political Civil Service serving governments of whatever political persuasion is more difficult because of this polarisation ... If the polarisation changes ... if the gap narrows again, then that problem will diminish in importance. I don't think it's impossible now. I think it makes the job a little more difficult to do.[192]

Armstrong was sometimes portrayed as a Thatcherite. That was wrong. It stemmed from his traditional and genuine conviction that a permanent secretary must, having given his advice plainly and fearlessly, do the bidding of his minister and, as he once put it in a television interview, in his job he was 'as near as we come in the British system to a permanent secretary to the Prime Minister'.[193] But in so far as he ever let his own political views slip to his friends they were old-fashioned 'one nation' Conservative of the kind that prevailed when as a young Treasury assistant principal he began his long ascent up the Civil Service ladder in the early fifties. In the mid-eighties he stood where the Earl of Stockton, for whom he retained a great affection, stood. His friends were in no doubt that in Mrs Thatcher's terms, he was not 'one of us'. As one old friend put it, 'He would feel very strongly that two nations were to be avoided. The whole north–south divide in Britain he finds awfully worrying. He would definitely want to keep the nation together. Unemployment would rather shock him. He hasn't got the aggression of the Thatcherite Tories.'[194] He was sympathetic to the spirit and tone of the *It Took a Riot* paper that Michael Heseltine prepared for his Cabinet colleagues in 1981. As somebody who knows him well remembered, 'Robert was shattered by Mrs Thatcher's insensitivity in handling the riots.'[195]

Like the true nineteenth-century professional he was, Armstrong subsumed private feelings to his high sense of duty. He had, he believed, 'a clear understanding of where the role of the civil servant stops and the role of the politician begins'.[196] It made him stoical when his advice was overridden as it was in 1984 when Mrs Thatcher refused to accept the Civil Service Unions' offer of a 'no-strike' agreement at GCHQ. (Armstrong thought de-unionisation should be held in reserve and imposed the moment one radio operator took unofficial action at GCHQ or its out-stations.[197]) Armstrong was not keen, either, on her disbanding of the CPRS.[198] As a result, as one well-placed observer put it, he was 'not as close to Mrs Thatcher as some Cabinet secretaries have been to their Prime Ministers. He's not a conviction man, or at least, not her convictions. They have a different style of going about things. She needs people [like Robert] who can fix things and make things happen.'[199]

Armstrong may not have been 'one of us' but he gave ministers no grounds for moving his profession down the road towards politicisation, which, in common with all his fellow permanent secretaries, he regarded as anathema. Doing ministers' ultimate bidding, after proper confidential discussion and debate, was crucial to this, he believed. Confidentiality, itself was another indispensable element in this. Armstrong, again contrary to popular belief, was not a total closed-government man. Asked by Marcel Berlins in 1984, 'are you secretive, do you think?', Armstrong replied, 'I think my family would probably say I was, yes.' But in the same interview he outlined his wider philosophy on public access to official information:

> I would like to see more open government and I've made no secret of that in a variety of respects. But I don't think that's government-in-a-goldfish-bowl. And I think it would be very difficult to conduct the business of government in a reasonably orderly fashion if you were conducting it ... in a goldfish bowl particularly where the onlookers could throw stones in all the time. So though ... I believe that governments ought to explain the decisions which they take as fully as possible to Parliament and the public, and, if possible, more fully than they do now, I don't think that that means the process of reaching the decision should be completely open.[200]

Armstrong was sure that if a mandatory right of public access to documents was enforced, decision-making would be driven into other channels – oral or written – which were not covered by such freedom-of-information provisions.[201] His private preference was for a code of practice, not a law, which would drive a more open approach down the Whitehall line.[202] This again was a divergence of opinion from Mrs Thatcher who did not see that there was any problem in this area and, when pressed on the issue, tended to declare how much more information was being made available thanks to the new system of select committees which her administration had fostered (which was true but missed the wider point).

Leaks of various kinds blighted Armstrong's Cabinet Secretaryship – the Ponting, Westland and Wright affairs revolved around them. A year before his cycle of torment began, Armstrong tried to fill the breach following a spate of minor but embarrassing disclosures during the June 1983 general election campaign. In a letter to his fellow permanent secretaries in July 1983, Armstrong, logically enough, drew a distinction between such practices and the authorised disclosure of more official information as part of a deliberately conceived policy of greater openness and emphasised the implications for creeping politicisation of the Civil Service if the flow was not stopped. 'It is not so much a matter of the Official Secrets Acts – though no doubt these were being breached,' he told his colleagues, it was also

> 'a matter of professional duty and loyalty'. In any walk of life an employee has a duty to keep his employer's confidences and the Civil Service is no exception to that. There can be no justification or excuse for passing out a document, or indeed for orally disclosing information which is entrusted to an employee in confidence. If it is done for money, it is an act of corruption. If it is done for political or personal motives, it is an act of disoloyalty which reflects a corrupt sense of values, and the person concerned had better seek employment where he can pursue the causes in which he believes without breaching his employer's confidences: it is not for Civil Servants to play politics. Whatever the motive, the perpetrator forfeits the trust placed in him when he accepts employment and with it the right to continue in that employment.
>
> If the Civil Service is to deserve the trust which Ministers, and those who may at some future date be Ministers, have traditionally placed in it, and if it is to retain the confidence of Parliament and the public as being a non-political service of Government, we have to reassert the values and the sense of professional obligation and loyalty which will make such leaks unacceptable and unthinkable at any time. And that applies not just to the deliberately leaked document, but also to the information communicated orally to the journalist or to someone else

> outside the Service, with the intention or in the knowledge that disclosure will be damaging or embarrassing to the Government.[203]

Inevitably, the letter leaked. Armstrong was funny about this when asked about it by Paul Greengrass of Granada Television's *World in Action*: 'I was very sad that it took so long as six weeks to leak. I hoped it would leak much sooner than that.'[204]

As that remark showed, Armstrong had a lightness of touch and a self-irony far removed from the inevitable pomposity of ancient certainties reprised in letters to fellow permanent secretaries. He was not, despite public caricature and the efforts of Mr Malcolm Turnbull in a Sydney court-room, a stuffed shirt. There was, too, a mild dash of eccentricity about the man. A truncheon rested upon his desk in the Cabinet Office, a memento of his Home Office phase, and, until fairly late in his career, he would use a quill pen to execute his neat calligraphic handwriting, building up words in a memo, as one colleague put it, 'as an artist paints strokes on a canvas'.[205] And there was more than a dose of artistic passion in him, too, brought out by music in particular. In the sixties he had conducted the Treasury Singers until the demands of running Roy Jenkins's private office precluded it. Armstrong was so much the prisoner of music that he once begged William Armstrong to postpone a discussion on monetary policy as the military bands outside in Parliament Square struck up an aria from *Figaro* as a State visit passed by on its way, via Whitehall and the Mall, to Buckingham Palace.[206] Covent Garden, where he was secretary to the Board of Directors of the Royal Opera House, was a constant solace. 'Covent Garden', he once said, 'is a good contrast to the Civil Service. At 7.30 each evening the curtain has to go up on a performance to be judged by 2000 people. There is no tomorrow. In the Civil Service there is always a tomorrow and a tomorrow.'[207]

Though 'happier . . . in a kind of backroom' than in what were for him regrettably frequent appearances before select committees at Westminster, the legal profession in Australia and cameramen at airports in between (in a rare lapse of self-control he belted a *Daily Express* photographer at Heathrow in November 1986,[208] an incident which amazed his friends), Armstrong was nevertheless quite candid about the job satisfaction which came from being at the heart of government:

> Whether it's as Principal Private Secretary at No. 10, or now as Secretary to the Cabinet, there you are at the centre where these decisions are being taken, and it's very hard work, and the hours are very long, and you can use any epithet you like to describe the activity except 'boring'. It's fascinating and sometimes it's infuriating. Sometimes it's frantic. A lot of it is tremendous fun in the sense that Edward Bridges, my

> predecessor, used to say that things were fun because they were very stimulating and exciting to do.[209]

But, behind the pleasure and the excitement, the boyishness and the mild eccentricity, lay a sense of his profession and its duties which was for Armstrong as timeless as it was pellucid:

> You need to be dispassionate, you need to be thorough, you need to be able to subordinate your personal and political views to the work of your department and to the service of the government of the day. And you need to be discreet.[210]

That was his personal code and he expected his fellow Crown servants to observe it while serving or retired. When a Ministry of Defence assistant secretary flouted those canons in 1984, Armstrong, as one colleague put it, shared 'no understanding that an official like Clive Ponting might, in this day and age, kick over the traces when dealing with slippery politicians, and he could not conceive that Ponting might be acquitted by a jury'.[211] In the aftermath of that acquittal he saw his job, as he told the Commons Treasury and Civil Service Committee in November 1985, as being to help 'to steady nerves which, perhaps, had been unsteadied by some events'.[212] For him it was sufficient to restate the old verities as practised and promulgated by Fisher and Bridges.

Between his first appearance before the Mitchell Committee inquiring into the duties and responsibilities of civil servants and ministers and his second four months later, Westland erupted and his post-Ponting guidelines had proved as effective as an ethical Maginot Line in the onrush of events. None of the five officials involved, in one way and another, in No 10 and in the Department of Trade and Industry in the leaking of the Solicitor-General's letter on 6 January 1986 followed his guidelines, though Miss Colette Bowe tried to do so. She attempted to contact her Permanent Secretary, Sir Brian Hayes, who was in transit between Whitehall and the Civil Service College at Sunningdale in his official car (Sir Brian relishes such moments as a chance to get on with his work and deliberately does not have a car phone.[213]) In 'giving cover' to DTI officials to leak parts of the letter, neither Bernard Ingham, Mrs Thatcher's Press Secretary, nor Charles Powell, her Private Secretary dealing with foreign affairs and defence matters, sought guidance from their professional head of department, Robert Armstrong. Despite this, and the humiliating leak inquiry he was obliged to conduct (there was a possibility that the Law Officers would have resigned if he had not),[214] Armstrong nonetheless told the Mitchell Committee when he reappeared before them in February 1986 that he thought there was no need for a code to guide ministers in how they should conduct relationships with their officials: 'No, I do not think there is a need for that. I think these matters are well understood and I do not think it would be advantageous to have a code for ministers; certainly not if I have to write it!'[215]

Armstrong was proud of his post-Westland performances before the Treasury and Civil Service and Defence select committees. He had donned his fire-proof asbestos suit and defended both his Prime Minister and his profession under intense questioning. He felt he had got Mrs Thatcher off the rack.[216]

But appearing before select committees was one thing. Standing up on oath day after day and taking an onslaught from a far from deferential Australian lawyer, Malcolm Turnbull, with unhelpful asides from a judge, Mr Justice Powell, who seemed bent on wreaking revenge for decades of Dominion status, was quite another. The principles Armstrong was defending were the same – his own personal ones and the traditional truths outlined in his 1983 letter to permanent secretaries and his post-Ponting memorandum in 1985. Again, in person, he was taking the flak for his PM and his profession. A longstanding colleague told me at the time: 'Robert should never have gone to Sydney . . . He should have said a legally qualified person must go. Robert has no experience of cross-examination . . . When you're on oath, you haven't got the protection you have before the select committees.'[217]

Under days of aggressive cross-questioning from Malcolm Turnbull, Armstrong seemed uncharacteristically badly prepared. The reason, according to one insider, was that 'for Robert this was just something he had to fit in with 250 other things and Turnbull had been preparing for months. I think the Government completely underestimated the kind of occasion it was going to be.'[218] He was hugely damaged by having to correct earlier testimony and his typically self-ironic remark that he had been 'economical with the truth' will dog him for ever.[219] He received a hugely hostile press at home. For a highly respected commentator like Hugo Young, events in that Australian courtroom had wrecked two great offices, Armstrong's and the Attorney-General's, which were 'dragged down from the pinnacle which both have occupied for most of their history'.[220] The leader-writers were savage. For *The Observer* it was brutally simple – 'Lying abroad for one's country gets a bad name.'[221] The cartoonists had a field-day. For Gale in *The Daily Telegraph* he was depicted as 'The Naked Civil Servant', complete with briefcase, copy of Peter Wright's *Spycatcher* and a bush hat, cork's a'dangling.[222] To me he looked like Sydney Carton on the scaffold suffering a dire penalty for a lady.[223] He became a household name, his face a nightly feature on the television screen. Horace Wilson's notoriety had been confined to a small section of the political nation, as had William Armstrong's. His was public property. It was comparable only to the fall of Wolsey.

Robert Armstrong, however, did not fall. I did not expect him to.[224] There was a political spin-off which affronted that other great Armstrong canon, the ability of a career civil servant to serve political chiefs of all hues. This had been compounded by an earlier event in the summer of 1986 when it was announced that Armstrong would be staying on beyond his retiring age (which came up at Easter 1987) to take care of events through an election period. At the time Armstrong had asked Mrs Thatcher to follow precedent and consult the Leader of the Opposition as had been traditional in the appointment of past Cabinet secretaries. She refused. When Callaghan had chosen Bancroft to replace Allen as Head of the Home Civil Service in 1977 he refused to consult her. Mrs Thatcher found out and took belated revenge.[225]

Neil Kinnock criticised the government's conduct of the Wright case but refrained from attacking Armstrong personally. David Steel and David Owen were less restrained. David Steel used the occasion of Armstrong's travails in Sydney to describe him as 'damaged goods' as a result of his involvement in the GCHQ, Westland and Wright affairs.[226] David Owen, in an interview with BBC Radio 4's *Analysis* about policy-making in Opposition, said of Armstrong that 'his credibility is at a very low ebb', that he had 'become a civil servant who's very much seen as a supporter of the government' and that he could not 'see any case' for seeing Armstrong in the run-up to a general election to discuss any machinery-of-government changes the Alliance might wish to make.[227] In the event, Armstrong was still there come election time in 1987. Kinnock called on him, as did Owen and Steel (the Alliance Leaders were even filmed entering the Cabinet Office).

Armstrong had been consistent in his convictions throughout the accumulating troubles which made the inconvenience caused to John Hunt by the Crossman diaries seem trifling.[228] It will haunt his reputation for decades. He seemed surprisingly unhurt to his friends when he returned from Australia. As one put it, 'He didn't realise he'd been wounded till he got back and people came up and said "Are you all right?" because out in Australia it had been news but it hadn't been given the prominence and the slant given it here. I did admire the way that on the surface he was unfazed. Deep down? Who's to know?'[229]

But the summer of 1987 saw a degree of vindication of Armstrong's principles and values which went far beyond what must have been the quiet satisfaction of having Dr Owen turn up to consult him after all. For in choosing Robin Butler to succeed him, Mrs Thatcher was following in many ways a natural apostolic succession and ensuring that the traditional values Armstrong cherished would be enshrined in the Cabinet secretaryship and the headship of the Civil Service until the late 1990s, way beyond any likely departure of Mrs Thatcher herself. Unless her successor deliberately tore it up, the Northcote–Trevelyan settlement would endure. There was particular satisfaction for Armstrong, too, in that the headship and Cabinet secretaryship were to remain united. This was another principle he had defended through thick and thin before critical select committees. So strongly did he feel about it that he made a point in his fond, warm obituary of Burke Trend (whose death he felt very deeply in the summer of 1987[230]) of recording that Trend had 'rejoiced when the two positions were brought together again in 1981'. It was not difficult to trace in that obituary the epitaph Armstrong thought proper for those who had spent their life in his profession. 'He [Trend] was a private person, who did not become, or aspire to be, a public figure ... He was content to be appreciated by his peers and by the Ministers whom he served with self-effacement for so many years ...'[231] I am sure that Armstrong's aspirations were identical. But a list of highly public events, from GCHQ through Ponting and Westland to Wright, had conspired to deprive him of their fulfilment.

His swansong, however, was altogether in character. Three weeks before his retirement in December 1987 two carefully crafted farewell encyclicals appeared. The first was a refinement of his post-Ponting guidelines on the duties and responsibilities of ministers and civil servants. The path of complaint to be taken by an official fearing improper behaviour on the part of his political chief was mapped with greater precision:

> In the very unlikely event of a civil servant being asked to do something which he or she believes would put him or her in clear breach of the law, the matter should be reported to a senior officer or to the principal establishment officer who should if necessary seek the advice of the legal adviser to the department. If legal advice confirms that the action would be likely to be held unlawful, the matter should be reported in writing to the permanent head of the department.[232]

An official plagued by problems of conscience rather than law could raise the matter with his permanent secretary with the right 'in the last resort' of having the issue referred by his head of department to the Head of the Home Civil Service. There was still to be no right of appeal to an impartial outside figure, members of security and intelligence services excepted (see p. 474). Whatever the outcome, the secret of the grievance had to be carried to the grave. To the sanctions for speaking in this world was added the possibility of civil law proceedings. To round off the revised rules, Armstrong, ever the tidy administator, had them incorporated in the *Civil Service Pay and Conditions of Service Code*.[233]

On a more personal level his farewell took the form of a paeon of praise to the public service ethic which he tacked on to the end of a lecture on the Rayner reforms.[234] Given the traumas he had endured in the previous three years, it was genuinely moving to witness his delivery of it at Regent's College in London's Regent's Park in early December 1987. Once more he quoted Elizabeth I's words to William Cecil, words that he said he could 'never get out of my mind'. That passage, he continued:

> encapsulates the standards that are expected of members of the public service to this day . . . One of the abiding strengths of the British Civil Service is that it retains a strong sense of the values of public service and of its importance and worth, which gives civil servants pride in the discharge of their duties and sustains them when the going is rough.[235]

People were in danger of taking such values for granted. 'It would be foolish and shortsighted to do so.' It could have been Bridges talking. Robin Butler was there to hear Armstrong. It was rather like a laying-on of hands, or perhaps a passing of the torch.

The torch, inevitably, passed against a turbulent background caused by a final flurry of criticism directed at Armstrong, who, as expected, became a life peer in the 1988 New Year Honours List, an event he marked by letting the cameras photograph him and his wife at home in Somerset.[236] Within a few days of his retirement, BBC 2's *Newsnight* ran an item on the Armstrong–Butler succession in which Armstrong had to endure Lord Havers, Attorney-General at the time of the *Spycatcher* hearings in Australia, describing him as 'the natural fall-guy, the one who knew the most'; his former colleague Sir Kenneth Clucas saying, 'I think that having the Cabinet Secretary in court undergoing cross-examination, yes, I think this is bound to have damaged the public concept of the Civil Service'; and, most significant of all, his former chief, Edward Heath, saying of the Westland affair and the select committee inquiry into it, 'I would never have dreamt of asking Sir Burke Trend to go and give evidence in this way, or handle the case in the way in which Sir Robert was asked.'[237] It was a retirement almost as controversial and uncomfortable as a forced ministerial resignation.

As so often with the apostolic succession of top Whitehall jobs, those departing and those arriving had a familiarity based on long years of friendship and shared experience. Robert Armstrong had worked with Robin Butler in No. 10 during the transition from Heath to Wilson. They made a formidable team. When Armstrong left Downing Street for the Home Office in 1975, Wilson, as we have seen, was not impressed by the slate of Treasury men he was offered instead and told Douglas Allen and John Hunt that if they could not do better than that he would bump up the thirty-seven year-old Butler to the number one slot in the Private Office.[238] Wilson was very fond of Butler. There is a charming photograph in Lady Falkender's memoir of No. 10 of the party Wilson threw for Butler when he was posted back to the Treasury in 1976 to help Pliatzky bring public spending under tighter control. [239] (He developed a financial information system, known as 'fizz', to monitor spending surges department by department, month by month.[240]) For the Bernard Donoughue–Joe Haines Downing Street partnership, no lover of civil servants they, Butler was *sans pareil*. For press officer and PM's speech writer Haines, 'The principal speech writer on the official side was Robin Butler, a young private secretary who brought astonishing energy and rigid discipline to his work. He would provide the facts and the framework for the speech. My task was then to do for them what Van Meegeren did for Vermeer: forge them into a style that only an expert [Harold Wilson] might detect.'[241] Haines also warmed to Butler because of the skill and enthusiasm he applied to Haines's pet ideas on housing policy.[242] For Donoughue, Butler was simply 'the most outstanding civil servant with whom I ever had to deal, at any level'.[243] It was entirely possible to foresee in 1976 that a decade or so later Butler would fill one or other of the three 'super' permanent secretaryships in the Home Civil Service, at the Treasury, the Cabinet Office or the CSD.

Why was this? The temperament and the attractive personality were obvious enough. He was, without doubt, a Renaissance prince, First Class Honours in Greats and a Rugby blue at Oxford, but he was Renaissance man without arrogance or hauteur. A Renaissance prince would not have continued to cycle to work, even as a permanent secretary, on a rusty old bike of the kind favoured by undergraduates in ancient universities. (The Butler bike became a bit of a legend: in 1983 he pedalled to the Palace on it to discuss the dissolution of Parliament prior to the election and was stopped by a policeman as he tried to ride back down the Mall during a rehearsal of Trooping the Colour.[244]) He never grew grand, either, remaining what in fact he had been, an enthusiastic public school head boy whose conversation was peppered with 'goshes' and 'supers'. He kept up the sport, too, captaining the Mandarins XI for several years as a stylish batsman ('You could tell he'd spent years playing on manicured wickets – that tranquil, effortless confidence', said one former opponent on the pitch),[245] and continued to play squash every week with his fellow permanent secretary, Sir Michael Quinlan.

A school friend from Harrow days said of Butler, 'He would never challenge authority. He would always keep a straight bat, never play across the line.'[246] For years I saved up a Harrow story for the day Robin Butler inherited one or other of the great bureaucratic kingdoms, and being no longer a daily journalist when it happened in the summer of 1987, I gave it to *The Independent*. It was this, as *The Independent*'s Andrew Marr reported it:

> Butler was captaining his house team in the obscure sport of Harrow football. They went one goal up early on and Butler spent the rest of the match sitting on the ball while both sides fought furiously over him. Eventually he was carried off, bloodied but unbowed, without another goal having been scored. No one was quite sure whether this was a splendid example of house spirit or sharp practice.[247]

It was entirely typical of the man, in this reply to a letter from me, for him to write:

> I can't remember whether I told you the story about Harrow football or you got it from someone else. Anyway it is true and I suppose that it is character-revealing. The point is that kneeling on the ball was within the rules. The convention was that you then stood up and struggled forward. My innovation was to notice that the rules didn't require you to do so. When I next see you I will demonstrate![248]

Butler's physical bravery, like that of his Prime Minister, is not in doubt. He was with her in the Grand Hotel, Brighton, the night the IRA tried to blow up the British Cabinet during the 1984 Conservative Party Conference. Indeed, his appetite for hard work is said to have saved her life when at ten to three in the morning he asked her to read just one extra brief which meant she was still in her sitting room when the bomb went off.[249]

To turn from the serious to the hilarious, it was a different kind of explosion which, metaphorically speaking, first brought the young Robin Butler, newly arrived at the Treasury from Oxford, into direct contact with the ultimate glittering prize of the Cabinet secretaryship. As Lawrence Marks, *The Observer*'s ace profile writer, described it:

> Butler was playing Peter Wimsey in the Treasury Players' production of Dorothy L. Sayers' 'Busman's Honeymoon'. Its dénouement occurred when a booby-trapped aspidistra plant shattered the glass bowl of a standard lamp on stage, surprising the murderer into confessing. Butler, a perfectionist, thought the smash insufficiently dramatic, and introduced some mechanical improvements.
>
> Their effect was impressive. The glass bowl catapulted into the second-row stalls where it exploded on Normanbrook's head. Fortunately, when the splinters were picked out of him, the great man was found to be unharmed, and Butler's career resumed its climb.[250]

But there was much more to Butler than the winnin' ways of a contemporary Peter Wimsey in the personal make-up which carried him to the Cabinet Office and the headship of his profession (though it was certainly a chivalrous spirit worthy of Wimsey which persuaded Butler to attend a *Private Eye* lunch to put them right about a friend they were unjustly pillorying – a *very* brave thing for an ambitious young official to do[251]. After all, he had a formidable and accomplished rival for the job in Sir Clive Whitmore who shone as Mrs Thatcher's Principal Private Secretary between the Stowe and the Butler years.

At the time of the 1983 general election one prescient senior man predicted, against the current informal odds, that Butler, not Whitmore, would eventually succeed Armstrong, though he reckoned it would be a close-run thing. 'Robin is a better all-rounder than Clive', he said.

> The personal qualities of Robin will just about tell. He's a more eager beaver. Ken and Clive had a relaxed style. Robin is a get-up-and-go man all the time. And he's different from Robert. Although Robert has a good manner with people, he doesn't identify with the rank-and-file in the manner that Robin does. Ken and Clive are at heart both big managers. Their forte is management. Robin's and Robert's forte is policy – it's partly their genesis in the Treasury – and the Cabinet Office is really a policy department.[252]

Intriguingly, Whitmore in the No. 10 Private Office was tougher with Mrs Thatcher than Butler, as one insider put it, 'because she was on a learning-curve, too, when he joined her in 1979'.[253] And, as Cooper's successor at Defence, he was still deemed to be the front-runner for the Cabinet Office when the choice of Butler was announced in the summer of 1987. Quite apart from Butler's qualities, the feeling within Whitehall was that Whitmore was pipped at the post for a number of reasons: there was no obvious successor at MOD and Quinlan had seemed too near retirement to return (though this is exactly what happened in the spring of 1988); there were suggestions that Mrs Thatcher was not pleased at Whitmore's failure to calm down Heseltine when the pressure was rising over Westland (which is most unfair, as a permanent secretary's loyalty must be to his secretary of state's cause); it was also suggested that it is most unlikely that a Defence man would ever get the senior umpire's job in the Cabinet Office, as the MOD is a controversial department whichever party is in power.[254]

It would, however, be wrong to assume that Butler is 'one of us' in Mrs Thatcher's terms. 'He doesn't fit any category,' says a friend, 'but he's certainly not a Thatcherite. He would regard it as slightly off-side to make a political value judgment in Whitehall. He's not a great philosopher, not a great original thinker.'[255] There was no question of Butler's conspicuous suitability for what Burke Trend once called 'the bread and butter of the job – ensuring that [the] flow of government business up through committees to the Cabinet itself goes forward as quickly and as smoothly as it possibly can'.[256] As a long-time Butler-watcher put it, 'Robin is very good at administration. If a minister says "I want this done," he is brilliant at calling a meeting, making it clear how he thinks business should proceed, consulting all the concerned departments represented round the table and parcelling out the work. He prides himself enormously on it.'[257]

Butler, like Armstrong, could have been picked as head of his profession at any time since 1870. He fitted the Northcote–Trevelyan specification to a tee, but, as one insider put it, 'he is sufficiently twentieth century to say we've got to have more efficiency and let's not be too squeamish about things like merit pay'.[258] He is thoroughly and admirably nineteenth-century, however, in his even-handed ability to get on with ministers of all possible hues. 'He looks at his political masters as men, not political puppets. He wouldn't go along with unethical behaviour, though, and he is prepared to tell ministers when they are being perverse.'[259] He does it with great charm, and charm is always a great seasoner of palatability, as Lord Rothschild knew when he picked Butler to put the more uncomfortable findings of the CPRS to its ministerial customers. He remained devoted to Rothschild and organised a party to cheer him up in 1987 when it seemed as if he might be prosecuted in connection with the Wright affair. And it was Rothschild who inspired Butler to declare his view of the job when he wrote on the 1972 team picture of the Tank, 'To Victor, who reminded me that government should be fun and should deal in big ideas'.[260]

Butler certainly cares about the condition of government. His friends believe that, ingrained though the traditional virtues of his profession were, he could not hand over his Service to his successor in the same condition as he found it. 'I think he does care about the Service', said one. 'He will be torn. It's an impossible task to be the Prime Minister's confidante *and* create the kind of Service she might not be happy with.'[261]

Robin Butler, after all, inherited a Civil Service with its morale at its lowest ebb in living memory. He knew that, and by no stretch of the imagination could he be content to maintain such a dismal, depressing *status quo*. One of his first acts as head of profession was to initiate visits to Civil Service establishments all over the country. Armstrong had given about a quarter of his time to his duties as Head of the Civil Service and three-quarters to the Cabinet Secretaryship. With Butler, the time devoted to the Civil Service in his first two months was 'closer to 50 per cent'.[262] The reason, as he explained to the Treasury and Civil Service Committee, was that the Prime Minister had relieved him of the so-called 'Sherpa' duties which precede an economic summit.

I have been relieved of those duties and that is a great help because one of the difficulties about combining the two jobs is that the Secretary to the Cabinet is, of course, the servant of the Cabinet and has to make himself available to the Cabinet and its committees. One of the times when one can be confident that one can be free to get out and go round the Civil Service and pay them visits – which is just one part of the job but quite an important part – is when the Prime Minister has commitments overseas.[263]

The Butler visits had a discernible impact on morale generally because they were reported in the press. The impression abroad, rightly or wrongly, was that he had made more visits in his first two months than Armstrong had managed in his entire period as Head of the Civil Service. But the problem about discussing morale is that it cannot be measured and, therefore, for some social scientists more attuned to counting than to reading, it does not exist. Mass Observation tried throughout the war to measure home front morale on behalf of the Ministry of Home Security.[264] Its presiding genius, Tom Harrisson, years later would treat laughter in the then packed cinemas as a key indicator and, on that basis, the greatest single contributor to morale was George Formby in *Let George Do It* when the moon-faced ukeleleist was parachuted into the middle of a Nuremberg Rally and socked Hitler on the jaw to the delight of assembled storm-troopers.[263] People like Tom Harrisson tend not to write about the public service. Such fun is not permitted. When Dr Chris Painter of Birmingham Polytechnic presented what I thought was an excellent paper on Whitehall morale at a scholarly conference in 1981 he was roundly critcised by some of his academic peers for being unscientific.[264]

Unmeasurable or not, it was a problem. In 1986, David Young, a former high-flyer in the MOD and the Cabinet Office, said in a television interview that 'the morale of the Civil Service is certainly at the lowest point that I've known it in twenty years and that can't be good'.[265] Shortly before Mr Young made this remark, Sir Robert Armstrong had gone as close as he dared to making the same point in an exchange with a Conservative MP, Mr John Townend, during a session of the Commons Treasury and Civil Service Committee:

'Whilst they were giving evidence to the Committee both Mr Callaghan and Mr Heath expressed concern at the morale at the present time in the Civil Service: do you feel there is a problem?'

'I think there is a problem, yes.'

'What do you think should be done about it?'

'I think that is a matter on which I have to advise Ministers. I find it rather difficult to speak on this without, as it were, appearing to disclose the advice I have given to Ministers or might give to Ministers.'

'We had better move on to another subject as you do not wish to answer that one.'

'Could I add it is one of the penalties, I think, of being a Permanent Secretary, let alone Head of the Civil Service, that you do feel a sense of responsibility for these matters but that the advice you give on them has to be, as it were, behind closed doors – that does not mean you do not give it.'[266]

That there was a morale problem which affected all ranks, including the topmost, was undeniable. The steady haemorrhage of top young talent demonstrated it beyond argument. The Prime Minister implicitly recognised it, too, when the Efficiency Unit undertook an examination of the problem in 1986 as part of its preparation of *The Next Steps*.[269]

And in September 1987 the Civil Service Commission launched a recruiting drive with the avowed intention of filling the gap left by the gifted departed. The most severe breaches needing to be filled were at Education and Environment. The Treasury and the DTI were also in the market. In all at least fifty-five recruits of principal rank were being sought with experience in education, local government and commerce.[270] The proposed pay scale – £15,000 to £21,000 – stimulated a 'We get what we pay for' leading article in *The Independent* which put its finger firmly on the 'market' problem such salaries were certain to create. 'The public image of the Civil Service will not start to recover', it declared, 'until the Government dares to vary rates of pay much more widely ... so that everyone gets what is needed to find and keep the right people.'[271] The outflow was both difficult to measure and potentially misleading when it was measured. It was more a matter of quality than of quantity, though in 1985 BBC Radio 4's *Analysis* had calibrated the Treasury's loss of 'crack troops' since 1981 as 'close to fifty'. As Hugo Young, presenter of that programme, *The Vanishing Mandarins*, put it:

Not long ago it was just about the smartest job in town. Mandarins, whether budding in their thirties or blooming in their fifties, were deeply respected, alike for their brains and their effortless self-esteem. To have managed to get into the Service was an achievement in itself. Once there, the ablest people, almost without exception, stayed for life. Until the tides of success carried them into a permanent secretary's chair. Upon this expectation rested a large part of the famous British administrative tradition. That remained true throughout the 1970s. But it's not true now. The Civil Service is no longer smart, no longer possessed of much self-esteem, no longer unfailingly respected – and can no longer keep its best people for life.[272]

The kind of people the Civil Service, and, therefore, the Efficiency Unit, were particularly concerned about losing were men like Norman Warner and Gerry Grimstone, the duo whose Rayner scrutiny on benefit payments had led to the rural post-masters making their Pilgrimage of Grace. The chief reason Warner left the DHSS to run Kent County Council's Social Services Department was his desire for 'more freedom of manoeuvre and more ability actually to manage things under my own control'.[273] The context in which he placed his decision to go was particularly worrying for Whitehall's management revolutionaries, as few people were more *au fait* with Raynerism than Norman Warner:

> I'd spent nearly $2\frac{1}{2}$ decades in the DHSS and I found the thing rather claustrophobic. I was beginning to feel that the Civil Service was not serious about rewarding people who were good managers and I didn't find it easy to practise the sort of management skills that I'd developed. So I thought it better to move out, plus the fact that I was able to get more money which is always a consideration.[274]

For Gerry Grimstone, who left the Treasury for a merchant bank, it was the equivalent of the nun's story, a powerful desire to climb over the wall:

> It was a case of having spent fourteen years in the same job. I thought it was time for a change. You are rather cut-off from outside influences in the Civil Service. I think you get to the point where you really want to see what life is like outside as well as having had a very good experience of what life is like inside.[275]

For some, the spur to evacuate was provided by the decline they perceived in the type and quality of policy work they were expected to provide after the Conservatives returned to power. Dr Charlie Bean was an economist who quit the Treasury for the London School of Economics, a move which, unlike a transfer to the City or even local government, would probably not have meant more money. Dr Bean told Hugo Young in 1985:

> I think the nature of the job of an economics adviser had changed quite substantially between early 1979 and my return from the United States. Morale in the Treasury was really very good, certainly among the economists. I may not be able to speak generally about the Treasury, but the economic forecasting divisions and the like were very happy places to work under the previous administration. And it was very noticeable when I came back two years later that morale had dropped quite significantly for the economists. They felt that the sort of work

they were doing was much more in the nature of justification of politics rather than serious analysis of different policy options.[276]

It was not just in the front line of economic policy-makers, Mrs Thatcher's priority, that disillusion was setting in. David Young, who left the MOD for the John Lewis Partnership, was crucially involved in the Whitehall battles over defence spending after 1979. He was regarded inside the Ministry as a near certainty for one of its top handful of jobs in the 1990s, yet he went in 1982. 'It's certainly true that the thought of going through another four or five defence reviews before I retired didn't thrill me and I wanted to do something different.'[277] The manner in which business was conducted did not appeal to him either:

> One of the things that bothered me was the way that Whitehall plays it as a game rather than trying to arrive at the best possible decision in the national interest. I can illustrate that by an occasion when we made a bit of an error in Defence over the calculation of a particular figure and it wasn't until close to publication that we realised what we'd done. And when I talked to my Treasury opposite number the reply was 'Ah, I wondered if you'd spot that'. That bothers me because it isn't a game. It is a very serious business ... There is too much fighting of the departmental case.[278]

There were a sizeable bundle of factors, largely though not wholly associated with 'de-privileging' the Civil Service, which sapped morale at all levels, not just at the top. Mrs Thatcher did not have it all her own way on the de-privileging front. The committee she established in 1981 under the industrialist, Sir Bernard Scott, to examine the value of public service pensions did not, to her dismay, come up with the recommendation that they should be de-indexed, and inflation-proofing remained,[279] though the issue lost its venom and its high profile as inflation was progressively squeezed out of the economy. Pay was a different matter.

An inquiry chaired by Sir John Megaw came up with the kind of recommendation Mrs Thatcher had been wanting – a decisive move away from the post-Priestley system of comparability with analogous work outside and its replacement with a more fluid decentralised arrangement embracing regional differences, productivity incentives and rewards related to performance.[280] In the envenomed circumstances of Whitehall industrial relations, it was inevitable that the Megaw recommendations should be seen by the Civil Service unions as another instrument of 'de-privileging' intended in the end to depress their relative remuneration still further. It took more than six years for a single union to make a deal which reflected, in part at least, the new ground-rules when the professionals' association, the IPCS, came to terms with the Treasury. They had the most to gain, given the often scarce skills of their members.

The possibility opened up of new deals with 55,000 tax specialists embracing performance pay, regional variations and annual comparability studies and of a further accommodation with 17,000 office support staff across the Civil Service. But by the end of 1987 there was still no prospect of long-term pay agreements with the big battalions represented by the NUCPS and the CPSA, and the new pay order covered a mere 80,000 officials, less than one-sixth of the Civil Service as a whole.[281] And given the morale and image problems besetting Whitehall as a whole, it remained a very moot point whether any of the new pay arrangements would adequately meet the Megaw requirement that 'the governing principle for a Civil Service pay system in the future should be to ensure that the Government as an employer pays civil servants enough, taking one year with another, to recruit, retain and motivate them to perform efficiently the duties required of them at an appropriate level of competence'.[287] The problem was acknowledged publicly by Robert Armstrong a few weeks before his retirement when he recognised that 'it is widely felt in the Civil Service that policies of pay restraint have borne with especial severity on the Civil Service, even when compared with other public services, and that as a result civil servants have fallen behind other people in terms of earnings. That perception, too, has a depressing effect on morale.'[283] The Government's withdrawal of the old-style pay system based on comparability provoked the 1981 strike and led to an unhappy, scrappy quinquennium of half-free collective bargaining, an outcome unsatisfactory to both sides.

Another, though delayed, casualty of the 1981 strike was the right of employees at the Government Communications Headquarters to belong to trade unions. Whatever the unions claimed, the strike *had* seriously disrupted the flow of signals intelligence into the Cheltenham headquarters and its outstations around the world and, understandably, enraged the United States National Security Agency with whom there were long-standing arrangements for pooling the product. Shortly after the dispute, the Director of GCHQ, Sir Brian Tovey, and his establishment officer, Mr Derek Wakefield, prepared a plan to rid GCHQ of unions and to bring it into line with MI5 and MI6.[284] The proposal reached the Permanent Secretaries' Intelligence Steering Committee. Its advice to the Prime Minister, in the framing of which Cooper and Wass were the dominant voices,[285] was that the benefits of de-unionisation were not worth the fuss it would cause. With the departure of Cooper and Wass into retirement, the PSIS's advice changed. De-unionisation of GCHQ was announced, to general surprise and widespread condemnation, in January 1984. Armstrong, who, as we have seen, favoured a no-strike agreement as a first step, conducted negotiations with the Council of Civil Service Unions, who with strong leadership from Bill McCall of the IPCS offered a no-strike agreement. It did not deflect Mrs Thatcher from her purpose. Unions were banned.

The de-unionisation of GCHQ caused genuine outrage and not just in the expected quarters of the TUC and the Labour Party. It seemed to many within the higher Civil Service itself to be an arbitrary and, given McCall's offer, an unnecessary step. There was great sympathy for the recusants of Cheltenham who enjoyed high calibre and dignified leadership from individuals such as Nancy Dufton, Michael King, Jeremy Windust and Kit Braunholtz. It did nothing to improve the relationship between employer and employed in Whitehall. The number holding out at Cheltenham dwindled to about thirty in three years, but, with successive appeals to courts in Britain and Europe, persistent sympathy from the entire trade union movement (which was split on virtually everything else) and pledges from all the Opposition parties to reverse the ban, the issue did not die. It will always be an item in any audit of the Thatcher years.

In overall Whitehall terms, that audit consists of contrasts. There was great turbulence among the personnel of the Civil Service and the methods used in fulfilling their routines. It is mistaken, in my view, to portray Mrs Thatcher as the politiciser of Whitehall and destroyer of the Gladstonian settlement. The reality was much less crude, except in the sense that it was all of a piece with what Rudolf Klein called 'the aggressive contempt which Mrs Thatcher reserves for all traditional institutions, whether the Civil Service or the professions, and leads her to deal with them like an obsessional housewife clearing out lumber from the attic',[286] though it was of considerable importance in what it might presage. After all, there *was* sufficient *prima facie* evidence of creeping politicisation to enable a future and less fastidious administration of Left or Right to make a fairly impressive fist of constructing a precedent from it. The reforms associated with Derek Rayner, however, did represent a substantial and seemingly long-lasting shift from previous practice and performance.

By contrast, the years after 1979 were a period of considerable stability in the structure of central government. Shortly after his retirement in 1987, Lord Hailsham disclosed 'that a radical reform of our constitution was not on her agenda in 1979 and the need for it has not reappeared since 1979'. He explained that 'after we got in in 1979, there were a number of more or less formal meetings of Ministers to discuss the question of constitutional change . . . The agenda was such that you had to choose between carrying out the programme which we'd been elected to carry out and indulging in some form of constitutional change.'[287]

The kind of constitutional change Lord Hailsham was discussing in October 1987 was reform of the House of Lords. But it is clear that the thinking among Mrs Thatcher and her ministers applied equally well to fundamental changes in the configuration of Whitehall, the structure of departments, and the relationship between ministers and officials. Indeed, change in the pattern of departments was minimal, almost, one suspects, as a deliberate symbol that it was no Wilson or Heath in No. 10. Where Wilson would have established a new ministry, Thatcher despatched her 'Overlord for all Seasons', Lord Young of Graffham, to take over the policy, spin a new one or reknit a skein of existing ones.[288] She became very fond, however, of setting up special task forces or seminars, as on crime prevention in 1986 and broadcasting in 1987, or creating new Cabinet committees for the purpose as with nationalised industries in 1981, Aids in 1986 and inner cities in 1987.

There were a few exceptions to the stability rule, as with the abolition of the Civil Service Department in 1981 and the re-merger of the Department of Trade and the Department of Industry after the 1983 general election. (The demise of the Central Policy Review Staff was in a different category.) Life was more precarious, however, in the secondary institutions of the bureaucratic fringe. A much publicised quango-cull was launched by the Prime Minister and led by Sir Leo Pliatzky in 1979. It bagged 30 executive bodies (out of 489), 211 advisory bodies (out of 1,561) plus a handful of tribunals. It got rid of 250 jobs and saved £11.6m a year.[289] And that government-funded Albert Memorial to the greatly decried corporatism of the sixties and seventies – the National Economic Development Council – was virtually dismantled by Mrs Thatcher as one of the first acts of her third term.[290] Perhaps only her wish to spare Neddy's progenitor, Harold Macmillan, unnecessary pain had stayed her hand so long (Macmillan had died six months earlier), as NEDC was the incarnation of everything she despised about the much parodied and, to my mind, overly-vilified, corporatist *ancien régime*.

She was, however, consistent in her convictions if usually cautious and gradualist in the application of them. As she proudly and now legendarily told her 1980 Party Conference, 'the Lady's not for turning'. The Whitehall version of the U-turn theory, as outlined to me by a permanent secretary in the late 1970s, used to run like this: 'For the first twelve months of a new Government, Ministers are very suspicious of us, convinced we are in the pockets of their outgoing rivals. Gradually they begin to realise both that that is not so and that they need us. If you're lucky you then get eighteen months to two years of good government. But as the shadow of the next election looms they start behaving in a political fashion again.'[291] It was possible to apply the permanent secretary's theory to the Heath administration (election 1970, U-turn 1972) and the last Wilson administration (election 1974, U-turn 1975). Callaghan was different, taking over in mid-administration very largely on the basis of business-as-usual. The theory, however, was in fragments by Budget Day 1981 which saw a further deflationary twist in an already deepening economic recession. By 1987 it was folk-memory.

She did not turn, either, on her two-lane approach to Whitehall reform – the de-privileging of the profession and the re-skilling of its professionals in a firmly managerial direction. But it was essentially a monochromatic view of reform. She turned her face firmly against major institutional change, though there was a brief flirtation with the idea of a Prime Minister's Department, which, had it happened, would have been an institutional and constitutional change of the first order comparable to Lloyd George's creation of the Cabinet Office in 1916. There was no systematic attempt seriously to alter the mix of regulars and irregulars or old and new blood. Nor were the hard tests of Raynerism applied to such areas as the policy-making process itself or to the performance of Cabinet government. These were 'no-go' areas in 1979 and remained so. Political will would be enough. Such matters, therefore, were 'non-problems' to the Prime Minister, the only figure in the constellation of power capable of challenging or altering them. Mrs Thatcher's approach to Whitehall reform was a classic manifestation of conviction politics: icons were there for the toppling but very little was done to create something new from the fragments. She was a singular politician. Professor Sammy Finer was right in his assessment of her: that 'she falls short of greatness, but she radiates dominance. I do not believe in our lifetime we shall ever look upon her like again.'[292] She dominated Whitehall but she did not, despite the genuine successes of Raynerism, transform it. That task would have to wait for other, more imaginative but equally determined hands. In Civil Service terms, twentieth-century Whitehall still awaits its second Lloyd George.

PART FIVE THE FUTURE

> Compare the story of Britain in the 20th century with that of her supposedly successful competitors, France or Germany or Japan. They made a ghastly hash of their countries, alongside which Britain, whether due to the qualities of her people and institutions or to her insular character or more likely to the combination of both, came relatively unscathed through immense transitions and vicissitudes: we defeated our aggressors, we preserved our constitution and we humbugged our way with self-satisfaction through everything. I say: beat that if you can.
> **Enoch Powell, 1987**[1]

Concluding sections of lengthy works are daunting prospects for authors. At the back of one's mind is the feeling that it ought to be like the fourth movement of Beethoven's Choral Symphony – an all-embracing crescendo which absorbs and then surpasses all the sensations and impressions that have gone before. No treatment of Whitehall, however, can expect to finish with an unambiguous ode to joy. Nor can it hope to strike resounding, unqualified themes that command universal approbation.

The way I have decided to tackle it is twofold: a fairly long assessment of performance and a short final burst laying out personal ideas for reform. Assessing performance is especially difficult as satisfactory comparative indicators are very hard to come by. I have three goes at it: another look at Whitehall's place in the 'Great Decline' debate; a pair of case-studies; and a section dealing with the late-1980s debate about the alleged postwar causes of current discontents and the rethink of the 1945 settlement which is beginning to chip away at even the most stone-clad of its artefacts, the National Health Service.

16 ASSESSING PERFORMANCE

The Civil Service is, in fact, all that its most ardent supporters crack it up to be, like the Brigade of Guards, the Bank of England, the judiciary, and many other typically British institutions. But it is very close to the seat of power, and because of the eclipse of Britain, its influence must be closely studied, for, despite its many virtues, its operations must bear some of the responsibility for what has been happening in the past thirty years.
Lord Hailsham, 1978[1]

Our present Civil Service is not interested in growth. It is geared to care and maintenance.
Tony Benn, 1965[2]

For a British civil servant, there is no problem so acute that it won't yield to a careful piece of drafting.
Senior Australian civil servant, 1984[3]

The Civil Service has stayed, at least as far as its top ranks are concerned, a civilised Oxbridge elite, free from party entanglement, but exercising vast political power.
David Butler, 1987[4]

When it comes to sniffing out the 'dilemmas of democracy', few have a more sensitive nose than Lord Hailsham. In a book of that title published in the late 1970s, remarkable for the urgency and intensity with which it diagnosed the contemporary ills of the British Constitution, he turned out to be a doughty defender of 'the morale, the discipline [and] the independence of our administrative civil servants'.[5] Nonetheless, he depicted in primary colours the core problem of our permanent politicians – their possession of power to a degree not balanced by their public responsibility.

His assessment of the career Civil Service, written after eleven years' experience as a Cabinet minister (he was to acquire another eight), is one of the finest expositions I have read of the power we place in the hands of our appointed rulers. The administrative class of the Civil Service, wrote Hailsham, is:

> surely one of the most talented bodies of men ever to be engaged in the art and science of civil government, recruited from the cream of the universities, selected by examination and interview, trained in political impartiality and secretiveness, rewarded for industry far beyond the calls of duty, advanced for efficiency, and gaining during the experience of a working lifetime more than the most able and experienced minister can summon to his task.[6]

After the panegyric came the barb:

> Of all political administrators they are most like the class of guardians in Plato's Republic, in all things save one. Unlike those guardians, they do not openly bear responsibility for what is done. That must be borne by the minister whom they tend and feed, and strip of the necessary decisions as the worker bees in the hive tend and strip the queen of her eggs as she is led with docility round the cells.[7]

Hailsham is right to assert that their constitutional position, sheltered behind the wall of ministerial responsibility, cannot shield the senior Civil Service from some of the culpability for Britain's postwar problems. Yet apportioning blame, even in crude terms, is extraordinarily difficult to do without falling into the distorting traps of prejudice and scapegoating. It is necessary, therefore, to begin by recognising what the British Civil Service is good at in comparison to some of its counterparts overseas. The most accurate, and impressive, tribute to its virtues I have encountered comes from Stephen Taylor, the management consultant and, though a former member of the profession, one of its most astringent critics in the 1980s. In LWT's *Whitehall* he said:

> It's not corrupt; it's not politicised; it's not grossly inefficient and it's not stupid and those are not things you can say about the civil service of most other countries . . . Those are positive things and we're at great danger if we take those things for granted.[8]

I would not quibble with a syllable of that assessment. But it is not a complete audit, as Mr Taylor knows better than most.

In the preceding chapters I have endeavoured to tell the story of the Civil Service, highlighting both its virtues and blemishes as I have done so. At risk of labouring the point, the downside of Stephen Taylor's audit would read something like this: Whitehall is closed, secretive, defensive, over-concerned with tradition and precedent, still too preoccupied with advising ministers on policy and enhancing their performance in Parliament, still insufficiently seized of the crucial importance of managing people and money and nothing like as good as it should be, given the proportion of prime British brainpower it possesses, at confronting hard long-term problems by thinking forward systematically and strategically.

Such sentiments, the stuff of countless leading articles in quality newspapers, roll off the pen with ease. Of themselves they are not enough. They are, however, all that is on offer because an assessment of the Civil Service's overall performance since 1945 is very difficult to make. There are a number of reasons for this. The story is a mixed one; the good, the bad and the mediocre combine in a fashion difficult to separate out. The best approach to the question is to tackle it at various levels.

The big question is the one posed by Lord Hailsham: to what extent must Whitehall 'bear some of the responsibility for what has been happening in the past thirty years?' In answering that question it would be possible to mount a quick, prejudiced dash over four decades and to scoop up a lorryload of howlers – Foreign Office's alleged advice against accepting Volkswagen's Wolfsburg plant as reparations after the war as, in sales terms, 'The Beetle' had meagre prospects;[9] the Treasury's confident advice in 1955–6 that nothing serious would come out of the negotiations about a putative Common Market of the six;[10] and the grim catalogue of political, intelligence and diplomatic failures laid out in the Franks Report on the origins of the Falklands War.[11] Again, this is as easy as it is facile. In general terms, it is impossible to winnow out Whitehall's share of culpability for forty years of relative economic and industrial under-achievement or failings in foreign and defence policy with any degree of certainty or objectivity.

The nearest I have ever come to laboratory conditions in which to pursue the Hailsham autopsy were created at Nuffield College, Oxford, in November 1987 at a conference on comparative postwar economic performance organised by the Institute of Contemporary British History.[12] After hearing from Dr Frances Lynch of the University of Manchester Institute of Science and Technology about the 'thirty glorious years of government sponsored investment' in France after 1945 and from Professor Ian Nish of the London School of Economics about the interventionist role of the bureaucracy in Japan's 'great transformation' between 1945 and 1962, I asked the assembled experts if the quality of a country's civil service was a crucial ingredient in its economic success.

Not one thought it was. I was especially interested in the verdict of David Henderson, a former chief economist at the Ministry of Aviation and now, as head of economics and statistics at OECD, very well placed to make comparisons. As Professor of Political Economy at University College, London, a decade ago, he launched the most devastating critique I have ever heard on the quality of analysis and decision-taking in Whitehall with a study of Concorde and the advanced gas-cooled reactor programme. In a series of broadcasts, entitled suggestively *The Unimportance of Being Right*, on BBC Radio 3 he called them two of the three worst civil procurements in the history of mankind (the third being the Russian version of Concorde).[13] Yet at Nuffield, even David Henderson gave the Whitehall mandarinate a conditional discharge. 'I'm not sure', he said, 'that in the British case it's been a major influence on economic performance. Insofar as it has been, it has been to do with ideas that were held outside the Civil Service as well . . . The British Civil Service has something to answer for in its closed nature and the way it has not reacted to evidence. But it is very easy to overdo the extent to which you can blame economic performance on the administrators.'

Certainly in setting the Whitehall of Sir Edward Bridges and Sir Norman Brook against the bureaucracies of Paris and Tokyo in the 1940s and 1950s, one is not comparing like with like. French and Japanese civil servants were decisive and impressive because the politicians were either transient as in France or inexperienced as in Japan. Postwar British governments were neither of these. The only way the mettle of Whitehall could be tested retrospectively against the bureaucracies of early postwar Japan and Fourth Republic France would be for the British ministerial class to go under. And that would be too high a price to pay for any experiment, however intriguing the results. I must admit, though, that the practical consequences of the Northcote–Trevelyan tradition make me sceptical about the capabilities of British civil servants as surrogate entrepreneurs, far-sighted long-term planners and versatile, successful interventionists had conditions comparable to postwar Japan or France prevailed in the United Kingdom during the first decade after the war. The occasional Otto Clarke apart, the British breed was deficient in people keen to seize or capable of seizing the initiative in such circumstances. The British tradition was geared to producing what officials said they were – servants rather than masterful figures.

Ironically, in the case of Concorde, which was an Anglo-French collaboration, the French technocracy pushed hard in favour of the project while their British equivalents, in the Treasury at least, strained every sinew in the vain attempt to stop it getting off the ground in the early 1960s.[14] By the mid-1970s when Labour returned to power *every* Whitehall ministry, including its sponsoring department, Industry, wanted to finish off Concorde.[15] Official Whitehall was overridden by a Cabinet decision which, constitutionally, is exactly as it should be. At the ICBH seminar in Nuffield College, David Henderson admitted that in the case of these two costly errors, 'both Concorde and the Advanced Gas Cooled Reactor were supported by both parties and by the public as well'.

In the energy field generally, forecasting has been a nightmare not confined to the 'Shiver with Shinwell and Starve with Strachey era'. Reginald Maudling, who as Paymaster-General spoke for the Macmillan government on energy matters in the House of Commons (the Minister of Fuel and Power, Percy Mills, was in the House of Lords), was characteristically candid in his memoirs about the inadequacy of the post-Suez rethink on energy supplies:

> Our plans were carefully laid on the best estimates available to us from public and private sources. I remember making a big speech in the House of Commons about the future pattern of Britain's energy consumption. It created a considerable impression as I was able to go into very detailed estimates of future consumption trends in a fairly lengthy speech, made, as was my custom then, without any use of notes.
>
> The only trouble was that all the figures I gave turned out in the event to be wrong. It was a salutary lesson in the dangers of economic forecasting, but it was also a lesson that private enterprise, in the shape of the great oil companies, could be just as far out in their predictions as government departments. We had been worried that there was a threat of a severe shortage of tankers in a few years' time ... but when the plans came to fruition, the whole market position had changed and we virtually had tankers running out of our ears.[16]

Maudling's problems in the late fifties were as nothing to those which faced officials in the mid-seventies and the late seventies as OPEC shoved the price of oil ever higher. Few could disagree with Sir Hermann Bondi, Chief Scientific Adviser at the Department of Energy 1976–80, when I asked him in 1987 for his assessment of the quality of Whitehall's energy forecasting since 1945. 'Total mess everytime', he said. 'You have a shortage, you build like mad. You have an excess, you stop. You are waiting for the next disaster.'[17] As we have seen from our historical chapters and the Cook's tour of the Treasury, the problems of Whitehall's energy forecasters were, if anything, surpassed by the difficulties of economic forecasting with which, naturally, they were closely linked. And life was no easier and the results no more impressive in any of the economics or energy ministries of the OECD nations – though in coping with the consequences of uncertainty, some countries proved far more ingenious and flexible than did others and, in some instances, such as Japan, after the oil shocks of the 1970s, the bureaucracy played a crucial part in this.[18]

Inevitably, any inquiry of this kind which is not a crude search for the purpose of naming the guilty men becomes beached upon the twin sandbanks of generality and imprecision. A more confined approach may be both fairer and more revealing. I have chosen two short case-studies for the purpose: one on Whitehall's policy-making for the inner cities spanning sixty years from 1928 to 1988; the other on the development and manufacture of nuclear weapons between 1945 and 1958, the period when Britain was forced to go it alone by the cessation of United States collaboration.

INNER CITIES, 1928–88

> These works brought all these people here. Something must be done to find them work.
> **King Edward VIII, Dowlais, 1936**[19]

> I cannot stress too strongly that my conclusions and proposals are not based on my fear of further riots. They are based on my belief that the conditions and prospects in the cities are not compatible with the traditions of social justice and national evenhandedness on which our Party prides itself.
> **Michael Heseltine, 1981**[20]

> But on Monday, you know, we've got a big job to do in some of those inner cities, a really big job. Our policies were geared – education and housing – to help the people in the inner cities to get more choice and, politically, we must get right back in there because we want them too, next time.
> **Mrs Margaret Thatcher, election night, June 1987**[21]

> It would be quite wrong to indicate that there is a pot of gold and all you have got to do is say 'Please, I want more [for the inner cities]'.
> **Mrs Margaret Thatcher, September 1987**[22]

Urban policy was only isolated as a problem in its own right as recently as 1968 but its roots lie deep in the relentless accumulation of difficulties since the mining and manufacturing activities which made Britain the world's first industrial nation moved into relative decline in the late nineteenth century. The first central-government initiative to cope with the consequences was taken sixty years ago with the Baldwin administration's industrial transference scheme of 1928 designed to assist the migration of workforces from depressed regions to more buoyant areas. It was a modest effort with limited results, not least because jobs were in such short supply elsewhere.[24] The first serious attempt to mitigate the worst effects of what was by now a deep-seated depression came with Neville Chamberlain's Special Areas Act of 1934. Chamberlain was Chancellor of the Exchequer at the time, and the Treasury, given today's complicated overlap of provision, must rue the day it started the process of selective grant-giving to attract industry to locations it would otherwise by-pass.

TABLE 9 CHRONOLOGY OF CENTRAL GOVERNMENT INITIATIVES FOR THE INNER CITIES

Date	*Government*	*Initiative*
1928	Baldwin (Con.)	Industrial Transference Scheme.
1934	MacDonald (Nat.)	Special Areas Act to encourage infrastructure projects, trading estates, advance factories and grants for incoming industry.
1939/45	Chamberlain/ Churchill (Nat. & after 1940 Coalition)	Ministry of Supply ran an effective regional policy by siting Royal Ordnance factories in depressed areas.
1945	Attlee (Lab.)	Distribution of Industry Act provided for the construction of estates and factories in depressed areas.
1946	Attlee (Lab.)	Location of labour-intensive government offices in the regions, e.g. Ministry of National Insurance in Newcastle.
1947	Attlee (Lab.)	Town & Country Planning Act established new towns.
1960	Macmillan (Con.)	Local Employment Act designated depressed areas 'development districts'.
1963	Macmillan (Con.)	The Hailsham Plan specifically for the North East created Washington New Town and designated Tyne and Wear as a 'regional growth zone'.
1966	Wilson (Lab.)	Industrial Development Act created development areas.
1967	Wilson (Lab.)	Regional employment premium introduced.
1968	Wilson (Lab.)	Urban programme established to combat inner-city deprivation.
1972	Heath (Con.)	Industry Act gave direct financial assistance through regional development grants.
1977	Callaghan (Lab.)	White Paper entitled *Policy for the Inner Cities.* Extra money found for the urban programme partly by reducing budget for New Towns; partnership arrangement with local authorities.
1978	Callaghan (Lab.)	Inner Urban Areas Act provided legal basis for 1977 rethink.
1980	Thatcher (Con.)	Local Government Act. Urban Development Corporations for London and Liverpool Docklands. Enterprise zones announced in budget.
1981	Thatcher (Con.)	Post-riots rethink boosts urban programme. Michael Heseltine becomes Minister for Merseyside.
1982	Thatcher (Con.)	Urban Development Grant created.
1984	Thatcher (Con.)	Review of Regional Policy targets. More selectivity proposed.
1986	Thatcher (Con.)	Housing & Planning Act establishes urban regeneration grant; five more urban development corporations created.
1987	Thatcher (Con.)	Conservative election manifesto promises mini-UDCs; Cabinet Committee on inner cities established to review policy.
1988	Thatcher (Con.)	*Action for Cities* published; inner city grant announced.[23]

For a policy to catch fire in the public's imagination it needs a catchphrase. British politicians never came up with a phrase to match Roosevelt's New Deal, partly, no doubt, because they were not in the business of creating one through the mixture of experimentation and investment applied by FDR in the 1930s. The one phrase which *has* stuck from that era sprang from the lips of a monarch rather than a premier. On 18 November 1936, less than a month before his abdication, King Edward VIII stood in the ruins of the Bessemer Steel Works in Dowlais above Merthyr Tydfil in South Wales. As he contemplated the dereliction of a workplace which, a few years before, had employed 9,000 men, several hundred of them, who had turned up to see him, arose as one and sang an old Welsh hymn. Visibly moved, the King turned to an official and said: 'These works brought all these people here. Something must be done to find them work.'[25] Decades of frivolous gossip-column living with the international glitterati never expunged those remarks. 'Something must be done' is the phrase for which the Duke of Windsor will be remembered. So deeply is it embedded in the nation's memory that even journalists, who are paid to report the words of the powerful, are convinced that Mrs Thatcher said the same thing about the inner cities on election night 1987. But she did not. As Colin Brown, who followed Mrs Thatcher to Teeside on the first of her post-election inner city tours, put it in *The Independent*, 'She was reminded that on her third election victory night, she had said: "We must do something about the inner cities." Mrs Thatcher said: "That was not quite what we said. We said we wanted to win back those inner cities to our cause." '[26]

In fact neither the politicians nor the monarchy had much impact on the interwar inner cities in the depressed regions of the United Kingdom. Rearmament and war did. Hitler had an enormous impact on the British economy. He revived Germany's economy with Keynesian methods. In a malign spin-off, the revival of the British economy was part of the multiplier effect. All the old staples flourished – every ounce of coal was needed, every pound of steel, every inch of shipyard. It was as if the pre-1914 world had been restored almost at a stroke. The merchants of death were also the bringers of economic recovery. And a mere glance at the list of Royal Ordnance factories on pp. 105–6 will show how precisely the Ministry of Supply seeded them in the areas of greatest employment need. In its way it was the most successful regional/inner cities policy ever designed by central government.

Labour tried very hard to replicate the policy in the peace. As Professor John Vincent has observed, the Attleean settlement of 1945 was designed to benefit poor manual workers (more than three-quarters of the adult male population were engaged in manual work at the time).[27] This was as true of its industrial and urban policies as of its welfare measures. In 1945 the Distribution of Industry Act made provision for the siting of factories and the building of industrial estates in depressed areas. The Government itself tried to set an example by locating its new clerical factories in areas of acute need such as Tyneside which housed the benefits bureaucracy of the Ministry of Pensions and National Insurance. And the Town and Country Planning Act of 1947 launched the New Towns, Whitehall's chosen vehicle for thirty years for easing the inner city problems by removing work and the workforce to greenfield sites. In its way, the new town initiative was the most dramatic of the inner city policies. It transformed considerable sections of the countryside. (Paul Addison's excellent documentary, *Now the War Is Over*, unearthed an unforgettable film clip of a charabanc load of gaberdine-macked, singing cockneys overshooting their destination on the Aylesbury road and having to seek directions to find the fields that were to become Hemel Hempstead.)[28] When the houses were up and the cockneys moved in, life was, in the main, dramatically changed for the better. The losers were those who remained behind in inner city areas which gradually lost their economic and social quality *and* became unrecognisable as the tower block and the huge estate replaced the familiar narrow streets of the old 'urban villages'.

Such was the pace of Britain's postwar economic miracle in the 1950s (glittering by our standards; somewhat tarnished compared to Western Europe's as a whole) that regional/inner city issues as a policy in their own right slipped way down the political agenda. In boom times, it was relatively easy to absorb the labour force released by the large-scale closure of coal mines even in the traditionally depressed areas of South Wales or the North-East. Economic growth, particularly in a period when it was still relatively labour intensive, can ease many of the more acute pains of industrial and social transition. Once again, the wider question of the country's economic performance – part, but only part of which can Whitehall be held to account for – is the crucial factor. If regional/urban policy appears to be a residual that will progressively ease, as it did in the fifties, it receives a relatively small portion of scarce ministerial and official time. Certainly, intense effort was applied to particular problems in these years. The Board of Trade in general and a promising official, Peter Carey, in particular, spent a great deal of effort, for example, on rationalising, with government assistance, the cotton trade, 'the first great British industry to rise, and the first to fall',[29] in the mill towns of Lancashire and Yorkshire in the late fifties.

It was the recession of 1960–1 which turned the Macmillan administration's attention to those areas which stubbornly resisted the economic take-off occurring in more favoured parts of the nation, favoured either because of their geographical location in the increasingly golden triangle of the south-east or because of their association with growth industries such as the motor manufacturing belt of the West Midlands. Macmillan was especially sensitive to the issue. The plight of his interwar constituency, Stockton-on-Tees, was one of his standard Cabinet monologues, as often repeated as it was genuinely felt. The 1960 Local Employment Act designated areas like Tyne and Wear 'development districts'. Where the National Government had first trodden thirty years earlier the Conservatives, whose postwar ascendancy was based on the politics of prosperity, were forced to follow.

For those who have lived through the oil shocks of the seventies and the ferocious recession of the early eighties, there now seems something inexorable about the deep, employment-shedding structural changes in the British economy and their disproportionate impact on those areas which increasingly appeared to be unwilling heritage museums to the country's first industrial revolution. Such a perspective was part and parcel of the politics of pessimism which set in in the mid-1970s. At the time attention was refocused on the depressed areas in the early 1960s this was not the feeling that held sway. There was a belief that the problem *was* residual, that with a bit of pump-priming by central government – advance factories, new roads, growth points around the second wave of new towns – such areas would, given time, be brought to share in the general prosperity of the nation. This was the reasoning behind the Hailsham Plan of 1963 for the north-east, drafted after his Lordship's famous cloth-capped foray to Geordieland. The roads were laid, Washington New Town was built. The problem was eased for a time but not solved. Whitehall was its meticulous self in devising rational, carefully costed and closely monitored schemes. The ministries concerned – the Board of Trade, Housing and Local Government and the Treasury – acted with enthusiasm and hope. It was not enough.

Wilson's growth strategy contained a strong regional element. The new prime minister and his ministerial team were enthusiastic interventionists. The Department of Economic Affairs fostered regional economic committees. The Industrial Development Act designated development areas and the regional employment premium provided the most direct incentives in peacetime for industry to relocate. The Wilson years, too, saw a tacit recognition of that tight bundle of interrelated urban problems, including the relative deprivation of inner city ethnic communities, which has stretched and vexed Whitehall policy-makers ever since. In 1968, shortly after Enoch Powell's 'River Tiber foaming with much blood' speech, the first custom-built initiative for tackling urban deprivation *per se* was unveiled by the Home Office (which was then the lead department on urban policy), though the bulk of the preliminary work had been done before Mr Powell's entry into the immigration debate. The urban programme of the late 1960s was modest in money terms and the bulk of it was spent on social amelioration rather than economic regeneration.[30]

After Labour lost office, Peter Walker, as Edward Heath's Environment Secretary, set in train a series of 'inner area studies' which, with some success, tried to disentangle the interlocking strands of deprivation, poor schooling, diminished job opportunities, inadequate housing and, where substantial ethnic populations were present, racial prejudice, which combined in a malign cycle to make the urban problem that much worse than the sum of its parts. Walker was transferred to the Department of Trade and Industry before he had a chance to apply his political and administrative skills to the information the research programme yielded.[31] Ironically, as Secretary of State for Trade and Industry he inherited responsibility for regional policy which, until the linkage problem was at last perceived in the 1980s, was treated in virtually total isolation from urban policy, even though its incentives to industry to move to greenfield sites could, as often as not, result in a further draining of economic life from the inner core of the great cities in the depressed areas. The Heath government after its U-turn in 1972 took considerable powers of intervention under its Industry Act of that year. The regional development grant was intended to be a key instrument in the alleviation of unemployment whose rise towards the then unacceptable level of one million was the main spur to Heath's change of direction.

Regional development grant has comprised by far the largest central government input into industrial assistance, totalling more than £4 billion in the decade between 1974 and 1984 when the Thatcher administration reviewed its regional policy. It tended to help large manufacturing companies keep up their levels of employment rather than foster newer, smaller employment-creating enterprises.[32] Like so many Whitehall schemes for mitigating the effects of economic under-performance, it relieved the symptoms but did little to foster a cure. No doubt, without RDG matters would have been even worse in inner city areas dependent on large, traditional manufacturing companies to sustain their populations.

From the oil shock and the winter crisis of 1973–4, the overall impression of Whitehall activity is that it has been of the finger-in-the-dyke variety. The raw figures of the larger shifts within the British economy in general and the large population centres in particular certainly buttress that view. In the thirty years between 1951 and 1981 employment in Britain's inner cities shrank by 45 per cent and a million manufacturing jobs were lost. And, in terms of joblessness, the position of the inner cities relative to the rest of the country was deteriorating in the same period. Unemployment rates among inner city residents were 33 per cent higher than the national average and 51 per cent higher in 1981.[33]

It was the Labour governments of the mid to late 1970s that first tackled the inner city problem for what it is, a deep-seated phenomenon rather than a transient residual difficulty of a society in mid-passage from an obsolescent to a modern economy. The information base that ministers and officials used for the rethink, which was steered by a special Cabinet committee on the inner cities,[34] was essentially the product of the inner area studies commissioned by Peter Walker five years earlier. It was an example of the fruits of continuity that could still ripen, on some policy issues at least, even in the increasingly chilly air of polarised politics.

Policy dilemmas were confronted. For example, the conflicting pull of urban programme money being pumped into the inner cities, and the new towns programme sucking people and industry out, was recognised. New towns, however, were not the only factor in this powerful centrifugal phenomenon which between 1951 and 1981 resulted in Britain's six largest conurbations losing some 35 per cent of their working-age population.[35] Luckily the conflict between new towns and urban policy could be resolved within a single department – Environment – whose Secretary of State, Peter Shore, was personally seized of the need for a rethink. Mr Shore continues, with justification, to regard the mid-seventies inner cities review as an example of the Cabinet system and its Whitehall back-up working to maximum advantage. Indeed, he used it in a conversation on Cabinet government in 1985 to rebut views of mine, about the difficulty of social policy-making in modern conditions. I reminded him of his involvement

> 'with inner cities – the progressive collapse of inner cities. It was after your time that we had the urban riots, but the problems were growing ... and there was a White Paper in your time ... implementing the Beveridge Report was a snip compared to what you have to do these days. Is that a fair impression on the social policy side?'
>
> 'If I take the inner cities one, I would say "No". I was struck by how much government could do when you clearly defined a new policy for the inner cities. It was a great advantage having a major spending department at the centre of it – it was my own department then, the Department of the Environment – and to be able to move resources, both people, because command of people, of civil servants, is terrifically important in getting any policy off the ground initially, and also having a big budget which one could switch money into. The fastest growing budget, although it was quite a small one to begin with, was indeed for the inner cities, even during a period of stringency. And we were able to get this new legislation through and changes in industrial-location policy, a whole range of things which you could develop and develop quite quickly. I only made my inner-city speech calling for a new inner-city policy in late 1976. We had legislation on the statute book by '77.
>
> 'And you had a Cabinet committee in the interim.'

'Absolutely. And, although there was some departmental resistance that had to be overcome, nevertheless they were pushed-pulled into line. So it shows ... government can move – and can move fairly swiftly to deal with what is certainly a very difficult and wide-ranging problem. Half the problems of government, as you well understand, are on the frontiers of a department, rather than centrally within it, and that co-ordination of policy ... covering the frontiers of different departments is of course one of the great difficulties in Cabinet government ...'[36]

Peter Shore's 1977 White Paper gave a sense of the depth of the inner city problem which 'has its roots in social and economic events reaching back to the last century and beyond. Much has been done to ease their problems since the Second World War, principally through the relief of overcrowding. But much remains to be done, and the regeneration of the inner areas will inevitably take some time.'[37] The thrust of the Shore strategy was 'to recast the urban programme and to extend it to cover industrial, environmental and recreational provision and other matters, as well as specifically social projects'.[38] Money was to be shifted from new towns to inner cities[39] and the urban programme's budget was to be quadrupled from £30 million to £125 million a year by 1980.[40]

Shore and the officials in his inner cities directorate deserve considerable credit for their 1976-7 policy review. It was conducted against the background of a barrage of intense and short-term crises associated with the currency collapse and the negotiation of the IMF loan. Yet it addressed the fundamentals and shifted the beginnings, at least, of the resources needed to tackle them. The White Paper recognised that 'the resources required for the inner cities will need to be found within the private sector as well as the public sector',[41] though in its implementation of the new policy, the Callaghan administration was heavily reliant on the largely Labour-controlled local authorities as the main delivery agency on the ground. At the Whitehall end, 'the bulk of the expenditure will have to be found within the main programmes of central and local government by giving a new priority to the inner urban areas'.[42] The new strategy was incorporated in the Inner Urban Areas Act of 1978.

Peter Shore placed great faith in the efficacy of shifting the emphasis of the Government's expenditure on social policy and rate support grant towards the inner cities. But an Economic and Social Research Council inquiry in the early 1980s was sceptical of the efficacy of this strategy. Victor Hausner and his colleagues claimed their 'local studies show that central government has not been successful in "bending" mainstream spending in support of urban policy objectives, despite the intentions of the Inner Urban Areas Act'.[43] The reasons, according to Hausner who had worked on President Carter's urban regeneration programme and was familiar with the tax regimes of American cities, were 'the limits on the fiscal powers of British local authorities and the lack of fiscal incentives to expand local tax bases [which] restrict the potential to use local fiscal policy as an instrument of urban economic development'.[44]

As is often the way, a shift in electoral fortunes changed the political landscape before the new policy had a chance to bite. The 1979 general election projected an equally committed inner cities man into the DOE in the person of Michael Heseltine, though he had very different ideas to Peter Shore about the nature of local government and the creation of local enterprise. Inner city policy was one of Heseltine's first priorities. It was number 4 on the 10 policy areas he listed on the famous envelope he passed to Sir John Garlick over the lunch table at their first meeting.[45]

He quickly reviewed the Shore approach of partnership with the local authorities. He concluded 'it was very much a process which took the form of central government adding to the expenditure of local government and the local authorities using the money to augment their existing programmes – in other words, it was just a little bit more of the same in certain selected stress areas'.[46]

The outcome of Heseltine's 1979 review was the reorientation of urban policy towards what he called 'a capital renovation programme and an environmental enhancement programme to try and change the nature of the [deprived] areas so that they attracted people and investment and talent'.[47] As part of recasting the policy he brought an ingredient of his own listed on the Garlick envelope as 'Development Corporations'. It was an idea which was to grow with the eighties. But it was conceived in the early seventies during Heseltine's ministerial apprenticeship. He later told me:

> It was born of an experience that I'd had as minister responsible for aerospace in Ted Heath's government and, in that capacity, I used to fly over the East End of London on my way to Maplin to take part in the preparation for the third London airport as it was then proposed. And, looking down, I was appalled at the thousands and thousands of acres of derelict land, under-used rotting areas in the East End of London . . .
>
> When I returned to the Department of the Environment one of the first things that I wanted to do was to create the new town corporation and use it to redevelop the inner urban area. Every sort of device had been used – consultation, reports, co-ordinating committees, dialogue of one sort or another – but nothing had actually happened to address this multiplicity of ownership and this inability to break through the public sector ownership, the lack of funds, the lack of commitment to the East End of London.[48]

Heseltine managed to persuade the Treasury to boost the urban programme to reflect his capital investment priorities (Fig. 22). Again it was an accomplished operation by DOE ministers and officials against a highly unfavourable background of general expenditure restraint. Urban development corporations for London Docklands and Liverpool were given a statutory basis in the Local Government Act, 1980 and the first enterprise zones – offering substantial tax and rates breaks to businessmen in particularly run-down areas like Gateshead – were announced in the Budget that year.

Civil disturbance, first in London, then in Liverpool and Manchester, changed the landscape of urban policy, probably for the foreseeable future, in 1981. Heseltine dropped everything and spent three weeks on Merseyside with a team of officials and, at one point, a charabanc-load of top people from industry and the financial institutions whom he had personally cajoled to join him and see for themselves. As he put it at the beginning of his report to the Cabinet:

> It took a riot. No sentiment was more frequently expressed to me during the time I spent with Tim Raison [Minister of State at the Home Office] in Merseyside. There is no escaping the uncomfortable implications.[49]

The implications of the long-term inner city decline of troubled conurbations such as Merseyside were converted by Heseltine into a six-part plan:

> 1. The economic and social decline evident in Merseyside, and other conurbations, requires a new priority for these areas in our policies.
> 2. A continued ministerial commitment to Merseyside is required for a specific period of, say, one year. A single regional office is needed in Liverpool comprising the main departments concerned with economic development. Similar arrangements should be adopted for other conurbations.
> 3. Our industrial, regional and training policies should be reassessed within the new context and administered with flexibility.
> 4. As part of this, we should involve the private sector and the financial institutions to a far greater degree than hitherto.
> 5. The future of the metropolitan counties and the GLC [Greater London Council] should be examined quickly.
> 6. Substantial additional public resources should be directed to Merseyside and other hard-pressed urban areas to create jobs on worthwhile schemes.[50]

There is no doubt that Heseltine's approach was very much in line with Whitehall's thinking – a 'one nation' style impulse towards the maintenance

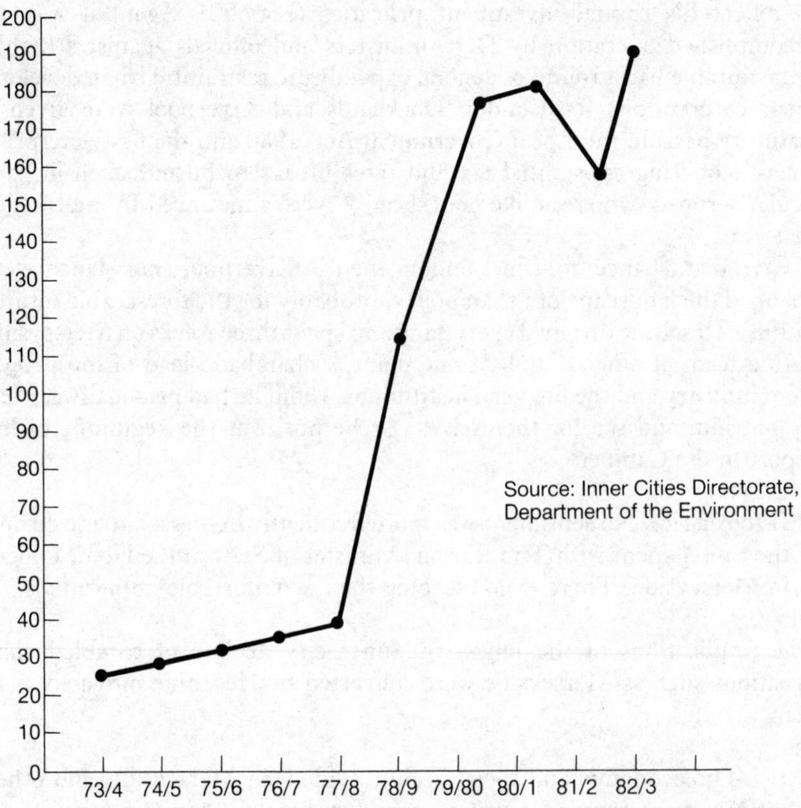

Fig. 22 Urban Aid Programme

of social peace, a centrally conceived rejigging of social and economic programmes to foster it, and the application of considerable public funds for the purpose, given the urgency of the issue. The sudden spasm of civil violence and riot shook those in authority in Whitehall who had grown up with the postwar settlement, a settlement which had been designed for the purpose of syphoning the venom from British society. (They shook me, too. I genuinely had not thought civil disturbance to be a serious possibility.) In an unacknowledged way, the postwar generation of senior civil servants were guardians of the 1945 settlement. Certainly, the select and exalted few invited to dine privately with Heseltine at Lockets shortly after the circulation of *It Took a Riot* (they included Robert Armstrong) lined up behind the Heseltine approach.

When it comes to Cabinet papers, however, the customer that counts is in No. 10, not the Cabinet Office. For Mrs Thatcher, Heseltine's report was peppered with irritations. For a start it seemed to suggest that rioters should be rewarded. The day Toxteth burned, the Cabinet was in session. Periodic reports from Kenneth Oxford, Chief Constable of Merseyside, would be brought to the Prime Minister which she would read aloud to her colleagues. One of them described widespread looting. 'Those poor shopkeepers', said Mrs Thatcher,[51] (a view with which I sympathised, though I have my reservations about the degree to which it apparently influenced the rest of her thinking). Equally important, Heseltine's prescriptions and the philosophy in which they were couched – 'the conditions and prospects in the cities are not compatible with the traditions of social justice and national evenhandedness on which our Party prides itself'[52] – seemed to the Prime Minister to be exactly what they were, a direct attack on the Government's tough economic strategy within months of Mrs Thatcher routing her Cabinet critics over the harshness of the 1981 Budget.

The Prime Minister convened an *ad hoc* ministerial group to consider *It Took a Riot*. She stacked it against Heseltine. Sir Geoffrey Howe at the Treasury was the guardian of tight public-expenditure control. In a letter to Mrs Thatcher prior to the meeting, he picked up an option raised (but rejected) in a CPRS report on Merseyside two months before. 'I cannot help feeling', Howe wrote, 'that the option of managed decline, which the CPRS reflected in its study of Merseyside, is one which we should not forget altogether. We must not expend all our resources in trying to make water flow uphill.'[53] As for the other members of the group, Sir Keith Joseph, then at the Department of Industry, was, as ever, a thoroughgoing Thatcher loyalist. Only William Whitelaw, then at the Home Office, might have been expected to place his formidable weight behind Heseltine. Instead he played the customary role he had taken upon himself as Deputy Prime Minister, that of mediator, and did not push for the policies in which, to a large extent, he believed (there are indications that he later regretted this).[54]

It Took a Riot had little hope in these circumstances when the ministerial group discussed it in September 1981. Heseltine, realistically, did not insist it went to a discussion in the full Cabinet because he would have lost there as well.[55] He did not leave No. 10 empty-handed, however. A modest increase in the urban programme was sanctioned and he, at least was allowed to become a kind of district commissioner for Merseyside, though no other Cabinet ministers were to be asked to head for the provinces as Heseltine had recommended.

Heseltine's subsequent actions are very illuminating about Whitehall in general, however, for a number of reasons. After his resignation from the Cabinet, he explained in a television interview how much the federal nature of Whitehall allows a minister to achieve even after the kind of experience he had endured in Mrs Thatcher's *ad hoc* group on the inner cities:

> A Cabinet minister of a large and wide-ranging department has very considerable powers, *particularly if he's going with what you might* ... [call] ... the grain of the bulk of the *people in his own department* [emphasis added]. And if he's pursuing and pushing at the frontiers ideas which are perhaps new, perhaps the sort of thing that some of his colleagues wouldn't have done, [that] some of his colleagues might even positively disapprove of as ... treading over some doctrinal divide – providing that he's sufficiently able to persuade his department, is making a competent job and not offending any of the proprieties of public accounting, there is very real discretion for a Cabinet minister to do his own thing within his own department. The trouble starts when he has to go and get agreement from other colleagues and has to get a collective discussion.[56]

Heseltine, acting on this practical philosophy of, as it were one nation 'in-a-single-department', returned to the DOE and, each Monday, to Merseyside, to experiment, to probe and to innovate. The idea was that he 'would come back to colleagues and say "Look, it works. Now let's do it on the scale that the crisis demands." Well, it so happened that I went to be Secretary of State for Defence about the time [New Year 1983] when I was beginning to show the sort of results which would have enabled me to say that.'[57]

In pursuing this strategy, Heseltine had his DOE officials firmly behind him. In this instance, there was not a trace of the problem in Tony Benn's days at the Department of Industry when civil servants were placed in a very awkward position as the signals poured in from No. 10 and the Cabinet Office about what the Government's industrial policy should be which were, in crucial instances, contrary to the wishes of their Secretary of State.

As part of his experiment within the DOE, Heseltine demonstrated another fruitful possibility for innovation within the Civil Service as it is currently constituted – the scope for putting together mixed teams of insiders and outsiders as a kind of task force dedicated to a specific practical purpose. During his evangelising of big industrial concerns and the financial institutions, Heseltine cajoled them into lending him skilled people to work within the DOE's Inner Cities Directorate alongside its regulars in helping create the new and enhanced urban policy he was seeking. Among those recruited was Howard Mallinson, a management consultant with Peat, Marwick McLintock. 'There was a deliberate policy,' he later recalled, 'and indeed, a policy executed with considerable enthusiasm by officials at the time, to recruit both chartered accountants and chartered surveyors. And a small group of us assembled in Marsham Street [site of the DOE headquarters] in September 1982 drawn largely from major firms of chartered accountants and from major firms of chartered surveyors.'[58] Mr Mallinson described in conversation with me the process which brought him from the City to Marsham Street:

> He [Heseltine] and his officials took a very early view that they needed outside skills, they needed skills which the Department did not have. They needed to be able to get inside the private sector mind. And my senior partner, along with the senior partners of most of the other big firms of chartered accountants, received a letter explaining what the policy was, saying they needed someone good and cheap to help him and his officials to get inside these applications for grant.
>
> ' "Cheap" meaning that some of the salary would have to be paid by the firm?'
>
> 'Indeed. The cost to my firm of my secondment was really quite significant not just in the difference between the remuneration which I actually earned and that which was refunded by the Department of the Environment, but, perhaps more importantly than that, the loss of opportunity which the firm suffered through my doing someone else's business instead of doing their own.'[59]

The lesson in Howard Mallinson's testimony is a crucial one: peacetime is not like the era of Beryl Power and the Central Register. Firms and professions cannot be expected to release their best people for temporary service in Whitehall on receipt of a letter through the post. The power and persuasion of a Secretary of State in person is required – plus the feeling that there is a *real* job to be done, as there undoubtedly was in the creation of urban development grant, the programme in which Mr Mallinson was involved.

As happened so often in the war, the mixture of the old and the new blood worked, with regulars and irregulars having a great deal to teach and to learn from each other. Howard Mallinson remembers: 'It was a very pioneering atmosphere in the Department of the Environment Inner Cities Directorate in 1982. The policy was being executed by ministers and their officials and by us private sector secondees with great enthusiasm. We were all charting very new ground. It hadn't really been done before.'[60] Mr Mallinson is fascinating about the practical effect of that part of the Whitehall culture which derives from traditional Civil Service accounting procedures. It emerged, once more, in a conversation for a BBC Radio 4 *Analysis* programme on the inner cities in the autumn of 1987:

> 'One of the things which I'm very disappointed to find is the way in which urban development grant is now administered [in that] there seems to be an attempt to very precisely measure the amount of grant which a capital project needs. Now, I think that is an objective which imposes too much on themselves ... The methodology now being used by the Department of the Environment tends to expect far too high levels of accuracy in project appraisal to a degree which is really just an illusion.'
>
> 'The Department of the Environment would say, would they not, that we may have sympathy with you, Mr Mallinson, but the Treasury never sleeps, to use a phrase of Michael Heseltine's. They are the ones that impose these disciplines on us, because it's public money, it's not like the City ...'
>
> 'I think that's a perfectly fair point. I think that sometimes, perhaps, we may expect too much of our civil servants when faced with some of the scandals that have taken place in th last few years. No one wants to be involved in another De Lorean [a Northern Ireland Office sponsored sports car venture in Belfast which went bust], and I sympathise with that point of view. But I think what it does demand is an ability, and the experience which fosters that ability, to be able to take the broad view. And I think it's a question really of how one's been brought up, how one's been trained.'[61]

Ironically, a joint DOE–Treasury value-for-money investigation of the urban programme after Heseltine's departure for Defence, led by David Edmonds, his former private secretary then heading the Inner Cities Directorate, concentrated on those aspects which Howard Mallinson thought were already the subject of excessive obsession.[62]

As we have seen, ministerial personality is crucial. None of Heseltine's successors at the DOE (and there was a profusion of them – Patrick Jenkin, Tom King, Kenneth Baker and Nicholas Ridley – one a year on average between 1983 and 1987) brought his passion or his commitment to urban policy. Ridley was keen on urban development corporations and characteristically candid about his disdain for local authorities as the deliverers or urban regeneration.[63] At the pre-election Conservative Party Conference of 1986, he announced five more UDCs which, with London Docklands and Liverpool, made seven in all. But he was not persuaded by Heseltine's argument that, with renewed growth in the economy, the funding of urban regeneration should be substantially boosted.[64]

Not until Mrs Thatcher delivered her 'Declaration of Smith Square' on election night 1987 did inner cities shoot up the political agenda once more. A new Cabinet Committee, Economy (Urban Policy) or E(UP), was created, with the Prime Minister herself in the chair at its monthly meetings. Lord Young, her favourite minister, was instructed to 'co-ordinate' inner city policy from the Department of Trade and Industry, though the great bulk of urban policy money – some £531 m in 1987–8 – remained within Mr Ridley's DOE bailiwick. (Total Whitehall spending on the inner cities amounted to £2 billion.) Mrs Thatcher spent the autumn of 1987 damping down expectations, insisting that 'It would be quite wrong to indicate there is a pot of gold' for the inner cities.[65] Eric Sorenson was transferred from the DOE's Inner Cities Directorate to head an Urban Policy Unit in the Cabinet Office to brief E(UP) and to prepare a review document on urban problems and government provision. Ridley fulfilled a manifesto pledge to create mini-UDCs, four of them to be precise.[66] But the prospects for a genuinely path-breaking White Paper looked meagre. Whitehall was simply not being commissioned to produce one. Existing achievements would be stressed and further exertions promised. It was to be a case of what William Solesbury, a DOE planner, once described as 'the Avis solution to difficult policy problems: you just try harder'.[67] But it did seem, at last, as if Mrs Thatcher would finally answer the 'who's in charge?' question by designating one of the multiplicity of colleagues involved as the lead minister,[68] and, just before Christmas 1987, she appointed Kenneth Clarke, Lord Young's deputy at DTI, to the task.[69]

The outcome of the much awaited review by E(UP) turned out to be a glossy brochure, *Action for Cities*,[70] launched at a press conference in March 1988 by Mrs Thatcher and a podium-full of ministers from relevant departments. ministers, it seems, spent very little time on the relative merits of a White Paper over an alternative type of prospectus. Though some senior civil servants, convinced that White Papers are of their nature a weightier genre within a longer shelf-life, expressed private disappointment.[71]

One reason, perhaps, for not having a White Paper to replace Peter Shore's 1977 document, *Policy for the Inner Cities*, was that there was very little new in *Action for Cities*. It was a reprise of existing policies and initiatives plus the announcement of more UDCs, new roads and the streamlining of the aid programme into a single City Grant which would absorb urban development grant and urban regeneration grant. Not a single FMI-related performance indicator was attached to the brochure, though these certainly existed across the range of departments involved.[72]

Somehow, too, the inner city budget had grown by one third in less than four months from the £2bn mentioned at the time of Mr Clarke's appointment as co-ordinator to £3bn, the figure mentioned by the Prime Minister at the *Action for Cities* press conference. The difference, it transpired, between the Thatcher and Clarke figures arose from his being based on 1987–8 estimates and hers on 1988–9 projections. His also excluded Scottish and Welsh money or any sum for housing associations while hers included them.[73] (For the breakdown of Mrs Thatcher's estimate, see Table 10.)

TABLE 10. PUBLIC SPENDING ON INNER CITIES; 1988–9 ESTIMATES

	£m
Training, enterprise, small firms	1,100
Housing associations	450
Urban programme	314
Roads	250
UDCs	203
Selective regional aid, innovation grants, English estates	200
Estate action	140
Derelict land reclamation	25
Task forces, city action teams	21
Scottish and Welsh equivalents	300
TOTAL	3,003

Urban policy is a good theme from which to draw lessons about the capability of the British Civil Service as it spans six decades and countless political administrations. For me it shows that what Disraeli called the 'condition of England' question is a genuine motivator of the British public servant. Whatever the policy approach tried – regional assistance, distribution of industry, new towns, urban development grants, urban development corporations – the push from Whitehall based on the impulse for improvement has been strong and sustained whether it be Evelyn Sharp on new towns or Edmonds and Sorenson on inner cities. The officials are at their least happy and, I suspect, least effective when it is business as usual with a dash of the Avis 'we try harder' principle. Nor has the

Whitehall machine been averse to the introduction of outsiders to their policy teams on the all too rare occasions that this has happened.

That said, the officials concerned in inner cities policy would be the first to admit that their efforts are about interim solutions, not final solutions. The world and the national economies have been passing some of the most blighted inner cities by since 1919 (with a brief respite in 1939–45). Structural changes of that.magnitude are beyond the reach of Whitehall to affect on anything except the slimmest of margins.

On his Monday visits to Merseyside Michael Heseltine would acknowledge the grim reality that all the best efforts of his Merseyside Task Force could be more than offset when, at the stroke of a chairman's pen in a multinational's board room far away from Liverpool or even from Britain, one of the area's big employers would be closed down, another victim to the vagaries of the so-called 'branch economy'. Quite apart from such mega forces, a problem – relative economic decline in its starkest and most geographically specific form – which had taken, in some cases and some places, the best part of a century to develop its malign chemistry is not going to be put right in the life of a Parliament, however well conceived the antidotes coming out of the Whitehall policy units and committee rooms. As so often, the judgement has to be that without Whitehall's efforts and the disbursement of public money, matters would be even worse in the 'Giro towns' of the old industrial areas and in the 'underclass' pockets of the towns and cities of the relatively prosperous south-east. It is not an heroic epitaph – but it is a virtuous one.

THE BRITISH NUCLEAR WEAPONS PROJECT, 1945–58

> We've got to have the bloody Union Jack on top of it.
> **Ernest Bevin, 1946**[74]

> We never had the resources we needed ... Attlee said to Portal [in 1947] 'They [the atomic bomb project] must have top priority'. Portal wrote it down and locked it in his safe ... It was comic opera really.
> **Lord Penney, 1987**[75]

> After twelve years of separation it is obvious that the laws of physics apply on both sides of the Atlantic and that the British, in scientific terms, know as much about the matter [the hydrogen bomb] as their American colleagues.
> **Edward Teller, 1957**[76]

TABLE 11. BRITAIN AND THE BOMB.
CHRONOLOGY OF POLICY AND DEVELOPMENT, 1940–58

1940	Peierls–Fisch memorandum 'on the properties of a radioactive super-bomb'.
1941	Whitehall committee produces the 'Maud Report' on the feasibility of a uranium bomb.
1943	Quebec Agreement concluded by Roosevelt and Churchill pledges Anglo–American atomic collaboration in war and peace. Bomb not to be used by either nation without the consent of the other.
1944	Hyde Park *aide-mémoire* confirms postwar US–UK atomic collaboration 'unless and until terminated by joint agreement'.
1945	Labour government elected. Attlee becomes prime minister. US Air Force drops atomic bombs on Hiroshima and Nagasaki. Cabinet committee, GEN 75, authorises construction of an atomic pile to produce plutonium. Chiefs of Staff instructed to assess British requirements for atomic weapons.
1946	McMahon Act passed by US Congress undoes the Quebec Agreement. Anglo-American collaboration ceases except for procurement of uranium supplies. Portal appointed controller of Production (Atomic Energy). Hinton appointed to lead atomic energy production organisation. GEN 75 authorises construction of a gaseous diffusion plant. Air Ministry draws up plans for V Bomber force.
1947	Cabinet committee, GEN 163, authorises the manufacture of a British atomic bomb. Attlee issues directive giving atomic energy priority over resources. Penney appointed to head weapons team. Work begins on construction of atomic piles at Windscale.
1948	'Modus vivendi' agreement with US. UK gives up its right to veto US use of atomic weapons. Collaboration agreed on detection of nuclear explosions, design of research reactors, health and safety. Atomic bomb decision announced in Parliament.
1949	Attlee issues second and third priority directives on atomic energy. Capenhurst chosen as site for gaseous diffusion plant. Soviet Union tests atomic weapon.
1950	Klaus Fuchs convicted of spying for Russia. US decides to develop hydrogen bomb. Aldermaston the new site for atomic weapons research. Windscale No. 1 pile goes critical.

1951 Chiefs of Staff agree a shipborne atomic weapons trial off north-west coast of Australia in late 1952.
Windscale No. 2 pile goes critical.
Conservatives win election. Attlee replaced by Churchill. Ministerial responsibility for atomic energy split between Sandys (Minister of Supply) and Cherwell (Paymaster-General).

1952 Windscale No. 1 pile shut down temporarily, owing to overheating.
British atomic weapon exploded on HMS *Plym* off the Monte Bello Islands.
US tests a thermonuclear device.

1953 Churchill announces decision to transfer responsibility for atomic energy to a new authority.
Construction of Calder Hall reactor begins.
Soviet Union tests hydrogen bomb.
Further British atomic tests near Woomera, South Australia.

1954 Atomic Energy Authority created.
Full Cabinet authorises the manufacture of a British hydrogen bomb.
US Atomic Energy Act makes minor modifications to the McMahon Act easing slightly restrictions on collaboration.

1955 Hydrogen bomb decision announced in Parliament.
Six more reactors of Calder Hall type to be built to meet increased needs for military plutonium.
Eden replaces Churchill as prime minister.

1957 Eden resigns. Replaced by Macmillan. Macmillan restores Anglo-US relations at meetings with Eisenhower in Bermuda and Washington.
V bomber squadrons operational.
British 'megaton' weapon tested at Christmas Island in the Indian Ocean.
US and UK scientists open talks on their respective nuclear research programmes.
Further tests at Maralinga.
Windscale accident: fire in the core of No. 1 Pile releases radioactivity into the surrounding countryside. No. 2 Pile shut down.

1958 Campaign for Nuclear Disarmament founded.
Completion of hydrogen bomb trials on Christmas Island.
Anglo-American atomic collaboration restored after Macmillan talks with Eisenhower in Washington. McMahon Act amended.[77]

As a case study, the British nuclear weapons programme is at the opposite end of the spectrum to inner cities policy for more than the obvious reason that it has to do with the power to destruct rather than construct. It has to do with a direct, hands-on Whitehall enterprise. The state cannot create a climate in which it hopes the private sector will go ahead with the R & D and the manufacture of an atomic bomb. And it is the kind of project which has very little to do with huge, unpredictable factors such as fluctuations or structural changes in the world economy, apart, perhaps, from such specific matters as the supply of uranium. ICI and other private companies were involved, but essentially the British bomb project in the period I have chosen, when we went it alone without American help, was state enterprise in the purest sense of the term.

It was, too, an enterprise on the frontier of scientific and technical knowledge conducted, particularly in its early postwar phase, against a background of acute shortages in money, materials and skilled manpower. The Attlee government, however, gave the bomb project top priority. It had, in theory at least, an overriding claim to the physical and human resources at the disposal of central government. And, unlike most Whitehall operations, it was crucially dependent upon a handful of individuals with the knowledge and skill to make things happen to a very tight deadline. In assessing it I have deliberately refrained from bringing in judgements about the validity of the programme in the first place. But to declare my own view, I am one of those who believes that the acquisition of a British nuclear weapons capability was the right decision in the circumstances of early 1947 when it was taken by Attlee and a small ministerial group, though, as a bit of a traditionalist on Cabinet government, I would have preferred the Prime Minister to have taken the decision to the full Cabinet where I am sure it would have been endorsed.

My main focus is on the 'standing alone' period of twelve years, 1946–58 (Table 11). But the story begins in England in the early years of the war when a pair of brilliant refugee scientists, Otto Frisch and Rudolf Peierls, prepared a memorandum in 1940 on the scientific feasibility of an atomic bomb. The possibility was assessed by a sub-committee of government scientists under Professor Sir George Thomson which produced the so-called Maud Report the following year. Its dramatic import – that an atomic bomb was possible – was apparent to all in the small circle who were privy to it, whether or not they had a scientific background. For example, Denis Rickett, the young Cabinet Office official who was secretary to Lord Hankey's Scientific Advisory Committee which considered Maud, told his chief, Edward Bridges, that 'this will make war impossible'.[78]

Initially British scientists pursued their own weapons research independently of the American programme commissioned by Roosevelt. But in 1943 the huge resources, financial and industrial, required to make a bomb and the vulnerability to German attack of atomic plants built in

Britain led to a pooling of resources and the transfer of key sections of the British scientific teams to Chalk River near Montreal and to Los Alamos in New Mexico.[79] The Anglo-American partnership was recognised in the Quebec Agreement of 1943 and in the *aide-mémoire* of a conversation between Roosevelt and Churchill at Hyde Park, the President's home in up-state New York (Table 11). It was a partnership that was intended to endure beyond the defeat of Germany and Japan. Matters turned out very differently.

With Roosevelt dead (the American bureaucracy had lost its copy of the Quebec Agreement; the code name of 'Tube Alloys' had led to its misfiling) and Churchill out of office, the human incarnations of the accord were removed from the scene when, in the very different postwar climate, a 'Fortress America' mentality asserted itself in atomic matters. The passage of the McMahon Act, named after its sponsor, Senator Brian McMahon of Connecticut, finally put paid to all postwar collaboration in 1946, though, in real terms, this had ceased when the British team came home from Los Alamos the year before.

Brief hopes were raised in 1945 that international control of atomic energy would be possible, though Bevin was always sceptical of this. Referring to the US sponsored Baruch Plan, he declared at one meeting of GEN 75, Attlee's atomic energy Cabinet committee, 'Let's forget about the Baroosh [Bevin always had trouble with foreign-sounding names] and get on with the fissile.'[80]

But 'getting on with the fissile' was a daunting task for austerity Britain. For Attlee's inner circle of ministers, it was what a senior official closely involved with nuclear matters later called an 'of course' decision.[81] British brainpower had been an important factor in the development of the uranium weapon dropped on Hiroshima and the plutonium bomb dropped on Nagasaki. Early British work on the atomic bomb had the effect of accelerating the American decision to make a weapon as soon as possible. A later decision might have resulted in the last stages of the war with Japan taking a very different course. Labour ministers, like the vast bulk of their fellow countrymen, still regarded their nation, so recently victorious in a total war, as a great power. Only Cripps and Dalton raised objections at the political level on the grounds that the project was likely to absorb scarce human and physical resources needed for economic recovery.[82]

It was undoubtedly an 'of course' decision for Attlee and most of his senior colleagues (Bevin was the one who really counted). But they took a long time to make it. As early as December 1945 ministers on GEN 75 approved the construction of an atomic pile to produce plutonium, the fissile material in the Nagasaki bomb. It was assumed from the start that there would eventually be a bomb with 'a bloody Union Jack on it', as Bevin put it at a subsequent meeting of the Cabinet committee. But it took a request from Lord Portal, wartime Chief of the Air Staff turned Controller of Production (Atomic Energy), that ministers take a formal decision to proceed, to finally prod Attlee and his colleagues to do so in another special committee, GEN 163. Attlee gave it top priority. But only four months later was Dr William (now Lord) Penney, who was mentioned in Portal's memorandum prepared for GEN 163 as knowing 'more than any other British scientist about the secrets of the bomb',[83] summoned by Portal to be told he would be leading the team which would design the weapon required so urgently by the Chiefs of Staff.[84] Penney, however, had been pretty certain Britain would make its own bomb since the winter of 1945 when Sir James Chadwick, a key figure in Washington during the wartime atomic collaboration, and C. P. Snow, Civil Service Commissioner with responsibility for the Scientific Civil Service, persuaded him to forego plans to return to academic life and to become an established official for the purposes of working on the weapon.

Lord Penney's description of events in the spring and early summer of 1947 is the best account I have ever heard (or am ever likely to) of the chaotic method with which the bomb project was initially pursued despite those priority instructions from No. 10. In a conversation at his home in East Hendred near Oxford in November 1987 he told me and my BBC producer, Mark Laity:

> 'For the whole of 1946 there was no mention to me of making a bomb. In May 1947 I got a telephone message from Portal's secretary saying would I go and see him. So I went to see Portal. He didn't mince words. He said "We're going to make an atomic bomb. The Prime Minister has asked me to co-ordinate the work. They want you to lead it. I am not going to worry about all the details. But I am very prepared to use my influence, with the Prime Minister if necessary, to get all the resources you need. In a few days bring me a plan saying what you need." He said "Write it out and type it yourself."
>
> 'I typed out two pages. I said the quickest way and the cheapest way was to do the explosive at Woolwich and the testing work at Foulness. I haven't got a workshop of any use. I must have electronics people to make a firing circuit. We'll need an air-burst fuse. Malvern can do that ... We'll need 100 scientists and engineers. We'll put up a fence in Woolwich ... Portal said "Fine" and made a few notes. I said "How do I get these things?" He said "I'll tell the Ministry of Supply you've got to have them." Settled.'
>
> 'What did you get, Lord Penney?'
>
> 'I got the fences!' he replied, with a smile.[85]

One of the problems, Lord Penney explained, was that the bomb project was so secret at that stage (it was not announced in Parliament for a further year) that Portal kept Attlee's directive giving it priority in his safe. This meant that if he (Penney) asked Harwell to acquire stainless steel, then in very short supply, they were very reluctant to pass it on to him once it appeared. Lord Penney added, 'We never had the resources we needed.' His account of his initial resources really does deserve the 'comic opera' description he gave it:

> I had a few excellent staff with the right skills to start with but there were some terrible gaps. Armaments Research had half a workshop ... half-a-dozen skilled men but ropy machines. It had one man with the lowest rank of engineer in the Civil Service – simply incredible. Two or three young men on electronics. We wanted 5000 square feet. I didn't have anything like that ...
>
> I didn't start till August–September 1947. For a year or so I was struggling to teach people what to do.[86]

Matters were equally Heath-Robinson at the policy-making level in the Ministry of Supply to which Portal and his small team were somewhat precariously attached. As Professor Margaret Gowing, the project's official historian, has written:

> Apart from Portal and his staff, there was in the Ministry of Supply's Division of Atomic Energy a small band of career civil servants who serviced the project – an under secretary, an assistant secretary and two principals. They were not the usual Civil Service birds of passage moving quickly between jobs, but remained connected with atomic energy for unusually long periods ...
>
> The project used the common services of the Ministry of Supply – contracts, housing, canteens, establishments – but otherwise it was an island unto itself within the Ministry. Its special security barriers made it known as 'the cage'.[87]

At the stratospheric decision-taking level matters were no better, with a messy overlap of advisory, ministerial and official committees, not to mention the Chiefs of Staff and their bodies.[88] The fact that a British atomic device was tested successfully in October 1952, five years and five months after Portal summoned Penney to the Ministry of Supply's 'cage', shows that practical success *can* be wrought in difficult circumstances despite an organisational structure that would have grossly offended any tidy-minded civil servant or management consultant.

It was, however, a classic example of management-by-objectives and the achievement of the objective – a British atomic bomb within a relatively short space of time – was largely due to personalities, a trio of them to be precise. All three were civil servants cast again in a classic role of fulfilling instructions laid upon them by ministers. In addition to Penney, they were Christopher Hinton, former head of ICI's Alkali Division who had been brought in to the Ministry of Supply as a wartime temporary, and Sir John Cockcroft, prewar splitter of the atom and, in wartime, the scientist-administrator who had held the sometimes fractious multinational team at Chalk River in Canada together.[89]

In simplified terms, the division of labour was as follows: Penney's team at, first, Fort Halstead in Kent (at Aldermaston from 1950) with out-stations at Woolwich and Shoeburyness, were charged with designing the weapon; Hinton's team based at Risley in Lancashire, with responsibility for the atomic piles at Windscale in Cumbria and the gaseous diffusion plant at Capenhurst in Cheshire, were to produce the fissile material for the bomb; Cockcroft's research laboratory at Harwell on the Berkshire Downs was responsible for advising Hinton on the methods of producing plutonium. All three were young by peacetime Whitehall standards (at the beginning of 1946 Cockcroft was 48, Hinton 44 and Penney 36), all three were meritocrats, scholarship boys *par excellence*, and all had had great responsibility thrust upon them young by war. As Margaret Gowing commented, 'it seemed that the special qualities and past experience of all three had combined to produce a very rare situation: the right men all arriving in the right jobs at the right moment'.[90]

It is true to say that without Penney the task could not have been achieved in time. The Americans had cut off collaboration. But, in the high days of wartime co-operation at Los Alamos, Penney, as *the* expert on blast, was a member of most if not all the scientific groups working on the bomb, organised as they were on a strict need-to-know basis. He probably knew as much as anybody about the workings of the Nagasaki plutonium bomb – the kind which the British project intended to replicate albeit with operational improvements. Penney may not have had access to the American files, but the detail, essentially, was in his head from whence neither the McMahon Act nor anything else could move it. Penney's unique position was recognised, as we have seen, in Portal's paper for GEN 163, and by Lord Cherwell, Churchill's minister responsible for 'Tube Alloys', and, once more, for matters atomic in a clumsy, unsatisfactory duumvirate with Duncan Sandys after 1951. Cherwell wrote of Penney to Churchill in 1952 before the Monte Bello trial:

> He is our chief – indeed our only – real expert in the construction of the bomb and I do not know what we should do without him. He played an outstanding part in designing the original American bombs at Los Alamos in the war and participated in the first tests. The Americans

admit frankly that they would give a great deal to get him back. But on an appeal to his patriotism he gave up the offer of a very attractive professorship and came into government service. He is not always tactful but his heart is in the right place.[91]

Penney, in addition to his gifts as a fine applied mathematician and the, by non-American standards, unique store of knowledge in his head, was a very capable technical administrator when it came to working out what was needed, from where, in what order and by when and converting all this into realistic but tight timetables. A scheme is one thing, finding the materials (as we have seen) and the manpower quite another. Lorna Arnold has written of Penney's early days on the British project:

> He had much greater difficulties of recruitment than did the already well-known Cockcroft at Harwell. A top secret weapons establishment was less appealing. There had to be tight security restrictions; deadlines were inexorable; the work was often difficult and dangerous; the scientists could not publish their results as Harwell staff were comparatively free to do; some potential recruits had conscientious objections, or a strong distaste for weapons. The weapons group was always short of staff, sometimes desperately so. Few of the returning Manhattan Project scientists, even those from Los Alamos, joined the weapons work.[92]

Penney's problems were real enough but Hinton's were more acute. Building huge, advanced industrial plants in the manpower, material and money starved late forties was a formidable undertaking. It is in this area that the McMahon Act probably had its greatest immediate effect. The Americans, with their genius for fast and large-scale production, had performed prodigious feats in their factories at Oak Ridge in Tennessee and Hanford in Washington State. Know-how from their production lines would have been a boon to Hinton had it been available. Lord Sherfield, the Foreign Office negotiator of the 1948 'Modus Vivendi' which restored a mite (though, as we shall see, an important mite) of collaboration, believes that even if Quebec and Hyde Park had been adhered to, 'we would not have had a British bomb on a plate [but] we might have got a diffusion plant' from the United States.[93] And, through no fault of the hard-driving Hinton, production of plutonium was the slowest part of the scientific and industrial convoy moving towards the Monte Bello test of 1952. His people only just met the deadline. But meet it they did. As the fleet assembled off the islands, there was a great deal of confidence that the huge device in the bowels of HMS *Plym* would work. Churchill, back in Downing Street, was more cautious. He had two telegrams drafted. 'Thank you, Dr Penney', if it failed. 'Well done, Sir William' if it went up.[94] Penney got his knighthood.

For the politicians, civil servants, chiefs of staff and diplomats back in Whitehall, the explosion off the north-west coast of Australia was an important event. Britain was now the world's third nuclear power. 'It did enhance our position', said that fine instrument for measuring diplomatic clout, Lord Sherfield. 'It was certainly important in terms of our relations with the Americans.'[95] But the dreadful programme of technological escalation was already well in train. In October 1952, British nuclear capability, was roughly speaking, where the Manhattan Project had been in July 1945 and Kurchatov's team in the Soviet Union in August 1949. Within weeks of Monte Bello, the Americans tested a thermonuclear device. In the summer of 1953 the Soviets exploded a device in the megaton range. British information about these two tests was meagre, but they caused Churchill and some of his ministers to want to place a Union Jack on an H-bomb. Penney and Cockcroft undertook preliminary work but thought the cost would be high. Lord Penney recalled:

> A new situation arose in early 1954, when the US ran a series of five enormous explosions. The world press reported heavy and extensive fall-out from the first test called 'Bravo'. The Americans had clearly made a big military advance and said so. We could not match the American resources but surely we could manage one or two tests in due course. We had to take a chance. Maybe we were not out of things.[96]

Accordingly, when the full Cabinet was briefed on the H-bomb in July 1954, ministers were told that the net additional cost to the existing programme 'would not be very substantial. The capital cost should not exceed £10 million, and the thermonuclear bombs would be made in lieu of atomic bombs at a relatively small additional production cost'.[97]

Another milestone was passed in 1955 when the Russians conducted further thermonuclear tests. High-flying RAF and US Air Force aircraft, flying far from Soviet territory, collected good samples of weapons débris on filter papers. The samples were analysed by the Americans and the British and the results were compared, as was permitted by the 1948 'Modus Vivendi'. The results tallied and the British weaponeers began to feel they were on the right track. They were now confident that most of the fall-out from an H-bomb came from the fission of natural uranium by the fast neutrons of fusion. Ironically, the Russians had helped the British, unintentionally, naturally. In a strange way it compensated a little for the treachery of Klaus Fuchs and the other atomic spies who, it has been estimated, between them saved Kurchatov some eighteen months in presenting Stalin with his atomic weapon.[98]

Penney's estimate was that 'we would do a big test in 1958'.[99] The team met the deadline, thanks in considerable part to another scientist-manager,

William Cook, brought in to Aldermaston as Penney's deputy from the Royal Naval Scientific Service in 1954.[100] In the event, the H-bomb project ran ahead of schedule. The series of tests, code-named *Grapple*, on Christmas Island in the Indian Ocean 1957–8, demonstrated Britain's capability as a thermonuclear power and provided the key to the restoration of collaboration with the United States, a priority goal for politicians and civil servants alike since 1946. During discussions in Washington in the autumn of 1957 between members of the British and American projects, there was great debate among the British team about whether or not to show the Americans their best H-bomb design. If they were unimpressed, the locker would be empty. The British team took the risk. It worked. The Americans were impressed. Edward Teller, the so-called 'father' of the United States H-bomb, said, 'it is obvious that the laws of physics apply on both sides of the Atlantic'.[101] It was, in its way, a huge compliment to the British scientific Civil Service. Circumstances had forced them to go it alone and they had succeeded.

In every sense they had fulfilled their remit. The Chiefs of Staff had been presented with their small stockpile of 'Blue Danube' atomic bombs, and the 'Yellow Suns', the hydrogen weapons, were now in prospect. It showed what a small number of capable and determined professionals could do *despite* a nightmare of a Whitehall machine and a confused system of political decision-taking. In reaching this judgement I have isolated the performance assessment from the question of whether Britain should be an atomic power or not, the very different matter of designing and building the delivery system of the early deterrent, the V-force, or the human costs of the Windscale accident of 1957 and the side-effects of the weapons tests in Australia and on Christmas Island, issues which I am not competent to judge. In many ways, the early British bomb project was a continuation into the peace of that formidable mixture of people and skills that made up the Second World War Civil Service. It is frequently said in Whitehall that only in wartime is it possible to recruit absolutely first-class scientific talent into the Service. Such judgements are impossible to quantify. But, if true, it buttresses my belief that the retention of Penney, Hinton, Cockcroft and some other talented staff after 1945 was crucial to the project's accomplishment.

No two case-studies come up with the same lesson. If, as I generally maintain, the British Civil Service in similar conditions could not have done what the Japanese or, particularly, the French bureaucracies did so brilliantly after the war on the economic and industrial fronts, it is largely because they were not designed for the purpose. The ethos of the British senior civil servant is that of the adviser-regulator, not of the original-thinker-doer. In both world wars, that changed. But when on automatic pilot in peacetime the Service is very largely a hands-off institution. To make it otherwise requires a deliberate change, the penning of a new blueprint, which no postwar government has yet attempted.

Strangely enough, the political language of the Thatcher era would imply that Britain *had* passed through a corporatist era, complete with interventionist bureaucracy and empire-minded civil servants building an ever larger state apparatus – a malign condition from which only the 1979 general election rescued us. A slimmer Civil Service, a rationalised benefits system (both achieved by the spring of 1988) and a reformed Health Service (on the horizon) were very much in accordance with this view of the country's political economy and its alleged maladies.

But is it an accurate view? Does it really reflect what happened in political, public and administrative life after 1945? It is a very wide and very complicated issue, but a crucial one for any overarching assessment of performance. Were – are – the Whitehall regulars the guardians of the 1945 settlement, keepers of a philosophy conceived by Beveridge out of Keynes, who placed the construction of a welfare state before the creation of an economic miracle thereby making both unachievable? This is important territory, not just a land fit for scholars to live in.

It has become a part of mainstream political debate in the late eighties. Whenever a politician on the Conservative side wishes to flaunt his deeper intellectual capabilities this is the field in which he tends to display himself. For example, Nigel Lawson, the Chancellor of the Exchequer, chose the Centre for Policy Studies as the audience in February 1988 for a disquisition on 'The New Britain: The Tide of Ideas from Attlee to Thatcher'. The Thatcher governments, Mr Lawson claimed, had

> transformed the politics of Britain – indeed Britain itself – to an extent no other Government has achieved since the Attlee Government of 1945 to 1951 . . . [which] . . . set the political agenda for the next quarter of a century. The two key principles which informed its actions and for which it stood, big government and the drive towards equality, remained effectively unchallenged for more than a generation, the very heart of the postwar consensus.
>
> The pursuit of equality . . . led to growing discord, and the exercise of big government had led to the point where it was widely felt that Britain had become ungovernable. Yet it was not until the final stages of this process, in the mid-1970s, as the tensions that had been building up in a holocaust of inflation, a disease as socially destructive as it is economically damaging, that the tide of ideas began to turn.[102]

This is Correlli Barnett turned into political conventional wisdom. It is this brand of political thought which has led to demolition experts in the Cabinet Room eyeing the monuments of the postwar settlement with a view to detonation, including, as I write, its most granite-clad artefact, the National Health Service, which, a decade after its foundation, a Harvard professor had described as 'accepted as an altogether natural feature of the British landscape, almost a part of the Constitution'.[103]

It is a view which, consciously or not, absorbs part of the American 'public choice' school of thought which sees the politicisation of professions as they grow into empires clashing clumsily in a web of private competitions for public power and public money. To those who accept this line of thought, senior civil servants are both referees and players in this particular corporatist game. As Nigel Lawson put it, 'The benefits from the transfer of decision-making from the state to the citizen, which accompanies this process [the reduction of taxation], are many. On the moral plane, as that admirable documentary, *Yes, Prime Minister*, has memorably illustrated, those who work in government are no more immune from self-interest than anyone else.'[104]

I am deeply sceptical of this all-embracing view of the Civil Service as the builder of bureaucratic empires, the construction engineers of a ruinously expensive welfare apparatus or the back-room fixers of deals between the corporate fiefdoms of Britain at the expense of its citizens. When a new regime for both central government and welfare state is in the process of erection – as it is in the late eighties – the temptation to parody the *ancien régime* for propaganda and self-motivation purposes is very strong. It should be resisted.

For example, it would be possible using those same Whitehall files quarried by Correlli Barnett in his *The Audit of War* to show that it was those much-maligned Whitehall officials in the Board of Trade who sent a stream of warnings to ministers about the parlous condition of British industry and productivity which would be exposed once the command economy of the Second World War had given way to a restored system of international competition and trade. Equally it was the Treasury which mobilised every statistic and every ounce of pessimism it could to persuade the Coalition ministers that the Beveridge proposals could all too easily prove financially unsupportable in the postwar years.

It would be quite wrong, too, to imagine that Britain was unique in developing a mixed economy/welfare state in the late forties and early fifties. The merest glance at Walter Lacquer's figures (see Table 12) show that, if anything, we were a relative sluggard in this area compared to other Western European nations whether they had participated in the war or not. The Lacquer league table which is at the root of the problem is the one dealing with productivity (see Table 13). A better performance here and funding the health service would have been a snip. But the causes of *this* failure go very deep and dwarf anything the postwar Civil Service may or may not have done.

TABLE 12. PER CAPITA SOCIAL SECURITY EXPENDITURE IN DOLLARS AT 1954 PRICES

	1930	*1957*
Belgium	12	148
France	17	136
Germany	54	132
Holland	10	56
Italy	5	54
Sweden	22	135
Switzerland	24	96
United Kingdom[105]	59	93

TABLE 13. GROWTH OF LABOUR PRODUCTIVITY 1949–59 (Compound annual percentage of growth)

West Germany	5.7
Italy	4.8
Austria	4.8
France	4.3
Spain	4.3
Switzerland	3.7
Holland	3.6
Sweden	2.9
Belgium	2.7
(United States	2.0)
United Kingdom[106]	1.8

A more finely-tuned critique of postwar Whitehall would, however, pick out some peculiarly British characteristics which are important. There were some important delusions sustained in governing circles – both political and official – in the first postwar years. Professor Eric Hobsbawm, our leading Marxist economic historian and a man deeply familiar with other advanced political economies, was surely right when he said in a radio conversation, *The Road From 1945*, that

> the whole of the world actually after 1945 used the same techniques which [were] a mixed economy very strongly governed by . . . public and government control. And even the ones that started off like the Germans trying to do it by the free market actually within a few years conformed to the basic pattern of a mixed economy led by government planning.
>
> Our problem wasn't that we had a different type of economy. Our problem was that we couldn't get used to the idea that we were declining as fast as we were. We thought somehow or other Britain must remain a major industrial power and it's quite clear that the Labour people in the 1940s it didn't cross their mind . . . And neither on the Conservative side. Paradoxically, the first Government which really thought in those terms, however ineffectively, was Wilson.[107]

There was another, linked illusion which affected Whitehall and its transient political chiefs – that Britain was still capable of sustaining a great-power role in the world. Paul Kennedy has described it in hard, comparative terms whose reality not even the stoutest patriot could sensibly dispute. He also explains why the delusion endured.

> The frailty of Britain's international and economic position was partially disguised in the early post-1945 period by the even greater weakness of other States, the prudent withdrawals from India and Palestine, the short-term surge in exports, and the maintenance of Empire in the Middle East and Africa. The humiliation at Suez in 1956 therefore came as a greater shock, since it revealed not only the weakness of sterling but also the blunt fact that Britain could not operate militarily in the Third World in the face of American disapproval.
>
> Nonetheless, it can be argued that the realities of decline were *still* disguised – in defence matters, by the post-1957 policy of relying upon the nuclear deterrent, which was far less expensive than large conventional forces yet suggested a continued Great Power status; and in economic matters by the boom of the 1950s and 1960s.[108]

Kennedy, a supreme calibrator of such things, assessed 1980s Britain as a nation where 'the decline seemed to be levelling off', leaving the country 'still with the world's sixth-largest economy, and with very substantial armed forces. By comparison with Lloyd George's time, or even with Clement Attlee's in 1945, however, it was now just an ordinary, moderately large power, not a Great Power.'[109] Even so, as we have seen, Professor Kennedy still regarded 1980s Britain as second only to the Soviet Union in the over-extension of her overseas and defence commitments which underpinned his conviction that another, thoroughgoing, defence review could not be long delayed.[110]

When examining the grand themes of relative power and the need to match aspirations to capabilities, it strikes me that the people who make up the permanent government cannot win. If they sustained ministers in their belief that postwar problems were temporary, that military and economic greatness were capable of restoration they can be accused of fostering delusion. If they spoke, as William Armstrong and Paul Gore-Booth did, of managing decline, they are branded as defeatist.

These matters are important. But the key question for me is the capability of the British Civil Service in terms of helping to formulate and deliver the kind of policies and strategies their ministers prescribe. The peculiar skill of the civil servant, as opposed to the minister, should be the ability to pick out the requirements needed to make things happen, to allow a policy to run. And here in the postwar years the Service can, I think, be partially faulted.

Professor David Marquand has, I reckon, identified a significant lacuna in arguing that the state machine failed to adapt itself to the requirements of putting real flesh on Keynesian social democracy in the years after 1945.[111] The Whitehall slice of the thesis contained in his *The Unprincipled Society* runs like this: the Second World War represented a success story with government managing a siege economy and a command society with skill and competence. In the postwar period, the senior Civil Service was very much a part of the Keynesian social democratic consensus of a mixed economy fine-tuned from Whitehall and the increasing use of neo-corporatist techniques of consultation with great interests in the land, the employers and the trade unions in particular.

But there was a flaw in the chemistry of the postwar settlement. No new theory of the state was developed to accommodate the *formal* constitution of parliamentary sovereignty and ministerial accountability with the *informal* one of extra-parliamentary dealings with the great powers of the real economy. Postwar ministers and officials were attempting to run the modern state with the same bureaucratic instruments and administrative culture that had served Gladstone and Salisbury.

What was needed to make Keynesianism work here, according to Professor Marquand, was a British version of what he calls 'developmental states' such as Japan or France in which central government was in the van of progress. And the failure to grow one here was a crucial, though by no means the sole, contributor to the eventual failure of the social democratic consensus and the slide into the political economy of the Thatcher era.

I would extend the thesis still further and argue that the nineteenth-century bureaucracy with modifications and refinements in Whitehall is ill-suited to *any* of the governments likely to be thrown up in future by the political parties solo or in combination – that a degree of reskilling and rejigging is needed if a flexible and effective instrument for converting political wishes into practical reality is to be in place in time for the twenty-first century, whether managing decline or (as I fervently hope) managing revival is the order of the day.

17 A SYSTEM FOR THE TWENTY-FIRST CENTURY

It cannot be necessary to enter into any lengthened argument for the purpose of showing the high importance of the Permanent Civil Service of the country in the present day. The great and increasing accumulation of public business, and the consequent pressure on the Government, need only be alluded to; and the inconveniences which are inseparable from the frequent changes which take place in the responsible administration are matters of sufficient notoriety.
Sir Stafford Northcote and Sir Charles Trevelyan, 1853[1]

One of the remarkable differences between the public and the private sector is that the former can take very clever people and put them in an environment where it is impossible to achieve anything, and the latter can take rather dull people, point them at the rabbit and have them achieve marvels.
Stephen Taylor, 1987[2]

We glimpse in operation a system which is extremely centralised without, however, being decisive; and procedures which are extraordinarily time-consuming, yet leave one with no confidence that the evidence has been systematically and objectively explored ... [it] is a process of decision-making which is ponderous, ritualised, secretive and highly unreliable in its results.
Professor David Henderson, 1977[3]

That the Whitehall system can be substantially improved I have no doubt despite my determination *not* to use the Civil Service as a scapegoat for more general national shortcomings. And in suggesting a series of reforms I think it is possible to be brief, as Northcote and Trevelyan were, and I propose to start where they did with the most important ingredient of change: people. In this I am deliberately setting my face against the belief of both Haldane and William Armstrong that machinery should come first. People build structures, not the other way round.

For me the history of post-Warren Fisher Whitehall, when Northcote–Trevelyanism set hard, shows that Whitehall failed to attract the rich mixture of human skills it needed, relying overmuch on a single if refined stream of generalist graduates, and that it failed to make full use – and still does – of the human capital already in its possession. The *great* flaw in Northcote–Trevelyan was the answer they gave to their own key question on recruitment policy, 'whether it is better to train young men for the discharge of the duties which they will afterwards perform, or to take men of mature age, who have already acquired experience in other walks of life'. The master builders of the British Civil Service declared:

> Our opinion is that, as a general rule, it is decidedly best to train young men. Without laying too much stress on the experience which a long official life necessarily brings with it, we cannot but regard it as an advantage of some importance. In many offices, moreover, it is found that the *superior docility* [emphasis added] of young men renders it much easier to make valuable public servants of them, than of those more advanced in life ... To these advantages must be added the important one of being able, by proper regulations, to secure the services of fit persons on much more economical terms.[4]

The priority of any serious attempt to reform Whitehall must be to undo that defective, time-honoured canon of Northcote–Trevelyanism.

It has been undone twice this century by force of circumstances when new blood was brought in during both world wars only to be leached and removed once peace returned. (It happened, too, on a minor scale during the period of the 'New Liberalism' in the past first years of this century.) What is needed is a peaceful alternative to wartime compulsion. The way to achieve in the 1990s what Hitler did for Whitehall in the 1940s is to deliberately scale down the Civil Service Commission's production line from which successor generation after successor generation rolls off. The Commission's aim in the 1987–8 recruiting season is to find a hundred administration trainees or HEODs from within the service and without. If that were reduced by ten a year until only twenty a year were entering as young men and women with the possibility of staying for life, if they so chose – and a cap was rigidly placed upon that figure to prevent it rising in subsequent years – as time goes by, Whitehall would be *forced* to look outside to fill more and more of its regular posts in policy divisions and line management.

Allied to that should be a policy of publicity advertising *all* posts at under secretary level and above so that an open competition was held between lifers wishing to proceed above the rank of assistant secretary and those experienced in outside professions. An 'open recruitment' policy would have the additional advantage of ending the absurdly self-defeating rule which forces officials, who have gone outside the Service to broaden their experience, to re-enter on their return the grade they left – a more powerful disincentive could not be imagined, particularly to the especially successful. Bringing people in – a score of ATs apart – to the senior ranks of the Civil Service on fixed-term contracts would require more competitive pay rates than are on offer at the present. It should not be beyond the wit of the Treasury's pay technicians to devise them once ministers had approved such a radical unfreezing of the Whitehall labour market. The gains would soon outweigh the temporary burden on the Civil Service pay bill. It is an extension of liberal labour market principles that any government, whatever its political colouration, could adopt. The conduct and efficiency of public business could only be enhanced as it was in the years of 'war socialism' between 1939 and 1945.

New men would bring new methods. Certainly there would remain a need for a small corps of regulars familiar with the arcana of Whitehall machinery and Westminster procedure. The twenty per year intake of ATs would take care of that. Where the new men and women would shine would be in the importation of the best techniques and working methods from outside, particularly where, as happened in the DOE's Inner Cities Directorate in 1981–2, a task force-teamwork approach was adopted in the search for solutions to special problems. With open competition the norm, the Civil Service Commission would be in a position to search for the particular skills its departmental clients required. Departmental needs alter when there is a change of government or a policy review shifts priorities or when a particular procurement decision is in the offing. At the moment, ministers and permanent secretaries have to make do with whatever mixture of skills and personalities the CSSB competition has endowed them with some ten, twenty or thirty years before. No sensible institution would hobble its personnel side in this way.

None of this need mean the politicisation of the Civil Service. The principle of recruitment would be demonstrated merit, not ideological soundness. 'Is he one of us?' is not a question that would or should pass anyone's lips. The Civil Service Commission, on a lesser scale, naturally, would be replicating the practices and achievements of Beryl Power's Central Register. The map of the way forward is already there in Whitehall's own files. They should examine the best of their past and see how it worked. A retasked Civil Service Commission would itself need new blood, as the Ministry of Labour did in 1938–40 when it was searching for a new generation. It would take good people from other professions to help guide the Whitehall regulars on recruitment boards empanelled by the Commission, as already happens to a limited extent. In some ways the Commission's task will be easier. Choosing an experienced professional – and professional skill is what would count, not all-round ability – is surely easier than picking future permanent secretaries from bright but raw graduates.

A reformed recruitment policy and a refashioned Civil Service Commission would meet the needs of both the policy-making *and* the management sides of Whitehall, though I am at one with Rayner in believing that distinctions between the two activities should be progressively diminished. The original Civil Service Commission was the instrument of a genuine administrative revolution in the late nineteenth century. It could be again in the late twentieth. Contemporary reformers need to start exactly where Gladstone did with people and recruitment. Central government has to deal with a range of problems and execute a variety of tasks which dwarf even the largest multinationals. If a way is not found of tapping the nation's talent which successfully meets that myriad of requirements the nation will, year in year out, skimp itself in an area where, for the well-being of the citizenry as a whole, only the best is good enough.

Even if such a reform were attempted tomorrow it would, as Gladstone's did, take decades to run itself in. There are a number of shorter-term expedients which could be adopted to hasten the achievement of desirable long-term goals. First of all, the Civil Service should make greater use of its existing pool of talent, particularly that held in the reservoirs of the scientific, professional and technology grades. The SPATS scheme is admirable but marginal. The Cabinet Office and the Treasury should follow the logic of the extension of unified grading to principal level achieved in 1986 and take active steps to encourage the lateral transfer of professionals into administrative work by designating as many jobs as possible 'opportunity posts' for which generalists and specialists alike could apply. Such transfers should not be once-and-for-all steps. A spell in administration or management should be a routine part of the experience of a professional or scientific civil servant likely to rise to the top of a research division or establishment. Fulton in many ways was the specialists' charter. Twenty years later they are still some way from being truly enfranchised in terms of wider opportunities.

The Rayner reforms have by no means run their full course. In career terms, the good manager has still to be recognised for what he or she is worth. Policy advice remains the royal route to the top, as Sir Robert Armstrong recognised in his last speech as Head of the Home Civil Service.[5] In terms of techniques, the extension of the scrutiny methods into the £100 billion of programme expenditure beyond the £13 billion of running costs has a very long way to go.[6] Until it is so extended, those 'greater prizes' of which Armstrong spoke will remain to be won.[7] The Rayner techniques have yet to mesh with the public expenditure cycle and the frenzy of ministerial horse-trading and power-playing which marks its climax. Until they do, Raynerism's capacity to provide performance surrogates for the signals the market transmits to the private sector will remain unproven.

The other area where Raynerism has yet to impinge is the one he singled out himself in his own farewell lecture, 'The Unfinished Agenda'. The fruits of the efficiency programme have been considerable but they have yet to spread to the workforce who grew them in the shape of better accommodation and working conditions. This remains a piece of the Marks & Spencer philosophy that the Government has yet to buy. And, in the absence of advances on the pay front, the lack of such improvements is a genuine disincentive to further exertion and a persistent dampener on morale. The position could be changed relatively easily and swiftly.

Another aspect of the Government-as-employer has the air of unfinished business about it – the ground-rules covering the relationship between ministers and officials. Robert Armstrong had two goes at this before retirement, but the position remained unsatisfactory. For the regular servants of the state concerned about the propriety of ministerial instructions or actions, the last port of appeal was the Head of the Home Civil Service himself. Beyond that the road involved resignation and the carrying of grievance to the grave. This was not good enough. At the very least the regulars should enjoy the facility available to Whitehall's specials in the secret services who have their own independent counsellor outside the ranks of the hierarchy. Ideally, they should have a written code of 'do's' and 'don'ts' along the lines drafted by the First Division Association, with, if all else fails, the right of access to a Parliamentary officer such as the Ombudsman, who, for his part, would be able to alert the chairman of the Commons select committee shadowing the work of a complainant's department. Without a genuinely *external* avenue of complaint, the possibility would persist that an official's permanent secretary and the head of his profession might themselves have a personal interest in the issue at stake.

The interim reforms I have mentioned so far could be implemented in a relatively short time at a cost that would neither break the Exchequer nor stoke inflation and without the need for legislation. Another which comes into this category involves a second traditional institution at least eight hundred years older than the Civil Service Commission itself – the much abused good and great in a revived, streamlined form. The old system was both over-used and ignored, the worst of all worlds. For the new model G and G to take and flourish, the Government would have to impose certain disciplines on itself from the outset. Respect for the royal commission and the committee of inquiry will only be forthcoming if they are seen to be an impressive, somewhat awesome institution – an instrument of last rather than first resort. The selection of people to man them would have to be rigorous, with proven merit and expertise and dominant criteria of choice. The Government would have to heed, too, Professor Bernard Williams's strictures about the credibility gap that widened as report after report was ignored in the 1970s. An undertaking would be needed that the Government would make a considered reply to a G and G report within six months of its publication. In this way new blood and fresh thought could be quickly fed into the mainstream of Whitehall policy-making long before a new in-house breed of policy-maker began to emerge thanks to the efforts of a retasked Civil Service Commission.

With such new ground-rules in place for the G and G, they could profitably be deployed on three types of enterprise:

1. Ground-breaking inquiries in which a corpus of evidence needs to be created where little or none already exists. The Warnock committee on human embryology was an example of this type.
2. Task forces to tackle a pressing problem where both technical skill and inside knowledge are required. Hybrid committees of insiders and outsiders can be very productive here. The Beveridge report on social insurance and the Plowden report on public expenditure were examples of these. They have the great advantage of having at least some of the people who may be charged with implementing the proposals around the table from the outset.
3. Grand consensus-forming exercises on contentious problems which span the life of several parliaments and where cross-party agreement in a fairly high degree is desirable. Examples would include central–local government relations, major changes to the system of state education and lasting reform in the tax and benefits field.

A remodelled Good and Great would help fill the high duty Haldane placed on Government of 'investigation and thought as preliminary to action'.[8]

To place human reform at a premium is not to dismiss other Haldanian preoccupations with structure and machinery of government. Wherever the boundary between the public and the private, the state and the citizen, is drawn, there will be a need once more to examine central government from a functional perspective as Haldane did. The twenty-first-century state, unless something truly dramatic and unforeseen intervenes, will be engaged in the following activities:

* short-term crisis management;
* medium-term planning for manifesto programmes to be implemented in the life of a Parliament;
* strategic thinking on such issues as defence, foreign policy, energy and the welfare state;

* management of huge in-house businesses such as tax gathering and the social security system;
* management at one stage removed of huge enterprises like the National Health Service or the education system;
* regulation of public order and civic behaviour as laid down by law;
* powerfully influencing the British economy as bulk buyer of military and civilian goods;
* employing people on a large scale.

None of these activities has ever been static. I suspect they will become more mobile still. A fluid labour policy, therefore, will be indispensable in matching skills to tasks in a way that has not happened before in peacetime. A strong case can be made, however, for saying that substantial institutional changes need to be made if the state as thinker and manager is to match up to the requirements of the next century. That is certainly my view, accepting as I do Clive Priestley's philosophy that the citizen who funds it and whom it exists to serve deserves nothing less than a well-managed state wherever its frontier lies.

To take Whitehall's traditional and much-prized activity of policy analysis and advice first: this is not as good as it could be in an institution which practises its own brand of insider trading in which the same small group of regulars revolve around the same policy circuit year after year, keeping out alternative supplies of thought and analysis except where, on occasion, management consultants or the rare committee of inquiry are invited to participate in the process on terms dictated by the insiders. This is Bernard Donoughue's 'velvet drainpipe' syndrome with a vengeance and it has to be broken. That will not be easy. It will take a dramatic lowering of Whitehall's secrecy defences. Nothing so strongly reduces the power of an outsider to contribute as enforced secrecy. It will take, too, the conscious adoption of a team approach to problem-solving which is not the same thing at all as establishing yet another inter-departmental committee of officials to find the lowest common denominator of agreement.

Reviving the CPRS and providing each Cabinet minister with a *cabinet*, though highly desirable developments in themselves, will not be sufficient to tackle this problem. Tacking on new capabilities to the existing machine is a partial solution. Something more fundamental is required. The machine needs to be rebuilt so that the multi-disciplinary team approach, involving a real mix of skills and experience, is built into the specification of policy formulation in the line divisions of every department, which is why the wholly new approach to recruitment with which I began this chapter is *the* crucial first step.

If this new-blood argument were accepted and implemented the gains would be considerable, but only if a substantial proportion of this enhanced capability in Whitehall-as-thinker were applied to long-term problems of immense difficulty that range beyond the horizon of a manifesto or a single Parliament – issues such as the inner cities, future energy needs, the safety of nuclear power, and funding and shape of the welfare state, defence and weapons procurement ten to twenty years ahead. If Whitehall does not tackle these problems, nobody will. They are beyond the range and resources of university departments, private think-tanks or party research departments. The citizen-as-taxpayer is right to expect the Government to devote a slice of its very best brainpower to matters that will be crucial for his or her grandchildren. Future generations have to live not only with the sins of commission of their forebears (shoddy buildings, crumbling roads, faulty power stations) but with their sins of omission as well. This is perhaps the hardest area of all confronting Whitehall-as-thinker, which is why all too often it is placed in, Frank Cooper's phrase, in the 'too difficult category' and 'put on the long finger'. But if this work is not done by top-flight people, ministers *and* their permanent secretaries are genuinely culpable.

Twenty years after Fulton and eight years after Rayner's *The Conventions of Government* it is, at last, surely beyond argument that large sections of the Civil Service, the vast bulk of its manpower in fact, are employed in one or other of the vast businesses that statute requires the state to provide. As Stephen Taylor in particular never tires of pointing out, the amount of human and financial resources entrusted to departments and their senior officials is immense and comparable, ministry by ministry, to the largest multi-nationals:

> The average main Government department's income and expenditure is of the same order of magnitude as that of, for example, British Aerospace, Sainsbury or Lonrho. The Scottish Office spends as much as Shell UK earns (£8 bn), Environment is the equivalent of Unilever (£7 bn), Employment the equivalent of Ford UK (£4 bn) . . .[9]

Similar comparisons could have been made at any time since 1945–6 when Bridges and his fellow permanent secretaries contemplated taking action on the implications and then allowed the thought to perish. The implications have *still* not been taken fully on board in Whitehall, as Robert Armstrong was candid enough to admit more than forty years on from Bridges's meetings. Armstrong, referring to the Fulton Report, said:

> It . . . gave a signal that the management road to the top should be regarded as no less important than the traditional policy one. We have made some progress in that, but I would not claim that the message has even now been fully taken on board in practice. This is something

> towards which I hope future management reforms will give greater attention.[10]

So resistant has the Civil Service been to the self-evident need to embrace the notion of Whitehall-as-manager despite Fulton and Rayner that I have come to believe it will not be taken on board until central government's great executive functions are treated as what they are – big businesses – and organised and staffed accordingly. This essentially is the thinking developed independently by Michael Heseltine and Robin Ibbs. This is not at all the same thing as saying they should be privatised. Tax collection and benefits payment are, to my mind, genuine state activities and should remain so. It does not mean they are doomed to inefficiency thereby. State enterprise can be efficient. It depends on good managers with the freedom to manage and *that* means an end to the skein of Treasury controls put in place by Warren Fisher seventy years ago. Block budgets should be agreed annually for pay and running costs; within them the managers of the revenue, customs, social security and vehicle licensing businesses, to single out but four, should be free to pay, structure and recruit according to their needs as they see them against performance and productivity indicators agreed centrally in advance. The staff would remain civil servants, however, subject to the public service ethos, ethic and disciplinary code.

For this to work, the central supervision now exercised jointly and untidily by the Treasury and the Cabinet Office would need to be placed in the hands of a Management Board for the Civil Service along the lines suggested by Ken Stowe in 1987. It would have the nature of a supervisory board overseeing the work of Whitehall as a whole and its big businesses in particular. It would advise the Civil Service Commission on recruitment needs and the Civil Service College on training needs. It should be chaired by a senior Cabinet minister, preferably the No. 2 in the Cabinet hierarchy. Its chief executive would be head of the Home Civil Service, who would *not* be the same person as the Cabinet Secretary. To be chief executive of a 600,000 strong, £150 bn a year enterprise is a fulltime job for any man or woman.

The board's membership, in addition to the senior Cabinet minister and the Head of the Civil Service, would consist of the Cabinet Secretary, the Permanent Secretary to the Treasury and three other heads of departments chosen on the basis of seniority. The insider element must be balanced by at least four outsiders, three of whom should have experience of running large enterprises in the private sector. The board would advise the Prime Minister and the Cabinet on Civil Service matters, report annually to Parliament and submit itself to a yearly public examination by the all-party Commons Treasury and Civil Service Committee. The board should be given the staff it needed and be entirely separate from the Treasury and the Cabinet Office, its permanent official being the Head of the Home Civil Service and its minister the Cabinet's No. 2 acting on behalf of the Prime Minister. Apart from at last providing the Civil Service with the leadership and guidance it needs, the board would end once and for all the perpetual debate about the locus of Whitehall responsibilities between the central departments. And, finally, for more than symbolic reasons, the headship of the Civil Service should be advertised, made subject to an open competition and awarded on the basis of a contract renewable after five years. The salary would be commensurate with responsibility and exceed that of the Cabinet Secretary and the Permanent Secretary to the Treasury. It should be performance-related. Personnel revolutions should start from the top.

Let us assume, and it is a titanic assumption, that a series of revolutions in recruitment, policy-making, management and central direction *had* been effected in Whitehall. It would be breathtaking and deserve to rank with the post-Northcote–Trevelyan achievement of the nineteenth century. But there would still be a missing dimension – the kind of openness and public accountability that keeps bureaucracies constitutional, clean, efficient and responsive. Openness is the point of departure here. The best way of achieving this, initially at any rate, is, I believe, to go with the constitutional grain and take the Parliamentary route. A code of practice, determining what areas should be open and which remain closed, should be agreed by negotiation between the Government and the Liaison Committee of Select Committee chairmen. It should be laid before Parliament for debate and approval. It should be monitored by an Information Ombudsman who would report routinely to a Select Committee on Official Information and to Parliament annually with a day set aside for a full Commons debate. It should be for the Commons to vote on how to proceed if a minister defied the select committee. The code of practice–select committee arrangement should be instituted for an experimental five-year period. When it was up, Parliament should decide whether or not open government needed to be placed on a statutory basis with a full-blooded Freedom of Information Act. But, without the minimum solution of a policeable code on access to information, neither the policy nor the managerial revolutions in Whitehall would succeed. The system would remain one of largely unaccountable insider trading with both Parliament and the public kept in the role of excluded paymaster instead of enfranchised shareholder.

Lines of accountability are crucial, but those to whom the public entrusts the job of calling the executive to account need a brain of their own. The National Audit Office, as we have seen, has enjoyed a new lease of life in the 1980s. It needs to be built upon. Here ideas developed independently by David Henderson and Norman Strauss are central. In 1977 Henderson argued for the creation of a 'new institution specifically created to analyse and review British public expenditure programmes, with a vested interest in the truth'.[11] This institution, Henderson suggested, should undertake top-flight policy analysis on current programmes and projects and disseminate them for public consumption in a timely and digestible fashion. Strauss in the mid-1980s developed his concept of an independent but publicly funded institution staffed on multi-disciplinary lines and making full use of information technology (he called it first 'the Computeracy' and later changed it to 'the Net'). It would have access to all government data and would publish its analysis and advice.[12]

Given my preference for using, wherever possible, traditional and familiar institutions for new purposes, I would follow Henderson in looking to Parliament as the patron and first customer of an institution 'with a vested interest in the truth' able to serve the Commons, the Lords and their select committees and, through them, the public. For me the National Audit Office would be the body on which to build these new current policy-analysis capabilities in addition to the retrospective skills and techniques its staff already possess. The Commons, acting on the recommendation of its own House of Commons Commission, already has the power to vote the money necessary for this which would be, at the most generous, no more than £10 m a year out of a total public expenditure tranche of £150 billion. It should use that power. If it did, at last it would have a chance of holding Whitehall and the executive properly and consistently to account.

The reforms I have sketched are ambitious but they go with the grain of Westminster and Whitehall and their traditions, as all lasting reforms should if they are to have any real prospect of taking and enduring. For any of them to happen two key elements must be in place: parties when in Opposition must take the condition of the instruments of government seriously. If you think it will be all right on the day, you can be certain of one thing – it won't be. Whitehall is the prize with which, if successful at the polls, the electorate endows them. Some prior thought about that trophy and its utility is a first-order problem for any serious Opposition. Secondly, a reform-minded prime minister once elected must take the lead in making change happen and keep at it until change is achieved. Unless that is done, little of serious value will result. The lesson of history, here at least, is uncontestable. From Gladstone through Lloyd George via Wilson and Heath to Thatcher, the message is plain: unless the individual in No. 10 wants it and presses for it, Whitehall will adapt but it will not shift. When it comes to reforming the Civil Service, one heart and one mind has to be convinced and captured before all others – the prime minister's. And if Britain is to have the Civil Service it needs in the twenty-first century, the sooner the capture is made the better for the nation's sake *and* Whitehall's.

NOTES

The following abbreviations are used in the notes.

CUP	Cambridge University Press
H of C	House of Commons
H of L	House of Lords
HMSO	Her Majesty's Stationery Office
LSE	London School of Economics and Political Science
LWT	London Weekend Television
OUP	Oxford University Press
PRO	Public Record Office
RIPA	Royal Institute of Public Administration
TUC	Trades Union Congress

PREFACE

1 Lord Radcliffe, *Power and the State*, The Reith Lectures, 1951, I, 'On Plato's Idea of the State', first broadcast on the BBC Home Service, 4 November 1951.
2 Lord Hailsham, *The Granada Guildhall Lecture 1987*, delivered at the Guildhall in the City of London, 10 November 1987.
3 Quoted in *Thatcher's 3000 Days*, BBC 1 *Panorama*, 4 January 1988.
4 Anthony Sampson, *Anatomy of Britain Today*, Hodder, 1965.
5 Ibid., p. 251.
6 London *Evening Standard*, 17 November 1964.
7 Sir Robert Armstrong interviewed by Marcel Berlins on LWT's *Questions*, Channel 4 Television, 1 July 1984.
8 Public Record Office, CO 267/159 quoted in Ronald Robinson and John Gallagher with Alice Denny, *Africa and the Victorians: The Official Mind of Imperialism*, Papermac, 1965, p. 16.
9 W. J. Braithwaite, *Lloyd George's Ambulance Wagon*, Cedric Chivers, 1970, p. 33.

10 For Fulton see *The Civil Service,* Vol. 1, *Report of the Committee 1966–68*, HMSO, 1968. Vol. I of Fulton very conveniently reprinted Northcote and Trevelyan in full as its Appendix B, pp. 108–31.
11 Maurice Kogan, *The Politics of Education*, Penguin, 1971.
12 See below pp. 162–3.
13 Samuel Brittan, *Steering the Economy: The Role of the Treasury*, Pelican, 1969.
14 Peter Hennessy, 'Abrasive Touch for a Silky Machine', *Times Higher Education Supplement*, 19 January 1973.
15 It was published as Peter Hennessy, 'The Think Tank gets a man with a talent for saying what he means', *The Times*, January 1975.
16 Richard Rose (ed.), *Policy-Making in Britain, A Reader in Government*, Macmillan, 1969.
17 Paul Addison, *The Road to 1945*, Cape, 1975.
18 Tom Harrisson, *Living through the Blitz*, Collins, 1976.
19 D. N. Chester (ed), *Lessons of the British War Economy*, Cambridge, 1951.
20 Hugh Heclo and Aaron Wildavsky, *The Private Government of Public Money*, Macmillan, 1974 (2nd edn, 1981).
21 Henry Roseveare, *The Treasury, The Evolution of a British Institution*, Allen Lane, 1969.
22 It is described from the inside by Richard Crossman in *The Diaries of a Cabinet Minister,* Vol. One, *Minister of Housing, 1964–66*, Hamish Hamilton, Jonathan Cape, 1977, p. 166, diary entry for 22 February 1965.
23 Anthony Verrier, *Through the Looking Glass: British Foreign Policy in the Age of Illusions*, Cape, 1983.
24 See below pp. 238–41.

INTRODUCTION

1 Sir Edward Bridges, 'Portrait of a Profession', Rede Lecture, University of Cambridge, 1950, printed by: CUP, 1950, p. 33.
2 Shirley Williams, 'The Decision Makers', in *Policy and Practice: The Experience of Government*, RIPA, 1980, p. 81.
3 Sidney Pollard, *The Wasting of the British Economy*, 2nd edn, Croom Helm, 1984, p. 159.
4 C. R. Attlee, *As It Happened,* Odhams, 1954, p. 251.
5 Douglas Jay, *Change and Fortune: A Political Record*, Hutchinson, 1980, p. 505.
6 Peter Kellner and Lord Crowther-Hunt, *The Civil Servants: An Inquiry into Britain's Ruling Class*, Macdonald, 1980.
7 Leslie Chapman, *Your Disobedient Servant*, Chatto, 1978.
8 Brian Sedgemore, *The Secret Constitution, An Analysis of the Political Establishment*, Hodder, 1980.
9 Hugo Young and Anne Sloman, *No, Minister: An Inquiry into the Civil Service*, BBC, 1982.

10 Hugo Young and Anne Sloman, *But, Chancellor: An Inquiry into the Treasury*, BBC, 1984.
11 Clive Ponting, *The Right to Know: The Inside Story of the Belgrano Affair*, Sphere, 1985.
12 Clive Ponting, *Whitehall: Tragedy and Farce*, Hamish Hamilton, 1986.
13 Martin Wiener, *English Culture and the Decline of the Industrial Spirit 1850–1980*, Cambridge, 1981, p. 3.
14 Dennis Kavanagh, *British Politics: Continuities and Change*, OUP, 1985, p. 1.
15 Correlli Barnett, *The Audit of War: The Illusion and Reality of Britain as a Great Nation*, Macmillan, 1986, p. 55.
16 Ibid., pp. 88, 104–5.
17 Ibid., p. 123.
18 Ibid., p. 55.
19 Michael Charlton, *The Price of Victory*, BBC, 1983, p. 117.
20 Young and Sloman, *No, Minister*, p. 71.
21 Private information.
22 Private information.
23 Bridges, *Portrait of a Profession*, p. 17.
24 Two of Sir John Hoskyns's lectures need to be read in full if the gravamen of his case is to be appreciated: 'Westminster and Whitehall: An Outsider's View', *Fiscal Studies*, Vol. 3, No. 3 (November 1982), pp. 162–72; 'Conservatism is not Enough', *Political Quarterly*, Vol. 55, No. 1 (January–March 1984), pp. 3–16.
25 Quoted in Richard Rose, 'Steering the Ship of State: One Tiller but Two Pairs of Hands', Treasury and Civil Service Committee, *Civil Servants and Ministers* (HMSO, 1986), 7th Report, HC 92-II, 301–14.
26 Letter from Sir Patrick Nairne to Peter Hennessy, 29 April 1977.
27 George W. E. Russell, *Collections and Recollections*, Nelson, 1904, p. 332.
28 A. J. P. Taylor, 'William Cobbett', in *Englishmen and Others*, Hamish Hamilton, 1956, p. 7.
29 Henry Fairlie, 'Political Commentary', *The Spectator*, 23 September 1955, p. 380.
30 Thomas Balogh, 'The Apotheosis of the Dilettante: The Establishment of Mandarins', in Hugh Thomas (ed.), *The Establishment: A Symposium*, Anthony Blond, 1959, p. 99.
31 Ibid., p. 111.
32 Ibid.
33 Correlli Barnett, *The Collapse of British Power*, Eyre Methuen, 1972, p. 41.
34 Quoted in O. R. McGregor, 'Admonishing the administrators', *The Times Literary Supplement*, 4 April 1986.
35 Wiener, *English Culture and the Decline of the Industrial Spirit*, pp. 16, 24.
36 Hannah Arendt, *The Origins of Totalitarianism*, Harcourt, Brace, 1951.
37 Conversation with Denis Healey, 16 March 1977.
38 The Hudson Report, *The United Kingdom to 1980*, Hudson Institute, 1973.
39 Anthony Sampson, *The Changing Anatomy of Britain*, Hodder, 1982.

40 Pollard, *The Wasting of the British Economy*, p. 156.
41 Ibid., p. 159.
42 Ibid., pp. 154–5.
43 Ibid., pp. 155–6.
44 Peter Hennessy and Sir Douglas Hague, *How Adolf Hitler Reformed Whitehall*, Strathclyde Papers on Government and Politics, No. 41, p. 31. Department of Politics, University of Strathclyde, 1985.
45 Eric Hobsbawm, *Industry and Empire*, Weidenfeld, 1969.
46 G. C. Allen, *The British Disease*, Hobart Papers 67, Institute of Economic Affairs, 1976.
47 Ibid.
48 Ibid.
49 Ibid.
50 Correlli Barnett, *The Audit of War: The Illusion and Reality of Britain as a Great Nation*, Macmillan, 1986, pp. 18–19. His Chapter 1 on 'The Dream of the New Jerusalem', pp. 11–38, is best taken in one gulp like a goblet brimming with bilious polemic.
51 Mancur Olson, *The Rise and Decline of Nations: Economic Growth, Stagflation and Rigidities*, Yale, 1982, p. 78.
52 Sir Robert Armstrong's tribute to Sir Anthony Rawlinson, Westminster Abbey, 8 April 1986, quoted in Peter Hennessy, 'The Listener Profile: Sir Robert Armstrong', *The Listener*, 26 June 1986, p. 14.
53 For Gladstone at Eton and Oxford see E. J. Feuchtwanger, *Gladstone*, Allen Lane, 1975, pp. 8–13. For his Civil Service reforms see Feuchtwanger's Chapter 1.
54 The easiest package tour can be found in the shape of David Coates and John Hillard (eds), *The Economic Decline of Modern Britain: The Debate Between Left and Right*, Wheatsheaf, 1986.
55 *Reskilling Government*, Institute of Directors, 1986, p. 4
56 Ministry of Reconstruction, *Report of the Machinery of Government Committee*, Cd. 9230, HMSO, 1918, p. 16.
57 G. R. Elton, *The Future of the Past*, CUP, 1968, pp. 24–5.
58 I was told this story by Sir Kenneth Stowe on 22 September 1987.
59 'Another Turn of the Mangle', Times Diary, *The Times*, 15 July 1980.
60 Figure supplied by the Prime Minister's Efficiency Unit, Spring 1988.

PART 1 ORIGINS

1 Edward Shils, *The Intellectuals and the Powers and Other Essays*, University of Chicago, 1972, p. 21.
2 Robert Skidelsky, *John Maynard Keynes, Hopes Betrayed 1883–1920*, Macmillan, 1983, p. 175.
3 Quoted in Sampson, *Anatomy of Britain*, pp. 227–8.
4 Hailsham, *Granada Guildhall Lecture, 1987*.

5 A. J. P. Taylor, *Englishmen and Others*, Hamish Hamilton, 1956, p. 21.
6 *House of Lords Official Report*, 2 March 1988, cols 181–4.

1 THE MAKING OF AN INSTITUTION

1 Sir Edward Bridges, 'Machinery of Government', Lecture to the Imperial Defence College, January, 1950, preserved in PRO, T 273/187.
2 Quoted in Asa Briggs, *Victorian People*, Pelican, 1965, p. 117.
3 James Winter, *Robert Lowe*, University of Toronto Press, 1976, p. 264.
4 A delightful geographic history of Whitehall can be found in Samuel McKechnie's deliciously titled, *The Romance of the Civil Service*, Sampson, Low, Marston. It is undated, but it is clearly from the early 1930s. Mr McKechnie was Editor of the *Civil Service Arts Magazine*. He has a sensitive appreciation of the spirit of place. See Chapter 1, pp. 1–14.
5 Neville Cardus, *Second Innings*, Collins, 1950, pp. 240.
6 The essay on Clive appeared in January 1940, that on Hastings in October 1841. They are reproduced in *Lord Macaulay's Essays and Lays of Ancient Rome*, Longman, 1889, pp. 502–46 and 602–67.
7 For the Northcote–Trevelyan Report see Fulton Report, Cmnd. 3638, Volume I, Appendix B, p. 108. For usage of the term 'Civil Service' see Sir Norman Chester, *The English Administrative System 1780–1870*, OUP, 1981, pp. 298–9 and Richard A. Chapman and J. R. Greenaway, *The Dynamics of Administrative Reform*, Croom Helm, 1980, p. 53.
8 Roseveare, *The Treasury*, p. 23.
9 Ibid., p. 23.
10 See Peter Hennessy, 'Permanent Government: The "Guilt" of the Treasury 1000', *New Statesman*, 23 January 1987.
11 Roseveare, *The Treasury*, p. 27.
12 Ibid., p.30.
13 G. R. Elton, *England under the Tudors*, Methuen, 1955, p. 54.
14 Ibid., p. 75.
15 Ibid., p. 180.
16 Chester, *The English Administrative System*, p. 229.
17 Elton, *England under the Tudors*, p. 183.
18 Susan Foreman, *Shoes and Ships and Sealing-Wax: An Illustrated History of the Board of Trade 1786–1986*, HMSO, 1986, p. 1.
19 See p. 345 above.
20 Roseveare, *The Treasury*, p. 44.
21 H of C Debates, 11 March 1980.
22 Elton, *England under the Tudors*, p. 406.
23 Roseveare, *The Treasury*, p. 47.
24 Ibid., p. 54.
25 Foreman, *Shoes and Ships and Sealing-Wax*, p. 1.
26 Ibid., p. 2.
27 Ibid.
28 Max Hastings and Simon Jenkins, *The Battle for the Falklands*, Michael

Joseph, 1983, p. 2; *Home Office 1782–1982*, Home Office, 1981, p. 3.
29 Roseveare, *The Treasury*, p. 58.
30 Christopher Jones, *No. 10 Downing Street: The Story of a House*, BBC, 1985, p. 14.
31 Roseveare, *The Treasury*, p. 63.
32 Ibid., p. 62.
33 G. M. Trevelyan, *England under Queen Anne*, Vol. 2, *Ramillies*, Longmans, 1932, p. 163.
34 Roseveare, *The Treasury*, p. 84.
35 *A Guide to the Inland Revenue*, HMSO, 1983, p. 3.
36 Roseveare, *The Treasury*, p. 84.
37 John Douglas, *Seasonal Hints from an Honest Man*, 1761, p. 38.
38 Chester, *English Administrative System*, p. 18.
39 *Northcote–Trevelyan Report*, as reproduced in Cmn. 3638, p. 109.
40 *Home Office 1782–1982*, p. 3.
41 James Callaghan, 'Cumber and Variableness', in *The Home Office: Perspectives on Policy and Administration, Bicentenary Lectures 1982,* RIPA, 1982, p. 9.
42 Ibid.
43 Ibid.
44 *Home Office 1782–1982*, p. 3.
45 Lord Allen of Abbeydale, 'State Service: Reflections of a Bureaucrat', *Bicentenary Lectures*, p. 23.
46 Valerie Cromwell and Zara S. Steiner, 'The Foreign Office before 1914: a Study in Resistance', in Gillian Sutherland (ed.), *Studies in the Growth of Nineteenth Century Government*, Routledge, 1972, p. 175.
47 Ibid., p. 49.
48 Algernon Cecil, *British Foreign Secretaries*, G. Bell & Sons Ltd, 1927, p. 229.
49 A. W. Ward and G. P. Gooch, *Cambridge History of British Foreign Policy*, Vol. 3, CUP, 1923, p. 599.
50 Extracts from Burke's philippic are reproduced in Foreman, *Shoes and Ships and Sealing-Wax*, pp. 2–3.
51 Richard Pares, *King George III and the Politicians*, OUP, 1953, pp. 148–9.
52 Foreman, *Shoes and Ships and Sealing-Wax*, p. 3.
53 Ibid.
54 Ibid., p. 4.
55 Winter, *Robert Lowe*, p. 96.
56 Ibid.
57 Quoted in Briggs, *Victorian People*, p. 117.
58 Quoted in Winter, *Robert Lowe*, p. 264.
59 Briggs, *Victorian People*, p. 117.
60 H. C. G. Matthew, *Gladstone 1809–1874*, Clarendon Press, 1986, p. 85.
61 *The Civil Service*, Vol. I, Report of the Committee 1966–68, HMSO, 1968, p. 9. Cmnd. 3638.
62 Chapman and Greenaway, *Dynamics of Administrative Reform*, p. 23.
63 Jenifer Hart, 'Sir Charles Trevelyan at the Treasury', *English Historical Review*, Vol. 75, 1960, p. 106.

64 Briggs, *Victorian People*, p. 169.
65 Ibid.
66 Chapman and Greenaway, *Dynamics of Administrative Reform*, p. 23.
67 Trevelyan to Lewis, 18 September 1848, Trevelyan Papers, CET 52.
68 Anthony Trollope, *The Three Clerks*, Richard Bentley, 1884, p. 59.
69 Raleigh Trevelyan, *The Golden Oriole*, Secker & Warburg, 1987, pp. 286–7.
70 Hart, 'Trevelyan at the Treasury', p. 102. Trevelyan's views on Ireland are in letters of 6 and 9 October 1846. His image of the English as improved Germans was committed to paper on 8 December 1852.
71 Trevelyan to Gladstone, 15 September 1853, Trevelyan Papers, CET 18.
72 Chapman and Greenaway, *Dynamics of Administrative Reform*, p. 24.
73 Matthew, *Gladstone*, p. 110.
74 Chapman and Greenaway, *Dynamics of Administrative Reform*, p. 25.
75 Roseveare, *The Treasury*, pp. 165–6.
76 The Treasury Minute is reproduced in Chapman and Greenaway, *Dynamics of Administrative Reform*, pp. 25–6.
77 Ibid., p.26.
78 Roseveare, *The Treasury*, pp. 168–9.
79 Trevelyan made this point in a letter to John Parker, former joint secretary to the Treasury, of 14 March 1854, quoted in Hart, 'Trevelyan at the Treasury', p. 106.
80 Ibid., p. 107.
81 Professor Kenneth Wheare, 'The Civil Service in the Constitution', Haldane Lecture, 1954, University of London, 1954, p. 14.
82 This and subsequent extracts are taken from the Northcote–Trevelyan Report as reprinted in Appendix B of the Fulton Report.
83 Bridges, *Portrait of a Profession*, p. 32.
84 H of L Debates, Cols 525–26, 10 July 1833.
85 Quoted in Chapman and Greenaway, *Dynamics of Administrative Reform*, pp. 40–1.
86 The Macaulay Report can also be most conveniently found in Appendix B to the Fulton Report, Vol. 1, pp. 119–28.
87 Chapman and Greenaway, *Dynamics of Administrative Reform*, p. 41–2.
88 See above pp. 629–35.
89 Chapman and Greenaway, *Dynamics of Administrative Reform*, p. 44.
90 Ibid., p. 42.
91 Ibid., p. 43.
92 Ibid.
93 *Iolanthe* was first performed at the Savoy Theatre in London in 1882.
94 John Morley, *The Life of William Ewart Gladstone*, Vol. I, Macmillan, 1903, p. 649.
95 Peter Gowan, 'The other face of administrative reform: the Northcote–Trevelyan programme and the "19th century revolution in Government"', unpublished MSc thesis, London School of Economics, 1987, has the best summary of the debate I have read. I am grateful to Professor George Jones for bringing it to my attention and to Peter Gowan for permission to quote from it.

96 Ibid., p. 34.
97 Trevelyan to Raglan 13 February 1854, quoted in Hart, 'Trevelyan at the Treasury', p. 103.
98 Ibid.
99 See Oliver Woods and James Bishop, *The Story of* The Times, Michael Joseph, 1983, pp. 67–79.
100 Roy Jenkins outlined his thesis on nineteenth-century reform to the SDP Annual Conference in Harrogate on 15 September 1986.
101 Olive Anderson, 'The Janus Face of Mid-Nineteenth Century English Radicalism: The Administrative Reform Association of 1855', *Victorian Studies*, Vol. 8, March 1965, p. 234.
102 Quoted in Chapman and Greenaway, *Dynamics of Administrative Reform*, p. 45.
103 Ibid., p. 46.
104 H of C Debates, 15 June 1855, Col. 2090.
105 Roseveare, *The Treasury*, p. 172.
106 Ibid.
107 Sir Algernon West, *Recollections, 1832 to 1886*, Vol. I, Smith, Elder, 1899, pp. 52–3.
108 Winter, *Robert Lowe*, p. 245.
109 Quoted in Michael Cockerell, Peter Hennessy and David Walker, *Sources Close to the Prime Minister*, Macmillan, 1984, p. 233.
110 Winter, *Robert Lowe*, p. 263.
111 Ibid.
112 Ibid., pp. 263–4.
113 Ibid., p. 264.
114 Roseveare, *The Treasury*, p. 177.
115 Lord Allen, 'Reflections of a Bureaucrat', p. 26.
116 Roseveare, *The Treasury*, p. 179.
117 Ibid., p. 180.
118 Bridges, *Portrait of a Profession*, p. 10.
119 PRO T 273/9.
120 *The Administrators: The Reform of the Civil Service*, Fabian Tract 355, Fabian Society, 1964, p. 2.
121 J. D. Gregory, *On the Edge of Diplomacy, Rambles and Reflections, 1902–28*, Hutchinson, 1929, p. 274.
122 Chapman and Greenaway, *Dynamics of Administrative Reform*, p. 57.
123 Herman Finer, *The British Civil Service: An Introductory Essay*, Fabian Society, 1927, p. 14.

2 WELFARE, WAR AND PEACE

1 Quoted by Sir John Martin in Sir John Wheeler-Bennett (ed.), *Action This Day: Working with Churchill*, Macmillan, 1968, p. 153.
2 John Turner, 'Experts and Interests: David Lloyd George and the Dilemmas of the Expanding State', in Rory Macleod (ed.), *Government and Expertise*

in Nineteenth Century Britain: Essays in Honour of Oliver Macdonagh, CUP, 1988.

3 Max Beloff, 'The Whitehall Factor: The Role of the Higher Civil Service 1919–39' in Gillian Peele and Chris Cook (eds), *The Politics of Reappraisal, 1918–39*, Macmillan, 1957, p. 210.
4 Foreman, *Shoes and Ship and Sealing-Wax*, p.53.
5 Ibid., pp. 54–5.
6 Harry Judge, 'R. L. Morant 1863–1920', in Paul Barker (ed.), *Founders of the Welfare State*, Heinemann Educational, 1984, p. 61.
7 E. J. R. Eaglesham, 'The Centenary of Sir Robert Morant', in The British Journal of Educational Studies, (Nov 1963), p. 7.
8 Ibid., pp. 17–18.
9 *Top Jobs in Whitehall: Appointments and Promotions in the Senior Civil Service*, Report of an RIPA Working Group, RIPA, 1987, p. 14.
10 Ibid., pp. 14–15. I am grateful to Dr Kevin Theakston, secretary of the RIPA Working Group, for identifying Kekewich. Other examples of the two-way movement are Reginald Brett, a Liberal MP 1880–5 and Permanent Secretary to the Office of Works 1895–1901; as Viscount Esher, he was a pillar of the prewar committee of Imperial Defence; and David Shackleton, Labour MP 1902–10, President of the TUC 1908–9, who was Permanent Secretary to the Ministry of Labour 1916–21. Letter from Dr Kevin Theakston 14 May 1987.
11 Ibid., p. 15.
12 Jill Pellew, *The Home Office 1848–1914: from Clerks to Bureaucrats*, Heinemann Educational, 1982.
13 Turner, 'Experts and Interests'.
14 Cromwell and Steiner, 'The Foreign Office before 1914', p. 183.
15 E. J. Hobsbawm, *The Age of Empire, 1875–1914*, Weidenfeld, 1987, p. 103.
16 Ibid.
17 Ibid.
18 Kenneth O. Morgan, 'Aneurin Bevan 1897–1960', in Barker (ed.), *Founders of the Welfare State*, p. 106.
19 Turner, 'Experts and Interests'.
20 John Grigg, *Lloyd George, The People's Champion 1902–1911*, Eyre Methuen, 1978, p. 102.
21 Keith Middlemas, *Politics in Industrial Society: The Experience of the British System since 1911*, Deutsch, 1979, p. 62.
22 Eric Hobsbawm, 'Offering a Good Society', *New Statesman*, 6 March 1987.
23 Grigg, *The People's Champion*, p. 335.
24 It became the title of Braithwaite's classic memoir, *Lloyd George's Ambulance Wagon*.
25 Ibid. pp. 84–5.
26 R. W. Harris, *Not so Humdrum: the Autobiography of a Civil Servant*, 1939, p. 123.
27 John W. Wheeler-Bennett, *John Anderson, Viscount Waveley*, Macmillan, 1962, p. 36.

28 Sir Henry Bunbury in the Introduction to Braithwaite, *Lloyd George's Ambulance Wagon*, p. 18.
29 Sir Richard Clarke, 'The Machinery of Government' in W. Thornhill (ed.), *The Modernisation of British Government*, Pitman, 1975, p. 66.
30 Ibid.
31 *Fourth Report of the Royal Commission on the Civil Service*, Cd. 7338, HMSO, 1914, xvi. 1.
32 Arthur Marwick, *Britain in the Century of Total Wars: War, Peace and Social Change 1900–1967*, Bodley Head, 1968, p. 17.
33 David French, 'The Rise and Fall of "Business as Usual"', in Kathleen Burk (ed.), *War and the State: The Transformation of British Government, 1914–1919*, Allen & Unwin, 1982, p. 18.
34 PRO T 181/50, 'Notes on Private Arms Manufacture in the Great War', May 1935.
35 Waley told this story to Burke Trend shortly after he joined the Treasury in 1937. Conversation with Lord Trend, 1 October 1986.
36 French, 'Business as Usual', p. 19.
37 PRO CAB 37/124/40.
38 H of C Debates, 10 March 1915, col. 1460.
39 Quoted in French, 'Business as Usual', p. 24.
40 A. J. P. Taylor, *Essays in English History*, Hamish Hamilton, 1977, p. 270.
41 Chris Wrigley, 'The Ministry of Munitions: an Innovatory Department', in Burk (ed.), *War and the State*, p. 32.
42 David Lloyd George, *War Memoirs, Vol. I*, Nicolson and Watson, 1933, p. 254.
43 Turner, 'Experts and Interests'.
44 Taylor, *Essays in English History*, p. 270.
45 Turner, 'Experts and Interests'.
46 D. A. Wilson, unpublished University of Bristol PhD Thesis, 'The economic development of the electricity supply industry in Great Britain 1919–1939', 1976, quoted in Wrigley, 'The Ministry of Munitions', p. 47.
47 Barnett, *The Collapse of British Power*, pp. 82–9, 114–16.
48 Collected wartime speeches of Lloyd George, *Through Terror to Triumph*, Hodder, 1915, p. 104.
49 Lord Hunt of Tanworth interviewed for Brook Productions's Channel 4 Television Programme, *All the Prime Minister's Men*, 29 May 1986.
50 John P. Mackintosh, *The British Cabinet*, 2nd ed., Methuen, 1968, p. 4.
51 Zara Steiner, 'Decision-making in American and British Foreign Policy: an open and shut case', *Review of International Studies* (1987), 13, p. 7.
52 See John Turner, 'Cabinets, Committees and Secretariats: the Higher Direction of War' in Burk, *War and the State*, pp. 57–83.
53 See David Howell in the lead book review in *Political Quarterly*, Vol. 58 (1), January–March 1987, p. 102.
54 John Grigg, *Lloyd George from Peace to War 1912–1916*, Methuen, 1985, p. 488.
55 W. S. Churchill, *Great Contemporaries*, Butterworth, 1939, p. 249.

56 Turner, 'Cabinets, Committees and Secretariats' in Burk, *War and the State*, p. 72.
57 Stephen Roskill, *Hankey, Man of Secrets,* Vol. I, *1877–1918*, Collins, 1970, pp. 320–1.
58 PRO CAB 23/1. Cabinet Conclusions 9 December 1916.
59 Roskill, *Hankey, Man of Secrets*, Vol. I, pp. 337–8.
60 Gerald Kaufman, *How to be a Minister*, Sidgwick & Jackson, 1980, p. 72.
61 Stephen Roskill, *Hankey, Man of Secrets,* Vol. II, *1919–1931*, Collins, 1972, Chapter 11, pp. 304–29.
62 Lord Vansittart, *The Mist Procession*, Hutchinson, 1958, p. 164.
63 Lord Beaverbrook, *Men and Power 1917–18*, Hutchinson, 1956, pp. xviii-ix.
64 Private information.
65 For the attempted suppression see Stephen Roskill, *Hankey, Man of Secrets*, Vol. III, *1931–1963*, Collins, 1974, pp. 615–21. For the offending memoir see Lord Hankey *The Supreme Command, 1914–1918*, 2 vols, Allen and Unwin, 1961.
66 John Turner, *Lloyd George's Secretariat*, CUP, 1980, p. 15.
67 H. W. Massingham, *The Nation*, 24 February 1917.
68 Turner, *Lloyd George's Secretariat*, pp. 2–3.
69 Ibid., p. 4.
70 Ibid., pp. 6–7.
71 Ibid., p. 190.
72 Ibid., p. 197.
73 See Peter Hennessy, Susan Morrison and Richard Townsend, *Routine Punctuated by Orgies: The Central Policy Review Staff, 1970–83*, Strathclyde Papers on Government and Politics, No. 31, 1985, p. 204.
74 Conversation with Professor George Jones, 5 May 1983. His assessment is quoted in Peter Hennessy, 'Whitehall brief: Shades of a Home Counties Boudicca', *The Times*, 17 May 1983.
75 Quoted in José Harris, *William Beveridge: A Biography*, Oxford, 1977, p. 235.
76 *Report of the Machinery of Government Committee*, Cd. 9230.
77 See Kathleen Burk, 'The Treasury: From Impotence to Power', in Burk, *War and the State*, p. 97.
78 Cmd. 7338, p. 86.
79 Parliamentary Papers 1917–18, Vol. III, First and Second Reports from the Select Committee on National Expenditure.
80 Michael Heseltine, *Where There's a Will*, Hutchinson, 1987, pp. 52–3.
81 Max Beloff, *Wars and Welfare Britain 1914–45*, Edward Arnold, 1984, p. 23.
82 Burk, 'The Treasury', p. 107.
83 Taylor, *English History, 1914–1945*, p. 183.
84 Roseveare, *The Treasury*, p. 252.
85 Eunan O'Halpin, 'Sir Warren Fisher and the Coalition, 1919–1922', *The Historical Journal*, 24, 4 (1981), p. 907.
86 Quoted in Roseveare, *The Treasury*, p. 253.
87 PRO T 199/506.
88 PRO CAB 23/20. Cabinet Conclusions for 11 February 1920.

88 Roseveare, *The Treasury*, p. 248.
89 PRO T 199/506. Fisher to MacDonald, Neville Chamberlain and Baldwin, 25 November 1931.
90 *First and Second Reports from the Committee of Public Accounts, Sessions 1935–36,* Vol. 5, Question 4480.
91 P. J. Grigg, *Prejudice and Judgement*, Cape, 1948, p. 52.
92 McKechnie, *Romance of the Civil Service*, p. 205.
93 Ibid., facing p. 203.
94 Grigg, *Prejudice and Judgement*, p. 51.
95 Balogh, 'Apotheosis of the Dilettante' in Thomas (ed.), *The Establishment*, pp. 86–7.
96 Zara Steiner, *The Foreign Office and Foreign Policy, 1898–1914,* CUP 1969, p. 168.
97 Balogh, 'Apotheosis of the Dilettante', p. 86.
98 *Top Jobs in Whitehall*, p. 15.
99 Grigg, *Prejudice and Judgement*, pp. 81–2.
100 Ibid., pp. 52–3.
101 For an excellent account of the making of Bridges including his service on the Tomlin Royal Commission see Sir John Winnifrith, 'Edward Ettingdean Bridges – Baron Bridges 1892–1969' in *Biographical Memoirs of Fellows of the Royal Society*, Vol. 16, 1970, pp. 37–56.
102 *Royal Commission on the Civil Service 1929–31*, Cmd. 3909, HMSO, 1931, p. 1269 and p. 1276.
103 House of Commons Committee on Public Accounts, 1935–36 session, Question 4611.
104 John S. Harris and Thomas V. Garcia, 'The Permanent Secretaries: Britain's Top Administrators', *Public Administration Review*, XXVI (March 1966), p. 35.
105 Cmd. 3909, p. 1276 and p. 1284.
106 Grigg, *Prejudice and Judgement*, p. 53.
107 Barnett, *The Collapse of British Power*, p. 63.
108 Ibid., p. 64.
109 H. E. Dale, *The Higher Civil Service of Great Britain*, OUP, 1941, pp. 96–7.
110 Bridges, *Portrait of a Profession*, p. 31.
111 Private information.
112 Beloff, 'The Whitehall Factor' in Peele and Cook (eds), *The Politics of Reappraisal*, p. 210.
113 Ibid.
114 G. C. Peden, *British Rearmament and the Treasury: 1932–1939*, Scottish Academic Press, 1979.
115 Private information.
116 PRO T 161/800. Note by Sir Warren Fisher, 20 February 1923.
117 Beloff, 'The Whitehall Factor', p. 225.
118 Ibid., p. 227.
119 Ibid., p. 218.
120 Ian M. Drummond, *Imperial Economic Policy 1917–1939*, Allen & Unwin, 1974, pp. 127–9.

121 PRO T 161/538. Treasury Memorandum for the Middle East Standing Official Committee (1931).
122 PRO T 161/291. Minute of 7 January 1929.
123 Robert Skidelsky, *Politicians and the Slump*, Penguin edn, 1970, pp. 39–40.
124 Douglas Jay, *Change and Fortune: A Politican Record*, Hutchinson, 1980, p. 94.
125 Valerie Cromwell and Zara Steiner, 'Reform and Retrenchment: The Foreign Office Between the Wars', p. 96.
126 *Memorandum by the Board of Trade and the Foreign Office with respect to the Future Organization of Commercial Intelligence*, Cd, 8715, HMSO, 1917.
127 *Report of the Royal Commission on the Civil Service*, Cmd. 3909, HMSO, 1930, x, 517.
128 Cromwell and Steiner, 'Reform and Retrenchment', pp. 86–7.
129 Cromwell and Steiner, 'The Foreign Office before 1914', p. 193.
130 H of C Report, 28 May 1930, col. 1269.
131 PRO FO 366/781, Hughe Knatchbull-Hugessen to Sir Alexander Cadogan, 20 January 1939.
132 Keith Middlemas, *Politics in Industrial Society: The Experience of the British System since 1911*, André Deutsch, 1979, p. 18.
133 The phrase was coined by Peter Jenkins, 'The forging of Pym's Rebellion', *The Sunday Times*, 12 May 1985.
134 Eric Wigham, *From Humble Petition to Militant Action: A History of the Civil and Public Services Association 1903–1978,* CPSA, 1980, p. 17.
135 Colin Cross, *Philip Snowden*, Barrie and Rockcliff, 1966, p. 9.
136 Wigham, *From Humble Petition*, p. 23.
137 Sub-Committee on Relations between Employers and Employed, *Interim Report on Joint Standing Industrial Councils*, Col. 8606, HMSO, 1917, xvii.
138 W. J. Brown, *So Far . . .*, Allen & Unwin, 1943, p. 90.
139 Quoted in Chapman and Greenaway, *Dynamics of Administrative Reform*, p. 95.
140 Roseveare, *The Treasury*, p. 272.
141 Blanche E. C. Dugdale, *Arthur James Balfour, II, 1906–1930*, Hutchinson, 1936, pp. 372–3.
142 Skidelsky, *Politicians and the Slump*, pp. 155–7.
143 David Marquand, *Ramsay MacDonald*, Cape, 1977, p. 523.
144 Ibid.
145 Ibid.
146 R. H. Tawney, *Religion and the Rise of Capitalism* (first published 1926; successive Pelican editions since 1938); *The Acquisitive Society*, Bell, 1921.
147 Marquand, *Ramsay MacDonald*, p. 523.
148 Keith Middlemas (ed.), *Thomas Jones, Whitehall Diary*, Vol. 2, *1926/1930*, OUP, 1969, p. 226.
149 Skidelsky, *Politicians and the Slump*, p. 158.
150 Marquand, *Ramsay MacDonald*, p. 524.
151 Taylor, *English History 1914–1945*, p. 206.
152 Douglas Jay, *The Socialist Case*, Faber and Faber, 1937, p. 317.
153 J. M. Keynes, *The General Theory of Employment, Interest and Money*, Macmillan, 1936.

154 See John Pinder (ed.), *Fifty Years of Political and Economic Planning*, Heinemann Educational, 1981.
155 For an excellent survey of all these harbingers of war and postwar policy-making see Paul Addison, *The Road to 1945*, Cape, 1975, Chapter I.
156 Harold Macmillan, *The Middle Way*, Macmillan, 1938.
157 Ben Pimlott, 'Building afresh from defeat', *The Times*, 16 June 1987.
158 David Dilks (ed.), *The Diaries of Sir Alexander Cadogan, 1938–1945*, Cassell, 1971, pp. 31–4.
159 Quoted in Martin Gilbert, 'Horace Wilson: Man of Munich?' *History Today*, Vol. 32, October 1982, p. 9.
160 Ibid. Dalton is quoted in Kenneth O. Morgan, *Labour People*, OUP, 1987, p. 119.
161 Conversation with Lord Armstrong of Sanderstead, 2 July 1976.
162 Gilbert, 'Horace Wilson', p. 9.
163 Quoted in ibid.
164 Harold J. Laski, *A Grammar of Politics*, 4th edn, Allen & Unwin, 1937, pp. 402–3.
165 James Callaghan, *Time and Chance*, Collins, 1987, p. 41.
166 Nick Clarke, *Legacy of Empire*, BBC Radio 4, 18 March 1987.

3 HITLER'S REFORM

1 Conversation with Lord Penney, 7 May 1985.
2 D. N. Chester, 'The Central Machinery for Economic Policy' in D. N. Chester (ed.), *Lessons of the British War Economy*, CUP, 1951, p. 33.
3 Conversation with Sir John Winnifrith, former Second Secretary HM Treasury and Permanent Secretary to the Ministry of Agriculture, 30 April 1985.
4 Clive Priestley, former chief of staff, Prime Minister's Efficiency Unit, interviewed on 3 March 1987 for London Weekend Television's programme *Whitehall* made for Channel 4 Television.
5 For an economic assessment of the UK's mobilisation in the Second World War see Alec Cairncross, *Years of Recovery: British Economic Policy 1945–51*, Methuen, 1985, pp. 6–8, and Lord Robbins, *Autobiography of an Economist*, Macmillan, 1971, p. 177.
6 C. P. Snow, *The New Men*, Macmillan, 1954, collected Penguin edn, *Strangers and Brothers*, 1984.
7 *Strangers and Brothers*, Vol. 2, pp. 282–3.
8 'Action to ensure use of the Central Register by Government Departments', PRO LAB 8/175.
9 *Strangers and Brothers*, Vol. 2, p. 284.
10 PRO T 162/641.
11 R. J. Q. Adams, *Arms and the Wizard: Lloyd George and the Ministry of Munitions 1915–1916*, Cassell, 1978, p. 187.
12 Harold Macmillan, *The Past Masters: Politics and Politicans 1906–1939*, Macmillan, 1975, p. 44.
13 PRO T 162/641.

14 Ibid.
15 Ibid.
16 See PRO LAB 8/223.
17 Ibid.
18 Ibid.
19 PRO FO 366/1059. 'Recruitment of Emergency Staff for the Code and Cypher School'.
20 PRO FO 366/1024. 'List of certain candidates to be kept by Commander Denniston'.
21 Ronald Lewin, *Ultra Goes to War*, Hutchinson, 1978, p. 51.
22 Taylor, *English History 1914–1945*, pp. 427–8.
23 Conversation with Lord Franks, 24 January 1977.
24 H. M. D. Parker, *Manpower. A Study of War-time Policy and Administration*, HMSO, 1957, p. 51.
25 Ibid., p. 318.
26 PRO LAB 8/214. 'Memorandum prepared by the Committee of Vice-Chancellors and Principals for the organisation of the universities for war-time services'.
27 PRO LAB 8/139. 'Central Register. National Emergency. Establishment of an Advisory Council. Central Bureau of personnel with scientific, technical, professional or administrative qualifications'.
28 Ibid.
29 PRO LAB 8/24.
30 Lewin, *Ultra Goes to War*, p. 52.
31 PRO LAB 8/214.
32 Conversation with Lord Franks, 11 December 1984.
33 Ibid.
34 *The Times*, 15 November 1974. A note from Mr Philip Mason.
35 *Who's Who*, Adam & Charles Black, 1975, p. 2542.
36 Private information.
37 Ibid.
38 Ibid.
39 Ibid.
40 Ibid.
41 Ibid.
42 Ibid.
43 Ibid.
44 Ibid.
45 Ibid.
46 *Imperial Calendar*, 1940.
47 PRO LAB 8/142.
48 PRO LAB 8/145.
49 See the Earl of Birkenhead, *The Prof in Two Worlds: The Official Life of Professor F. A. Lindemann, Viscount Cherwell*, Collins, 1961, pp. 211–68, and G. D. A. MacDougall, 'The Prime Minister's Statistical Section', in Chester (ed.), *Lessons of the British War Economy*, pp. 58–68.

50 Philip Williams, *Hugh Gaitskell*, Cape, 1979, p. 93.
51 PRO LAB 8/145.
52 Ibid.
53 PRO LAB 8/175.
54 Lord Franks interviewed for LWT's *Whitehall*, 17 March 1977.
55 PRO LAB 8/175.
56 PRO LAB 8/145.
57 Ibid.
58 Ibid.
59 Ibid.
60 See Peter Hennessy and Gail Brownfeld, 'Britain's Cold War Security Purge: The Origins of Positive Vetting', *The Historical Journal*, 25, 4 (1982), pp. 965–73.
61 PRO LAB 8/175, Minute from Alan Hitchman (Brown's private secretary), to Sir Thomas Phillips, the Permanent Secretary, 18 September 1939.
62 PRO LAB 8/145.
63 Ibid.
64 Ibid.
65 Taylor, *English History, 1914–1945*, p. 452.
66 Letter from Mr Anthony Sutherland, 25 June 1985.
67 Ibid.
68 PRO FO 366/1059. Denniston to T. J. Wilson, 3 September 1939.
69 Ibid.
70 Ibid.
71 Winston S. Churchill, *The Second World War: The Commonwealth Alone* (Cassell, paperback edn, 1964), p. 55. For an excellent summary of scientific manpower (minus GC & CS) mobilised for war, see 'The Playing Fields of Malvern (1)' in Angus Calder, *The People's War: Britain 1939–45*, Cape, 1969, pp. 457–77. For the GC & CS see Lewin, *Ultra Goes to War*. For a particularly gripping individual account see R. V. Jones, *Most Secret War*, Hamish Hamilton, 1978.
72 Peter Hennessy, 'The Lord who sits in Judgement', *The Times*, 17 January 1983.
73 PRO LAB 8/145.
74 Lord Franks, interviewed for LWT's *Whitehall*, 17 March 1987.
75 Ibid.
76 PRO LAB 8/175.
77 Ibid.
78 Ibid.
79 Ibid.
80 Ibid.
81 Conversation with Lord Penney, 7 May 1985.
82 Ibid.
83 Conversation with Lord Croham, 4 March 1985.
84 Conversation with Lord Wilson, 27 February 1985.
85 Harris, *William Beveridge*, p. 367. For an account of Walter Layton's spell

in the Ministry of Supply, where he worked with Geoffrey Crowther, his successor as Editor of *The Economist*, see David Hubback, *No Ordinary Press Baron, A Life of Walter Layton*, Weidenfeld, 1985, Chapter 11.
86 Harris, *William Beveridge*, p. 368.
87 Ibid.
88 Ibid., p. 370.
89 Ibid., pp. 376–7.
90 Harold Wilson, *The Making of a Prime Minister, Memoirs 1916–1964*, Weidenfeld and Michael Joseph, 1986, p. 59.
91 Bernard Donoughue, *Prime Minister, The Conduct of Policy under Harold Wilson and James Callaghan, 1974–79*, Cape, 1987, p. 10.
92 Kellner and Crowther-Hunt, *The Civil Servants*, p. 27.
93 W. L. Wilson, 'Engineering in H. M. Office of Works and its Successors', unpublished manuscript, 1978, p. 18. I am grateful to Mr Wilson for lending me a copy.
94 Ibid., p. 19.
95 *The Times*, 6 May 1985.
96 Ibid.
97 Obituary of Sir Martin Roseveare, *The Times*, 2 April 1985.
98 Ibid.
99 Ibid.
100 Conversation with Lord Penney, 7 May 1985.
101 Lord Franks interviewed for *Whitehall*, 17 March 1987.
102 Douglas Jay, *Change and Fortune: A Political Record*, Hutchinson, 1980, p. 85.
103 Taylor, *English History 1914–1945*, p. 444.
104 Jay, *Change and Fortune*, p. 86.
105 Ibid., p. 93.
106 Ibid.
107 Ibid., p. 99.
108 Ibid.
109 Ibid.
110 Robbins, *Autobiography of an Economist*, p. 168.
111 Ibid., p. 170.
112 Ibid.
113 Ibid., p. 171.
114 Ibid., p. 172.
115 D. N. Chester, 'The Central Machinery for Economic Policy', in Chester (ed.), *Lessons of the British War Economy*, p. 23.
116 Cromwell and Steiner, 'Reform and Retrenchment', p. 101.
117 Ernest Bevin Papers, Churchill College Archives Centre, Cambridge, 2/1.
118 Ibid.
119 He used the phrase in a conversation with Lord Franks. See Peter Hennessy, 'Lord who sits in Judgement', *The Times*, 17 January 1983.
120 PRO FO 366/975/ × 1455.
121 Cromwell and Steiner, 'Reform and Retrenchment', p. 102.
122 PRO FO 336/1202/ × 4186. 12 May 1941.

123 Cromwell and Steiner, 'Reform and Retrenchment', p. 102.
124 PRO FO 366/1202/ × 4002. 20 June 1941.
125 PRO FO 366/1202/ × 3621. 25 April 1941.
126 PRO FO 366/883/ × 7586. Dalton to Montgomery, 1 August 1930.
127 Ernest Bevin Papers, 3/2. Bevin to Eden, 5 June 1941.
128 *Proposals for the Reform of the Foreign Service*, Cmd. 6420, HMSO, 1943.
129 For a detailed account of the genesis of selection changes see Richard A. Chapman, *Leadership in the British Civil Service*, Croom Helm, 1984, Chapter 2, pp. 30–68.
130 Geoffrey Moorhouse, *The Diplomats: The Foreign Office Today*, Cape, 1977, p. 24.
131 Bevin delivered these remarks to the annual conference of the TUC at Southport in October 1940. See Ernest Bevin, *The Trade Unions and the War*, TUC, 1940.
132 R. J. Hammond, *Food,* Vol. II, *Studies in Administration and Control*, HMSO, 1956, p. 445.
133 Ibid., p. 6.
134 Ibid., p. 109.
135 Marion Yass, *This Is Your War: Home Front Propaganda in the Second World War*, HMSO, 1983, pp. 50–1.
136 Alan Bennett, *A Private Function*, Faber, 1984.
137 PRO INF 1/292.
138 PRO INF 1/284.
139 Hammond, *Food*, Vol. II, p. 753.
140 Susan Briggs, *Keep Smiling Through, The Home Front 1939–45*, Fontana, 1976, p. 148.
141 A. J. P. Taylor, *Politics in Wartime*, Hamish Hamilton, 1964, p. 202.
142 J. D. Scott and Richard Hughes, *The Administration of War Production*, HMSO, 1955, p. 219.
143 Ibid., pp. 216–17.
144 Ibid., p. 215.
145 Ibid., p. 232.
146 For a vivid account of this see Hubback, *No Ordinary Press Baron*, Chapter 11, pp. 167–95.
147 Barnett, *Audit of War*, pp. 61–2.
148 David Hubback, 'Sir Richard Clarke, 1910–1975. A Most Unusual Civil Servant', *Public Policy and Administration*, Vol. 3, No. 1 (Spring 1988), p. 19.

4 THE MISSED OPPORTUNITY

1 Lord Franks interviewed for LWT's *Whitehall*, 17 March 1987.
2 Lord Bancroft, 'The Art of Management', Three Cantor Lectures, 'II, Whitehall and Management: A Retrospect', Royal Society of Arts, 30 January 1984.
3 PRO T 215/306.
4 Cairncross, *Years of Recovery*, p. 55.
5 Ibid.

6 PRO T 273/9.
7 Ibid.
8 Ibid.
9 Ibid., Robinson to Bridges, 1 March 1946.
10 Ibid.
11 Ibid.
12 Ibid.
13 Lord Franks interviewed for LWT's *Whitehall*, 17 March 1987.
14 PRO T 273/9.
15 I have been unable to verify this phrase and Ben Pimlott, Dalton's biographer and the editor of his Diaries, has been unable to confirm it except to say that it sounds typically Daltonian.
16 PRO T 273/9. Undated memo for Dalton, Chancellor of the Exchequer, from Bridges.
17 Hugh Dalton, *The Fateful Years*, Muller, 1957, pp. 407–8.
18 See J. M. Lee, *Reviewing the Machinery of Government 1942–1952: An Essay on the Anderson Committee and its Successors*, 1977, pp. 43–4 (available from Professor Michael Lee, Department of Politics, University of Bristol).
19 His 1932 Essay is reproduced as the 'Short Note' in Appendix III of Kenneth Harris, *Attlee*, Weidenfeld, 1984, paperback edn, pp. 593–5.
20 Ben Pimlott (ed.), *The Political Diary of Hugh Dalton, 1918–40, 1945–60*, Cape, 1987, p. 361.
21 See Peter Hennessy, 'The Attlee Governments 1945–51', in Peter Hennessy and Anthony Seldon (eds), *Ruling Performance: British Governments from Attlee to Thatcher*, Blackwell, 1987, p. 50.
22 Lord Attlee, 'Civil Servants, Ministers, Parliament and the Public', in *The Civil Service in Britain and France*, William A. Robson (ed.), Hogarth Press, 1956, p. 16.
23 'Quotes of the Day', *The Independent*, 23 May 1987.
24 Kenneth O. Morgan, *Labour People, Leaders and Lieutenants: Hardie to Kinnock*, OUP, 1987, pp. 94–5.
25 J. M. Lee, *The Churchill Coalition 1940–1945*, Batsford Academic, 1980.
26 Lee, *Reviewing the Machinery of Government*, p. 8.
27 Morgan, *Labour People*, p. 116.
28 Douglas Jay, 'Trade Winds', *Financial Times*, 29 August 1987.
29 Lee, *Reviewing the Machinery of Government*, pp. 11–16. Cripps's mental furniture is described in Roy Jenkins, *Nine Men of Power*, Hamish Hamilton, 1974, p. 104.
30 PRO PREM 4/63/2. Prime Minister's minute of 27 August 1942.
31 James Margach, *The Abuse of Power*, W. H. Allen, 1978, p. 1.
32 Lee, *Reviewing the Machinery of Government*, p. 139.
33 Ibid., pp. 139–40.
34 Harris, *William Beveridge*, p. 420.
35 Lee, *Reviewing the Machinery of Government*, p. 23. Anderson's Romanes Lectures, '*The Machinery of Government*', delivered at Oxford in 1946, was published in Public Administration, Vol. xxiii, 1945–46, pp. 147–56.
36 Lord Hunt interviewed for *All the Prime Minister's Men*, 29 May 1987.

37 Bancroft, 'The Art of Management'.

38 For a fascinating account of the original War Office Selection Board see Macdonald Hastings, 'A New Way to Choose our Army Officers', *Picture Post*, 19 September 1942, in Tom Hopkinson (ed.), *Picture Post, 1938–50*, Penguin, 1970, pp. 122–6. For Waterfield's adaptation of it see Richard A. Chapman, *Leadership in the British Civil Service: A Study of Sir Percival Waterfield and the Creation of the Civil Service Selection Board*, Croom Helm, 1984.

39 Douglas Wass, *Government and the Governed*, Routledge, 1984, p. 43.

40 Alan Bullock, *Ernest Bevin, Foreign Secretary*, Heinemann, 1983, p. 73.

41 The description is Lord Bullock's. Ibid.

42 Pimlott (ed.), *The Political Diary of Hugh Dalton*, p. 367.

43 Bullock, *Ernest Bevin, Foreign Secretary*, p. 74 footnote.

44 Christopher Mayhew, *Time to Explain*, Hutchinson, 1987, p. 120.

45 Moorhouse, *The Diplomats*, p. 325.

46 Speech to the Labour Party Conference, Bournemouth, 12 June 1946, quoted in Bullock, *Ernest Bevin, Foreign Secretary*, p. 74 footnote.

47 Alan Bullock, *The Life and Times of Ernest Bevin*, Vol. 2, *Minister of Labour, 1940–1945*, Heinemann, 1967, p. 103.

48 Nicholas Henderson, *The Private Office*, Weidenfeld, 1984, p. 25.

49 Ibid.

50 Bullock, *Ernest Bevin, Foreign Secretary*, p. 833.

51 Conversation with Sir Douglas Wass, 1 May 1987.

52 Leo Pliatzky, *Getting and Spending: Public Expenditure, Employment and Inflation*, rev. edn, Blackwell, 1984, p. 3.

53 Kenneth O. Morgan, *Labour in Power, 1945–51*, OUP, 1984, p. 368.

54 Pliatzky, *Getting and Spending*, pp. 5–6.

55 Peter Hennessy, 'Whitehall brief: Counter-puncher quits the subfusc ring', *The Times*, 5 February 1980.

56 PRO ADM 1/21121.

57 Foreign office material preserved in PRO FO 371/75588. The Treasury archive is huge but Bridges had the key devaluation papers bound together in PRO T 269/1.

58 PRO T 299/136.

59 Letter from Sir Frank Figgures to Peter Hennessy, August 1979.

60 Cairncross, *Years of Recovery*, p. 20.

61 Pimlott, *The Political Diary of Hugh Dalton*, p. 367.

62 Ibid., p. 398.

63 Ibid., pp. 453–4.

64 Private information.

65 Pimlott (ed.), *The Political Diary of Hugh Dalton*, p. 437, entry for 11 July 1948.

66 Paul Addison, *Now the War is Over*, Cape–BBC, 1985, p. 2.

67 Bullock, *Ernest Bevin, Foreign Secretary*; pp. 65–6.

68 See a fascinating and full account of this programme in Stuart Maclure, *Educational Development and School Building: Aspects of Public Policy 1945–73*, Longman, 1984.

69 Introduction to Chester (ed.), *Lessons of the British War Economy*, p. 2.
70 Sadly, no such picture was taken. Lord Ismay, *The Memoirs of Lord Ismay*, Heinemann, 1960, pp. 395–6. The group picture is reproduced in Bullock, *The Life and Times of Ernest Bevin,* Vol. 2, opposite p. 339.
71 The photograph outside St Paul's is reproduced as illustration 38.
72 Private information.
73 Sir Harold S. Kent, *In On the Act: Memoirs of a Lawmaker*, Macmillan, 1979, p. 231.
74 Private information.
75 George Mallaby, *Each in His Office: Studies of Men in Power*, Leo Cooper, 1972, p. 51.
76 Peter Hennessy, 'Whitehall Watch: Ethics of a Formidable Maiden Aunt', *The Independent*, 9 May 1988.
77 Pliatzky, *Getting and Spending*, p. 13.
78 Kent, *In On the Act*, pp. 243–4.
79 Private information.
80 Private information.
81 Conversation with Lord Armstrong of Sanderstead, 17 February 1976.
82 Ibid.
83 Lord Bridges, *The Treasury*, 2nd edn, Allen & Unwin, 1966, pp. 176–7.
84 Brittan, *Steering the Economy*, p. 37.
85 W. K. Hancock, *Country and Calling*, Faber, 1954, pp. 196–7.
86 For an assessment of their output see Denys Hay, 'British Historians and the Beginnings of the Civil History of the Second World War', in M. R. D. Foot (ed.), *War and Society: Essays on Honour and Memory of J. R. Western*, Elek, 1973, pp. 39–55.
87 See Peter Hennessy, 'Whitehall Watch: Unlocking Treasures of the Kew Archives', *The Independent*, 28 December, 1987.
88 Winnifrith, *Edward Ettingdean Bridges,* p. 47.
89 He wrote an account of their wartime relationship in Wheeler-Bennett (ed.), *Action This Day*, pp. 218–40.
90 Ibid., p. 218.
91 Ibid., p. 219.
92 Winnifrith, *Edward Ettingdean Bridges,* p. 47.
93 Ibid.
94 Ibid., p. 53.
95 Ibid.
96 Gardner, *Sterling-Dollar Diplomacy*, p. 206.
97 PRO T 269/1.
98 John Colville, *The Churchillians*, Weidenfeld, 1981, p. 131.
99 Lord Butler, *The Art of the Possible*, Penguin edn, 1973, pp. 158–9.
100 Peter Hennessy, 'Rab: politics as a matter of heart', *The Independent*, 8 May 1987.
101 Churchill's biographer, Martin Gilbert, has assured me the old man actually said this.

102 See Anthony Howard, *Rab: The Life of R. A. Butler*, Cape, 1987, p. 182.
103 Colville, *The Churchillians*, p. 131.
104 Ibid., pp. 131–2.
105 Anthony Seldon, *Churchill's Indian Summer: The Conservative Government 1951–55*, Hodder, 1981, p. 169.
106 Ibid., p. 100.
107 Evelyn Shuckburgh, *Descent to Suez 1951–56*, Weidenfeld, 1986, p. 61.
108 Conversation with Sir Roger Makins (now Lord Sherfield), 20 January 1987.
109 PRO T 236/4188.
110 See Peter Hennessy and Mark Laity, 'Suez – What the Papers Say', *Contemporary Record*, Vol. 1, No. 1 (Spring 1987), p. 4.
111 Peter Hennessy, 'Suez 30 years on: the secrets which will stay secret for ever', *The Listener*, 11 September 1986, pp. 8–9.
112 Lord Moran, *Winston Churchill: The Struggle for Survival 1940–65*, Sphere, 1968, pp. 795–6, Moran's diary entry for 3 August 1959.
113 Hugh Lloyd-Jones (ed.), *Maurice Bowra: A Celebration*, Duckworth, 1974, p. 61.
114 Ibid., p. 26.
115 Private information.
116 Mallaby, *Each in His Office*, p. 49.
117 Kent, *In On the Act*, pp. 28–9.
118 'Lord Normanbrook', *The Times*, 16 June 1967.
119 Winnifrith, *Edward Ettingdean Bridges*, p. 48.
120 PRO PREM 8/1482 part 2. Brook to Attlee, 29 May 1948.
121 PRO CAB 21/2248, Brook to Attlee, 'Overseas Operations (Security of Forces) Bill', 15 November 1950.
122 Colville, *The Churchillians*, p. 132.
123 PRO CAB 21/2654.
124 Hennessy, *Cabinet*, pp. 47–9.
125 Colville, *The Churchillians*, pp. 132–3.
126 Ibid., p. 133.
127 The doctored minute is reproduced as a photograph in Cockerell, Hennessy, Walker, *Sources Close to the Prime Minister*, between pp. 96 and 97.
128 John Colville, *The Fringes of Power, Downing Street Diaries 1939–1955*, Hodder, 1985, pp. 668–70.
129 Ibid., p. 670.
130 Douglas Dodds-Parker, *Political Eunuch*, Springwood, 1986, p. 68.
131 Shuckburgh, *Descent to Suez*, diary entry for 5 March 1954, pp. 141–2.
132 Jay, *Change and Fortune*, p. 95.
133 Private information.
134 The occasion was a meeting of the St Alban's Baconian Society, 9 March 1975.
135 Sir Douglas Wass interviewed for LWT's *Whitehall*, 23 March 1987.
136 Ibid.
137 Wass, *Government and the Governed*, pp. 52–3.
138 Bridges, *Portrait of a Profession*, p. 31.
139 For Lord Bancroft's evocation of Bridges see Peter Hennessy, 'Sir Ian

Bancroft is anxious to dispel the public's hostile attitude to Whitehall,' *The Times*, 7 December 1977. For his wider thoughts see Lord Bancroft, 'Whitehall: Some Personal Reflections', LSE, Suntory-Toyota Lecture, 1 December 1983.

140 Hennessy, *Cabinet*, pp. 39–43.
141 PRO CAB 21/1701. Brook to Bridges, 13 September 1946.
142 PRO CAB 21/1701. CP (46)357: 'Cabinet Committees', note by the Prime Minister, 26 September 1946.
143 PRO CAB 21/1626. Brook to Bridges, 21 April 1950.
144 Hennessy, *Cabinet*, p. 45.
145 Bernard Donoughue and G. W. Jones, *Herbert Morrison: Portrait of a Politician*, Weidenfeld, 1973, pp. 406–7.
146 Jay, *Change and Fortune*, p. 171.
147 PRO T 273/139.
148 Butler, *The Art of the Possible*, p. 159.
149 Charles Andrew, 'The Central Economic Planning Staff', unpublished thesis for Part II of the Cambridge Historical Tripos, 1986. At the time of writing, a PhD on the CEPS is in preparation by Mr N. Rollings.
150 Cairncross, *Years of Recovery*, p. 303.
151 Joan Mitchell, *Groundwork to Economic Planning*, Secker & Warburg, 1966, p. 75.
152 Andrew, *The Central Economic Planning Staff*, pp. 3, 5.
153 Pollard, *Wasting of the British Economy*, p. 33.
154 Eric Roll, *Crowded Hours*, Faber, 1985, pp. 46–9.
155 Ibid., pp. 56–7.
156 PRO T 273/141.
157 PRO T 273/139.
158 Butler, *Art of the Possible*, p. 159.
159 Andrew, *The Central Economic Planning Staff*, pp. 3, 10.
160 Lee, *Reviewing the Machinery of Government*, p. 149.
161 Paul Gore-Booth, *With Great Truth and Respect*, Constable, 1974, p. 232.
162 Callaghan, *Time and Chance*, p. 341.
163 The description used by a senior Ministry of Defence official in the late 1970s. Hennessy, *Cabinet*, p. 125.
164 Margaret Gowing, *Independence and Deterrence: Britain and Atomic Energy 1945–1952,* Vol. I, *Policy Making*, Macmillan, 1974, p. 230.
165 Ibid., p. 229.
166 See Rothschild, *Meditations of a Broomstick*, pp. 89–95.
167 'Mammon: the new face of Labour', *The Observer*, 17 May 1987.
168 Gerry Grimstone, 'Privatisation: the unexpected crusade', *Contemporary Record*, Vol. 1, No. 1 (Spring 1987), p. 25.
169 Pelling, *The Labour Governments 1945–51*, p. 90.
170 Donoughue and Jones, *Herbert Morrison*, pp. 184–8.
171 Hennessy, 'The Attlee Governments 1945–51', in Hennessy and Seldon (eds), *Ruling Performance*, p. 36.
172 James Griffiths, *Pages from Memory*, Dent, 1969, pp. 80–1.

173 Michael Foot, *Aneurin Bevan 1945–1960*, Davis-Poynter, 1973, p. 108; Kenneth O. Morgan, 'The State of Welfare', *New Society*, 7 February 1986.
174 Ibid.
175 Ibid., pp. 78–80.
176 H. V. Rhodes, 'Setting up a new government department', Ministry of National Insurance, 1948.
177 Griffiths, *Pages from Memory*, p. 80.
178 Private information.
179 Wigham, *From Humble Petition to Militant Action*, p. 100.
180 Ibid., Chapter 17, 'The First Strikes', pp. 148–58.
181 For an authoritative account of the industrial side of the British atomic weapons programme see Margaret Gowing, *Independence and Deterrence*, Vol. 2, *Policy Execution*, Macmillan, 1974.
182 *Statement on the Defence Estimates 1987*, Vol. I, Cm. 101–1, HMSO, 1987, p. 48.
183 Angus Calder, *The People's War, Britain 1939–1945*, paperback edn, Granada, 1971, p. 530.
184 I was told this story during a visit to RSRE Malvern in the summer of 1977.
185 *Science in War*, Penguin, 1940.
186 Calder, *The People's War*, p. 534.
187 Lee, *Reviewing the Machinery of Government*, pp. 71, 77.
188 The Earl of Birkenhead, *The Prof in Two Worlds*, Collins, 1961, p. 211.
189 *The Times*, 19 June 1943.
190 Macmillan was speaking about Britain's attitude to the nascent European Coal and Steel Community. Nora Beloff, *The General Says No*, Penguin special, 1963, p. 59.
191 Lee, *Reviewing the Machinery of Government*, p. 71.
192 Cmd. 6679.
193 Stephen Roskill, *Hankey: Man of Secrets*, Vol. III, *1931–1963*, Collins, 1974, p. 601.
194 PRO T 215/306.
195 Conversation with Lord Croham, 29 May 1987.
196 For Sir Frank Lee's views on Europe see Britain, *Treasury Under the Tories*, pp. 213–14.
197 Anthony Sampson, *Anatomy of Britain*, Hodder, 1962, p. 273.
198 Brian Lapping at an Institute of Contemporary British History Sixth Form Conference at LSE, 26 March 1987.
199 Brian Lapping, *End of Empire*, Granada/Channel 4, 1985, p. 369.
200 See the obituary of Sir Frank Lee, *The Times*, 20 April 1971.
201 Michel Debré, *Reforme de la Fonction Publique*, 1945.
202 Bancroft, 'Whitehall: Some Personal Reflections'.
203 Wass, *Government and the Governed*, pp. 52–3.
204 Private information.
205 For an account of Morrell's career at the DES see Kogan (ed.), *The Politics of Education*, 1971, pp. 29, 73, 150, 180, 187. For his inner cities and deprivation work at the Home Office see Peter Hall (ed.), *The Inner City in Context*, Heinemann Educational, 1981, p. 93.

206 The text of Mr Morrell's speech, which has no title, has been preserved in their files by the First Division Association. I am grateful to the association's assistant general secretary, Sue Corby, for supplying me with a copy.
207 Foot, *Aneurin Bevan 1945–1960*, pp. 450–2.
208 Richard Norton-Taylor and Seumas Milne, 'Bomb order refused', *The Guardian*, 2 January 1987. Their article was based on newly declassified papers for 1956.
209 Armstrong was interviewed for BBC 2's *Man Alive*. The transcript was published in *The Listener*, 28 March 1974.
210 Lord Sherfield interviewed for the BBC Radio 3 programme, *A Canal Too Far*, 20 January 1987.
211 Lord Bancroft interviewed for *All the Prime Minister's Men*, 10 April 1986.
212 Pliatzky, *Getting and Spending*, p. 27.
213 Sir Anthony Nutting interviewed for *A Canal Too Far*, 13 January 1987.
214 Ibid.
215 Clark's fascinating posthumous account of the Suez crisis was published as *From Three Worlds*, Sidgwick & Jackson, 1986, see Chapter 6, pp. 146–215.
216 Conversation with Lord Thomas of Swynnerton, 30 May 1987.
217 Hugh Thomas, *The World's Game*, Eyre & Spottiswoode, 1957.
218 Hugh Thomas, *The Suez Affair*, first published by Weidenfeld in 1967 and reissued by them as a paperback in 1987. Paperback edn p. 154.
219 Gore-Booth, *With Great Truth and Respect*, pp. 227–31.
220 Gore-Booth MS, Bodleian Library, Oxford. I am grateful to Helen Langley of its Department of Western Manuscripts for providing me with a copy.
221 PRO PREM 11/1090.
222 Conversation with Lord Sherfield, 20 January 1987.
223 Shuckburgh, *Descent to Suez*, diary entry for 24 September 1956, p. 360.
224 Gore-Booth, *With Great Truth and Respect*, p. 230.
225 Sir Richard Powell interviewed for *A Canal Too Far*, 13 January 1987.
226 Ibid. Sir Richard said, 'I very strongly feel that if you take a pledge of confidence, you should observe that confidence throughout your life. And it's only because the documents have now been published and they're in the public domain that I would feel able to go beyond that.'
227 Shuckburgh, *Descent to Suez*, diary entry 5 December 1956, p. 366. Brook disclosed this at the Imperial Defence College after delivering a lecture. Shuckburgh at this stage of his career was an instructor at the IDC.
228 Clark, *From Three Worlds*, diary entry for 9 August 1956, p. 172.
229 Ibid.
230 Unnamed 'very senior figure from the official world' quoted in Hennessy, 'Suez 30 years on: the secrets which will say secret for ever', *The Listener*, 11 September 1986.
231 H of C Official Report, 20 December 1956, col. 1493.
232 Sir Donald Logan interviewed for *A Canal Too Far*, 8 January 1987.
233 Now available at the Public Record Office in FO 800/728. Marked for 'UK EYES ONLY' it is unsigned but entitled 'Memorandum on relations between the United Kingdom, the United States and France in the months

following Egyptian nationalisation of the Suez Canal Company in 1956' and dated 21 October 1957.

234 Sir Guy Millard interviewed for *A Canal Too Far*, 8 January 1987. A full account of the exchange is published in Peter Hennessy, 'The scars of Suez: reopening the wounds of the end of Empire', *The Listener*, 5 February 1987.

235 Sir Guy Millard to Mark Laity, 13 February 1987. I have Sir Guy's permission to quote him.

236 Anthony Nutting, *No End of A Lesson: The Story of Suez*, Constable, 1967.

237 See Peter Hennessy, 'No end of an argument: How Whitehall tried and failed to suppress Sir Anthony Nutting's Suez memoir', *Contemporary Record*, Vol. 1, No. 1 (Spring 1987), pp. 12–13.

238 Merry and Serge Bromberger, *Les Secrets de Suez*, editions des 4 fils Aymon, 1957.

239 Moshe Dayan, *Diary of the Sinai Campaign*, Weidenfeld, 1966.

240 See Peter Hennessy, 'Permanent government: Suez and the Ponting factors', *New Statesman*, 6 February 1987.

5 CRITICISM, INQUIRY AND REFORM

1 Balogh, 'Apotheosis of the Dilettante' in Thomas (ed.), *The Establishment*, p. 111.

2 Wilson, *Memoirs 1916–1964*, p. 193.

3 Lord Lever interviewed for *All the Prime Minister's Men*, 7 May 1986.

4 John Garrett, *Managing the Civil Service*, Heinemann, 1980, p. 11.

5 Lord Armstrong, evidence to the General Sub-Committee of the Commons Select Committee on Expenditure, 24 January 1977, reproduced in *Eleventh Report from the Expenditure Committee Session 1976–77*, vol. II, Part II, HMSO, 1977, p. 656.

6 The phrase is Michael Foot's. See Foot, *Aneurin Bevan, 1945–1960*, p. 515.

7 The title of a series of Penguin specials which captured the spirit of the age.

8 Their progression was as follows: *Anatomy of Britain*, Hodder, 1962; *Anatomy of Britain Today*, Hodder, 1965; *The New Anatomy of Britain*, Hodder, 1971; and *The Changing Anatomy of Britain*, Hodder, 1982.

9 Sampson, *The Changing Anatomy of Britain*, Chapter 10.

10 Roll, *Crowded Hours*, p. 46.

11 PRO CAB 21/1729 and CAB 130/8.

12 Bridges, *Portrait of a Profession*, p. 33.

13 John Le Carré, *Tinker, Tailor, Soldier, Spy*, (1974), p. 113.

14 John Le Carré, *A Perfect Spy*, Coronet edn, 1987, p. 518.

15 Balogh, 'Apotheosis of the Dilettante', p. 99.

16 Ibid.

17 Ibid., p. 109.

18 Ibid., p. 110.

19 Ibid., p. 109.

20 Ibid., p. 126.

21 See, for example, Barbara Castle, *The Castle Diaries 1964–70*, Weidenfeld, 1984, pp. 51, 91–3, 117, 720.

22 Richard Crossman, *The Diaries of a Cabinet Minister*, Vol. Two, *Lord President of the Council and Leader of the House of Commons 1966–68*, Hamish Hamilton and Cape, 1976, p. 200, diary entry for 17 January 1967.

23 The Fabian Society's archives are preserved in the Library of Nuffield College, Oxford. The papers of the Civil Service inquiry of 1963–4 are preserved in boxes K65–67. The 'two permanent secretaries' wish to remain anonymous to this day.

24 *The Administrators*, pp. 15–16.

25 Ibid., p. 5.

26 Ibid., p. 41.

27 Ibid., p. 15.

28 Ibid., p. 9.

29 See Hennessy, *Cabinet*, p. 168.

30 Private information.

31 *The Administrators*, p. 23.

32 Ibid., pp. 41–2.

33 Ibid., p. 42.

34 Roseveare, *The Treasury*, p. 303.

35 The words were part of Sir Douglas's eulogy at Clarke's memorial service in 1975 and are quoted by Sir Alec Cairncross in his Foreword to Sir Richard Clarke's posthumous *Public Expenditure Management and Control: The Development of the Public Expenditure Survey Committee*, Macmillan, 1978, p.x.

36 Ibid.

37 Pliatzky, *Getting and Spending*, pp. 42–3.

38 He made the remark in an interview with Peter Kellner recorded in Kellner and Crowther-Hunt, *The Civil Servants*, p. 183.

39 PRO CAB 129/ , C (53) 355, 'Civil Supply 1954–55', Memorandum by the Chancellor of the Exchequer, 16 December 1953, is but one of several examples.

40 Clarke, *Public Expenditure Management and Control.*

41 Brittan, *Steering the Economy*, p. 41.

42 Clarke, *Public Expenditure Management and Control.*

43 A flavour of these high investing times is found in the memoirs of John Boyd-Carpenter, Minister of Transport and Civil Aviation in the mid-fifties, *Way of Life*, Sidgwick & Jackson, 1980, particularly Chapter 9, pp. 107–21. For railway modernisation, see also T. R. Gourvish, *British Railways 1948–73: A Business History*, Cambridge, 1986, Chapter 8, pp. 256–304.

44 *The Administrators*, p. 38.

45 Ibid., p. 16.

46 Lord Hailsham describes this commonly held view as the 'Svengali' theory though he does not believe it himself. Lord Hailsham interviewed for *All the Prime Minister's Men*, 14 May 1986.

47 See Alan Thompson, *The Day Before Yesterday*, Sidgwick & Jackson, 1971, pp. 166–7.

48 Nearly thirty years later Lord Thorneycroft recalled, 'It was said that the limits we were arguing about at the time, £50 million, was too small to

resign on ... Ministers who resign are always forced in the last resort to resign over things which look too small. But those small things represent the principles that they were battling for.' Lord Thorneycroft interviewed for *All the Prime Minister's Men*, 21 March 1986.

49 Pliatzky, *Getting and Spending*, p. 34. Sir Leo is right to say that the then Permanent Secretary, Sir Roger Makins, was 'not in his natural element in this affair'. Ibid.

50 H of C, *Sixth Report from the Select Committee on Estimates*, 1957–8, House of Commons Paper, 254, 1958.

51 Clarke, *Public Expenditure Management and Control*, p. 1.

52 W. J. M. MacKenzie, 'The Plowden Report: A translation', *The Guardian*, 25 May 1963. It is reproduced in Rose (ed.), *Policy-Making in Britain*, pp. 273–82.

53 Clarke, *Public Expenditure Management and Control*, p. 25.

54 Pliatzky, *Getting and Spending*, p. 44. An edited version of the Plowden Report was published as *Control of Public Expenditure*, Cmnd. 1432, HMSO, 1961.

55 Clarke, *Public Expenditure Management and Control*, pp. 25–6.

56 Brittan, *The Treasury Under the Tories*, p. 222.

57 Though Armstrong was appointed to succeed Lee in running the reorganised Treasury, he gave the lion's share of the credit for the new design to Otto Clarke. Conversation with Lord Armstrong, 17 February 1976.

58 Quoted in Hennessy, *Cabinet*, p. 70. Lord Wilson originally imparted this information when interviewed for BBC Radio 3's *The Quality of Cabinet Government*, 27 February 1985.

59 Ibid., p. 69.

60 Donoughue, *Prime Minister*, pp. 9–10.

61 Hennessy, *Cabinet*, p. 70.

62 Tony Benn, *Out of the Wilderness: Diaries 1963–67*, Hutchinson, 1987, p. 25. Diary entry for 25 May 1963.

63 Ibid., pp. 25–6.

64 An authoritative account of Wilson's changes can be found in Christopher Pollitt, *Manipulating the Machine: Changing the Pattern of Ministerial Departments 1960–83*, Allen & Unwin, 1984, Chapter 5, pp. 46–81.

65 Lord Lever interviewed for *All the Prime Minister's Men*, 7 May 1986.

66 Sir James Callaghan interviewed for *All the Prime Minister's Men*, 30 April 1986.

67 Ibid.

68 Wilson, *The Making of a Prime Minister*, p. 193.

69 George Brown, *In My Way*, Penguin, 1972, p. 89.

70 Roll, *Crowded Hours*, pp. 149–50.

71 Ibid., p. 150.

72 Susan Crosland, *Tony Crosland*, Cape, 1982, p. 129.

73 Samuel Brittan, 'The Irregulars', *Crossbow*, xxxxvii, 1966, pp. 30–3. An expanded version of the article is published in Rose (ed.), *Policy-Making in Britain*, pp. 329–39.

74 My phrase, not his, which I propose to use for convenience of reference.

75 Samuel Brittan, *Diary of an Irregular*, entry for 2 November 1964.
76 Ibid., diary entry for 9 November 1964.
77 Ibid.
78 Callaghan, *Time and Chance*, p. 218.
79 Samuel Brittan, *Diary of an Irregular*, entry for 19 November 1964.
80 Norman Hunt, *Whitehall and Beyond*, BBC, 1964, pp. 12–15.
81 Lord Bridges in ibid., p. 71.
82 Conversation with Sir John Burgh, 23 June 1987.
83 Donald MacDougall, *Don and Mandarin: Memoirs of an Economist*, John Murray, 1987, p. 159.
84 Bridges in Hunt, *Whitehall and Beyond*, p. 71.
85 Pollard, *Wasting of the British Economy*; it is the title of his Chapter 4, pp. 71–101.
86 Brown, *In My Way*, pp. 98–9.
87 Susan Crosland, *Tony Crosland*, Cape, 1982, p. 136.
88 Tony Benn, *Out of the Wilderness*, diary entry for 28 August 1967, p. 510.
89 Lord Lever interviewed for *All the Prime Minister's Men*, 7 May 1986.
90 Brittan, *Diary of an Irregular*, 6 October 1965.
91 Sir Douglas Wass interviewed for *All the Prime Minister's Men*, 8 April 1986.
92 The phrase is Ian Bancroft's, who was private secretary to the Chancellor at the time. Lord Bancroft interviewed by Michael Crick for *Channel 4 News*.
93 Sir Douglas Wass interviewed for *All the Prime Minister's Men*, 8 April 1986.
94 Hennessy, *Cabinet*, p. 70, drawn from a conversation with Lord Wilson of 27 February 1985.
95 Morgan, *Labour People*, p. 256.
96 Susan Crosland, *Tony Crosland*, Cape, 1982, p. 137.
97 Private information.
98 Lord Bancroft interviewed by Michael Crick, May 1987.
99 Private information.
100 Hunt, *Whitehall and Beyond*, p. 19.
101 Ibid., p. 14.
102 Ibid., p. 13.
103 Ibid., pp. 17–18.
104 Ibid., p. 18.
105 Ibid.
106 C. P. Snow, *Corridors of Power*, Macmillan, 1964.
107 Private information.
108 Private information.
109 Brittan, *Diary of an Irregular*, entry for 18 September 1965.
110 H of C, *Sixth Report from the Estimates Committee, 1964–65*, HMSO, 1965, p. xxxv.
111 Quoted in *The Sunday Times*, 5 September 1965.
112 H of C, *Sixth Report from the Estimates Committee, 1964–65*, p. xvi.
113 H of C Debates, 8 February 1966, col. 210.

114 Kellner and Crowther-Hunt, *The Civil Servants*, p. 27.
115 Ibid., pp. 27–8.
116 Memorandum No. 139 in *The Civil Service,* Vol. 5(2), *Proposals and Opinions Parts 3 and 4. Organisations and Individuals*, pp. 998–1004.
117 Ibid. 'Whitehall's Brain Drain', Memorandum No. 132, pp. 930–6.
118 Ibid. 'The Role of the Civil Service in Modern Society', Memorandum No. 144, p. 1085.
119 Ibid., p. 1086.
120 Nicholas Wapshott and George Brock, *Thatcher, The Major New Biography*, Futura, 1983, p. 84.
121 Ryrie, 'The Role of the Civil Service in Modern Society', p. 1088.
122 Ibid.
123 Letter from Sir William Ryrie, 7 July 1987.
124 Ryrie, 'The Role of the Civil Service in Modern Society', p. 1088.
125 Ibid., p. 1089.
126 Ibid., pp. 1090–1.
127 Ibid., p. 1091.
128 Ibid., p. 1092.
129 Cmnd. 3638, pp. 104–6.
130 Ibid., p. 101.
131 Ibid., p. 103.
132 Private information. Some of these views were expressed non-attributably in Peter Hennessy, 'The Civil Service: Whitehall's loyal executors of ordained error', *The Times*, 28 July 1985. The two permanent secretaries on Fulton, Allen and Dunnett poured cold water on this interpretation at the joint ICBH/RIPA seminar on 'Fulton: 20 Years On' in London on 7 March 1988 (for an edited transcript see Contemporary Record, Vol 2, No 2, Summer 1988, pp. 44–51).
133 Sir William Armstrong quoted in Kellner and Crowther-Hunt, *The Civil Servants*, p. 62.
134 Barbara Castle, *The Castle Diaries 1964–70*, Weidenfeld, 1984, p. 464.
135 Richard Crossman, *The Diaries of a Cabinet Minister,* Vol. III, *Secretary of State for the Social Services 1968–1970*, p. 98, diary entry for 17 June 1968.
136 Ibid., p. 107, diary entry for 25 June 1968.
137 Ibid., pp. 101–2, diary entry for 19 June 1968.
138 Ibid., p. 103, diary entry for 20 June 1968.
139 Ibid.
140 Kellner and Crowther-Hunt, *The Civil Servants*, p. 77.
141 Castle, *The Castle Diaries 1964–70*, p. 464, diary entry for 20 June 1987.
142 Kellner and Crowther-Hunt, *The Civil Servants*, p. 56.
143 Castle, *The Castle Diaries 1964–70,* p. 467, diary entry for 24 June 1987.
144 Ibid., p. 468.
145 Crossman, *Diaries of a Cabinet Minister,* Vol. III, p. 107, diary entry for 25 June 1968.
146 Ibid.
147 Clarke, *Public Expenditure, Management and Control*, p. 105.

148 Kellner and Crowther-Hunt, *The Civil Servants*, p. 63.
149 Quoted ibid.
150 Ibid., pp. 63–4.
151 Ibid., p. 64.
152 Ibid.
153 *Eleventh Report from the Expenditure Committee, 1976–77*, p. 656.
154 For the most brilliant attack see Ian Robinson, *The Survival of English*, CUP, 1973, Chapter 3, pp. 66–98.
155 H of C Official Report, 26 June 1968, col. 456.
156 Garrett, *Managing the Civil Service*, see Chapter II, pp. 11–27.
157 Harold Wilson, *The Governance of Britain*, Weidenfeld and Michael Joseph, 1976, p. 91.
158 Ibid., Appendix V, pp. 202–5.
159 Conversation with Sir Harold Wilson, 20 May 1976; Peter Hennessy, 'New Inland Revenue Chairman', *The Times*, 4 March 1976.
160 In the mid-1970s I was asked if I would help Armstrong on this endeavour by Harold Evans, Editor of *The Sunday Times*, who was keen to serialise the memoirs in his paper. Though I had a considerable affection for William Armstrong, I declined, preferring to continue working full-time on *The Times*.
161 See his reply to John Garrett when giving evidence to the Expenditure Committee in 1977. *Eleventh Report from the Expenditure Committee*, Vol. II, Part II, p. 656.
162 Ibid., pp. 657–8.
163 Kellner and Crowther-Hunt, *The Civil Servants*, Chapter 4, 'How Armstrong Defeated Fulton', pp. 59–77.
164 Harold Wilson, *The Labour Government 1964–70*, Pelican edn, 1974, p. 684.
165 'Fulton 20 Years On', *Contemporary Record*.
166 Private information.
167 Quoted in Pollitt, *Manipulating the Machine*, p. 78.
168 Conversation with Lord Shackleton, 24 June 1987.
169 MacDougall, *Don and Mandarin*, p. 193.
170 Kellner and Crowther-Hunt, *The Civil Servants*, p. 59.
171 H of L Official Report, 24 July 1968, Col. 1105.
172 Derek Morrell. Address to the 1969 Annual Conference of the First Division Association.
173 Hennessy, 'Whitehall's loyal executors of ordained error', *The Times*, 28 July 1975.
174 Ibid.
175 Sir Robert Armstrong, 'Taking stock of our achievements'. Joint RIPA–Peat Marwick McLintock seminar on the 'Future Shape of Reform in Whitehall', Regent's College, London, 4 December 1987.
176 The title of Chapter 5 of Kellner and Crowther-Hunt's *The Civil Servants*.
177 Private information.
178 Cmnd. 3638, p. 104.
179 R. N. Heaton and Sir Leslie Williams, *Civil Service Training*, Civil Service Department, 1974.

180 Private information.
181 Cmnd. 3638, p. 106.
182 Ibid.
183 Castle, *The Castle Diaries 1964–70*, pp. 785–6, diary entry for 13 April 1970.
184 *Reskilling Government: Proposals for the Experimental Introduction of Departmental Cabinets*, Institute of Directors, 1987, p. 6.

6 EXPERIMENT, CRISIS AND DISILLUSION

1 Edward Heath, *My Style of Government*, Evening Standard Publications, 1972, p. 3.
2 Dr David Owen interviewed for BBC Radio 3's *Routine Punctuated by Orgies*, 10 November 1983.
3 Quoted in Phillip Whitehead, *The Writing on the Wall*, Channel 4 Books and Michael Joseph, 1985, p. 52.
4 Quoted in William Plowden (ed.), *Advising the Rulers*, Blackwell, 1987, p. 67.
5 Sir Douglas Wass, *Government and the Governed*, p. 38.
6 Bernard Donoughue, *Prime Minister*, p. 173.
7 George Hutchinson, *Edward Heath: A Personal and Political Biography*, Longman, 1970, p. 46.
8 Peter Hennessy, 'Surprising slants on reforming Whitehall', *Financial Times*, 12 June 1976.
9 Private information.
10 *Eleventh Report from the Expenditure Committee*, Vol. II, Part II, p. 657.
11 Pollitt, *Manipulating the Machine*, p. 83.
12 Ibid.
13 Ibid.
14 Edward Heath, *My Style of Government*, p. 5.
15 Pollitt, *Manipulating the Machine*, p. 84.
16 Conversation with Lord Plowden, 13 October 1983.
17 Pollitt, *Manipulating the Machine*, p. 85.
18 Ibid., p. 86.
19 Ibid., p. 87.
20 Ibid., p. 88.
21 *A Better Tomorrow*, Conservative Central Office, 26 May 1970.
22 Pollitt, *Manipulating the Machine*, p. 88.
23 Bridges, *Portrait of a Profession*, p. 19.
24 I have heard him use the phase.
25 Winnifrith, *Edward Ettingdean Bridges*, pp. 52–3.
26 Private information.
27 Private information.
28 Quoted in Peter Hennessy, 'The Cabinet Office: A magnificent piece of powerful bureaucratic machinery', *The Times*, 8 March 1976.
29 John Le Carré, *A Perfect Spy*, Coronet edn, 1987, p. 13.

30 Private information.
31 Private information.
32 For Lord Trend's endeavours see the Prime Minister's statement to the Commons, Official Report 26, March 1981, cols 1079 et seqs; for George Smiley's see John Le Carré, *Tinker, Tailor, Soldier, Spy*, Hodder, 1974, p. 125 et seq.
33 Private information.
34 Private information.
35 Private information.
36 Private information.
37 Private information.
38 Peter Hennessy, 'No end of an argument: How Whitehall tried and failed to suppress Sir Anthony Nutting's Suez Memoir', *Contemporary Record*, Vol. 1, No. 1, pp. 12–13.
39 Richard Crossman, *Diaries of a Cabinet Minister*, Vol. II, pp. 343–4.
40 Private information.
41 'Lord Trend', *The Times*, 30 July 1987.
42 Henry Kissinger, *Years of Upheaval*, Weidenfeld and Michael Joseph, 198, pp. 191–2.
43 Private information.
44 Private information.
45 R. F. Harrod, *The Life of John Maynard Keynes*, Pelican edn, 1972, first published 1951.
46 Conversation with Lord Armstrong, 2 July 1976.
47 Ibid.
48 Private information.
49 Harold Wilson, *The Labour Government 1964–70*, p. 45.
50 Barbara Castle, *The Castle Diaries: 1964–70*, p. 115, diary entry for 19 April 1966.
51 Richard Crossman, *Diaries of a Cabinet Minister*, Vol. I, pp. 103–4, diary entry for 15 December 1964.
52 Richard Crossman, *Diaries of a Cabinet Minister*, Vol. II, pp. 159–60, diary entry for 11 December 1966.
53 Ibid., pp. 167–8, diary entry for 16 December 1966.
54 Ibid., p. 296, diary entry for 27 March 1967.
55 Reginald Maudling, *Memoirs*, Sidgwick & Jackson, 1978, p. 27.
56 As I drove him from Cambridge station to give the Johnian Society Lecture for 1979.
57 Interview with Desmond Wilcox for BBC 2's *Man Alive* reproduced in *The Listener*, 28 March 1974.
58 See Anthony Howard, *RAB: The Life of R. A. Butler*, Cape, 1987, p. 203.
59 Conversation with Lord Armstrong, 2 July 1976.
60 It was 25 June 1975.
61 I have described the scene in Peter Hennessy, 'An inside story of political suicide', *The Independent*, 29 May 1987.
62 Speech to the annual conference of the Society of Civil Servants, Bournemouth, 15 May 1968.

63 Quoted in Stephen Fay and Hugo Young, 'The Fall of Heath', *The Sunday Times*, 22 February 1976.
64 Ibid.
65 Samuel Brittan, 'A passion for rationality', *Financial Times*, 14 July 1980.
66 Pollitt, *Manipulating the Machine*, p. 90.
67 *The Reorganisation of Central Government*, HMSO, 1970, Cmnd. 4506.
68 Conversation with Lord Trend, 7 November 1983, for BBC Radio 3's *Routine Punctuated by Orgies.*
69 Conversation with Hector Hawkins, 2 October 1983, for *Routine Punctuated by Orgies.*
70 Douglas Hurd, *An End to Promises: Sketch of a Government 1970–74*, Collins, 1979, p. 39.
71 Quoted in Hennessy, *Cabinet*, p. 77.
72 Edward Heath, The First Keeling Memorial Lecture, Royal Institute of Public Administration, 7 May 1980.
73 Conversation with Lord Trend, 7 November 1983, for BBC Radio 3's *Routine Punctuated by Orgies.*
74 James Fox, 'The brains behind the throne', in Valentine Herman and James E. Alt (eds), *Cabinet Studies: A Reader*, Macmillan, 1975, p. 287.
75 Cmnd. 4506.
76 Private information.
77 Private information.
78 Conversation with Lord Trend, 7 November 1983, for BBC Radio 3's *Routine Punctuated by Orgies.*
79 Private information.
80 Ivan Yates, 'Lord of the Think Tank', *The Observer*, 1 November 1970.
81 Ibid.
82 Private information.
83 Lord Rothschild, *Random Variables*, Collins, 1984, p. 81.
84 Ibid.
85 Ibid., pp. 75–6.
86 Ibid., p. 74.
87 Ibid.
88 Dr Tessa Blackstone, 'Ministers, Advisers and Civil Servants', 1979 Gaitskell Memorial Lecture, Nottingham University.
89 Private information.
90 In *Meditations of a Broomstick*, Collins, 1977, pp. 112–13, Lord Rothschild does not identify Wade-Gery by name but refers to him as 'a brilliant member of the Think Tank'.
91 Private information.
92 Conversation with Lord Hunt, 24 October 1983, for BBC Radio 3's *Routine Punctuated by Orgies.*
93 Ibid.
94 Private information.
95 Private information.

96 Private information.
97 James Fox, 'The brains behind the throne', in Herman and Alt (eds), *Cabinet Studies: A Reader*, Macmillan, 1975, pp. 277–92.
98 Private information.
99 Private information.
100 Private information.
101 Quoted in Bernard Donoughue and Peter Hennessy, 'Why policy dynamo slowed down', *The Times*, 15 July 1981.
102 Conversation with Lord Rothschild for BBC Radio 3's *The Politics of Thinking*, 20 May 1984.
103 Private information.
104 Private information.
105 *The Levin Interviews*, BBC 2, 12 August 1984.
106 Conversation with Lord Rothschild, 25 October 1983.
107 Private information.
108 Conversation with Lord Rothschild for BBC Radio 3's *The Politics of Thinking*, 20 May 1984.
109 *Framework for Government Research and Development*, Cmnd. 5406, HMSO, 1972.
110 Private Information.
111 Conversation with Sir Frank Cooper for *Routine Punctuated by Orgies*, 31 October 1983.
112 Ibid.
113 The letter is published in full in Peter Hennessy, Susan Morrison and Richard Townsend, *Routine Punctuated by Orgies: The Central Policy Review Staff, 1970–83*, Strathclyde Papers on *Government and Politics No. 31*, Politics Department, Strathclyde University, 1985, Appendix A, pp. 104–8.
114 Ibid.
115 Private information.
116 Private information.
117 Private information.
118 Private information.
119 As he told me when I interviewed him for *The Politics of Thinking*, 20 May 1984.
120 Ibid.
121 Rothschild, *Meditations of a Broomstick*, pp. 89–96.
122 Ibid.
123 Ibid.
124 Rothschild interviewed for *The Politics of Thinking*, 20 May 1984.
125 Rothschild, *Meditations of a Broomstick*, pp. 89–90.
126 Private information.
127 H of C Paper, 147, Expenditure Committee, 1971–72 Session, p. 14.
128 Hugh Heclo and Aaron Wildavsky, *The Private Government of Public Money: Community and Policy Inside British Politics*, Macmillan, 2nd edn, 1981. See Chapter 6, 'There Must be a Better Way', pp. 264–303.

129 Andrew Gray and William I. Jenkins, *Administrative Politics in British Government*, Wheatsheaf, 1985, pp. 102–13.
130 Colin Campbell, *Governments Under Stress: Political Executives and Key Bureaucrats in Washington, London and Ottawa*, University of Toronto Press, 1983.
131 Clive Priestley, Rayner's former chief of staff, speaking in *The Good and the Great*, BBC Radio 3, 4 February 1985.
132 Peter Hennessy, 'Surprising slants on reforming Whitehall', *Financial Times*, 22 February 1976.
133 Stephen Fay and Hugo Young, 'The Fall of Heath', *The Sunday Times*, 22 February 1976.
134 For a full account of the Whitehall emergency machine, see Keith Jeffery and Peter Hennessy, *States of Emergency: British Governments and Strikebreaking Since 1919*, Routledge, 1983.
135 Ibid., p. 236.
136 Quoted in Hennessy, *Cabinet*, p. 79.
137 Stephen Fay and Hugo Young, 'The Fall of Heath', *The Sunday Times*, 22 February 1976.
138 Private information.
139 Private information.
140 Private information.
141 Private information.
142 Hurd, *An End to Promises*, p. 118.
143 Ibid.
144 Ibid., pp. 117–18.
145 Hennessy, 'Surprising slants on reforming Whitehall'.
146 M. S. Schreiber and T. A. A. Hart, 'Cabinets Ministériels in France', Civil Service Department, 1972, unpublished report, p. 11.
147 Wigham, *From Humble Petition to Militant Action*, p. 154.
148 Fay and Young, 'The Fall of Heath'.
149 Interview with BBC 2's *Man Alive*.
150 Roy Blackman, 'Silly Season Stuff says Sir William', *Daily Express*, 25 August 1972.
151 Private information.
152 Quoted in Whitehead, *The Writing on the Wall*, p. 83.
153 Interview with BBC 2's *Man Alive*.
154 Quoted in Whitehead, *The Writing on the Wall*, p. 89.
155 Conversation with Lord Armstrong, 2 July 1976.
156 Hurd, *An End of Promises*, p. 131.
157 Quoted in Whitehead, *The Writing on the Wall*, p. 110.
158 Private information.
159 Stephen Fay and Hugo Young, 'The Red Alert', *The Sunday Times*, 29 February 1976.
160 Joe Haines, *The Politics of Power*, Cape, 1977, p. 18.
161 Michael Horsnell, 'Discord in Whitehall as Sir William goes', *The Times*, 28 June 1974.
162 Interview with BBC 2's *Man Alive*.

163 Conversation with Lord Armstrong, 2 July 1976.
164 Peter Hennessy, 'The Think Tank gets a man with a talent for saying what he means', *The Times*, 6 January 1975.
165 Quoted in Hennessy, *Cabinet*, p. 170.
166 Ibid.
167 Ibid., p. 171.
168 Peter Jenkins, 'Seventies show takes the middle road', *The Independent*, 19 May 1987.
169 Donoughue, *Prime Minister*, pp. 46–7.
170 Ibid., p. 1.
171 Ibid., pp. 47–8.
172 Pliatzky, *Getting and Spending*, p. 118.
173 Ibid.
174 Sir Douglas Wass interviewed for *All the Prime Minister's Men*, 8 April 1986.
175 Hurd, *An End to Promises*, p. 38.
176 Lord Rothschild, *Random Variables*, p. 80.
177 Lord Rothschild, 'In and Out of the Think Tank', an address to the Press Club, 7 September 1979, reproduced in *Random Variables*, pp. 73–9.
178 Conversation with Dr Donoughue, 4 July 1984.
179 Ibid.
180 Wilson, *The Governance of Britain*, p. 95.
181 Ibid., pp. 97–8.
182 Conversation with Dr Donoughue, 4 July 1984.
183 Ibid.
184 It is reproduced in Rothschild *Meditations of a Broomstick*, pp. 121–3.
185 Ibid.
186 Reproduced in ibid., pp. 163–79.
187 Ibid.
188 Fay and Young, 'The Red Alert'.
189 *The Times*, 22 December 1974. The article is reproduced in Rothschild *Meditations of a Broomstick*, pp. 144–7.
190 Conversation with Lord Rothschild for *The Politics of Thinking*, BBC Radio 3, 20 May 1984.
191 *The Times*, 22 May 1984.
192 Private information.
193 Private information.
194 Private information.
195 Hennessy, 'The Think Tank gets a man with a talent for saying what he means'.
196 Conversation with Dr Donoughue, 4 July 1984.
197 *The Times*, 6 January 1975.
198 Private information.
199 Quoted in Whitehead, *The Writing on the Wall*, p. 128.
200 Ibid.

201 Pliatzky, *Getting and Spending*, p. 131.
202 Ibid., p. 131.
203 Ibid.
204 Ibid., p. 133.
205 Ibid., p. 134.
206 Jocelyn Davey, *A Treasury Alarm*, Chatto & Windus, 1976, p. 23.
207 Pliatzky, *Getting and Spending*, p. 135.
208 Wilson used the expression in conversation with Pliatzky. Ibid., p. 136.
209 Ibid.
210 Private information.
211 This should be attributed to 'folklore' but I have had it confirmed privately.
212 Peter Hennessy, *The Last Edwardian*, BBC Radio 4, 30 December 1986.
213 Hugo Young and Ann Sloman, *No, Minister*, p. 73.
214 Lord Rothschild, 'Too Old?', the Melchett Lecture, 8 November 1972, reproduced in *Meditations of a Broomstick*, pp. 124–37.
215 Bancroft, 'The Art of Management'.
216 Sir Richard Clarke, *New Trends in Government*, HMSO, 1971. The book was based on a series of lectures at the Civil Service College.
217 Private information.
218 John Bourne, 'He gets on with things', *Financial Times*, 21 April 1973.
219 Hennessy, 'A magnificent piece of bureaucratic machinery'.
220 Ibid.
221 Private information.
222 The view of Wilson's Downing Street Press Secretary, Joe Haines. Picture caption opposite p. 97 in *The Politics of Power*.
223 Sir John Hunt, 'Do's and Don'ts of Chairmanship', *Management Services in Government*, May 1977, Vol. 32, No. 2, Civil Service Department, 1977, p. 63.
224 Desmond Quigley, 'Sir John Hunt – keeper of secrets', *Financial Weekly*, 2 November 1979.
225 Lord Hunt of Tanworth interviewed for *All the Prime Minister's Men*, 29 May 1986.
226 Ibid.
227 Ibid.
228 Ibid.
229 See Plowden (ed.), *Advising the Rulers*, p. 69.
230 'Grasping the cable', *Sunday Times*, 10 October 1982.
231 Arthur Sandles, 'Midwife of the Cable Age', *Financial Times*, 8 October 1982.
232 'The new Trend', *Financial Times*, 3 April 1973.
233 Lord Hunt of Tanworth, 'Cabinet strategy and management', CIPFA/RIPA Conference, Eastbourne, 9 June 1983. For a fuller account of the speech see Hennessy, *Cabinet*, pp. 189–90.
234 He used this phrase at a Wilton Park seminar organised by RIPA, PSI and the European Centre for Political Studies, 22–25 November 1984. See Plowden (ed.), *Advising the Rulers*, p. 67.
235 Lord Hunt of Tanworth interviewed for LWT's *Whitehall*, 10 April 1987.

236 Private information.
237 Quoted in Peter Hennessy, 'Whitehall brief: The civil servant who is more like a politician', *The Times*, 14 July 1981.
238 Denis Healey interviewed for *All the Prime Minister's Men*, 14 May 1987.
239 Sir Frank used these words before the Public Accounts Committee. *Ninth Report from the Committee of Public Accounts, Session 1981–82*, 'Ministry of Defence. Chevaline Improvement to Polaris Missile System'. H of C Paper 269, April 1982, p. 13.
240 'Spectrum: Our men behind the truce, Troubles' shooters', *The Sunday Times*, 16 February 1975.
241 The John Mortimer Interview, 'The Man from the Ministry on: – dangerous women – low-grade spies – and illogical wars', *The Sunday Times*, 2 January 1983.
242 Ibid.
243 Figure supplied by Ministry of Defence Press Office.
244 Hennessy, 'Squaddie's friend', *The Times*, 16 December 1982.
245 Hennessy, 'The civil servant who is more like a politician'.
246 The John Mortimer Interview, 'The Man from the Ministry . . .'
247 Peter Hennessy, 'The civil servant who is more like a politician'.
248 Ivan Rowan, 'Whitehall's frankest mandarin bows out', *Sunday Telegraph*, 2 January 1983.
249 Private information.
250 Pliatzky, *Getting and Spending*, pp. 130–1.
251 Hennessy, *Cabinet*, p. 91.
252 Whitehead, *The Writing on the Wall*, p. 191.
253 Ibid., p. 197.
254 Ibid.
255 Lord Hunt of Tanworth interviewed for *All the Prime Minister's Men*, 29 May 1987.
256 Callaghan described it as 'a group to keep a watch on the interplay of our domestic fiscal and monetary policy with that of overseas countries', *Time and Chance*, p. 476.
257 Donoughue, *Prime Minister*, p. 9.
258 Lord Callaghan interviewed for *All the Prime Minister's Men*, 30 April 1986.
259 Peter Hennessy, 'Committee decided Callaghan economic policy', *The Times*, 17 March 1980.
260 Margaret Drabble, *The Ice Age*, Weidenfeld, 1977, p. 36.
261 Ibid., p. 78.
262 *Civil Servants and Change*, Civil Service Department, 1975.
263 Peter Hennessy, '£140 m cuts in Whitehall would end 35,000 jobs', *Financial Times*, 4 May 1976.
264 Peter Hennessy, 'Civil Service staffing inquiry by Commons', *The Times*, 10 January 1976.
265 *Eleventh Report from the Expenditure Committee, Session 1976–77*, 'The Civil Service', Vol. II, Part II, pp. 782–3.

266 Ibid., p. 787.
267 Ibid., p. 788.
268 Ibid., p. 764.
269 Ibid., p. 777.
270 Conversation with Lord Rayner for *All the Prime Minister's Men*, 21 May 1986.
271 *Eleventh Report from the Expenditure Committee, Session 1976–77*, 'The Civil Service', Vol. II, Part II, p. 659.
272 Ibid.
273 Ibid., p. 661.
274 Ibid., p. 664.
275 See Peter Hennessy, 'Whitehall brief: Man who fights a personal war with the Civil Service', *The Times*, 27 May 1980.
276 *Eleventh Report from the Expenditure Committee, Session 1976–77*, 'The Civil Service', Vol. I, Report, p. lxxxiii.
277 Ibid., p. lxxii.
278 Ibid.
279 Ibid., p. lxxiv.
280 Ibid., p. lxxiii.
281 Ibid., p. lxxix.
282 Ibid., p. lxxxii.
283 Ibid., p. lxxxiii.
284 Mr Sedgemore kept a diary during his time as Tony Benn's Parliamentary Private Secretary at the Department of Energy, extracts from which are the most fascinating contents of *The Secret Constitution*.
285 *Eleventh Report from the Expenditure Committee, Session 1976–77*, 'The Civil Service', Vol. II, Part II, p. 747.
286 On Granada Television's *Under Fire*, 9 February 1987.
287 Peter Hennessy, 'Dismantling the Treasury is suggested', *The Times*, 15 February 1977.
288 Private information.
289 Quigley, 'Sir John Hunt – Keeper of secrets'.
290 Peter Hennessy, 'Treasury break-up unlikely while Mr Healey remains', *The Times*, 21 March 1977.
291 Donoughue, *Prime Minister*, p. 93.
292 Private information.
293 Conversation with David Young for BBC Radio 3's *Routine Punctuated by Orgies*, 2 November 1983.
294 Conversation with Sir Kenneth Berrill for *Routine Punctuated by Orgies*, 14 October 1983.
295 Ibid.
296 Ibid.
297 Ibid.
298 *Review of Overseas Representation. Report by the Central Policy Review Staff*, HMSO, 1977, p. v.
299 Haines, *The Politics of Power*, p. 37.
300 Private information.

301 Private information.
302 Private information.
303 Conversation with Dr Tessa Blackstone for *Routine Punctuated by Orgies*, 11 November 1983.
304 Private information.
305 Private information.
306 Private information. For an account of the 'Fortress Britain' exercise see Hennessy, Morrison and Townsend, *Routine Punctuated by Orgies*, pp. 54–5.
307 Private information.
308 Roger Berthoud, 'Think Tank suggests closing at least 55 diplomatic posts overseas', *The Times*, 4 August 1977.
309 Peter Hennessy, '"Parody" staff associations say', *The Times*, 5 August 1977.
310 Ibid.
311 The existence of GEN 89 was disclosed in *The Times*, on 5 July 1978.
312 *Routine Punctuated by Orgies*, BBC Radio 3, 13 December 1983.
313 Ibid.
314 Ibid.
315 Private information.
316 *The United Kingdom's Overseas Representation*, Cmnd. 7308, 1978.
317 Ibid.
318 Ibid.
319 Conversation with Sir Frank Cooper for *Routine Punctuated by Orgies*, 31 October 1983.
320 Conversation with David Young, 2 November 1983.
321 Plowden (ed.), *Advising the Rulers*, p. 66.
322 Peter Hennessy, 'A PM's dislike of "Jumbos"', *Financial Times*, 17 September 1976.
323 Peter Hennessy, 'Some of the leading candidates for the succession', *The Times*, 5 October 1977.
324 Private information.
325 Sir Frank Cooper, Book Review, *Public Administration*, Vol. 65, No.3, Autumn 1986.
326 Hennessy, 'Sir Ian Bancroft's axioms.'
327 Hennessy, 'Some of the leading candidates for the succession'.
328 Ibid.
329 Peter Hennessy, 'Whitehall campaign to improve tarnished image of Civil Service', *The Times*, 31 August 1978.
330 Jeffery and Hennessy, *States of Emergency*, p. 245.
331 Callaghan, *Time and Chance*, p. 538.
332 William Rodgers, 'A winter's tale of discontent', *The Guardian*, 7 January 1984.
333 Donoughue, *Prime Minister*, p. 173.
334 Rodgers, 'A winter's tale of discontent'.

PART 2 SYSTEM

1 Lord Hailsham, *The Dilemma of Democracy*, Collins, 1978, p. 155.

7 POLICY-MAKING IN OPPOSITION

1 *RIPA Report*, Winter 1985, Vol. 6, No. 4, p. 1.
2 William Wallace, 'Preparing for Government', 'Most confidential' document, June 1985. Not generally available but its contents were widely reported in September 1985. See Robert Carvel, 'Steel's adviser says Liberals not ready for power', *The Guardian*, 7 September 1985.
3 Quoted in Peter Hennessy, 'The Berlin Wall between the Opposition and the Civil Service', *The Listener*, 27 November 1986.
4 Dr John Cunningham, speaking on *The Shadows' Dummy Run*, BBC Radio 4's *Analysis*, 26 November 1986.
5 'Agenda for the third phase of Thatcherism', *The Independent*, 14 September 1987.
6 Lord Rothschild, 'The Best Laid Plans . . .', The First Israel Sieff Memorial Lecture, 4 May 1976, reproduced in *Meditations of a Broomstick*, p. 171.
7 Conversation with Professor S. E. Finer for *The Shadows' Dummy Run*, 14 November 1986.
8 Sir James delivered his view when interviewed by Brian Walden for London Weekend Television's *Callaghan* programme, Channel 4 Television, 10 April 1987.
9 Conversation with Professor John Ashworth for *The Shadows' Dummy Run*, 19 November 1986.
10 Private information. For Heath as a young assistant principal, see George Hutchinson, *Edward Heath, A Personal and Political Biography*, Longman, 1970, pp. 45–52.
11 Private information.
12 Hennessy, *Cabinet*, p. 169.
13 Cmnd, 4506.
14 It is reproduced as an appendix in John Ramsden, *The Making of Conservative Party Policy: The Conservative Research Department Since 1929*, Longman, 1980, pp. 279–81.
15 Conversation with Professor Finer for *The Shadows' Dummy Run*, 14 November 1986.
16 Ibid.
17 Letter from Sir Adam Ridley to Peter Hennessy, 27 November 1986.
18 Conversation with Dr David Owen for *The Shadows' Dummy Run*, 18 November 1986.
19 Ibid.
20 Private information.
21 Private information.
22 Conversation with Dr William Wallace for *The Shadows' Dummy Run*, 19 November 1986.
23 John Le Carré, *Smiley's People*, Hodder, 1979, p. 58.
24 Conversation with Dick Taverne, 18 November 1986.

25 Conversation with Sir Adam Ridley, 18 November 1986.
26 Conversation with Dr David Owen for *The Shadows' Dummy Run*, 18 November 1986.
27 Conversation with Sir Frank Cooper for *The Shadows' Dummy Run*, 12 November 1986.
28 Ibid.
29 See Peter Hennessy, 'The Attlee Governments 1945–51', in Hennessy and Seldon (eds), *Ruling Performance*, p. 32.
30 Conversation with Conservative Central Office Press Office, 10 December 1986.
31 Private information.
32 Figures supplied by Labour Party Office, 18 December 1986.
33 Figures supplied by SDP Party Department, 11 December 1986.
34 Figures supplied by Liberal Party Research Department, 11 December 1986.
35 H of C Debates, 23 January 1985, cols 1097–8.
36 Conversation with Dr John Cunningham, 18 November 1986.
37 Conversation with Dr David Owen for *The Shadows' Dummy Run*, 18 November 1986.
38 Peter Kellner, 'It wasn't the campaign, it was the product', *New Statesman*, 10 July 1987.
39 Geoff Bish interviewed for LWT's *Whitehall*, 20 March 1987.
40 Peter Hennessy, 'Civil Service challenger', *Financial Times*, 12 May 1976.
41 Ibid.
42 Parliamentary answer by Mr Nigel Lawson, Chancellor of the Exchequer, 6 July 1987 as reported in The *Financial Times*, 7 July 1987.
43 *Top Salaries Review Body: Report No. 24, Review of Parliamentary Allowances*, Vol. I, H of C 131–1, April 1987, p. 12.
44 Letter from Geoffrey Lock, Head of Research Division, H of C Library, 7 July 1987.
45 Conversation with Sir Adam Ridley, 18 November 1986.
46 Conversation with Dick Taverne, 18 November 1986.
47 Ibid.
48 *Merging Tax and Benefits, Attacking Poverty*, SDP, 1986.
49 Conversation with Dick Taverne for *The Shadows' Dummy Run*, 18 November 1986.
50 Conversation with Sir Adam Ridley for *The Shadows' Dummy Run*, 18 November 1986.
51 Conversation with Sir Frank Cooper for *The Shadows' Dummy Run*, 12 November 1986.

8 CABINET, PARLIAMENT AND PRESSURE

1 Sir Frank Cooper, 'Changing the Establishment', LSE, Suntory Toyota Lecture, 12 March 1986. An abridged version of Sir Frank's lecture was published in *The Political Quarterly*, Vol. 57, No. 3 (July–September 1986), pp. 267–77.

2 Burke Trend, 'Machinery under pressure,' *Times Literary Supplement*, 26 September 1986, p. 1076.
3 Conversation with Lord Trend, 1 October 1986.
4 Ibid.
5 *World as Will and Idea*, Trübner, 1883; *Life of Adam Smith*, Walter Scott, 1887.
6 Paul Johnson writing in the Preface to George Dangerfield, *The Strange Death of Liberal England*, Paladin edn, 1983, p. 9.
7 Roy Jenkins, *Asquith*, Fontana, 1967, p. 34.
8 Stephen Koss, *Asquith*, Allen Lane, 1976, pp. 191–2.
9 Conversation with Lord Trend, 1 October 1986.
10 For Haldane's paternity of Britain's prototype national security apparatus see Christopher Andrew, *Secret Service, The Making of the British Intelligence Community*, Heinemann, 1985, pp. 52–3, 56–8.
11 *Richard Burdon Haldane, An Autobiography*, Hodder, 1929, pp. 216–17. Haldane had died the summer before the book was published.
12 Ibid., p. 224.
13 Margaret Cole (ed.), *Beatrice Webb's Diaries, 1912–1924*, Longman, 1952, p. 98.
14 Ibid., p. 98 footnote.
15 Ibid., p. 87.
16 Ibid., pp. 97–8.
17 Ibid., p. 98.
18 Ibid., pp. 137–8.
19 Ibid., p. 138.
20 Ibid.
21 *Report of the Machinery of Government Committee*, p. 4.
22 Arthur Marwick, *Britain in the Century of Total Wars: War, Peace and Social Change 1900–1967*, Bodley Head, 1968, p. 17.
23 Olson, *Rise and Decline of Nations*, p. 78.
24 *Report of the Machinery of Government Committee*, p. 4.
25 Lord Bridges, 'Haldane and the Machinery of Government,' *Public Administration*, Vol. XXXV, Autumn 1956, p. 261.
26 *Report of the Machinery of Government Committee*, p. 4.
27 Ibid.
28 Ibid., p. 5.
29 Ibid., p. 6.
30 Conversation with Lord Trend, 1 October 1986.
31 *Report of the Machinery of Government Committee,* p. 6.
32 Ibid., p. 30. For Haldane's desire for a 'trained thinker' see Bridges, 'Haldane and the Machinery of Government', p. 261.
33 Ibid.
34 Ibid., p. 7.
35 Ibid., p. 14.
36 See John Wheeler Bennett, *John Anderson, Viscount Waverley*, Macmillan 1962, and below pp. 558–65.
37 *Beatrice Webb's Diaries*, p. 126.

38 *Report of the Machinery of Government Committee*, p. 15.
39 Letter from Haldane to his mother, 7 December 1918, preserved in the Haldane Papers, National Library, Edinburgh.
40 Stephen Koss, *Lord Haldane, Scapegoat for Liberalism*, Columbia University Press, 1969, p. 231.
41 Michael Posner, 'Do We Need Research Councils?' *The Political Quarterly*, Vol. 57, No. 2 (April–June 1986), p. 156.
42 PRO, CAB 66/67, CP (45) 100, II: 'Proceedings in Cabinet Committees'.
43 Colin Seymour-Ure, 'The "Disintegration" of the Cabinet and the Neglected Question of Cabinet Reform', *Parliamentary Affairs*, XXIV, 3 (1971), p. 196.
44 David Howell, lead book review in *The Political Quarterly*, Vol. 58(1) (January–March 1987), p. 102.
45 Lord Whitelaw, Deputy Prime Minister, interviewed for *The Other Opposition*, BBC Radio 4's *Analysis*, 19 October 1987.
46 Trend, 'Machinery under pressure'.
47 See Philip Norton, 'Introduction, Parliament in Perspective', in Philip Norton (ed.), *Parliament in the 1980s*, Blackwell, 1985, pp. 3–4.
48 Russell, *Collections and Recollections*, p. 324. He produced this definition in 1897 when Lord Salisbury was Prime Minister.
49 *Report of the Machinery of Government Committee*, p. 4.
50 Hennessy, *Cabinet* (1986). Two previous volumes remain a must on any student's reading list: John Mackintosh, *The British Cabinet* (3rd edn Stevens, 1977), and Patrick Gordon-Walker, *The Cabinet*, (2nd edn, Fontana, 1972). The great 1960s debate on prime-ministerial government versus Cabinet government should also be sampled. This can be tasted most conveniently by reading Mackintosh, and R. H. S. Crossman's 'Prime Ministerial Government' and G. W. Jones's 'The Prime Minister's Power' in Anthony King (ed.), *The British Prime Minister* (2nd edn, Macmillan, 1985) pp. 175–94 and 195–220.
51 Lord Home interviewed in 'The Unknown Premiership', *The Quality of Cabinet Government*, BBC Radio 3, 25 July 1985.
52 Seymour-Ure, '"Disintegration" of the Cabinet,' p. 196.
53 Ibid.
54 Sir Frank Cooper interviewed for *All the Prime Minister's Men*, 8 April 1986.
55 Lord Hunt of Tanworth, 'Cabinet Strategy and Management,' CIPFA/RIPA Conference, Eastbourne, 9 June 1983.
56 Dangerfield, *Strange Death of Liberal England*, p. 44.
57 E. C. S. Wade and G. Godfrey Phillips, *Constitutional and Administrative Law*, 9th edn by A. W. Bradley, Longman, 1977, p. 244.
58 For the Ministerial Salaries Act see ibid., p. 253–4; for the Chequers statute see ibid., p. 244 footnote.
59 Mr Kinnock used this phrase on the Thames Television programme, *This Week*, on 2 October 1986 to describe speculation that the United States would withdraw from Europe if Labour's defence programme was implemented.
60 H of C Debates, 8 February 1960, Col. 70.
61 See Hennessy, *Cabinet*, pp. 7–8. *Questions* expanded almost fourfold in thirty years from 37 paragraphs in 1945 to 132 paragraphs in 1976.

62 Conversation with Lord Trend, 1 October 1986.
63 I have written at greater length on this theme. See Peter Hennessy, 'Michael Heseltine, Mottram's Law and the Efficiency of Cabinet Government', *The Political Quarterly*, Vol. 57, No. 2 (April–June 1986), pp. 137–43, and 'Helicopter Crashes into Cabinet: Prime Minister and Constitution Hurt', *Journal of Law and Society*, Vol. 13, No. 3 (Winter 1986), pp. 423–32.
64 The most recent version of *Questions* to have seen the light of day was Mr Callaghan's edition of April 1976 disclosed in the *New Statesman*, 14 February 1986, p. 11.
65 Interview with Lord Hunt of Tanworth for *All the Prime Minister's Men*, 29 May 1986.
66 Private information.
67 For a critique of this system see Michael Cockerell, Peter Hennessy and David Walker, *Sources Close to the Prime Minister*, Papermac, 1985.
68 H of C, Fourth Report from the Defence Committee, Session 1985–6, *Westland plc: The Government's Decision-Making*, HMSO, 1986, p. xi.
69 H of C Debates, Col. 652, 27 January 1986.
70 John Cole, 'Westland – an unexploded bomb', *The Listener*, 31 July 1986, p. 6.
71 The Commons Treasury and Civil Service Committee was already examining the duties and responsibilities of civil servants to ministers.
72 Cole, 'Westland – an unexploded bomb'.
73 He was speaking under 'Chatham House' rules of non-attribution at a seminar on 'The Constitutional Position of Civil Servants', organised by the Constitutional Reform Centre and the Royal Institute of Public Administration, held in London on 30 July 1986.
74 *Civil Servants and Ministers: Duties and Responsibilities*, Cmnd. 9841, HMSO, 1986, p. 3.
75 John Ward, 'Civil Servants and Ministers', *FDA News*, September 1986.
76 Richard Norton-Taylor, 'Civil Service concern at evasive Ministers', *The Guardian*, 10 October 1986.
77 Graham Turner, 'How Lord Hailsham judges himself and his peers', *Sunday Telegraph*, 13 April 1986.
78 Private information.
79 See Peter Hennessy, 'The secrets that will stay secret for ever', *The Listener*, 11 September 1986.
80 Lord Hailsham delivered this opinion after I had finished a television interview with him on 14 May 1986.
81 Lord Hailsham interviewed for *All the Prime Minister's Men*, 14 May 1986.
82 Interview with Kenneth Harris, *The Observer*, 25 February 1979.
83 It is reproduced in Alan Thompson, *The Day Before Yesterday: An Illustrated History of Britain from Attlee to Macmillan*, Sidgwick & Jackson, 1971, p. 163.
84 Norman St John-Stevas, 'Prime Ministers rise and fall but the Cabinet abides', *Daily Telegraph*, 7 August 1986.
85 Quoted in Peter Hennessy, 'From Woodshed to Watershed', *The Times*, 5 March 1984.

86 *Nine O'Clock News*, BBC 1, 10 January 1986.
87 *News At Ten*, ITN, 10 January 1986.
88 Ian Gilmour, *The Body Politic*, Hutchinson, 1969.
89 'Friday People', The *Guardian*, 22 November 1985.
90 Lord Bancroft interviewed for *All the Prime Minister's Men*, 10 April 1986.
91 'At Last Someone Says No, Prime Minister', leading article, *The Observer*, 12 January 1986.
92 See his introduction to *Re-skilling Government: The Boundaries of the Reform Process*, a discussion paper prepared for a conference on 8 September 1986. Available from the Institute of Directors.
93 Sir John Hoskyns interviewed for *All the Prime Minister's Men*, 26 March 1986.
94 Ibid.
95 Sir John Nott interviewed for *All the Prime Minister's Men*, 22 April 1986.
96 Leon Brittan interviewed for *All the Prime Minister's Men*, 26 March 1986.
97 Quoted in Hennessy, *Cabinet*, p. 105.
98 *The Times*, 1 September 1984.
99 London Weekend Television, *Weekend World*, 26 January 1986.
100 Tyne Tees Television, *Face the Press*, 26 January 1986.
101 Lord Hailsham interviewed for *All the Prime Minister's Men*, 14 May 1986.
102 See Peter Hennessy, 'The Quality of Cabinet Government in Britain', *Policy Studies*, Vol. 6, Part 2 (October 1985), p. 16.
103 Hunt, 'Cabinet Strategy and Management'.
104 I have drawn heavily in this section on Chapter 3, 'Conviction Cabinet 1979–86', in Hennessy, *Cabinet*, pp. 99–101 in particular.
105 The committees of which I have learned are listed in Table I, 'Mrs Thatcher's engine room', Hennessy, *Cabinet*, pp. 27–30.
106 Ibid., pp. 95–6.
107 Lord Rothschild, *Meditations of a Broomstick*, Collins, 1977, p. 171.
108 Quoted in Hennessy, Morrison and Townsend, *Routine Punctuated by Orgies: The Central Policy Review Staff 1970–83*, p. 85.
109 Sir Frank Cooper inteviewed for *All the Prime Minister's Men*, 8 April 1986.
110 *Re-Skilling Government: The Boundaries of the Reform Process.*
111 Mr Hurd delivered his views on the need for a small new CPRS on *All the Prime Ministers' Men: The Shape of Things to Come*, Channel 4 Television, 24 July 1986.
112 Private information.
113 For the genesis and function of Mr Callaghan's 'Economic Seminar' see Hennessy, *Cabinet*, p. 92.
114 Private information.
115 Private information.
116 Private information.
117 Private information.
118 Private information.
119 Private information.

120 Quoted in Hennessy, *Cabinet*, pp. 103–4.
121 Private information.
122 Robert Harris, 'Blazing June for high-noon Thatcher', *The Observer*, 10 May 1987. In fact, it turned out to be one of the wettest Junes on record.
123 'Quotes of the Day', *The Independent*, 22 May 1987.
124 Neil Kinnock interviewed by Peter Murphy of Independent Radio News, 31 May 1987.
125 John Pienaar and Andrew Marr, 'Thatcher the target of more personal attacks', *The Independent*, 2 June 1987.
126 Denis Healey on the *Six O'Clock News*, BBC Television, 1 June 1987.
127 See Peter Hennessy, 'Permanent Government: Queen Boadicea at the Cabinet door', *New Statesman*, 19 June 1987.
128 Quoted from an original interview in *The Mail on Sunday* by Anthony Bevins, 'Kinnock calls for curbs on private schools', in *The Independent*, 1 June 1987.
129 Anthony King, 'Overload: problems of Governing in the 1970s', *Political Studies*, xxii, 2–3, June-September, 1975.
130 Anthony Sampson, *Anatomy of Britain Today*, Hodder, 1965, p. 105.
131 Francis Pym (one of the objectors) interviewed for *All the Prime Minister's Men*, 25 March 1986.
132 Adam Raphael, Simon Hoggart, Peter Pringle and Robin Smyth, 'The Winning of Thatcher', *The Observer*, 20 April 1986.
133 Postcard from Lord Hailsham to Peter Hennessy, 16 June 1987.
134 Lord Hailsham interviewed by Jon Snow, ITV *News At One*, 17 June 1987.
135 Lord Hailsham's judgement was broadcast in *All the Prime Minister's Men: Conviction Cabinet*, Channel 4 Television, 17 July 1986.
136 John Gallagher, *The Decline, Revival and Fall of the British Empire*, CUP, 1982, p. 73. For pre-Thatcher moves towards a more dominant premiership see Hennessy, *Cabinet*, Chapter 2, 'Overloading the Engine', pp. 34–93.
137 Vernon Bogdanor, 'The Crossman Diaries', *Political Studies*, Vol. XXV, No. 1, 1976, p. 120.
138 Ibid.
139 Richard Crossman, *The Diaries of a Cabinet Minister*, Vol. I, *Minister of Housing 1964–66*, Hamish Hamilton and Cape, 1975.
140 King, 'Overload', p. 164.
141 See the evidence of Dr Bernard Donoughue, Head of Wilson's Downing Street Policy Unit, in Phillip Whitehead, *The Writing on the Wall*, Michael Joseph, 1985, p. 128.
142 Barbara Castle, *The Castle Diaries, 1974–76*, Weidenfeld, 1980, pp. 219–24.
143 When I published an article on the 'overload' theme which drew on this extract from the Castle Diaries – 'Does the Elderly Cabinet Machine Need Oiling?' *The Listener*, 27 June 1985 – Callaghan's office at Westminster telephoned to say he was joking when he made his remarks about emigrating.
144 Castle, *Diaries, 1974–76*, p. 223.
145 Hennessy, *Cabinet*, p. 86.

146 Castle, *Diaries, 1974–76*, p. 223.
147 See Peter Hennessy, 'The Attlee Governments, 1945–51', in Peter Hennessy and Anthony Seldon (eds), *Ruling Performance*, pp. 28–52.
148 King, 'Overload', p. 163.
149 Hennessy, *Cabinet*, pp. 39–43.
150 Diary entry for 14 October 1947. Philip M. Williams (ed.), *The Diary of Hugh Gaitskell, 1945–1956*, Cape, 1983, p. 36.
151 For the 1947 reorganisation see Alec Cairncross, *Years of Recovery, British Economic Policy 1945–51*, Methuen, 1985, pp. 52–3.
152 Conversation with Sir John Hoskyns, 18 September 1986.
153 Peter Riddell, 'Privatisation momentum to be kept up, says Lamont', *Financial Times*, 8 October 1986.
154 See 'Table 5.1 Nationalisation Measures, 1945–51', in Henry Pelling, *The Labour Governments 1945–51*, Macmillan, 1984, p. 90.
155 S. E. Finer, 'Thatcherism and British Political History', in Kenneth Minogue and Michael Biddiss, *Thatcherism: Personality and Politics*, Macmillan, 1987, p. 127.
156 Stephen Taylor, 'Is politics compatible with management', paper delivered at the RIPA Conference on Politics and Administration, Durham, 20 September 1986.
157 Robin Pauley, 'Health Minister to head management of NHS', *Financial Times*, 3 October 1986.
158 Chris Patten interviewed for *All the Prime Minister's Men*, 8 April 1986.
159 Crossman, *Diaries of a Cabinet Minister*, Vol. I, pp. 352–3.
160 Private information.
161 Roy Gregory, 'Executive Power and Constituency Representation in the United Kingdom', *Political Studies*, XXVII, 1 (March 1980), pp. 63–83.
162 William Rees-Mogg, 'Time for the BBC gentlemen to hand over to the players', *The Independent*, 7 October 1986.
163 Hennessy, *Cabinet*, p. 67.
164 Harold Evans, *Downing Street Diary: The Macmillan Years 1957/63*, Hodder, 1981, p. 264.
165 Lord Hailsham interviewed for *All the Prime Minister's Men*, 14 May 1986.
166 Lord Hailsham, *The Dilemma of Democracy, Diagnosis and Prescription*, Collins, 1978, pp. 208–9.
167 'Home Secretary's Lecture to Royal Institute of Public Administration', Durham University, 19 September 1986, available from the Home Office Press office.
168 Ibid.
169 Ibid.
170 Sir John Hoskyns, 'Conservatism is not enough', Institute of Directors Annual Lecture, 25 September 1983.
171 Aneurin Bevan, *In Place of Fear*, Heinemann, 1952, p. 6.
172 The phrase is Kenneth O. Morgan's. See his 'Bevan, Architect of the NHS', *New Society*, 17 February 1983, p. 256.

173 'Scargill in call for direct action', *The Observer*, 21 June 1987.
174 Charles Headlam (ed.), *The Milner Papers*, Vol. II, 1931–33, p. 291.
175 Lord Hailsham interviewed by Jon Snow, ITN *News at One*, 17 June 1987.
176 Michael Foot, *Aneurin Bevan*, Vol. I, *Four Square*, 1966, pp. 71–2.
177 Ronald Butt, *The Power of Parliament*, 2nd edn, Constable, 1969, p. 34.
178 'Watchman', *Right Honourable Gentlemen*, Hamish Hamilton, 1939, p. 102.
179 G. Almond and S. Verba, *The Civil Culture*, Princeton University Press, 1963, p. 102.
180 Private information.
181 Norton *Parliament in the 1980s*, p. 137.
182 Sir John Hoskyns, 'Conservatism is not enough'.
183 Sir Frank Cooper, 'Changing the Establishment'.
184 Susan Crosland, *Tony Crosland*, pp. 288–97.
185 Lord Whitelaw gave these figures in a speech to the Parliamentary Press Gallery on 11 November 1987.
186 Norton, *Parliament in the 1980s*, pp. 4–9.
187 H of C Select Committee on Procedure, First Report, Session 1977–78, House of Commons Paper No. 588.
188 Mr St John-Stevas's own account can be found in Norman St John-Stevas, *The Two Cities*, Faber, 1984, pp. 54–7, 104–7. For a comprehensive account of the background to the 1979 reform see Priscilla Baines, 'History and Rationale of the 1979 Reforms' in Gavin Drewry (ed.), *The New Select Committees: A Study of the 1979 Reforms,* OUP, 1985, pp. 13–36.
189 H of C Debates, 25 June 1979, Vol. 969, Col. 36.
190 *Report of the Machinery of Government Committee.*
191 Gavin Drewry, 'The New Select Committees – A Constitutional Non-Event?' in Dilys M. Hill (ed.), *Parliamentary select Committees in Action: A symposium*, Strathclyde Papers on Government and Politics, No. 24, 1984, p. 30.
192 Ibid., p. 52.
193 *Politics Without Power*, BBC Radio 4's, *Analysis*, 13 August 1980.
194 *Westland plc: The Defence Implications of the Future of Westland plc, The Government's decision-making Government. Response to the Third and Fourth Reports from the Defence Committee Session 1985–86, HC 518 and 519*, Cmnd. 9916, HMSO, October 1986, p. 10.
195 Simon Jenkins, 'The Price of Survival', *The Sunday Times*, 19 October 1986.
196 John Ward, 'In the Wake of Westland', *FDA News*, November 1986.
197 'The powers of Parliament', *Financial Times*, 28 October 1986.
198 Hugo Young, 'Westland's black hole of non-accountability', *The Guardian*, 23 October 1986.
199 H of C Report, 29 October 1986, col. 386.
200 H of C Report, Ibid. col. 415.
201 Peter Hennessy, 'Dr John Gilbert – Grand Inquisitor', *Contemporary Record*, Vol. 1, No. 1 (Spring 1987), p. 19.
202 Ibid.

203 Martin Fletcher, 'MPs' watchdogs will be stronger', *The Times*, 6 November 1987.

204 The speech is reproduced in Andrew Roth, *Enoch Powell: Tory Tribune*, Macdonald, 1970, pp. 350–7.

205 I am grateful to Mr Vernon Bogdanor of Brasenose College, Oxford, for this statistic which he likes to compare to the 10,000 letters the SDP received after its launch in 1981.

206 Lord Hailsham, 'Elective Dictatorship', the 1976 Richard Dimbleby Lecture, *The Listener*, 21 October 1976.

207 Donald Shell, 'The House of Lords and the Thatcher Government', *Parliamentary Affairs*, Vol. 38, No. 1 (Winter 1985), p. 30.

208 He made his prediction on *The Other Opposition*, BBC Radio 4's *Analysis*, on 5 November 1985. It did not go down well in No. 10, see Anthony Bevins, 'Rebuke expected for Lord Whitelaw', *The Independent*, 6 November 1987.

209 Lord Cledwyn, Leader of the Labour peers, interviewed for *The Other Opposition*, 28 October 1987.

210 S. E. Finer, *Anonymous Empire, A Study of the Lobby in Great Britain*, Pall Mall, 1958, p. 133.

211 Des Wilson, *Pressure: The A to Z of Campaigning in Britain*, Heinemann Educational, 1984, p. 21.

212 Douglas Hurd, 'Home Secretary's Lecture to Royal Institute of Public Administration'.

213 *Report of the Departmental Committee on Section 2 of the Official Secrets Act, 1911*, Vol. 4, Oval Evidence, Home Office, 1972, p. 187.

214 I am grateful to Professor Sammy Finer for this story which he told me during a 'Government and Opposition' Conference on 'Thatcherism' at LSE on 1 October 1986.

215 *Grey Matters*, BBC Radio 4's *Analysis*, 14 October 1987.

216 For an excellent short summary see Geoffrey Alderman, *Pressure Groups and Government in Great Britain*, Longman, 1984.

217 Wilson, *Pressure*, p. 5.

218 Quoted in Part 4 of Michael Charlton's BBC Radio 3 Documentary series, *The Little Platoon – The Long Struggle for the Falklands*, broadcast on 17 May 1987.

219 Ibid.

220 As quoted in the preamble to the broadcast.

221 For a vigorously argued case *against* 'Buy British' see Keith Hartley, Farooq Hussain and Ron Smith, 'The UK defence industrial base', in *The Political Quarterly*, Vol. 58 (1) (January–March 1987), pp. 62–72.

222 *Bangs to the Buck*, BBC Radio 4's *Analysis*, 27 May 1987.

223 Hartley, Hussain and Smith, 'The UK defence industrial base', p. 63.

224 Sir Frank Cooper interviewed for *Bangs to the Buck*, 11 May 1987.

225 Lord Weinstock interviewed for *Bangs to the Buck*, 19 May 1987.

226 Private information.

227 Laurence Marks, 'Civil boorishness at the Opera House', *The Observer*, 5 July 1987.

228 Conversation with Sir Adam Ridley, 18 November 1986.

229 J. M. Ashworth, 'On the Giving and Receiving of Advice (in Whitehall and Salford)', Manchester Statistical Society, 16 November 1982.
230 Michael Davie, 'Man of property with a mission', *The Observer*, 5 July 1987.
231 He used the phrase at a Public Policy Consultant's seminar on 'Influencing Government' at the Painters' Hall in the City of London on 27 January 1987. I have to declare an interest: not only was I present but I was paid as well for acting as moderator during the hypothetical case-study.
232 Charles Miller, *Lobbying Government, Understanding and Influencing the Corridors of Power*, Blackwell, 1987.
233 Ibid., pp. 56–9.
234 Ibid., p. 56.

9 SECRECY, NEUTRALITY, PROBITY

1 Sir Robert Armstrong, *The Duties and Responsibilities of Civil Servants in Relation to Ministers, Note by the Head of the Home Civil Service*, Cabinet Office, 25 February 1985, p. 3.
2 *Report of the Committee of Privy Counsellors on Ministerial Memoirs*, Cmnd. 6386, HMSO, 22 January 1976, p. 13.
3 Sir John Hoskyns, 'Conservatism is not enough'.
4 Two accounts of the Ponting Affair are available: Clive Ponting, *The Right to Know*, Sphere, 1985, and Richard Norton-Taylor, *The Ponting Affair*, Cecil Woolf, 1985.
5 Hennessy, 'Whitehall Watch: Ethics of a Formidable Maiden Aunt.'
6 *The Vanishing Mandarins*, BBC Radio 4, *Analysis*, 13 February 1985.
7 'The monarchy adapts', *Financial Times*, 22 April 1986.
8 Lord Bancroft, 'The Art of Management', *Three Cantor Lectures*, II, *Whitehall and Management: A Retrospects* Royal Society of Arts, 30 January 1984.
9 On freedom of information Lord Bancroft said, 'I see no advantage and considerable disadvantage in immediately making public *how* the decisions are reached, disclosing confidential exchanges between Minister and Minister, and between Minister and adviser'. And, referring to the case of Ian Willmore, an administration trainee at the Department of Employment, he said: 'I am relieved that a leaker has been dismissed'.
10 I had this story from a retired intelligence officer.
11 See Peter Hennessy and Colin Bennett, *A Consumer's Guide to Open Government, Techniques for Penetrating Whitehall*, Outer Circle Policy Unit, 1980, p. 3.
12 Quoted in H. A. Gerth and C. Wright Mills, *From Max Weber: Essays in Sociology*, paperback edition, Routledge, 1970, pp. 233–4.
13 Sonia Orwell and Ian Angus, *The Collected Essays, Journalism and Letters of George Orwell*, Vol. II, *My Country Right or Left 1940–1943*, Penguin ed, 1970, p. 77.
14 Edward Shils, *The Torment of Secrecy*, Heinemann, 1956, pp. 48–9.
15 Conversation with D'Arcy Finn, Privy Council Office, Ottawa, 3 October 1980.

16 See Cockerell, Hennessy and Walker, *Sources Close to the Prime Minister*, p. 16.
17 Richard Crossman, *Diaries of a Cabinet Minister,* Vol. II, p. 44, diary entry for 20 September 1966.
18 The text of the oath was published in the aftermath of the Crossman Affair in the Radcliffe Report on Ministerial memoirs, Cmnd. 6386.
19 Private information.
20 Evidence of a Labour Cabinet minister.
21 George Blair, *Mind's Eye*, 'Collective Responsibility', undated. In author's possession.
22 Richard Pares, *King George III and the Politicians*, OUP, 1953, pp. 148–9.
23 Clive Priestley, 'Promoting the efficiency of central government', in Arthur Shenfield *et al.*, *Managing the Bureaucracy*, Adam Smith Institute, 1986, p. 117.
24 *Home Office, Departmental Committee on Section 2 of the Official Secrets Act 1911,* Vol. I, *Report of the Committee*, Cmnd. 5104, HMSO, 1972, p. 120.
25 Ibid.
26 Ibid., p. 21.
27 Ibid., p. 122.
28 Jonathan Steinberg, *Yesterday's Deterrent*, Macdonald, 1965.
29 See 'We want eight, and we won't wait', in A. J. P. Taylor, *Essays in English History*, Book Club Associates, 1977, pp. 199–203.
30 See Peter Hennessy, 'This culture of closed government is overdue for dynamiting', *The Daily Telegraph*, 14 August 1986, and Peter Hennessy, 'Opinion', in *Index in Censorship*, Vol. 15, No. 6 (June 1986), p. 2.
31 Andrew, *Secret Service*, pp. 63–4, and James Michael, *The Politics of Secrecy*, Penguin, 1982, pp. 36–43.
32 Section 2 can be read in full in Appendix I of the Franks Report, Cmnd. 5014, pp. 112–14.
33 Ibid., p. 14.
34 David Hooper, *Official Secrets: The Use and Abuse of the Act*, Secker & Warburg, 1987. See particularly Appendix 1, 'Selected Official Secrets Acts cases', pp. 243–73.
35 Michael, *The Politics of Secrecy*, p. 41.
36 Cmnd. 5104, p. 123.
37 Kent, *In on the Act,* p. 108.
38 Cmnd. 5104, p. 123.
39 Kent, *In on the Act*, p. 110.
40 I wrote an account of this episode while a member of the Britain Section of *The Economist* in 1982.
41 For the Prussian analogy and that of the Russo-Japanese War of 1905 which also haunted the CID see Alasdair Palmer, 'The history of the D-Notice Committee', in Christopher Andrew and David Dilks (eds), *The Missing Dimension, Governments and Intelligence Communities in the Twentieth Century*, Macmillan, 1984, p. 228.

42 Ibid., pp. 234–6.
43 Cmnd. 5104, pp. 123–4.
44 *The Civil Service Pay and Conditions of Service Code* can be consulted in the Cabinet Office's Library.
45 See Hennessy, *Cabinet*, pp. 12–13; Clive Ponting, 'Hopeless hypocrisy of propriety rules', *New Statesman*, 21 February 1986, pp. 13–14.
46 *Talking about the Office* is classified 'restricted' and is unavailable to the public.
47 My copy of *Talking about the Office* predates the Franks Report on the Falklands Islands which makes public a great deal of information about the JIC and its supporting apparatus. *Falkland Islands Review: Report of a Committee of Privy Counsellors*, Cmnd. 8787, HMSO, 1983, Annexe B, pp. 93–5.
48 H of C Debates, 4 July 1983, written answers.
49 Colin Hughes, 'Cabinet takes up the battle against Aids', *The Independent*, 3 November 1986.
50 Colin Brown, 'Aids warning will go to every home', *The Independent*, 12 November 1986.
51 David Leigh, 'I'll fight to the finish', *The Observer*, 16 November 1986.
52 Brittan, *Diary of an Irregular*, entry for 11 September 1965.
53 Letter to *The Times*, 7 January 1988.
54 'When courts strike the balance on behalf of the nation', *The Guardian*, 22 December 1987.
55 H of C, *Official Report*, 15 January 1988, Col. 584.
56 Douglas Hurd interviewed for *The Need to Know*, BBC Radio 4's *Analysis*, 25 January 1988.
57 I have to plead guilty to this. It was my story in *The Times* which started it. Peter Hennessy, 'Whitehall men told what not to disclose,' *The Times*, 22 May 1980.
58 *Memorandum of Guidance for Officials Appearing Before Select Committees*, Civil Service Department, 1980.
59 Ibid.
60 They made their pledges in the first edition of the newspaper of the Campaign for Freedom of Information, *Secrets*, No. 1, January 1984.
61 James Margach, *The Abuse of Power: The War Between Downing Street and the Media from Lloyd George to James Callaghan*, W. H. Allen, 1978, p. 1.
62 Quoted in Cockerell, Hennessy and Walker, *Sources Close to the Prime Minister*, p. 233.
63 Quoted as the frontispiece to Hennessy, *What the Papers Never Said*.
64 Stephen Koss, *The Rise and Fall of the Political Press in Britain,* Vol. I, *The Nineteenth Century*, Hamish Hamilton, 1981, pp. 238–9.
65 For the best history of the Lobby see James Margach, *The Anatomy of Power: An Enquiry into the Personality of Leadership*, W. H. Allen, 1979, Chapter 9, 'The Lobby', pp. 125–56.
66 Humbert Wolfe, 'Over the fire', in *The Uncelestial City*, Gollancz, 1930, pp. 30–1.

67 Francis Williams, *Parliament, Press and the Public*, Heinemann, 1946, p. 136.
68 Ibid., p. 137.
69 Kaufman, *How to Be a Minister*, p. 171.
70 PRO PREM 11/732.
71 See John Hunt, 'Whitelaw pledge on Tory plans in Lords', *Financial Times*, 12 November 1987.
72 PRO PREM 11/732.
73 It is reproduced in Cockerell, Hennessy and Walker, *Sources Close to the Prime Minister*, opposite p. 96.
74 The Prime Minister's speech at the Savoy on 18 January 1984 is reproduced as Appendix B in Hennessy, *What the Papers Never Said*, pp. 153–63.
75 Quoted in Cockerell, Hennessy and Walker, *Sources Close to the Prime Minister*, p. 122.
76 Ibid., p. 126.
77 Peter Hennessy, 'The case of the visible spokesman: the Lobby reforms itself', *New Statesman*, 3 October 1986.
78 For an account of the Lobby's to'ings and fro'ings in 1986–7 see Peter Hennessy, 'The Quality of Political Journalism', in *The Royal Society of Arts, Journal*, Vol. CXXXV, No. 5376, (November 1987), pp. 926–34.
79 Bridges, *Portrait of a Profession*, pp. 29–30.
80 I have found it impossible to source this one-liner which has long been a cherished part of Whitehall folklore.
81 For an audit of the effectiveness of the Croham Directive see Bennett and Hennessy, *A Consumer's Guide to Open Government*, pp. 5–14.
82 *Pay and Conditions of Service Code*, Paragraph 9923.
83 *Committee on the Political Activities of Civil Servants, Report*, Cmnd. 7057, HMSO, 1978.
84 See J. C. Masterman, *On the Chariot Wheel*, OUP, 1975, pp. 266–70.
85 Ibid. *Pay and Conditions of Service Code*, Paragraph 9925.
86 Ibid., Paragraph 9926.
87 Ibid., Paragraph 9929.
88 Ibid., Paragraph 9934.
89 Ibid.
90 Ibid., Paragraphs 9952, 9953 and 9954.
91 Private information.
92 Private information.
93 Private information.
94 Private information.
95 Heseltine, *Where There's a Will*, p. 46.
96 Civil Service Commission, *Annual Report 1985*, Civil Service Commission, 1986, p. 7.
97 *The Civil Service Order in Council 1982*, HMSO, 1982, p. 1.
98 Civil Service Commission, *Annual Report 1985*, p. 8.
99 *The Civil Service Order in Council 1985*, HMSO, 1985.
100 Civil Service Commission, *Annual Report 1985*, p. 8.
101 Ibid.

102 Ibid., p. 9.
103 *Report of the Royal Commission on the Private Manufacture of and Trading in Arms*, Cmd. 5292, HMSO, 1936.
104 Cmd. 5517, HMSO, 1937.
105 *Report of the Royal Commission on Standards of Conduct in Public Life*, Cmnd. 6524, HMSO, 1976, p. 7.
106 Written Parliamentary Answer from the Prime Minister, Official report, 3 July 1975, cols 495–6.
107 *Eleventh Report from the Expenditure Committee, Session 1976–77*, HC 535–1, para. 42.
108 *Fourth Report from the Treasury and Civil Service Committee, Session 1980–81*, HC 215, Appendix 2, Annexe 7.
109 Ibid., Appendix 5.
110 Ibid., pp. xiii–xiv.
111 Ibid., p. xiv.
112 *Eighth Report from the Treasury and Civil Service Committee, Session 1983–84*, HC 302, HMSO, 1884.
113 *Government Observations on the Eighth Report from the Treasury and Civil Service Committee*, Cmnd. 9465, HMSO, 1985.
114 *Pay and Conditions of Service Code*, para. 9870.
115 Ibid., para. 9882.
116 Ibid.
117 Ibid., paras 9884–5.
118 Ibid., para. 9893.
119 These are reproduced as Appendix 16 in the *Report of the Royal Commission on Standards of Conduct in Public Life*, pp. 198–200.
120 *Wardale Inquiry*, Report to the Secretary of State for the Environment, August 1983.
121 Figures supplied by the PSA press office, 11 December 1986.
122 Mueller, 'The public sector – present and future'.
123 Cmnd. 6524, 1974, p. 5.
124 Ibid., pp. 6–7.
125 Charles Batchelor and Clay Harris, 'Inquiries into inside dealing spread to DTI's own officials', *Financial Times*, 19 December 1986.
126 'Home Secretary's Lecture to the RIPA'.
127 Ibid.
128 The latest refinement of it can be found in Annexe A, *Seventh Report from the Treasury and Civil Service Committee*, HC 92–II, Vol. II, HMSO, 1986, pp. 64–6.
129 *Pay and Conditions of Service Code*, para. 9870.
130 Armstrong, *Duties and Responsibilities of Civil Servants*, para 2.
131 Cd. 9230, p. 4.

10 THE GEOGRAPHY OF ADMINISTRATION

1 Sir William Armstrong, 'The Civil Service and its Tasks', *O and M Bulletin*, Vol. 25, No. 2, HMSO, May 1970, pp. 63–79.
2 Williams, 'The Decision Makers', in *Policy and Practice*, p. 92.
3 A. J. P. Taylor, *A Personal History*, Hamish Hamilton, 1983, p. 210.
4 A. J. P. Taylor, *The Troublemakers, Dissent over Foreign Policy 1792–1939*, Hamish Hamilton, 1957, p. 11.
5 Haines, *The Politics of Power*, p. 1.
6 Donoughue, *Prime Minister*, p. 1.
7 Pliatzky, *Getting and Spending*, 1st edn 1982, p. 38.
8 Lord Callaghan interviewed for *All the Prime Minister's Men*, 30 April 1986.
9 Ibid.
10 Richard Rose, *Ministers and Ministries: A Functional Analysis*, OUP, 1987, p. 90.
11 Miller, *Lobbying Government*, p. 57.
12 See the various country chapters in Plowden (ed.), *Advising the Rulers.*
13 Miller, *Lobbying Government*, p. 4.
14 Donoughue, *Prime Minister*, p. 17.
15 Ibid., pp. 17–18.
16 Peter Hennessy, 'Why the best job in the Civil Service means carrying the Prime Minister's bag', *The Times*, 10 November 1976.
17 Ibid.
18 G. W. Jones, 'The Prime Minister's Aides', in King (ed.), *The British Prime Minister,* 2nd edn 1986, p. 85.
19 Donoughue, *Prime Minister*, p. 2.
20 Colville, *The Churchillians*, pp. 54–5.
21 Mallaby, *From My Level*, pp. 53–4.
22 Jones, 'The Prime Minister's Aides', p. 85.
23 Ibid.
24 Quoted in Plowden (ed.), *Advising the Rulers*, p. 69.
25 Wilson, *The Governance of Britain*, p. 96.
26 *How Cabinet Government Works*, BBC Radio 3, 12 March 1976.
27 Sir Robert Armstrong, 'Keepers of the Cabinet', *The Daily Telegraph*, 8 December 1986.
28 Donoughue, *Prime Minister*, p. 5.
29 Hennessy, 'A magnificent piece of powerful bureaucratic machinery'.
30 Donoughue, *Prime Minister*, pp. 29–30.
32 For a full account of the origins and work of the CCU see Jeffery and Hennessy, *States of Emergency*.
33 Quoted in 'The Winter of Discontent Symposium', *Contemporary Record*, Vol. 1, No. 3, Autumn 1987, p. 41.
34 *Civil Research and Development*, Cm 185, HMSO, 1987, p. 2.
35 Hennessy, *Cabinet*, pp. 25–6.
36 Private information.
37 Peter Hennessy, 'Whitehall brief: Mr John Boreham, a character and a measurer,' *The Times*, 1 August 1978.

38 Private information.
39 In the mid-eighties, the gongs and ribbons of the Honours system were unceremoniously ripped away by two excellent volumes: Michael De-La-Noy, *The Honours System*, Allison and Busby, 1985; John Walker, *The Queen Has Been Pleased: The British Honours System at Work*, Secker & Warburg, 1986.
40 For example, Sir Michael Palliser did not follow his predecessors from the headship of the Diplomatic Service to the House of Lords when he retired in 1982 nor did Sir Douglas Wass follow previous heads of the Civil Service there a year later, though Sir Frank Lee, the last permanent secretary to the Treasury till Wass not to become sole head of his profession, retired to Corpus Christi, Cambridge, without a trace of ermine.
41 Heseltine, *Where There's a Will*, p. 147.
42 Sir Douglas Wass interviewed for *All the Prime Minister's Men*, 8 April 1986.
43 John Pienaar, 'Senior Tory peer attacks curbs on science budget', *The Independent*, 19 November 1987.
44 Quoted in Les Metcalfe and Sue Richards, *Improving Public Management*, Sage, 1987, p. 200.
45 Tom Caulcott interviewed for *Decline or Rise of the Inner Cities*, BBC Radio 4's *Analysis*, 8 September 1987.
46 Enoch Powell interviewed for *All the Prime Minister's Men*, April 1986.
47 Private information.
48 James Callaghan interviewed for *All the Prime Minister's Men*, 30 April 1986.
49 Peter Hennessy, 'Economists multiply and thrive', *The Times*, 24 November 1975.
50 Quoted in Hennessy, *Cabinet*, pp. 103, 164.
51 John Smith interviewed for *The Shadows' Dummy Run*, BBC Radio 4's *Analysis*, 19 November 1986.
52 See Heseltine, *Where There's a Will*, Chapter 5, pp. 96–129.
53 Jenkins, 'On Being a Minister,' in Herman and Alt (eds), *Cabinet Studies*, p. 212.
54 The sequence was not used in the subsequent television programmes, but I was present during filming and heard Mr. Folger say it.
55 Quoted in Sampson, *Anatomy of Britain Today*, p. 291.
56 Quoted in Peter Hennessy, 'Bank manager and probation officer rolled into one', *The Times*, 28 March 1977.
57 Les Metcalfe and Sue Richards, *Improving Public Management*, Sage, 1987, p. 200.
58 Sir Leo Pliatzky interviewed for *All the Prime Minister's Men*, 26 March 1986.
59 Private information.
60 I have the 'old warlord's' permission to attribute this remark in his obituary but not before.
61 Steiner, 'Decision-making in American and British Foreign Policy', p. 16.
62 Gore-Booth, *With Great Truth and Respect*, p. 425.

63 David Owen, *Personally Speaking to Kenneth Harris*, Weidenfeld, 1987, p. 131.
64 *Eleventh Report from the Expenditure Committee, Session 1976–77*, p. lxxxi.
65 *The Little Platoon*, Part Four; 'A totally Uncompromising Lobby', BBC Radio 3, 17 May 1987.
66 See the debate between Professor Anthony Low of Cambridge University and Brian Lapping of Granada Television in 'Controversy: Did Suez Hasten the End of Empire?', *Contemporary Record*, Vol. 1, No. 2, (Summer 1987), pp. 31–3.
67 *The Little Platoon*, Part Five, 'Argentine Attitudes', BBC Radio 3, 24 May 1987.
68 Kissinger, *Years of Upheaval*, p. 708.
69 Gore-Booth, *With Great Truth and Respect*, p. 424.
70 Tony Benn, *Out of the Wilderness*, diary entry for 5 January 1966, p. 367.
71 Owen, *Personally Speaking*, p. 129.
72 Ibid., p. 110.
73 Jenkins and Sloman, *With Respect, Ambassador*, p. 103.
74 Anthony Bevins and Colin Hughes, 'Kinnock spells out unilateralist approach', *The Independent*, 29 May 1987.
75 Michael Evans, 'Defence chiefs pledge silence', *The Times*, 9 June 1987.
76 Neil Kinnock, interviewed in *Under Fire*, Granada Television, 21 October 1985.
77 Young and Sloman, *No, Minister*, p. 73.
78 Ibid., p. 80.
79 Ibid., p. 81.
80 Norman Kirkham, 'Thatcher–Howe split on Minister for Europe', *Sunday Telegraph*, 12 July 1987.
81 Gore-Booth, *With Great Truth and Respect*, pp. 397–8.
82 Peter Hennessy, 'Whitehall Watch: Recruitment the key to better FO career structure', *The Independent*, 18 January 1988.
83 Ibid.
84 Private information.
85 Peter Hennessy, 'Whitehall Watch: FO reform of recruitment merits debate', *The Independent*, 14 March 1988.
86 Peter Hennessy, 'Whitehall Watch: Sober message for defence chiefs', *The Independent*, 26 March 1988.
87 Paul Kennedy, *The Rise and Fall of the Great Powers*, Unwin Hyman, 1988, p. 482.
88 *Report of the Committee on Representational Services Overseas*, HMSO, 1964.
89 *Report of the Review Committee on Overseas Representation*, Cmnd. 4107, HMSO, 1969.
90 *Review of Overseas Representation*, HMSO, 1977.
91 Castle, *The Castle Diaries, 1964–70*, p. xiii.
92 Ibid., p. xii.
93 Ibid., pp. 45–6.
94 Quoted in Owen, *Personally Speaking*, p. 144.
95 Heseltine, *Where There's a Will*, p. 30.

96 Peter Levene interviewed for the BBC Radio 4's *Analysis* programme, *Bangs to the Buck*, 30 April 1987.

97 Sir Frank Cooper, 'The Problems of Resources for Defence', Eurogroup Seminar, Odense, Denmark, December 1986.

98 According to MOD legend, Ismay produced this unforgettable job description while explaining NATO's functions to a private meeting of Conservative backbenchers in 1949.

99 Anthony Bevins, 'Benn to call for distinct left-wing party stance', *The Independent*, 28 September 1987.

100 William Appleman Williams, *The Tragedy of American Diplomacy*, 2nd edn, Dell, 1962.

101 Walter La Feber, *America, Russia and the Cold War, 1945–75*, 3rd edn, Wiley, 1976.

102 Gar Alperovitz, *Atomic Diplomacy, Hiroshima and Potsdam*, Vintage, 1967.

103 Bullock, *Ernest Bevin, Foreign Secretary*, pp. 844–5.

104 PRO, DEFE 6/14; 'The Spread of Russian Communism', 7 July 1950.

105 I wrote a piece for *The Times* based on the briefing, Peter Hennessy, 'Whitehall brief: Why 95 per cent of defence budget is devoted to containing the Soviet Union', 14 April 1981.

106 *Civil Research and Development*, Cm 185, HMSO, 1987, p. 1.

107 Hartley, Hussain and Smith, 'The UK Defence Industrial Base'.

108 Peter Hennessy, 'Permanent Government; Waiting for Defence Review No. 8', *New Statesman*, 17 July 1987.

109 Ibid.

110 Heseltine, *Where There's a Will*, p. 46.

111 Mr Levene declines to confirm this story, but it is true and was told on *Bangs to the Buck*, BBC Radio 4's *Analysis*, 27 May 1987.

112 Ibid.

113 Eric J. Grove, *Vanguard to Trident. British Naval Policy since World War II*, Bodley Head, 1987, p. 260.

114 Ibid., p. 261.

115 Peter Hennessy, 'Whitehall brief: Viceroy Heseltine charts the bounds of his empire', *The Times*, 8 March 1983.

116 Heseltine, *Where There's a Will*, p. 29.

117 Ibid.

118 Ibid.

119 He reproduced it in ibid.

120 Ibid., p. 31.

121 *Statement on the Defence Estimates, 1984–85*, Vol. 1, Cmnd. 9227, HMSO, 1984.

122 Grove, *Vanguard to Trident*, p. 393.

123 Heseltine, *Where There's a Will*, p. 31.

124 Crossman, *Diaries of a Cabinet Minister*, Vol. III, p. 225, diary entry for 16 October 1968. It has been suggested that Her Majesty was joking and that Crossman's sense of humour was insufficiently developed to catch it.

125 *Eleventh Report from the Expenditure Committee, Session 1976–77*, 'The Civil Service', Vol. II, Part II, p. 786.

126 Private information.
127 Quoted in David Donnison, *The Politics of Poverty*, Martin Robertson, 1982, p. 58.
128 Sir Kenneth Stowe, 'Managing a Great Department of State', Royal Society of Arts, 21 April 1986.
129 Stowe, 'Managing a Great Department of State'.
130 Ibid.
131 Ibid.
132 For a superb account of the building of the Attleean Welfare State see Morgan, *Labour in Power*, Chaper 4, pp. 142–87.
133 Stowe, 'Managing a Great Department of State'.
134 Ibid.
135 Andrew Marr, 'The case for a new think tank', *The Independent*, 12 November 1987.
136 See Robert Harris, 'Tarnishing of a golden boy', *The Observer*, 17 April 1988.
137 Nicholas Timmins, 'Child benefit to be frozen in wide-ranging reforms', *The Independent*, 28 Octover 1987.
138 Carmel Fitzsimons, 'Breadline Britain', *The Observer*, 17 April 1988.
139 Quoted in Kogan, (ed), *The Politics of Education*, p. 100.
140 Susan Crosland, *Tony Crosland*, p. 148.
141 Donoughue, *Prime Minister*, pp. 109–10.
142 Speech to the North of England Conference, Rotherham, 9 January 1987. Text supplied by the DES press office.
143 Addison, *The Road to 1945*, p. 172.
144 Butler, *The Art of the Possible*, p. 91.
145 *Grey Matters*, BBC Radio 4's *Analysis*, 14 October 1987.
146 Peter Hennessy, 'Whitehall Watch: Education finds a Bismarck,' *The Independent*, 25 January 1988.
147 Benn, *Out of the Wilderness*, p. 264, diary entry for 28 May 1965.
148 Lord Young, speech to the Conservative Party Conference, Blackpool, 8 October 1987.
149 Pollard, *The Wasting of the British Economy*, p. 73.
150 Heseltine, *Where There's a Will*, p. 116.
151 Neil Kinnock, *Making Our Way*, Blackwell, 1986, p. 106.
152 'New Role for the DTI announced by Lord Young', DTI Press Notice, 13 October, 1987.
153 Sarah Hogg, 'Young issues "upmarket" blueprint for the DTI', *The Independent*, 14 October 1987.
154 Department of Trade and Industry, *DTI – The Department for Enterprise*, Cm. 278, HMSO, 1988.
155 Mr Benn made this point during a discussion of his *Out of the Wilderness* at the Riverside Studios in Hammersmith on 10 October 1987.
156 Brian W. Hogwood, 'The Rise and Fall and Rise of the Department of Trade and Industry', in Colin Campbell SJ, and B. Guy Peters (eds), *Organising Governance Governing Organizations*, University of Pittsburgh, 1988, pp. 209–32.

157 Private information.
158 Nicholas Wood, 'Young orders radical boost for business', *The Times*, 13 October 1987.
159 DTI Press Notice, 13 October 1987.
160 Heseltine, *Where There's A Will*, Chapter 5, pp. 96–129.
161 Hennessy, 'The "Guilt" of the Treasury 1000'.
162 Peter Hennessy, 'Whitehall Watch: Minister with a Mission', *The Independent*, 7 March 1988.
163 Cm. 278, p. 1.
164 Crossman, *The Diaries of a Cabinet Minister*, Vol. I, diary entry for 22 October 1964, pp. 24–5.
165 Harold Macmillan in conversation with Ludovic Kennedy, *Reflections*, BBC 2, 20 October 1983.
166 Sampson, *Anatomy of Britain*, pp. 240–1.
167 Crossman, *Diaries of a Cabinet Minister*, Vol. I. p. 24.
168 Peter Jenkins, *Mrs Thatcher's Revolution: The Ending of the Socialist Era*, Cape, 1987, p. 179.
169 Michael Whitbread, 'Department of the Environment', in Harrison and Gretton (eds), *Reshaping Central Government*, p. 100.
170 Heseltine, *Where There's a Will*, p. 14.
171 Peter Hennessy, 'The devolution effort "was all worthwhile" ', *The Times*, 16 May 1981.
172 Conversation with Sir John Garlick, 15 May 1981.
173 Quoted in Jenkins, *Mrs Thatcher's Revolution*, p. 285.
174 Nicholas Holgate (ed.), *Careers in the Civil Service – An Alternative View*, FDA, 1987, p. 20.
175 Morgan, *Labour in Power*, pp. 303–5.
176 Peter Self, 'A Policy for Agriculture', *The Political Quarterly*, Vol. xix, No. 2 (April–June 1948), p. 138.
177 Quoted in Whitehead, *The Writing on the Wall*, p. 394.
178 Mr John MacGregor interviewed by David Wheeler for *The Lie of the Land*, BBC Radio 4's *Analysis*, 12 November 1987.
179 Quoted in Sissons and French (eds), *The Age of Austerity*, p. 258.
180 Jenkins, *Mrs Thatcher's Revolution*, p. 175.
181 *Nuclear Power and the Environment, Sixth Report of the Royal Commission on Environmental Pollution*, HMSO, 1976, paragraph 338.
182 Ibid., paragraph 511.
183 Richard Marsh, *Off the Rails: An Autobiography*, Weidenfeld, 1978, pp. 124–5.
184 Susan Crosland, *Tony Crosland*, p. 308.
185 Ibid.
186 Boyd-Carpenter, *Way of Life*, Chapter 9, pp. 107–21.
187 *Transport Policy: A Consultation Document*, Vol. 1, HMSO, 1976, p. 49.
188 Terry Coleman 'The Warship Holds Station,' *The Guardian*, 13 April 1987. For Callaghan's account, see Callaghan, *Time and Chance*, p. 97.
189 It was Mr Gunter's most famous one-liner as Minister of Labour, 1964–8.
190 Castle, *The Castle Diaries 1964–70*, p. 420, diary entry for 3 April 1968.
191 *Report of the Royal Commission on Trades Union and Employers Organisations*,

Cmnd 3623, HMSO, 1968, Appendix VI, Written Evidence of Sir Harold Emmerson, 'Mass Prosecution in Wartime', pp. 340–1.

192 See for example Richard Lamb, *The Failure of the Eden Government*, Sidgwick & Jackson, 1987, pp. 24–8.

193 In many ways the first account remains the best. See Peter Jenkins, *The Battle of Downing Street*, Charles Knight, 1970.

194 *Corporate Plan for 1975* (Manpower Services Commission, 1975), p. 1.

195 Evidence before the House of Commons Employment Committee, 21 March 1984; *The Manpower Services Commission's Corporate Plan, 1984–88, Second Report from the Employment Committee, Session 1983–84*, HC 340.

196 David Walker and Peter Hennessy, 'Plenty of money to spend – but who is minding the child-minders?', *The Times*, 21 October 1981.

197 The phrase is used by Denys Hay in *British Historians and the Beginnings of the Civil History of the Second World War*, p. 295, footnote 15.

198 Walker and Hennessy, 'Plenty of money to spend'.

199 John Vincent, 'The Thatcher Governments 1979–1987', in Hennessy and Seldon (eds), *Ruling Performance*, pp. 291–2.

200 Nicholas Wood, 'Renamed MSC in shake-up', *The Times*, 21 October 1987.

201 Butler, *The Art of the Possible*, p. 199.

202 Jenkins, *On Being a Minister*, pp. 215–16.

203 Rejected alternative introduction to the Commons Expenditure report on 'The Civil Service', p. lxxxi.

204 Quoted in Young and Sloman, *No, Minister*, p. 47.

205 Butler, *The Art of the Possible*, p. 199.

206 Ibid.

207 Jenkins, *On Being a Minister*, p. 215.

208 Ibid., p. 219.

209 Stephen Taylor, for example, in his 'Future Shape of Reform in Whitehall: Radical Structures and Systems', RIPA/Peat Marwick McLintock seminar, Regent's College, London, 4 December 1987.

210 *Crime, Policy and the Public View*, Leon Brittan in conversation with Peter Hennessy, BBC Radio 3, 11 September 1987.

211 *Home Office 1782–1982*, p. 42.

212 Ibid.

213 Lord Boothby, *My Yesterday, Your Tomorrow*, Hutchinson, 1962, p. 140.

214 Conversation with Lord Home for BBC Radio 3's *The Quality of Cabinet Government*, 6 February 1985.

215 *Royal Commission on Scottish Affairs Report*, HMSO, 1954, Cmd. 9212, p. 12.

216 Michael Fry, *Patronage and Principle*, Aberdeen University Press, 1981, p. 239.

217 Boothby, *My Yesterday, Your Tomorrow*, p. 140.

218 Conversation with Mrs Sheila McNeil, 11 January 1988.

219 Richard Parry, 'The Centralization of the Scottish Office', in Rose, *Ministers and Ministries*, pp. 120–5.

220 These remarks are taken from an interview given by Sir Charles in 1980 and preserved in the 'Scotland's Record' oral archive in the National Library of Scotland, Edinburgh.

221 For a fascinating account of Johnston's tartan state building, see Thomas Johnston, *Memories*, Collins, 1952, Chapter XVIII, 'Secretary of State', pp. 147–70.
222 Michael Fry interviewed for *Adam Smith's Children*, BBC Radio 4's *Analysis*, 25 February 1988.
223 Bob Calderwood interviewed for *Adam Smith's Children*, 24 February 1988.
224 Malcolm Rifkind interviewed for *Adam Smith's Children*, 8 March 1988.
225 Neville Chamberlain to Morgan Jones MP, 27 July 1938, quoted in Griffiths, *Pages from Memory*, p. 159.
226 Ibid., p. 165.
227 Jan Morris, *A Matter of Wales, Epic Views of a Small Country*, OUP, 1984, p. 208.
228 Griffiths, *Pages from Memory*, p. 162.
229 I owe this piece of information to Professor John Griffith of the London School of Economics.
230 Griffiths, *Pages from Memory*, p. 166.
231 Ian C. Thomas, 'Giving Direction to the Welsh Office', in Rose, *Ministers and Ministries*, p. 146.
232 John Grigg, *The Young Lloyd George*, Eyre Methuen, 1973, pp. 17–18.
233 'The Observer Profile', *The Observer*, 25 July 1982.
234 Quoted in Hennessy, *Cabinet*, p. 168.
235 P. N. Bell, 'Direct Rule in Northern Ireland', in Rose, *Ministers and Ministries*, p. 193.
236 Ibid., pp. 190–1.
237 Ibid., p. 198.
238 John A. Oliver, *Working at Stormont*, Institute of Public Administration, Dublin, 1978.
239 William Rees-Mogg, *An Humbler Heaven*, Hamish Hamilton, 1977, p. 33.
240 M. R. D. Foot, 'Roger Hesketh', obituary, *The Independent*, 23 November 1987.
241 Heather Mills, 'Judge Rules in favour of Press on "Spycatcher"', *The Independent*, 22 December 1987.
242 Peter Hennessy, 'How to control the secret state', *The Independent*, 3 December 1986.
243 I have compiled this assessment as best I could on the basis of private information.
244 Gardner, *Sterling-Dollar Diplomacy*, p. xvii.
245 Private information.
246 Private information.
247 Roseveare, *The Treasury*, p. 215.
248 Callaghan, *Time and Chance*, p. 39.
249 Roseveare, *The Treasury*, p.215.
250 Barnett, *Inside the Treasury*, p. 24.
251 Young and Sloman, *But, Chancellor*, p. 78.
252 *Careers in the Civil Service: An Alternative View*, FDA, 1986, p. 23.
253 *A Guide to the Inland Revenue*, pp. 3–4.

254 Dorothy Johnstone, *A Tax Shall be Charged, Some Aspects of the Introduction of the British Value Added Tax*, Civil Service Studies 1, HMSO, 1975, p. 3.
255 Jock Bruce Gardyne, *Ministers and Mandarins,* p. 214.
256 Johnstone, *A Tax Shall be Charged*, pp. 7–8.

PART THREE PEOPLE

1 Sir Patrick Nairne interviewed for LWT's *Whitehall*, March 1987.
2 Vansittart, *The Mist Procession*, p. 313.
3 Sir Reginald Hibbert Interviewed for BBC Radio 3's *The Good and the Great*, November 1984.

11 MINISTERS

1 As quoted (via Randolph Churchill) after losing the 1945 General Election in Boyd-Carpenter, *Way of Life*, pp. 86–7.
2 Quoted in Hennessy, *Cabinet*, p. 172. Mr Shore originally delivered his remarks on 12 March 1985 when interviewed for BBC Radio 3's *The Quality of Cabinet Government*.
3 Bancroft, 'Whitehall: Some personal reflections'.
4 Yehezkel Dror, 'Conclusions', in Plowden (ed.), *Advising the Rulers*, pp. 191 and 196.
5 Dudley Seers, evidence to Fulton, *The Civil Service*, Vol. 5 (2), Parts 3 and 4, Memorandum No. 145, p. 1095.
6 Jenkins, *Nine Men of Power*, p. 64.
7 Peter Hennessy, 'Whitehall brief: timely reminder of a bulldog presence', *The Times*, 1 November 1983.
8 Alan Bullock, *The Life and Times of Ernest Bevin*, Vol. Two, *Minister of Labour 1940–1945*, Heinemann, 1967, p. 103.
9 Lord Croham interviewed for LWT's *Whitehall*, 21 March 1987.
10 Peter Hennessy, 'Permanent Government: 'How to be "viewy" and survive', *New Statesman*, 28 August 1987.
11 Dror, 'Conclusions', in Plowden (ed.), *Advising the Rulers*, p. 189.
12 Jean Blondel, *Government Ministers in the Contemporary World*, Sage, 1985, Appendix II, Table: Country Characteristics of Ministers, 1945–81, p. 277.
13 Rose, *Ministers and Ministries,* pp. 73–4.
14 Hoskyns, 'Conservatism is not enough'.
15 'UK squanders its management talent', *Chief Executive*, November 1984, pp. 10–11.
16 Rose, *Ministers and Ministries*, p. 77.
17 Ibid., p. 80.
18 Rothschild, *Meditations of a Broomstick*, p. 173–4.

19 Benn, *Out of the Wilderness*, diary entry for 30 June 1966, p. 441.
20 Ibid., diary entry for 15 September 1966, p. 474.
21 This was the theme of Wilson's famous speech to the 1963 Labour Party Conference at Scarborough. See Wilson, *Memoirs, 1916–1964*, pp. 197–8.
22 Benn, *Out of the Wilderness*, diary entry for 5 August 1966, p. 466.
23 Bruce Headey, *British Cabinet Ministers: The Roles of Politicians in Executive Office*, Allen & Unwin, 1974, Part III, pp. 191–248.
24 Heclo and Wildavsky, *The Private Government of Public Money*, Chapter 3, pp. 76–128.
25 Eric Clark, *Corps Diplomatique*, Allen Lane, 1973, p. 8.
26 Owen, *Personally Speaking*, p. 54.
27 Lord Croham interviewed for LWT's *Whitehall*, 21 March 1987.
28 *Seventh Report from the Treasury and Civil Service Committee: Session 1985–86*, 'Civil Servants and Ministers: Duties and Responsibilities', Vol. II, p. 19.
29 Ibid., p. 225.
30 Ibid.
31 Lord Croham interviewed for LWT's *Whitehall*, 21 March 1987.
32 Wass, *Government and the Governed*, p. 25.
33 Ibid., p. 26.
34 Quoted in Peter Hennessy, 'Permanent Government: Underlord of all he surveys', *New Statesman*, 3 July 1987.
35 Lord Croham interviewed for LWT's *Whitehall*, 21 March 1987.
36 The Terry Coleman interview, 'A Man at Home with Fact and Fiction', *Guardian*, 30 November 1985.
37 Rose, *Ministers and Ministries*, p. 88.
38 Ibid.
39 Peter Riddell, 'Big Thatcher shuffle aims to sharpen team', *Financial Times*, 16 June 1987.
40 Rodney Tyler, *Campaign! The Selling of the Prime Minister*, Grafton, 1987, p. 250.
41 Ibid., pp. 250–1.
42 Henderson, *The Private Office*, p. 73.
43 Howard, *RAB*, p. 369.
44 Ibid.
45 Ibid., p. 404, footnote 17.
46 Ibid., p. 336.
47 Roy Jenkins, *Mr Attlee: An Interim Biography*, Heinemann, 1948; *Sir Charles Dilke, A Victorian Tragedy*, Collins, 1958; *Asquith*, Collins, 1964.
48 'The Tolerant Community', *The Sunday Times*, 26 April 1966.
49 Roy Jenkins, 'Castle Battlements', *The Observer*, 4 November 1984.
50 Jenkins, 'On Being a Minister', in Herman and Alt (eds), *Cabinet Studies*, p. 218.
51 Ibid.
52 Gore-Booth, *With Great Truth and Respect*, p. 231.
53 Ibid.
54 Ibid.
55 Ibid.

56 The ICBH seminar was held on 27 May 1987. Its proceedings were published as 'Symposium: The Crossman Diaries Reconsidered', in *Contemporary Record*, Vol. 1, No. 2 (Summer 1987), pp. 22–30.
57 Ibid.
58 Ibid.
59 Ibid.
60 Benn, *Arguments for Democracy*, p. 50.
61 Ibid.
62 Sedgemore, *The Secret Constitution*, p. 70, pp. 139–40.
63 *The Regeneration of British Industry*, Cmnd. 5710, HMSO, 1974.
64 Whitehead, *The Writing on the Wall*, pp. 131–2.
65 Benn, *Arguments for Democracy*, Chapter 2, pp. 18–43.
66 Ibid., pp. 46–67.
67 Bullock, *Ernest Bevin: Minister of Labour*, p. 124.
68 Sir David Hunt interviewed for *All the Prime Minister's Men*, 8 April 1986.
69 'A Tory wet who made it to the top', *Observer* profile, *The Observer*, 8 September 1985.
70 'At Home with Kenneth Baker', *You Magazine*, *The Mail on Sunday*, 15 February 1987.
71 Richard Norton-Taylor 'Baker provokes civil servants', *The Guardian*, 21 May 1987.
72 Private information.
73 Bruce-Gardyne, *Ministers and Mandarins.*
74 Crossman, *The Diaries of a Cabinet Minister,* Vol. I, diary entry for 10 August 1966, p. 618.
75 Kaufman, *How to be a Minister*, pp. 42–3.
76 Barnett, *Inside the Treasury*, p. 21.
77 I can also remember him refusing, somewhat testily, to say how much that personal budget was to be at the press conference announcing the results of the review on 25 June 1981.
78 'Spending – The Thatcher Years', *The Guardian*, 15 January 1987.
79 I. F. Nicolson, *The Mystery of Crichel Down*, OUP, 1986, p. 193.
80 J. A. G. Griffith, xxxx, *Modern Law Review*, 1955, Vol. 18, p. 557 ff.
81 Lord Boyle, 'Ministers and the Administrative Process' *Public Administration*, Vol. 58, No. 1 (Spring 1980), pp. 1–11.
82 Tom Williams, *Digging for Britain*, Hutchinson, 1965, p. 182.
83 H of C Debates, 20 July 1954, col. 1283.
84 John Griffith, 'Crichel Down, The Most Famous Farm in British Constitutional History', *Contemporary Record*, Vol. 1, No. 1 (Spring 1987), pp. 35–40.
85 House of Commons, *First Report from the Treasury and Civil Service Committee, Session 1986–87*, 'Ministers and Civil Servants', p. vii.
86 H of C Debates, 20 July 1954, col. 1284.
87 *Report of the Tribunal appointed to inquire into certain issues in relation to the circumstances leading up to the cessation of trading by the Vehicle and General Insurance Company Limited*, HL 80, HC 133, HMSO, 1972, p. 133.

88 Peter Hennessy, 'The Ministers and the Mandarins', *Financial Times*, 10 May 1976.
89 HL 80, HC 133, p. 125.
90 Hennessy, 'The Ministers and the Mandarins', *Financial Times*, 10 May 1976.
91 Nicolson, *The Mystery of Crichel Down*, p. 205.
92 Lord Carrington, *News at Ten*, 5 April 1982.
93 Hastings and Jenkins, *The Battle for the Falklands*, pp. 79–80.
94 Private information.
95 Prior, *A Balance of Power*, p. 232.
96 Ibid., pp. 232–3.
97 Julian Critchley, 'Political diary: the case for the cameras', *The Observer*, 23 August 1987.
98 Quoted in Sampson, *The New Anatomy of Britain*, p. 369.

12 REGULARS

1 Quoted in Gerth and Wright Mills, *From Max Weber*, p. 209.
2 Lord Zuckerman, 'Scientists, Bureaucrats and Ministers', in The Maxwell-Pergamon Discourse Proceedings of the Royal Institution, Vol. 56, 1984, pp. 205–29.
3 Lord Armstrong quoted in 'London Diary', *The Times*, 15 July 1980.
4 Enoch Powell interviewed for Brook Productions' Channel 4 Television programme, *The Writing on the Wall*, I am grateful to Phillip Whitehead for supplying me with a transcript of the interview.
5 Sir Robert Armstrong in an aside from his prepared text, 'Taking Stock of Our Achievements', RIPA-Peat Marwick McLintock Seminar on 'The Future Shape of Reform in Whitehall', Regents College, London, 4 December 1987.
6 David Walker, 'Whitehall Brief: The Master Servant Takes His Leave,' *The Times*, 4 April 1988.
7 Ibid.
8 See Peter Hennessy, 'Whitehall brief: Government machine goes over to automatic pilot', *The Times*, 31 May 1983.
9 Conversation with John Biffen, 13 May 1983, which he granted me permission to quote on 21 October 1987.
10 *The Shadows' Dummy Run*, BBC Radio 4's *Analysis*, 26 November 1986.
11 Lord Bancroft interviewed by Michael Crick, May 1987.
12 Peter Hennessy, 'Foot spurns Whitehall talks', *The Times*, 31 May 1983.
13 Lord Bancroft interviewed by Michael Crick, May 1987.
14 Ibid.
15 Quoted in Young and Sloman, *No, Minister*, pp. 21–2.
16 Tony Benn, *Arguments for Democracy*, Penguin, 1982, p. 54.
17 Young and Sloman, *No, Minister*, pp. 19–20.
18 Cmnd. 3638, Vol. I, p. 108.
19 Crossman, *The Diaries of a Cabinet Minister*, Vol. I, p. 616.
20 Noel Annan, 'Betrayal', *The New York Review of Books*, 24 September 1987.

21 Lord Donoughue, 'The Prime Minister's Diary', Jubilee Lecture, Nuffield College, Oxford, 16 October 1987.
22 Lord Donoughue interviewed for LWT's *Whitehall*, 25 March 1987.
23 The programme, *The Chosen Few*, Produced by Chris Curling for the BBC 2 *40 Minutes* series was transmitted in two parts on 4 and 11 December 1986.
24 Michael Davie (ed.), *The Diaries of Evelyn Waugh*, Weidenfeld, 1976, p. 518, diary, entry for 5 January–7 February 1942.
25 Ibid., p. 543.
26 Christopher Sykes, *Evelyn Waugh, a Biography*, Collins, 1975, pp. 244–56.
27 PRO PREM 11/1742. Macmillan to Brook, 20 July 1957.
28 Peter Hennessy, 'The two-day "mangling experience" that decides the men who will run Whitehall', *The Times*, 3 March 1976.
29 Ibid.
30 Private information.
31 Sir Alec Atkinson, *Selection of Fast-Stream Graduate Entrants to the Home Civil Service, the Diplomatic Service and the Tax Inspectorate; and of Candidates from within the Service, Management and Personnel Office, 1983*, p. 47.
32 Ibid., p. 3.
33 Ibid., p. 47.
34 Ibid., p. 48.
35 Ibid.
36 Nick Gurney interviewed for LWT's *Whitehall*, 5 March 1987.
37 Lord Donoughue interviewed for *Whitehall*, 25 March 1987.
38 Nick Gurney interviewed for *Whitehall*, 5 March 1987.
39 Ibid.
40 Letter from Nick Gurney to the author.
41 Teddy Morgan interviewed for *Whitehall*, 5 March 1987.
42 Nick Gurney interviewed for *Whitehall*, 5 March 1987.
43 Teddy Morgan interviewed for *Whitehall*, 5 March 1987.
44 Peter Hennessy, 'Civil Service selection test "best in any country"', *The Times*, 5 November 1976.
45 Nick Gurney interviewed for *Whitehall*, 5 March 1987.
46 Bancroft, 'Whitehall and Management: A Retrospect'.
47 This has been a constant refrain of Sir John's since his IFS lecture in 1982.
46 Mr Strauss has used this phrase many times in my presence.
49 Lord Donoughue interviewed for *Whitehall*, 25 March 1987.
50 *Interchange of Staff Between the Civil Service and Other Organisations* 1986 Report., Management and Personnel Office, 1987, p. 1.
51 Ibid., Annexe C.
52 Ibid., p. 2.
53 Will Peddar interviewed for *Whitehall*, 24 March 1987.
54 Ibid.
55 Ibid.
56 John Taylor interviewed for *Whitehall*, 14 March 1987.
57 Ibid.
58 I heard him say this on at least one occasion.

59 Civil Service College, *Principal's Annual Report, 1986–7*, Cabinet Office, 1987, p. 1.
60 Ibid.
61 Ibid., p. 17.
62 Peter Hennessy, 'Whitehall brief: Training the tribes to talk to each other', *The Times*, 24 April 1984.
63 Lord Rayner interviewed for *All the Prime Minister's Men*, 21 May 1986.
64 Hayden Phillips interviewed for *Whitehall*, 17 March, 1987.
65 Ibid.
66 Ibid.
67 Ibid.
68 Roger Jackling interviewed for *Whitehall*, 7 March 1987.
69 Ibid.
70 Ibid.
71 Peter Hennessy, 'Whitehall brief: seeing if "spats" has found its feet', *The Times*, 12 May 1981.
72 I spoke on the course.
73 Roger Jackling interviewed for *Whitehall*, 7 March 1987.
74 Private information.
75 Explanatory Note, Council of Civil Service Unions, 1986, p. 1.

13 AUXILIARIES

1 Samson, *Anatomy of Britain Today*, p. 312.
2 Rothschild, *Meditations of a Broomstick*, p. 170.
3 H of C, Parliamentary Debates, 4 August 1980, col. 320.
4 William Haley, *Times Literary Supplement*, 18 March 1977.
5 Sir William Rees-Mogg, 'A farce with old friends and a chorus of madmen', *The Independent*, 2 December 1986.
6 Peter B. Boyden, 'The Making of Domesday Book', *History Today*, Vol. 36, January 1986, p. 23.
7 Lord Radcliffe, 'Censors', The Rede Lecture, Cambridge University, 4 May 1961, reproduced in Radcliffe, *Not in Feather Beds*, pp. 161–82. This particular quotation is on p. 175.
8 Ibid.
9 David Cecil, *The Young Melbourne*, Constable, 1939, p. 2.
10 Ibid., pp. 2–3.
11 Ibid., p. 5.
12 Ibid., p. 1.
13 Quoted in *Supplement to the Oxford English Dictionary*, Vol. 1, OUP, 1972, p. 976.
14 Henry Fairlie, 'Political Commentary', *The Spectator*, 23 September 1955, p. 380.
15 PRO, CAB 129/78, CP (55) 161, 'Disappearance of two Foreign Office officials, Burgess and Maclean', 19 October 1955.
16 PRO, CAB 128/29, CM (55) 36, 20 October 1955, Item 6.

17 Richard Norton-Taylor, 'Memoirs "attempt to end mass spy penetration"', *The Guardian*, 9 December 1986.
18 Peter Hennessy, 'Permanent Government: Sir Sidney Carton of the Cabinet Office', *New Statesman*, 19 December 1986.
19 Rees-Mogg, 'A farce with old friends and a chorus of madmen'.
20 'Duke' Hussey's appointment stimulated an explosion of near identical headlines, stories and profiles – Peter Fiddick, 'The Duke at the Helm', *The Guardian*, 2 October 1986, Charles Clover, 'The Duke tackles "a hell of a job"', *The Daily Telegraph*, 1 October 1986.
21 Peter Hennessy and Gail Brownfeld, 'Britain's Cold War Security Purge: The Origins of Positive Vetting', *The Historical Journal*, 25, 4 (1982), p. 965.
22 Ibid., p. 972.
23 *National and English Review*, 10 September 1957, p. 8.
24 C. P. Snow, *Conscience of the Rich*, Macmillan, 1958, p. 254.
25 Thomas (ed.), *The Establishment*.
26 Hugh Thomas, *The Spanish Civil War*, Harper & Row, 1961.
27 Thomas, *The Establishment*, p. 23.
28 Ibid., p. 191.
29 Michael De-la-Noy, 'Arise, Sir...', *New Society*, 10 January 1986, p. 69.
30 *The Good and the Great*, BBC Radio 3, 4 February 1985.
31 Alan Watkins, 'Diary', *The Spectator*, 15 June 1985, p. 7.
32 Ronald Butt, 'Why Mrs Thatcher could win again', *The Times*, 20 June, 1985.
33 Tim Heald, *Networks. Who We Know and How We Use Them*, Hodder, 1983.
34 Peter Jenkins, 'The forging of Pym's Rebellion', *The Sunday Times*, 12 May 1985.
35 This delightful analogy was made in Richard H. Rovere, *The American Establishment and Other Reports, Opinions and Speculations*, Hart-Davis, 1963, pp. 233–4.
36 Peter Hall, 'How Other People Run Their Cities', *New Society*, 10 January 1985, p. 44.
37 Conversation with Lord Franks, 24 January 1977.
38 PRO PREM 11/952. C(53)322. Memorandum on Smog by the Minister of Housing and Local Government, 18 November 1953.
39 Mr Schuller made his highly useful remark during a seminar on 'The Demise of the Good and the Great', part of Dr Jim Sharpe's 'Government in Crisis?' series at Nuffield College, Oxford, on 29 November 1985.
40 PRO PREM 11/824, 'Colonial Policy – Immigrants', Brook to the Prime Minister, 14 June 1955.
41 PRO CAB CP (55) 32. 11 June 1955.
42 Ibid.
43 PRO PREM 11/824. Brook to the Prime Minister, 14 June 1955.
44 Ibid.
45 Hennessy, *Cabinet*, p. 54.
40 See P. J. Madgwick, D. Steeds and L. J. Williams, *Britain since 1945*, Hutchinson, 1982, pp. 321–5.

47 Private information.
48 Private information.
49 Private information. This particular passage was not used in Clive Ponting's three-part article on the 1976 edition of *Questions* in the *New Statesman* in Feburary–March 1986, but I have seen it privately.
50 Castle, *Castle Diaries 1974–76*, p. 541.
51 *The Good and the Great*, BBC Radio 3, 4 February 1985.
52 Sir Michael Edwardes, 'UK squanders its management talent', *Chief Executive*, November 1984, pp. 10–11.
53 PRO CAB 128/27, CC (54) 53. 26 July 1954, Item 6.
54 Private information.
55 Lord Wolfenden, *Turning Points*, Bodley Head, 1976, pp. 137–8.
56 Ibid., p. 129.
57 Ibid., p. 132.
58 Conversation with Lord Plowden, February 10 1977.
59 Lorna Arnold, *A Very Special Relationship: British Atomic Weapons Trials in Australia*, HMSO, 1987, p. 14.
60 Conversation with Sir John Winnifrith, 30 April 1985.
61 Conversation with Lord Redcliffe-Maud, 18 November 1974. As Sir John Maud he was the permanent secretary to the Lord President's office when Morrison arrived in 1945. Morrison was making it plain that there would not be a wholesale purge of what was then known as the 'Old Gang'. He was big enough to recognise capability where he saw it.
62 Private information.
63 Private information.
64 Rothschild, *Random Variables*, p. 74.
65 Rothschild, *Meditations of a Broomstick*, p. 170.
66 Private information.
67 Conversation with Dr Bernard Donoughue, 4 July 1984.
68 Private information.
69 Private information.
70 Cabinet Office, Management and Personnel Office, *Management Documents 1985–6*, available in the Cabinet Office Library since August 1985.
71 Jonathan Charkham, 'Board Structure and Appointments in the Public and Private Sectors', Royal Institute of Public Administration, 14 February 1986.
72 *The Good and the Great*, BBC Radio 3, 4 February 1985.
73 His picture appears in Peter Hennessy, *The Great and the Good, an Inquiry into the British Establishment*, Policy Studies Institute, 1986, p. 20.
74 Private information.
75 Figures provided by the Public Appointments Unit.
76 *The Good and the Great*, BBC Radio 3, 4 February 1985.
77 Peter Hennessy, 'Whitehall Brief: The chosen few, Britain ruled by "permanent coalition" since 1945', *The Times*, 12 February 1980.
78 H of C Parliamentary Debates, 4 August 1980, col. 320.
79 Peter Hennessy, 'Mr Channon requests more names for the "Great and the Good"', *The Times*, 30 August 1980.

80 Peter Hennessy, 'Invitation still open to public', *The Times*, 18 September 1983.
81 Peter Hennessy, 'Good and Great list attracts 600', *The Times*, 11 November 1981.
82 Peter Hennessy, 'Whitehall Brief: Red letter day for good and great', *The Times*, 18 January 1983.
83 G. W. Jones, 'The Prime Minister's Aides' in Anthony King (ed.), *The British Prime Minister*, 2nd edn, Macmillan, 1985, p. 85.
84 Private information.
85 Figures supplies by the Public Appointments Unit.
86 Ibid.
87 Private information.
88 Private information.
89 Private information.
90 C. R. Attlee, *As It Happened*, 1954, Odhams, p. 149.
91 Conversation with Dennis Trevelyan, 16 January 1986.
92 Quoted in Peter Hennessy, 'The Lord who sits in judgement', *The Times*, 17 January 1983.
93 Ian Bradley, *The Call to Seriousness, Evangelical Impact on the Victorians*, Cape, 1976.
94 Anderson is described thus by Sir Harold Kent, *In on the Act*, p. 232.
95 John Wheeler-Bennett, *John Anderson, Viscount Waverley*, Macmillan, 1962, p. 316.
96 Ibid., p. 185.
97 J. C. Masterman, *On the Chariot Wheel*, Oxford University Press, 1975, p. 216.
98 Wheeler-Bennett, *John Anderson*, p. 187.
99 According to political folklore, Bevan applied the phrase to his rival, Hugh Gaitskell. Bevan denied this. He said that the phrase, delivered in a speech during the 1954 Labour Party Conference in Scarborough, was directed at a 'synthetic figure'. Bevan's actual words were 'I know that the right kind of leader for the Labour Party is a desiccated calculating machine who must not in any way permit himself to be swayed by indignation.' See Michael Foot, *Aneurin Bevan 1945–60*, Davis-Poynter, 1973, pp. 450–2.
100 Quoted in Rothschild, *Meditations of a Broomstick*, p. 167.
101 Wheeler-Bennett, *John Anderson*, p. 17.
102 Ibid., p. 18.
103 Braithwaite, *Lloyd George's Ambulance Wagon*, pp. 36, 281, 302.
104 Jeffery and Hennessy, *States of Emergency*, pp. 72–4, 111, 120–5.
105 Roy Jenkins, 'On Being a Minister', in Herman and Alt (eds), *Cabinet Studies*. p. 211.
106 Wheeler-Bennett, *John Anderson*, p. 172.
107 Ibid., p. 276.
108 Ibid., p. 290.
109 Gowing, *Independence and Deterrence*, Vol. 1, p. 5.

110 Ibid., p. 25.
111 Ibid.
112 For a discussion of the bomb and collective reponsibility see Hennessy, *Cabinet*, Chapter 4, 'Cabinets and the Bomb'.
113 Gowing, *Independence and Deterrence*, Vol. 1, p. 25.
114 Wheeler-Bennett, *John Anderson*, pp. 352–3.
115 Hennessy, 'The most elevated and distinguished casualties of the Thatcher years', *The Listener*, 7 February 1985, p. 3.
116 Wheeler-Bennett, *John Anderson*, p. 381.
117 Ibid., p. 384.
118 Ibid., p. 403.
119 Quoted in Peter Hennessy, 'The eternal fireman who always answers the call to duty', *The Times*, 30 January 1976.
120 Conversation with Lord Radcliffe, 27 January 1976.
121 *Report of the Committee of Privy Counsellors on Ministerial Memoirs*, Cmnd. 6386, HMSO, 22 January 1976.
122 Ibid., p. 22.
123 Hugh Noyes, 'D Notices White Paper Savaged, Scathing Attack by Lord Radcliffe', *The Times*, 7 July 1967.
124 Ibid.
125 Latest wills, *The Times*, 17 June 1977.
126 Latest wills, *The Sunday Telegraph*, 8 August 1982.
127 Hennessy, 'The eternal fireman', *The Times*, 30 January 1986.
128 Conversation with Lord Radcliffe, 27 January 1976.
129 *Report of the Committee of Privy Counsellors on Ministerial Memoirs*, p. 13.
130 Ibid., p. 29.
131 Ibid., p. 31.
132 Private information.
133 'The Dissolving Society' was the title of Lord Radcliffe's Annual Oration at LSE, 10 December 1965. It is reproduced in *Not in Feather Beds*, pp. 229–46.
134 Private information.
135 Private information.
136 Private information.
137 Hennessy, 'The eternal fireman', *The Times*, 30 January 1976.
138 'Highest brow in Whitehall', *Daily Mail*, 16 February 1948.
139 Quoted in Paul Bareau, 'Sir Oliver Just Keeps Climbing', *News Chronicle*, 1 November 1954.
140 Moorhouse, *The Diplomats*.
141 Hennessy and Hague, *How Adolf Hitler Reformed Whitehall*, p. 26.
142 Hennessy, 'Lord who sits in judgement', *The Times*, 17 January 1983.
143 Ibid.
144 Conversation with Lord Franks, 11 January 1983.
145 Dean Acheson, *Present at the Creation, My Years in the State Department*, Hamish Hamilton, 1970.

146 Hennessy and Hague, *How Adolf Hitler Reformed Whitehall*, p. 36.
147 Lord Franks at a seminar on his Washington Embassy, London University Institute of Historical Research, 12 October 1983.
148 Private information.
149 Conversation with Lord Franks, 24 January 1977.
150 Hoskyns, 'Conversatism is not enough'.
151 Conversation with Lord Franks, 24 January 1977.
152 'Basis of Britain's Greatness, Partnership Replaces Isolation', *The Times*, 8 November 1954.
153 *The Good and the Great*, BBC Radio 3, 4 February 1985.
154 Ibid.
155 Private information.
156 Civil Service College, *CSC Working Paper No. 5*, January 1979, p. 1.
157 Cmnd. 5014.
158 *CSC Working Paper No. 5*, p. 9.
159 *Open Government*, Cmnd. 7250, HMSO, April 1979.
160 Private information.
161 Isaiah Berlin, *Personal Impressions*, OUP, 1982, p. 32.
162 Ibid., p. 33.
163 Correlli Barnett, *The Audit of War*. Chapter 1, 'The Dream of the New Jerusalem', is devoted to this theme.
164 Whitehead, *Writing on the wall*, p. 54.
165 *The Good and the Great*, BBC Radio 3, 4 February 1985.
166 Norman Stone, 'Margot and the ruling class', *The Sunday Times*, 10 June 1984.
167 This gem first appeared in A. P. Herbert, *Mild and Bitter*, Methuen, 1936. Herbert's last squib on the subject, which reproduced it, was *Anything but Action?*, Hobart Paper 5, Institute of Economic Affairs/Barrie and Rockliff, 1960, p. 6. There was quite a spate of publications on the Royal commission–committee of inquiry theme. The most useful general guide is probably T. J. Cartwright, *Royal Commissions and Departmental Committees in Britain*, Hodder, 1975. Also valuable are *Advisory Committees in British Government*, a PEP report, Allen & Unwin 1960; Gerald Rhodes, *Committees of Inquiry*, Allen & Unwin, 1975; Richard Chapmen (ed.), *The Role of Commissions in Policy Making*, Allen & Unwin, 1973; and Martin Bulmer (ed.), *Social Research and Royal Commissions*, Allen & Unwin, 1980.
168 Letter from Mr Leon Brittan to Mr Tim Eggar MP, 25 January 1985, available in the House of Commons Library.
169 Mr George Younger, Written Parliamentary Answer No. 65, 16 April 1985, in reply to a question from Mr Tim Eggar MP.
170 PRO, CAB 129/70 C (54) 264, 'Royal Commissions. Note by the Prime Minister', 4 August 1954.
171 For the complete list of post-war royal commissions see Leon Brittan's letter to Tim Eggar on 25 January 1985 and George Younger's written answer of 16 April 1985.

172 Peter Hennessy ('a Staff Reporter'), 'Royal Commissions' value questioned by Lord Rothschild', *The Times*, 30 June 1978.
173 Ibid. The full text of 'Royal Commissions' is reproduced in Lord Rothschild, *Random Variables*, Collins, 1984, pp. 85–91.
174 Ibid., p. 86.
175 The author was present at the occasion.
176 Conversation with Dr Bernard Donoughue, 29 November 1984.
177 'The Terry Coleman Interview', *The Guardian*, 8 September 1984.
178 *The Good and the Great*, BBC Radio 3, 4 February 1985.
179 See Jay, *Change and Fortune*, pp. 80ff.
180 See *CC41. Utility Furniture and Fashion 1941–1951*, ILEA, 1974, pp. 25–6.
181 Hennessy and Hague, *How Adolf Hitler Reformed Whitehall*, pp. 40–1.
182 Wolfenden, *Turning Points*, p. 144.
183 Peter Hennessy 'Some inquiry committees "meant to achieve nothing"', *The Times*, 11 April 1981.
184 Bernard Williams, 'Pathways to the pigeonhole', outline of a paper to the RIPA Conference, April 1981, p. 1.
185 Ibid., pp. 2–3.
186 Rothschild, *Random Variables*, p. 88.
187 *Report to the Departmental Committee on the Procedure of Royal Commissions*, Cmnd 5235, HMSO, 1910.
188 Lord Benson and Lord Rothschild, 'Royal Commissions: A Memorial', *Public Administration*, Vol. 60, Autumn 1982, pp. 339–48.
189 Ibid., p. 340.
190 Ibid., p. 341.
191 Ibid., p. 347.
192 Ibid., p. 348.
193 See Peter Hennessy and Andrew Arends, 'Whitehall brief: From Domesday to Falklands', *The Times*, 14 December 1982. The seminar discussion is summarised in Martin Bulmer, *Royal Commissions and Departmental Committees of Inquiry*, RIPA, 1983.
194 Hennessy, 'The most elevated and distinguished casualties of the Thatcher years', *The Listener*, 7 February 1985.
195 Ibid.
196 Anthony Bevins, 'Few Women in quangos', *The Independent*, 18 December 1986.
197 Ronald Butt, 'Why Mrs Thatcher could win again', *The Times*, 20 June 1985.
198 Ibid.
199 Thomas (ed.), *The Establishment*, p. 191.
200 David Watt, 'Not old-fashioned – commonsense', *The Times*, 3 January 1986.
201 David Watt, 'Reform the BBC, don't wreck it', *The Times*, 22 February 1985.
202 'The BBC's own power game', *The Observer*, 11 August 1985.
203 Conversation with Dr Bernard Donoughue, 29 November 1984.

204 Conversation with Clive Priestley, 28 November 1984.
205 Richard Hoggart, 'The gravy train runs amok', *The Observer*, 29 December 1985.
206 Richard Hoggart, 'Middle ground', *New Statesman*, 1 February 1985, pp. 31–2.
207 Hoggart, 'The gravy train runs amok'.
208 Private information.
209 Hoggart, 'The gravy train runs amok'.
210 Ibid.
211 Peter Fiddick, 'TV champion urges resistance to political pressure', *The Guardian*, 15 July 1987.
212 Ibid.
213 Michael Davie, 'Notebook: Inquiring Peacock will dance to his own tune', *The Observer*, 8 September 1985, p. 44.
214 I worked with him on the *Financial Times* and have seen him in action at Ditchley Park.
215 *Report of the Committee on Financing the BBC*, Cmnd. 9824, HMSO, 1986.
216 Ian Aitken, 'Franks "a bucket of whitewash" says scornful Callaghan', *The Guardian*, 27 January 1983.
217 *The Good and the Great*, BBC Radio 3, 4 February 1985.
218 Samuel Brittan, 'Lombard: The fundamentals of committees', *Financial Times*, 23 June 1986.

PART FOUR MRS THATCHER'S WHITEHALL

1 Conversation with Lord Jenkins, 23 March 1988.

14 RAYNERISM

1 Lord Rayner interviewed for *All the Prime Minister's Men*, 21 May 1986.
2 Quoted in Peter Hennessy, 'Sir Derek Rayner presses for Civil Service Department's merger with the Treasury', *The Times*, 14 August 1980.
3 Lord Rayner interviewed for LWT's *Whitehall*, 10 April 1987.
4 Clive Priestley, 'Promoting the Efficiency of Central Government', in Shenfield *et. al.*, *Managing the Bureaucracy*, pp. 124–5.
5 Ibid., p. 115.
6 Ibid., p. 116.
7 Ibid., p. 117.
8 Patrick Cosgrave, *Thatcher: The First Term*, Bodley Head, 1985, p. 169.
9 Ibid., p. 170.
10 Sir Keith described himself as 'a Correlli Barnett supporter' when inter-

viewed by Dr Anthony Seldon in 1987. See 'Escaping the Chrysalis of Statism', *Contemporary Record*, Vol. 1, No.1 (Spring 1987), p. 27.

11 Private information.
12 Shenfield *et al.*, *Managing the Bureaucracy*, pp. 116–17.
13 Les Metcalfe and Sue Richards, *Improving Public Management*, Gower, 1987, p. 5.
14 Shenfield *et al.*, *Managing the Bureaucracy*, p. 119.
15 Peter Hennessy, 'Permanent Government: Whitehall signals from the lecture hall', *New Statesman*, 21 November 1986.
16 Lord Rayner interviewed for *All the Prime Minister's Men*, 21 May 1986.
17 Lord Rayner interviewed for LWT's *Whitehall*, 10 April 1987.
18 Ibid.
19 Lord Rayner, 'The Unfinished Agenda', The Stamp Memorial Lecture, University of London, 6 November 1984.
20 The phrase was Clive Priestley's when interviewed for BBC Radio 3's *The Good and the Great*, 28 November 1984.
21 Rayner, 'The Unfinished Agenda'.
22 Metcalfe and Richards, *Improving Public Management*, p. 211.
23 Lord Rayner interviewed for LWT's *Whitehall*, 10 April 1987.
24 Ibid.
25 Lord Rayner interviewed for *All the Prime Minister's Men*, 21 May 1986.
26 Peter Hennessy, 'Whitehall brief: Cut down the rules, Sir Derek says', *The Times*, 11 March 1980.
27 Gray and Jenkins, *Administrative Politics in British Government*, p. 116.
28 Hennessy, 'Cut down the rules'.
29 'The Scrutiny Programme: A Note of Guidance by Sir Derek Rayner', p. 2.
30 Ibid.
31 Peter Hennessy, 'Whitehall talent "wasted"', *The Times*, 28 August 1981.
32 Private information.
33 'The Scrutiny Programme: A Note of Guidance by Sir Derek Rayner', p. 2.
34 Ibid., pp. 2–3.
35 Ibid., p. 3.
36 Ian Beesley interviewed for LWT's *Whitehall*, 4 March 1987.
37 Ibid.
38 Norman Warner interviewed for *Whitehall*, 13 March 1987.
39 Ibid.
40 Ibid.
41 See 'Exit Sir Derek', *The Times*, 15 December 1982, and Hargreaves and Pauley, 'Rayner: why his reforms may prove short-lived'.
42 Rose, *Ministers and Ministries*, p. 258.
43 Peter Hennessy, 'Whitehall to get £35 m Aid', *The Times*, 28 September 1983.
44 Lord Rayner interviewed for *All the Prime Minister's Men*, 21 May 1986.
45 Letter from Alan Cogbill of the Efficiency Unit to Peter Hennessy, 26 August 1987.
46 Peter Hennessy, 'Permanent Government: Raynerising the Whitehall Princes', *New Statesman*, 11 September 1987.

47 Letter from Alan Cogbill to Peter Hennessy, 26 August 1987.
48 National Audit Office, *Report by the Comptroller and Auditor General: The Rayner Scrutiny Programmes 1979 to 1983*, HMSO, 1986, p. 1.
49 Ibid.
50 Ibid., pp. 2–3.
51 George Clark, 'Civil Service to be cut by further 75,000 spread over 4 years', *The Times*, 15 May 1980.
52 Lord Rayner interviewed for LWT's *Whitehall*, 10 April 1987.
53 *Report by the Comptroller and Auditor General: The Rayner Scrutiny Programmes, 1979 to 1983*, p. 6.
54 Peter Hennessy, 'Sir Derek ready to tell secrets', *The Times*, 24 January 1980.
55 Peter Hennessy, 'Cost of Civil Service £8,335 m last year', *The Times*, 2 July 1981.
56 'Rayner's Raiders', *The Economist*, 3–9 July 1982.
57 Lord Rayner interviewed for *All the Prime Minister's Men*, 21 May 1986.
58 *Administrative Forms in Government*, Cmnd. 8504, HMSO, 1982, p. 4.
59 Lord Salter, *Memoirs of a Public Servant*, Faber, 1961, pp. 36–7.
60 *Administrative Forms in Government*, p. 4.
61 Ibid., p. 2.
62 Ibid., p. 1.
63 Ibid.
64 *In Good Form*, Office of the Minister for the Civil Service, 1987, p. 1.
65 Ponting, *Whitehall: Tragedy and Farce*, pp. 215–16.
66 Ibid., p. 216.
67 Ponting, *The Right to Know*, p. 181.
68 Lord Rayner interviewed for *All the Prime Minister's Men*, 21 May 1986.
69 Peter Hennessy, 'Whitehall brief: An unsung hero of Civil Service comes into the public view', *The Times*, 28 October 1980.
70 At the request of Mr Richard Shepherd MP, Michael Heseltine, then Environment Secretary, declassified Eric Turtle's *Maintenance Economy Review of the Bath District Works Office*, Property Services Agency, 1980.
71 Hennessy, 'Unsung hero of the Civil Service'.
72 Peter Hennessy, 'Rayner regrets his lack of impact on Whitehall', *The Times*, 20 June 1981.
73 Lord Rayner interviewed for *All the Prime Minister's Men*, 21 May 1986.
74 Ibid.
75 'Civil Service Department retained', *The Times*, 30 January 1981.
76 Robin Pauley and Philip Bassett, 'Thatcher disbands Civil Service Department and cuts staff', *Financial Times*, 13 November 1981.
77 Lord Rayner interviewed for LWT's *Whitehall*, 10 April 1987.
78 Ibid.
79 Rayner, 'The Unfinished Agenda'.
80 Rose, *Ministers and Ministries*, p. 53.
81 Lord Rayner interviewed for *All the Prime Minister's Men*, 21 May 1986.
82 David Felton, '£3 m Civil Service cuts found in a month', *The Times*, 21 December 1979.

83 *Progress in Financial Management in Government Departments*, Cmnd. 9297, HMSO, 1984.
84 'Must Efficiency be Dull?' *The Times*, 30 July 1984.
85 I heard him say it.
86 Hastings and Jenkins, *The Battle for the Falklands*, p. 342.
87 The FMI charter was published in a Government White Paper, *Efficiency and Effectiveness in the Civil Service*, Cmnd. 8616, Appendix 3, pp. 21–7.
88 Harrison and Gretton (eds), *Reshaping Central Government*, p. 125.
89 Peter Hennessy, 'Whitehall brief: The new hunters take over', *The Times*, 13 January 1983.
90 Cmnd. 8616, pp. 21–2.
91 Heseltine, *Where There's a Will*, p. 22.
92 Peter Hennessy, 'Permanent Government: Tarzan in the Whitehall game park', *New Statesman*, 27 May 1987.
93 Hennessy, 'Rayner regrets his lack of impact on Whitehall'.
94 Sir Peter Carey, 'Management in the Civil Service', *Management in Government*, Vol. 39, No. 2 (May 1984) p. 85.
95 Lord Hunt of Tanworth interviewed for *All the Prime Minister's Men*, 29 May 1987.
96 Sir Frank Cooper interviewed for *All the Prime Minister's Men*, 8 April 1986.
97 Ibid.
98 Ian Hargreaves and Robin Pauley, 'Moves to replace Rayner run into political trouble', *Financial Times*, 19 January 1983.
99 Private information.
100 Lord Rayner interviewed for *All the Prime Minister's Men*, 21 May 1986.
101 Cooper, 'Ministry of Defence', in Harrison & Gretton (eds), *Reshaping Central Government*, pp. 122–3.
102 Cmnd. 8616, p. 24.
103 *Treasury and Civil Service Committee, Third Report, Session 1981–82*, 'Efficiency and Effectiveness in the Civil Service', HMSO, 1982.
104 National Audit Office, *Report by the Comptroller and Auditor General, The Financial Management Initiative*, HMSO, 1986, p. 3.
105 *Financial Management in Government Departments,* Cmnd. 9058, HMSO, 1983.
106 Ibid., p. 3.
107 Metcalfe and Richards, *Improving Public Management*, pp. 14–15.
108 Efficiency Unit, *Making Things Happen: A Report on the Implication of Government Efficiency Scrutinies*, HMSO, 1985.
109 Ibid., p. 1.
110 Letter from Ian Beesley to Peter Hennessy, 28 October 1985.
111 *Making Things Happen*, pp. 4–5.
112 Ibid., p. 5.
113 Ibid., signed 'Foreword' by Mrs Thatcher.
114 Metcalfe and Richards, *Improving Public Management*, pp. 18–19.
115 Ibid., p. 20.

116 *Making Things Happen*, p. 3.
117 Ibid., p. 6.
118 Ibid., p. 1.
119 Metcalfe and Richards, *Improving Public Management*, p. 14.
120 Private information.
121 NAO, *The Financial Management Initiative*, p. 11.
122 LWT's *Whitehall*, was broadcast on Channel 4 Television on 25 May and 1 June 1988.
123 Ibid.
124 Ibid. Shortage of time presented Mr Young's explanation being broadcast.
125 Ibid.
126 NAO, *The Financial Management Initiative*, p. 1.
127 Ibid., p. 10.
128 Peter Hennessy, 'Whitehall brief: Running the empire that has come home', *The Times*, 20 June 1984.
129 Ibid.
130 For the best account of this see Simon Jenkins, 'The "Star Chamber", PESC and the Cabinet', *Political Quarterly*, Vol. 56, No. 2. (April–June 1985), pp. 113–21.
131 Hennessy, 'Whitehall brief: the new hunters take over'.
132 Private information.
133 Valerie Strachan interviewed for LWT's *Whitehall*, 4 March 1987.
134 NAO, *The Financial Management Initiative*, p. 10.
135 LWT, *Whitehall*, programme two, Channel 4 Television June 1988.
136 Ian Beesley interviewed for LWT's *Whitehall*, 4 March 1987.
137 *The Next Moves Forward*, Conservative Central Office, 1987, p. 41.
138 Private information.
131 *Government Purchasing, Progress Report to the Prime Minister*, HMSO, 1987, p. 1.
132 Metcalfe and Richards, *Improving Public Management*, p. 212.
133 Ibid.
134 Private information.
135 Efficiency Unit, *Improving Management in Govenment: The Next Steps*, HMSO, 1988.
136 H of C, *Official Report*, 18 February 1988.
137 Peter Hennessy, 'Whitehall Watch: Civil Service revolution that fell short', *The Independent*, 22 February 1988.
138 Sir Robin Butler, evidence to the Treasury and Civil Service Committee, 9 March 1988.
139 Clive Priestley, 'Government management must no longer be left to chance', *The Independent*, 26 February 1988.
140 Peter Hennessy, 'Whitehall Watch: Careful steps towards greater efficiency', *The Independent*, 18 April 1988.

15 THE THATCHER EFFECT

1 Mr Priestley delivered this judgement at the Anglo-American Seminar at St George's House, Windsor, organised by the Adam Smith Institute, 1–2 May 1984.
2 Mrs Thatcher delivered this verdict on 16 June 1987. Tyler, *Campaign! The Selling of the Prime Minister*, p. 247.
3 Lord Bancroft interviewed for *All the Prime Minister's Men*, 10 April 1986.
4 'Agenda for the third phase of Thatcherism', *The Independent*, 14 September 1987.
5 Hugo Young, 'The convictions that will not serve the full term', *The Guardian*, 21 July 1987.
6 The paper was leaked to *The Sunday Times*. See Peter Stothard, 'Secret documents reveal Tory strategy', *The Sunday Times*, 18 November 1979.
7 Ibid.
8 Sir Frank Cooper.
9 Lord Bancroft interviewed for *All the Prime Minister's Men*, 10 April 1986.
10 Ibid.
11 Lord Bancroft interviewed for Granada Television's 'Civil Unrest' *World in Action* programme, broadcast on 21 January 1985.
12 Lord Bancroft interviewed for *All the Prime Minister's Men*, 10 April 1986.
13 The occasion was a meeting of the Conservative Philosophy Group. Private Information.
14 See Peter Hennessy, 'From Woodshed to Watershed', *The Times*, 5 March 1984.
15 Private information.
16 Prior, *A Balance of Power*, p. 117.
17 Hugo Young and Anne Sloman, *The Thatcher Phenomenon*, p. 24.
18 Richard Jameson, 'Election Campaigns and Civil Service Neutrality', *Contemporary Record*, Vol. 1, No. 2 (Summer 1987), p. 4.
19 Young and Sloman, *The Thatcher Phenomenon*, p. 25.
20 Ibid., pp. 22–3.
21 Dennis Kavanagh, *Thatcherism and British Politics, The End of Consensus?*, OUP, 1987.
22 G. W. Jones, 'Cabinet Government and Mrs Thatcher', *Contemporary Record*, Vol. 1, No. 3 (Autumn 1987), p. 8–12.
23 Private information.
24 Peter Hennessy, 'Whitehall brief', *The Times*, 22 September 1984.
25 Cosgrave, *Thatcher: The First Term*, p. 71.
26 Prior, *A Balance of Power*, p. 136.
27 Ibid.
28 Ibid., p. 137.
29 Peter Hennessy, 'Permanent Government: The Prime Minister's Chemistry Test', *New Statesman*, 20 February 1987.
30 Private information.
31 Peter Riddell, *The Thatcher Government*, Blackwell, rev. edn, 1985, p. 53.
32 Private information.

33 Private information.
34 Private information.
35 Peter Hennessy, 'The Listener Profile: Sir Robert Armstrong', *The Listener*, 26 June 1986.
36 Private information.
37 Private information.
38 I heard him do so during a lecture at Nottingham University in 1985.
39 Sir Douglas Wass interviewed for *All the Prime Minister's Men*, 8 April 1986.
40 Ibid.
41 Address by Sir Robert Armstrong to the Centenary Conference of the Chartered Institute of Public Finance and Accountancy, 15 June 1985.
42 Lord Rayner interviewed for *All the Prime Minister's Men*, 21 May 1986.
43 Lord Bancroft interviewed for *All the Prime Minister's Men*, 10 April 1986.
44 Ibid.
45 Sir Frank Cooper interviewed for *All the Prime Minister's Men*, 8 April 1986.
46 Ibid.
47 For the members of the Williams Committee see *Top Jobs in Whitehall*, p. 7.
48 Ibid., 43
49 Brook Productions's *A Week in Politics*, Channel 4 Television, 24 May 1985.
50 Address to the CIPFA Centenary Conference, 18 June 1985.
51 Private information.
52 Hennessy, Morrison and Townsend, *Routine Punctuated by Orgies*, p. 69.
53 Conversation with Sir John Hoskyns, 3 November 1983.
54 Ibid.
55 Private information.
56 Conversation with Sir John Hoskyns, 3 November 1983.
57 Private information.
58 Private information.
59 Private information.
60 Private information.
61 Private information.
62 Private information.
63 Stothard, 'Secret documents reveal Tory strategy'.
64 Private information.
65 Private information.
66 Private information.
67 Conversation with Sir Kenneth Berrill, 14 October 1983.
68 Sir John Hoskyns *In Conversation* with David Dimbleby, BBC 1 Television, 7 December 1982.
69 Ibid.
70 Peter Hennessy, 'Whitehall brief: Anti-establishment strategist', *The Times*, 24 January 1984.
71 Hoskyns, *In Conversation*, 7 December 1982.
72 Ibid.
73 Sir John Hoskyns interviewed for *All The Prime Minister's Men*, 26 March 1986.

74 In fact it was Baldwin's doctrine.
75 Sir John Hoskyns, letter to *The Times*, 2 July 1987.
76 Hoskyns, *In Conversation*, 7 December 1982.
77 Ibid.
78 Ibid.
79 Ibid.
80 Ibid.
81 Letter to *The Times*, 2 July 1987.
82 Private information.
83 David Willetts, 'The Role of the Prime Minister's Policy Unit', *Public Administration*, Vol. 65, No. 4 (Winter 1987), pp. 443–55.
84 Norman Strauss interviewed for *All the Prime Minister's Men*, 10 April 1986.
85 Norman Strauss interviewed for *The Shadows' Dummy Run*, BBC Radio 4's *Analysis*, 13 November 1986.
86 Hoskyns, *In Conversation*, 7 December 1982.
87 Hennessy, Morrison and Townsend, *Routine Punctuated by Orgies*, p. 79.
88 Ibid.
89 Sir John Hoskyns interviewed for *All the Prime Minister's Men*, 26 March 1986.
90 David Norris, 'Maggie's money man travels second class', *Daily Mail*, 18 July 1981.
91 Private information.
92 Alan Walters, *The Economic Adviser's Role, Scope & Limitations*, Centre for Policy Studies, 1981, pp. 7–8.
93 Conversation with Sir John Hoskyns, 3 November 1983.
94 Professor John Ashworth speaking on BBC Radio 3's *Routine Punctuated by Orgies*, 13 December 1983.
95 Private information.
96 Private information.
97 Peter Hennessy, 'Striking Lessons from History', *The Times*, 24 July 1984.
98 Simon Jenkins, 'The Battle of Britain's Dinosaurs', *The Economist*, 6 March 1982.
99 Ibid.
100 Ibid.
101 Ibid.
102 Peter Hennessy, 'Whitehall brief: History Men Wrestling with Morrison's Monsters', *The Times*, 3 May 1983.
103 For Ibbs's refusal to discuss Merseyside and the inner cities see Hennessy, Morrison and Townsend, *Routine Punctuated by Orgies*, p. 75.
104 See Peter Hennessy and David Walker, *The Times*, 27 July 1981.
105 Private information.
106 Private information.
107 Quoted in Peter Hennessy, 'The highbrow with the low profile', *The Times*, 22 July 1981.
108 Peter Hennessy, 'Permanent Government: Will she take on the Foreign Office?', *New Statesman*, 31 July 1987.

109 Private information.
110 See Anthony Parsons, *The Pride and the Fall, Iran 1974–1979*, Cape, 1984.
111 Private information.
112 Letter from Sir Anthony Parsons to Peter Hennessy, 5 October 1987.
113 Observer Profile, 'Intruder in Downing Street', *The Observer*, 7 November 1982.
114 Ibid.
115 Sir Anthony Parsons interviewed for BBC Radio 3's *The Good and the Great*, 13 December 1984.
116 David Tonge, 'Decline of a proud department', *Financial Times*, 26 October 1982.
117 Private information.
118 Private information.
119 Private information.
120 Private information.
121 Peter Hennessy, 'Duff gets top security job', *The Times*, 28 February 1983.
122 Bancroft, 'The Art of Management'.
123 'Think Tank: more buoyancy needed', *The Economist*, 6 March 1982.
124 Ibid.
125 Peter Hennessy, 'Think Tank paper outlines new assault on the state monopolies', *The Times*, 1 November 1982.
126 Ibid.
127 Private information.
128 *The Economist*, 18 September 1984.
129 Private information.
130 Private information.
131 Hennessy, 'Think tank paper outlines new assault on the state monopolies'.
132 Private information.
133 Private information.
134 Private information.
135 Private information.
136 Private information.
137 Private information.
138 Professor John Ashworth Speaking on BBC Radio 3's *Routine Punctuated by Orgies*, 13 December 1983.
139 Private information.
140 Peter Hennessy, 'Unlucky 13 for think tank', *The Times*, 21 June 1983.
141 Willetts, 'The Role of the Prime Minister's Policy Unit'.
142 Ibid.
143 Ibid.
144 Ibid.
145 Ibid.
146 Ferdinant Mount, *The Subversive Family, An Alternative History of Love and Marriage*, Cape, 1982.
147 Willetts, 'The Role of the Prime Minister's Policy Unit'.
148 Ibid.
149 Ibid.

150 Written Parliamentary Question to the Prime Minister from Tim Eggar MP, answered 27 June 1983.
151 Written Parliamentary Question to the Prime Minister from Bruce George MP, answered 24 June 1987.
152 Willetts, 'The Role of the Prime Minister's Policy Unit'.
153 Ibid.
154 Ibid.
155 Ibid.
156 Ibid.
157 Ibid.
158 Private information.
159 Stowe, 'Managing a great department of state'.
160 Peter Hennessy, 'Whitehall brief: Cycling to dizzy heights in the Civil Service'. *The Times*, 23 June 1981.
161 Ibid.
162 Ibid.
163 Ibid.
164 Donoughue, *Prime Minister*, p. 18.
165 Callaghan, *Time and Chance*, p. 406.
166 Ibid., p. 21.
167 Donoughue, *Prime Minister*, p. 18.
168 Hazel Duffy, 'Treasury control of Civil Service Strengthened', *Financial Times*, 8 August 1987.
169 Hennessy, *Cabinet*, p. 100.
170 Peter Hennessy, 'Whitehall brief: Thatcher's new-style man for all summits', *The Times*, 24 November 1981.
171 Private information.
172 Private information.
173 Hennessy, *Cabinet*, p. 105.
174 Sir Frank Cooper interviewed for *All the Prime Minister's Men*, 6 April 1986.
175 Ibid.
176 Private information.
177 I heard him deliver it in February 1978.
178 Private information
179 Private information.
180 Wass, *Government and the Governed*, p. 52.
181 Private information.
182 The photograph was published in *The Guardian* alongside Michael White's article 'First Lord's old-time treat at the Treasury', *The Guardian*, 2 April 1983.
183 Wass, *Government and Governed*, p. 50.
184 Private information.
185 Private information.
186 Private information.
187 Private information.
188 Private information.

189 Sir Robert Armstrong, *Questions*, Channel 4 Television, 1 July 1984.
190 Donoughue, *Prime Minister*, p. 18.
191 Ibid.
192 Sir Robert Armstrong in *The Vanishing Mandarins*, BBC Radio 4's *Analysis*, 13 February 1985.
193 Sir Robert Armstrong interviewed for Granada Television's 'Civil Unrest'.
194 Private information.
195 Private information.
196 Sir Robert Armstrong interviewed for 'Civil Unrest'.
197 Private information.
198 Private information.
199 Private information.
200 Sir Robert Armstrong, *Questions*, 1 July 1984.
201 Ibid.
202 Private information.
203 Private information.
204 Sir Robert Armstrong interviewed for 'Civil Unrest'.
205 Quoted in Peter Hennessy, 'The Listener Profile: Sir Robert Armstrong', *The Listener*, 26 June 1986.
206 Sir Robert Armstrong, *Questions*, 1 July 1984.
207 Linda Christmas, 'The Man who will be with the PM in 1987', *Guardian Weekly*, 22 July 1979.
208 John Burns, 'Sir Robert blows his top', *Daily Express*, 13 November 1986.
209 Sir Robert Armstrong, *Questions*, 1 July 1984.
210 Ibid.
211 Quoted in Hennessy, 'The Listener Profile: Sir Robert Armstrong'.
212 *Seventh Report, Treasury and Civil Service Committee, Session 1985–86*, 'Civil Servants and Ministers: Duties and Responsibilities', Vol. II, p. 31.
313 Private information.
314 John Cole, 'Westland – an unexploded bomb', *The Listener*, 31 July 1986.
215 *Seventh Report, Treasury and Civil Service Committee, Session 1985–6*, Vol. II, p. 230.
216 Private information.
217 Private information.
218 Private information.
219 On his very last day in office, Armstrong wrote to *The Times* to remind readers that the phrase was Edmund Burke's, not his. '"Economy with truth" in context', *The Times*, 5 January 1988.
220 Hugo Young, 'Two great offices dethroned at a stroke', *The Guardian*, 2 December 1986.
221 'Lying abroad for one's country gets a bad name,' *The Observer*, 30 November 1986.
222 'The Naked Civil Servant', *The Daily Telegraph*, 26 November 1986.
223 Peter Hennessy, 'Permanent Government: Sir Sydney Carton of the Cabinet Office', *New Statesman*, 19–26 December 1986.
224 Ibid.

225 Ibid.
226 Adam Raphael, 'Pressure mounts on Britain to pull out', *The Observer*, 30 November 1986.
227 Colin Hughes, 'Armstrong out of favour with Owen', *The Independent*, 27 November 1986.
228 Hugo Young, chronicler of the Crossman affair, drew a sharp and contrasting picture of the two men's experiences in 'The upside down view of Sir Robert in Sydney', *The Guardian*, 20 November 1986.
229 Private information.
230 Private information.
231 Robert Armstrong, 'Obituary: Lord Trend', *The Independent*, 24 July 1987.
232 *The Duties and Responsibilities of Civil Servants in Relation to Ministers, Note by the Head of the Home Civil Service*, Cabinet Office, December 1987.
233 Ibid.
234 Peter Hennessy, 'Whitehall Watch: Swan-song of a public civil servant,' *The Independent*, 7 December 1987.
235 Armstrong, 'Taking Stock of Our Achievements'.
236 Philip Webster, 'New Year peerage for controversial Cabinet Secretary', *The Times*, 31 December 1987.
237 Andrew Marr, 'Heath attacks questioning of Armstrong', *The Independent*, 5 January 1988.
238 Private information.
239 Marcia Falkender, *Downing Street in Perspective*, Weidenfeld, 1983, photos between pp. 152 and 153.
240 The Times Business Diary, 'Fizz', *The Times*, 13 April 1977.
241 Haines, *The Politics of Power*, p. 33.
242 Ibid. pp. 100–2.
243 Donoughue, *Prime Minister*, p. 19.
244 'T-rusty servant', *Daily Mail*, 17 July 1987.
245 Private information.
246 Peter Hennessy, 'Whitehall brief: Head boy of Downing Street', *The Times*, 7 June 1983.
247 Andrew Marr, 'Butler named as the new head of Civil Service', *The Independent*, 9 July 1987.
248 Robin Butler to Peter Hennessy, 11 July 1987.
249 William Russell, 'Butler: a civil servant for all seasons', *Glasgow Herald*, 14 July 1987.
250 'The Mandarin who glided to the top', *The Observer*, 12 July 1987.
251 Hennessy, 'Whitehall brief: Head Boy of Downing Street'.
252 Private information.
253 Hennessy, 'Whitehall brief: Head Boy of Downing Street'.
254 Private information.
255 Private information.
256 *How Cabinet Government Works*, BBC Radio 3, 12 March 1976.
257 Private information.
258 Private information.

259 Private information.
260 Hennessy, Morrison and Townsend, *Routine Punctuated by Orgies*, p. 10.
261 Private information.
262 Evidence to the H of C Treasury and Civil Service Committee, 9 March 1988.
263 Ibid.
264 Tom Harrisson, *Living Through the Blitz*, pp. 42, 129, 134.
265 Peter Hennessy, 'How George Formby Won the War', *Times Higher Education Supplement*, 13 July 1973.
266 Peter Hennessy, 'Whitehall brief: Morale on the slide but does it matter?', *The Times*, 15 September 1981.
267 David Young interviewed for *All the Prime Minister's Men*, May 1986.
268 *Seventh Report from the Treasury and Civil Service Committee, Session 1985–86*, 'Civil Servants and Ministers: Duties and Responsibilities', Vol. II, p. 231.
269 *The Next Steps*, p. 29.
270 Richard Norton-Taylor, 'Whitehall tackles high-flyer shortage', *The Guardian*, 4 September 1987.
271 'We get what we pay for', *The Independent*, 4 September 1987.
272 *The Vanishing Mandarins*, BBC Radio 4's *Analysis*, 13 February 1985.
273 Norman Warner interviewed for LWT's *Whitehall*, 13 March 1987.
274 Ibid.
275 Gerry Grimstone interviewed for *Whitehall*, 19 March 1987.
276 *The Vanishing Mandarins*, BBC Radio 4's *Analysis*, 13 February 1985.
277 David Young interviewed for *All the Prime Minister's Men*, May 1986.
278 Ibid.
279 *Inquiry into the Value of Pensions*, Cmnd. 8147, HMSO, 1981.
280 *Inquiry into Civil Service Pay*, two vols, Cmnd. 8590, HMSO, 1982.
281 Armstrong, 'Taking Stock of Our Achievements'.
282 Cmnd. 8590, p. 93.
283 Armstrong, 'Taking Stock of Our Achievements'.
284 Peter Hennessy, 'Whitehall brief: Peacemaker of Cheltenham', *The Times*, 14 February 1984.
285 Private information.
286 Rudolf Klein, 'Inside the Ivory Tower', *New Society*, 17 April 1987.
287 Lord Hailsham interviewed for *The Other Opposition*, BBC Radio 4's *Analysis*, 15 October 1987.
288 Peter Hennessy, 'Permanent Government: "Underlord" of all he surveys', *New Statesman*, 3 July 1987.
289 See Anthony Barker, 'Quango: a word and a campaign', Anthony Barker (ed.), *Quangos in Britain*, Macmillan, 1982, pp. 228–9.
290 Hazel Duffy, 'Lawson reduces status of NEDC', *Financial Times*, 2 July 1987.
291 Private information.
292 S. E. Finer, 'Thatcherism and British Political History', in Minogue and Biddiss (eds), *Thatcherism, Personality and Politics*, p. 140.

PART FIVE THE FUTURE

1 J. Enoch Powell, 'The causes of the English Revolution', *The Spectator*, 5 December 1987.

16 ASSESSING PERFORMANCE

1 Hailsham, *The Dilemma of Democracy*, p. 156.
2 Benn, *Out of the Wilderness*, diary entry for 28 May 1965, p. 264.
3 Private information.
4 David Butler, 'An Independent Perspective', in Hennessy and Seldon (eds), *Ruling Performance*, p. 325.
5 Hailsham, *The Dilemma of Democracy*, p. 161.
6 Ibid., pp. 157–8.
7 Ibid., p. 158.
8 Mr Taylor's words were broadcast on Channel 4 Television on 1 June 1988.
9 This is part of Whitehall folklore but I have yet to read a document at the PRO which corroborates it.
10 In May 1956, Leslie Rowan, head of the Treasury's Overseas Finance Division, told the Chancellor, Macmillan, that 'it is quite likely that the Six will not progress very much further in fact at Venice, and it may be thought that the risk is negligible of our receiving any embarrassing invitation to join'. PRO T 234/183.
11 Cmnd. 8787.
12 See Peter Hennessy, 'Whitehall Watch: A Conditional Discharge for the Mandarins', *The Independent*, 30 November 1987. The conference itself took place on 20 November.
13 David Henderson, 'Two Costly British Errors', *The Unimportance of Being Right*, BBC Radio 3, 24 Octoer 1977.
14 Jock Bruce-Gardyne and Nigel Lawson, *The Power Game*, Macmillan, 1976, pp. 19, 27–8.
15 Tony Benn interviewed for *All the Prime Minister's Men*, 16 May 1986.
16 Maudling, *Memoirs*, p. 66.
17 Sir Hermann made his remarks at a seminar on 'Energy and the World' organised by the Institute of Contemporary British History at Chatham House on 24 November 1987.
18 Professor Ian Nish at the ICBH seminar on 'Comparative Postwar Economic Performance'. Speaking of the Japanese Civil Service and the post-1973 oil crises, he said: 'ingenious measures were initiated from the top down'.
19 Frances Donaldson, *Edward VIII*, Weidenfeld, 1974, p. 253.
20 From an unpublished paper, *It Took a Riot*, circulated to the Cabinet in August 1981.
21 She delivered them on the steps at Conservative Central Office at 3.30 a.m. The exact text is important as it has often been misquoted, see Peter Hennessy, 'No gold at the end of the rainbow', *The Listener*, 8 October 1987.

22 Peter Jenkins, 'Agenda for the third phase of Thatcherism', *The Independent*, 14 September 1987.
23 A version of this chart first appeared in Hennessy, 'No gold at the end of the rainbow.'
24 John Goddard, Fred Robinson and Colin Wren, 'Urban and Regional Policies and the Economic Development of the Newcastle Metropolitan Region', in Victor Hausner and members of the ESRC Inner Cities Research Programme, *Urban Economic Change; Five City Studies*, Oxford, Clarendon Press, 1987, p. 136.
25 Donaldson, *Edward VIII*, p. 253.
26 Colin Brown, 'Thatcher uses inner cities visit for private enterprise crusade', *The Independent*, 17 September 1987.
27 Quoted in the Introduction to Hennessy and Seldon (eds), *Ruling Performance*, pp. 1–2.
28 Addison, *Now the War Is Over*, see Chapter 3.
29 Peter Pagnamenta and Richard Overy, *All Our Working Lives*, BBC, 1984, p. 45.
30 Peter Hall (ed.), *The Inner City in Context*, p. 92.
31 Ibid., p. 94.
32 Goddard, Robinson and Wren, '*Urban and Regional Policies and the Economic Development of the Newcastle Metropolitan Region*', in Hausner *et al.*, *Urban Economic Change*, pp. 150, 150, 163, 170.
33 Victor Hausner and Brian Robson, *Changing Cities*, ESRC, 1985, p. 8.
34 Hennessy, *Cabinet*, p. 172.
35 Hausner and Robson, *Changing Cities*, p. 9.
36 Hennessy, *Cabinet*, pp. 171–2.
37 *Policy For the Inner Cities*, Cmnd, 6845, HMSO, 1977, p. 25.
38 Ibid., p. 15.
39 Ibid., p. 16.
40 Ibid., p. 15.
41 Ibid., p. 24.
42 Ibid.
43 Hausner and Robson, *Changing Cities*, p. 28.
44 Ibid.
45 Heseltine, *Where There's a Will*, p. 15.
46 Michael Heseltine interviewed for *Decline or Rise of the Inner Cities*, BBC Radio 4's *Analysis*, 15 September 1987.
47 Ibid.
48 Ibid.
49 Private information.
50 Private information.
51 Private information.
52 Private information.
53 Private information.
54 Private information.
55 Private information.

56 Michael Heseltine interviewed for *All the Prime Minister's Men*, 17 April 1986.
57 Ibid.
58 Howard Mallinson interviewed for *Decline or Rise of the Inner Cities*, BBC Radio 4's *Analysis*, 8 September 1987.
59 Ibid.
60 Ibid.
61 Ibid.
62 Peter Hennessy and David Walker, 'Urban plan review to remain secret', *The Times*, 23 April 1984.
63 *Decline or Rise of the Inner Cities*, BBC Radio 4's *Analysis*, 30 September 1987.
64 Ibid.
65 Peter Jenkins, 'Thatcher seeks school opt-out on large scale', *The Independent*, 14 September 1987.
66 *The Next Moves Forward*, Conservative Central Office, 1987, p. 64. Richard Evans, 'Government plans "mini" urban development areas', *Financial Times*, 8 December 1987.
67 William Solesbury, 'The Dilemmas of Inner City Policy', *Public Administration*, Vol. 64, Winter 1986, p. 396.
68 James Naughtie and Alan Travis, 'Thatcher relents on Inner Cities minister', *The Guardian*, 2 December 1987.
69 Peter Riddell, 'Clarke chosen as inner-cities minister', *Financial Times*, 19 December 1987.
70 *Action For Cities*, Cabinet Office, 1988.
71 Private information.
72 Private information.
73 Peter Hennessy, 'Whitehall Watch: Precision lacking in latest plan to end urban blight', *The Independent*, 21 March 1988.
74 Peter Hennessy, 'How Bevin saved Britain's Bomb', *The Times*, 30 September 1982.
75 Conversation with Lord Penney, 19 November 1987.
76 Quoted by Victor Macklen (who was present when Teller spoke) interviewed for BBC Radio 4's *A Bloody Union Jack on Top of It*, 1 December 1987.
77 In preparing this chronology I have found *The Development of Atomic Energy 1939–84, Chronology of Events,* prepared for the UKAEA by Lorna Arnold and Margaret Gowing, to be an invaluable source.
78 Conversation with Sir Denis Rickett, 2 December 1987.
79 The full story has been told in the first volume of what I consider to be a magnificent official history of the project, Margaret Gowing's *Britain and Atomic Energy 1939–45*, Macmillan, 1964.
80 Conversation with Lord Sherfield, 17 November 1987.
81 Private information.
82 Hennessy, *Cabinet*, p. 126.
83 PRO CAB 130/16.
84 Conversation with Lord Penney, 19 November 1987.
85 Ibid.

86 Ibid.
87 Gowing, *Independence and Deterrence*, Vol. I, pp. 44–5.
88 Ibid., pp. 19–32.
89 A full biography and character assessment of the three men can be found in Margaret Gowing, *Independence and Deterrence, Vol. 2. Policy Execution*, Macmillan, 1974, Chapter 13, pp. 3–36.
90 Ibid., p. 9.
91 Quoted in Lorna Arnold, *A Very Special Relationship, British Atomic Weapon Trials in Australia*, HMSO, 1987, pp. 14–15.
92 Ibid., p. 15.
93 Conversation with Lord Sherfield, 17 November 1987.
94 Gowing, *Independence and Deterrence*, Vol. 2. pp. 494–5.
95 Conversation with Lord Sherfield, 17 November 1987.
96 Conversation with Lord Penney, 27 November 1987.
97 PRO, CAB 128/27, CC (54) 48, Item 2.
98 H. Montgomery Hyde, *The Atom Bomb Spies*, Hamish Hamilton, 1980, p. 222.
99 Conversation with Lord Penney, 27 November 1987.
100 V. J. B. Macklen, 'Sir William Cook', *The Independent*, 29 September 1987.
101 Conversation with Victor Macklen, 1 December 1987.
102 I am grateful to the Centre for Policy Studies for providing me with a copy of Mr Lawson's 'The New Britain' speech.
103 Harry Eckstein, *The English Health Service*, Harvard, 1959, p. 72.
104 Lawson 'The New Britain'.
105 Walter Laqueur, *Europe since Hitler*, Pelican edn, 1972, p. 251.
106 Ibid., p. 269.
107 Professor Eric Hobsbawm speaking on *The Road From 1945*, BBC Radio 4 *Analysis*, 31 March 1988.
108 Kennedy, *The Rise and Fall of the Great Powers*, p. 424.
109 Ibid., p. 425.
110 Ibid., pp. 482–3.
111 The Marquand thesis is one of those which, to be properly understood, requires a full reading of the volume adumbrating it. David Marquand, *The Unprincipled Society, New Demands and Old Policies*, Cape, 1988.

17 A SYSTEM FOR THE TWENTY-FIRST CENTURY

1 Cmd. 3638, Appendix B, p. 108.
2 Taylor, 'Future Shape of Reform in Whitehall'.
3 Professor David Henderson, 'The British Way of Administration', *The Unimportance of Being Right*, Programme 4, BBC Radio 3, 14 November 1977.
4 Cmnd, 3638, Appendix B, p. 111.

5 Armstrong, 'Taking Stock of Our Achievements'.
6 Peter Hennessy, 'Whitehall Watch: Scrutinies bring savings, but bigger prizes await', *The Independent*, 21 December 1987.
7 Armstrong, 'Taking Stock of Our Achievements'.
8 Cmnd. 9230, p. 6.
9 Taylor, 'Future Shape of Reform in Whitehall'.
10 Armstrong, 'Taking Stock of Our Achievements'.
11 Henderson, 'A Vested Interest in the Truth', Programme 5 of *The Unimportance of Being Right*, BBC Radio 3, 21 November 1977.
12 The development of Strauss's thinking is most easily sampled by reading Norman Strauss, 'The Computeracy: Watchdog of the Future', *Intermedia*, July–September 1984, Vol. 12, No. 4/5, pp. 70–2, and Norman Strauss, 'New Ethos Needed', *The Illustrated London News*, April 1986, p. 34.

INDEX